S0-ASG-547

SOMETHING ABOUT THE AUTHOR®

Something about the Author *was named an* ***"Outstanding Reference Source,"*** *the highest honor given by the American Library Association Reference and Adult Services Division.*

ISSN 0276-816X

SOMETHING ABOUT THE AUTHOR®

Facts and Pictures about Authors
and Illustrators of Books for Young People

volume 241

Detroit • New York • San Francisco • New Haven, Conn • Waterville, Maine • London

Something about the Author, Volume 241

Project Editor: Lisa Kumar

Permissions: Sheila Spencer

Imaging and Multimedia: Sheila Spencer, John Watkins

Composition and Electronic Capture: Amy Darga

Manufacturing: Rhonda Dover

Product Manager: Mary Onorato

Gale, Cengage Learning
27500 Drake Rd.
Farmington Hills, MI, 48331-3535

LIBRARY OF CONGRESS CATALOG CARD NUMBER 62-52046

ISBN-13: 978-1-4144-8097-8
ISBN-10: 1-4144-8097-0

ISSN 0276-816X

This title is also available as an e-book.
ISBN-13: 978-1-4144-8243-9
ISBN-10: 1-4144-8243-4
Contact your Gale, Cengage Learning sales representative for ordering information.

Printed in Mexico
1 2 3 4 5 6 7 16 15 14 13 12

Contents

Authors in Forthcoming Volumes . . . vii
Introduction . . . ix
SATA Product Advisory Board . . . xi
Illustrations Index . . . 179
Author Index . . . 217

A

Anderson, Derek 1969- . . . 1
Ashburn, Boni . . . 4

B

Barrows, Annie 1962- . . . 6
Bass, Guy . . . 8
Berkley, Elizabeth 1972- . . . 9
Bliss, Frederick
See Card, Orson Scott . . . 12
Burgis, Stephanie . . . 10

C

Card, Orson Scott 1951- . . . 12
Chow, Cara 1972- . . . 21
Clarke, J.
See Clarke, Judith . . . 23
Clarke, Judith 1943- . . . 23
Cohen, Joshua C. 1970- . . . 27
Colgan, Lynda 1953- . . . 28
Cornell, Kevin . . . 29

D

Daly, Cathleen . . . 31
DeMatteis, J.M. 1953- . . . 32
DeMatteis, John Marc
See DeMatteis, J.M. . . . 32
DePalma, Mary Newell 1961- . . . 36
DeStefano, Lauren 1984- . . . 40

F

Fisher, Catherine 1957- . . . 42
Fleming, Denise 1950- . . . 47
Fliess, Sue . . . 51
Frossard, Claire . . . 51

G

Gay, Kelly
See Keaton, Kelly . . . 77
Gelbwasser, Margie 1976- . . . 53
Golio, Gary . . . 54
Gollub, Matthew 1960- . . . 56
Gormley, Greg 1966- . . . 60
Green, Brian
See Card, Orson Scott . . . 12
Gump, P.Q.
See Card, Orson Scott . . . 12

H

Hand, Cynthia 1978- . . . 62
Harmer, Wendy 1955- . . . 63
Harper, Jamie . . . 65
Hart, Sam 1973- . . . 68
Hodson, Ben . . . 70
Holbrook, Sara . . . 72
Hubbard, Kirsten 1983- . . . 74

J

James, Kelle . . . 76

K

Keaton, Kelly . . . 77
Kennedy, Kim . . . 78
Kirby, Matthew J. 1976- . . . 80
Kurisu, Jane 1952- . . . 82

L

Lamut, Sonja 84

Laughead, Mike 1978- 86

Lobel , Anita 1934- 86

Luna, James 1962- 93

M

Mack, Steve 95

Magoon, Kekla 1980- 96

Mason, Margaret H. 1954- 98

Matthies, Janna 99

Metzger, Steve 1949- 100

Mooney, Melissa Duke 1968-2009 103

Morales, Yuyi 1968- 104

N

Newbound, Andrew 1969- 109

Nolan, Han 1956- 110

Norman, Kim 114

Novesky, Amy 116

P

Peot, Margaret 118

Pittman, Rickey E. 119

Power, Timothy 1960- 120

R

Reeve, Philip 1966- 122

Restrepo, Bettina 1972- 127

Richards, Scott
See Card, Orson Scott 12

Rosenstock, Barb 1960- 129

Rudnicki, Richard 131

Runton, Andy 133

Rylant, Cynthia 1954- 134

S

Sales, Leila 146

Scales, Simon 148

Schreiber, Ellen 148

Scieszka, Casey 1984- 151

Simone, Ni-Ni 152

Stevenson, Sarah Jamila 1977- 153

Szpirglas, Jeff 155

T

Thompson, Kate 1956- 157

V

Van Cleave, Ryan G. 1972- 162

W

Walley, Byron
See Card, Orson Scott 12

Watson, Wendy 1942- 164

White, Kiersten 1983(?)- 170

Whittemore, Jo 1977- 171

Williamson, Pete 173

Wood, Frances M. 173

Wummer, Amy 1955- 175

Authors in Forthcoming Volumes

Below are some of the authors and illustrators that will be featured in upcoming volumes of *SATA*. These include new entries on the swiftly rising stars of the field, as well as completely revised and updated entries (indicated with *) on some of the most notable and best-loved creators of books for children.

***Marc Aronson** ▮ Inspired in his writing career by his love of history and literature, Aronson has made a career of crafting thought-provoking nonfiction for young adults. In addition to historical books such as *Sir Walter Ralegh and the Quest for El Dorado, Art Attack: A Short Cultural History of the Avant-Garde,* and *Sugar Changed the World: A Story of Magic, Spice, Slavery, Freedom, and Science*, he has also explored contemporary topics in the essay collections *Exploding the Myths: The Truth about Teenagers and Reading* and *Beyond the Pale: New Essays for a New Era.* In 2006, Aronson was appointed as spokesman for Save Our History, a national history education and preservation initiative sponsored by television's History Channel.

***Cecil Castellucci** ▮ Writing is just one of Castellucci's many interests; a Los Angeles-based author, she is also a film director, performance artist and indie rock musician. With *Boy Proof* she began the career that has brought her a devout audience. Her more recent novels have included the teen-centered *The Queen of Cool* and *Beige,* as well as the "P.L.A.I.N. Jane" graphic novels. She has also joined with fellow writer Holly Black to coedit *Geektastic: Stories from the Nerd Herd.*

Mike Deas ▮ Based in Canada, Deas is perhaps best known for his contributions to the "Graphic Guide Adventure" series written by Liam O'Donnell, which includes the preteen-friendly *Wild Ride* and *Ramp Rats,* as well as *Media Meltdown. Dalen and Gole: Scandal in Port Angus,* Deas's first original graphic novel, offers a humorous take on extraterrestrial life that is brought to life in his quirky sequential art.

Dianne Eastman ▮ After a successful career as an advertising art director, Eastman began designing and illustrating children's books, among them *Wow, Canada! Exploring This Land from Coast to Coast to Coast* and *Only in Canada! From the Colossal to the Kooky,* both written by Vivien Bowers. Eastman's award-winning illustration projects have also included several books by author Lyn Thomas, as well as stories by Marilyn Helmer and Cynthia Pratt Nicolson.

***Anne Isaacs** ▮ Isaacs is an award-winning author of picture books for young readers, among them *Treehouse Tales* and *Pancakes for Supper!* She is perhaps best known for *Swamp Angel,* an imaginative historical tale spotlighting a young female heroine who sometimes appears larger than life. Isaacs returns to the wild and untamed west in *The Ghosts of Luckless Gulch,* a picture book illustrated by Dan Santat, while her novel *Torn Thread* is based on the true story of a young girl imprisoned in a Nazi labor camp during World War II.

Tony Lee ▮ Well known in the comic-book world, Lee is a comics writer whose credits include titles for DC Comics, Marvel Comics, Del Rey, MTV Comics, and Titan, where he has written for series such as "X-Men Unlimited," "Spider-Man", "The Gloom," and "Doctor Who." Other projects have included adapting the King Arthur myths into a graphic-novel format and joining artist Cliff Richards in creating the graphic novel *Pride and Prejudice and Zombies.* Turning to teens, Lee has teamed up with artist Dan Boultwood to craft the four-volume "Baker Street Irregulars" graphic novel series, which is based on the Sherlock Holmes character created by Sir Arthur Conan Doyle.

Susan Lynn Meyer ▮ A professor of English at a women's college, Meyer was inspired to write her first fictional story, the picture book *Matthew and Tall Rabbit Go Camping,* during a holiday taken with her husband and young son. Her young-adult novel *Black Radishes* was inspired by her father's childhood experiences as a young Jew living in France during the 1940s and earned Meyer a Sydney Taylor Award Honor Book commendation as well as several other literary honors.

***Jane Ray** ▮ With a body of work that has drawn comparisons to that of noted nineteenth-century children's book illustrator Arthur Rackham, Ray is a British illustrator whose work has appeared in books as varied as Vikram Seth's *Arion and the Dolphin* and the collected stories of the Brothers Grimm. Other writers whose works have been brought to life in her art include Jeanette Winterson, Malachy Doyle, Margaret Mayo, Rachel Anderson, Joyce Dunbar, and Berlie Doherty. In addition, Ray has also produced luminous paintings to accompany her own renditions of classic fairy tales and favorite Biblical passages.

Gillian Tyler ▮ Tyler can recall many of the small details that made up her childhood, and she draws on such memories in creating her watercolor-and-ink illustrations for children's books. Her colorful drawings, which evoke the work of illustrator Janet Ahlberg in their detail and good-natured humor, bring to life stories that range from a new edition of Ursula Moray Williams' *The Good Little Christmas Tree* and Dori Chaconas's *Hurry down to Derry Fair* to the traditional folk-lyric *Froggy Went A-Courtin'* as well as stories by popular children's author Allan Ahlberg.

***Laurence Yep** ▮ The author of such award-winning novels as *Dragonwings, Child of the Owl, Sea Glass,* and *Dragon Steel,* as well as of illustrated stories for younger readers, novelist and playwright Yep is noted for penning fiction that brings the history and culture of Chinese Americans into realistic view. In his books he exchanges the exaggerated, stereotyped images of characters such as Dr. Fu Manchu and Charley Chan for portraits of the real-life Chinese-American men and women who have enriched North America with both their labor and their willingness to share their cultural heritage.

Introduction

Something about the Author (*SATA*) is an ongoing reference series that examines the lives and works of authors and illustrators of books for children. *SATA* includes not only well-known writers and artists but also less prominent individuals whose works are just coming to be recognized. This series is often the only readily available information source on emerging authors and illustrators. You'll find *SATA* informative and entertaining, whether you are a student, a librarian, an English teacher, a parent, or simply an adult who enjoys children's literature.

What's Inside *SATA*

SATA provides detailed information about authors and illustrators who span the full time range of children's literature, from early figures like John Newbery and L. Frank Baum to contemporary figures like Judy Blume and Richard Peck. Authors in the series represent primarily English-speaking countries, particularly the United States, Canada, and the United Kingdom. Also included, however, are authors from around the world whose works are available in English translation. The writings represented in *SATA* include those created intentionally for children and young adults as well as those written for a general audience and known to interest younger readers. These writings cover the entire spectrum of children's literature, including picture books, humor, folk and fairy tales, animal stories, mystery and adventure, science fiction and fantasy, historical fiction, poetry and nonsense verse, drama, biography, and nonfiction. Obituaries are also included in *SATA* and are intended not only as death notices but also as concise overviews of people's lives and work. Additionally, each edition features newly revised and updated entries for a selection of *SATA* listees who remain of interest to today's readers and who have been active enough to require extensive revisions of their earlier biographies.

Autobiography Feature

Beginning with Volume 103, many volumes of *SATA* feature one or more specially commissioned autobiographical essays. These unique essays, averaging about ten thousand words in length and illustrated with an abundance of personal photos, present an entertaining and informative first-person perspective on the lives and careers of prominent authors and illustrators profiled in *SATA*.

Two Convenient Indexes

In response to suggestions from librarians, *SATA* indexes no longer appear in every volume but are included in alternate (odd-numbered) volumes of the series, beginning with Volume 57.

SATA continues to include two indexes that cumulate with each alternate volume: the Illustrations Index, arranged by the name of the illustrator, gives the number of the volume and page where the illustrator's work appears in the current volume as well as all preceding volumes in the series; the Author Index gives the number of the volume in which a person's biographical sketch, autobiographical essay, or obituary appears in the current volume as well as all preceding volumes in the series.

These indexes also include references to authors and illustrators who appear in *Gale's Yesterday's Authors of Books for Children, Children's Literature Review,* and *Something about the Author Autobiography Series.*

Easy-to-Use Entry Format

Whether you're already familiar with the *SATA* series or just getting acquainted, you will want to be aware of the kind of information that an entry provides. In every *SATA* entry the editors attempt to give as complete a picture of the person's life and work as possible. A typical entry in *SATA* includes the following clearly labeled information sections:

PERSONAL: date and place of birth and death, parents' names and occupations, name of spouse, date of marriage, names of children, educational institutions attended, degrees received, religious and political affiliations, hobbies and other interests.

ADDRESSES: complete home, office, electronic mail, and agent addresses, whenever available.

CAREER: name of employer, position, and dates for each career post; art exhibitions; military service; memberships and offices held in professional and civic organizations.

MEMBER: professional, civic, and other association memberships and any official posts held.

AWARDS, HONORS: literary and professional awards received.

WRITINGS: title-by-title chronological bibliography of books written and/or illustrated, listed by genre when known; lists of other notable publications, such as plays, screenplays, and periodical contributions.

ADAPTATIONS: a list of films, television programs, plays, CD-ROMs, recordings, and other media presentations that have been adapted from the author's work.

WORK IN PROGRESS: description of projects in progress.

SIDELIGHTS: a biographical portrait of the author or illustrator's development, either directly from the biographee—and often written specifically for the *SATA* entry—or gathered from diaries, letters, interviews, or other published sources.

BIOGRAPHICAL AND CRITICAL SOURCES: cites sources quoted in "Sidelights" along with references for further reading.

EXTENSIVE ILLUSTRATIONS: photographs, movie stills, book illustrations, and other interesting visual materials supplement the text.

How a *SATA* Entry Is Compiled

SATA editors examine a wide variety of published sources to gather information for an entry. Biographical and bibliographic sources are consulted, as are book reviews, feature articles, published interviews, and material sometimes obtained from the biographee's family, publishers, agent, or other associates. Whenever possible, the author or illustrator is sent a copy of the entry to check for accuracy and completeness.

Entries that have not been verified by the biographees or their representatives are marked with an asterisk (*).

Contact the Editor

We encourage our readers to examine the entire *SATA* series. Please write and tell us if we can make *SATA* even more helpful to you. Give your comments and suggestions to the editor:

Editor
Something about the Author
Gale, Cengage Learning
27500 Drake Rd.
Farmington Hills MI 48331-3535

Toll-free: 800-877-GALE
Fax: 248-699-8070

Something about the Author Product Advisory Board

The editors of *Something about the Author* are dedicated to maintaining a high standard of excellence by publishing comprehensive, accurate, and highly readable entries on a wide array of writers for children and young adults. In addition to the quality of the content, the editors take pride in the graphic design of the series, which is intended to be orderly yet inviting, allowing readers to utilize the pages of *SATA* easily and with efficiency. Despite the longevity of the *SATA* print series, and the success of its format, we are mindful that the vitality of a literary reference product is dependent on its ability to serve its users over time. As literature, and attitudes about literature, constantly evolve, so do the reference needs of students, teachers, scholars, journalists, researchers, and book club members. To be certain that we continue to keep pace with the expectations of our customers, the editors of *SATA* listen carefully to their comments regarding the value, utility, and quality of the series. Librarians, who have firsthand knowledge of the needs of library users, are a valuable resource for us. The *Something about the Author* Product Advisory Board, made up of school, public, and academic librarians, is a forum to promote focused feedback about *SATA* on a regular basis. The nine-member advisory board includes the following individuals, whom the editors wish to thank for sharing their expertise:

SOMETHING ABOUT THE AUTHOR

ANDERSON, Derek 1969-

Personal

Born March 21, 1969; son of Marvin (a physicist) and Carol (a teacher) Anderson. *Education:* Iowa State University, B.F.A. (drawing and painting).

Addresses

Home—Minneapolis, MN.

Career

Children's book writer and illustrator. Designer and sculptor of figurines for Warner Brothers and Disney.

Awards, Honors

Children's Choice Award, International Reading Association/Children's Book Council (IRA/CBC), and National Parenting Publication Gold Award, both c. 2003, both for *Little Quack* by Lauren Thompson; National Parenting Publication Gold Award, 2005, for *Little Quack's Bedtime* by Thompson; IRA/CBC Children's Choice selection, 2006, for *Little Quack's New Friend* by Thompson; Best Children's Book selection, Bank Street College of Education, 2009, for *Ballyhoo Bay* by Judy Sierra; Best Children's Books of the Year selection, Bank Street College of Education, and Parents' Choice Award, both 2010, and South Carolina Picture Book Award, 2012, all for *Hot Rod Hamster* by Cynthia Lord; Best Children's Book selection, 2012, for *Happy Birthday, Hamster* by Lord.

Writings

SELF-ILLUSTRATED

Gladys Goes out to Lunch, Simon & Schuster Books for Young Readers (New York, NY), 2005.

Over the River: A Turkey's Tale, Simon & Schuster Books for Young Readers (New York, NY), 2005.

Blue Burt's Bluff, Simon & Schuster Books for Young Readers (New York, NY), 2006.

How the Easter Bunny Saved Christmas, Simon & Schuster Books for Young Readers (New York, NY), 2006.

Blue Burt and Wiggles, Simon & Schuster Books for Young Readers (New York, NY), 2006.

Romeo and Lou Blast Off, Simon & Schuster Books for Young Readers (New York, NY), 2007.

Story County: Here We Come!, Orchard Books (New York, NY), 2011.

ILLUSTRATOR

Vaunda Micheaux Nelson, *Ready? Set. Raymond!,* Random House (New York, NY), 2002.

Lydia Maria Child, *Over the River: A Turkey Tale, Hot Rod Hamster* Simon & Schuster Books for Young Readers (New York, NY), 2005.

David Hochman and Ruth Kennison, *The Potty Train,Hot Rod Hamster* by Cynthia Lord2008.

Judy Sierra, *Ballyhoo Bay,* Simon & Schuster Books for Young Readers (New York, NY), 2009.

Cynthia Lord, *Hot Rod Hamster,* Scholastic Press (New York, NY), 2010.

Cynthia Lord, *Happy Birthday, Hamster,* Scholastic Press (New York, NY), 2011.
Jane Yolen, *Waking Dragons,* Simon & Schuster Books for Young Readers (New York, NY), 2012.

ILLUSTRATOR; "LITTLE QUACK" PICTURE-BOOK SERIES

Lauren Thompson, *Little Quack,* Simon & Schuster Books for Young Readers (New York, NY), 2003.
Lauren Thompson, *Little Quack's Hide and Seek,* Simon & Schuster Books for Young Readers (New York, NY), 2004.
Lauren Thompson, *Little Quack's Bedtime,* Simon & Schuster Books for Young Readers (New York, NY), 2005.
Lauren Thompson, *Little Quack's New Friend,* Simon & Schuster Books for Young Readers (New York, NY), 2006.
Lauren Thompson, *Little Quack Dial-a-Duck,* Little Simon (New York, NY), 2006.
Lauren Thompson, *Little Quack's Bath Book,* Little Simon (New York, NY), 2006.
Lauren Thompson, *Little Quack Counts,* Little Simon (New York, NY), 2009.
Lauren Thompson, *Little Quack Loves Colors,* Little Simon (New York, NY), 2009.
Lauren Thompson, *Little Quack's ABC's,* Little Simon (New York, NY), 2010.
Lauren Thompson, *Little Quack's Opposites,* Little Simon (New York, NY), 2010.

Sidelights

Perhaps best known for his work as the illustrator of Lauren Thompson's "Little Quack" series of picture books about a tiny duckling, Derek Anderson has also created several original self-illustrated stories, among them *Gladys Goes out to Lunch, How the Easter Bunny Saved Christmas,* and *Story County: Here We Come!* Anderson recognized that he had a passion for drawing when he was in kindergarten; as he told *SATA* regarding his career decision, "Somehow I don't think I ever really had a choice. Writing and painting chose me." Praising his artwork for *Little Quack,* Connie Fletcher noted in *Booklist* that the volume's "charm is in Anderson's comical, eye-commanding acrylics."

Derek Anderson's illustrations for Lauren Thompson's* Little Quack *follows the story of a little duckling that is encouraged to leave the safety of his nest for adventures in the outside world. (Illustration copyright © 2003 by Derek Anderson. Reprinted with the permission of Simon & Schuster Books for Young Readers, an imprint of Simon & Schuster Children's Publishing Division.)

In *Over the River: A Turkey's Tale* the author/illustrator's "amusing acrylic artwork provides a new twist on a favorite holiday song," according to *School Library Journal* reviewer Roxanne Burg. As a family of turkeys makes its way through the woods on the way to Grandma Turkey's house, it encounters a wide array of characters, some comical and some mischievous. "Children will enjoy looking at the entertaining illustrations and comparing the chaos pictured there to the words of the old song," predicted Burg, while a *Kirkus Reviews* critic maintained that "young readers will be . . . captivated by the fracas in Anderson's big, exuberant cartoons."

In *Gladys Goes out to Lunch* Anderson once again captivates story-hour audiences with his bright, vibrantly colored illustrations. When Gladys, a purple-and-blue gorilla with a passion for bananas, catches a whiff of something wonderful in the air, she is determined to find out what it is. Readers follow Gladys as she visits a variety of restaurants, none of which proves to be the source of the intriguing and appetizing smell. As the gorilla meanders back to the zoo, the answer is revealed: a vendor's cart parked near Gladys's home is filled to the brim with banana bread! "This humorous book will tickle children and could also fit well into a unit of the five senses," stated Judith Constantinides in her review of *Gladys Goes out to Lunch* for *School Library Journal.* A *Kirkus Reviews* critic commented that, "like Gladys's bananas, Anderson's story is simple comfort food, with eye-candy artwork providing a welcome dash of spice."

Another self-illustrated story by Anderson, *Blue Burt and Wiggles* concerns the efforts of two animal friends who wish to delay the onset of winter. Determined to extend the summer season, Blue Burt the bird and Wiggles the worm use their artistic talents to keep the forest looking green and the sky sunny . . . until a change in the weather renders their efforts futile. A writer in *Kirkus Reviews* applauded the "expressive and adorable main characters" in *Blue Burt and Wiggles* and described the picture book as "pure pleasure."

Another humorous tale, *How the Easter Bunny Saved Christmas,* finds Mrs. Claus calling for help when Santa injures himself just before the holiday. Although Easter Bunny is a willing worker, he makes a slew of mis-

***Anderson mixes a humorous story with his whimsical line-and-wash art in his original picture book* Story Country.** (Copyright © 2011 by Derek Anderson. Reproduced with permission of Orchard Books, an imprint of Scholastic, Inc.)

takes—including placing gifts under the wrong trees—until the reindeer team up and set things right. "A fast pace, broad humor and silly puns add to the effort," remarked a *Kirkus Reviews* critic in reviewing Anderson's holiday-themed tale, and a *Publishers Weekly* contributor suggested that *How the Easter Bunny Saved Christmas* will "tickle younger readers' funnybones."

A penguin and his polar bear pal take a trip aboard a rocket ship in *Romeo and Lou Blast Off,* another self-illustrated tale. After building a rocket ship from snow, the two friends are magically transported to a strange "planet" (in reality, a large city) where they encounter "walruses" (mustachioed construction workers) and a "shark" (a toothy policeman). "The big bold depictions of the characters have plenty of detail," Catherine Callegari observed in her *School Library Journal* review of the book, and Carolyn Phelan stated in *Booklist* that *Romeo and Lou Blast Off* "resembles an old-fashioned animated kids' cartoon."

Anderson's whimsical illustrations take center stage in *Story County,* as a farmer and four barnyard animals transform the book's empty pages into a colorful working farm. A *Kirkus Reviews* writer praised the author/illustrator's "metafictional worldbuilding," and a contributor in *Publishers Weekly* commented that "Anderson demonstrates that storytelling is much more than just what happens."

In addition to illustrating Thompson's "Little Quack" books, Anderson has contributed artwork to stories by several other authors. Judy Sierra's *Ballyhoo Bay* centers on an art teacher who tries to save a pristine beach from developers. Here Anderson's pictures "have a buoyancy that captures the sparkle of the seaside setting," according to *School Library Journal* contributor Sally R. Dow.

Hot Rod Hamster, a story by Cynthia Lord, finds a confident and energetic rodent entering his homemade car in a big race. According to *Booklist* critic Daniel Kraus, "Anderson's acrylics are boisterously large, colorful, and off-kilter—just like his swaggering protagonist." In Lord's companion story, *Happy Birthday, Hamster,* the rodent's friends plan a surprise party right under his unsuspecting nose. "Loud, exaggerated acrylics burst off the pages," explained Julie Roach in her *School Library Journal* review of this picture book.

"I've found my purpose," Anderson told *SATA*. "I knew from a very early age that I wanted to tell stories with words and pictures. And when I re-discovered children's picture books shortly before graduating from college, I found the outlet I was after. It took years of hard work and rejection to finally break through and get published, but I've never once second-guessed my decision to pursue the world of children's books.

"There is nothing more exciting to me than making books. Sitting down with a new story and my sketchbook at the beginning of the process is both overwhelming and an endless thrill. I don't like being off balance and out of control any more than anyone else, but I've found it to be a necessary part of the journey. If I knew where I was going, it would ruin the process of discovery that I've come to enjoy so much. I've learned to trust my own persistence. I have faith that every time I start work on a new book, I will find a way—that if I stick with it long enough, I'll stumble onto something wonderful and conjure a world and characters that didn't exist before I came along.

"The most important quality I can think of when coming to a new book is retaining a sense of wonder about the world. Deep inside me lives the six-year-old boy that I once was. He's a boy who still believes in magic, refuses to accept that he doesn't have super powers, and looks at the world with a sense of great awe. That's who I make my books for. I know that if I continue to push myself and explore new approaches with story, characters, and how I describe them in paint—that boy will enjoy my books and others will too."

Biographical and Critical Sources

PERIODICALS

Booklist, February 1, 2003, Connie Fletcher, review of *Little Quack,* p. 1002; November 1, 2007, Carolyn Phelan, review of *Romeo and Lou Blast Off,* p. 55; December 1, 2009, Daniel Kraus, review of *Hot Rod Hamster,* p. 50.

Kirkus Reviews, June 1, 2005, review of *Gladys Goes out to Lunch,* p. 632; September 15, 2005, review of *Over the River: A Turkey's Tale,* p. 1019; July 1, 2006, review of *Blue Burt and Wiggles,* p. 673; November 1, 2006, review of *How the Easter Bunny Saved Christmas,* p. 1126; October 15, 2007, review of *Romeo and Lou Blast Off*; December 15, 2009, review of *Hot Rod Hamster*; December 15, 2010, review of *Story County: Here We Come!*

Publishers Weekly, November 11, 2002, review of *Little Quack,* p. 62; June 30, 2003 "Flying Starts," p. 18; February 9, 2004, "More Duck and Bunny Tales," p. 83; September 25, 2006, review of *How the Easter Bunny Saved Christmas,* p. 69; January 11, 2010, review of *Hot Rod Hamster,* p. 46; November 15, 2010, review of *Story County,* p. 55; June 27, 2011, review of *Happy Birthday, Hamster,* p. 156.

School Library Journal, December, 2002, Kay Bowes, review of *Ready? Set. Raymond!,* p. 104; August, 2005, Judith Constantinides, review of *Gladys Goes out to Lunch,* p. 84; October, 2005, Roxanne Burg, review of *Over the River,* p. 102; October, 2006, Lisa Falk, review of *How the Easter Bunny Saved Christmas,* p. 94; January, 2008, Catherine Callegari, review of *Romeo and Lou Blast Off,* p. 80, and Gay Lynn Van Vleck, review of *The Potty Train,* p. 88; February, 2009, Sally R. Dow, review of *Ballyhoo Bay,* p. 86; January, 2010, Sara Paulson-Yarovoy, review of *Hot Rod Hamster,* p. 77; October, 2011, Julie Roach, review of *Happy Birthday, Hamster,* p. 112.

ONLINE

Derek Anderson Home Page, http://www.derekanderson.net (May 15, 2012).

* * *

ASHBURN, Boni

Personal

Children: four. *Education:* University of Colorado, degree.

Addresses

Home—Houghton, MI. *E-mail*—boni@charter.net.

Career

Writer. Manager of family grocery store.

Member

Society of Children's Book Writers and Illustrators.

Awards, Honors

Best Children's Books of the Year selection, Bank Street College of Education, 2011, for *Over at the Castle,* 2012, for *I Had a Favorite Dress.*

Writings

Hush, Little Dragon, illustrated by Kelly Murphy, Abrams Books for Young Readers (New York, NY), 2008.

Over at the Castle, illustrated by Kelly Murphy, Abrams Books for Young Readers (New York, NY), 2010.

I Had a Favorite Dress, illustrated by Julia Denos, Abrams Books for Young Readers (New York, NY), 2011.

Builder Goose: It's Construction Rhyme Time!, illustrated by Sergio De Giorgi, Sterling (New York, NY), 2012.

Sidelights

An avid reader who once dreamed of becoming a librarian, Boni Ashburn decided to write her own stories after falling in love with picture books when her children were young. Since the publication of her debut story, *Hush, Little Dragon,* Ashburn has created several other tales, among them *I Had a Favorite Dress, Over at the Castle,* and *Builder Goose: It's Construction Rhyme Time!,* the last featuring colorful artwork by Argentine illustrator Sergio De Giorgi.

Inspired by the traditional lullaby "Hush, Little Baby," Ashburn's humorous bedtime story *Hush, Little Dragon* centers on a mother dragon's efforts to settle her dragonling down for the night. When Baby Dragon demands a treat before going to bed, Mama offers him a host of deliciously human options, including a princess, a magician, and a musketeer. The dragons make a return appearance in *Over at the Castle,* a counting book set to the rhythm of the folk song "Over in the Meadow." As they keep watch over an ever-increasing number of soldiers, servants, and jesters, Mama and Baby Dragon wait patiently for their chance to amaze the castle's inhabitants with their fire-breathing skills. Ashburn's "comedic touches" in *Over at the Castle* "deepen the story and will have children flipping back through the pages," remarked *Booklist* critic Patricia Austin.

In *I Had a Favorite Dress* a young girl discovers that the beloved frock she wears every Tuesday has become too small for her. With her mother's help, the girl redesigns the dress into a comfortable shirt, and as she continues to grow the fabric of the dress is reworked as a tank top, a skirt, a scarf, and eventually a hair ribbon. *I Had a Favorite Dress* "is sure to capture the imaginations of would-be seamstresses," Catherine Callegari predicted in her *School Library Journal* review, and Pamela Paul praised the story in the *New York Times Book Review,* stating that "What could have been yet another example of kindergarten consumerism instead becomes one of resourcefulness and resilience."

Boni Ashburn's story in* I Had a Favorite Dress *is brought to life in colorful art by Julia Denos. (Illustration © copyright 2011 by Julia Denos. Reproduced by permission of Abrams Books for Young Readers, an imprint of ABRAMS.)

Biographical and Critical Sources

PERIODICALS

Booklist, March 1, 2010, Patricia Austin, review of *Over at the Castle,* p. 80; March 1, 2012, John Peters, review of *Builder Goose: It's Construction Rhyme Time!,* p. 71.

Children's Bookwatch, May, 2008, review of *Hush, Little Dragon*; September, 2011, review of *I Had a Favorite Dress.*

Kirkus Reviews, July 15, 2011, review of *I Had a Favorite Dress.*

New York Times Book Review, September 22, 2011, Pamela Paul, review of *I Had a Favorite Dress.*

School Librarian, summer, 2010, Jayne Gould, review of *Over at the Castle,* p. 87.

School Library Journal, May, 2010, Amy Rowland, review of *Over at the Castle,* p. 79; August, 2011, Catherine Callegari, review of *I Had a Favorite Dress,* p. 67.

ONLINE

Boni Ashburn Home Page, http://www.boniashburn.com (March 15, 2012).

Seven Impossible Things before Breakfast Web log, http://sevenimpossiblethings.blaine.com/ (August 31, 2010), interview with Ashburn.

BARROWS, Annie 1962-

Personal

Born 1962, in San Diego, CA; married; children: two. *Education:* University of California, Berkeley, B.A. (medieval history); Mills College, M.F.A. (creative writing).

Addresses

Home—Berkeley, CA. *E-mail*—annie@anniebarrows.com.

Career

Author and editor.

Awards, Honors

100 Titles for Reading and Sharing inclusion, New York Public Library, and Best New Books for the Classroom designation, *Booklinks,* both 2006, and American Library Association Notable Children's Book designation, and *Booklist* Editor's Choice and Best Books designations, all 2007, all for *Ivy and Bean;* Maud Hart Lovelace Award nominee, and nomination for several state book awards, all 2011, all for *The Magic Half.*

Writings

(With aunt Mary Ann Shaffer) *The Guernsey Literary and Potato Peel Pie Society* (adult novel), Dial Press (New York, NY), 2008.

The Magic Half, Bloomsbury Children's Books (New York, NY), 2008.

"IVY AND BEAN" CHAPTER-BOOK SERIES

Ivy and Bean, illustrated by Sophie Blackall, Chronicle Books (San Francisco, CA), 2006.

Ivy and Bean and the Ghost That Had to Go, illustrated by Sophie Blackall, Chronicle Books (San Francisco, CA), 2006.

Ivy and Bean Break the Fossil Record, illustrated by Sophie Blackall, Chronicle Books (San Francisco, CA), 2007.

Ivy and Bean Take Care of the Babysitter, illustrated by Sophie Blackall, Chronicle Books (San Francisco, CA), 2008.

Ivy and Bean: Bound to Be Bad, illustrated by Sophie Blackall, Chronicle Books (San Francisco, CA), 2008.

Ivy and Bean: Doomed to Dance, illustrated by Sophie Blackall, Chronicle Books (San Francisco, CA), 2009.

Ivy and Bean: What's the Big Idea?, illustrated by Sophie Blackall, Chronicle Books (San Francisco, CA), 2010.

Ivy and Bean: No News Is Good News, illustrated by Sophie Blackall, Chronicle Books (San Francisco, CA), 2011.

Annie Barrows (Photograph by Annie Frantzeskos. Reproduced by permission.)

Sidelights

Annie Barrows worked as a professional editor before beginning her career as an author. She began writing for children when she realized that some stories captured her daughters' interest and others did not. In her popular and award-winning "Ivy and Bean" chapter-book series, Barrows captures the ups and downs of a special type of childhood friendship: one that weathers differences and disagreements with lightheartedness, loyalty, and affection. Illustrated by Sophie Blackall, the "Ivy and Bean" stories include *Ivy and Bean, Ivy and Bean Break the Fossil Record, Ivy and Bean Take Care of the Babysitter,* and *No News Is Good News,* among others.

Readers first meet quiet and imaginative Ivy and fun-loving, mischievous, and energetic Bean in *Ivy and Bean,* which captures the early days of their relationship as neighbors living on Pancake Court. Although their moms are good friends, Ivy and Bean do not share the same affinity. Things change when Bean gets in trouble with her sister Nancy and Ivy uses her ability as a witch-in-training to cast the spell that solves the problem. It is then that the two girls realize that they go together like salt goes with pepper.

Ivy and Bean return in *Ivy and Bean and the Ghost That Had to Go,* which finds a spectre haunting the halls of the girls' elementary school, and Bean's ambition to see her name in the world-record books fuels *Ivy and Bean Break the Fossil Record.* Being baby-sat by an older sister is truly torture, at least according to Bean in *Ivy and Bean Take Care of the Babysitter,* and Ivy convinces her bff to join her in her challenge to be really, really GOOD in *Ivy and Bean: Bound to Be Bad.* The trials of ballet class, teaming up to create an entry in the school science fair, and finding ways to make money provide the drama in other stories in Barrows' "Ivy and Bean" series.

Calling Barrows and Blackall an "inspired writer-artist team" in the same league as Eleanor Estes and Louis Slobodkin, who produced such classic stories as *The Hundred Dresses* during the mid-twentieth century, a *Kirkus Reviews* writer added that *Ivy and Bean Take Care of the Babysitter* "celebrates the joys and thrills of friendship, unrestricted play and unfettered imagination." *Ivy and Bean Break the Fossil Record* captures the girls' "wonderful, positive relationship" as well as their unique personalities, according to *School Library Journal* critic Sharon R. Pearce, and the black-and-white illustrations highlight Barrows' entertaining story "with wry, spiky visuals that capture the kids' personalities perfectly," according to another *Kirkus Reviews* contributor. Calling *Bound to Be Bad* "another laugh-out-loud . . . romp" from the author/illustrator team, a third *Kirkus Reviews* critic added that the story "derives its humor from the very believable characters and chemistry" of the childhood friends. "Ivy and Bean are bound to satisfy fans and garner new ones," predicted *Horn Book* contributor Jennifer M. Brabander of the same series installment, while in *School Library Journal* Adrienne Furness asserted that *Ivy and Bean and the Ghost That Had to Go* "defies expectations of what an early chapter book can be."

In addition to her "Ivy and Bean" chapter books, Barrows has written *The Magic Half,* the story of an eleven-year-old girl whose older and younger siblings are twins. Although Miri feels lonely with no twin companion of her own, a move to a new house leads her into a time-travel adventure that bonds her to a new friend in need of her help. In *The Magic Half* "Barrows conjures up a delightful tale brimming with mystery, magic, and adventure," asserted *School Library Journal* critic Laura Butler, the reviewer predicting that Barrows' story "will surely enchant readers everywhere."

Barrows' skills as an editor also allowed her to help her aunt, Mary Ann Shaffer, complete the manuscript of an historical novel set on the British Channel Islands during World War II. Written when Shaffer was elderly and infirm, the novel was completed and edited by Barrows and published after Shaffer's death as *The Guernsey Literary and Potato Peel Pie Society.*

***Barrows teams up with artist Sophie Blackall on her "Ivy and Bean" series, which includes* Ivy and Bean Take Care of the Babysitter.** (Illustration © copyright by Sophie Blackall. Used with permission of Chronicle Books, LLC, San Francisco. Visit ChronicleBooks.com.)

Biographical and Critical Sources

PERIODICALS

Booklist, April 1, 2006, Ilene Cooper, review of *Ivy and Bean,* p. 42; October 15, 2006, Ilene Cooper, review of *Ivy and Bean and the Ghost That Had to Go,* p. 44; July 1, 2007, Kay Weisman, review of *Ivy and Bean Break the Fossil Record,* p. 58; February 1, 2008, Ilene Cooper, review of *The Magic Half,* p. 46; July 1, 2008, Mary Ellen Quinn, review of *The Guernsey Literary and Potato Peel Pie Society,* p. 34; February 1, 2009, Ilene Cooper, review of *Ivy and Bean: Bound to Be Bad,* p. 44.

Bulletin of the Center for Children's Books, June, 2006, Deborah Stevenson, review of *Ivy and Bean,* p. 440.

Horn Book, July-August, 2008, Jennifer M. Brabander, review of *Ivy and Bean Take Care of the Babysitter,* p. 438; March-April, 2009, Jennifer M. Brabander, review of *Ivy and Bean: Bound to Be Bad,* p. 191; January-February, 2010, Jennifer M. Brabander, review of *Ivy and Bean: Doomed to Dance,* p. 80; November-December, 2010, Jennifer M. Brabander, review of *Ivy and Bean: What's the Big Idea?,* p. 85.

Kirkus Reviews, May 1, 2006, review of *Ivy and Bean,* p. 454; June 1, 2007, review of *Ivy and Bean Break the Fossil Record*; December 1, 2007, review of *The*

Magic Half; August 1, 2008, review of *Ivy and Bean Take Care of the Babysitter*; December 15, 2008, review of *Ivy and Bean: Bound to Be Bad.*

Library Journal, July 1, 2008, Susan Clifford Braun, review of *The Guernsey Literary and Potato Peel Pie Society,* p. 67.

Publishers Weekly, May 15, 2006, review of *Ivy and Bean,* p. 72; December 17, 2007, review of *The Magic Half,* p. 51; April 21, 2008, review of *The Guernsey Literary and Potato Peel Pie Society,* p. 30.

School Library Journal, July, 2006, Even Ottenberg Stone, review of *Ivy and Bean,* p. 68; February, 2007, Adrienne Furness, review of *Ivy and Bean and the Ghost That Had to Go,* p. 84; July, 2007, Sharon R. Pearce, review of *Ivy and Bean Break the Fossil Record,* p. 67; December, 2008, Laura Butler, review of *The Magic Half,* p. 118; January, 2010, Sarah Polace, review of *Ivy and Bean: Doomed to Dance,* p. 68.

Tribune Books (Chicago, IL), January 7, 2007, Mary Harris Russell, review of *Ivy and Bean and the Ghost That Had to Go,* p. 7.

ONLINE

Annie Barrows Home Page, http://www.anniebarrows.com (May 1, 2012).

* * *

BASS, Guy

Personal

Born in England; married.

Addresses

Home—London, England. *Office*— *Agent*—Stephanie Thwaites, Curtis Brown Groups, Ltd., Haymarket House, 28-29 Haymarket, London SW1Y 4SP, England. *E-mail*—guy@guybass.com.

Career

Author. Worked as an actor and theatrical producer.

Awards, Honors

Blue Peter Book Award for Most Fun Book with Pictures, 2010, for *Dinkin Dings and the Frightening Things;* two Portsmouth (UK) Book Awards for Shorter Novel, for "Dinkin Dings" series.

Writings

Secret Santa, Agent of X.M.A.S., illustrated by David Lopez, Stripes (London, England), 2010, Scholastic (New York, NY), 2011.

Alien Invasion!, Scholastic (London, England), 2010.

Alien Escape!, Scholastic (London, England), 2010.

Stitch Head, illustrated by Pete Williamson, Stripes (London, England) 2011.

Stitch Head: The Pirate's Eye, illustrated by Pete Williamson, Stripes (London, England) 2012.

Atomic: The Vengeance of Vinister Vile, illustrated by Jamie Littler, Scholastic (London, England), 2012.

Atomic: The Madness of Madame Malice, illustrated by Jamie Littler, Scholastic (London, England), 2012.

Author of stage plays for children. Contributor to books, including *The Vesuvius Club Graphic Edition,* by Mark Gatiss, Simon & Schuster (London, England), 2005.

Work has been translated into seven languages.

"GORMY RUCKLES" SERIES

Monster Boy, illustrated by Ross Collins, Scholastic (London, England), 2008.

Monster Mischief, illustrated by Ross Collins, Scholastic (London, England), 2008.

Monster Hero, illustrated by Ross Collins, Scholastic (London, England), 2008.

Monster Trouble, illustrated by Ross Collins, Scholastic (London, England), 2009.

Monster Birthday, illustrated by Ross Collins, Scholastic (London, England), 2009.

Monster Contest, illustrated by Ross Collins, Scholastic (London, England), 2009.

Monster Madness (omnibus), illustrated by Ross Collins, Scholastic (London, England), 2011.

Monster Mayhem (omnibus), illustrated by Ross Collins, Scholastic (London, England), 2011.

"DINKIN DINGS" SERIES

Dinkin Dings and the Frightening Things, illustrated by Pete Williamson, Stripes (London, England), 2009, Grosset & Dunlap (New York, NY), 2011.

Dinkin Dings and the Curse of Clawfingers, illustrated by Pete Williamson, Stripes (London, England), 2009.

Dinkin Dings and the Revenge of the Fish-Men, illustrated by Pete Williamson, Stripes (London, England), 2009.

Dinkin Dings and the Double from Dimension 9, illustrated by Pete Williamson, Stripes (London, England), 2010, Grosset & Dunlap (New York, NY), 2011.

Biographical and Critical Sources

PERIODICALS

Kirkus Reviews, February 15, 2011, review of *Dinkin Dings and the Frightening Things.*

School Library Journal, April, 2011, Elizabeth Swistock, review of *Dinkin Dings and the Frightening Things,* p. 139.

ONLINE

Guy Bass Home Page, http://www.guybass.com (May 1, 2012).
Guy Bass Web log, http://guybass.blogspot.com (May 1, 2012).
Scholastic Web site, http://www5.scholastic.co.uk/ (May 1, 2012), "Guy Bass."

* * *

BERKLEY, Elizabeth 1972-

Personal

Born July 28, 1972, in Farmington Hills, MI; daughter of Fred (a lawyer) and Jere (a business owner) Berkley; married Greg Lauren (an artist and actor), November 1, 2003.

Addresses

Home—New York, NY; and Los Angeles, CA.

Career

Actor, motivational speaker, and writer. Founder of Ask-Elizabeth (nonprofit organization), 2006—. Actor in films, including *Showgirls,* 1995, *Any Given Sunday,* 1999; *The Curse of the Jade Scorpion,* 2001; *Roger Dodger,* 2002; *Meet Market,* 2008; and *S. Darko,* 2009. Actor in television series, including *Saved by the Bell,* 1988-93; *CSI: Miami,* 2008-09; and *The L Word,* 2009. Actor in plays, including *Lenny,* 1999; and *Sly Fox,* 2003.

Writings

Ask Elizabeth: Real Answers to Everything You Secretly Wanted to Ask about Love, Friends, Your Body . . . and Life in General, G.P. Putnam's Sons (New York, NY), 2011.

Sidelights

Perhaps best known for her role as the brainy and opinionated Jessie Spano on the wildly popular 1990s sitcom *Saved by the Bell,* Elizabeth Berkley is also the founder of Ask Elizabeth, a nonprofit organization devoted to the well being of teenage girls. Through her Web site, www.Ask-Elizabeth.com, and self-esteem workshops held in middle schools and high schools across the United States, Berkley counsels teens on a variety of issues, including body image, family dynamics, sex, nutrition, and beauty.

The origins of Ask Elizabeth can be traced to Berkley's television career. After *Saved by the Bell* began airing in syndication, it reached a new generation of viewers. Soon the actress was approached by autograph seekers, often young women who sought her advice on personal matters. Berkley's husband suggested that she begin writing an advice column for teens, and this led to an interactive workshop that proved popular in classrooms. "The whole thing spread completely through word-of-mouth," Berkley told *New York* interviewer Alyssa Giacobbe. "Teachers started telling each other about me, and I started finding myself on planes. I just kept showing up."

Ask Elizabeth workshops are a collaborative experience: participants share their questions and concerns with one another and Berkley openly discusses experiences from her own life. As she remarked to *Teenreads.com* interviewer Jordana Frankel, "I am there as a facilitator—to guide the girls and to create a safe space for them to feel heard and to remind them they have value. The spirit in which I do this is speaking with them—never at them. Think big sister-style girl talk, but always leading/guiding the dialogue."

Repeated requests to share her advice in a book prompted Berkley to gather testimonials and questions into the self-help guide *Ask Elizabeth: Real Answers to Everything You Secretly Wanted to Ask about Love, Friends, Your Body . . . and Life in General.* The book

Cover of Elizabeth Berkley's teen self-help guide* Ask Elizabeth, *an outgrowth of the author's work with adolescent girls. (Copyright © 2011 by Elizabeth Berkley. Reproduced by permission of G.P. Putnam's Sons, a division of Penguin Group (USA), Inc.)

includes material drawn from Berkley's workshops as well as from social media like Skype and iChat. "At every step, girls were moved and empowered to share their stories to help another girl they may never meet in their life," the author/actress told Frankel. "I think we were all transformed from the experience together—knowing the impact our past stories might have on empowering another's present."

Formatted like a diary, complete with collage elements, *Ask Elizabeth* offers guidance on topics from romance to bullying to self-identity. "Berkley maintains a chatty, direct voice throughout that contributes to the accessibility of the work," a writer in *Kirkus Reviews* observed, and a *Publishers Weekly* critic stated that the author's honesty about her own life "lends the project qualities of rare intimacy and grace." Asked what she hopes readers gain from the work, Berkley remarked to Frankel: "I hope they are filled with comfort, own their power, and feel strengthened, seen and gotten. I also hope they know they are a part of a sisterhood of girls who support them with me—they are not alone and they are now armed with tools to make the path a bit more gentle and clear."

Biographical and Critical Sources

PERIODICALS

Kirkus Reviews, February 15, 2011, *Ask Elizabeth: Real Answers to Everything You Secretly Wanted to Ask about Love, Friends, Your Body . . . and Life in General.*

New York, May 2, 2011, Alyssa Giacobbe, "59 Minutes With Elizabeth Berkley; In Towering Heels, the Former Teen Star Talks Body Image, Mean Girls, and Her Unlikely New Calling as a Professional Teen Advice-Giver."

Philadelphia Inquirer, April 21, 2011, Tirdad Derakhshani, Former Sitcom Star Berkley Turns to Helping Teens."

Publishers Weekly, February 7, 2011, review of *Ask Elizabeth,* p. 59.

School Library Journal, May, 2011, Elaine Baran Black, review of *Ask Elizabeth,* p. 129.

Voice of Youth Advocates, June, 2011, review of *Ask Elizabeth,* p. 198.

ONLINE

Ask-Elizabeth Web site, http://ask-elizabeth.com/ (April 15, 2012).

Teenreads.com, http://www.teenreads.com/ (May, 2011), Jordana Frankel, interview with Berkley.*

* * *

BLISS, Frederick
See CARD, Orson Scott

BURGIS, Stephanie

Personal

Born in East Lansing, MI; immigrated to United Kingdom; married Patrick Samphire (a writer and Web designer); children: one son. *Education:* Attended Michigan State University; Oberlin College, B.M.; graduate study at University of Vienna; University of Pittsburgh, M.A. (music history).

Addresses

Home—Wales. *Agent*—Barry Goldblatt Literary, LLC, 320 7th Ave., No. 266, Brooklyn, NY 11215.

Career

Writer. Worked as an English-language teacher in Vienna, Austria, and as a Web-site editor for an opera company in England.

Awards, Honors

Fulbright scholarship; Fountain Award nomination, Speculative Literature Foundation, 2004, for "Giant"; Small Press Award finalist, Washington Science Fiction Association, 2007, for "Ivy and Thorn"; British Fantasy Award nomination, Branford Boase Award nomination, Best Children's Books of the Year selection, Bank Street College of Education, and Notable Children's Book nominee, American Library Association, all 2011, all for *Kat, Incorrigible.*

Writings

"UNLADYLIKE ADVENTURES OF KAT STEPHENSON" SERIES

A Most Improper Magick, Templar Publishing (Dorking, England), 2010, published as *Kat, Incorrigible,* Atheneum Books for Young Readers (New York, NY), 2011.

A Tangle of Magicks, Templar Publishing (Dorking, England), 2011, published as *Renegade Magic,* Atheneum Books for Young Readers (New York, NY), 2012.

OTHER

Contributor of short stories to anthologies, including *White Knuckles: Tales of Terror by American Teen Writers,* edited by Kathryn Kulpa, Merlyn's Pen, 1995. Contributor to periodicals, including *Aeon, Flytrap, Grendelsong,* and *Strange Horizons.*

Sidelights

An American-born writer now living in Wales, Stephanie Burgis is the creator of the "Unladylike Adventures of Kat Stephenson" series, featuring a clever and scrappy

heroine who possesses the gift of magic. Set in the Regency era, Burgis's novels are equally influenced by J.R.R. Tolkien's "Lord of the Rings" saga and Jane Austen's *Pride and Prejudice,* which her father read to her as a child. As the author recalled on her home page, "Writing the 'Kat' books was my chance to finally combine the two kinds of stories I love best."

Born and raised in Michigan, Burgis decided to become a writer at age seven and she sold her first short story as a teenager. Despite her interest in literature, she studied music in college, eventually pursuing her doctorate. "The best thing I did as preparation for the 'Kat' books was to become a Ph.D. student in music history," she told R.L. LaFevers in an *Enchanted Inkpot* online interview. While working at the University of Leeds, Burgis noted, "I kept getting hopelessly sidetracked by the eighteenth-century literature section, devouring letters and diaries of Regency-era British women instead of working on my dissertation. It was like an addiction I couldn't overcome!"

Although she never completed her dissertation, Burgis used this research in writing *A Most Improper Magick,* a novel published in the United States as *Kat, Incorrigible.* Here readers are introduced to Kat Stephenson, a twelve year old who rebels against the strict social customs of her times. After learning that her late mother was a witch, Kat decides to practice magic to prevent her older sister, Elissa, from entering a disastrous marriage engineered by their controlling stepmother. While the girl also intends to help another sibling, Angeline, find her true love, her untamed and misdirected energy draws the attention of the Order of the Guardians, a secret society devoted to the magical arts.

"Regency romance and fantasy adventure all in one, this is a satisfying read," Kathleen Isaacs noted in her *School Library Journal* review of *Kat, Incorrigible.* Debbie Carton, writing in *Booklist,* offered praise for "the delightfully feisty Kat, whose fearless and frequently impulsive actions will have readers cheering her on."

Kat makes a return appearance in *A Tangle of Magicks,* a story known to U.S. readers as *Renegade Magic.* When a scandal threatens to ruin Angeline's reputation, the Stephenson clan heads to the fashionable city of Bath, where Kat's stepmother hopes to find a proper suitor for her middle daughter. Unfortunately, Angeline falls for a notorious womanizer, while Kat's roguish brother Charles joins a group attempting to harness the wild magic of the area's hot springs. Worse still, Kat has been denied admittance to the Order of the Guardians, yet she must employ her still untrained magic to save her family members.

A writer in *Kirkus Reviews* applauded *Renegade Magic* as a "rollicking tale," and *School Library Journal* contributor Misti Tidman remarked that Burgis's "research into early-19th-century England shines through without detracting from the nimble plotting." Taryn Bush, writing in *Voice of Youth Advocates,* complimented the author's fully realized portrayal of Kat, describing her as "fiercely loyal, stubborn, funny, and incredibly likable. Readers will root for her throughout her magical adventures."

Biographical and Critical Sources

PERIODICALS

Booklist, February 15, 2010, Debbie Carton, review of *A Most Improper Magick,* p. 71; March 15, 2012, Debbie Carton, review of *Renegade Magic,* p. 60.

School Librarian, winter, 2010, Janet Sumner, review of *A Most Improper Magick.*

School Library Journal, December, 2010, Kathleen Isaacs, review of *Kat, Incorrigible,* p. 104; March, 2012, Misti Tidman, review of *Renegade Magic,* p. 150.

Voice of Youth Advocates, April, 2012, Taryn Bush, review of *Renegade Magic,* p. 69.

ONLINE

Enchanted Inkpot Web log, http://enchantedinkpot.livejournal.com/ (May 24, 2011), R.L. LaFevers, interview with Burgis.

Shimmer Online, http://www.shimmerzine.com/ (March 26, 2009), interview with Burgis.

Simon & Schuster Web site, http://www.simonandschuster.com/ (April 15, 2012), "Stephanie Burgis."

Stephanie Burgis Home Page, http://www.stephanieburgis.com (April 15, 2012).

Stephanie Burgis Web log, http://stephanieburgis.livejournal.com (April 15, 2012).*

C

CARD, Orson Scott 1951- (Frederick Bliss, Brian Green, P.Q. Gump, Scott Richards, Byron Walley)

Personal

Born August 24, 1951, in Richland, WA; son of Willard Richards (a teacher) and Peggy Jane (a secretary and administrator) Card; married Kristine Allen, May 17, 1977; children: Michael Geoffrey, Emily Janice, Charles Benjamin (deceased), Zina Margaret, Erin Louisa. *Education:* Brigham Young University, B.A. (with distinction), 1975; University of Utah, M.A., 1981; Attended University of Notre Dame. *Politics:* "Moderate Democrat." *Religion:* Church of Jesus Christ of Latter-day Saints (Mormon).

Addresses

Home—Greensboro, NC. *Agent*—Barbara Bova, 3951 Gulf Shore Blvd., No. PH1B, Naples, FL 33940.

Career

Writer, editor, and educator. Volunteer Mormon missionary in Brazil, 1971-73; operated repertory theater in Provo, UT, 1974-75; Brigham Young University Press, Provo, proofreader, 1974, editor, 1974-76; *Ensign* magazine, Salt Lake City, UT, assistant editor, 1976-78; freelance writer and editor, beginning 1978; Compute! Books, Greensboro, NC, senior editor 1983. Teacher at writers' workshops and universities, including University of Utah, 1979-80, 1981, Brigham Young University, 1981, and Clarion Writers Workshop, East Lansing, MI, 1982; writing workshop leader, beginning 2001; Southern Virginia University, distinguished professor, beginning 2005.

Member

Science Fiction Writers of America.

Awards, Honors

John W. Campbell Award for Best New Writer, World Science Fiction Convention, 1978; Hugo Award nominations, World Science Fiction Convention, 1978, 1979, 1980, for short stories, and 1986, for novelette "Hatrack River"; Nebula Award nominations, Science Fiction Writers of America, 1979, 1980, for short stories; Utah State Institute of Fine Arts prize, 1980, for epic poem "Prentice Alvin and the No-Good Plow"; Nebula Award, 1985, and Hugo Award, 1986, both for *Ender's Game;* Nebula Award, 1986, and Hugo Award, and Locus Award, both 1987, all for *Speaker for the Dead;* World Fantasy Award, 1987, for novelette "Hatrack River"; Hugo Award, and Locus Award nomination, both 1988, both for novella "Eye for Eye"; Locus Award for Best

Orson Scott Card (Photograph © Bassouls Sophie/Corbis. Reproduced by permission.)

Fantasy, Hugo Award nomination, World Fantasy Award nomination, and Mythopoeic Fantasy Award, Mythopoeic Society, all 1988, all for *Seventh Son;* Locus Award, 1989, for *Red Prophet;* Hugo Award, 1991, for *How to Write Science Fiction and Fantasy;* Locus Award, 1996, for *Alvin Journeyman;* Geffen Award for Best Science Fiction Book (Israel), 1999, for *Pastwatch;* Grand Prix de L'Imaginaire, 2000, for *Heartfire;* Margaret A. Edwards Award, 2008, for *Ender's Game* and *Ender's Shadow;* Whitney Award for Lifetime Achievement, 2008.

Writings

SCIENCE FICTION AND FANTASY

A Planet Called Treason, St. Martin's Press (New York, NY), 1979, revised edition, Dell (New York, NY), 1980, published as *Treason,* 1988.

Songmaster, Dial (New York, NY), 1980, reprinted, Orb (New York, NY), 2002.

Unaccompanied Sonata, and Other Stories, Dial (New York, NY), 1980.

(Editor) *Dragons of Darkness,* Ace (New York, NY), 1981.

Hart's Hope, Berkley (New York, NY), 1983, reprinted, Orb (New York, NY), 2003.

(Editor) *Dragons of Light,* Ace (New York, NY), 1983.

(With others) *Free Lancers,* Baen (New York, NY), 1987.

Wyrms, Arbor House (New York, NY), 1987, reprinted, Orb (New York, NY), 2003.

Folk of the Fringe (short stories), Phantasia Press (Huntington Woods, MI), 1989.

The Abyss (novelization; based on the screenplay by James Cameron), Pocket Books (New York, NY), 1989.

Eye for Eye (bound with *The Tunesmith* by Lloyd Biggle, Jr.), Tor (New York, NY), 1990.

(Editor) *Future on Fire,* Tor (New York, NY), 1991.

(With Kathryn H. Kidd) *Lovelock* (first novel in "Mayflower" trilogy), Tor (New York, NY), 1994.

Black Mist, and Other Japanese Futures (novella), DAW (New York, NY), 1997.

(Editor) *Future on Ice* (sequel to *Future on Fire*), Tor (New York, NY), 1998.

Magic Mirror, illustrated by Nathan Pinnock, Gibbs Smith (Salt Lake City, UT), 1999.

(Editor) *Masterpieces: The Best Science Fiction of the Century,* Ace Books (New York, NY), 2001.

(Editor, with Keith Olexa) *Empire of Dreams and Miracles: The Phobos Science-Fiction Anthology,* foreword by Lawrence Krauss, Phobos Books (New York, NY), 2002.

(Editor with Keith Olexa) *Hitting the Skids in Pixeltown: The Phobos Science-Fiction Anthology,* volume 1, Phobos Books (New York, NY), 2003, volume 2, with Christian O'Toole, 2003.

(With Doug Chiang) *Robota: Reign of Machines,* Chronicle Books (San Francisco, CA), 2003.

(Under name Scott Richards) *Zanna's Gift: A Life in Christmases,* Forge Books (New York, NY), 2004.

Magic Street, Del Rey/Ballantine Books (New York, NY), 2005.

Empire, Tor (New York, NY), 2006.

The Space Boy, Subterranean Press (New York, NY), 2007.

Keeper of Dreams (short fiction), Tor (New York, NY), 2008.

Orson Scott Card's InterGalactic Medicine Show (story collection; originally published online), Tor (New York, NY), 2008.

The Stonefather (novella; prequel to *The Lost Gate*), Subterranean Press (New York, NY), 2008.

Hidden Empire (sequel to *Empire*) Tor (New York, NY), 2009.

Pathfinder, ("Pathfinder" series), Simon Pulse (New York, NY), 2010.

The Lost Gate ("Mither Mages" series), Tor (New York, NY), 2011.

(With Aaron Johnston) *Dragon Age* (graphic novel; originally published in comic-book form), illustrated by Mark Robinson, IDW, 2011.

Hamlet's Father (novella; originally anthologized in *The Ghost Quartet*), Subterranean (New York, NY), 2011.

(With daughter Emily Janice Card) *Laddertop* (graphic novel), art by Honoel A. Ibardolaza, Tor/Seven Seas (New York, NY), 2011.

Ruins ("Pathfinder" series), Simon Pulse (New York, NY), 2012.

(With Aaron Johnston) *Earth Unaware* ("First Formic War" series), Tor (New York, NY), 2012.

Also author of novelette "Hatrack River," 1986. Work included in numerous anthologies, including *The Bradbury Chronicles: Stories in Honor of Ray Bradbury,* edited by William F. Nolan and Martin H. Greenberg, New American Library (New York, NY), 1991; *The Ghost Quartet,* edited by Marvin Kaye, Tor, 2008; and *Wasteland: Stories of the Apocalypse,* edited by John Joseph Adams, Night Shade Books, 2008.

"WORTHING CHRONICLE" SERIES

Capitol (short stories), Ace (New York, NY), 1978.

Hot Sleep, Baronet (New York, NY), 1978, revised as *The Worthing Chronicle,* Ace (New York, NY), 1983.

The Worthing Saga (omnibus), Tor (New York, NY), 1990.

"ENDER" SCIENCE-FICTION NOVEL SERIES

Ender's Game (also see below), Tor (New York, NY), 1985, published with *Speaker for the Dead,* 1987.

Speaker for the Dead (also see below), Tor (New York, NY), 1986, published with *Ender's Game,* 1987.

Xenocide, Tor (New York, NY), 1991.

Children of the Mind, Tor (New York, NY), 1996.

First Meetings: In the Enderverse (short stories; includes "Ender's Game," "The Polish Boy," and "Teacher's Pest"), Tor (New York, NY), 2003.

A War of Gifts: An Ender Story, Tor (New York, NY), 2007.

Ender in Exile, Tor (New York, NY), 2008.

(Supervising editor) Jake Black, *The Authorized Ender Companion,* Tor (New York, NY), 2009.

Also author, with Aaron Johnston, of comic-book prequel *Formic Wars: Burning Earth,* illustrated by Giancarlo Caracuzzo, Marvel Comics (New York, NY), 2011.

"MAPS IN MIRROR" NOVEL SERIES

Maps in a Mirror: The Short Fiction of Orson Scott Card (includes stories originally published as Byron Walley), Tor (New York, NY), 1990.
The Changed Man, Tor (New York, NY), 1992.
Flux, Tor (New York, NY), 1992.
Cruel Miracles, Tor (New York, NY), 1992.
Monkey Sonatas, Tor (New York, NY), 1993.

"HEGEMON"/"SHADOW" NOVEL SERIES

Ender's Shadow, Tor (New York, NY), 1999.
Shadow of the Hegemon, Tor (New York, NY), 2001.
Shadow Puppets, Tor (New York, NY), 2002.
The Shadow Saga, Orbit (New York, NY), 2003.
Shadow of the Giant, Tor (New York, NY), 2005.
Shadows in Flight, Tor (New York, NY), 2012.

Published in omnibus form, as *Ender's Shadow/Shadow of the Hegemon,* 2002; *Ender's Shadow/Shadow of the Hegemon/Shadow Puppets,* 2003: and *The Ender's Shadow Series Box Set,* 2008.

"TALES OF ALVIN MAKER" NOVEL SERIES

Seventh Son, St. Martin's Press (New York, NY), 1987.
Red Prophet, Tor (New York, NY), 1988.
Prentice Alvin, Tor (New York, NY), 1989.
Hatrack River (originally published in comic-book form), Science Fiction Book Club (Rantoul IL), 1989.
Alvin Journeyman, Tor (New York, NY), 1995.
Heartfire, Tor (New York, NY), 1998.
The Crystal City, Tor (New York, NY), 2003.

Published in omnibus form as *Tales of Alvin Maker: Seventh Son, Red Prophet, and Prentice Alvin,* 1995; and *Alvin Wandering,* 1998.

"HOMECOMING" NOVEL SERIES

The Memory of Earth (also see below), Tor (New York, NY), 1992.
The Call of the Earth (also see below), Tor (New York, NY), 1993.
The Ships of Earth (also see below), Tor (New York, NY), 1993.
Earthfall, Tor (New York, NY), 1994.
Homecoming: Harmony (contains *The Memory of Earth, The Call of Earth,* and *The Ships of Earth*), Science Fiction Book Club (Rantoul IL), 1994.
Earthborn, Tor (New York, NY), 1995.

PLAYS

Tell Me That You Love Me, Junie Moon (adaptation of novel by Marjorie Kellogg), produced in Provo, UT, 1969.
The Apostate, produced in Provo, UT, 1970.
In Flight, produced in Provo, UT, 1970.
Across Five Summers, produced in Provo, UT, 1971.
Of Gideon, produced in Provo, UT, 1971.
Stone Tables, produced in Provo, UT, 1973.
A Christmas Carol (adapted from the story by Charles Dickens), produced in Provo, UT, 1974.
Father, Mother, Mother, and Mom (produced in Provo, UT, 1974), published in *Sunstone,* 1978.
Liberty Jail, produced in Provo, UT, 1975.
Fresh Courage Take, produced in Salt Lake City, UT, 1978.
Elders and Sisters (adaptation of novel by Gladys Farmer), produced in American Fork, UT, 1979.
(Author of book and lyrics) *Barefoot to Zion* (musical), music composed by Arlen L. Card, produced in North Salt Lake City, UT, 1997.

"WOMEN OF GENESIS" NOVEL SERIES

Sarah, Shadow Mountain (Salt Lake City, UT), 2000.
Rebekah, Shadow Mountain (Salt Lake City, UT), 2001.
Rachel and Leah, Shadow Mountain (Salt Lake City, UT), 2004.

"ULTIMATE IRON MAN" GRAPHIC-NOVEL SERIES

Ultimate Iron Man, Volume 1, illustrated by Andy Kubert and Pasqual Ferry, Marvel Comics (New York, NY), 2001.
Ultimate Iron Man, Volume 2, illustrated by Andy Kubert and Pasqual Ferry, Marvel Comics (New York, NY), 2006.
Ultimate Iron Man: Ultimate Collection (omnibus), illustrated by Andy Kubert and Pasqual Ferry, Marvel Comics (New York, NY), 2010.

OTHER

Listen, Mom and Dad, Bookcraft (Salt Lake City, UT), 1978.
Saintspeak: The Mormon Dictionary, Signature Books (Midvale, UT), 1981.
Ainge, Signature Books (Midvale, UT), 1982.
A Woman of Destiny (historical novel), Berkley (New York, NY), 1983, published as *Saints,* Tor (New York, NY), 1988.
Compute's Guide to IBM PCjr Sound and Graphics, Compute (Greensboro, NC), 1984.
Cardography, Hypatia Press, 1987.
Characters and Viewpoint, Writer's Digest (Cincinnati, OH), 1988, revised edition, 2010.

(Author of introduction) Susan D. Smallwood, *You're a Rock, Sister Lewis,* Hatrack River Publications, 1989.
How to Write Science Fiction and Fantasy (also see below), Writer's Digest (Cincinnati, OH), 1990.
Lost Boys, HarperCollins (New York, NY), 1992.
A Storyteller in Zion: Essays and Speeches, Bookcraft (Salt Lake City, UT), 1993.
(Editor, with David C. Dollahite) *Turning Hearts: Short Stories on Family Life,* Bookcraft (Salt Lake City, UT), 1994.
How to Write a Million, Robinson Publishing (Great Britain), 1995.
Treasure Box (novel), HarperCollins (New York, NY), 1996.
Pastwatch: The Redemption of Christopher Columbus, Tor (New York, NY), 1996.
Stone Tables (novel), Deseret Book Co. (Salt Lake City, UT), 1997.
Homebody (novel), HarperCollins (New York, NY), 1998.
Enchantment, Del Rey (New York, NY), 1999.
An Open Book (poetry), Subterranean Press/Hatrack River Publications (Burton, MI), 2003.
Les to Live by, Subterranean Press (Burton, MI), 2005.
(Editor) *Getting Lost: Survival, Baggage, and Starting over in J.J. Abrams' Lost,* BenBella Books (Dallas, TX), 2006.
(With Amy Berner and Joyce Millman) *The Great Snape Debate: Is Snape Innocent or Guilty?,* Benbella Books (New York, NY), 2007.
(With Aaron Johnston) *Invasive Procedures* (based on Card's short story "Malpractice"), Tor (New York, NY), 2007.

Author of audio plays for Living Scriptures; coauthor of animated videotapes. Author of review columns, including "You Got No Friends in This World," *Science Fiction Review,* 1979-86; "Books to Look For," *Fantasy and Science Fiction,* 1987-94; "Gameplay," *Compute!,* 1988-89; and "Uncle Orson Reviews Everything," for *Rhinoceros Times* (Greensboro, NC). Contributor to *The Writer's Digest Guide to Science Fiction and Fantasy,* Writer's Digest Books (Cincinnati, OH), 2010; contributor of columns and editorials to Web sites, including *Hauvoo* and *Ornery American,* and of articles and reviews to periodicals, including *Washington Post Book World, Science Fiction Review, Destinies,* and *Rhinoceros Times.* Author of works under pseudonyms Frederick Bliss and P.Q. Gump.

Author's manuscripts are housed at Brigham Young University.

Author's works have been translated into Catalan, Danish, Dutch, Finnish, French, German, Hebrew, Italian, Japanese, Polish, Portuguese, Romanian, Russian, Slovakian, Spanish, and Swedish.

Adaptations

Ender's Game, Seventh Son, Speaker for the Dead, The Memory of Earth, Lost Boys, and *The Call of Earth* were adapted as audiobooks. *Xenocide* was adapted for audiobook, read by Mark Rolston, Audio Renaissance, 1991. *The Ender Wiggin Saga* was adapted for audiobook, Audio Renaissance, 2000. *Laddertop* was adapted for audiobook, read by Stefan Rudnicki and Emily Janice Card, Blackstone Audio, 2010. *Ender's Game* was adapted for film, produced, 2013.

Sidelights

Although best known for his science fiction, award-winning author Orson Scott Card has also authored books in genres as disparate as fantasy, history, religious studies, and suspense. Best known for his "Ender" series of science-fiction novels, Card has also created other memorable series, including his "Tales of Alvin Maker" saga and the "Homecoming" novels. His fantasy stories include the quest novel *Wyrms* and the mythic *Enchantment,* while mainstream novels include *Lost Boys, Treasure Box, Homebody,* and the medical thriller *Invasive Procedures.* Blending his devout Mormon faith with an interest in history, Card has also written the historical novels *A Woman of Destiny* and *Stone Tables* as well as the stories in his "Women of Genesis" series. As if such a literary output is not enough for one imagination, Card is also a proficient playwright, columnist, and poet.

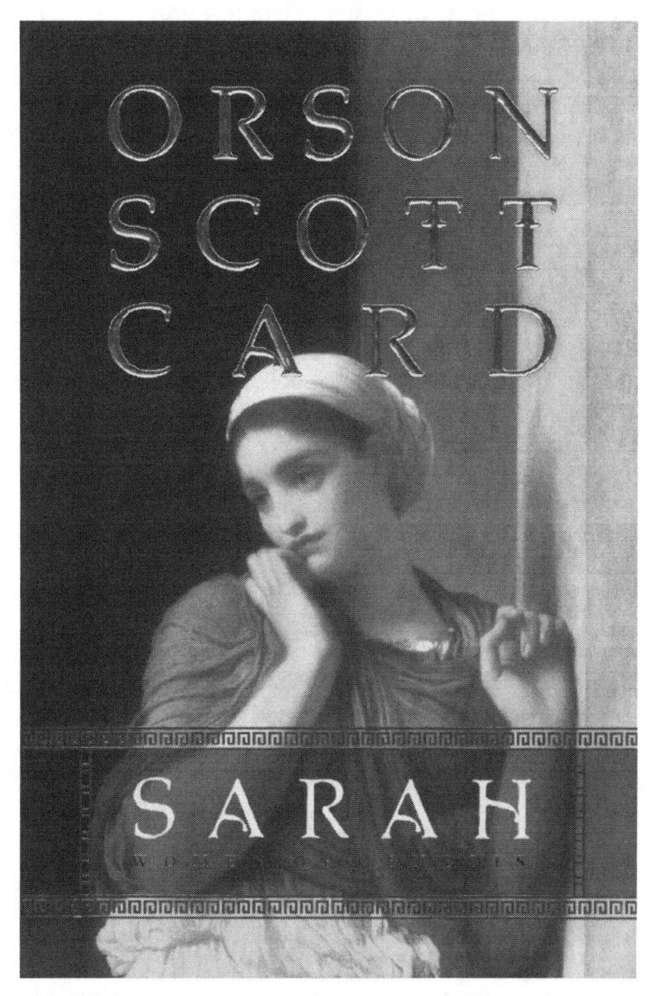

***Card focuses on inspirational women from history in his "Women of the Bible" series, which includes the novel* Sarah.** (Cover painting by Frederic Leighton. Reproduced by Christie's Images/The Bridgeman Art Library.)

While growing up in Richland, Washington, Card became an early fan of both the theater and science fiction. Entering Brigham Young University at age sixteen, he produced his first play while still an undergraduate, focusing on religious and biblical themes. He began writing short fiction after returning from a mission trip to Brazil and editing a Mormon magazine. His early science-fiction story "Ender's Game" would eventually be expanded into his breakthrough novel of the same title.

Winner of several awards, *Ender's Game* takes place in the near future, as Earth is facing invading Formics and Bugger aliens. Gifted children are located and sent to an elite training school where they learn warfare strategies and intelligence gathering. Among these children is Ender Wiggin, a six-year-old genius who may be the planet's only hope. *New York Times Book Review* critic Gerald Jonas observed of *Ender's Game* that "Card has shaped this unpromising material into an affecting novel full of surprises that seem inevitable once they are explained." According to several reviewers, the author's protagonist remains sympathetic despite his acts of violence. Although a *Kirkus Reviews* contributor noted several weaknesses in the plot, "the long passages focusing on Ender are nearly always enthralling" and make *Ender's Game* "a . . . solid, mature, and persuasive effort." Deeming *Ender's Game* to be "the best novel I've read in a long time," *West Coast Review of Books* contributor Dan K. Moran added that "Ender Wiggin is a unique creation": "a character who deserves to be remembered with the likes of Huckleberry Finn."

Cover of Card's award-winning* Ender's Game, *part one of his "Ender" series and a novel featuring cover art by John Harris. (Copyright © 1977, 1985, 1991 by Orson Scott Card. Reproduced by permission of Tom Doherty Associates, LLC, an imprint of St. Martin's Press.)

Written as a sequel to *Ender's Game, Ender in Exile* follows Ender and the other super-children—now teenagers—as they return to normal life on Earth. Estranged from their families and with no experience in normal social interaction, they are now viewed with suspicion due to their former life as ruthless warriors. Ender, most feared even though he is only twelve years old, decides to leave Earth and join a group of colonists on a new world. He travels into space with his sister Valentine, and eventually rules this new society as governor; meanwhile his brother attempts to establish political control on Earth. Ender's journey covers 3,000 years, although Ender ages only two decades during his travels to far-flung stars.

A *Publishers Weekly* contributor cited *Ender in Exile* for its focus on the "ethical ramifications" of Ender's youthful heroism and predicted that "fans will find [it] . . . illuminating," while in *Horn Book* Jonathan Hunt praised Card's story as "deeply involving" and "replete with suspenseful action, sympathetic characters, and provocative action." Noting that *Ender in Exile* weaves together plot threads from both *Ender's Game* and subsequent novels in the series, Sally Estes added in *Booklist* that the teen's "angst" as well as his "handling of the intrigue swirling around him, ensures the depth for which the series is famous."

Considered by some critics to be among Card's best novels, *Speaker for the Dead* finds Ender Wiggin traveling the galaxy to interpret the lives of the deceased for their families and neighbors. While working as a "Speaker for the Dead," he also searches for a home for the eggs of the lone surviving Formic "hive queen" whose race he destroyed as a child. Ender's appointment on the colony planet of Lusitania coincides with the discovery of another intelligent race, re-opening the question of co-existence versus survival.

Card's "constantly escalating storyline" in *Speaker for the Dead* "deals with religion, alien/human viewpoints and perspectives on instinctual and cultural levels, the fate of three alien species . . . , and quite possibly the fate of mankind itself," according to *Science Fiction Review* contributor Richard E. Geis. Unlike *Ender's Game, Speaker for the Dead* "deals with issues of evil and empathy" in a less-polarized manner, observed Tom Easton in his *Analog* review, and *Washington Post Book*

World contributor Janrae Frank commented on the "quasi-religious images and themes" that can be found in both *Ender's Game* and *Speaker for the Dead.*

Card continues his "Ender" series with *Xenocide,* as Ender works feverishly with his adopted Lusitanian family to neutralize a deadly virus. "The real action is philosophical," observed Gerald Jonas in the *New York Times Book Review:* "long, passionate debates about ends and means among people who are fully aware that they may be deciding the fate of an entire species, entire worlds." In the final volume of the "Ender" quartet, *Children of the Mind,* Ender plays a relatively minor role as colonists attempt to stop the destruction of Lusitania at the orders of the Starways Congress. "Card's prose is powerful here," commented a reviewer for *Publishers Weekly,* "as is his consideration of mystical and quasi-religious themes." In *Booklist* Roland Green praised *Children of the Mind* as "a worthy ending to what might be stylized a saga of the ethical evolution of humanity, a concept seldom attempted before and never realized with the success Card achieves here."

Card continues to ponder similar themes in his "Hegemon"/"Shadow" novels, which include *Ender's Shadow, Shadow of the Hegemon, Shadow Puppets, Shadow of the Giants,* and *Shadow in Flight.* In *Ender's Shadow* readers meet gifted child Bean who, like Ender, is taken from the streets of Rotterdam and sent to Battle School to learn to fight the insect-like Buggers. At the school he learns how to battle the enemy and also comes to understand what makes him human. In *Shadow of the Hegemon* Bean is a young man, and with the wars over he must make the crucial decision of which leader to support in creating a new world. A reviewer for *Publishers Weekly* praised *Ender's Shadow* as an "immensely involving SF novel" and dubbed Card's portrait of Bean at once "strange and wonderful, tragic yet hopeful." In *Booklist* Estes found *Shadow of the Hegemon* to be "so nicely integrated into the rest of the Ender canon that readers will be completely enthralled and left anxiously awaiting the next installment."

In *Shadow Puppets* Bean and his fellow Battle School alumni return after proving themselves against the Buggers, only to find Earth in chaos. Bean had thwarted young mastermind Achilles' efforts in battle, but now the evil teen teams up with Ender's brother Peter to wrest control of all life on the planet. Together with wife Petra, Bean attempt to stop these efforts while their battle-hardened friends turn their attention to the predations of the Chinese government. Including in his story "a far-flung, pan-Islamic shadow government" and focusing on the thoughtful musings of both Bean and Peter Wiggin, "Card keeps the action, danger, and intrigue levels high" in *Shadow Puppets,* according to Estes. "Fans of Card's bestselling 'Ender' series will be delighted with this tale of teen empowerment," asserted a *Publishers Weekly* contributor in a review of the novel.

Continuing the "Hegemon"/"Shadow" saga, *Shadow of the Giant* finds Bean facing his own mortality as the genetic engineering that gave him atypical size, strength, and genius now threatens to kill him although he is only twenty. To continue his bloodline, he and Petra have created eight fertilized embryos that will hopefully not contain the deformity. Now that these embryos have fallen into the hands of Achillles, Petra and Bean must retrieve them while also stalling Peter Wiggin's efforts at ruling the world. Three of his children join Bean in fleeing from Earth in *Shadows in Flight,* the hope being that their time-slowing trip through space will allow science time to develop a cure for the condition. A discovery by the Delphikis may be Bean's only hope, however, as an abandoned Formic space transport is located that contains the advanced scientific facility needed to effect a cure.

In *Shadow of the Giant* Card "does a superlative job of dramatically portraying the maturing process of child into adult," according to a *Publishers Weekly* contributor, and readers "will marvel" at the series' "clever resolution." With "several balls in the air," the author

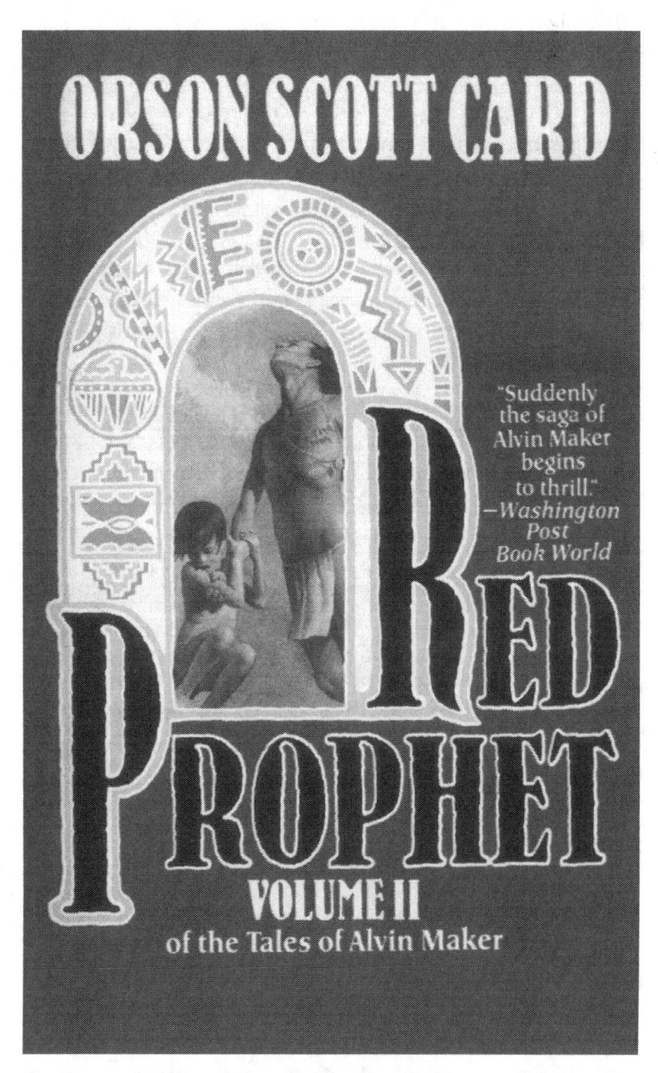

Card's sequel to* Seventh Son, Red Prophet *finds young Alvin traveling through an America alive with mystery. (Copyright © 1988 by Orson Scott Card. Reprinted by permission of Tom Doherty Associates, LLC, an imprint of St. Martin's Press.)

focuses primarily on Peter Wiggin as he works "to bring the apparently runaway geopolitical forces back under control," wrote a *Kirkus Reviews* writer, and in *Library Journal* Jackie Cassada praised *Shadow of the Giant* as a "story of love, sacrifice, and duty" that makes a fitting addition to a "brilliant" series.

Seventh Son is the first volume in Card's "Tales of Alvin Maker" series. With its genesis in an epic poem he wrote during graduate studies at the University of Utah, the "Tales of Alvin Maker" saga is set in an alternate pioneer America, a nation of inchoate states to which witches have been exiled by the Puritans. *Seventh Son* details the early years of the series' protagonist, Alvin Miller is a "Maker," one endowed with magical powers because of his distinctive status as the seventh son of a seventh son. Although many people possess mystical powers in Card's America—such as dowsing, hexing, and healing—Alvin owns the supreme talent of being able to control reality, and his demise is the goal of the evil and patient Unmaker.

In *Red Prophet* Card shifts the focus away from Alvin to the issue of the interfacing between colonists and Native Americans as represented by three individuals: Ta-Kumsaw, a Shawnee who wishes to reserve all lands east of the Mississippi River for the whites while keeping all lands to the west for the Indians; William Henry "White Murderer" Harrison, who desires to slaughter all Native Americans; and Lolla-Wossiky, Ta-Kumsaw's brother and a "Red Prophet" preaching of a land where all people can live in harmony. *Prentice Alvin,* the third volume in Card's "Tales of Alvin Maker" series, follows Alvin as he matures to nineteen years of age and presages his future.

Alvin Journeyman continues the cycle, as Alvin reaches manhood, returns to the isolated town of Vigor Church, and takes up work as a blacksmith while also sharing his knowledge of the Maker's art. Love comes to Alvin in *Heartfire,* as he marries Peggy, who is able to see people's hearts as well as their future. As Alvin moves north to New England, Peggy is called southward to the court of an exiled king, where she hopes to avert a future war. A childhood vision and the threat of war work together to forge Alvin's own path south in *The Crystal City,* and a trip to New Orleans in Spanish-occupied territory leads him and his brother-in-law Arthur to a fateful meeting.

Throughout the course of the "Alvin Maker" series, Card presents "alternative American history," explained a reviewer for *Publishers Weekly.* Another critic for the magazine wrote that "a large part of the appeal" of the series "lies in the . . . homegrown characters using their powers for ordinary purposes," while in *Kliatt* Sherry Hoy noted of *The Crystal City* that Card's "long-awaited" series installment will appeal to even middle-grade readers.

Card's "Homecoming" series begins with *The Memory of Earth,* a novel mixing philosophy, futuristic technology, and biblical lore. The story is set on the planet Harmony, where for millions of years humans have been controlled by Oversoul, a powerful computer programmed to prevent humanity from destroying itself through needless wars. When Oversoul falls into disrepair and requires restoration, Earth's inhabitants have lost the technological ability to travel into space, let alone repair the computer. To save itself as well as Harmony, Oversoul engages the aid of Wetchik and his son Nafai, members of an extended family of nomadic traders.

David E. Jones, in his Chicago *Tribune Books* appraisal of *The Memory of Earth,* wrote that "Card gives us . . . an interaction between supreme intelligence and human mental capability that is at once an intellectual exercise, a Biblical parable and a thoroughly enjoyable piece of storytelling." Joel Singer noted in his *Voice of Youth Advocates* appraisal of the same novel that "Card has recaptured the originality and grace that so enthralled readers of *Ender's Game*" and "expertly weaves

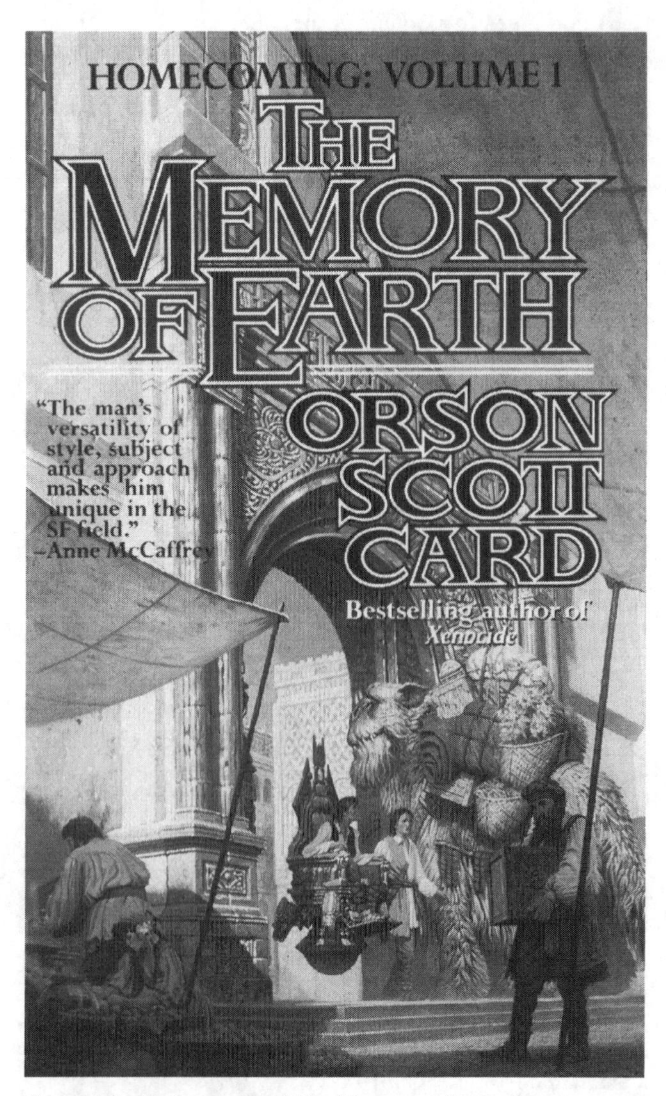

Cover of Card's fantasy novel* The Memory of Earth, *featuring cover art by Keith Parkinson. (Copyright © 1992 by Orson Scott Card. Reproduced by permission of Tom Doherty Associates, LLC, an imprint of St. Martin's Press.)

Biblical imagery, modern science, philosophy, and emotion in a tale of a young man . . . growing and maturing."

Card's "Homecoming" series continues with *The Call of Earth* and *The Ships of Earth,* as the Harmony city of Basilica is still regulated by the powerful Oversoul. The computer uses the faith of its followers to communicate its demise, for without it humans will regain their memories and spawn the re-creation of both technological understanding and their instinctual aggression. *The Ships of Earth* explores the intricacies of man vs. man. *Earthfall* and *Earthborn* conclude the series, as the travelers from Harmony return to Earth, thereby becoming the first humans to set foot on the planet in forty million years.

Writing in the *Voice of Youth Advocates,* Singer stated of *The Call of Earth* that "one of Card's major strengths as an author is characterization, and [here] he introduces some extremely interesting and engaging ones." Hoy, writing in the *Voice of Youth Advocates,* judged *The Ships of Earth* to be "classic Card—solid, careful character development and interplay plus a clearly defined setting." "This action-packed, plot-rich installment features Card's typical virtues," wrote a contributor in a *Publishers Weekly* review of *Earthfall:* "well-drawn characters, and a story driven by complex moral issues."

In his novella *Stonefather* and his novel *The Lost Gate* Card sets the stage for his "Mithermages" fantasy saga, which follows a young man with magical abilities as he learns to use his talent. In *Stonefather* Runnel, a village peasant, travels to Mitherhome, a thriving city, where he becomes the servant of a local mage. Although the young man quickly learns that he has magic powers of his own, his compassion and his naiveté allow others to use him for their own purposes. *The Lost Gate* expands the story of these Mithermages, extended families with inherited magical talents. Modern-day teen Danny North lives in a world of magic where he feels like an outsider in a family of talented mages. When he discovers his special gift—the ability to create portals between worlds—Danny's problems increase: such a gift has been outlawed and those who practice it are sentenced to death. Determined to fulfil his destiny as a Gate mage, the thirteen year old leaves home and begins his grand adventure, befriending fellow gatemage Wad along the way.

Noting the mix of magic and urban fantasy in Card's "Mithermage" saga, a *Publishers Weekly* contributor deemed *The Lost Gate* an "ambitious tale [that] is well crafted, highly detailed, and pleasantly accessible." In *Library Journal* Jackie Cassada also enjoyed the story, writing that Danny's "coming of age resonates with depth and meaning," and *Voice of Youth Advocates* contributor Donna Phillips observed that Card salts his story with enough "close calls to keep the parallel stories [in *The Lost Gate*] moving toward their final collision."

In addition to his series fiction, Card has written several stand-alone novels, such as the fantasies *Wyrms, Enchantment,* and *Magic Street. Wyrms* is a traditional quest adventure involving a deposed princess, while the story in *Enchantment* blends Sleeping Beauty with the Russian folk tales about Baba Yaga. "An often intriguing story told with Card's usually impeccable skills" and based on Shakespeare's *Midsummer Night's Dream,* according to a *Kirkus Reviews* writer, *Magic Street* is set in an affluent California suburb and follows a boy from his strange birth and adoption through his childhood as he discovers his gift for making the wishful dreams of others come true . . . in a slightly askew fashion. Card also mined Shakespeare's work in writing *Hamlet's Father,* an imaginative story in which the young hero of *Hamlet* questions the visitation of his dead father and the assertion that his uncle Claudius was in fact his father's killer.

Card turns to science fiction in *Pathfinder,* a novel for younger readers that a *Kirkus Reviews* writer dubbed "a brain-bending bildungsroman." The first installment in the planned "Serpent World" series, *Pathfinder* intro-

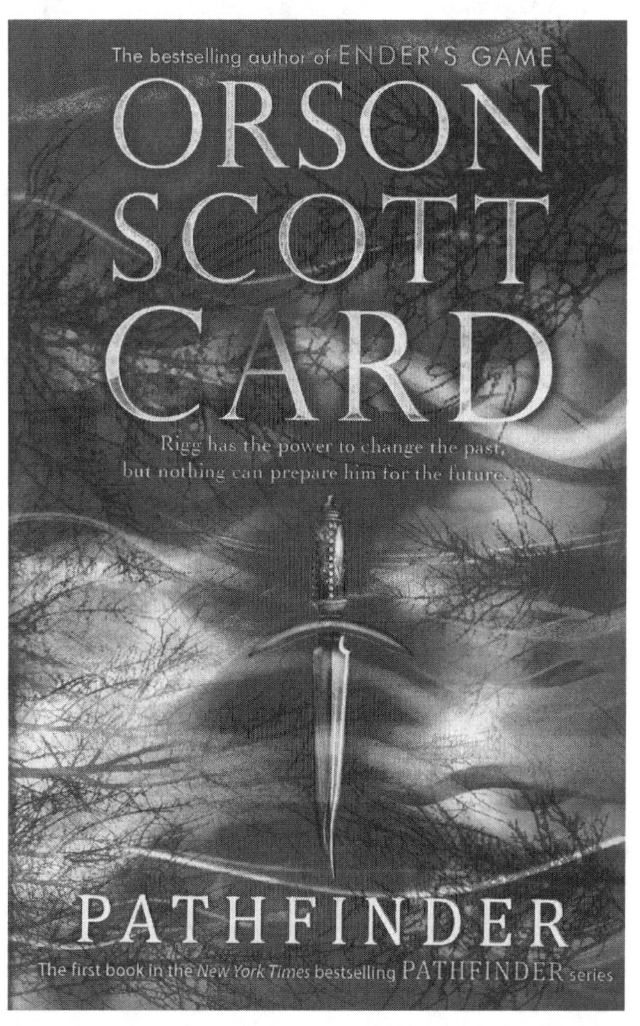

Cover of Card's young-adult novel* Pathfinder, *featuring artwork by Sammy Yuen, Jr. (Copyright © 2010 by Orson Scott Card. Reprinted with permission of Simon Pulse, an imprint of Simon & Schuster's Children's Publishing Division.)

duces a teen named Rigg, who has the ability to see people's pasts. At his father's death Rigg learns the secret of his own past as well as of the destiny his father had kept hidden. While searching for his sister, he also realizes that he can sometimes change people's pasts as well as see them. In *Ruins* Rigg's journey toward his ultimate fate continues. When he is joined by Umbo, another teen with a special power, both boys realize that they are capable of far different things separately than they can accomplish together.

Dubbed "a brain-bending bildungsroman" by a *Kirkus Reviews* writer, *Pathfinder* chronicles Rigg and Umbo's journey against a backdrop of "Machiavellian political intrigue" and leads to "a pulse-pounding climax." In *Booklist* Debbie Carton praised the same novel as "fast paced and thoroughly engrossing, . . . challenging readers to [ponder] . . . sophisticated, confusing, and captivating ideas" about political power as well as time and space. "Ever the master storyteller," according to *Horn Book* contributor Jonathan Hunt, Card gathers together several conventional elements of science fiction in *Pathfinder,* then "weaves them together seamlessly and in startling ways."

Teaming up with daughter Emily Janice Card, Card has also experimented with manga in a two-volume series that begins with *Laddertop.* Featuring artwork by Honoel A. Ibardolaza, the series opener introduces Roberta and Azure, two preteens who jump at the chance to work as part of the maintenance crew on the technologically advanced space station Laddertop. Constructed with the help of alien Givers for the benign purpose of conserving resources and providing power, Laddertop has another purpose that has been kept secret. Once the two girls climb the heights to the station and begin their training, they realize that there are reasons why little about Laddertop is know to the Earthlings down below. Noting that the Cards effectively lay out the framework of their "extended story" in *Laddertop,* a *Publishers Weekly* critic recommended the manga as "a worthy young-adult adventure novel." A *Kirkus Reviews* contributor remarked positively on the story's "strong and intelligent" female cast, praising the saga as "a wonderful departure from male-dominated extraterrestrial offerings."

Card has long been praised for the moral messages delivered in his books, but he is careful to keep his personal and political views out of his fiction. As he told Laura Ciporen in a *Publishers Weekly* interview, "I hate black and white representations of good versus evil, that's so boring. . . . My characters wrestle with real moral dilemmas where all the choices have steep prices." Remarking on his choice of science fiction as the vehicle for his stories, Card concluded to Ciporen, "Mainstream literature is so stultifyingly rigid. I don't just want to talk to people who believed everything their English teacher told them. I want to reach people who read books for the sheer pleasure of it, because those are the people who are open to having their lives changed by what they read."

Biographical and Critical Sources

BOOKS

Collings, Michael R., *Storyteller: The Official Orson Scott Card Bibliography and International Reader's Guide,* Overlook Connection Press (New York, NY), 2001.

Tyson, Edith S., *Orson Scott Card: Writer of the Terrible Choice,* Scarecrow Press (Lanham, MD), 2003.

PERIODICALS

Analog, June, 1986, Tom Easton, review of *Speaker for the Dead,* p. 183.

Booklist, June 1-15, 1996, Roland Green, review of *Children of the Mind,* p. 1629; March 1, 1999, Roberta Johnson, review of *Enchantment,* p. 1103; November 1, 2000, Sally Estes, review of *Shadow of the Hegemon,* p. 490; October 1, 2001, Roland Green, review of *Masterpieces: The Best Science Fiction of the Century,* p. 306; July, 2002, Sally Estes, review of *Shadow Puppets,* p. 1796; April 15, 2005, Ray Olson, review of *Magic Street,* p. 1413; August, 2007, Roland Green, review of *Invasive Procedures,* p. 55; September 15, 2007, Sally Estes, review of *A War of Gifts: An Ender Story,* p. 54; March 1, 2008, Roland Green, review of *Keeper of Dreams,* p. 56; June 1, 2008, Roland Green, review of *Orson Scott Card's InterGalactic Medicine Show,* p. 58; August 1, 2008, Roland Green, review of *Stonefather,* p. 53; October 1, 2008, Sally Estes, review of *Ender in Exile,* p. 4; November 1, 2010, Debbie Carton, review of *Pathfinder,* p. 53.

Fantasy Review, April, 1986, Michael R. Collings, "Adventure and Allegory," p. 20.

Horn Book, May-June, 2009, Jonathan Hunt, review of *Ender in Exile,* p. 293; January-February, 2011, Jonathan Hunt, review of *Pathfinder,* p. 90.

Kirkus Reviews, November 1, 1984, review of *Ender's Game,* p. 1021; February 2, 1998, review of *Homebody;* March 1, 2005, review of *Shadow of the Giant,* p. 266; April 15, 2005, review of *Magic Street,* p. 455; November 1, 2009, review of *Hidden Empire*; October 15, 2010, review of *Pathfinder;* August 15, 2011, review of *Laddertop.*

Kliatt, March, 2002, Sherry S. Hoy, review of *Shadow of the Hegemon,* p. 20; March, 2003, Claire Rosser, review of *Rebekah,* p. 20; March, 2005, Sherry Hoy, review of *The Crystal City,* p. 24; November, 2006, Sherry Hoy, review of *Magic Street,* p. 26; November, 2007, Paula Rohrlick, review of *A War of Gifts,* p. 6.

Library Journal, September 15, 2003, Jackie Cassada, review of *First Meetings in the Enderverse,* p. 96; April 15, 2005, Jackie Cassada, review of *Shadow of the Giant,* p. 78; May 15, 2005, Jackie Cassada, review of *Magic Street,* p. 111; September 1, 2007, A.J. Wright, review of *Invasive Procedures,* p. 124; June 15, 2008, Jackie Cassada, review of *Orson Scott Card's InterGalactic Medicine Show,* p. 59; November 15, 2009, Jackie Cassada, review of *Hidden Empire,* p. 58; January, 2011, Jackie Cassada, review of *The Lost Gate,* p. 86.

Locus, February, 1992, Faren Miller, review of *The Memory of Earth,* pp. 17, 57; December, 1993, Faren Miller, review of *The Ships of Earth,* p. 19.

Los Angeles Times Book Review, July 22, 1984, Kristiana Gregory, review of *A Woman of Destiny,* p. 8; August 9, 1987, Ingrid Rimland, review of *Wyrms,* p. 11; February 14, 1988, Sue Martin, "Battling the Natives along the Mississippi".

New York Times Book Review, June 16, 1985, Gerald Jonas, review of *Ender's Game,* p. 18; September 1, 1991, Gerald Jonas, review of *Xenocide,* p. 13.

Publishers Weekly, November 30, 1990, Graceanne A. DeCandido and Keith R.A. DeCandido, interview with Card, pp. 54-55; January 30, 1995, review of *Earthfall,* p. 89; June 24, 1996, review of *Children of the Mind,* pp. 45, 49; February 2, 1998, review of *Homebody,* p. 79; June 29, 1998, review of *Heartfire,* p. 40; March 8, 1999, review of *Enchantment,* p. 52; November 1, 1999, review of *Ender's Shadow,* p. 48; September 11, 2000, review of *Sarah,* p. 71; November 20, 2000, Laura Ciporen, interview with Card, p. 51; November 20, 2000, review of *Shadow of the Hegemon,* p. 50; July 15, 2002, review of *Shadow Puppets,* p. 59; October 27, 2003, review of *The Crystal City,* p. 48; February 21, 2005, review of *Shadow of the Giant,* p. 162; May 30, 2005, review of *Magic Street,* p. 44; May 7, 2007, review of *Space Boy,* p. 46; July 9, 2007, review of *Invasive Procedures,* p. 30; August 27, 2007, review of *A War of Gifts,* p. 65; February 18, 2008, review of *Keeper of Dreams,* p. 140; June 2, 2008, review of *Orson Scott Card's InterGalactic Medicine Show,* p. 33; August 18, 2008, review of *Stonefather,* p. 49; September 29, 2008, review of *Ender in Exile,* p. 63; November 8, 2010, review of *The Lost Gate,* p. 47; February 28, 2011, review of *Hamlet's Father,* p. 39; August 1, 2011, review of *Laddertop,* p. 33.

School Library Journal, January, 2004, Mara Alpert, review of *First Meetings in the Enderverse,* p. 124; February, 2008, Matthew L. Moffett, review of *A War of Gifts,* p. 140; July, 2008, Charli Osborne, review of *Keeper of Dreams,* p. 125.

Science Fiction Review, February, 1986, Richard E. Geis, review of *Speaker for the Dead,* p. 14.

Tribune Books (Chicago, IL), March 1, 1992, David E. Jones, "Trapped in a Serial Universe."

Voice of Youth Advocates, October, 1992, Joel Singer, review of *The Memory of Earth,* p. 236; August, 1993, Joel Singer, review of *The Call of Earth,* p. 236; June, 1994, Sherry Hoy, review of *The Ships of Earth,* p. 98; June, 2011, Donna Phillips, review of *The Lost Gate,* p. 179.

Washington Post Book World, February 23, 1986, Janrae Frank, "War of the Worlds," p. 10; August 30, 1987, John Clute, review of *Seventh Son.*

West Coast Review of Books, July, 1986, Dan K. Moran, review of *Ender's Game,* p. 20.

ONLINE

Goodreads Web site, http://www.goodreads.com/ (January, 2011), interview with Card.

Orson Scott Card Home Page, http://www.hatrack.com (December 10, 2001).*

* * *

CHOW, Cara 1972-

Personal

Born 1972, in Hong Kong; immigrated to United States; married; children: one son. *Education:* University of California, Los Angeles, B.A. (English).

Addresses

Home—Los Angeles, CA. *E-mail*—cara@carachow.com.

Career

Writer.

Awards, Honors

PEN Emerging Voices fellow; Best Fiction for Young Adults designation, American Library Association, 2012, for *Bitter Melon.*

Writings

Bitter Melon, Egmont (New York, NY), 2011.

Adaptations

Bitter Melon was adapted as an audiobook, Brilliance Audio, 2011.

Sidelights

In her debut novel, the semi-autobiographical *Bitter Melon,* Cara Chow offers "a searing, contemporary story of timeless parent-child friction across cultural and generational borders," observed *Booklist* critic Gillian Engberg. *Bitter Melon* centers on the often difficult relationship between a high-school senior and her mother, a woman who seems demanding and sometimes even abusive. "When creating the scenes between Frances and Gracie, I drew upon the dynamic my mom and I had and the turbulent emotions I felt during my teens," Chow remarked to *Voice of Youth Advocates* contributor Rebecca Hill.

Chow was born in Hong Kong and immigrated to the United States with her parents, who held academic achievement in high esteem. "Though my mother and I enjoy a very positive relationship today," she related in an interview for the Public Broadcasting System Web log, "we definitely struggled a lot when I was a teen. My mom wanted me to be the best, and her way of mo-

Cara Chow (Photograph by Laura Joyce. Reproduced by permission.)

tivating me was by being very hard on me. Unfortunately, her parenting strategy did not have the effect on me that she had intended. I wanted to make her proud, but I always felt like a disappointment to her, and this really affected my confidence and self-image as a teen."

Bitter Melon was also inspired by Chow's memories of her maternal grandmother, who alternately lived with Chow's mother and Chow's uncle. "On the one hand, I deeply respected and admired this family style," the author remarked on her home page. "On the other hand, I pondered its potential pitfalls. What if the aging parent was difficult, dysfunctional, or even abusive? Should the adult child fulfill her obligation to the parent, or should she break free of that obligation? Should she betray her parent or herself? That question became the seed for *Bitter Melon*."

In *Bitter Melon* high-school senior Frances and her mother Gracie share a cramped, one-room apartment in San Francisco. Gracie is embittered by her husband's abandonment of the family and exhausted from working long hours; her frustrations prompt her to push Frances to earn the top grades she hopes will lead to a college scholarship and a remunerative career as a physician. When Frances is accidentally placed in a speech class instead of calculus, she feels liberated and discovers a talent for public speaking. She hides the truth from her mother, however, and lies about her academic pursuits. When Gracie learns about the deceit, Frances comes to the realization that she must assert her independence and take control of her own life.

"Chow skillfully describes the widening gulf between mother and daughter," Suzanne Gordon commented in her *School Library Journal* review of *Bitter Melon.* In *Publishers Weekly* a critic also enjoyed the coming-of-age story, writing that the author's "descriptions, dialogue, and details of Chinese-American life in 1980s San Francisco shine, and Frances's growth is rewarding."

Biographical and Critical Sources

PERIODICALS

Booklist, December 1, 2010, Gillian Engberg, review of *Bitter Melon,* p. 52.

Kirkus Reviews, November 15, 2010, review of *Bitter Melon.*

Publishers Weekly, November 22, 2010, review of *Bitter Melon,* p. 59.

School Library Journal, January, 2011, Suzanne Gordon, review of *Bitter Melon,* p. 102.

Cover of Chow's coming of age novel* Bitter Melon, *a story based on her own experiences growing up between two cultures. (Jacket photo courtesy Getty Images. Jacket design by Alison Chamberlain. Reproduced with permission of Egmont USA.)

Voice of Youth Advocates, February, 2011, Kathleen Beck, review of *Bitter Melon,* p. 550; October, 2011, Rebecca Hill, review of *Bitter Melon,* p. 332.

ONLINE

Cara Chow Home Page, http://www.carachow.com (March 15, 2012).

PBS Kids Web log, http://pbskids.org/itsmylife/blog/ (February 1, 2011), interview with Chow.

School Library Journal Online, http://www.schoollibraryjournal.com/ (January 19, 2011), Dodie Ownes, review of *Bitter Melon.**

* * *

CLARKE, J.
See CLARKE, Judith

* * *

CLARKE, Judith 1943-
(J. Clarke)

Personal

Born August 24, 1943, in Sydney, New South Wales, Australia; daughter of Kenneth Edward (a production supervisor) and Sheila Iris Clarke; married Rashmi Desai (an anthropologist), December 27, 1968; children: Yask. *Education:* University of New South Wales, B.A. (with honors), 1964; Australian National University, M.A. (with honors), 1966.

Addresses

Home—Melbourne, Victoria, Australia.

Career

Teacher, librarian, lecturer, and writer.

Awards, Honors

New South Wales Premier's Award shortlist, 1989, and Best Book for Young Adults designation, American Library Association, both 1990, both for *The Heroic Life of Al Capsella;* New South Wales Premier's Award shortlist, 1990, Talking Book of the Year designation, Variety Club, 1991, and Best Book for Young Adults designation, New York Public Library, 1992, all for *Al Capsella and the Watchdogs;* Children's Book Council of Australia (CBCA) Book of the Year shortlist, 1994, for *Friend of My Heart;* CBCA Notable Book designation, 1995, for *Big Night Out,* 1996, for *The Ruin of Kevin O'Reilly,* and 1997, for *The Lost Day;* Victorian Premier's Award for Young-Adult Novel, and CBCA Honour Book designation, both 1998, both for *Night Train;* Family Therapy Award, 1999, for *Angels Passing By;* CBCA Book of the Year designation, 2001, for *Wolf on the Fold; Boston Globe/Horn Book* Honor Book designation in fiction and poetry, 2004, for *Kalpana's Dream.*

Judith Clarke (Reproduced by permission.)

Writings

The Boy on the Lake (stories), University of Queensland Press (St. Lucia, Queensland, Australia), 1989, revised edition published as *The Torment of Mr. Gully: Stories of the Supernatural,* Henry Holt (New York, NY), 1990.

Teddy B. Zoot, illustrated by Margaret Hewitt, Henry Holt (New York, NY), 1990.

Luna Park at Night, Pascoe Publishing (Apollo Bay, Victoria, Australia), 1991.

Riff Raff, Henry Holt (New York, NY), 1992.

Friend of My Heart, University of Queensland Press (St. Lucia, Queensland, Australia), 1994.

Big Night Out, Shorts (Norwood, South Australia, Australia), 1995.

Panic Stations (short stories), University of Queensland Press (St. Lucia, Queensland, Australia), 1995.

Night Train, Penguin (Ringwood, Victoria, Australia), 1998, Henry Holt (New York, NY), 2000.

The Lost Day, Henry Holt (New York, NY), 1999.

Angels Passing By, Puffin (Ringwood, Victoria, Australia), 1999.

Wolf of the Fold, Allen & Unwin (Crows Nest, New South Wales, Australia), 2000, Front Street (Asheville, NC), 2002.

Starry Nights, Allen & Unwin (Crows Nest, New South Wales, Australia), 2001, Front Street (Asheville, NC), 2003.

Kalparna's Dream, Front Street (Ashville, NC) 2004.

One Whole and Perfect Day, Front Street (Asheville, NC), 2006.

The Winds of Heaven, Allen & Unwin (Crows Nest, New South Wales, Australia), 2009, Henry Holt (New York, NY), 2010.

"AL CAPSELLA" NOVEL SERIES

The Heroic Life of Al Capsella, University of Queensland Press (St. Lucia, Queensland, Australia), 1988, Henry Holt (New York, NY), 1990.

Al Capsella and the Watchdogs, University of Queensland Press (St. Lucia, Queensland, Australia), 1990, Henry Holt (New York, NY), 1991.

Al Capsella on Holidays, University of Queensland (St. Lucia, Queensland, Australia), 1992, published as *Al Capsella Takes a Vacation,* Henry Holt (New York, NY), 1993.

The Heroic Lives of Al Capsella (abridged omnibus), University of Queensland Press (St. Lucia, Queensland, Australia), 2000.

Sidelights

Judith Clarke writes incisive novels for teens that have earned praise for their humor and deft handling of weighty issues. A former teacher and librarian as well as a parent, Clarke enjoyed her first taste of success as an author with *The Heroic Life of Al Capsella,* a 1988 novel set in the author's native Australia. Two other novels featuring the likable teen have followed, as well as other young-adult novels that feature universal adolescent concerns and issues. Since the success of Clarke's debut as a writer, nearly all of her novels have made their way to U.S. bookstore shelves.

Born in Sydney, Clarke "never made a conscious decision to be a writer," as she recalled in an essay posted on the Front Street Books Web site. "I never saw it as a profession or career. Writing was something I began doing when I was a child in the western suburbs of Sydney in the 1950s. . . . All of the kids in my neighborhood were boys, and though they let my sister and I play with them, they pinched our marbles and comics and bashed us up. Writing stories was less dangerous." Clarke earned an advanced degree from the Australian National University in 1966, and two years later she married an anthropologist, with whom she has raised a son, Yask.

"Although I didn't write much during the period when my own family was young . . . I can remember very clearly my first attempt at writing," Clarke once told *SATA.* "I was very young, probably about four, had not gone to school yet, and had no idea of how to 'write' in the sense of forming actual letters. My mother had given me an empty notebook to draw in, and I used it to write a 'book' (it even had chapters) about a doll who'd fallen from her pram and had a series of horrendous adventures. The actual 'writing' was a kind of scribble—long wavy lines—but the story itself was a heartrending tale, and when I finished it, I gave it to my uncle to read. I watched him closely, expecting him to dissolve into sympathetic tears, but to my amazement and fury he burst out laughing. Perhaps this unsettling experience is what turned me toward comedy so many years after."

The hero of Clarke's "Al Capsella" series is actually named Almeric, and this odd name provides the first in a series of burdens dogging the lad in *The Heroic Life of Al Capsella.* Fourteen-year-old Al wishes his parents were conformist and "normal" rather than intellectual and decidedly different from the parents of his friends. His mother writes romance novels and wears second-hand clothes, while his father is a university professor who finds it difficult to keep up on the yard work that is the hallmark of perfection in their suburban community. During a visit to the home of his grandparents—whose household is a veritable model of the ordinary—"Al discovers what 'normal' is with a vengeance," noted Ronald A. Van De Voorde in his review of the novel for *School Library Journal.* Stephanie Zvirin, reviewing *The Heroic Life of Al Capsella* for *Booklist,* wrote that "beneath the comic veneer" of Clarke's story "lurks a fondness and respect for people—even parents—despite their strange ways."

In *Al Capsella and the Watchdogs* Al attempts to forge a more independent life. He feels that parents worry far too much—they give him permission to attend a party, for instance, but then his mother borrows a dog and takes it for a walk in order to spy on him and his friends. When his grandparents come for a visit, Al realizes that his mother endured—and still endures—the same constant, overprotective hovering he now experiences. Zvirin, reviewing *Al Capsella and the Watchdogs* for *Booklist,* again praised Clarke as a writer with a unique ability to relate to teens; the cast of adult characters in the series "ring true in surprising, subtle ways," according to the critic.

In the third and final book in the series, *Al Capsella Takes a Vacation,* sixteen-year-old Al convinces his parents that he and his friend are mature enough to take their own holiday at Christmastime, when it is summer in Australia. Lured by another friend's exaggerations, they cart their surfboards off to what they envision will be a beachfront party paradise. Instead they find themselves in a deadly dull rural nightmare hundreds of miles inland; a leech-filled pond awaits, and they are forced to fend for themselves even to the point of cooking their own food. "Al's wry, almost deadpan narrative is the perfect vehicle for describing a fantasy vacation gone awry," remarked Zvirin, while *School Library*

Journal reviewer Kathy Piehl noted that "the maturing Al has grown a bit reflective, and a new poignancy surfaces in his consideration of the world" in *Al Capsella Takes a Vacation.*

In her standalone novel *The Lost Day* Clarke explores what happens when a friend mysteriously disappears. Australian teens Vinny and Jasper spend a Saturday evening at the Hanging Gardens, but Jasper is preoccupied over a breakup with his girlfriend and does not notice when Vinny disappears. Vinny is still missing the following day, and the effect this has on Jasper and several other friends makes up the bulk of the action in the novel. As the concern and worry mount, Clarke paints a realistic picture of the stress and strain teens face from parents, school, and peers. Anne Briggs, who reviewed *The Lost Day* for *Magpies,* called it a "clever and memorable book" in which Clarke merges "the most original and lyrical language with perfectly realised teenage slang."

The novel *Night Train* won unstinting praise for presenting teen depression and suicide in an empathetic manner. Luke, Clarke's young protagonist, feels increasingly isolated from those around him. Introduced to him at the end of Luke's life, readers retrace the teen's final weeks. Because of a learning disability, Luke does poorly in school despite the fact that he is intelligent. Teachers and school officials fail to recognize the depth of his problem, and Luke's bad grades and expulsions lead to harsh treatment at the hands of his father. His mother and sister fail to sympathize while mired in their own problems, and it is only his youngest sister, Naomi, who tries to show Luke that someone needs him. Luke's sole comfort comes from the sound of the night train, but he begins to question his own sanity when he learns that no one else hears it.

Jane Connolly, reviewing *Night Train* for *Magpies,* commended the author's deft handling of a difficult subject matter. "By providing the end before the beginning, Clarke changes this story from simply one of despair and ultimate death to an examination of the care we provide or deny young people in obvious need," the critic declared, asserting that "the story becomes a powerful question about responsibility." Frances Bradburn, writing in *Booklist,* called *Night Train* "a well-written but devastating book," while a *Publishers Weekly* reviewer commented that, "at the root of this tale is the compelling idea of one person's power to reach out—to make a difference in or even potentially save, someone's life."

Wolf on the Fold collects six interrelated short stories that refer to the poem by Alfred, Lord Byron, from which the book's title is drawn. As a *Kirkus Reviews* contributor observed, Clarke's 'well-crafted vignettes and convincing dialogue" span four generations of the same family: between 1935 and 2002 members cope with the economic depression in Australia, wars in Vietnam and Israel, divorce, death, emigration, and poverty. "Clarke's quiet wisdom and keen understanding will touch hearts and stimulate the imagination," praised a reviewer for *Publishers Weekly,* while *School Library Journal* contributor Alison Follos wrote that the novel's "subject matter is haunting and evocative." Readers "will be intrigued by Clarke's style and anxious to get the puzzle pieces to fit together by the end of the book," predicted *Kliatt* reviewer Claire Rosser, and Frances Bradburn wrote in *Booklist* that Clarke's "spare, though-provoking novels . . . challenge teen readers to think of elemental issues."

An eerie ghost story intertwines with a family drama in *Starry Nights,* as Jess's family moves into a strange new house after something bad happened in the family. In their new home, Jess's sister Vida suddenly becomes obsessed with magic, her brother Clem becomes increasingly uncommunicative, and her mother lies sick in bed without moving. Worse, Jess thinks she hears footsteps following her, and occasionally she glimpses a pair of legs or a blue skirt hem out of the corner of her eye. Knowing that she will get no help from her family, the teen decides to go about solving the mystery herself, and as she does, the mystery of what happened to her family to cause them to move becomes clear.

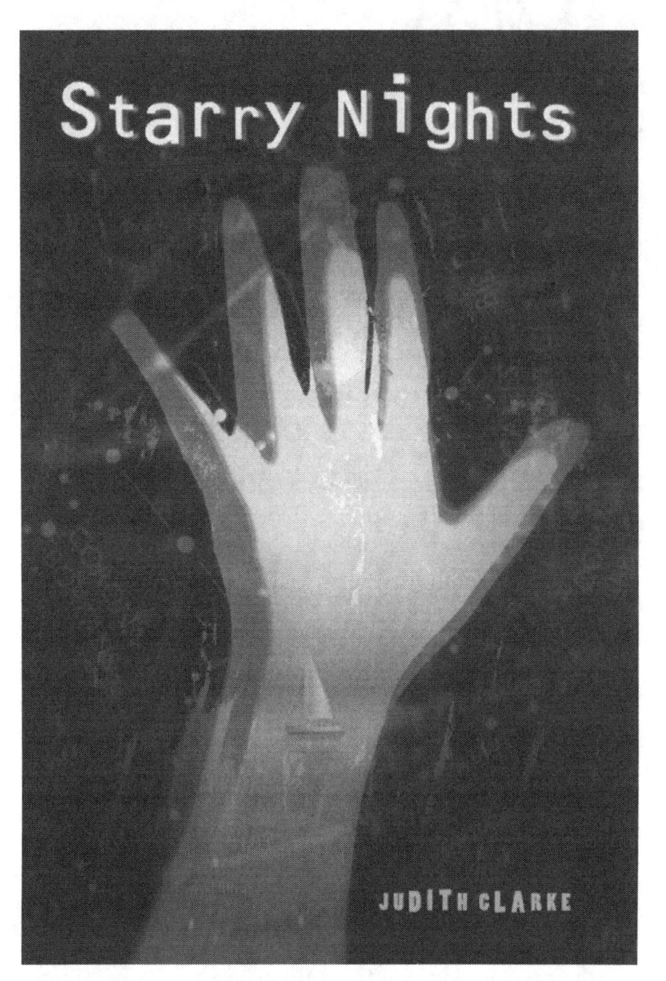

***A preteen finds emotional support from a supernatural source in Clarke's occult novel* Starry Nights.** (Copyright © by Judith Clarke. Reproduced by permission of Boyds Mills Press, Inc.)

Taking place in Australia, Clarke's novel* Kalpana's Dream *focuses on a teen who gains a new perspective on her own life by spending time with her Hindi-speaking grandmother. (Copyright © 2004 by Judith Clarke. Reproduced by permission of Boyds Mills Press, Inc.)

Sally Murphy, writing for *AussieReviews.com,* dubbed Clark's tale "a haunting mystery of a family caught in the Twilight Zone," while a *Publishers Weekly* contributor commented that, "with masterly skill," the author "sprinkles in just enough [clues] to fuel the audience's interest." A *Kirkus Reviews* contributor described *Starry Nights* as "a touching tale" and *Booklist* reviewer Anne O'Malley called it "a fine tale of grief and mystery." According to Joanna Rudge Long in *Horn Book,* "In Clarke's capable hands, the resolution, when it comes at last, is as satisfying as it is surprising."

Kalpana's Dream also mixes elements of the supernatural with a family drama. Neema's great-grandmother, Kalpana, comes from India to live with Neema's family in Australia. Kalpana has trouble communicating with the family and none of the Australian family members speak Hindi particularly well, so there is much confusion when the elderly woman first arrives. Australian culture is also difficult for the Indian woman to comprehend; when she sees Neema's friend Gull on his skateboard, for example, she is convinced that he is flying. *Kalpana's Dream* "is moving—and funny, too," according to *Kliatt* contributor Claire Rosser. While a *Publishers Weekly* critic wrote that "the surreal and realistic elements do not interweave as comfortably here as they did in . . . *Starry Nights,*" a *Kirkus Reviews* critic considered Clarke's novel to be an "intricate blend of fairy tale elements, Indian culture, school story, friendship and family tensions."

Set during 1952 in rural Australia, *The Winds of Heaven* allows Clarke to focus on the choices and experiences that shape a young woman's life. Clementine and Fan are cousins who have grown up very differently. A city girl, Clementine is nine years old when she travels with her mother out to the countryside to meet her beautiful, free-spirited cousin and her taciturn Aunt Rene. Although they are inseparable during their summer together and vow to be friends forever, the second two visits, years apart, show their paths to be diverging. Clementine is bound for college and a career while Fan finds her adventurous spirit crushed by a husband and two children. Told in a third-person text from the perspective of many years, *The Winds of Heaven* provides a "moving" story featuring "introspective, quiet prose [and] . . . authentic coming-of-age characters," according to a *Kirkus Reviews* writer. Readers appreciative of a nuanced story will be "rewarded by the original poetic language" in *The Winds of Heaven,* as well as by "Clarke's achingly spot-on emotional insights," observed Gillian Engberg in *Booklist.* According to Sarah Ellis in *Horn Book,* the author's "baroque, metaphor-rich" text captures "the high emotional pitch of early adolescence."

Clarke takes a more lighthearted approach in her novel *One Whole and Perfect Day,* which is told through a succession of narrators, all related and each with an unique point of view. Central to the story is sixteen-year-old Lily Samson, who feels like the only normal person in her family. Her older brother aspires to be a perennial student, much to the chagrin of Lily's volatile grandfather. Lily's mom dedicates herself to the elderly clients at the senior center where she works, ignoring her home and family in the process and leaving Lily to handle the day-to-day chores. Assorted other relatives also spice up the family, to the point where family gatherings like the one being planned by her strident grandmother are a cause for worry. And Lily does worry: she worries that she could morph from teenager to middle-aged hausfrau overnight. When she meets handsome Daniel Steadman she senses that love may help ground her in the sea of family craziness, but so would her delight at a single day of normalcy. "Filled with surprising turns of events and serendipitous encounters with strangers," according to a *Publishers Weekly* critic, *One Whole and Perfect Day* "celebrates rekindled friendship and blossoming romance."

Clarke defends the realism she injects in her fiction for teen readers. "I want people to read my books and feel a kind of empathy, to feel that they understand how it is," the author explained to Margot Hillel in *Magpies.* "That's what I want really, I want a child to read a

book and think that's just like me or that's how it is for me, and there is somebody who understands. I do believe that something you read in a book can change your life for good."

Biographical and Critical Sources

PERIODICALS

Booklist, March 15, 1990, Stephanie Zvirin, "Guffaws, Giggles, and Good Old-Fashioned Roars," p. 1429; August, 1991, Stephanie Zvirin, review of *Al Capsella and the Watchdogs,* p. 2140; July, 1993, Stephanie Zvirin, review of *Al Capsella Takes a Vacation,* p. 1957; June 1, 2001, Frances Bradburn, review of *Night Train,* p. 1880; September 1, 2002, Frances Bradburn, review of *Wolf on the Fold,* p. 112; June 1, 2003, Anne O'Malley, review of *Starry Nights,* p. 1759; May 1, 2005, Ilene Cooper, review of *Kalpana's Dream,* p. 1586; May 1, 2007, Heather Booth, review of *One Whole and Perfect Day,* p. 81; October 15, 2010, Gillian Engberg, review of *The Winds of Heaven,* p. 52.

Bulletin of the Center for Children's Books, May, 2000, review of *Night Train,* p. 310; October, 2002, review of *Wolf on the Fold,* p. 52.

Horn Book, September-October, 2003, Joanna Rudge Long, review of *Starry Nights,* p. 608; January-February, 2006, review of *Kalpana's Dream,* p. 22; May-June, 2007, Deirdre F. Baker, review of *One Whole and Perfect Day,* p. 279; September-October, 2009, review of *The Miles Between,* p. 572; September-October, 2010, Sarah Ellis, review of *The Winds of Heaven,* p. 74.

Kirkus Reviews, May 15, 2002, review of *Wolf on the Fold,* p. 729; May 15, 2003, review of *Starry Nights,* p. 747; April 1, 2005, review of *Kalpana's Dream,* p. 414; August 15, 2010, review of *The Winds of Heaven.*

Kliatt, July, 2002, Claire Rosser, review of *Wolf on the Fold,* p. 7; March, 2005, Claire Rosser, review of *Kalpana's Dream,* p. 8.

Magpies, May, 1998, Jane Connolly, review of *Night Train,* pp. 36-37; March, 1999, Margot Hillel, interview with Clarke, pp. 14-16; March, 2002, review of *Starry Nights,* p. 32.

Publishers Weekly, June 26, 2000, review of *Night Train,* p. 75; June 10, 2002, review of *Wolf on the Fold,* p. 61; May 12, 2003, review of *Starry Nights,* p. 67; April 25, 2005, review of *Kalpana's Dream,* p. 57; March 12, 2007, review of *One Whole and Perfect Day,* p. 59; October 4, 2010, review of *The Winds of Heaven,* p. 50.

School Librarian, summer, 2000, review of *Al Capsella and the Watchdogs,* p. 97.

School Library Journal, July, 1990, Ronald A. Van De Voorde, review of *The Heroic Life of Al Capsella,* p. 88; August, 1991, Anne Briggs, review of *The Lost Day,* p. 195; May, 1993, Kathy Piehl, review of *Al Capsella Takes a Vacation,* p. 124; May, 2000, Joel Shoemaker, review of *Night Train,* p. 170; September, 2002, Alison Follos, review of *Wolf on the Fold,* p. 220; August, 2005, Christine McGinty, review of *Kalpana's Dream,* p. 122; August, 2007, Heather E. Miller, review of *One Whole and Perfect Day,* p. 112.

Times Educational Supplement, May 4, 2001, review of *Wolf on the Fold,* p. 20.

Voice of Youth Advocates, August, 2000, review of *Night Train,* p. 186; October, 2002, review of *Wolf on the Fold,* p. 270; February, 2004, review of *Starry Nights,* p. 455; August, 2010, Francisca Goldsmith, review of *The Winds of Heaven,* p. 244; February, 2011, Courtney Huse Wika, review of *The Winds of Heaven,* p. 550.

ONLINE

Allen & Unwin Web site, http://www.allenandunwin.com/ (May 1, 2012), "Judith Clarke."

AussieReviews.com, http://www.aussiereviews.com/ (December 4, 2001), Sally Murphy, review of *Starry Nights.*

Front Street Books Web site, http://www.frontstreetbooks.com/ (September 18, 2005), "Judith Clarke."

O'Brien Books Web site, http://www.obrien.ie/ (September 18, 2005), "Judith Clarke."

Penguin Books Australia Web site, http://www.penguin.com.au/ (May 1, 2012), "Judith Clarke."*

* * *

COHEN, Joshua C. 1970-

Personal

Born March 8, 1970, in MN. *Education:* Attended University of Wisconsin.

Career

Writer. Also performed with professional dance companies and in musical theater productions.

Awards, Honors

Top Ten Best Fiction for Young Adults selection, American Library Association, 2012, for *Leverage.*

Writings

Leverage (novel), Dutton Children's Books (New York, NY), 2011.

Sidelights

Joshua C. Cohen explores a host of compelling issues, including bullying, peer pressure, and high-stakes athletics, in *Leverage,* his debut novel for young adults. The idea for the work was a news account detailing a vicious attack by a group of high-school football play-

ers on their younger teammates. When the victims reported the assault, they became pariahs in their community, blamed for tarnishing the school's reputation as well as for the cancellation of the team's remaining games. "My fascination with that part of human nature—the need to keep quiet when awful things occur and how that leads to victims getting wronged twice—is what started the whole story that eventually led to *Leverage,*" Cohen explained on his home page.

Leverage centers on the unlikely relationship between Danny Meehan, an undersized and insecure gymnast at Oregrove High School, and Kurt Brodsky, a gargantuan football player with a troubled past. A rivalry between the school's two athletic squads escalates into tragedy when three steroid-fueled members of the celebrated football team rape a freshman gymnast, Ronnie Gunderson. Kurt and Danny are witnesses to the attack. Kurt is reminded of the abuse he suffered in his foster home and puts a halt to the aggression while Danny hides, too frightened to intervene. After Ronnie commits suicide, Kurt and Danny first remain silent, worried about the repercussions they could face for speaking out against the assailants. With the help of a sympathetic classmate, however, the boys devise a method to expose the crime.

Cover of Joshua Cohen's novel* Leverage, *featuring a cover photograph by Loginov Alexander Vladimirovich. (Reproduced by permission of Dutton Books, a member of Penguin Group (USA) Inc.)

In the words of *School Library Journal* contributor Richard Luzer, *Leverage* "is thought-provoking and well-written, and . . . about as dark and disturbing as YA literature gets." Comparing the novel to Robert Cormier's acclaimed *The Chocolate War,* Sonja Bolle observed in the *Los Angeles Times* that Cohen's novel "draws a connection between the attraction of team sports and the thrill of aggression, and . . . makes the ferocious *Chocolate War* seem almost genteel." A number of critics applauded Cohen's portrayal of Brodsky, the pained, gentle giant. "The central tragedy is gripping, as is Kurt's heartbreaking past," a critic noted in reviewing *Leverage* for *Publishers Weekly,* and a *Kirkus Reviews* writer wrote that Kurt's tribulations "are heartbreakingly real, and readers will pull for him long after the story ends."

Biographical and Critical Sources

PERIODICALS

Booklist, December 15, 2010, Daniel Kraus, review of *Leverage,* p. 45.

Kirkus Reviews, December 15, 2010, review of *Leverage.*

Los Angeles Times, February 20, 2011, Sonja Bolle, review of *Leverage.*

Publishers Weekly, December 6, 2010, review of *Leverage,* p. 50.

School Library Journal, April, 2011, Richard Luzer, review of *Leverage,* p. 170.

Voice of Youth Advocates, February, 2011, Cindy Faughnan and Jenna Yee, review of *Leverage,* p. 550.

ONLINE

Joshua C. Cohen Home Page, http://www.leveragethebook.com (April 15, 2012).

Joshua C. Cohen Web log, http://joshuacohenbooks.wordpress.com (April 15, 2012).*

* * *

COLGAN, Lynda 1953-

Personal

Born 1953, in Canada. *Education:* University of Toronto, B.Sc. (biology and mathematics; with honours), 1976, B.Ed., 1977; Ontario Institute for Studies in Education, M.Ed. (computer applications), 1988, Ph.D. (computer applications), 1992.

Addresses

Home—Kingston, Ontario, Canada. *E-mail*—lynda.colgan@queensu.ca.

Career

Educator and author. Mathematics and science teacher of grades 5 through 9 in Scarborough, Ontario, Canada, 1977-83, consultant in computers in education, 1983-

90, K-12 mathematics coordinator, 1992-98, vice principal of Dr. Norman Bethune school, 1998; York University, North York, Ontario, adjunct professor, then visiting assistant professor of education, 1983-86; Associated Hebrew Schools, Toronto, Ontario, mathematics consultant, 1988-90; Queen's University, Kingston, Ontario, assistant professor, 1998-2004, associate professor of education, beginning 2004, and coordinator of Community Outreach Centre, beginning 2009. Educational consultant and researcher. Developer, *Prime Radicals* (television program), beginning 2008.

Awards, Honors

Marshall McLuhan Distinguished Teaching Award, McLuhan Institute for Global Communications, 1987; Award of Excellence in Education, Ontario Secondary School Teachers' Federation, 1988; Golden Apple Teaching Award, Queen's University Faculty of Education, 2001, and several nominations; Ontario Association for Mathematic Education honor for outstanding contribution to mathematics education, 2007; 3M MacLeans National Teaching fellowship nomination, 2007; Silver Birch Award nomination for Children's Non-Fiction Book, Ontario Library Association, 2011, for *Mathemagic!;* recipient of numerous grants.

Writings

Mathemagic! Number Tricks, illustrated by Jane Kurisu, Kids Can Press (Toronto, Ontario, Canada), 2011.

Contributor to periodicals, including *Ontario Mathematics Gazette* and *Teaching and Teacher Education* and of biweekly column for *Kingston Whig-Standard,* 2006-09. Contributor to books, including *Helping Children Learn Mathematics,* John Wiley & Sons, 2010, and *Elementary Mathematics in Canada: Research Summary and Classroom Implications,* Pearson Education Canada.

Author's work has been translated into Slovenian.

Biographical and Critical Sources

PERIODICALS

Booklist, May 1, 2011, Carolyn Phelan, review of *Mathemagic! Number Tricks,* p. 75.

Kirkus Reviews, February 15, 2011, review of *Mathemagic!*

School Library Journal, May, 2011, Grace Oliff, review of *Mathemagic!,* p. 95.

ONLINE

Kid's Can Press Web site, http://www.kidscanpress/ (May 1, 2012), "Lynda Colgan."

Prime Radicals Web site, http://www.primeradicals.com (May 1, 2012).

Queen's University Web site, http://educ.queensu.ca/ (May 1, 2012), "Lynda Colgan."*

* * *

CORNELL, Kevin

Personal

Born in New York, NY.

Addresses

Home—Philadelphia, PA. *Agent*—Steven Malk, Writers House, 7660 Fay Ave., No. 338H, La Jolla, CA 92037.

Career

Animator, designer, and illustrator.

Writings

SELF-ILLUSTRATED

(With Matthew Sutter) *The Superest: Who Is the Superest Hero of Them All?,* Rebel Base Books (New York, NY), 2010.

Author/illustrator of *Six-Penny Anthems I, Six-Penny Anthems II, Curriculum Vitae, The Story of Eh, Ambidextrous, The Wippins Campaign,* and *The Bearskinrug Swap Meat Scrapbook.*

ILLUSTRATOR

F. Scott Fitzgerald, *The Curious Case of Benjamin Button* (graphic novel), adapted by Nunzio DeFilippis and Christina Weir, Quirk Books (Philadelphia, PA), 2008.

Doreen Cronin, *The Trouble with Chickens,* Laura Geringer Books (New York, NY), 2011.

Mac Barnett, *Mustache!,* Disney/Hyperion Books (New York, NY), 2011.

Contributor to Web sites, including *Birthday Street, The Superest,* and *A List Apart.* Contributor to periodicals, including *McSweeney's* and *Maisonneuve.*

Sidelights

A respected animator, designer, and illustrator, Kevin Cornell has also created artwork for children's books such as *The Trouble with Chickens* by Doreen Cronin and *Mustache!* by Mac Barnett. In addition to Web sites and periodicals, Cornell's illustrations can also be found in *The Superest: Who Is the Superest Hero of Them All?,* a book cocreated by Matthew Sutter.

***Kevin Cornell teams up with author Doreen Cronin to entertain children in the picture book* The Trouble with Chickens.** (Illustration copyright © by Kevin Cornell. Reproduced by permission of Balzer + Bray, an imprint of HarperCollins Publishers.)

The Trouble with Chickens centers on the adventures of J.J. Tully, a retired search-and-rescue dog that agrees to locate a pair of missing chicks for a distraught mother hen. Tully must match wits with Vince the Funnel, an obnoxious, indoor canine who sports a plastic cone around his head and who is believed to be the kidnapper. "Cornell's black-and-white cartoon illustrations add to the hilarity," observed *School Library Journal* critic Michele Shaw, and a *Publishers Weekly* reviewer noted that the illustrations in *The Trouble with Chickens* "have a mix of energy and humor that adds to the fun."

In Barnett's *Mustache!* a narcissistic and mustachioed ruler cares more about his appearance than the health of his kingdom. His frustrated subjects resort to graffiti as a form of rebellion, drawing mustaches on every poster, billboard, and statue in the land. According to a writer in *Kirkus Reviews,* "Cornell ushers the story forward with cinematic [sequential] artwork, framed in elaborate medieval-like." A *Publishers Weekly* contributor applauded the humor in Barnett's narrative for *Mustache!,* adding that Cornell "holds his own in scenes filled with visual gags."

The Curious Case of Benjamin Button, a graphic-novel adaptation of a short story by F. Scott Fitzgerald, tells the fantastical tale of a man who ages in reverse. Born a septuagenarian in 1860, Benjamin grows younger (and shorter) as the years pass, during which time he goes to war, heads a business, raises a son, and eventually attends kindergarten as his memory fades. In *Booklist* Ian Chipman complimented Cornell's "sepia-toned art" for the book, writing that it "lends itself to the late nineteenth-and early twentieth-century time period." A *Publishers Weekly* reviewer maintained that the illustrations "are especially clever at showing physical and emotional changes as Benjamin moves backward through life," and *School Library Journal* critic Benjamin Russell stated that "Cornell depicts not just the transformation of Benjamin's face, but also his changing poise and confidence with well-rendered body language."

Biographical and Critical Sources

PERIODICALS

Booklist, January 1, 2009, Ian Chipman, review of *The Curious Case of Benjamin Button,* p. 66; February 1, 2011, review of *The Trouble with Chickens,* p. 80.

Horn Book, March-April, 2011, review of *The Trouble with Chickens,* p. 113.

Kirkus Reviews, April 15, 2011, and September 15, 2011, review of *Mustache!*

New York Times Book Review, March 13, 2011, Pamela Paul, review of *The Trouble with Chickens,* p. 15.

Publishers Weekly, September 29, 2008, review of *The Curious Case of Benjamin Button,* p. 65; January 17, 2011, review of *The Trouble with Chickens,* p. 49; September 5, 2011, review of *Mustache!,* p. 46.

School Library Journal, January, 2009, Benjamin Russell, review of *The Curious Case of Benjamin Button,* p. 135; February, 2011, Michele Shaw, review of *The Trouble with Chickens,* p. 78; September, 2011, Marianne Saccardi, review of *Mustache!,* p. 112.

ONLINE

Kevin Cornell Home Page, http://www.bearskinrug.co.uk (April 15, 2011).*

D

DALY, Cathleen

Personal

Born in Palo Alto, CA.

Addresses

Home—Berkeley, CA. *Agent*—Meredith Kaffel, Charlotte Sheedy Literary Agency, 928 Broadway, Ste. 901, New York, NY 10010; meredith@sheedylit.com.

Career

Performance artist, writer, and educator. Teaches theater for children; San Francisco Children of Incarcerated Parents Project, Berkeley, CA, member of staff.

Awards, Honors

Best of the San Francisco Fringe Festival selection, for play *How to be a Secret Agent Girl as Seen on American Television and in Movies;* Notable Children's Books selection, American Library Association, 2012, for *Prudence Wants a Pet.*

Writings

Flirt Club (novel), Roaring Brook Press (New York, NY), 2011.

Prudence Wants a Pet, illustrated by Stephen Michael King, Roaring Brook Press (New York, NY), 2011.

Author of plays, including *How to be a Secret Agent Girl as Seen on American Television and in Movies.* Also author of *Ode to the Unhinged* (poetry chapbook). Contributor of poetry to anthologies, including *Literary Mama: Reading for the Maternally Inclined,* edited by Andrea J. Buchanan and Amy Hudock, Seal Press, 2005, and to periodicals, including *Palo Alto Times, Seeker,* and *Slow Trains.*

Sidelights

Educator and performance artist Cathleen Daly earned critical acclaim for her debut young-adult novel, *Flirt Club,* which was inspired by her love of the theatre. "When I teach I create stories with and for kids," she explained to *Publishers Weekly* interviewer Donna Freitas. "Performing and being in front of people, you get a sense of what's entertaining—or not. The stuff I do on stage is very character-driven and so are my books." Daly has also produced a children's book, *Prudence Wants a Pet,* which features illustrations by Stephen Michael King.

Flirt Club centers on a pair of boy-crazy but insecure eighth graders and was based in part on the author's own experiences in middle school. Best friends Izzy and Annie—known as Cisco and the Bean, respectively—desperately want to attract the attention of their male classmates, but they do not have a clue how to go about it. Tired of blushing and stammering every time a boy approaches, the girls form the secretive and exclusive Flirt Club as a way to improve their communication skills and boost their confidence. Cisco and the Bean are soon joined by three members of their school's drama club, and although their hard work pays off the girls also discover that dating has pitfalls, including cheating boyfriends and broken hearts.

Daly tells *Flirt Club* through journal entries and notes exchanged between the main characters. According to a critic in *Publishers Weekly,* the author's "debut sparkles with wit, and her protagonists brim with enthusiasm and heart." In *School Library Journal* Mariela Siegert observed that "the girls' friendships are authentic and the situations are definitely on target for middle schoolers," and Marilyn Beebe stated in *Voice of Youth Advocates* that "the importance of honesty, family, and female friendships is transmitted to readers in a relatively painless manner."

An imaginative and determined girl seeks companionship in *Prudence Wants a Pet,* "a lighthearted read about never giving up on one's dreams," according to *School*

Library Journal reviewer Maryann H. Owen. When her parents refuse to purchase a pet for her, Prudence adopts an unlikely alternative: a tree limb. When Branch becomes a nuisance for Prudence's father (he trips over it eight times), she begins caring for a series of equally unusual yet ultimately disappointing "pets" that include an old shoe and a car tire. Prudence's mother and father come to admire her persistence, resulting in a wonderful surprise for the youngster. "This sly story suggests nonwhiny—if sometimes mischievous—ways to bend the most stubborn wills," a critic maintained in *Publishers Weekly,* and a writer in *Kirkus Reviews* stated that the "classic theme" in *Prudence Wants a Pet* "feels fresh as a squiggling kitten."

Biographical and Critical Sources

PERIODICALS

Booklist, December 15, 2010, Shelle Rosenfeld, review of *Flirt Club,* p. 48; June 1, 2011, Angela Leeper, review of *Prudence Wants a Pet,* p. 97.

Horn Book, May-June, 2011, Tanya D. Auger, review of *Flirt Club,* p. 86; July-August, 2011, Tanya D. Auger, review of *Prudence Wants a Pet,* p. 126.

Kirkus Reviews, December 1, 2010, review of *Flirt Club*; May 1, 2011, review of *Prudence Wants a Pet.*

Publishers Weekly, November 22, 2010, review of *Flirt Club,* p. 58; May 9, 2011, review of *Prudence Wants a Pet,* p. 50; June 20, 2011, Donna Freitas, "Flying Starts."

School Library Journal, April, 2011, Mariela Siegert, review of *Flirt Club,* p. 170; May, 2011, Maryann H. Owen, review of *Prudence Wants a Pet,* p. 74.

Voice of Youth Advocates, February, 2011, Marlyn Beebe, review of *Flirt Club,* p. 551.

ONLINE

Cathleen Daly Web log, http://cathleenadaly.blogspot.com (April 15, 2012).*

* * *

DeMATTEIS, J.M. 1953-
(John Marc DeMatteis)

Personal

Born December 15, 1953, in New York, NY; married; children: one son, one daughter. *Education:* Empire State College, degree. *Religion:* Hindu. *Hobbies and other interests:* Travel, playing guitar and piano, spending time with family.

Addresses

Home—Upstate New York.

Career

Comic-book writer, scriptwriter, and novelist. Formerly worked as a music critic; DC Comics, New York, NY, writer, beginning c. 1970s; Marvel Comics, New York, NY, writer, beginning 1980s; Ardden Entertainment, editor in chief, beginning 2008. Story consultant; host of Imagination 101 (writing workshop). Musician, performing on *How Many Lifetimes?,* produced 1997.

Awards, Honors

American Library Association Ten Best Graphic Novels designation, 2001, for *Brooklyn Dreams;* (with others) Eisner Award for Best Humor Publication, 2004, for *Formerly Known as the Justice League.*

Writings

GRAPHIC NOVELS

Greenberg the Vampire, illustrated by Mark Badger, Marvel Comics (New York, NY), 1986.

Stan Lee Presents Spider Man: Fearful Symmetry—Kraven's Last Hunt (originally published in comic-book form), illustrated by Mike Zeck and others, Marvel Comics (New York, NY), 1989.

Moonshadow (originally published in comic-book form), illustrated by Jon J. Muth and others, Marvel/Epic Comics (New York, NY), 1989, published as *The Compleat Moonshadow*, DC Comics (New York, NY), 1998.

Blood (originally published in comic-book form), illustrated by Kent Williams, Marvel/Epic Comics (New York, NY), 1989, reprinted, 2004.

(With Keith Giffen) *Justice League International: The Secret Gospel of Maxwell Lord,* illustrated by Bill Willingham and others, DC Comics (New York, NY), 1992.

Mercy, illustrated by Paul Johnson, DC Comics (New York, NY), 1993.

Brooklyn Dreams (originally published in comic-book form by Paradox, 1994–1995), illustrated by Glenn Barr, Vertigo/DC Comics (New York, NY), 2003.

(With Sherilyn Van Valkenburgh) *Wings,* DC Comics (New York, NY), 2001.

Green Lantern: Willworld, illustrated by Seth Fisher, DC Comics (New York, NY), 2001.

Batman: Absolution, illustrated by Brian Ashmore, DC Comics (New York, NY), 2002.

(With Phil Jimenez and Joe Kelly) *Wonder Woman: Paradise Lost* (originally published in comic-book form), illustrated by Jimenez and others, DC Comics (New York, NY), 2002.

(With others) *Superman: President Lex,* DC Comics (New York, NY), 2003.

(With Keith Giffen) *Formerly Known as the Justice League* (originally published in comic-book form), DC Comics (New York, NY), 2004.

(With Keith Giffen) *I Can't Believe It's Not the Justice League* (originally published in comic-book form), DC Comics (New York, NY), 2005.

Stardust Kid (originally published in comic-book form), illustrated by Mike Ploog, Boom! Studios, 2008.

Batman: Going Sane, illustrated by Joe Staton, DC Comics (New York, NY), 2008.

Justice League International, five volumes, illustrated by Kevin Maguire, DC Comics (New York, NY), 20082011.

(With Keith Giffen) *Booster Gold: Past Imperfect* (originally published in comic-book form), illustrated by Chris Batista, Giffen, and Pat Olliffe, DC Comics (New York, NY), 2011.

(With Fred van Lente and Michael Oeming) *Chaos War: Avengers* (originally published in comic-book form), illustrated by Tom Grummett, Stephen Segovia, and Brian Ching, Marvel (New York, NY), 2011.

Author, with Giffen, of comic-book series "Hero Squared," for Atomeka Press; and "Planetary Brigade," for Boom! Studios, 2006. Author of graphic miniseries "Into Shambhala," 1986; "Farewell, Moonshadow"; "The Last One"; "Seekers into the Mystery"; and "The Life and Times of Savior 28," IDW, 2009. Contributor to ongoing comic-book series, including "The Amazing Spider-Man," "The Defenders," "Superman," "Captain America," "Justice League," "Doctor Strange," "Daredevil," "Man-Thing," "The Silver Surfer," "Wonder Woman," "Doctor Fate," "Spectre," "Batman," and "Doom Patrol."

"ABADAZAD" GRAPHIC-NOVEL SERIES; FOR CHILDREN

The Road to Inconceivable (originally published in comic-book form by CrossGen), illustrated by Mike Ploog, Hyperion Books for Children (New York, NY), 2006.

The Dream Thief (originally published in comic-book form by CrossGen), illustrated by Mike Ploog, Hyperion Books for Children (New York, NY), 2006.

The Puppet, the Professor, and the Prophet (originally published in comic-book form by CrossGen), illustrated by Mike Ploog, Hyperion Books for Children (New York, NY), 2007.

OTHER

Imaginalis (middle-grade novel), Katherine Tegen Books (New York, NY), 2010.

Author of episodes for television series, including *The Twilight Zone, The Adventures of Superboy, Batman, Earth: Final Conflict, The Real Ghostbusters, Justice League Unlimited, Thundercats,* and *Legion of Super-Heroes.* Author of unproduced screenplays and of installments in *Justice League* (animated television program), for Cartoon Network. Contributor of reviews to periodicals, including *Rolling Stone.*

Adaptations

Author's teleplay *The Eyes of Despero!* was adapted by Jake Black, Grosset & Dunlap (New York, NY), 2010.

Sidelights

Considered among the most versatile writers working in contemporary comics, J.M. DeMatteis is noted for creating compelling characters and plots involving complex themes. Starting as a music critic, the Brooklyn-born DeMatteis moved into writing texts for comic books in the late 1970s. In the years since, he has contributed to numerous ongoing comic-book series as well as creating acclaimed original stories that have been published in graphic-novel format. In his work for DC Comics and Marvel DeMatteis has made his creative mark on such series as "The Defenders," "Spider-Man," "Superman," "Batman," and the superhero spoof "Justice League International," while in *Brooklyn Dreams, Moonshadow,* and *Abadazad* he presents original stories that appeal to both teens and adult fans of the graphic-novel medium. He has also worked for indie comics publishers such as Boom! Studios, which published DeMatteis' children's comic "Stardust Kid" as well as its graphic-novel adaptation.

DeMatteis played a significant role in founding DC's Vertigo imprint, which began publishing adult-themed

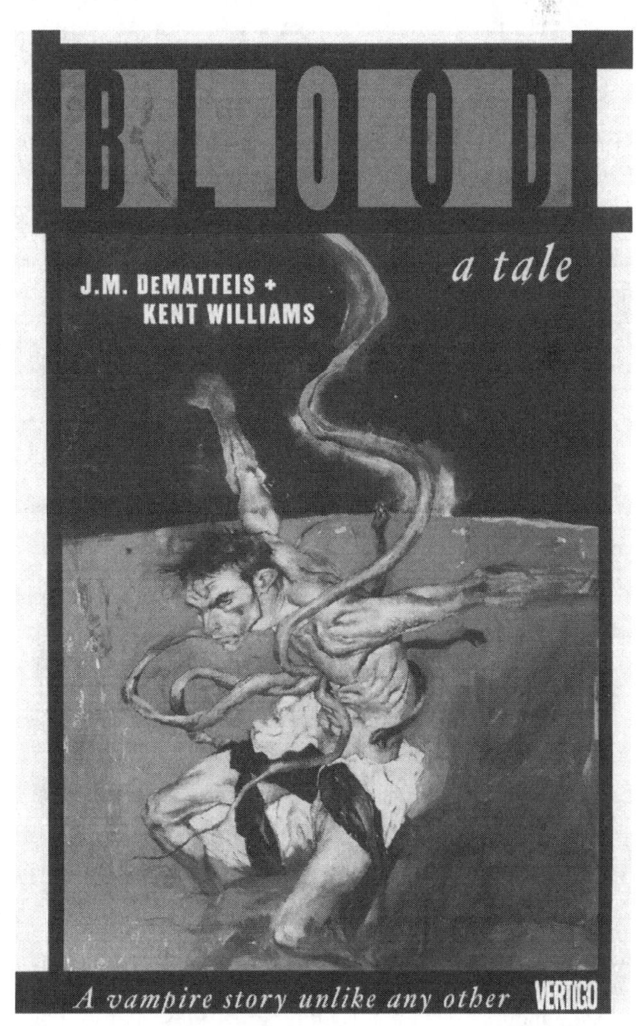

Cover of J.M. DeMatteis' graphic novel* Blood, *which was originally published as a comic-book series and features artwork by Kent Williams. (Cover copyright © 2004 by DC Comics. Used with permission of DC Comics, Inc.)

horror comics during the 1970s. He then went on to collaborate with artist Mike Zeck on Marvel's "Captain America" series, as well as on a story arc that ran in "Spider-Man" before appearing in graphic-novel format as *Stan Lee Presents Spider Man: Fearful Symmetry—Kraven's Last Hunt.* DeMatteis also worked with artist Jon J. Muth to produce *Moonshadow,* a series produced in book form by Marvel that was noted for being the first fully painted comic series.

Remaining with Marvel throughout much of the 1980s, DeMatteis followed *Moonshadow* with *Blood,* a vampire story with mythic undertones that features art by Kent Williams. Returning to DC by the time *Blood* hit bookstores, he took over the reins of the long-running "Justice League of America" superhero saga. When characters from that series, such as G'nort, Mr. Nebula, and Mister Miracle, were recast in the more-humorous "Justice League International," he worked with coauthor Keith Giffen on developing both the series and its various spin-offs. In 2003 DeMatteis joined with Giffen to receive an Eisner award recognizing the story arc published in book form as *Formerly Known as the Justice League.* After five years, he returned to Marvel and shepherded the "Spider-Man" series down a darker path in story arcs such as "The Child Within," working with artist Sal Buscema.

In DeMatteis' autobiographical miniseries *Brooklyn Dreams,* a collaboration with artist Glenn Bart that was issued by DC Comics in 1994, forty-something narrator Carl Santini looks back on his high-school years in the late 1960s. Issues in the teen's tumultuous multicultural family, his questions of faith, as well as his friendships, experimental drug use, and romantic entanglements highlight the memoir, bubbling to the story's surface in the form of what *Booklist* contributor Ray Olson described as "richly detailed" and humorous "digressions." Against Santini's teen reality is the narrator's memory of meeting with his guardian angel, a scruffy, stray hound, and this memory also resonates throughout DeMatteis' story. Praising *Brooklyn Dreams* as "a classic of the [comic-book] form," Olson deemed the work "as graphically distinguished and creatively novelistic a graphic novel as has ever been." In *Publishers Weekly* a critic called DeMatteis' tale "hypnotic," adding that Barr's illustrations follow "the plot's twists, . . . captur[ing] . . . the wild enthusiasms and fears of Carl's world." First published by DC Comics' Paradox Press imprint, *Brooklyn Dreams* was reissued in one volume by Vertigo in 2003.

In 2004 DeMatteis teamed with veteran British artist Mike Ploog to create "Abadazad," a fantasy comic published by Florida-based publisher CrossGen. Two installments appeared in soft-cover editions before CrossGen went bankrupt, leaving both author and illustrator in a quandary. Fortunately, the series was acquired by Walt Disney Corporation, and the media giant allowed DeMatteis and Ploog to return to the proverbial drawing table and reconfigure their story as a hybrid meld-

DeMatteis teams up with artist Mike Ploog to adapt a popular comic-book series into the graphic novel **Abadazad: The Road to Inconceivable.** (Hyperion Books for Children, 2006. Reprinted by permission of Disney-Hyperion, an imprint of Disney Book Group LLC. All rights reserved.)

ing picture book and comic book. The saga is an amalgam of *The Wizard of Oz, Alice in Wonderland,* and the Arabian Nights, with nine-year-old Katie Jameson its Shaharazad. In the story, Katie is a fan of the book series "Martha in Abadazad," and she shares these books with her younger brother Matt. The two have a close relationship until Matt mysteriously vanishes while on a ride at a local carnival. Guilt over Matt's fate transforms Katie's nature, and by her early teens she has become glum and taciturn. A meeting with a quirky neighbor who claims that Martha's Abadazadian adventures were, in fact, real rekindles Katie's fascination with the fantasy world. When the woman provides the fourteen year old with the means by which she can enter Abadazad, Katie willingly takes a chance, propelled by the belief that there she will discover Matt's fate.

Discussing the initial comic-book version of the "Abadazad" saga in a *Magazine of Fantasy and Science Fiction* review, Charles de Lint noted that it engages

readers due to DeMatteis' "inventiveness" and "attention to real world detail and problems [which] . . . slightly subvert everything in the magical land." Calling the series "kid-friendly," de Lint also noted that DeMatteis' story contains "enough meat and sly asides and bits of humor that adults will enjoy it as well."

The "Abadazad" series was repackaged in 2006 as the illustrated novels *The Road to Inconceivable, The Dream Thief,* and *The Puppet, the Professor, and the Prophet. The Road to Inconceivable* follows fourteen-year-old Katie into the fantasy world, where the Brooklyn teen confirms that younger brother Matt is being held hostage there. DeMatteis' text is multi-level; it alternates between Katie's diary entries and the overarching story line and is cemented by Ploog's animé-style art. Although her search proves fruitless, by the end of the book Katie has started down the path she will follow in *The Dream Thief.* Helped by the benevolent Little Martha in the saga's second installment, the teen learns that her little brother is being held captive by the sinister Lanky Man.

While Sharon R. Pearce wrote in *School Library Journal* that the format of the "Abadazad" books might be "too confusing" for some readers, a *Publishers Weekly* reviewer maintained that the series "expertly blends art and text" and "Katie's emotionally messy but honest diary" is enhanced by Ploog's "deft brushwork." Writing that the series' "black-and-white art is an appealing mix of realism and exaggeration," Jesse Karp added in *Booklist* that DeMatteis' heroine "makes the story shine," resulting in a "thoughtful read with surprising psychological nuance."

DeMatteis reconnected with his young fans in *Imaginalis,* a middle-grade novel that finds twelve-year-old Mehera Beatrice Crosby totally addicted to the "Imaginalis" book series. Each book has taken her on a new adventure, and she is crestfallen when she learns that no new "Imaginalis" novels are scheduled for publication. For Mehera, the story's cast of characters—Prince Imagos, Prognostica, the regal elephant Lord Nossyss, and other residents of Nolandia—are real, and she is determined to help them resolve the dilemmas they each faced at the cliffhanger close of the final volume. When she finds a way to travel into Imaginalis, the preteen faces another dilemma: if she can travel between worlds, so can Pralaya, the arch villain of the "Imaginalis" series.

Reviewing *Imaginalis* in *Publishers Weekly,* a critic cited DeMatteis' story for its "well-drawn characters, abundant action and humor, and hopeful message." In *Booklist* John Peters remarked on the Hindu/East Indian roots of the "Imaginalis" saga and concluded that the author's "fluently written metafiction features . . . enough action to keep the philosophical underpinnings in their place." Likening the novel to a Hindu version of C.S. Lewis's Christian-inspired "Chronicles of Narnia," Karen E. Brooks-Reese added in her *School Library Journal* review of *Imaginalis* that DeMatteis' "premise is intriguing and will delight readers who imagine themselves in the pages of their favorite books."

Cover of DeMatteis' middle-grade fantasy* Imaginalis, *featuring artwork by Dominic Hartman. (Reproduced by permission of Katherine Tegen Books, an imprint of HarperCollins Publishers.)

Speaking with Mike Jozic in an online interview for Silver Bullet Comics, DeMatteis noted: "When I look at fantasy books I've enjoyed—from *Alice in Wonderland* to *Oz,* from [J.R.R.] Tolkien to Ray Bradbury—I think it comes down to one essential ingredient: the sense of wonder. Whether you're seven years old or a jaded adult, if your sense of wonder is blown open, if you're drawn into a world that intrigues and excites you and if you believe in that world, then the story is going to appeal. Which is why the best fantasy seems to work on so many levels, for so many age groups."

Biographical and Critical Sources

PERIODICALS

Booklist, July, 2003, Ray Olson, review of *Brooklyn Dreams,* p. 1855; July 1, 2006, Jesse Karp, review of

The Road to Inconceivable, p. 55; June 1, 2008, Jesse Karp, review of *Stardust Kid,* p. 82; May 15, 2010, John Peters, review of *Imaginalis,* p. 53.
Kirkus Reviews, May 15, 2006, review of *The Road to Inconceivable,* p. 516; June 1, 2010, review of *Imaginalis.*
Magazine of Fantasy and Science Fiction, September, 2004, Charles de Lint, review of *Abadazad,* p. 32.
Publishers Weekly, September 29, 2003, review of *Superman: President Lex,* p. 45; August 11, 2003, review of *Brooklyn Dreams,* p. 259; June 12, 2005, review of *The Road to Inconceivable,* p. 53; July 12, 2010, review of *Imaginalis,* p. 47.
School Library Journal, November, 2006, Sharon R. Pearce, reviews of *The Road to Inconceivable* and *The Dream Thief,* both p. 166; November, 2010, Karen E. Brooks-Reese, review of *Imaginalis,* p. 110.
Wilson Library Bulletin, October, 1993, review of *Moonshadow,* p. 136.

ONLINE

ComicFanatic.com, http://www.comicfanatic.com/ (December 9, 2004), interview with DeMatteis.
Comicon.com, http://www.comicon.com/ (May 5, 2005), Jennifer M. Contino, interview with DeMatteis.
J.M. DeMatteis Home Page, http://www.jmdematteis.com (May 1, 2012).
Silver Bullet Comics Web site, http://www.silverbulletcomicbooks.com/ (January 14, 2004), Mike Jozic, interview with DeMatteis.*

* * *

DeMATTEIS, John Marc
See DeMATTEIS, J.M.

See DeMATTEIS, J.M.

* * *

DePALMA, Mary Newell 1961-

Personal

Born August 20, 1961, in Pittsburgh, PA; daughter of Francis and Joan Newell; married Alphonse DePalma III; children: Kepley Therese, Alphonse IV. *Education:* Rochester Institute of Technology, B.F.A. (medical illustration), 1983. *Hobbies and other interests:* Gardening, knitting, reading.

Addresses

Home and office—Boston, MA. *E-mail*—mary@marynewelldepalma.com.

Career

Freelance illustrator, Boston, MA, beginning 1984. Has worked as an interpreter for the deaf, a calligrapher, and a hand-knitter of designer sweaters. *Exhibitions:*

Mary Newell DePalma (Photograph by Alphonse DePalma III. Reproduced by permission.)

Work exhibited at Huntington House Museum, Windsor, CT, 2002; Concord Museum, Concord, MA, 2002; Chemer's Gallery, Tustin, CA, 2004; and Elizabeth Stone Gallery, Alexandria, VA, 2007, and included in Society of Illustrators annual exhibition, 2000, and Original Art Exhibition, 2001. Work included in permanent collection at Mazza Museum of International Art from Picture Books, Findlay, OH.

Member

Society of Children's Book Writers and Illustrators.

Awards, Honors

Best Children's Book selection, Bank Street College of Education, 2004, for *Now It Is Winter* by Eileen Spinelli; Best Children's Book selection, New York Public Library, 2004, and Children's Choice selection, International Reading Association (IRA), 2005, both for *My Chair* by Betsy James; Best Children's Book selection, *Washington Post Book World,* 2006, for *The Squeaky Door* by Margaret Read MacDonald; IRA/Children's Book Council Choice selection, 2006, for *A Grand Old Tree;* Oppenheim Toy Portfolio Gold Medal, 2010, for *The Perfect Gift.*

Writings

SELF-ILLUSTRATED

The Strange Egg, Houghton Mifflin (Boston, MA), 2001.
A Grand Old Tree, Arthur A. Levine (New York, NY), 2005.
The Nutcracker Doll, Arthur A. Levine (New York, NY), 2007.
The Perfect Gift, Arthur A. Levine Books (New York, NY), 2010.
Uh-oh!, Eerdmans Books for Young Readers (Grand Rapids MI), 2011.
Bow-wow Wiggle Waggle, Eerdmans Books for Young Readers (Grand Rapids, MI), 2012.

Author's work has been translated into French, Japanese, and Korean.

ILLUSTRATOR

Ilona Kemeny Stashko and Carol Whiting Bowen, retellers, *Goldilocks and the Three Bears,* Come Alive Publications (Concord, MA), 1992.
Miriam Aroner, *Giraffes Aren't Half as Fat,* Millbrook Press (Brookfield, CT), 1995.
Matt Curtis, *Six Empty Pockets,* Children's Press (New York, NY), 1997.
Patricia Hubbell, *Black Earth, Gold Sun* (poems), Marshall Cavendish (New York, NY), 2001.
Susan Blackaby, *Rembrandt's Hat,* Houghton Mifflin (Boston, MA), 2002.
Marc Harshman, *Roads,* Marshall Cavendish (New York, NY), 2002.
Betsy James, *My Chair,* Arthur A. Levine (New York, NY), 2004.
Eileen Spinelli, *Now It Is Winter,* Eerdmans (Grand Rapids, MI), 2004.
Jan Wahl, *Knock! Knock!,* Henry Holt (New York, NY), 2004.
Jill Esbaum, *Estelle Takes a Bath,* Henry Holt (New York, NY), 2006.
Margaret Read MacDonald, *The Squeaky Door,* HarperCollins (New York, NY), 2006.
Susan Milord, *Happy School Year!,* Scholastic (New York, NY), 2008.
Carol Molski, *Swimming Sal,* Eerdmans Books for Young Readers (Grand Rapids, MI), 2009.
Susan Milord, *Happy 100th Day!,* Scholastic Press (New York, NY), 2011.
Eileen Spinelli, *Now It Is Summer,* Eerdmans Books for Young Readers (Grand Rapids, MI), 2011.

Sidelights

Mary Newell DePalma began her picture-book career as an illustrator, producing colorful art for stories by authors that include Jan Wahl, Betsy James, Patricia Hubbell, Margaret Read Macdonald, Susan Milord, and Eileen Spinelli. In reviewing an early work, *Rembrandt's Hat* by Susan Blackaby, Robin L. Gibson suggested in *School Library Journal* that "children will want to take a closer look, as the illustrations deserve careful inspection." Noting the growing number of children that populate the illustrations in James's *My Chair* from first page to last, one *Kirkus Reviews* contributor predicted that "young viewers will pore over the actively posed figures and sometimes-surprising details" DePalma features in her colorful art, while another suggested that her brightly colored illustrations for Susan Milord's *Happy 100th Day!* helps make the work "a refreshing change from the usual ruck of 100th-day-[in-school] books." In more recent years, the illustrator has paired her art with original stories, producing picture books such as *The Strange Egg, The Nutcracker Doll, Uh-oh!,* and *Bow-wow Waggle.*

DePalma worked in a number of fields, from advertising to textbook illustration, before entering the children's book market. Her unique, brightly colored art first appeared in *Goldilocks and the Three Bears,* a retelling by Ilona Kemeny Stashko and Carol Whiting Bowen, and other illustration projects quickly followed. Her contribution to Wahl's spooky folk-tale adaptation *Knock! Knock!* includes "creepy details and atmospheric shadows," according to *School Library Journal* contributor Susan Weitz, and a *Kirkus Reviews* writer noted that, "with their exaggerated perspectives and spooky shadows," DePalma's characters "seal the deal."

Macdonald's retelling of a traditional tale in *The Squeaky Door* features a humorous cast of pajama-clad animals in a story about a youngster moving to a big-

***DePalma's illustrations have appeared in picture books such as Patricia Hubbell's rural-themed* Black Earth, Gold Sun.** (Marshall Cavendish. Illustration copyright 2001 © Mary Newell DePalma. Reproduced by permission of the publisher.)

boy bed. DePalma's "diminutive and detailed" art for the story "envision[s] a cozy home and loving grandma," noted Stephanie Zvirin in her review of *The Squeaky Door* for *Booklist.* Equally whimsical pictures bring to life *Estelle Takes a Bath,* as a child interrupts her bubble bath to chase a mouse around the house. Calling the illustrations for Jill Esbaum's story "lighthearted," Blair Christolon added in *School Library Journal* that they are "filled with humor as bubbles, steam, and an assortment of strategically placed household objects" preserve the young girl's modesty. DePalma's work on Spinelli's companion picture books *Now It Is Winter* and *Now It Is Summer* also earned kudos, *Booklist* critic Carolyn Phelan noting of the latter that the "nicely detailed acrylic paintings create an effective visual counterpoint" to the text.

Featuring the combination of a naive bird and a wise little monkey, DePalma's first self-illustrated children's book, *The Strange Egg,* focuses on the joy of new friends and the value in sharing dreams and ideas. With few words and short sentences, the book describes the antics of a small black bird that finds a round, orange object and tries to determine what it is. Finally, deciding that the object must be an egg, the bird sits on it, to the great amusement of a monkey, who shows the bird how to peel and eat the orange. After the two enjoy the

Cover of DePalma's picture book* A Grand Old Tree, *a gentle nature story featuring her colorful graphic art. (Illustration © 2005 by Mary Newell DePalma. Reproduced by permission of Scholastic, Inc.)

fruit, the bird returns the favor by teaching the monkey how to plant the orange's seeds. Soon the two are fast friends and enjoy many oranges together.

A contributor to *Kirkus Reviews* dubbed *The Strange Egg* "an odd little tale of fruit and friendship," and Susan Marie Pitard pointed out in *School Library Journal* that the story "underlines issues important to children: cooperation, friendship, using your individual talents," and others. Both reviewers noted that the exuberance of DePalma's mixed-media illustrations provide much of the humor and fun of the story. "There is real humor in the illustrations," the *Kirkus Reviews* critic observed, while a contributor to *Publishers Weekly* credited much of the book's success to the author/illustrator's "quirky" and "postmodern" illustrations. "This offbeat riff on the joys of the unexpected as well as the give-and-take of friendship is eggs-actly right," the critic concluded of *The Strange Egg.*

DePalma's *A Grand Old Tree* is the story of a tree's life cycle, and her illustrations show the many creatures that live in the tree while it is alive and healthy, as well as those who move in after it is dead. Carolyn Phelan, writing in *Booklist,* commented that DePalma's "well-chosen words . . . are poetic in the economy of their expression and the precision of their imagery." Maura Bresnahan, reviewing the book for *School Library Journal,* wrote that the "art superbly complements the writing." Noting the variety of collage materials that accompany DePalma's watercolors, a *Kirkus Reviews* contributor found the illustrations "winningly simple," adding that "her big-eyed animals are sweetly comical." Also favorably reviewing *A Grand Old Tree,* a *Publishers Weekly* critic felt that "the stylized shapes of the watercolor and torn-paper art emanate a carefree, child-like feel."

The inspiration for DePalma's story for *The Nutcracker Doll* was found close to home and involved "daughter Kepley and everyone involved with Boston Ballet's *The Nutcracker,*" as she explained to an online interviewer for *Book Page.* The tale is based on third grader Kepley's experiences as part of the Boston Ballet's annual production of *The Nutcracker.* Both text and illustrations "incorporate the details that authenticate the story and make readers feel like insiders," wrote a contributor to *Publishers Weekly.* In *Horn Book,* Jennifer M. Brabander concluded that *The Nutcracker Doll* is "a book that's as sweet and delectable as a Christmas cookie."

Friendship is DePalma's focus in *The Perfect Gift,* as a little bird attempts to carry a ripe strawberry home as a gift for her grandmother. When the strawberry accidentally falls into the river, a chipmunk, a goose, and a frog help retrieve it. Just as they have the strawberry safely in hand, a crocodile attempts to eat not only the berry but the four animal friends as well. The bird must sacrifice the berry, but with the help of the three friends she creates a far-more-lasting present. "Lots of action and a satisfying ending will please young readers," pre-

***Colorful art by DePalma adds exuberance to Susan Milord's upbeat school story* Happy 100th Day!** (Illustration copyright © 2011 by Mary Newell DePalma. Reproduced by permission of Scholastic Press, an imprint of Scholastic, Inc.)

dicted a *Publishers Weekly* critic in reviewing *The Perfect Gift,* while in *Kirkus Reviews* a contributor hailed the brightly illustrated story as "a solid salute to friendship, the power of creativity and the wonder of a homemade gift."

Young dinosaur fans are the particular audience for *Uh-Oh!,* which finds a young triceratops causing a steady stream of unintended mischief. In cartoon-style art and a text that consists of a repetition of the title word, DePalma follows the spiky-tailed toddler stand-in as he goes from kicking a pillow to jumping on the couch to knocking over a potted plant. His attempts at cleaning things up create even more chaos and culminate in a sea of soap bubbles issuing from his mother's dishwasher. Praising *Uh-Oh!* as an "entertaining romp," a *Kirkus Reviews* writer added that the author/artist's "lively watercolor illustrations. . . . comically animate each episode almost like cartoon strips." In *School Library Journal* Amy Lilien-Harper noted the book's appeal to even beginning readers, writing that "the plot is humorously appealing, if deceptively sophisticated."

Biographical and Critical Sources

PERIODICALS

Booklist, April 15, 2002, Kay Weisman, review of *Rembrandt's Hat,* p. 1405; October 15, 2002, Helen Rosenberg, review of *Roads,* p. 412; September 15, 2004, Karin Snelson, review of *My Chair,* p. 250 October 15, 2004, Julie Cummins, review of *Now It Is Winter,* p. 411; December 1, 2004, Karin Snelson, review of *Knock! Knock!,* p. 664; November 15, 2005, review of *A Grand Old Tree,* p. 51; December 1, 2005, Stephanie Zvirin, review of *The Squeaky Door,* p. 54; January 1, 2007, Janice Del Negro, review of *Estelle Takes a Bath,* p. 114; November 1, 2007, Jennifer Mattson, review of *The Nutcracker Doll,* p. 62; April 15, 2009, Patricia Austin, review of *Swimming Sal,* p. 48; April 15, 2011, Carolyn Phelan, review of *Now It Is Summer,* p. 60.

Bulletin of the Center for Children's Books, September, 2004, Deborah Stevenson, review of *My Chair,* p. 23, and Timnah Card, review of *Knock! Knock!,* p. 43; March, 2006, Elizabeth Bush, review of *The Squeaky Door,* p. 319.

Horn Book, November-December, 2007, Jennifer M. Brabander, review of *The Nutcracker Doll,* p. 628.

Kirkus Reviews, March 15, 2001, review of *The Strange Egg,* p. 406; June 15, 2004, review of *My Chair,* p. 577; July 15, 2004, review of *Knock! Knock!,* p. 695; August 15, 2004, review of *Now It Is Winter,* p. 813; November 1, 2005, review of *A Grand Old Tree,* p. 1183; December 15, 2005, review of *The Squeaky Door,* p. 1325; September 15, 2006, review of *Estelle Takes a Bath,* p. 952; June 15, 2008, reviews of *Happy School Year!* and *Happy 100th Day!*; December 15, 2009, review of *The Perfect Gift;* February 15, 2011, review of *Now It Is Summer;* June 15, 2011, review of *Uh-Oh!*

Library Media Connection, February, 2006, Barbara B. Freehrer, review of *A Grand Old Tree,* p. 82.

Publishers Weekly, February 19, 2001, review of *The Strange Egg,* p. 90; January 14, 2002, review of *Rembrandt's Hat,* p. 59; December 19, 2005, review of *A Grand Old Tree,* p. 62; January 16, 2006, review of *The Squeaky Door,* p. 63; October 22, 2007, review of *The Nutcracker Doll,* p. 53; December 7, 2009, review of *The Perfect Gift,* p. 48.

School Library Journal, April, 1995, Lisa Wu Stowe, review of *Giraffes Aren't Half as Fat,* p. 121; May, 2001, Susan Marie Pitard, review of *The Strange Egg,* p. 114; November, 2001, Nina Lindsay, review of *Black Earth, Gold Sun,* p. 146; July, 2002, Robin L. Gibson, review of *Rembrandt's Hat,* p. 83; September, 2002, Roxanne Burg, review of *Roads,* p. 193; July, 2004, Marianne Saccardi, review of *My Chair,* p. 78; August, 2004, Susan Weitz, review of *Knock! Knock!,* p. 97; September, 2004, Kathleen Kelly MacMillan, review of *Now It Is Winter,* p. 181; December, 2005, Maura Bresnahan, review of *A Grand Old Tree,* p. 126; January, 2006, Elaine Lesh Morgan, review of *The Squeaky Door,* p. 108; November, 2006, Blair Christolon, review of *Estelle Takes a Bath,* p. 92; July, 2008, Donna Cardon, review of *Happy School Year!,* p. 78; March, 2009, Linda M. Kenton, review of *Swimming Sal,* p. 123; February, 2010, Rachel G. Payne, review of *The Perfect Gift,* p. 80; February, 2011, Gloria Koster, review of *Happy 100th Day!,* p. 87; May, 2011, Julie R. Ranelli, review of *Now It Is Summer,* p. 90; August, 2011, Amy Lilien-Harper, review of *Uh-Oh!,* p. 71.

Tribune Books (Chicago, IL), May 13, 2007, Maria Pontillas, review of *The Squeaky Door,* p. 6.

ONLINE

Mary Newell DePalma Home Page, http://www.marynewelldepalma.com (April 15, 2012).
Book Page Web site, http://www.bookpage.com/ (July 12, 2007), "Mary Newell DePalma."
Scholastic Web site, http://content.scholastic.com/ (December 3, 2007), "Mary Newell DePalma."

* * *

DeSTEFANO, Lauren 1984-

Personal
Born 1984, in New Haven, CT. *Education:* Albertus Magnus College, B.A. (English), 2007.

Addresses
Agent—Barbara Poelle, Irene Goodman Literary Agency, 27 W. 24th St., Ste. 700B, New York, NY 10010. *E-mail*—lauren@laurendestefano.com.

Career
Writer. Worked variously as a receptionist, barista, tax collector, and English tutor.

Awards, Honors
Best Fiction for Young Adults designation, American Library Association, 2012, for *Wither.*

Writings

"CHEMICAL GARDEN" NOVEL TRILOGY

Wither, Simon & Schuster Books for Young Readers (New York, NY), 2011.
Fever, Simon & Schuster Books for Young Readers (New York, NY), 2012.

Adaptations
Wither was adapted as an audiobook, Recorded Books, 2011.

Sidelights
In *Wither* and *Fever,* the first two works in her "Chemical Garden" trilogy, Lauren DeStefano depicts a dystopian world in which genetic engineering has gone awry, threatening the survival of the human race. "The idea of altering nature fascinates me," DeStefano commented on her home page. "Eliminating one problem might create a different problem. Maybe stripping the carbs from a potato means introducing a new sort of food allergy. Maybe altering human genetics to eradicate cancer will make humans more vulnerable to other ailments, or new ailments entirely. I don't stand on any particular side of the argument. I'm just a weaver of what ifs."

Growing up in Connecticut, DeStefano began writing at an early age, often jotting down her thoughts in notebooks during long car rides. She drew particular inspiration from a fifth-grade teacher who convinced her that "Author" was a legitimate career choice. After majoring in English and creative writing at Albertus Magnus College, DeStefano began *Wither,* which expanded from a short story into a novel-length work.

Earning comparisons to Margaret Atwood's *The Handmaid's Tale, Wither* introduces Rhine Ellery, a sixteen year old living in a frightening future America. Although genetically engineering has created a generation of virtually immortal humans, their offspring and succeeding generations are ravaged by a virus and must confront their mortality as young adults: males die at age twenty-five, females at twenty. Kidnapped by Gatherers, who collect girls for brothels and polygamous marriages, Rhine is sold to Vaughan Ashby, a scientist and a wealthy member of the immortal "First Generation." Along with two other teens, Rhine becomes a sister wife to Vaughn's son, Linden, who is as much as a captive as the girls are. After Rhine falls in love with a house servant, Gabriel, and discovers that Vaughan is performing gruesome experiments in his efforts to find a cure for the virus, she decides to escape.

According to Krista Hutley in *Booklist,* the "arresting premise" of *Wither* "succeeds because of Rhine's poignant, conflicted narrative and DeStefano's evocative prose." "This beautifully-written debut fantasy, with its intriguing world-building, well-developed characters and . . . edge-of-the-seat suspense, will keep teens riveted," Bonnie Kunzel asserted in her *Voice of Youth Advocates* review, while Eric Norton commented in *School Library Journal* that Rhine "proves herself to be a heroine who faces her situation with spirit and cleverness."

In *Fever* Rhine and Gabriel make their way from Florida to New York, hoping to reunite with Rhine's twin brother, Rowan. On arrival, however, they discover that Rowan has disappeared. Rhine now shows the signs of illness although it is years before the virus should attack her, and her illness may be a result of Vaughn's medical experiments. Although some critics noted that *Fever* lacks the energy *Wither, Booklist* reviewer Cindy Welch asserted that "DeStefano's rich use of language helps set this dystopian tale apart."

Asked if she had any advice for aspiring writers, DeStefano told Maryann Yin in a *Galleycat* online interview: "Writing is a deeply personal journey, and the only voice a writer should mind is his or her own. . . . As a

reader, I seek out stories that are told with bravery and honesty, by an author who was more concerned with telling the story than anything else. Those things really shine through."

Biographical and Critical Sources

PERIODICALS

Booklist, February 1, 2011, Krista Hutley, review of *Wither,* p. 79; February 1, 2012, Cindy Welch, review of *Fever,* p. 85.

Journal of Adolescent and Adult Literacy, September, 2011, Risha Mullins, review of *Wither,* p. 84.

Kirkus Reviews, February 1, 2011, review of *Wither;* January 15, 2012, review of *Fever.*

Publishers Weekly, January 10, 2011, review of *Wither,* p. 51.

School Library Journal, April, 2011, Eric Norton, review of *Wither,* p. 170; April, 2012, Erik Carlson, review of *Fever,* p. 158.

Voice of Youth Advocates, April, 2011, Bonnie Kunzel, review of *Wither,* p. 79.

ONLINE

ALAN Online, http://www.alan-ya.org/ (May 23, 2011), Pam Cole, interview with DeStefano.

Chemical Garden Books Web site, http://thechemicalgardenbooks.com/ (March 22, 2012).

Galleycat Web log, http://www.mediabistro.com/galleycat/ (February 21, 2012), Maryann Lin, "Lauren DeStefano and Moira Young Share Advice on Writing Dystopian Fiction."

Lauren DeStefano Home Page, http://laurendestefano.com (March 22, 2012).*

F

FISHER, Catherine 1957-

Personal

Born October 28, 1957, in Wales. *Education:* University of Wales, B.A. (English), 1980. *Religion:* Roman Catholic.

Addresses

Home—Newport, Wales. *Agent*—Lesley Pollinger, Pollinger Ltd., 9 Staple Inn, Holborn, London WC1V 7QH, England.

Career

Writer and educator. Worked as a school teacher, archaeologist, broadcaster, and adjudicator. University of Glamorgan, Glamorgan, Wales, visiting lecturer of children's literature; teacher in Newport, Gwent, Wales.

Member

Welsh Academy (fellow).

Awards, Honors

Welsh Arts Council Young Writers Award, 1988, for *Immrama;* Welsh Arts Council Young Writers' Prize, and Cardiff International Poetry Competition prize, both 1989, both for poetry; Cardiff International Poetry Prize, 1990; Smarties' Book Prize shortlist, 1990, for *The Conjuror's Game;* Tir na n'Og Prize, 1995, for *The Candle Man;* Whitbread Prize shortlist, 2003, for *The Oracle;* Mythopoeic Society Children's Fiction Award, 2007, for *Corbenic;* London *Times* Children's Book of the Year selection, and Carnegie Medal longlist, both 2008, both for *Incarceron;* named Wales' Young People's Laureate, 2011.

Catherine Fisher (Photograph by Ross Pierson/Alamy. Reproduced by permission.)

Writings

FICTION

The Conjuror's Game (also see below), Bodley Head (London, England), 1990.

Fintan's Tower (also see below), Bodley Head (London, England), 1991.

Saint Tarvel's Bell, Swift Children's (London, England), 1992.

The Hare and Other Stories, Pont Books (Llandysul, Wales), 1994.

The Candleman (also see below), Bodley Head (London, England), 1994.

Scared Stiff: Stories, Dolphin Books (London, England), 1997.

Magical Mystery Stories, Red Fox (London, England), 1999.

The Lammas Field, Hodder Children's (London, England), 1999.

Darkwater Hall, Hodder Children's (London, England), 2000.
Old Enough and Other Stories, Cló Iar-Chonnachta, (Indreabhán, Conamara, Wales), 2002.
The Glass Tower (contains *The Conjuror's Game, Fintan's Tower,* and *The Candleman*), Red Fox (London, England), 2004.
Corbenic, Greenwillow Books (New York, NY), 2006.
Darkhenge, Greenwillow Books (New York, NY), 2006.
The Weather Dress, Pont Books (Llandysul, Wales), 2006.
Incarceron, Hodder Children's Books (London, England), 2007, Dial Books (New York, NY), 2010.
Sapphique (sequel to *Incarceron*), Hodder Children's Books (London, England), 2008, Dial Books (New York, NY), 2011.
The Pickpocket's Ghost (novella), Barrington Stoke (London, England), 2008.
Crown of Acorns, Hodder Children's Books (London, England), 2010.
The Magic Thief (novella), illustrated by Peter Clover, Barrington Stoke (London, England), 2011.
The Ghost Box (novella), illustrated by Peter Clover, Barrington Stoke (London, England), 2012.
The Cat with Iron Claws, illustrated by Nicola Robinson, Pont (Ceredigion, Wales), 2012.
The Obsidian Mirror, Hodder Children's (London, England), 2012.

Author's works have been translated into over twenty languages.

"SNOW-WALKER TRILOGY"

The Snow-Walker's Son, Bodley Head (London, England), 1993.
The Empty Hand, Bodley Head (London, England), 1995.
The Soul Thieves, Bodley Head (London, England), 1996.
The Snow-Walker Trilogy (omnibus), Red Fox (London, England), 2003, published as *Snow-Walker,* Greenwillow Books (New York, NY), 2004.

"BOOK OF THE CROW"/"RELIC MASTER" NOVEL SERIES

The Relic Master, Bodley Head (London, England), 1998, published as *The Dark City,* Dial Books (New York, NY), 2011.
The Interrex, Bodley Head (London, England), 1999, published as *The Lost Heiress,* Dial Books (New York, NY), 2011.
Flain's Coronet, Bodley Head (London, England), 2000, published as *The Hidden Coronet,* Dial Books (New York, NY), 2011.
The Margrave, Red Fox (London, England), 2001, Dial Books (New York, NY), 2011.

"ORACLE" TRILOGY

The Oracle, Hodder Children's Books (London, England), 2003, published as *The Oracle Betrayed,* Greenwillow Books (New York, NY), 2004.
The Archon, Hodder Children's Books (London, England), 2004, published as *The Sphere of Secrets,* Greenwillow Books (New York, NY), 2005.
The Scarab, Hodder Children's Books (London, England), 2005, published as *Day of the Scarab,* Greenwillow Books (New York, NY), 2006.

POETRY

Immrama, Seren (Bridgend, Wales), 1988.
The Unexplored Ocean, Seren (Bridgend, Wales), 1994.
Altered States, Seren (Bridgend, Wales), 1999.
Folklore, Smith/Doorstep Books (Wakefield, England), 2003.

Contributor to poetry anthologies, including *Twentieth-Century Anglo-Welsh Poetry,* Seren (Bridgend, Wales); *Oxygen,* Seren (Bridgend, Wales), and *The Forward Book of Poetry, 2001.*

Adaptations

Sapphique was adapted for audiobook, read by Kim Mai Guest, Listening Library, 2010. *Incarceron* was optioned for film by Twentieth Century-Fox.

Sidelights

Familiar to middle-grade fantasy buffs in her native United Kingdom, fiction writer and poet Catherine Fisher has become increasingly well known since novels such as her Whitbread Award-winning *The Oracle* were published in the United States as well as in translation. Named as the first young-adult laureate in her native Wales in 2011, Fisher has also gained praise for books that include *Darkhenge, Corbenic, Crown of Acorns,* and *Incarceron* as well as for her "Snow-Walker" and "Book of the Crow/Relic Master" series. In addition to writing fantasy novels, she has also penned short fiction and has published several highly praised volumes of poetry.

Fisher was born and still lives in an area of Wales called the Gwent Levels, and she fell in love with fantasy after discovering Lewis Carroll's *Alice in Wonderland* as a child. Inspired by sources as various as Icelandic sagas and the Welsh bardic tradition, she credits her love of writing to her homeland. "A basic love of words (rich, ornamented words) and poetry is very Celtic," Fisher noted in an interview for the HarperChildrens Web site. "Also I have a great interest in spirituality and in the landscape—woods and trees and the history of how people have lived on the earth. Both of those are highly Celtic obsessions." Reflecting these interests, her first novel, *The Conjurer's Game,* was published in 1990.

Released in the United States as *The Oracle Betrayed, The Oracle* introduces readers to Fisher's "Oracle" trilogy, which is set in the Two Lands amid a mix of ancient Greek and Egyptian cultures. In *The Oracle Be-*

trayed Mirany is appointed one of the nine guardians of the Oracle of the One God. As handmaiden to High Priestess Hermia, she learns that the words of the One God, as delivered to the priestess, are being twisted to benefit both Hermia and Hermia's ally, the cunning General Argelin. Determined to both thwart Argelin's plot to assume control of the Two Lands and fulfill the true wishes of the One God, Mirany teams up with Seth, a scribe familiar with the pyramid's underground passages. Another ally, a musician named Oblek, also comes to her aid as she searches for the whereabouts of Alexos, a boy destined by the One God to be his new Archon, or representative on Earth. Unknown to the young Alexos, his life is threatened by Hermia and Argelin, who wish to put another, more easily manipulated, Archon in his place.

Describing *The Oracle Betrayed* as a "sprawling, atmospheric adventure," a *Publishers Weekly* contributor praised Fisher for creating a "crisp, quickly moving narrative and fully fleshed-out characters" that combine to "keep readers hooked." A *Kirkus Reviews* critic also found much to enjoy in the novel, citing its "genuinely chilling" ending and noting that the author's "heroes are likable but realistically flawed, her villains despicable and menacing without being stupid." Michele Winship, writing for *Kliatt,* recommended the development of awkward and immature Mirany into a self-assured young woman as among the novel's strengths, deeming *The Oracle Betrayed* as a "fast-paced and intriguing tale," while in *Horn Book* Anita L. Burkam wrote that "the mythology that underpins Mirany's world is richly imagined." Due to Fisher's skill as a writer, Burkam added in *Horn Book,* "thoughtful readers will delight in the interplay of the allegorical with the literal, expertly balanced against each other."

The "Oracle" trilogy continues in *The Archon*—published in the United States as *The Sphere of Secrets*—as young Alexos takes on his role of ruler and diplomat while also hoping to avoid the ritual sacrifice planned by Hermia that would end his life. Together with Seth and Oblek, he leads a pilgrimage across the desert to the Well of Songs, hoping to end a long drought credited to the angry Rain Queen. However, this is a pilgrimage some do not wish the Archon to survive. In the concluding volume, *Day of the Scarab,* Akexos returns to the Two Lands to find that Argelin has made his move and is now using terror to control the land of the one god, whom the general denounces. From a place of safety, Mirany must now work to counter Argelin's sacrilege in order to avert further retaliation from the powerful Rain Queen. The only way to accomplish this is to undertake a terrifying journey, which the ten-year-old Archon must make with her.

Reviewing *The Sphere of Secrets,* Tasha Saecker noted in *School Library Journal* that "Fisher has created an incredible, detailed, and believable setting" and her characters "are vivid and complex." "Richly imagined," according to Burkam, *The Sphere of Secrets* benefits from the author's characterization of the Archon as "a believable intersection of a human boy and an ineffable, infinitely powerful being." "Assassination attempts, double-crosses and plots within plots enliven this breathlessly paced" installment in the "Oracle" trilogy, wrote a *Kirkus Reviews* writer, and in *Booklist* Carolyn Phelan concluded that, while "vividly described" in *The Oracle Prophecies,* "the world of the Two Lands becomes increasingly well realized" in *The Sphere of Secrets.* "Vivid, complicated, and thoroughly engrossing," the "fast-paced adventure" in *Day of the Scarab* "keeps readers evidly turning pages until the majestic conclusion" to Fisher's "Oracle" trilogy, asserted Burkam in her *Horn Book* review.

The Dark City is the first novel in Fisher's "Book of the Crow"/"Relic Master" series. Published in the United Kingdom as *The Relic Master, The Dark City* finds Galen Harn relying on his teenage apprentice, Raffi, after he loses his ability to locate, secure, and protect the relics of his waning culture. While on an assignment which requires his journey to the city of Tasceron, Relic Master Galen also hopes to locate the powerful Crow and regain his power; in the interim he relies on Raffi's still-unrefined skills. On their journey Galen and Raffi are joined by several fellow travelers, all who worry about the overlords of the city, the sinister Watch.

Reviewing *The Dark City* in *School Library Journal,* Eric Norton characterized Fisher's story as "moody" and "full of mist, swamps, and darkness" before recommending it as "a great read." A *Publishers Weekly* reviewer deemed Fisher's series opener a "gritty and enjoyable tale of adventure" that will appeal to fans of dystopian fiction. In his *Voice of Youth Advocates* review, Walter Hogan noted that the use of a "deep, Tolkien-esque back history and [a] third-person narration from multiple viewpoints" help make the first "Relic Master" novel "approachable for young readers" and "will please fantasy lovers of both sexes." Fisher's "detailed and exotic worldbuilding" results in "a tale redolent with humor, wonder and suspense," asserted a *Kirkus Review* writer in a laudatory appraisal of *The Dark City.*

The "Book of the Crow" saga continues in *The Lost Heiress* (originally published as *The Interrex*), *The Hidden Coronet* (*Flain's Coronet* in its U.K. edition), and *The Margrave,* all which follow Raffi and Galen on further adventures. As revolution brews among the leaders of the land, the Keepers are charged with locating the young heir of a once-powerful emperor, a lad known as the Interrex. As Galen builds an alliance to support this future leader, he must acquire several other relics in order to match the power of the Margrave, who commands the sinister Watch. Although some would test their loyalty to the Interrex, Galen and Raffi ultimately risk everything to journey into the Pit of Maar, where combat with the Margrave is assured.

Reviewing *The Lost Heiress* for *Kirkus Reviews,* a writer cited the novel's "flashes of brilliance" and added

Cover of Fisher's dystopian fantasy **Sapphique,** *a sequel to her highly acclaimed novel* **Incarceron.** (Reproduced by permission of Firebird, an imprint of Penguin Group (USA) Inc.)

that Fisher's interwoven plot lines present "puzzles to keep readers ensnared while providing pleasing narrative momentum." Her artful intermixing of "visionary mysticism and gee-whiz gadgetry" in *The Hidden Coronet* is "rendered bittersweet by all-too-human failures," asserted another *Kirkus Reviews* writer, the contributor predicting that readers "will be on tenterhooks" while awaiting the final installment in the "Book of the Crow" saga. Those "who came for the adventure will be left pondering the fragile alliance" that exists among "mercy, justice, duty and responsibility," concluded still another *Kirkus Reviews* writer, this reviewer noting the thoughtful resolution in *The Margrave.*

In *Incarceron* Fisher weaves another dystopian yarn, this time mixing in a touch of romance. Set in the distant future, the novel follows two stories: the frustrations of Finn and his brother Keiro as they survive life in the vast, sentient prison called Incarceron; and the experiences of Claudia, daughter of the prison's warden, as she navigates a society that eschews technology in favor of a seventeenth-century standard of living. Finn has learned to live by his wits and can hold his own amid the prison's murderous population, while Claudia is trapped by society's entropy. Finn and Claudia's lives intersect when they both acquire keys to Incarceron, and by teaming up they begin preparations to flee from both their prisons.

"Complex and inventive, with numerous and rewarding mysteries, [*Incarceron*] . . . is sure to please," according to a *Publishers Weekly* contributor, and in *Booklist* Hutley cited both the novel's "killer ending" and its "emotionally resonant, flawed, [and] determined" young characters. "Like the finest chocolate," wrote a *Kirkus Reviews* critic, Fisher serves up "a rich confection of darkness, subtlety and depth" in *Incarceron,* while Burkam concluded that "reader attention never flags through this elegant, gritty, often surprising novel."

Finn's saga concludes in *Sapphique,* as he feels guilt over the fact that Keiro was left behind in Incarceron. While Claudia encourages him to believe that his destiny is to rule, he remains confused as to whether his childhood memories of being a prince are merely a reaction to his lengthy stay in a sensory-deprived environment. Meanwhile, Keiro plans a daring escape of his own, one that requires them to steal a well-guarded talisman: the Glove of Sapphique, the only prisoner ever to escape from Incarceron. In *Sapphique* the author maintains the "intensely original world building" of her first novel while "further explor[ing] . . . themes of reality, illusion, and freedom," according to Hutley, and a *Kirkus Reviews* contributor dubbed the novel a "dark, brilliant sequel" to *Incarceron.* As the tension ratchets higher, the plot of *Sapphique* "builds to an inexorable climax," wrote Burkam: "a fitting finial on Fisher's grand invention." While *Voice of Youth Advocates* contributor Judy Brink-Drescher recommended that readers begin with *Incarceron,* the "well-written, fast-paced" sequel "is highly recommended for audiences from middle school and up."

Often featuring strong female protagonists, Fisher's standalone stories are also frequently influenced by Britain's past; for instance, her novel *Corbenic* retells the story of the Holy Grail. "*Corbenic* is perhaps my favourite book of those I've written," the author admitted on her home page, citing her main character, Cal. A modern-day teen escaping a chaotic home life with an alcoholic mother, Cal is taking the train to his uncle Trevor's house when he gets off at the wrong station. The seventeen year old now finds himself in the time of Camelot, standing before the sickly Fisher King, a wounded knight who guarded the Holy Grail in ancient legends. But then, in a blink, he returns to the present, but now with a knight's sword in his hand. The weapon has a life of its own and leads the way back to the ancient land. Cal follows and is joined by several companions, but doubts plague him as to whether his supernatural journey is actually occurring or only the product of the same mental illness that destroyed his mother's life.

For Burkam, *Corbenic* is enriched by Fisher's juxtaposition of Arthurian England and a "depressingly industrial modern setting," and the author "handily exploits the Fisher King's motifs of sacrifice, self-discovery, and ultimate healing." While Cal is a sullen and less-than-likeable hero, "minor characters are portrayed with subtle wit and sweetness," wrote Johanna Lewis in her review of the novel for *School Library Journal.* "Fisher ably splices the Arthurian legend into Cal's very modern quest for self-determination," observed a *Kirkus Reviews* writer, and in *Booklist* Holly Koelling suggested that thoughtful teens will "relish the immersion in Cal's complex relationships, choices, and fantasy-fueled journey toward adult understanding."

The strong Welsh storytelling tradition that began with the ancient stories collectively known as the Mabinogion, has also inspired Fisher's fiction, particularly her "Snow-Walker" trilogy, which includes *The Snow-Walker's Son, The Empty Hand,* and *The Soul Thieves.* Published in a single volume as *Snow-Walker,* the saga focuses on Gudrun, a sorceress who emerges from the snows at the world's edge and aggressively takes over leadership of the Jarl people. Yearning for freedom, cousins Jessa and Thorkil of the Wulfling clan look to the possibility that Gudrun's son Kari may be the key to ending her dominion, but Kari lives in mysterious isolation in a fortress in the frigid north. After Gudrun is deposed, she uses her magic to cause chaos among the Jarl. As Jessa and companions Skapti and Hakon Empty Hand attempt to difuse Gudrun's spells, rumors circulate stating that Kari is coming into his own as a fearsome mage. An enchanted bride, a challenging quest, and an epic battle culminate Fisher's saga.

Reviewing *Snow-Walker* in *Kirkus Reviews,* a contributor praised Fisher's saga as a "richly atmospheric Nordic fantasy aswirl with snow and magic." Salted with Norse mythology, the Celtic-inspired story interweaves "all the classical elements" of myth, according to Cindy Dobrez, the *Booklist* critic adding that the "description of the icy backdrop and . . . mythological beings" in *Snow-Walker* showcase "the beauty of Fisher's prose." A *Publishers Weekly* reviewer also cited the story's "atmospheric setting" and suggested that "fans of Norse myths and magic may be swept up in this frosty tale," while *School Library Journal* reviewer Margaret A. Chang asserted that the novel shows Fisher to be "a skillful storyteller" who employs "clear language and plenty of action to keep the plot moving."

Darkhenge also takes its setting and inspiration from Welsh tradition, although its mystery is centered in the present day. In the novel, artistic teen Rob Drew worries when his sister Chloe falls into a mysterious coma. To keep busy, he volunteers at a nearby archaeological site, and the findings at this Bronze Age henge cause Rob to suspect that the site might be affecting his sister's health. Braving the ancient powers and led by a strange man named Vetch, Rob crosses the portal into the supernatural realm and valiantly attempts to rescue Chloe from the mythic King of Annwn. Unfortunately a childhood hurt caused by her brother causes Chloe to welcome this unearthly and sinister alliance. In addition to being a Celtic fantasy, *Darkhenge* is also "an exploration of the responsibility of families to speak honestly to one another," asserted *School Library Journal* contributor Sharon Grover, and "the portrayal is delicate and poetic, . . . with suspense that builds," according to a *Kirkus Reviews* writer. By interjecting "the psychological underpinnings of myth" and its "ties to pagan nature," Fisher crafts "a complex fantasy that resonates with strangeness, mysticism, and magic," according to Burkam, while in *Booklist* Jennifer Mattson predicted that fans of Susan Cooper's stories will enjoy "the magical, atmospheric setting" of *Darkhenge.*

A mystery couched in the history of Bath, England—a city familiar to most U.K. residents due to its circular, townhouse-lined street called the Royal Crescent—*Crown of Acorns* interweaves three stories. The first takes place in ancient times, as King Blalud, a leper, discovers a sacred spring he believes to have healing powers and orders that a massive temple be built to honor its resident deity. Flash forward to 1740, as visionary architect Jonathan Forrest is inspired by his interest in ancient druid rituals to design Bath's Royal Crescent. Forrest's teen apprentice, Zac, dislikes the tempermental architect and as events play out he is drawn into a scheme to sabotage the construction effort. The third intertwined story is set in contemporary times and follows a girl named Sulis as she arrives in the city of Logria to stay with a foster family, one in a series she has stayed with since witnessing a murder and going into hiding. Praising *Crown of Acorns* in *School Librarian,* Marzena Currie described it as "a sophisticated and beautifully written novel with a beautiful climax."

Fisher continues to live in Wales where, in addition to reading, writing, and teaching, she enjoys fencing, walking, and exploring the ruined castles that dot the British landscape. Although she enjoys futuristic writing, she does not mix technology with her work as an author; she does not own a computer and does her research the old-fashioned way: without the Internet. Enthusiastic about the fantasy genre, Fisher offered this advice to beginning authors during an interview posted on the Random House Web site: "Read a lot of the sort of book you want to write. Then read behind those books, from the older layers of story they come from. Write what you want to write. Don't be put off by uninformed comment, but if someone knows what they're talking about and gives you advice, listen to them. Believe in yourself. We can all do a lot more than we know."

Biographical and Critical Sources

PERIODICALS

Booklist, June 1, 2000, Patricia Monaghan, review of *Altered States,* p. 1839; February 15, 2004, Carolyn Phelan, review of *The Oracle Betrayed,* p. 1059; Sep-

tember 1, 2004, Cindy Dobrez, review of *Snow-Walker,* p. 106; March 15, 2005, Carolyn Phelan, review of *The Sphere of Secrets,* p. 1292; January 1, 2006, Jennifer Mattson, review of *Darkhenge,* p. 81; May 15, 2006, Carolyn Phelan, review of *Day of the Scarab,* p. 61; August 1, 2006, Holly Koelling, review of *Corbenic,* p. 65; January 1, 2010, Krista Hutley, review of *Incarceron,* p. 80; October 1, 2010, Krista Hutley, review of *Sapphique,* p. 81.

Horn Book, March-April, 2004, Anita L. Burkam, review of *The Oracle Betrayed,* p. 181; September-October, 2004, Anita L. Burkam, review of *Snow-Walker,* p. 581; March-April, 2005, Anita L. Burkam, review of *The Sphere of Secrets,* p. 200; March-April, 2006, Anita L. Burkam, review of *Darkhenge,* p. 187; May-June, 2006, Anita L. Burkam, review of *Day of the Scarab,* p. 315; September-October, 2006, Anita L. Burkam, review of *Corbenic,* p. 582; January-February, 2010, Anita L. Burkam, review of *Incarceron,* p. 86; January-February, 2011, Anita L. Burkam, review of *Sapphique,* p. 93.

Kirkus Reviews, February 1, 2004, review of *The Oracle Betrayed,* p. 132; July 15, 2004, review of *Snow-Walker,* p. 684; February 1, 2005, review of *The Sphere of Secrets,* p. 176; February 1, 2006, review of *Darkhenge,* p. 131; May, 2006, review of *Day of the Scarab,* p. 457; August 1, 2006, review of *Corbenic,* p. 785; January 15, 2010, review of *Incarceron;* October 15, 2010, review of *Sapphique;* April 15, 2011, review of *The Dark City;* May 1, 2011, review of *The Lost Heiress*; June 1, 2011, review of *The Hidden Coronet*; June 15, 2011, review of *The Margrave.*

Kliatt, March, 2004, Michele Winship, review of *The Oracle Betrayed,* p. 10; September, 2004, Michele Winship, review of *Snow-Walker,* p. 10; March, 2006, Lesley Farmer, review of *Darkhenge,* p. 10; May, 2006, Michele Winship, review of *Day of the Scarab,* p. 8; September, 2006, Claire Rosser, review of *Corbenic,* p. 11.

Publishers Weekly, June 26, 1995, review of *The Unexplored Ocean,* p. 102; January 19, 2004, review of *The Oracle Betrayed,* p. 77; November 15, 2004, review of *Snow-Walker,* p. 61; April 10, 2006, review of *Darkhenge,* p. 73; November 6, 2006, review of *Corbenic,* p. 62; December 7, 2009, review of *Incarceron,* p. 49; March 7, 2011, review of *The Dark City,* p. 65.

School Librarian, autumn, 2010, Marzena Currie, review of *Crown of Acorns,* p. 176.

School Library Journal, March, 2004, Margaret A. Chang, review of *The Oracle Betrayed,* p. 210; November, 2004, Margaret A. Chang, review of *Snow-Walker,* p. 143; March, 2005, Tasha Saecker, review of *The Sphere of Secrets,* p. 210; March, 2006, Sharon Grover, review of *Darkhenge,* p. 220; July, 2006, Coop Renner, review of *Day of the Scarab,* p. 101; November, 2006, Johanna Lewis, review of *Corbenic,* p. 134; February, 2010, Karen E. Brooks-Reese, review of *Incarceron,* p. 110; December, 2010, Jessica Miller, review of *Sapphique,* p. 113; July, 2011, Eric Norton, review of *The Dark City,* p. 97.

South Wales Echo, October 18, 2011, Karen Price, "Writer Hopes to Inspire Children," p. 13.

Times (London, England), April 28, 2007, Amanda Craig, interview with Fisher, p. 15; December 7, 2007, Amanda Craig, review of *Incarceron;* June 19, 2010, Amanda Craig, review of *Crown of Acorns,* p. 12.

Voice of Youth Advocates, December, 2010, Judy Brink-Drescher, review of *Sapphique,* p. 468; August, 2011, Walter Hogan, review of *The Relic Master,* p. 287.

ONLINE

Catherine Fisher Home page, http://www.catherine-fisher.com (May 1, 2012).

HarperChildren's Web site, http://www.harperchildrens.com/ (November 22, 2004), interview with Fisher.

* * *

FLEMING, Denise 1950-

Personal

Born January 31, 1950, in Toledo, OH; daughter of Frank (a realtor) and Inez (a homemaker) Fleming; married David Powers (a designer), October 9, 1971; children: Indigo (daughter). *Education:* Kendall College of Art and Design, degree, 1970. *Hobbies and other interests:* Gardening, natural habitats.

Addresses

Home—Toledo, OH. *E-mail*—denise@denisefleming.com.

Career

Children's book author and illustrator.

Awards, Honors

Notable Book designation, American Library Association (ALA), *American Bookseller* Pick-of-the-List designation, and *Redbook* Children's Picture Book Award, all 1991, and *Boston Globe/Horn Book* Award Honor Book designation, and Children's Choices selection, International Reading Association/Children's Book Council (IRA/CBC), both 1992, all for *In the Tall, Tall Grass;* ALA Notable Book designation, 1992, for *Lunch; American Bookseller* Pick-of-the-List designation, 1993, and Caldecott Honor Book designation, and ALA Notable Book designation, both 1994, all for *In the Small, Small Pond; American Bookseller* Pick-of-the-List designation, 1994, for *Barnyard Banter;* Silver Medal, Society of Illustrators, One Hundred Titles for Reading and Sharing selection, New York Public Library, and Charlotte Zolotow Award highly commended selection, all 1998, all for *Time to Sleep;* ALA Notable Book designation, One Hundred Titles for Reading and Sharing selection, IRA/CBC Children's Choices selection, and Charlotte Zolotow Award highly commended title, all 1998, all for *Mama Cat Has Three Kittens;* One Hun-

dred Titles for Reading and Sharing selection, 2000, for *The Everything Book;* Best Children's Books of the Year selection, Bank Street College of Education, 2001, for *Pumpkin Eye;* ALA Notable Children's Book selection, and Oppenheim Toy Portfolio Gold Medal, both 2003, and Best of the Best listee, Chicago Public Library, 2004, all for *Alphabet under Construction;* Best of the Best listee, Chicago Public Library, and One Hundred Titles for Reading and Sharing selection, both 2004, both for *Buster;* One Hundred Titles for Reading and Sharing selection Choices selection, Cooperative Children's Book Center (CCBC), and Oppenheim Toy Portfolio Best Book Award, all 2006, all for *The First Day of Winter;* CCBC Choices selection, Best Children's Books of the Year selection, Bank Street College of Education, and Best of the Best listee, Chicago Public Library, all 2007, all for *The Cow Who Clucked;,* Best of the Best listee, Chicago Public Library, 2008, for *Beetle Bop;* ALA Notable Children's Book selection, and Best of the Best listee, Chicago Public Library, both 2009, both for *Buster Goes to Cowboy Camp.*

Writings

SELF-ILLUSTRATED

In the Tall, Tall Grass, Henry Holt (New York, NY), 1991.
Count!, Henry Holt (New York, NY), 1992.
Lunch, Henry Holt (New York, NY), 1992.
In the Small, Small Pond, Henry Holt (New York, NY), 1993.
Barnyard Banter, Henry Holt (New York, NY), 1994.
Denise Fleming's Painting with Paper, Henry Holt (New York, NY), 1994.
Where Once There Was a Wood, Henry Holt (New York, NY), 1996.
Time to Sleep, Henry Holt (New York, NY), 1997.
Mama Cat Has Three Kittens, Holt (New York, NY), 1998.
The Everything Book, Henry Holt (New York, NY), 2000.
Pumpkin Eye, Henry Holt (New York, NY), 2001.
Maker of Things, photographs by Karen Bowers, Richard C. Owen (Katonah, NY), 2002.
Alphabet under Construction, Henry Holt (New York, NY), 2002.
Buster, Henry Holt (New York, NY), 2003.
The First Day of Winter, Henry Holt (New York, NY), 2005.
The Cow Who Clucked, Henry Holt (New York, NY), 2006.
Beetle Bop, Harcourt (Orlando, FL), 2007.
Buster Goes to Cowboy Camp, Henry Holt (New York, NY), 2008.
Sleepy, Oh So Sleepy, Henry Holt (New York, NY), 2010.
Shout! Shout It Out!, Henry Holt (New York, NY), 2011.

ILLUSTRATOR

Edith Adams, *The Charmkins Discover Big World,* Random House (New York, NY), 1983.
The Charmkins' Sniffy Adventure, Random House (New York, NY), 1983.
Alice Low, *All through the Town,* Random House (New York, NY), 1984.
It Feels like Christmas! A Book of Surprises to Touch, See, and Sniff, Random House (New York, NY), 1984.
Peggy Kahn, *The Care Bears Help Santa,* Random House (New York, NY), 1984.
Ernie's Sesame Street Friends, Random House (New York, NY), 1985.
This Little Pig Went to Market, Random House (New York, NY), 1985.
Count in the Dark with Glo Worm, Random House (New York, NY), 1985.
Deborah Shine, *Little Puppy's New Name,* Random House (New York, NY), 1985.
Teddy's Best Toys, Random House (New York, NY), 1985.
The Merry Christmas Book: A First Book of Holiday Stories and Poems, Random House (New York, NY), 1986.
Linda Hayward, *This Is the House,* Random House (New York, NY), 1988.
Linda Hayward, *D Is for Doll,* Random House (New York, NY), 1988.
Linda Hayward, *Tea Party Manners,* Random House (New York, NY), 1988.
Natalie Standiford, *Dollhouse Mouse,* Random House (New York, NY), 1989.

Adaptations

In the Small, Small Pond was adapted as an animated video by Weston Woods/Scholastic (New York, NY), 2001.

Sidelights

Denise Fleming has earned a host of honors for the children's books featuring her signature pulp-painting technique, among them *In the Tall, Tall Grass, Beetle Bop,* and *Shout! Shout It Out!* She started her illustration career in the 1980s, when she illustrated stories by other authors. When she and her sister enrolled in a papermaking class, Fleming found the subject so fascinating that she took a further course. With mastery of this new skill, she found a way to integrate it into book illustration, developing a way of forcing cotton pulp through hand-cut stencils and create the distinctive art that now accompanies her original picture-book stories.

Although their techniques are completely different, Fleming has been compared to collage-artist and author Eric Carle, and critics often cite the stunningly vibrant colors in her creations. "Papermaking for me is cathartic," Fleming stated on her home page. "What other medium requires that you be up to your elbows in brilliant color? It's wet, messy, and wonderful—I haven't picked up a brush or a colored pencil since I discovered papermaking."

Fleming's first book to feature her stenciled art technique, *In the Tall, Tall Grass,* follows a caterpillar through a backyard jungle from afternoon until evening.

"Bold, bright, stylized . . . illustrations" offer the caterpillar's point of view on the myriad of other creatures in the yard, from hummingbirds to bees, ants, and snakes, according to Virginia Opocensky in *School Library Journal.* As a *Publishers Weekly* reviewer commented, "the ultimate kaleidoscope effect makes this title ideal for sharing with young explorers." Each of Fleming's illustrations pairs with a simple rhyming text that emphasizes the activity of the creature depicted. Ellen Fader, writing in *Horn Book,* remarked that *In the Tall, Tall Grass* "holds appeal for a wide range of children."

A related volume, *In the Small, Small Pond* presents a close-to-the-ground view of a contained natural system. In this work, Fleming focuses on a frog and its interaction with other creatures associated with pond life. Her rhyming text again emphasizes the activities of each of the animals depicted while accompanying illustrations lead readers through the seasons from spring to winter. Like many other critics, *Booklist* contributor Ilene Cooper emphasized Fleming's compositions in her review, concluding that the author/illustrator's "art has both a fluidity of design and a precision of definition that make it a pleasure to view." As Judy Constantinides commented in *School Library Journal, In the Small, Small Pond* serves as "another truly stunning picture book from Fleming."

Animal life is also the focus of *Barnyard Banter,* in which a variety of creatures tend to business on the farm . . . except for a missing goose. *Time to Sleep* finds Bear preparing to hibernate for the winter, and the news travels to Snail, who tells Skunk, who tells Turtle, and so on until Ladybug wakes up already-slumbering Bear to inform him that it is indeed, time to sleep. "Lush colors, startled, wide-eyed animals, and bold, black print make each page" of *Barnyard Banter* "jump with activity," according to a *Kirkus Reviews* writer, while *School Library Journal* critic Marcia Hupp called *Time to Sleep* "a gem of a picture book." "Subtly informative and poetic in its simplicity," according to Hupp, *Time to Sleep* will be useful in afternoon story-hours in the autumn months.

Like *Barnyard Banter,* Fleming's *The Cow Who Clucked* reverberates with barnyard noises. Cow has lost her moo and she is determined to find out where it has gone! She interviews several other barnyard animals, asking if they have acquired her moo, but all each can utter is their own unique sound until Hen solves the mystery. "The layers of subtle humor and visual splendor are truly impressive," remarked Susan Weitz in her *School Library Journal* review of *The Cow Who Clucked,* while a *Kirkus Reviews* writer cited artwork that is "vintage Fleming, [with] Van Gogh-inspired endpapers framing the jewel-toned daytime action." A *Publishers Weekly* critic similarly found that Fleming's "signature cotton fiber illustrations are as sumptuous as ever" in the farm-themed picture book.

In *Where Once There Was a Wood* readers learn that, while a new housing development will provide a new community for humans, it displaces existing communities of animals and other creatures. Here Fleming pairs her gently rhyming text with vibrantly colored and richly textured illustrations that compare and contrast animal habitats with those of humans. "An ecology lesson it surely is," remarked a contributor to *Kirkus Reviews,* "but it's also a celebration of the earth and its creatures." Fleming does not abandon her audience to the dilemma she has exposed; the conclusion of *Where once There Was a Wood* includes simple suggestions that encourage the wildlife in one's own yard, such as planting butterfly or hummingbird gardens. In *School Library Journal,* Sarabeth Kalajian recommended the picture book as one that should "be shared and enjoyed by a wide audience."

Fleming addresses a younger audience in *The Everything Book,* a compendium of nursery rhymes, games, and basic concepts that will prove useful and amusing pastimes for parents and toddlers alike. "All the first concepts children learn are endearingly presented in Fleming's vibrant, distinctively textured style," recounted Julie Yates Walton in the *New York Times Book Review.* Walton also compared *The Everything Book* to adult "Everything You Need to Know" books and concluded that, "with her warm, intuitively childlike touch, Fleming's volume could be properly billed as 'What Every Pre-Kindergartner Wants to Know.'"

Halloween becomes the author/illustrator's focus in *Pumpkin Eye,* as her rhyming text follows a young group of trick-or-treaters on a walk through their neighborhood. Stephanie Zvirin complimented the book's "spectacularly atmospheric pictures" in her review for *Booklist,* and a *Publishers Weekly* critic dubbed *Pumpkin Eye* "pleasingly spooky." Another seasonal tale, *The First Day of Winter,* uses "The Twelve Days of Christmas" as a child's guide to finding the perfect gift for a snowman. Fleming's "clever new words to a favorite old tune might become a new winter favorite in music classrooms," predicted a *Kirkus Reviews* contributor, and *Horn Book* critic Lauren E. Raece noted that the art is "filled with energy and movement." *Booklist* contributor Gillian Engberg found *The First Day of Winter* to be a "counting exercise with winter magic," while Shawn Brommer described it in *School Library Journal* as "quietly told and thoughtfully illustrated."

Life changes dramatically for the family dog when a new pet enters the household in *Buster.* At first, Buster wants nothing to do with the strange cat that has invaded his space, despite the feline's friendly ways. When the canine runs away from home in search of alone time, he becomes lost, but Buster ultimately arrives home safely by following a familiar white puff that turns out to be the very cat he has been trying to avoid. Fleming "brings a cheerful childlike tone to her text" for *Buster,* augmenting it "with abundant touches of humor and tenderness," according to a *Publishers*

Weekly critic. Joy Fleishhacker, writing in *School Library Journal,* noted that the book's "format, as well as the use of repetitive language, makes this heartwarming tale a good choice for emergent readers," and a *Kirkus Reviews* critic wrote that with *Buster* "Fleming barks up the right tree."

Fleming's sensitive canine makes a return appearance in *Buster Goes to Cowboy Camp.* When Buster's owner goes on vacation, the pup is left at Sagebrush Kennels, a doggy dude ranch. After an initial bout of nerves, Buster learns to embrace the rustic setting by gathering wood for a fire and enjoying a sing-along with his fellow campers. "Fleming's masterly control of her paper-pulp medium shows" in the artwork for *Buster Goes to Cowboy Camp,* as a *Kirkus Reviews* writer observed, and *School Library Journal* contributor Mary Hazelton cited the book's illustrations for their "sun-baked colors and dry, sandy textures with personality on every dog's face."

In *Beetle Bop* Fleming examines one of the largest groups of insects on the planet. The rhythmic narrative celebrates the diversity of the creatures . . . , while characteristically colorful artwork adds to the reader's knowledge of the insects' habitat. A *Publishers Weekly* critic applauded Fleming's illustrations, remarking that "young readers will especially want to pore over her bursting-with-color, dyed-paper-pulp compositions," and Gillian Engberg commented in *Booklist* that "both words and pictures vibrate with the relentless energy of her subject" in *Beetle Bop.*

A bedtime tale, *Sleepy, Oh So Sleepy* focuses on the nocturnal habits of baby animals which include an ostrich, a panda, and an anteater. A writer in *Kirkus Reviews* commented that "the simple, patterned text and repeated refrain make it easy for [youngsters] to join in the reading," and Phelan stated in *Booklist* that Fleming's "large-scale illustrations are bold in form and rich in color."

In *Shout! Shout It Out!* the author/illustrator goes to the opposite extreme, offering preschoolers a chance to loudly demonstrate their knowledge of numbers, letters, colors, and animals, among other topics. According to a contributor in *Kirkus Reviews,* her "illustrations are peopled with a multicultural cast of rosy-cheeked, wide-eyed preschoolers," while Maryann H. Owen commented in *School Library Journal* that the use of "wild shades and patterns add[s] to the fun of simply letting loose." Kay Weisman wrote in her *Booklist* review of *Shout! Shout It Out!* that "Fleming's signature style—brightly colored mixed-media artwork—is well suited to the exuberant text."

Biographical and Critical Sources

BOOKS

Evans, Dilys, *Show and Tell: Exploring the Fine Art of Children's Book Illustration,* Chronicle Books (San Francisco, CA), 2008.

PERIODICALS

Booklist, November 1, 1992, Kathryn Broderick, review of *Lunch,* p. 519; September 1, 1993, Ilene Cooper, review of *In the Small, Small Pond,* p. 67; April 1, 1997, review of *Where Once There Was a Wood,* p. 1296; September 15, 2001, review of *Pumpkin Eye,* p. 237; August, 2002, GraceAnne A. DeCandido, review of *Alphabet under Construction,* p. 1962; September 1, 2003, Lauren Peterson, review of *Buster,* p. 128; September 1, 2006, Carolyn Phelan, review of *The Cow Who Clucked,* p. 135; August, 2007, Gillian Engberg, review of *Beetle Bop,* p. 81; May 15, 2008, Thom Barthelmes, review of *Buster Goes to Cowboy Camp,* p. 47; June 1, 2010, Carolyn Phelan, review of *Sleepy, Oh So Sleepy,* p. 69; March 1, 2011, Kay Weisman, review of *Shout! Shout It Out!,* p. 66.

Childhood Education, summer, 2004, Sue Grossman, review of *Buster,* p. 214.

Horn Book, January-February, 1992, Ellen Fader, review of *In the Tall, Tall Grass,* pp. 56-57; January-February, 1993, Ellen Fader, review of *Lunch,* pp. 74-75; September-October, 2003, Lauren Adams, review of *Buster,* p. 597; November-December, 2005, Lauren E. Raece, review of *The First Day of Winter,* p. 693; September-October, 2006, Martha V. Parravano, review of *The Cow Who Clucked,* p. 565; July-August, 2010, Kitty Flynn, review of *Sleepy, Oh So Sleepy,* p. 88; March-April, 2011, Ashley Waring, review of *Shout! Shout It Out!,* p. 100.

Kirkus Reviews, March 15, 1994, review of *Barnyard Banter,* p. 395; April 1, 1996, review of *Where Once There Was a Wood,* p. 528; July 1, 2002, review of *Alphabet under Construction,* p. 954; August 15, 2003, review of *Buster,* p. 1072; September 15, 2005, review of *The First Day of Winter,* p. 1025; August 15, 2006, review of *The Cow Who Clucked,* p. 840; July 1, 2007, review of *Beetle Bop*; April 15, 2008, review of *Buster Goes to Cowboy Camp*; July 15, 2010, review of *Sleepy, Oh So Sleepy*; February 15, 2011, review of *Shout! Shout It Out!*

New York Times Book Review, November 19, 2000, Julie Yates Walton, "Everything You Always Wanted to Know," p. 36.

Publishers Weekly, September 13, 1991, review of *In the Tall, Tall Grass,* p. 78; December 13, 1991, review of *Count!,* p. 55; December 20, 1991, Shannon Maughan, interview with Denise Fleming, p. 24; October 10, 1994, review of *Painting with Paper,* p. 71; January 27, 1997, review of *Count!,* p. 108; July, 1998, review of *Mama Cat Has Three Kittens,* p. 217; September 24, 2001, review of *Pumpkin Eye,* p. 42; June 24, 2002, review of *Alphabet under Construction,* p. 54; July 14, 2003, review of *Buster,* p. 75; July 2, 2006, review of *Alphabet under Construction,* p. 60; July 10, 2006, review of *The Cow Who Clucked,* p. 80; July 23, 2007, review of *Bettle Bop,* p. 66; July 19, 2010, review of *Sleepy, Oh So Sleepy,* p. 126; January 10, 2011, review of *Shout! Shout It Out!,* p. 48.

School Library Journal, September, 1991, Virginia Opocensky, review of *In the Tall, Tall Grass,* pp. 232-233; March, 1992, Liza Bliss, review of *Count!,* p. 228;

December, 1992, Karen James, review of *Lunch,* pp. 81-82; September, 1993, Judy Constantinides, review of *In the Small, Small Pond,* pp. 206-207; June, 1996, Sarabeth Kalajian, review of *Where Once There Was a Wood,* p. 116; November, 1997, Lisa Falk, review of *Time to Sleep,* p. 80; November, 1998, Blair Christolon, review of *Mama Cat Has Three Kittens,* p. 84; September, 2002, Jody McCoy, review of *Alphabet under Construction,* p. 190; September, 2003, Joy Fleishhacker, review of *Buster,* p. 178; December, 2005, Shawn Brommer, review of *The First Day of Winter,* p. 112; August, 2006, Susan Weitz, review of *The Cow Who Clucked,* p. 81; August, 2007, Carolyn Janssen, review of *Beetle Bop,* p. 80; July, 2008, Mary Hazelton, review of *Buster Goes to Camp,* p. 72; July, 2010, Barbara Elleman, review of *Sleepy, Oh So Sleepy,* p. 59; February, 2011, Maryann H. Owen, review of *Shout! Shout It Out!,* p. 78.

Teacher Librarian, June, 2009, John Peters, review of *Buster Goes to Cowboy Camp,* p. 63.

Tribune Books (Chicago, IL), August 25, 2002, review of *Alphabet under Construction,* p. 5.

ONLINE

Denise Fleming Home Page, http://www.denisefleming.com (March 22, 2012).

Denise Fleming Web log, http://blog.denisefleming.com (March 22, 2012).

Harcourt Books Web site, http://www.harcourtbooks.com/ (March 22, 2012), interview with Fleming.

National Center for Children's Illustrated Literature Web site, http://nccil.org/ (March 22, 2012), "Denise Fleming."

Reading Rockets Web site, http://www.readingrockets.org/ (March 22, 2012), video interview with Fleming (includes transcript).*

* * *

FLIESS, Sue

Personal

Born in Modesto, CA; married; children: two sons. *Education:* College degree. *Hobbies and other interests:* Running, playing tennis, travel, singing.

Addresses

Home—Mountain View, CA. *Agent*—Jennifer Unter, Unter Agency, 23 W. 73rd St., Ste. 100, New York, NY 10023. *E-mail*—fliess1@yahoo.com.

Career

Writer, copywriter, and marketing consultant. eBay, Inc., San Jose, CA, junior copywriter; Penguin Publishing, New York, NY, former publicist of adult paperback division; worked variously as a copywriter, marketing communications manager, and director of marketing. Volunteer at schools.

Member

Society of Children's Book Writers and Illustrators, Author's Guild.

Awards, Honors

Society of Children's Book Writers and Illustrators Letters of Commendation, 2007, 2008.

Writings

Shoes for Me!, illustrated by Mike Laughead, Marshall Cavendish (New York, NY), 2011.

A Dress for Me!, illustrated by Mike Laughead, Marshall Cavendish Children (New York, NY), 2012.

Tons of Trucks, illustrated by Betsy Snyder, Harcourt Children's Books (New York, NY), 2012.

Celebrate Me, Gluten-Free!, Albert Whitman (Morton Grove, IL), 2012.

Robots, Robots, Everywhere!, Little Golden Books (New York, NY), 2013.

Contributor to print and online periodicals, including *Bay Area Parent, Education.com, Travelmuse.com, Circleofmoms.com,* and *Writer's Digest.*

Biographical and Critical Sources

PERIODICALS

Kirkus Reviews, February 15, 2011, review of *Shoes for Me!*

School Library Journal, April, 2011, Blair Christolon, review of *Shoes for Me!,* p. 142.

ONLINE

Sue Fliess Home Page, http://www.suefliess.com (May 1, 2012).

* * *

FROSSARD, Claire

Personal

Born in Versailles, France. *Education:* Ècole d'Arts Décoratif (Strasbourg), degree, 2002.

Addresses

Home—France. *Agent*—Emmanuelle Serroy Leaf, French Touch Agency, 1366 21st. Ave., San Francisco, CA 94122. *E-mail*—clairefrossard@yahoo.fr.

Career

Children's author and illustrator. Creator of art for postage stamps.

Writings

SELF-ILLUSTRATED

Emma's Journey, photographs by uncle, Etienne Frossard, Enchanted Lion Books (New York, NY), 2010.

ILLUSTRATOR

Orianne Lallemand, *Petite Taupe ouvre-moi ta porte,* Editions Auzou, 2009.

Armelle Renoult, *Croquette devient grand frère,* Editions Auzou, 2010.

Contributor to educational material and to books, including *Mon premier livre à grandir,* Editions Auzou, and *La ronde des contes,* Editions Flies France. Contributor to periodicals, including *Abricot, Histoire por les petits, l'École des Parents, Toupie,* and *Tralalire.*

Biographical and Critical Sources

PERIODICALS

Kirkus Reviews, October 1, 2010, review of *Emma's Journey.*

Publishers Weekly, October 11, 2010, review of *Emma's Journey,* p. 42.

School Library Journal, March, 2011, Kristine M. Casper, review of *Emma's Journey,* p. 122.

ONLINE

Claire Frossard Home Page, http://clairefrossard.ultra.book.com (May 1, 2012).*

G

GAY, Kelly
See KEATON, Kelly

* * *

GELBWASSER, Margie 1976-

Personal
Born 1976, in Minsk, Belarus; immigrated to United States, 1979; married; husband's name Stu; children: Noah. *Education:* Trenton State College, B.A. (English and secondary education), 1998; William Paterson University, M.A. (English), 2003. *Religion:* Jewish.

Addresses
Home—Fair Lawn, NJ. *Agent*—Jennifer Laughran, Andrea Brown Literary Agency; jennL@andreabrownlit.com.

Career
Writer. Worked as a teacher in Rockaway Township, NJ.

Awards, Honors
Sydney Taylor Notable Books for Teen Readers selection, Association of Jewish Libraries, 2011, for *Inconvenient.*

Writings

NOVELS

Inconvenient, Flux (Woodbury, MN), 2010.
Pieces of Us, Flux (Woodbury, MN), 2012.

Contributor to periodicals, including *Self, Ladies' Home Journal,* and *New Jersey Monthly.*

Sidelights
Margie Gelbwasser explores sensitive issues—including bullying, alcoholism, and parental neglect—in her highly regarded young-adult novels *Inconvenient* and *Pieces of Us.* A native of eastern Europe who now lives and works in northern New Jersey, Gelbwasser notes that her books are based in part on her experiences growing up in a Russian-Jewish immigrant family. "Regardless of what you write about, you put something you know into the book," she remarked to *Jewish Standard* online contributor Lois Goldrich. "I don't see how you can avoid it."

Born in Belarus, Gelbwasser immigrated to the United States as a child and grew up in Fair Lawn, New Jersey, where she still lives. She first became interested in writing in elementary school and as a teen edited her school's literary magazine while dabbling in poetry and short stories. At age fifteen, while attending a national poetry festival that included workshops with published authors, Gelbwasser experienced an epiphany. "To sit in a tent with other writers and be treated by the moderator as a real writer, not some kid who has a cute little dream was inspiring," she remarked to *Cynsations* online interviewer Cynthia Leitich Smith. "Seeing so many people who wrote for a living and realizing they were just people . . . made me see my dream was possible too."

After graduating from college, Gelbwasser taught language arts and wrote magazine articles before producing her first novel. *Inconvenient* centers on Alyssa Bondar, the fifteen-year-old daughter of hard-working Russian immigrants. While coping with her first romance as well as her best friend's decision to renounce her heritage so she can run with the popular crowd, Alyssa has a more serious concern: her mother is becoming an alcoholic. The teen's father unfortunately ignores the problem, leaving Alyssa to manage her mother's increasingly erratic behavior. "Gelbwasser realistically portrays the shifting emotions of a teenager navigating complicated situations and conflicting loyal-

Cover of Margie Gelbwasser's young-adult novel* Inconvenient, *which focuses on a young Eastern-European immigrant. (Cover design by Adrienne Zimiga. Cover images: (girl) © Design Pics/Punchstock; (rain) © Enviroman/Alamy; (butterfly) © iStockphoto/Janis Litavnieks. Reproduced with permission of Flux, an imprint of Llewellyn Worldwide Ltd.)

ties," observed *Voice of Youth Advocates* critic Amy Fiske in a review of *Inconvenient,* while Hazel Rochman commented in *Booklist* that "the story is both hilarious and heartbreaking, and the situations are universal."

Pieces of Us, Gelbwasser's second novel, is told through the alternating perspectives of four adolescents whose lives intersect during summer vacation. Alex, a damaged and brutish Pennsylvania teen, hates his mother, whom he blames for his father's suicide, and he often takes out his anger on sensitive younger brother Kyle. In New Jersey, studious Julie plays second fiddle to her older sister Katie, a popular cheerleader. During the school year, Katie is the victim of a date rape that is captured on video and used to humiliate her. When the four young people meet during a summer retreat in the Catskills, Katie's secret is revealed, prompting a disturbing response from Alex. *Pieces of Us* "is a very grim portrayal of teen bullying, sexual abuse, and misogyny," a contributor noted in *Publishers Weekly,* and Beth Karpas stated in the *Voice of Youth Advocates* that, although the novel explores a difficult subject matter, "it does not feel as if a single issue is forced into the tale." "Suspenseful, disturbing and emotionally fraught," according to a *Kirkus Reviews* writer, *Pieces of Us* is "a strong novel for a strong stomach."

Biographical and Critical Sources

PERIODICALS

Booklist, November 1, 2010, Hazel Rochman, review of *Inconvenient,* p. 64.

Kirkus Reviews, October 1, 2010, review of *Inconvenient;* January 1, 2012, review of *Pieces of Us.*

Publishers Weekly, January 23, 2012, review of *Pieces of Us,* p. 165.

School Library Journal, January, 2011, Jennifer Miskec, review of *Inconvenient,* p. 106; March, 2012, Diana Pierce, review of *Pieces of Us,* p. 156.

Voice of Youth Advocates, December, 2010, Amy Fiske, review of *Inconvenient,* p. 452; April, 2012, Beth Karpas, review of *Pieces of Us,* p. 56.

ONLINE

Cynsations Web log, http://cynthialeitichsmith.blogspot.com/ (January 24, 2011), Cynthia Leitich Smith, interview with Gelbwasser.

Jewish Standard Online, http://www.jstandard.com/ (December 3, 2010), Lois Goldrich, "When Caring Isn't Enough: Book by Local Author Shows a Teen's 'Inner Strength.'"

Margie Gelbwasser Home Page, http://www.margiewrites.com (April 15, 2012).*

* * *

GOLIO, Gary

Personal

Married Susanna Reich (a children's book author); children: Laurel. *Education:* B.F.A.; M.S.W. *Hobbies and other interests:* Playing guitar, painting and drawing, studying foreign languages, hiking, watching *Star Trek.*

Addresses

Home—Ossining, NY. *E-mail*—gary@garygolio.com.

Career

Social worker, writer, and artist. Worked as a fine artist and museum exhibitions installer; clinical social worker and psychotherapist; high-tension electrician; arts instructor.

Awards, Honors

One Hundred Titles for Reading and Sharing selection, New York Public Library, Notable Children's Books in the English Language Arts selection, National Council

of Teachers of English, and Nonfiction Picture Book Award, New York Book Show, all 2011, all for *Jimi* illustrated by Javaka Steptoe; National Parenting Publications Award, 2011, and Choices listee, Children's Cooperative Book Center, 2012, both for *When Bob Met Woody.*

Writings

Jimi: Sounds like a Rainbow: A Story of the Young Jimi Hendrix, illustrated by Javaka Steptoe, Clarion Books (Boston, MA), 2010.

When Bob Met Woody: The Story of the Young Bob Dylan, illustrated by Marc Burckhardt, Little, Brown (New York, NY), 2011.

Spirit Seeker: John Coltrane's Musical Journey, illustrated by Rudy Gutierrez, Clarion Books (Boston, MA), 2012.

Sidelights

A former landscape painter who now works as a psychotherapist, Gary Golio is also the author of the picture-book biographies *Jimi: Sounds like a Rainbow: A Story of the Young Jimi Hendrix, When Bob Met Woody: The Story of the Young Bob Dylan,* and *Spirit Seeker: John Coltrane's Musical Journey,* the last illustrated by Rudy Gutierrez. "The reason I always enjoyed reading about the lives of artists . . . was because I wanted to know how to become an artist, and how other people had done it," Golio remarked on his home page. "By writing books about great artists (musicians, songwriters, painters, actors), I've tried to lay out some maps for young people interested in the arts, and to show how the arts can make for a richer life."

Golio became interested in writing a children's book about Hendrix, who is considered to be one of the greatest musical artists in history, after reading *Jimi Hendrix: Electric Gypsy,* an exhaustive biography by Harry Shapiro and Caesar Glebbeek. "I was moved by the tender details of Jimi's childhood, and began to imagine a story for kids that was both inspiring and child-friendly," as he told *Cynsations* online interviewer Cynthia Leitich Smith.

Some eight years in the making, *Jimi* focuses on the young musician's formative years in Seattle, Washington, where he learned to play a one-string ukulele before graduating to the acoustic and electric guitars. Golio, an amateur musician, gives special attention to Hendrix's innate sense of creativity, particularly his ability to translate the sounds of his vibrant neighborhood into music. "Jimi's is a hopeful tale, about the value of imagination and making dreams real," the author stated in an interview on the *Embracing the Child* Web site. "It's also a story about the roots of artistry, and how creative people develop their interests and abilities early on."

"Golio's lyrical text sings with delicious description," Kathleen Kelly MacMillan reported in a review of *Jimi* for *School Library Journal.* The book presents a "convincing portrait of a boy who . . . heard the world very differently from anyone else," Ian Chipman stated in *Booklist,* and a writer in *Kirkus Reviews* observed that Golio's picture-book story shows "that a path to creative excellence is not only possible for young people but self-actualizing."

Two folk-music legends are at the heart of *When Bob Met Woody,* a "sensitively written, meticulously researched" work, in the words of a *Kirkus Reviews* contributor. In his story, Golio recounts a seminal 1961 encounter between Bob Dylan—at the time an unknown singer-songwriter named Bob Zimmerman who was struggling to define his musical identity—and his idol, troubador Woody Guthrie, who lay sick in a New York hospital. "Golio excels at portraying Zimmerman's angst as he flounders for meaning," Daniel Kraus remarked in *Booklist.* Writing in the *New York Times Book Review,* Sean Wilentz commented that the author "charmingly delivers the boy behind the ragamuffin troubadour, doing justice to young Zimmerman's jumbled early musical interests, including rock 'n' roll, however off kilter it seems in the familiar folk romance. *When Bob Met Woody* should stick in young readers' minds, especially if accompanied by the musicians' recordings."

Biographical and Critical Sources

PERIODICALS

Booklist, November 1, 2010, Ian Chipman, review of *Jimi: Sounds like a Rainbow: A Story of the Young Jimi Hendrix,* p. 57; March 1, 2011, Daniel Kraus, review of *When Bob Met Woody: The Story of the Young Bob Dylan,* p. 47.

Horn Book, July-August, 2011, review of *Jimi,* p. 178.

Kirkus Reviews, October 1, 2010, review of *Jimi*; April 1, 2010, review of *When Bob Met Woody.*

New York Times Book Review, May 15, 2011, Sean Wilentz, review of *When Bob Met Woody,* p. 22.

Publishers Weekly, October 4, 2010, review of *Jimi,* p. 47; March 14, 2011, review of *When Bob Met Woody,* p. 73.

School Library Journal, September, 2010, Kathleen Kelly MacMillan, review of *Jimi,* p. 172.

ONLINE

Cynsations Web log, http://cynthialeitichsmith.blogspot.com/ (January 11, 2011), Cynthia Leitich Smith, interview with Golio.

Embracing the Child Web site, http://www.embracingthechild.org/ (October, 2010), interview with Golio.

Gary Golio Home Page, http://www.garygolio.com (March 22, 2012).

* * *

GOLLUB, Matthew 1960-

Personal

Born September 29, 1960, in Hollywood, CA; son of Irving (an accountant) and Lorraine (an attorney) Gollub; married; children: Jacob. *Education:* University of the Pacific (Stockton, CA), B.A., 1982; postgraduate study in Taipei, Taiwan, 1982; attended I.S.S. Interpreting Institute (Torrance, CA), 1990-91. *Hobbies and other interests:* Jazz and ethnic (Taiko) drumming, swimming, travel.

Addresses

Home—Santa Rosa, CA. *Office*—Tortuga Press, 181 2777 Yulupa Ave., Santa Rosa, CA 95405.

Career

Writer and translator, performer, and publisher. Kansai Television Inc., Osaka, Japan, newscaster, 1983-85; Standard Advertising, Inc., Osaka, 1983-85; North Carolina Japan Center, Raleigh, editor and translator, 1986-87; Northern Telecom, Inc., Research Triangle Park, NC, translator and advisor, 1986-87; Project "X" Productions, Studio City, CA, translator, 1990; Matthew Gollub Communications, Santa Rosa, CA, freelance writer and translator, beginning 1990. Tortuga Press, Santa Rosa, founder, 1997. Member of Nohso Daiko drum troupe. *Exhibitions:* Work exhibited at Art Institute of Chicago, 1994-95.

Awards, Honors

The Twenty-five Mixtec Cats named to New York Public Library list of 100 Children's Titles for Reading and Sharing, 1993, Américas Commended selection, 1995, for *Uncle Snake;* American Library Association Notable Books selection and *Horn Book* Fanfare Best Book of the Year selection, both 1998, both for *Cool Melons—Turn to Frogs!; Writer's Digest* National Self-published Book Award, 2000, for *The Jazz Fly;* Benjamin Franklin Award for Best Children's Book/Audio Book, 2000, for *The Jazz Fly,* 2002, for *Gobble, Quack, Moon;* National Best Books Awards finalist in parenting/family category, 2007, for *Give the Gift!; ForeWord* Best Books Gold Award, Parents' Choice Award, and Moonbeam Children's Book Award Gold Medal, all c. 2010, all for *Jazz Fly 2.*

Writings

FOR CHILDREN

The Twenty-five Mixtec Cats, illustrated by Leovigildo Martinez, Tambourine Books (New York, NY), 1993.

Matthew Gollub (Reproduced by permission.)

The Moon Was at a Fiesta, illustrated by Leovigildo Martinez, Tambourine Books (New York, NY), 1994.

Uncle Snake, illustrated by Leovigildo Martinez, Tambourine Books (New York, NY), 1995.

(And translator of haiku poems) *Cool Melons—Turn to Frogs! The Life and Poems of Issa,* illustrated by Kazuko G. Stone, calligraphy by Keiko Smith, Lee & Low (New York, NY), 1998.

(And performer) *The Jazz Fly: Starring the Jazz Bugs,* illustrated by Karen Hanke, Tortuga Press (Santa Rosa, CA), 2000.

Ten Oni Drummers, illustrated by Kazuko G. Stone, Lee & Low Books (New York, NY), 2000.

Gobble, Quack, Moon (includes audio CD), illustrated by Judy Love, Tortuga Press (Santa Rosa, CA), 2002.

Supergrandpa, illustrated by Bert Dodson, Tortuga Press (Santa Rosa, CA), 2005.

Jazz Fly 2: The Jungle Pachanga (with audio CD), illustrated by Karen Hanke, Tortuga Press (Santa Rosa, CA), 2010.

Author's works have been translated into Spanish.

OTHER

Give the Gift! Ten Fulfilling Ways to Raise a Lifetime Reader, illustrated by Larry Nolte, Tortuga Press (Santa Rosa, CA), 2007.

Adaptations

The Moon Was at a Fiesta and *The Twenty-five Mixtec Cats* were adapted for video, narrated by Gollub and featuring illustrations from the original books.

Sidelights

Widely traveled and a one-time resident of both South America and Japan, Matthew Gollub brings an international spirit to both his stories and presentation for children. A storyteller who frequently appears at schools and libraries, Gollub enjoys punctuating his tales with drumming and other rhythmic sounds, as well as interaction in several languages. While many a story hour has been enlivened by his award-winning picture book *The Jazz Fly: Starring the Jazz Bugs,* his published stories also include *Supergrandpa,* illustrated by Bert Dodson, *Gobble, Quack, Moon,* with artwork by Judy Love, and *Ten Oni Drummers,* a story featuring illustrations by Kazuko G. Stone. In *Give the Gift! Ten Fulfilling Ways to Raise a Lifetime Reader,* Gollub also comes to the aid of parents by presenting suggestions regarding ways to inspire children to put down the video-game controller, switch off the television, and develop the "reading habit."

Hoping to capture an authentic style in his stories *The Twenty-five Mixtec Cats, The Moon Was at a Fiesta,* and *Uncle Snake,* Gollub teamed up with Leovigildo Martinez, an Oaxacan artist who also contributed the illustrations. Their picture-book debut, *The Twenty-five Mixtec Cats,* was lauded by Donna J. Murray in *School Library Journal* for its smooth narrative and lively, colorful illustrations, both of which combine to create "fine picture-book storytelling."

In *The Moon Was at a Fiesta* Gollub narrates a tale about a Mexican fiesta that is accompanied by Martinez's full-page illustrations. Reviewing this work for *School Library Journal,* Selene S. Vasquez characterized it as "an excellent read-aloud introduction to the famous fiestas of Mexico" and made special note of the seamless partnership between text and pictures. In *Uncle Snake* a young boy ventures into a forbidden cave that is full of human heads. Although the story is based on an old Mexican folk story, Gollub modified it for

Gollub's* Ten Oni Drummers *pairs a rhyming bedtime story with detailed artwork by Kazuko G. Stone. (Illustration copyright © 2000 by Kazuko G. Stone. Reproduced by permission of Lee & Low Books, Inc.)

Music is at the heart of Gollub's story for* The Jazz Fly, *featuring artwork by Karen Hanke. (Illustration copyright © 2000 by Karen Hanke. Reproduced by permission of Tortuga Press.)

younger children, creating a "captivating tale," according to a critic for *Kirkus Reviews.* The same critic went on to note that Martinez's "delightfully comic illustrations place readers solidly in the enchanted world" of the story. Reviewing *Uncle Snake* for *Booklist,* Annie Ayers also commented that the story's mix of "authentic ethnic flavor and richly complex watercolor illustrations" combine to create a "dramatically compelling" tale.

Gollub's more-recent stories have been brought to life by other artists. Stone creates the colorful art for *Cool Melons—Turn to Frogs!,* which collects translations of works by the eighteenth-century haiku poet Issa. Accompanied by a brief biography and illustrations that include Japanese calligraphy, the work was lauded as an "eloquent, concise and inspiring approach to understanding . . . this deceptively simple art form" by a critic for *Publishers Weekly.*

Another collaboration with Stone, *Ten Oni Drummers,* was inspired by Gollub's interest in Taiko drumming. Framed as a bedtime story about a little boy whose bad dreams are chased away by one, then two, then three and more likeable goblin drummers, the book's text introduces both Japanese drumming and numbers. Although *Ten Oni Drummers* is intended to carry listeners off to dreamland, the onis' lively drumming makes the book a "delightful and unique offering," in the view of *School Library Journal* contributor Beth Tegart.

The Jazz Fly and *Jazz Fly 2: The Jungle Pachanga* focus on a jazz-playing insect that has trouble finding its way to a performance. The fly fumbles across the countryside, seeking help from animals it meets along the way, until it finally buzzes its way into the band to close out what a *Publishers Weekly* critic characterized as a "feel-good" picture book. Karen Hanke created the digital illustrations for both books, and the combination

of text and art in *The Jazz Fly* "give[s] the whole enterprise the feel of jazz," according to Tim Wadham in his *School Library Journal* review.

Jazz Fly 2 finds the fly and his instrument-toting bandmates on the way to a tropical dance party. Several rain-forest animals are there to help, but the bandmates must ask for assistance in Spanish. In reviewing the fly' s second outing, a *Kirkus Reviews* writer stated that the "cross-cultural interplay of scat and Latin rhythms wins out" in *Jazz Fly 2.*

Sound also plays a significant role in *Gobble, Quack, Moon,* in which Love's colorful watercolor illustrations bring to life Gollub's story about a cow with big dreams. Not only does Katie the cow want to be a ballerina in a pink tutu, she wants to wear that tutu while dancing on the moon. Fortunately, Donkey, Turkey, and Duck are undeterred by distance, and the space ship they tinker together through teamwork transports Katie and friends skyward for a night of moonlit revelry. Released with an accompanying audio CD, *Gobble, Quack, Moon* features a "rhyming text that bounces along agreeably," according to *Booklist* contributor Carolyn Phelan, and in *Publishers Weekly* a critic wrote that "Gollub's rhyming text exudes a buoyant energy."

"Though I wasn't what you would call a bookish kid, I knew from the fifth grade that I liked to write," Gollub once told *SATA*. "I'd discovered the joys of alliterative phrasing, the excitement of satire and composing words that elicited snorts and guffaws from my peers. Next to shooting baskets on the playground, writing was the activity for me.

"When I was fourteen, I summered with a family in Quito, Ecuador, learning for the first time to get along in Spanish. A voyage to the Galapagos and bus journeys through the jungle ignited my life-long love of travel. Later, I graduated from college with majors in international studies and Japanese. Overseas studies led to overseas jobs: as a copywriter, newscaster, and touring member of a Japanese *taiko* drum troupe.

Gollub's popular insect hero returns for another musical adventure in* Jazz Fly 2: The Jungle Pachanga, *featuring Hanke's colorful art. (Illustration copyright © 2010 by Karen Hanke. Reproduced by permission of Tortuga Press.)

"In 1990, I went to Oaxaca, Mexico, where a friend introduced me to Leovigildo Martinez. A jovial spirit and a magnificent painter, Leo introduced me to Oaxacan markets and villages. A fine artist, he had never illustrated books but suggested we collaborate on a book of Oaxacan tales. The region's phenomenal array of indigenous cultures, their pyramids, textiles, customs, and crafts posed too delicious a challenge to turn down.

"Although I had never written for children, I told Leo, '*Me gusta la idea.*' Writing children's books has led to visits to many schools, where I enjoy presenting my stories in English and Spanish, playing bongo drums, conga drums, and showing slides for effect."

Biographical and Critical Sources

PERIODICALS

Booklist, April 25, 1994, Julie Corsaro, review of *The Moon Was at a Fiesta,* p. 1607; October 1, 1996, Annie Ayers, review of *Uncle Snake,* p. 355; December 1, 1998, GraceAnne A. DeCandido, review of *Cool Melons—Turn to Frogs! The Life and Poems of Issa,* p. 663; June 1, 2002, Carolyn Phelan, review of *Gobble, Quack, Moon,* p. 1737.

Children's Bookwatch, October, 2011, review of *Jazz Fly 2: The Jungle Pachanga.*

Horn Book, May-June, 1994, Ellen Fader, review of *The Moon Was at a Fiesta,* pp. 314-315.

Kirkus Reviews, June 15, 1996, review of *Uncle Snake,* p. 898; May 15 2010, review of *Jazz Fly 2.*

Publishers Weekly, April 19, 1993, review of *Twenty-five Mixtec Cats,* p. 61; March 28, 1994, review of *The Moon Was at a Fiesta,* p. 27; July 15, 1996, review of *Uncle Snake,* p. 74; October 12, 1998, review of *Cool Melons—Turn to Frogs!,* p. 76; March 20, 2000, review of *The Jazz Fly,* p. 90; April 1, 2002, review of *Gobble, Quack, Moon,* p. 81.

School Library Journal, November, 1997, Donna J. Murray, review of *The Twenty-five Mixtec Cats,* p. 136; November, 1998, Selene S. Vasquez, review of *The Moon Was at a Fiesta,* pp. 148, 150; August, 2000, Tim Wadham, review of *The Jazz Fly,* p. 155; January, 2001, Beth Tegart, review of *Ten Oni Drummers,* p. 100; July, 2005, Coop Renner, review of *Uncle Snake,* p. 44; August, 2010, Mary Landrum, review of *Jazz Fly 2,* p. 76.

ONLINE

Folkart and Craft Exchange Web site, http://www.folkart.com/ (February 11, 2002), "Matthew Gollub."

Matthew Gollub Home Page, http://www.matthewgollub.com (May 1, 2012).*

GORMLEY, Greg 1966-

Personal

Born 1966, in Stourbridge, England; partner's name Ana; children: Pepa (daughter). *Education:* Studied art in Belfast, Ireland, and Liverpool, England.

Addresses

Home—Cambridge, England. *E-mail*—info@greggormley.com.

Career

Author and illustrator.

Writings

(Self-illustrated) *Cat Trap!,* Scholastic (London, England), 2004.

Stick with Me, illustrated by James Croft, Gullane Children's Books (London, England), 2006.

Rocky and the Lamb, illustrated by Lynne Chapman, Barron's Educational Series (Hauppauge, NY), 2006.

(Self-illustrated) *The Yawning Game,* Gullane Children's Books (London, England), 2006, published as *The Yawn That Wouldn't Stop,* Gingham Dog Press (Columbus, OH), 2007.

(Self-illustrated) *Daddy's Day at Work,* Bloomsbury (London, England), 2007.

(Self-illustrated) *Mummy's Big Day Out,* Bloomsbury (London, England), 2007.

(Self-illustrated) *Grandad's Busy Day,* Bloomsbury (London, England), 2007.

(Self-illustrated) *Grandma Goes to Tea,* Bloomsbury (London, England), 2007.

Dog in Boots, illustrated by Roberta Angaramo, Holiday House (New York, NY), 2011.

ILLUSTRATOR

Pat Moon, *The Stare,* Mammoth (London, England), 1997.

Greg Gormley (Reproduced by permission.)

Penny McKinlay, *Escape from Germany: A Tale of Wartime Refugees,* Franklin Watts (London, England), 1998.
Penny McKinlay, *The Prisoner,* Franklin Watts (London, England), 1998.
Mary Hooper, *The Great Raj,* Franklin Watts (London, England), 1998.
Malachy Doyle, *Farewell to Ireland,* Franklin Watts (London, England), 1998.
Malachy Doyle, *The Great Hunger,* Franklin Watts (London, England), 1998.
Karen Wallace, *Stop, Thief!,* Franklin Watts (London, England), 1999.
Karen Wallace, *Penny Post Boy,* Franklin Watts (London, England), 1999.
Mary Hooper, *Bodies for Sale,* Franklin Watts (London, England), 1999.
Malachy Doyle, *12,000 Miles from Home,* Franklin Watts (London, England), 1999.
Jon Blake, *Down the Drain: A Tale of the Victorian Sewers,* Franklin Watts (London, England), 1999.
Charlotte Hudson, *Monkey Words,* Bodley Head (London, England), 2003.
Lou Kuenzler, *The Runaway Bannock,* A & C Black (London, England), 2010.

Sidelights

Greg Gormley is a British author and illustrator of children's books who has garnered critical acclaim for his humorous and energetic stories. In addition to original picture books such as *Cat Trap!, Stick with Me, Dog in Boots,* and *The Yawning Game,* Gormley also provides artwork for stories by others, including Malachy Doyle's *12,000 Miles from Home,* Lou Kuenzler's *The Runaway Bannock,* and *Monkey Words,* Charlotte Hudson's picture book about an insolent jungle dweller.

In *Monkey Words* Monkey delights in teasing its fellow creatures and pointing out their physical imperfections, such as Bushbaby's huge eyes and Anteater's long nose. The frustrated animals cleverly strike back against the satirical simian, in the process teaching Monkey a valuable lesson that Gormley's pictures reinforce "in a playful and original way," according to London *Guardian* reviewer Julia Eccleshare.

Inspired by the classic fairy tale "Puss in Boots," Gormley's *Dog in Boots* concerns an energetic pup's search for some magnificent footwear. Venturing to the local shoe store, Dog purchases a set of four boots that ultimately proves too impractical while digging in the backyard. During his return visit into the store, he finds another set of boots that improves his digging skills, but these boots are a hindrance when Dog attempts to paddle around in a pond. Flippers solve the swimming problem, but they get in the way of a good scratch. After Dog experiments with several other types of footwear, a helpful salesman provides a simple solution to the canine's dilemma. Reviewing *Dog in Boots* for *Booklist,* Andrew Medlar applauded Gormley's "repetitive text filled with sly, kid-friendly jokes," and a writer for *Kirkus Reviews* predicted that young readers will "laugh out loud at the satisfying ending."

Gormley's story in the picture book* Dog in Boots *comes to life in Robert Angaramo's animation-style art. (Illustration copyright © 2011 by Roberta Angaramo. Reproduced by permission of Holiday House, Inc.)

Biographical and Critical Sources

PERIODICALS

Booklist, March 15, 2011, Andrew Medlar, review of *Dog in Boots,* p. 63.
Guardian (London, England), June 7, 2003, Julia Eccleshare, review of *Monkey Words,* p. 33.
Kirkus Reviews, August 1, 2006, review of *Rocky and the Lamb,* p. 786; February 1, 2011, review of *Dog in Boots.*
School Library Journal, March, 2011, Anne Beier, review of *Dog in Boots,* p. 122.

ONLINE

Greg Gormley Home Page, http://greggormley.com (May 1, 2012).
Greg Gormley Web log, http://greggormley.blogspot.com (May 1, 2012).*

* * *

GREEN, Brian
See CARD, Orson Scott

* * *

GUMP, P.Q.
See CARD, Orson Scott

H

HAND, Cynthia 1978-

Personal

Born 1978, in ID; married; husband's name John; children: two. *Education:* College of Idaho, B.A. (English), 2000; Boise State University, M.F.A. (fiction writing), 2003; University of Nebraska, Ph.D. (English), 2006.

Addresses

Home—CA. *Agent*—Katherine Fausset, Curtis Brown, Ltd., Ten Astor Pl., New York, NY 10003. *E-mail*—writercynthiahand@gmail.com.

Career

Writer. Pepperdine University, Malibu, CA, teacher of creative writing.

Member

Society of Children's Book Writers and Illustrators.

Writings

"UNEARTHLY" NOVEL SERIES

Unearthly, HarperTeen (New York, NY), 2011.
Hallowed, HarperTeen (New York, NY), 2012.

Sidelights

A teenager who is descended from angels discovers the extent of her supernatural powers in Cynthia Hand's debut novel *Unearthly,* a critically acclaimed paranormal romance. "I think *Unearthly* is different from the other angel-related books in that it is, at heart, a human story," Hand stated in a HarperCollins online interview. "My story is about a girl who wants to understand her purpose on this earth. Her situation is a metaphor, I think, for a basic question all human beings ask themselves at some point: Why am I here?"

Unearthly introduces Clara Gardner, a sixteen-year-old Quartarius (one-quarter angel) whose visions of a young man standing in a raging fire reveal her divine purpose: to find the teen and save his life. After Clara learns more about her vision, she relocates from California to Wyoming with her half-angel mom and younger brother,

Cover of Cynthia Hand's paranormal fantasy* Unearthly, *featuring photography by Howard Huang. (Jacket photo © 2011 by Howard Huang. Reproduced by permission of HarperTeen, an imprint of HarperCollins Publishers.)

and there she meets Christian Prescott, the boy she is fated to rescue. As a student at Christian's high school, Clara befriends Angela, a brooding loner who similarly possesses an angelic nature. Angela warns Clara about the Black Wings, fallen angels who wish to steal her powers. When Clara falls in love with schoolmate Tucker Avery, their relationship ultimately threatens her ability to complete her destined mission.

In *Unearthly* "Hand has crafted a story of angels among us that is intriguing and believable," Deborah L. Dubois observed in her review for *Voice of Youth Advocates.* Several critics applauded the novel's well-developed characters, a *Kirkus Reviews* writer remarking that "Clara struggles with her mother's expectations of her purpose . . . and her desire to acknowledge her human side." *School Library Journal* contributor Samantha Larsen Hastings also recommended *Unearthly,* writing that "Hand does an excellent job of creating and sustaining the mood of teenage angst mixed with first love."

Clara's story continues in *Hallowed,* as her ability to help Tucker and her knowledge that Christian is also an angel move her slowly toward her divine purpose. After she begins having visions that someone close to her will die, Clara attempts to learn more about her special powers while also keeping watch for Samjeeza, a threatening Black Wing. "Themes of destiny and free will are explored, giving the reader much to think about," Dubois commented in a review of Hand's third "Unearthly" installment.

Biographical and Critical Sources

PERIODICALS

Booklist, December 1, 2010, Karen Cruze, review of *Unearthly,* p. 55; January 1, 2012, Karen Cruze, review of *Hallowed,* p. 108.

Kirkus Reviews, November 15, 2010, review of *Unearthly;* December 1, 2011, review of *Hallowed.*

Publishers Weekly, November 15, 2010, review of *Unearthly,* p. 58.

School Library Journal, January, 2011, Samantha Larsen Hastings, review of *Unearthly,* p. 106.

Voice of Youth Advocates, February, 2011, Deborah L. Dubois, review of *Unearthly,* p. 569; February, 2012, Deborah L. Dubois, review of *Hallowed,* p. 609.

ONLINE

Cynthia Hand Home Page, http://www.cynthiahandbooks.com (March 22, 2012).

Cynthia Hand Web log, http://www.cynthiahand.blogspot.com (March 22, 2012).

HarperTeen Web site, http://www.harperteen.com/ (March 22, 2012), interview with Hand.

Open Book Society Web site, http://openbooksociety.com/ (March 2, 2011), interview with Hand.*

* * *

HARMER, Wendy 1955-

Personal

Born October 10, 1955, in Yarram, Victoria, Australia; married; husband's name Brendan; children: one son, one daughter.

Addresses

Home—Collaroy, New South Wales, Australia. *Agent*—Kate Richter, HLA Management, P.O. Box 1536, Strawberry Hills, New South Wales 2012, Australia.

Career

Writer, journalist, radio-show host, and comedian. *Sun News-Pictorial,* Melbourne, Victoria, Australia, journalist for twelve years; stand-up comedian in Australia, beginning 1985; *The Hoopla* (online magazine), cofounder and editor in chief, 2011—. Television work includes *The Video Comedy Show,* 1985; (host) *The Big Gig,* 1989-91; *The Glass House,* 2002-03; *Greeks on the Roof,* 2003; *Australian Story,* 2005; *20 to 1,* 2006; and *Agony Aunts,* 2012. Host of radio shows, including *Radio National,* beginning 1991, and *2-Day FM,* 1993-2004.

Awards, Honors

Pick of the Fringe award, 1990, for *Love Gone Wrong* (one-woman show).

Writings

"PEARLIE" READER SERIES; FOR CHILDREN

Pearlie in the Park (also see below), illustrated by Mike Zarb, Random House Australia (Milsons Point, New South Wales, Australia), 2003.

Pearlie and the Big Doll (also see below), illustrated by Mike Zarb, Random House Australia (Milsons Point, New South Wales, Australia), 2004.

Pearlie and Opal (also see below), illustrated by Mike Zarb, Random House Australia (Milsons Point, New South Wales, Australia), 2004, published as *Deluxe Pearlie and Opal,* 2012.

Very, Very Pearlie (contains *Pearlie in the Park, Pearlie and the Big Doll,* and *Pearlie and Opal*), illustrated by Mike Zarb, Random House Australia (Milsons Point, New South Wales, Australia), 2005.

Pearlie and the Lost Handbag, illustrated by Mike Zarb, Random House Australia (Milsons Point, New South Wales, Australia), 2005.

Pearlie and Jasper, illustrated by Mike Zarb and Gypsy Taylor, Random House Australia (Milsons Point, New South Wales, Australia), 2006.

Pearlie and the Christmas Angel, illustrated by Gypsy Taylor, Random House Australia (North Sydney, New South Wales, Australia), 2006.

Really, Really Pearlie, illustrated by Gypsy Taylor, Random House Australia (North Sydney, New South Wales, Australia), 2007.

Pearlie and Great Aunt Garnet, illustrated by Gypsy Taylor, Random House Australia (North Sydney, New South Wales, Australia), 2007.

Pearlie and Sapphire (also see below), illustrated by Gypsy Taylor, Random House Australia (North Sydney, New South Wales, Australia), 2007.

Pearlie and Her Pink Shell (also see below), illustrated by Gypsy Taylor, Random House Australia (North Sydney, New South Wales, Australia), 2008.

Pearlie and the Fairy Queen (also see below), illustrated by Gypsy Taylor, Random House Australia (North Sydney, New South Wales, Australia), 2008.

Truly Ruly Pearlie (contains *Pearlie and Sapphire, Pearlie and Her Pink Shell,* and *Pearlie and the Fairy Queen*), illustrated by Gypsy Taylor, Random House Australia (North Sydney, New South Wales, Australia), 2009.

Pearlie and the Cherry Blossom Fairy, illustrated by Gypsy Taylor, Random House Australia (North Sydney, New South Wales, Australia), 2010.

Pearlie in Central Park, illustrated by Gypsy Taylor, Random House Australia (North Sydney, New South Wales, Australia), 2010.

Pearlie and the Silver Fern Fairy, illustrated by Gypsy Taylor, Random House Australia (North Sydney, New South Wales, Australia), 2011.

Pearlie in Paris, illustrated by Gypsy Taylor, Random House Australia (North Sydney, New South Wales, Australia), 2011.

Author of stage play *Pearlie in the Park* (adapted from the book of the same title), produced in Sydney, New South Wales, Australia.

Author's works have been translated into ten languages.

FOR ADULTS

It's a Joke, Joyce: Australia's Funny Women, Pan Books (Sydney, New South Wales, Australia), 1989.

So Anyway . . .: Wendy's Words of Wisdom (collected columns), Pan MacMillan (Sydney, New South Wales, Australia), 1997.

Farewell My Ovaries, Allen & Unwin (Crows Nest, New South Wales, Australia), 2005.

Nagging for Beginners, Allen & Unwin (Crows Nest, New South Wales, Australia), 2006.

Love and Punishment, Allen & Unwin (Crows Nest, New South Wales, Australia), 2006.

Roadside Sisters, Allen & Unwin (Crows Nest, New South Wales, Australia), 2010.

Friends like These, Allen & Unwin (Crows Nest, New South Wales, Australia), 2011.

PLAYS

(Coauthor) *Faking It . . . One, Two, and Two and a Half* produced in Melbourne, Victoria, Australia, 1983.

(Coauthor) *Sunburn, Bloody Sunburn,* produced in Melbourne, Victoria, Australia, 1984.

(Coauthor) *Sunburn, the Day After,* produced in Melbourne, Victoria, Australia, 1984.

(Coauthor) *Harmer and Stubbs,* produced in Melbourne, Victoria, Australia, 1985.

(Coauthor) *Stop Laughing This Is Serious,* produced in Melbourne, Victoria, Australia, 1985.

(With Jane Clifton) *On a Clear Day You Can See Jane Clifton* (cabaret show), produced in Melbourne, Victoria, Australia, 1985.

I Only Wanna Be with You, produced in Sydney, New South Wales, Australia, 1987.

(Author of libretto) *Lake Lost* (opera), produced in Australia, 1990.

Backstage Pass (produced in Adelaide, South Australia, Australia, 1990), Currency Press (Sydney, New South Wales), 1991.

Love Gone Wrong (one-woman show; produced in Australia, 1990), illustrated by Bruce Currie, Macmillan (Chippendale, New South Wales, Australia), 1991.

(And director) *What Is the Matter with Mary Jane?* (adapted from a story by Sancia Robinson; produced in Sydney, New South Wales, Australia, 1995), Currency Press (Sydney, New South Wales), 1996.

TELEVISION SCRIPTS

(With others) *The Gillies Report,* Australian Broadcasting Company, produced 1984–1994.

While You're Down There, Australian Broadcasting Company, produced 1986.

(With others; and performer) *The Big Gig,* Australian Broadcasting Company, produced 1989–1991.

(With Patrick Cooks) *In Harmer's Way,* Australian Broadcasting Company, produced 1990.

(With Andrew Denton) *World Series Debating,* Australian Broadcasting Company, produced 1993–1994.

(And executive producer and presenter) *Stuff* (documentary), Australian Broadcasting Company, 2008.

OTHER

I Lost My Mobile at the Mall: Teenager on the Edge of Technological Breakdown (young-adult fiction), Random House Australia (North Sydney, New South Wales, Australia), 2009, Kane Miller (San Diego, CA), 2011.

Contributor to periodicals, and to books, including *The Best Ever Australian Sports Writing: A 200 Year Collection,* 2001, and *What Women Want,* 2002. Contributing columnist for *Australian Women's Weekly, Good Weekend, HQ,* and *New Weekly.*

Adaptations

The "Pearlie" series was adapted as the animated television series *Pearlie,* Network Ten, 2009.

Sidelights

A popular Australian humorist, Wendy Harmer has enjoyed a successful career as a journalist, radio host, author, and comedian. Demonstrating her versatility, Harmer has written television scripts, cabaret shows, the libretto for an opera, adult novels, fantasy tales for children, and the young-adult novel *I Lost My Mobile at the Mall: Teenager on the Edge of Technological Breakdown.* "I don't try to force gags," Harmer remarked to *Boomerang Books* online interviewer William Kostakis in discussing her use of humor in her work. "If you do that you lose the empathy for a character. I like it when readers have a laugh and then, hopefully a tear or two."

Harmer's popular "Pearlie" series, which is aimed at young readers, includes *Pearlie and Opal, Pearlie and the Lost Handbag, Pearlie and the Fairy Queen,* and *Pearlie in Paris* and chronicles the adventures of an energetic urban fairy. Discussing her inspiration for the works, the author told Kostakis: "I was sick of reading my daughter fairy stories about characters that were no more than Paris Hilton with wings—all frocking up to go to parties. Yawn! Pearlie is feisty—a bit of a detective, an overachiever, and bossy. She has been successful because she has a bit of 'get up and go' about her. She's not a soppy character. And each book has a real story—suspense and humour."

In *I Lost My Mobile at the Mall* Harmer homes in on 'tween and younger teen readers. After losing her cherished cell phone, fourteen-year-old Elly Pickering becomes convinced that death is preferable to the punishment she will receive from her parents, who have replaced two previous phones, and the ribbing she will take from her best friend, who has stored one of her precious photographs on the device. Worse still, Elly and her family soon face a variety of technology-related disasters that leads them to question their reliance on modern conveniences. According to a writer in *Kirkus Reviews,* in *I Lost My Mobile at the Mall* Harmer "clearly wants readers to consider whether we really want to make our distracted, fleeting lives move even faster."

Biographical and Critical Sources

PERIODICALS

Kirkus Reviews, February 1, 2011, review of *I Lost My Mobile at the Mall: Teenager on the Edge of Technological Breakdown.*

School Library Journal, May, 2011, Christi Esterle, review of *I Lost My Mobile at the Mall,* p. 114.

ONLINE

Boomerang Books Web log, http://content.boomerangbooks.com.au/blog/ (May 28, 2009), William Kostakis, interview with Harmer.

HLA Management Web site, http://www.hlamgt.com.au/ (April 15, 2012), "Wendy Harmer."

Wendy Harmer Home Page, http://www.wendyharmer.com (April 15, 2012).*

* * *

HARPER, Jamie

Personal

Married; children: Grace, Lucy, Georgia Rose. *Education:* Attended Bryn Mawr College; attended Massachusetts College of Art.

Addresses

Home—Weston, MA. *E-mail*—jharper109@gmail.com.

Career

Author and illustrator. Formerly worked as a business consultant in San Francisco, CA, as a pastry chef, and in educational publishing.

Member

Society of Children's Book Writers and Illustrators.

Awards, Honors

Choices listee, Cooperative Children's Book Center, 2007, for *Night-night, Baby Bundt.*

Writings

SELF-ILLUSTRATED PICTURE BOOKS

Don't Grown-ups Ever Have Fun?, Little, Brown (New York, NY), 2003.

Me Too!, Little, Brown (New York, NY), 2005.

Miss Mingo and the First Day of School, Candlewick Press (Cambridge, MA), 2006.

Night-night, Baby Bundt: A Recipe for Bedtime, Candlewick Press (Cambridge, MA), 2007.

Splish Splash, Baby Bundt: A Recipe for Bath Time, Jamie Harper, Candlewick Press (Cambridge, MA), 2007.

Blast off, Baby Bundt: A Recipe for Playtime, Candlewick Press (Cambridge, MA), 2009.

Miss Mingo and the Fire Drill, Candlewick Press (Somerville, MA), 2009.

Yum Yum, Baby Bundt, Candlewick Press (Cambridge, MA), 2009.

Miles to Go, Candlewick Press (Somerville, MA), 2010.

ILLUSTRATOR

Sally Warner, *Only Emma,* Viking (New York, NY), 2005.

Sally Warner, *Not-So-Weird Emma,* Viking (New York, NY), 2005.

Sally Warner, *Super Emma,* Viking (New York, NY), 2006.

Sally Warner, *Best Friend Emma,* Viking (New York, NY), 2007.

Sally Warner, *Excellent Emma,* Viking (New York, NY), 2009.

Sally Warner, *Happily Ever Emma,* Viking (New York, NY), 2010.

Sally Warner, *EllRay Jakes Is Not a Chicken!,* Viking (New York, NY), 2011.

Sally Warner, *EllRay Jakes Is Not a Rock Star!,* Viking (New York, NY), 2011.

Sally Warner, *EllRay Jakes Walks the Plank!,* Viking (New York, NY), 2012.

Contributor of illustrations to periodicals, including *Click* and *American Girl.*

Sidelights

A former pastry chef, Jamie Harper has gained a reputation among youngsters as the author/illustrator of children's picture books such as *Miss Mingo and the Fire Drill, Miles to Go,* and the humorous stories featuring Baby Bundt. Drawing heavily on the experiences of her own children, Harper focuses her stories on sibling rivalry, parents, and other topics of universal concern to the very young.

In *Don't Grown-ups Ever Have Fun?* three siblings try to bring a little fun into their parents' lives. Through their efforts they help their dad avoid "boring" television programs like the news and give their mom a home-made spa holiday that features beautification ingredients such as "diaper goo." Despite the chaotic efforts of the children, the patient parents show their appreciation by having fun with their enthusiastic offspring. "This high-spirited romp will elicit both giggles and groans of recognition," wrote Kathleen Kelly MacMillan in a *School Library Journal* review of *Don't Grown-ups Ever Have Fun?* A *Publishers Weekly* critic cited the same book for containing "laughs for everyone," and *Booklist* contributor Diane Foote noted that Harper's "scratchy, hyperactive art puts a cheerful face on chaos." According to a *Kirkus Reviews* contributor, *Don't Grown-ups Ever Have Fun?* "lets the pictures tell the story . . . , with text kept at a comfortable minimum."

Inspired by Harper's daughters, *Me Too!* focuses on Grace, whose little sister Lucy tries to copy everything

***Jamie Harper introduces readers to a new feathered friend in her self-illustrated picture book* Miss Mingo and the First Day of School.** (Copyright © 2006 by Jamie Harper. Reproduced by permission of the publisher Candlewick Press, Inc., Cambridge, MA.)

***Harper's illustration projects include creating the artwork for Sally Warner's* Happily Ever Emma.** (Illustration copyright © 2010 by Jamie Harper. Used by permission of Viking Children's Books, a division of Penguin Young Readers Group, a member of Penguin Group (USA), Inc.)

her older sibling does. It is not until Grace realizes that she also has someone she admires and tries to imitate that she begins to understand Lucy's perspective. "With its compassionate ending," *Me Too!* "is a must for any multi-child home," wrote a *Kirkus Reviews* contributor, while Judith Constantinides noted in *School Library Journal* that Harper's "humorous ink-and-watercolor cartoons mirror Grace's frustration and Lucy's determination." *Booklist* critic Jennifer Mattson wrote that young audiences will "feel reassured by the honest portrayal of . . . [a] sibling relationship" in *Me Too!,* and a *Publishers Weekly* critic predicted that "readers of all ages will find plenty to chuckle about in this tale that touches on both the highs and lows of having a sibling."

Miss Mingo and the First Day of School focuses on a classroom of inquisitive kindergartners and their creative teacher, a pink flamingo. Miss Mingo asks her students—which include an alligator, a koala, and an octopus—to share one interesting thing about themselves, leading to a discussion about similarities and differences. A *Publishers Weekly* contributor noted that "young animal enthusiasts won't soon forget these unique students or Miss Mingo's enthusiastic celebration of their diversity," and a *Kirkus Reviews* critic deemed *Miss Mingo and the First Day of School* "a cute combination of animal fact book and a lesson in kindergarten preparedness."

In *Miss Mingo and the Fire Drill* the teacher reassures nervous students while they practice safety measures. When one animal unleashes a loud sneeze at lunchtime, the cafeteria empties quickly as the students mistakenly believe they have heard the signal to evacuate the building. Harper's silliness helps deliver the well-articulated and important lessons about emergency behavior," Mary Hazelton remarked in her *School Library Journal* review of *Miss Mingo and the First Day of School.*

Harper's "Baby Bundt" picture books take a lighthearted look at the relationship between an energetic toddler and his older sister. *Yum Yum, Baby Bundt: A Recipe for Mealtime* presents step-by-step instructions for feeding a little one, while other sibling interactions are the focus of *Night-night, Baby Bundt: A Recipe for Bedtime* and *Splish Splash, Baby Bundt: A Recipe for Bath Time.* "The writing is clear and simple," Amelia Jenkins wrote in her *School Library Journal* review of *Yum, Yum, Baby Bundt,* the critic also complimenting the "playful, expressive watercolor-and-ink illustrations" in Harper's other "Baby Bundt" stories.

In *Miles to Go* young Miles carefully "drives" his foot-propelled car to preschool, treating his commute as seriously as any adult driver. Besides making a number of safety checks before he takes off, Miles alertly avoids a collision with a baby stroller and ends his day by fixing a broken horn. "The rosy-cheeked Miles marvelously

embodies the exuberance, imagination and passions of a preschool boy," observed a writer in *Kirkus Reviews,* and Carolyn Phelan, critiquing *Miles to Go* for *Booklist,* reported that Harper "tells a simple story in a satisfying way."

In addition to her self-illustrated titles, Harper has contributed artwork to several stories by author Sally Warner, among them the "Emma" chapter books which follow the exploits of a sensitive but strong-willed third grader. *Booklist* critic Jennifer Locke praised the "charming ink-and-wash drawings" featured in *Only Emma,* and *School Library Journal* contributor Carol L. MacKay observed that "Harper's spunky black-and-white illustrations work well with the text" in *Not-So-Weird Emma.* Reviewing *Excellent Emma,* for *School Library Journal,* Lucinda Snyder Whitehurst commented that Harper's "watercolors add to the humor of the story."

Harper and Warner have also collaborated on the "EllRay Jakes" series of tales, which feature Emma's likable but often-bullied classmate. Here "Warner creates a humorous voice for EllRay, amplified by Harper's winsome illustrations," as Erin Anderson remarked in her *Booklist* review of *EllRay Jakes Is Not a Chicken!* The youngster's interest in geology is at the heart of *EllRay Jakes Is a Rock Star!,* and Harper's "charming cartoon illustrations make this beginning chapter book approachable for reluctant readers," according to *School Library Journal* contributor Sarah Polace.

Biographical and Critical Sources

PERIODICALS

Booklist, July, 2003, Diane Foote, review of *Don't Grown-ups Ever Have Fun?,* p. 1896; March 1, 2005, Jennifer Locke, review of *Only Emma,* p. 1199; April 1, 2005, Jennifer Mattson, review of *Me Too!,* p. 1366; September 1, 2005, Debbie Carton, review of *Not-So-Weird Emma,* p. 137; December 15, 2010, Carolyn Phelan, review of *Miles to Go,* p. 58; June 1, 2011, Erin Anderson, review of *EllRay Jakes Is Not a Chicken!,* p. 85.

Kirkus Reviews, April 1, 2003, review of *Don't Grown-ups Ever Have Fun?,* p. 534; January 15, 2005, review of *Me Too!,* p. 120; March 1, 2005, review of *Only Emma,* p. 297; August 1, 2005, review of *Not-So-Weird Emma,* p. 860; June 15, 2006, review of *Miss Mingo and the First Day of School,* p. 634; August 1, 2006, review of *Super Emma,* p. 797; May 15, 2009, review of *Yum Yum, Baby Bundt*; September 15, 2010, review of *Miles to Go*; April 15, 2011, review of *EllRay Jakes Is Not a Chicken!*

Publishers Weekly, February 3, 2003, review of *Don't Grown-ups Ever Have Fun?,* p. 74; April 18, 2005, review of *Me Too!,* p. 61; June 12, 2006, review of *Miss Mingo and the First Day of School,* p. 50; October 11, 2010, review of *Miles to Go,* p. 40; March 14, 2011, review of *EllRay Jakes Is Not a Chicken!,* p. 73.

School Library Journal, April, 2003, Kathleen Kelly MacMillan, review of *Don't Grown-ups Ever Have Fun?,* p. 122; February, 2005, Judith Constantinides, review of *Me Too!,* p. 97; April, 2005, Linda Zeilstra Sawyer, review of *Only Emma,* p. 114; November, 2005, Carol L. MacKay, review of *Not-So-Weird Emma,* p. 110; August, 2006, Christine Markley, review of *Miss Mingo and the First Day of School,* p. 88; October, 2006, Debbie Lewis O'Donnell, review of *Super Emma,* p. 129; July, 2007, Debbie Whitbeck, review of *Best Friend Emma,* p. 87; January, 2008, Amelia Jenkins, reviews of *Night Night, Baby Bundt* and *Splish Splash, Baby Bundt,* both p. 87; March, 2009, Lucinda Snyder Whitehurst, review of *Excellent Emma,* p. 130; September, 2009, Mary Hazelton, review of *Miss Mingo and the Fire Drill,* p. 122; November, 2009, Amelia Jenkins, review of *Yum Yum, Baby Bundt,* p. 79; May, 2011, Sara Lissa Paulson, review of *Miles to Go,* p. 78; August, 2011, Kari Allen, review of *EllRay Jakes Is Not a Chicken!,* p. 87; September, 2011, Sarah Polace, review of *EllRay Jakes Is a Not Rock Star!,* p. 132.

ONLINE

Jamie Harper Home Page, http://www.jamieharper.com (March 22, 2012).

Wellesley Weston Online, http://www.wellesleyweston magazine.com/ (summer, 2006), Winky Merrill, "Jamie Harper."*

* * *

HART, Sam 1973-

Personal

Born 1973, in England; married; children: Kaya.

Addresses

Home—São Paulo, Brazil. *E-mail*—sam@samhartgraph ics.com.

Career

Illustrator.

Awards, Honors

Children's Choices listee, International Reading Association/Children's Book Council, Oppenheim Toy Portfolio Gold Award, Books for the Teen Age selection, New York Public Library, and Best Books for Young Adults designation, Great Graphic Novels for Teens designation, and Popular Paperbacks for Young Adults designation, all American Library Association (ALA), all 2009, all for *Outlaw;* Great Graphic Novels for Teens designation, ALA, 2011, for *Excalibur.*

Illustrator

COMICS AND GRAPHIC NOVELS

Tony Lee, *Outlaw: The Legend of Robin Hood,* Candlewick Press (Somerville, MA), 2009.

Tony Lee, *Excalibur: The Legend of King Arthur,* Candlewick Press (Somerville, MA), 2011.

Antony Johnson, *The Coldest City,* Oni Press (Portland, OR), 2012.

Contributor to comic-book series, including *Abiding Perdition,* 2005; *2000 AD,* 2006; *Brothers: The Fall of Lucifer,* 2006; *Starship Troopers: Blaze of Glory,* 2006; *Starship Troopers: Damaged Justice,* 2006; *Starship Troopers: Dead Man's Hand,* 2006; and *The Three-Minute Sketchbook,* 2007. Contributor to newspapers and magazines published in Brazil.

Sidelights

A British-born illustrator who now makes his home in São Paulo, Brazil, Sam Hart has enjoyed a successful career as a sequential artist. Among Hart's best-known works are his collaborations with writer Tony Lee on the award-winning graphic novels *Outlaw: The Legend of Robin Hood* and *Excalibur: The Legend of King Arthur.*

In *Outlaw,* Lee offers his version of the life of the celebrated figure from English folklore, presenting Robin as a soldier who returns from the Crusades to avenge

***Sam Hart creates the stylized sequential art that accompany Tony Lee's chronicle of a time-honored monarch in* Excalibur: The Legend of King Arthur.** (Illustration copyright © 2011 by Sam Hart. Reproduced by permission of Candlewick Press, on behalf of Walker Books, London.)

the murder of his father and eventually leads a band of rebels who challenge the authority of the tyrannical Sheriff of Nottingham. Andrea Lipinski, writing in *School Library Journal,* praised "Hart's expressive illustrations, featuring lots of close-ups and dramatic lighting and a beautiful jewel-toned palette." According to Snow Wildsmith, reviewing *Outlaw* for the *Graphic Novel Reporter* online, "Hart's drawings are realistic and take their material seriously. People and settings look the way they . . . would have looked in the Middle Ages, and he's careful not to make things too clean or too orderly. On top of that, the action scenes are exciting and easy to follow, deadly without being too gory."

Hart and Lee also joined forces on *Excalibur,* which presents "a fresh take on the Arthurian legends" according to a *Publishers Weekly* critic. Lee's story focuses on Arthur's adversarial relationship with his half-sister, the sorceress Morgana, as well as on his betrayal by Sir Lancelot and Lady Guinevere. "Hart captures it all with intense, shadow-and light-filled artwork," Ian Chipman maintained in a *Booklist* review of the work. Douglas P. Davey, critiquing *Excalibur* for *School Library Journal,* reported that "the artist's use of color does a fantastic job of creating different moods."

Biographical and Critical Sources

PERIODICALS

Booklist, August 1, 2009, Jesse Karp, review of *Outlaw: The Legend of Robin Hood,* p. 59; March 15, 2011, Ian Chipman, review of *Excalibur: The Legend of King Arthur,* p. 32.

Publishers Weekly, April 4, 2011, review of *Excalibur,* p. 55.

School Library Journal, September, 2009, Andrea Lipinski, review of *Outlaw,* p. 188; May, 2011, Douglas P. Davey, review of *Excalibur,* p. 142.

ONLINE

Candlewick Press Web site, http://www.candlewick.com/ (March 22, 2012), "Sam Hart."

Graphic Novel Reporter Online, http://graphicnovel reporter.com/ (March 22, 2012), Now Wildsmith, review of *Outlaw.*

Sam Hart Home Page, http://www.samhartgraphics.com (March 22, 2012).*

* * *

HODSON, Ben

Personal

Born in Guelph, Ontario, Canada; married; wife's name May; children: Zoe.

Addresses

Home and office—Silver Lake, Ontario, Canada. *E-mail*—benjhodson@hotmail.com.

Career

Illustrator and graphic artist. Clients include environmental and social-justice organizations. Owner of a greeting card company in Waterloo, Ontario, Canada.

Member

Society of Children's Book Writers and Illustrators, Canadian Society of Children's Authors, Illustrators and Performers, Canadian Children's Book Centre.

Awards, Honors

Best Books for the Teen Age listee, New York Public Library, 2004, for *I Love Yoga* by Ellen Schwartz; Glass Slipper Award, Society of Children's Book Writers and Illustrators' Canadian Conference, 2004; Our Choice selection, Canadian Children's Book Centre, 2005, for *Pigs Aren't Dirty, Bears Aren't Slow, and Other Truths about Misunderstood Animals* by Joanne Boutilier; Society of Illustrators' Original Art selection 2006, and Benjamin Franklin Award, Children's Choices listee, International Reading Association/Children's Book Council, Moonbeam Children's Book Award, and Patricia Gallagher Picture Book Award, Oregon Reading Association, all c. 2007, all for *How the Moon Regained Her Shape* by Janet Ruth Heller; Best Bets listee, Ontario Library Association, 2008, for *Jeffrey and Sloth* by Kari-Lynn Winters.

Illustrator

Ellen Schwartz, *I Love Yoga: A Guide for Kids and Teens,* Tundra Books (Toronto, Ontario, Canada), 2003.

Anne Patton, *Tyler's New Friends,* Scholastic Canada (Markham, Ontario, Canada), 2003.

Anne Patton, *Tyler's Teacher,* Scholastic Canada (Markham, Ontario, Canada), 2005.

Anne Patton, *Tyler's First Sleepover,* Scholastic Canada (Markham, Ontario, Canada), 2005.

Joanna Boutilier, *Pigs Aren't Dirty, Bears Aren't Slow, and Other Truths about Misunderstood Animals,* Annick Press (Toronto, Ontario, Canada), 2005.

Wendy A. Lewis, *Dress Up,* Scholastic Canada (Markham, Ontario, Canada), 2005.

Wishes and Worries: A Story to Help Children Understand a Parent Who Drinks Too Much Alcohol, Centre for Addiction & Mental Health (Toronto, Ontario, Canada), 2005.

Janet Ruth Heller, *How the Moon Regained Her Shape,* Sylvan Dell Publishing (Mt. Pleasant, SC), 2006.

Laura Crawford, *In Arctic Waters,* Sylvan Dell Publishing (Mount Pleasant, SC), 2007.

Kari-Lynn Winters, *Jeffrey and Sloth,* Orca Book Publishers (Custer, WA), 2007.

Caroline Everson, *Ali Runs with the Pack,* Scholastic Canada (Markham, Ontario, Canada), 2007.

Shannon Stewart, *Captain Jake,* Orca Book Publishers (Custer, WA), 2008.
Catherine Ipcizade, *'Twas the Day before Zoo Day,* Sylvan Dell Publishing (Mount Pleasant, SC), 2008.
Gillian Watts, *Hear My Roar: A Story of Family Violence,* Annick Press (Toronto, Ontario, Canada), 2009.
Carolyn Peck, *Richard Was a Picker,* Orca Book Publishers (Custer, WA), 2010.

Sidelights

A self-taught Canadian artist, Ben Hodson has provided the illustrations for children's books that include *Pigs Aren't Dirty, Bears Aren't Slow, and Other Truths about Misunderstood Animals* by Joanne Boutilier and *How the Moon Regained Her Shape* by Janet Ruth Heller. In an interview on the Orca Books Web site, Hodson noted that helping to bring a narrative to life is a "tricky business. Maintaining the same characters in different poses from a variety of angles with consistent colours, moving the action from page to page with some sort of flow and continuity, and all the while adding smaller visual stories within and around the main story are not small feats! Each book is a marathon for my imagination."

In *Pigs Aren't Dirty, Bears Aren't Slow, and Other Truths about Misunderstood Animals,* Boutilier clears up a number of misconceptions about the natural world. The author notes, for instance, that while wolves are remarkable hunters, they are not as big and bad as fairy tales would suggest. "Cartoony pencil crayon drawings by . . . Hodson are fun, and add humour to the text," commented Evette Berry in her *Resource Links* review of the whimsical work.

Hodson's mixed-media illustrations were cited as a highlight of Heller's *How the Moon Regained Her Shape,* a story based on a native North American legend. "An intriguing fore-and middle-ground palette of muted colours complements the dominant background colours," observed *Canadian Review of Materials* reviewer Gregory Bryan, the critic adding that the variety of colors and materials in the book's art "result[s] in a visual feast and readers will be fascinated by the illustrations."

A cumulative tale, Laura Crawford's *In Arctic Waters* follows the amusing adventures of a beluga whale, a narwhal, a seal, a walrus, a polar bear, and a fish. "Both the animals and their habitat are rendered in textured, vibrant colours that give the images a nearly three-dimensional effect," wrote *Quill & Quire* reviewer Etta Kaner. According to Tanya Boudreau in *Resource Links,* "each mammal has a personality of its own that comes across in the text and in its facial expressions. The many shades of blue and white found in the ice, water, and sky create a beautiful Arctic environment" in the pages of the picture book.

In *Jeffrey and Sloth,* with a story by Kari-Lynn Winters, a youngster finishes a homework fiction-writing assignment by cleverly manipulating his story's main character, a lazy creature that comes to life on the page. *School Library Journal* critic Rachael Vilmar maintained that Hodson's illustrations "add an element of silly fun" to *Jeffrey and Sloth,* while Michelle Gowans described the artwork in her *Resource Links* review as "punchy and colourful."

A treasure-loving youngster stands up to a bully with the help of a pirate in Shannon Stewart's *Captain Jake,* another of Hodson's illustration projects. Praising the artwork for this story, Jonine Bergen stated in the *Canadian Review of Materials* that "Hodson tickles the funny bone while providing excellent clues to the surrounding text."

Gross-out humor is at the core of Carolyn Peck's *Richard Was a Picker,* which concerns a boy's unfortunate fascination with picking his nose. "Hodson's sticky green acrylics-and-colored-pencil illustrations hearken back to the anything-for-a-gag Garbage Pail Kids gross-outs of the 1980s," *Booklist* reviewer Daniel Kraus observed. Further praise for Hodson's work here came from Mike Crisolago, who predicted in *Quill & Quire* that "kids will love how he splashes every page . . . with enormous green boogers that actually draw readers in instead of repelling them."

Biographical and Critical Sources

PERIODICALS

Booklist, November 1, 2010, Daniel Kraus, review of *Richard Was a Picker,* p. 78.
Canadian Review of Materials, March 7, 2008, Gregory Bryan, review of *How the Moon Regained Her Shape*; February 20, 2009, Jonine Bergen, review of *Captain Jake.*
Children's Bookwatch, March, 2006, review of *How the Moon Regained Her Shape*; February, 2007, review of *In Arctic Waters.*
Kirkus Reviews, July 1, 2005, review of *Pigs Aren't Dirty, Bears Aren't Slow, and Other Truths about Misunderstood Animals,* p. 731.
Publishers Weekly, July 19, 2010, Sally Lodge, review of *Richard Was a Picker,* p. 83.
Quill & Quire, May, 2003, Bridget Donald, review of *I Love Yoga: A Guide for Kids and Teens*; April, 2007, Etta Kaner, review of *In Arctic Waters*; December, 2010, Mike Crisolago, review of *Richard Was a Picker.*
Resource Links, October, 2005, Denise Parrott, review of *Wishes and Worries: A Story to Help Children Understand a Parent Who Drinks Too Much Alcohol,* p. 2, and Evette Berry, review of *Pigs Aren't Dirty, Bears Aren't Slow, and Other Truths about Misunderstood Animals,* p. 24; February, 2007, Tanya Boudreau, review of *In Arctic Waters,* p. 2, and *How the Moon Regained Her Shape,* p. 3; April, 2007, Michelle Gowans, review of *Jeffrey and Sloth,* p. 11; February, 2010, Linda Ludke, review of *Hear My Roar: A Story of Family Violence,* p. 60.

School Library Journal, December, 2003, Diane Olivo-Posner, review of *I Love Yoga,* p. 174; April, 2007, Amanda Moss, review of *In Arctic Waters,* p. 96; January, 2008, Barbara Wysocki, review of *In Arctic Waters,* p. 55; March, 2008, Rachael Vilmar, review of *Jeffrey and Sloth,* p. 180; June, 2008, Linda Staskus, review of *'Twas the Day before Zoo Day,* p. 106; December, 2009, Sadie Mattox, review of *Hear My Roar,* p. 93.

ONLINE

Annick Press Web site, http://www.annickpress.com/ (March 22, 2012), "Ben Hodson."

Ben Hodson Home Page, http://benhodson.ca (March 22, 2012).

Ben Hodson Web log, http://www.spacejunk1971.blogspot.com (March 22, 2012).

Orca Books Web site, http://www.orcabook.com/ (March 22, 2012), "Ben Hodson."*

* * *

HOLBROOK, Sara

Personal

Children: Katie, Kelly. *Education:* Mount Union College (Alliance, OH), B.A. (English).

Addresses

Home—Mentor, OH. *E-mail*—sara@saraholbrook.com.

Career

Writer and performance poet. Formerly worked as part-time teacher and in public relations, law, public housing, and drug prevention fields. Presenter of poetry and writing workshops at schools and teacher meetings.

Writings

POETRY

The Dog Ate My Homework, privately published (Bay Village, OH), 1990, revised edition, Boyds Mills Press (Honesdale, PA), 1996.

Kid Poems for the Not-So-Bad, privately published (Bay Village, OH), 1992, published as *I Never Said I Wasn't Difficult,* Boyds Mills Press (Honesdale, PA), 1997.

Nothing's the End of the World, illustrated by J.J. Smith-Moore, Boyds Mills Press (Honesdale, PA), 1995.

Am I Naturally This Crazy?, Boyds Mills Press (Honesdale, PA), 1996.

Which Way to the Dragon? Poems for the Coming-on-Strong, Boyds Mills Press (Honesdale, PA), 1996.

Walking on the Boundaries of Change: Poems of Transition, Boyds Mills Press (Honesdale, PA), 1998.

By Definition: Poems of Feelings, illustrated by Scott Mattern, Wordsong/Boyds Mills Press (Honesdale, PA), 2003.

(With Allan Wolf) *More than Friends: Poems from Him and Her,* Wordsong (Honesdale, PA), 2008.

Weird? (Me, Too!): Let's Be Friends, illustrated by Karen Sandstrom, Wordsong (Honesdale, PA), 2010.

Zombies! Evacuate the School, illustrated by Karen Sandstrom, Wordsong (Honesdale, PA), 2010.

OTHER

Feelings Make Me Real, privately published (Bay Village, OH), 1990.

Some Families, privately published (Bay Village, OH), 1990.

What's So Big about Cleveland, Ohio? (picture book), illustrated by Ennis McNulty, Gray & Co. (Cleveland, OH), 1997.

Chicks up Front (poetry; for adults), Cleveland State University Poetry Center (Cleveland, OH), 1998.

Wham! It's a Poetry Jam: Discovering Performance Poetry (for children), foreword by Jane Yolen, Boyds Mills Press (Honesdale, PA), 2002.

Isn't She Ladylike? (for children), Collinwood Media (Mentor, OH), 2002.

Practical Poetry: A Nonstandard Approach to Meeting Content-area Standards, Heinemann (Portsmouth, NH), 2005.

(With Michael Salinger) *Outspoken!: How to Improve Writing and Speaking Skills through Poetry Performance,* Heinemann (Portsmouth, NH), 2006.

(With Michael Salinger) *High Definition: Unforgettable Vocabulary-Building Strategies across Genres and Subjects,* Heinemann (Portsmouth, NH), 2010.

Contributor to periodicals, including *Journal of Children's Literature.*

Sidelights

Poet and educator Sara Holbrook does not think poetry should be confined to the printed page. Referring to herself as a "performance poet," Holbrook dedicates much of her time to reading her works—collected in books such as *Isn't She Ladylike?, The Dog Ate My Homework, Am I Naturally This Crazy?,* and *More than Friends: Poems from Him and Her*—before young audiences as well as in writing workshops and other creative settings throughout the United States and internationally. "I write about two things, mostly," Holbrook noted on her home page: "What I know and what I wonder about. Reading and writing poetry helps me understand my life, the world, and the people I care about. Whether I am writing funny or serious poems, writing poetry helps me see what's true." Praising Holbrook's *Wham! It's a Poetry Jam: Discovering Performance Poetry,* which illustrates creative, inspiring ways in which young poets can share their verses with others, James Blasingame noted in the *Journal of Adolescent & Adult Literacy* that the book reflects "Holbrook's firm

Cover of Sara Holbrook's entertaining poetry collection* The Dog Ate My Homework, *which focuses on a perennial childhood excuse, among other issues. (Illustration copyright © 1996 by The Reuben Group. Reproduced by permission of Wordsong, an imprint of Boyds Mills Press, Inc.)

belief that poetry should be heard, not just read." "Guaranteed to get even confirmed classroom drones out of their seats . . . , this high-energy manual is a poetry slam-dunk," concluded a *Kirkus Reviews* writer in reviewing the same work.

While some of her poetry collections are intended for adults, much of Holbrook's published verse addresses topics of interest to school-aged children: neglecting to complete homework assignments; frustrations with parents and siblings; living with a bad haircut, or glasses, or braces; annoying babysitters; ups and downs with friends; and making important life choices. As the poet noted on her home page, even the simplest of her poems, such as those in *Which Way to the Dragon? Poems for the Coming-on-Strong,* are relevant to children of all ages, even older high school students. "Just remember for a moment how scary it was to get stuck in the port-a-potty at a T-ball game and it will all come back to you," she noted.

In *Am I Naturally This Crazy?* the poet takes a lighthearted approach to such topics as pets, school, divorcing parents, and school issues. According to *School Library Journal* contributor Marjorie Lewis, here Holbrook's "inventive wordplay and bouncy rhythms give some of the short pieces a surprising punch." More serious in focus, *By Definition: Poems of Feeling* delves into the world of emotions, where feelings can sometimes mutate in confusing ways. Bad moods, avoidance, a rush of excitement, sadness, and frustration: all play a part in adolescent life: the forty poems in *By Definition* crystallize "the changeable emotional skies of early adolescence" within Holbrook's "clear-eyed observations," according to a *Kirkus Reviews* writer.

Two of Holbrook's poetry collections feature illustrations by Karen Sandstrom. A collection of school-themed poems, *Zombies! Evacuate the School!,* addresses everything from worries over a surprise quiz to bullying, to getting caught daydreaming during class. Within the book's forty-one verses, the author also includes suggestions to jump-start the imagination of budding poets as well as information about traditional poetry forms. A related volume, *Weird? (Me, Too!): Let's Be Friends* homes in on friendship in its many forms, from a child's relationship with a beloved pet to a team-

***Holbrook continues her verse chronicle of the ups and downs and adventures of childhood in* I Never Said I Wasn't Difficult.** (Illustration copyright © 1996 by The Reuben Group. Reproduced by permission of Wordsong, an imprint of Boyds Mills Press, Inc.)

mate at school to a bff, subtly illustrating the difference between a true friendship and a relationship that feels out of balance. The topics Holbrook addresses in *Zombies!* "will resonate," predicted a *Kirkus Reviews* writer, "and the hints and tips will excite young writers." In her review of the same collection for *School Library Journal,* Shawn Brommer cited the poet's "breezy and comedic touch," adding that "many of the poems utilize an inner voice and encourage self-reflection." In *Weird?* the author and illustrator pair "quirky, accessible verses with lively digital cartoons," according to another *Kirkus Reviews* writer, and a *Publishers Weekly* critic wrote that Holbrook's poems "tenderly articulate the complexities of identity and social dynamics."

Holbrook's collections *Nothing's the End of the World, More than Friends,* and *Walking on the Boundaries of Change: Poems of Transition* are geared toward middle-grade readers and focus on themes of interest to budding adolescents. Calling the fifty-plus poems in *Walking on the Boundaries of Change* "energetic," *Voice of Youth Advocates* contributor Debra Lynn Adams praised in particular the poems "My Plan," "The Runaway," and "On the Verge." "Holbrook's poems have universal appeal," Adams added in her review of *Walking on the Boundaries of Change,* "and readers who discover her book will find themselves within its pages."

Described by *New York Times Book Reviews* contributor Katie Roiphe as "a lively verse novella," *More than Friends* was the result of a collaboration between Holbrook and fellow poet Allan Wolf. Using a variety of poetic forms (which are identified in descriptive notes throughout the volume), the two authors take on the role of a young girl and boy as they meet, feel the pangs of first love, defend their relationship to protective parents, attempt to balance their desire for each others' company with the demands of friendships, and ultimately fall out of love and experience heartbreak before reestablishing their relationship as fast friends. *More than Friends* was suggested by a *Kirkus Reviews* writer as a "top choice" for educators hoping to introduce older teens to "poetry and . . . its forms," and Hazel Rochman asserted in *Booklist* that the book's "simple language" distills "the edgy truth of romance in all its joy and confusion." In "deliciously readable" verse, *More than Friends* takes an "innovative approach to an ever-popular topic," according to *School Library Journal* contributor Marilyn Taniguchi.

Biographical and Critical Sources

PERIODICALS

Booklist, September 15, 2008, Hazel Rochman, review of *More than Friends: Poems from Him and Her,* p. 59.

Journal of Adolescent & Adult Literacy, December, 2002, James Blasingame, review of *Wham! It's a Poetry Jam: Discovering Performance Poetry,* p. 367, and *Isn't She Ladylike?,* p. 368.

Kirkus Reviews, March 1, 2002, review of *Wham! It's a Poetry Jam,* p. 336; April 1, 2003, review of *By Definition: Poems of Feelings,* p. 535; September 1, 2008, review of *More than Friends*; July 1, 2010, review of *Zombies! Evacuate the School!*; March 1, 2011, review of *Weird? (Me, Too!): Let's Be Friends.*

New York Times Book Review, April 12, 2009, Katie Roiphe, review of *More thatn Friends,* p. 14.

Publishers Weekly, October 12, 1998, review of *Walking on the Boundaries of Change,* p. 79; January 13, 2003, review of *By Definition,* p. 60; August 9, 2010, review of *Zombies!,* p. 50; February 14, 2011, review of *Weird?,* p. 55.

School Library Journal, February, 1995, Sally R. Dow, review of *Nothing's the End of the World,* p. 107; April, 1997, Marjorie Lewis, reviews of *Am I Naturally This Crazy?* and *Which Way to the Dragon!,* both p. 126; May, 2002, Nina Lindsay, review of *Wham! It's a Poetry Jam,* p. 138; April, 2003, Sally R. Dow, review of *By Definition,* p. 183; October, 2005, review of *Practical Poetry: A Nonstandard Approach to Meeting Content-Area Standards,* p. 84; November, 2008, review of *More than Friends,* p. 146; November, 2010, Shawn Brommer, review of *Zombies!,* p. 139; April, 2011, Lauralyn Persson, review of *Weird?,* p. 192.

Voice of Youth Advocates, February, 1999, Debra Lynn Adams, review of *Walking on the Boundaries of Change,* pp. 454-455.

ONLINE

Sara Holbrook Home Page, http://www.saraholbrook.com (May 1, 2012).

Sara Holbrook Web log, http://saraholbrook.blogspot.com (May 1, 2012).*

* * *

HUBBARD, Kirsten 1983-

Personal

Born 1983, in CA; married, 2008. *Education:* University of California, San Diego, B.A. (literature and writing), 2004.

Addresses

Home—San Diego, CA. *Agent*—Michelle Andelman, Regal Literary Inc., Capitol Building, 236 W. 26th St., No. 801, New York, NY 10001. *E-mail*—kirstenhubbard@gmail.com.

Career

Travel writer and novelist. Central America travel writer for About.com. Editor-in-chief for DiscoverSD.com; managing editor for *Pacific Beach* magazine.

Writings

NOVELS

Like Mandarin, Delacorte Press (New York, NY), 2011.

Wanderlove, Delacorte Press (New York, NY), 2012.

OTHER

Contributor to periodicals, including *Bellissima, Destination Weddings and Honeymoons, Luxury Latin America, Luxveria, Pology,* and *Southwest Airlines Spirit.* Contributor to Web sites, including *YA Highway* and *Figment;* columnist for *AOL City Guide.*

Sidelights

A travel writer best known for her articles about the wonders of Central America, Kirsten Hubbard is also the author of the young-adult novels *Like Mandarin* and *Wanderlove.* In the former, Hubbard introduces Grace Carpenter, a fourteen year old living unhappily in the tiny, rural town of Washokey, Wyoming. Sensitive and studious, Grace is an outsider both at school, where she is a year younger than her classmates, and at home, where her mother dotes on Grace's younger sister. For a school project, the teen is paired with Mandarin Ramey, a wild child whose fearless attitude has always fascinated her. While Grace begins to emulate Mandarin's reckless ways, she also learns that the older girl leads a troubled life steeped in deceit, and their friendship takes a dangerous turn.

Reviewing *Like Mandarin*, Pam Carlson noted in the *Voice of Youth Advocates* that "Hubbard's writing exposes the deep emotions and conflicts that have rippled through most of Grace and Mandarin's lives." "The portrayal of the complexities and tensions of friendships between teenaged girls is spot on," Kathleen E. Gruver commented of the same novel in *School Library Journal,* and Shelle Rosenfeld predicted in *Booklist* that Hubbard's readers "will appreciate this sensitive portrayal of the ambiguities of relationships and the challenges of growing up."

Hubbard's travels in Guatemala and Belize inform her second novel, *Wanderlove,* "a story of healing and growth," according to *Voice of Youth Advocates* critic Alissa Lauzon. The work centers on Bria Sandoval, a recent high-school graduate who embarks on a trip to Central America after her boyfriend dumps her and her dreams of attending art school fail to materialize. Abandoning her tour group, Bria joins an adventurous globetrotter, Starling, and Starling's charming but troubled brother, Rowan, a teen struggling with his own past mistakes. "Hubbard has crafted delightfully complex characters who are fresh and realistic," Lauzon stated in her review of *Wanderlove,* and a *Kirkus Reviews* writer maintained that the work will appeal to audiences "willing to take the time to get to know characters whose motives they might not always understand." The complex relationship between Bria and Rowan "and the vast emotional and physical territory Hubbard covers make for an evocative and romantic read," a contributor concluded in praising the novel for *Publishers Weekly.*

Biographical and Critical Sources

PERIODICALS

Booklist, March 1, 2011, Shelle Rosenfeld, review of *Like Mandarin,* p. 57; April 1, 2012, Melissa Moore, review of *Wanderlove,* p. 70.

Kirkus Reviews, February 1, 2011, review of *Like Mandarin;* January 15, 2012, review of *Wanderlove.*

Publishers Weekly, February 6, 2012, review of *Wanderlove,* p. 63.

School Library Journal, April, 2011, Kathleen E. Gruver, review of *Like Mandarin,* p. 175; April, 2012, Nina Sachs, review of *Wanderlove,* p. 165.

Voice of Youth Advocates, April, 2011, Pam Carlson, review of *Like Mandarin,* p. 60; February, 2012, Alissa Lauzon, review of *Wanderlove,* p. 592.

ONLINE

About.com, http://www.about.com/ (March 13, 2012), "Kirsten Hubbard, Travel Writer."

Kirsten Hubbard Home Page, http://www.kirstenhubbard.com (May 1, 2012).

Kirsten Hubbard Web log, http://kirstenhubbard.blogspot.com (May 1, 2012).*

J-K

JAMES, Kelle

Personal

Female.

Addresses

Home—Los Angeles, CA. *E-mail*—author@kellejames.com.

Career

Writer. Worked as a fashion model in New York, NY, beginning c. 1970s.

Writings

Smile for the Camera: A Memoir, Simon & Schuster Books for Young Readers (New York, NY), 2010.

Sidelights

In *Smile for the Camera: A Memoir* Kelle James chronicles her often-disturbing experiences working as a young fashion model during the 1970s. At the age of sixteen, hoping to escape her abusive father, James left her home in rural Maryland and boarded a bus bound for New York City to begin a modeling career. Convinced that she would find instant success, the teen instead found herself homeless and broke within days. She survived with the help of friends who were equally desperate, and spent her time attempting to drum up work while living in a series of squalid apartments and hotels and fending off the advances of lecherous older men. James' experiences also included a bizarre and short-lived relationship with Buddy Jacobson, a landlord and agent who was convicted of murdering his ex-girlfriend's fiancée.

"James's depiction of the underbelly and excesses of . . . New York is fascinating," Johanna Lewis commented in her *School Library Journal* review of *Smile for the Camera,* and a writer for *Kirkus Reviews* observed that the memoir "propels readers forward with a sense of suspense worthy of a thriller." A number of

Cover of Kelle James' memoir* Smile for the Camera, *which chronicles her experiences pursing a modeling career in a harsh city. (Cover photograph by Jon Pack, copyright © 2010 by Simon & Schuster, Inc. Reprinted by permission of Simon & Schuster BFYR, an imprint of Simon & Schuster Children's Publishing Division.)

critics remarked on James's perseverance, *Booklist* contributor John Peters stating that the former model "delivers healthy doses of humor and poignancy in fluent present-tense prose." *Voice of Youth Advocates* contributor Ellen Frank maintained that *Smile for the Camera* "is another stark reminder of the brutality young women face when they leave one desperate situation and find themselves trapped in another."

Biographical and Critical Sources

BOOKS

James, Kelle, *Smile for the Camera: A Memoir,* Simon & Schuster Books for Young Readers (New York, NY), 2010.

PERIODICALS

Booklist, November 1, 2010, John Peters, review of *Smile for the Camera: A Memoir,* p. 40.
Kirkus Reviews, October 1, 2010, review of *Smile for the Camera.*
Publishers Weekly, November 1, 2010, review of *Smile for the Camera,* p. 46.
School Library Journal, December, 2010, Johanna Lewis, review of *Smile for the Camera,* p. 138.
Voice of Youth Advocates, February, 2011, Ellen Frank, review of *Smile for the Camera,* p. 583.

ONLINE

Galleycat Web log, http://www.mediabistro.com/galleycat/ (November 23, 2010), Maryann Yin, interview with James.
Kelle James Home Page, http://www.kellejames.com (March 22, 2012).*

* * *

KEATON, Kelly (Kelly Gay)

Personal

Has children.

Addresses

Home—NC. *Agent*—Miriam Kriss, Irene Goodman Literary Agency, 27 W. 24 St., Ste. 700B, New York, NY 10010. *E-mail*—kelly@kellykeaton.net.

Career

Writer. Worked variously as an equine neo-natal nurse, a waitress, a theater manager, and a copy editor.

Awards, Honors

Awards from numerous screenwriting contests; North Carolina Arts Council grant in literature; Book Award finalist, Southern Independent Booksellers Alliance, and finalist for Rita awards for Best First Book and Best Novel with Strong Romantic Elements, both Romance Writers of America, all 2010, all for *The Better Part of Darkness;* Australian Romance Readers Association Award finalist, 2011, for *The Darkest Edge of Dawn;* three-time Golden Heart finalist, Romance Writers of America.

Writings

Darkness Becomes Her, Simon Pulse (New York, NY), 2011.
A Beautiful Evil (sequel to *Darkness Becomes Her*), Simon Pulse (New York, NY), 2012.

"CHARLIE MADIGAN" SERIES; AS KELLY GAY

The Better Part of Darkness, Pocket Books (New York, NY), 2009.
The Darkest Edge of Dawn, Pocket Books (New York, NY), 2010.
The Hour of Dust and Ashes, Pocket Books (New York, NY), 2011.
Shadows before the Sun, Pocket Books (New York, NY), 2012.

Sidelights

Kelly Keaton blends elements of horror and Greek mythology in her young-adult novel *Darkness Becomes Her* and its sequel, *A Beautiful Evil.* In the former title, Keaton, who also writes adult fiction under the name Kelly Gay, introduces Ari Selkirk, a seventeen year old searching for answers to her clouded past. Raised by foster parents who work as bail bondsmen, Ari has cultivated a tough demeanor that is reflected in her teal-green eyes and silvery hair that resists cutting. After Ari discovers a note from her birth mother urging the teen to flee for safety, she journeys to her birthplace, the city of New 2. Built over the hurricane-ravaged ruins of New Orleans, New 2 is now run by the Novem, a cadre of witches, vampires, shapeshifters, and other supernatural creatures. Once there, Ari learns about the centuries-old curse plaguing her family and faces a threat from the goddess Athena.

In *Darkness Becomes Her* "Keaton paints richly detailed scenes of the New Orleans landscape," observed *School Library Journal* critic Jill Heritage Maza, the critic adding that the fiction debut is peopled with "fully realized, sympathetic characters." Writing in *Booklist,* Francisca Goldsmith stated that Keaton "allows Ari to discover, articulate, and explore a range of political and ethical questions without ever striking a didactic note."

Cover of Kelly Keaton's* Darkness Becomes Her, *a horror novel that incorporates elements of Greek mythology. (Jacket photograph of gate © Eudora Welty/Corbis, tree © iStockphoto.com/Fenykepez.)

Ari's adventures continue in *A Beautiful Evil.* After learning that she has inherited the Medusa curse, which will change her into a monstrous gorgon when she turns twenty-one, the young woman hopes to learn how to harness her powers. Meanwhile, she seeks help from her boyfriend, aristocratic vampire Sebastian, to rescue friend Violet from Athena's realm. "Ari's gruff but introspective narration serves to nicely flesh out her character, allowing her to be both brave and vulnerable," remarked a writer in *Kirkus Reviews.* Adrienne Amborski, reviewing *A Beautiful Evil* for *Voice of Youth Advocates,* remarked that "elements of Greek mythology are woven into this story, which is filled with action and suspense."

Biographical and Critical Sources

PERIODICALS

Booklist, April 15, 2011, Francisca Goldsmith, review of *Darkness Becomes Her,* p. 52; March 1, 2012, Francisca Goldsmith, review of *A Beautiful Evil,* p. 83.

Kirkus Reviews, January 1, 2012, review of *A Beautiful Evil.*

School Library Journal, February, 2011, Jill Heritage Maza, review of *Darkness Becomes Her,* p. 110.

Voice of Youth Advocates, February, 2011, Beth Karpas, review of *Darkness Becomes Her,* p. 571; December, 2011, Adrienne Amborski, review of *A Beautiful Evil,* p. 513.

ONLINE

Kelly Gay Home Page, http://www.kellygay.com (May 1, 2012).

Kelly Keaton Home Page, http://kellykeaton.net (May 1, 2012).

Simon & Schuster Web site, http://www.simonandschuster.com/ (March 22, 2012), "Kelly Keaton."

* * *

KENNEDY, Kim

Personal

Born in LA; daughter of I.G. (a physician) and Carole (an artist) Kennedy. *Religion:* Methodist.

Addresses

Home—Monroe, LA.

Career

Children's book author.

Writings

PICTURE BOOKS

Napoleon, illustrated by brother, Doug Kennedy, Viking (New York, NY), 1995.

Mr. Bumble, illustrated by Doug Kennedy, Hyperion (New York, NY), 1997.

Mr. Bumble Buzzes through the Year, illustrated by Doug Kennedy, Hyperion (New York, NY), 1998.

Frankenfrog, illustrated by Doug Kennedy, Hyperion (New York, NY), 1999.

Pirate Pete, illustrated by Doug Kennedy, Harry Abrams (New York, NY), 2002.

Pirate Pete's Giant Adventure, illustrated by Doug Kennedy, Harry Abrams (New York, NY), 2006.

Pirate Pete's Talk like a Pirate, illustrated by Doug Kennedy, Harry Abrams (New York, NY), 2007.

Hee-Haw-Dini and the Great Zambini, illustrated by Doug Kennedy, Abrams Books for Young Readers (New York, NY), 2009.

Misty Gordon and the Mystery of the Ghost Pirates, illustrated by Greg Call, Amulet Books (New York, NY), 2010.

Sidelights

Along with illustrator Doug Kennedy, Kim Kennedy is one half of the creative brother-and-sister partnership that has produced a number of entertaining picture

Kim and Doug Kennedy's picture-book collaborations include* Talk like a Pirate, *part of a series that takes readers on amusing high-seas adventures. (Illustration copyright © 2007 by Doug Kennedy. Reproduced by permission of Abrams Books for Young Readers, an imprint of ABRAMS.)

books. Louisiana natives, the Kennedys began their career in children's books with *Napoleon,* in which a small white dog is faced with the dilemma of how to occupy himself on a rainy day. Going to the attic, the pudgy pup finds collected treasures to explore, old clothes to try on, and bubbles to blow. Eventually, Napoleon settles down for a nap, allowing the rhythm of the rain to lull him to sleep. A *Publishers Weekly* contributor wrote that Kim Kennedy's technique of stretching single sentences over several pages enhances the story's suspense and hailed *Napoleon* as "an unusual and arresting debut." Similarly, *Booklist* critic Michael Cart praised the tale's "minimalist pictures" and deemed the picture book "cutting-edge" withing its genre and age group.

Both *Mr. Bumble* and *Mr. Bumble Buzzes through the Year* feature a bumble bee who is the clumsiest and most fearful in his hive. In the first story readers learn that the bucket with which he attempts to collect honey for his queen has never been filled. Even worse, it is scarred by dents incurred in the clumsy bee's various misadventures. When the queen bee announces the discovery of an especially bountiful clover field, Mr. Bumble goes forth despite his fears and feelings of inadequacy. In the midst of a spectacular display of clumsiness, he is rescued by a group of friendly fairies who give him a crash course in flying skills and help him return triumphantly to his queen with his bucket overflowing. Although Dawn Amsberry, writing in *School Library Journal,* cautioned that the bee's speedy "transformation from clumsy to graceful" in *Mr. Bumble* "may leave young readers wondering why they can't overcome their own problems" with the same ease, a *Kirkus Reviews* writer applauded Mr. Bumble as "a winning dweeb with pluck and heart enough to inspire readers." A *Horn Book* reviewer commented on Doug Kennedy's "droll figures of bees and fairies," and a critic for the *New York Times Book Review* cited *Mr. Bumble* for its "very pretty illustrations."

In *Frankenfrog* a mad scientist named Dr. Franken concocts a potion designed to "hyper-size" lollipops. Unfortunately, the tonic also spawns a multitude of oversized flies, which the doctor zaps with Frankenfrog, his gigantic amphibious creation. A critic for the *Children's Book Review Service* praised *Frankenfrog* for its "lively text and humorous illustrations," and a *Horn Book* reviewer noted that while some of Kim Kennedy's "puns feel forced," the book's "illustrations add amusing details."

A donkey and a mouse take on starring roles in the Kennedys' *Hee-Haw-Dini and the Great Zambini,* which is set in an unusual farmyard. Hee-Haw the donkey and tiny rodent friend Chester have dreams of making a name as magicians, and they suffer the ridicule of their barn-mates while practicing their act. When a leather-bound trunk belonging to The Great Zambini falls off a passing circus train and lands in their farmyard, Hee-Haw and Chester have a chance to polish and practice their act before real-life magic helps them realize their dream. *Hee-Haw Dini and the Great Zambini* pairs a story about "the power of advertising and the gulibility of the public" with "cheerful" cartoon art, according to *Booklist* critic Patricia Austin.

In the Kennedys' "Pirate Pete" series the brother-and-sister team introduce a roly poly, peg-legged, red-bearded pirate who behaves in typical pirate fashion. *Pirate Pete* finds the old salt and his trusty parrot sailing the seas in search of gold and booty after pilfering a treasure map from the queen. On course for Mermaid Island and the spot marked with a large "X," the pirate stops to scout for gold on other islands along the way, ultimately bringing aboard trouble in the form of a small

***The Kennedy siblings continue Pirate Pete's story in the picture book* Pirate Pete's Giant Adventure.** (Illustration copyright © 2006 by Doug Kennedy. Reproduced by permission of Abrams Books for Young Readers, an imprint of Harry N. Abrams, Inc.)

but testy fire-breathing dragon. Describing *Pirate Pete* as "inventive," *Booklist* contributor Julie Cummins had special praise for Doug Kennedy's "appealing, richly colored, cartoonlike paintings," which were based on clay models created especially for the purpose.

Readers meet up with Pete again in *Pirate Pete's Giant Adventure* as the portly swashbuckler sits, stranded, in a rowboat off the coast of Mermaid Island. His wish for a ship is answered in a roundabout way when a genie agrees to provide a pirate ship if Pete is able to locate a magic sapphire that has been lost by the sea fairies. This seemingly simple task holds significant challenges, however, when Pirate Pete learns that the jewel is in the possession of a very large and very angry giant. According to *Booklist* contributor Gillian Engberg, "the silly adventure" combines with "rhymes, . . . repetitive songs, and Pete's salty-dog dialogue" to make *Pirate Pete's Giant Adventure* "a natural for reading aloud." Praising the "cartoon pictures," a *Kirkus Reviews* writer concluded of the same book that the Kennedys' "follow-up to *Pirate Pete* . . . should keep young mateys anchored to their seats."

Pete has earned his ship in *Pirate Pete: Talk like a Pirate!,* but now the task is to sail to Rascal Island and locate shipmates able to walk the pirate walk and talk the pirate talk, such as a hearty "aaaargh!" or "shiver me timbers." Noting that *Pirate Pete: Talk like a Pirate* is characteristic of the series, Randal Enos concluded in *Booklist* that the "varied cast of cartoonlike characters" combines with Kim Kennedy's story "to make this a natural for readalouds." "Chock-full of fun rhymes and expressive illustrations, this book is sure to please," predicted *School Library Journal* critic Catherine Callegari.

Pirates are also a main feature of Kennedy's first middle-grade novel, *Misty Gordon and the Mystery of the Ghost Pirates,* which features artwork by Greg Call. Eleven-year-old Misty lives in Ashcrumb, a coastal town with a long and mysterious past. Her parents are in the antique business and Misty has been surrounded by very old things as long as she can remember. When her father is hired to dispose of the estate of Miss Zaster, a wealthy clairvoyant who is now communing with her spiritual associates, Misty finds a diary dating back to the town's founding as well as a pair of eyeglasses that allow the wearer to see into the spiritual dimension. Sharing her secret with best friend Yoshi, Misty realizes that the pirate ghosts who seem to be converging on Ashcrumb are actually those of the town's founders, come to claim a powerful buried treasure. But is it in the town's best interest that they find it?

Deeming Kennedy's fiction debut "a delightful read," Melissa Moore added in *Booklist* that *Misty Gordon and the Mystery of the Ghost Pirates* pairs "engaging and fun" characters with a story that is "equal parts craziness and humor." In *School Library Journal* Caitlin Augusta had particular praise for the story's setting, writing that the "quirky" town of Ashcrumb "reeks with ghostly surprises and odd souls." Shrouded with several different plot threads, *Misty Gordon and the Mystery of the Ghost Pirates* serves as "an appealing adventure" for fans of the genre, Augusta added.

Biographical and Critical Sources

PERIODICALS

Booklist, June 1, 2002, Julie Cummins, review of *Pirate Pete,* p. 1740; June 1, 2006, Gillian Engberg, review of *Pirate Pete's Giant Adventure,* p. 84; December 1, 2007, Randall Enos, review of *Pirate Pete's Talk like a Pirate,* p. 49; April 1, 2009, Patricia Austin, review of *Hee-Haw-Dini and the Great Zambini,* p. 43; September 1, 2010, Melissa Moore, review of *Misty Gordon and the Mystery of the Ghost Pirates,* p. 106.

Bulletin of the Center for Children's Books, October, 1999, Janice M. Del Negro, review of *Frankenfrog,* p. 57.

Children's Book Review Service, August, 1999, review of *Frankenfrog,* p. 160.

Kirkus Reviews, July 1, 2006, review of *Pirate Pete's Giant Adventure,* p. 678; March 1, 2009, review of *Hee-Haw-Dini and the Great Zambini;* July 1, 2010, review of *Misty Gordon and the Mystery of the Ghost Pirates.*

Publishers Weekly, October 2, 1995, review of *Napoleon,* p. 73; August 11, 1997, review of *Mr. Bumble,* p. 401; August 2, 1999, review of *Frankenfrog,* p. 83.

School Library Journal, February, 1996, Virginia Opocensky, review of *Napoleon,* p. 86; September, 1997, Dawn Amsberry, review of *Mr. Bumble,* p. 184; August, 1999, Christine A. Moesch, review of *Frankenfrog,* p. 138; April, 2008, Catherine Callegari, review of *Pirate Pete's Talk like a Pirate,* p. 114; April, 2009, Mary Elam, review of *Hee-Haw-Dini and the Great Zambini,* p. 108; October, 2010, Caitlin Augusta, review of *Misty Gordon and the Mystery of the Ghost Pirates,* p. 120.

ONLINE

Doug and Kim Kennedy Home Page, http://petesadventures.com (May 1, 2012).*

* * *

KIRBY, Matthew J. 1976-

Personal

Born 1976, in UT; father in the military; married Azure Midzinski. *Education:* Utah State University, B.S. (history), M.S., Ed.S. (school psychology).

Addresses

Home—Layton, UT. *Agent*—Stephen Fraser, Jennifer De Chiara Literary Agency, 31 E. 32nd St., Ste. 300, New York, NY 10015. *E-mail*—matthew.kirby@hotmail.com.

Career

School psychologist and author. Workshop leader.

Member

Society of Children's Book Writers and Illustrators.

Awards, Honors

Parents' Choice Gold Award in Fiction Category, 100 Titles for Reading and Sharing selection, New York Public Library, CYBILS Award finalist in Middle-Grade Science Fiction and Fantasy category, and Edgar Allan Poe Award for Best Juvenile Fiction nomination, all 2011, all for *Icefall.*

Writings

The Clockwork Three, Scholastic Press (New York, NY), 2010.

Icefall, Scholastic Press (New York, NY), 2011.

Author's work has been translated into several languages, including Italian.

Adaptations

The Clockwork Three was adapted for audiobook, read by Mark Thompson, Scholastic Audio, 2010. *Icefall* was adapted for audiobook, ready by Jenna Lamia, Scholastic Audio, 2011.

Sidelights

In addition to his work as a school psychologist, Matthew J. Kirby writes for middle graders and is best known for his novels *The Clockwork Three* and *Icefall.* Mixing fantasy, history, and steampunk elements, *The Clockwork Three* attracted comparisons to Brian Selznick's *The Invention of Hugo Cabret,* while the award-winning *Icefall* draws readers into a frozen northern world wherein three siblings must survive the treachery of their kingly father's hidden enemies.

Born in Utah, Kirby moved several times while growing up due to his father's career in the U.S. Navy. He returned to his home state to attend college, earning a bachelor's degree in history before embarking on the graduate programs that would qualify him for his intended career as a school psychologist. As a child, he discovered *The Hobbit* and other novels by J.R.R. Tolkien, and also reading enjoyed fantasy and science-fiction stories by Natalie Babbit, Elizabeth George Speare, and Ursula K. Le Guin. An interest in comic books inspired him to write one of his own during high school, but it was the more-recent encouragement of his wife, Azure Midzinski, that inspired Kirby to use weekends and school vacations to complete the manuscript of his first middle-grade novel.

That novel, *The Clockwork Three*, is set in a mythical industrial-age city and focuses on three children who have been forced into work due to adverse circumstances. Orphaned Giuseppe is a street musician whose protector pockets all the money he earns performing for passersby. Frederick is an apprentice clockmaker whose free time is spent creating a mechanical man, an automaton, and Hannah works as a hotel chambermaid to help support her destitute family. When each child encounters something magical, it sparks their curiosity and their puzzlement and their paths intersect. As problems—and even threats—cause each child distress, their growing connection helps them realize that they are not alone, especially as they face the greatest challenge of all. "A compelling read," according to *Voice of Youth Advocates* contributor Karen Jensen, *The Clockwork Three* features young characters who "are rich and rewarding" and discover "that each of them has the key to helping the other."

In writing *Icefall,* Kirby took his inspiration from Norse mythology, telling the story of the three children of a powerful king. With war threatening, crown prince Harald and his older sisters Asa and Solveig are sent up into the mountains, where they are guarded by trusted

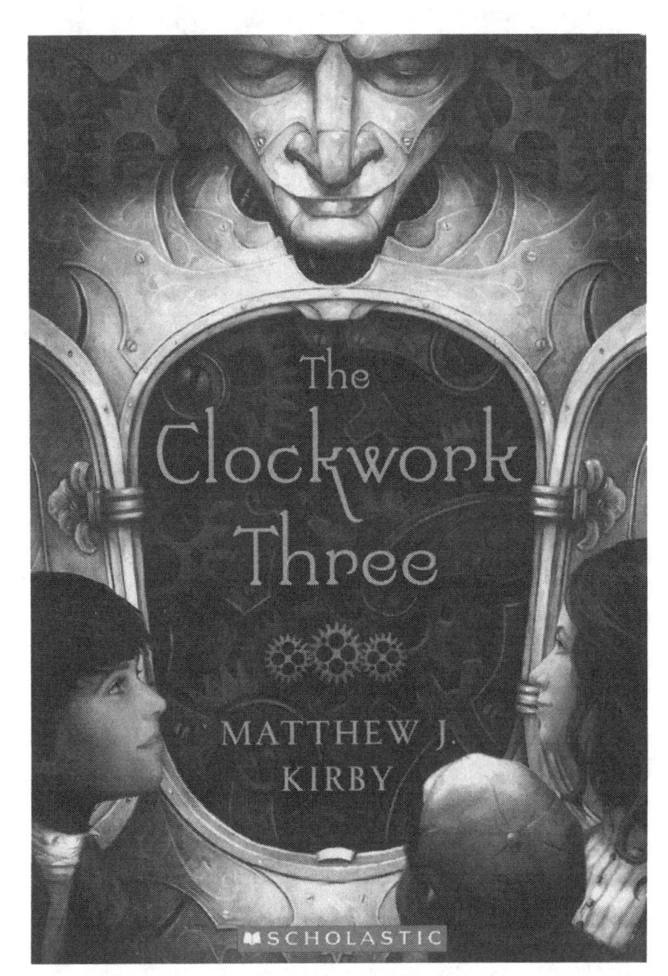

Cover of Matthew J. Kirby's middle-grade adventure* The Clockwork Three, *featuring cover art by Brian Despain. (Cover art © 2010 by Brian Despain. Reproduced by permission of Scholastic, Inc.)

warriors. The only way to reach them is across a fjord, but as their store of supplies dwindles and the waters turn to ice, their refuge becomes a prison. When a group of rowdy soldiers arrive, Solveig finds a use for her talent as an apprentice storyteller, and her tales of the gods keep the men from becoming restless. Her quick intelligence also proves useful when the prince's life is threatened and the members of the encampment must battle an epic foe. "Battle and survival scenes are vividly portrayed," noted Vicki Reutter in her *School Library Journal* review of *Icefall,* and a *Publishers Weekly* critic praised Kirby's novel as "a tense mystery that blends history and Norse myth" while also illuminating Solveig's growing sense of her own talents and abilities. In *Voice of Youth Advocates* Jennifer Miskec recommended *Icefall* to fans of steampunk fiction, adding that "the pace and tone is even; the characters and their reactions lovingly drawn."

Biographical and Critical Sources

PERIODICALS

Bulletin of the Center for Children's Books, December, 2010, Elizabeth Bush, review of *The Clockwork Three,* p. 192.

Publishers Weekly, December 20, 2010, "Flying Starts," p. 18; September 26, 2011, review of *Icefall,* p. 73.

School Library Journal, November, 2011, Vicki Reutter, review of *Icefall,* p. 128.

Voice of Youth Advocates, February, 2011, Karen Jensen, review of *The Clockwork Three,* p. 571; October, 2011, Jennifer Miskec, review of *Icefall,* p. 405.

ONLINE

Matthew J. Kirby Web log, http://www.matthewjkirby.com (May 15, 2012).*

* * *

KURISU, Jane 1952-

Personal

Born 1952, in Canada.

Addresses

Home—Toronto, Ontario, Canada. *E-mail*—kurisu@rogers.com.

Career

Illustrator.

Awards, Honors

Silver Birch Book Award nomination, Ontario Libraries Association, 2011, for *Mathemagic!* by Lynda Colgan.

Illustrator

Frank Etherington, *The General,* Annick Press (Toronto, Ontario, Canada), 1983.

Debora Pearson, *Cookie Count and Bake: A Cookbook and Cutter Set,* Dutton Children's Books (New York, NY), 1996.

Harold Myra, *Halloween, Is It for Real?,* Tommy Nelson (Nashville, TN), 1997.

Harold Myra, *Santa, Are You for Real?,* Tommy Nelson (Nashville, TN), 1997.

Harold Myra, *Easter Bunny, Are You for Real?,* Tommy Nelson (Nashville, TN), 1998.

Joan Holub, *Backwards Day,* Scholastic (New York, NY), 2000.

Margot Griffin, *The Sleepover Book,* Scholastic (New York, NY), 2001.

Lynn Thomas, *My Pet Hamster,* Kids Can Press (Toronto, Ontario, Canada), 2002.

Harold Myra, *Thanksgiving: What Makes It Special?,* Tommy Nelson (Nashville, TN), 2002.

Fantastic Feats and Failures, Kids Can Press (Toronto, Ontario, Canada), 2004.

Marilyn Helmer, *Funtime Riddles,* Kids Can Press (Toronto, Ontario, Canada), 2004.

Marilyn Helmer, *Recess Riddles,* Kids Can Press (Toronto, Ontario, Canada), 2004.

Marilyn Baillie, *My Pet Kitten,* Kids Can Press (Toronto, Ontario, Canada), 2005.

Marilyn Baillie, *My Pet Puppy,* Kids Can Press (Toronto, Ontario, Canada), 2005.

Marsha Heckman, Cathy Obiedo, and Claudia Allin, *How to Cut Your Own Hair (or Anyone Else's!),* Workman Pub. Co. (New York, NY), 2008.

Lynda Colgan, *Mathemagic! Number Tricks,* Kids Can Press (Toronto, Ontario, Canada), 2011.

"KIDS CAN DO IT" SERIES

Karyn Morris, *The Kids Can Press Jumbo Book of Gardening,* Kids Can Press (Toronto, Ontario, Canada), 2000.

Amanda Lewis, *The Jumbo Book of Paper Crafts,* Kids Can Press (Toronto, Ontario, Canada), 2002.

Deborah Dunleavy, *The Jumbo Book of Drama,* Kids Can Press (Toronto, Ontario, Canada), 2004.

Judith Ann Sadler, *Simply Sewing,* Kids Can Press (Toronto, Ontario, Canada), 2004.

Rachel Di Salle and Ellen Warwick, *Junk Drawer Jewelry,* photographs by Ray Boudreau, Kids Can Press (Toronto, Ontario, Canada), 2006.

Biographical and Critical Sources

PERIODICALS

Booklist, July, 2000, Catherine Andronik, review of *The Kids Can Press Jumbo Book of Gardening,* p. 2022; December 15, 2002, Carolyn Phelan, review of *The Jumbo Book of Paper Crafts,* p. 762; May 1, 2004,

Chris Sherman, review of *The Jumbo Book of Drama,* p. 1556; June 1, 2004, Hazel Rochman, reviews of *Funtime Riddles* and *Recess Riddles,* both p. 1735; December 15, 2004, Carolyn Phelan, review of *Simply Sewing,* p. 748; May 1, 2011, Carolyn Phelan, review of *Mathemagic! Number Tricks,* p. 75.

Kirkus Reviews, September 1, 2004, review of *Fantastic Feats and Failures,* p. 863; February 15, 2011, review of *Mathemagic!*

Publishers Weekly, April 16, 2001, review of *The Sleepover Book,* p. 67.

Resource Links, June, 2001, Linda Irvine, review of *The Sleepover Book,* p. 18; October, 2002, Karen MacKinnon, review of *The Jumbo Book of Paper Crafts,* p. 20, and *My Pet Hamster,* p. 23; April, 2004, Antonia Gisler, review of *The Jumbo Book of Drama,* p. 26; December, 2004, Gail Lennon, review of *Simply Sewing,* p. 29.

School Library Journal, June, 2001, Jane Halsall, review of *The Sleepover Book,* p. 174; December, 2002, Susannah Price, review of *The Jumbo Book of Paper Crafts,* p. 164; May, 2004, Cynde Suite, reviews of *Funtime Riddles* and *Recess Riddles,* both p. 132; June, 2004, Nancy Menaldi-Scanlan, review of *The Jumbo Book of Drama,* p. 126; November, 2006, Augusta R. Malvagno, review of *Junk Drawer Jewelry,* p. 158; May, 2011, Grace Oliff, review of *Mathemagic!,* p. 95.*

L

LAMUT, Sonja

Personal

Born in Yugoslavia; immigrated to United States; married; children: one daughter. *Education:* University of Arts (Belgrade, Yugoslavia), B.F.A.; Hunter College, M.A.

Addresses

Home—New York, NY. *E-mail*—Sonja@sonjalamut.com.

Career

Painter, printmaker, illustrator, and educator. Fashion Institute of Technology, State University of New York, professor of illustration beginning 1988. *Exhibitions:* Works have been exhibited at Norwegian International Print Biennale, Finnish International Print Biennale, and Lujubljana International Print Biennale; Alternative Museum, New York, NY, and at galleries in New York, NY, Boston, MA, Miami, FL, Greenwich, CT, and cities including Stockholm, Sweden, Geneva, Switzerland, and Ljubljana, Slovenia. Work included in permanent collections at Brooklyn Museum, Brooklyn, NY; Grafiska Sallskapet, Stockholm; museums of modern art in Fredrikstad, Norway, Belgrade, Serbia, and Ljubljana; Utubo Gallery, Kyoto, Japan; and the National Museum, Krakow, Poland.

Awards, Honors

Grand Prix, Mediterranean Art Biennale; American Bookseller Pick-of-the-List selection; Best Children's Book selection, Bank Street College of Education, 1998, 2000; Parent's Choice Recommended selection, 2000; Sydney Taylor Award Notable Book for Younger Readers selection, Association of Jewish Libraries, 2001, for *Lemuel, the Fool* by Myron Uhlberg.

Writings

SELF-ILLUSTRATED

Too Noisy!, Grosset & Dunlap (New York, NY), 1996.

1, 2, Peek-a-boo!, Grosset & Dunlap (New York, NY), 1997.

Turn and Learn Colors, Grosset & Dunlap (New York, NY), 1997.

Turn and Learn Numbers, Grosset & Dunlap (New York, NY), 1997.

Turn and Learn Shapes, Grosset & Dunlap (New York, NY), 1997.

Turn and Learn Christmas Numbers, Grosset & Dunlap (New York, NY), 2000.

Turn and Learn Christmas Rhyme Time, Grosset & Dunlap (New York, NY), 2000.

ILLUSTRATOR

Amy Hest, *The Private Notebook of Katie Roberts, Age 11,*Candlewick Press (Cambridge, MA), 1995.

Jennifer Dussling, *A Very Strange Dollhouse,* Grosset & Dunlap (New York, NY), 1996.

Portia Aborio, *King Big Wig,* Grosset & Dunlap (New York, NY), 1996.

Helen V. Griffith, *Alex and the Cat,* Greenwillow Books (New York, NY), 1997.

Nicholas Heller, *This Little Piggy,* Greenwillow Books (New York, NY), 1997.

Helen V. Griffith, *Dinosaur Habitat,* Greenwillow Books (New York, NY), 1998.

Amy Hest, *The Great Green Notebook of Katie Roberts: Who Just Turned 12 on Monday,* Candlewick Press (Cambridge, MA), 1998.

Hugh Lofting, *The Voyages of Doctor Dolittle,* new edition, Grosset & Dunlap (New York, NY), 1998.

Helen V. Griffith, *How Many Candles?,* Greenwillow Books (New York, NY), 1999.

Mildred Phillips, *And the Cow Said Moo!,* Greenwillow (New York, NY), 2000.

Amy Hest, *Love You, Soldier,* Candlewick Press (Cambridge, MA), 2000.

Margaret Sutherland, *Thanksgiving Is for Giving Thanks,* Grosset & Dunlap (New York, NY), 2000.

Myron Uhlberg, *Lemuel, the Fool,* Peachtree Pub. (Atlanta, GA), 2001.

Berlie Doherty, *The Famous Adventures of Jack,* Greenwillow Books (New York, NY), 2001.

Melissa Tyrrell, *Aladdin: A Fairytale Foil Book,* Price Stern Sloan (New York, NY), 2002.

Melissa Tyrrell, reteller, *Cinderella,* Price Stern Sloan (New York, NY), 2002.

Melissa Tyrrell, reteller, *Snow White and the Seven Dwarfs,* Price Stern Sloan (New York, NY), 2002.

Melissa Tyrrell, reteller, *The Little Mermaid,* Price Stern Sloan (New York, NY), 2002.

Charles Toscano, *Papa's Pastries,* Zonderkidz (Grand Rapids, MI), 2010.

Sidelights

Trained in both her native Yugoslavia and the United States, Sonja Lamut is an award-winning illustrator and artist whose work has appeared in picture books by writers such as Berlie Doherty, Myron Uhlberg, Hugh Lofting, Helen V. Griffiths, Amy Hest, and Melissa Tyrrell. One of her illustration projects, Margaret Sutherland's *Thanksgiving Is for Giving Thanks,* was included on the *New York Times* best-seller lists seasonally for eight years in a row. Lamut shares her knowledge and experience with new generations of illustrators as well by teaching at New York's prestigious Fashion Institute of Technology.

With a text by Uhlberg, *Lemuel, the Fool* is based on a Yiddish folktale about a man who longs to experience life far away from his small village. In a review for *Booklist,* Hazel Rochman praised the "lively pictures" Lamut contributes to the book, and a *Publishers Weekly* critic wrote that her "graceful" and textured images "are jazzed up by the variety in presentation" and help make *Lemuel, the Fool* "fresh and diverting." The "albumlike quality" the artist evokes through her intricately framed, tempera-and-oil paintings "heightens the sense of old-world fantasy" in Uhlberg's story, according to *School Library Journal* critic Martha Link.

This Little Piggy, a story by Nicholas Heller, "gets its life from Lamut's fresh, bright artwork," according to *Booklist* critic Ilene Cooper, while a *Publishers Weekly* critic maintained that the artist "adds . . . energy through skillful visual pacing, alternating full-page illustrations with insets, panel art," and several double-page spreads. Energy also emanates from her paintings for *Papa's Pastries,* a story by Charles Toscano. Here the family-centered tale comes to life in "idealized" images featuring "warm characters in traditional costumes, dancing, singing, and marketing," according to *Booklist* critic Karen Cruze, and in *Publishers Weekly* a critic wrote that Lamut's use of "earth-toned hues" evokes Toscano's themes of "communal warmth and industry against a backdrop of poverty and looming fear." These same "soft colors suit the quiet message" in *Papa's Pastries,* noted a *Kirkus Reviews* writer, and in *School Library Journal* Mary N. Oluonye praised the "soft, sweet illustrations [that] accompany this gentle story."

***Sonja Lamut's illustration projects include creating the artwork for Charles Toscano's picture book* Papa's Pastries.** (Illustration copyright © 2010 by Sonja Lamut. Reproduced by permission of Zondervan.)

Biographical and Critical Sources

PERIODICALS

Booklist, February 15, 1997, Ilene Cooper, review of *This Little Piggy,* p. 1026; October 15, 1997, Lauren Peterson, review of *Alex and the Cat,* p. 406; October 15, 1999, GraceAnn A. DeCandido, review of *How Many Candles?,* p. 452; April 15, 2001, Hazel Rochman, review of *Lemuel, the Fool,* p. 1567; October 1, 2001, GraceAnne A. DeCandido, review of *The Famous Adventures of Jack,* p. 318; November 1, 2010, Karen Cruze, review of *Papa's Pastries,* p. 78.

Horn Book, November-December, 2001, Jennifer M. Brabander, review of *The Famous Adventures of Jack,* p. 760.

Kirkus Reviews, August 1, 2010, review of *Papa's Pastries.*

Publishers Weekly, April 7, 1997, review of *This Little Piggy,* p. 91; March 9, 1998, review of *Dinosaur Habitat,* p. 68; August 2, 1999, review of *How Many Candles?,* p. 84; February 5, 2001, review of *Lemuel, the Fool,* p. 88; August 23, 2010, review of *Papa's Pastries,* p. 46.

School Library Journal, July, 2000, Sally R. Dow, review of *And the Cow Said Moo!,* p. 86; August, 2001, Martha Link, review of *Lemuel, the Fool,* p. 164; January, 2002, Susan M. Moore, review of *The Famous Adventures of Jack,* p. 117; November, 2010, Mary N. Oluonye, review of *Papa's Pastries,* p. 86.

ONLINE

Fashion Institute of Technology Web log, http://blog.fitnyc.edu/ (December 7, 2011), "Sonja Lamut."

Sonja Lamut Home Page, http://www.sonjalamut.com (May 15, 2012).

* * *

LAUGHEAD, Mike 1978-

Personal

Born 1978; married; children: two daughters. *Education:* Brigham Young University, B.F.A. (art), 2005; Columbus College of Art and Design, M.F.A. (visual art), 2013. *Religion:* Jesus Christ of Latter-Day Saints (Mormon).

Addresses

Home—Columbus, OH. *Agent*—Justin Ricker, Shannon Associates, 333. W. 57th St., Ste. 809, New York, NY 10019; justin@shannonassociates.com. *E-mail*—mike@mikelaughead.com.

Career

Illustrator and sequential artist. Mike Tyson Design, partner, 2004-09; Kalamazoo Valley Community College, Kalamazoo, MI, instructor in art, 2008-11.

Illustrator

Sue Fliess, *Shoes for Me!,* Marshall Cavendish (New York, NY), 2011.

Sue Fliess, *A Dress for Me!,* Marshall Cavendish Children (New York, NY), 2012.

Anara Guard, *What If You Need to Call 911?,* Picture Window Books (Mankato, MN), 2012.

"ROBOT AND RICO" READER SERIES BY ANASTASIA SUEN

A Prize Inside, Stone Arch Books (Minneapolis, MN), 2010.

Dino Hunt, Stone Arch Books (Mankato, MN), 2010.

Skate Trick, Stone Arch Books (Minneapolis, MN), 2010.

Snow Games, Stone Arch Books (Mankato, MN), 2010.

Test Drive, Stone Arch Books (Mankato, MN), 2010.

The Big Catch, Stone Arch Books (Minneapolis, MN), 2010.

The Pirate Map, Stone Arch Books (Mankato, MN), 2010.

The Scary Night, Stone Arch Books (Minneapolis, MN), 2010.

Biographical and Critical Sources

PERIODICALS

Booklist, April 1, 2010, Hazel Rochman, review of *Snow Games,* p. 48.

Kirkus Reviews, February 15, 2011, review of *Shoes for Me!*

School Library Journal, June, 2010, Lora Van Marel, review of *Snow Games,* p. 66; April, 2011, Blair Christolon, review of *Shoes for Me!,* p. 142.

ONLINE

Mike Laughead Home Page, http://www.mikelaughead.com (May 15, 2012).

Mike Laughead Web log, http://mikelaughead.blogspot.com (May 15, 2012).

Shannon Assoociates Web site, http://www.shannonassociates.com/ (May 15, 2012), "Mike Laughead."*

* * *

LOBEL, Anita 1934-

Personal

Surname pronounced "*Lo*-bel"; born June 3, 1934, in Cracow, Poland; immigrated to United States, 1952; naturalized citizen, 1956; daughter of Leon and Sofia Kempler; married Arnold Stark Lobel (an author and illustrator) April, 1955 (died December 4, 1987); children: Adrianne, Adam. *Education:* Pratt Institute, B.F.A., 1955; attended Brooklyn Museum Art School, 1975-76.

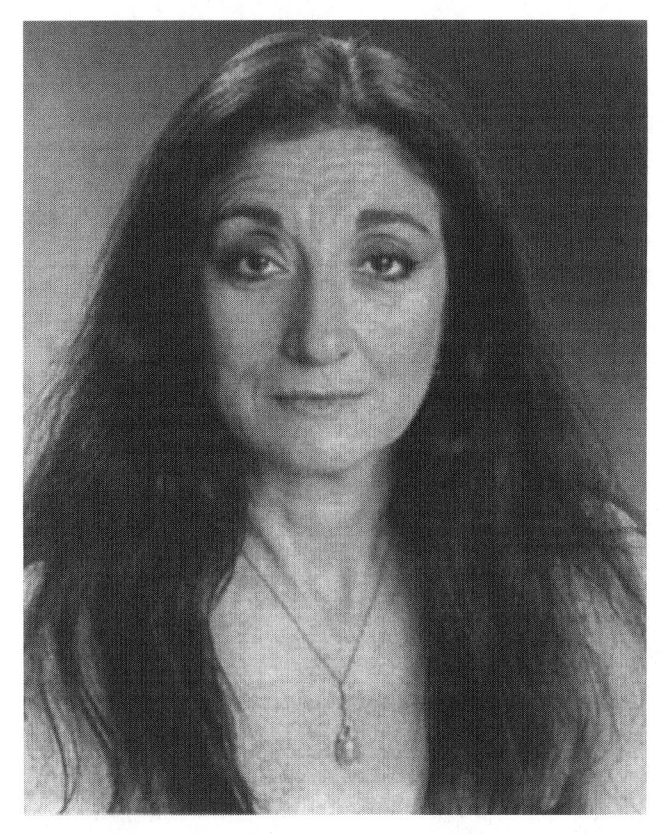

Anita Lobel (Reproduced by permission.)

Addresses

Home—New York, NY. *E-mail*—anitalobel@verizon.net.

Career

Author and illustrator. Freelance textile designer, 1957-64; writer and illustrator of children's books, beginning 1964. *Exhibitions:* Work exhibited at National Center for Children's Literature, Abilene, TX, 2011, and Chrysler Museum of Art, Norfolk, VA. Works included in private collections in the United States and Japan.

Awards, Honors

Best Illustrated Book selection, *New York Times Book Review,* 1965, for *Sven's Bridge,* 1981, for *Market Street,* and 2000, for *One Lighthouse, One Moon;* Spring Book Festival Award for Picture Book, 1972, for *Little John;* Children's Book Showcase Award, 1974, for *A Birthday for the Princess,* and 1977, for *Peter Penny's Dance;* Outstanding Book selection, *New York Times,* 1976, for *Peter Penny's Dance,* 1977, for *How the Rooster Saved the Day,* and 1981, for *On Market Street; Boston Globe/Horn Book* Award for Illustration, 1981, for *On Market Street,* and 1984, for *The Rose in My Garden;* Caldecott Honor Book selection, and American Book Award finalist, both 1982, both for *On Market Street;* National Book Award finalist, Judy Lopez Memorial Medal for Children's Literature, Orbis Pictus Award, Golden Kite Award, Sydney Taylor Award Honor Book selection, Association of Jewish Libraries, *River Bank Review* Children's Books of Distinction finalist, American Library Association Best Books for Young Adults citation, and Gradiva Award for Best Memoir, all c. 1998, all for *No Pretty Pictures;* One Hundred Titles for Reading and Sharing selection, New York Public Library, 2008, for *Hello, Day!;* Choices listee, Cooperative Children's Book Center, and Best Children's Books of the Year designation, Bank Street College of Education, both 2010, both for *Nini Lost and Found.*

Writings

SELF-ILLUSTRATED

Sven's Bridge, Harper (New York, NY), 1965, reprinted, Greenwillow Books (New York, NY), 1992.

The Troll Music, Harper (New York, NY), 1966.

Potatoes, Potatoes, Harper (New York, NY), 1967, reprinted, Greenwillow Books (New York, NY), 2004.

The Seamstress of Salzburg, Harper (New York, NY), 1970.

Under a Mushroom, Harper (New York, NY), 1970.

A Birthday for the Princess, Harper (New York, NY), 1973.

(Reteller) *King Rooster, Queen Hen,* Greenwillow Books (New York, NY), 1975.

(Reteller) *The Pancake,* Greenwillow Books (New York, NY), 1978.

(Adapter) *The Straw Maid,* Greenwillow Books (New York, NY), 1983.

Alison's Zinnia, Greenwillow Books (New York, NY), 1990.

The Dwarf Giant, Holiday (New York, NY), 1991.

Pierrot's ABC Garden, Golden Books (New York, NY), 1992.

Away from Home, Greenwillow Books (New York, NY), 1994.

One Lighthouse, One Moon, Greenwillow Books (New York, NY), 2000.

Animal Antics A to Z, Greenwillow Books (New York, NY), 2005.

Nini Here and There, Greenwillow Books (New York, NY), 2007.

Hello, Day!, Greenwillow Books (New York, NY), 2008.

Nini Lost and Found, Knopf (New York, NY), 2010.

Ten Hungry Rabbits: Counting and Color Concepts for the Very Young, Knopf (New York, NY), 2012.

ILLUSTRATOR

Paul Kapp, *Cock-a-Doodle Doo! Cock-a-Doodle Doo!,* Harper (New York, NY), 1966.

Meindert de Jong, *Puppy Summer,* Harper (New York, NY), 1966.

The Wishing Penny and Other Stories, (anthology), Parents Magazine Press 1967.

F.N. Monjo, *Indian Summer,* Harper (New York, NY), 1968.

Alice Dalgliesh, *The Little Wooden Farmer,* Macmillan (New York, NY), 1968.

Benjamin Elkin, *The Wisest Man in the World,* Parents Magazine Press (New York, NY), 1968.

Barbara Borack, *Someone Small,* Harper (New York, NY), 1969.

Doris Orgel, *The Uproar,* McGraw (New York, NY), 1970.

Mirra Ginsburg, editor, *Three Rolls and One Doughnut: Fables from Russia,* Dial (New York, NY), 1970.

Benjamin Elkin, *How the Tsar Drinks Tea,* Parents Magazine Press (New York, NY), 1971.

Theodore Storm, *Little John,* retold by Doris Orgel, Farrar, Straus (New York, NY), 1972.

John Langstaff, editor, *Soldier, Soldier, Won't You Marry Me?,* Doubleday, 1972.

Cynthia Jameson, *One for the Price of Two,* Parents Magazine Press (New York, NY), 1972.

Elizabeth Shub, adapter, *Clever Kate,* Macmillan (New York, NY), 1973.

Carolyn Meyer, *Christmas Crafts: Things to Make the Days before Christmas,* Harper (New York, NY), 1974.

Janet Quin-Harkin, *Peter Penny's Dance,* Dial (New York, NY), 1976.

Arnold Lobel, *How the Rooster Saved the Day,* Greenwillow Books (New York, NY), 1977.

Arnold Lobel, *A Treeful of Pigs,* Greenwillow Books (New York, NY), 1979.

Penelope Lively, *Fanny's Sister,* Dutton (New York, NY), 1980.

Arnold Lobel, *On Market Street,* Greenwillow Books (New York, NY), 1981, twenty-fifth-anniversary edition,2006.

Jane Hart, compiler, *Singing Bee! A Collection of Favorite Children's Songs,* Lothrop (New York, NY), 1982, published as *Sing a Song of Sixpence! The Best Song Book Ever,* Gollancz (London, England), 1983.

Clement Clarke Moore, *The Night before Christmas,* Knopf (New York, NY), 1984.

Arnold Lobel, *The Rose in My Garden,* Greenwillow Books (New York, NY), 1984.

Harriet Ziefert, *A New Coat for Anna,* Knopf (New York, NY), 1986.

B.P. Nichol, *Once: A Lullaby,* Greenwillow Books (New York, NY), 1986.

Steven Kroll, *Looking for Daniela: A Romantic Adventure,* Holiday House (New York, NY), 1988.

Charlotte S. Huck, reteller, *Princess Furball,* Greenwillow Books (New York, NY), 1989.

Charlotte Zolotow, *This Quiet Lady,* Greenwillow Books (New York, NY), 1992.

Ethel L. Heins, reteller, *The Cat and the Cook and Other Fables of Krylov,* Greenwillow Books (New York, NY), 1995.

Charlotte S. Huck, reteller *Toads and Diamonds,* Greenwillow Books (New York, NY), 1995.

Charlotte Pomerantz *Mangaboom,* Greenwillow Books (New York, NY), 1997.

Carl Sandburg, *Not Everyday an Aurora Borealis for Your Birthday: A Love Poem,* Knopf (New York, NY), 1998.

Miela Ford, *My Day in the Garden,* Greenwillow Books (New York, NY), 1999.

Charlotte S. Huck, reteller, *The Black Bull of Norroway: A Scottish Tale,* Greenwillow Books (New York, NY), 2001.

Julia Cunningham, *The Stable Rat and Other Christmas Poems,* Greenwillow Books (New York, NY), 2001.

Adèle Geras, *My Grandmother's Stories: A Collection of Jewish Folk Tales,* Knopf (New York, NY), 2003.

Rebecca Piatt Davidson, *All the World's a Stage,* Greenwillow Books (New York, NY), 2003.

Kevin Henkes, *So Happy!,* Greenwillow Books (New York, NY), 2005.

OTHER

No Pretty Pictures: A Child of War (memoir), Greenwillow Books (New York, NY), 1998.

Lobel's art and papers are included in the Kerlan Collection at the University of Minnesota.

Adaptations

The Little Wooden Farmer was adapted for filmstrip with audiocassette, Threshold Filmstrips, 1974. *Peter Penny's Dance* was adapted for filmstrip with audiocassette, Weston Woods, 1978. *A New Coat for Anna* was adapted for filmstrip with audiocassette, Random House, 1987. *A Treeful of Pigs* and *On Market Street* were adapted for filmstrip with audiocassette, Random House. *King Rooster, Queen Hen* and *The Rose in My Garden* were adapted for audiocassette, Random House. *On Market Street* was adapted for videocassette, Random House.

Sidelights

Drama and design are hallmarks of Anita Lobel's many books for children. Celebrated as both a talented artist and the creator of charming texts, Lobel is the author and illustrator of picture books, fantasies, retellings, and concept books that have as their hallmarks a theatrical approach and a keen sense of design. She has also provided the pictures for dozens of stories by acclaimed writers such as Meindert de Jong, Doris Orgel, Clement Clarke Moore, Penelope Lively, John Langstaff, Kevin Henkes, and Charlotte Zolotow.

As an artist, Lobel is well known for creating evocative, detailed paintings in line-and-wash or watercolor and gouache, all which feature her characteristic use of richly patterned landscapes, opulent costumes and tapestries, and colorful flowers. As a writer, she is inspired by traditional folk stories and fairy tales, using "once-upon-a-time" settings and happy endings as well as humor. Several of Lobel's tales are underscored by serious themes, such as the nature of war and the results of parental neglect. As a creator of concept books, she has been credited for her originality and inventiveness, especially in her contributions to the alphabet-book genre.

Lobel was born in Poland into a family of well-off Jewish merchants, but her life changed quickly when German chancellor Adolf Hitler rose to power. "My parents separated for practical reasons, believing we would all have better chances for survival, which proved to be true," she stated in *Books Are by People.* A kind Polish nanny took Lobel and her brother under her wing, eventually relocating the children to the countryside. Tragically, the children were discovered by the Nazis and sent to a German concentration camp. At the war's end in 1945 they were rescued by the Swedish Red Cross and, after two years, were reunited with their parents through the efforts of a relief organization based in Stockholm.

Lobel's award-winning memoir *No Pretty Pictures: A Child of War* shares her childhood experiences. Beginning in 1939 when she was five years old, *No Pretty Pictures* follows the author/illustrator's life through her liberation from the concentration camp and her family's reunion in Sweden. "This piercing and graceful account is rewarding for readers of all ages," praised a *Publishers Weekly* reviewer, while in *Booklist* Hazel Rochman noted that "the truth of the child's viewpoint is the strength of this Holocaust survivor story." Mary M. Burns, in her *Horn Book* review, considered *No Pretty Pictures* to be "notable both as an account of survival and as a revelation of a remarkable human being."

***Drawing from her childhood memories as an European Jew during the Holocaust, Lobel presents a dramatic statement on the futility of war and the human capacity to survive in* No Pretty Pictures.** (Cover photo courtesy of Anita Lobel. Cover copyright © 1998 by HarperCollins Publishers. Used by permission of HarperCollins Publishers.)

This encounter with war reshaped Lobel's childhood. "I did not go to school until I was thirteen, but was taught how to read and write," she recalled in *Books Are by People.* "I came from Sweden to New York against my will because my parents wanted to reclaim some long-lost relatives they had in this country." Immigrating to the United States in 1952, she grew up in the city and entered Pratt Institute to study for her B.F A. in fine arts. Although she received encouragement to become an artist, Lobel was also interested in the theater and she took part in stage productions at Pratt. She met her future husband, Arnold Lobel, when she was cast in a play he directed, and they were married in 1955. The couple created four books together before Arnold's death in 1987; their third, *On Market Street,* received the *Boston Globe/Horn Book* Award for illustration.

After graduating from Pratt, Lobel worked as a textile designer for several years; then, at the urging of editor Susan Hirschman, she decided to try her hand at writing and illustrating a children's book. "I didn't know if I could do it," Lobel remarked her 2010 Zena Sutherland lecture, reprinted in *Horn Book.* "But would it not be thrilling to find words, and then have words and pictures marching one after another, illuminating each other? And, not only that, I would have my name in print on the cover of the book." That first book, *Sven's Bridge,* grew from an idea about a goodhearted man; the artwork incorporates examples of Swedish folk design that Lobel remembered from her childhood.

Another early self-illustrated picture book, *Potatoes, Potatoes,* was inspired by Lobel's childhood memories. The story describes how two brothers become enemies during wartime but are reunited by their mother, who refuses to give them each something to eat until they and their comrades stop fighting. A reviewer for the *Times Literary Supplement* called *Potatoes, Potatoes* "beautifully executed," and *New York Times Book Review* critic Barbara Wersba praised Lobel's artwork as "excellent picture-book fare, finely drawn and colored."

The Dwarf Giant, a story set in ancient Japan, finds an evil dwarf intent upon taking over a peaceful kingdom until he is defeated by the resourcefulness of the country's princess. Although the dwarf is stopped, the story ends in a minor key, as other potential immigrants wait outside the palace. A *Kirkus Reviews* contributor called *The Dwarf Giant* "a deeply felt variant on a classic theme that more often ends in tragedy," noting that the book's "graceful paintings . . . reflect Japanese art and architecture, . . . their allusive power reinforcing the Faustian subtext" of the story.

Alison's Zinnias links a girl's name with a verb and a flower, all starting with the same letter of the alphabet,

***Lobel captures the architecture of coastal regions in her self-illustrated picture book* One Lighthouse One Moon..** (Greenwillow Books, 2000. Copyright © 2000 by Anita Lobel. Used by permission of HarperCollins Publishers.)

before coming back to the beginning; each page features a painting and a line of type, below which is a large letter and a smaller storyboard that shows the flower chosen by each child. Caroline Ward, in a review for *School Library Journal,* described *Alison's Zinnias* as "luscious-looking," while *Bulletin of the Center for Children's Books* contributor Zena Sutherland called it "an unusual alphabet book" and a "dazzling display of floral painting." In *Horn Book* Burns recommended Lobel's imaginative work as "a book to brighten the dreariest of days." "What could have been just another clever idea becomes . . . a tour de force," Burns added.

A companion piece to *Alison's Zinnias, Away from Home* focuses on little boys rather than little girls and, in the words of a *Publishers Weekly* reviewer, "takes the reader on a globe-trotting adventure as Lobel sets the stage—literally—to introduce letters and various world cities as well." A *Publishers Weekly* contributor commended the accuracy, romanticism, and informativeness of the illustrations in *Away from Home,* while *Booklist* reviewer Rochman noted that "an all-male cast pulls you into imagining each character's story and making the journey to each exciting place."

Lobel celebrates both the familiar—camels, elephants, and rabbits—as well as the unusual—quetzals and xenopuses—in *Animal Antics A to Z,* a "charming and literary frolic through a carnival of letters . . . and critters," according to a *Kirkus Reviews* writer. In the work, acrobatic human figures introduce a host of creatures in festive attire. Sheep, cows, and other barnyard animals greet the morning sun in *Hello, Day!,* a read-aloud story featuring Lobel's mixed-media illustrations. "The luxuriantly hued, playfully textured portraits will rivet preschoolers and invite them to make animal sounds of their own," a contributor in *Publishers Weekly* stated of this illustrated story.

One Lighthouse, One Moon turns to counting by focusing on days of the week and months of the year. In the text, a young girl selects different colored shoes for each day of the week, while her cat becomes the focus of the section on months of the year, The feline's activities adapting to the changes in the passing months as all await the birth of her kittens in December. Noting the three different themes, a *Publishers Weekly* reviewer wrote that "Lobel segues seamlessly from one theme to the next." Jonas JoAnn commented in *School Library Journal* that "the book combines text and illustration quite successfully and really works," while a *Horn Book* reviewer predicted that *One Lighthouse, One Moon* "will reward reading and rereading, again and again."

An imaginative feline is the star of both *Nini Here and There* and *Nini Lost and Found.* In the first, Nini the cat falls asleep while in her pet carrier, dreaming of wild adventures enjoyed aboard a hot-air balloon and the back of an elephant until she arrives at her family's country home. *Nini Lost and Found* centers on the feline's misadventures in the woods after she wanders away from home. "Lobel's hallmark art and design paint a charming tale told by the striped tabby," a *Kirkus Reviews* critic stated in reviewing *Nini Here and There,* and a *Publishers Weekly* contributor remarked that the artist's "realistic renderings of the endearing tabby's visage reveal a range of emotions that cat-familiar readers will recognize." According to a *Kirkus Reviews* writer, *Nini Lost and Found* "captures a cat's clear, opinionated and lovably hedonistic thinking in her simple storytelling," and *Booklist* reviewer Ilene Cooper applauded the book's "endearing" illustrations, "with big swirls of emotion and the tiniest nod of relief in a little cat's upturned lip."

In her illustrations for Charlotte Zolotow's *The Quiet Lady* Lobel brings to life a tender story in which a little girl views photographs of her mother at various stages of her life, ending with the birth and baby picture of the young narrator. Each double-page spread features a small, darkly hued painting of the child along with richly colored paintings of her mother. A *Publishers Weekly* critic called *The Quiet Lady* an "excellent choice for quiet mother-child sharing [that is] sure to invite genealogy lessons filled with fond memories," while Phelan noted that "the exceptional talents of Zolotow and Lobel combine in this celebration of life."

In *The Cat and the Cook and Other Fables of Krylov,* Lobel creates illustrations for twelve Russian fables retold by Ethel L. Heins, several based on poems by popular fabulist Ivan Andreevich Krylov. Her folk-art paintings for the book are noted both for their theatrical quality and evocation of the works of Marc Chagall. In *Booklist* Julie Corsaro claimed that Lobel "outdoes herself" with "paintings that are brilliantly colored and wonderfully composed," while *School Library Journal* reviewer Cheri Estes maintained that "the artist adeptly captures the essence of each tale" in "paintings [that] will entice youngsters to read this collection independently."

With a text by Charlotte S. Huck, *Toads and Diamonds* retells a classic French folktale in which lovely Renée lives with her nasty stepmother and stepsisters and is treated as a lowly servant. When she goes to the well and brings water to an elderly woman, Renée is rewarded with flowers and jewels every time she speaks; she wins the heart of a handsome prince, who appreciates her for herself and not for her jewels. "Full of life, color, and grace, Lobel's paintings create a sense of magic within everyday reality," wrote Phelan in *Booklist,* while Maria B. Salvadore concluded in *Horn Book* that "this is some of Anita Lobel's best work, each picture in close harmony with the text to move quickly to a satisfying conclusion."

Another picture book by Huck, *The Black Bull of Norroway* features a "Beauty and the Beast"-style story in which a young woman marries a hideous black bull only to discover that the creature is in fact a cursed prince. Marie Orlando commented in *School Library Journal* that Lobel's watercolor-and-black-pen illustrations for *The Black Bull of Norroway* "provide a dynamic visual presentation" of the story.

All the World's a Stage provides young readers with snippets from several of Shakespeare's plays, all written in rhyme. A *Kirkus Reviews* contributor commented on Lobel's "marvelously integrated spreads," which create a tableaux of Shakespearean characters. A *Publishers Weekly* critic praised the artwork for the volume, noting that it "ranks among her best. Here she gleefully follows her own theater muse, staging dramatic montages of the famous plays." Nancy Menaldi-Scanlan also cited the artwork in her *School Library Journal* review, writing that Lobel's "stunning illustrations are the highlight of the book."

The artist also joins forces with celebrated author Henkes on *So Happy!,* a story about a magical seed, a wandering rabbit, and a restless young boy. Her "vigorous artwork, a riot of color that pays homage to [Vincent] Van Gogh, locates events in a sun-toasted, south-of-the-border landscape," Jennifer Mattson commented in *Booklist,* and a *Publishers Weekly* reviewer noted of *So Happy!* that the illustrator "uses deliberate, heavy brush strokes to depict the desert's flora and fauna . . . and vividly evokes the movement of sky and water."

***Lobel captures the life of a much-loved cat in her self-illustrated picture book* Nini Lost and Found.** (Copyright © 2010 by Anita Lobel. Used by permission of Alfred A. Knopf, an imprint of Random House Children's Books, a division of Random House, Inc.)

***Lobel's colorful, detailed illustrations capture the energy in Rebecca Piatt Davidson's rhyming text about the characters, plays, and Elizabethan age of English dramatist William Shakespeare in* All the World's a Stage.** (Illustration copyright © 2003 by Anita Lobel. Used by permission of Greenwillow Books, an imprint of HarperCollins Publishers.)

Biographical and Critical Sources

BOOKS

Cummins, Julie, editor, *Children's Book Illustration and Design,* PBC International, 1992.

Hopkins, Lee Bennett, editor, *Books Are by People,* Citation Press, 1969.

Kingman, Lee, and others, editors, *Illustrators of Children's Books: 1957-1966,* Horn Book (Boston, MA), 1968.

Kingman, Lee, and others, editors, *Illustrators of Children's Books, 1967-1976,* Horn Book (Boston, MA), 1978.

Lanes, Selma G., *Down the Rabbit Hole,* Atheneum (New York, NY), 1971.

Lobel, Anita, *No Pretty Pictures: A Child of War* Greenwillow Books (New York, NY), 1998.

St. James Guide to Children's Writers, St. James Press (Detroit, MI), 1999.

Silvey, Anita, editor, *Children's Books and Their Creators,* Houghton Mifflin (Boston, MA), 1995.

PERIODICALS

Booklist, May 1, 1992, Carolyn Phelan, review of *This Quiet Lady,* p. 1599; November 15, 1993, Carolyn Phelan, review of *Pierrot's ABC Garden,* p. 632; August, 1994, Hazel Rochman, review of *Away from Home,* p. 2054; March 15, 1995, Julie Corsaro, review of *The Cat and the Cook and Other Fables of Krylov,* p. 1330; November 1, 1996, Carolyn Phelan, review of *Toads and Diamonds,* p. 496; August, 1998, Hazel Rochman, "Anita Lobel's War" and review of *No Pretty Pictures: A Child of War,* p. 1988; January 1, 1999, review of *No Pretty Pictures,* p. 782; April 1, 1999, Stephanie Zvirin, review of *No Pretty Pictures,* p. 1382; April 1, 2000, Gillian Engberg, review of *One Lighthouse, One Moon,* p. 1463; January 1, 2004, Carolyn Phelan, review of *Potatoes, Potatoes,* pp. 876-877; February 1, 2005, Jennifer Mattson, review of *So Happy!,* p. 960; November 1, 2005, Gillian Engberg, review of *Animal Antics A to Z,* p. 50; May 1, 2007, Gillian Engberg, review of *Nini Here and There,* p. 88; April 1, 2008, Janice Del Negro, review of *Hello, Day!,* p. 54; August 1, 2010, Ilene Cooper, review of *Nini Lost and Found,* p. 55.

Bulletin of the Center for Children's Books, October, 1990, Zena Sutherland, review of *Alison's Zinnia,* p. 36.

*Horn Book,*November-December, 1990, Mary M. Burns, review of *Alison's Zinnia,* p. 730; July-August, 1995; November-December, 1996, Maria B. Salvadore, review of *Toads and Diamonds,* p. 751; November-December, 1998, Mary M. Burns, review of *No Pretty Pictures,* p. 755; July-August, 2000, review of *One Lighthouse, One Moon,* p. 437; November-December, 2000, Anita Lobel, "Future Classics," p. 684; March-April, 2005, Susan Dove Lempke, review of *So Happy!,* p. 188; March-April, 2008, Joanna Rudge Long, review of *Hello, Day!,* p. 205; November-December, 2010, Anita Lobel, "I Did It Sideways: The Zena Sutherland Lecture," p. 10, and Roger Sutton, review of *Nini Lost and Found,* p. 77.

Kirkus Reviews, April 15, 1991, review of *The Dwarf Giant,* p. 537; October 1, 1993, review of *Pierrot's ABC Garden,* p. 1276; April 1, 2003, review of *All the World's a Stage,* p. 532; August 1, 2005, review of *Animal Antics A to Z,* p. 853; April 15, 2007, review of *Nini Here and There*; August 15, 2010, review of *Nini Lost and Found.*

New York Times Book Review, October 1, 1967, Barbara Wersba, review of *Potatoes, Potatoes*; October 14, 2007, J.D. Biersdorfer, review of *Nini Here and There,* p. 21; October 17, 2010, Julie Just, review of *Nini Lost and Found,* p. 17.

Publishers Weekly, May 17, 1971, Pamela Bragg, "Authors & Editors," pp. 11-13; June 1, 1992, review of *This Quiet Lady,* p. 61; July 4, 1994, review of *Away from Home,* pp. 60-61; August 10, 1998, review of *No Pretty Pictures,* p. 389; September 7, 1998, Elizabeth Devereaux, "Telling Their Own Stories," p. 28; April 17, 2000, review of *One Lighthouse, One Moon,* p. 80; April 28, 2003, review of *All the World's a Stage,* p. 70; February 21, 2005, review of *So Happy!,* p. 173; June 4, 2007, review of *Nini Here and There,* p. 48; February 25, 2008, review of *Hello, Day!,* p. 77; September 13, 2010, review of *Nini Lost and Found,* p. 44.

School Library Journal, October, 1990, Caroline Ward, review of *Alison's Zinnia,* p. 96; May, 1991; June, 1992; April, 1995, Cheri Estes, review of *The Cat and the Cook and Other Tales of Krylove,* pp. 142-143; September, 1996; May, 2000, Jonas JoAnn, review of *One Lighthouse, One Moon,* p. 148; June, 2001, Marie Orlando, review of *The Black Bull of Norroway: A Scottish Tale,* p. 137; May, 2003, Nancy Menaldi-Scanlan, review of *All the World's a Stage,* p. 165; November, 2003, Carol Fazioli, review of *No Pretty Pictures,* p. 83; March, 2005, Wendy Lukehart, review of *So Happy!,* p. 172; September, 2005, Kathy Krasniewicz, review of *Animal Antics A to Z,* p. 176; June, 2007, Marian Creamer, review of *Nini Here and There,* p. 114; March, 2008, Carolyn Janssen, review of *Hello, Day!,* p. 170; September, 2010, Kara Schaff Dean, review of *Nini Lost and Found,* p. 130.

Times Literary Supplement, June 26, 1969, review of *Potatoes, Potatoes.*

Washington Post Book World, June 13, 1982, John F. Berry, "The Lobels: A Marriage of Two Drawing Boards."

***Lobel's delicately colored illustrations bring to life Julia Cunningham's holiday verse collection* The Stable Rat, and Other Christmas Poems.** (Illustration copyright © 2001 by Anita Lobel. Reproduced by permission of Greenwillow Books, an imprint of HarperCollins Publishers.)

ONLINE

Anita Lobel Home Page, http://www.anita-lobel.com (March 22, 2012).*

* * *

LUNA, James 1962-

Personal

Born 1962; married; children: three. *Education:* University of California, Riverside, B.A. (liberal studies), 1985; National University, M.F.A. (creative writing: Fiction), 2011. *Hobbies and other interests:* Baking.

Addresses

Home—Riverside, CA. *E-mail*—jluna@moonstories.com.

Career

Educator and author. Madison Elementary School, Riverside, CA, teacher.

Member

Society of Children's Book Writers and Illustrators.

Writings

The Runaway Piggy/El cochinito fugitivo, illustrated by Laura Lacámara, Piñata Books (Houston, TX), 2010.

Contributor of stories to *My Friend* magazine.

Biographical and Critical Sources

PERIODICALS

Kirkus Reviews, October 15, 2010, review of *The Runaway Piggy/El cochinito fugitivo.*

School Library Journal, March, 2011, Tim Wadham, review of *The Runaway Piggy,* p. 151.

ONLINE

James Luna Home Page, http://www.moonstories.com (May 15, 2012).*

M

MACK, Steve

Personal

Born in Canada; married; children: two.

Addresses

Home—Lumsden, Saskatchewan, Canada. *E-mail*—steve@stevemack.com; steve@illustrationfarm.com.

Career

Illustrator. Freelance illustrator and graphic artist, beginning 1998; American Greetings, Cleveland, OH, former in-house artist.

Illustrator

Jacob Berkowitz, *Jurassic Poop: What Dinosaurs (and Others) Left Behind,* Kids Can Press (Tonawonda, NY), 2006.

Betty Ann Schwartz, *Hide-and-Seek Dinosaurs!,* Chronicle Books (San Francisco, CA), 2008.

So Many Animals! (board-book set), Peaceable Kingdom Press, 2008.

The Leaves Fall All Around! ("Rookie Reader" series), Scholastic (New York, NY), 2009.

Christina Rosetti, *The Pancake,* Oxford University Press (New York, NY), 2009.

Debbie Wagenbach, *The Grouchies,* Magination Press (Washington, DC), 2010.

Brian P. Cleary, *Six Sheep Sip Thick Shakes, and Other Tricky Tongue Twisters,* Millbrook Press (Minneapolis, MN), 2011.

Illustrator of novelty and activity books, including "Flash Kids Preschool Activity Books" series, Barnes & Noble, and "Sight Word Stories" series, Scholastic. Contributor to periodicals, including *Kayak, National Geographic Kids,* and *Popular Mechanics.*

Sidelights

Based in rural Canada, Steve Mack is an artist whose retro-inspired collage images can be found on everything from greeting cards to sticker and flip books to children's story books. With an addiction for drawing that was fed by the stacks of printed-on-one-side computer paper his mother brought home from work, while he was a child. Mack trained in art and started working professionally during the late 1990s. Like many artists, he found work with greeting-card companies and eventually signed on as a staff artist for American Greetings. Soon American Greetings signed Mack to an exclusive freelance contract: they made him an offer to work in-house in Cleveland, Ohio. Several years later, in 2006, Mack made his picture-book debut as illustrator of Jacob Berkowitz's quirky *Jurassic Poop: What Dinosaurs (and Others) Left Behind.*

In *Jurassic Poop* Berkowitz appeals to young science buffs with what a *Kirkus Reviews* critic characterized as "the 'e-e-eew factor,'" and Mack's colorful artwork helps make the book a "lively introduction to . . . fossil feces." Another illustration project, Debbie Wagenbach's *The Grouchies,* finds his "simple cartoon drawings" contributing to a story that will "engage children." "Mack's brightly colored madcap cartoon illustrations match the tongue-in-cheek humor" of Brian P. Cleary's text for *Six Sheep Sip Thick Shakes, and Other Tricky Tongue Twisters,* wrote another *Kirkus Reviews* writer, and in *Booklist* Diane Foote cited the "hilarious" details Mack incorporates into its "colorful, stylized illustrations."

Biographical and Critical Sources

PERIODICALS

Booklist, March 15, 2011, Diane Foote, review of *Six Sheep Sip Thick Shakes, and Other Tricky Tongue Twisters,* p. 51.

Kirkus Reviews, August 1, 2006, review of *Jurassic Poop: What Dinosaurs (and Others) Left Behind,* p. 781; February 15, 2011, review of *Six Sheep Sip Thick Shakes, and Other Tricky Tongue Twisters.*

***Steve Mack's work as an illustrator includes creating the colorful illustrations for Brian P. Cleary's* Six Sheep Sip Thick Shakes, and Other Tricky Tongue Twisters.** (Text copyright © 2011 by Brian P. Cleary. Illustrations copyright © 2011 by Steve Mack. Reproduced by permission of Millbrook Press, a division of Lerner Publishing Group.)

Publishers Weekly, November 22, 2010, review of *Six Sheep Sip Thick Shakes, and Other Tricky Tongue Twisters,* p. 56.

School Library Journal, March, 2010, Teresa Pfeifer, review of *The Grouchies,* p. 135.

ONLINE

Steve Mack Home Page, http://www.stevemack.com (May 1, 2012).*

* * *

MAGOON, Kekla 1980-

Personal

Born 1980, in MI. *Education:* Northwestern University B.A. (history), 2001; Vermont College, M.F.A. (writing for children and young adults), 2005.

Addresses

Home—New York, NY. *E-mail*—keklamagoon@gmail.com.

Career

Author and educator. Formerly worked in nonprofit sector, including for Girl Scouts, Salvation Army, and Brotherhood/Sister Sol. Teacher of writing in New York, NY. *Hunger Mountain Arts Journal,* co-editor of teen and children's literature. Member of board, VIDA: Women in Literary Arts. Presenter to youth groups; speaker at schools.

Member

Society of Children's Book Writers and Illustrators, Editorial Freelancers Association, Freelancers Union, Women's Mosaic Society.

Awards, Honors

Coretta Scott King/John Steptoe Award for New Talent, American Library Association (ALA), and Image Award nomination, National Association for the Advancement of Colored People (NAACP), both 2009, ALA Notable Book designation and YALSA Best Books for Young Adults designations, both 2010, and Best Book selection, Bank Street College School of Education, all for *The Rock and the River;* Image Award nomination, NAACP, for *Camo Girl.*

Writings

NONFICTION

Abraham Lincoln, ABDO Publishing (Edina, MN), 2008.

Gun Control, ABDO Publishing (Edina, MN), 2008.

Nelson Mandela: A Leader for Freedom, ABDO Publishing (Edina, MN), 2008.

The Salem Witch Trials, ABDO Publishing (Edina, MN), 2008.

Media Censorship, ABDO Publishing (Edina, MN), 2009.

Sex Education in Schools, ABDO Publishing (Edina, MN), 2009.

The Welfare Debate, ABDO Publishing (Edina, MN), 2009.

The Zebulon Pike Expedition, ABDO Publishing (Edina, MN), 2009.

Cesar Chavez: Crusader for Labor Rights, ABDO Publishing (Edina, MN), 2011.

Today the World Is Watching You: The Little Rock Nine and the Fight for School Integration, 1957, Twenty-first Century Books (Minneapolis, MN), 2011.

YOUNG-ADULT FICTION

The Rock and the River, Aladdin (New York, NY), 2009.

Camo Girl, Aladdin (New York, NY), 2011.

37 Things I Love (in No Particular Order), Henry Holt (New York, NY), 2012.

Fire in the Streets (sequel to *The Rock and the River*), Aladdin (New York, NY), 2012.

Adaptations

The Rock and the River was adapted for audiobook, Brilliance Audio, 2010.

Sidelights

With a first name that means "morning star" in the Bassa language of her father's native Cameroon, Kekla Magoon draws on her biracial heritage and her many travels in her work as a writer. Magoon's nonfiction books focus on history and social issues and include *Media Censorship, Nelson Mandela: A Leader for Freedom,* and *The Zebulon Pike Expedition,* as well as *Today the World Is Watching You: The Little Rock Nine and the Fight for School Integration,* the last an "extensively researched" study of an event that "forever changed the landscape of [U.S.] race relations," according to *School Library Journal* contributor Rita Meade. With her award-winning *The Rock and the River,* along with its sequel, *Fire in the Streets,* Magoon drew on similar themes and issues while also revealing her skills as a young-adult novelist.

Born in Michigan, Magoon inherited a rich cultural and racial heritage from her African, Dutch, and Scottish ancestors. Raised in Fort Wayne, Indiana, she loved reading and writing and completed her first novel while still in high school. At Northwestern University she majored in history, focusing on the complexities of the Middle East and Africa, and she moved to New York City in 2001, to work in the nonprofit sector while honing her skills as a writer. Magoon also worked to complete an M.F.A. in writing, producing several nonfiction books for ABDO Publishing along the way. With *The Rock and the River* she revealed her calling in fiction and was awarded the American Library Association's prestigious Coretta Scott King New Talent Award.

Cover of Kekla Magoon's young-adult novel* The Rock and the River, *which focuses on a family torn by conflicting passions. (Jacket photograph copyright © 2008 by Getty Images. Reproduced by permission of Aladdin, an imprint of Simon & Schuster Macmillan.)

Set in Chicago in 1968 and reflecting the tensions of the civil-rights era, *The Rock and the River* finds thirteen-year-old Sam Childs respectful of the pacifist approach of his minister father, a colleague of the Reverend Martin Luther King, Jr. The teen is confused, therefore, when older brother Stick leaves home in the wake of Reverend King's assassination and joins the radical Black Panther organization. Although he loves Stick, Sam has stood alongside his father at many nonviolent demonstrations, and his brother's action seems disrespectful in light of his father's pacifism. When Sam and friend Maxie witness another friend's brutal treatment at the hands of the Chicago police, he begins to question his father's approach. With their militaristic presence in his community, the Panthers make Sam feel secure, and their demands for better housing, education, and justice echo his own frustrations over the inequities he sees around him. Tragically, the growing tensions in Sam's community will ultimately lead to more tragedy.

Calling *The Rock and the River* a "taut, eloquent first novel," *Booklist* critic Hazel Rochman added that Magoon illuminates for readers "what it was like to be young, black, and militant" at the height of the civil-rights struggle. The story's "well drawn" characters add depth to the drama of the Childs family, maintained Kristin Anderson in her *School Library Journal* review, the critic praising the novel as "an important book about a[n] historical reality that has not been dealt with in juvenile literature." Calling the novel "unflinching" when dealing with the "police brutality and racism" that characterized the era, a *Kirkus Reviews* writer added that *The Rock and the River* "offers readers a perspective that is rarely explored."

In *Camo Girl* Magoon focuses on two friends who find their relationship changing during middle school. Bonding in elementary school while they each mourned the loss of their fathers, Ella and Z have gained a joint reputation as outsiders by the time they reach sixth grade, Ella because she is the only black student in class and Z because he is immersed in a medievalesque fantasy world where he is Sir Zachariah to her Lady Eleanor. When a second African-American student, Bailey, joins their class, Z realizes that the new boy's presence will change his relationship with Ella. Befriended by Bailey, who is also popular with her white classmates, Ella is able to throw off the nickname "Camo-Face" and feel accepted. However, she also recognizes a responsibility to Z, who remains on the outside, and her reflections on friendship, loyalty, and the value of fitting in provide the tension in Magoon's coming-of-age tale.

Cover of Magoon's novel* Camo Girl, *in which three multiracial teens develop a dynamic friendship that empowers each differently. (Jacket photographs copyright © 2011 by Getty Images. Reproduced by permission of Aladdin, an imprint of Simon & Schuster Macmillan.)

A "poetic and nuanced story," according to a *Publishers Weekly* critic, *Camo Girl* "addresses the courage it takes to truly know and support someone." Through the interactions of Bailey, Ella, and Z, the author weaves "a sensitive, quietly powerful look at discovering inner strength, coping, and thriving" in the face of adversity, asserted *Booklist* contributor Heather Booth. In *Kirkus Reviews* a writer praised the story's "full and richly textured narrative," recommending *Camo Girl* as an "elegantly crafted" showcase of both "strong writing and solid characterizations."

Biographical and Critical Sources

PERIODICALS

Booklist, February 1, 2009, Hazel Rochman, review of *The Rock and the River,* p. 50; February 1, 2011, Heather Booth, review of *Camo Girl,* p. 74.

Bulletin of the Center for Children's Books, March, 2011, Karen Coats, review of *Camo Girl,* p. 337.

Kirkus Reviews, December 15, 2008, review of *The Rock and the River;* December 1, 2010, review of *Camo Girl.*

New York Times Book Review, April 12, 2009, review of *The Rock and the River,* p. 15.

Publishers Weekly, December 6, 2010, review of *Camo Girl,* p. 48.

School Library Journal, February, 2009, Kristin Anderson, review of *The Rock and the River,* p. 104; May, 2011, Rita Meade, review of *Today the World Is Watching You: The Little Rock Nine and the Fight for School Integration,* p. 134; January, 2011, Gerry Larson, review of *Camo Girl,* p. 112.

ONLINE

Kekla Magoon Home Page, http://www.keklamagoon.com (May 1, 2012).*

* * *

MASON, Margaret H. 1954-

Personal

Born March 15, 1954, in Wilmington, DE; married; husband's name Roger; children: Kammy, Isaac, Eliza. *Education:* Hampshire College, bachelor's degree; University of Michigan, M.S. *Hobbies and other interests:* Gardening.

Addresses

Home—Ferndale, MI.

Career

Author. Works in field of public health.

Writings

Inside All, illustrated by Holly Welch, Dawn Publications (Nevada City, CA), 2008.

These Hands, illustrated by Floyd Cooper, Houghton Mifflin Harcourt (Boston, MA), 2010.

Contributor to periodicals, including *Skipping Stones.*

Sidelights

Margaret H. Mason augments her work in public health by creating engaging and reassuring stories for young children. In *Inside All* she teamed with artist Holly Welch to show young children that they occupy a secure place within a multilayered universe, while *These Hands* inspires children with a sense of possibilities through Mason's story and evicatuve paintings by bited artist Floyd Cooper.

In *Inside All* Mason's rhythmic text describes a vast universe that is structured like an onion: readers can peel apart the layers—galaxy, solar system, planet, con-

tinent, and country—down to their own neighborhood, home, and cozy bedroom. Praising Welch's "richly colored mixed-media" paintings and Mason's "sweet" rhyming text, a *Kirkus Reviews* writer recommended the work as a "moving bedtime story." *Inside All* is effective at communicating "the idea of interconnectedness" at "a level young children can understand," wrote *Booklist* critic Ilene Cooper, and in *School Library Journal* Judith Constantinides asserted that the "artistic" picture book "succeed[s] in . . . giving children a sense of belonging to the universe."

Mason was inspired to write *These Hands* after learning that African-American bakery workers at Wonder Bread factories around the United States were prohibited from handling bread dough during the mid-twentieth century because timid owners feared that whites would not purchase a food product touched by black hands. In the story, a grandfather teaches his young grandson how to do many things with his hands, from tying shoelaces and playing the piano to gripping a baseball bat. Their closeness allows the man to recall his many life tasks, among them the accomplishment of protesting in the hope of expanding employment opportunities at the bakery where he worked as a young man.

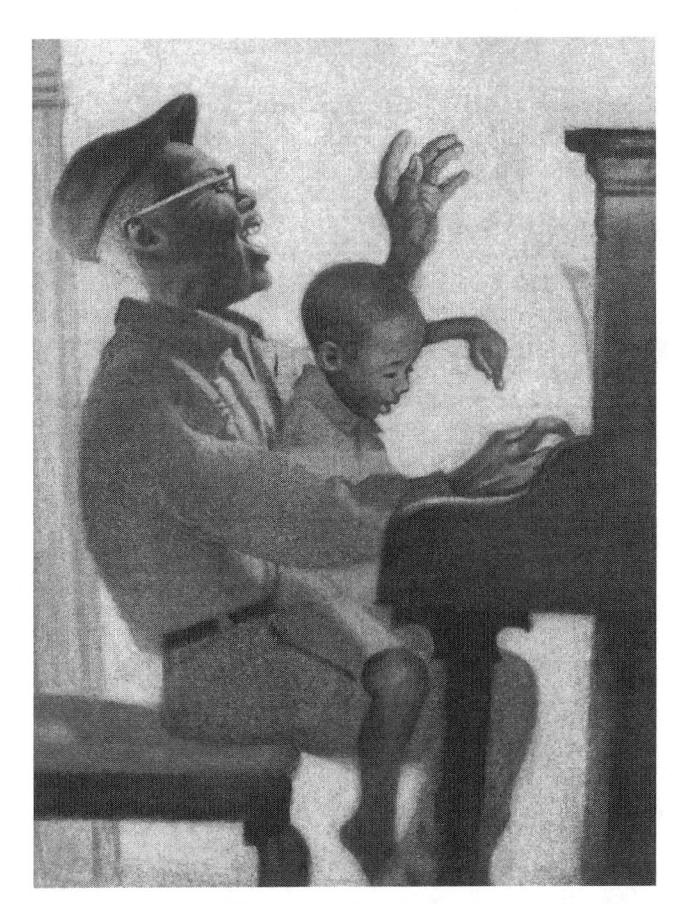

Margaret H. Mason tells a rich multigenerational story in her picture book* These Hands, *featuring artwork by Floyd Cooper. (Illustration copyright © 2010 by Floyd Cooper. Reproduced with permission of Houghton Mifflin Books for Children, an imprint of Houghton Mifflin Harcourt Publishing Company.)

Cooper's "softly blurred," earth-toned artwork joins with Mason's rhyming text to make *These Hands* a "rarely told history" of the civil-rights era, according to Hazel Rochman in *Booklist.* A *Kirkus Reviews* writer asserted that Mason's story "stands tall . . . for its ability to relate history with heart and resonance," and a *Publishers Weekly* critic recommended *These Hands* as "a moving study of multigenerational relationships and triumph over discrimination."

Biographical and Critical Sources

PERIODICALS

Booklist, October 1, 2008, Ilene Cooper, review of *Inside All,* p. 51; February 1, 2011, Hazel Rochman, review of *These Hands,* p. 75.

Kirkus Reviews, August 1, 2008, review of *Inside All*; February 1, 2011, review of *These Hands.*

Publishers Weekly, January 31, 2011, review of *These Hands,* p. 48.

School Library Journal, November, 2008, Judith Constantinides, review of *Inside All,* p. 96; March, 2011, Sara Lissa Paulson, review of *These Hands,* p. 130.

ONLINE

Margaret H. Mason Home Page, http://www.callingmrtoad.com (May 1, 2012).*

* * *

MATTHIES, Janna

Personal

Married; children: one daughter, two sons.

Addresses

Home—Indianapolis, IN. *E-mail*—jannamatthies@yahoo.com.

Career

Writer and preschool music teacher. Presenter at schools.

Awards, Honors

Best Books of Indiana finalist, Indiana Center for the Book, 2010, for *Peter, the Knight with Asthma;* Best English-Language Children's Book award, Sharjah International Book Fair, and CCBC Choice selection, both 2012, both for *The Goodbye Cancer Garden.*

Writings

Monster Trucks, illustrated by Gene Barretta, Piggy Toes Press (Santa Monica, CA), 2009.

Peter, the Knight with Asthma, illustrated by Anthony Lewis, Albert Whitman (Chicago, IL), 2009.
The Goodbye Cancer Garden, illustrated by Kristi Valiant, Albert Whitman (Chicago, IL), 2011.

Contributor to periodicals, including *Spider.*

Sidelights

A writer as well as a storyteller who entertains young listeners with her guitar, Janna Matthies has an upbeat perspective on life that has enriched her stories for children. Although two of her picture books—*Peter, the Knight with Asthma* and *The Goodby Cancer Garden*—deal with subjects that youngsters usually find challenging, Matthies finds a way to curb worries and fears with humor and an imaginative approach.

In *Peter, the Knight with Asthma* Matthies introduces a boy whose games of make-believe are interrupted by a persistent cough. An imaginative child, Peter pretends that he is a knight in shining armor, and his mother is a gentlewoman who comes to his aide with an inhaler when he feels unwell. When a trip to the doctor diagnoses his condition as asthma, the boy's imaginative perspective allows him to view the medical tests he must undergo as part of his knightly duties, then get home in time to battle a dragon. "The inside peek at the medical appointment will reassure . . . readers facing similar office visits," asserted a *Kirkus Reviews* writer, and in *Booklist* Randall Enos wrote of *Peter, the Knight with Asthma* that Anthony Lewis's "bright watercolor illustrations . . . juxtapose Peter's fantasies with scenes in the doctor's office." *Peter, the Knight with Asthma* "introduces useful information" via "the dragon-slaying metaphor," asserted Mary Hazelton in *School Library Journal,* and Matthies supplements her "helpful text" with a note from an asthma specialist.

Janna Matthies tells a family-centered story of resilience in* The Goodbye Cancer Garden, *featuring artwork by Kristi Valiant. (Illustration copyright © 2011 by Kristi Valiant. Reproduced by permission of Albert Whitman & Company.)

Dealing with a family member suffering from cancer can be one of childhood's greatest traumas, and in *The Goodbye Cancer Garden* Matthies draws on her own two children's way of dealing with her diagnosis of breast cancer. Featuring artwork by Kristi Valiant, the book begins in January, as Janie and Jeffrey learn that their mother has cancer. During a trip to the doctor, many questions are answered and the children are left feeling reassured that their mother will recover. The doctor's prediction that Mom will be out of treatment by fall and harvest time inspires Janie to plant a vegetable garden as a way of visualizing growth and healing as well as providing the family with healthy food.

Praising *The Goodbye Cancer Garden* as a "heartening and informed story," a *Publishers Weekly* critic added that Valiant's artwork captures "the family's energy and hopefulness" in a way that will "reassure children facing similar ordeals." "An unexpectedly upbeat text and delicate illustrations distinguish this story," noted Kara Dean in her *Booklist* review of Matthies' picture book, and in *School Library Journal* Heidi Estrin praised *The Goodbye Cancer Garden* as "an uplifting, hopeful story, well told and beautifully illustrated."

Biographical and Critical Sources

PERIODICALS

Booklist, November 1, 2009, Randall Enos, review of *Peter, the Knight with Asthma,* p. 55; February 15, 2011, Kara Dean, review of *The Goodbye Cancer Garden,* p. 77.
Kirkus Reviews, August 15, 2009, review of *Peter, the Knight with Asthma.*
Publishers Weekly, January 31, 2011, review of *The Goodbye Cancer Garden,* p. 49.
School Library Journal, January, 2010, Mary Hazelton, review of *Peter, the Knight with Asthma,* p. 78; February, 2011, Heidi Estrin, review of *The Goodbye Cancer Garden,* p. 86.

ONLINE

Janna Matthies Web log, http://jannamatthies.blogspot.com (May 1, 2012).

* * *

METZGER, Steve 1949-

Personal

Born 1949, in New York, NY; married Nancy Novick; children: Julia. *Education:* Baruch College, degree; Bank Street College, M.A. (education), 1981.

Steve Metzger (Reproduced by permission.)

Addresses

Home—New York, NY. *E-mail*—stevemet@yahoo.com.

Career

Children's author. Worked variously as a cab driver, dish washer, and hotel clerk; Preschool teacher for ten years; worked in school administration; Scholastic, Inc., New York, NY, writer, beginning 1992, vice president and editorial director of Scholastic Book Clubs. Presenter at schools.

Awards, Honors

Children's Choice selection, International Reading Association/Children's Book Council, 2012, and Bill Martin, Jr., Picture Book Award nomination, Kansas Reading Association, 2013, both for *Detective Blue.*

Writings

Ladybug's Birthday, illustrated by James Williamson, Scholastic (New York, NY), 1998.

(Adaptor) *Little Red Caboose,* illustrated by Jill Dubin, Scholastic (New York, NY), 1998.

(Adaptor) *You Are My Sunshine,* illustrated by Jill Dubin, Scholastic (New York, NY), 2001.

The Falling Leaves, illustrated by Jill Dubin, Scholastic (New York, NY), 2002.

I'll Always Come Back!, illustrated by Joy Allen, Scholastic (New York, NY), 2002.

The Biggest Leaf Pile, illustrated by Jill Dubin, Scholastic (New York, NY), 2003.

The Little Snowflake, illustrated by Monica Wellington, Scholastic (New York, NY), 2003.

The Falling Leaves and the Scarecrow, illustrated by Jill Dubin, Scholastic (New York, NY), 2004.

Five Little Bats Flying in the Night, illustrated by Laura Bryant, Scholastic (New York, NY), 2004.

Little Snowflake's Big Adventure, illustrated by Monica Wellington, Scholastic (New York, NY), 2005.

Big Shark's Lost Tooth, Scholastic (New York, NY), 2005.

Five Spooky Ghosts Playing Tricks at School, illustrated by Laura Bryant, Scholastic (New York, NY), 2005.

Big Shark's Valentine Surprise, illustrated by Cedric Hohnstadt, Scholastic (New York, NY), 2005.

The Easter Bunny Is Missing!, illustrated by Barbara Spurll, Scholastic (New York, NY), 2005.

Five Little Bunnies Hopping up a Hill, illustrated by Laura Bryant, Scholastic (New York, NY), 2006.

My Bossy Dolly, illustrated by Chris Demarest, Scholastic (New York, NY), 2006.

When the Leaf Blew In, illustrated by Kellie Lewis, Scholastic (New York, NY), 2006.

The Great Turkey Race, illustrated by Jim Paillot, Scholastic (New York, NY), 2006.

We're Going on a Nature Hunt, illustrated by Miki Sakamoto, Scholastic (New York, NY), 2007.

The Mixed-up Alphabet, illustrated by Jennie Ho, Scholastic (New York, NY), 2007.

The Amazing Turkey Rescue, illustrated by Jim Paillot, Scholastic (New York, NY), 2007.

Big Shark's Halloween Mystery, illustrated by Cedric Hohnstadt, Scholastic (New York, NY), 2007.

Autumn's First Leaf, illustrated by Aaron Zenz, Scholastic (New York, NY), 2008.

Easter Eggs Everywhere, Scholastic (New York, NY), 2008.

We're Going on a Leaf Hunt, illustrated by Miki Sakamoto, Scholastic (New York, NY), 2008.

Under the Apple Tree, illustrated by Alessia Girasole, Scholastic (New York, NY), 2009.

Five Little Penguins Slipping on the Ice, illustrated by Laura Bryant, Scholastic (New York, NY), 2009.

The Silly Turkey Party, illustrated by Jim Paillot, Scholastic (New York, NY), 2009.

Wise Up, Silly Owl!, illustrated by Hans Wilhelm, Scholastic (New York, NY), 2009.

Five Little Sharks Swimming in the Sea, illustrated by Laura Bryant, Scholastic (New York, NY), 2010.

I Love You All Year Long, illustrated by Claire Keay, Tiger Tales (Wilton, CT), 2010.

The Leaves Are Falling One by One, illustrated by Miriam Sagasti, Scholastic (New York, NY), 2010.

Detective Blue, illustrated by Tedd Arnold, Scholastic (New York, NY), 2011.

The Ice Cream King, illustrated by Julie Downing, Tiger Tales (Wilton, CT), 2011.
The Way I Act, illustrated by Janan Cain, Parenting Press (New York, NY), 2011.
Give Thanks for Each Day, illustrated by Robert McPhillips, Scholastic (New York, NY), 2011.
Skeleton Meets the Mummy, illustrated by Aaron Zenz, Scholastic (New York, NY), 2011.
The Dancing Clock, illustrated by John Abbott Nez, Tiger Tales (Wilton, CT), 2011.
Huggapotamus, illustrated by Gabriele Antonini, Scholastic (New York, NY), 2011.
Pluto Visits Earth!, illustrated by Jared Lee, Tiger Tales (Wilton, CT), 2012.
Will Princess Isabel Ever Say Please?, illustrated by Amanda Haley, Holiday House (New York, NY), 2012.
The Turkey Train, illustrated by Aaron Zenz, Scholastic (New York, NY), 2012.
Lincoln and Grace: Why Abraham Lincoln Grew a Beard, illustrated by Ann Kronheimer, Scholastic (New York, NY), 2012.

"DINOFOURS" PRESCHOOL SERIES; ILLUSTRATED BY HANS WILHELM

I'm Not Your Friend!, Scholastic (New York, NY), 1996.
It's Time for School!, Scholastic (New York, NY), 1996.
It's Class Trip Day, Scholastic (New York, NY), 1997.

***Miki Sakamoto created the humorous art for Metzger's story in* We're Going on a Leaf Hunt.** (Illustration copyright © 2005 by Miki Sakamoto. Reproduced by permission of Scholastic Inc.)

I'm Super Dino!, Scholastic (New York, NY), 1997.
It's Fire Drill Day!, Scholastic (New York, NY), 1997.
Where's Mommy?, Scholastic (New York, NY), 1997.
I'm Having a Bad Day!, Scholastic (New York, NY), 1998.
It's Beach Day!, Scholastic (New York, NY), 1998.
I'm the Boss!, Scholastic (New York, NY), 1998.
It's Apple Picking Day!, Scholastic (New York, NY), 1998.
It's Time-out Time!, Scholastic (New York, NY), 1998.
I'm the Winner!, Scholastic (New York, NY), 1999.
It's Halloween, Scholastic (New York, NY), 1999.
It's Thanksgiving!, Scholastic (New York, NY), 1999.
It's Snowing, Scholastic (New York, NY), 1999.
I'm So Grumpy!, Scholastic (New York, NY), 2000.
Let Me Play!, Scholastic (New York, NY), 2000.
My Seeds Won't Grow!, Scholastic (New York, NY), 2001.
We Love Bugs!, Scholastic (New York, NY), 2001.
It's Pumpkin Day!, Scholastic (New York, NY), 2001.
We Love Mud, Scholastic (New York, NY), 2002.
It's My Birthday!, Scholastic (New York, NY), 2002.
Rain! Rain! Go Away, Scholastic (New York, NY), 2002.
I'm Sorry! I'm Sorry!, Scholastic (New York, NY), 2003.
Our Holiday Show, Scholastic (New York, NY), 2003.

Author's works have been translated into Spanish.

Sidelights

Vice president and editorial director of Scholastic Press Book Clubs, Steve Metzger is also a prolific author of books for young children, and his stories include *The Great Turkey Race, Detective Blue,* and *Pluto Visits Earth.* Metzger has also teamed up with illustrator Hans Wilhelm to create the entertaining "Dinofours" preschool book series, which focus on the fun, challenges, and developmental issues of typical four year olds through its cast of young dinosaurs and their teacher, Mrs. Dee. A teacher himself for over ten years, Metzger makes a point of taking time to visit his young audiences. "I enjoy visiting schools and giving presentations where I share my stories, discuss the process of creating a picture book . . . and telling traditional folktales," he noted on his home page.

Raised in Queens, New York, Metzger earned a degree at Baruch College, but he graduated unsure of what his career might be. While working a series of odd jobs around the city, he realized that his true calling was working with children. After earning a teaching degree, he taught preschool for a decade, until a move from the classroom into the administrative sector led him to a job at Scholastic, Inc. Although he was not hired as a writer, Metzger became one after he remarked on the need for more preschool books during a staff meeting. Tapping the popularity of dinosaurs among preschool boys, he came up with the idea for "Dinofours", and the first books in the series were published in 1996. With engaging illustrations by Wilhelm, twenty-eight "Up" books were in print by the time the series came to a close in 2003.

While many of Metzger's stories are published for Scholastic's various book clubs, several have attracted the attention of reviewers, and the roster of illustrators

Metzger's quirky story in **Detective Blue** *comes to life in cartoon-style art by Tedd Arnold.* (Illustration copyright © 2011 by Tedd Arnold. Reproduced by permission of Orchard Books, an imprint of Scholastic Inc.)

who have brought these stories to life include Tedd Arnold, Joy Allen, Laura Bryant, Jill Dubin, Jim Paillot, and Jared Lee. Featuring colorful art by John Abbott Nez, *The Dancing Clock* features Metzger's rhyming story about a New York City landmark—the musical clock at the Central Park Zoo—and a young snow monkey who is captivated by it. Another story, *The Ice Cream King,* pairs a story about an imaginative ice-cream lover with artwork by Julie Downing. Writing in *School Library Journal,* Meg Smith praised Metzger's "bouncy rhyming text" for taking readers on a "feel-good journey [that] maintains its sweetness . . . without being saccharine."

Arnold creates the comic-book-style illustrations for *Detective Blue,* Metzger's story about how Little Boy Blue spent his time after growing up. Clad in traditional secret-agent attire that is blue from fedora to trench coat to wing-tip shoes, the former nursery-rhyme star now solves "nursery crimes," such as catching the Dish who ran away with the Spoon, solving the mystery of Little Miss Muffet, and tracking down Mary's little lamb. "Metzger and Arnold display a consistent wit on every page," asserted a *Publishers Weekly* contributor in a review of *Detective Blue,* and Marge Loch-Wouters remarked in *School Library Journal* that the "madcap mystery"—which draws on over twenty classic nursery rhymes—"will keep children . . . intrigued with [clues] . . . that point the detective and readers in the right direction." Metzger tells his "clever story" in "deadpan, *Dragnet*-style prose," according to *Booklist* critic Kay Weisman, and his humorous tale "will entertain anyone with knowledge of Mother Goose." A *Kirkus Reviews* critic quipped that the text of *Detective Blue* is "aided and abetted by Arnold's illustrations" featuring round-eyed characters rendered in "black outlines and translucent blocks of color."

Biographical and Critical Sources

PERIODICALS

Booklist, August 1, 2011, Kay Weisman, review of *Detective Blue,* p. 51.

Horn Book, September-October, 2011, Roger Sutton, review of *Detective Blue,* p. 72.

Kirkus Reviews, May 15, 2011, review of *Detective Blue*; August 1, 2011, review of *The Dancing Clock.*

Publishers Weekly, May 16, 2011, review of *Detective Blue,* p. 69.

School Library Journal, April, 2011, Meg Smith, review of *The Ice Cream King,* p. 150, and Meg Smith, review of *The Way I Act,* p. 162; July, 2011, Marge Loch-Wouters, review of *Detective Blue,* p. 72.

ONLINE

Steve Metzger Home Page, http://www.stevemetzgerbooks.com (May 15, 2012).

* * *

MOONEY, Melissa Duke 1968-2009

Personal

Born 1968, in Baton Rouge, LA; daughter of William Duke and Delores Blankenship; died February 18, 2009, in Nashville, TN; married Neil Mooney (a musician), 1999; children: Nola Belle, Tallulah Jane.

Career

Publicist and musician. Junket Productions, Los Angeles, CA, publicist. Vocalist for country-western band Junebug. Volunteer at elementary school and for neighborhood events in Nashville, TN.

Writings

The ABC's of Rock, illustrated by Print Mafia, Tricycle Press (Berkeley, CA), 2010.

Biographical and Critical Sources

PERIODICALS

Kirkus Reviews, October 1, 2010, review of *The ABC's of Rock.*

Publishers Weekly, October 18, 2010, review of *The ABC's of Rock,* p. 42.

ONLINE

Nashville Scene Online, http://www.nashvillescene.com/ (October 14, 2010), "Melissa Duke Mooney Couldn't Find a Rock 'n' Roll Alphabet Book for Kids, So She Made One Herself."*

* * *

MORALES, Yuyi 1968-

Personal

Born 1968, in Xalapa, Veracruz, Mexico; immigrated to United States, 1994; married; husband's name Tim; children: Kelly (son). *Education:* University of Xalapa, B.A.; graduate study in creative writing.

Addresses

Home—San Francisco, CA. *E-mail*—yuyi@yuyimorales.com.

Career

Children's writer and illustrator. Swimming coach in Mexico; KPOO Radio, San Francisco, CA, host of children's radio show, 1997-2000.

Yuyi Morales (Photograph by Tim O'Meara. Reproduced by permission.)

Awards, Honors

Don Freeman Memorial grant-in-aid, Society of Children's Book Writers and Illustrators, 2000; Américas Award for Children's and Young-Adult Literature, Consortium of Latin American Studies Programs, Parent's Choice Award, Northern California Book Award nomination, Best of the Best selection, Chicago Public Library, and Best Children's Books of the Year selection, Bank Street College of Education, all 2003, Pura Belpré Illustrator Award, and Notable Books for Children selection, both American Library Association (ALA), California Book Award Silver Medal for juvenile fiction, Tomás Rivera Mexican-American Children's Book Award, Golden Kite Honor Book selection, Latino Book Award, Latino Literary Award for Best Children's Book, Cooperative Children's Book Center (CCBC) Choices selection, and Notable Books for a Global Society selection, International Reading Association, all 2004, all for *Just a Minute;* Américas Award honorable mention, *San Francisco Chronicle* Best of Year selection, and Lasting Connections selection, all 2003, and Christopher Award, Jane Addams Children's Book Award, Pura Belpré Illustrator Award, ALA Notable Children's Book designation, CCBC Choices selection, and Notable Social Studies Trade Books for Young People designation, National Council for Social Studies, all 2004, all for *Harvesting Hope* by Kathleen Krull; Golden Kite Award, 2007, and ALA Notable Children's Book selection, 2008, both for *Little Night;* Notable Children's Book designation and Pura Belpré Illustrator Award, both 2008, both for *Los Gatos Black on Halloween* by Marisa Montes; Américas Award for Children's and Young-Adult Literature, 2008, and ALA Notable Children's Book designation, and Pura Belpré Illustrator Award, both 2009, all for *Just in Case;* ALA Notable Children's Book designation, 2009, for *My Abuelita* by Tony Johnston.

Writings

SELF-ILLUSTRATED

Just a Minute: A Trickster Tale and Counting Book, Chronicle Books (San Francisco, CA), 2003.

Little Night, Roaring Brook Press (New Milford, CT), 2006.

Just in Case: A Trickster Tale and Spanish Alphabet Book, Roaring Brook Press (New York, NY), 2008.

ILLUSTRATOR

F. Isabel Campoy, *Todas las buenas manos,* Harcourt (San Diego, CA), 2002.

Kathleen Krull, *Harvesting Hope: The Story of Cesar Chavez,* Harcourt (San Diego, CA), 2003.

Amanda White, *Sand Sister,* Barefoot Books (Cambridge, MA), 2004.

Marisa Montes, *Los Gatos Black on Halloween,* Holt (New York, NY), 2006.

Tony Johnston, *My Abuelita,* Harcourt (Boston, MA), 2009.

Laura Lacámara, *Floating on Mama's Song/Flotando con la canción de mamá,* Katherine Tegen Books (New York, NY), 2010.

Maya Soetoro-Ng, *Ladder to the Moon,* Candlewick Press (Somerville, MA), 2011.

Amy Novesky, *Georgia in Hawai'i: When Georgia O'Keeffe Painted What She Pleased,* Houghton Mifflin Harcourt (Boston, MA), 2012.

Adaptations

Just a Minute was adapted for DVD, Nutmeg, 2007. *Los Gatos Black on Halloween* was adapted for DVD, Weston Woods, 2009.

Sidelights

A four-time recipient of the Pura Belpré Illustrator Award, Yuyi Morales celebrates Latino culture in such highly regarded works as *Little Night* and *Just in Case: A Trickster Tale and Spanish Alphabet Book.* Noted for her bright, child-friendly art, Morales has also provided the illustrations for books by Marisa Montes, Tony Johnston, and Laura Lacámara, among other writers. Often working with bilingual texts, the artist stated in a *Worlds of Words* online interview with Jeanne Fain and Julia López-Robertson that "I can declare that both English and Spanish are powerful and inspiring elements of the creation of my art, and I will make use of them as they beautifully serve their own purpose in the telling of stories."

Morales was born in Xalapa, Mexico, the eldest of four children. As a child she loved drawing, and she often paired her pictures with stories. Although her father recognized her talent for drawing, he encouraged her to follow a career in architecture. Instead, she drew on her skill as a competitive swimmer and majored in physical education at the University of Xalapa, working as a swimming coach for two years following graduation.

While coaching, Morales met her future husband, Tim, an American, got married, and had a son, Kelly. Following a move to California, Morales was challenged by her minimal understanding of English. The collection of children's books at her local library rekindled her love of bookmaking, and she began creating handmade picture books for Kelly. Learning to read English along with her son, she used picture-book illustrations to decipher the simple texts. Writers' and illustrators' conferences helped Morales learn the skills of the trade, and a meeting with author F. Isabel Campoy resulted in an offer to illustrate Campoy's book, *Todas las buenas manos.*

***Morales's self-illustrated picture books include the engaging* Just a Minute: A Trickster Tale and Counting Book.** (Illustration copyright © 2003 by Maria de Lourdes Morales O'Meara. Used with permission of Chronicle Books LLC, San Francisco. Visit ChronicleBooks.com.)

Morales's first English-language picture-book project was Kathleen Krull's text for *Harvesting Hope: The Story of Cesar Chavez.* Chavez, a labor organizer who worked on behalf of California's migrant farm workers, made gains in the mid-1960s by organizing boycotts and strikes that ultimately improved working conditions and pay rates for farm workers. Reviewing Morales's work for the volume, *School Library Journal* contributor Sue Morgan praised her "beautifully rendered earth-tone illustrations," while Traci Todd, writing in *Booklist,* cited the book's "gorgeous paintings, with their rounded, organic forms and lush, gemstone hues." *Horn Book* contributor Susan Dove Lempke noted that the illustrator "suffused" her acrylic paintings "with a variety of emotions, especially fear and sorrow," while a *Kirkus Reviews* critic compared Morales's artwork to that of noted twentieth-century Mexican muralist Diego Rivera.

Morales's first self-illustrated title, *Just a Minute,* was published in 2003. In the book, an old woman is summoned by Death to the afterlife. Death, a skeleton who calls himself Señor Calavera, arrives at Grandma Beetle's door and requests that she come with him. Although the old woman agrees, she has one small task to complete, then another, and then another, leaving Death increasingly impatient and frustrated. The reason for all the woman's work is soon revealed: Grandma Beetle's nine children are on their way to her house to celebrate her birthday. After the party, the woman prepares to go, but Señor Calavera has enjoyed himself so much during the festivities that he decides not to take her right now; instead, he leaves her a note saying that he is looking forward to coming to her next birthday party. "Morales's personification of death is never forbidding or scary," Catherine Threadgill commented in the *School Library Journal,* while a *Publishers Weekly* critic wrote that Death's "ghoulish, goofy gallantry would make him the comic lead of any Day of the Dead festivity."

Señor Calavera makes a return appearance in *Just in Case.* After the skeleton secures an invitation to Grandma Beetle's birthday party, Zelmiro the Ghost reminds him that he needs to bring an appropriate gift. With the spirit's help, Calavera gathers a variety of items, from *una acordeon* (an accordion) to satisfy her musical cravings to *una yerba buena* (a soothing herb). Although Calavera overloads his bicycle basket with presents, which are ruined when they spill onto the ground, he still manages to make Grandma's birthday a memorable one. "Part ghost story and part alphabet book, this trickster tale transcends both," Mary Jean Smith noted in *School Library Journal.* "Drenched in rich hues, the light-filled illustrations add a whimsical dimension" to the work, remarked *Booklist* critic Patricia Austin, and Joanna Rudge Long observed in *Horn Book* that Morales's artwork, "in brilliant sunset hues, portrays an amiable, dreamlike world where weightless, comfortably rounded figures swirl joyously among the creative assemblage of gifts."

In *Little Night* Morales celebrates the special bonds between children and their mothers. In her self-illustrated story Little Night hides from Mother Sky and readers follow the mother's search for her child across dusky hills and in dark caves. Ultimately, Little Night is discovered and must bathe in falling stars, pin glowing planets in her hair, and have a bedtime glass of milk from the Milky Way before playing games with the moon at bedtime. Noting the book's "mystical effect," a *Kirkus Reviews* writer dubbed *Little Night* "lovely" while Randall Enos wrote in *Booklist* that Morales presents readers with "a sumptuous feast of metaphors," both in her serene text and "equally splendid illustrations." "Creating what amounts to a new myth may seem an ambitious project," noted a *Publishers Weekly* reviewer in appraising *Little Night,* "but Morales succeeds by combining intimacy and grandeur."

In addition to her self-illustrated books, Morales takes on illustration duties for Amanda White's *Sand Sister* and *Los Gatos Black on Halloween,* the latter a holiday-themed picture book with an English/Spanish text by Marisa Montes. *Sand Sister* finds a shy child wishing for a playmate at the beach while other children play with their brothers and sisters. When the lonely girl finds a stick and draws a picture of a playmate in the wet sand, her drawing magically comes alive. The two play together for the rest of the day, but when the tide turns the "sand sister" must leave and go back to the sea. Moving from the sunlit seashore to a shadow-filled haunted house, *Los Gatos Black on Halloween* invites

***Morales's illustration projects include creating the art for Tony Johnston's story in* My Abuelita.** (Illustration © 2009 by Yuyi Morales. Reproduced by permission of Houghton Mifflin Harcourt Publishing Company. All rights reserved.)

readers to join a Halloween party where witches, skeletons, vampires, and black cats join in the scary fun. Reviewing *Sand Sister* for *Booklist,* Jennifer Mattson noted that Morales's "sun-drenched paintings," are filled with "vigor and fantastical sensibility," while her illustrations for *Los Gatos Black on Halloween* make the book "an atmospheric, bilingual romp" according to a *Publishers Weekly* contributor. Noting that the frightening creatures depicted in the illustrations might be too scary for smaller readers, Ilene Cooper wrote in *Booklist* that Morales's "soft-edged paintings glow with the luminosity of jewels." The illustrator's "dark, glowing pictures of inventively proportioned ghosts and other sinister night creatures provide the ideal accompaniment" for Montes' tale, concluded a *Kirkus Reviews* critic.

Morales employs puppet-like, clay polymer figures to illustrate *My Abuelita,* a story by Tony Johnston that focuses on the loving relationship between a young boy and his grandmother. Shelle Rosenfeld, writing in *Booklist,* applauded "the eye-catching, mixed-media illustrations, sparked with bright patterns, textures, and color," and a contributor in *Publishers Weekly* commented that Morales's "vignettes seamlessly knit together realism and fantasy, giving every spread a dreamy physicality."

A bilingual tale by Laura Lacámara, *Floating on Mama's song/Flotando con la canción de mamá* centers on a girl's efforts to help her mother recover a special type of magic. According to a *Kirkus Reviews* critic, "Morales's lyrical illustrations, done in a warm, soothing palette, work well with the dual-language text," and Angelica Sauceda maintained in *School Library Journal* that the book's brightly colored collage illustrations "will help children's imaginations take flight."

Ladder to the Moon, a mystical story of healing and peace by Maya Soetoro-Ng, also features the artist's "lovely, folk-art-style illustrations," according to a *Kirkus Reviews* writer. "It's hard to imagine a more perfect illustrator for this text than Morales, whose rounded shapes, sunset colors, and softness . . . mirror the words," Ilene Cooper explained in *Booklist.*

Speaking with *PaperTigers* online interviewer Aline Pereira, Morales maintained that "books are like magic crystal balls. Looking inside them, I have seen my past, my present, and my future. When I open a book, there! There! I see myself. In books I have discovered what I love and what I hate, what makes me powerful and what makes me weak, what I want to be and, even more importantly, what I don't want to be. And anybody else can do that too."

***Morales' stylized art captures the whimsy in Laura Lacámara's bilingual story for* Floating on Mama's Song.** (Illustration copyright © 2010 by Yuyi Morales. Reproduced by permission of Katherine Tegen Books, an imprint of HarperCollins Publishers.)

Biographical and Critical Sources

PERIODICALS

Booklist, June 1, 2003, Traci Todd, review of *Harvesting Hope: The Story of Cesar Chavez,* p. 1795; December 1, 2003, Jennifer Mattson, review of *Just a Minute: A Trickster Tale and Counting Book,* p. 668; March 15, 2004, Jennifer Mattson, review of *Sand Sister,* p. 1311; February 1, 2007, Randall Enos, review of *Little Night,* p. 46; March 1, 2008, Lucinda Whitehurst, review of *Just a Minute,* p. 75; September 15, 2008, Patricia Austin, review of *Just in Case: A Trickster Tale and Spanish Alphabet Book,* p. 57; August 1, 2009, Shelle Rosaenfeld, review of *My Abuelita,* p. 80; August 1, 2010, Karen Cruze, review of *Floating on Mama's song/Flotando con la canción de mamá,* p. 59; March 1, 2011, Ilene Cooper, review of *Ladder to the Moon,* p. 48.

Horn Book, July-August, 2003, Susan Dove Lempke, review of *Harvesting Hope,* p. 480; January-February, 2009, Joanna Rudge Long, review of *Just in Case,* p. 81.

Kirkus Reviews, July 1, 2003, review of *Harvesting Hope,* p. 911; October 15, 2003, review of *Just a Minute,* p. 1274; August 15, 2006, review of *Los Gatos Black on Halloween,* p. 848; April 1, 2007, review of *Little Night;* September, 2008, Mary Jean Smith, review of *Just in Case,* p. 155; August 1, 2009, review of *My Abuelita*; August 15, 2010, review of *Floating on Mama's Song*; March 1, 2011, review of *Ladder to the Moon.*

Publishers Weekly, May 5, 2003, review of *Harvesting Hope,* p. 221; December 1, 2003, review of *Just a*

Minute, p. 55; August 14, 2006, review of *Los Gatos Black on Halloween,* p. 204; March 26, 2007, review of *Little Night,* p. 93; August 31, 2009, review of *My Abuelita,* p. 55; February 21, 2011, review of *Ladder to the Moon,* p. 130.

School Library Journal, June, 2003, Sue Morgan, review of *Harvesting Hope,* p. 129; December, 2003, Catherine Threadgill, review of *Just a Minute,* p. 136; October, 2004, Maryann H. Owen, review of *Sand Sister,* p. 136; July, 2005, Coop Renner, review of *Just a Minute,* p. 44; September, 2006, Joy Fleishhacker, review of *Los Gatos Black on Halloween,* p. 180; May, 2007, DoAnn Okamura, review of *Little Night,* p. 106; August, 2009, Mary Landrum, review of *My Abuelita,* p. 78; September, 2010, Angelica Sauceda, review of *Floating on Mama's Song,* p. 144; April, 2011, Marianne Saccardi, review of *Ladder to the Moon,* p. 154.

ONLINE

Cynsations Web log, http://cynthialeitichsmith.blogspot.com/ (September 7, 2006), Cynthia Leitich Smith, interview with Morales.

PaperTigers.org, http://www.papertigers.org/ (October, 2005), Aline Pereira, interview with Morales.

Society of Children's Book Writers and Illustrators Web site, http://www.scbwi.org/ (June 10, 2007), "Yuyi Morales."

Worlds of Words Web log, http://wowlit.org/blog/ (February 1, 2010), Jeanne Fain and Julia López-Robertson, interview with Morales.

Yuyi Morales Home Page, http://www.yuyimorales.com (May 1, 2012).

Yuyi Morales Web log, http://yuyimorales.blogspot.com/ (May 1, 2012).

N

NEWBOUND, Andrew 1969-

Personal

Born 1969, in Yorkshire, England; children. *Education:* Attended college. *Hobbies and other interests:* Visiting the seaside.

Addresses

Home—Yorkshire, England.

Career

Author. Worked variously as a journalist, debt collector, salesman, private investigator, rock-band manager, and advertising copywriter. Presenter at schools.

Writings

Ghoul Strike!, Chicken House/Scholastic (New York, NY), published as *Demon Strike!,* Chicken House (London, England), 2010.

Author of *I Spy, Sport S.P.I.E.S.: Not So United,* 2011, and *Space A.C.E.S.: Grakk Attack!!!,* 2012. Author of *Vampire's Nemesis* (e-book; first volume of "Elven Chronicles" series), 2012.

Sidelights

Working as a writer is just one aspect of Andrew Newbound's long and varied career. Raised in Yorkshire, England, Newbound dreamed of becoming a private investigator but studied journalism in college and then left school to work a succession of jobs that included debt collector, rock-band manager, and a stint writing copy for an advertising agency. His first book for children, the middle-grade novel *Demon Strike!,* was released to U.S. readers under the title *Ghoul Strike!* and is only one of the ways he has found to help encourage the reading habit. As a frequent guest at schools and libraries in his native England, Newbound morphs into the "Word Wizard." His Word Wizard Loving Literacy program introduces children to the fascinating history of the English language as well as the amazing variety of underutilized vocabulary waiting to be mined from the pages of the average dictionary.

Cover of Andrew Newbound's middle-grade adventure novel* Ghoul Strike!, *featuring artwork by Martin Simpson. (Cover art copyright © 2010 by Martin Simpson. Reproduced by permission of Scholastic, Inc.)

In *Ghoul Strike!* Newbound introduces Alannah Malarra, a twelve-year-old psychic who was destined to add "ghost hunter" to her resumé after her ghostbusting parents disappeared three years ago. Teaming up with eleven-year-old housebreaker Worley Flint, Alannah now runs the family business, funding her operation by contractually laying claim to any treasure discovered during the de-ghosting process. The preteen finds herself on the front line of a supernatural battle when she learns that villainous Gnarl Krot is leading demonic beings from the Dark Dimension to nearby Pittingham Manor with the goal of invading the human world. Fortunately, several agents of the Attack-ready Network of Global Evanescent Law-Enforcers (ANGEL) are on the ready, and soon Alannah and Worley are standing shoulder to shoulder with Inspector Flhi Swift and his loyal officers Yell and Gloom.

Ghoul Strike! "effectively" establishes the setting for Newbound's proposed novel series, according to a *Kirkus Reviews* writer, and Alannah's adventures "keep . . . the pages turning with laughs and suspense." Although the *Kirkus Reviews* critic found the "avarice" of Newbound's story's heroine to be "a bit alarming," *School Library Journal* contributor Julie G. Shatterly dubbed Alannah "a great female hero." Newbound's "descriptions of the [story's] various creatures are detailed and entertaining," Shatterly added, recommending *Ghoul Strike!* to fans of Eoin Colfer's "Artemis Fowl" series.

Biographical and Critical Sources

PERIODICALS

Booklist, October 15, 2010, Todd Morning, review of *Ghoul Strike!,* p. 64.
Kirkus Reviews, October 1, 2010, review of *Ghoul Strike!*
School Library Journal, January, 2011, Julie G. Shatterly, review of *Ghoul Strike!,* p. 113.

ONLINE

Andrew Newbound Home Page, http://www.andrewnewbound.com (May 1, 2012).
Go Away Ghosts Web site, http://www.goawayghosts.com/ (May 1, 2012).
KidsReadsWeb site, http://www.kidsreads.com/ (October, 2010), interview with Newbound.*

* * *

NOLAN, Han 1956-

Personal

Born August 25, 1956, in Birmingham, AL; married September 12, 1981; children: three (adopted). *Education:* University of North Carolina at Greensboro, B.S. (dance), 1979; Ohio State University, M.S. (dance), 1981. *Hobbies and other interests:* Traveling, hiking, running, swimming, attending plays and concerts.

Addresses

E-mail—han@hannolan.com.

Career

Writer. Teacher of dance, 1981-84. Hollins University, Roanoke, VA, writer in residence, 2002, visiting associate professor, 2004-05.

Member

Society of Children's Book Writers and Illustrators, Author's Guild.

Awards, Honors

International Reading Association (IRA)/Children's Book Council (CBC) Young Adults' Choice selection, 1994, for *If I Should Die before I Wake;* Books for the Teen Age selection, New York Public Library, 1994, for *If I Should Die before I Wake,* 1996, for *Send Me down a Miracle,* 1997, for *Dancing on the Edge,* 1999, for *A Face in Every Window,* 2001, for *Born Blue,* 2003, for *When We Were Saints,* 2006, for *A Summer of Kings;* People's Choice Award, Parent's Choice Book Award, and National Book Award finalist, all 1996, all for *Send Me down a Miracle;* National Book Award, 1997, and YALSA Best Books for Young Adults, American Library Association (ALA), 1998, both for *Dancing on the Edge;* Eliot Rosewater Award nomination, 1999, for *A Face in Every Window;* YALSA Best Books for Young Adults selection, and IRA/CBC Young Adults' Choice selection, both 2002, both for *Born Blue.*

Writings

If I Should Die before I Wake, Harcourt (San Diego, CA), 1994.
Send Me down a Miracle, Harcourt (San Diego, CA), 1996.
Dancing on the Edge, Harcourt (San Diego, CA), 1997.
A Face in Every Window, Harcourt (San Diego, CA), 1999.
Born Blue, Harcourt (San Diego, CA), 2001.
When We Were Saints, Harcourt (San Diego, CA), 2003.
A Summer of Kings, Harcourt (Orlando, FL), 2006.
Crazy, Harcourt (Boston, MA), 2010.
Pregnant Pause, Harcourt (Boston, MA), 2011.

Contributor of fiction to anthology *Don't Cramp My Style: Stories about That Time of the Month,* edited by Lisa Rowe Fraustino, Simon & Schuster Books for Young Readers (New York, NY), 2004.

Sidelights

In her novels for young adults, Han Nolan speaks directly to readers in a voice at once empathic and down-home humorous. Within her stories, which include *Born*

Han Nolan (Photograph by Brian Nolan. Reproduced by permission.)

Blue, Dancing on the Edge, When We Were Saints, A Summer of Kings, and *Crazy,* Nolan weaves themes of tolerance and understanding, and her youthful protagonists gain a crucial understanding of who they are and what they want from their lives. Her stories have dealt with neo-Nazis, religious zealotry, and the lies that families promulgate to supposedly protect their members. Her characters are young men and women emerging from shaky adolescence to an uncertain adulthood. In the course of the challenges Nolan puts before them they learn to stand up for themselves—to throw off the influences of adults and peers and find their own center in a turbulent universe. "I'm always searching for the truth in my stories," the author commented in an interview on the Harcourt Books Web site. "That truth has led me to the characters that I have created."

One of five children, Nolan moved with her family several times during her childhood, but a constant was a shared love of books and the arts. "One of my favorite books as a child was *Harriet the Spy,*" the author recalled on her home page. "I wanted to be a spy, so I started spying on my family, especially my older sister. It turned out I was a terrible spy because I kept getting caught, but I kept a spy notebook, just like Harriet. I quickly gave up on the spying, but writing thoughts and stories in a notebook has been a habit for me ever since."

After graduating from high school, Nolan studied dance at the University of North Carolina at Greensboro, and she subsequently completed a master's program in dance at Ohio State University. It was there that she met her future husband, who was working on his doctorate in the classics. In 1981 she graduated, married, and began teaching dance. Several years later, the shared decision to start a family prompted Nolan to make a career change. "I decided to return to my first love, writing," she noted on her home page. "Soon after that we adopted three children and I knew for sure that staying home and writing instead of dancing was the best decision for me."

Thus began Nolan's literary career. She studied not only markets, but every book on writing technique that she could get her hands on. She wrote stories and sent some out with no success. Then she tackled lengthier projects, writing a mystery that won some attention with a publisher but was not purchased. Nonetheless, there was encouragement in the fact that an editor had taken an interest in her work. She joined or formed writers' groups wherever she happened to be living. She began another mystery, but one of the characters was stubbornly going off on her own, dreaming about the Holocaust.

The discovery that a Ku Klux Klan group was active in a neighboring town and that hate crimes were being reported inspired Nolan's debut novel *If I Should Die before I Wake.* As the story begins, gentile Hilary Burke is lying in a coma in a Jewish hospital, the result of a motorcycle accident. Hilary's family has a history: her father died years before, presumably at the hand of a Jew, and her Bible-thumping mother temporarily abandoned her. Hilary has subce found a replacement family in the neo-Nazi group led by her current boyfriend. While in a coma state, she sees a fellow patient, an elderly Jewish Holocaust survivor named Chana, enter her room in her mind. Propelled back in time to World War II Europe, Hilary experiences Chana's life as a young Polish Jew. Her father is shot just before the family is forced to abandon their home and find a place to live in the Warsaw ghetto. Successful in their effort to escape from the ghetto, Hilary/Chana and her grandmother are eventually captured, tortured, and sent to Auschwitz-Birkenau.

Roger Sutton, reviewing *If I Should Die before I Wake* for the *Bulletin of the Center for Children's Books,* commented that Nolan is forthright in dealing with her material, "and her graphic descriptions of camp life have a morbid interest . . . but come . . . down on the side of the truth." *Booklist* critic Mary Harris Veeder stated that Nolan's debut novel "has great strengths," although the time-travel episodes and certain contemporary characterizations are problematic. "Chana's story, however, is brilliantly rendered," Veeder added, and it "carries memorable emotional impact." A *Kirkus Reviews* critic described *If I Should Die before I Wake* as "ambitious indeed," concluding that "the book as a whole is deeply felt and often compelling."

Nolan taps her family's Southern roots in *Send Me down a Miracle*, which follows the fortunes of fourteen-year-

old Charity Pittman as she battles for a sense of self in her insular hometown. Now that her mother has abandoned the family, Charity feels trapped at home with her younger sister Grace and her preacher father. Rebelling against her father's strict interpretation of Christianity, Charity is attracted to the cosmopolitan Adrienne Dabney, a teen who has returned to town from New York City with the intention of attempting a deprivation experiment. For three weeks Adrienne locks herself away in her inherited home, without visitors, light, or food. Emerging after twenty-one days, she claims that Jesus visited her and spent time sitting across from her in a chair in her living room. This proclamation splits the small town asunder: Charity and many others believe the chair has miraculous powers while Charity's father labels Adrienne both a blasphemer and evil incarnate. Caught between the father whom she loves and Adrienne, who she views as both a friend and a fellow artist, Charity must finally learn to make up her own mind.

In her *School Library Journal* review of *Send Me down a Miracle,* Jana R. Fine noted that Nolan explores the "heart of a young girl" who learns to meld her religious background with compassion and forgiveness. A critic in *Kirkus Reviews* described the novel as a "busy, hilarious, tragic story" in which "readers will be dizzied by the multiple subplots and roller-coaster highs and lows." In *Booklist* Ilene Cooper praised the author's storytelling as "intricate, sharp, and invigorating," and the 1996 National Book Award jury agreed, nominating *Send Me down a Miracle* for its prestigious award.

While *Send Me down a Miracle* was honored with a nomination, *Dancing on the Edge* earned Nolan the National Book Award. The story's ten-year-old protagonist, Miracle McCloy, was so named because she was delivered after her birth mother died in an accident. Although her maternal grandmother Gigi calls her "the greatest miracle to ever come down the pike," Miracle feels like a misfit in a family of misfits: Her father, Dane, was once a child prodigy but now spends his days shuffling around the basement in his bathrobe, and Gigi spends her time immersed in the occult. When Dane disappears, the older woman takes Miracle to live with Opal, Gigi's ex-husband, and the gruff grandfather provides stability by buying her a bicycle and enrolling her in dancing lessons. Dance becomes a temporary salvation for Miracle, but problems arise when she takes up her grandmother's occult hobby and begins casting spells and making love potions for classmates. A desperate cry for attention results in her commitment to a mental hospital, where she slowly comes to terms with the facts of her life.

"Nolan skillfully discloses" the nature of her cast of offbeat characters, a *Kirkus Reviews* critic noted in a review of *Send Me down a Miracle,* the critic calling the novel both "intense" and "exceptionally well-written." Miriam Lang Budin, writing in *School Library Journal,* dubbed the same work "extraordinary" and concluded that "Nolan does a masterful job of drawing readers into the girl's mind and making them care deeply about her chances for the future."

Described by a *Publishers Weekly* critic as a "sometimes outlandish, often poignant exploration of a chaotic household," *A Face in Every Window* is narrated by teenager JP O'Brien, who cares for his mentally ill father and his emotionally fragile mom. Determined to give her family a fresh start, JP's mother moves them to a ramshackle farmhouse which she won in an essay contest. The dwelling is soon filled with an odd collection of musicians, artists, and misfits that Mam has invited into her home, fulfilling her dream of being welcomed by "a face at every window." Although JP is disturbed by the situation and withdraws into his room, he eventually comes to know the strangers as individuals and begins to accept them as his new "family."

"Only a writer as talented as Nolan could make this improbable story line and bizarre cast of characters not only believable but also ultimately uplifting, intriguing, and memorable," noted *Booklist* contributor Frances Bradburn in a review of *A Face in Every Window.* According to a reviewer for *Publishers Weekly,* the novel "delivers a profound and heartwarming message about the various manifestations of love."

Cover of Nolan's novel* Born Blue, *in which a girl moves through several foster families before finding comfort in singing the blues music she heard as a child. (Reproduced by permission of Houghton Mifflin Harcourt Publishing Company.)

Janie, the abused daughter of a heroin-addicted mother, is the central character in *Born Blue.* Living in a foster home, Janie builds a friendship with African-American foster brother Harmon, who loves soulful blues singers such as Etta James and Billie Holiday. Janie's fascination with black culture grows so strong that she changes her name to Leshaya. Meanwhile, her biological mother remains a disruptive presence, at one point kidnaping the girl and selling her to a drug dealer. Although Janie finds solace in drugs and alcohol and relationships with men, her magnificent singing voice gives her a path to salvation, allowing her to join a blues band and sparking the romantic interest of a gifted songwriter.

Born Blue "is raw, rough, and riveting," stated Alison Follos in *School Library Journal.* "The writing is superb; like the blues, it bores down through the soul, probing at unpleasant truths and wringing out compassion." According to a reviewer in *Publishers Weekly,* while readers "gain . . . an understanding of the tragic heroine's fears, desires and warped perception of family, . . . Janie herself remains hauntingly elusive, adding to the impact of the book." Gillian Engberg, writing in *Booklist,* stated that, "with themes of race, talent, family, love, control, and responsibility, the novel asks essential questions about how to reclaim oneself and build a life."

In *When We Were Saints* southern farm boy Archie Caswell believes himself to be a saint after his grandfather declares the fourteen year old to be so while on his deathbed. Archie interprets the dying man's words literally after meeting beautiful, charismatic newcomer Claire, whose strange religious rituals both intrigue and confuse him. When Claire convinces Archie that God has called them to undertake a pilgrimage to the Cloisters Museum in New York City, he steals his grandfather's truck to make the journey north. "Nolan's novel of spiritual exploration is both exceptionally grounded and refreshingly open," remarked *Horn Book* contributor Lauren Adams, and *School Library Journal* reviewer Joel Shoemaker described *When We Were Saints* as "powerfully written" and "outstanding in terms of the intensity of the experience described." A *Publishers Weekly* critic praised Nolan's skillful portrayal of Archie while adding that Clare's character "is what keeps the pages turning; audience members are left to ponder whether she is truly a Christ figure or an emotionally disturbed teen bent on self-destruction."

Set during the summer of 1963, *A Summer of Kings* finds fourteen-year-old Esther Young feeling ignored and unhappy. Growing up in a posh New York City suburb in affluence, Esther has not discovered a creative talent that will make her blossom within her artistic family. When eighteen-year-old runaway King-Roy is given refuge by her parents for the summer, she gravitates to him as a way to gain attention. King-Roy is one step ahead of a murder charge: he is black and he is accused of killing a white man in Alabama. As friendship grows between the two, Esther shares King-Roy's exposure to the violent teachings of Malcolm X as the only way to achieve racial equality, a stark contrast to the philosophy of the Reverend Martin Luther King, Jr. As the young man's fear, anger, and frustration are tapped, Esther realizes the power that frustration has had in forming her own life and vows to make changes.

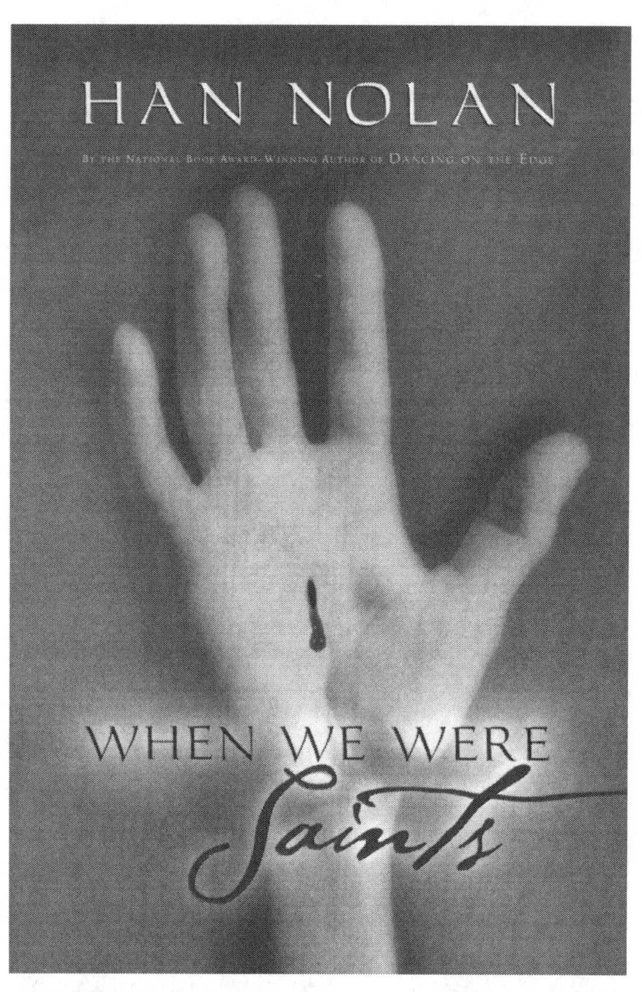

Cover of Nolan's novel* We Were Saints, *in which a teen saddened by several losses finds solace in a friend's belief that the two are saints destined for spiritual greatness. (Copyright © 2003. Reproduced by permission of Houghton Mifflin Harcourt Publishing Company. All rights reserved.)

Calling *A Summer of Kings* an "intimate story" that also presents readers with an "introduction to the civil rights movement," a *Publishers Weekly* critic praised Nolan for creating "a convincing, admirable heroine" in Esther. "Brilliantly portrayed," according to a *Kirkus Reviews* writer, the novel's diverse characters bring to life "the gut-wrenching history of the time, making tangible the sorrow and hurt that is always personal." *A Summer of Kings* achieves a "powerful mix of triumph and tragedy," concluded John Peters in his *School Library Journal* appraisal, and it "also displays Nolan's brilliant gift for crafting profoundly appealing protagonists."

For Jason Papadopoulos, the central character in *Crazy,* adult responsibilities are too weighty to handle. Now that his mother is dead, the fifteen year old is the sole caretaker of his mentally ill father, a man whose condition is deteriorating. As a way of coping with the unfolding emotional and economic tragedy that is his life,

Jason has created several imaginary friends to witness and provide perspective on his situation. Among them are sympathetic aunt, a sexy woman, a portly, balding middle-aged man, and a sarcastic voice called Crazy Glue that leavens the teen's sense of deepening tragedy with humor. As readers watch Jason skirt the edges of his own madness, they also witness his resolve to keep things together and ultimately discern the point where he must look for help in the real world. In framing her story as a dialogue between the boy and his internal voices, Nolan "draws readers inside the psyche of a troubled teenager to experience the chaos, panic and isolation he feels," according to a *Publishers Weekly* critic. A *Kirkus Reviews* critic noted the "distinct and effective blend of sorrow and humor" that is woven into the author's first-person narrative. With "spot-on humor and a well-developed cast of characters," *Crazy* reveals "with moving clarity the emotional costs of mental illness," Cindy Dobrez concluded in her *Booklist* review.

Teen motherhood is Nolan's focus in *Pregnant Pause.* The fact that her parents are Christian missionaries makes the pregnancy of sixteen-year-old Elly Crowe that much more fraught with emotion, and she reacts to their anger by stubbornly marrying Lam, the young man who fathered her child. Lam's parents, less rigid in their beliefs, allow the newlyweds to live at their summer camp for overweight children. Working with the pudgy young campers while awaiting her baby, Elly is able to lose her defensiveness and take stock of her situation, gaining a sense of her own abilities as well as assessing the shortcomings of a young man she once thought she loved. "Elly is passionate, smart-mouthed, rebellious and completely endearing," asserted a *Kirkus Reviews* writer, the critic adding that in *Pregnant Pause* "Nolan proves once again that she can take a familiar story to surprising new heights." The teen's growing maturity in untangling her life "makes for not only a strong story but a subtle object lesson as well," according to *Booklist* contributor Frances Bradburn, while in *School Library Journal* Allison Tran dubbed *Pregnant Pause* "an uplifting page-turner with a great deal of heart."

Biographical and Critical Sources

BOOKS

St. James Guide to Young-Adult Writers, 2nd edition, St. James Press (Detroit, MI), 1999.

PERIODICALS

Booklist, April 1, 1994, Mary Harris Veeder, review of *If I Should Die before I Wake,* p. 1436; March 15, 1996, Ilene Cooper, review of *Send Me down a Miracle,* p. 1263; October 1, 1997, Ilene Cooper, review of *Dancing on the Edge,* p. 331; November 1, 1999, Frances Bradburn, review of *A Face in Every Window,* p. 525; May 1, 2001, Stephanie Zvirin, review of *Send Me Down a Miracle,* p. 1611; September 15, 2001, Gillian Engberg, review of *Born Blue,* p. 217; October 1, 2003, Ilene Cooper, review of *When We Were Saints,* p. 330; August 1, 2010, Cindy Dobrez, review of *Crazy,* p. 54; August 1, 2011, Frances Bradburn, review of *Pregnant Pause,* p. 48.

Bulletin of the Center for Children's Books, April, 1994, Roger Sutton, review of *If I Should Die before I Wake,* pp. 267-268.

Horn Book, January-February, 2002, Lauren Adams, review of *Born Blue,* pp. 82-83; January-February, 2004, Lauren Adams, review of *When We Were Saints,* p. 87; November-December, 2010, Jennifer M. Brabander, review of *Crazy,* p. 100.

Kirkus Reviews, March 1, 1994, review of *If I Should Die before I Wake,* p. 308; March 15, 1996, review of *Send Me down a Miracle,* p. 451; August 1, 1997, review of *Dancing on the Edge,* p. 1227; October 1, 2003, review of *When We Were Saints,* p. 1228; March 15, 2006, review of *A Summer of Kings,* p. 297; August 15, 2010, review of *Crazy.*

Kliatt, July, 2003, Claire Rosser, review of *Born Blue,* pp. 24-25; September, 2003, Claire Rosser, review of *When We Were Saints,* pp. 9-10; March 15, 2006, review of *A Summer of Kings,* p. 297; August 1, 2011, review of *Pregnant Pause.*

Publishers Weekly, November 1, 1999, review of *A Face in Every Window,* p. 85; October 8, 2001, review of *Born Blue,* p. 66; October 20, 2003, *When We Were Saints,* p. 55; March 27, 2006, review of *A Summer of Kings,* p. 80; September 13, 2010, review of *Crazy,* p. 46; July 4, 2011, review of *Pregnant Pause,* p. 67.

School Library Journal, April, 1996, Jana R. Fine, review of *Send Me down a Miracle,* p. 157; September, 1997, Miriam Lang Budin, review of *Dancing on the Edge,* p. 223; November, 2001, Alison Follos, review of *Born Blue,* p. 162; November, 2003, Joel Shoemaker, review of *When We Were Saints,* p. 144; April, 2006, John Peters, review of *A Summer of Kings,* p. 145; October, 2006, review of *A Summer of Kings*; September, 2010, Johanna Lewis, review of *Crazy,* p. 160; September, 2011, Allison Tran, review of *Pregnant Pause,* p. 164.

Voice of Youth Advocates, June, 1994, Susan Levine, review of *If I Should Die before I Wake,* p. 88; October, 2010, review of *Crazy,* p. 380.

ONLINE

Han Nolan home page, http://www.hannolan.com (May 15, 2012).

Harcourt Books Web site, http://www.harcourtbooks.com/ (January 6, 2005), interview with Nolan.

* * *

NORMAN, Kim

Personal

Born in CA; married; children: two sons. *Hobbies and other interests:* Gardening, singing, acting.

Addresses

Home—Smithfield, VA. *E-mail*—kimnorman@mac.com.

Career

Author and illustrator of children's books. Graphic artist. Presenter at schools. Performer in community theatre.

Writings

Jack of All Tails, illustrated by David Clark, Dutton Children's Books (New York, NY), 2007.
Crocodaddy, illustrated by David Walker, Sterling Publishing (New York, NY), 2009.
Ten on the Sled, illustrated by Liza Woodruff, Sterling Publishing (New York, NY), 2010.
All Kinds of Kittens, illustrated by Betina Ogden, Sterling Publishing (New York, NY), 2010.
Whales, illustrated by Carol Schwartz, Sterling Publishing (New York, NY), 2012.
Dinosaurs and Other Prehistoric Animals, illustrated by Julius Csotonyi, Sterling Publishing (New York, NY), 2012.
I Know a Wee Piggy, illustrated by Henry Cole, Dial Children's Books (New York, NY), 2012.
The Great Christmas Crisis, illustrated by Janni Ho, Sterling Publishing (New York, NY), 2012.

OTHER

(Illustrator) Verne Edwards, *The Museum Duck,* Pearl Line Press, 2000.

Contributor to books, including *Rolling in the Aisles: A Collection of Laugh-out-loud Poems,* edited by Bruce Lansky, Meadowbrook Press, 2004.

Sidelights

Kim Norman worked for several years as a graphic artist before shifting her creative focus to crafting stories for children. Norman also worked as a performer, writing and performing original songs, stories, and poems on "The Eyewitness Radio Show" as well as during author visits to schools and libraries. Her first published picture book, *Jack of All Tails,* pairs an entertaining story about a young pet lover with whimsical artwork by David Clark, while *Crocodaddy* was based on a game from Norman's own childhood. Other books by Norman include *All Kinds of Kittens, Ten on the Sled,* and *I Know a Wee Piggy,* the last a color concept book featuring humorous illustrations by Henry Cole.

In *Crocodaddy* Norman transports readers to a sultry summer day as a young boy and his father stay cool by splashing in a nearby lake. In their imaginative play, Daddy becomes a crocodile lurking in wait and the boy becomes a brave hunter. After the boy spots the crocodile, he leaps on its back and is taken for a ride punctuated by gleeful giggles. The illustrations David Walker contributes to *Crocodaddy* feature "vibrant colors and expressive characters" that match Norman's "percussive rhyming text" to produce a "celebration of imaginative play," according to *School Library Journal* contributor Kathleen Kelly MacMillan.

Set in the cold lands of the north, where the sun rarely sets in winter, *Ten on the Sled* finds a group of Arctic animals pulling a toboggan up hill in order to ride it back down. Set to the rhythm of a popular children's counting chant, Norman's text begins with ten toboggan riders aboard the fast-moving sled, but as each animal in turn requests that others slide over, another animal falls off the end. After Seal, Hare, Sheep, Moose, Fox, Walrus, Squirrel, and several others land on the snowy hillside, their momentum rollling down causes them to combine in a giant snowball that creates humorous chaos when it collides with the toboggan and its riders at the bottom. Chock full of concepts such as "animal identification, counting, vocabulary building, and [animal] print awareness," *Ten on the Sled* also features a "can't-lose rhyme" that makes Norman's story "a keeper," according to a *Kirkus Reviews* writer. Praising Liza Woodruff's pastel-and-colored pencil art for the book, Lissa Sara Paulson noted in *School Library Journal* that the "comic-style illustrations" match the alliterative text for *Ten on the Sled* and feature "characters . . . [that] exhibit a playful, cheery spirit."

A young boy loses control of his playful pig in Norman's farmyard story *I Know a Wee Piggy.* At a country fair Piggy becomes covered in brown mud, rolls in red tomatoes, splashes in white milk, and ultimately makes contact with some sticky pink cotton candy. As brought to life in humorous artwork by Henry Cole, *I Know a Wee Piggy* pairs what a *Publishers Weekly* critic described as a "catchy cumulative verse that riffs on 'I Know an Old Lady' with Cole's depiction of the "eager-eyed, grinning, leaping, prancing, filthy pig."

Biographical and Critical Sources

PERIODICALS

Kirkus Reviews, October 1, 2010, review of *Ten on the Sled.*
Publishers Weekly, April 30, 2012, review of *I Know a Wee Piggy.*
School Library Journal, May, 2009, Kathleen Kelly MacMillan, review of *Crocodaddy,* p. 84; December, 2010, Lissa Sara Paulson, review of *Ten on the Sled,* p. 86.

ONLINE

Kim Norman Home Page, http://www.kimnormanbooks.com (May 1, 2012).

NOVESKY, Amy

Personal

Born in CA; daughter of Roger (a pharmaceuticals development executive) and Bonny (a jewelry designer) Novesky; married N.D. Koster (an editor), November, 2003; children: one son. *Education:* University of California at San Diego, B.A. (literature and creative writing), 1992; University of San Francisco, M.A. (creative writing), 1996.

Addresses

Home—San Francisco Bay area, CA. *E-mail*—anovesky@earthlink.net.

Career

Children's book editor and author. Chronicle Books, San Francisco, CA, children's book editor, 1994-2000; Paper Hat Press (publishing company), creative director, beginning 2009; Goosebottom Books, Foster City, CA, editor; Ever After Studio (book production company), cofounder. Presenter at workshops.

Awards, Honors

FOCAL Award, Los Angeles Public Library, Notable Book Selection, American Library Association, Best Picture Book selection, International Latino Book Awards, Choice selection, Cooperative Children's Book Center, Children's Picture Book Award finalist, Society of Children's Book Writers and Illustrators, and Pura Belpré Honor designation, all 2011, all for *Me, Frida* illustrated by David Diaz.

Writings

FOR CHILDREN

Elephant Prince: The Story of Ganesh, illustrated by Belgin K. Wedman, Mandala (San Rafael, CA), 2004.
Me, Frida, illustrated by David Diaz, Abrams Books for Young Readers (New York, NY), 2010.
Cloud's Best Worst Day Ever, illustrated by Hanako Wakiyama, Tricycle Press (Berkeley, CA), 2011.
Bug Makes a Big Splash, illustrated by Hanako Wakiyama, Tricycle Press (Berkeley, CA), 2011.
Georgia in Hawai'i: When Georgia O'Keeffe Painted What She Pleased, illustrated by Yuyi Morales, Houghton Mifflin Harcourt (Boston, MA), 2012.
Imogen, illustrated by Lisa Congdon, Cameron & Company, 2012.
Cat's Just Right Sandcastle, illustrated by Hanako Wakiyama, Tricycle Press (Berkeley, CA), 2012.
Huggtopus Makes Way for Play, illustrated by Hanako Wakiyama, Tricycle Press (Berkeley, CA), 2012.
Mister and Lady Day, illustrated by Vanessa Newton, Harcourt (New York, NY), 2012.

Sidelights

Based in northern California, Amy Novesky is involved in many phases of children's book production, from coordinating relationships with authors and publishers to editing, directing the creative efforts of small publishers, and co-founding her own small publisher. Drawing on this wealth of expertise, Novesky has also shared her talent as a writer, producing biographical-themed picture books that include *Elephant Prince: The Story of Ganesh, Me, Frida, Georgia in Hawai'i: When Georgia O'Keeffe Painted What She Pleased,* and *Imogen,* the last focusing on noted twentieth-century photographer Imogen Cunningham.

Based on a traditional East Indian tale and illustrated by Belgin K. Wedman, *Elephant Prince* introduces children to the legend of the jolly, rotund, and elephant-headed god Ganesh, who figures largely in Hindu worship. Raised high in the Himalayas, the much-loved infant son of Shiva and her beloved Parvati loses his head to powerful flames when he is looked upon by the powerful god Shanaishchara. Vishnu restores the infant to life by giving Ganesh the head of an elephant, symbolizing the greatness that is part of his being. Although there are several different versions of this story, Novesky retells "the less-popular but authentic version," noted Grace Oliff in *School Library Journal,* and the love between mother and son "is captured beautifully in both text and illustrations." Praising Wedman's "glittering gouache paintings," which evoke intricate Indian miniatures, *Booklist* contributor Gillian Engberg added that *Elephant Prince* is a "accessible and well-paced" story perfectly designed "for read-alouds."

Mexican artist Frida Kahlo is Novesky's focus in *Me, Frida,* which features colorful charcoal-and-acrylic artwork by award-winning illustrator David Diaz. As the young wife of noted muralist Diego Rivera, Kahlo moved with him to San Francisco in 1930 while he worked on a project there. Rivera's fame and forceful personality left her in the shadows until she began painting herself and developed the unique style that tapped both her personality and her colorful Mexican heritage. While noting that Novesky's approach to Kahlo's complex history is unusually sophisticated for a picture book, Carolyn Phelan added in her *Booklist* review of *Me, Frida* that "the writing is lucid, the emotions are universal, and the illustrations soar." A *Publishers Weekly* contributor wrote that the author's prose is "overflowing with compelling imagery" while Diaz's use of "intense hues and folk/naive style recall[s] . . . Kahlo's [own] work." *Me, Frida* "is a book that should be seen by any secondary student studying art," recommended Beverley Mathias in a review of Novesky's biography for *School Librarian,* and in *School Library Journal* Jody Kopple described the text as "succinct and careful."

Georgia O'Keeffe, another renowned twentieth-century artist, takes center stage in *Georgia in Hawai'i.* Paired with "lush, almost sensual art" by Yuyi Morales that

***Amy Novesky teams with artist David Diaz to capture the life of artist Frida Kahlo in the picture-book biography* Me, Frida.** (Illustration copyright © 2010 by David Diaz. Reproduced with permission of Abrams Books for Young Readers, an imprint of ABRAMS.)

"recalls O'Keefe's," according to *Booklist* critic Ilene Cooper, Novesky's text takes readers to 1939, the year the artist accepted a commission to paint pineapples for use in advertising the Hawaiian Pineapple Company. Traveling to Hawai'i, the single-minded woman painted seascapes, flowers, and other natural features of the tropical paradise, but pineapples were a focus of only one of her paintings: an image of a pineapple budding out on a tree.

Praising *Georgia in Hawai'i, Booklist* critic Ilene Cooper deemed Novesky's prose "often lovely," while a *Kirkus Reviews* contributor characterized the picturebook as "an appealing and slightly humorous portrayal of O'Keeffe's artistic vision and determination" that will strike readers as "accessible, unfussy and visually charming."

Biographical and Critical Sources

PERIODICALS

Booklist, January 1, 2005, Gillian Engberg, review of *Elephant Prince: The Story of Ganesh,* p. 872; November 1, 2010, Carolyn Phelan, review of *Me, Frida,* p. 60; February 1, 2012, Ilene Cooper, review of *Georgia in Hawai'i: When Georgia O'Keeffe Painted What She Pleased,* p. 98.

Kirkus Reviews, October 1, 2010, review of *Me, Frida;* December 15, 2011, review of *Georgia in Hawai'i.*

Publishers Weekly, October 4, 2010, review of *Me, Frida,* p. 46.

School Librarian winter, 2010, Beverley Mathias, review of *Me, Frida,* p. 251.

School Library Journal, February, 2005, Grace Oliff, review of *Elephant Prince,* p. 126; December, 2010, Jody Kopple, review of *Me, Frida,* p. 96.

ONLINE

Amy Novesky Home Page, http://amynovesky.com (May 1, 2012).

Children's Book Review Web log, http://www.thechildrensbookreview.com/ (March 21, 2012), Nicki Richesin, interview with Novesky.

P

PEOT, Margaret

Personal

Married Daniel Levy; children: Sam. *Education:* Miami University (OH), B.F.A. (cum laude), 1986.

Addresses

Home—New York, NY. *E-mail*—margaretannpeot@verizon.net.

Career

Author and illustrator. Printmaker; theatrical scenic artist and costume painter and dyer, beginning 1989, including for stage productions *Spiderman: Turn off the Dark, Shrek the Musical, Spamalot, The Lion King, Wicked, Titanic, Cats, Phantom of the Opera,* and *Kiss of the Spiderwoman,* as well as for dance productions, circus and music acts, and film. Tisch School of the Arts, New York University, instructor in costume painting, 1993-2005; teacher at Creative Center, University of North Carolina, USITT-SE, Athens, GA, and various art-education conferences, including Artworks 2011 and New York Education Roundtable's Face to Face conference. *Exhibitions:* Work exhibited at New York City galleries, including Grady Alexis Gallery at El Taller Latinoamericano, Center for Book Arts, Fashion Institute of Technology, and Galleries at Saint Peter's as well as at Lake Placid Center for the Arts, Lake Placid, NY, and Ocean City Artists Guild, Island Heights, NJ. Decorative painter, as part of Tromploy, Inc., creating installations for Los Angeles Museum of Science and Technology, for restaurants in Japan, and for private residences.

Member

United Scenic Artists, Authors Guild.

Awards, Honors

Orbis Pictus Recommended title, and Eureka! Honor Book Silver Medal, California Reading Association, both 2012, both for *Inkblot.*

Writings

Make Your Mark: Explore Your Creativity and Discover Your Inner Artist, Chronicle Books (San Francisco, CA), 2004.

Inkblot: Drip, Splat, and Squish Your Way to Creativity, Boyds Mills Press (Honesdale, PA), 2011.

The Successful Artist's Career Guide: Finding Your Way in the Business of Art, North Light Books (Blue Ash, OH), 2012.

Sidelights

Based in New York City, Margaret Peot has used her creativity to develop a dynamic career that incorporates printmaking and painting, writing, teaching, and theatre crafts: she has created painted costumes for Broadway productions of *The Lion King, Wicked, Shrek the Musical,* and *Spamalot* as well as for dance and circus performances and films. Peot helps others tap into creative talents that may be latent or just budding through her writing, producing both *Make Your Mark: Explore Your Creativity and Discover Your Inner Artist* and *Inkblot: Drip, Splat, and Squish Your Way to Creativity.* She also shares her expertise in developing a sustainable career as an artist in *The Successful Artist's Career Guide: Finding Your Way in the Business of Art.*

Full of inspiring artwork and other visuals, *Make Your Mark* shares Peot's method of developing individual creative talents by allowing readers to sample artistic media ranging from stenciling and print-making to collage, incorporating sketching and painting but not requiring a mastery of these traditional mediums. Containing instructions for fifty-five art projects, the book is designed "for those who are serious about expressing visual creativity," according to *Library Journal* contributor Daniel Lombardo.

Although Peot confines herself to a single, time-honored technique in *Inkblot,* the use of unconstrained splatters, splashes, and blots yields limitless opportunities to tap

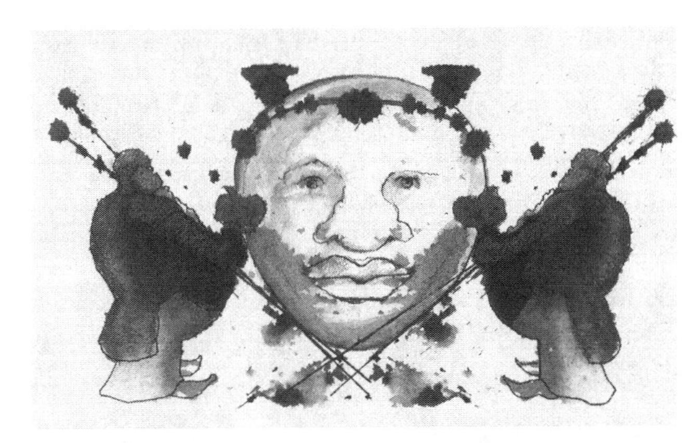

***Margaret Peot finds an intriguing way to tap personal creativity in her book* Inkblot.** (Illustration copyright © 2011 by Margaret Peot. Reproduced with permission of Boyds Mills Press, Inc.)

creativity. Beginning with basic instructions in paper and ink selection, she discusses folding methods to generate more complex patterns as well as techniques employing colored inks and other basic tools. Readers learn to see creative opportunities in every inkblot and are shown how to use various media—markers, pens, paints, and colored pencils—to reveal beetles, butterflies, fish, faces, flowers, and other objects in the blots.

Recommending *Inkblot* as "equally cool for kids and parents, art classes or casual groups," a *Kirkus Reviews* writer added that Peot's book combines "clear directions and lively encouragement." In *Booklist* Carolyn Phelan dubbed *Inkblot* "upbeat, practical, and nearly irresistible," while Donna Cardon noted in *School Library Journal* that "Peot's enthusiasm is contagious and her idea about using images to develop creativity is intriguing."

Biographical and Critical Sources

PERIODICALS

Booklist, May 1, 2011, Carolyn Phelan, review of *Inkblot: Drip, Splat, and Squish Your Way to Creativity,* p. 74.

Bulletin of the Center for Children's Books, May, 2011, Elizabeth Bush, review of *Inkblot,* p. 435.

Kirkus Reviews, February 15, 2011, review of *Inkblot.*

Library Journal, July, 2004, Daniel Lombardo, review of *Make Your Mark: Explore Your Creativity and Discover Your Inner Artist,* p. 81.

School Library Journal, May, 2011, Donna Cardon, review of *Inkblot,* p. 136.

Voice of Youth Advocates, June, 2011, Elaine Gass Hirsch, review of *Inkblot,* p. 200.

ONLINE

Art Career Project Web site, http://www.theartcareerproject.com/ (May 1, 2012), interview with Peot.

Inkblot the Book Web site, http://theinkblotbook.com (May 1, 2012).

Margaret Peot Home Page, http://www.margaretpeot.com (May 1, 2012).

* * *

PITTMAN, Rickey E.

Personal

Born in Dallas, TX. *Education:* Abilene Christian University, B.A. (New Testament Greek), M.A. (English literature).

Addresses

Home—Monroe, LA. *E-mail*—rickeyp@bayou.com.

Career

Author, storyteller, educator, and musician. Performer/presenter at schools, libraries, museums, festivals, and U.S. civil war reenactments. Louisiana Delta Community College, instructor in writing on the college level.

Awards, Honors

Ernest Hemingway Short-story Competition winner, 1998.

Writings

Stories of the Confederate South, Pelican Pub. Co. (Gretna, LA), 2006.

Jim Limber Davis: A Black Orphan in the Confederate White House, illustrated by Judith Hierstein, Pelican Pub. Co. (Gretna, LA), 2007.

Scottish Alphabet, illustrated by Connie McLennan, Pelican Pub. Co. (Gretna, LA), 2008.

Confederate Alphabet, illustrated by Jane Duplechin, Pelican Pub. Co. (Gretna, LA), 2010.

Stonewall Jackson's Black Sunday School, illustrated by Lynn Hosegood, Pelican Pub. Co. (Gretna, LA), 2010.

Irish Alphabet, illustrated by Connie McLennan, Pelican Pub. Co. (Gretna, LA), 2011.

Also author of *Red River Fever* and *Just Write for Dinner: Planning, Producing, and Presenting Dinner Theatre* (e-books). Editor of *Biography of a Sea Captain's Life: Written by Himself* (e-book), by W.C. Flanders.

Biographical and Critical Sources

PERIODICALS

Booklist, March 1, 2010, Hazel Rochman, review of *Stonewall Jackson's Black Sunday School,* p. 75.

Kirkus Reviews, April 15, 2010, review of *Stonewall Jackson's Black Sunday School*; February 15, 2011, review of *Irish Alphabet*; August 1, 2011, review of *Confederate Alphabet.*

Publishers Weekly, January 31, 2011, review of *Irish Alphabet,* p. 46.

School Library Journal, September, 2007, Anne Chapman Callaghan, review of *Jim Limber Davis: A Black Orphan in the Confederate White House,* p. 185; March, 2010, Alyson Low, review of *Stonewall Jackson's Black Sunday School,* p. 143; May, 2011, C.J. Connor, review of *Irish Alphabet,* p. 100.

ONLINE

Rickey E. Pittman Home Page, http://www.rickeypittman.com (May 1, 2012).*

* * *

POWER, Timothy 1960-

Personal

Born 1960. *Education:* California Institute of the Arts, degree.

Addresses

Home—Los Angeles, CA. *Agent*—Jennifer De Chiara Literary Agency, 31 E. 32nd St., Ste. 300, New York, NY 10016.

Career

Educator and author. Formerly worked in animation; substitute teacher. Musician, performing keyboards.

Writings

The Boy Who Howled, Bloomsbury (New York, NY), 2010.

Sidelights

Timothy Power was inspired by a true story in creating his middle-grade novel *The Boy Who Howled.* In the eighteenth century, a strange boy was found living in the woods near a town in rural France. Due to his strange behavior and general wildness, it was determined that the lad had in fact been kept alive and raised by wolves since infancy. In fictionalizing this compelling story, Power transports the tale to the United States, where young Callum Firehead toddles off into the wilderness during a family outing after wriggling out of his car seat undetected. Discovered by a wolf pack, the little boy is allowed to join the group, protected by a female wolf from her more-aggressive (and hungry) male partner. With an intuitive sense that the wolves might be dangerous, Callum learns to appease the pack's alpha male and enthusiastically joins in with their cacophonous nightly howling. He also tolerates "Father" wolf's efforts to lay claim to him by scenting him with urine, but eventually "Mother" wolf realizes that the lad will be safer among his own kind. A quirky chain of events allow Callum to reacclimate to human society at the Hargrove Academy for the Gifted, Bright, and Perceptive Child before being reunited with his human family.

"Power writes formally," noted Patty Saldenberg in her *School Library Journal* review of *The Boy Who Howled,* and this stylistic conceit allows his tale to gain the literary veneer of a story dating to "the early 20th century." In *Booklist* Abby Nolan noted the mix of humor and pathos in the novel, writing that *The Boy Who Howled* "is comical but also poignant." An "amiable satire," Callum's story is related with "an overriding sweetness," concluded a *Kirkus Reviews* writer, and Power's young hero ultimately "brings a good dose of humanity to the civilized world."

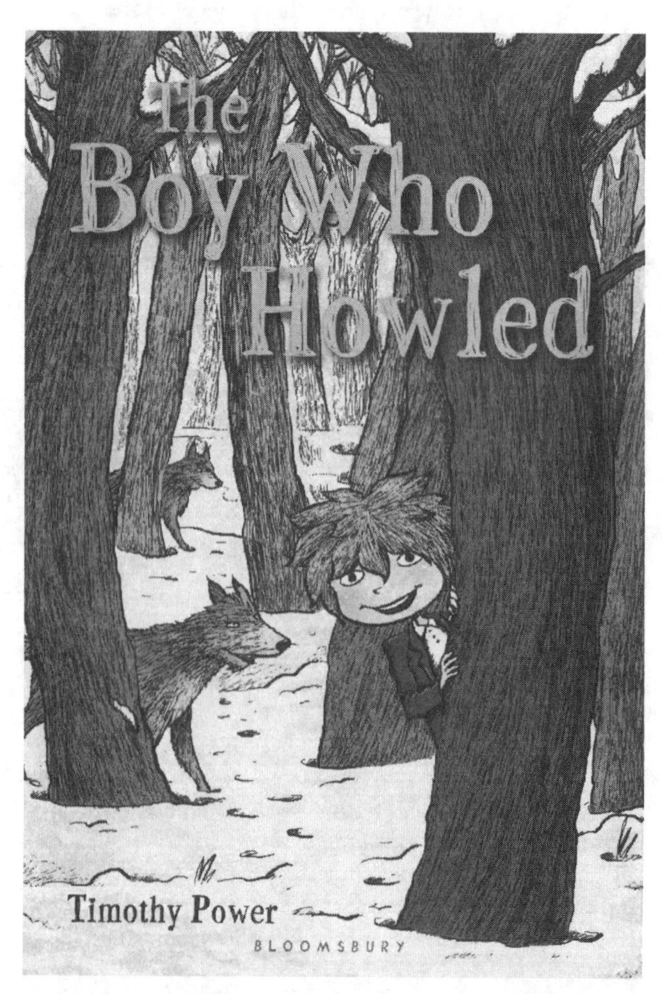

Timothy Power was inspired by a true story in his middle-grade novel* The Boy Who Howled, *featuring cover art by Victor Rivas. (Illustration © 2010 by Victor Rivas. Reproduced by permission of Bloomsbury Books for Young Readers.)

Biographical and Critical Sources

PERIODICALS

Booklist, October 15, 2010, Abby Nolan, review of *The Boy Who Howled,* p. 63.

Kirkus Reviews, October 1, 2010, review of *The Boy Who Howled.*

School Library Journal, November, 2010, Patty Saldenberg, review of *The Boy Who Howled,* p. 125.

ONLINE

Timothy Power Web log, http://timothypower.me (May 1, 2012).*

R

REEVE, Philip 1966-

Personal

Born 1966, in Brighton, England; married; wife's name Sarah; children: Samuel. *Education:* Attended Cambridgeshire College of Arts and Technology (now Anglia Ruskin University) and Brighton Polytechnic (now University of Brighton). *Hobbies and other interests:* Walking, drawing, writing, reading.

Addresses

Home—Devon, England.

Career

Illustrator, author, and bookseller. Children's book illustrator, 1994—. Producer and director of stage plays.

Awards, Honors

Whitbread Children's Book Award shortlist, and Gold Award, Nestlé Smarties Book Prize, both 2002, and Best Book of the Year designation, *Washington Post,* Best Book for Young Adults designation, American Library Association (ALA), and Blue Peter Book of the Year Award, all 2003, all for *Mortal Engines;* Best Book for Young Adults designation, ALA, and W.H. Smith People's Choice Award shortlist, 2004, for *Predator's Gold;* London *Guardian* Children's Fiction Prize, 2006, and *Los Angeles Times* Book Prize for Young-Adult Fiction, 2007, both for *A Darkling Plain;* Carnegie Medal, 2008, for *Here Lies Arthur;* Carnegie Medal shortlist, 2010, for *Fever Crumb.*

Writings

FOR CHILDREN

(Self-illustrated) *Horatio Nelson and His Victory* ("Dead Famous" series), Hippo (London, England), 2003.

Philip Reeve (Alamy Images. Reproduced by permission.)

Here Lies Arthur, Scholastic (London, England), 2007, Scholastic (New York, NY), 2008.

No Such Thing as Dragons, Scholastic (New York, NY), 2010.

Goblins, Marion Lloyd (London, England), 2012.

Coauthor, with Brian P. Mitchell, of musical *The Ministry of Biscuits.* Coauthor, with Sarah McIntyre, of Web comics.

"MORTAL ENGINES/HUNGRY CITY CHRONICLES"; YOUNG-ADULT NOVEL SERIES

Mortal Engines, Scholastic (London, England), 2001, HarperCollins (New York, NY), 2003.

Predator's Gold, Scholastic (London, England), 2003, Eos (New York, NY), 2004.
Infernal Devices, Eos (New York, NY), 2006.
A Darkling Plain, Eos (New York, NY), 2006.
(With Chris Priestley) *Traction City: A World Day Flip Book* (distributed to U.K. school children), Scholastic (London, England), 2011.

Series also published in an "adult" edition

"LARKLIGHT" NOVEL TRILOGY; ILLUSTRATED BY DAVID WYATT

Larklight: A Rousing Tale of Dauntless Pluck in the Farthest Reaches of Space, Bloomsbury (New York, NY), 2006.
Starcross; or, The Coming of the Moobs!; or, Our Adventures in the Fourth Dimension!: A Stirring Tale of British Vim upon the Seas of Space and Time, Bloomsbury (London, England), 2007, published as *Starcross: A Stirring Adventure of Spies, Time Travel, and Curious Hats,* Bloomsbury (New York, NY), 2007.
Mothstorm; or, The Horror from beyond Georgium Sidus!; or, A Tale of Two Shapers: A Rattling Yarn of Danger, Dastardy, and Derring-do upon the Far Frontiers of British Space!, Bloomsbury (London, England), 2007, published as *Mothstorm: The Horror from beyond Georgium Sidus!,* Bloomsbury (New York, NY), 2008.

"FEVER CRUMB" YOUNG-ADULT NOVEL SERIES

Fever Crumb, Scholastic (London, England), 2009, Scholastic (New York, NY), 2010.
A Web of Air, Scholastic (London, England), 2010, Scholastic (New York, NY), 2011.
Scrivener's Moon, Scholastic (London, England), 2011.

"BUSTER BAYLISS" SERIES; FOR CHILDREN

Night of the Living Veg, illustrated by Graham Philpot, Scholastic Children's Books (London, England), 2002, new edition, illustrated by Steve May, 2006.
The Big Freeze, illustrated by Graham Philpot, Scholastic Children's Books (London, England), 2002, new edition, illustrated by Steve May, 2006.
Day of the Hamster, illustrated by Graham Philpot, Scholastic Children's Books (London, England), 2002.
Custardfinger, illustrated by Graham Philpot, Scholastic Children's Books (London, England), 2003.

ILLUSTRATOR

Terry Deary, *Wicked Words* ("Horrible Histories" series), Andre Deutsch (London, England), 1996.
Terry Deary, *Dark Knights and Dingy Castles* ("Horrible Histories" series), Andre Deutsch (London, England), 1997.
Terry Deary, *The Angry Aztecs* ("Horrible Histories" series), Andre Deutsch (London, England), 1997, published with *The Incredible Incas* (also see below), 2001.
Chris D'Lacey, *Henry Spaloosh!,* Hippo (London, England), 1997.
Michael Cox, *Awful Art* ("The Knowledge" series), Hippo (London, England), 1997.
Michael Cox, *Mind-blowing Music* ("The Knowledge" series), Hippo (London, England), 1997.
Peter Corey, *Coping with Love,* Hippo (London, England), 1997.
Michael Cox, *Smashin' Fashion* ("The Knowledge" series), Hippo (London, England), 1998.
Kjartan Poskitt, *More Murderous Maths,* Hippo (London, England), 1998, published as *Desperate Measures,* Scholastic (London, England), 2008.
Chris D'Lacey, *Snail Patrol,* Hippo (London, England), 1998.
Terry Deary and Barbara Allen, *Space Race* ("Spark Files" series), Faber (London, England), 1998.
Terry Deary and Barbara Allen, *Shock Tactics* ("Spark Files" series), Faber (London, England), 1998.
Terry Deary and Barbara Allen, *Chop and Change* ("Spark Files" series), Faber (London, England), 1998.
Terry Deary and Barbara Allen, *Bat and Bell* ("Spark Files" series), Faber (London, England), 1998.
Kjartan Poskitt, *Isaac Newton and His Apple* ("Dead Famous" series), Hippo (London, England), 1999.
Hayden Middleton, *Come and Have a Go If You Think You're Cool Enough!,* Hippo (London, England), 1999.
Hayden Middleton, *Come and Have a Go If You Think You're Mad Enough!,* Hippo (London, England), 1999.
Alan MacDonald, *Henry VIII and His Chopping Block,* Scholastic (London, England), 1999.
Alan MacDonald, *Al Capone and His Gang,* Scholastic (London, England), 1999.
Terry Deary, *Rowdy Revolutions* ("Horrible Histories" series), Scholastic (London, England), 1999.
Terry Deary and Barbara Allen, *Magical Magnets* ("Spark Files" series), Faber (London, England), 1999.
Terry Deary, *The Incredible Incas,* Hippo (London, England), 2000.
Margaret Simpson, *Cleopatra and Her Asp,* Hippo (London, England), 2000.
Alan MacDonald, *Oliver Cromwell and His Warts* ("Dead Famous" series), Hippo (London, England), 2000.
Terry Deary and Barbara Allen, *The Secrets of Science* ("Spark Files" series), Faber (London, England), 2000.
Margaret Simpson, *Elizabeth I and Her Conquests,* Hippo (London, England), 2001.
Margaret Simpson, *Mary, Queen of Scots and Her Hopeless Husbands,* Hippo (London, England), 2001.
Kjartan Poskitt, *Do You Feel Lucky? The Secrets of Probability* ("Murderous Maths" series), Hippo (London, England), 2001.
Mike Goldsmith, *Albert Einstein and His Inflatable Universe* ("Dead Famous" series), Hippo (London, England), 2001.
Michael Cox, *Elvis and His Pelvis,* Hippo (London, England), 2001.
Phil Robins, *Joan of Arc and Her Marching Orders* ("Dead Famous" series), Scholastic (London, England), 2002.
Kjartan Poskitt, *Vicious Circles and Other Savage Shapes* ("Murderous Maths" series), Hippo (London, England), 2002.

Kjartan Poskitt, *Professor Fiendish's Book of Diabolical Brainbenders* ("Murderous Maths" series), Hippo (London, England), 2002.

Kjartan Poskitt, *Numbers: The Key to the Universe* ("Murderous Maths" series), Hippo (London, England), 2002.

Kjartan Poskitt, *The Phantom X* ("Murderous Maths" series), Hippo (London, England), 2003.

Kjartan Poskitt, *The Fiendish Angletron* ("Murderous Maths" series), Hippo (London, England), 2004.

Kjartan Poskitt, *The Magic of Pants: A Conjuror's Compendium of Underpants Tricks to Delight All Ages (and Sizes),* Scholastic (London, England), 2004, published as *Pantsacadabra! A Conjuror's Compendium of Underpants Tricks to Delight All Ages,* 2007.

Kjartan Poskitt, *A Brief History of Pants, or, The Rudiments of Pantology,* Scholastic (London, England), 2005, published as *Pantology: A Brief History of Pants,* 2008.

Kjartan Poskitt, *Urgum the Axeman,* Scholastic (London, England), 2006.

Kjartan Poskitt, *The Perfect Sausage,* Hippo (London, England), 2007.

Kjartan Poskitt, *Urgum and the Seat of Flames,* Scholastic (London, England), 2007.

Kjartan Poskitt, *Urgum and the Goo Goo Bah!,* Scholastic (London, England), 2008.

Adaptations

The "Buster Bayliss" novels were adapted as audiobooks by Chivers Children's Audio Books, 2003. *Larklight* was adapted for a film, produced by Denise Di Novi, for Warner Brothers. *Fever Crumb* was adapted for audiobook, read by Reeve, Scholastic Audio, 2010.

Sidelights

With his "Hungry City Chronicles," former bookseller and illustrator Philip Reeve amassed some of England's top honors for children's literature, among them a Nestlé Children's Gold award, a Blue Peter Book of the Year award, and the London *Guardian*'s annual Children's Fiction Prize. The series, which includes the novels *Mortal Engines, Predator's Gold, Infernal Devices,* and *A Darkling Plain,* is a notable examples of "steampunk" fiction, a genre in which science fiction and fantasy stories play out in post-apocalyptic or alternate-history settings in which mechanized, clockwork elements become sinister forces. Imaginative and clever, Reeve's novels have been compared to Philip Pullman's "His Dark Materials" trilogy and have attracted a large and loyal readership. In addition to his work as a writer, which includes stories in the "Fever Crumb" and "Larklight" series as well as the Carnegie Medal-winning novel *Here Lies Arthur,* Reeve is a popular cartoonist and illustrator who has contributed substantially to Terry Deary's popular "Horrible Histories" nonfiction series.

The first novel in Reeve's "Hungry City Chronicles" series (collected in the United Kingdom as the "Mortal Engines" novels), *Mortal Engines* takes place in a bleak age thousands of years in the future, "in which larger, faster cities literally gobble up the resources of smaller towns in order to feed the never-ending need for fuel," as Janice M. Del Negro explained in the *Bulletin of the Center for Children's Books.* In a floating London, scavenger Thaddeus Valentine has discovered an ancient energy source that will enable his mobile city to overwhelm the stationery but well-defended cities of Asia. When a horribly disfigured girl named Hester attempts to take Valentine's life, loyal young apprentice historian Tom Natsworthy saves his mentor. To Tom's surprise, instead of rewarding him, Valentine shoves both he and Hester down a waste chute and out of London. Learning several unpleasant truths about Valentine—including that the man killed Hester's parents—Tom joins the girl's quest for vengeance as the two set out across a landscape rife with pirates and slave traders in pursuit of east-bound London.

"The grimy yet fantastical post-apocalyptic setting; the narrow escapes, deepening loyalties, and not-infrequent bitter losses—all keep readers' attention riveted," commented Anita L. Burkam in a review of *Mortal Engines* for *Horn Book. Kliatt* reviewer Paula Rohrlick described Reeve's "wildly imaginative British tale" as "full of marvelous details . . . humor, and grand adventures," and *Chronicle* contributor Don D'Ammassa judged the book to be "well worth the time of readers of any age."

The second book in the "Hungry City Chronicles" series, *Predator's Gold,* finds Tom and Hester in Anchorage, Alaska, a city that, like many in Reeve's futuristic world, moves from place to place, searching for comfortable climes and incorporating smaller cities that cross its path. Anchorage is now under the control of a pretty young woman named Freya, and when she discovers the town's history as part of the old continental United States and the lush fields it once controlled in its original stationary site, she decides to take Anchorage on the perilous journey back across the ice wastes. When Hester sees Tom kissing Freya, a jealous rage causes her to betray Anchorage's location to the predatory city of Arkangel. At the same time, a gang of baddies known as the Lost Boys are spying on the city and trying to kidnap Tom, while the Anti-Traction League seeks to destroy Anchorage altogether with the help of a horrible cyborg.

For *Horn Book* contributor Burkam, "the technological wizardry" in *Predator's Gold* "will gratify young sci-fi gearheads, while the intense emotions drive the thrilling plot at top speed." In *Kliatt,* Rohrlick commended Reeve's "marvelous imagination and emotional depth, the sympathetic young protagonists, and the thrilling adventures," while *Booklist* contributor Sally Estes noted that, despite a complex plot and multiple characters, *Predator's Gold* "is still easy to follow [and] gripping enough to leave readers anxious to find out what's to come."

Infernal Devices and *A Darkling Plain* finish up Reeve's "Hungry City Chronicles" saga. In *Infernal Devices* two

decades have passed since the action in *Predator's Gold,* and Tom and Hester now have a teenaged daughter, Wren, who is being threatened by the same Lost Boys who once pursued her father. As the middle-aged Tom watches, Earth's population fractures into the competing Traction League and Green Storm in *A Darkling Plain*; meanwhile, a powerful weapon created by humans prior to the apocalyptic war that destroyed their civilization hangs in the sky, poised to destroy everything. "Reeve keeps the multiple plots moving with surprises, tragedy, and multiple betrayals," noted Tim Wadhams, reviewing *Infernal Devices* for *School Library Journal,* and in *Booklist* Sally Estes praised the book's culmination in "a thrilling climax and hint of more battles to come."

While commenting on the "fabulous streak of frivolity running through absolutely everything Reeve writes," London *Guardian* contributor Josh Lacey added that the author also has a more serious side: "Municipal Darwinism. A perfect expression of the true nature of the world: that the fittest survive," as one character explains. While noting that the author's prose alternates between complex and "sparkling and witty," Lacey concluded that in the "Hungry City Chronicles" "Reeve has created an extraordinary imaginative achievement" that ends with a "cunning twist."

Described by *Guardian* contributor Frank Cottrell Boyce as "a sci-fi Dickens, full of orphans, villains, chases and mysteries," Reeve's "Fever Crumb" novels include *Fever Crumb, A Web of Air,* and *Scrivener's Moon.* A prequel to the "Mortal Engines" books, this series finds the city of London still earthbound amid the detritus of the technologically advanced civilization that collapsed thousands of years before. In *Fever Crumb* readers meet the titular fourteen year old, an orphan who has been taken in and educated by Dr. Crumb, a member of the Order of Engineers who is living a protected life inside a vast but never-completed statue. While women are considered ill fit for rational, scientific work, Fever Crumb has shown herself to be unusually analytical, pragmatic, and unflappable. Following in the footsteps of her mentor, Fever leaves the safety of her isolated home to work on a secret archaeological site in the city that is being overseen by Kit Solent. These new surroundings—characterized by London *Daily Telegraph* contributor Philip Womack as "a shabby, quasi-18th-century hellhole"—tap something in Fever's memory that involves Godshawk, a former leader of London who among the Scriven, a highly intelligens people capable of restarting the machines that now sit idle.

Fever's story continues in *A Web of Air* and *Scrivener's Moon,* which find the young woman experiencing life outside of London and gradually coming to terms with her own destiny. In *A Web of Air* Fever is now sixteen and traveling with a troupe of peripatetic actors, using her knowledge of science and the elements to create lighting and theatrical special effects. Arriving at Mayda, a city far south of London, she learns that a reclusive young scientist named Arlo Thursday resides there and is attempting to build a flying machine. While Fever's intellect and her Scriven abilities make her an ideal workmate for Arlo, her inability to relate emotionally dooms any deeper relationship between the two. The effort to get London airborne continues in *Scrivener's Moon,* as do the machinations of those who would stop it. As the city readies for launch, Fever journeys north to discover once and for all the secret of her birth.

"Reeve evokes his world masterfully," asserted Womack in appraising the first "Fever Crumb" novel, and his story "is both a thrilling slice of retro science fiction and an involving fable about a young girl coming to terms with herself." A *Kirkus Reviews* writer recommended *Fever Crumb* as "an essential read for ["Hungry City Chronicles"] fans and a great entry point for newcomers" to Reeve's fictional universe. "Always excellent," according to another *Kirkus Reviews* writer, "Reeve's writing [in *A Web of Air*] shines . . . as he turns his attention to the romantic," although Ian Chipman noted in *Booklist* that the novel's "high-wire action and inventive writing" culminates in a "downer of an ending." Fever's experience of love does make the ending "bittersweet," wrote *School Library Journal* critic Misti Tidman of the second "Fever Crumb" novel, but the "intricately imagined world" evoked in the novel "offers a rich, rewarding reading experience." "It's clear that Reeve . . . is building toward an epic," asserted Jonathan Hunt in his *Horn Book* review of *A Web of Air,* and his storytelling continues to reveal "a trenchant understanding of human nature."

Featuring illustrations by David Wyatt, Reeve's middle-grade "Larklight" trilogy—*Larklight: A Rousing Tale of Dauntless Pluck in the Farthest Reaches of Space,* as well as *Starcross; or, The Coming of the Moobs!; or, Our Adventures in the Fourth Dimension!: A Stirring Tale of British Vim upon the Seas of Space and Time* and *Mothstorm; or, The Horror from beyond Georgium Sidus!; or, A Tale of Two Shapers: A Rattling Yarn of Danger, Dastardy, and Derring-do upon the Far Frontiers of British Space!*—take readers on a more lighthearted excursion into the author's imagination. Set in a Victorian alternate world where houses float in space, *Larklight* introduces siblings Myrtle and Art Mumby, who live in a floating house called Larklight along with their father. Separated from their home during an attack of space spiders, the children begin an adventure that leads them from the moon and Venus to the pirate ship of Captain Jack Havock. From there, they travel to a scientific institute where they uncover a plot by a mad scientist that involves the invasion of hoards of the pesky spiders. With the help of Wyatt's detailed ink drawings, *Larklight* "melds deadpan comedy, anticolonial political satire, sci-fi epic, and pirate caper with aplomb," maintained Gross, while a contributor to *Kirkus Reviews* dubbed the novel "jolly good fun, all around." Calling Reeve's story "utterly entertaining," a

Publishers Weekly critic added that the conclusion of *Larklight* "is an absolute hoot" and will leave readers craving more.

Dubbed a "dashing and outrageous sequel" by a *Publishers Weekly* writer, *Starcross* reunites readers with Art and Myrtle and sends them off on another fanciful adventure in Reeve's alternate universe. Together with their half-alien-and-older-that-dirt Mum, the children travel to Starcross, a space resort, where they hope to find time to rest. Such is not to be, however, when vicious sand crabs appear and another plot surfaces that threatens their free-floating world. The children's adventures conclude in *Mothstorm,* as Art and Myrtle look forward to a Christmas spent with Jack Havock until an alert sends the group spaceward. On the planet Georgium Sidus (a.k.a. Uranus) an evil Shaper called the Mothmaker has marshaled an army of blue lizard creatures known as Snilth, Under the leadership of Captain Jack, the Mumbys decipher the complex history of the Mothmaker, and ultimately save the British Empire from being overtaken.

"Tongue-in-cheek, hilarious, and wildly imaginative," according to Connie Tyrell Burns in *School Library Journal, Starcross* compelled readers to eagerly await the conclusion to Reeve's archly British saga. In reviewing *Mothstorm,* a *Kirkus Reviews* writer was equally enthusiastic, writing that "Reeve's imagination seems to know no bounds as he conjures up ever more ridiculous and hilarious predicaments" for his young adventurers. "A clever blending of genres . . . with a liberal dash of British humor and style," according to *School Library Journal* contributor Jennifer D. Montgomery, *Mothstorm* is also "simply a jolly good read."

In addition to his series fiction, Reeve has also created several stand-alone novels, among them *Here Lies Arthur* and the middle-grade story *No Such Things as Dragons.* In *Here Lies Arthur* Reave intrigues readers with a new version of the legend of King Arthur. As narrated by a perceptive girl named Gwyna, his medieval Britain is a dark, unsettling place where a subtle magic and evil exist side by side. In this world Arthur claims himself to be king of a band of marauders, while Myddrin (Merlin) is a woman with a talent for disguise, subterfuge, and storytelling. Citing the "deep cynicism" that undergirds Reeve's tale, a *Publishers Weekly* contributor maintained that *Here Lies Arthur* resonates in the present, "neatly skewering the modern-day cult of spin and the age-old trickery behind it." Calling the novel "a study in balance and contradiction," *Horn Book* reviewer Claire E. Gross expressed a similar view, deeming Reeve's story "bleak yet tender; impeccably historical, yet distinctly timely in its driving sense of disillusionment." The legends of Camelot have "inspired many novels for young people," concluded *Booklist* critic Carolyn Phelan in her review of *Here Lies Arthur,* "but few as arresting as this."

Described by Chipman as an exploration of "the cracks between life and lore," *No Such Things as Dragons* focuses on Ansel, a mute ten year old who is the apprentice of dragon-hunter Johannes von Brock. Together the two travel the countryside, alerting those who will listen that dragons do exist and showing them a purported dragon scull as proof. Ansel is a perceptive lad, and he soon suspects that Brock may be nothing more than a huckster, using people's superstitious fears to separate them from their money. Brock admits as much and reveals the evidentiary skull to be that of a large crocodile, so when a dragon-like creature DOES appear on the scene both Brock and Ansel must summon real courage as well as wisdom in order to deal with it.

Cover of Reeve's fanciful story **No Such Things as Dragons,** ***which features cover art by David Wyatt.*** (Cover art copyright © 2009 by David Wyatt. Reproduced by permission of Scholastic Press, an imprint of Scholastic, Inc.)

In *Publishers Weekly* a contributor praised *No Such Things as Dragons* as a "somber but rewarding tale," noting that it is uncharacteristically "understated" when compared to Reeve's body of work. For Chipman, such understatement does not detract: *No Such Things as Dragons* "still has all the excitement of a thrilling adventure," the critic asserted. A *Kirkus Reviews* contributor described Reeve's middle-grade novel as "a gem" in which "Ansel's growth provides a heart beneath the adventure," and for Burkam the story "is taut with tension and flowing with Reeve's commanding language."

Biographical and Critical Sources

PERIODICALS

Booklist, November 1, 2003, Sally Estes, review of *Mortal Engines,* p. 491; August, 2004, Sally Estes, review of *Predator's Gold,* p. 1920; May 15, 2006, Sally Estes, review of *Infernal Devices,* p. 61; November 1, 2007, Todd Morning, review of *Starcross; or, The Coming of the Moobs!; or, Our Adventures in the Fourth Dimension!: A Stirring Tale of British Vim upon the Seas of Space and Time,* p. 48; August 1, 2008, Carolyn Phelan, review of *Here Lies Arthur,* p. 69; January 1, 2010, Ian Chipman, review of *Fever Crumb,* p. 80; August 1, 2010, Ian Chipman, review of *No Such Thing as Dragons,* p. 51; Ocotber 15, 2011, Ian Chipman, review of *A Web of Air,* p. 47.

Bookseller, August 10, 2001, Tara Stephenson, review of *Mortal Engines,* p. 33; June 27, 2008, Caroline Horn, interview with Reeve, p. 10.

Bulletin of the Center for Children's Books, March, 2004, Janice M. Del Negro, review of *Mortal Engines,* p. 294; November, 2004, Timnah Card, review of *Predator's Gold,* p. 141.

Chronicle, January, 2004, Don D'Ammassa, review of *Mortal Engines,* p. 31.

Daily Telegraph (London, England), June 13, 2009, Philip Womack, review of *Fever Crumb,* p. 14.

Guardian (London, England), June 2, 2007, Kathryn Hughes, review of *Here Lies Arthur,* p. A&E 20; April 8, 2006, Josh Lacey, review of *A Darkling Plain;* June 27, 2009, Frank Cottrell Boyce, review of *Fever Crumb,* p. A&E 14.

Horn Book, November-December, 2003, Anita L. Burkam, review of *Mortal Engines,* p. 755; September-October, 2004, Anita L. Burkam, review of *Predator's Gold,* p. 596; November-December, 2006, Claire E. Gross, review of *Larklight: A Rousing Tale of Dauntless Pluck in the Farthest Reaches of Space,* p. 724; November-December, 2008, Claire E. Gross, review of *Here Lies Arthur,* p. 713; March-April, 2010, Claire E. Gross, review of *Fever Crumb,* p. 68; September-October, 2010, Anita Burkham, review of *No Such Thing as Dragons,* p. 92; September-October, 2011, Jonathan Hunt, review of *A Web of Air,* p. 98.

Kirkus Reviews, October 15, 2003, review of *Mortal Engines,* p. 1275; August 15, 2004, review of *Predator's Gold,* p. 216; September 15, 2006, review of *Larklight,* p. 965; October 1, 2007, review of *Starcross;* October 15, 2008, reviews of *Here Lies Arthur* and *Mothstorm: The Horror from beyond Georgium Sidus!;* March 1, 2010, review of *Fever Crumb;* August 15, 2010, review of *No Such Thing as Dragons;* September 1, 2011, review of *A Web of Air.*

Kliatt, November, 2003, Paula Rohrlick, review of *Mortal Engines,* p. 10; September, 2004, Paula Rohrlick, review of *Predator's Gold,* p. 16; May, 2006, Paula Rohrlick, review of *Infernal Devices,* p. 13; November, 2008, Paula Rohrlick, review of *Here Lies Arthur,* p. 17.

Magpies, May, 2002, review of *Mortal Engines,* p. 38; March, 2004, Rayma Turton, review of *Predator's Gold,* p. 43.

Publishers Weekly, October 27, 2003, review of *Mortal Engines,* p. 70; August 16, 2004, review of *Predator's Gold,* p. 64; August 28, 2006, review of *Larklight,* p. 54; November 5, 2007, review of *Starcross,* p. 64; October 6, 2008, review of *Here Lies Arthur,* p. 55; February 15, 2010, review of *Fever Crumb,* p. 133; July 19, 2010, review of *No Such Thing as Dragons,* p. 130.

School Librarian, winter, 2001, review of *Mortal Engines,* p. 214; winter, 2002, review of *Night of the Living Veg,* p. 202; spring, 2004, Michael Holloway, review of *Predator's Gold,* p. 34; winter, 2010, Karen King, review of *A Web of Air,* p. 247.

School Library Journal, December, 2003, Sharon Rawlins, review of *Mortal Engines,* p. 864; September, 2004, Sharon Rawlins, review of *Predator's Gold,* p. 216; June, 2006, Tim Wadham, review of *Infernal Devices,* p. 164; November, 2006, Rick Margolis, interview with Reeve, p. 33; December, 2007, Connie Tyrrell Burns, review of *Starcross,* p. 142; December, 2008, Jennifer D. Montgomery, review of *Mothstorm,* p. 136; September, 2011, Misti Tidman, review of *A Web of Air,* p. 168.

Tribune Books (Chicago, IL), November 23, 2003, review of *Mortal Engines,* p. 4.

Voice of Youth Advocates, October, 2004, Sarah Flowers, review of *Predator's Gold,* p. 318.

ONLINE

British Broadcasting Corporation Web site, http://www.bbc.co.uk/ (September 29, 2004), interview with Reeve.

ContemporaryWriters.com, http://www.contemporarywriters.com/ (June 8, 2009), "Philip Reeve."

Philip Reeve Home Page, http://www.philip-reeve.com (May 1, 2012).

Philip Reeve Web log, http://philipreeve.blogspot.com (May 1, 2012).*

* * *

RESTREPO, Bettina 1972-

Personal

Born April, 1972, in Lawton, OK; father in the U.S. Army; married; husband's name Tom (an engineer); children: Thomas Allen. *Education:* University of Texas at Austin, B.S. (speech communications).

Addresses

Home—Frisco, TX. *Agent*—John M. Cusick, Scott Treimel Agency, 434 Lafayette St., New York, NY 10003. *E-mail*—Bettina@bettinarestrepo.com.

Career

Author. Worked as an internal auditor for ten years; full-time writer. Presenter at schools and conferences.

Bettina Restrepo (Photograph by H. Green Photography. Reproduced by permission.)

Member

Authors Guild, Society of Children's Book Writers and Illustrators.

Awards, Honors

Mom's Choice Awards Silver Medal, 2009, for *Moose and Magpie;* YALSA Quick Pick for Reluctant Readers, American Library Association (ALA), 2011, and TAYSHAS listee, Texas Library Association Young-Adult Roundtable, and ALA Amelia Bloomer listee, both 2012, all for *Illegal.*

Writings

Moose and Magpie, illustrated by Sherry Rogers, Sylvan Dell Pub. (Mount Pleasant, SC), 2009.
Illegal, Katherine Tegen Books (New York, NY), 2011.

Contributor of over one hundred articles to periodicals.

Sidelights

Bettina Restrepo worked in business for fifteen years before shifting her focus to more creative pursuits. Her first published work, the picture book *Moose and Magpie,* was inspired by her reading of numerous stories to her growing son, and her young-adult novel *Illegal* was inspired by her experiences as a first-generation American.

Featuring illustrations by Sherry Rogers, *Moose and Magpie* tells the story of a young moose and his friend Magpie. From the summer, as Moose grows taller and begins to sprout his first antlers, through the fall and into winter as both creatures migrate to warmer climes, Moose and Magpie are joined by several other animal friends in taking stock of the changing world around them.

A journey of an entirely different sort is the focus of *Illegal,* which introduces fourteen-year-old Nora. Life in Cedula, Nora's Mexican farming village, is difficult for the family. Because there was no market for the family's crop of grapefruits, Nora's father travels north into Texas in search of paid work that will allow him to support his family. A job with a construction company has meant money coming home to his family, along with letters. Now, three years have passed and the letters and the money no longer come. Worried that harm

Cover of Restrepo's thoughtful and timely young-adult novel* Illegal, *which features cover art by Jonathan Barkat. (Jacket art © 2011 by Jonathan Barkat. Reproduced by permission of Katherine Tegen Books, an imprint of HarperCollins Publishers.)

has befallen the man, Nora and her mother use the family's remaining savings to make an illegal border-crossing journey hidden in a truck conveying mangos into the United States. The search for Nora's father is made all the more difficult because the two women have few friends and few resources, and finding food and shelter are as much a challenge as searching for the missing man. While some are willing to help the mother and daughter, others attempt to take advantage of them, and the challenges Nora faces cause her to reconsider her strong Christian faith as well as wish for circumstances that would allow her to celebrate her upcoming quinceañera in the traditional Mexican fashion.

Citing *Illegal* for its "depth and detail" in her *Booklist* review, Hazel Rochman added that Restrepo's young-adult fiction debut avoids sentimentality in favor of a first-person narration in which "unsparing language keeps the tension mounting as well as the heartbreak." A *Kirkus Reviews* writer commented on the novel's "searing realism," adding that Nora's "memorable coming-of-age story will awaken readers to the overlooked struggles of immigrants." Reviewing *Illegal* in the *Voice of Youth Advocates,* Angie Hammond praised Restrepo's tale as "thoroughly engaging and thought-provoking," recommending the novel as a provocative choice for both book groups and classroom discussion of immigration policy.

Biographical and Critical Sources

PERIODICALS

Booklist, March 15, 2011, Hazel Rochman, review of *Illegal,* p. 52.

Bulletin of the Center for Children's Books, March, 2011, Hope Morrison, review of *Illegal,* p. 343.

Kirkus Reviews, February 15, 2011, review of *Illegal.*

School Library Journal, September, 2009, Maryann H. Owen, review of *Moose and Magpie,* p. 132; May, 2011, Jessie Spalding, review of *Illegal,* p. 122.

Voice of Youth Advocates, February, 2011, Angie Hammond, review of *Illegal,* p. 559.

ONLINE

Bettina Restrepo Home Page, http://bettinarestrep.com (May 1, 2012).

Class of 2k11 Web site, http://www.classof2k11.com/ (May 1, 2012), "Bettina Restrepo."

Cynsations Web log, http://cynthialeitichsmith.blogspot.com/ (April 27, 2011), Cynthia Leitich Smith, interview with Restrepo.

* * *

RICHARDS, Scott

See CARD, Orson Scott

ROSENSTOCK, Barb 1960-

Personal

Born April 1, 1960, in Chicago, IL; married; children: three children. *Education:* Loyola University, B.S.; National Louis University, M.A.T. *Religion:* Roman Catholic. *Hobbies and other interests:* History, music, gardening.

Addresses

Home—Chicago, IL. *Agent*—Stimola Literary Studio, 308 Livingston Ct., Edgewater, NJ 07020. *E-mail*—barb@barbrosenstock.com.

Career

Author and educator. Worked in advertising and marketing; teacher. Presenter at schools.

Member

Society of Book Writers and Illustrators.

Awards, Honors

Amelia Bloomer listee, American Library Association, and Best Children's Book selection, New York Public Library, both 2010, both for *Fearless;* Sydney Taylor Book Award Notable Book designation, Association of Jewish Libraries, and Best Book selection, Bank Street College of Education, both 2011, both for *The Littlest Mountain.*

Writings

Fearless: The Story of Racing Legend Louise Smith, illustrated by Scott Dawson, Dutton Children's Books (New York, NY), 2010.

Barb Rosenstock (Photograph by Kris Hildy. Reproduced by permission.)

The Littlest Mountain, illustrated by Melanie Hall, Kar-Ben Pub. (Minneapolis, MN), 2011.

The Camping Trip That Changed America: Theodore Roosevelt, John Muir, and Our National Parks, illustrated by Mordicai Gerstein, Dial Books for Young Readers (New York, NY), 2012.

Sidelights

A love of history inspires much of Barb Rosenstock's writing for children. Her first book, *Fearless: The Story of Racing Legend Louise Smith,* was based on a true-life story about an adventurous young woman, and *The Camping Trip That Changed America: Theodore Roosevelt, John Muir, and Our National Parks* also has its roots in a person from America's past. A native of Illinois, Rosenstock also shares a story from the Jewish faith in *The Littlest Mountain,* an award-winning picture book illustrated by Melanie Hall. Reviewing this story of God's presentation of the Ten Commandments on Mount Sinai, Heidi Estrin noted in *School Library Journal* that Rosenstock's story will make a "great read-aloud for the holiday of Shavuot" and "may be enjoyed in a secular setting as well."

Featuring illustrations by Scott Dawson, *Fearless* profiles the long career of Louise Smith, a woman who, born in 1906, first drove a car at age seven and became a professional stock-car racer in the early days of auto racing. In capturing Smith's eventful life, which included both excitement and danger, Dawson's "realistic, action-filled" illustrations bring to life the story of "a person once called 'the craziest woman we know,'" according to *Booklist* critic Andrew Medlar. "Rosenstock tells her story in a simple but animated way," noted a *Kirkus Reviews* writer, and her use of a refrain "conveys movement and energy." The "upbeat prose" in *Fearless* "finishes on a high note," asserted a *Publishers Weekly* contributor, the reviewer concluding that "this debut for both author and illustrator is a winner."

In 1903 U.S. President Theodore Roosevelt joined conservationist John Muir on a tour of the western wilderness that would one day become Yosemite National Park, and their few days spent exploring this mountainous land inspired Roosevelt to further support the system of national parks that now protect and preserve pristine sections of the United States. In her "very readable text" for *The Camping Trip That Changed America,* Rosenstock "focuses . . . on the men's enjoyment of the outdoors" by creating fictional dialogue based on archived writings, while artist Mordicai Gerstein contributes "wonderfully varied . . . line-and-watercolor" art, according to *Booklist* critic Carolyn Phelan. In *Horn Book* Joanna Rudge Long also recommended the artist's characteristic "verve," noting that *The Camping Trip That Changed America* captures an instance wherein "an effective government respond[ed] . . . to a vital need in a timely manner." A *Kirkus Reviews* contributor dubbed the same picture book "wonderfully simple, sweet and engaging."

Biographical and Critical Sources

PERIODICALS

Booklist, December 1, 2010, Andrew Medlar, review of *Fearless: The Story of Racing Legend Louise Smith,*

***Rosenstock's biography of a noted female athlete gains added energy from Scott Dawson's artwork for* Fearless: The Story of Racing Legend Louise Smith.** (Illustration copyright © 2010 by Scott Dawson. Used by permission of Dutton Children's Books, a division of Penguin Group (USA), Inc.)

p. 43; December 15, 2011, Carolyn Phelan, review of *The Camping Trip That Changed America: Theodore Roosevelt, John Muir, and Our National Parks,* p. 48.
Bulletin of the Center for Children's Books, November, 2010, Elizabeth Bush, review of *Fearless,* p. 145.
Horn Book, January-February, 2012, Joanna Rudge Long, review of *The Camping Trip That Changed America,* p. 118.
Kirkus Reviews, October 1, 2010, review of *Fearless;* December 1, 2011, review of *The Camping Trip That Changed America.*
Publishers Weekly, October, 11, 2010, review of *Fearless,* p. 42.
School Library Journal, December, 2010, Patricia Manning, review of *Fearless,* p. 97; April, 2011, Heidi Estrin, review of *The Littlest Mountain,* p. 152.

ONLINE

Barb Rosenstock Home Page, http://barbrosenstock.com (May 1, 2012).
Society of Children's Book Writers and Illustrators—Illinois Web site, http://www.scbwi-illinois.org/ (May 1, 2012), "Barb Rosenstock."

* * *

RUDNICKI, Richard

Personal
Born in Yorkton, Saskatchewan, Canada; married Susan Tooke (an artist). *Education:* Attended art school.

Addresses
Home—Halifax, Nova Scotia, Canada. *E-mail*—richard@chebucto.ns.ca.

Career
Fine-art painter, author, and illustrator. Formerly worked as a graphic designer.

Member
Canadian Society of Children's Authors, Illustrators, and Performers, Canadian Children's Book Centre, Writer's Federation of Nova Scotia, Visual Arts Nova Scotia.

Awards, Honors
Lillian Sheppard Award for Excellence in Illustration, and Atlantic Book Publishers Award nomination, both c. 2007, both for *Gracie, the Public Gardens Duck* by Judith Meyrick; Mayor's Award for Excellence in Illustration, 2007, for *I Spy a Bunny* by Judy Dudar; Norma Fleck Award nomination, Shining Willow Award nomination, and Golden Oak Award nomination, all 2010, all for *Viola Desmond Won't Be Budged!* by Jody Nyasha Warner.

Richard Rudnicki (Photograph by Susan Tooke. Reproduced by permission.)

Writings

SELF-ILLUSTRATED

A Christmas Dollhouse, Nimbus Pub. (Halifax, Nova Scotia, Canada), 2011.

ILLUSTRATOR

Judith Meyrick, *Gracie, the Public Gardens Duck,* Nimbus Pub. (Halifax, Nova Scotia, Canada), 2007.
Judy Dudar, *I Spy a Bunny,* Nimbus Pub. (Halifax, Nova Scotia, Canada), 2009.
Jody Nyasha Warner, *Viola Desmond Won't Be Budged!,* Groundwood Books (Toronto, Ontario, Canada), 2010.
James Laxer, *Tecumseh,* Groundwood Books (Toronto, Ontario, Canada), 2012.
Erin Arsenault, *Gus the Tortoise Takes a Walk,* Nimbus Pub. (Halifax, Nova Scotia, Canada), 2012.

Sidelights
Richard Rudnicki worked as a graphic designer for several years after completing art school, until his love of painting won out, and he now works as an artist in the studio he shares with his wife, Susan Tooke, in Nova Scotia, Canada. In his paintings for picture books, which are rendered in acrylics, Rudnicki shows his mastery of color and light and his work has appeared in award-winning picture books such as Jody Nyasha Warner's *Viola Desmond Won't Be Budged!* and Judith Meyrick's *Gracie, the Public Gardens Duck.*

Rudnicki's first illustration project, *Gracie, the Public Gardens Duck,* captures the life of a duck that lives a rarified life in the Halifax Public Gardens where treats are tossed by passersby who enjoy the ducks in the well-cared-for setting. When a sign is installed requesting that visitors refrain from feeding the "wild" animals, Gracie must learn how to search for food in the traditional way: like a duck. Featuring "soft, light hues" that pair well with the "quiet feel" of Meyrick's story, Rudnicki's images for *Gracie, the Public Gardens Duck* "are realistic and detailed," according to Tanya Boudreau in her *Resource Links* review of the picture book.

Rudnicki teams up with another Canadian author, Judy Dudar, in *I Spy a Bunny,* in which a little girl and her aunt visit a seaside park in Nova Scotia and pass the time playing "I Spy." Here the artist's "large and colourful" images for *I Spy a Bunny* introduce readers to a cast of "white-nosed rabbits on almost every page," asserted *Canadian Review of Materials* critic Helen Norrie. In *Quill & Quire* Nathan Whitlock praised the book's mix of a "straightforward" story by Dudar and illustrations by Rudnicki "that are filled with colour and sunlight."

A picture-book biography by Warner, *Viola Desmond Won't Be Budged!* is set in 1946 and focuses on the time when Viola Desmond, a black businesswoman on a driving trip, waited for her car to be repaired by taking in a movie at the cinema in downtown New Glasgow, Nova Scotia. After she chose a seat on the main floor, Viola was asked to move to the balcony, where people of color were segregated. Viola's refusal resulted in time in jail, but her willingness to stand up against racism inspired many other black Canadians, much as Rosa Parks did in the United States through her refusal to move to the back of a city bus. In *Quill & Quire* Joanne Findon described *Viola Desmond Won't Be Budged!* as "a wonderful marriage of text and image," while a *Kirkus Reviews* contributor cited Rudnicki's "bold acrylics in vivid colors" as effective in evoking "the style, dress and look of the period." The "vivid, dramatic art" in *Viola Desmond Won't Be Budged!* "intensifies the danger that Desmond's stubborn determination brought her," according to *Booklist* contributor Courtney Jones, and in *School Library Journal* Lucinda Snyder Whitehurst wrote that the artist's use of "varying perspectives heighten the emotional intensity" of Warner's story.

With *A Christmas Dollhouse* Rudnicki also turned author, creating nostalgic-themed illustrations to accompany his retelling of a true-to-life Christmas tale set in Canada during the 1930s. The book finds a young girl's imagination captivated by a beautiful dollhouse displayed in a local shop window; her reality consists of helping her older brother care for their infirm mother during trying economic times. Reviewing *A Christmas*

Rudnicki's paintings include the light-filled "Quaker Meeting House." (Reproduced by permission.)

Dollhouse in the *Canadian Review of Materials,* Rebecca King cited Rudnicki's "straightforward telling" as "smooth and fluent," and his illustrations "beautiful and evocative of the period" as experienced in "a tightly knit and generous small community."

Biographical and Critical Sources

PERIODICALS

Booklist, November 15, 2010, Courtney Jones, review of *Viola Desmond Won't Be Budged!,* p. 34.
Canadian Review of Materials, June 26, 2009, Helen Norrie, review of *I Spy a Bunny;* September 3, 2010, Crystal Sutherland, review of *Viola Desmond Won't Be Budged!;* May 4, 2012, Rebecca King, review of *A Christmas Dollhouse.*
Publishers Weekly, October 11, 2010, review of *Viola Desmond Won't Be Budged!,* p. 42.
Quill & Quire, June, 2009, Nathan Whitlock, review of *I Spy a Bunny;* October, 2010, review of *Viola Desmond Won't Be Budged!*
Resource Links, October, 2007, Tanya Boudreau, review of *Gracie, the Public Gardens Duck,* p. 6.
School Library Journal, December, 2010, Lucinda Snyder Whitehurst, review of *Viola Desmond Won't Be Budged!,* p. 98.

ONLINE

Richard Rudnicki Home Page, http://www.richardrudnicki.com (May 1, 2012).

* * *

RUNTON, Andy

Personal

Born in GA. *Education:* Georgia Tech, M.A. (industrial design).

Addresses

Home—Lilburn, GA. *E-mail*—Owly@mac.com.

Career

Author and illustrator. Computer programmer; Motorola Corp, creator of user interfaces (icons) for eight years.

Awards, Honors

Howard E. Day Memorial Prize; Harvey Award for Best New Talent, 2004, two Ignatz Awards, and Eisner Award for Best Publication for a Younger Audience, 2006, all for "Owly" series.

Writings

SELF-ILLUSTRATED GRAPHIC NOVELS

Owly: The Only Way Home; and, The Bittersweet Summer, Top Shelf Comics (Marietta, GA), 2004.
Owly: Just a Little Blue, Top Shelf Comics (Marietta, GA), 2005.
Flying Lessons, Top Shelf Comics (Marietta, GA), 2005.
Owly and Wormy, Friends All Aflutter!, Atheneum Books for Young Readers (New York, NY), 2011.

Creator of "Owly" mini-comics series, published by Top Shelf Comics (Marietta, GA), beginning 2004.

Sidelights

After earning a master's degree in industrial design and working for ten years in a major corporation, Andy Runton found himself at a career crossroads. Recalling the reason why he studied art and design, he rekindled his interest in cartoon art and discovered a new use for a cartoon character he had invented years before. Runton's award-winning "Owly" graphic-novel series has gained the particular affection of beginning readers who can master Runton's "text" with its mix of emoticons and symbols in place of words. In addition to the graphic novels *Owly: The Only Way Home; and, The Bittersweet Summer, Owly: Just a Little Blue,* and *Flying Lessons,* Runton's likeable round-eyed character also stars in the picture book *Owly and Wormy, Friends All Aflutter!*

Runton first developed his cartoon character Owly while attending college and living at home, where his irregular schedule required that he leave his mother notes when he stayed up late into the night working on school assignments. Remarks about his night-owl lifestyle in-

***Andy Runton's popular cartoon creations Owly and Wormy star take center state in their picture-book debut* Owly and Wormy, Friends All Aflutter!** (Copyright © 2011 by Andy Runton. Reprinted by permission of Atheneum Books for Young Readers, an imprint of Simon & Schuster, Inc.)

spired Runton to invent the cartoon owl that became his alter ego in notes to his mom and eventually morphed into Owly. Making his comic-book appearance in 2004, Owly is a friendly, gentle owl who enjoys making friends and experiencing new things, especially out of doors with his woodland animal friends. Because the speech balloons in an "Owly" story are filled with symbols signifying emotions and other information that helps move the story forward logically, Runton's books have been credited with building confidence among children still mastering letter sounds and also tapping their storytelling skills by giving them the chance to add telling details to the obvious action.

Owly makes his debut in *Owly: The Only Way Home; and, The Bittersweet Summer,* two stories in which Owly and friend Wormy share adventures. Their friendship is forged in "The Only Way Home," wherein Wormy fears that Owly will eat rather than befriend him; in "The Bittersweet Summer" the two become sad when their new hummingbird friends leave for their fall migration to warmer climes. *Owly: Just a Little Blue* finds Owly and Wormy attempting to help a bluebird family when its home in a rotting tree stump is threatened. A friendship with a flying squirrel provides readers with a lesson in prejudice in *Flying Lessons,* as a new friend must get over its fear of owls and also recognize Wormy's limitations when it comes to becoming airborne.

Reviewing Runton's first "Owly" story, Tina Coleman remarked in *Booklist* that readers of all ages "will appreciate the book's simple charm, wisdom, and warmth," while *School Library Journal* critic Steve Weiner called the book's loosely drawn cartoon art "warm and poignant." The artist's "deceptively simple" ink-and-brush illustrations have "a flair and subtlety that makes words unnecessary," asserted Coleman in a review of *Owly: Just a Little Blue,* and in *Flying Lessons* his "expressive, animated . . . art breathes life into the [story's] loveable characters."

Owly and Wormy make their full-color debut in *Owly and Wormy, Friends All Aflutter!,* a picture book in which "the huge-eyed bird radiates appeal even more strongly than . . . as a line drawn figure," according to a *Kirkus Reviews* writer. In Runton's story, Owly and Wormy hope to attract butterflies to their garden and a raccoon suggests adding a milkweed plant which is known to attract the fluttering creatures. Although the plant attracts only a pair of caterpillars, the four become friends and play together throughout the spring. Sadness over the disappearance of the two worms turns to joy when the pair returns in a far-more colorful form in Runton's characteristically good-hearted story.

Paired with large-scale drawings that Ian Chipman characterized as "a blast" in his *Booklist* review, the "dialogue visuals" make *Owly and Wormy, Friends All Aflutter!* a "gently challenging offering," according to the critic, "Runton's colors are unabashedly cheerful . . . and clever, rewarding touches abound," noted a *Publishers Weekly* critic, and in *School Library Journal* Suzanne Myers Harold concluded that, "with its cheerful palette, cartoon characters, and humorous . . . details," *Owly and Wormy, Friends All Aflutter!* "is a thoroughly endearing story."

Biographical and Critical Sources

PERIODICALS

Booklist, February 1, 2005, Tina Coleman, review of *Owly: The Only Way Home; and, The Bittersweet Summer,* p. 959; July, 2005, Tina Coleman, review of *Owly: Just a Little Blue,* p. 1927; March 15, 2006, Tina Coleman, review of *Flying Lessons,* p. 60; March 15, 2007, Michael Cart, "You Go, Graphic!," p. 43; February 15, 2011, Ian Chipman, review of *Owly and Wormy, Friends All Aflutter!,* p. 78.

Kirkus Reviews, February 1, 2011, review of *Owly and Wormy, Friends All Aflutter!*

Publishers Weekly, August 30, 2004, review of *Owly: The Only Way Home; and, The Bittersweet Summer,* p. 34; January 10, 2011, review of *Owly and Wormy, Friends All Aflutter!,* p. 49.

School Library Journal, December, 2004, Steve Weiner, review of *Owly: The Way Home; and, The Bittersweet Summer,* p. 25; May, 2011, Suzanne Myers Harold, review of *Owly and Wormy, Friends All Aflutter!,* p. 88.

ONLINE

Andy Runton Home Page, http://www.andyrunton.com (May 1, 2012).

Comic Book Resources Web site, http://www.comicbookresources.com/ (December 11, 2007), Shaun Manning, interview with Runton.

Daily Cross Hatch Web log, http://thedailycrosshatch.com/ (November 26, 2008), interview with Runton.

School Library Journal Web log, http://blog.schoollibraryjournal.com/ (November 10, 2011), interview with Runton.*

* * *

RYLANT, Cynthia 1954-

Personal

Surname pronounced "Rye-*lunt*"; born June 6, 1954, in Hopewell, VA; daughter of John Tune (an army sergeant) and Leatrel (a nurse) Smith; twice married (divorced); children (first marriage): Nathaniel. *Education:* Morris Harvey College (now University of Charleston), B.A., 1975; Marshall University (Huntington, WV), M.A., 1976; Kent State University, M.L.S., 1982. *Politics:* Democrat. *Religion:* Christian. *Hobbies and other interests:* Pets, reading, going to movies, going to the seashore.

Addresses

Home—Eugene, OR. *Agent*—Steven Malk, Writers House, 7660 Fay Ave., No. 338H, La Jolla, CA 92037.

Career

Writer, educator, and librarian. Marshall University, Huntington, WV, part-time English instructor, 1979-80; Akron Public Library, Akron, OH, children's librarian, 1983; University of Akron, Akron, part-time English lecturer, 1983-84; Northeast Ohio Universities College of Medicine, Rootstown, part-time lecturer, beginning 1991.

Awards, Honors

American Book Award nomination, and Notable Book designation, American Library Association (ALA), both 1983, and English-Speaking Union Book-across-the-Sea Ambassador of Honor Award, 1984, all for *When I Was Young in the Mountains;* National Council for Social Studies Best Book designation, and Notable Book designation, ALA, both 1984, and Society of Midland Authors Best Children's Book designation, 1985, all for *Waiting to Waltz: A Childhood;* Children's Book of the Year designation, Child Study Association of America (CSA), 1985, for *The Relatives Came;* Children's Book of the Year designation, CSA, 1985, for *A Blue-eyed Daisy;* Parents' Choice Award, 1986, and Newbery Medal Honor Book designation, 1987, both for *A Fine White Dust;* Best Book for Young Adults citation, ALA, 1988, for *A Kindness;* Ohioana Award, 1990, for *But I'll Be Back Again;* Best Book for Young Adults citation, ALA, 1990, for *A Couple of Kooks and Other Stories about Love;* Parents' Choice Award in picture-book category, and *Boston Globe/Horn Book* Honor Book for Nonfiction designation, both 1991, and Ohioana Award, 1992, all for *Appalachia; Boston Globe/Horn Book* Award for Children's Fiction, Reading Magic Award, and Parents' Choice Award, all 1992, and John Newbery Medal and *Hungry Mind Review* Award, both 1993, all for *Missing May;* Notable Children's Book designation, ALA, 1996, for *The Van Gogh Café;* Notable Children's Book designation, ALA, 2006, for *Henry and Mudge and the Great Grandpas; Boston Globe/Horn Book* Honor Book designation, 2004, and Best Books for Young Adults citation, ALA, both 2004, both for *God Went to Beauty School.* Several of Rylant's "Henry and Mudge" books received child-selected awards, including Garden State Children's Book Award, Children's Services Section of the New Jersey Library Association, and Children's Choice Award, Association of Booksellers for Children. *When I Was Young in the Mountains* was named a Caldecott Honor Book for its illustrations by Diane Goode, 1983; *The Relatives Came* was named a *New York Times* Best Illustrated Book, 1985, and a Caldecott Medal Honor Book, 1986, both for illustrations by Stephen Gammell.

Writings

FOR CHILDREN; PICTURE BOOKS AND EARLY FICTION, EXCEPT AS NOTED

When I Was Young in the Mountains, illustrated by Diane Goode, Dutton (New York, NY), 1982.

Miss Maggie, illustrated by Thomas DiGrazia, Dutton (New York, NY), 1983.

This Year's Garden, illustrated by Mary Szilagyi, Bradbury (New York, NY), 1984.

The Relatives Came, illustrated by Stephen Gammell, Bradbury (New York, NY), 1985.

Night in the Country, illustrated by Mary Szilagyi, Bradbury (New York, NY), 1986.

Birthday Presents, illustrated by Suçie Stevenson, Orchard Books (New York, NY), 1987.

All I See, illustrated by Peter Catalanotto, Orchard Books (New York, NY), 1988.

Mr. Griggs' Work, illustrated by Julie Downing, Orchard Books (New York, NY), 1989.

An Angel for Solomon Singer, illustrated by Peter Catalanotto, Orchard Books (New York, NY), 1992.

Best Wishes (autobiographical picture book), photographs by Carlo Ontal, Richard C. Owen (Katonah, NY), 1992.

The Dreamer, illustrated by Barry Moser, Blue Sky Press (New York, NY), 1993.

(Self-illustrated) *Dog Heaven,* Blue Sky Press (New York, NY), 1995.

Gooseberry Park, illustrated by Arthur Howard, Harcourt (San Diego, CA), 1995.

The Van Gogh Café (middle-grade fiction), Harcourt (San Diego, CA), 1995.

The Bookshop Dog, Blue Sky Press (New York, NY), 1996.

The Whales, Blue Sky Press (New York, NY), 1996.

The Old Woman Who Named Things, illustrated by Kathryn Brown, Harcourt (San Diego, CA), 1996.

(Self-illustrated) *Cat Heaven,* Blue Sky Press (New York, NY), 1997.

An Everyday Book, Simon & Schuster (New York, NY), 1997.

Bear Day, illustrated by Jennifer Selby, Harcourt (San Diego, CA), 1998.

Tulip Sees America, illustrated by Lisa Desimini, Blue Sky Press (New York, NY), 1998.

The Bird House, illustrated by Barry Moser, Blue Sky Press (New York, NY), 1998.

Scarecrow, illustrated by Lauren Stringer, Harcourt (San Diego, CA), 1998.

The Heavenly Village, Blue Sky Press (New York, NY), 1999.

The Cookie-Store Cat, Blue Sky Press (New York, NY), 1999.

Bunny Bungalow, illustrated by Nancy Hayashi, Harcourt (San Diego, CA), 1999.

The Troublesome Turtle, Greenwillow (New York, NY), 1999.

Puzzling Possum, Greenwillow (New York, NY), 1999.

Let's Go Home: The Wonderful Things about a House, illustrated by Wendy Anderson Halperin, Simon & Schuster (New York, NY), 2000.

In November, illustrated by Jill Kastner, Harcourt (San Diego, CA), 2000.

Thimbleberry Stories, illustrated by Maggie Kneen, Harcourt (San Diego, CA), 2000.

The Ticky-Tacky Doll, illustrated by Harvey Stevenson, Harcourt (San Diego, CA), 2000.

The Great Gracie Chase, illustrated by Mark Teague, Blue Sky Press (New York, NY), 2001.

Good Morning Sweetie Pie, and Other Poems for Little Children, illustrated by Jane Dyer, Simon & Schuster (New York, NY), 2001.

Old Town in the Green Groves: The Lost Little-House Years, illustrated by Jim LaMarche, HarperCollins (New York, NY), 2002.

Christmas in the Country, illustrated by Diane Goode, Blue Sky Press (New York, NY), 2002.

Moonlight, the Halloween Cat, illustrated by Melissa Sweet, HarperCollins (New York, NY), 2003.

Long Night Moon, illustrated by Mark Siegel, Simon & Schuster (New York, NY), 2004.

The Stars Will Still Shine, illustrated by Tiphanie Beeke, HarperCollins (New York, NY), 2005.

Miracles in Motion, illustrated by Lambert Davis, Blue Sky Press (New York, NY), 2005.

If You'll Be My Valentine, illustrated by Fumi Kosaka, HarperCollins (New York, NY), 2005.

The Case of the Desperate Duck, illustrated by G. Brian Karas, Greenwillow Books (New York, NY), 2005.

The Journey: Stories of Migration, illustrated by Lambert Davis, Blue Sky Press (New York, NY), 2006.

(Adaptor) *Walt Disney's Cinderella,* Disney Press (New York, NY), 2007.

Alligator Boy, illustrated by Diane Goode, Harcourt (Orlando, FL), 2007.

Snow, illustrated by Lauren Stringer, Harcourt (Orlando, FL), 2008.

Puppies and Piggies, illustrated by Ivan Bates, Harcourt (Orlando, FL), 2008.

(Reteller) *Hansel and Gretel,* illustrated by Jen Corace, Hyperion (New York, NY), 2008.

The Beautiful Stories of Life: Six Greek Myths, Retold, illustrated by Carson Ellis, Harcourt (Orlando, FL), 2008.

Baby Face: A Book of Love for Baby, illustrated by Diane Goode, Simon & Schuster (New York, NY), 2008.

All in a Day, illustrated by Nikki McClure, Abrams Books for Young Readers (New York, NY), 2009.

Walt Disney's Snow White and the Seven Dwarfs, illustrated by Gustaf Tenggren, Disney Press (New York, NY), 2009.

Rylant's papers are housed in Special Collections at Kent State University, Kent, OH.

"HENRY AND MUDGE" SERIES; BEGINNING READERS

Henry and Mudge: The First Book of Their Adventures, illustrated by James Stevenson, Macmillan (New York, NY), 1987.

Henry and Mudge in Puddle Trouble: The Second Book of Their Adventures, illustrated by James Stevenson, Macmillan (New York, NY), 1987.

Henry and Mudge in the Green Time: The Third Book of Their Adventures, illustrated by Suçie Stevenson, Macmillan (New York, NY), 1987.

Henry and Mudge under the Yellow Moon: The Fourth Book of Their Adventures, illustrated by Suçie Stevenson, Macmillan (New York, NY), 1987.

Henry and Mudge in the Sparkle Days: The Fifth Book of Their Adventures, illustrated by Suçie Stevenson, Macmillan (New York, NY), 1988.

Henry and Mudge and the Forever Sea: The Sixth Book of Their Adventures, illustrated by Suçie Stevenson, Macmillan (New York, NY), 1989, reprinted, Simon and Schuster Books for Young Readers (New York, NY), 2012.

Henry and Mudge Get the Cold Shivers: The Seventh Book of Their Adventures, illustrated by Suçie Stevenson, Macmillan (New York, NY), 1989.

Henry and Mudge and the Happy Cat: The Eighth Book of Their Adventures, illustrated by Suçie Stevenson, Macmillan (New York, NY), 1990.

Henry and Mudge and the Bedtime Thumps: The Ninth Book of Their Adventures, illustrated by Suçie Stevenson, Macmillan (New York, NY), 1991.

Henry and Mudge Take the Big Test: The Tenth Book of Their Adventures, illustrated by Suçie Stevenson, Macmillan (New York, NY), 1991.

Henry and Mudge and the Long Weekend: The Eleventh Book of Their Adventures, illustrated by Suçie Stevenson, Macmillan (New York, NY), 1992.

Henry and Mudge and the Wild Wind: The Twelfth Book of Their Adventures, illustrated by Suçie Stevenson, Macmillan (New York, NY), 1992, reprinted, Simon Spotlight (New York, NY), 2012.

Henry and Mudge and the Careful Cousin: The Thirteenth Book of Their Adventures, illustrated by Suçie Stevenson, Macmillan (New York, NY), 1994.

Henry and Mudge and the Best Day of All: The Fourteenth Book of Their Adventures, illustrated by Suçie Stevenson, Bradbury Press (New York, NY), 1995.

Henry and Mudge in the Family Trees: The Fifteenth Book of Their Adventures, illustrated by Suçie Stevenson, Simon & Schuster (New York, NY), 1997.

Henry and Mudge and the Sneaky Crackers: The Sixteenth Book of Their Adventures, illustrated by Suçie Stevenson, Simon & Schuster (New York, NY), 1998.

Henry and Mudge and the Starry Night: The Seventeenth Book of Their Adventures, illustrated by Suçie Stevenson, Simon & Schuster (New York, NY), 1998.

Henry and Mudge and Annie's Good Move: The Eighteenth Book of Their Adventures, illustrated by Suçie Stevenson, Simon & Schuster (New York, NY), 1998.

Henry and Mudge and the Snowman Plan: The Nineteenth Book of Their Adventures, illustrated by Suçie Stevenson, Simon & Schuster (New York, NY), 1999.

Henry and Mudge and Annie's Perfect Pet: The Twentieth Book of Their Adventures, illustrated by Suçie Stevenson, Simon & Schuster (New York, NY), 2000.

Henry and Mudge and the Tall Tree House: The Twenty-first Book of Their Adventures, illustrated by Carolyn Bracken, Simon & Schuster (New York, NY), 2002.
Henry and Mudge and Mrs. Hopper's House: The Twenty-second Book of Their Adventures, illustrated by Carolyn Bracken, 2003.
Henry and Mudge and the Wild Goose Chase: The Twenty-third Book of Their Adventures, illustrated by Carolyn Bracken, Simon & Schuster (New York, NY), 2003.
Henry and Mudge and the Funny Lunch: The Twenty-fourth Book of Their Adventures, illustrated by Carolyn Bracken, Simon & Schuster (New York, NY), 2004.
Henry and Mudge and a Very Special Merry Christmas: The Twenty-fifth Book of Their Adventures, illustrated by Suçie Stevenson, Simon & Schuster (New York, NY), 2005.
Henry and Mudge and the Great Grandpas: The Twenty-sixth Book of Their Adventures, illustrated by Suçie Stevenson, Simon & Schuster (New York, NY), 2005.
Henry and Mudge and the Tumbling Trip: The Twenty-seventh Book of Their Adventures, illustrated by Carolyn Bracken, Simon & Schuster (New York, NY), 2005.
Henry and Mudge and the Big Sleepover: The Twenty-eighth Book of Their Adventures, illustrated by Suçie Stevenson, Simon & Schuster (New York, NY), 2006.

Selected "Henry and Mudge" books were translated into Spanish and published in Braille.

"ANNIE AND SNOWBALL" CHILDREN'S BOOKS; ILLUSTRATED BY SUÇIE STEVENSON

Annie and Snowball and the Dress-up Birthday: The First Book of Their Adventures, Simon & Schuster (New York, NY), 2007.
Annie and Snowball and the Prettiest House: The Second Book of Their Adventures, Simon & Schuster (New York, NY), 2007.
Annie and Snowball and the Teacup Club: The Third Book of Their Adventures, Simon & Schuster (New York, NY), 2008.
Annie and Snowball and the Pink Surprise: The Fourth Book of Their Adventures, Simon & Schuster (New York, NY), 2008.
Annie and Snowball and the Cozy Nest: The Fifth Book of Their Adventures, Simon & Schuster (New York, NY), 2009.
Annie and Snowball and the Shining Star: The Sixth Book of Their Adventures, Aladdin (New York, NY), 2009.
Annie and Snowball and the Magical House: The Seventh Book of Their Adventures, Aladdin (New York, NY), 2010.
Annie and Snowball and the Wintry Freeze: The Eighth Book of Their Adventures, Simon Spotlight (New York, NY), 2010.
Annie and Snowball and the Book Bugs Club: The Ninth Book of Their Adventures, Simon Spotlight (New York, NY), 2011.
Annie and Snowball and the Thankful Friends: The Tenth Book of Their Adventures, Simon Spotlight (New York, NY), 2011.
Annie and Snowball and the Surprise Day: The Eleventh Book of Their Adventures, Simon Spotlight (New York, NY), 2012.
Annie and Snowball and the Grandmother Night: The Twelfth Book of Their Adventures, Simon Spotlight (New York, NY), 2012.

"BROWNIE AND PEARL" CHILDREN'S BOOKS; ILLUSTRATED BY BRIAN BIGGS

Brownie and Pearl Step Out, Harcourt (Orlando, FL), 2009.
Brownie and Pearl Get Dolled Up, Beach Lane Books (New York, NY), 2010.
Brownie and Pearl See the Sights, Beach Lane Books (New York, NY), 2010.
Brownie and Pearl Step Out, Beach Lane Books (New York, NY), 2010.
Brownie and Pearl Grab a Bite, Beach Lane Books (New York, NY), 2011.
Brownie and Pearl Hit the Hay, Peach Lane Books (New York, NY), 2011.
Brownie and Pearl Take a Dip, Beach Lane Books (New York, NY), 2011.
Brownie and Pearl Go for a Spin, Beach Lane Books (New York, NY), 2012.
Brownie and Pearl Make Good, Beach Lane Books (New York, NY), 2012.

"PUPPY MUDGE" SERIES; BEGINNING READERS; ILLUSTRATED BY ISIDRE MONES

Puppy Mudge Takes a Bath, Simon & Schuster (New York, NY), 2002.
Puppy Mudge Has a Snack, Simon & Schuster (New York, NY), 2003.
Puppy Mudge Loves His Blanket, Simon & Schuster (New York, NY), 2005.
Puppy Mudge Wants to Play, Simon & Schuster (New York, NY), 2005.
Puppy Mudge Finds a Friend, Simon & Schuster (New York, NY), 2005.

"EVERYDAY BOOKS" SERIES; SELF-ILLUSTRATED BOARD BOOKS

The Everyday Pets, Macmillan (New York, NY), 1993.
The Everyday Children, Macmillan (New York, NY), 1993.
The Everyday Garden, Macmillan (New York, NY), 1993.
The Everyday House, Macmillan (New York, NY), 1993.
The Everyday School, Macmillan (New York, NY), 1993.
The Everyday Town, Macmillan (New York, NY), 1993.

"MR. PUTTER AND TABBY" SERIES; BEGINNING READERS; ILLUSTRATED BY ARTHUR HOWARD

Mr. Putter and Tabby Walk the Dog, Harcourt (San Diego, CA), 1994.
Mr. Putter and Tabby Pour the Tea, Harcourt (San Diego, CA), 1994.

Mr. Putter and Tabby Bake the Cake, Harcourt (San Diego, CA), 1994.

Mr. Putter and Tabby Pick the Pears, Harcourt (San Diego, CA), 1995.

Mr. Putter and Tabby Fly the Plane, Harcourt (San Diego, CA), 1997.

Mr. Putter and Tabby Row the Boat, Harcourt (San Diego, CA), 1997.

Mr. Putter and Tabby Toot the Horn, Harcourt (San Diego, CA), 1998.

Mr. Putter and Tabby Take the Train, Harcourt (San Diego, CA), 1998.

Mr. Putter and Tabby Paint the Porch, Harcourt (San Diego, CA), 2000.

Mr. Putter and Tabby Feed the Fish, Harcourt (San Diego, CA), 2001.

Mr. Putter and Tabby Catch the Cold, Harcourt (San Diego, CA), 2002.

Mr. Putter and Tabby Stir the Soup, Harcourt (San Diego, CA), 2003.

Mr. Putter and Tabby Write the Book, Harcourt (San Diego, CA), 2004.

Mr. Putter and Tabby Make a Wish, Harcourt (San Diego, CA), 2005.

Mr. Putter and Tabby Spin the Yarn, Harcourt (San Diego, CA), 2006.

Mr. Putter and Tabby See the Stars, Harcourt (San Diego, CA), 2007.

Mr. Putter and Tabby Run the Race, Harcourt (San Diego, CA), 2008.

Mr. Putter and Tabby Spill the Beans, Harcourt (San Diego, CA), 2009.

Mr. Putter and Tabby Clear the Decks, Harcourt (Boston, MA), 2010.

Mr. Putter and Tabby Ring the Bell, Houghton Mifflin Harcourt (Boston, MA), 2011.

"BLUE HILL MEADOWS" SERIES; MIDDLE-GRADE FICTION; ILLUSTRATED BY ELLEN BEIER

The Blue Hill Meadows, Harcourt (San Diego, CA), 1997.

The Blue Hill Meadows and the Much-loved Dog, Harcourt (San Diego, CA), 1997.

"POPPLETON" SERIES; BEGINNING READERS; ILLUSTRATED BY MARK TEAGUE

Poppleton, Blue Sky Press (New York, NY), 1997.

Poppleton and Friends, Blue Sky Press (New York, NY), 1997.

Poppleton Everyday, Blue Sky Press (New York, NY), 1998.

Poppleton Forever, Blue Sky Press (New York, NY), 1998.

Poppleton in Fall, Blue Sky Press (New York, NY), 1999.

Poppleton in Spring, Blue Sky Press (New York, NY), 1999.

Poppleton in Winter, Blue Sky Press (New York, NY), 2001.

"COBBLE STREET COUSINS" SERIES; MIDDLE-GRADE FICTION; ILLUSTRATED BY WENDY ANDERSON HALPERIN

In Aunt Lucy's Kitchen, Simon & Schuster (New York, NY), 1998.

A Little Shopping, Simon & Schuster (New York, NY), 1998.

Some Good News, Simon & Schuster (New York, NY), 1999.

Special Gifts, (also published as *Winter Gifts*), Simon & Schuster (New York, NY), 1999.

Spring Deliveries, Simon & Schuster (New York, NY), 1999.

Summer Party, Simon & Schuster (New York, NY), 2001.

Wedding Flowers, Simon & Schuster (New York, NY), 2002.

"HIGH-RISE PRIVATE EYES" SERIES; ILLUSTRATED BY G. BRIAN KARAS

The Case of the Missing Monkey, Greenwillow (New York, NY), 2000.

The Case of the Climbing Cat, Greenwillow (New York, NY), 2000.

The Case of the Puzzling Possum, Greenwillow (New York, NY), 2001.

The Case of the Troublesome Turtle, Greenwillow (New York, NY), 2001.

The Case of the Sleepy Sloth, Greenwillow (New York, NY), 2002.

The Case of the Fidgety Fox, Greenwillow (New York, NY), 2003.

The Case of the Baffled Bear, Greenwillow (New York, NY), 2004.

The Case of the Desperate Duck, Greenwillow (New York, NY), 2005.

"LITTLE WHISTLE" SERIES; ILLUSTRATED BY TIM BOWERS

Little Whistle, Harcourt (San Diego, CA), 2000.

Little Whistle's Dinner Party, Harcourt (San Diego, CA), 2001.

Little Whistle's Medicine, Harcourt (San Diego, CA), 2002.

Little Whistle's Christmas, Harcourt (San Diego, CA), 2003.

"LIGHTHOUSE FAMILY" SERIES; ILLUSTRATED BY PRESTON MCDANIELS

The Storm, Simon & Schuster (New York, NY), 2002.

The Whale, Simon & Schuster (New York, NY), 2003.

The Eagle, Simon & Schuster (New York, NY), 2004.

The Turtle, Simon & Schuster (New York, NY), 2005.

The Octopus, Simon & Schuster (New York, NY), 2005.

YOUNG-ADULT FICTION

A Blue-eyed Daisy (novel), Bradbury (New York, NY), 1985, published as *Some Year for Ellie,* illustrated by Kate Rogers, Viking Kestrel (London, England), 1986.

Every Living Thing (short stories), illustrated by S.D. Schindler, Bradbury (New York, NY), 1985.
A Fine White Dust (novel), Bradbury (New York, NY), 1986, reprinted, Aladdin (New York, NY), 2007.
A Kindness (novel), Orchard Books (New York, NY), 1988.
A Couple of Kooks, and Other Stories about Love, Orchard Books (New York, NY), 1990.
Missing May (novel), Orchard Books (New York, NY), 1992.
I Had Seen Castles (novel), Harcourt Brace (San Diego, CA), 1993.
The Islander (novel), DK Ink (New York, NY), 1998.
Ludie's Life, Harcourt (Orlando, FL), 2006.

FOR YOUNG ADULTS; POETRY

Waiting to Waltz: A Childhood, illustrated by Stephen Gammell, Bradbury (New York, NY), 1984.
Soda Jerk, illustrated by Peter Catalanotto, Orchard Books (New York, NY), 1990.
Something Permanent, photographs by Walker Evans, Harcourt (San Diego, CA), 1994.
God Went to Beauty School, HarperCollins (New York, NY), 2003.
Boris, Harcourt (Orlando, FL), 2005.

OTHER

Children of Christmas: Stories for the Season, illustrated by S.D. Schindler, Orchard Books (New York, NY), 1987, published as *Silver Packages and Other Stories,* [London, England], 1987, selection published as *Silver Packages: An Appalachian Christmas Story,* illustrated by Chris K. Soentpiet, Orchard Books, 1997.
But I'll Be Back Again: An Album (autobiography), Orchard Books (New York, NY), 1989.
Appalachia: The Voices of Sleeping Birds, illustrated by Barry Moser, Harcourt (San Diego, CA), 1991.
Margaret, Frank, and Andy: Three Writers' Stories (biography) Harcourt (San Diego, CA), 1996, published in three volumes as *A Story of Margaret Wise Brown, A Story of L. Frank Baum,* and *A Story of E.B. White.*
Bless Us All: A Child's Yearbook of Blessings, Simon & Schuster (New York, NY), 1998.
Give Me Grace: A Child's Daybook of Prayers, Simon & Schuster (New York, NY), 1999.

Author's papers are collected at the Kent State University Libraries Department of Special Collections and Archives.

Adaptations

Filmstrip adaptations by Random House include *When I Was Young in the Mountains,* 1983, *This Year's Garden,* 1983, and *The Relatives Came,* 1986. Audiobook adaptations by SRA McGraw-Hill include *When I Was Young in the Mountains* and *The Relatives Came,* both 1985, *This Year's Garden,* 1987, and *Henry and Mudge in the Green Time,* 1988. *Children of Christmas* and *Every Living Thing* were released as book-and-audio versions and as audiobooks by Chivers North America, 1993 and 1997, respectively. *Missing May* was released as an audiobook by BDD Audio, 1996, Recorded Books, 1997. *A Fine White Dust* was released as an audiobook by Recorded Books, 1997. Many of Rylant's "Henry and Mudge" books were adapted as audiobooks by Recorded Books and Live Oak Media, 1997-98. The stage play *Henry and Mudge,* produce in New York, NY, 2007, is based on Rylant's books.

Sidelights

An author of fiction, nonfiction, and poetry for children and young adults, Cynthia Rylant is recognized as a gifted writer who has contributed memorably to several genres of juvenile literature. With a writing style that has been described as unadorned, clear, and lyrical, the author presents young people's experiences with sensitivity and perceptiveness, branding her protagonists' concerns as legitimate and equally important as those of adults. She often bases her works on her own background, especially on her childhood in the Appalachian region of West Virginia. "Rylant has tackled such issues as crises of religious faith, war, death and grief, but the things that matter most to her—family, friends, pets—are the recurring themes that resound throughout her work," Heather Vogel Frederick commented in *Publishers Weekly.*

Cynthia Rylant's text for **Appalachia: The Voices of Sleeping Birds** *is brought to life in Barry Moser's sun-filled paintings.* (Illustration copyright © 1991 by Pennyroyal Press. Reprinted by permission of Houghton Mifflin Harcourt Publishing Company. All rights reserved.)

Many of Rylant's books for beginning readers are published in series, such as her beloved "Henry and Mudge" books about a small boy and his very large dog. She has also earned recognition for the "Annie and Snowball" series of children's books, her "Brownie and Pearl" picture books, and her "Mr. Putter and Tabby" series of beginning readers. The author began illustrating some of her picture books in the early 1990s and has developed a folk-art style that is usually thought to complement her texts nicely. She has also worked with a number of outstanding illustrators, such as Peter Catalanotto, Barry Moser, James and Suçie Stevenson, and Walker Evans.

While her elementary-school-aged fans are legion, Rylant is perhaps best known as a novelist. Characteristically, she portrays introspective, compassionate young people who live in rural settings or in small towns and who tend to be set apart from their peers. Her young male and female protagonists meet challenges with the help of their families and friends as well as from within their strong, supportive communities. She often focuses on relationships between the old and the young and between people and animals. In addition, she underscores her works with such themes as the act of creation, both by God and by human artists; the transforming power of love; and the importance of all living things.

Writing in *Children's Books and Their Creators,* Eden K. Edwards noted that Rylant "demonstrates an inimitable ability to evoke the strongest of emotions from the simplest of words. . . . In her work, Rylant gives depth and dignity to a litany of quiet characters and sagaciously reflects on some of life's most confusing mysteries." Miriam Lang Budin noted in *School Library Journal* that readers "have come to expect resonant, deeply felt work from Rylant," while Hollis Lowery-Moore concluded in the *St. James Guide to Young-Adult Writers* that "all of Rylant's stories, including her picture story books marketed for younger readers, create memorable characters and places and provide teens with a window on the world."

Many of Rylant's works are rooted in the memories and images of her childhood. Her parents had a stormy marriage and separated when the author was four years old. The author and her mother moved to West Virginia, where Rylant was left in her grandparents' care while her mother earned a nursing degree. She lost contact with her father for several years, and he died when she was thirteen. As the author later recalled in her autobiography *But I'll Be Back Again: An Album,* "I did not have a chance to know him or to say goodbye to him, and that is all the loss I needed to become a writer."

Unhappiness, however, did not dominate the author's childhood. Rylant enjoyed the rustic West Virginia environment while living with her grandparents in a mountain town where many houses had neither electricity nor running water. The lack of amenities did not bother young Rylant; she felt secure surrounded by equally poor yet friendly, church-going neighbors. When the author was eight years old, she and her mother moved to another West Virginia town named Beaver.

During her early years, Rylant was not much of a reader. In fact, as she recalled in *Something about the Author Autobiography Series* (*SAAS*), "I did not *see* many books." After enrolling at Morris Harvey College (now the University of Charleston), she initially planned to go into nursing like her mother, but she switched her major after taking her first college English class. As she recalled in *SAAS,* "I heard and read stories I had never heard or read before, and I was in love with words." She became editor of the campus newspaper and was active in a variety of other campus activities. "I liked college so much that when I finished I didn't want to stop being a student," Rylant later admitted in *SAAS.*

Rylant's first year of graduate school at Marshall University in Huntington, West Virginia, was "without a doubt the happiest year of my life. . . . I loved literature so much and every day all I had to do was attend class and listen to it and talk about it and write about it." After receiving her master's degree in 1976, she found work in a public library and began composing her own stories. *When I Was Young in the Mountains,* her debut work, was published in 1982.

A picture book describing Rylant's childhood spent with her grandparents in Appalachia, *When I Was Young in the Mountains* is a collection of vignettes about the busy, joyous life of a small community. The book was favorably received by critics such as a *Publishers Weekly* reviewer who stated that Rylant "proves she knows precisely how to tell a story that brings the reader into the special world of her recollecting. . . . These are memories of a way of living that will entrance readers and broaden their outlook." Released in 1984, Rylant's *Waiting to Waltz: A Childhood* includes thirty autobiographical free-verse poems that outline the author's memories of growing up in Beaver, West Virginia. Ethel R. Twichell predicted in *Horn Book* that the poems "will gently pluck a long-forgotten memory or awaken a shared experience."

In her autobiographical *But I'll Be Back Again,* Rylant also reflects on the region where she was raised, and her picture book *Appalachia: The Voices of Sleeping Birds* poetically evokes the spirit of Appalachia in a tribute to that region and its people. *Appalachia* describes the living conditions, hard work, customs, activities, and personalities of the Appalachian people. The book's lyrical prose is paired with realistic paintings by artist Barry Moser who, like Rylant, has roots in Appalachia. Praising the book as an excellent marriage of text and picture, Barbara Chatton noted in *School Library Journal* that *Appalachia* should "encourage original writing or art as it reveals how illustrations and words can interact, how prose can illuminate a painting, and how simple paintings can bring power to prose."

Published in 1985, Rylant's first novel, *A Blue-eyed Daisy,* chronicles a year in the life of Ellie Farley, an eleven year old living in the hills of West Virginia. Ellie recounts several memorable moments that occur over the course of her eleventh year, such as getting kissed at her first co-ed party and attending the funeral of a classmate. Throughout the narrative, Ellie deepens her relationship with her father, Okey, a former miner who lost his job in an accident. A reviewer in *Publishers Weekly* wrote of *A Blue-eyed Daisy:* "No reader will be able to resist Ellie or her kith and kin. Their ability to live life and endure ills is the core of an exquisite novel, written with love." Katherine Bruner, writing in *School Library Journal,* added that Rylant's "low-key, evocative style . . . is the shining quality which sets this book apart."

Winner of a Newbery Medal Honor designation, *A Fine White Dust* finds seventh-grader Pete living in the rural South. Pete becomes a born-again Christian after being converted by charismatic preacher James W. Carson. When Carson offers Pete the chance to go with him as his disciple, the boy decides, after much soul-searching, to leave his parents and his best friend, Rufus. Carson, who is viewed by Pete as God in the flesh, eventually runs off with Darlene, a young woman who works at the town soda fountain. Although Pete feels betrayed, he comes through his experience with an unshaken faith in God and a more realistic view of human nature. Calling the novel "an achingly resonant portrayal of a naive youth," Denise M. Wilms added in her *Booklist* review that *A Fine White Dust* is "poignant and perceptive, with almost all of the characters subtly drawn."

In *Missing May* Rylant outlines how twelve-year-old Summer, who came to stay with her Aunt May and Uncle Ob in West Virginia after the death of her mother six years before, attempts to save her uncle from despair after the death of his beloved wife. In the midst of his mourning, Ob senses May's presence. Looking for an interpreter, Ob and Summer settle on Cletus, an unusual boy from Summer's class who once had a near-death experience and is, according to *Voice of Youth Advocates* reviewer Caroline S. McKinney, "as full of the energy for living as Ob is with the numbness of grieving." Through the boy's suggestion, the trio goes to Charleston to find a medium at the Spiritualist Church, and the trip begins a personal quest for each of them. McKinney concluded that "*Missing May* will be passed around by many of us who love beautiful words. It will speak in that warm, flowing West Virginia tongue to young people and old." *Missing May* earned Rylant a Newbery medal in 1993.

Another novel that draws from Appalachia and Rylant's family history, *Ludie's Life,* evokes the life of a young girl facing struggles as she attempts to survive the challenges of rural West Virginia in a life spanning most of the twentieth century. Married to a coal miner in 1925 at age fifteen, Ludie raises six children and watches as their lives stretch beyond her beloved Appalachia. With

A family-centered story, **The Relatives Came** *features engaging pastel art by Stephen Gammell.* (Illustration copyright © 1985 by Stephen Gammell. Reprinted with permission of Simon & Schuster Children's Publishing Division.)

an introspective nature, Ludie grows in her understanding of life while never regretting the limitations that have tied her to her rural home. In *Booklist* Cooper described *Ludie's Life* as "infused with poetry, pathos, and an everyday heroism."

Henry and Mudge: The First Book of Their Adventures made its appearance in 1987. Based on her own son and a dog Rylant once knew, the book introduces Henry, an only child. When Henry receives a pet, Mudge, a three-foot-tall dog that appears to be a cross between a Saint Bernard and a Great Dane, the two form a deep attachment. Tension comes when Mudge is lost, but happiness is restored when he is found again. Rylant presents lots of humorous details, such as Mudge's drooling and love of dirty socks, in prose that is designed for beginning readers. Reviewing *Henry and Mudge* and the second volume of the series, *Henry and Mudge in Puddle Trouble,* a critic for *Kirkus Reviews* called the author's language "easy to read but vividly evocative" and concluded: "Warm, loving, and gently philosophical, these stories about an only child and his closest companion deserve a place in every library collection."

Rylant has written dozens of other volumes in the "Henry and Mudge" series, easy-reading books that feature illustrations by noted cartoonist James Stevenson as well as by his artist daughter, Suçie Stevenson. In *Henry and Mudge and the Bedtime Thumps: The Ninth Book of Their Adventures* the pair take a trip to Grandmother's house in the country. When Mudge is deemed too large for the small home and is made to sleep out-

side, Henry is afraid both for Mudge and for himself. However, the large hound finds a spot under a large table on the porch, and both he and Henry curl up happily and fall sleep. In *Henry and Mudge and the Funny Lunch: The Twenty-fourth Book of Their Adventures* Henry and his dad cook up something incredible for Mother's Day. Writing in *Horn Book,* Elizabeth S. Watson noted that in *Henry and Mudge and the Bedtime Thumps* Rylant "has developed a fresh, warm, imaginative, and yet absolutely realistic tale for the beginning reader." Hazel Rochman praised *Henry and Mudge and the Funny Lunch,* noting that the book is "bound to get kids laughing, reading, and maybe cooking, too."

Since the early 1990s, with the success of the "Henry and Mudge" books, Rylant has increasingly concentrated on developing series titles for younger readers, such as the "Lighthouse Family," High-rise Private Eyes," and self-illustrated "Everyday Books" series. "Short sentences, peppy dialogue, and well developed characters" are the hallmarks of the "High-rise Private Eyes" series, according to *Horn Book* reviewer Kitty Flynn. The first of Rylant's works to include her own illustrations, the "Everyday Books" feature child-friendly collages.

Rylant's other self-illustrated titles include *The Whales, The Cookie-Store Cat,* and *Dog Heaven.* A playful book, *Dog Heaven* depicts the author/illustrator's idea of what dogs experience in the afterlife, such as fields to run in, plenty of angel children to pet them, and appetizing cat-shaped biscuits to eat. The book is illustrated in bright acrylics that blend naïve forms with unusual colors. *Bulletin of the Center for Children's Books* reviewer Roger Sutton concluded that Rylant maintains "a plain, conversational tone that resists gooeyness" while her "paintings allow viewers to imagine their own pets at play in the fields of the Lord." Another self-illustrated work, *Cat Heaven,* describes a kitty afterlife that is full of trees and clouds to perch on, soft angel laps to sit on, lots of toys to play with, and full dishes of food to eat. A critic in *Kirkus Reviews* called the book "every bit as rich in eye-dimming sentiment as *Dog Heaven*" and a work sure to "kindle sighs even from the feline-indifferent."

A love of cats figures prominently in several of Rylant's works, including her multi-book series "Mr. Putter and Tabby," as well as the "Brownie and Pearl" titles. The "Mr. Putter and Tabby" series features the domestic duo engaged in riveting adventures that are set forth in titles such as *Mr. Putter and Tabby Spill the Beans* and *Mr. Putter and Tabby Ring the Bell.* Each of these easy-to read volumes features the man and his pet attending to simple activities only to be thwarted by unruly appliances or other silly obstructions. In *Mr. Putter and Tabby Spill the Beans,* for instance, an invitation to a cooking class leads to chaos when neighbor Mrs. Teaberry's dog, Zeke, frightens a student. According to *School Library Journal* contributor Nancy Baumann, Rylant's "hilarious story is told with a minimal text that's perfect for beginning readers." In *Mr. Putter and Tabby Ring the Bell* the title characters pay a friendly visit to a local school, only to have the occasion spoiled by the rambunctious Zeke. Writing in *Booklist,* Carolyn Phelan stated that Rylant "tells an appealing story in simple language."

The "Brownie and Pearl" series, aimed at emerging readers, focuses on the adventures of a charming young lass named Brownie and her spunky feline companion. In *Brownie and Pearl Step Out* the youngster shies away from a birthday party until Pearl slips into the celebration, encouraging her owner to join the fun. "Rylant addresses the challenges and rewards of facing new social situations in short, conversational text," Kristen McKulski noted in *Booklist,* and Horn Book critic Betty Carter explained that the story "is perfect for toddlers and preschoolers wanting a straightforward narrative complete with familiar objects to identify." The engaging duo makes a return appearance in *Brownie and Pearl Grab a Bite,* which follows their efforts to prepare their own lunch. According to a *Kirkus Reviews* writer, Rylant's "short, carefully crafted sentences can . . . support beginning readers in their efforts to decode text."

Boris joins works such as Rylant's award-winning *God Went to Beauty School* as an acclaimed collection of verse that presents the author's more reflective side. Containing nineteen poems, *Boris* comprises what *Horn Book* reviewer Jennifer M. Brabander praised as an "accessible, compelling story" describing a beloved gray cat and its many adventures after arriving at Rylant's door.

***Rylant teams up with artist Brian Biggs to create a series of toddler-themed tales that include* Brownie and Pearl Hit the Hay.** (Illustration copyright © 2011 by Brian Biggs. Reprinted with permission of Beach Lane Books, an imprint of Simon & Schuster Children's Publishing Division.)

***Seattle-based artist Nikki McClure creates the intricate cut-paper art for Rylant's story in* All in a Day.** (Illustration copyright © 2009 by Nikki McClure. Reproduced by permission of Abrams Books for Young Readers, an imprint of ABRAMS.)

In *Baby Face: A Book of Love for Baby,* illustrated by Diane Goode, the author offers six poems about the joys of infancy. "Rylant's verse is as cute as a newborn," observed Cooper, and a *Publishers Weekly* critic maintained that the book "turns on the 'awww' factor." Also told in verse, *All in a Day,* follows a boy's adventures on his family's farm. Illustrated with cut-paper art by Nikki McClure, the work "introduce[es] children to the perennial promise of tomorrow through lithe language and honed imagery," in the words of a *Kirkus Reviews* writer.

Rylant has collaborated with a number of gifted artists in the process of creating her children's stories. *Snow,* a lyrical ode to winter, features illustrations by Lauren Stringer. "This is a gentle gem," maintained *School Library Journal* critic Marianne Saccardi, and Ilene Cooper, writing in *Booklist,* applauded "Rylant's evocative words and Stringer's entrancing paintings."

Carson Ellis provides the artwork for *The Beautiful Stories of Life: Six Greek Myths, Retold,* which offers Rylant's take on such well-known characters as Pandora, Orpheus, and Pygmalion. The author's "language is economical and straightforward; and her tone is one of tender melancholy," Deirdre F. Baker commented in *Horn Book.* A reviewer in *Publishers Weekly* deemed the collection "a pleasurable sampling of some well-known Greek myths, their ideas and morals distilled to their core."

In an interview with Anita Silvey for *Horn Book,* Rylant once commented that writing "has given me a sense of self-worth that I didn't have my whole childhood. I am really proud of that. The [books] have carried me through some troubled times and have made me feel that I am worthy of having a place on this earth." In *SAAS,* the author concluded: "I will write, because I have to earn my way and because it seems to be what God put me here to do. I hope one day to write a great book, a magnificent book, which people will buy for those they love best, which they will place in someone else's hands and say: 'Before you do anything else, *you must read this.*'"

Biographical and Critical Sources

BOOKS

Authors & Artists for Young Adults, Volume 45, Gale (Detroit, MI), 2002.

Children's Books and Their Creators, edited by Anita Silvey, Houghton Mifflin (Boston, MA), 1995.

Children's Literature Review, Gale (Detroit, MI), Volume 15, 1988, Volume 86, 2003.

Rylant, Cynthia, *Best Wishes,* Richard C. Owen, 1992.

Rylant, Cynthia, *But I'll Be Back Again: An Album,* Beech Tree Books/Orchard Books (New York, NY), 1993.

St. James Guide to Children's Writers, 5th edition, St. James Press (Detroit, MI), 1999.

St. James Guide to Young Adult Writers, edited by Tom and Sara Pendergast, St. James Press (Detroit, MI), 1999.

Something about the Author Autobiography Series, Volume 13, Gale (Detroit, MI), 1991.

PERIODICALS

Booklist, September 1, 1986, Denise M. Wilms, review of *A Fine White Dust,* p. 67; May 15, 1989, Denise M. Wilms, review of *But I'll Be Back Again: An Album,* p. 1655; February 15, 1992, Ilene Cooper, "The Other Side of Good-bye," p. 1105; May 15, 2001, Gillian Engberg, review of *The Case of the Troublesome Turtle,* p. 1753; June 1, 2001, Ilene Cooper, review of *Summer Party,* p. 1884; September 15, 2001, Ilene Cooper, review of *Good Morning, Sweetie Pie, and Other Poems for Children,* p. 229; February, 15, 2002, Lauren Peterson, review of *Wedding Flowers,* p. 1015; March 1, 2002, Gillian Engberg, review of *Little Whistle's Medicine,* p. 1144; April 15, 2002, Ilene Cooper, review of *Let's Go Home: The Wonderful Things about a House,* p. 68; May 1, 2002, Kay Weisman, review of *Old Town in the Green Groves,* p. 1527; September 1, 2002, Ilene Cooper, review of *The Ticky-Tacky Doll,* p. 137; September 15, 2002, Diane Foote, review of *Christmas in the Country,* p. 247; November 1, 2002, Ilene Cooper, review of *Mr. Putter and Tabby Catch the Cold,* p. 509; January 1, 2003, Hazel Rochman, review of *Henry and Mudge and the Tall Tree House: The Twenty-first Book of Their Adventures,* p. 910; January 1, 2003, Connie Fletcher, review of *The Case of the Sleepy Sloth,* p. 893; March 15, 2003, Gillian Engberg, review of *Henry and Mudge and Mrs. Hopper's House: The Twenty-second Book of Their Adventures,* p. 1333; September 1, 2003, Kay Weisman, review of *The Whale,* p. 121; October 1, 2003, Carolyn Phelan, review of *Henry and Mudge and the Wild Goose Chase: The Twenty-third Book of Their Adventures,* p. 329; March 15, 2004, Hazel Rochman, review of *Henry and Mudge and the Funny Lunch: The Twenty-fourth Book of Their Adventures,* p. 1310; July, 2004, Carolyn Phelan, review of *The Case of the Baffled Bear,* p. 1852; November 15, 2004, Ilene Cooper, review of *Long Night Moon,* p. 591; February 15, 2005, Ilene Cooper, review of *Boris,* p. 1074; May 15, 2005, Hazel Rochman, review of *Puppy Mudge Wants to Play,* p. 1667; October 15, 2006, Ilene Cooper, review of *Ludie's Life,* p. 41; May 15, 2007, Randall Enos, review of *Alligator Boy,* p. 48; March 1, 2008, Ilene Cooper, review of *Baby Face: A Book of Love for Baby,* p. 72; April 1, 2008, Julie Cummins, review of *Puppies and Piggies,* p. 57, and Carolyn Phelan, review of *Mr. Putter and Tabby Run the Race,* p. 58; August 1, 2008, Carolyn Phelan, review of *Hansel and Gretel,* p. 78; October 15, 2008, Ilene Cooper, review of *Snow,* p. 41; August 1, 2009, Carolyn Phelan, review of *Mr. Putter and Tabby Spill the Beans,* p. 78; December 1, 2009, Kristen McKulski, review of *Brownie and Pearl Step Out,* p. 48; September 1, 2011, Carolyn Phelan, review of *Brownie and Pearl Grab a Bite,* p. 126; October 1, 2011, Carolyn Phelan, review of *Mr. Putter and Tabby Ring the Bell,* p. 84.

Bulletin of the Center for Children's Books, April, 1982, Zena Sutherland, review of *When I Was Young in the Mountains,* p. 157; July-August, 1989, Betsy Hearne, review of *But I'll Be Back Again,* p. 283; October, 1990, Betsy Hearne, review of *Henry and Mudge and the Happy Cat: The Eighth Book of Their Adventures,* pp. 43-44; March, 1992, Betsy Hearne, review of *Missing May,* p. 192; October, 1995, Roger Sutton, review of *Dog Heaven,* pp. 66-67; November, 1997, Pat Mathews, review of *Cat Heaven,* p. 100; December, 2001, review of *Poppleton in Winter,* p. 152; July, 2003, review of *God Went to Beauty School,* p. 461.

Children's Book Review Service, November, 1984, Leigh Dean, review of *Waiting to Waltz: A Childhood,* p. 32.

Horn Book, January-February, 1985, Ethel R. Twichell, review of *Waiting to Waltz,* p. 64; November-December, 1987, Anita Silvey, interview with Rylant, pp. 695-703; May-June, 1991, Elizabeth S. Watson, review of *Henry and Mudge and the Bedtime Thumps,* pp. 328-329; March-April, 1992, p. 206; May, 2001, review of *The Case of the Troublesome Turtle,* p. 337; November-December, 2002, Mary M. Burns, review of *Christmas in the Country,* p. 738; September-October, 2004, Kitty Flynn, review of *The Case of the Baffled Bear,* p. 599; January-February, 2005, review of *God Went to Beauty School,* p. 30; May-June, 2005, Jennifer M. Brabander, review of *Boris,* p. 341; November-December, 2005, Jeannine M. Chapman, review of *The Stars Will Still Shine,* p. 696; January-February, 2008, Christine M. Heppermann, review of *Walt Disney's Cinderella,* p. 100; November-December, 2008, Joanna Rudge Long, review of *Hansel and Gretel,* p. 720; May-June, 2009, Deirdre F. Baker, review of *The Beautiful Stories of Life,* p. 314; March-April, 2010, Betty Carter, review of *Brownie and Pearl Step Out,* p. 50.

Kirkus Reviews, July 1, 1986, review of *A Fine White Dust,* pp. 1023-1024; February 15, 1987, reviews of *Henry and Mudge* and *Henry and Mudge in Puddle Trouble,* both p. 300; February 1, 1991, review of *Henry and Mudge and the Bedtime Thumps,* p. 184; March 1, 1991, review of *Appalachia: The Voices of Sleeping Birds,* p. 322; July 1, 1995, review of *Dog Heaven,* p. 951; July 1, 1997, review of *Cat Heaven,* p. 1035; January 15, 2002, review of *Little Whistle's*

Medicine, p. 108; April 15, 2002, review of *Let's Go Home,* p. 577; June 15, 2002, review of *The Case of the Sleepy Sloth,* p. 888; August 1, 2002, review of *The Ticky-Tacky Doll,* p. 141; October 15, 2002, review of *Mr. Putter and Tabby Catch the Cold,* p. 1538; November 1, 2002, review of *Christmas in the Country,* p. 135; March 1, 2003, review of *The Case of the Fidgety Fox,* p. 397; June 15, 2003, review of *God Went to Beauty School,* p. 864; December 15, 2004, review of *If You'll Be My Valentine,* p. 1207; March 1, 2005, review of *The Turtle,* p. 294; March 15, 2005, review of *Boris,* p. 357; February 1, 2006, review of *The Journey: Stories of Migration,* p. 36; November 1, 2006, review of *Ludie's Life,* p. 1124; May 15, 2007, review of *Alligator Boy;* January 1, 2008, review of *Puppies and Piggies;* September 15, 2008, review of *Snow;* February 15, 2009, review of *All in a Day*; December 15, 2009, review of *Brownie and Pearl Step Out*; April 15, 2010, review of *Brownie and Pearl Get Dolled Up*; July 15, 2011, review of *Brownie and Pearl Grab a Bite.*

Kliatt, May, 2002, Paula Rohrlick, "The Heavenly Village," p. 29.

New York Times Book Review, June 3, 1990, Valerie Sayers, review of *Soda Jerk,* p. 24; May 30, 1993, review of *Henry and Mudge and the Wild Wind,* p. 19; December 7, 2008, review of *Snow,* p. 52.

Publishers Weekly, March 19, 1982, review of *When I Was Young in the Mountains,* pp. 70-71; August 17, 1984, review of *Waiting to Waltz,* p. 60; March 8, 1985, review of *A Blue-eyed Daisy,* p. 91; March 1, 1991, review of *Appalachia,* p. 74; July 21, 1997, Heather Vogel Frederick, "Cynthia Rylant: A Quiet and Reflective Craft," p. 178; April 2, 2001, review of *Little Whistle,* p. 63; September, 3, 2001, review of *Good Morning, Sweetie Pie,* p. 86; April 22, 2002, review of *Let's Go Home,* p. 68; August 5, 2002, review of *The Ticky-Tacky Doll,* p. 71; August 26, 2002, review of *The Storm,* p. 69; June 89, 2003, review of *God Went to Beauty School,* p. 53; October 6, 2003, review of *The Whale,* p. 86; January 17, 2005, review of *Long Night Moon,* p. 54; February 20, 2006, review of *The Journey,* p. 156; February 18, 2006, review of *Baby Face,* p. 152; October 6, 2008, review of *Snow,* p. 53; January 19, 2009, review of *All in a Day,* p. 59; May 11, 2009, review of *The Beautiful Stories of Life: Six Greek Myths, Retold,* p. 51.

Quill & Quire, December, 1990, Susan Perren, review of *Henry and Mudge and the Happy Cat,* p. 19.

School Library Journal, November, 1984, Margaret C. Howell, review of *Waiting to Waltz,* p. 138; April, 1985, Katherine Bruner, review of *A Blue-eyed Daisy,* p. 92; September, 1986, Julie Cummins, review of *A Fine White Dust,* p. 138; July, 1989, Amy Kellman, review of *But I'll Be Back Again,* p. 97; August, 1990, Trev Jones, review of *Henry and Mudge and the Happy Cat,* p. 134; April, 1991, Nancy Seiner, review of *Henry and Mudge and the Bedtime Thumps,* p. 101; April, 1991, Barbara Chatton, review of *Appalachia,* p. 137; October, 1995, Joy Fleishhacker, review of *Dog Heaven,* p. 115; January, 1999, Miriam Lang Budin, review of *Bear Day,* pp. 101-102; October, 2001, Patricia Manning, review of *Poppleton in Winter,* p. 130; April, 2002, Carol A. Edwards, review of *Old Town in the Green Groves,* p. 156; June, 2002, Blair Christolon, review of *Let's Go Home,* p. 124; August, 2002, Pat Leach, review of *Wedding Flowers,* p. 166; October, 2002, Susan Patron, review of *Christmas in the Country,* p. 63, and Lynda S. Poling, review of *Mr. Putter and Tabby Catch the Cold,* p. 130; November, 2002, Sheilah Kosco, review of *The Ticky-Tacky Doll,* p. 134; December, 2002, Laura Scott, review of *The Case of the Sleepy Sloth,* p. 108; February, 2003, Lee Bock, review of *The Old Woman Who Named Things,* p. 97; April, 2003, Marilyn Taniguchi, review of *Puppy Mudge Takes a Bath,* p. 137; May, 2003, Doris Losey, review of *The Case of the Fidgety Fox,* p. 129; July, 2003, Maura Smith, review of *Henry and Mudge and the Snowman Plan,* p. 59; October, 2003, Maureen Wade, review of *Little Whistle's Christmas,* p. 67, Maren Ostergard, review of *The Case of the Troublesome Turtle,* p. 87, and Laura Scott, review of *Henry and Mudge and the Wild Goose Chase,* p. 137; November, 2003, Barbara Buckley, review of *The Whale,* p. 115; January, 2004, Laura Scott, review of *Puppy Mudge Has a Snack,* p. 104; September, 2004, Susan Lissim, review of *Mr. Putter and Tabby Write the Book,* and Bethany L.W. Hankinson, review of *The Case of the Baffled Bear,* p. 178; November, 2004, Debbie Steward Hoskins, review of *The Eagle,* p. 117; December, 2004, Rhona Campbell, review of *Long Night Moon,* p. 120; April, 2005, Cris Riedel, review of *Boris,* p. 156; April, 2007, Kathleen Pavin, review of *Mr. Putter and Tabby Spin the Yarn,* p. 126; April, 2007, Pat Leach, review of *Ludie's Life,* p. 148; June, 2007, Marianne Saccardi, review of *Alligator Boy,* p. 123; September, 2007, Erika Qualls, review of *Mr. Putter and Tabby See the Stars,* p. 175; February, 2008, Kelly Roth, review of *Mr. Putter and Tabby Run the Race,* p. 96; April, 2008, Madeline Walton-Hadlock, review of *Puppies and Piggies,* p. 122; August, 2008, Amelia Jenkins, review of *Baby Face,* p. 101; December, 2008, Marianne Saccardi, review of *Snow,* p. 101; May, 2009, Kathleen Kelly MacMillan, review of *All in a Day,* p. 88; December, 2009, Nancy Baumann, review of *Mr. Putter and Tabby Spill the Beans,* p. 90; April, 2010, Carrie Rogers-Whitehead, review of *Brownie and Pearl Get Dolled Up,* p. 139; October, 2010, Ieva Bates, review of *Brownie and Pearl See the Sights,* and Loreli Stochaj, review of *Mr. Putter and Tabby Clear the Decks,* p. 93; March, 2011, Martha Simpson, review of *Brownie and Pearl Take a Dip,* p. 134; August, 2011, Lora Van Marel, review of *Mr. Putter and Tabby Ring the Bell,* and Laura Scott, review of *Brownie and Pearl Grab a Bite,* p. 83; September, 2011, Catherine Callegari, review of *Brownie and Pearl Hit the Hay,* p. 129.

Voice of Youth Advocates, April, 1992, Caroline S. McKinney, review of *Missing May,* pp. 35-36; April, 2005, Jan Chapman, review of *Boris,* p. 48; February, 2007, Debbie Clifford, review of *Ludie's Life,* p. 531.

ONLINE

Kent State University Library Web site, http://speccoll.library.kent.edu/ (May 1, 2012), "Cynthia Rylant Papers."*

S

SALES, Leila

Personal

Born April 20, in MA. *Education:* University of Chicago, B.A. (psychology).

Addresses

Home—Brooklyn, NY. *E-mail*—Leila@leilasales.com.

Career

Children's book editor and author. Viking Children's Books, New York, NY, editor.

Writings

Mostly Good Girls, Simon Pulse (New York, NY), 2010.
Past Perfect, Simon Pulse (New York, NY), 2011.

Sidelights

Writing occupied much of Leila Sales's free time when she was a child, and princesses took center stage in many of her illustrated stories. By the time she reached the ninth grade Sales was tackling novel-length works and, although she majored in psychology during college, she also won a collegiate writing award for an unpublished young-adult novel. Her move to New York City landed her an editorial position at a mainstream publisher, and her continued writing has produced the young-adult novels *Mostly Good Girls* and *Past Perfect.*

Leila Sales (Photograph by Dan Dry. Reproduced by permission.)

"For almost as long as I can remember, I wanted to write children's books, and I wanted to write humor," Sales told *SATA.* "I was raised in a family that valued humor a great deal, and I've always surrounded myself with books and friends who could make me laugh. In college I wrote a regular humor column for my school paper, and I joined my school's improvisational and sketch comedy troupe, Off-Off Campus. After that, I thought, 'I wonder if I could write a novel that felt like a collection of humor columns or comedy sketches.' So I did. That's how *Mostly Good Girls* came to be."

In *Mostly Good Girls* Sales introduces readers to Violet Tunis, a junior at a prestigious East Coast prep school

who has always been committed to academic success and her job editing Westfield School's literary magazine. Violet has also been committed to best friend Katie, a popular and super-smart classmate who shares her interests and goals. This year is different, however: Katie has quit the crew team and begun taking chances and exhibiting risky behavior. And she wants Violet to come along for the ride. Soon the partying starts, along with the pressure to get drunk and experiment with drugs, and then Katie begins dating an older teen who is definitely out of her league. Violet's reluctant participation in one of Katie's schemes ultimately threatens her role on the literary magazine. When Katie drops out of school Violet is left to deal with Westfield's principal, salvage her social and academic reputations, and reflect on the true cost of relationships.

Reviewing *Mostly Good Girls* in *Voice of Youth Advocates,* Marlyn Beebe asserted that Sales's "exploration of growing up, personal change and angst is well written." Lori A. Guenthner described Violet's first-person narrative as "witty and unpretentious" and the novel as "a strong debut that is not to be missed" in her *School Library Journal* review. Noting that readers will be intrigued as Violet attempts to justify Katie's actions against "her own internal barometer of right and wrong," a *Kirkus Reviews* writer dubbed *Mostly Good Girls* "an enjoyable, light read," and in *Booklist* Kara Dean suggested that Sales's fiction debut will appeal "to fans of Meg Cabot's novels and academy-based stories."

Friendship also guides the summer activities of Chelsea Glaser, the narrator of *Past Perfect.* It is the summer after junior year and Chelsea was hoping to land a job at the local mall. However, best-friend Fiona convinces her to put in one last year as part of the staff of reenactors at Colonial Essex Village, the Virginia-based living-history museum where Chelsea has worked alongside her parents since she was a child. the teen's expectation of spending another lackluster summer dressed in seventeenth-century costume and assisting museum patrons is shattered when former boyfriend Ezra shows up to work at the village. Things become even more complicated because Chelsea has already focused her romantic sights on Dan, a cute teen working at a Civil War-era reenactor encampment across the street from Essex Village.

Past Perfect gains its realism and detail from Sales's own experience working in a living-history museum. A *Kirkus Reviews* writer noted that the first-person narrative of the novel's heroine "is peppered with sharp and witty observation" that includes Chelsea's perceptions of typical tourists and the degree of authenticity that causes some reenactors to be held in more esteem than others. While the teen entertains readers with her "acerbically funny voice," *Past Perfect* also contains "serious meditations on the nature of history, memory, heartbreak and love," according to *Horn Book* contributor Rachel L. Smith. Caught up in Chelsea's romantic dilemma, "readers will tear through this novel," predicted Rachael Myers-Ricker, the *School Library Journal* contributor deeming *Past Perfect* "a satisfying and fun read."

Cover of Sales' young-adult novel* Mostly Good Girls, *which finds a teen forced to reexamine the meaning of true friendship. (Jacket photograph of legs by Evan Schwartz, copyright © 2010 by Simon & Schuster, Inc. Reprinted with permission of Simon Pulse, an imprint of Simon & Schuster Children's Publishing Division.)

Biographical and Critical Sources

PERIODICALS

Booklist, October 15, 2010, Kara Dean, review of *Mostly Good Girls,* p. 61.

Horn Book, November-December, 2011, Rachel L. Smith, review of *Past Perfect,* p. 111.

Kirkus Reviews, October 1, 2010, review of *Mostly Good Girls*; September 15, 2011, review of *Past Perfect.*

School Library Journal, October, 2010, Lori A. Guenthner, review of *Mostly Good Girls,* p. 124; October, 2011, Rachael Myers-Ricker, review of *Past Perfect,* p. 147.

Voice of Youth Advocates, December, 2010, Marlyn Beebe, review of *Mostly Good Girls,* p. 460.

ONLINE

Leila Sales Home Page, http://leilasales.com (May 1, 2012).

* * *

SCALES, Simon

Personal

Born in Adelaide, South Australia, Australia. *Education:* University of Southern Australia, degree (illustration; with honors); attended Concept Design Academy (Pasadena, CA).

Addresses

Home—Victoria, Australia. *Agent*—Shannon Associates, 333 W. 57th St., Ste. 809, New York, NY 10019. *E-mail*—simon@simonscales.com.au.

Career

Illustrator, educator, and artist. Concept artist; clients include Blue Tongue Entertainment, End Game Studios, and LEGO Group; Concept Design Workshop, Melbourne, Victoria, Australia, founder and instructor, beginning 2011.

Member

Society of Digital Artists.

Illustrator

Jill McDougall, *The Terrible Unbearable Giant,* Era Publications (Flinders Park, South Australia, Australia), 2004.

Phil Cummings, *The Wild Whirlpool,* Era Publications (Flinders Park, South Australia, Australia), 2007.

Jill McDougall, *Good Luck, Lilly,* Era Publications (Flinders Park, South Australia, Australia), 2007.

Nigel Gray, *Don't Be Afraid!,* Koala Books (Mascot, New South Wales, Australia), 2008.

Clayton Perry, *Gnarly Grom Marley!,* Nelipot Productions (Innaloo, West Australia, Australia), 2009.

Elizabeth Spurr, *Monsters, Mind Your Manners!,* Albert Whitman (Chicago, IL), 2011.

Also illustrator of educational readers and privately published picture books.

Biographical and Critical Sources

PERIODICALS

Kirkus Reviews, February 15, 2011, Elizabeth Spurr, review of *Monsters, Mind Your Manners!*

School Library Journal, April, 2011, Jayne Damron, review of *Monsters, Mind Your Manners!,* p. 154.

ONLINE

Concept Design Workshop Web site, http://www.conceptdesignworkship.com/ (May 15, 2012), "Simon Scales."

Simon Scales Home Page, http://www.simonscales.com.au (May 1, 2012).*

* * *

SCHREIBER, Ellen

Personal

Married January, 2008; husband's name Edward. *Education:* B.A. (theatre); attended Royal Academy of Dramatic Arts (London, England) and Second City Training Center (Chicago, IL).

Addresses

E-mail—ellenschreiber@mac.com.

Career

Actress and author. Performer on improv and aboard cruise ships; stand-up comedienne at comedy clubs.

Member

Society of Children's Book Writers and Illustrators.

Awards, Honors

Quick Pick for Reluctant Young-Adult Readers selection, American Library Association (ALA), New York Public Library Book for the Teen Age selection, and Young Adults' Choice selection, International Reading Association/Children's Book Council, 2003, all for *Vampire Kisses.*

Writings

Teenage Mermaid, HarperCollins (New York, NY), 2003.

Comedy Girl, Katherine Tegen Books (New York, NY), 2004.

"VAMPIRE KISSES" NOVEL SERIES

Vampire Kisses, Katherine Tegen Books (New York, NY), 2003.

Kissing Coffins, Katherine Tegen Books (New York, NY), 2005.

Vampireville, Katherine Tegen Books (New York, NY), 2006.

Dance with a Vampire, Katherine Tegen Books (New York, NY), 2007.

Blood Relatives: Volume 1 (manga), artwork by Rem, Katherine Tegen Books (New York, NY), 2007.

Blood Relatives: Volume 2 (manga), artwork by Rem, Katherine Tegen Books (New York, NY), 2008.

The Coffin Club, Katherine Tegen Books (New York, NY), 2008.

Blood Relatives: Volume 3 (manga), artwork by Rem and Elisa Kwon, Katherine Tegen Books (New York, NY), 2009.

Royal Blood, Katherine Tegen Books (New York, NY), 2009.

Vampire Kisses: The Beginning (includes *Vampire Kisses, Kissing Coffins,* and *Vampireville*), HarperCollinsPublishers (New York, NY), 2009.

Love Bites, Katherine Tegen Books (New York, NY), 2010.

Cryptic Cravings, Katherine Tegen Books (New York, NY), 2011.

Immortal Hearts, Katherine Tegen Books (New York, NY), 2012.

Graveyard Games (manga; sequel to *Blood Relatives*), illustrated by Xian Nu Studio, Katherine Tegen Books (New York, NY), 2012.

Copy of Ellen Schreiber's* Once in a Full Moon, *the first volume in her "Full Moon" paranormal romance series. (Cover photograph © 2011 by Gustavo Marx/MergeLeft Reps. Reproduced with permission of Katherine Tegen Books, an imprint of HarperCollins Publishers.)

Author's novels have also been published in Dutch.

"FULL MOON" NOVEL SERIES

Once in a Full Moon, Katherine Tegen Books (New York, NY), 2011.

Magic of the Moonlight, Katherine Tegen Books (New York, NY), 2012.

Sidelights

Although she has always enjoyed writing, Ellen Schreiber trained as an actor and spent five years in Chicago, where she mastered the art of improv at the Second City Training Center. Performing a two-woman show and stand-up comedy followed, and then came the point in her career where Schreiber realized that she had "outgrown" Chicago and could best further her career by moving to Los Angeles. On a flight to check out her West-Coast options, she read a young-adult book recommended by her older brother, writer Mark Schreiber, and had an "I could write that!" moment. She found a Dutch publisher for her first young-adult novel before connecting with a U.S. editor taken by the originality and humor in Schreiber's stories. In the years since she has crafted a two-tiered career writing for teens: Her novels *Teenage Mermaid* and *Comedy Girl* are based on real-life experiences while her popular "Vampire Kisses" and "Full Moon" series are—fortunately—not.

One of the first of Schreiber's novels to find a U.S. publisher, *Vampire Kisses* proved to be so popular that it quickly morphed into a nine-volume series. The story focuses on sixteen-year-old Raven Madison, whose Goth persona is totally at odds with her mundane home town, which she refers to as Dullsville. Things in Dullsville begin to look up when handsome Alexander Sterling and his family move into an old mansion that has been vacant and rumored to be haunted. Because of their secretive behavior, the Sterlings quickly become the focus of rumors, and when Raven learns that Alexander may be a vampire she knows that they are destined to be lovers.

Reviewing *Vampire Kisses* in *Kirkus Reviews,* a critic dubbed Schreiber's paranormal fiction debut an "awkwardly endearing tale of teen angst" in which Raven's love interest "is perfect . . . a dark and broody knight of night." "Raven's voice is immediately charming," asserted *Booklist* contributor Francesca Goldsmith, while Claire Rosser noted in *Kliatt* that the author's "talent with humor is apparent" throughout, and her "lighthearted novel will be fun to read for many YAs." Enlivened by "comic timing [that] is dead-on," according to a *Publishers Weekly* critic, *Vampire Kisses* treats teens to an "ill-fated flirtation [that] will bring more laughs than heartache."

Schreiber continues her "Vampire Kisses" saga in several other novels. *Kissing Coffins* finds Raven searching for Alexander, whose vampirism has made him the fo-

cus of evil, while vampire twins Jagger and Luna Maxwell create problems for the two teens in *Vampireville* as they scheme to prey on the complacent residents of Dullsville. Little brother Valentine Maxwell becomes the problem in *Dance with a Vampire* as he sets his sights on Raven's brother Billy and reveals his menacing intent. *The Coffin Club* finds Raven partying at a Goth-themed nightclub, only to discover that it is also a hangout for local vampires. Alexander may be moving from the family manse back to Romania in *Royal Blood,* and an introduction to his mysterious parents looms in Raven's future, while *Love Bites* allows her to learn more about her boyfriend's back story from visiting friend Sebastian. Jagger opens an alluring vampire night club in Dullsville in *Cryptic Cravings,* and Raven hopes to have input into both the club's decor and its ultimate goal, while in series finale *Immortal Hearts* Alexander's younger sis Athena comes for a visit and helps Raven decide once and for all whether becoming a vampire is worth the cost.

Recommending that teens read *Vampire Kisses* to understand the series cast, *School Library Journal* critic Lynn Evarts deemed *Vampireville* a "fun, fast read for vampire fans," and Jennifer Mattson wrote in *Booklist* that the third novel in Schreiber's series benefits from a "tender outsiders-in-love theme." Noting the appeal of *Dance with a Vampire* among Goth-affected teens, Donna Rosenblum added in *School Library Journal* that "Raven's character continues to develop," fully revealing "her needs, attitude, and desires."

Schreiber turns to werewolves in her "Full Moon" series, which includes *Once in a Full Moon* and *Magic of the Moonlight.* In the series opener, seventeen-year-old Celeste Parker lives in the town of Legend's Run, where werewolves are said to roam. When Brandon Maddox shows up in the halls at the local high school Celeste is immediately attracted to the darkly handsome new student, despite the fact that she has Nash, a crushworthy boyfriend. When she crosses paths with a pack of wolf-like animals one winter's night during a full moon, Brandon serves as her rescuer and is bitten. Although she suspects that he is no longer altogether human, Brandon now exudes an even greater magnetism now that danger is part of the romantic mix. This romance heats up further in *Magic of the Moonlight,* as Brandon's scientist father becomes an ally in the battle to keep his son's wolven side from taking total control. With the school ball scheduled for the night of a full moon, Celeste knows that she has to make a choice: go public about her romance or find a way to avert potential tragedy.

With its "undeniable" romance, *Once in a Full Moon* recrafts "the myth of werewolves . . . with just enough ingenuity to make it into a sumptuous series," asserted Alicia Abdul in a review of Schreiber's novel for *Voice of Youth Advocates.* Although Hayden Bass wrote in *School Library Journal* that Celeste's "good girl" persona may disappoint fans of "spunky goth protagonist" Raven in Schreiber's "Vampire Kisses" series, a *Publishers Weekly* reviewer maintained that *Once in a Full Moon* "pushes all the right paranormal, romantic buttons . . . with its target audience."

In addition to her "Vampire Kisses" and "Full Moon" books, Schreiber has also authored several stand-alone novels. Geared for 'tweens, *Teenage Mermaid* focuses on modern-day mermaid Waterlilly, who mixes with the "Earthee" students at Pacific Reefs High School. Spunky and flamboyant, Lilly falls in love with fellow student Spencer after she saves the human surfer from drowning. After a magical kiss, Lilly vows to embrace being mortal in order to join her landlocked true love, but once her flippers transform permanently into a pair of human legs she has serious second thoughts. "The details of Lilly's ocean life may be the biggest lure to readers," noted a *Publishers Weekly* critic, the reviewer adding that Schreiber's lighthearted story is "loaded with fun." In *Booklist* Todd Morning also praised the novel, dubbing *Teenage Mermaid* "a sharp, funny novel that includes a super-sized serving of over-the-top romance."

Schreiber sets the stage of *Comedy Girl* in her native Chicago, as high schooler Trixie Shapiro works hard at staying in the shadows. Hoping to help her painfully shy best friend shine, Jazzy signs Trixie up to perform during Senior Talent Night, knowing that her friendstalent for stand-up comedy will impress. Practice on local "open mic" nights helps the self-conscious Trixie gain confidence, and her star performance at school lands her a gig at a local comedy club as well as the attention of long-time crush Gavin Baldwin. Along with her newfound popularity comes numerous demands on her time, and Trixie soon realizes that she is in a place where her choices will have real importance going forward. *Comedy Girl* "is just the sort of light, bubbly coming-of-age novel that may appeal to young teens," wrote *School Library Journal* contributor Amy Patrick, and in *Kliatt* Claire Rosser commended Schreiber's obvious "abilities as a comic" and her willingness to share "believable details of life as a performer." "Trixie will keep her audience amused" while her story in *Comedy Girl* "teaches something about the cost—and rewards—of pursuing a dream," concluded a *Publishers Weekly* critic.

Biographical and Critical Sources

PERIODICALS

Booklist, July, 2003, Todd Morning, review of *Teenage Mermaid,* p. 1881; November 15, 2003, Francesca Goldsmith, review of *Vampire Kisses,* p. 593; August 1, 2006, Jennifer Mattson, review of *Vampireville,* p. 70.

Kirkus Reviews, July 1, 2003, review of *Vampire Kisses,* p. 914; July 1, 2004, review of *Comedy Girl,* p. 636; November 15, 2010, review of *Once in a Full Moon.*

Kliatt, July, 2003, Claire Rosser, review of *Vampire Kisses,* p. 18; July, 2004, Claire Rosser, review of *Comedy Girl,* p. 13.

Publishers Weekly, June 16, 2003, review of *Teenage Mermaid,* p. 72; August 4, 2003, review of *Vampire Kisses,* p. 81; September 13, 2004, review of *Comedy Girl,* p. 79; November 8, 2010, review of *Once in a Full Moon,* p. 62.

School Library Journal, August, 2003, Molly S. Kinney, review of *Vampire Kisses,* p. 166; September, 2004, Amy Patrick, review of *Comedy Girl,* p. 218; December, 2005, Kimberly L. Paone, review of *Kissing Coffins,* p. 154; November, 2006, Lynn Evarts, review of *Vampireville,* p. 151; November, 2007, Donna Rosenblum, review of *Dance with a Vampire,* p. 137; May, 2011, Hayden Bass, review of *Once in a Full Moon,* p. 123.

Voice of Youth Advocates, December, 2010, Alicia Abdul, review of *Once in a Full Moon,* p. 475; February, 2012, Dotsy Harland, review of *Graveyard Games,* p. 614.

ONLINE

Ellen Schreiber Home Page, http://www.ellenschreiber.com (May 1, 2012).*

* * *

SCIESZKA, Casey 1984-

Personal

Born 1984, in NY; surname pronounced "ShEH-ska"; daughter of Jon Scieszka (a children's author); partner of Steven Weinberg (an illustrator). *Education:* Pitzer College, degree, 2006. *Hobbies and other interests:* Travel.

Addresses

Home—Brooklyn, NY. *Agent*—Steve Malk, Writers House; smalk@writershouse.com.

Career

Writer. Local Language Literacy (nonprofit), cofounder, with Steven Weinberg, 2008. Teacher of English in Beijing, China, 2006.

Writings

To Timbuktu: Nine Countries, Two People, One True Story, illustrated by Steven Weinberg, Roaring Brook Press (New York, NY), 2011.

Contributor to periodicals, including *Huffington Post* online.

Sidelights

As the daughter of children's book author Jon Scieszka, it seems only natural that Casey Scieszka would use writing as one avenue for her own creativity. She does just this in creating her book *To Timbuktu: Nine Countries, Two People, One True Story. To Timbuktu* is a graphic memoir that follows Scieszka's travels throughout Asia with boyfriend and artist Steven Weinberg, and Weinberg tells his side of the story in his cartoon illustrations. In addition to their work as a writer/illustrator team, Scieszka and Weinberg have founded the nonprofit Local Language Literacy, which publishes and distributes stories in the native language of students in West and North Africa.

Scieszka and Weinberg met while she attended school in California and he attended school in New England. It was during their junior year, while they attended a foreign-exchange program in Morocco, that romance blossomed. In 2006, following graduation, the adventure-seeking duo decided to spend eighteen months on a travel adventure, during which time they would teach English and Scieszka would conduct research funded by a Fulbright grant. Their travels took them to China, Vietnam, Laos, Thailand, Mali, and several other countries, all which the outgoing Scieszka described in her journal and Weinberg captured visually in his sketchbook. "We shared a big desk, and decided together how we'd tell each story," Scieszka explained while describing how the book was compiled to *Publishers Weekly* online interviewer Sally Lodge. "We knew we didn't want traditional words and pictures. It was a new world for us, and a lot of trial and error. And a lot of fun."

Reviewing *To Timbuktu* for *School Library Journal,* Sharon Senser KcKellar characterized the collaboration as "often humorous, and occasionally heartbreaking" as readers are exposed to "the difficulties and beauties of friendships that span different cultures and language." The "present-tense" text by Scieszka is "witty, perceptive, and candid," in the opinion of a *Publishers Weekly* critic, and the authors' enthusiasm for her journey is echoed in "Weinberg's fluid cartoon sketches." Recommending the travelogue to young people anticipating continent-jumping in their own future, *Booklist* contributor Ian Chipman dubbed *To Timbuktu* "a great road map" and the coauthors "eminently pleasant traveling companions."

Biographical and Critical Sources

PERIODICALS

Booklist, January 1, 2011, Ian Chipman, review of *To Timbuktu: Nine Countries, Two People, One True Story,* p. 70.

Publishers Weekly, February 21, 2011, review of *To Timbuktu,* p. 135.

School Library Journal, June, 2011, Sharon Senser McKellar, review of *To Timbuktu,* p. 146.

Voice of Youth Advocates, April, 2011, Molly Krichten, review of *To Timbuktu,* p. 93.

ONLINE

All the Way to Timbuktu Web site, http://www.alltheway totimbuktu.com (May 1, 2012).

Publishers Weekly Online, http://www.publishersweekly .com/ (February 17, 2011), Sally Lodge, interview with Scieszka and Steven Weinberg.*

* * *

SIMONE, Ni-Ni

Personal

Born in Ahoskie, NC; married; children: three. *Education:* B.A. (English). *Religion:* Baptist. *Hobbies and other interests:* Antiquing, traveling with family, reading, watching reality television.

Addresses

Home—Northern NJ. *E-mail*—ninisimone@yahoo.com.

Career

Novelist for teens and adults, beginning c. 2003.

Awards, Honors

YALSA Quick Pick for Reluctant Young-Adult Readers, American Library Association, 2008, for *Shortie like Mine.*

Writings

A Girl like Me, Dafina Books (New York, NY), 2008.

Shortie like Mine, Kensington (New York, NY), 2008.

If I Was Your Girl, Kensington (New York, NY), 2008.

Teenage Love Affair, Dafina Books (New York, NY), 2010.

(With Kelli London) *The Break-Up Diaries* (includes novelette "Hot Boyz"), Dafina Books (New York, NY), 2011.

Upgrade U, Dafina Books (New York, NY), 2011.

No Boyz Allowed, Dafina Books (New York, NY), 2012.

(With Amir Abrams) *Hollywood High,* Kensington (New York, NY), 2012.

Also author of novels for adults.

Sidelights

After studying writing during college, where she edited the school literary magazine, Ni-Ni Simone decided to make a career of it. While pursuing a living as a social worker following graduation, Simone has found writing for young women of color to be an opportunity to share her upbeat attitude and encouragement. In addition to her novels, which include *A Girl like Me, Shortie like Mine, If I Was Your Girl,* and *Upgrade U,* she has collaborated with fellow authors Kelli London on *The Break-Up Diaries,* which includes her novelette "Hot Boyz," and Amir Abrams, with whom she wrote *Hollywood High.* Praising *The Break-Up Diaries,* which focuses on teen dating relationships, a *Kirkus Reviews* writer noted that "the language in both stories is fresh and appealing," while in *School Library Journal* Miranda Doyle asserted that Simone's "main characters are memorable, there are plenty of plot twists and turns, and readers will enjoy the pop culture and fashion references."

Each of Simone's young-adult novels focuses on a spirited young woman who is focused on dealing with family issues, navigating her social sphere, and attracting or cultivating the affections of a particular love interest. In *A Girl like Me,* for example, talented teen vocalist Elite must decide whether or not to come clean about her crack-addicted mom and the three siblings she is trying to raise when she meets a handsome pop singer and sparks fly. Zsa-Zsa, the narrator of *Teenage Love Affair,* takes pride in her independence and self-reliance but is trapped in an abusive relationship with Ameen until

Cover of Ni-Ni Simone's teen romance* Upgrade U, *which follows a savvy young woman from high school into college. (Cover photograph © Shutterstock. Reproduced with permission of Dafina Books, an imprint of Kensington Publishing Corp.)

former boyfriend Malachi gives her a reason to take flight. Talented student Seven McKnight is the focus of Simone's novels *Shortie like Mine, If I Was Your Girl,* and *Upgrade U,* as readers follow her through her final years of high school and into college where academic stresses are matched by worries over a troubled twin sister, various crushes, and the need to keep one eye on her future.

Reviewing *A Girl like Me* for *Kirkus Reviews,* a critic praised Simone's "rich characterization" of her sixteen-year-old heroine and suggested that the book's "formula plot and raw dialogue will attract many young readers." Another *Kirkus Reviews* writer commended *Shortie like Mine* for its "strong characterizations and colorful contemporary language," while "shouting matches, door slamming, trash talk, bitch slaps, and baby-daddy drama all reign supreme" in *If I Was Your Girl.* Citing Simone's use of "snappy dialogue and one-liners," a *Publishers Weekly* contributor added that *Upgrade U* "mixes romantic drama with empowering messages."

Biographical and Critical Sources

PERIODICALS

Kirkus Reviews, July 1, 2008, review of *Shortie like Mine*; September 15, 2008, review of *If I Was Your Girl;* November 15, 2008, review of *A Girl like Me;* April 15, 2011, review of *The Break-Up Diaries.*

Publishers Weekly, January 17, 2011, review of *Upgrade U,* p. 51; April 11, 2011, review of *The Break-Up Diaries,* p. 55.

School Library Journal, August, 2011, Miranda Doyle, review of *The Break-Up Diaries,* p. 122.

ONLINE

Brown Bookshelf Web site, http://thebrownbookshelf.com (February 15, 2012), interview with Simone.

Ni-Ni Simone Home Page, http://www.ninisimone.com (May 1, 2012).

* * *

STEVENSON, Sarah Jamila 1977-

Personal

Born 1977, in CA; married; husband an artist and professor of art. *Education:* University of California—Berkeley, B.A. (art practice and psychology); San Francisco Art Institute, certificate (printmaking); Mills College, M.F.A. (creative writing). *Hobbies and other interests:* Video Games, Welsh language, blogging, role-playing games, traveling, music, cooking.

Addresses

Home—Modesto, CA. *Agent*—Jennifer Laughran, Andrea Brown Literary Agency; jennL@andreabrownlit.com. *E-mail*—sjs@sarahjamilastevenson.com.

Sarah Jamila Stevenson (Photograph by Lee R. Bailey. Reproduced by permission.)

Career

Author, artist, and graphic designer. *Exhibitions:* Work included in group shows at San Francisco Art Institute, San Francisco, CA, 1999; Sebastopol Center for the Arts, Sebastopol, CA, 1999; Downtown Art Center, San Rafael, CA, 1999; Modesto Junior College Gallery, Modesto, CA, 2006; Gallery of Urban Art, Oakland, Ca, 2007; and Thoreau Center Seed Gallery, San Francisco, 2010. Work included in permanent collections at Metropolitan Museum of Art and History San Jose.

Writings

The Latté Rebellion, Flux (Woodbury, MN), 2011.

Underneath, Flux (Woodbury, MN), 2013.

Contributor to periodicals and Web sites, including *San Joaquin Woman, Mills Quarterly, Suite101.com,* and *IGN.com.*

Sidelights

Sarah Jamila Stevenson has found several outlets for her creativity, and each has brought her success. A practicing artist, she has exhibited her prints, artist's books, and drawings and paintings as well as building a career as a graphic artist. As a writer, Stevenson has contributed to magazines and Web sites as well as producing the young-adult novels *The Latté Rebellion* and *Underneath.*

In *The Latté Rebellion* readers become immersed in the senior-year exploits of narrator Asha Jamison, a mixed-race student whose focus has been on earning the grades to get into a top college. Asha's focus shifts when she attends a friend's pool party and another guest thoughtlessly calls her a "towel head." Although she did indeed have a towel wrapped around her head at the time, Asha and Amer-Asian best friend Carey Wong interpret the remark as a racial slur and decide to start a club for mixed-race students called the Latté Rebellion. By putting their "manifesto" online, the girls calculate that they can also sell T-shirts and earn money for a vacation they have planned for the summer after graduation. Their initial success is encouraging, but when the rebellion becomes a viral Internet sensation both Asha and Carey are caught off guard. Soon the stresses of off-the-chart T-shirt sales begin fracturing their friendship and threaten to erode Asha's grade-point average. Out in the public domain, the Latté Rebellion also turns radical, sparking the concern of school administrators and resulting in a disciplinary hearing during which Asha must decide how much she is willing to sacrifice.

Far more than examining "the complexities of mixed ethnicity," *The Latté Rebellion* also "offers a thought-provoking account of a girl's search for identity," asserted a *Publishers Weekly* critic in appraising Stevenson's fiction debut. The author "expertly handles complex issues around race and ethnic identity without seeming pedantic," noted Lalitha Nataraj in her *School Library Journal* review of the novel. For *Booklist* contributor Courtney Jones, *The Latté Rebellion* is enriched by the author's "portrayal of Asha's initially misguided but relatable social awakening," and a *Kirkus Reviews* writer characterized the narrator's maturation as "a realistic mess of vague hopes, serendipitous events, serious missteps and gutsy choices."

"I didn't initially plan on becoming a writer," Stevenson told *SATA*. "I've always enjoyed writing, ever since I was a kid and used my mom's old manual typewriter to make my own 'magazines'. But for most of my life I was focused on visual art. In fact, I was pretty sure I was going to end up illustrating the covers of books rather than writing their contents! But I had always written stories and poems, so I suppose the possibility of a writing career was always lurking in the background.

"The first time I thought about writing as a career was in 2000, when I was working at the Web site IGN.com and doing a little freelance humor writing for them on the side. I realized how much I was enjoying it, and decided to take a fiction-writing class online to see whether I might be interested in pursuing it further. As it turned out, I really wanted to keep doing it, and felt strongly about writing fiction in particular, but I felt like I needed a lot more practice and guidance to know where I wanted to take it, so I applied to graduate school for creative writing. After finishing an M.F.A. at Mills

***Two multiracial friends start a trend that turns into a movement in Stevenson's young-adult novel* The Latté Rebellion.** (Cover design by Lisa Novak. Reproduced with permission of Flux, an imprint of Llewellyn Worldwide Ltd.)

College in Oakland, I felt a lot more comfortable with my own skills and I started sending my work out into the world.

"It took about four years of sending out my novels and getting rejections before my first book was accepted for publication. I credit hard work, humility, persistence, a great support system, and a lot of luck."

Biographical and Critical Sources

PERIODICALS

Booklist, January 1, 2011, Courtney Jones, review of *The Latté Rebellion,* p. 96.

Kirkus Reviews, December 1, 2010, review of *The Latté Rebellion.*

Kliatt, December 1, 2010, review of *The Latté Rebellion.*

Publishers Weekly, November 22, 2010, review of *The Latté Rebellion,* p. 57.

School Library Journal, February, 2011, Lalitha Nataraj, review of *The Latté Rebellion,* p. 120.
Voice of Youth Advocates, December, 2010, Ursula Adams, review of *The Latté Rebellion,* p. 462.

ONLINE

Sarah Jamila Stevenson Home Page, http://www.sarahjamilastevenson.com (May 1, 2012).

* * *

SZPIRGLAS, Jeff

Personal

Born in Hamilton, Ontario, Canada. *Education:* College degree.

Addresses

Home—Toronto, Ontario, Canada.

Career

Educator and author. Worked in a steelyard and as a kid's page editor for children's magazines; currently teacher of elementary school in Toronto, Ontario, Canada. Producer of radio programming for *Out Front,* Canadian Broadcasting Corporation.

Writings

NONFICTION

Gross Universe: Your Guide to All Disgusting Things under the Sun, illustrated by Michael Cho, Maple Tree Press (Toronto, Ontario, Canada), 2004.
They Did What?! Your Guide to Weird and Wacky Things People Do, illustrated by Dave Whamond, Maple Tree Press (Toronto, Ontario, Canada), 2005.
Fear This Book: Your Guide to Fright, Horror, and Things That Go Bump in the Night, illustrated by Ramón Pérez, Maple Tree Press (Toronto, Ontario, Canada), 2006.
Just a Minute! A Crazy Adventure in Time, illustrated by Stephen MacEachern, Maple Tree Press (Toronto, Ontario, Canada), 2009.
(With Danielle Saint-Onge) *Something's Fishy* (chapter book), illustrated by Dave Whamond, Orca Book Publishers (Custer, WA), 2011.
You Just Can't Help It! Your Guide to the Wild and Wacky World of Human Behavior, illustrated by Josh Holinaty, Owlkids (Berkley, CA), 2011.

Contributor to periodicals, including *Chirp, chickaDEE, Owl,* and *Rue Morgue.* Author of scripts for television series *Polka Dot Shorts, Ricky's Room,* and *System Crash.*

Author's work has been translated into French.

Sidelights

Beginning his writing career with the mesmerizingly titled *Gross Universe: Your Guide to All Disgusting Things under the Sun,* Canadian teacher Jeff Szpirglas has continued to attract young readers with his nonfiction books *They Did What?! Your Guide to Weird and Wacky Things People Do, Just a Minute! A Crazy Adventure in Time,* and *You Just Can't Help It! Your Guide to the Wild and Wacky World of Human Behavior.* In addition to these storehouses of quirky facts, Szpirglas also joined Danielle Saint-Onge as coauthor of the beginning chapter book *Something's Fish,* about a second-grade boy's misadventure with the class pet.

Illustrated by Dave Whamond, *They Did What?!* highlights the triumphs of human will—and whimsy—that have not made it into the history books. From merchandising marvels such as pet rocks to strange inventions and unsuccessful scientific experiments that ultimately produced something useful (think penicillin), Szpirglas provides a wealth of trivia about "perpetrators of hoaxes, tall tales, extreme sports, amusing misunderstandings, and ridiculous fads," as Laura Reilly observed in her *Resource Links* appraisal. "Puns and lively wordplay are sprinkled about," noted *School Library Journal* reviewer Wendy Woodfill, and the author's high-energy approach will inspire young readers with "enthusiasm and curiosity" as they follow the history of everything from worm-charming championships to the story of Orson Welles' 1938 *War of the Worlds* radio broadcast. "Kids love oddities," asserted Carol L. MacKay in *Quill & Quire,* and in *They Did What?!* Szpirglas and Whamond have produced "engrossing leisure reading material."

Moving from the intentional to the unintentional, Szpirglas discusses reflex responses and other odd un-

Jeff Szpirglas treats readers to a wealth of human-interest trivia in* You Just Can't Help It, *featuring line art by Josh Holinaty.

conscious human behaviors in *You Just Can't Help It.* Why do people use hand gestures while talking? Why do they smile or frown? Why do some people cry when they are happy? Why do people love sweets? Or know when they are being secretly watched? "Energetic, educational and fun," the book "explores the quirks of human nature from both a scientific and cultural perspective," according to Gail Hamilton in *Canadian Review of Materials.* In *Quill & Quire* Kate Watson recommended *You Just Can't Help It* as "a fun way to introduce young readers to many aspects of human behaviour," while Meg Smith asserted in *School Library Journal* that Szpirglas's well-researched compilation of "snazzy trivia snippets" also yields "succinct answers" to reader questions that "convey both brevity and clarity."

Szpirglas presents another compendium of strangeness in *Fear This Book: Your Guide to Fright, Horror, and Things That Go Bump in the Night,* which features artwork by illustrator Ramón Pérez. Adopting the approach that we fear that which we do not understand, the author homes in on commonly held phobias such as fear of the dark, fear of spiders, fear of ghosts, and fear of snakes as well as on superstitions that hold out the promise of seven years' bad luck or other undesired consequences. A history of time and the way humans have sought to measure and control it is Szpirglas's focus in *Just a Minute! A Crazy Adventure in Time,* as artist Stephen MacEachern uses comic-style illustrations about how long things take during a typical day to tap into all manner of time-related factoids. In *Resource Links* Heather Empey dubbed *Fear This Book* "easy to read" and "fun and interesting," while *Quill & Quire* critic Paul Challen noted that *Just a Minute* is effective at "relating time to everyday events" by using "examples that young readers will understand and enjoy."

Biographical and Critical Sources

PERIODICALS

Canadian Review of Materials, June 4, 2004, Linda Ludke, review of *Gross Universe: Your Guide to All Disgusting Things under the Sun;* December 9, 2005, Lee Anne Smith, review of *They Did What?! Your Guide to Weird and Wacky Things People Do;* October 14, 2011, Gail Hamilton, review of *You Just Can't Help It! Your Guide to the Wild and Wacky World of Human Behavior.*

Quill & Quire, April, 2004, Nathan Whitlock, review of *Gross Universe;* December, 2005, Carol L. MacKay, review of *They Did What?!;* May, 2009, Paul Challen, review of *Just a Minute! A Crazy Adventure in Time;* March, 2011, Kate Watson, review of *You Just Can't Help It!*

Resource Links, February, 2006, Laura Reilly, review of *They Did What?!,* p. 79; December, 2006, Heather Empey, review of *Fear This Book: Your Guide to Fright, Horror, and Things That Go Bump in the Night,* p. 28.

School Library Journal, November, 2004, Kathryn Kosiorek, review of *Gross Universe,* p. 132; March, 2006, Wendy Woodfill, review of *They Did What?!,* p. 248; June, 2009, Kathleen Kelly MacMillan, review of *Just a Minute!,* p. 100; June, 2011, Meg Smith, review of *You Just Can't Help It!,* p. 147; July, 2011, Debbie Whitbeck, review of *Something's Fishy,* p. 74.

Voice of Youth Advocates, February, 2011, Matthew Weaver, review of *You Just Can't Help It!,* p. 584.

ONLINE

Open Book Toronto Web site, http://www.openbooktoronto.com/ (May 1, 2012), interview with Szpirglas.

Owlkids Books Web site, http://owlkids.rightbrainmedia.com/ (May 1, 2012), "Jeff Szpirglas."*

T-V

THOMPSON, Kate 1956-

Personal

Born July 23, 1956, in Halifax, Yorkshire, England; daughter of E.P. (an historian and social activist) and Dorothy (an historian and social activist) Thompson; children: Cliodhna and Dearbhla (daughters). *Education:* Studied law. *Hobbies and other interests:* Playing Irish fiddle, restoring fiddles.

Addresses

Home—Kinvara, Galway, Ireland. *Agent*—Sophie Hicks, Ed Victor Ltd., 6 Bayley St., Bedford Sq., London WC1B 3HE, England; sophie@victor.com. *E-mail*—kate@katethompson.info.

Career

Writer. Trained racehorses for several years; operated a smallholding in Inagh, Ireland, 1984-94. Wild Goat Fiddles (violin restoration and sales), owner.

Awards, Honors

Bisto Book Prize, Children's Books Ireland, 2002, for *The Beguilers,* 2003, for *The Alchemist's Apprentice,* 2004, for *Annan Water,* and 2006, for *The New Policeman;* London *Guardian* Children's Fiction Prize, Whitbread Children's Book Award, and Dublin Airport Authority Children's Book of the Year Award, all 2005, all for *The New Policeman;* Arts and Ecology residency, Royal Society for the Encouragement of Arts, Manufactures, and Commerce, 2007; Tyrone Guthrie Centre and Varuna Writers' Centre exchange bursary, 2008; Booktrust Teenage Prize shortlist, 2008, and Bisto Honour Award, Children's Books Ireland, and Carnegie Medal shortlist, both 2009, all for *Creature of the Night;* Judges Special Recognition Award, Children's Books Ireland, 2009, for *Highway Robbery.*

Kate Thompson (Photograph © Reuters/Toby Melville/Corbis.Reproduced by permission.)

Writings

JUVENILE FICTION

The Alchemist's Apprentice, Bodley Head (London, England), 2001.

The Beguilers, Dutton Children's Books (New York, NY), 2001.

Annan Water, Bodley Head (London, England), 2004.

The Fourth Horseman, Bodley Head (London, England), 2006.

Creature of the Night, Bodley Head (London, England), 2008, Roaring Brook Press (New York, NY), 2009.

Highway Robbery, illustrated by Johnny Duddle and Robert Dress, Bodley Head (London, England), 2008, Greenwillow Books (New York, NY), 2009.

Wanted!, illustrated by Jonny Duddle, Bodley Head (London, England), 2010, published as *Most Wanted!,* Greenwillow Books (New York, NY), 2010.

Contributor to anthologies, including *Just When Stories,* Beautiful Books; and *Tales from the Tower,* Allen & Unwin, 2011.

"SWITCHERS" NOVEL TRILOGY

Switchers (also see below), Bodley Head (London, England), 1997, Hyperion Books for Children (New York, NY), 1998.

Midnight's Choice (also see below), Bodley Head (London, England), 1998, Hyperion Books for Children (New York, NY), 1999.

Wild Blood (also see below), Bodley Head (London, England), 1999, Hyperion Books for Children (New York, NY), 2000.

The Switchers Trilogy (omnibus), Red Fox (London, England), 2004.

"MISSING LINK" NOVEL TRILOGY

The Missing Link, Bodley Head (London, England), 2000, published as *Fourth World,* Bloomsbury (New York, NY), 2005.

Only Human, Bodley Head (London, England), 2001, Bloomsbury (New York, NY), 2006.

Origins, Bodley Head (London, England), 2003, Bloomsbury (New York, NY), 2007.

"NEW POLICEMAN" NOVEL TRILOGY

The New Policeman, Bodley Head (London, England), 2005, Greenwillow Books (New York, NY), 2007.

The Last of the High Kings, Bodley Head (London, England), 2007, Greenwillow Books (New York, NY), 2008.

The White Horse Trick, Bodley Head (London, England), 2009, Greenwillow Books (New York, NY), 2010.

OTHER

There Is Something (poetry), Signpost Press (Bellingham, WA), 1992.

Down among the Gods (for adults), Virago (London, England), 1997.

Thin Air (for adults), Sceptre (London, England), 1999.

An Act of Worship (for adults), Sceptre (London, England), 2000.

Contributor of book reviews to London *Guardian.*

Adaptations

A number of Thompson's works have been adapted as audiobooks.

Sidelights

As a writer, Kate Thompson draws on the lore and locales of her adopted Ireland in award-winning novels such as *The New Policeman* and its sequels *The Last of the High Kings* and *The White Horse Trick.* Crafted from a mix of fantasy and several other elements, Thompson's books for young adults include *Creature of the Night* as well as installments in the "Switchers" and "Missing Link" series, all which also mix fantasy into a story grounded in science. She also entertains younger readers with her horse stories *Highway Robbery* and *Wanted!,* the latter which was published in the United States as *Most Wanted.*

Thompson was born in England to renowned historians E.P. and Dorothy Thompson, and she spent much of her free time riding and racing horses. She traveled the world, including the United States and India, before moving to Ireland in 1981 and settling down to write poetry and novels. Her first novel for young adults, *Switchers,* follows teenagers Tess and Kevin in their mission to prevent jelly-fish-like creatures known as krool from sending Earth into another ice age. The krool devour anything in their path, but the two teens hope to battle them through their ability to morph into any animal, real or imaginary. While a *Publishers Weekly* critic praised Thompson for her ability to interweave "elements from mythology and science fiction with insights into animal nature," *Rambles* online critic Donna Scanlon deemed *Switchers* "completely engrossing, and the characters of Tess and Kevin . . . very well drawn and sympathetic." The author rounds out her "Switchers" series with the novels *Midnight's Choice* and *Wild Blood.*

Thompson's "Missing Link" novels begin with *Fourth World* which, like the "Switchers" books, plays on the link between humans and animals. In her story, Christie accompanies his mentally impaired foster brother Danny on a trip to Scotland to meet his birth mother, a scientist named Maggie. Christie is suspicious, however, when Maggie sends a talking bird and dog to travel with them. He later finds out that Maggie is a neo-Dr. Moreau who has been splicing human DNA with that of animals to create a range of hybrids, Danny included. In her *Horn Book* review of *Fourth World,* Vicky Smith questioned Thompson's genetic arguments, but added of the novel that, even "if the exact nature of the genetic work is rather sketchily developed, the characters are not." Susan L. Rogers wrote in *School Library Journal* that, although "Christie's narrative voice seems far too sophisticated for his age," it gives Thompson's story "more heft than the average plot-driven series opener." A contributor to *Kirkus Reviews* concluded of *Fourth World* that the author "weaves some stimulating ideas into this suspenseful tale and leaves plenty of unanswered questions for future installments."

Thompson continues her "Missing Link" series with *Only Human* and *Origins.* In *Only Human* Christie encounters one of the world's mythic creatures and is

given a stone that contains a powerful, alien presence. Dubbed "a post-apocalyptic stunner" by a *Publishers Weekly* critic, follow-up novel *Origins* finds the teen living at the science lab in Scotland along with brother Danny and a rag-tag adopted family of human and creature hybrids. As the shadows lengthen on humanity's dominance, Christie records in his diary the days leading up to the disaster that will bring about the end of mankind. In a parallel story, future-born humanoids begin to form a rough new civilization while also dividing into warring factions. Fleeing from the fighting, two young people attempt to broker peace by searching for the common origin of their competing tribes. "When the storylines [in *Origins*] finally connect," wrote the *Publishers Weekly* critic, "SF fans will be blown away," and *Horn Book* critic Vicky Smith wrote that the novels' "characters are sympathetic, the narrative tension is thick, and the moral ambiguities are profound."

The first part of a fiction trilogy that includes *The Last of the High Kings* and *The White Horse Trick,* Thompson's *The New Policeman* won several top awards, among them the Bisto Book Prize and the Whitbread Children's Book Award. In this novel, fifteen-year-old Irish fiddle player J.J. Liddy discovers a bridge between his world and the world of eternal youth that can literally give his musician mother more time to perform her music. While exploring the fantastic world across the bridge—a place akin to the legendary Tir na n'Og—J.J. faces dark rumors about his family and attempts to fix a threatening leak in time between the two worlds.

***Cover of Thompson's award-winning science-fiction novel* The New Policeman.** (Cover art © 2007 by Marc Tauss/Getty Images. Used by permission of HarperCollins Children's Books, a division of HarperCollins Publishers.)

Judith A. Hayn, writing in the *Journal of Adolescent & Adult Literacy,* commented that with *The New Policeman* "Thompson takes the reader into a dreamland, coupled with the reality of Ireland as part of the European Union . . . , and captivates . . . until the charming tale ends in surprise." *Booklist* contributor Gillian Engberg predicted that readers will likely "overlook any creaky plot connections and fall eagerly into the rich, comic language and the captivating characters and scenes" of the novel, while in *School Library Journal* Heather M. Campbell maintained that "those who follow [*The New Policeman*] . . . through to the end will not be disappointed."

Praised by a *Publishers Weekly* reviewer as "just as well crafted" as its predecessor, *The Last of the High Kings* finds J.J. a few years older, married, and working as a luthier to support his wife and four children. When he is offered some special maple wood for fiddle-making, J.J. covets the rare lumber so much that he agrees to exchange one of his children for a changeling from the fairy world. As the changeling, Jenny, grows older, she begins to exhibit several surprising behaviors; she also develops a strong friendship with J.J.'s musician son Donal Liddy. Jenny ultimately uses the human boy as an ally when she takes up her preordained changeling mission to defend Earth in what Engberg described as "an ancient, epic battle between supernatural forces." Noting that the characters in *The Last of the High Kings* are "often humorous but far from whimsical," *Horn Book* writer Betsy Hearne added that Thompson's "skill" in crafting a "plot puzzle leads to peaks of narrative surprise and . . . emotional satisfaction." In *Kliatt* Paula Rohrlick deemed the sequel to *The New Policeman* as "well-plotted," "delightful," and with "a fey but admirable heroine." "Fans of *The New Policeman* will relish it all," Rohrlick predicted.

As Earth's surface is scoured by violent storms and hurricanes, its mortal human population searches for food and shelter in *The White Horse Trick.* Decades have passed since Jenny returned to Tir na n'Og, the faerie kingdom where time stands still. Donal is now older and working in the service of brother Aidan, whose accumulation of stored supplies and powerful troops has made him all-powerful. As the timeless world of the fae looks increasingly hospitable to humans, a scattered few push for migration as a way to save the race from destruction in an environmental collapse. When an Irish lad named Pup grudgingly accepts the assignment to find a way into that feudal realm, his path crosses that of an elderly J.J. as well as Jenny, who remains a young and energetic ally to the human race.

***Jonny Duddle creates the detailed artwork in Thompson's middle-grade fantasy adventure* Most Wanted.** (Illustration copyright © 2010 by Jonny Duddle. Reproduced with permission of Shannon Associates.)

Describing *The White Horse Trick* as "a compelling if slightly message-heavy story about global warming," a *Publishers Weekly* critic added that Thompson leavens her "weighty concerns" with "humor" and a conclusion that highlights "the planet's ultimate resilience." The concluding novel in the trilogy "offers readers a taste of genre-blending that is both challenging and successful," asserted Francisca Goldsmith in her *Booklist* review, while in *Horn Book* Jonathan Hunt announced that with *The White Horse Trick* "Thompson has simply outdone herself." Praising the author as "a supreme storyteller and gifted writer, *School Librarian* contributor Audrey Baker added that the "humour, action and tension" add up to "a real page turner" that will best be enjoyed by those readers familiar with the first two books in the series.

Turning to younger readers in *Highway Robbery,* Thompson takes readers back to 1700s London and a young orphan's tale of mystery and magic. As the boy relates, he was promised a gold coin if he agreed to stay on the street and watch the horse of a mysterious stranger on a mission. The horse, a sleek black mare, obviously does not belong to the beggarly lad, and soon others offer to buy it. After hours go by, several soldiers arrive and assert that the horse is actually Black Bess and her mysterious owner none other than the notorious highwayman Dick Turpin. As Thompson's young narrator weighs his options and attempts to negotiate his position, his story "introduces a host of ambiguities" that involve loyalty and self-preservation, according to a *Publishers Weekly* contributor. "A fine exercise in storytelling," in the view of *Booklist* critic Ian Chipman, *Highway Robbery* "delivers a delicious twist" to close the boy's rousing adventure, while Joanna Rudge Long described Thompson's illustrated novel as "a narrative rich in language, told with panache and begging to be shared aloud."

Horses are also the focus of *Most Wanted,* which takes readers back to the realm of the cruel Roman emperor Gaius (a fictionalized Caligula). As with *Highway Robbery,* young Marcus is also caught unaware when he suddenly finds the reins of a powerful horse thrust into his grasp by a slave. In this case, the horse is Incitatus, the stallion of the emperor himself, and Marcus is but a baker's son. When the slave is subsequently killed, Marcus recognizes that his actions will either bring honor or death upon his family. Reviewing *Most Wanted* in *Booklist,* Krista Hutley praised Thompson's "short,

fast-paced historical adventure" as perfect for readers transitioning to longer books, while *School Librarian* contributor Martin Axford described the tale as "beautifully paced . . . and delightfully illustrated" with black-and-white drawings by Jonny Duddle. Calling Marcus "clever, resourceful and observant," a *Kirkus Reviews* writer added that the "short page count" and "fast-paced plot" of *Most Wanted* will add appeal to a story "significantly more sophisticated" than standard chapter-book fare.

The tragic life of a troubled modern-day teen plays out against a backdrop of faerie interference in Thompson's critically acclaimed stand-alone novel *Creature of the Night*. Set in Dublin, the story focuses on Bobby, a fourteen-year-old ne'er-do-well whose activities alternate among stealing cars, abusing alcohol and drugs, and getting into fights. Desperate to change her son's future, Bobby's mother moves the family to the countryside, unaware that a different sort of threat awaits. Noting that *Creature of the Night* is a change of pace for the author, Hunt wrote in *Horn Book* that Thompson's "gritty crime thriller" employs the characteristic Irish setting that "works its own kind of magic." As the novelist explained in an interview with *School Library Journal* contributor Rick Margolis, both Ireland and its stories continue to be a strong influence on her fiction. "On a very basic level," she noted, "if you walk around [County Galway] . . . , in some of the very empty and unused countryside, you almost get a sense of that magic in the air."

Biographical and Critical Sources

PERIODICALS

Booklist, March 15, 1998, John Peters, review of *Switchers,* p. 1245; April 15, 2000, Sally Estes, review of *Wild Blood,* p. 1543; May 15, 2005, Jennifer Mattson, review of *Fourth World,* p. 1660; May 15, 2006, Jennifer Mattson, review of *Only Human,* p. 61; February 1, 2007, Gillian Engberg, review of *The New Policeman,* p. 47; May 15, 2008, Gillian Engberg, review of *The Last of the High Kings,* p. 56; April 1, 2009, Ian Chipman, review of *Creature of the Night,* p. 38; June 1, 2009, Ian Chipman, review of *Highway Robbery,* p. 55; August 1, 2010, Francisca Goldsmith, review of *The White Horse Trick,* p. 50; October 15, 2010, Krista Hutley, review of *Most Wanted,* p. 53.

Bookseller, February 18, 2005, review of *The New Policeman,* p. 40; February 17, 2006, review of *The Fourth Horseman,* p. 32.

Children's Bookwatch, July, 2005, review of *Fourth World.*

Globe & Mail (Toronto, Ontario, Canada), March 31, 2007, O.R. Melling, review of *The New Policeman,* p. D12.

Guardian (London, England), July 29, 2006, Adélè Geras, review of *The Fourth Horseman,* p. 16; August 3, 2008, Philip Ardagh, review of *Creature of the Night,* p. 25.

Horn Book, January-February, 2002, Anita L. Burkam, review of *The Beguilers,* p. 85; May-June, 2005, Vicky Smith, review of *Fourth World,* p. 333; May-June, 2006, Vicky Smith, review of *Only Human,* p. 332; March-April, 2007, Betsy Hearne, review of *The New Policeman,* p. 206; January-February, 2008, Vicky Smith, review of *Origins,* p. 95; May-June, 2008, Betsy Hearne, review of *The Last of the High Kings,* p. 331; May-June, 2009, Jonathan Hunt, review of *Creature of the Night,* p. 309; July-August, 2009, Joanna Rudge Long, review of *Highway Robbery,* p. 432; September-October, 2010, Jonathan Hunt, review of *The White Horse Trick,* p. 96; January-February, 2011, Joanna Rudge Long, review of *Most Wanted,* p. 102.

Independent (London, England), October 11, 2008, Jayne Howarth, review of *Creature of the Night,* p. 20.

Journal of Adolescent & Adult Literacy, May, 2007, Judith A. Hayn, review of *The New Policeman,* p. 690.

Kirkus Reviews, April 1, 2005, review of *Fourth World,* p. 427; May 1, 2006, review of *Only Human,* p. 468; December 15, 2006, review of *The New Policeman,* p. 1273; May 1, 2008, review of *The Last of the High Kings;* November 1, 2010, review of *Most Wanted.*

Kliatt, January, 2007, Paula Rohrlick, review of *The New Policeman,* p. 19; May, 2008, Paula Rohrlick, review of *The Last of the High Kings,* p. 17.

Observer (London, England), August 3, 2008, Stephanie Merritt, review of *Creature of the Night,* p. 25.

Publishers Weekly, June 8, 1998, review of *Switchers,* p. 61; October 29, 2001, review of *The Beguilers,* p. 65; November 26, 2007, review of *Origins,* p. 54; May 12, 2008, review of *The Last of the High Kings,* p. 54; June 8, 2009, review of *Highway Robbery,* p. 44; September 27, 2010, review of *The White Horse Trick,* p. 62.

School Librarian, spring, 2010, Audrey Baker, review of *The White Horse Trick,* p. 55; winter, 2010, Martin Axford, review of *Wanted!,* p. 232.

School Library Journal, July, 2000, Patricia A. Dollisch, review of *Wild Blood,* p. 111; October, 2001, Steven Engelfried, review of *The Beguilers,* p. 173; October, 2005, Susan L. Rogers, review of *Fourth World,* p. 175; March, 2007, Heather M. Campbell, review of *The New Policeman,* p. 220; December, 2007, Sharon Rawlins, review of *Origins,* p. 145; July, 2008, Robin Henry, review of *The Last of the High Kings,* p. 108; August, 2009, Kat Redniss, review of *Creature of the Night,* p. 115.

Times (London, England), June 21, 2008, Amanda Craig, review of *Creature of the Night,* p. 15.

ONLINE

Contemporary Writers in the UK Web site, http://www.contemporarywriters.com/ (May 1, 2012), "Kate Thompson."

Rambles Online, http://www.rambles.net/ (October 8, 2007), Donna Scanlon, review of *Switchers.*

School Library Association Web site, http://www.sla.org.uk/ (January 5, 2006), "Kate Thompson Wins Whitbread Children's Book Award."

VAN CLEAVE, Ryan G. 1972-

Personal

Born May 20, 1972, in Neenah, WI; married; children: two daughters. *Education:* Northern Illinois University, B.A. (English), 1994; Florida State University, M.A. (American literature), 1997, Ph.D. (American literature), 2001.

Addresses

Home—Sarasota, FL. *Agent*—Claire Gerus, Claire Gerus Literary Agency; gerus.claire@gmail.com, *E-mail*—rvcleave@c.ringling.edu.

Career

Author, educator, editor, and writing coach. Clemson University, assistant professor of English, 2002-07; Eckerd College, member of writing faculty, 2009-10; Ringling College, Sarasota, FL, member of writing faculty, beginning 2009. Edward H. and Marie C. Kingsbury fellow, Florida State University, 2000; Anastasia C. Hoffman poetry fellow, University of Wisconsin—Madison, 2000-01; Jenny McKean Moore Writer-in-Washington, George Washington University, 2007-08. C. & R. Press (publisher and literary nonprofit), Chattanooga, TN, cofounder with Chad Prevost, 2006. Teacher of creative writing at prisons, community centers, and urban youth centers. Speaker on video-game addiction.

Member

Society of Children's Book Writers and Illustrators, Poetry Society of America, Southeast College Art Conference.

Awards, Honors

Theodore Christian Hoepfner Award, *Southern Humanities Review*, 2000; American Poetry Anthology Award, 2003, for *Like Thunder: Poets Respond to Violence in America;* Quick Pick for Reluctant Readers selection, American Library Association, 2012, for *Unlocked.*

Writings

Unplugged: My Journey into the Dark World of Video Game Addiction, foreword by Mark Griffiths, Health Communications (Deerfield Beach, FL), 2010.

Unlocked (young-adult novel), Walker & Co. (New York, NY), 2011.

You Know You're a Video-Game Addict If . . . , Running Press (Philadelphia, PA), 2012.

POETRY

The Florida Letters, Dream Horse Press (San Jose, CA), 2001.

Ha Ha Tonka: A Book of Rune, Higganum Hill Books (Higganum, CT), 2003.

Imagine the Dawn: The Civil War Sonnets, Turning Point (Cincinnati, OH), 2005.

Also author of poetry collection *The Magical Breasts of Britney Spears.*

OTHER

(Editor with Virgil Suárez) *American Diaspora: Poetry of Displacement,* University of Iowa Press (Iowa City, IA), 2001.

(Editor with Virgil Suárez) *Like Thunder: Poets Respond to Violence in America,* University of Iowa Press (Iowa City, IA), 2002.

(Compiler) *Contemporary American Poetry: Behind the Scenes* (textbook), Longman (New York, NY), 2003.

(Editor with Virgil Suárez) *Vespers: Contemporary American Poems of Religion and Spirituality,* University of Iowa Press (Iowa City, IA), 2003.

(Editor with Virgil Suárez) *Red, White, and Blues: Poets on the Promise of America,* University of Iowa Press (Iowa City, IA), 2004.

(Editor with Todd James Pierce) *Behind the Short Story: From First to Final Draft,* Pearson Longman (New York, NY), 2007.

(Editor with Chad Prevost) *Breathe: 101 Contemporary Odes,* C&R Press (Chattanooga, TN), 2009.

(Editor) *City of the Big Shoulders: An Anthology of Chicago Poetry,* University of Iowa Press (Iowa City, IA), 2012.

Contributor of poems, articles, and reviews to periodicals, including *Boston Review, California Literary Review, Christian Science Monitor, Clean Eating, Harvard Review, Iowa Review, Mid-American Review, Missouri Review, National Geographic Adventures, New York Times Book Review, People, Ploughshares, Progressive, Psychology Today, Puerto del Sol, Scene, Scott Stamp Monthly, Southern Humanities Review, TriQuarterly,* and *Writers' Digest.* Contributor to anthologies, including *Mooring against the Tide: Writing Fiction and Poetry,* Prentice Hall, 2000; *Year's Best Fantasy and Horror,* St. Martin's Press, 2002; *Never Before: Poems about First Experiences,* Four Way Books, 2005; and *In a Fine Frenzy: Poetry Inspired by Shakespeare,* University of Iowa Press, 2005.

Sidelights

In college, Ryan G. Van Cleave trained to become a teacher of creative writing, and he has also found success as a poet and the editor of a number of prose and poetry anthologies. Reviewing Van Cleave's collaboration with fellow editor Virgil Suárez, *Like Thunder: Poets Respond to Violence in America, Booklist* contributor Donna Seaman praised the work as "deeply resonant" and full of "fresh, searching, and necessary poems that together create a compassionate and momentous anthology." In addition to his work as a poet and anthologist, Van Cleave also shares his experience

as a life-long World of Warcraft gamer in *Unplugged: My Journey into the Dark World of Video Game Addiction,* and he has also produced a verse novel, *Unlocked,* intended for young adults.

In *Unplugged* Van Cleave recalls his own relationship with video games, one that started when he was a boy. "Many gamers feel trapped by their love of games," he noted in an interview with Randolph Carter for *Grinding to Valhalla* online. While parents have difficulty understanding why their child is drawn into interactive online gaming, they sense that the compulsion is an unhealthy one, as well as being disruptive to families. While noting that "video games provide some terrific and useful experiences" and even enhance "memory and motor function," they "are doing something to us emotionally, socially, and intellectually. I'm including information about some of those things in this book to help wake people up about the true costs. If they then still choose to make an informed choice to play, great."

In Van Cleave's novel, *Unlocked* readers meet Andy, a fourteen year old whose father is the janitor of his school. As the janitor's son, Andy has resigned himself to being a social pariah. However, when a rumor circulates that another social outcast, Blake, has a handgun hidden in his school locker, Andy senses the opportunity to become a school hero. Taking his father's master keys, he opens Blake's locker, but when no gun is found the taunting directed his way escalates. As fellow outsiders, Blake and Andy gradually strike up a friendship, and it turns out that Blake does indeed have a handgun. Firing the gun at targets gives Andy a rush of power as well as a rush of mixed feelings: both a fear of what the gun can do and the realization that the gun could be a way to balance the social scales after years of bullying.

Cover of Ryan G. Van Cleave's coming-of-age novel* Unlocked, *which finds an insecure teen battling class differences. (Reproduced by permission of Walker Publishing Company, a division of Bloomsbury Publishing, Inc.)

Noting that the "suspenseful ending and short" length of *Unlocked* will attract even reluctant readers, Shawna Sherman added in *School Library Journal* that Van Cleave's young-adult novel "is strong on insight into the lives of those bullied in high school." In *Voice of Youth Advocates* Christina Fairman recommended the author's "compelling free verse" in which "sparse words and vivid phrases reveal the multilayered dilemma confronting Andy." Michael Cart also weighed in on *Unlocked* in a *Booklist* review, concluding that Van Cleave focuses on an "all-too-familiar" situation in writing that reveals "both empathy and authority."

Biographical and Critical Sources

BOOKS

Van Cleave, Ryan G., *Unplugged: My Journey into the Dark World of Video Game Addiction,* Health Communications (Deerfield Beach, FL), 2010.

PERIODICALS

Booklist, March 1, 2002, Donna Seaman, review of *Like Thunder: Poets Respond to Violence in America,* p. 1079; March 1, 2011, Michael Cart, review of *Unlocked,* p. 59.

Bulletin of the Center for Children's Books, April, 2011, Claire Gross, review of *Unlocked,* p. 395.

Kliatt, January, 2002, James Beschta, review of *American Diaspora: Poetry of Displacement,* p. 22.

Library Journal, April 1, 2002, Rochelle Ratner, review of *Like Thunder,* p. 112.

School Library Journal, April, 2011, Shawna Sherman, review of *Unlocked,* p. 187.

Voice of Youth Advocates, April, 2011, Christina Fairman, review of *Unlocked,* p. 71.

ONLINE

Grinding to Valhalla Web log, http://grindingtovalhalla.wordpress.com/ (March 24, 2010), Randolph Carter, interview with Van Cleave.

Ryan G. Van Cleave Home Page, http://www.ryanvancleave.com (May 1, 2012).

Unplugged Web site, http://www.unpluggedthebook.com/ (May 1, 2012).

WALLEY, Byron
See CARD, Orson Scott

* * *

WATSON, Wendy 1942-

Personal

Born July 7, 1942, in Patterson, NJ; daughter of Aldren Auld (an art editor, illustrator, and writer) and Nancy (a writer) Watson; married Michael Donald Harrah (an actor and opera singer), December 19, 1970; children: Mary Cameron Harrah, one other child. *Education:* Bryn Mawr College, B.A. (Latin literature; magna cum laude; with honors), 1964; studied painting with Jerry Farnsworth in Cape Cod, MA, 1961-62; attended National Academy of Design, 1966-67. *Religion:* Society of Friends (Quaker). *Hobbies and other interests:* Theater, music (plays the piano and cello), reading, gardening.

Addresses

Home—Phoenix, AZ; Truro, MA. *Agent*—Curtis Brown, Ltd., 10 Astor Pl., New York, NY10003.

Career

Illustrator and author of children's books. Hanover Press, Hanover, NH, compositor and designer, 1965-66; freelance illustrator, beginning 1966. *Exhibitions:* Work exhibited at American Institute of Graphic Arts Children's Book Show, 1967-68, 1972; Biennial of Illustrations, Bratislava, 1973, 1981; City Gallery, New York, NY, 1984; Bush Galleries, Boston, MA, 1989; Society of Illustrators Original Art Show, 1990, 1994, 1999, 2002, 2004; Green Mountain Art Gallery, Bradford, VT, 1993; and Brattleboro Museum and Art Center, Brattleboro, VT, 1994; in "Myth, Magic, and Mystery" touring exhibition, 1995-97; and elsewhere. Work represented in private collections.

Member

Authors Guild, Society of Children's Book Writers and Illustrators.

Awards, Honors

New York Times Outstanding Books citation, and Notable Book selection, American Library Association (ALA), both 1971, and Children's Book Showcase award, Children's Book Council (CBC), and National Book Award finalist, Association of American Publishers, both 1972, all for *Father Fox's Pennyrhymes* by Clyde Watson; Outstanding Science Trade Book for Children, National Science Teacher's Association/CBC, 1974, for *Sleep Is for Everyone* by Paul Showers, 1996, for *Maps, Tracks, and the Bridges of Konigsberg* by Michael Holt, 1977, for *Binary Numbers* by Watson; Notable Children's Trade Book in the Field of Social Studies, CBC, 1982 for both *Winding Valley Farm* and *First Farm in the Valley* by Anne Pellowski, 1987, for *Doctor Coyote* by John Bierhorst; One Hundred Books for Reading and Sharing selection, New York Public Library, Sydney Taylor Honor Book selection, Association of Jewish Libraries, and Koret Jewish Book Award, all 2004, and California Young Readers Medal, 2007, all for *The Cats in Krasinski Square* by Karen Hesse.

Writings

FOR CHILDREN; SELF-ILLUSTRATED

Very Important Cat, Dodd (New York, NY), 1958.
(Editor) *Fisherman Lullabies,* music by sister Clyde Watson, World Publishing (Cleveland, OH), 1968.
(Adapter) Jacob Grimm and Wilhelm Grimm, *The Hedgehog and the Hare,* World Publishing (Cleveland, OH), 1969.
Lollipop, Crowell (New York, NY), 1976.
Moving, Crowell (New York, NY), 1978.
Has Winter Come?, Philomel (New York, NY), 1978.

Jamie's Story, Philomel (New York, NY), 1981.
The Bunnies' Christmas Eve, Philomel (New York, NY), 1983.
Christmas at Bunny's Inn: A Three-Dimensional Advent Calendar with Twenty-four Windows and Doors to Open from December First to Christmas Eve, Philomel (New York, NY), 1984.
Little Brown Bear, Western Publishing (New York, NY), 1985.
Tales for a Winter's Eve (short stories), Farrar, Straus & Giroux (New York, NY), 1988.
Wendy Watson's Mother Goose, Lothrop, Lee & Shepard (New York, NY), 1989.
Wendy Watson's Frog Went A-Courting, Lothrop, Lee & Shepard (New York, NY), 1990.
Thanksgiving at Our House, Houghton (Boston, MA), 1991.
A Valentine for You, Houghton (Boston, MA), 1991.
Boo! It's Halloween, Clarion (New York, NY), 1992.
Hurray for the Fourth of July!, Clarion (New York, NY), 1992.
Happy Easter Day!, Clarion (New York, NY), 1993.
Fox Went out on a Chilly Night, Lothrop, Lee & Shepard (New York, NY), 1994.
Holly's Christmas Eve, HarperCollins (New York, NY), 2002.
Bedtime Bunnies, Clarion Books (New York, NY), 2010.

ILLUSTRATOR

Yeta Speevach, *The Spider Plant,* Atheneum (New York, NY), 1965.
A Comic Primer, Peter Pauper (Mount Vernon, NY), 1966.
Love Is a Laugh, Peter Pauper (Mount Vernon, NY), 1967.
The Country Mouse and the City Mouse, Stinehour Press (Lunenburg, VT), 1967.
Alice E. Christgau, *Rosabel's Secret,* W.R. Scott, 1967.
Paul Tripp, *The Strawman Who Smiled by Mistake,* Doubleday (New York, NY), 1967.
Edna Boutwell, *Daughter of Liberty,* World Publishing (Cleveland, OH), 1967.
Ogden Nash, *The Cruise of the Aardvark,* M. Evans (New York, NY), 1967.
Henry Wadsworth Longfellow, *Henry Wadsworth Longfellow: Selected Poems,* edited by Clarence Merton Babcock, Peter Pauper Press (Mount Vernon, VT), 1967.
Miska Miles, *Uncle Fonzo's Ford,* Little, Brown (Boston, MA), 1968.
The Best in Offbeat Humor, Peter Pauper (Mount Vernon, NY), 1968.
Kathryn Hitte, *When Noodlehead Went to the Fair,* Parents' Magazine Press (New York, NY), 1968.
Nancy Dingman Watson (mother), *Carol to a Child,* music by Clyde Watson, World Publishing (Cleveland, OH), 1969.
Louise Bachelder, compiler, *God Bless Us, Every One,* Peter Pauper (Mount Vernon, NY), 1969.
The Jack Book, Macmillan (New York, NY), 1969.
Margaret Davidson, *Helen Keller,* Scholastic (New York, NY), 1969.
Mary H. Calhoun, *Magic in the Alley,* Atheneum (New York, NY), 1970.
Mabel Harmer, *Lizzie, the Lost Toys Witch,* Macrae Smith (Philadelphia, PA), 1970.
Louise Bachelder, compiler, *Happy Thoughts,* Peter Pauper Press (Mount Vernon, VT), 1970.
How Dear to My Heart, Peter Pauper (Mount Vernon, NY), 1970.
Clyde Watson, *Father Fox's Pennyrhymes* (verse; also see below), Crowell (New York, NY), 1971, HarperCollins (New York, NY), 2001.
Life's Wondrous Ways, Peter Pauper (Mount Vernon, NY), 1971.
America! America!, Peter Pauper (Mount Vernon, NY), 1971.
A Gift of Mistletoe, Peter Pauper (Mount Vernon, NY), 1971.
Charles Linn, *Probability,* Crowell (New York, NY), 1972.
Clyde Watson, *Tom Fox and the Apple Pie,* Crowell (New York, NY), 1972.
Clyde R. Bulla, *Open the Door and See All the People,* Crowell (New York, NY), 1972.
Bobbie Katz, *Upside Down and Inside Out: Poems for All Your Pockets,* F. Watts (New York, NY), 1973.
Nancy Dingman Watson, *The Birthday Goat,* Crowell (New York, NY), 1974.
Paul Showers, *Sleep Is for Everyone,* Crowell (New York, NY), 1974.
Clyde Watson, *Quips and Quirks,* Crowell (New York, NY), 1975.
Michael Holt, *Maps, Tracks, and the Bridges of Königsberg,* Crowell (New York, NY), 1975.
Nancy Dingman Watson, *Muncus Agruncus: A Bad Little Mouse,* Golden Press (New York, NY), 1976.
Clyde Watson, *Hickory Stick Rag* (verse), Crowell (New York, NY), 1976.
Florence Pettit, *Christmas All around the House: Traditional Decorations You Can Make,* Crowell (New York, NY), 1976.
Clyde Watson, *Binary Numbers* (nonfiction), Crowell (New York, NY), 1977.
Clyde Watson, *Catch Me and Kiss Me and Say It Again* (verse; also see below), Philomel (New York, NY), 1978.
Miska Miles, *Jenny's Cat,* Dutton (New York, NY), 1979.
Clyde Watson, *How Brown Mouse Kept Christmas,* Farrar, Straus & Giroux (New York, NY), 1980.
Jan Wahl, *Button Eye's Orange,* Warne (New York, NY), 1980.
Anne Pellowski, *Stairstep Farm: Anna Rose's Story,* Philomel (New York, NY), 1981.
Anne Pellowski, *Willow Wind Farm: Betsy's Story,* Philomel (New York, NY), 1981.
Clyde Watson, *Applebet: An ABC,* Farrar, Straus & Giroux (New York, NY), 1982.
Anne Pellowski, *Winding Valley Farm: Annie's Story,* Philomel (New York, NY), 1982.
Anne Pellowski, *First Farm in the Valley: Anna's Story,* Philomel (New York, NY), 1982.
Rebecca C. Jones, *The Biggest, Meanest, Ugliest Dog in the Whole Wide World,* Macmillan (New York, NY), 1982.

Clyde Watson, *Father Fox's Feast of Songs* (musical adaptations of poems from *Father Fox's Pennyrhymes* and *Catch Me and Kiss Me and Say It Again*), Philomel (New York, NY), 1983.

Anne Pellowski, *Betsy's Up-and-Down Year,* Philomel (New York, NY), 1983.

Carolyn Haywood, *Happy Birthday from Carolyn Haywood,* Morrow (New York, NY), 1984.

Elaine Edelman, *I Love My Baby Sister (Most of the Time),* Lothrop, Lee & Shepard (New York, NY), 1984.

Elizabeth Winthrop, *Belinda's Hurricane,* Dutton (New York, NY), 1984.

John Bierhorst, *Doctor Coyote: A Native American Aesop's Fables,* Macmillan (New York, NY), 1987.

Marcia Leonard, *Angry,* Bantam (New York, NY), 1988.

Marcia Leonard, *Happy,* Bantam (New York, NY), 1988.

Marcia Leonard, *Scared,* Bantam (New York, NY), 1988.

Marcia Leonard, *Silly,* Bantam (New York, NY), 1988.

Clyde Watson, *Valentine Foxes,* Orchard Books (New York, NY), 1989.

B.G. Hennessy, *A, B, C, D, Tummy, Toes, Hands, Knees,* Viking Kestrel (New York, NY), 1989.

Clement Clarke Moore, *The Night before Christmas,* Clarion (New York, NY), 1990.

Clyde Watson, *Love's a Sweet,* Viking Penguin (New York, NY), 1998.

John Bierhorst, *Is My Friend at Home?: Pueblo Fireside Tales,* Farrar Straus & Giroux (New York, NY), 2001.

***Wendy Watson created the line art for John Bierhorst's Native-American-themed story* Doctor Coyote.** (Illustration copyright © 1987 by Wendy Watson. Reproduced by permission of illustrator's agent, Curtis Brown, Ltd.)

Patricia Hubbell, *Rabbit Moon: A Book of Holidays and Celebrations,* Marshall Cavendish (New York, NY), 2002.

Clyde Watson, *Father Fox's Christmas Rhymes,* Farrar Straus & Giroux (New York, NY), 2003.

Karen Hesse, *The Cats in Krasinski Square,* Scholastic Press (New York, NY), 2004.

Karen Hesse, *Spuds,* Scholastic Press (New York, NY), 2008.

Sidelights

An esteemed author and illustrator of books for children under the age of ten, Wendy Watson is most often recognized for her artistic work, especially when it accompanies stories written by her sister Clyde Watson. The sisters' award-winning collaboration *Father Fox's Pennyrhymes* was widely praised by critics, *New York Times Book Review* contributor George A. Woods dubbing the picture book "an American original." Watson has contributed to dozens of illustrated stories by other writers as well as creating original self-illustrated tales such as *Lollipop, Has Winter Come,* and *Bedtime Bunnies.*

From foxes to chaotic and happy families, Watson's artwork brings to life myriad characters and activities that engage readers. Blending humor and traditional scenes, she has created a body of work that has been praised by critics and honored by awards committees. Watson's "honest, often wise stories and detailed country illustrations are full of joy and life," concluded an essayist in *Children's Books and Their Creators.*

"My parents provided, indirectly, a great deal of my basic training in drawing and books in general" Watson once told *SATA.* Born in New Jersey, she grew up on a farm in Putney, Vermont, one of seven children born to an artist father and writer mother. Surrounded by animals—goats, horses and chickens—Watson also grew up in the company of art, for her father, Aldren Watson, had his studio on the third floor of the house. Books were present everywhere as well, including those published by her mother, Nancy. Watson's "cheerful, homey illustrations reflect this rural upbringing," according to the *Children's Books and Their Creators* writer.

Watson attended Bryn Mawr College, majoring in Latin literature and graduating in 1964. However, from the time she was a young child, she knew she wanted to become an illustrator; during her college summers and thereafter, she received formal training from Jerry Farnsworth, Helen Sawyer, and Daniel Greene both on Cape Cod and at the National Academy of Design in 1966 and 1967. Her father also helped in her art training. Following college graduation, Watson worked for a time at a small press in New Hampshire where she was a compositor and designer and gained the knowledge of typography and design that would be invaluable to her in her book-illustrating career. In 1970 Watson married opera singer and actor Michael Donald Harrah.

***Watson's collaboration with sister and author Clyde Watson include their picture book* Father Fox's Pennyrhymes.** (Illustration copyright © 1971 by Wendy Watson. Reproduced by permission of illustrator's agent, Curtis Brown, Ltd.)

Watson's career as a professional author and illustrator got underway in 1958 when, at age sixteen, she published her self-illustrated *Very Important Cat.* Throughout the 1960s she focused on illustrating stories by other authors before firmly establishing her reputation with *Father Fox's Pennyrhymes,* written by her sister Clyde. In the story, Fox entertains his large family around the fire on wintry nights with rhymes, telling of love and family life as well as topics including gluttony and his love of song. Watson's illustrations for the book were warmly received by critics and *Father Fox's Pennyrhymes* was nominated for a National Book Award as well as inclusion in the 1972 Children's Book Showcase.

The drawings for *Father Fox's Pennyrhymes* are typical of Watson's work. Inspired by her life in Vermont, her work exudes a New England country charm: "cheerful, old-fashioned illustrations," as one *Publishers Weekly* contributor characterized them in a review of *A Valentine for You.* "Her colors have a real integrity that seems to derive from the New England light," Christina Olson observed in her review of *Wendy Watson's Mother Goose* for the *New York Times Book Review.*

Another characteristic of Watson's work is her attention to small details. Her images are often filled with objects and bustling with activity that catches the reader's eye. This aspect of her work is especially evident in *Wendy Watson's Frog Went A-Courting,* a self-illustrated work that prompted a *Publishers Weekly* reviewer to remark that "youngsters will enjoy seeking out the many droll details" to be found on every page. Also noting the artist's interest in detail, Olson wrote in the *New York Times Book Review* that "Watson is . . . an illustrator who knows what she is doing. There is a sweetness in her work that is unfailingly appealing, and she produces thoughtful and well-made books."

Other collaborative efforts between Watson and her sister include *Tom Fox and the Apple Pie, Love's a Sweet, Catch Me and Kiss Me and Say It Again, How Brown Mouse Kept Christmas, Father Fox's Feast of Songs, Love's a Sweet,* and *Father Fox's Christmas Rhymes.* Most of these books have a simple rhyming text designed to be easily memorized by young readers or listeners. The compilation of Clyde Watson's stories and Wendy Watson's watercolor illustrations reveal an appreciation for family life and the fine details of childhood. A reviewer for *Horn Book,* for example, praised the "jolly, decorative illustrations" to be found in *Father Fox's Feast of Songs.* In *Love's a Sweet,* a collection of poems showing the ups and downs of love, Watson supplies "lively colored pencil drawing that skip across the pages," according to *Booklist* reviewer Kathy Broderick, while a *Publishers Weekly* critic described the book's art as "sweetly misted but witty" as well as "serene and soothing."

Watson provides her own take on foxes in *Fox Went out on a Chilly Night,* a retelling of an old folk song. A fox leaves its burrow in the dark of night in order to find food to feed its young brood of kits, evading and eluding all the townsfolk who soon follow it in hot pursuit. A contributor for *Kirkus Reviews* found Watson's adaptation of this song to be a worthwhile addition, especially because of the artwork "that gives the classic a heft you can almost bite into." In *Publishers Weekly* a reviewer suggested of *Fox Went out on a Chilly Night* that "Watson's timeless illustrations offer abundant particulars to pore over."

Woodland animals also star in *Bedtime Bunnies*, which finds Mother and Father Rabbit calling their five fluffy-tailed offspring back into the home for the night. In chronicling the parents' efforts to get the five frisky bunnies fed, washed, dressed, and tucked into bed, Watson assembles what a *Publishers Weekly* critic characterized as "a punchy, onomatopoeic selection of [action] words" that pair with the artist's "buoyant, gauzy" watercolor and acrylic illustrations. Praising the book for providing "a warm glimpse of family life, *Booklist* critic Ilene Cooper dubbed *Bedtime Bunnies* "short, sweet, and smart," while a *Kirkus Reviews* writer asserted that the "charmingly executed" illustrations let "individual bunnies' personalities shine through."

With *Holly's Christmas Eve* Watson returns to holiday themes in a tale of a painted wooden ornament that leaves the Christmas tree to goes in search of her missing arm. Holly is the most recent addition to a family's colorful collection of ornaments, but when the household cat crawls up the tree, Holly is knocked down, los-

ing her arm in the process. The vacuum cleaner proceeds to gobble it up, but Holly, joined by other ornaments, including Tin Horse and Cloth Bear, makes an expedition to retrieve the missing appendage. She finds the arm and, with the help of Santa, manages to repair it. In a *School Library Journal* review, Maureen Wade praised *Holly's Christmas Eve,* noting that the book's "vivid, full page . . . artwork captures the drama and satisfying ending." In *Booklist* Ilene Cooper also commended Watson's illustrations, writing that they possess "the exuberance and simplicity of children's own art." A *Kirkus Reviews* critic focused on the text, noting that, although the story is "simple," the author/illustrator blends "amusing characters" and a "folksy narrative voice . . . into a satisfying, if unusual, Christmas Eve tale."

Watson draws on her rural background, growing up in a large, loving, and boisterous family, as inspiration for her illustrations for stories by Anne Pellowski that introduce farm families in Wisconsin: *First Farm in the Valley: Anna's Story, Stairstep Farm: Anna Rose's Story,* and *Willow Wind Farm: Betsy's Story.* With John Bierhorst, she has worked on a duet of books involving the Native American trickster, Coyote. *Doctor Coyote: A Native American Aesop's Fables* presents a bevy of Aztec interpretations of Aesop's fables. Bierhorst returns to such Coyote tales with *Is My Friend at Home?: Pueblo Fireside Tales,* a compilation of seven trickster tales from the Hopi tradition. Rosalyn Pierini, writing in *School Library Journal,* noted that Watson's "child-centered, humorous illustrations enliven the text and lend a great deal of personality to these archetypal characters." Similarly, *Horn Book* critic Nell D. Beram asserted that Watson's cartoon-like illustrations "capture the spirit of these disarmingly absurd, unexpectedly touching tales."

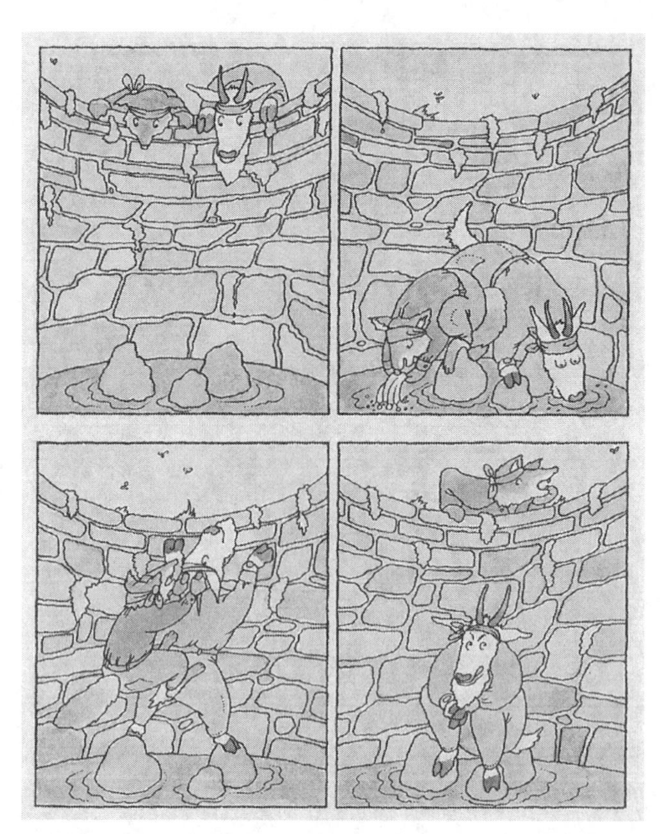

***Watson's sequential line-drawn elements add humor to Bierhorst's text for* Doctor Coyote.** (Illustration copyright © 1987 by Wendy Watson. Reproduced by permission of the illlustrator's agent, Curtis Brown Ltd.)

***Watson introduces a family ready for fun in her colorful self-illustrated picture book* Bedtime Bunnies.** (Copyright © 2010 by Wendy Watson. Reproduced with permission of Clarion Books, an imprint of Houghton Mifflin Harcourt Publishing Company.)

Rabbits take center stage in a collaborative effort with writer Patricia Hubbell for *Rabbit Moon: A Book of Holidays and Celebrations.* Piper L. Nyman wrote in *School Library Journal* that the "adorable characters cavort over the spreads" of this entertaining picture book.

Another exceptional collaboration has been that between Watson and Karen Hesse, author of both *Spuds* and the award-winning *The Cats in Krasinski Square.* In *Spuds* three children growing up during the Great Depression of the 1930s are determined to locate enough potatoes to feed their poor-off farming family. Here "Hesse's spare . . . poetry is beautifully extended in Watson's uncluttered pictures," according to *Booklist* reviewer Gillian Engberg. Praising Hesse's ability to evoke a "mood of tender nostalgia," a *Kirkus Reviews* writer added that the artist's "soft, muted" line, watercolor, and gouache illustrations in warm earthy tones "perfectly complement the text," and Marilyn Taniguchi concluded her *School Library Journal* review that *Spuds* serves up a "sweetly understated affirmation of hard work and honesty, neighborliness and family love [that] . . . will resonate with a wide audience."

The Cats in Krasinski Square is perhaps Watson's best-known illustration project. Hesse's story transports readers back to 1942, where a young Jewish girl joins sev-

eral other children helping the resistance to smuggle food to Polish Jews still living as captives in the Warsaw ghetto. As the true-life story has been remembered, the German Gestapo discover the plan and lear the exact time the resistance plans to bring the food to Warsaw via train. They wait in hiding at the station, bringing with them several dogs that are able to sniff out the parcels of food. Fortunately, the resistance learns of the ambush, and the little girl helps collect all the wild cats living in the city's Krasinski Square, put them into baskets, and carry them to the station. There they are let loose to distract the dogs and ultimately allow the food to be distributed.

In her work for *The Cats in Krasinski Square,* Watson makes "an arresting departure from her usual style," according to Harriett Fargnoli, the *School Library Journal* contributor adding that her earth-toned pictures resonate with "a kind of innocent luminescence of hope that belies the evil that is being done" by the Gestapo. Her renderings "reveal the girl's sensitivity and delicacy" and the numerous cats in her pictures "pay homage to Wanda Gag's *Millions of Cats,* in the opinion of *Horn Book* contributor Susan Dove Lempke. Noting that Watson's line-drawn images capture "the starkness of the Ghetto's confines," a *Publishers Weekly* contributor wrote that *The Cats in Krasinski Square* "take[s] a complex situation and make[s] its most important aspects comprehensible to a child." Praising Hesse's text, with its "luminous free verse," Engberg added in her *Booklist* review that "Watson's arresting images echo the pared-down language." As a *Kirkus Reviews* writer concluded, in their creative collaboration, Hesse and Watson introduce children to "a grave subject" in a way that is "accessible, gently humorous, and affectingly triumphant."

Among her many other illustration projects, Watson has worked on books focusing on holidays and celebrations. Christmas is featured in her version of Clement Clarke Moore's traditional poem *The Night before Christmas,* producing an "utterly charming" book as a contributor for *Publishers Weekly* observed. Gathering several well-known rhymes and songs about love in *A Valentine for You,* the artist presents "a fetching gift for a young Valentine," according to a reviewer for *Publishers Weekly.*

In *Thanksgiving at Our House* Watson crafts an original story containing a mix of traditional songs and rhymes and pairs it with full-page artwork in "a pleasantly cluttered book," as another *Publishers Weekly* contributor noted. The extended family featured in *Thanksgiving at Our House* prepares for the traditional holiday feast, and Watson's illustrations "capture the high-spirited anticipation," according to the same critic.

Independence Day receives a similar treatment in *Hurray for the Fourth of July!,* and here the same family stars a "heartening portrait of a holiday celebration in a small American town," as a contributor for *Publishers Weekly* commented. Watson reprises the same family in *Happy Easter Day,* as the clan prepares hot-cross buns and Easter eggs for the upcoming holiday, unaware that the birth of five kittens will be the best Easter surprise of all. Virginia Opocensky, writing in *School Library Journal,* dubbed *Happy Easter Day* "a delightful addition for holiday shelves" due to illustrations that are "bustling with activity and details."

Biographical and Critical Sources

BOOKS

Children's Books and Their Creators, edited by Anita Silvey, Houghton Mifflin (Boston, MA), 1995, pp. 670-671.

Continuum Encyclopedia of Children's Literature, edited by Bernice E. Cullinan and Diane G. Person, Continuum (New York, NY), 2001, p. 808.

Kingman, Lee, et al., compilers, *Illustrators of Children's Books,* Horn Book (Boston, MA), 1978, p. 167.

PERIODICALS

Booklist, March 1, 1993, Deborah Abbott, review of *Happy Easter Day!,* p. 1233; September 1, 1994, Mary Harris Veeder, review of *Fox Went out on a Chilly Night,* p. 47; August, 1997, Hazel Rochman, review of *Sleep Is for Everyone,* p. 1904; December 1, 1998, Kathy Broderick, review of *Love's a Sweet,* p. 668; September 15, 2002, Ilene Cooper, review of *Holly's Christmas Eve,* p. 247; September 1, 2003, Carolyn Phelan, review of *Father Fox's Christmas Rhymes,* p. 136; October 15, 2004, Gillian Engberg, review of *The Cats in Krasinski Square,* p. 404; September 15, 2008, Gillian Engberg, review of *Spuds,* p. 55; December 1, 2010, Ilene Cooper, review of *Bedtime Bunnies,* p. 62.

Horn Book, March-April, 1993, review of *Father Fox's Feast of Songs,* p. 232; September-October, 2001, Nell D. Beram, review of *Is My Friend Home?,* p. 600; November-December, 2003, Joanna Rudge Long, review of *Father Fox's Christmas Rhymes,* p. 760; September-October, 2004, Susan Dove Lempke, reveiw of *The Cats in Krasinski Square,* p. 569; November-December, 2010, Kitty Flynn, review of *Bedtime Bunnies,* p. 81.

Kirkus Reviews, October 15, 1994, review of *Fox Went out on a Chilly Night,* p. 1418; November 1, 2002, review of *Holly's Christmas Eve,* p. 1627; August 1, 2004, review of *The Cats in Krasinski Square,* p. 742; August 15, 2008, review of *Spuds;* October 15, 2010, review of *Bedtime Bunnies.*

New York Times Book Review, August 15, 1971, George A. Woods, review of *Father Fox's Pennyrhymes,* p. 8; May 27, 1990, Christina Olson, review of *Wendy Watson's Frog Went A-Courting,* p. 18.

Publishers Weekly, April 27, 1990, review of *Wendy Watson's Frog Went A-Courting,* p. 60; September 14, 1990, review of *The Night before Christmas,* p. 123; January 25, 1991, review of *A Valentine for You,* p. 56; July 25, 1991, review of *Thanksgiving at Our*

House, pp. 52-53; March 9, 1992, review of *Hurray for the Fourth of July!,* p. 55; October 17, 1994, review of *Fox Went out on a Chilly Night,* p. 80; October 26, 1998, review of *Love's a Sweet,* p. 65; September 22, 2003, review of *Father Fox's Christmas Rhymes,* p. 69; August 23, 2004, review of *The Cats in Krasinski Square,* p. 54; August 25, 2008, review of *Spuds,* p. 73; October 25, 2010, review of *Bedtime Bunnies,* p. 48.

School Library Journal, April, 1993, Virginia Opocensky, review of *Happy Easter Day!,* p. 116; August, 1997, Marsha McGrath, review of *Sleep Is for Everyone,* pp. 150-151; October, 1994, Roseanne Cerny, review of *Fox Went out on a Chilly Night,* p. 116; January, 1999, Marlene Gawron, review of *Love's a Sweet,* p. 122; September, 2001, Rosalyn Pierini, review of *Is My Friend Home?,* p. 211; June, 2002, Piper L. Nyman, review of *Rabbit Moon: A Book of Holidays and Celebrations,* pp. 97-98; October, 2002, Maureen Wade, review of *Holly's Christmas Eve,* pp. 64-65; October, 2003, Evas Mitnick, review of *Father Fox's Christmas Rhymes,* p. 69; November, 2004, Harriett Fargnoli, review of *The Cats in Krasinski Square,* p. 106; September, 2008, Marilyn Taniguchi, review of *Spuds,* p. 148; December, 2010, Maryann H. Owen, review of *Bedtime Bunnies,* p. 90.

ONLINE

VisitingAuthors.com, http://www.visitingauthors.com/ (June 29, 2003), "Wendy Watson."

Wendy Watson Home Page, http://www.wendy-watson.com (May 1, 2012).

Wendy Watson Web log, http://thewendywatsonblog.blogspot.com (May 1, 2012).*

* * *

WHITE, Kiersten 1983(?)-

Personal

Born c. 1983, in UT; married, 2002; children: two. *Education:* Brigham Young University, degree. *Religion:* Church of Jesus Christ of Latter-Day Saints (Mormon). *Hobbies and other interests:* Reading, blogging.

Addresses

Home—San Diego, CA. *Agent*—Michelle Wolfson, Wolfson Literary Agency, michelle@wolfsonliterary.com. *E-mail*—kierstenwhite@yahoo.com.

Career

Writer.

Writings

"PARANORMALCY" YOUNG-ADULT NOVEL SERIES

Paranormalcy, HarperTeen (New York, NY), 2010.

Supernaturally, HarperTeen (New York, NY), 2011.

Contributor to anthology *Corsets and Clockwork,* Running Press, 2011.

Adaptations

Paranormalcy was adapted for film by Mitch Klebanoff, directed by Ray Kay, produced 2013.

Sidelights

Kiersten White began writing while raising her children, and she became a published author by honing her skills and being persistent. After completing two novels, White attracted the attention of an agent with her third, a middle-grade story that was never published. While shopping that third novel, she began writing her fourth, the young-adult *Paranormalcy,* which hit best-seller status and became the first of a trilogy that includes *Supernaturally* and *Endlessly.* Observing that magical creatures such as witches, fairies, vampires, zombies, and werewolves "are essentially personifications of adolescent problems," White told *Publishers Weekly* contributor that including these creatures when writing for a young-adult audience "is just plain . . . fun."

Tapping the popular urban fantasy trend, White's high-action "Paranormalcy" series follows a teenager charged with keeping faeries, shape-shifters, and other creatures below the human radar while also navigating romance and following her preordained destiny. In *Paranormalcy* readers meet Evie, a sixteen year old who has worked for the International Paranormal Containment Agency (IPCA) since age eight, when her special gift for sensing the presence of vampires, werewolves, and other paranormal creatures was revealed. The IPCA has dedicated itself to detecting and cataloguing such creatures, and also neutralizing those that it deems to be a threat, but Evie finds her job veering into a more-sinister realm when it is learned that the world's paranormal population is being decimated by a mysterious force. Things become increasingly complex for the teen when she tracks down Lend, a shape-shifting non-human who captures her romantic interest and attracts the jealousy of her former (faerie) flame Reth.

Calling *Paranormalcy* "a fast-paced, entertaining debut," Kara Dean suggested that White's story will appeal to fans of the popular *Buffy the Vampire Slayer* television series, and a *Publishers Weekly* critic asserted that "the technique and polish of . . . this absorbing romance . . . comes closer than most to hitting the *Buffy* mark." A *Kirkus Reviews* writer had a similar perspective on the novel, citing "the play between this imagined wold and Evie's desire for . . . normal teen amusements" as contributing to the story's "good, romantic—and a little weird—entertainment [value.]" Evie is "a thoroughly modern adolescent heroine," asserted Laura Woodruff in her review of *Paranormalcy* for *Voice of Youth Advocates:* "Perky, insolent, fearless, and insecure," she will appeal to many teen readers who "will

Cover of Kiersten White's urban fantasy/romance* Paranormalcy, *the first novel in an ongoing trilogy focusing on a talented teen vampire hunter. (Cover art © 2010 by Karen Pearson/MergeLeft Reps, Inc. Reproduced with permission of HarperTeen, an imprint of HarperCollins Publishers.)

recognize themselves" in her everyday worries and concerns. A "clever, must-have debut," *Paranormalcy* "will likely fly off library shelves," predicted *School Library Journal* contributor Danielle Serra.

Evie continues to deal with atypical adolescent challenges in *Supernaturally.* No longer working for the IPCA, she now "passes" for normal in high school as Evie Green, but she misses the excitement of her former life. The chance comes to return to active paranormal-hunting duty and she takes it, only to realize that the problems roiling within the faerie realm may involve her. While teaming up with a new hunter, Jack, helps Evie deal with the increasingly malignant fae, she loses her focus when the persuasive Reth tries to insinuate himself back into her life.

Featuring White's characteristic lighthearted humor, *Supernaturally* treats readers to "a goofy, amusing ride," according to a *Kirkus Reviews* critic. "Evie's voice is the best part of the story," the critic added, noting the teen's efforts to juggle her mission to preserve earthly balance with "typical teen concerns and obsessions." In *Voice of Youth Advocates* Suanne B. Roush wrote that *Supernaturally* continues to slowly unravel Evie's complex past and present, and White salts her story with "enough action and plot twists to keep the reader engaged."

Biographical and Critical Sources

PERIODICALS

Booklist, October 15, 2010, Kara Dean, review of *Paranormalcy,* p. 61.

Kirkus Reviews, October 1, 2010, review of *Paranormalcy;* June 1, 2011, review of *Supernaturally.*

Publishers Weekly, September 13, 2010, review of *Paranormalcy,* p. 47; December 20, 2010, "Flying Starts," p. 18.

School Library Journal, December, 2010, Danielle Serra, review of *Paranormalcy,* p. 130.

Voice of Youth Advocates, October, 2010, Laura Woodruff, review of *Paranormalcy,* p. 374; August, 2011, Suanne B. Roush, review of *Supernaturally,* p. 300.

ONLINE

Kiersten White Home Page, http://www.kierstenwhite.com (May 1, 2012).

Kiersten White Web log, http://kierstenwrites.blogspot.com (May 1, 2012).*

* * *

WHITTEMORE, Jo 1977-

Personal

Born October 31, 1977, in Fort Campbell, KY; married. *Education:* Texas A&M University, B.A. (business marketing).

Addresses

Home—Austin, TX. *Agent*—Jennifer Laughran, Andrea Brown Literary Agency; jennL@andreabrownlit.com. *E-mail*—jo_whittemore@hotmail.com.

Career

Novelist and executive assistant.

Member

Society of Children's Book Writers and Illustrators, Authors Supporting Intellectual Freedom, Texas Sweethearts and Scoundrels (writing group; co-founder).

Writings

Front Page Face-Off (Aladdin "M!X" novel series), Aladdin Mix (New York, NY), 2010.

Jo Whittemore (Photograph by Sonya Sones. Reproduced by permission.)

Odd Girl In (Aladdin "M!X" novel series), Aladdin Mix (New York, NY), 2011.
D Is for Drama (Aladdin "M!X" novel series), Aladdin Mix (New York, NY), 2012.

Work include in anthology *Dear Teen Me,* Zest Books, 2012.

"SILVERSKIN LEGACY" NOVEL SERIES

Escape from Arylon, Llewellyn Publications (Woodbury, MN), 2006.
Curse of Arastold, Llewellyn Publications (Woodbury, MN), 2006.
Onaj's Horn, Llewellyn Publications (Woodbury, MN), 2007.

Sidelights

Jo Whittemore is a Texas-based writer who began her career writing fantasy fiction. Her "Silverskin Legacy" novels—which include *Escape from Arylon, Curse of Arastold,* and *Onaj's Horn*—follow Megan and Ainsley as a strange neighbor sends both teens into a strange and magical world called Arylon, where mages rule, curses are all-powerful, and dragons and unicorns wander. Growing up as a Korean American, Whittemore has become keenly aware of the way perceived differences can shape a teen's experiences. In addition to her fantasy fiction, she encourages teens to embrace their uniqueness in several stories for Aladdin's "M!X" preteen novel series, among them *Front Page Face-Off, Odd Girl In,* and *D Is for Drama*, the last in which a twelve year old watches her dream of directing a simple one-act play morph into an overblown Broadway-esque musical when she allows several classmates to help her.

In *Front Page Face-Off* Delilah James has big plans: to move from reporting for her middle-school newspaper to a coveted position as a Junior Global Journalist. Stiff competition comes from fellow student Ava, who happens to be smart, French, and dating the newspaper's editor. Romance and a misguided effort to report on matters beyond her understanding also challenge the twelve-year-old reporter in a novel that a *Publishers Weekly* contributor praised for its "quick-witted banter" and a plot that ranges in focus from "breaking gender stereotypes" to humorous preteen missteps.

Another twelve year old stars in *Odd Girl In,* but for Alexis Evins the goal is to make news, not report on it. Teaming up with her twin brothers, Alexis' pranks are usually harmless, but every once in a while she crosses the line, and now their professor father hopes to end the nonsense by enrolling both twins in an after-school life-skills program. Threatened with private school if she does not pass, Alexis is resolved to do well, but team-building with her middle-school nemesis and an uber-annoying classmate named Chloe may be more than she can bear. "There's plenty of humor along the way to redemption" in Whittemore's 'tween novel, noted *School Library Journal* critic Brenda Kahn, and even minor "characters have surprising depth." A *Kirkus Reviews* writer dubbed *Odd Girl In* "fun and perky," noting that the author "handles not only the comedy but deftly portrays Alex[is]'s and her brother's advancement into a more mature state of mind."

On her home page, Whittemore offers advice for newbie writers. "Before you even think about submitting your manuscript, . . . you need to understand how the publishing industry works and what they are looking for," she explained. "Publishers aren't in the business to make your dreams come true. They are in it to make money (though they'd also like to make your dreams come true in the process)." Writers should follow the markets, and also have a clearly defined audience. "A particular genre might be more popular than another," she added, "but if you hate aliens, don't try to write about them just because it's what's selling. It can be difficult enough to pull together a story on a topic you love, but pulling together a story about something you have no interest in?

"Write about what you enjoy (unless it's mitochondria)."

Biographical and Critical Sources

PERIODICALS

Kirkus Reviews, February 15, 2011, review of *Odd Girl In.*

Publishers Weekly, March 1, 2010, review of *Front Page Face-Off,* p. 50.
School Library Journal, March, 2011, Brenda Kahn, review of *Odd Girl In,* p. 175.
Voice of Youth Advocates, December, 2007, Amy Luedtke, review of *Onaj's Horn,* p. 456.

ONLINE

Cynsations Web log, http://cynthialeitichsmith.blogspot.com/ (April 5, 2006), Cynthia Leitich Smith, interview with Whittemore.
I Am Korean American Web site, http://iamkoreanamerican.com/ (February 4, 2011), "Jo Whittemore."
Jo Whittemore Home Page, http://www.jowhittemore.com (May 1, 2012).
Jo Whittemore Web log, http://jo-no-anne.livejournal.com (May 1, 2012).

* * *

WILLIAMSON, Pete

Personal

Born in Derby, England.

Addresses

Home—South London, England. *E-mail*—info@petewilliamson.co.uk.

Career

Illustrator, animator, and writer. Loose Moose Productions, London, England, head of design, 1996-2009, and head of art; formerly worked as a psychiatric nurse.

Member

Association of Authors.

Awards, Honors

(With Marcus Sedgwick) Blue Peter Most Fun Story with Pictures Prize, 2011, for *Lunatics and Luck.*

Writings

(Coauthor and director, with Emma Burch) *Being Bradfrod Dillman* (animated short film), Loose Moose Productions, 2011.

Author of short fiction.

ILLUSTRATOR

Dominik Diamond's Guide to Video Games and How to Survive Them, HarperCollins Children's Books (London, England), 1994.
Guy Bass, *Stitch Head,* Stripes (London, England), 2011.
Guy Bass, *Stitch Head: The Pirate's Eye,* Stripes (London, England) 2012.

ILLUSTRATOR; "RAVEN MYSTERIES" CHAPTER-BOOK SERIES BY MARCUS SEDGWICK

Flood and Fang, Orion Children's (London, England), 2009.
Ghosts and Gadgets, Orion Children's (London, England), 2009.
Lunatics and Luck, Orion Children's (London, England), 2010.
Vampires and Volts, Orion Children's (London, England), 2010.

ILLUSTRATOR; "DINKIN DINGS" CHAPTER-BOOK SERIES BY GUY BASS

Dinkin Dings and the Frightening Things, Stripes (London, England), 2009, Grosset & Dunlap (New York, NY), 2011.
Dinkin Dings and the Curse of Clawfingers, Stripes (London, England), 2009.
Dinkin Dings and the Revenge of the Fish-Men, Stripes (London, England), 2009.
Dinkin Dings and the Double from Dimension 9, Stripes (London, England), 2010, Grosset & Dunlap (New York, NY), 2011.

Biographical and Critical Sources

PERIODICALS

Kirkus Reviews, February 15, 2011, review of *Dinkin Dings and the Frightening Things.*
School Librarian, summer, 2010, D. Telford, review of *Lunatics and Luck,* p. 101; summer, 2011, Kathryn Tyson, review of *Vampires and Volts,* p. 105.
School Library Journal, April, 2011, Elizabeth Swistock, review of *Dinkin Dings and the Frightening Things,* p. 139.

ONLINE

Pete Williamson Home Page, http://www.petewilliamson.co.uk (May 1, 2012).
Loose Moose Productions Web site, http://www.loosemoose.net/ (May 1, 2012), "Pete Williamson."*

* * *

WOOD, Frances M.

Personal

Born in WA; married. *Education:* Attended Brown University; Stanford University, B.A.; University of California, Berkeley, M.L.S. *Hobbies and other interests:* Hiking, music, pets (currently a rescue parrot), sewing.

Frances M. Woods (Photography by Brian J. Morton. Reproduced by permission.)

Addresses

Agent—Jennifer Weltz, Jean V. Naggar Agency, 216 E. 75th St., New York, NY 10021. *E-mail*—fmw@francesmwood.com.

Career

Writer. Former reference librarian at public and university libraries.

Awards, Honors

Best Children's Book selection, Bank Street College of Education, 1998, for *Becoming Rosemary;* North Carolina Artist grant, 1999-2000; One Hundred Titles for Reading and Sharing selection, New York Public Library, and Best Books selection, Center for Children's Books, both 2002, and Best Books for the Teen Age selection, New York Public Library, and Friends of Children and Literature Award, Los Angeles Public Library, both 2004, all for *Daughter of Madrugada:* Notable Social Studies Trade Book for Young People selection, National Council of Social Studies, Best Children's Book selection, Bank Street College of Education, and Amelia Bloomer Project nominee, American Library Association, all 2011, and Lamplighter Award nomination, 2012, all for *When Molly Was a Harvery Girl.*

Writings

Becoming Rosemary, Delacorte (New York, NY), 1997.

Daughter of Madrugada, Delacorte Press (New York, NY), 2002.

When Molly Was a Harvey Girl, Kane Miller (Tulsa, OK), 2010.

Author's work has been translated into Danish and Turkish.

Adaptations

Becoming Rosemary was adapted for audiobook by Recorded Books, 1998.

Sidelights

Frances M. Wood was born in the Pacific Northwest, grew up in California, and now lives in North Carolina, the state that inspired her first novel, *Becoming Rosemary.* Wood continues to share her fascination for history in the other novels she writes for young readers, among them *Daughter of Madrugada* and *When Molly Was a Harvey Girl.*

Becoming Rosemary is set in a small North Carolina farming village and takes place during the late eighteenth century. The eponymous twelve-year-old heroine must reconcile her family's magical gifts of healing and telepathy with her community's perception of what is "normal." *Booklist* contributor Hazel Rochman maintained that "readers will be caught by the witch-hunting history and by the universal outsider story" in Wood's fiction debut, and a *Publishers Weekly* commentator described *Becoming Rosemary* as "a hymn to the pains and joys of special gifts." A *Kirkus Reviews* critic similarly lauded Wood's tale as "nearly flawless" and "an auspicious debut."

Wood turns her focus west to California in *Daughter of Madrugada,* which is set in 1848 as gold-rush fever hits the region. Thirteen-year-old narrator Cesa de Haro is a lucky girl: in addition to being the only daughter, she has been raised among her extended family on the de Haro's 150,000-acre Mexican land-grant estate. Called El Rancho de la Valle de la Madrugada, the ranch employs a staff of *vaqueros* to tend the cattle and a staff of Native-American servants to keep the family living in comfort. As news comes that gold can be found by those who are willing to look for it, many of the ranch employees abandon the family in search of a better life. When California is ceded to the United States following their victory in the Mexican-American War, Cesa realizes that her family's traditional way of life is over.

"Vividly realized scenes, rich in the details of daily life, convey a . . . perspective not often found in American children's literature," noted a *Kirkus Reviews* writer in a review of *Daughter of Madrugada.* Writing in *Booklist,* Hazel Rochman noted Wood's focus on the prejudices held by differing groups—the Mexican elite, the Native Americans, the homesteaders from the East—and her overriding theme "about what it means to be American." In addition to praising *Daughter of Madrugada* as a sensitive coming-of-age story, Carol A. Edwards noted in *School Library Journal* that Wood's novel treats readers to "a vivid work of historical fiction" that reflects "a genuine love of the land and the time."

Wood was inspired by her great-grandmother's experiences traveling westward during the 1880s in writing *When Molly Was a Harvey Girl.* The year is 1886 when their father dies and sisters Molly and Colleen Gerry are forced to survive on their own. The sisters have heard of the Harvey Eating House restaurants, a chain started by Fred Harvey to serve the customers of the new Santa Fe Railroad. Because trains did not then have dining cars, passengers took their meals at stops along the way, and Harvey's restaurants guaranteed good food and a comfortable dining experience. Although Harvey waitresses must be at least eighteen, thirteen-year-old Molly fibs about her age and both sisters are hired by a restaurant in New Mexico, living with other waitresses in a dormitory. "A vivid portrayal" of a young woman surviving trying times in a "wild west" where outlaws still roamed free, *When Molly Was a Harvey Girl* benefits from "entertaining characters and a fast-paced plot [that] will keep readers engaged," according to a *Kirkus Reviews* writer. In *Booklist,* Melissa Moore also praised Wood's historical novel, noting that "the values of education, courage, and simplicity all come together in this delightful tale."

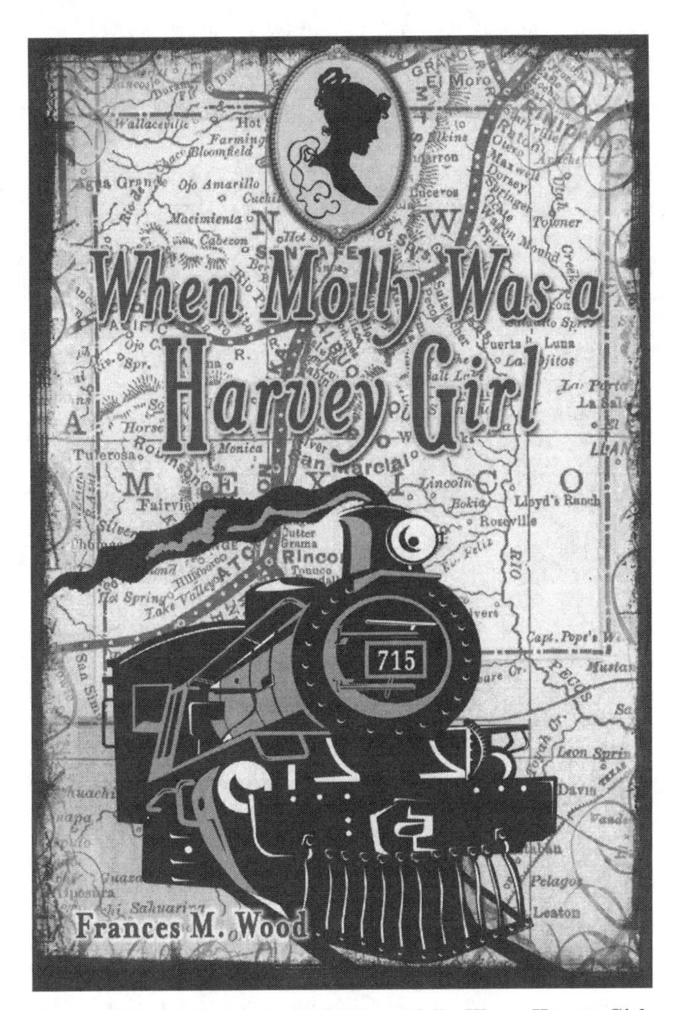

Cover of Woods' historical novel* When Molly Was a Harvey Girl, *which is based on a family story. (Copyright © 2010 by Frances M. Wood. Reproduced by permission of Kane Miller, a division of EDC Publishing.)

Biographical and Critical Sources

PERIODICALS

Booklist, January 1, 1997, Hazel Rochman, review of *Becoming Rosemary,* p. 846; May 15, 2002, Hazel Rochman, review of *Daughter of Madrugada,* p. 1606; September 15, 2010, Melissa Moore, review of *When Molly Was a Harvey Girl,* p. 65.

Bulletin of the Center for Children's Books, May, 1997, review of *Becoming Rosemary,* p. 338.

Kirkus Reviews, November 1, 1996, review of *Becoming Rosemary,* p. 1610; May 15, 2002, review of *Daughter of Madrugada,* p. 744; July 15, 2010, review of *When Molly Was a Harvey Girl.*

Publishers Weekly, December 9, 1996, review of *Becoming Rosemary,* p. 69.

School Library Journal, February, 1997, review of *Becoming Rosemary,* p. 106; May, 2002, Carol A. Edwards, review of *Daughter of Madrugada,* p. 163.

Voice of Youth Advocates, April, 1997, review of *Becoming Rosemary,* p. 34.

ONLINE

Frances M. Wood Home Page, http://francesmwood.com (May 1, 2012).

North Carolina Arts Council Web site, http://www.ncarts.org/ (May 1, 2012), "Frances M. Wood."

Writers and Illustrators of North Carolina Web site, http://www.wincbooks.com/ (May 1, 2012), "Frances M. Wood."

* * *

WUMMER, Amy 1955-

Personal

Born 1955; married; husband's name Mark; children: three.

Addresses

Home—Reading, PA. *Agent*—Deborah Wolfe, Ltd.; info@illustrationOnLine.com.

Career

Illustrator of books for children, beginning mid-1990s.

Illustrator

Patti Farmer, *Bartholomew's Dream,* Barron's (Hauppauge, NY), 1994.

Catherine McMarrow, *The Jellybean Principle,* Random House (New York, NY), 1994.

Jennifer Dussling, *Bug Off!,* Grosset & Dunlap (New York, NY), 1997.

Sid Fleischman, *McBroom Tells the Truth,* Price Stern Sloan (New York, NY), 1998.

Sid Fleischman, *McBroom's Ghost,* Price Stern Sloan (New York, NY), 1998.

Sid Fleischman, *McBroom Tells a Lie,* Price Stern Sloan (New York, NY), 1999.

Sid Fleischman, *McBroom the Rainmaker,* Price Stern Sloan (New York, NY), 1999.

Louis Sachar, *Marvin Redpost: A Flying Birthday Cake,* Random House (New York, NY), 1999.

Louis Sachar, *Marvin Redpost: Class President,* Random House (New York, NY), 1999.

Susan Hood, *Look! I Can Read!,* Grosset & Dunlap (New York, NY), 2000.

Louis Sachar, *A Magic Crystal?,* Random House (New York, NY), 2000.

Louis Sachar, *Marvin Redpost: Super Fast, out of Control!,* Random House (New York, NY), 2000.

Rita Book, *My Soccer Mom from Mars,* Grosset & Dunlap (New York, NY), 2001.

Marcia Thornton Jones and Debbie Dadey, *Ghost Dog,* Volo (New York, NY), 2001.

Marcia Thornton Jones and Debbie Dadey, *Playground Bully,* Volo (New York, NY), 2001.

Marcia Thornton Jones and Debbie Dadey, *Puppy Trouble,* Volo (New York, NY), 2001.

Marcia Thornton Jones and Debbie Dadey, *Snow Day,* Volo (New York, NY), 2001.

Marcia Thornton Jones and Debbie Dadley, *Top Dog,* Volo (New York, NY), 2001.

Johnny Ray Moore, *The Story of Martin Luther King, Jr.,* Candy Cane Press (Nashville, TN), 2001.

Barbara J. Neasi, *Listen to Me,* Children's Press (New York, NY), 2001.

Marcia Thornton Jones and Debbie Dadey, *Tattle Tales,* Volo (New York, NY), 2002.

Johnny Ray Moore, *Meet Martin Luther King, Jr.,* Ideals Children's Books (Nashville, TN), 2002.

Jennie Bishop, *Jesus Must Be Really Special,* Standard (Cincinnati, OH), 2002.

Susan Hood, *Look, I Can Tie My Shoes!,* Grosset & Dunlap (New York, NY), 2002.

Marcia Thornton Jones and Debbie Dadey, *Blue-Ribbon Blues,* Volo (New York, NY), 2002.

Marcia Thornton Jones and Debbie Dadey, *Buried Treasure,* Volo (New York, NY), 2002.

Marcia Thornton Jones and Debbie Dadey, *Puppies on Parade,* Volo (New York, NY), 2002.

Marcia Thornton Jones and Debbie Dadey, *Puppy Love,* Volo (New York, NY), 2002.

Marcia Thornton Jones and Debbie Dadey, *Santa Dog,* Volo (New York, NY), 2002.

Marcia Thornton Jones and Debbie Dadey, *Sticks and Stones and Doggie Bones,* Volo (New York, NY), 2002.

Michelle Knudsen, *The Case of Vampire Vivian,* Kane Press (New York, NY), 2003.

Karen Ann Moore, *Dear God, Let's Talk about You,* Standard (Cincinnati, OH), 2003.

Karen Ann Moore, *Hi God, Let's Talk about My Life,* Standard (Cincinnati, OH), 2003.

Jennifer Dussling, *Whatcha Got?,* Kane Press (New York, NY), 2004.

Pansie Hart Flood, *It's Test Day, Tiger Turcotte,* Carolrhoda Books (Minneapolis, MN), 2004.

Pamela Kennedy, *Five-Minute Devotions for Children: Celebrating God's World as a Family,* Ideals Childrens Books (Nashville, TN), 2004.

Pamela Kennedy, *More Five-Minute Devotions for Children: Celebrating God's World as a Family,* Ideals Childrens Books (Nashville, TN), 2004.

Lynn Plourde, *Mother, May I?,* Dutton Children's Books (New York, NY), 2004.

Sarah Willson, *Hocus Focus,* Kane Press (New York, NY), 2004.

Michelle Medlock Adams, *What Is Easter?,* Candy Cane Press (Nashville, TN), 2005.

Chris Auer, *Molly and the Good Shepherd,* Zonderkidz (Grand Rapids, MI), 2005.

Pansie Hart Flood, *Tiger Turcotte Takes on the Know-It-All,* Carolrhoda (Minneapolis, MN), 2005.

Taylor Jordan, *Movin' on In,* Kane Press (New York, NY), 2005.

Marie Karns, *The Incredible Peepers of Penelope Budd,* Gibbs Smith Publisher (Salt Lake City, UT), 2005.

Lynn Plourde, *Dad, Aren't You Glad?,* Dutton Children's Books (New York, NY), 2005.

Michelle Medlock Adams, *What Is Christmas?,* Candy Cane Press (Nashville, TN), 2006.

Laura Driscoll, *Sally's Big Save,* Kane Press (New York, NY), 2006.

Jamie Gilson, *Gotcha!,* Clarion Books (New York, NY), 2006.

Pamela Kennedy, *Granny's Cozy Quilt of Memories: Remembering Grandmother's Love through Her Lasting Gift,* GPKids (Nashville, TN), 2006.

Pamela Kennedy, *A Sister for Matthew: A Story about Adoption,* GPKids (Nashville, TN), 2006.

Jill Roman Lord, *If Jesus Lived inside My Heart,* Candy Cane Press (Nashville, TN), 2006.

Nan Walker, *Stressbusters,* Kane Press (New York, NY), 2006.

Michelle Medlock Adams, *What Is Halloween?,* Candy Cane Press (Nashville, TN), 2007.

Jennie Bishop, *Jesus Must Be Really Special,* Standard (Cincinnati, OH), 2007.

Laura Driscoll, *Real Heroes Don't Wear Capes,* Kane Press (New York, NY), 2007.

Denise Eliana Gruska, *The Only Boy in Ballet Class,* Gibbs Smith (Layton, UT), 2007.

Pamela Kennedy and Douglas Kennedy, *My Book of Five-Minute Devotions: Celebrating God's World,* Ideals Children's Books (Nashville, TN), 2007.

Eleanor May, *Ty's Triple Trouble,* Kane Press (New York, NY), 2007.

Margaret Sutherland, *Valentines Are for Saying I Love You,* Grosset & Dunlap (New York, NY), 2007.

Jamie Gilson, *Chess! I Love It, I Love It, I Love It!,* Clarion Books (New York, NY), 2008.

Pamela Kennedy, *Two Homes for Tyler: A Story about Understanding Divorce,* GPKids (Nashville, TN), 2008.

Suzy Kline, *Horrible Harry and the Dead Letters,* Viking Childrens Books (New York, NY), 2008.

Eleanor May, *Keesha's Bright Idea,* Kane Press (New York, NY), 2008.

Nan Walker, *The Bay School Blogger,* Kane Press (New York, NY), 2008.

Toni Buzzeo, *Adventure Annie Goes to Work,* Dial Books for Young Readers (New York, NY), 2009.

Suzy Kline, *Horrible Harry on the Ropes,* Viking Children's Books (New York, NY), 2009.

Lewis B. Montgomery (pen name of Myra Rockcliff), *The Case of the Amazing Zelda,* Kane Press (New York, NY), 2009.

Lewis B. Montgomery, *The Case of the Haunted Haunted House,* Kane Press (New York, NY), 2009.

Lewis B. Montgomery, *The Case of the Poisoned Pig,* Kane Press (New York, NY), 2009.

Lewis B. Montgomery, *The Case of the Stinky Socks,* Kane Press (New York, NY), 2009.

Natasha Wing, *The Night before New Year's,* Grosset & Dunlap (New York, NY), 2009.

Natasha Wing, *The Night before St. Patrick's Day,* Grosset & Dunlap (New York, NY), 2009.

Michelle Medlock Adams, *What Is Thanksgiving?,* Candy Cane Press (Nashville, TN), 2009.

Toni Buzzeo, *Adventure Annie Goes to Kindergarten,* Dial Books for Young Readers (New York, NY), 2010.

Suzy Kline, *Horrible Harry Goes Cuckoo,* Viking (New York, NY), 2010.

Mark Elkin, *Samuel's Baby,* Tricycle Press (Berkeley, CA), 2010.

Lewis B. Montgomery, *The Case of the July 4th Jinx,* Kane Press (New York, NY), 2010.

Natasha Wing, *The Night before Mother's Day,* Grosset & Dunlap (New York, NY), 2010.

Suzy Kline, *Horrible Harry and the June Box,* Viking (New York, NY), 2011.

Suzy Kline, *Horrible Harry and the Secret Treasure,* Viking (New York, NY), 2011.

Lewis B. Montgomery, *The Case of the Missing Moose,* Kane Press (New York, NY), 2011.

Lewis B. Montgomery, *The Case of the Purple Pool,* Kane Press (New York, NY), 2011.

Natasha Wing, *The Night before Preschool,* Grosset & Dunlap (New York, NY), 2011.

Pamela Kennedy and Anne Kennedy Brady, *Five-minute Bible Devotions for Children: Stories from the Old Testament,* Ideals Children's Books (Nashville, TN), 2012.

Suzy Kline, *Horrible Harry and the Scarlet Scissors,* Viking (New York, NY), 2012.

Lewis B. Montgomery, *The Case of the Diamonds in the Desk,* Kane Press (New York, NY), 2012.

Natasha Wing, *The Night before Father's Day,* Grosset & Dunlap (New York, NY), 2012.

Sidelights

A prolific artist, Amy Wummer has contributed her amusing cartoon images to picture books, chapter books, and easy readers since the mid-1990s. Often working on several books at the same time, Wummer creates illustrations that have been paired with texts by writers ranging from Sid Fleishman and Louis Sachar to Eleanor May and Suzy Kline, the last for whom she has brought to life the amusing "Horrible Harry" easy-reader series.

Commenting on Wummer's work for *It's Test Day, Tiger Turcotte,* a chapter book by Pansie Hart Flood, Sharon R. Pearce wrote in *School Library Journal* that the artist's pencil illustrations capture the characters' emotions." In her artwork for Jamie Gilson's *Gotcha!,* Wummer "spices up" the text by contributing "humorous line drawings, engaging readers in the zany story," according to Debbie Whitbeck, also in *School Library Journal.*

A story about a boy named Tucker whose love of dance allows him to brave socially trying circumstances, Denise Gruska's *The Only Boy in Ballet Class* features "sprightly" pen-and-ink and water-color illustrations "that capture Tucker's fancy footwork and the characters' varied expressions," according to *School Library Journal* critic Linda Ludke. The "cheerful cartoons" Wummer creates for Marie Karns' *The Incredible Peepers of Penelope Budd* "capture the child's free spirit . . . [and] the beauty in everyday objects," Suzanne Myers Harold concluded in another *School Library Journal* review, while in *Booklist* Ilene Cooper wrote that the book's "delightful watercolor-and-ink" cartoon renderings leap off the page "and match . . . the gusto of the text." *Samuel's Baby,* a picture book by Mark Elkin that focuses on a boy's anticipation of a new sibling, benefits from illustrations that "charmingly portray the innocence and enthusiasm of [Elkin's] . . . multicultural cast," the artist employing equal parts "sweetness and humor," according to a *Kirkus Reviews* writer.

***Amy Wummer's illustrations are a feature of Louis Sachar's popular "Marvin Redpost" chapter books, which include* Marvin Redpost: Super Fast, Out of Control.** (Illustration copyright © 2000 by Amy Wummer. Used by permission of Random House Children's Books, a division of Random House, Inc.)

Many of Wummer's illustration projects involve work on ongoing series. In addition to Kline's "Horrible Harry" books, she has also worked on Sachar's "Marvin Redpost" stories and Natasha Wing's "The Night before" picture books, the last which include *The Night before New Year's, The Night before Preschool,* and *The Night before Father's Day.* Another series, Toni Buzzeo's "Adventure Annie" tales, focuses on a spunky kindergartner whose preschool adventures include accompanying her mother to work. "Wummer gives the curly-mopped tyke all the visual verse she deserves," asserted a *Kirkus Reviews* writer in reviewing *Adventure Annie Goes to Kindergarten,* and *Booklist* critic Hazel Rochman concluded of *Adventure Annie Goes to Work* that the artist's "colorful, child-friendly pencil-and-watercolor pictures . . . are filled with movement and zip."

Biographical and Critical Sources

PERIODICALS

Booklist, December 1, 2000, Ilene Cooper, review of *Look! I Can Read!,* p. 725; March 15, 2004, Carolyn Phelan, review of *Hocus Focus,* p. 1312; March 1, 2008, Carolyn Phelan, review of *Chess! I Love It I Love It I Love It!,* p. 70; February 1, 2009, Hazel Rochman, review of *Adventure Annie Goes to Work,* p. 45; May 1, 2009, Ilene Cooper, review of *The Case of the Stinky Socks,* p. 42; May 1, 2010, Carolyn Phelan, review of *Adventure Annie Goes to Kindergarten,* p. 94; May 1, 2011, Linda Sawyer, review of *The Case of the Missing Moose,* p. 45.

Kirkus Reviews, January 1, 2004, review of *Mother May I?,* p. 40; February 15, 2008, review of *Chess!;* January 15, 2009, review of *Adventure Annie Goes to Work;* June 1, 2010, review of *Adventure Annie Goes to Kindergarten;* June 15, 2010, review of *Samuel's Baby.*

Wummer's artwork is a feature of Toni Buzzeo's* Adventure Annie Goes to Kindergarten, *one of several books featuring a fun-loving youngster. (Illustration copyright © 2010 by Amy Wummer. Used by permission of Dial Books for Young Readers, a division of Penguin Group (USA), Inc.)

***Wummer teams up with author Margaret Sutherland to create the warmhearted picture-book* Valentines Are for Saying I Love You.** (Illustration copyright © 2007 by Amy Wummer. All rights reserved. Used by permission of Philomel Books, a division of Penguin Group (USA), Inc.)

Publishers Weekly, September 3, 2007, review of *The Only Boy in Ballet Class,* p. 58; June 14, 2010, review of *Samuel's Baby,* p. 50.

School Library Journal, February, 2003, Nancy Gifford, review of *Look! I Can Tie My Shoes!,* p. 113; March, 2004, Rosalyn Pierini, review of *Mother May I?,* p. 180; July, 2004, Sharon R. Pearce, review of *It's Test Day, Tiger Turcotte,* p. 75; March, 2005, Wendy Woodfill, review of *Dad, Aren't You Glad?,* p. 186; January, 2006, Suzanne Myers Harold, review of *The Incredible Peepers of Penelope Budd,* p. 104; April, 2006, Debbie Whitbeck, review of *Gotcha!,* p. 106; June, 2007, Gina Powell, review of *Ty's Triple Trouble,* p. 94; September, 2007, Linda L. Walkins, review of *Real Heroes Don't Wear Capes,* p. 164; November, 2007, Linda Ludke, review of *The Only Boy in Ballet Class,* p. 92; May, 2008, Sarah O'Holla, review of *Chess!,* p. 98; July, 2008, Laura Scott, review of *The Bay School Blogger,* p. 76; January, 2009, Marge Loch-Wouters, review of *Adventure Annie Goes to Work,* p. 73; July, 2009, Bethany A. Lafferty, review of *The Case of the Poisoned Pig,* p. 66; May, 2010, Kim T. Ha, review of *Adventure Annie Goes to Kindergarten,* p. 80; July, 2010, Richelle Roth, review of *Samuel's Baby,* p. 58; September, 2010, Lora Van Marel, review of *The Case of the July 4th Jinx,* p. 132.

ONLINE

Directory of Illustration Web site, http://www.directoryofillustration.com/ (May 1, 2012), "Amy Wummer."*

Illustrations Index

(In the following index, the number of the *volume* in which an illustrator's work appears is given *before* the colon, and the *page number* on which it appears is given *after* the colon. For example, a drawing by Adams, Adrienne appears in Volume 2 on page 6, another drawing by her appears in Volume 3 on page 80, another drawing in Volume 8 on page 1, and so on and so on. . . .)

YABC

Index references to *YABC* refer to listings appearing in the two-volume *Yesterday's Authors of Books for Children,* also published by Gale, Cengage Learning. *YABC* covers prominent authors and illustrators who died prior to 1960.

A

Aas, Ulf *5:* 174
Abbe, S. van
See van Abbe, S.
Abel, Raymond *6:* 122; *7:* 195; *12:* 3; *21:* 86; *25:* 119
Abelliera, Aldo *71:* 120
Abolafia, Yossi *60:* 2; *93:* 163; *152:* 202
Abrahams, Hilary *26:* 205; *29:* 24, 25; *53:* 61
Abram, Amanda *240:* 12
Abrams, Kathie *36:* 170
Abrams, Lester *49:* 26
Abulafia, Yossi *154:* 67; *177:* 3
Accardo, Anthony *191:* 3, 8
Accornero, Franco *184:* 8
Accorsi, William *11:* 198
Acedera, Kei *235:* 110
Acs, Laszlo *14:* 156; *42:* 22
Acuna, Ed *198:* 79
Adams, Adrienne *2:* 6; *3:* 80; *8:* 1; *15:* 107; *16:* 180; *20:* 65; *22:* 134, 135; *33:* 75; *36:* 103, 112; *39:* 74; *86:* 54; *90:* 2, 3
Adams, Connie J. *129:* 68
Adams, John Wolcott *17:* 162
Adams, Kathryn *224:* 1
Adams, Lynn *96:* 44
Adams, Norman *55:* 82
Adams, Pam *112:* 1, 2
Adams, Sarah *98:* 126; *164:* 180
Adams, Steve *209:* 64
Adamson, George *30:* 23, 24; *69:* 64
Addams, Charles *55:* 5
Addison, Kenneth *192:* 173; *231:* 166
Addy, Sean *180:* 8; *222:* 31
Ade, Rene *76:* 198; *195:* 162
Adinolfi, JoAnn *115:* 42; *176:* 2; *217:* 79
Adkins, Alta *22:* 250
Adkins, Jan *8:* 3; *69:* 4; *144:* 2, 3, 4; *210:* 11, 17, 18, 19
Adl, Shirin *225:* 2
Adler, Kelynn *195:* 47
Adler, Peggy *22:* 6; *29:* 31
Adler, Ruth *29:* 29
Adlerman, Daniel *163:* 2
Adragna, Robert *47:* 145
Adria, Miranda *240:* 11
Agard, Nadema *18:* 1
Agee, Jon *116:* 8, 9, 10; *157:* 4; *196:* 3, 4, 5, 6, 7, 8
Agre, Patricia *47:* 195
Aguirre, Alfredo *152:* 218
Ahl, Anna Maria *32:* 24
Ahlberg, Allan *68:* 6, 7, 9; *165:* 5; *214:* 9
Ahlberg, Janet *68:* 6, 7, 9; *214:* 9
Ahlberg, Jessica *229:* 2, 191
Aicher-Scholl, Inge *63:* 127
Aichinger, Helga *4:* 5, 45
Aitken, Amy *31:* 34
Ajhar, Brian *207:* 126; *220:* 2
Akaba, Suekichi *46:* 23; *53:* 127
Akasaka, Miyoshi *YABC 2:* 261
Akib, Jamel *181:* 13; *182:* 99; *220:* 74
Akino, Fuku *6:* 144
Alain *40:* 41
Alajalov *2:* 226
Albert, Chris *200:* 64
Alborough, Jez *86:* 1, 2, 3; *149:* 3
Albrecht, Jan *37:* 176
Albright, Donn *1:* 91
Alcala, Alfredo *91:* 128
Alcantará, Felipe Ugalde *171:* 186
Alcorn, John *3:* 159; *7:* 165; *31:* 22; *44:* 127; *46:* 23, 170
Alcorn, Stephen *110:* 4; *125:* 106; *128:* 172; *150:* 97; *160:* 188; *165:* 48; *201:* 113; *203:* 39; *207:* 3; *226:* 25
Alcott, May *100:* 3
Alda, Arlene *44:* 24; *158:* 2
Alden, Albert *11:* 103
Aldridge, Andy *27:* 131
Aldridge, George *105:* 125
Aldridge, Sheila *192:* 4
Alejandro, Cliff *176:* 75
Alex, Ben *45:* 25, 26
Alexander, Claire *228:* 2
Alexander, Ellen *91:* 3
Alexander, Lloyd *49:* 34
Alexander, Martha *3:* 206; *11:* 103; *13:* 109; *25:* 100; *36:* 131; *70:* 6, 7; *136:* 3, 4, 5; *169:* 120; *230:* 78
Alexander, Paul *85:* 57; *90:* 9
Alexeieff, Alexander *14:* 6; *26:* 199
Alfano, Wayne *80:* 69
Aliki
See Brandenberg, Aliki
Alko, Selina *218:* 2; *235:* 187
Allamand, Pascale *12:* 9
Allan, Judith *38:* 166
Alland, Alexandra *16:* 255
Allen, Gertrude *9:* 6
Allen, Graham *31:* 145
Allen, Jonathan *131:* 3, 4; *177:* 8, 9, 10
Allen, Joy *168:* 185; *217:* 6, 7
Allen, Pamela *50:* 25, 26, 27, 28; *81:* 9, 10; *123:* 4, 5
Allen, Raul *207:* 94
Allen, Rick *236:* 174
Allen, Rowena *47:* 75
Allen, Thomas B. *81:* 101; *82:* 248; *89:* 37; *104:* 9
Allen, Tom *85:* 176
Allender, David *73:* 223
Alley, R.W. *80:* 183; *95:* 187; *156:* 100, 153; *169:* 4, 5; *179:* 17
Allison, Linda *43:* 27
Allon, Jeffrey *119:* 174
Allport, Mike *71:* 55
Almquist, Don *11:* 8; *12:* 128; *17:* 46; *22:* 110
Aloise, Frank *5:* 38; *10:* 133; *30:* 92
Alsenas, Linas *186:* 2
Alter, Ann *206:* 4, 5
Althea
See Braithwaite, Althea
Altmann, Scott *238:* 78
Altschuler, Franz *11:* 185; *23:* 141; *40:* 48; *45:* 29; *57:* 181
Alvin, John *117:* 5
Ambrus, Victor G. *1:* 6, 7, 194; *3:* 69; *5:* 15; *6:* 44; *7:* 36; *8:* 210; *12:* 227; *14:* 213; *15:* 213; *22:* 209; *24:* 36; *28:* 179; *30:* 178; *32:* 44, 46; *38:* 143; *41:* 25, 26, 27, 28, 29, 30, 31, 32; *42:* 87; *44:* 190; *55:* 172; *62:* 30, 144, 145, 148; *86:* 99, 100, 101; *87:* 66, 137; *89:* 162; *134:* 160
Ames, Lee J. *3:* 12; *9:* 130; *10:* 69; *17:* 214; *22:* 124; *151:* 13; *223:* 69
Amini, Mehrdokht *211:* 119
Amini-Holmes, Liz *239:* 119; *240:* 8
Amon, Aline *9:* 9
Amoss, Berthe *5:* 5
Amstutz, André *152:* 102; *214:* 11, 16; *223:* 99
Amundsen, Dick *7:* 77
Amundsen, Richard E. *5:* 10; *24:* 122
Ancona, George *12:* 11; *55:* 144; *145:* 7; *208:* 13
Anderson, Alasdair *18:* 122
Andersen, Bethanne *116:* 167; *162:* 189; *175:* 17; *191:* 4, 5; *218:* 20
Anderson, Bob *139:* 16
Anderson, Brad *33:* 28

Anderson, Brian *211:* 8
Anderson, C.W. *11:* 10
Anderson, Carl *7:* 4
Anderson, Catherine Corley *72:* 2
Anderson, Cecil *127:* 152
Anderson, David Lee *118:* 176
Anderson, Derek *169:* 9; *174:* 180; *241:* 2, 3
Anderson, Doug *40:* 111
Anderson, Erica *23:* 65
Anderson, G.E. *223:* 181
Anderson, Laurie *12:* 153, 155
Anderson, Lena *99:* 26
Anderson, Peggy Perry *179:* 2
Anderson, Sara *173:* 3
Anderson, Scoular *138:* 13; *201:* 6
Anderson, Stephanie *225:* 3
Anderson, Susan *90:* 12
Anderson, Tara *188:* 132; *211:* 115
Anderson, Wayne *23:* 119; *41:* 239; *56:* 7; *62:* 26; *147:* 6; *202:* 4, 5
Andreasen, Daniel *86:* 157; *87:* 104; *103:* 201, 202; *159:* 75; *167:* 106, 107; *168:* 184; *180:* 247; *186:* 9; *212:* 101; *220:* 110, 111; *221:* 56; *227:* 3, 4, 5, 6; *234:* 214
Andrew, Ian *111:* 37; *116:* 12; *166:* 2
Andrew, John *22:* 4
Andrews, Benny *14:* 251; *31:* 24; *57:* 6, 7; *183:* 8
Andrews, Vaughn *166:* 28
Anelay, Henry *57:* 173
Angaramo, Robert *241:* 61
Angel, Marie *47:* 22
Angelo, Valenti *14:* 8; *18:* 100; *20:* 232; *32:* 70
Anglund, Joan Walsh *2:* 7, 250, 251; *37:* 198, 199, 200
Anholt, Catherine *74:* 8; *131:* 7; *141:* 5
Anholt, Laurence *141:* 4
Anno, Mitsumasa *5:* 7; *38:* 25, 26, 27, 28, 29, 30, 31, 32; *77:* 3, 4; *157:* 10, 11
Antal, Andrew *1:* 124; *30:* 145
Antram, David *152:* 133
Apostolou, Christy Hale
See Hale, Christy
Apple, Margot *33:* 25; *35:* 206; *46:* 81; *53:* 8; *61:* 109; *64:* 21, 22, 24, 25, 27; *71:* 176; *77:* 53; *82:* 245; *92:* 39; *94:* 180; *96:* 107; *152:* 4, 5; *162:* 192, 194; *173:* 44; *214:* 21, 22, 23, 24; *238:* 3
Appleyard, Dev *2:* 192
Aragones, Sergio *48:* 23, 24, 25, 26, 27
Araneus *40:* 29
Arbo, Cris *103:* 4; *220:* 4, 5
Archambault, Matt *85:* 173; *138:* 19, 20; *143:* 33; *145:* 144; *179:* 103; *187:* 7; *219:* 2
Archer, Janet *16:* 69; *178:* 156
Ardizzone, Edward *1:* 11, 12; *2:* 105; *3:* 258; *4:* 78; *7:* 79; *10:* 100; *15:* 232; *20:* 69,178; *23:* 223; *24:* 125; *28:* 25, 26, 27, 28, 29, 30, 31,33, 34, 35, 36, 37; *31:* 192, 193; *34:* 215, 217; *60:* 173; *64:* 145; *87:* 176; *YABC 2:* 25
Arena, Jill *176:* 49
Arenella, Roy *14:* 9
Argemi, David *197:* 2
Argent, Kerry *103:* 56; *138:* 17; *158:* 134
Arihara, Shino *201:* 98
Arisman, Marshall *162:* 50
Armer, Austin *13:* 3
Armer, Laura Adams *13:* 3
Armer, Sidney *13:* 3
Armitage, David *47:* 23; *99:* 5; *155:* 4
Armitage, Eileen *4:* 16
Armstrong, George *10:* 6; *21:* 72
Armstrong, Shelagh *102:* 114; *224:* 4
Armstrong-Ellis, Carey *185:* 196
Arno, Enrico *1:* 217; *2:* 22, 210; *4:* 9; *5:* 43; *6:* 52; *29:* 217, 219; *33:* 152; *35:* 99; *43:* 31, 32, 33; *45:* 212, 213, 214; *72:* 72; *74:* 166; *100:* 169
Arnold, Alli *187:* 40, 41
Arnold, Andrew *219:* 155; *221:* 155
Arnold, Caroline *174:* 5
Arnold, Emily *76:* 7, 9, 10
Arnold, Katya *115:* 11; *168:* 2, 3
Arnold, Tedd *116:* 14; *133:* 152; *160:* 5; *208:* 24, 25, 26, 176; *241:* 103
Arnosky, Jim *22:* 20; *70:* 9, 10, 11; *118:* 3, 5; *160:* 8, 10; *189:* 5, 7, 8, 9, 10; *217:* 11, 12, 13, 14
Arnsteen, Katy Keck *105:* 97; *116:* 145
Arsenault, Isabelle *207:* 7; *226:* 109
Arrowood, Clinton *12:* 193; *19:* 11; *65:* 210
Artell, Mike *89:* 8
Arting, Fred J. *41:* 63
Artzybasheff, Boris *13:* 143; *14:* 15; *40:* 152, 155
Aruego, Ariane *6:* 4
Aruego, José *4:* 140; *6:* 4; *7:* 64; *33:* 195; *35:* 208; *68:* 16, 17; *75:* 46; *93:* 91, 92; *94:* 197; *109:* 65, 67; *125:* 2, 3, 4, 5; *127:* 188; *143:* 25; *178:* 17, 19, 74; *188:* 166; *202:* 164; *231:* 176; *239:* 155
Arzoumanian, Alik *177:* 12; *194:* 115
Asare, Meshack *86:* 9; *139:* 19
Ascensios, Natalie *105:* 139
Asch, Frank *5:* 9; *66:* 2, 4, 6, 7, 9, 10; *102:* 18, 19,21; *154:* 12
Ashby, Gail *11:* 135
Ashby, Gil *146:* 4
Ashby, Gwynneth *44:* 26
Ashley, C.W. *19:* 197
Ashmead, Hal *8:* 70
Ashton, Tim *211:* 204
Aska, Warabe *56:* 10
Assel, Steven *44:* 153; *77:* 22, 97
Astrop, John *32:* 56
Atene, Ann *12:* 18
Atherton, Lisa *38:* 198
Atkinson, Allen *60:* 5
Atkinson, J. Priestman *17:* 275
Atkinson, Janet *86:* 147; *103:* 138
Atkinson, Mike *127:* 74
Atkinson, Wayne *40:* 46
Attard, Karl *196:* 22, 23
Attebery, Charles *38:* 170
Atwell, Debby *150:* 6
Atwood, Ann *7:* 9
Aubrey, Meg Kelleher *77:* 159
Auch, Herm *173:* 7, 8
Auch, Mary Jane *173:* 7
Augarde, Steve *25:* 22; *159:* 7; *210:* 43, 44
Austerman, Miriam *23:* 107
Austin, Cary *234:* 171
Austin, Margot *11:* 16
Austin, Dawn *234:* 117
Austin, Robert *3:* 44
Austin, Virginia *81:* 205; *127:* 221; *232:* 190
Auth, Tony *51:* 5; *192:* 18
Avendano, Dolores *158:* 74
Avedon, Richard *57:* 140
Averill, Esther *1:* 17; *28:* 39, 40, 41
Avilés, Martha *218:* 6
Axeman, Lois *2:* 32; *11:* 84; *13:* 165; *22:* 8; *23:* 49; *61:* 116; *101:* 124
Axtel, David *155:* 110
Ayer, Jacqueline *13:* 7
Ayer, Margaret *15:* 12; *50:* 120
Ayers, Alan *91:* 58; *107:* 169
Ayliffe, Alex *95:* 164; *237:* 68
Ayto, Russell *111:* 5; *112:* 54; *206:* 7, 8; *213:* 56
Azarian, Mary *112:* 9, 10; *114:* 129; *117:* 171; *137:* 163; *171:* 4, 5; *181:* 161; *188:* 128; *232:* 174

B

B.T.B.
See Blackwell, Basil T.
Baasansuren, Bolormaa *216:* 40
Babbitt, Bradford *33:* 158
Babbitt, Natalie *6:* 6; *8:* 220; *68:* 20; *70:* 242, 243; *194:* 8, 9
Baca, Maria *104:* 5
Bacchus, Andy *94:* 87
Bacha, Andy *109:* 169
Bachelet, Gilles *196:* 18
Bachem, Paul *48:* 180; *67:* 65; *144:* 206; *234:* 113
Back, Adam *63:* 125
Back, George *31:* 161
Backes, Nick *190:* 72
Backhouse, Colin *78:* 142
Bacon, Bruce *4:* 74
Bacon, Paul *7:* 155; *8:* 121; *31:* 55; *50:* 42; *56:* 175; *62:* 82, 84
Bacon, Peggy *2:* 11, 228; *46:* 44
Baek, Matthew J. *169:* 95; *202:* 8
Baer, Julie *161:* 2
Baeten, Lieve *238:* 5
Baicker-McKee, Carol *177:* 15; *180:* 215
Bailey, Peter *58:* 174; *87:* 221; *194:* 12
Bailey, Sheila *155:* 11
Baker, Alan *22:* 22; *61:* 134; *93:* 11, 12; *146:* 6, 7, 10
Baker, Charlotte *2:* 12
Baker, Garin *89:* 65
Baker, Jeannie *23:* 4; *88:* 18, 19, 20
Baker, Jim *22:* 24
Baker, Joe *82:* 188; *111:* 55; *124:* 70; *197:* 73
Baker, Keith *179:* 6, 7; *222:* 36
Baker, Leslie *112:* 214; *132:* 103, 246; *180:* 74, 246; *234:* 213
Baker-Smith, Grahame *223:* 10; *225:* 132
Baldacci, Rudy *184:* 9
Baldridge, Cyrus LeRoy *19:* 69; *44:* 50
Baldus, Jackie *216:* 81
Baldus, Zachary *152:* 231; *187:* 60
Balet, Jan *11:* 22
Balian, Lorna *9:* 16; *91:* 16
Balit, Christina *102:* 24; *159:* 9; *162:* 118, 119; *212:* 2, 3
Ballantyne, R.M. *24:* 34
Ballis, George *14:* 199
Balouch, Kristen *176:* 11
Baltzer, Hans *40:* 30
Banbery, Fred *58:* 15
Bancroft, Bronwyn *216:* 42
Banfill, A. Scott *98:* 7; *112:* 59
Bang, Molly *24:* 37, 38; *69:* 8, 9, 10; *111:* 7,9, 10, 11; *140:* 11; *158:* 37, 38, 39; *195:* 3; *215:* 11, 12, 13, 14
Banik, Yvette Santiago *21:* 136
Banks, Erin Bennett *211:* 12
Banner, Angela
See Maddison, Angela Mary
Bannerman, Helen *19:* 13, 14
Banning, Greg *202:* 98
Bannon, Laura *6:* 10; *23:* 8
Bantock, Nick *74:* 229; *95:* 6
Banyai, Istvan *185:* 209; *193:* 14, 16; *209:* 155; *223:* 166, 167; *238:* 87
Baptist, Michael *37:* 208
Baracca, Sal *135:* 206
Baranaski, Marcin *182:* 113
Barasch, Lynne *126:* 16; *186:* 15
Barbarin, Lucien C., Jr. *89:* 88
Barbour, Karen *96:* 5; *74:* 209; *170:* 16
Bare, Arnold Edwin *16:* 31
Bare, Colleen Stanley *32:* 33
Barger, Jan *147:* 11
Bargery, Geoffrey *14:* 258
Barkat, Jonathan *149:* 177; *164:* 254; *181:* 106; *184:* 186; *196:* 11; *198:* 148; *239:* 176; *240:* 85; *241:* 128
Barker, Carol *31:* 27
Barker, Cicely Mary *49:* 50, 51
Barkley, James *4:* 13; *6:* 11; *13:* 112
Barks, Carl *37:* 27, 28, 29, 30, 31, 32, 33, 34
Barling, Joy *62:* 148
Barling, Tom *9:* 23

Barlow, Gillian *62:* 20
Barlow, Perry *35:* 28
Barlowe, Dot *30:* 223
Barlowe, Wayne *37:* 72; *84:* 43; *105:* 5
Barnard, Bryn *88:* 53; *13:* 55; *169:* 13; *193:* 194
Barneda, David *206:* 11
Barner, Bob *29:* 37; *128:* 33; *136:* 19, 20; *177:* 27; *238:* 8
Barnes, Hiram P. *20:* 28
Barnes, Tim *137:* 28
Barnes-Murphy, Rowan *88:* 22
Barnett, Charles II *175:* 150
Barnett, Ivan *70:* 14
Barnett, Moneta *16:* 89; *19:* 142; *31:* 102; *33:* 30, 31, 32; *41:* 153; *61:* 94, 97
Barney, Maginel Wright *39:* 32, 33, 34; *YABC 2:* 306
Barnum, Jay Hyde *11:* 224; *20:* 5; *37:* 189, 190
Baron, Alan *80:* 3; *89:* 123
Barr, George *60:* 74; *69:* 64
Barragán, Paula S. *134:* 116; *186:* 158; *216:* 43, 44, 197; *232:* 133
Barrall, Tim *115:* 152
Barraud, Martin *189:* 38
Barrauds *33:* 114
Barrer-Russell, Gertrude *9:* 65; *27:* 31
Barret, Robert *85:* 134
Barrett, Angela *40:* 136, 137; *62:* 74; *75:* 10; *76:* 142; *144:* 137; *145:* 14; *223:* 14
Barrett, Jennifer *58:* 149
Barrett, John E. *43:* 119
Barrett, Moneta *74:* 10
Barrett, Peter *55:* 169; *86:* 111
Barrett, Robert *62:* 145; *77:* 146; *82:* 35
Barrett, Ron *14:* 24; *26:* 35
Barron, John N. *3:* 261; *5:* 101; *14:* 220
Barrow, Ann *136:* 27
Barrows, Walter *14:* 268
Barry, Ethelred B. *37:* 79; *YABC 1:* 229
Barry, James *14:* 25
Barry, Katharina *2:* 159; *4:* 22
Barry, Robert E. *6:* 12
Barry, Scott *32:* 35
Barshaw, Ruth McNally *203:* 9
Bartenbach, Jean *40:* 31
Barth, Ernest Kurt *2:* 172; *3:* 160; *8:* 26; *10:* 31
Bartholomew, Caty *208:* 153
Bartholomew, Marie *200:* 66
Bartlett, Alison *101:* 88; *165:* 93; *209:* 51
Barton, Byron *8:* 207; *9:* 18; *23:* 66; *80:* 181; *90:* 18, 19, 20, 21; *126:* 29, 30
Barton, Harriett *30:* 71
Barton, Jill *129:* 108; *135:* 120; *145:* 185, 189; *184:* 177; *224:* 142, 143
Barton, Patrice *226:* 14
Bartram, Robert *10:* 42
Bartram, Simon *218:* 8
Bartsch, Jochen *8:* 105; *39:* 38
Bascove, Barbara *45:* 73
Base, Graeme *101:* 15, 16, 17, 18; *162:* 8, 10, 12
Baseman, Gary *174:* 12
Bash, Barbara *132:* 9
Basic, Zdenko *235:* 176
Baskin, Leonard *30:* 42, 43, 46, 47; *49:* 125, 126, 128, 129,133; *173:* 120
Bass, Saul *49:* 192
Bassett, Jeni *40:* 99; *64:* 30
Basso, Bill *99:* 139; *189:* 134
Batchelor, Joy *29:* 41, 47, 48
Bate, Norman *5:* 16
Bates, Amy June *188:* 170; *189:* 27, 28; *239:* 8, 9
Bates, Leo *24:* 35
Batet, Carmen *39:* 134
Batherman, Muriel *31:* 79; *45:* 185
Battaglia, Aurelius *50:* 44
Batten, John D. *25:* 161, 162
Batten, Mary *162:* 14, 15
Battles, Asa *32:* 94, 95
Bauer, Carla *193:* 6
Bauer, Jutta *150:* 32
Bauernschmidt, Marjorie *15:* 15
Baum, Allyn *20:* 10
Baum, Willi *4:* 24, 25; *7:* 173
Bauman, Leslie *61:* 121
Baumann, Jill *34:* 170
Baumhauer, Hans *11:* 218; *15:* 163, 165, 167
Baxter, Glen *57:* 100
Baxter, Leon *59:* 102
Baxter, Robert *87:* 129
Bayer, Herbert *181:* 16
Bayley, Dorothy *37:* 195
Bayley, Nicola *40:* 104; *41:* 34, 35; *69:* 15; *129:* 33, 34, 35
Baylin, Mark *158:* 233
Baynes, Pauline *2:* 244; *3:* 149; *13:* 133, 135,137, 141; *19:* 18, 19, 20; *32:* 208, 213, 214; *36:* 105, 108; *59:* 12, 13, 14, 16, 17, 18, 20; *100:* 158, 159, 243; *133:* 3, 4
Beach, Lou *150:* 150; *207:* 117, 118
Beaky, Suzanne *232:* 11
Beame, Rona *12:* 40
Bean, Jonathan *196:* 102
Bear's Heart *73:* 215
Beard, Alex *222:* 40
Beard, Dan *22:* 31, 32
Beard, J.H. *YABC 1:* 158
Bearden, Romare *9:* 7; *22:* 35
Beardshaw, Rosalind *169:* 22; *190:* 22; *224:* 12; *225:* 6, 7, 8; *226:* 71
Beardsley, Aubrey *17:* 14; *23:* 181; *59:* 130, 131
Bearman, Jane *29:* 38
Beaton, Cecil *24:* 208
Beaton, Clare *125:* 28; *208:* 67; *220:* 10, 11, 12
Beauce, J.A. *18:* 103
Beaujard, Sophie *81:* 54
Beavers, Ethen *225:* 9
Beccia, Carlyn *189:* 29
Bechtold, Lisze *208:* 29
Beck, Andrea *226:* 16
Beck, Charles *11:* 169; *51:* 173
Beck, Ian *138:* 27; *182:* 150; *190:* 25; *225:* 130
Beck, Melinda *203:* 112
Beck, Ruth *13:* 11
Becker, Harriet *12:* 211
Beckerman, Jonathan *208:* 194
Beckett, Sheilah *25:* 5; *33:* 37, 38
Beckhoff, Harry *1:* 78; *5:* 163
Beckhorn, Susan Williams *189:* 32
Beckman, Kaj *45:* 38, 39, 40, 41
Beckman, Per *45:* 42, 43
Beddows, Eric *72:* 70
Bedford, F.D. *20:* 118, 122; *33:* 170; *41:* 220, 221,230, 233
Bee, Joyce *19:* 62
Bee, William *188:* 6
Beeby, Betty *25:* 36
Beech, Carol *9:* 149
Beech, Mark *192:* 122
Beek *25:* 51, 55, 59
Beeke, Tiphanie *177:* 127; *204:* 140; *212:* 178; *218:* 102
Beekman, Doug *125:* 146, 148
Beerbohm, Max *24:* 208
Beeson, Bob *108:* 57
Begin, Mary Jane *82:* 13; *206:* 13
Beha, Philippe *172:* 85
Behr, Joyce *15:* 15; *21:* 132; *23:* 161
Behrens, Hans *5:* 97
Beier, Ellen *135:* 170; *139:* 47; *183:* 164; *221:* 177; *222:* 151
Beingessner, Laura *220:* 14
Beinicke, Steve *69:* 18
Beisner, Monika *46:* 128, 131; *112:* 127
Belden, Charles J. *12:* 182
Belina, Renate *39:* 132
Bell, Corydon *3:* 20
Bell, Graham *54:* 48
Bell, Julia *151:* 214
Bell, Julie *159:* 172; *165:* 18
Bell, Thomas P. *76:* 182
Bellamy, Glen *127:* 15
Beltran, Alberto *43:* 37
Bemelmans, Ludwig *15:* 19, 21; *100:* 27
Ben-Ami, Doron *75:* 96; *84:* 107; *108:* 132; *110:* 63; *159:* 157; *197:* 142; *233:* 122
Bendall-Brunello, John *150:* 4; *157:* 163; *185:* 3, 4; *203:* 5; *237:* 101
Benda, Wladyslaw T. *15:* 256; *30:* 76, 77; *44:* 182
Bender, Robert *77:* 162; *79:* 13; *160:* 23
Bendick, Jeanne *2:* 24; *68:* 27, 28
Benioff, Carol *121:* 42; *175:* 23; *232:* 12
Benner, Cheryl *80:* 11
Bennett, Charles H. *64:* 6
Bennett, Erin Susanne *165:* 216
Bennett, F.I. *YABC 1:* 134
Bennett, James *146:* 240
Bennett, Jill *26:* 61; *41:* 38, 39; *45:* 54
Bennett, Rainey *15:* 26; *23:* 53
Bennett, Richard *15:* 45; *21:* 11, 12, 13; *25:* 175
Bennett, Susan *5:* 55
Benny, Mike *142:* 78; *203:* 13, 14; *207:* 85
Benoit, Elise *77:* 74
Benson, Linda *60:* 130; *62:* 91; *75:* 101; *79:* 156; *134:* 129
Benson, Patrick *68:* 162; *147:* 17, 18, 19, 20
Bentley, Carolyn *46:* 153
Bentley, James *149:* 30
Bentley, Roy *30:* 162
Benton, Jim *172:* 22
Benton, Thomas Hart *2:* 99
Bereal, JaeMe *228:* 16
Berelson, Howard *5:* 20; *16:* 58; *31:* 50
Berenstain, Jan *12:* 47; *64:* 33, 34, 36, 37, 38, 40, 42, 44; *135:* 25, 28, 31, 35
Berenstain, Stan *12:* 47; *64:* 33, 34, 36, 37, 38, 40, 42, 44; *135:* 25, 28, 31, 35
Berenzy, Alix *65:* 13; *73:* 6; *78:* 115
Berg, Joan *1:* 115; *3:* 156; *6:* 26, 58
Berg, Ron *36:* 48, 49; *48:* 37, 38; *67:* 72
Bergen, David *115:* 44; *207:* 34
Berger, Barbara *77:* 14
Berger, Carin *185:* 6; *232:* 14
Berger, Joe *221:* 9
Berger, William M. *14:* 143; *YABC 1:* 204
Bergherr, Mary *74:* 170; *151:* 123
Bergin, Mark *114:* 8, 9; *143:* 95; *160:* 26, 27
Bergstreser, Douglas *69:* 76
Bergum, Constance R. *121:* 14, 15; *208:* 31, 32, 33; *209:* 176
Bering, Claus *13:* 14
Berkeley, Jon *139:* 218
Berkowitz, Jeanette *3:* 249
Berman, Paul *66:* 14
Berman, Rachel *217:* 26
Bernal, Richard *154:* 176
Bernadette
See Watts, Bernadette
Bernard, Gary *216:* 71
Bernardin, James *112:* 24; *167:* 94; *227:* 14, 15
Bernasconi, Pablo *183:* 10, 11
Bernatene, Poly *235:* 193
Bernath, Stefen *32:* 76
Berner, Rotraut Susanne *214:* 32
Bernhard, Durga *80:* 13
Bernstein, Michel J. *51:* 71
Bernstein, Ted *38:* 183; *50:* 131
Bernstein, Zena *23:* 46
Berridge, Celia *86:* 63
Berrill, Jacquelyn *12:* 50
Berry, Erick
See Best, Allena
Berry, Holly *205:* 116; *210:* 49, 50

Berry, William D. *14:* 29; *19:* 48
Berry, William A. *6:* 219
Berson, Harold *2:* 17, 18; *4:* 28, 29, 220; *9:* 10; *12:* 19; *17:* 45; *18:* 193; *22:* 85; *34:* 172; *44:* 120; *46:* 42; *80:* 240
Bertholf, Bret *187:* 9; *189:* 32, 33
Berton, Patsy *99:* 16
Bertschmann, Harry *16:* 1
Besco, Don *70:* 99
Beskow, Elsa *20:* 13, 14, 15
Bess, Clayton *63:* 94
Best, Allena *2:* 26; *34:* 76
Betera, Carol *74:* 68
Bethell, Thomas N. *61:* 169
Bethers, Ray *6:* 22
Betteridge, Deirdre *214:* 34
Bettina
See Ehrlich, Bettina
Betts, Ethel Franklin *17:* 161, 164, 165; *YABC 2:* 47
Betz, Rudolf *59:* 161
Bewick, Thomas *16:* 40, 41, 43, 44, 45, 47; *54:* 150; *YABC 1:* 107
Beyer, Paul J. III *74:* 24
Bezencon, Jacqueline *48:* 40
Biamonte, Daniel *40:* 90
Bianchi, John *91:* 19
Bianco, Pamela *15:* 31; *28:* 44, 45, 46
Bible, Charles *13:* 15
Bice, Clare *22:* 40
Biedrzycki, David *186:* 170; *219:* 7
Bierman, Don *57:* 184
Biggers, John *2:* 123
Biggs, Brian *192:* 38; *196:* 15; *207:* 170; *241:* 142
Bikadoroff, Roxanna *201:* 74
Bileck, Marvin *3:* 102; *40:* 36, 37
Bilibin, Ivan *61:* 8, 9, 12, 13, 14, 15, 151, 152, 154, 162
Billington, Patrick *98:* 71
Billout, Guy *144:* 38, 39
Bimen, Levent *5:* 179
Binch, Caroline *81:* 18; *140:* 15, 16; *144:* 115; *211:* 82
Binder, Hannes *169:* 163
Bing, Christopher *126:* 34
Binger, Bill *121:* 46
Binks, Robert *25:* 150
Binzen, Bill *24:* 47
Birch, Reginald *15:* 150; *19:* 33, 34, 35, 36; *37:* 196,197; *44:* 182; *46:* 176; *YABC 1:* 84; *2:* 34, 39
Birch, Wendy *223:* 70
Birchall, Mark *123:* 188
Bird, Esther Brock *1:* 36; *25:* 66
Birdsong, Keith *167:* 85; *219:* 105
Birkett, Georgie *204:* 121
Birkett, Rachel *78:* 206
Birling, Paul *109:* 30
Birmingham, Christian *132:* 243; *143:* 114; *209:* 58; *220:* 20
Birmingham, Lloyd P. *12:* 51; *83:* 13
Biro, Val *1:* 26; *41:* 42; *60:* 178; *67:* 23, 24; *84:* 242, 243
Bischoff, Ilse *44:* 51
Bishop, Don *199:* 133; *239:* 146
Bishop, Gavin *97:* 17, 18; *144:* 42, 44; *216:* 52, 55, 56, 57
Bishop, Kathleen Wong *115:* 67
Bishop, Rich *56:* 43
Bite, I. *60:* 14
Bittinger, Ned *93:* 117; *205:* 115
Bjorklund, Lorence *3:* 188, 252; *7:* 100; *9:* 113; *10:* 66; *19:* 178; *33:* 122, 123; *35:* 36, 37, 38, 39,41, 42, 43; *36:* 185; *38:* 93; *47:* 106; *66:* 194; *YABC 1:* 242
Björkman, Steve *91:* 199; *160:* 110; *198:* 18; *218:* 188; *223:* 20, 21; *236:* 56
Blabey, Aaron *214:* 35
Black Sheep *164:* 100
Blackburn, Loren H. *63:* 10
Blackall, Sophie *194:* 140; *209:* 157; *231:* 31, 115; *237:* 172; *241:* 7
Blackford, John *137:* 105; *180:* 36
Blackwell, Basil T. *YABC 1:* 68, 69
Blackwood, Freya *199:* 9
Blackwood, Gary L. *118:* 17
Blades, Ann *16:* 52; *37:* 213; *50:* 41; *69:* 21; *99:* 215
Blair, Jay *45:* 46; *46:* 155
Blaisdell, Elinore *1:* 121; *3:* 134; *35:* 63
Blake, Anne Catharine *189:* 71
Blake, Francis *198:* 4
Blake, Quentin *3:* 170; *10:* 48; *13:* 38; *21:* 180; *26:* 60; *28:* 228; *30:* 29, 31; *40:* 108; *45:* 219; *46:* 165, 168; *48:* 196; *52:* 10, 11, 12,13, 14, 15, 16, 17; *73:* 41, 43; *78:* 84, 86; *80:* 250, 251; *84:* 210, 211, 212; *87:* 177; *96:* 24, 26, 28; *124:* 79; *125:* 32, 34; *181:* 139; *211:* 26, 27; *227:* 176; *229:* 167
Blake, Robert J. *37:* 90; *53:* 67; *54:* 23; *160:* 28, 29
Blake, William *30:* 54, 56, 57, 58, 59, 60
Blakeslee, Lys *218:* 11, 105
Blanchard, N. Taylor *82:* 140
Blass, Jacqueline *8:* 215
Blazek, Scott R. *91:* 71
Blecha, Aaron *233:* 17
Bleck, Cathie *118:* 116
Bleck, Linda *204:* 124
Blegvad, Erik *2:* 59; *3:* 98; *5:* 117; *7:* 131; *11:* 149; *14:* 34, 35; *18:* 237; *32:* 219; *60:* 106; *66:* 16, 17, 18, 19; *70:* 233; *76:* 18; *82:* 106; *87:* 45; *100:* 188; *129:* 125; *132:* 17, 18, 19, 20; *176:* 14; *200:* 100; *YABC 1:* 201
Blessen, Karen *93:* 126
Bliss, Corinne Demas *37:* 38
Bliss, Harry *196:* 27, 28, 29
Blitt, Barry *179:* 199; *187:* 13; *225:* 198
Bloch, Lucienne *10:* 12
Blondon, Herve *129:* 48; *183:* 22
Bloom, Lloyd *35:* 180; *36:* 149; *47:* 99; *62:* 117; *68:* 231; *72:* 136; *75:* 185; *83:* 99; *108:* 19; *229:* 114
Bloom, Suzanne *172:* 23, 24; *232:* 17
Blossom, Dave *34:* 29
Blumen, John *239:* 106
Blumenschein, E.L. *YABC 1:* 113, 115
Blumer, Patt *29:* 214
Blundell, Kim *29:* 36
Bluthenthal, Diana Cain *93:* 32; *104:* 106; *177:* 26; *232:* 21
Blythe, Benjamin *128:* 7
Blythe, Gary *112:* 52; *181:* 166; *182:* 64; *185:* 7; *186:* 116, 117; *238:* 163
Boake, Kathy *176:* 185
Board, Perry *171:* 99
Boardman, Gwenn *12:* 60
Boase, Susan *224:* 53
Boatwright, Phil *211:* 195
Bober, Richard *125:* 145; *132:* 40
Bobri *30:* 138; *47:* 27
Bock, Vera *1:* 187; *21:* 41
Bock, William Sauts *8:* 7; *14:* 37; *16:* 120; *21:* 141; *36:* 177; *62:* 203
Bodecker, N(iels) M(ogens) *8:* 13; *14:* 2; *17:* 55, 56, 57; *73:* 22, 23, 24
Boehm, Linda *40:* 31
Bogacki, Tomek *138:* 31, 32; *144:* 123; *202:* 13
Bogan, Paulette *197:* 152; *201:* 17
Bogdan, Florentina *107:* 43
Bohdal, Susi *22:* 44; *101:* 20
Bohlen, Nina *58:* 13
Boies, Alex *96:* 53
Bok, Chip *205:* 16
Bolam, Emily *101:* 216; *159:* 12; *205:* 59
Bolian, Polly *3:* 270; *4:* 30; *13:* 77; *29:* 197
Bolle, Frank *87:* 100; *208:* 101
Bollen, Roger *79:* 186; *83:* 16
Bolling, Vickey *114:* 44
Bollinger, Peter *101:* 7; *128:* 198; *172:* 26
Bolognese, Don *2:* 147, 231; *4:* 176; *7:* 146; *17:* 43; *23:* 192; *24:* 50; *34:* 108; *36:* 133; *71:* 24, 25; *103:* 131; *129:* 39, 40
Bolster, Rob *186:* 169
Bolton, A.T. *57:* 158
Bond, Arnold *18:* 116
Bond, Barbara Higgins *21:* 102
Bond, Bruce *52:* 97
Bond, Felicia *38:* 197; *49:* 55, 56; *89:* 170; *90:* 171; *126:* 37
Bond, Higgins *177:* 22, 23; *209:* 175; *220:* 22, 23, 24
Bone, J. *230:* 11, 181
Bonn, Pat *43:* 40
Bonner, Hannah *197:* 13, 14
Bonners, Susan *41:* 40; *85:* 36; *94:* 99, 100; *151:* 105, 106
Bonnet, Rosalinde *230:* 79
Bono, Mary *184:* 73
Bonsall, Crosby *23:* 6
Booker, Philip *225:* 16
Boon, Debbie *103:* 6; *144:* 188
Boon, Emilie *86:* 23, 24
Boone, Debbie *165:* 77
Boore, Sara *60:* 73
Bootman, Colin *155:* 13; *159:* 35; *174:* 192; *222:* 128; *239:* 13, 14, 15
Booth, Franklin *YABC 2:* 76
Booth, George *191:* 13
Booth, Graham *32:* 193; *37:* 41, 42
Borda, Juliette *102:* 188
Bordier, Georgette *16:* 54
Boren, Tinka *27:* 128
Borges, Jose Francisco *119:* 62
Borja, Robert *22:* 48
Born, Adolf *49:* 63
Bornstein, Ruth *14:* 44; *88:* 45, 46; *107:* 30
Borten, Helen *3:* 54; *5:* 24
Bosin, Blackbear *69:* 104
Bossom, Naomi *35:* 48
Bostock, Mike *83:* 221; *114:* 14; *188:* 205
Boston, Peter *19:* 42
Bosustow, Stephen *34:* 202
Boszko, Ron *75:* 47
Bottner, Barbara *14:* 46
Boucher, Joelle *41:* 138
Boulat, Pierre *44:* 40
Boulet, Susan Seddon *50:* 47
Bouma, Paddy *118:* 25; *128:* 16
Bour, Daniele *66:* 145
Bourke-White, Margaret *15:* 286, 287; *57:* 102
Boutavant, Marc *200:* 136
Boutet de Monvel, M. *30:* 61, 62, 63, 65
Bowen, Betsy *105:* 222
Bowen, Richard *42:* 134
Bowen, Ruth *31:* 188
Bower, Ron *29:* 33
Bowers, David *95:* 38; *115:* 20; *127:* 169, 170; *165:* 57; *207:* 11
Bowers, Tim *185:* 35; *201:* 41; *218:* 13
Bowman, Claire *174:* 177
Bowman, Eric *151:* 23
Bowman, Leslie *85:* 203; *105:* 108; *116:* 76; *128:* 234; *182:* 24, 25
Bowman, Peter *146:* 214, 215; *150:* 115
Bowser, Carolyn Ewing *22:* 253
Boxall, Ed *178:* 28
Boyd, Aaron *158:* 242; *240:* 169
Boyd, Patti *45:* 31
Boyden, Linda *238:* 39
Boyle, Eleanor Vere *28:* 50, 51
Boynton, Sandra *57:* 13, 14, 15; *107:* 36, 37; *152:* 12, 13, 14
Bozzo, Frank *4:* 154
Brabbs, Derry *55:* 170
Brace, Eric *132:* 193, 194; *152:* 71; *184:* 195; *197:* 6; *201:* 54; *233:* 160
Brackers de Hugo, Pierre *115:* 21
Bradford, June *158:* 138
Bradford, Ron *7:* 157
Bradley, David P. *69:* 105

Bradley, Richard D. *26:* 182
Bradley, William *5:* 164
Brady, Irene *4:* 31; *42:* 37; *68:* 191
Bragg, Michael *32:* 78; *46:* 31
Bragg, Ruth Gembicki *77:* 18
Brainerd, John W. *65:* 19
Braithwaite, Althea *23:* 12, 13; *119:* 16
Brak, Syd *146:* 187
Bralds, Braldt *90:* 28; *91:* 151
Bram, Elizabeth *30:* 67
Bramley, Peter *4:* 3
Brandenberg, Aliki *2:* 36, 37; *24:* 222; *35:* 49, 50, 51,52, 53, 54, 56, 57; *75:* 15, 17; *92:* 205; *113:* 18, 19, 20; *157:* 28; *156:* 111
Brandenburg, Alexa *75:* 19
Brandenburg, Jim *47:* 58; *150:* 212
Brandi, Lillian *31:* 158
Brandon, Brumsic, Jr. *9:* 25
Brannen, Sarah S. *202:* 15; *216:* 199; *240:* 38
Bransom, Paul *17:* 121; *43:* 44
Braren, Loretta Trezzo *87:* 193
Brassard, France *186:* 22
Braun, Wendy *80:* 17, 18; *213:* 14
Brautigam, Don *115:* 175, 176; *225:* 109
Brazell, Derek *75:* 105; *79:* 9
Breathed, Berkeley *86:* 27, 28, 29; *161:* 13, 14; *229:* 10, 11, 12
Breckenreid, Julia *192:* 209
Breen, Steve *186:* 23
Brennan, Steve *83:* 230; *101:* 184
Brenner, Fred *22:* 85; *36:* 34; *42:* 34
Brett, Bernard *22:* 54
Brett, Harold M. *26:* 98, 99, 100
Brett, Jan *30:* 135; *42:* 39; *71:* 31, 32; *130:* 23, 24, 25, 26, 27; *171:* 15, 16; *234:* 32, 34, 35, 36, 37
Brewer, Paul *106:* 115; *145:* 202; *230:* 13
Brewer, Sally King *33:* 44
Brewster, Patience *40:* 68; *45:* 22, 183; *51:* 20; *66:* 144; *89:* 4; *97:* 30, 31; *212:* 99
Brick, John *10:* 15
Brickman, Robin D. *131:* 88; *142:* 150; *155:* 18; *178:* 109; *184:* 32
Bridge, David R. *45:* 28
Bridgman, L.J. *37:* 77
Bridwell, Norman *4:* 37; *138:* 36, 37, 40
Brierley, Louise *91:* 22; *96:* 165; *183:* 51
Briggs, Harry *172:* 187
Briggs, Raymond *10:* 168; *23:* 20, 21; *66:* 29, 31, 32; *131:* 28, 29; *184:* 15, 16
Brigham, Grace A. *37:* 148
Bright, Robert *24:* 55
Brighton, Catherine *107:* 39; *206:* 23
Brinckloe, Julie *13:* 18; *24:* 79, 115; *29:* 35; *63:* 140; *81:* 131
Brion *47:* 116
Brisley, Joyce L. *22:* 57
Brisson, James F. *110:* 60
Brittingham, Geoffrey *88:* 37
Brix-Henker, Silke *81:* 194
Broadway, Hannah *208:* 104
Brock, Charles E. *15:* 97; *19:* 247, 249; *23:* 224, 225; *36:* 88; *42:* 41, 42, 43, 44, 45; *100:* 189; *YABC 1:* 194, 196, 203
Brock, Emma *7:* 21
Brock, Henry Matthew *15:* 81; *16:* 141; *19:* 71; *34:* 115; *40:* 164; *42:* 47, 48, 49; *49:* 66
Brocksopp, Arthur *57:* 157
Broda, Ron *136:* 180; *174:* 123
Brodkin, Gwen *34:* 135
Brodovitch, Alexi *52:* 22
Bromhall, Winifred *5:* 11; *26:* 38
Bromley, Lizzy *159:* 179; *237:* 150
Bronson, Linda *150:* 210; *174:* 133; *203:* 16, 17; *225:* 178
Brooke, L. Leslie *16:* 181, 182, 183, 186; *17:* 15, 16, 17; *18:* 194
Brooker, Christopher *15:* 251
Brooker, Kyrsten *111:* 94; *140:* 28; *162:* 111; *175:* 108; *186:* 42, 225; *199:* 12; *201:* 30; *219:* 98
Brooks, Erik *166:* 52; *182:* 30; *232:* 139; *236:* 40, 41
Brooks, Karen Stormer *186:* 110; *220:* 65
Brooks, Maya Itzna *92:* 153
Brooks, Ron *94:* 15; *197:* 188; *212:* 6, 7, 8, 9
Brooks, S.G. *178:* 127
Broomfield, Maurice *40:* 141
Brotman, Adolph E. *5:* 21
Brown, Bill *235:* 139
Brown, Buck *45:* 48
Brown, Calef *179:* 18; *210:* 206; *217:* 30, 31; *225:* 201
Brown, Christopher *62:* 124, 125, 127, 128
Brown, Craig *73:* 28; *84:* 65; *224:* 18
Brown, Dan *61:* 167; *115:* 183, 184; *116:* 28, 29; *193:* 190; *200:* 21, 23
Brown, David *7:* 47; *48:* 52
Brown, Denise *11:* 213
Brown, Don *172:* 29
Brown, Elbrite *195:* 39; *198:* 5
Brown, Ford Madox *48:* 74
Brown, Gayle *224:* 184
Brown, Hunter *191:* 111, 112; *234:* 105, 107
Brown, Judith Gwyn *1:* 45; *7:* 5; *8:* 167; *9:* 182, 190; *20:* 16, 17, 18; *23:* 142; *29:* 117; *33:* 97; *36:* 23, 26; *43:* 184; *48:* 201, 223; *49:* 69; *86:* 227; *110:* 188; *153:* 7
Brown, Kathryn *98:* 26
Brown, Lisa *187:* 175; *234:* 39
Brown, Laurie Krasny *99:* 30
Brown, Leo *225:* 18
Brown, Marc (Tolon) *10:* 17, 197; *14:* 263; *51:* 18; *53:* 11, 12, 13, 15, 16, 17; *75:* 58; *80:* 24, 25, 26; *82:* 261; *99:* 29; *145:* 22, 23, 25, 27; *162:* 198; *224:* 136
Brown, Marcia *7:* 30; *25:* 203; *47:* 31, 32, 33, 34, 35,36, 37, 38, 39, 40, 42, 43, 44; *YABC 1:* 27
Brown, Margery W. *5:* 32, 33; *10:* 3
Brown, Martin *101:* 43
Brown, Mary Barrett *97:* 74
Brown, Palmer *36:* 40
Brown, Paul *25:* 26; *26:* 107
Brown, Richard *61:* 18; *67:* 30
Brown, Rick *78:* 71; *150:* 154; *224:* 16
Brown, Robert S. *85:* 33
Brown, Rod *157:* 142; *232:* 32, 33
Brown, Ruth *55:* 165; *86:* 112, 113; *105:* 16, 17, 18; *171:* 178
Brown, Trevor *99:* 160; *139:* 247; *189:* 206
Browne, Anthony *45:* 50, 51, 52; *61:* 21, 22, 23, 24, 25; *105:* 21, 22, 23, 25
Browne, Dik *8:* 212; *67:* 32, 33, 35, 37, 39
Browne, Gordon *16:* 97; *64:* 114, 116, 117, 119, 121
Browne, Hablot K. *15:* 65, 80; *21:* 14, 15, 16, 17, 18, 19,20; *24:* 25
Browne, Jane *165:* 222
Browning, Coleen *4:* 132
Browning, Diane *233:* 30
Browning, Mary Eleanor *24:* 84
Bruce, Robert *23:* 23
Brude, Dick *48:* 215
Bruel, Nick *166:* 41; *205:* 17, 18
Brule, Al *3:* 135
Brumbeau, Jeff *157:* 29
Bruna, Dick *43:* 48, 49, 50; *76:* 27, 28
Brundage, Frances *19:* 244
Brunhoff, Jean de *24:* 57, 58
Brunhoff, Laurent de *24:* 60; *71:* 35, 36, 37
Brunkus, Denise *84:* 50; *123:* 117; *178:* 209; *193:* 99; *204:* 10, 11, 12; *209:* 202
Brunson, Bob *43:* 135
Bryan, Ashley *31:* 44; *72:* 27, 28, 29; *107:* 92; *116:* 192; *132:* 24; *178:* 33, 34, 35; *208:* 83
Bryant, Laura J. *176:* 36; *183:* 168; *214:* 141; *222:* 49, 152; *240:* 27, 28
Bryant, Michael *93:* 74
Brychta, Alex *21:* 21
Bryer, Diana *107:* 121
Bryson, Bernarda *3:* 88, 146; *39:* 26; *44:* 185; *131:* 40
Buba, Joy *12:* 83; *30:* 226; *44:* 56
Buchanan, George *166:* 198
Buchanan, Lilian *13:* 16
Buchanan, Rachel *171:* 71
Bucholtz-Ross, Linda *44:* 137
Buchs, Thomas *40:* 38
Buck, Margaret Waring *3:* 30
Buckhardt, Marc *172:* 59
Buckley, Mike *166:* 180
Budwine, Greg *175:* 172
Buehner, Mark *104:* 12, 15; *105:* 160; *119:* 98; *157:* 188; *159:* 39, 40, 43; *192:* 111; *219:* 13, 14, 15, 16; *221:* 17, 18, 19
Buehr, Walter *3:* 31
Buell, Carl *222:* 68
Buff, Conrad *19:* 52, 53, 54
Buff, Mary *19:* 52, 53
Bull, Charles Livingston *18:* 207; *88:* 175, 176
Bullen, Anne *3:* 166, 167
Buller, Jon *205:* 21
Bullock, Kathleen *77:* 24
Bumgarner-Kirby, Claudia *77:* 194
Burbank, Addison *37:* 43
Burchard, Peter Duncan *3:* 197; *5:* 35; *6:* 158, 218; *143:* 17
Burckhardt, Marc *94:* 48; *110:* 89; *196:* 41; *199:* 116
Burden, Andrea *227:* 26
Burger, Carl *3:* 33; *45:* 160, 162
Burgeson, Marjorie *19:* 31
Burgess, Anne *76:* 252
Burgess, Gelett *32:* 39, 42
Burgess, Mark *157:* 31
Burke, Jim *179:* 19; *185:* 63
Burke, Phillip *95:* 117
Burkert, Nancy Ekholm *18:* 186; *22:* 140; *24:* 62, 63,64, 65; *26:* 53; *29:* 60, 61; *46:* 171; *YABC 1:* 46
Burkhardt, Bruce *142:* 86
Burkhardt, Melissa A. *142:* 86
Burleson, Joe *104:* 35; *172:* 139; *227:* 124
Burn, Doris *6:* 172
Burn, Jeffrey *89:* 125; *152:* 132
Burn, Ted
See Burn, Thomas E.
Burn, Thomas E. *151:* 41; *232:* 40
Burnard, Damon *115:* 23
Burnett, Lindy *210:* 59
Burnett, Virgil *44:* 42
Burningham, John *9:* 68; *16:* 60, 61; *59:* 28, 29, 30,31, 32, 33, 35; *111:* 18, 19, 21; *160:* 37; *225:* 21, 24
Burns, Howard M. *12:* 173
Burns, Jim *47:* 70; *86:* 32; *91:* 197; *123:* 16
Burns, M.F. *26:* 69
Burns, Raymond *9:* 29
Burns, Robert *24:* 106
Burr, Dan *65:* 28; *108:* 134; *164:* 203; *182:* 68
Burr, Dane *12:* 2
Burra, Edward *YABC 2:* 68
Burrell, Galen *56:* 76
Burri, Rene *41:* 143; *54:* 166
Burridge, Marge Opitz *14:* 42
Burris, Burmah *4:* 81
Burroughs, John Coleman *41:* 64
Burroughs, Studley O. *41:* 65
Burton, Marilee Robin *46:* 33
Burton, Virginia Lee *2:* 43; *44:* 49, 51; *100:* 46, 47; *YABC 1:* 24; *147:* 56
Buscema, Stephanie *232:* 34
Bush, Timothy *228:* 138
Busoni, Rafaello *1:* 186; *3:* 224; *6:* 126; *14:* 5; *16:* 62, 63
Butchkes, Sidney *50:* 58
Butler, Geoff *94:* 20
Butler, Ralph *116:* 212
Butterfield, Ned *1:* 153; *27:* 128; *79:* 63
Butterworth, Ian *184:* 48, 49
Butterworth, Nick *106:* 43, 44; *149:* 34

Buxton, John *123:* 12
Buzelli, Christopher *105:* 149
Buzonas, Gail *29:* 88
Buzzell, Russ W. *12:* 177
Byard, Carole *39:* 44; *57:* 18, 19, 20; *60:* 60; *61:* 93, 96; *69:* 210; *78:* 246; *79:* 227
Byars, Betsy *46:* 35
Byfield, Barbara Ninde *8:* 18
Byfield, Graham *32:* 29
Bynum, Janie *176:* 50
Byrd, Robert *13:* 218; *33:* 46; *158:* 70; *212:* 100; *226:* 39, 40; *229:* 102; *232:* 167
Byrd, Samuel *123:* 104

C

Cabat, Erni *74:* 38
Cabban, Vanessa *138:* 73; *176:* 39; *185:* 65; *227:* 70
Cabrera, Jane *103:* 24; *152:* 27; *182:* 33, 34
Caceres, Ana Palmero *198:* 106
Caddy, Alice *6:* 41
Cady, Harrison *17:* 21, 23; *19:* 57, 58
Caffrey, Aileen *72:* 223; *141:* 154
Cairns, Julia *177:* 37; *239:* 18, 19
Caldecott, Randolph *16:* 98, 103; *17:* 32, 33, 36, 38, 39; *26:* 90; *100:* 49, 50; *YABC 2:* 172
Calder, Alexander *18:* 168
Calderón, Gloria *179:* 5
Calderon, W. Frank *25:* 160
Caldwell, Ben *105:* 75; *149:* 60; *195:* 61
Caldwell, Clyde *98:* 100; *116:* 39; *208:* 145
Caldwell, Doreen *23:* 77; *71:* 41
Caldwell, John *46:* 225
Call, Greg *126:* 135; *165:* 49; *182:* 105, 163; *197:* 18, 19; *200:* 159; *209:* 166; *212:* 161; *229:* 122; *236:* 129
Callahan, Kevin *22:* 42
Callahan, Philip S. *25:* 77
Callan, Jamie *59:* 37
Callen, Liz *231:* 37
Calo, Marcos *236:* 151
Calvert, Rosemary *218:* 96
Calvin, James *61:* 92
Camburn-Bracalente, Carol A. *118:* 22
Cameron, Chad *190:* 144
Cameron, Julia Margaret *19:* 203
Cameron, Scott *99:* 18
Camm, Martin *140:* 208, 209, 210
Campbell, Ann *11:* 43; *123:* 182; *183:* 68
Campbell, Bill *89:* 39
Campbell, Ken *126:* 143; *205:* 162
Campbell, Robert *55:* 120
Campbell, Rod *51:* 27; *98:* 34
Campbell, Walter M. *YABC 2:* 158
Camps, Luis *28:* 120, 121; *66:* 35
Canga, C.B. *187:* 165
Caniglia, Jeremy *201:* 89
Cann, Helen *124:* 50; *141:* 78; *170:* 138; *179:* 22, 23
Cannell, Jon *196:* 43
Cannon, Janell *78:* 25; *128:* 40
Canright, David *36:* 162
Cantone, AnnaLaura *182:* 146; *196:* 80
Canty, Thomas *85:* 161; *92:* 47; *113:* 192; *134:* 60; *185:* 117
Canyon, Christopher *150:* 44; *151:* 112
Cáparo, Antonio Javier *204:* 128; *218:* 88; *220:* 114; *221:* 167; *227:* 125; *231:* 154; *240:* 45
Caple, Laurie *228:* 9
Caporale, Wende *70:* 42
Capp, Al *61:* 28, 30, 31, 40, 41, 43, 44
Cappon, Manuela *154:* 64; *218:* 149
Caras, Peter *36:* 64
Caraway, Caren *57:* 22
Caraway, James *3:* 200, 201
Carbe, Nino *29:* 183
Cardinale, Christopher *231:* 38
Cares, Linda *67:* 176
Carigiet, Alois *24:* 67
Carle, Eric *4:* 42; *11:* 121; *12:* 29; *65:* 32,33, 34, 36; *73:* 63, 65; *163:* 55, 56
Carling, Amelia Lau *164:* 46
Carlino, Angela *168:* 43; *188:* 20
Carlson, Nancy L. *41:* 116; *56:* 25; *90:* 45; *144:* 48, 50; *213:* 24, 25, 26
Carluccio, Maria *175:* 129; *221:* 119
Carmi, Giora *79:* 35; *149:* 40; *208:* 126
Carpenter, Nancy *76:* 128; *86:* 173; *89:* 171; *131:* 186; *134:* 8; *138:* 215; *153:* 204; *159:* 93; *165:* 232; *211:* 134; *216:* 113; *238:* 183
Carr, Archie *37:* 225
Carrick, Donald *5:* 194; *39:* 97; *49:* 70; *53:* 156; *63:* 15, 16, 17, 18, 19, 21; *80:* 131; *86:* 151; *118:* 24
Carrick, Malcolm *28:* 59, 60
Carrick, Paul *118:* 26; *194:* 28
Carrick, Valery *21:* 47
Carrier, Lark *71:* 43
Carroll, Jim *88:* 211; *140:* 177; *153:* 99; *195:* 75; *236:* 88
Carroll, Lewis
See Dodgson, Charles L.
Carroll, Michael *72:* 5
Carroll, Pamela *84:* 68; *128:* 214; *199:* 130
Carroll, Ruth *7:* 41; *10:* 68
Carter, Abby *81:* 32; *97:* 121; *102:* 61; *163:* 139; *164:* 125; *184:* 22, 23; *191:* 85; *222:* 51; *233:* 84, 94
Carter, Barbara *47:* 167, 169
Carter, David A. *114:* 24, 25; *170:* 42, 43; *228:* 29
Carter, Don *124:* 54; *184:* 100; *192:* 43, 44, 45
Carter, Harry *22:* 179
Carter, Helene *15:* 38; *22:* 202, 203; *YABC 2:* 220, 221
Carter, Penny *173:* 91
Cartlidge, Michelle *49:* 65; *96:* 50, 51
Cartwright, Reg *63:* 61, 62; *78:* 26; *143:* 4
Cartwright, Shannon *176:* 81
Carty, Leo *4:* 196; *7:* 163; *58:* 131
Cary *4:* 133; *9:* 32; *20:* 2; *21:* 143
Cary, Page *12:* 41
Casale, Paul *71:* 63; *109:* 122; *136:* 28
Case, Chris *209:* 23
Case, Sandra E. *16:* 2
Caseley, Judith *87:* 36; *159:* 47, 48, 49
Casilla, Robert *78:* 7; *167:* 124; *211:* 41; *212:* 165
Casino, Steve *85:* 193
Cassel, Lili
See Wronker, Lili Cassel
Cassel-Wronker, Lili
See Wronker, Lili Cassel
Cassels, Jean *8:* 50; *150:* 119; *173:* 37; *186:* 182
Cassen, Melody *140:* 51
Cassity, Don *104:* 24
Cassler, Carl *75:* 137, 138; *82:* 162
Casson, Hugh *65:* 38, 40, 42, 43
Castellon, Federico *48:* 45, 46, 47, 48
Castle, Jane *4:* 80
Castro L., Antonio *84:* 71; *226:* 43
Casu, Danny "casroc" *201:* 10
Catalano, Dominic *94:* 79; *163:* 60, 61; *162:* 54
Catalanotto, Peter *63:* 170; *70:* 23; *71:* 182; *72:* 96; *74:* 114; *76:* 194, 195; *77:* 7; *79:* 157; *80:* 28, 67; *83:* 157; *85:* 27; *108:* 11; *113:* 30, 31, 33, 34, 36; *114:* 27, 28, 29; *117:* 53; *124:* 168; *159:* 54, 55; *195:* 19, 20, 21, 22, 24, 174; *200:* 156; *207:* 103; *209:* 184; *226:* 4
Catania, Tom *68:* 82
Cather, Carolyn *3:* 83; *15:* 203; *34:* 216
Catlin, George *214:* 172
Catrow, David *117:* 179; *152:* 31, 33; *173:* 24; *206:* 29; *231:* 107; *236:* 154
Catusanu, Mircea *222:* 53
Cauley, Lorinda Bryan *44:* 135; *46:* 49
Cayard, Bruce *38:* 67
Cazet, Denys *52:* 27; *99:* 39, 40; *163:* 65, 66; *191:* 25, 27, 28
Ceccoli, Nicoletta *181:* 39; *188:* 99; *199:* 118; *209:* 6
Cecil, Randy *127:* 132, 133; *187:* 16, 17; *191:* 168; *209:* 5; *223:* 37, 38; *224:* 83; *233:* 156
Cellini, Joseph *2:* 73; *3:* 35; *16:* 116; *47:* 103
Cepeda, Joe *90:* 62; *109:* 91; *134:* 172; *159:* 57, 58, 164; *197:* 157; *203:* 69, 95; *215:* 38, 39, 40
Chabrian, Debbi *45:* 55
Chabrian, Deborah *51:* 182; *53:* 124; *63:* 107; *75:* 84; *79:* 85; *82:* 247; *89:* 93; *101:* 197; *212:* 13
Chagnon, Mary *37:* 158
Chalmers, Mary *3:* 145; *13:* 148; *33:* 125; *66:* 214
Chamberlain, Christopher *45:* 57
Chamberlain, Margaret *46:* 51; *106:* 89; *188:* 193; *212:* 16, 17; *224:* 181
Chamberlain, Nigel *78:* 140
Chambers, C.E. *17:* 230
Chambers, Dave *12:* 151
Chambers, Jill *134:* 110
Chambers, Mary *4:* 188
Chambliss, Maxie *42:* 186; *56:* 159; *93:* 163, 164; *103:* 178; *186:* 33, 34; *196:* 39; *223:* 182; *235:* 21
Champlin, Dale *136:* 124
Chan, Harvey *96:* 236; *99:* 153; *143:* 218; *179:* 144; *211:* 219
Chan, Peter *207:* 21; *221:* 39; *235:* 110
Chandler, David P. *28:* 62
Chaney, Howard *139:* 27
Chang, Warren *101:* 209
Chapel, Jody *68:* 20
Chapman, C.H. *13:* 83, 85, 87
Chapman, Frederick T. *6:* 27; *44:* 28
Chapman, Gaye *203:* 133
Chapman, Gaynor *32:* 52, 53
Chapman, Jane *145:* 186; *150:* 56; *166:* 220; *174:* 202; *176:* 43, 44; *179:* 131; *202:* 189; *212:* 20, 21, 22; *216:* 123, 225; *221:* 181, 182
Chapman, Lynne *175:* 31; *197:* 25; *208:* 44
Chapman-Crane, Jeff *220:* 101
Chappell, Warren *3:* 172; *21:* 56; *27:* 125
Charles, Donald *30:* 154, 155
Charlip, Remy *4:* 48; *34:* 138; *68:* 53, 54; *119:* 29, 30; *210:* 63, 64
Charlot, Jean *1:* 137, 138; *8:* 23; *14:* 31; *48:* 151; *56:* 21
Charlot, Martin *64:* 72
Charlton, Michael *34:* 50; *37:* 39
Charmatz, Bill *7:* 45
Chartier, Normand *9:* 36; *52:* 49; *66:* 40; *74:* 220; *145:* 169; *168:* 91; *177:* 108
Chase, Lynwood M. *14:* 4
Chast, Roz *97:* 39, 40; *212:* 25
Chastain, Madye Lee *4:* 50
Chateron, Ann *152:* 19
Chatterton, Martin *68:* 102; *152:* 19; *225:* 42
Chau, Tungwai *140:* 35
Chauncy, Francis *24:* 158
Chavarri, Elisa *240:* 29, 30
Chayka, Doug *145:* 97; *177:* 150; *196:* 46; *212:* 58
Chee, Cheng-Khee *79:* 42; *81:* 224; *180:* 245; *234:* 212
Chen, Chih-sien *90:* 226
Chen, Tony *6:* 45; *19:* 131; *29:* 126; *34:* 160
Chen, Wendy *221:* 76
Chen, Yong *183:* 34
Cheney, T.A. *11:* 47
Cheng, Andrea *205:* 28
Cheng, Judith *36:* 45; *51:* 16
Chermayeff, Ivan *47:* 53
Cherry, David *93:* 40

Cherry, Lynne *34:* 52; *65:* 184; *87:* 111; *99:* 46, 47
Chesak, Lina *135:* 118
Chess, Victoria *12:* 6; *33:* 42, 48, 49; *40:* 194; *41:* 145; *69:* 80; *72:* 100; *92:* 33, 34; *104:* 167
Chessa, Francesca *233:* 40
Chessare, Michele *41:* 50; *56:* 48; *69:* 145
Chesterton, G.K. *27:* 43, 44, 45, 47
Chestnutt, David *47:* 217
Chesworth, Michael *75:* 24, 152; *88:* 136; *94:* 25; *98:* 155; *160:* 42; *207:* 23, 24, 25; *214:* 145
Chetham, Celia *134:* 34
Chetwin, Grace *86:* 40
Cheung, Irving *158:* 96
Chevalier, Christa *35:* 66
Chew, Ruth *7:* 46; *132:* 147
Chewning, Randy *92:* 206
Chichester Clark, Emma *72:* 121; *77:* 212; *78:* 209; *87:* 143; *117:* 37, 39, 40; *144:* 138; *156:* 24, 25; *209:* 26
Chifflart *47:* 113, 127
Child, Lauren *119:* 32; *183:* 30, 31
Chin, Alex *28:* 54
Chitwood, Susan Tanner *163:* 16
Cho, Shinta *8:* 126
Chodos-Irvine, Margaret *52:* 102, 103, 107; *152:* 44
Choi, Yangsook *171:* 134; *173:* 135; *178:* 38, 39, 40
Choksi, Nishant *222:* 54
Chollat, Emilie *170:* 203
Chollick, Jay *25:* 175
Choma, Christina *99:* 169
Chomey, Steve *188:* 53
Chong, Vincent *238:* 105
Chorao, Kay *7:* 200, 201; *8:* 25; *11:* 234; *33:* 187; *35:* 239; *69:* 35; *70:* 235; *123:* 174; *193:* 179; *215:* 43, 44, 45, 46; *229:* 174
Chorney, Steve *221:* 63
Chow, Frances J. Soo Ping *206:* 36
Chowdhury, Subrata *62:* 130; *162:* 22, 23
Christelow, Eileen *38:* 44; *83:* 198, 199; *90:* 57, 58; *184:* 26
Christensen, Bonnie *93:* 100; *153:* 67; *213:* 29, 30
Christensen, Gardell Dano *1:* 57
Christensen, James C. *140:* 226
Christiana, David *90:* 64; *135:* 13; *171:* 7; *195:* 26, 27; *237:* 12; *239:* 84
Christiansen, Per *40:* 24
Christie, R. Gregory *116:* 107; *127:* 20, 21; *162:* 179; *164:* 114; *165:* 137; *174:* 157; *179:* 172; *185:* 17, 18, 19; *200:* 2; *204:* 85; *215:* 207; *218:* 57; *220:* 80, 130; *225:* 45, 46, 47; *226:* 211; *231:* 113; *235:* 167; *240:* 5
Christy, Howard Chandler *17:* 163, 164, 165, 168, 169; *19:* 186, 187; *21:* 22, 23, 24, 25
Christy, Jana *194:* 21
Chronister, Robert *23:* 138; *63:* 27; *69:* 167
Chu, Carol *237:* 108
Church, Caroline Jayne *179:* 27; *219:* 28, 29
Church, Frederick *YABC 1:* 155
Chute, Marchette *1:* 59
Chwast, Jacqueline *1:* 63; *2:* 275; *6:* 46, 47; *11:* 125; *12:* 202; *14:* 235
Chwast, Seymour *3:* 128, 129; *18:* 43; *27:* 152; *92:* 79; *96:* 56, 57, 58; *146:* 32, 33; *197:* 99
Cieslawski, Steve *101:* 142; *127:* 116; *158:* 169, 171; *190:* 174; *212:* 85; *228:* 123
Cinelli, Lisa *146:* 253
Cirlin, Edgard *2:* 168
Clairin, Georges *53:* 109
Clapp, John *105:* 66; *109:* 58; *126:* 7; *129:* 148; *130:* 165; *195:* 48; *220:* 102
Clark, Brenda *119:* 85; *153:* 55
Clark, David *77:* 164; *134:* 144, 145; *216:* 66, 67
Clark, Emma Chichester
See Chichester Clark, Emma
Clark, Robert *227:* 170
Clark, Victoria *35:* 159
Clarke, Greg *169:* 134; *215:* 47, 115; *237:* 119
Clarke, Gus *72:* 226; *134:* 31
Clarke, Harry *23:* 172, 173
Clarke, Peter *75:* 102
Claverie, Jean *38:* 46; *88:* 29
Clavis, Philippe Goossens *182:* 167
Clay, Wil *203:* 29
Clayton, Elaine *159:* 60; *209:* 32
Clayton, Robert *9:* 181
Cleary, Brian P. *186:* 37
Cleaver, Elizabeth *8:* 204; *23:* 36
Cleland, Janet *225:* 111; *226:* 48
Cleland, T.M. *26:* 92
Clemens, Peter *61:* 125
Clement, Charles *20:* 38
Clement, Gary *186:* 79; *191:* 32
Clement, Janet *182:* 50
Clement, Nathan *200:* 30
Clement, Rod *97:* 42; *234:* 68, 69
Clement, Stephen *88:* 3
Clementson, John *84:* 213
Clemesha, David *192:* 49, 50
Cleminson, Kate *221:* 26
Clevin, Jorgen *7:* 50
Clifford, Judy *34:* 163; *45:* 198
Clokey, Art *59:* 44
Clouse, Dennis *187:* 158
Clouse, James *84:* 15
Clouse, Nancy L. *78:* 31; *114:* 90; *225:* 117
Clover, Peter *152:* 45
Cneut, Carll *156:* 166; *165:* 67; *197:* 26
Coalson, Glo *9:* 72, 85; *25:* 155; *26:* 42; *35:* 212; *53:* 31; *56:* 154; *94:* 37, 38, 193
Cober, Alan E. *17:* 158; *32:* 77; *49:* 127
Cober-Gentry, Leslie *92:* 111
Cocca-Leffler, Maryann *80:* 46; *136:* 60; *139:* 193; *194:* 31, 33, 34
Cochran, Bobbye *11:* 52
Cochran, Josh *221:* 27
CoConis, Ted *4:* 41; *46:* 41; *51:* 104
Cocozza, Chris *87:* 18; *110:* 173; *111:* 149
Cockroft, Jason *152:* 20
Coerr, Eleanor *1:* 64; *67:* 52
Coes, Peter *35:* 172
Cogancherry, Helen *52:* 143; *69:* 131; *77:* 93; *78:* 220; *109:* 204; *110:* 129; *203:* 92
Coggins, Jack *2:* 69
Cohen, Alix *7:* 53
Cohen, Lisa *225:* 49
Cohen, Miriam *155:* 23, 24
Cohen, Nancy R. *165:* 35
Cohen, Santiago *164:* 26; *215:* 52, 199
Cohen, Sheldon *105:* 33, 34; *166:* 46, 47
Cohen, Vincent O. *19:* 243
Cohen, Vivien *11:* 112
Coker, Paul *51:* 172
Colbert, Anthony *15:* 41; *20:* 193
Colby, C.B. *3:* 47
Cole, Babette *58:* 172; *96:* 63, 64; *155:* 29
Cole, Brock *68:* 223; *72:* 36, 37, 38, 192; *127:* 23; *136:* 64, 65; *197:*
Cole, Gwen *87:* 185
Cole, Henry *178:* 120; *181:* 42, 43; *189:* 60; *213:* 35, 36; *222:* 139; *238:* 84
Cole, Herbert *28:* 104
Cole, Michael *59:* 46
Cole, Olivia H.H. *1:* 134; *3:* 223; *9:* 111; *38:* 104
Cole, Rachael *209:* 39
Colin, Paul *102:* 59; *123:* 118; *126:* 152; *192:* 129; *234:* 129
Colley, Jacqui *202:* 20
Collicott, Sharleen *98:* 39; *143:* 29, 30
Collier, Bryan *126:* 54; *151:* 166; *174:* 16, 17, 18; *204:* 18, 19; *208:* 84; *211:* 143; *228:* 128
Collier, David *13:* 127
Collier, John *27:* 179; *208:* 154
Collier, Steven *50:* 52
Collier-Morales, Roberta *168:* 61
Collins, Heather *66:* 84; *67:* 68; *81:* 40; *98:* 192, 193; *129:* 95, 96, 98
Collins, Matt *167:* 90; *231:* 9
Collins, Ross *140:* 23, 24; *200:* 36, 37; *209:* 54; *239:* 24, 26, 27, 28
Colman, Audrey *146:* 161
Colón, Raul *108:* 112; *113:* 5; *117:* 167; *134:* 112; *146:* 23; *159:* 92; *166:* 73; *180:* 107; *186:* 156; *190:* 6; *193:* 24, 205; *202:* 21, 22, 23; *217:* 68; *220:* 126, 157; *226:* 118; *227:* 165; *232:* 122
Colonna, Bernard *21:* 50; *28:* 103; *34:* 140; *43:* 180; *78:* 150
Comport, Sally Wern *117:* 169; *169:* 104; *190:* 42; *207:* 50
Conahan, Carolyn *215:* 17
Conde, J.M. *100:* 120
Condon, Grattan *54:* 85 *Condon, Ken 161:* 44; *195:* 28, 29
Cone, Ferne Geller *39:* 49
Cone, J. Morton *39:* 49
Conklin, Paul *43:* 62
Connelly, Gwen *212:* 30
Connelly, James *198:* 12
Connolly, Howard *67:* 88
Connolly, Jerome P. *4:* 128; *28:* 52
Connolly, Peter *47:* 60
Conoly, Walle *110:* 224
Conover, Chris *31:* 52; *40:* 184; *41:* 51; *44:* 79; *213:* 39
Conroy, Melissa *226:* 54
Constantin, Pascale *207:* 159
Contreras, Gerry *72:* 9
Converse, James *38:* 70
Conway *62:* 62
Conway, Michael *69:* 12; *81:* 3; *92:* 108
Cook, Ande *188:* 135
Cook, G.R. *29:* 165
Cook, Joel *108:* 160
Cook, Lynette *228:* 211
Cookburn, W.V. *29:* 204
Cooke, Donald E. *2:* 77
Cooke, Tom *52:* 118
Coomaraswamy, A.K. *50:* 100
Coombs, Charles *43:* 65
Coombs, Deborah *139:* 175
Coombs, Patricia *2:* 82; *3:* 52; *22:* 119; *51:* 32, 33, 34, 35, 36, 37, 38, 39, 40, 42, 43
Cooney, Barbara *6:* 16, 17, 50; *12:* 42; *13:* 92; *15:* 145; *16:* 74, 111; *18:* 189; *23:* 38, 89, 93; *32:* 138; *38:* 105; *59:* 48, 49, 51, 52, 53; *74:* 222; *81:* 100; *91:* 25; *96:* 71, 72, 74; *100:* 149; *YABC2:* 10
Cooper, Elisha *157:* 38, 39; *234:* 45, 46, 47
Cooper, Floyd *79:* 95; *81:* 45; *84:* 82; *85:* 74; *91:* 118; *96:* 77, 78; *103:* 149; *144:* 54; *145:* 151; *159:* 198; *176:* 133, 134; *187:* 26, 27, 28, 29; *188:* 22; *199:* 175; *219:* 66; *227:* 38, 39, 40, 42; *241:* 99
Cooper, Heather *50:* 39
Cooper, Helen *102:* 42, 43, 44
Cooper, Mario *24:* 107
Cooper, Marjorie *7:* 112
Cope, Jane *61:* 201; *108* 52
Copeland, Mark *180:* 12
Copelman, Evelyn *8:* 61; *18:* 25
Copley, Heather *30:* 86; *45:* 57
Corace, Jen *208:* 48
Corbett, Grahame *30:* 114; *43:* 67
Corbett, Tom *234:* 99
Corbino, John *19:* 248
Corcos, Lucille *2:* 223; *10:* 27; *34:* 66
Cordell, Matthew *197:* 93; *199:* 20, 21; *238:* 50
Córdova, Amy *220:* 194
Corey, Robert *9:* 34
Corlass, Heather *10:* 7
Cornell, James *27:* 60
Cornell, Jeff *11:* 58

Cornell, Kevin *241:* 30
Cornell, Laura *94:* 179; *95:* 25
Corr, Christopher *204:* 98
Corral, Ridrigs *212:* 87
Corrigan, Barbara *8:* 37
Corrigan, Patrick *145:* 149
Corwin, Judith Hoffman *10:* 28
Corwin, Oliver *191:* 119
Cory, Fanny Y. *20:* 113; *48:* 29
Cosentino, Ralph *169:* 32
Cosgrove, Margaret *3:* 100; *47:* 63; *82:* 133
Costabel, Eva Deutsch *45:* 66, 67
Costanza, John *58:* 7, 8, 9
Costello, Chris *86:* 78
Costello, David F. *23:* 55
Côté, Geneviéve *184:* 37, 39; *210:* 256; *211:* 151; *240:* 68
Cote, Nancy *126:* 139; *156:* 101; *174:* 101; *182:* 53, 54, 55; *222:* 49
Cottenden, Jeff *190:* 45
Couch, Greg *94:* 124; *110:* 13; *162:* 31; *168:* 149; *199:* 22; *216:* 144; *229:* 103
Coulson, David *239:* 132
Councell, Ruth Tietjen *79:* 29
Courtney, Cathy *58:* 69, 144; *59:* 15; *61:* 20, 87
Courtney, R. *35:* 110
Counihan, Claire *133:* 106
Cousineau, Normand *89:* 180; *112:* 76; *227:* 75
Cousins, Lucy *172:* 53, 54; *205:* 34, 35
Couture, Christin *41:* 209
Covarrubias, Miguel *35:* 118, 119, 123, 124, 125
Coville, Katherine *32:* 57; *36:* 167; *92:* 38
Covington, Neverne *113:* 87
Cowdrey, Richard *169:* 170; *178:* 205; *204:* 22, 23; *215:* 31
Cowell, Cressida *140:* 39
Cowell, Lucinda *77:* 54
Cowles, Rose *203:* 164, 167
Cox *43:* 93
Cox, Charles *8:* 20
Cox, David *56:* 37; *90:* 63; *119:* 38
Cox, Palmer *24:* 76, 77
Cox, Paul *226:* 57, 58
Cox, Steve *140:* 96
Coxe, Molly *69:* 44
Coxon, Michele *158:* 80
Crabb, Gordon *70:* 39
Crabtree, Judith *98:* 42
Craft, Kinuko *22:* 182; *36:* 220; *53:* 122, 123, 148,149; *74:* 12; *81:* 129; *86:* 31; *89:* 139; *127:* 27, 28, 29; *132:* 142; *139:* 38
Craig, Daniel *177:* 67; *180:* 11; *185:* 203; *211:* 212; *224:* 27; *229:* 59
Craig, David *136:* 198; *205:* 37; *236:* 188
Craig, Helen *49:* 76; *62:* 70, 71, 72; *69:* 141; *94:* 42, 43, 44; *112:* 53; *135:* 101, 102; *213:* 45, 46, 47, 55, 81, 82
Crane, Alan H. *1:* 217
Crane, H.M. *13:* 111
Crane, Jack *43:* 183
Crane, Jordan *174:* 21
Crane, Walter *18:* 46, 47, 48, 49, 53, 54, 56, 57, 59, 60, 61; *22:* 128; *24:* 210, 217; *100:* 70, 71
Cravath, Lynne Avril *98:* 45; *182:* 58, 59; *216:* 48; *219:* 61; *220:* 124; *224:* 183; *228:* 74; *229:* 89
Crawford, Allen *212:* 181
Crawford, Denise *137:* 213
Crawford, Will *43:* 77
Credle, Ellis *1:* 69
Czekaj, Jef *217:* 44; *218:* 77
Czernecki, Stefan *154:* 104; *178:* 68, 69
Cresci, Anne *232:* 148
Crespi, Francesca *87:* 90
Cressy, Michael *124:* 55; *203:* 132
Crews, Donald *32:* 59, 60; *76:* 42, 43, 44
Crews, Nina *97:* 49
Crichlow, Ernest *74:* 88; *83:* 203
Crilley, Mark *210:* 71
Croft, James *150:* 57
Crofut, Bob *80:* 87; *81:* 47
Crofut, Susan *23:* 61
Croll, Carolyn *80:* 137; *102:* 52; *235:* 166
Cross, Peter *56:* 78; *63:* 60, 65
Crossman, David A. *219:* 38
Crowe, Elizabeth *88:* 144
Crowell, Pers *3:* 125
Cruikshank, George *15:* 76, 83; *22:* 74, 75, 76, 77, 78, 79,80, 81, 82, 84, 137; *24:* 22, 23
Crump, Fred H. *11:* 62
Cruz, Ray *6:* 55; *70:* 234; *123:* 173; *172:* 192
Csatari, Joe *44:* 82; *55:* 152; *63:* 25, 28; *102:* 58
Cuetara, Mittie *158:* 85
Cuffari, Richard *4:* 75; *5:* 98; *6:* 56; *7:* 13,84, 153; *8:* 148, 155; *9:* 89; *11:* 19; *12:* 55, 96,114; *15:* 51, 202; *18:* 5; *20:* 139; *21:* 197; *22:* 14, 192; *23:* 15, 106; *25:* 97; *27:* 133; *28:* 196; *29:* 54; *30:* 85; *31:* 35; *36:* 101; *38:* 171; *42:* 97; *44:* 92, 192; *45:* 212, 213; *46:* 36, 198; *50:* 164; *54:* 80, 136, 137, 145; *56:* 17; *60:* 63; *66:* 49, 50; *70:* 41; *71:* 132; *77:* 157; *78:* 58, 149; *79:* 120; *85:* 2, 152
Cugat, Xavier *19:* 120
Cumings, Art *35:* 160
Cummings, Chris *29:* 167
Cummings, Michael *159:* 142
Cummings, Pat *42:* 61; *61:* 99; *69:* 205; *71:* 57,58; *78:* 24, 25; *93:* 75; *107:* 49, 50; *164:* 259; *203:* 45, 46
Cummings, Richard *24:* 119
Cummings, Terrance *227:* 49, 172
Cummings, Troy *236:* 83
Cunette, Lou *20:* 93; *22:* 125
Cunningham, Aline *25:* 180
Cunningham, David *11:* 13
Cunningham, Imogene *16:* 122, 127
Cunningham, Kelley *176:* 159
Cupples, Pat *107:* 12; *126:* 109; *182:* 13; *198:* 68; *217:* 21, 22
Curlee, Lynn *98:* 48; *141:* 39; *190:* 48
Currey, Anna *190:* 145; *202:* 130, 132
Curry, John Steuart *2:* 5; *19:* 84; *34:* 36; *144:* 126
Curry, Tom *127:* 131; *185:* 25, 26
Curtis, Bruce *23:* 96; *30:* 88; *36:* 22
Curtis, Neil *167:* 30
Curtis, Stacy *205:* 38
Cusack, Margaret *58:* 49, 50, 51
Cushman, Doug *65:* 57; *101:* 39, 40; *133:* 179; *157:* 45; *186:* 157; *210:* 76, 77; *232:* 132
Cutting, Ann *196:* 194
Cyrus, Kurt *132:* 39; *179:* 36, 37; *236:* 61, 62
Czechowski, Alicia *95:* 21; *171:* 37
Czernecki, Stefan *117:* 173

D

Dabcovich, Lydia *25:* 105; *40:* 114; *99:* 75, 76
Dacey, Bob *82:* 175; *152:* 65
d'Achille, Gino *127:* 175, 176
Daigneault, Sylvie *236:* 65
Daily, Don *78:* 197; *220:* 154
Dain, Martin J. *35:* 75
Dale, Penny *127:* 224; *151:* 57; *160:* 89; *197:* 75; *232:* 188
Dale, Rae *72:* 197
Daley, Joann *50:* 22
Dalton, Anne *40:* 62; *63:* 119
Dalton, Max *234:* 2, 52
Daly, Deborah M. *74:* 213
Daly, Jim *103:* 60; *150:* 48
Daly, Jude *138:* 118, 119; *213:* 41; *222:* 56, 57
Daly, Nicholas *37:* 53; *76:* 48, 49
Daly, Niki *107:* 15; *114:* 38, 39, 40; *164:* 86; *192:* 53; *198:* 26, 27
Daly, Paul *97:* 205
Dalziel, Brothers *33:* 113
D'Amato, Alex *9:* 48; *20:* 25
D'Amato, Janet *9:* 48; *20:* 25; *26:* 118
D'Amico, Steve *170:* 52
Danalis, Johnny *167:* 27
D'Andrade, Hugh *240:* 61
D'Andrea, Domenick *183:* 108
Daniel, Alan *23:* 59; *29:* 110; *76:* 50, 53, 55, 56; *153:* 76 *115:* 74; *134:* 70
Daniel, Lea *76:* 53, 55; *153:* 76
Daniel, Lewis C. *20:* 216
Daniels, Beau *73:* 4
Daniels, Steve *22:* 16
Daniels, Stewart *56:* 12
Dann, Bonnie *31:* 83
Dann, Penny *82:* 128
Danska, Herbert *24:* 219
Danyell, Alice *20:* 27
Darbyshire, Kristen *218:* 41
Dardik, Helen *208:* 200
Darley, F.O.C. *16:* 145; *19:* 79, 86, 88, 185; *21:* 28,36; *35:* 76, 77, 78, 79, 80, 81; *YABC 2:* 175
Darling, Lois *3:* 59; *23:* 30, 31
Darling, Louis *1:* 40, 41; *2:* 63; *3:* 59; *23:* 30,31; *43:* 54, 57, 59; *121:* 53
Darnell, K.L. *210:* 247
Darrow, David R. *84:* 101
Darrow, Whitney, Jr. *13:* 25; *38:* 220, 221
Darwin, Beatrice *43:* 54
Darwin, Len *24:* 82
Dastolfo, Frank *33:* 179
Dauber, Liz *1:* 22; *3:* 266; *30:* 49
Daugherty, James *3:* 66; *8:* 178; *13:* 27, 28, 161; *18:* 101; *19:* 72; *29:* 108; *32:* 156; *42:* 84; *YABC 1:* 256; *2:* 174
d'Aulaire, Edgar Parin *5:* 51; *66:* 53
d'Aulaire, Ingri Parin *5:* 51; *66:* 53
Davalos, Felipe *99:* 197; *159:* 66; *174:* 163; *235:* 52
Davenier, Christine *125:* 88; *127:* 32; *128:* 152; *179:* 39, 40; *216:* 84, 85, 86, 87; *218:* 62, 63; *224:* 73; *237:* 51
Davick, Linda *151:* 124; *208:* 187
David, Jacques-Louis *193:* 22
David, Jonathan *19:* 37
Davidson, Kevin *28:* 154
Davidson, Raymond *32:* 61
Davie, Helen K. *77:* 48, 49
Davies, Andy Robert *205:* 169
Davies, Lottie *214:* 69
Davis, Allen *20:* 11; *22:* 45; *27:* 222; *29:* 157; *41:* 99; *47:* 99; *50:* 84; *52:* 105
Davis, Bette J. *15:* 53; *23:* 95
Davis, Dimitris *45:* 95
Davis, Eleanor *209:* 33
Davis, Hendon *151:* 122
Davis, Jack E. *145:* 139; *175:* 84, 85; *208:* 102; *210:* 81, 82; *213:* 151
Davis, Jim *32:* 63, 64
Davis, Katie *152:* 52, 53, 54; *208:* 52
Davis, Lambert *110:* 23, 24; *176:* 58; *237:* 20
Davis, Marguerite *31:* 38; *34:* 69, 70; *100:* 34; *YABC 1:* 126, 230
Davis, Natalie *235:* 196
Davis, Nelle *69:* 191
Davis, Paul *78:* 214
Davis, Rich *206:* 38
Davis, Stuart *211:* 69
Davis, Yvonne LeBrun *94:* 144
Davisson, Virginia H. *44:* 178
DaVolls, Andy *85:* 53
Dawson, Diane *24:* 127; *42:* 126; *52:* 130; *68:* 104
Dawson, Janine *215:* 198
Dawson, Scott *241:* 130
Dawson, Willow *208:* 54; *216:* 119
Day, Alexandra *67:* 59; *97:* 54; *166:* 65; *169:* 40; *197:* 50, 51, 52, 54
Day, Larry *169:* 88; *185:* 59; *227:* 55

Day, Rob *94:* 110; *127:* 24; *197:* 32
Dean, Bob *19:* 211
Dean, David *192:* 55; *239:* 55
de Angeli, Marguerite *1:* 77; *27:* 62, 65, 66, 67, 69, 70, 72; *100:* 75, 76; *YABC 1:* 166
DeArmond, Dale *70:* 47
Deas, Michael *27:* 219, 221; *30:* 156; *67:* 134; *72:* 24; *75:* 155; *84:* 206; *88:* 124
Deas, Rich *191:* 87; *193:* 10; *212:* 79
deBarros, Jim *196:* 60
Debon, Nicolas *151:* 60; *177:* 46
de Bosschere, Jean *19:* 252; *21:* 4; *186:* 44, 45
De Bruyn, M(onica) G. *13:* 30, 31
Decker, C.B. *172:* 120; *215:* 94
De Cuir, John F. *1:* 28, 29
Deeter, Catherine *74:* 110; *103:* 150; *137:* 50
Degen, Bruce *40:* 227, 229; *57:* 28, 29; *56:* 156; *75:* 229; *76:* 19; *81:* 36, 37; *92:* 26; *93:* 199; *97:* 56, 58, 59; *124:* 40; *147:* 39, 40, 41; *168:* 23; *205:* 45, 46; *231:* 46, 47, 48, 49
De Grazia *14:* 59; *39:* 56, 57
DeGrazio, George *88:* 40
deGroat, Diane *9:* 39; *18:* 7; *23:* 123; *28:* 200, 201; *31:* 58, 59; *34:* 151; *41:* 152; *43:* 88; *46:* 40, 200; *49:* 163; *50:* 89; *52:* 30, 34; *54:* 43; *63:* 5; *70:* 136; *71:* 99; *73:* 117,156; *77:* 34; *85:* 48; *86:* 201; *87:* 142; *90:* 72, 73, 143; *95:* 182; *111:* 123; *118:* 160; *126:* 8; *130:* 130; *138:* 93, 94; *169:* 46, 47
de Groot, Lee *6:* 21
Deines, Brian *110:* 139; *220:* 36, 37
DeJohn, Marie *89:* 78
Dekhteryov, B. *61:* 158
de Kiefte, Kees *94:* 107
Delacre, Lulu *36:* 66; *156:* 35; *202:* 10, 53; *209:* 36
Delaney, A. *21:* 78
Delaney, Michael *180:* 16
Delaney, Molly *80:* 43
Delaney, Ned *28:* 68; *56:* 80; *102:* 11
DeLapine, Jim *79:* 21
De La Roche Saint Andre, Anne *75:* 37
de Larrea, Victoria *6:* 119, 204; *29:* 103; *72:* 203; *87:* 199
Delehanty, Joan W. *223:* 165
DeLeon, Melanie *210:* 43
Delessert, Étienne *7:* 140; *46:* 61, 62, 63, 65, 67, 68; *130:* 38, 39, 40, 41, 42; *179:* 46, 47, 48, 49; *YABC 2:* 209
Delezenne, Christine *186:* 126
Delinois, Alix *228:* 40
Del Negro, Janice *196:* 161
Delon, Melanie *216:* 30
DeLorenzo, Christopher *154:* 149
Delulio, John *15:* 54
DeLuna, Tony *88:* 95
Demarest, Chris L. *45:* 68, 69, 70; *73:* 172, 173, 176; *78:* 106; *82:* 48, 49; *89:* 212; *92:* 86; *128:* 57, 58; *175:* 46, 48
De Mejo, Oscar *40:* 67
De Muth, Roger *205:* 184; *221:* 35
Demi *11:* 135; *15:* 245; *66:* 129, 130; *89:* 216; *102:* 66, 67, 68; *210:* 86, 87, 89
Denetsosie, Hoke *13:* 126; *82:* 34
Denise, Christopher *147:* 43, 44; *176:* 101; *193:* 35, 36, 37; *201:* 37; *238:* 56
Dennis, Morgan *18:* 68, 69; *64:* 89
Dennis, Wesley *2:* 87; *3:* 111; *11:* 132; *18:* 71, 72, 73, 74; *22:* 9; *24:* 196, 200; *46:* 178; *69:* 94, 96; *129:* 62
Denos, Julia *202:* 26; *241:* 5
Denslow, W.W. *16:* 84, 85, 86, 87; *18:* 19, 20, 24; *29:* 211; *100:* 21
Denton, Kady MacDonald *110:* 82; *130:* 70; *181:* 54, 55, 56; *192:* 75
Denton, Phil *220:* 6
Denton, Terry *72:* 163; *174:* 26; *186:* 52; *196:* 83, 84
DePalma, Mary Newell *132:* 114; *139:* 75; *185:* 30, 31; *186:* 121; *213:* 62; *241:* 37, 38, 39
dePaola, Tomie *8:* 95; *9:* 93; *11:* 69; 25; 103; *28:* 157; *29:* 80; *39:* 52, 53; *40:* 226; *46:* 187; *59:* 61, 62, 63, 64, 65, 66, 67, 68, 69, 71, 72, 74; *62:* 19; *108:* 63, 67, 68, 70; *155:* 62, 64, 66; *180:* 105; *200:* 47, 48, 49, 50; *226:* 116
Deraney, Michael J. *77:* 35; *78:* 148
deRosa, Dee *70:* 48; *71:* 210; *91:* 78
Dervaux, Isabelle *111:* 117
DeSaix, Deborah Durland *180:* 15; *188:* 24
De Saulles, Tony *119:* 39
de Sève, Peter *146:* 261; *207:* 78; *219:* 42
Deshaprabhu, Meera Dayal *86:* 192
Despain, Brian *241:* 81
Desimini, Lisa *86:* 68; *94:* 47; *96:* 7; *104:* 107; *125:* 194; *131:* 180; *172:* 56; *216:* 89, 90; *240:* 6
de St. Menin, Charles *70:* 17
Detmold, Edward J. *22:* 104, 105, 106, 107; *35:* 120; *64:* 5; *YABC 2:* 203
Detrich, Susan *20:* 133
Deutermann, Diana *77:* 175
Deutsch, Barry *239:* 34
DeVelasco, Joseph E. *21:* 51
de Veyrac, Robert *YABC 2:* 19
DeVille, Edward A. *4:* 235
de Visser, John *55:* 119
Devito, Bert *12:* 164
Devlin, Harry *11:* 74; *74:* 63, 65; *136:* 77, 78
Dewan, Ted *108:* 73; *157:* 55; *165:* 129; *226:* 67, 68, 69
Dewar, Ken *238:* 180
Dewar, Nick *133:* 122
Dewdney, Anna *184:* 43, 44; *232:* 46, 47, 48
Dewey, Ariane *7:* 64; *33:* 195; *35:* 208; *68:* 16,17; *75:* 46; *93:* 91; *94:* 197; *109:* 65, 66, 67; *125:* 2, 3, 4, 5; *127:* 188; *143:* 25; *178:* 17, 19, 74; *188:* 166; *202:* 164; *231:* 176; *239:* 155
Dewey, Jennifer (Owings) *58:* 54; *64:* 214; *65:* 207; *88:* 169; *103:* 45
Dewey, Kenneth *39:* 62; *51:* 23; *56:* 163
de Zanger, Arie *30:* 40
Diakité, Baba Wagué *174:* 28
Diamond, Donna *21:* 200; *23:* 63; *26:* 142; *35:* 83, 84, 85, 86, 87, 88, 89; *38:* 78; *40:* 147; *44:* 152; *50:* 144; *53:* 126; *69:* 46, 47, 48, 201; *71:* 133; *123:* 19
Dias, Ron *71:* 67
Diaz, David *80:* 213; *96:* 83, 84; *108:* 228; *110:* 29; *149:* 106; *150:* 63; *179:* 160; *184:* 95, 97; *189:* 51, 52, 53; *221:* 86; *229:* 37, 38, 39, 40; *241:* 117
di Bartolo, Jim *225:* 53
Dibley, Glin *138:* 83; *141:* 128; *211:* 162; *221:* 61
DiCesare, Joe *70:* 38; *71:* 63, 106; *79:* 214; *93:* 147; *116:* 217; *143:* 111; *166:* 57
Dick, John Henry *8:* 181
Dickens, Frank *34:* 131
Dickey, Robert L. *15:* 279
Dickson, Mora *84:* 21
Didier, Sam *166:* 114
Dietz, James *128:* 223; *193:* 136
di Fate, Vincent *37:* 70; *90:* 11; *93:* 60; *109:* 219, 220
Di Fiori, Lawrence *10:* 51; *12:* 190; *27:* 97; *40:* 219; *93:* 57; *130:* 45
Digby, Desmond *97:* 180
Dignan, James *196:* 143; *234:* 136
Di Grazia, Thomas *32:* 66; *35:* 241
Dillard, Annie *10:* 32
Dillard, Sarah *136:* 186; *217:* 53
Dillon, Corinne B. *1:* 139
Dillon, Diane *4:* 104, 167; *6:* 23; *13:* 29; *15:* 99; *26:* 148; *27:* 136, 201; *51:* 29, 48, 51, 52, 53, 54,55, 56, 57, 58, 59, 60, 61, 62; *54:* 155; *56:* 69; *58:* 127,128; *61:* 95; *62:* 27; *64:* 46; *68:* 3; *69:* 209; *74:* 89; *79:* 92; *86:* 89; *92:* 28, 177; *93:* 7, 210; *94:* 239, 240; *97:* 167; *106:* 58, 59,61, 64; *107:* 3; *139:* 246; *167:* 77; *189:* 202; *191:* 191; *194:* 45, 46, 48, 49
Dillon, Leo *4:* 104, 167; *6:* 23; *13:* 29; *15:* 99; *26:* 148; *27:* 136, 201; *51:* 29, 48, 51, 52, 53, 54,55, 56, 57, 58, 59, 60, 61, 62; *54:* 155; *56:* 69; *58:* 127,128; *61:* 95; *62:* 27; *64:* 46; *68:* 3; *69:* 209; *74:* 89; *79:* 92; *86:* 89; *92:* 28, 177; *93:* 7, 210; *94:* 239, 240; *97:* 167; *106:* 58, 59,61, 64; *107:* 3; *139:* 246; *167:* 77; *189:* 202; *191:* 191; *194:* 45, 46, 48, 49
Dillon, Sharon Saseen *59:* 179, 188
DiMaccio, Gerald *121:* 80
DiMaggio, Joe *36:* 22
DiMassi, Gina *169:* 17
Dinan, Carol *25:* 169; *59:* 75
Dines, Glen *7:* 66, 67
Dinesen, Thomas *44:* 37
Dinh, Pham Viet *167:* 184
Dinnerstein, Harvey *42:* 63, 64, 65, 66, 67, 68; *50:* 146
Dinsdale, Mary *10:* 65; *11:* 171
Dinyer, Eric *86:* 148; *109:* 163; *110:* 239; *124:* 11; *150:* 69; *170:* 4; *171:* 30
Dion, Nathalie *170:* 124; *213:* 52
DiPucchio, Kelly *230:* 3
DiRocco, Carl *181:* 23
DiSalvo-Ryan, DyAnne *59:* 77; *62:* 185; *117:* 46; *144:* 64; *150:* 153; *186:* 162
Disney, Walt *28:* 71, 72, 73, 76, 77, 78, 79, 80, 81, 87, 88, 89,90, 91, 94
DiTerlizzi, Tony *105:* 7; *147:* 22; *154:* 31, 32, 33; *214:* 74; *236:* 33
Divito, Anna *83:* 159
Dixon, Don *74:* 17; *109:* 196
Dixon, Larry *127:* 125
Dixon, Maynard *20:* 165
Dizin, Pascal *230:* 25, 26
Doares, Robert G. *20:* 39
Dob, Bob *205:* 14
Dobias, Frank *22:* 162
Dobrin, Arnold *4:* 68
Dobson, Steven Gaston *102:* 103
Docherty, Thomas *218:* 45, 46
Dockray, Tracy *139:* 77
Docktor, Irv *43:* 70
Dodd, Ed *4:* 69
Dodd, Emma *203:* 57; *239:* 37
Dodd, Julie *74:* 73
Dodd, Lynley *35:* 92; *86:* 71; *132:* 45, 46, 47
Dodge, Bill *96:* 36; *118:* 7, 8, 9; *133:* 135
Dodgson, Charles L. *20:* 148; *33:* 146; *YABC 2:* 98
Dodson, Bert *9:* 138; *14:* 195; *42:* 55; *54:* 8; *60:* 49; *101:* 125
Dodson, Emma *235:* 43
Dodson, Liz Brenner *105:* 117; *111:* 15
Dohanos, Stevan *16:* 10
Dolce, J. Ellen *74:* 147; *75:* 41
Dolch, Marguerite P. *50:* 64
Dolesch, Susanne *34:* 49
Dollar, Diane *57:* 32
Dolobowsky, Mena *81:* 54
Dolson, Hildegarde *5:* 57
Domanska, Janina *6:* 66, 67; *YABC 1:* 166
Domi *134:* 113
Dominguez, El *53:* 94
Domjan, Joseph *25:* 93
Domm, Jeffrey C. *84:* 69; *135:* 70
Donahey, William *68:* 209
Donahue, Dorothy *76:* 170
Donahue, Vic *2:* 93; *3:* 190; *9:* 44
Donald, Elizabeth *4:* 18
Donalty, Alison *149:* 195, 196, 197
Donato *85:* 59; *149:* 204; *191:* 19
Donato, Michael A. *200:* 143
Doner, Kim *208:* 57

Doney, Todd L.W. *87:* 12; *93:* 112; *98:* 135; *101:* 57; *104:* 40; *118:* 163; *135:* 162, 163; *151:* 18; *227:* 79; *236:* 74
Donna, Natalie *9:* 52
Donohue, Dorothy *95:* 2; *132:* 30; *176:* 54, 55; *178:* 77, 78, 79
Donovan, Jane Monroe *237:* 28
Dooling, Michael *82:* 19; *105:* 55; *106:* 224; *125:* 135; *171:* 46; *172:* 12; *176:* 120; *197:* 89; *220:* 39, 40
Doran, Ben-Ami *128:* 189
Doran, Colleen *211:* 48
Dore, Gustave *18:* 169, 172, 175; *19:* 93, 94, 95, 96, 97, 98,99, 100, 101, 102, 103, 104, 105; *23:* 188; *25:* 197, 199
Doremus, Robert *6:* 62; *13:* 90; *30:* 95, 96, 97; *38:* 97
Dorfman, Ronald *11:* 128
Doriau *86:* 59; *91:* 152
Dorman, Brandon *197:* 35; *204:* 6; *210:* 104; *212:* 95; *216:* 156; *222:* 133; *234:* 92; *237:* 117
Dormer, Frank W. *200:* 55; *222:* 48; *237:* 124
Dorros, Arthur *78:* 42, 43; *91:* 28
Doruyter, Karel *165:* 105
dos Santos, Joyce Audy *57:* 187, 189
Doty, Roy *28:* 98; *31:* 32; *32:* 224; *46:* 157; *82:* 71; *142:* 7
Doucet, Bob *132:* 238; *169:* 159
Dougherty, Charles *16:* 204; *18:* 74
Doughty, Rebecca *177:* 174; *222:* 159
Doughty, Thomas *118:* 31; *140:* 60
Douglas, Aaron *31:* 103
Douglas, Allen *223:* 53; *230:* 148
Douglas, Carole Nelson *73:* 48
Douglas, Goray *13:* 151
Dow, Brian *150:* 92
Dowd, Jason *132:* 51, 52; *164:* 244
Dowd, Vic *3:* 244; *10:* 97
Dowden, Anne Ophelia *7:* 70, 71; *13:* 120
Dowdy, Mrs. Regera *29:* 100
Downard, Barry *202:* 32
Downes, Belinda *180:* 29
Downing, Julie *60:* 140; *81:* 50; *86:* 200; *99:* 129
Doyle, Janet *56:* 31
Doyle, Richard *21:* 31, 32, 33; *23:* 231; *24:* 177; *31:* 87
Draper, Angie *43:* 84
Drath, Bill *26:* 34
Drawson, Blair *17:* 53; *126:* 65
Dray, Matt *177:* 47
Drescher, Henrik *105:* 60, 62, 63; *172:* 72
Drescher, Joan *30:* 100, 101; *35:* 245; *52:* 168; *137:* 52
Dressell, Peggy *186:* 41
Drew, Janet *201:* 177
Drew, Patricia *15:* 100
Dronzek, Laura *199:* 28, 29; *207:* 69
Drummond, Allan *209:* 41
Drummond, V.H. *6:* 70
Drury, Christian Potter *105:* 97; *186:* 224
Dubanevich, Arlene *56:* 44
Dubin, Jill *205:* 56; *217:* 25
Dubois, Claude K. *196:* 2
Dubois, Gerard *182:* 9
DuBurke, Randy *187:* 89; *222:* 136; *224:* 35
Ducak, Danilo *99:* 130; *108:* 214
Duchesne, Janet *6:* 162; *79:* 8
Duda, Jana *102:* 155; *209:* 134
Dudash, C. Michael *32:* 122; *77:* 134; *82:* 149; *212:* 93, 94
Duddle, Jonny *233:* 118; *240:* 94; *241:* 160
Duer, Douglas *34:* 177
Duewell, Kristina *195:* 76
Duffy, Daniel Mark *76:* 37; *101:* 196; *108:* 147, 148
Duffy, Joseph *38:* 203
Duffy, Pat *28:* 153
Dugan, Karen *181:* 26; *202:* 35
Dugin, Andrej *77:* 60
Dugina, Olga *77:* 60
Duke, Chris *8:* 195; *139:* 164
Duke, Kate *87:* 186; *90:* 78, 79, 80, 81; *192:* 21, 59, 60, 61, 63
Duke, Marion *165:* 87
Dulac, Edmund *19:* 108, 109, 110, 111, 112, 113, 114, 115, 117; *23:* 187; *25:* 152; *YABC 1:* 37; *2:* 147
Dulac, Jean *13:* 64
Dumas, Philippe *52:* 36, 37, 38, 39, 40, 41, 42, 43, 45; *119:* 40, 41, 42
Dunaway, Nancy *108:* 161
Dunbar, James *76:* 63
Dunbar, Polly *181:* 60, 61; *211:* 51, 52, 53; *212:* 42; *233:* 6
Duncan, Beverly *72:* 92
Duncan, John *116:* 94
Dunn, H.T. *62:* 196
Dunn, Harvey *34:* 78, 79, 80, 81
Dunn, Iris *5:* 175
Dunn, Phoebe *5:* 175
Dunne, Jeanette *72:* 57, 173, 222
Dunnick, Regan *176:* 51; *178:* 83, 84; *219:* 36; *224:* 144; *229:* 83
Dunnington, Tom *3:* 36; *18:* 281; *25:* 61; *31:* 159; *35:* 168; *48:* 195; *79:* 144; *82:* 230
Dunn-Ramsey, Marcy *117:* 131
Dunrea, Olivier *59:* 81; *118:* 53, 54; *124:* 43; *233:* 63, 64, 66
Duntze, Dorothee *88:* 28; *160:* 76
Dupasquier, Philippe *86:* 75; *104:* 76; *151:* 63
duPont, Lindsay Harper *207:* 39
DuQuette, Keith *90:* 83; *155:* 73, 74
Durand, Delphine *200:* 56
Durham, Sarah *192:* 248
Durney, Ryan *208:* 122
Duroussy, Nathalie *146:* 150
Durrell, Julie *82:* 62; *94:* 62
Dusíková, Maja *223:* 49
Dutz *6:* 59
Duvoisin, Roger *2:* 95; *6:* 76, 77; *7:* 197; *28:* 125; *30:* 101, 102, 103, 104, 105, 107; *47:* 205; *84:* 254
Dyer, Dale *141:* 71
Dyer, Brooke *238:* 65
Dyer, Jane *75:* 219; *129:* 28; *147:* 49, 50, 51; *168:* 121; *190:* 4; *191:* 57, 59, 60; *203:* 4; *238:* 65
Dyer, Sarah *212:* 40
Dypold, Pat *15:* 37

E

E.V.B.
See Boyle, Eleanor Vere (Gordon)
Eachus, Jennifer *29:* 74; *82:* 201; *164:* 153
Eadie, Bob *63:* 36
Eagle, Bruce *95:* 119
Eagle, Ellen *82:* 121; *89:* 3
Eagle, Jeremy *141:* 71
Eagle, Michael *11:* 86; *20:* 9; *23:* 18; *27:* 122; *28:* 57; *34:* 201; *44:* 189; *73:* 9; *78:* 235; *85:* 43
Earl-Bridges, Michele *159:* 128
Earle, Edwin *56:* 27
Earle, Olive L. *7:* 75
Earle, Vana *27:* 99
Earley, Lori *132:* 2; *186:* 4; *195:* 8
Early, Margaret *72:* 59
East, Jacqueline *218:* 198; *224:* 38
East, Stella *131:* 223
Eastman, P.D. *33:* 57
Easton, Reginald *29:* 181
Eaton, Tom *4:* 62; *6:* 64; *22:* 99; *24:* 124
Eaves, Edward *224:* 13
Ebbeler, Jeffrey *193:* 62; *206:* 45; *236:* 55
Ebel, Alex *11:* 89
Eberbach, Andrea *192:* 115
Ebert, Len *9:* 191; *44:* 47
Echevarria, Abe *37:* 69
Echo Hawk, Bunky *187:* 192
Eckersley, Maureen *48:* 62
Eckert, Horst *72:* 62
Ede, Janina *33:* 59
Edens, Cooper *49:* 81, 82, 83, 84, 85; *112:* 58
Edens, John *109:* 115
Edgar, Sarah E. *41:* 97
Edgerton, Perky *195:* 144
Edliq, Emily S. *131:* 107
Edrien *11:* 53
Edwards, Freya *45:* 102
Edwards, George Wharton *31:* 155
Edwards, Gunvor *2:* 71; *25:* 47; *32:* 71; *54:* 106
Edwards, Jeanne *29:* 257
Edwards, Linda Strauss *21:* 134; *39:* 123; *49:* 88, 89
Edwards, Michelle *152:* 62, 63
Edwards, Wallace *170:* 55
Egan, Tim *155:* 76, 77, 78
Egge, David *102:* 71
Eggenhofer, Nicholas *2:* 81
Eggleton, Bob *74:* 40; *81:* 190, 191; *105:* 6; *121:* 183; *149:* 203; *166:* 215
Egielski, Richard *11:* 90; *16:* 208; *33:* 236; *38:* 35; *49:* 91, 92, 93, 95, 212, 213, 214, 216; *79:* 122; *106:* 67, 68, 69; *134:* 135; *144:* 244; *163:* 82, 84; *207:* 125; *225:* 200
Ehlert, Lois *35:* 97; *69:* 51; *112:* 7; *113:* 208; *128:* 63, 64, 65; *172:* 77, 79, 80; *220:* 43, 44, 45, 46, 47, 48; *237:* 33, 34, 35, 36, 37, 38
Ehrlich, Bettina *1:* 83
Eitan, Ora *160:* 165
Eichenberg, Fritz *1:* 79; *9:* 54; *19:* 248; *23:* 170; *24:* 200; *26:* 208; *50:* 67, 68, 69, 70, 71, 72, 73,74, 75, 77, 79, 80, 81; *60:* 165; *100:* 137; *YABC 1:* 104, 105; *2:* 213
Einsel, Naiad *10:* 35; *29:* 136
Einsel, Walter *10:* 37
Einzig, Susan *3:* 77; *43:* 78; *67:* 155; *129:* 154
Eisner, Will *165:* 82, 83
Eitzen, Allan *9:* 56; *12:* 212; *14:* 226; *21:* 194; *38:* 162; *76:* 218
Eldridge, H. *54:* 109
Eldridge, Harold *43:* 83
Elgaard, Greta *19:* 241
Elgin, Kathleen *9:* 188; *39:* 69
Eliopoulos, Chris *234:* 56; *238:* 116
Ellacott, S.E. *19:* 118
Elliot, David *192:* 26; *208:* 62, 63
Elliott, Mark *93:* 69; *105:* 108; *107:* 123; *140:* 53; *165:* 189; *173:* 67; *195:* 95; *203:* 67; *210:* 99; *221:* 57, 70; *230:* 147; *236:* 186; *239:* 80, 81
Elliott, Sarah M. *14:* 58
Ellis, Carson *216:* 210
Ellis, Dianne *130:* 208
Ellis, Jan Davey *88:* 50; *115:* 80
Ellis, Richard *130:* 47, 48
Ellison, Chris *196:* 66; *199:* 131; *207:* 193
Ellison, Pauline *55:* 21
Ellwand, David *213:* 60
Elmer, Richard *78:* 5
Elmore, Larry *90:* 8
Elschner, Géraldine *183:* 38
Elwell, Peter *195:* 150
Elwell, Tristan *110:* 39; *121:* 182; *127:* 46; *137:* 144; *141:* 173; *151:* 236; *158:* 264; *167:* 119, 120, 121; *169:* 20; *190:* 12; *202:* 16; *226:* 6; *233:* 181
Elzbieta *88:* 80, 81
Ember, Kathi *214:* 147; *234:* 58
Emberley, Ed *8:* 53; *70:* 53, 54; *146:* 65, 69, 70; *218:* 50
Emberley, Rebecca *218:* 50
Emberley, Michael *34:* 83; *80:* 72; *119:* 47, 48; *147:* 100; *158:* 115; *189:* 62, 64; *203:* 87, 89; *232:* 51, 52, 54
Emerling, Dorothy *104:* 27

Emery, Leslie *49:* 187
Emmett, Bruce *49:* 147; *80:* 175; *101:* 206; *220:* 200
Emond, Stephen *231:* 59
Emry-Perrott, Jennifer *61:* 57
Emshwiller, Ed *174:* 45
Endle, Kate *191:* 167; *207:* 41; *233:* 155
Engel, Christiane *231:* 61
Engel, Diana *70:* 57
Engle, Mort *38:* 64
Englebert, Victor *8:* 54
English, Mark *101:* 207; *220:* 201
Enik, Ted *142:* 39
Enos, Randall *20:* 183
Enright, Maginel Wright *19:* 240, 243; *39:* 31, 35, 36
Enrique, Romeo *34:* 135
Ensor, Barbara *180:* 30
Epstein, Stephen *50:* 142, 148
Erdogan, Buket *174:* 179
Erdrich, Louise *141:* 62
Erhard, Walter *1:* 152
Erickson, Jim *196:* 190; *233:* 173
Erickson, Phoebe *11:* 83; *59:* 85
Erikson, Mel *31:* 69
Eriksson, Eva *63:* 88, 90, 92, 93; *203:* 99; *207:* 44
Ering, Timothy Basil *131:* 100; *176:* 63, 64; *202:* 29; *204:* 8
Erlbruch, Wolf *181:* 66
Ernst, Lisa Campbell *47:* 147; *95:* 47; *154:* 46, 47, 48; *164:* 88; *212:* 45
Esco, Jo *61:* 103
Escourido, Joseph *4:* 81
Escrivá, Viví *119:* 51; *181:* 36
Essakalli, Julie Klear *200:* 58
Este, Kirk *33:* 111
Estep, David *73:* 57
Estes, Eleanor *91:* 66
Estoril, Jean *32:* 27
Estrada, Pau *74:* 76
Estrada, Ric *5:* 52, 146; *13:* 174
Etchemendy, Teje *38:* 68
Etheredges, the *73:* 12
Etienne, Kirk-Albert *145:* 184
Ets, Marie Hall *2:* 102
Ettlinger, Doris *171:* 98; *186:* 106; *197:* 126; *214:* 125
Eulalie *YABC 2:* 315
Eustace, David *224:* 24
Evangelista, Theresa M. *213:* 67
Evans, Greg *73:* 54, 55, 56; *143:* 40, 41
Evans, Katherine *5:* 64
Evans, Leslie *144:* 227; *207:* 57; *214:* 88; *221:* 28
Evans, Shane W. *159:* 142; *160:* 190; *168:* 39; *188:* 88; *189:* 66, 67, 68; *229:* 150; *240:* 49, 50, 51
Everitt, Betsy *151:* 110
Ewart, Claire *76:* 69; *145:* 59, 60
Ewing, Carolyn *66:* 143; *79:* 52
Ewing, Juliana Horatia *16:* 92
Eyolfson, Norman *98:* 154

F

Fabian, Limbert *136:* 114
Facklam, Paul *132:* 62
Falconer, Ian *125:* 66; *179:* 59
Falconer, Pearl *34:* 23
Falkenstern, Lisa *70:* 34; *76:* 133; *78:* 171; *127:* 16; *191:* 151
Fallone, Gianluca *231:* 23
Falls, C.B. *1:* 19; *38:* 71, 72, 73, 74
Falter, John *40:* 169, 170
Falwell, Cathryn *118:* 77; *137:* 185; *196:* 71, 72
Fancher, Lou *138:* 219; *141:* 64; *144:* 199; *177:* 51; *214:* 95; *221:* 63; *228:* 42, 43, 44; *230:* 44, 45, 46
Fanelli, Sara *89:* 63; *126:* 69
Faria, Rosana *150:* 143
Faricy, Patrick *185:* 182; *212:* 61
Farooqi, Musharraf Ali *207:* 46
Farmer, Andrew *49:* 102
Farmer, Peter *24:* 108; *38:* 75
Farnsworth, Bill *93:* 189; *116:* 147; *124:* 8; *135:* 52; *146:* 242, 243, 244; *182:* 176; *186:* 31, 83, 84, 85; *191:* 197; *222:* 2
Farquharson, Alexander *46:* 75
Farrell, Darren *228:* 45
Farrell, David *40:* 135
Farrell, Russell *196:* 38
Farris, David *74:* 42
Fasolino, Teresa *118:* 145
Fatigati, Evelyn *24:* 112
Fatus, Sophie *182:* 74; *190:* 218; *225:* 131
Faul-Jansen, Regina *22:* 117
Faulkner, Jack *6:* 169
Faulkner, Matt *161:* 174; *167:* 75
Faust, Anke *230:* 166
Fava, Rita *2:* 29
Fax, Elton C. *1:* 101; *4:* 2; *12:* 77; *25:* 107
Fay *43:* 93
Fearing, Mark *223:* 142; *224:* 39, 40
Fearnley, Jan *153:* 82, 83; *205:* 63, 64, 65
Fearrington, Ann *146:* 80
Federspiel, Marian *33:* 51
Fedorov, Nickolai Ivanovich *110:* 102
Feelings, Tom *5:* 22; *8:* 56; *12:* 153; *16:* 105; *30:* 196; *49:* 37; *61:* 101; *69:* 56, 57; *93:* 74; *105:* 88
Fehr, Terrence *21:* 87
Feiffer, Jules *3:* 91; *8:* 58; *61:* 66, 67, 70, 74, 76,77, 78; *111:* 47, 48, 49, 50; *132:* 122; *157:* 62; *201:* 48, 49, 50; *230:* 66
Feigeles, Neil *41:* 242
Feldman, Elyse *86:* 7
Feller, Gene *33:* 130
Fellows, Muriel H. *10:* 42
Felstead, Cathie *116:* 85
Felts, Shirley *33:* 71; *48:* 59
Fennell, Tracy *171:* 69
Fennelli, Maureen *38:* 181
Fenton, Carroll Lane *5:* 66; *21:* 39
Fenton, Mildred Adams *5:* 66; *21:* 39
Ferguson, Peter *177:* 30, 31; *181:* 154; *197:* 4; *199:* 40; *215:* 104; *221:* 66; *229:* 15, 16; *236:* 98; *237:* 153
Ferguson, Walter W. *34:* 86
Fernandes, Eugenie *77:* 67; *205:* 68
Fernandes, Stanislaw *70:* 28
Fernandez, Fernando *77:* 57
Fernandez, Laura *77:* 153; *101:* 117; *131:* 222; *170:* 119; *175:* 182
Ferrari, Alex *188:* 121
Ferrington, Susan *172:* 22
Fetz, Ingrid *11:* 67; *12:* 52; *16:* 205; *17:* 59; *29:* 105; *30:* 108, 109; *32:* 149; *43:* 142; *56:* 29; *60:* 34; *85:* 48; *87:* 146
Fiammenghi, Gioia *9:* 66; *11:* 44; *12:* 206; *13:* 57, 59; *52:* 126, 129; *66:* 64; *85:* 83; *91:* 161; *166:* 169
Fiedler, Joseph Daniel *96:* 42; *113:* 173; *129:* 164; *146:* 17; *159:* 68; *162:* 104
Field, Rachel *15:* 113
Fielding, David *70:* 124
Fieser, Stephen *152:* 36
Fine, Howard *145:* 159; *159:* 64; *165:* 134; *174:* 129; *181:* 68
Fine, Peter K. *43:* 210
Finger, Helen *42:* 81
Fink, Sam *18:* 119
Finlay, Winifred *23:* 72
Finney, Pat *79:* 215
Fiore, Peter *99:* 196; *125:* 139; *144:* 225; *160:* 169; *180:* 72; *212:* 103
Fiorentino, Al *3:* 240
Firehammer, Karla *174:* 202; *221:* 183; *228:* 84
Firmin, Charlotte *29:* 75; *48:* 70
Firmin, Peter *58:* 63, 64, 65, 67, 68, 70, 71
Firth, Barbara *81:* 208; *127:* 218; *179:* 62; *232:* 189
Fischel, Lillian *40:* 204
Fischer, Hans *25:* 202
Fischer, Scott M. *207:* 37; *217:* 29
Fischer-Nagel, Andreas *56:* 50
Fischer-Nagel, Heiderose *56:* 50
Fisher, Carolyn *154:* 50
Fisher, Chris *79:* 62; *158:* 248; *188:* 195
Fisher, Cynthia *117:* 45; *137:* 118; *195:* 40; *235:* 126
Fisher, Jeffrey *142:* 80
Fisher, Leonard Everett *3:* 6; *4:* 72, 86; *6:* 197; *9:* 59; *16:* 151, 153; *23:* 44; *27:* 134; *29:* 26; *34:* 87, 89, 90, 91, 93, 94, 95, 96; *40:* 206; *50:* 150; *60:* 158; *73:* 68, 70, 71, 72, 73; *176:* 71, 72, 73; *208:* 131; *YABC 2:* 169
Fisher, Lois *20:* 62; *21:* 7
Fisher, Valorie *177:* 55; *214:* 92
Fisk, Nicholas *25:* 112
Fitschen, Marilyn *2:* 20, 21; *20:* 48
Fitz-Maurice, Jeff *175:* 2
Fitzgerald, F.A. *15:* 116; *25:* 86, 87
Fitzgerald, Joanne *157:* 153, 154; *198:* 34, 35
Fitzgerald, Royce *205:* 5
Fitzhugh, Louise *1:* 94; *9:* 163; *45:* 75, 78
Fitzhugh, Susie *11:* 117
Fitzpatrick, Jim *109:* 130
Fitzpatrick, Marie-Louise *125:* 69, 70; *189:* 72, 73
Fitzsimmons, Arthur *14:* 128
Fix, Philippe *26:* 102
Flack, Marjorie *21:* 67; *100:* 93; *YABC 2:* 122
Flagg, James Montgomery *17:* 227
Flavin, Teresa *132:* 115; *186:* 119
Flax, Zeona *2:* 245
Fleetwood, Tony *171:* 51
Fleishman, Seymour *14:* 232; *24:* 87
Fleming, Denise *71:* 179; *81:* 58; *126:* 71, 72, 73; *173:* 52, 53
Fleming, Guy *18:* 41
Flesher, Vivienne *85:* 55
Fletcher, Claire *80:* 106; *157:* 159
Flint, Russ *74:* 80
Floate, Helen *111:* 163
Floca, Brian *155:* 88, 89; *190:* 10, 66, 67
Floethe, Richard *3:* 131; *4:* 90
Floherty, John J., Jr. *5:* 68
Flook, Helen *160:* 81
Flora, James *1:* 96; *30:* 111, 112
Florczak, Robert *166:* 51
Florian, Douglas *19:* 122; *83:* 64, 65; *125:* 71, 72, 74, 76; *128:* 130; *177:* 58, 60; *226:* 119
Flory, Jane *22:* 111
Flower, Renee *125:* 109
Floyd, Gareth *1:* 74; *17:* 245; *48:* 63; *62:* 35,36, 37, 39, 40, 41; *74:* 245; *79:* 56
Fluchere, Henri A. *40:* 79
Flynn, Alice *183:* 2
Flynn, Barbara *7:* 31; *9:* 70
Fogarty, Thomas *15:* 89
Foley, Greg *190:* 69
Folger, Joseph *9:* 100
Folkard, Charles *22:* 132; *29:* 128, 257, 258
Foott, Jeff *42:* 202
Forberg, Ati *12:* 71, 205; *14:* 1; *22:* 113; *26:* 22; *48:* 64, 65
Ford, A.G. *230:* 40; *231:* 69
Ford, George *24:* 120; *31:* 70, 177; *58:* 126; *81:* 103; *107:* 91; *136:* 100; *194:* 47; *208:* 81; *218:* 56; *237:* 57, 58
Ford, Gilbert *199:* 10
Ford, H.J. *16:* 185, 186
Ford, Jason *174:* 119
Ford, Pamela Baldwin *27:* 104
Fordham, John *168:* 160, 161

Foreman, Michael *2:* 110, 111; *67:* 99; *73:* 78, 79, 80,81, 82; *93:* 146; *135:* 55, 56, 57; *184:* 58, 59; *216:* 100, 101, 102, 103; *225:* 144
Forrester, Victoria *40:* 83
Forsey, Chris *140:* 210
Fortnum, Peggy *6:* 29; *20:* 179; *24:* 211; *26:* 76, 77, 78; *39:* 78; *58:* 19, 21, 23, 27; *YABC 1:* 148
Fortune, Eric *191:* 52
Foster, Brad W. *34:* 99
Foster, Genevieve *2:* 112
Foster, Gerald L. *7:* 78; *198:* 40
Foster, Jon *146:* 18; *198:* 7; *237:* 140
Foster, Laura Louise *6:* 79
Foster, Marian Curtis *23:* 74; *40:* 42
Foster, Sally *58:* 73, 74
Fotheringham, Edwin *219:* 32
Foucher, Adele *47:* 118
Foust, Mitch *168:* 50
Fowler, Jim *184:* 190
Fowler, Mel *36:* 127
Fowler, Richard *87:* 219
Fowles, Shelley *165:* 127; *205:* 72
Fox, Charles Phillip *12:* 84
Fox, Christyan *188:* 36
Fox, Jim *6:* 187
Fox, Nathan *208:* 64
Fox-Davies, Sarah *76:* 150; *182:* 63; *199:* 42, 43
Frace, Charles *15:* 118
Frailey, Joy *72:* 108
Frame, Paul *2:* 45, 145; *9:* 153; *10:* 124; *21:* 71; *23:* 62; *24:* 123; *27:* 106; *31:* 48; *32:* 159; *34:* 195; *38:* 136; *42:* 55; *44:* 139; *60:* 39, 40, 41, 42, 43, 44, 46; *73:* 183
Frampton, David *85:* 72; *102:* 33; *139:* 182; *152:* 37; *189:* 171
Francis, Guy *198:* 164; *224:* 91; *225:* 65
Francois, Andre *25:* 117
Francoise
See Seignobosc, Francoise
Frank, Lola Edick *2:* 199
Frank, Mary *4:* 54; *34:* 100
Franke, Phil *45:* 91
Frankel, Alona *66:* 70
Frankel, Julie *40:* 84, 85, 202
Frankenberg, Robert *22:* 116; *30:* 50; *38:* 92, 94, 95; *68:* 111
Frankfeldt, Gwen *84:* 223; *110:* 92
Frankland, David *169:* 137; *182:* 164; *201:* 159; *224:* 7; *231:* 27; *236:* 37; *237:* 152
Franklin, Ashton *165:* 144; *225:* 107
Franklin, John *24:* 22
Franson, Leanne R. *111:* 57, 58; *151:* 7; *223:* 63, 64, 158
Frascino, Edward *9:* 133; *29:* 229; *33:* 190; *48:* 80, 81, 82, 83, 84, 85, 86
Frasconi, Antonio *6:* 80; *27:* 208; *53:* 41, 43, 45, 47,48; *68:* 145; *73:* 226; *131:* 68
Fraser, Betty *2:* 212; *6:* 185; *8:* 103; *31:* 72,73; *43:* 136; *111:* 76
Fraser, Eric *38:* 78; *41:* 149, 151
Fraser, F.A. *22:* 234
Fraser, James *171:* 68
Fraser, Mary Ann *137:* 63; *214:* 98
Frasier, Debra *69:* 60; *112:* 67; *182:* 81, 82, 83
Fraustino, Lisa Rowe *146:* 87
Frazee, Marla *72:* 98; *105:* 79, 80; *151:* 67, 68; *164:* 165; *171:* 190, 191; *187:* 53, 54, 55, 56, 143; *222:* 173; *225:* 68, 69, 70; *226:* 180
Frazetta, Frank *41:* 72; *58:* 77, 78, 79, 80, 81, 82, 83
Frazier, Craig *177:* 63; *221:* 47
Freas, John *25:* 207
Fredrickson, Mark *103:* 33
Freeland, Michael J. *118:* 115
Freeman, Don *2:* 15; *13:* 249; *17:* 62, 63, 65, 67, 68; *18:* 243; *20:* 195; *23:* 213, 217; *32:* 155; *55:* 129
Freeman, Irving *67:* 150
Freeman, Laura *144:* 111; *200:* 62, 63
Freeman, Pietri *140:* 223
Freeman, Tom *167:* 118
Freeman, Tor *164:* 93
Fregosi, Claudia *24:* 117
Fremaux, Charlotte Murray *138:* 29; *141:* 95
French, Fiona *6:* 82, 83; *75:* 61; *109:* 170; *132:* 79, 80, 81, 82
French, Martin *163:* 4
French, S. Terrell *216:* 106
Frendak, Rodney *126:* 97, 98
Freschet, Gina *175:* 73
Freynet, Gilbert *72:* 221
Friar, Joanne *237:* 41
Fried, Janice *202:* 121
Frieden, Sarajo *213:* 119
Friedman, Judith *43:* 197; *131:* 221
Friedman, Marvin *19:* 59; *42:* 86
Frinta, Dagmar *36:* 42
Frith, Michael K. *15:* 138; *18:* 120
Fritz, Ronald *46:* 73; *82:* 124
Fromm, Lilo *29:* 85; *40:* 197
Frost, A.B. *17:* 6, 7; *19:* 123, 124, 125, 126, 127, 128, 129,130; *100:* 119; *YABC 1:* 156, 157, 160; *2:* 107
Frost, Helen *183:* 51
Frost, Kristi *118:* 113; *231:* 114
Frost, Michael *151:* 209; *209:* 44; *212:* 70
Froud, Brian *150:* 82, 83
Froud, Wendy *151:* 237
Fry, Guy *2:* 224
Fry, Rosalie *3:* 72; *YABC 2:* 180, 181
Fry, Rosalind *21:* 153, 168
Fryer, Elmer *34:* 115
Fuchs, Bernie *110:* 10; *162:* 46
Fuchs, Erich *6:* 84
Fuchshuber, Annegert *43:* 96
Fucile, Tony *221:* 48
Fufuka, Mahiri *32:* 146
Fuge, Charles *144:* 91, 93
Fujikawa, Gyo *39:* 75, 76; *76:* 72, 73, 74
Fulford, Deborah *23:* 159
Fuller, Margaret *25:* 189
Fulweiler, John *93:* 99
Funai, Mamoru *38:* 105
Funfhausen, Christian *196:* 30
Funk, Tom *7:* 17, 99
Furchgott, Terry *29:* 86
Furness, William Henry, Jr. *94:* 18
Furukawa, Mel *25:* 42
Fusari, Erika *164:* 227

G

Gaadt, David *78:* 212; *121:* 166; *201:* 171
Gaadt, George *71:* 9
Gaber, Susan *99:* 33; *115:* 57, 58; *164:* 195; *169:* 61, 62, 63; *185:* 50, 51; *188:* 124
Gaberell, J. *19:* 236
Gable, Brian *195:* 68, 69
Gabler, Mirko *99:* 71; *195:* 32
Gabor, Tim *216:* 61
Gackenbach, Dick *19:* 168; *41:* 81; *48:* 89, 90, 91, 92,93, 94; *54:* 105; *79:* 75, 76, 77
Gad, Victor *87:* 161
Gaetano, Nicholas *23:* 209
Gaffney-Kessell, Walter *94:* 219; *174:* 188
Gag, Flavia *17:* 49, 52
Gag, Wanda *100:* 101, 102; *YABC 1:* 135, 137, 138, 141, 143
Gagnon, Cecile *11:* 77; *58:* 87
Gaillard, Jason *200:* 69; *204:* 74
Gal, Laszlo *14:* 127; *52:* 54, 55, 56; *65:* 142; *68:* 150; *81:* 185; *96:* 104, 105
Gal, Susan *228:* 58
Galazinski, Tom *55:* 13
Galbraith, Ben *200:* 70
Galdone, Paul *1:* 156, 181, 206; *2:* 40, 241; *3:* 42,144; *4:* 141; *10:* 109, 158; *11:* 21; *12:* 118, 210; *14:* 12; *16:* 36, 37; *17:* 70, 71, 72, 73, 74; *18:* 111, 230; *19:* 183; *21:* 154; *22:* 150, 245; *33:* 126; *39:* 136, 137; *42:* 57; *51:* 169; *55:* 110; *66:* 80, 82, 139; *72:* 73; *100:* 84
Gale, Cathy *140:* 22; *143:* 52; *213:* 166
Gall, Chris *176:* 79, 80
Gallagher, Jack *187:* 100
Gallagher, S. Saelig *105:* 154; *198:* 91
Gallagher, Sears *20:* 112Gallagher-Cole, Mernie *206:* 56
Galloway, Ewing *51:* 154
Galouchka, Annouchka Gravel *95:* 55; *182:* 40
Galster, Robert *1:* 66
Galsworthy, Gay John *35:* 232
Galvez, Daniel *125:* 182
Gamble, Kim *112:* 64, 65; *124:* 77; *183:* 40, 42, 43, 56, 57; *187:* 170
Gammell, Stephen *7:* 48; *13:* 149; *29:* 82; *33:* 209; *41:* 88; *50:* 185, 186, 187; *53:* 51, 52, 53, 54, 55, 56,57, 58; *54:* 24, 25; *56:* 147, 148, 150; *57:* 27, 66; *81:* 62, 63; *87:* 88; *89:* 10; *106:* 223; *126:* 2; *128:* 71, 73, 74, 77; *154:* 34; *211:* 210; *226:* 80, 81, 82; *241:* 141
Gamper, Ruth *84:* 198
Gampert, John *58:* 94
Ganly, Helen *56:* 56
Gannett, Ruth Chrisman *3:* 74; *18:* 254; *33:* 77, 78
Gannon, Ned *205:* 6
Gantschev, Ivan *45:* 32
Garafano, Marie *73:* 33
Garbot, Dave *131:* 106
Garbutt, Bernard *23:* 68
Garcia *37:* 71
Garcia, Geronimo *222:* 73
Garcia, Manuel *74:* 145
Garcia-Franco, Rebecca *173:* 46
Gardiner, Lindsey *178:* 128; *186:* 137
Gardner, Earle *45:* 167
Gardner, Joan *40:* 87
Gardner, Joel *40:* 87, 92
Gardner, John *40:* 87
Gardner, Lucy *40:* 87
Gardner, Richard
See Cummings, Richard
Gardner, Sally *171:* 177; *177:* 66, 68; *229:* 58
Gargiulo, Frank *84:* 158
Garland, Michael *36:* 29; *38:* 83; *44:* 168; *48:* 78, 221, 222; *49:* 161; *60:* 139; *71:* 6, 11; *72:* 229; *74:* 142; *89:* 187; *93:* 183; *104:* 110; *131:* 55; *139:* 209; *168:* 56; *208:* 72, 73, 75
Garland, Peggy *60:* 139
Garland, Sarah *62:* 45; *135:* 67, 68; *171:* 118
Garn, Aimee *75:* 47
Garner, Joan *128:* 170
Garneray, Ambroise Louis *59:* 140
Garnett, Eve *3:* 75
Garnett, Gary *39:* 184
Garns, Allen *80:* 125; *84:* 39; *165:* 231; *209:* 44
Garófoli, Viviana *186:* 123
Garraty, Gail *4:* 142; *52:* 106
Garrett, Agnes *46:* 110; *47:* 157
Garrett, Edmund H. *20:* 29
Garrett, Tom *107:* 194; *215:* 179
Garrick, Jacqueline *67:* 42, 43; *77:* 94
Garrison, Barbara *19:* 133; *104:* 146; *109:* 87
Garro, Mark *108:* 131; *128:* 210
Garvey, Robert *98:* 222
Garza, Carmen Lomas *80:* 211; *182:* 86
Garza, Xavier *184:* 64
Gates, Frieda *26:* 80
Gaughan, Jack *26:* 79; *43:* 185
Gaver, Becky *20:* 61
Gavril, David *211:* 196
Gawing, Toby *72:* 52

Gay, Marie-Louise 68: 76, 77, 78; 102: 136; 126: 76, 78, 81, 83; 127: 55, 56; 179: 70, 72, 73, 74; 224: 81
Gay, Zhenya 19: 135, 136
Gaydos, Tim 62: 201
Gazsi, Ed 80: 48
Gazso, Gabriel 73: 85
Geary, Clifford N. 1: 122; 9: 104; 51: 74
Geary, Rick 142: 44, 46
Gee, Frank 33: 26
Geehan, Wayne 157: 181
Geer, Charles 1: 91; 3: 179; 4: 201; 6: 168; 7: 96; 9: 58; 10: 72; 12: 127; 39: 156,157, 158, 159, 160; 42: 88, 89, 90, 91; 55: 111, 116
Geerinck, Manuel 173: 128
Gehm, Charlie 36: 65; 57: 117; 62: 60, 138
Geis, Alissa Imre 189: 77; 233: 93
Geisel, Theodor Seuss 1: 104, 105, 106; 28: 108, 109, 110,111, 112, 113; 75: 67, 68, 69, 70, 71; 89: 127, 128; 100: 106, 107, 108
Geisert, Arthur 92: 67, 68; 133: 72, 73, 74; 165: 97, 98; 171: 64, 65; 237: 45, 46, 47, 48
Geldart, William 15: 121; 21: 202
Genia 4: 84
Gentry, Cyrille R. 12: 66
Genzo, John Paul 136: 74
George, Jean 2: 113
George, Lindsay Barrett 95: 57; 155: 97, 98
Geraghty, Paul 130: 60, 61
Gerard, Jean Ignace 45: 80
Gerard, Justin 239: 20
Gerard, Rolf 27: 147, 150
Gerber, Mark 61: 105
Gerber, Mary Jane 112: 124; 171: 56
Gerber, Stephanie 71: 195
Gerdstein, Mordecai 169: 105
Gergely, Tibor 54: 15, 16
Geritz, Franz 17: 135
Gerlach, Geff 42: 58
Gerrard, Roy 47: 78; 90: 96, 97, 98, 99
Gerritsen, Paula 177: 69; 217: 166
Gershinowitz, George 36: 27
Gerstein, Mordicai 31: 117; 47: 80, 81, 82, 83, 84, 85, 86; 51: 173; 69: 134; 107: 122; 142: 49, 52; 165: 209; 176: 119; 178: 95, 97, 99; 215: 173; 222: 76
Gervase 12: 27
Geter, Tyrone 146: 249; 150: 86
Getz, Arthur 32: 148
Gévry, Claudine 188: 47
Gewirtz, Bina 61: 81
Giancola, Donato 95: 146; 164: 226; 229: 181
Gibala-Broxholm, Scott 205: 76; 219: 186
Gibbons, Gail 23: 78; 72: 77, 78, 79; 82: 182; 104: 65; 160: 99, 100; 201: 59, 60, 62
Gibbs, Tony 40: 95
Gibran, Kahlil 32: 116
Gibson, Barbara Leonard 205: 77; 212: 151
Gider, Iskender 81: 193
Giebfried, Rosemary 170: 135
Giesen, Rosemary 34: 192, 193
Giffard, Hannah 83: 70
Gifford, Carrie 236: 67, 68
Giguere, George 20: 111
Gilbert, John 19: 184; 54: 115; YABC 2: 287
Gilbert, W.S. 36: 83, 85, 96
Gilbert, Yvonne 116: 70; 128: 84; 149: 119; 185: 69; 192: 25; 195: 81
Gilchrist, Jan Spivey 72: 82, 83, 84, 85, 87; 77: 90; 105: 89, 91; 130: 63, 64; 155: 105, 107; 182: 67
Giles, Will 41: 218
Gili, Phillida 70: 73
Gill, Margery 4: 57; 7: 7; 22: 122; 25: 166; 26: 146, 147
Gillen, Denver 28: 216
Gillette, Henry J. 23: 237
Gilliam, Stan 39: 64, 81
Gillies, Chuck 62: 31
Gilliland, Jillian 87: 58
Gillman, Alec 98: 105
Gilman, Esther 15: 124
Gilman, Phoebe 104: 70, 71
Gilpin, Stephen 213: 68; 236: 116
Ginsberg, Sari 111: 184
Ginsburg, Max 62: 59; 68: 194 Girard, Roge 161: 30
Girouard, Patrick 155: 100; 218: 165
Giovanopoulos, Paul 7: 104; 60: 36
Giovine, Sergio 79: 12; 93: 118; 139: 118; 205: 114
Gist, E.M. 206: 60
Githens, Elizabeth M. 5: 47
Gladden, Scott 99: 108; 103: 160; 193: 46, 47
Gladstone, Gary 12: 89; 13: 190
Gladstone, Lise 15: 273
Glanzman, Louis S. 2: 177; 3: 182; 36: 97, 98; 38: 120, 122; 52: 141, 144; 71: 191; 91: 54, 56
Glaser, Byron 154: 59, 60
Glaser, Milton 3: 5; 5: 156; 11: 107; 30: 26; 36: 112; 54: 141; 151: 70
Glass, Andrew 36: 38; 44: 133; 48: 205; 65: 3; 68: 43, 45; 90: 104, 105; 150: 89; 223: 73, 74
Glass, Marvin 9: 174
Glasser, Judy 41: 156; 56: 140; 69: 79; 72: 101
Glasser, Robin Preiss 123: 176; 152 40; 172: 194; 235: 78
Glattauer, Ned 5: 84; 13: 224; 14: 26
Glauber, Uta 17: 76
Gleeson, J.M. YABC 2: 207
Glegg, Creina 36: 100
Glienke, Amelie 63: 150
Gliewe, Unada 3: 78, 79; 21: 73; 30: 220
Gliori, Debi 72: 91; 138: 82; 162: 37; 189: 79, 81, 82; 238: 70, 72
Glovach, Linda 7: 105
Gobbato, Imero 3: 180, 181; 6: 213; 7: 58; 9: 150; 18: 39; 21: 167; 39: 82, 83; 41: 137, 251; 59: 177
Goble, Paul 25: 121; 26: 86; 33: 65; 69: 68, 69; 131: 79, 80
Goble, Warwick 46: 78, 79; 194: 143
Godal, Eric 36: 93
Godbey, Cory 221: 154
Godkin, Celia 145: 84, 86
Godfrey, Michael 17: 279
Godon, Ingrid 166: 163; 186: 99
Goede, Irene 208: 87
Goembel, Ponder 42: 124; 237: 171
Goffe, Toni 61: 83, 84, 85; 89: 11; 90: 124; 178: 118
Goffstein, M.B. 8: 71; 70: 75, 76, 77
Golbin, Andre 15: 125
Gold, Robert 166: 151, 152
Goldfeder, Cheryl 11: 191
Goldfinger, Jennifer P. 185: 71
Goldin, David 240: 63, 64
Goldman, Todd H. 221: 50, 51
Goldsborough, June 5: 154, 155; 8: 92, 14: 226; 19: 139; 54: 165
Goldsmith, Robert 110: 77
Goldstein, Barry 198: 147
Goldstein, Leslie 5: 8; 6: 60; 10: 106
Goldstein, Nathan 1: 175; 2: 79; 11: 41, 232; 16: 55
Goldstrom, Robert 98: 36; 145: 51, 52; 233: 56
Golembe, Carla 79: 80, 81; 136: 91; 144: 113; 193: 53
Golin, Carlo 74: 112
Gomez, Elena 188: 122; 191: 72
Gomez, Elizabeth 127: 70; 133: 76
Gomi, Taro 64: 102; 103: 74, 76
Gon, Adriano 101: 112
Gonsalves, Ron 178: 213; 212: 196
Gonzalez, Maya Christina 104: 3; 136: 92; 215: 4, 5
Gonzalez, Thomas 226: 157
Gonzalez, Yolanda 212: 65
Good, Karen Hillard 212: 143; 214: 103
Goodall, John S. 4: 92, 93; 10: 132; 66: 92, 93; YABC 1: 198
Goode, Diane 15: 126; 50: 183; 52: 114, 115; 76: 195; 84: 94; 99: 141; 114: 76, 77, 78; 170: 99, 101; 225: 80, 81, 82, 83, 84
Goodelman, Aaron 40: 203
Goodenow, Earle 40: 97
Goodfellow, Peter 62: 95; 94: 202
Goodman, Joan Elizabeth 50: 86
Goodman, Vivienne 82: 251; 146: 181, 182
Goodnow, Patti 117: 33
Goodrich, Carter 221: 52, 53
Goodwin, Harold 13: 74
Goodwin, Philip R. 18: 206
Goor, Nancy 39: 85, 86
Goor, Ron 39: 85, 86
Goossens, Philippe 195: 71
Gorbachev, Valeri 89: 96; 112: 97; 143: 63, 64; 184: 66, 67, 68, 101; 222: 84, 85, 86, 87
Gordon, David 216: 159
Gordon, Gwen 12: 151
Gordon, Margaret 4: 147; 5: 48, 49; 9: 79
Gordon, Mike 101: 62, 63, 64
Gordon, Russell 136: 204; 137: 214; 228: 34
Gordon, Walter 138: 9
Gore, Leonid 89: 51; 94: 74; 136: 8; 158: 117; 166: 136; 168: 36; 170: 107; 181: 94; 185: 73; 222: 89, 90, 91, 92; 235: 10, 11; 240: 74
Gorecka-Egan, Erica 18: 35
Gorey, Edward 1: 60, 61; 13: 169; 18: 192; 20: 201; 29: 90, 91, 92, 93, 94, 95, 96, 97, 98, 99, 100; 30: 129; 32: 90; 34: 200, 65: 48; 68: 24, 25; 69: 79; 70: 80, 82, 83, 84; 85: 136; 127: 62
Gorman, Mike 222: 167
Gorsline, Douglas 1: 98; 6: 13; 11: 113; 13: 104; 15: 14; 28: 117, 118; YABC 1: 15
Gorton, Julia 108: 94; 178: 81, 82; 234: 145
Gosfield, Josh 118: 165, 166; 149: 67
Gosner, Kenneth 5: 135
Gosney, Joy 167: 142
Gotlieb, Jules 6: 127
Goto, Scott 115: 86; 136: 69; 203: 77, 78
Gott, Barry 197: 95; 212: 102
Gottlieb, Dale 67: 162; 107: 16; 149: 6
Goudey, Ray 97: 86
Gough, Alan 91: 57
Gough, Philip 23: 47; 45: 90
Gould, Chester 49: 112, 113, 114, 116, 117, 118
Gould, Jason 151: 232
Gourbault, Martine 177: 159
Govern, Elaine R. 26: 94
Gower, Teri 102: 184
Gowing, Toby 60: 25; 63: 33; 78: 70, 252; 83: 228; 86: 187; 93: 145; 108: 133; 110: 217; 184: 125; 225: 142
Grabianski 20: 144
Grabianski, Janusz 39: 92, 93, 94, 95
Graboff, Abner 35: 103, 104
Graef, Renée 61: 188; 72: 207; 204: 45; 210: 249
Grafe, Max 156: 173; 178: 237; 192: 240; 198: 51
Graham, A.B. 11: 61
Graham, Bob 101: 66, 67, 68; 151: 74, 75; 187: 65, 67, 68, 70
Graham, Georgia 188: 3; 190: 75
Graham, L. 7: 108
Graham, Margaret Bloy 11: 120; 18: 305, 307
Graham, Mark 88: 208; 159: 153; 182: 3
Grahame-Johnstone, Janet 13: 61
Grahame-Johnstone, Anne 13: 61
Grainger, Sam 42: 95
Gralley, Jean 166: 86
Gramatky, Hardie 1: 107; 30: 116, 119, 120, 122, 123
Gran, Julie 168: 118
Granahan, Julie 84: 84

GrandPré, Mary *84:* 131; *109:* 199; *118:* 76; *180:* 65; *184:* 70, 71, 180; *192:* 87; *215:* 24; *229:* 68, 69, 70
Grandström, Brita *176:* 139
Grandville, J.J. *45:* 81, 82, 83, 84, 85, 86, 87, 88; *47:* 125; *64:* 10
Granger, Paul *39:* 153
Granström, Brita *162:* 35; *167:* 46; *224:* 56, 57
Grant, (Alice) Leigh *10:* 52; *15:* 131; *20:* 20; *26:* 119; *48:* 202
Grant, Gordon *17:* 230, 234; *25:* 123, 124, 125, 126; *52:* 69; *YABC 1:* 164
Grant, Melvyn *159:* 186, 187; *170:* 48, 49; *213:* 168, 169; *226:* 163
Grant, Michelle *210:* 95
Grant, Renee *77:* 40
Grant, Shirley *109:* 45
Graves, Elizabeth *45:* 101
Graves, Keith *167:* 89; *191:* 74; *216:* 34; *223:* 103
Gray, Harold *33:* 87, 88
Gray, Les *82:* 76; *83:* 232
Gray, Reginald *6:* 69
Gray, Steve *226:* 206; *231:* 77, 78
Greco, Tony *184:* 6
Greder, Armin *76:* 235
Green, Ann Canevari *62:* 48
Green, Eileen *6:* 97
Green, Elizabeth Shippen *139:* 109
Green, Jonathan *86:* 135; *105:* 109; *221:* 73
Green, Ken *111:* 68
Green, Michael *32:* 216
Green, Robina *87:* 138
Green, Jonathan *157:* 105
Greene, Jeffrey *117:* 93
Greenaway, Kate *17:* 275; *24:* 180; *26:* 107; *41:* 222, 232; *100:* 115, 116; *YABC 1:* 88, 89; *2:* 131, 133, 136,138, 139, 141
Greenberg, Melanie Hope *72:* 93; *80:* 125; *101:* 174; *133:* 180; *186:* 189; *214:* 105
Greenseid, Diane *178:* 106, 107
Greenstein, Elaine *150:* 100
Greenwald, Sheila *1:* 34; *3:* 99; *8:* 72
Greger, Carol *76:* 86
Gregorian, Joyce Ballou *30:* 125
Gregory, Emilian *177:* 146; *187:* 10
Gregory, Fran *130:* 4; *140:* 93
Gregory, Frank M. *29:* 107
Greiffenhagen, Maurice *16:* 137; *27:* 57; *YABC 2:* 288
Greiner, Robert *6:* 86
Gretter, J. Clemens *31:* 134
Gretz, Susanna *7:* 114
Gretzer, John *1:* 54; *3:* 26; *4:* 162; *7:* 125; *16:* 247; *18:* 117; *28:* 66; *30:* 85, 211; *33:* 235; *56:* 16
Grey, Mini *166:* 90; *192:* 71; *239:* 57
Grey Owl *24:* 41
Gri *25:* 90
Grieder, Walter *9:* 84
Griesbach/Martucci *59:* 3
Grifalconi, Ann *2:* 126; *3:* 248; *11:* 18; *13:* 182; *46:* 38; *50:* 145; *66:* 99, 100, 101, 104, 106; *69:* 38; *70:* 64; *87:* 128; *90:* 53; *93:* 49; *128:* 48; *133:* 79, 81; *210:* 111
Griffin, Gillett Good *26:* 96
Griffin, James *30:* 166
Griffin, John Howard *59:* 186
Griffin, Rachel *131:* 23
Griffith, Gershom *94:* 214
Griffiths, Dave *29:* 76
Griffiths, Dean *168:* 180; *169:* 182
Grimly, Gris *186:* 102; *192:* 112; *197:* 86; *219:* 34
Grimsdell, Jeremy *83:* 75
Grimwood, Brian *82:* 89
Gringhuis, Dirk *6:* 98; *9:* 196
Gripe, Harald *2:* 127; *74:* 98
Grisha *3:* 71
Grobler, Piet *201:* 100
Grohmann, Susan *84:* 97
Gropper, William *27:* 93; *37:* 193
Gros *60:* 199
Grose, Helen Mason *YABC 1:* 260; *2:* 150
Grossman, Nancy *24:* 130; *29:* 101
Grossman, Robert *11:* 124; *46:* 39
Groth, John *15:* 79; *21:* 53, 54; *83:* 230
Grover, Lorie Ann *168:* 59
Grubb, Lisa *160:* 116
Grue, Lisa *187:* 193
Gruelle, Johnny *35:* 107
Gschwind, William *11:* 72
Guarnaccia, Steven *201:* 170, 173; *233:* 73
Guay-Mitchell, Rebecca *110:* 95, 96; *135:* 240; *180:* 76; *181:* 71, 73; *216:* 77
Guback, Georgia *88:* 102
Gudeon, Karla *212:* 67
Guerguerion, Claudine *105:* 73
Guevara, Susan *97:* 87; *167:* 49; *194:* 54
Guggenheim, Hans *2:* 10; *3:* 37; *8:* 136
Guhathaakurta, Ajanta *183:* 199
Guida, Lisa Chauncy *172:* 188
Guilbeau, Honore *22:* 69
Guillette, Joseph *137:* 37
Guisewite, Cathy *57:* 52, 53, 54, 56, 57
Gukova, Julia *95:* 104; *154:* 103; *168:* 195
Gundersheimer, Karen *35:* 240; *82:* 100
Gunderson, Nick *57:* 120
Gunnella *192:* 144
Gurney, James *76:* 97; *86:* 32
Gurney, John Steven *75:* 39, 82; *110:* 175; *143:* 67, 68; *169:* 172; *217:* 50, 88; *227:* 86, 87, 88; *228:* 139, 140, 141
Gusman, Annie *38:* 62
Gustafson, Scott *34:* 111; *43:* 40
Gustavson, Adam *104:* 10; *171:* 183; *176:* 87; *197:* 94; *204:* 35; *219:* 187
Guthridge, Bettina *108:* 79; *186:* 92
Guthrie, R. Dale *64:* 143
Guthrie, Robin *20:* 122
Gutierrez, Akemi *172:* 87; *205:* 135
Gutierrez, Alan *136:* 31, 32
Gutierrez, Rudy *97:* 162; *203:* 79; *216:* 158
Gutmann, Bessie Pease *73:* 93, 94
Gwynne, Fred *41:* 94, 95
Gyberg, Bo-Erik *38:* 131

H

Haagensen, Per *238:* 88
Haas, Irene *17:* 77; *87:* 46; *96:* 117
Hack, Konrad *51:* 127
Hader, Berta H. *16:* 126
Hader, Elmer S. *16:* 126
Haeffele, Deborah *76:* 99
Haemer, Alan *62:* 109
Hafner, Marylin *22:* 196, 216; *24:* 44; *30:* 51; *35:* 95; *51:* 25, 160, 164; *86:* 16; *105:* 196; *121:* 93, 94; *149:* 208, 209; *179:* 82, 83, 84, 115; *190:* 200; *201:* 29; *217:* 91
Hagerty, Sean *62:* 181
Hague, Michael *32:* 128; *48:* 98, 99, 100, 101, 103, 105,106, 107, 108, 109, 110; *49:* 121; *51:* 105; *64:* 14, 15; *79:* 134; *80:* 91, 92; *83:* 135; *100:* 241; *102:* 29; *129:* 101, 103, 104; *185:* 80, 81, 82; *215:* 89
Hair, Jonathan *115:* 135
Halas, John *29:* 41, 47, 48
Haldane, Roger *13:* 76; *14:* 202
Hale, Bruce *203:* 83
Hale, Christy *79:* 124; *84:* 200; *114:* 201; *128:* 2, 3; *146:* 203; *158:* 243; *167:* 99; *179:* 87; *240:* 81, 167, 168
Hale, Irina *26:* 97
Hale, James Graham *88:* 207
Hale, Kathleen *17:* 79; *66:* 114, 116, 118
Hale, Nathan *210:* 115, 116; *214:* 179
Haley, Amanda *205:* 82, 83
Haley, Gail E. *43:* 102, 103, 104, 105; *78:* 65, 67; *136:* 106, 107
Hall, Amanda *96:* 110
Hall, Angus *224:* 192
Hall, August N. *217:* 74; *238:* 104
Hall, Chuck *30:* 189
Hall, Douglas *15:* 184; *43:* 106, 107; *86:* 100; *87:* 82; *129:* 72
Hall, H. Tom *1:* 227; *30:* 210
Hall, Melanie *116:* 48, 49; *169:* 77, 78; *219:* 170; *228:* 65, 66, 67
Hall, Michael *228:* 69
Hall, Sydney P. *31:* 89
Hall, Tim *164:* 196; *202:* 41
Hall, Vicki *20:* 24
Hallinan, P.K. *39:* 98
Hallman, Tom *98:* 166
Hally, Greg *101:* 200; *151:* 224
Halperin, Wendy Anderson *96:* 151; *125:* 96, 97, 98, 99; *139:* 22; *140:* 84; *200:* 77, 78; *210:* 157; *215:* 65; *228:* 24, 76
Halpern, Joan *10:* 25
Halpern, Shari *174:* 172
Halpin, Abigail *236:* 94
Halsey, Megan *96:* 172; *114:* 185; *180:* 8; *185:* 85
Halstead, Virginia *125:* 105
Halverson, Janet *49:* 38, 42, 44
Hallensleben, Georg *134:* 5, 6; *172:* 17
Hallett, Mark *220:* 63
Hamanaka, Sheila *71:* 100
Hamann, Brad *78:* 151
Hamann, Sigune *104:* 115
Hamberger, John *6:* 8; *8:* 32; *14:* 79; *34:* 136; *88:* 78
Hamil, Tom *14:* 80; *43:* 163
Hamilton, Bill and Associates *26:* 215
Hamilton, Helen S. *2:* 238
Hamilton, J. *19:* 83, 85, 87
Hamilton, Laurie *116:* 210
Hamilton, Todd Cameron *84:* 15
Hamlin, Janet *97:* 136; *124:* 90; *137:* 157; *182:* 117
Hamlin, Louise *71:* 135
Hammill, Matt *206:* 65
Hammond, Chris *21:* 37
Hammond, Elizabeth *5:* 36, 203
Hampshire, Michael *5:* 187; *7:* 110, 111; *48:* 150; *51:* 129
Hampson, Denman *10:* 155; *15:* 130
Hampton, Blake *41:* 244
Handford, Martin *64:* 105, 106, 107, 109
Handforth, Thomas *42:* 100, 101, 102, 103, 104, 105, 107
Handville, Robert *1:* 89; *38:* 76; *45:* 108, 109
Hane, Roger *17:* 239; *44:* 54
Haney, Elizabeth Mathieu *34:* 84
Hanke, Karen *234:* 71; *241:* 58, 59
Hanke, Ted *71:* 10
Hankinson, Phil *181:* 164; *238:* 160
Hanley, Catherine *8:* 161
Hann, Jacquie *19:* 144
Hanna, Cheryl *91:* 133
Hanna, Wayne A. *67:* 145
Hannon, Mark *38:* 37
Hanrahan, Kelly-Anne *203:* 142
Hansen, Gaby *159:* 11; *186:* 25; *224:* 11
Hansen, Mia *149:* 76
Hanson, Glen *229:* 84
Hanson, Joan *8:* 76; *11:* 139
Hanson, Peter E. *52:* 47; *54:* 99, 100; *73:* 21; *84:* 79; *116:* 144
Hansson, Gunilla *64:* 111, 112
Harbour, Elizabeth *221:* 68
Hardcastle, Nick *121:* 82; *175:* 185; *222:* 135
Hardy, David A. *9:* 96; *119:* 74
Hardy, Paul *YABC 2:* 245
Hargis, Wes *219:* 70; *239:* 175 *Haring, Keith 145:* 65
Harlan, Jerry *3:* 96
Harlin, Greg *89:* 194; *103:* 82; *118:* 161; *121:* 167; *182:* 76; *201:* 172; *215:* 76
Harman, Dominic *206:* 48

Harness, Cheryl *106:* 80; *131:* 87; *178:* 111; *200:* 39
Harnischfeger *18:* 121
Harper, Arthur *YABC 2:* 121
Harper, Betty *126:* 90
Harper, Jamie *174:* 71; *214:* 212; *241:* 66, 67
Harper, Piers *79:* 27; *105:* 102; *161:* 67
Harrington, Glenn *82:* 18; *94:* 66, 68; *185:* 118
Harrington, Jack *83:* 162
Harrington, Richard *5:* 81
Harris, Andrew N. *191:* 78
Harris, Jim *127:* 130; *183:* 4
Harris, John *83:* 25; *241:* 16
Harris, Nick *86:* 177
Harris, Susan Yard *42:* 121
Harrison, Florence *20:* 150, 152
Harrison, Harry *4:* 103
Harrison, Jack *28:* 149
Harrison, Mark *105:* 157; *165:* 190
Harrison, Ted *56:* 73
Harsh, Fred *72:* 107
Harston, Jerry *105:* 143
Hart, Lewis *98:* 115
Hart, Sam *241:* 69
Hart, Thomas *181:* 165; *238:* 161
Hart, William *13:* 72
Hartland, Jessie *171:* 80, 81; *186:* 165; *223:* 58
Hartman, Dominic *241:* 35
Hartung, Susan Kathleen *150:* 107, 108; *173:* 106; *175:* 106; *192:* 78; *211:* 19
Hartelius, Margaret *10:* 24
Hartshorn, Ruth *5:* 115; *11:* 129
Harvey, Amanda *145:* 44
Harvey, Bob *48:* 219
Harvey, Gerry *7:* 180
Harvey, Lisa *97:* 21
Harvey, Paul *88:* 74
Harvey, Roland *71:* 88; *123:* 63; *179:* 94; *218:* 94; *219:* 74
Haskamp, Steve *195:* 36; *229:* 29
Hassall, Joan *43:* 108, 109
Hassell, Hilton *YABC 1:* 187
Hassett, John *162:* 59
Hasselriis, Else *18:* 87; *YABC 1:* 96
Hastings, Glenn *89:* 183
Hastings, Ian *62:* 67
Hauman, Doris *2:* 184; *29:* 58, 59; *32:* 85, 86, 87
Hauman, George *2:* 184; *29:* 58, 59; *32:* 85, 86, 87
Hausherr, Rosmarie *15:* 29
Haverfield, Mary *225:* 87
Hawkes, Kevin *78:* 72; *104:* 198; *105:* 197; *112:* 109; *126:* 87; *144:* 88; *149:* 210; *150:* 110, 135; *156:* 94; *164:* 35; *186:* 18; *190:* 197; *198:* 152; *201:* 70, 71, 72; *220:* 99; *221:* 90, 92, 93; *234:* 195
Hawkins, Jacqui *112:* 86; *162:* 64
Hawkinson, John *4:* 109; *7:* 83; *21:* 64
Hawkinson, Lucy *21:* 64
Hawthorne, Mike *140:* 228
Haxton, Elaine *28:* 131
Haydock, Robert *4:* 95
Hayes, Geoffrey *26:* 111; *44:* 133; *91:* 85; *207:* 63
Hayes, Karel *207:* 65
Haynes, Max *72:* 107
Hays, Michael *73:* 207; *83:* 93; *139:* 197; *146:* 202, 250; *202:* 47
Haywood, Carolyn *1:* 112; *29:* 104
Heale, Jonathan *104:* 117
Healy, Daty *12:* 143
Healy, Deborah *58:* 181, 182; *101:* 111
Heap, Sue *102:* 207; *150:* 113, 114; *187:* 84, 85, 87
Hearn, Diane Dawson *79:* 99; *113:* 13; *209:* 71, 72; *211:* 106
Hearon, Dorothy *34:* 69
Heaslip, William *57:* 24, 25
Hechtkopf, H. *11:* 110
Heck, Ed *173:* 81
Hector, Julian *205:* 85
Hedderwick, Mairi *30:* 127; *32:* 47; *36:* 104; *77:* 86; *145:* 91, 93, 95
Heffernan, Phil *146:* 197; *195:* 172; *218:* 123
Hefter, Richard *28:* 170; *31:* 81, 82; *33:* 183
Hehenberger, Shelly *126:* 91
Heigh, James *22:* 98
Heighway, Richard *25:* 160; *64:* 4
Heighway-Bury, Robin *159:* 89
Heine, Helme *67:* 86; *135:* 91, 92
Heinly, John *45:* 113
Helakoski, Leslie *238:* 85
Hellard, Susan *81:* 21; *204:* 82; *209:* 92
Hellebrand, Nancy *26:* 57
Heller, Linda *46:* 86
Heller, Ruth M. *66:* 125; *77:* 30, 32
Hellmuth, Jim *38:* 164
Helms, Georgeann *33:* 62
Helquist, Brett *142:* 203; *146:* 133, 134; *156:* 10; *173:* 25; *180:* 106; *187:* 90, 91; *193:* 12; *224:* 186; *226:* 117; *229:* 76, 77, 78; *239:* 5, 161
Helweg, Hans *41:* 118; *50:* 93; *58:* 22, 26
Hemingway, Edward *212:* 71
Hemphill, Helen *179:* 95
Henba, Bobbie *90:* 195
Henderling, Lisa *214:* 65
Henderson, Dave *73:* 76; *75:* 191, 192, 193, 194; *82:* 4
Henderson, D.F. *216:* 77
Henderson, Douglas *103:* 68
Henderson, Kathy *55:* 32; *155:* 118
Henderson, Keith *35:* 122
Henderson, Meryl *127:* 58, 60; *169:* 81; *228:*
Hendra, Sue *235:* 95
Hendricks, Donald *235:* 142
Hendrix, John *187:* 133; *208:* 106, 107, 108; *216:* 115
Hendry, Linda *80:* 104; *83:* 83; *164:* 216; *233:* 11
Hengeveld, Dennis *142:* 86
Henkes, Kevin *43:* 111; *108:* 106, 107, 108
Henneberger, Robert *1:* 42; *2:* 237; *25:* 83
Henriksen, Harold *35:* 26; *48:* 68
Henriquez, Celeste *103:* 137
Henriquez, Elsa *82:* 260
Henriquez, Emile F. *89:* 88; *211:* 56
Henry, Everett *29:* 191
Henry, Matthew *117:* 58
Henry, Paul *93:* 121; *194:* 125
Henry, Rohan *217:* 77
Henry, Thomas *5:* 102
Hensel *27:* 119
Henshaw, Jacqui *141:* 127
Henstra, Friso *8:* 80; *36:* 70; *40:* 222; *41:* 250; *73:* 100, 101
Henterly, Jamichael *93:* 4
Heo, Yumi *89:* 85, 86; *94:* 89, 90; *146:* 40, 137, 138; *163:* 227; *201:* 192
Hepple, Norman *28:* 198
Herbert, Helen *57:* 70
Herbert, Jennifer *189:* 47
Herbert, Wally *23:* 101
Herbster, Mary Lee *9:* 33
Herder, Edwin *182:* 104
Herge
See Remi, Georges
Hermansen, Pal *133:* 113
Hermanson, Dennis *10:* 55
Hermes, Gertrude *54:* 161
Herr, Margo *57:* 191
Herr, Susan *83:* 163
Herriman, George *140:* 74, 75, 76, 77, 78
Herriman, Lisa *87:* 190
Herring, Michael *121:* 76; *182:* 103
Herrington, Roger *3:* 161
Herscovici, C. *165:* 240
Hescox, Richard *85:* 86; *90:* 30; *139:* 35
Heslop, Mike *38:* 60; *40:* 130
Hess, Lydia J. *85:* 17
Hess, Mark *111:* 146; *113:* 207
Hess, Paul *134:* 47; *166:* 133; *193:* 13
Hess, Richard *42:* 31
Hester, Ronnie *37:* 85
Heuser, Olga J. *121:* 116
Heusser, Sibylle *168:* 195
Heustis, Louise L. *20:* 28
Hewgill, Jodi *201:* 90
Hewitson, Jennifer *74:* 119; *124:* 167
Hewitt, Kathryn *80:* 126; *149:* 105; *184:* 93; *196:* 36; *229:* 99
Hewitt, Margaret *84:* 112
Heyduck-Huth, Hilde *8:* 82
Heyer, Carol *74:* 122; *130:* 72, 73; *192:* 35; *203:* 78
Heyer, Hermann *20:* 114, 115
Heyer, Marilee *102:* 108
Heyman, Ken *8:* 33; *34:* 113
Heyne, Ulrike *146:* 151
Heywood, Karen *48:* 114
Hickling, P.B. *40:* 165
Hickman, Stephen *85:* 58; *136:* 33; *171:* 128
Hierstein, Judith *56:* 40; *162:* 168; *212:* 72; *227:* 46
Higashi, Sandra *154:* 59, 60
Higginbottom, J. Winslow *8:* 170; *29:* 105, 106
Higgins, Chester *101:* 79
Higham, David *50:* 104
Hilb, Nora *176:* 8
Hild, Anja *215:* 194
Hildebrandt, Greg *8:* 191; *55:* 35, 36, 38, 39, 40, 42, 46; *172:* 110
Hildebrandt, Tim *8:* 191; *55:* 44, 45, 46
Hilder, Rowland *19:* 207
Hill, Eric *66:* 127, 128; *133:* 91
Hill, Gregory *35:* 190
Hill, Pat *49:* 120
Hillenbrand, Will *84:* 115; *92:* 76, 80; *93:* 131; *104:* 168; *128:* 137; *145:* 187; *146:* 184; *147:* 105, 106, 107; *152:* 59; *184:* 179; *195:* 34, 180; *196:* 125; *210:* 122, 123, 124; *217:* 62; *224:* 145; *239:* 151
Hilliard, Richard *183:* 74
Hillier, Matthew *45:* 205
Hillman, Priscilla *48:* 115
Hills, Tad *113:* 4; *137:* 147; *173:* 83; *208:* 199
Himler, Ronald *6:* 114; *7:* 162; *8:* 17, 84, 125; *14:* 76; *19:* 145; *26:* 160; *31:* 43; *38:* 116; *41:* 44, 79; *43:* 52; *45:* 120; *46:* 43; *54:* 44, 83; *58:* 180; *59:* 38; *68:* 146; *69:* 231; *70:* 98; *71:* 177, 178; *77:* 219; *79:* 212; *83:* 62; *89:* 5; *91:* 160; *92:* 91, 92, 93; *94:* 93; *95:* 69, 174, 194; *99:* 99, 112; *113:* 92; *118:* 114; *137:* 73, 74, 77, 167; *163:* 99; *165:* 138; *178:* 9, 220; *183:* 77, 79, 80, 81; *184:* 80, 83; *215:* 151; *231:* 11, 112; *234:* 76, 77, 78, 80; *237:* 54, 55
Himmelman, John *47:* 109; *65:* 87; *94:* 96, 97; *159:* 85; *221:* 79, 80, 81, 82
Hinds, Bill *37:* 127, 130
Hines, Anna Grossnickle *51:* 90; *74:* 124; *95:* 78, 79,80, 81
Hines, Bob *135:* 149, 150
Hirao, Amiko *203:* 98
Hiroko *99:* 61
Hiroshige *25:* 71
Hirsh, Marilyn *7:* 126
Hiscock, Bruce *137:* 80, 81; *204:* 51, 53
Hissey, Jane *103:* 90; *130:* 81
Hitch, Jeff *99:* 206; *128:* 86
Hitz, Demi *11:* 135; *15:* 245; *66:* 129, 130; *152:* 94, 95
Hnizdovsky, Jacques *32:* 96; *76:* 187
Ho, David *227:* 32
Ho, Kwoncjan *15:* 132
Hoban, Lillian *1:* 114; *22:* 157; *26:* 72; *29:* 53; *40:* 105, 107, 195; *41:* 80; *69:* 107, 108; *71:* 98; *77:* 168; *106:* 50; *113:* 86; *136:* 118
Hoban, Tana *22:* 159; *104:* 82, 83, 85

Hobbie, Holly *225:* 90, 91
Hobbie, Jocelyn *190:* 78; *196:* 92
Hobbie, Nathaniel *196:* 92
Hobbs, Leigh *166:* 95
Hoberman, Norman *5:* 82
Hobson, Sally *77:* 185
Hockerman, Dennis *39:* 22; *56:* 23
Hodgell, P.C. *42:* 114
Hodges, C. Walter *2:* 139; *11:* 15; *12:* 25; *23:* 34; *25:* 96; *38:* 165; *44:* 197; *45:* 95; *100:* 57; *YABC 2:* 62, 63
Hodges, David *9:* 98
Hodgetts, Victoria *43:* 132
Hofbauer, Imre *2:* 162
Hoff, Syd *9:* 107; *10:* 128; *33:* 94; *72:* 115,116, 117, 118; *138:* 114, 115
Hoffman, Rosekrans *15:* 133; *50:* 219; *63:* 97
Hoffman, Sanford *38:* 208; *76:* 174; *88:* 160, 161; *151:* 156
Hoffmann, Felix *9:* 109
Hoffnung, Gerard *66:* 76, 77
Hofsinde, Robert *21:* 70
Hogan, Inez *2:* 141
Hogan, Jamie *192:* 94; *198:* 177; *237:* 107; *240:* 19
Hogarth, Burne *41:* 58; *63:* 46, 48, 49, 50, 52, 53, 54, 55,56
Hogarth, Paul *41:* 102, 103, 104; *YABC 1:* 16
Hogarth, William *42:* 33
Hogenbyl, Jan *1:* 35
Hogner, Nils *4:* 122; *25:* 144
Hogrogian, Nonny *3:* 221; *4:* 106, 107; *5:* 166; *7:* 129; *15:* 2; *16:* 176; *20:* 154; *22:* 146; *25:* 217; *27:* 206; *74:* 127, 128, 129, 149, 152; *127:* 99; *YABC 2:* 84, 94
Hokanson, Lars *93:* 111; *172:* 137; *212:* 88
Hokusai *25:* 71
Hol, Colby *126:* 96
Holberg, Richard *2:* 51
Holbrook, Kathy *107:* 114
Holdcroft, Tina *38:* 109; *227:* 99, 100, 160
Holden, Caroline *55:* 159
Holder, Heidi *36:* 99; *64:* 9
Holder, Jim *204:* 163
Holder, Jimmy *151:* 224; *233:* 175; *234:* 82, 83
Holderness, Grizelda *215:* 107
Hole, Stian *204:* 55
Holiday, Henry *YABC 2:* 107
Holinaty, Josh *241:* 155
Holl, F. *36:* 91
Holland, Brad *45:* 59, 159
Holland, Gay W. *128:* 105; *225:* 76
Holland, Janice *18:* 118
Holland, Marion *6:* 116
Holland, Richard *216:* 109, 124
Holldobler, Turid *26:* 120
Holliday, Keaf *144:* 236
Holling, Holling C. *15:* 136, 137
Hollinger, Deanne *12:* 116
Holm, Sharon Lane *114:* 84; *115:* 52
Holmes, B. *3:* 82
Holmes, Bea *7:* 74; *24:* 156; *31:* 93
Holmes, Dave *54:* 22
Holmes, Lesley *135:* 96
Holmgren, George Ellen *45:* 112
Holmlund, Heather D. *150:* 140
Holt, Norma *44:* 106
Holt, Pater *151:* 188
Holtan, Gene *32:* 192
Holub, Joan *149:* 72; *229:* 82
Holyfield, John *149:* 231; *227:* 101; *230:* 9
Holz, Loretta *17:* 81
Hom, Nancy *79:* 195
Homar, Lorenzo *6:* 2
Homer, Winslow *128:* 8; *YABC 2:* 87
Honey, Elizabeth *112:* 95, 96; *137:* 93, 94
Honeywood, Varnette P. *110:* 68, 70
Hong, Lily Toy *76:* 104
Honigman, Marian *3:* 2
Honore, Paul *42:* 77, 79, 81, 82
Hood, Alun *69:* 145, 218; *72:* 41; *80:* 226; *87:* 4; *95:* 139
Hood, Susan *12:* 43
Hook, Christian *104:* 103
Hook, Frances *26:* 188; *27:* 127
Hook, Jeff *14:* 137; *103:* 105
Hook, Richard *26:* 188
Hooks *63:* 30
Hooper, Hadley *177:* 145
Hoover, Carol A. *21:* 77
Hoover, Russell *12:* 95; *17:* 2; *34:* 156
Hope, James *141:* 116
Hopkins, Chris *99:* 127
Hopkinson, Leigh *202:* 70
Hopman, Philip *178:* 184
Hoppe, Paul *209:* 85
Hoppin, Augustus *34:* 66
Horacek, Judy *211:* 86
Horacek, Petr *163:* 117; *214:* 113
Horder, Margaret *2:* 108; *73:* 75
Horen, Michael *45:* 121
Horne, Daniel *73:* 106; *91:* 153; *109:* 127; *110:* 232; *164:* 176
Horne, Richard *111:* 80
Horowitz, Dave *204:* 58
Horse, Harry *128:* 195; *169:* 86
Horstman, Lisa *219:* 79
Horton, Anthony *211:* 98
Horvat, Laurel *12:* 201
Horvath, David *192:* 95
Horvath, Ferdinand Kusati *24:* 176
Horvath, Maria *57:* 171
Horwitz, Richard *57:* 174
Hotchkiss, De Wolfe *20:* 49
Hough, Charlotte *9:* 112; *13:* 98; *17:* 83; *24:* 195
Houlihan, Ray *11:* 214
House, Caroline *183:* 121
Housman, Laurence *25:* 146, 147
Houston, James *13:* 107; *74:* 132, 134, 135
Hovland, Gary *88:* 172; *171:* 148
Hoyt, Eleanor *158:* 231
How, W.E. *20:* 47
Howard, Alan *16:* 80; *34:* 58; *45:* 114
Howard, Arthur *165:* 111, 112; *190:* 5; *229:* 30
Howard, J.N. *15:* 234
Howard, John *33:* 179
Howard, Kim *116:* 71
Howard, Paul *142:* 126, 129; *144:* 187
Howard, Rob *40:* 161
Howarth, Daniel *170:* 34; *222:* 97, 98; *224:* 20; *225:* 77; *234:* 189
Howe, John *79:* 101; *80:* 150; *115:* 47; *176:* 106; *207:* 32, 35
Howe, Phillip *79:* 117; *175:* 115
Howe, Stephen *1:* 232
Howell, Karen *119:* 123
Howell, Pat *15:* 139
Howell, Troy *23:* 24; *31:* 61; *36:* 158; *37:* 184; *41:* 76, 235; *48:* 112; *56:* 13; *57:* 3; *59:* 174; *63:* 5; *74:* 46; *89:* 188; *90:* 231; *95:* 97; *98:* 130; *99:* 189; *153:* 156, 157, 158; *176:* 104; *199:* 96, 98; *222:* 65
Howells, Tania *229:* 87
Howes, Charles *22:* 17
Hoyt, Ard *145:* 141; *190:* 82; *207:* 148
Hranilovich, Barbara *127:* 51
Hu, Ying-Hwa *116:* 107; *152:* 236; *173:* 171
Huang, Benrei *137:* 55
Huang, Zhong-Yang *117:* 30, 32; *213:* 18
Hubbard, Woodleigh Marx *98:* 67; *115:* 79; *160:* 138; *214:* 120
Hubbell, Patricia *222:* 31
Hubley, Faith *48:* 120, 121, 125, 130, 131, 132, 134
Hubley, John *48:* 125, 130, 131, 132, 134
Hudak, Michal *143:* 74
Hudnut, Robin *14:* 62
Huerta, Catherine *76:* 178; *77:* 44, 45; *90:* 182; *210:* 202
Huffaker, Sandy *10:* 56
Huffman, Joan *13:* 33
Huffman, Tom *13:* 180; *17:* 212; *21:* 116; *24:* 132; *33:* 154; *38:* 59; *42:* 147
Hughes, Arthur *20:* 148, 149, 150; *33:* 114, 148, 149
Hughes, Darren *95:* 44
Hughes, David *36:* 197
Hughes, Neal *238:* 142
Hughes, Shirley *1:* 20, 21; *7:* 3; *12:* 217; *16:* 163; *29:* 154; *63:* 118; *70:* 102, 103, 104; *73:* 169; *88:* 70; *110:* 118, 119; *159:* 103
Hugo, Victor *47:* 112
Huliska-Beith, Laura *204:* 108; *220:* 137; *232:* 97, 98
Hull, Cathy *78:* 29
Hull, Richard *95:* 120; *123:* 175; *172:* 195
Hulsmann, Eva *16:* 166
Hume, Lachie *189:* 93
Hummel, Berta *43:* 137, 138, 139
Hummel, Lisl *29:* 109; *YABC 2:* 333, 334
Humphrey, Henry *16:* 167
Humphreys, Graham *25:* 168
Humphries, Tudor *76:* 66; *80:* 4; *124:* 4, 5; *226:* 112
Huneck, Stephen *183:* 88, 89
Hunt, James *2:* 143
Hunt, Jonathan *84:* 120
Hunt, Paul *119:* 104; *129:* 135; *139:* 160; *173:* 112
Hunt, Robert *110:* 206, 235; *147:* 136, 137; *170:* 3; *211:* 76; *226:* 189
Hunt, Scott *190:* 143; *233:* 172
Hunter, Anne *133:* 190; *178:* 150
Huntington, Amy *180:* 99
Hurd, Clement *2:* 148, 149; *64:* 127, 128, 129, 131, 133, 134,135, 136; *100:* 37, 38
Hurd, Peter *24:* 30, 31,; *YABC 2:* 56
Hurd, Thacher *46:* 88, 89; *94:* 114, 115, 116; *123:* 81, 82, 84; *219:* 82
Hurlimann, Ruth *32:* 99
Hurst, Carol Otis *185:* 92
Hurst, Elise *221:* 98
Hurst, Philip *196:* 79
Hurst, Tracey *192:* 238
Hussar, Michael *114:* 113; *117:* 159
Hustler, Tom *6:* 105
Hutchins, Laurence *55:* 22
Hutchins, Pat *15:* 142; *70:* 106, 107, 108; *178:* 131, 132
Hutchinson, Sascha *95:* 211
Hutchinson, William M. *6:* 3, 138; *46:* 70
Hutchison, Paula *23:* 10
Hutton, Clarke *YABC 2:* 335
Hutton, Kathryn *35:* 155; *89:* 91
Hutton, Warwick *20:* 91
Huyette, Marcia *29:* 188
Hyatt, John *54:* 7
Hyatt, Mitch *178:* 162
Hyde, Maureen *82:* 17; *121:* 145, 146
Hyman, David *117:* 64
Hyman, Miles *210:* 132
Hyman, Trina Schart *1:* 204; *2:* 194; *5:* 153; *6:* 106; *7:* 138, 145; *8:* 22; *10:* 196; *13:* 96; *14:* 114; *15:* 204; *16:* 234; *20:* 82; *22:* 133; *24:* 151; *25:* 79, 82; *26:* 82; *29:* 83; *31:* 37, 39; *34:* 104; *38:* 84, 100, 128; *41:* 49; *43:* 146; *46:* 91, 92, 93, 95, 96, 97, 98, 99, 100, 101, 102, 103, 104, 105,108, 109, 111, 197; *48:* 60, 61; *52:* 32; *60:* 168; *66:* 38; *67:* 214; *72:* 74; *75:* 92; *79:* 57; *82:* 95, 238; *89:* 46; *95:* 91, 92, 93; *100:* 33, 199; *132:* 12; *147:* 33, 35, 36; *167:* 58, 60; *177:* 189, 190; *211:* 188; *236:* 128

I

Ibarra, Rosa *147:* 91
Ibatoulline, Bagram *156:* 48; *174:* 33, 82; *202:* 30; *211:* 213; *224:* 84; *225:* 98, 99; *232:* 60; *237:* 163; *239:* 6

Ichikawa, Satomi *29:* 152; *41:* 52; *47:* 133, 134,135, 136; *78:* 93, 94; *80:* 81; *146:* 143, 145, 146; *208:* 117, 118, 119
Ide, Jacqueline *YABC 1:* 39
Idle, Molly Schaar *223:* 95
Ignatow, Amy *233:* 91
Ilsley, Velma *3:* 1; *7:* 55; *12:* 109; *37:* 62; *38:* 184
Imai, Ayano *190:* 85, 86
in den Bosch, Nicole *150:* 204
Inga *1:* 142
Ingman, Bruce *134:* 50; *182:* 91, 92; *214:* 10
Ingpen, Robert *109:* 103, 104; *132:* 138; *137:* 177; *166:* 103; *181:* 140; *229:* 169
Ingraham, Erick *21:* 177; *84:* 256; *103:* 66
Inkpen, Mick *99:* 104, 105; *106:* 44
Innerst, Stacy *149:* 104; *232:* 101, 102
Innocenti, Roberto *21:* 123; *96:* 122; *159:* 111, 197; *199:* 176
Inoue, Yosuke *24:* 118
Iofin, Michael *97:* 157
Iosa, Ann *63:* 189
Ipcar, Dahlov *1:* 124, 125; *49:* 137, 138, 139, 140, 141, 142,143, 144, 145; *147:* 122, 124, 126
Irvin, Fred *13:* 166; *15:* 143, 144; *27:* 175
Irving, Jay *45:* 72
Irving, Laurence *27:* 50
Isaac, Joanne *21:* 76
Isaacs, Gary *170:* 188
Isadora, Rachel *43:* 159, 160; *54:* 31; *79:* 106, 107,108; *121:* 100, 102; *165:* 116, 117; *204:* 61, 63, 64
Ishmael, Woodi *24:* 111; *31:* 99
Isol *220:* 73
Ives, Ruth *15:* 257
Iwai, Melissa *149:* 233; *183:* 92; *199:* 115
Iwamura, Kazuo *213:* 87

J

Jabar, Cynthia *101:* 201; *210:* 134, 135
Jack, Colin *234:* 53
Jackness, Andrew *94:* 237
Jackson, Julian *91:* 104, 106
Jackson, Michael *43:* 42
Jackson, Shelley *79:* 71; *99:* 109; *187:* 82
Jacob, Murv *89:* 30
Jacobi, Kathy *62:* 118
Jacobs, Barbara *9:* 136
Jacobs, Lou, Jr. *9:* 136; *15:* 128
Jacobsen, Laura *176:* 98; *177:* 85, 86
Jacobson, Rick *131:* 222; *170:* 119; *222:* 52
Jacobus, Tim *79:* 140; *109:* 126; *129:* 180
Jacques, Robin *1:* 70; *2:* 1; *8:* 46; *9:* 20; *15:* 187; *19:* 253; *32:* 102, 103, 104; *43:* 184; *73:* 135; *YABC 1:* 42
Jaeggi, Yoshiko *186:* 184
Jaffee, Al *66:* 131, 132
Jago *216:* 122; *240:* 39
Jagr, Miloslav *13:* 197
Jahn-Clough, Lisa *88:* 114; *152:* 104; *193:* 70, 71
Jahnke, Robert *84:* 24
Jainschigg, Nicholas *80:* 64; *91:* 138; *95:* 63; *99:* 25; *108:* 50; *171:* 41
Jakesevic, Nenad *85:* 102; *226:* 215
Jakobsen, Kathy *116:* 83
Jakubowski, Charles *14:* 192
Jambor, Louis *YABC 1:* 11
James, Ann *73:* 50; *82:* 113; *158:* 61; *183:* 44
James, Brian *140:* 91
James, Curtis E. *182:* 93
James, Derek *35:* 187; *44:* 91; *61:* 133; *74:* 2; *80:* 57; *86:* 88; *130:* 30; *179:* 29; *218:* 31
James, Gilbert *YABC 1:* 43
James, Gordon C. *195:* 89
James, Harold *2:* 151; *3:* 62; *8:* 79; *29:* 113; *51:* 195; *74:* 90
James, Kennon *126:* 211
James, Rhian Nest *234:* 63
James, Robin *50:* 106; *53:* 32, 34, 35
James, Simon *202:* 73, 74; *233:* 161
James, Will *19:* 150, 152, 153, 155, 163
Janosch
See Eckert, Horst
Janovitch, Marilyn *68:* 168
Janovitz, Marilyn *87:* 187; *130:* 198; *194:* 91
Jansons, Inese *48:* 117
Jansson, Alexander *216:* 59; *234:* 29
Jansson, Tove *3:* 90; *41:* 106, 108, 109, 110, 111, 113, 114
Jaques, Faith *7:* 11, 132, 133; *21:* 83, 84; *69:* 114,116; *73:* 170
Jaques, Frances Lee *29:* 224
Jarka, Jeff *221:* 94
Jarrett, Clare *201:* 77
Jarrie, Martin *219:* 86
Jauss, Anne Marie *1:* 139; *3:* 34; *10:* 57, 119; *11:* 205; *23:* 194
Jay, Alison *158:* 97, 98; *183:* 126, 127; *196:* 95, 96, 97, 98; *200:* 72, 73, 74; *212:* 39
Jeffers, Oliver *175:* 111; *213:* 89
Jeffers, Susan *17:* 86, 87; *25:* 164, 165; *26:* 112; *50:* 132, 134, 135; *70:* 111, 112, 113; *137:* 107, 108, 109, 110, 111; *202:* 77, 78
Jefferson, Louise E. *4:* 160
Jenkin-Pearce, Susie *78:* 16
Jenkins, Debra Reid *85:* 202; *114:* 89; *173:* 134; *225:* 116
Jenkins, Jean *98:* 79, 102
Jenkins, Leonard *157:* 169; *167:* 128; *189:* 96, 97; *190:* 89
Jenkins, Patrick *72:* 126
Jenkins, Steve *124:* 177; *154:* 90, 91, 92, 93; *185:* 194; *188:* 81, 82, 83, 84, 85, 86; *218:* 67, 69, 70, 71, 72
Jenkins, Ward *238:* 91
Jenks, Aleta *73:* 117; *124:* 225
Jenkyns, Chris *51:* 97
Jensen, Bruce *95:* 39
Jensinius, Kirsten *56:* 58
Jeram, Anita *89:* 135; *102:* 122, 123; *129:* 112; *154:* 96, 97, 98; *164:* 154; *203:* 123, 124; *219:* 88, 89, 90, 91
Jernigan, E. Wesley *85:* 92
Jerome, Elaine *227:* 45
Jerome, Karen A. *72:* 194
Jeruchim, Simon *6:* 173; *15:* 250
Jeschke, Susan *20:* 89; *39:* 161; *41:* 84; *42:* 120
Jessel, Camilla *29:* 115
Jessell, Tim *159:* 3; *177:* 87; *181:* 95; *205:* 4; *213:* 74; *223:* 187; *225:* 102; *226:* 190
Jeyaveeran, Ruth *182:* 100
Jiang, Cheng An *109:* 108
Jiang, Wei *109:* 108
Jimenez, Maria *77:* 158; *93:* 127
Jobling, Curtis *138:* 74
Jocelyn, Marthe *118:* 83; *137:* 219; *163:* 119, 120; *198:* 62
Joerns, Consuelo *38:* 36; *44:* 94
John, Diana *12:* 209
John, Helen *1:* 215; *28:* 204
Johns, Elizabeth *127:* 33
Johns, Jasper *61:* 172
Johns, Jeanne *24:* 114
Johnson, Adrian *143:* 50
Johnson, Bruce *9:* 47
Johnson, Cathy *92:* 136; *218:* 112
Johnson, Crockett
See Leisk, David
Johnson, D. William *23:* 104
Johnson, D.B. *183:* 98, 139
Johnson, David A. *175:* 18; *191:* 91; *218:* 19
Johnson, Gillian *119:* 175; *164:* 217; *215:* 99
Johnson, Harper *1:* 27; *2:* 33; *18:* 302; *19:* 61; *31:* 181; *44:* 46, 50, 95
Johnson, Ingrid *37:* 118
Johnson, James Ralph *1:* 23, 127
Johnson, James David *12:* 195
Johnson, Jane *48:* 136
Johnson, Joel Peter *98:* 18; *128:* 111; *201:* 13; *213:* 189; *234:* 172
Johnson, John E. *34:* 133
Johnson, Kevin *72:* 44
Johnson, Kevin Eugene *109:* 215
Johnson, Larry *47:* 56; *123:* 107; *159:* 203
Johnson, Layne *187:* 94; *209:* 63; *222:* 100, 101; *233:* 123
Johnson, Margaret S. *35:* 131
Johnson, Meredith Merrell *71:* 181; *83:* 158; *89:* 103; *104:* 88
Johnson, Milton *1:* 67; *2:* 71; *26:* 45; *31:* 107; *60:* 112; *68:* 96
Johnson, Pamela *16:* 174; *52:* 145; *62:* 140; *73:* 116; *85:* 64
Johnson, Paul Brett *83:* 95; *132:* 119
Johnson, Stephen T. *80:* 15; *131:* 35; *141:* 96; *145:* 40; *164:* 187; *175:* 32; *189:* 99, 100; *208:* 43
Johnson, Steve *138:* 219; *141:* 64; *144:* 199; *177:* 51; *214:* 95; *221:* 63; *228:* 42, 43, 44; *230:* 44, 45, 46
Johnson, William R. *38:* 91
Johnson-Petrov, Arden *115:* 206
Johnston, David McCall *50:* 131, 133
Johnston, Lynne *118:* 85, 87, 89; *216:* 127, 128, 131
Johnstone, Anne *8:* 120; *36:* 89
Johnstone, Janet Grahame *8:* 120; *36:* 89
Jolivet, Joëlle *231:* 71
Jonas, Ann *50:* 107, 108, 109; *135:* 113
Jones, Bob *71:* 5; *77:* 199
Jones, Carol *5:* 131; *72:* 185, 186; *153:* 111, 112
Jones, Chuck *53:* 70, 71
Jones, Curtis *211:* 144
Jones, Davy *89:* 176
Jones, Douglas B. *185:* 192; *202:* 82
Jones, Elizabeth Orton *18:* 124, 126, 128, 129
Jones, Harold *14:* 88; *52:* 50
Jones, Holly *127:* 3
Jones, Jeff *41:* 64
Jones, Laurian *25:* 24, 27
Jones, Margaret *74:* 57
Jones, Noah Z. *182:* 37; *203:* 159
Jones, Randy *131:* 104
Jones, Richard *127:* 222
Jones, Robert *25:* 67
Jones, Tim *237:* 104
Jones, Wilfred *35:* 115; *YABC 1:* 163
Jordan, Charles *89:* 58
Jordan, Jess *158:* 136; *203:* 111
Jordan, Martin George *84:* 127
Jordan, Richard *84:* 36
Jorgenson, Andrea *91:* 111
Jorisch, Stéphane *153:* 56, 193; *177:* 29; *178:* 138, 139; *187:* 23; *211:* 182
Joseph, James *53:* 88
Josse, Annabelle *234:* 88
Joudrey, Ken *64:* 145; *78:* 6
Joyce, William *72:* 131, 132, 133, 134; *73:* 227; *145:* 37
Joyner, Jerry *34:* 138
Joyner, Loraine M. *209:* 17
Joysmith, Brenda *210:* 237
Juan, Ana *175:* 38; *179:* 111, 112; *213:* 9
Juarez, Fernando *233:* 26
Jucker, Sita *5:* 93
Judge, Lita *192:* 99; *234:* 97
Judkis, Jim *37:* 38
Juhasz, Victor *31:* 67
Julian, Russell *238:* 36
Julian, Sean *236:* 113
Jullian, Philippe *24:* 206; *25:* 203
Jung, Tom *91:* 217
Junge, Alexandra *183:* 37
Junge, Walter *67:* 150

Jupo, Frank *7:* 148, 149
Jurisch, Stephane *154:* 105
Justice, Martin *34:* 72

K

Kabatova-Taborska, Zdenka *107:* 153
Kachik, John *165:* 230
Kaczman, James *156:* 98; *235:* 86
Kadair, Deborah Ousley *184:* 45, 89
Kahl, David *74:* 95; *97:* 35; *109:* 174; *110:* 213; *198:* 15
Kahl, M.P. *37:* 83
Kahl, Virginia *48:* 138
Kahn, Katherine Janus *90:* 135; *211:* 155; *218:* 75, 76; *220:* 89,90
Kakimoo, Kozo *11:* 148
Kalett, Jim *48:* 159, 160, 161
Kalin, Victor *39:* 186
Kalis, Jennifer *207:* 82; *219:* 62
Kalman, Maira *96:* 131, 132; *137:* 115
Kalmenoff, Matthew *22:* 191
Kalow, Gisela *32:* 105
Kamen, Gloria *1:* 41; *9:* 119; *10:* 178; *35:* 157; *78:* 236; *98:* 82
Kaminsky, Jef *102:* 153
Kandell, Alice *35:* 133
Kane, Henry B. *14:* 90; *18:* 219, 220
Kane, Robert *18:* 131
Kanfer, Larry *66:* 141
Kangas, Juli *200:* 88
Kappes, Alfred *28:* 104
Karalus, Bob *41:* 157
Karas, G. Brian *80:* 60; *99:* 179; *115:* 41; *118:* 50; *136:* 168; *145:* 166; *149:* 245; *159:* 65; *171:* 192; *178:* 142, 143; *202:* 38; *209:* 142; *222:* 106, 107, 108, 109; *225:* 62; *235:* 53
Karasz, Ilonka *128:* 163
Karlin, Eugene *10:* 63; *20:* 131
Karlin, Nurit *63:* 78; *103:* 110
Karpinski, Tony *134:* 160
Kasamatsu, Shiro *139:* 155
Kasparavicius, Kestutis *139:* 210
Kassian, Olena *64:* 94
Kastner, Jill *79:* 135; *117:* 84, 85
Kasuya, Masahiro *41:* 206, 207; *51:* 100
Kasza, Keiko *191:* 99, 100, 101, 102, 103
Katona, Robert *21:* 85; *24:* 126
Katz, Avi *199:* 55
Katz, Karen *158:* 123; *232:* 108, 109, 110
Kauffer, E. McKnight *33:* 103; *35:* 127; *63:* 67
Kaufman, Angelika *15:* 156
Kaufman, Joe *33:* 119
Kaufman, John *13:* 158
Kaufman, Stuart *62:* 64; *68:* 226; *137:* 44
Kaufmann, John *1:* 174; *4:* 159; *8:* 43, 1; *10:* 102; *18:* 133, 134; *22:* 251
Kaye, Graham *1:* 9; *67:* 7, 8
Kaye, M.M. *62:* 95
Kazalovski, Nata *40:* 205
Keane, Bil *4:* 135
Kearney, David *72:* 47; *121:* 83
Keating, Pamel T. *77:* 37
Keats, Ezra Jack *3:* 18, 105, 257; *14:* 101, 102; *33:* 129; *57:* 79, 80, 82, 83, 84, 87
Keegan, Charles *166:* 211
Keegan, Marcia *9:* 122; *32:* 93
Keeler, Patricia A. *81:* 56; *183:* 102, 103
Keely, Jack *119:* 95
Keely, John *26:* 104; *48:* 214
Keen, Eliot *25:* 213
Keep, Richard C. *170:* 122
Keeping, Charles *9:* 124, 185; *15:* 28, 134; *18:* 115; *44:* 194, 196; *47:* 25; *52:* 3; *54:* 156; *69:* 123, 124; *74:* 56; *155:* 9
Keeter, Susan *168:* 46; *183:* 192; *237:* 64
Keith, Eros *4:* 98; *5:* 138; *31:* 29; *43:* 220; *52:* 91, 92, 93, 94; *56:* 64, 66; *60:* 37; *79:* 93
Keleinikov, Andrei *65:* 101, 102
Kelen, Emery *13:* 115
Keller, A.J. *62:* 198
Keller, Arthur I. *26:* 106
Keller, Dick *36:* 123, 125
Keller, Holly *45:* 79; *76:* 118, 119, 120, 121; *108:* 137, 138, 140; *157:* 117, 118, 119; *216:* 136
Keller, Katie *79:* 222; *93:* 108
Keller, Laurie *196:* 105, 106
Keller, Ronald *45:* 208
Kelley, Gary *183:* 105; *216:* 78; *217:* 95, 96, 97
Kelley, Marty *211:* 91
Kelley, True *41:* 114, 115; *42:* 137; *75:* 35; *92:* 104, 105; *124:* 62; *130:* 100, 101; *179:* 120, 121, 122; *192:* 251
Kellogg, Steven *8:* 96; *11:* 207; *14:* 130; *20:* ; *201:* 38 58; *29:* 140, 141; *30:* 35; *41:* 141; *57:* 89, 90, 92,93, 94, 96; *59:* 182; *73:* 141; *77:* 129; *130:* 105, 106; *177:* 94, 95, 96, 97; *199:* 57; *217:* 61; *239:* 137 *YABC 1:* 65, 73
Kelly, Billy *158:* 143
Kelly, Geoff *97:* 196; *112:* 25
Kelly, Irene *147:* 134; *210:* 144, 145
Kelly, Jennifer *230:* 137
Kelly, John *194:* 186
Kelly, Joseph *174:* 94
Kelly, Kathleen M. *71:* 109
Kelly, Laura *89:* 217
Kelly, True *163:* 87
Kelly, Walt *18:* 136, 137, 138, 139, 140, 141, 144, 145, 146, 148, 149
Kemble, E.W. *34:* 75; *44:* 178; *YABC 2:* 54, 59
Kemly, Kathleen *209:* 165
Kemp-Welsh, Lucy *24:* 197; *100:* 214
Kendall, Jane *150:* 105; *186:* 109
Kendall, Peter *152:* 85
Kendrick, Dennis *79:* 213
Kennaway, Adrienne *60:* 55, 56; *171:* 88, 89
Kennedy, Anne *212:* 34
Kennedy, Doug *189:* 104; *241:* 79
Kennedy, Paul Edward *6:* 190; *8:* 132; *33:* 120
Kennedy, Richard *3:* 93; *12:* 179; *44:* 193; *100:* 15; *YABC 1:* 57
Kent, Jack *24:* 136; *37:* 37; *40:* 81; *84:* 89; *86:* 150; *88:* 77
Kent, Rockwell *5:* 166; *6:* 129; *20:* 225, 226, 227,229; *59:* 144
Kenyon, Tony *81:* 201; *127:* 74; *231:* 86
Kepes, Juliet *13:* 119
Kerins, Anthony *76:* 84
Kerr, Judity *24:* 137
Kerr, Phyllis Forbes *72:* 141
Kessler, Leonard *1:* 108; *7:* 139; *14:* 107, 227; *22:* 101; *44:* 96; *67:* 79; *82:* 123
Kest, Kristin *168:* 99; *173:* 23
Kesteven, Peter *35:* 189
Ketcham, Hank *28:* 140, 141, 142
Kettelkamp, Larry *2:* 164
Key, Alexander *8:* 99
Khalsa, Dayal Kaur *62:* 99
Kiakshuk *8:* 59
Kid, Tom *207:* 54
Kidd, Chip *94:* 23
Kidd, Richard *152:* 110
Kidd, Tom *64:* 199; *81:* 189; *185:* 173
Kiddell-Monroe, Joan *19:* 201; *55:* 59, 60; *87:* 174; *121:* 112
Kidder, Harvey *9:* 105; *80:* 41
Kidwell, Carl *43:* 145
Kieffer, Christa *41:* 89
Kiesler, Kate *110:* 105; *136:* 142
Kiff, Ken *40:* 45
Kilaka, John *223:* 107
Kilbride, Robert *37:* 100
Kilby, Don *141:* 144
Killen, Nicola *236:* 115
Kim, David *201:* 79; *202:* 97
Kim, Glenn *99:* 82
Kimball, Anton *78:* 114; *119:* 105
Kimball, Yeffe *23:* 116; *37:* 88
Kimber, Murray *171:* 91
Kimmel, Warren *176:* 112
Kincade, Orin *34:* 116
Kindersley, Barnabas *96:* 110
Kindred, Wendy *7:* 151
King, Colin *53:* 3
King, Robin *10:* 164, 165
King, Stephen Michael *141:* 31; *197:* 191; *218:* 81, 82
King, Tara Calahan *139:* 172
King, Tony *39:* 121
Kingman, Dong *16:* 287; *44:* 100, 102, 104
Kingsley, Charles *YABC 2:* 182
Kingston, Julie *147:* 14
Kingston, Maxine Hong *53:* 92
Kinney, Jeff *187:* 97
Kipling, John Lockwood *YABC 2:* 198
Kipling, Rudyard *YABC 2:* 196
Kipniss, Robert *29:* 59
Kirchherr, Astrid *55:* 23
Kirchhoff, Art *28:* 136
Kirk, Daniel *153:* 115, 116, 117; *173:* 101; *196:* 113, 114, 115, 116
Kirk, David *117:* 88, 89; *161:* 97, 98
Kirk, Ruth *5:* 96
Kirk, Steve *170:* 37
Kirk, Tim *32:* 209, 211; *72:* 89; *83:* 49
Kirmse, Marguerite *15:* 283; *18:* 153
Kirsch, Vincent X. *124:* 207
Kirschner, Ruth *22:* 154
Kirwan, Wednesday *198:* 73
Kish, Ely *73:* 119; *79:* 2
Kitamura, Satoshi *62:* 102; *98:* 91; *101:* 147; *138:* 2; *143:* 83, 85, 86; *201:* 83; *223:* 3, 4
Kiss, Andrew *168:* 115
Kitchel, JoAnn E. *133:* 32
Kitchen, Bert *70:* 126; *193:* 49
Kittelsen, Theodor *62:* 14
Kiuchi, Tatsuro *114:* 71
Kiwak, Barbara *172:* 135
Klahr, Susan *176:* 196
Klapholz, Mel *13:* 35
Klassen, J. *234:* 196
Klee, Jutte *209:* 136
Klein, Bill *89:* 105
Klein, Robert *55:* 77
Klein, Suzanna *63:* 104
Kleinman, Zalman *28:* 143
Kleven, Elisa *173:* 96, 97; *217:* 100, 102
Kliban, B. *35:* 137, 138
Kline, Michael *127:* 66
Klinger, Shula *230:* 55
Klise, M. Sarah *180:* 117, 118; *181:* 97; *221:* 100, 102; *235:* 117, 118
Knabel, Lonnie *73:* 103; *75:* 187, 228; *194:* 216
Kneen, Maggie *140:* 139; *221:* 104, 105
Knight, Ann *34:* 143
Knight, Christopher *13:* 125
Knight, Hilary *1:* 233; *3:* 21; *15:* 92, 158, 159; *16:* 258, 259, 260; *18:* 235; *19:* 169; *35:* 242; *46:* 167; *52:* 116; *69:* 126, 127; *132:* 129; *YABC 1:* 168, 169, 172
Knorr, Laura *200:* 91
Knorr, Peter *126:* 92, 93
Knotts, Howard *20:* 4; *25:* 170; *36:* 163
Knutson, Barbara *112:* 134; *202:* 108
Knutson, Kimberley *115:* 90
Kobayashi, Ann *39:* 58
Kober, Shahar *240:* 40
Kochalka, James *196:* 120, 121, 122
Kocsis, J.C.
See Paul, James
Kodman, Stanislawa *201:* 85; *224:* 72
Koehler, Hanne Lore *176:* 203
Koehn, Ilse *34:* 198; *79:* 123
Koelsch, Michael *99:* 182; *107:* 164; *109:* 239; *138:* 142; *150:* 94; *176:* 105; *187:* 63; *198:* 63; *230:* 204

Koering, Ursula *3:* 28; *4:* 14; *44:* 5; *64:* 140,141; *85:* 46
Koerner, Henry
See Koerner, W.H.D.
Koerner, W.H.D. *14:* 216; *21:* 88, 89, 90, 91; *23:* 211
Koetsch, Mike *166:* 68
Koffler, Camilla *36:* 113
Kogan, Deborah Ray *161:* 101, 102
Koide, Yasuko *50:* 114
Kolado, Karen *102:* 228
Kolesova, Juliana *217:* 81; *222:* 185; *229:* 183; *237:* 16; *239:* 173
Komarck, Michael *227:* 48
Komoda, Kiyo *9:* 128; *13:* 214
Kompaneyets, Marc *169:* 92
Konashevich, Vladimir *61:* 160
Konashevicha, V. *YABC 1:* 26
Konigsburg, E.L. *4:* 138; *48:* 141, 142, 144, 145; *94:* 129, 130; *126:* 129, 130, 131; *194:* 95, 98
Kono, Erin Eitter *177:* 99
Kooiker, Leonie *48:* 148
Koonook, Simon *65:* 157
Koontz, Robin Michal *136:* 155
Koopmans, Loek *101:* 121
Kopelke, Lisa *154:* 107
Kopper, Lisa *72:* 152, 153; *105:* 135, 136
Korach, Mimi *1:* 128, 129; *2:* 52; *4:* 39; *5:* 159; *9:* 129; *10:* 21; *24:* 69
Koren, Edward *5:* 100; *65:* 65, 67
Kosaka, Fumi *164:* 130
Koscielniak, Bruce *99:* 122; *153:* 120, 121, 122
Koshkin, Alexander *92:* 180
Kossin, Sandy *10:* 71; *23:* 105
Kostin, Andrej *26:* 204
Kosturko, Bob *164:* 56
Kotzky, Brian *68:* 184
Kovacevic, Zivojin *13:* 247
Kovalski, Maryann *58:* 120; *84:* 88; *97:* 124, 125, 126; *158:* 3; *186:* 80
Kozjan, Drazen *209:* 99; *231:* 130; *236:* 28
Krahn, Fernando *2:* 257; *34:* 206; *49:* 152
Krall, Dan *218:* 84, 85
Kramek, Oren *231:* 119
Kramer, Anthony *33:* 81
Kramer, David *96:* 162; *109:* 132; *150:* 220
Kramer, Frank *6:* 121
Krantz, Kathy *35:* 83
Kratter, Paul *139:* 65
Kraus, Robert *13:* 217; *65:* 113; *93:* 93, 94
Krause, Jon *176:* 62
Krauss, Trisha *174:* 10
Kredel, Fritz *6:* 35; *17:* 93, 94, 95, 96; *22:* 147; *24:* 175; *29:* 130; *35:* 77; *YABC 2:* 166, 300
Kreloff, Eliot *189:* 107, 108; *205:* 182
Krementz, Jill *17:* 98; *49:* 41
Krenina, Katya *117:* 106; *125:* 133; *176:* 117; *221:* 107
Kresin, Robert *23:* 19
Kretschmar, Sonia *226:* 97
Krieger, Salem *54:* 164
Kriegler, Lyn *73:* 29
Krinitz, Esther Nisenthal *193:* 196
Krommes, Beth *128:* 141; *149:* 136; *181:* 100, 101; *184:* 105; *188:* 125; *208:* 135; *209:* 185
Krone, Mike *101:* 71
Kronheimer, Ann *135:* 119
Krosoczka, Jarrett J. *155:* 142; *200:* 93, 94
Kruck, Gerald *88:* 181
Krudop, Walter Lyon *199:* 19
Krug, Nora *240:* 80, 125
Krupinski, Loretta *67:* 104; *102:* 131; *161:* 105, 106
Krupp, Robin Rector *53:* 96, 98
Krush, Beth *1:* 51, 85; *2:* 233; *4:* 115; *9:* 61; *10:* 191; *11:* 196; *18:* 164, 165; *32:* 72; *37:* 203; *43:* 57; *60:* 102, 103, 107, 108, 109
Krush, Joe *2:* 233; *4:* 115; *9:* 61; *10:* 191; *11:* 196; *18:* 164, 165; *32:* 72, 91; *37:* 203; *43:* 57; *60:* 102, 103, 107, 108, 109
Krych, Duane *91:* 43
Krykorka, Vladyana *96:* 147; *143:* 90, 91; *168:* 14
Kubick, Dana *165:* 91; *212:* 104, 105, 212
Kubinyi, Laszlo *4:* 116; *6:* 113; *16:* 118; *17:* 100; *28:* 227; *30:* 172; *49:* 24, 28; *54:* 23; *167:* 149
Kubricht, Mary *73:* 118
Kucharik, Elena *139:* 31
Kuchera, Kathleen *84:* 5
Kuhn, Bob *17:* 91; *35:* 235
Kulikov, Boris *163:* 185; *185:* 23; *205:* 99, 100; *217:* 160; *235:* 190
Kulka, Joe *188:* 110
Kukalis, Romas *90:* 27; *139:* 37
Kuklin, Susan *63:* 82, 83, 84
Kunhardt, Dorothy *53:* 101
Kunhardt, Edith *67:* 105, 106
Kunstler, Mort *10:* 73; *32:* 143
Kurchevsky, V. *34:* 61
Kurczok, Belinda *121:* 118
Kurelek, William *8:* 107
Kuriloff, Ron *13:* 19
Kurisu, Jane *160:* 120
Kurilla, Renée *231:* 117
Kuskin, Karla *2:* 170; *68:* 115, 116; *111:* 116
Kutzer, Ernst *19:* 249
Kuzma, Steve *57:* 8; *62:* 93
Kuznetsova, Berta *74:* 45
Kvasnosky, Laura McGee *93:* 103; *142:* 83; *182:* 108
Kwas, Susan Estelle *179:* 116; *217:* 90
Kyong, Yunmee *165:* 139

L

LaBlanc, Andre *24:* 146
Laboccetta, Mario *27:* 120
LaBrose, Darcie *157:* 134
Labrosse, Darcia *58:* 88; *108:* 77; *178:* 89; *236:* 126
LaCava, Vince *95:* 118
Laceky, Adam *32:* 121
Lacis, Astra *85:* 117
Lacome, Julie *174:* 96, 97
La Croix *YABC 2:* 4
Ladd, London *206:* 50
Ladwig, Tim *98:* 212; *117:* 76; *215:* 32; *223:* 111, 112
La Farge, Margaret *47:* 141
LaFave, Kim *64:* 177; *72:* 39; *97:* 146; *99:* 172; *106:* 123; *149:* 126; *196:* 128, 129
Lafontaine, Roger *167:* 158
Lafrance, Marie *197:* 109
Lagarrigue, Jerome *136:* 102; *187:* 81
Laimgruber, Monika *11:* 153
Laínez, René Colato *226:* 50
Laio, Jimmy *213:* 57
Laite, Gordon *1:* 130, 131; *8:* 209; *31:* 113; *40:* 63; *46:* 117
Laliberté, Louise-Andrée *169:* 98
LaMarche, Jim *46:* 204; *61:* 56; *94:* 69; *114:* 22; *129:* 163; *162:* 78, 80; *239:* 61, 72, 73, 74, 75
Lamb, Jim *10:* 117
Lambase, Barbara *101:* 185; *150:* 221; *166:* 234
Lambert, J.K. *38:* 129; *39:* 24
Lambert, Sally Anne *133:* 191
Lambert, Saul *23:* 112; *33:* 107; *54:* 136
Lambert, Stephen *109:* 33; *174:* 99
Lambo, Don *6:* 156; *35:* 115; *36:* 146
Lamont, Priscilla *236:* 182
Lamontagne, Jacques *166:* 227
Lamut, Sonja *57:* 193; *85:* 102; *241:* 85
Landa, Peter *11:* 95; *13:* 177; *53:* 119
Landau, Jacob *38:* 111
Landis, Joan *104:* 23; *203:* 32; *235:* 33
Landon, Lucinda *79:* 31
Landshoff, Ursula *13:* 124
Landström, Lena *146:* 165, 166
Landström, Olof *146:* 166, 168; *170:* 22; *232:* 22
Lane, Daniel *112:* 60
Lane, John R. *8:* 145
Lane, John *15:* 176, 177; *30:* 146
Lane, Nancy *166:* 74
Lang, G.D. *48:* 56
Lang, Gary *73:* 75
Lang, Glenna *221:* 113
Leng, Qin *239:* 162; *240:* 89
Lang, Jerry *18:* 295
Langdo, Bryan *186:* 187; *191:* 113, 114, 115; *233:* 98, 100
Lange, Dorothea *50:* 141
Langley, Jonathan *162:* 128
Langner, Nola *8:* 110; *42:* 36
Lanino, Deborah *105:* 148
Lantz, Paul *1:* 82, 102; *27:* 88; *34:* 102; *45:* 123
Larkin, Bob *84:* 225
Laroche, Giles *126:* 140; *146:* 81; *221:* 116, 117
LaRochelle, David *171:* 97
Larrañaga, Ana Martín *229:* 106
Larrecq, John *44:* 108; *68:* 56
Larsen, Suzanne *1:* 13
Larson, Gary *57:* 121, 122, 123, 124, 125, 126, 127
Larsson, Carl *35:* 144, 145, 146, 147, 148, 149, 150, 152, 153, 154
Larsson, Karl *19:* 177
Lartitegui, Ana G. *105:* 167
LaRue, Jenna *167:* 20
La Rue, Michael D. *13:* 215
Lasker, Joe *7:* 186, 187; *14:* 55; *38:* 115; *39:* 47; *83:* 113, 114, 115
Latham, Barbara *16:* 188, 189; *43:* 71
Lathrop, Dorothy *14:* 117, 118, 119; *15:* 109; *16:* 78, 79, 81; *32:* 201, 203; *33:* 112; *YABC 2:* 301
Latimer, Miriam *234:* 205; *235:* 122
Lattimore, Eleanor Frances *7:* 156
Lauden, Claire *16:* 173
Lauden, George, Jr. *16:* 173
Laune, Paul *2:* 235; *34:* 31
Laure, Jason *49:* 53; *50:* 122
Lauter, Richard *63:* 29; *67:* 111; *77:* 198
Lavallee, Barbara *74:* 157; *92:* 154; *96:* 126; *145:* 193; *166:* 125, 126; *186:* 155; *192:* 172; *231:* 165; *232:* 131
Lave, Fitz Hugh *59:* 139
Lavis, Steve *43:* 143; *87:* 137, 164, 165; *222:* 161; *225:* 121
Layton, Neal *152:* 120, 121; *182:* 65; *187:* 103, 105, 106
Law, Jenny *201:* 31
Lawrason, June *168:* 30
Lawrence, John *25:* 131; *30:* 141; *44:* 198, 200; *214:* 7
Lawrence, Stephen *20:* 195
Lawson, Carol *6:* 38; *42:* 93, 131; *174:* 56; *189:* 89; *209:* 59
Lawson, George *17:* 280
Lawson, Robert *5:* 26; *6:* 94; *13:* 39; *16:* 11; *20:* 100, 102, 103; *54:* 3; *66:* 12; *100:* 144, 145; *YABC 2:* 222, 224, 225, 227, 228, 229, 230, 231, 232, 233, 234, 235, 237, 238, 239, 240, 241
Layfield, Kathie *60:* 194
Lazare, Jerry *44:* 109; *74:* 28
Lazarevich, Mila *17:* 118
Lazarus, Claire *103:* 30
Lazarus, Keo Felker *21:* 94
Lazzaro, Victor *11:* 126
Lea, Bob *166:* 208; *203:* 108
Lea, Tom *43:* 72, 74

Leacroft, Richard *6:* 140
Leaf, Munro *20:* 99
Leake, Donald *70:* 41
Leander, Patricia *23:* 27
Lear, Edward *18:* 183, 184, 185
Lear, Rebecca *149:* 46
Lebenson, Richard *6:* 209; *7:* 76; *23:* 145; *44:* 191; *87:* 153
Le Cain, Errol *6:* 141; *9:* 3; *22:* 142; *25:* 198; *28:* 173; *68:* 128, 129; *86:* 49
Lechon, Daniel *113:* 211
Leder, Dora *129:* 172
Ledger, Bill *181:* 58
Leduc, Bernard *102:* 36
Lee, Alan *62:* 25, 28
Lee, Bryce *99:* 60; *101:* 195; *196:* 53
Lee, Chinlun *181:* 138; *182:* 112
Lee, Declan *191:* 20
Lee, Dom *83:* 118, 120; *93:* 123; *121:* 121, 126; *146:* 174, 175, 206, 207; *174:* 204
Lee, Doris *13:* 246; *32:* 183; *44:* 111
Lee, Hector Viveros *115:* 96
Lee, Ho Baek *200:* 160
Lee, Huy Voun *217:* 106
Lee, Jeanne M. *158:* 56
Lee, Jared *93:* 200; *157:* 229; *215:* 113, 191, 192, 193; *228:* 177
Lee, Jody *81:* 121; *82:* 225; *91:* 155; *100:* 182
Lee, Jody A. *127:* 124, 126, 127
See also Lee, Jody
Lee, Manning de V. *2:* 200; *17:* 12; *27:* 87; *37:* 102, 103, 104; *YABC 2:* 304
Lee, Margaret *213:* 179
Lee, Marie G. *138:* 157
Lee, Paul *97:* 100; *105:* 72, 209; *109:* 177; *128:* 113; *202:* 45
Lee, Robert J. *3:* 97; *67:* 124
Lee, Victor *96:* 228; *105:* 182; *140:* 196; *208:* 191
Lee, Virginia *208:* 139, 140; *218:* 28
Leech, Dorothy *98:* 76
Leech, John *15:* 59
Leedy, Loreen *84:* 142; *128:* 144, 145, 146; *175:* 125, 126, 127; *238:* 100, 101, 102
Leeman, Michael *44:* 157
Leeming, Catherine *87:* 39
Lees, Harry *6:* 112
LeFever, Bill *88:* 220, 221
Legenisel *47:* 111
Legrand, Edy *18:* 89, 93
Lehman, Barbara *73:* 123; *170:* 130
Lehrman, Rosalie *2:* 180
Leichman, Seymour *5:* 107
Leick, Bonnie *205:* 104
Leighton, Clare *25:* 130; *33:* 168; *37:* 105, 106, 108,109
Leisk, David *1:* 140, 141; *11:* 54; *30:* 137, 142, 143,144
Leister, Bryan *89:* 45; *106:* 37; *114:* 67; *149:* 236; *222:* 181; *237:* 142
Leloir, Maurice *18:* 77, 80, 83, 99
Lemaître, Pascal *144:* 175; *176:* 130; *189:* 135; *225:* 124, 125
Lemieux, Michele *100:* 148; *139:* 153
Lemke, Horst *14:* 98; *38:* 117, 118, 119
Lemke, R.W. *42:* 162
Lemon, David Gwynne *9:* 1
LeMoult, Adolph *82:* 116
Lenn, Michael *136:* 89
Lennon, John *114:* 100
Lennox, Elsie *95:* 163; *143:* 160
Lenski, Lois *1:* 144; *26:* 135, 137, 139, 141; *100:* 153, 154
Lent, Blair *1:* 116, 117; *2:* 174; *3:* 206, 207; *7:* 168, 169; *34:* 62; *68:* 217; *133:* 101; *183:* 60
Leon, Jana *226:* 214
Leonard, David *212:* 149
Leonard, Richard *91:* 128
Leonard, Tom *207:* 95; *219:* 55
Leone, Leonard *49:* 190
Lerner, Carol *86:* 140, 141, 142
Lerner, Judith *116:* 138
Lerner, Sharon *11:* 157; *22:* 56
Leroux-Hugon, Helene *132:* 139
Leslie, Cecil *19:* 244
Lessac, Frané *80:* 182, 207; *96:* 182; *202:* 58; *209:* 104
Lessing, Erich *167:* 52; *173:* 60
Lester, Alison *50:* 124; *90:* 147, 148; *129:* 130; *218:* 91, 93
Lester, Mike *208:* 50
Lethcoe, Jason *191:* 116, 117
Le Tord, Bijou *49:* 156; *95:* 112
Leutz, Emanuel *165:* 27
Levai, Blaise *39:* 130
Levert, Mireille *211:* 101
Levin, Ted *12:* 148
Levine, David *43:* 147, 149, 150, 151, 152; *64:* 11
Levine, Joe *71:* 88; *219:* 74
Levine, Marge *81:* 127
Levinson, David *178:* 232
Levit, Herschel *24:* 223
Levstek, Ljuba *131:* 192; *134:* 216; *149:* 65; *168:* 180
Levy, Jessica Ann *19:* 225; *39:* 191
Levy, Lina *117:* 126
Lewin, Betsy *32:* 114; *48:* 177; *90:* 151; *91:* 125; *92:* 85; *115:* 105; *169:* 110, 111; *178:* 47; *186:* 188; *194:* 201; *222:* 120; *226:* 139
Lewin, Ted *4:* 77; *8:* 168; *20:* 110; *21:* 99,100; *27:* 110; 28; 96, 97; *31:* 49; *45:* 55; *48:* 223; *60:* 20, 119, 120; *62:* 139; *66:* 108; *71:* 12; *72:* 21; *74:* 226; *76:* 139, 140; *77:* 82; *79:* 87; *85:* 49, 177; *86:* 55; *88:* 182; *93:* 28, 29; *94:* 34, 182, 194; *99:* 156; *104:* 8; *115:* 123; *118:* 74; *119:* 114, 116; *131:* 54; *145:* 99; *165:* 151; *177:* 75; *178:* 42; *190:* 30; *192:* 86; *195:* 101, 102; *203:* 52; *222:* 119; *226:* 136, 137, 138, 139; *238:* 135
Lewis, Allen *15:* 112
Lewis, Anthony *227:* 114
Lewis, E.B. *88:* 143; *93:* 109; *119:* 79; *124:* 113; *128:* 49; *151:* 167; *168:* 110; *173:* 121; *174:* 66; *176:* 7; *184:* 150; *185:* 191; *211:* 108, 109, 110, 111; *223:* 17
Lewis, H.B. *170:* 124
Lewis, J. Patrick *162:* 83
Lewis, Jan *81:* 22
Lewis, Kim *136:* 165; *217:* 109, 111
Lewis, Richard W. *52:* 25
Lewis, Robin Baird *98:* 193
Lew-Vriethoff, Joanne *225:* 181
Leydon, Rita Floden *21:* 101
Li, Xiojun *187:* 172
Liao, Jimmy *202:* 100
Lichtenheld, Tom *152:* 125, 126; *222:* 160; *224:* 9
Lieblich, Irene *22:* 173; *27:* 209, 214
Lieder, Rick *108:* 197; *199:* 58, 59, 60
Lies, Brian *92:* 40; *141:* 101; *150:* 138; *190:* 97, 98, 99,
Liese, Charles *4:* 222
Liew, Sonny *219:* 108
Life, Kay *79:* 49
Lifton, Robert Jay *66:* 154
Lightburn, Ron *86:* 153; *91:* 122
Lightfoot, Norman R. *45:* 47
Lignell, Lois *37:* 114
Lill, Debra *121:* 70
Lilly, Charles *8:* 73; *20:* 127; *48:* 53; *72:* 9,16; *77:* 98; *102:* 94
Lilly, Ken *37:* 224
Lim, John *43:* 153
Limona, Mercedes *51:* 183
Lin, Grace *143:* 217; *162:* 86, 87; *174:* 185
Lincoln, Patricia Henderson *27:* 27; *78:* 127
Lindahn, Ron *84:* 17
Lindahn, Val *84:* 17
Lindberg, Howard *10:* 123; *16:* 190
Lindberg, Jeffrey *64:* 77; *77:* 71; *79:* 54; *80:* 149; *174:* 109; *179:* 52
Linden, Seymour *18:* 200, 201; *43:* 140
Lindenbaum, Pija *144:* 143; *183:* 113
Linder, Richard *27:* 119
Lindman, Maj *43:* 154
Lindsay, Norman *67:* 114
Lindsay, Vachel *40:* 118
Lindstrom, Jack *145:* 118
Line, Les *27:* 143
Linell
See Smith, Linell
Lintern, Tom *228:* 101
Lionni, Leo *8:* 115; *72:* 159, 160, 161
Lipinsky, Lino *2:* 156; *22:* 175
Lippincott, Gary A. *70:* 35; *119:* 118; *220:* 105, 106, 107
Lippman, Peter *8:* 31; *31:* 119, 120, 160
Lisi, Victoria *89:* 145
Lisker, Emily *169:* 114
Lisker, Sonia O. *16:* 274; *31:* 31; *44:* 113, 114
Lisowski, Gabriel *47:* 144; *49:* 157
Lissim, Simon *17:* 138
Little, Ed *89:* 145; *151:* 53
Little, Harold *16:* 72
Little, Mary E. *28:* 146
Littlewood, Karen *165:* 126; *211:* 112
Litty, Julie *111:* 63
Litwin, Mike *235:* 59, 136
Litzinger, Rosanne *151:* 101; *176:* 118; *196:* 133, 134, 135; *208:* 129; *209:* 147
Liu, Lesley *143:* 72
Livesly, Lorna *19:* 216
Livingston, Susan *95:* 22
Liwska, Renata *164:* 113; *199:* 25, 69; *220:* 79; *240:* 90, 91, 92
Ljungkvist, Laura *180:* 120
Llerena, Carlos Antonio *19:* 181
Lloyd, Errol *11:* 39; *22:* 178
Lloyd, Megan *77:* 118; *80:* 113; *97:* 75; *117:* 94, 95; *189:* 121, 122; *208:* 128; *211:* 72; *239:* 87, 88, 89
Lloyd, Sam *183:* 116, 117
Lo, Beth *165:* 154
Lo, Koon-chiu *7:* 134
Loates, Glen *63:* 76
Lobel, Anita *6:* 87; *9:* 141; *18:* 248; *55:* 85,86, 87, 88, 93, 104; *60:* 67; *78:* 263; *82:* 110; *96:* 157, 159; *101:* 84; *132:* 35; *162:* 93, 94; *241:* 90, 91, 92, 93
Lobel, Arnold *1:* 188, 189; *5:* 12; *6:* 147; *7:* 167, 209; *18:* 190, 191; *25:* 39, 43; *27:* 40; *29:* 174; *52:* 127; *55:* 89, 91, 94, 95, 97, 98, 99, 100, 101, 102,103, 105, 106; *60:* 18, 31; *66:* 181, 183; *75:* 57; *82:* 246; *136:* 146
Lobel, Gillian *190:* 21
Lobo, Jen *229:* 53
Locker, Thomas *109:* 134
Lodge, Bernard *107:* 125, 126; *153:* 93
Loeb, Jeph *153:* 177
Lodge, Jo *112:* 119
Loefgren, Ulf *3:* 108
Loescher, Ann *20:* 108
Loescher, Gil *20:* 108
Loew, David *93:* 184; *171:* 120; *211:* 187
Lofting, Hugh *15:* 182, 183; *100:* 161, 162
Lofts, Pamela *60:* 188
Loh, George *38:* 88
Lomberg, Jon *58:* 160
Lonette, Reisie *11:* 211; *12:* 168; *13:* 56; *36:* 122; *43:* 155
Long, Ethan *168:* 146; *178:* 12; *182:* 120, 121; *196:* 124; *223:* 116, 117; *235:* 127; *239:* 102
Long, Laurel *162:* 135; *190:* 11; *203:* 113, 114; *228:* 212
Long, Loren *99:* 176; *172:* 65; *182:* 78; *188:* 114, 115; *239:* 82
Long, Melinda *152:* 128
Long, Miles *115:* 174
Long, Sally *42:* 184
Long, Sylvia *74:* 168; *132:* 63; *179:* 134

Longoni, Eduardo *73:* 85
Longtemps, Ken *17:* 123; *29:* 221; *69:* 82
Looser, Heinz *YABC 2:* 208
Lopez, Loretta *190:* 100
López, Rafael *197:* 160; *198:* 85
Lopshire, Robert *6:* 149; *21:* 117; *34:* 166; *73:* 13; *233:* 103
Lord, John Vernon *21:* 104; *23:* 25; *51:* 22
Lorenz, Albert *40:* 146; *115:* 127
Lorenzen, Geoffrey *229:* 24
Loretta, Sister Mary *33:* 73
Lorraine, Walter H. *3:* 110; *4:* 123; *16:* 192; *103:* 119
Los, Marek *146:* 22; *193:* 23
Loss, Joan *11:* 163
Louderback, Walt *YABC 1:* 164
Loughridge, Stuart *214:* 131
Louis, Catherine *212:* 186
Lousada, Sandra *40:* 138
Louth, Jack *149:* 252; *151:* 191, 192
Love, Judy *173:* 43; *196:* 40; *235:* 24
Lovelock, Brian *214:* 132, 197
Low, Joseph *14:* 124, 125; *18:* 68; *19:* 194; *31:* 166; *80:* 239
Low, William *62:* 175; *80:* 147; *112:* 194; *150:* 202; *169:* 175; *177:* 110; *192:* 27
Lowe, Vicky *177:* 130
Lowenheim, Alfred *13:* 65, 66
Lowenstein, Sallie *116:* 90, 91
Lowery, Mike *227:* 115
Lowitz, Anson *17:* 124; *18:* 215
Lowrey, Jo *8:* 133
Loxton, Daniel *229:* 109
Lubach, Vanessa *142:* 152
Lubell, Winifred *1:* 207; *3:* 15; *6:* 151
Lubin, Leonard B. *19:* 224; *36:* 79, 80; *45:* 128, 129,131, 132, 133, 134, 135, 136, 137, 139, 140, 141; *70:* 95; *YABC2:* 96
Lucas, David *208:* 148
Lucht, Irmgard *82:* 145
Ludwig, Helen *33:* 144, 145
Luebs, Robin *212:* 109
Lufkin, Raymond *38:* 138; *44:* 48
Luhrs, Henry *7:* 123; *11:* 120
Lujan, Tonita *82:* 33
Lum, Bernice *230:* 70
Lupo, Dom *4:* 204
Lustig, Loretta *30:* 186; *46:* 134, 135, 136, 137
Lutes, Jason *210:* 163
Luthardt, Kevin *172:* 125, 126; *217:* 2
Luxbacher, Irene *153:* 145; *219:* 112, 113
Luzak, Dennis *52:* 121; *99:* 142
Lydbury, Jane *82:* 98
Lydecker, Laura *21:* 113; *42:* 53
Lynch, Charles *16:* 33
Lynch, Marietta *29:* 137; *30:* 171
Lynch, P.J. *126:* 228; *129:* 110; *132:* 247; *183:* 64; *207:* 184; *213:* 100, 101, 102; *237:* 164
Lyne, Alison Davis *188:* 118, 198
Lyon, Carol *102:* 26
Lyon, Elinor *6:* 154
Lyon, Fred *14:* 16
Lyon, Lea *212:* 110
Lyon, Tammie *175:* 170
Lyons, Oren *8:* 193
Lyster, Michael *26:* 41

M

Maas, Dorothy *6:* 175
Maas, Julie *47:* 61
Macaulay, David *46:* 139, 140, 141, 142, 143, 144, 145, 147, 149, 150; *72:* 167, 168, 169; *137:* 129, 130, 131, 132
MacCarthy, Patricia *69:* 141
Macdonald, Alister *21:* 55
Macdonald, Roberta *19:* 237; *52:* 164
MacDonald, Norman *13:* 99
MacDonald, Ross *201:* 103
MacDonald, Suse *54:* 41; *109* 138; *130:* 156; *193:* 106, 107, 109, 110
Mace, Varian *49:* 159
MacEachern, Stephen *206:* 2
Macguire, Robert Reid *18:* 67
Machetanz, Fredrick *34:* 147, 148
MacInnes, Cat *236:* 51
MacInnes, Ian *35:* 59
MacIntyre, Elisabeth *17:* 127, 128
Mack, Jeff *161:* 128; *194:* 119, 120; *219:* 67; *225:* 135
Mack, Stan *17:* 129; *96:* 33
Mack, Steve *241:* 96
Mackay, Donald *17:* 60
MacKaye, Arvia *32:* 119
Mackenzie, Robert *204:* 78
Mackenzie, Stuart *73:* 213
MacKenzie, Garry *33:* 159
Mackie, Clare *87:* 134
Mackinlay, Miguel *27:* 22
MacKinstry, Elizabeth *15:* 110; *42:* 139, 140, 141, 142, 143,144, 145
MacLeod, Lee *91:* 167
Maclise, Daniel *YABC 2:* 257
Macnaughton, Tina *182:* 145; *218:* 106, 107
MacRae, Tom *181:* 112
Madden, Don *3:* 112, 113; *4:* 33, 108, 155; *7:* 193; *78:* 12; *YABC 2:* 211
Maddison, Angela Mary *10:* 83
Madrid, Erwin *229:* 117
Madsen, Jim *146:* 259; *152:* 237; *184:* 106; *197:* 21; *202:* 103, 104; *233:* 38
Maestro, Giulio *8:* 124; *12:* 17; *13:* 108; *25:* 182; *54:* 147; *59:* 114, 115, 116, 117, 118, 121, 123, 124, 125,126, 127; *68:* 37, 38; *106:* 129, 130, 131, 136, 137, 138
Maffia, Daniel *60:* 200
Maggio, Viqui *58:* 136, 181; *74:* 150; *75:* 90; *85:* 159; *90:* 158; *109:* 184; *193:* 113
Magnus, Erica *77:* 123
Magnuson, Diana *28:* 102; *34:* 190; *41:* 175
Magoon, Scott *181:* 104; *217:* 165; *222:* 126
Magovern, Peg *103:* 123; *218:* 164
Maguire, Sheila *41:* 100
Magurn, Susan *91:* 30
Mahony, Will *37:* 120
Mahony, Will *85:* 116
Mahood, Kenneth *24:* 141
Mahurin, Matt *164:* 225; *175:* 95; *189:* 37; *196:* 14; *209:* 163; *229:* 179; *240:* 170
Maik, Henri *9:* 102
Maione, Heather *106:* 5; *178:* 8; *189:* 126, 127; *193:* 58
Mair, J. Sonia *237:* 84
Maisto, Carol *29:* 87
Maitland, Antony *1:* 100, 176; *8:* 41; *17:* 246; *24:* 46; *25:* 177, 178; *32:* 74; *60:* 65, 195; *67:* 156; *87:* 131; *101:* 110
Majewski, Dawn W. *169:* 95
Mak, Kam *72:* 25; *75:* 43; *87:* 186; *97:* 24; *102:* 154; *149:* 195; *186:* 28; *209:* 132
Makie, Pam *37:* 117
Maktima, Joe *116:* 191
Maland, Nick *99:* 77
Male, Alan *132:* 64
Malone, James Hiram *84:* 161
Malone, Nola Langner *82:* 239
Malone, Peter *191:* 121, 122, 123
Malsberg, Edward *51:* 175
Malvern, Corinne *2:* 13; *34:* 148, 149
Manchess, Gregory *165:* 241; *203:* 119
Mancusi, Stephen *63:* 198, 199
Mandelbaum, Ira *31:* 115
Manders, John *138:* 152, 155; *188:* 171; *190:* 92; *199:* 5; *217:* 52; *219:* 35; *219:* 115, 116, 117; *240:* 112
Mandine, Selma *228:* 103
Manet, Edouard *23:* 170
Mangelsdorf, Tyson *240:* 35
Mangiat, Jeff *173:* 127
Mangurian, David *14:* 133
Manham, Allan *42:* 109; *77:* 180; *80:* 227
Manley, Matt *103:* 167; *117:* 98; *172:* 49; *212:* 207
Manna, Giovanni *178:* 44
Manniche, Lise *31:* 121
Manning, Jane *96:* 203; *233:* 107
Manning, Jo *63:* 154
Manning, Lawrence *191:* 153
Manning, Maurie J. *211:* 116
Manning, Mick *176:* 139; *224:* 57
Manning, Samuel F. *5:* 75
Mantel, Richard *57:* 73; *63:* 106; *82:* 255
Mantha, John *205:* 164; *217:* 117
Maraja *15:* 86; *YABC 1:* 28; *2:* 115
Marcellino, Fred *20:* 125; *34:* 222; *53:* 125; *58:* 205; *61:* 64, 121, 122; *68:* 154, 156, 157, 158, 159; *72:* 25; *86:* 184; *98:* 181; *118:* 129, 130, 131; *149:* 218; *194:* 7
Marchesi, Stephen *34:* 140; *46:* 72; *50:* 147; *66:* 239; *70:* 33; *73:* 18, 114, 163; *77:* 47, 76,147; *78:* 79; *80:* 30; *81:* 6; *89:* 66; *93:* 21,130; *94:* 94; *97:* 66; *98:* 96; *114:* 115, 116
Marchiori, Carlos *14:* 60
Marciano, John Bemelmans *118:* 133; *167:* 110, 111, 112; *240:* 97, 98, 99
Marconi, Guilherme *220:* 143
Marcus, Barry David *139:* 248; *145:* 18
Maren, Julie *199:* 73
Margules, Gabriele *21:* 120
Mariana
See Foster, Marian Curtis
Mariano, Michael *52:* 108
Marino, Dorothy *6:* 37; *14:* 135
Mario, Heide Stetson *101:* 202
Maris, Ron *71:* 123
Maritz, Nicolaas *85:* 123
Mark, Mona *65:* 105; *68:* 205; *116:* 213
Markham, R.L. *17:* 240
Marklew, Gilly *211:* 118
Marks, Alan *104:* 104; *109:* 182; *164:* 92; *185:* 134; *187:* 120, 121, 122; *218:* 114, 115; *230:* 165
Marks, Cara *54:* 9
Marks, Colin *203:* 129
Marokvia, Artur *31:* 122
Marquez, Susan *108:* 121; *219:* 95
Marrella, Maria Pia *62:* 116
Marriott, Pat *30:* 30; *34:* 39; *35:* 164, 165, 166; *44:* 170; *48:* 186, 187, 188, 189, 191, 192, 193; *91:* 92
Mars, W.T. *1:* 161; *3:* 115; *4:* 208, 225; *5:* 92, 105, 186; *8:* 214; *9:* 12; *13:* 121; *27:* 151; *31:* 180; *38:* 102; *48:* 66; *62:* 164, 165; *64:* 62; *68:* 229; *79:* 55
Marschall, Ken *85:* 29
Marsh, Christine *3:* 164
Marsh, James *73:* 137
Marsh, Reginald *17:* 5; *19:* 89; *22:* 90, 96
Marshall, Anthony D. *18:* 216
Marshall, Felicia *170:* 190
Marshall, James *6:* 160; *40:* 221; *42:* 24, 25, 29; *51:* 111, 112, 113, 114, 115, 116, 117, 118, 119, 120, 121; *64:* 13; *75:* 126, 127, 128, 129; *102:* 10, 12; *216:* 26, 28
Marshall, Janet *97:* 154
Marstall, Bob *55:* 145; *84:* 153, 170; *104:* 145; *154:* 166, 167, 168
Martchenko, Michael *50:* 129, 153, 155, 156, 157; *83:* 144,145; *154:* 137, 138, 139
Marten, Ruth *129:* 52
Martin, Brad *199:* 186
Martin, Charles E. *70:* 144
Martin, Courtney A. *214:* 28
Martin, David Stone *24:* 232; *62:* 4
Martin, Fletcher *18:* 213; *23:* 151
Martin, Rene *7:* 144; *42:* 148, 149, 150
Martin, Richard E. *51:* 157; *131:* 203
Martin, Ron *32:* 81
Martin, Stefan *8:* 68; *32:* 124, 126; *56:* 33

Martin, Whitney *166:* 137
Martinez, Ed *58:* 192; *72:* 231; *77:* 33; *80:* 214; *167:* 123
Martinez, John *6:* 113; *118:* 13; *139:* 143
Martinez, Sergio *158:* 190; *220:* 156
Martini, Angela *183:* 161; *226:* 195
Martiniere, Stephan *171:* 130
Marton, Jirina *95:* 127, 128; *144:* 145; *230:* 73, 74, 75
Martorell, Antonio *84:* 6; *97:* 161
Martucci, Griesbach *52:* 106
Marvin, Frederic *83:* 86
Marx, Robert F. *24:* 143
Marzollo, Jean *190:* 127
Masefield, Judith *19:* 208, 209
Masheris, Robert *78:* 51
Masiello, Ralph *186:* 171; *214:* 134
Mason, George F. *14:* 139
Mason, Robert *84:* 96
Masse, Josée *208:* 45; *217:* 19; *221:* 134; *234:* 184
Massey, Barbara *68:* 142
Massie, Diane Redfield *16:* 194
Massie, Kim *31:* 43
Massini, Sarah *213:* 79
Mataya, David *121:* 66
Mathers, Petra *119:* 135; *163:* 104; *176:* 143, 144; *187:* 142; *196:* 101
Mathewuse, James *51:* 143
Mathieu, Joseph *14:* 33; *39:* 206; *43:* 167; *56:* 180; *79:* 126; *94:* 147; *185:* 140; *236:* 57
Matje, Martin *169:* 177, 178; *172:* 180
Matsubara, Naoko *12:* 121
Matsuda, Shizu *13:* 167
Matsuoka, Mei *192:* 135; *214:* 84
Matte, L'Enc *22:* 183
Mattelson, Marvin *36:* 50, 51
Mattheson, Jenny *180:* 132; *222:* 153
Matthews, Elizabeth *194:* 128; *223:* 35
Matthews, F. Leslie *4:* 216
Matthews, Tina *190:* 130
Mattingly, David *71:* 76, 77; *82:* 64; *91:* 216, 217; *109:* 25
Matulay, Laszlo *5:* 18; *43:* 168
Matus, Greta *12:* 142
Maughan, Bill *181:* 31; *211:* 211
Mauldin, Bill *27:* 23
Mauterer, Erin Marie *119:* 5
Mawicke, Tran *9:* 137; *15:* 191; *47:* 100
Mawson, Matt *74:* 115
Max, Peter *45:* 146, 147, 148, 149, 150
Maxie, Betty *40:* 135
Maxwell, John Alan *1:* 148
May, Katie *225:* 128
May, Steve *204:* 30
Mayan, Earl *7:* 193
Maydak, Michael S. *220:* 117
Mayer, Bill *200:* 138
Mayer, Danuta *117:* 103
Mayer, Marianna *32:* 132
Mayer, Mercer *11:* 192; *16:* 195, 196; *20:* 55, 57; *32:* 129, 130, 132, 133, 134; *41:* 144, 248, 252; *58:* 186; *73:* 140, 142, 143; *137:* 137, 138
Mayforth, Hal *166:* 77
Mayhew, James *85:* 121; *138:* 187; *149:* 140; *204:* 81
Mayhew, Richard *3:* 106
Mayo, Gretchen Will *38:* 81; *84:* 166
Mays, Victor *5:* 127; *8:* 45, 153; *14:* 245; *23:* 50; *34:* 155; *40:* 79; *45:* 158; *54:* 91; *66:* 240
Mazal, Chanan *49:* 104
Maze, Deborah *71:* 83
Mazellan, Ron *75:* 97, 98; *210:* 169
Mazetti, Alan *112:* 72
Mazille, Capucine *96:* 168
Mazza, Adriana Saviozzi *19:* 215
Mazzella, Mary Jo *82:* 165
Mazzetti, Alan *45:* 210
McAfee, Steve *135:* 146; *167:* 176; *191:* 84; *210:* 117; *218:* 34; *233:* 86
McAlinden, Paul *112:* 128
McBride, Angus *28:* 49; *103:* 40
McBride, Will *30:* 110
McCaffery, Janet *38:* 145
McCall, Bruce *209:* 119
McCallum, Graham *78:* 78
McCallum, Stephen *141:* 143; *156:* 5; *166:* 228
McCann, Gerald *3:* 50; *4:* 94; *7:* 54; *41:* 121
McCarthy, Dan *174:* 74
McCarthy, Linda *177:* 128; *218:* 104
McCarthy, Meghan *168:* 134; *199:* 74
McCauley, Adam *157:* 36; *184:* 199; *193:* 100; *209:* 122
McCay, Winsor *41:* 124, 126, 128, 129, 130, 131; *134:* 77, 79
McClary, Nelson *1:* 111
McClements, George *196:* 146
McClennan, Connie *210:* 181
McClintock, Barbara *57:* 135; *95:* 130; *146:* 190; *213:* 3, 5, 107, 108
McClintock, Theodore *14:* 141
McCloskey, Robert *1:* 184, 185; *2:* 186, 187; *17:* 209; *39:* 139, 140, 141, 142, 143, 146, 147, 148; *85:* 150, 151; *100:* 172, 173, 174
McClung, Robert *2:* 189; *68:* 166, 167
McClure, Gillian *31:* 132; *150:* 53
McClure, Nikki *218:* 120; *241:* 143
McConnel, Jerry *31:* 75, 187
McConnell, Mary *102:* 49
McCord, Kathleen Garry *78:* 236
McCormack, John *66:* 193
McCormick, A.D. *35:* 119
McCormick, Dell J. *19:* 216
McCoy, Glenn *212:* 132
McCrady, Lady *16:* 198; *39:* 127
McCrea, James *3:* 122; *33:* 216
McCrea, Ruth *3:* 122; *27:* 102; *33:* 216
McCue, Lisa *65:* 148, 149; *77:* 54; *80:* 132; *175:* 33; *177:* 133, 135; *212:* 136, 137, 138
McCully, Emily Arnold *2:* 89; *4:* 120, 121, 146, 197; *5:* 2, 129; *7:* 191; *11:* 122; *15:* 210; *33:* 23; *35:* 244; *37:* 122; *39:* 88; *40:* 103; *50:* 30,31, 32, 33, 34, 35, 36, 37; *52:* 89, 90; *57:* 6; *62:* 3; *70:* 195; *86:* 82; *96:* 192; *97:* 93; *110:* 143,144; *117:* 47; *167:* 96; *210:* 175, 176; *225:* 179; *231:* 157; *240:* 3
McCurdy, Michael *13:* 153; *24:* 85; *81:* 160; *82:* 157, 158; *86:* 125; *97:* 92; *117:* 178; *132:* 6; *147:* 159, 160; *237:* 92, 93, 94
McCusker, Paul *99:* 19
McDaniel, Jerry *132:* 135
McDaniel, Preston *160:* 206; *170:* 139
McDermott, Beverly Brodsky *11:* 180
McDermott, Gerald *16:* 201; *74:* 174, 175; *163:* 150, 151
McDermott, Mike *96:* 187
McDonald, Jill *13:* 155; *26:* 128
McDonald, Mercedes *169:* 118
McDonald, Ralph J. *5:* 123, 195
McDonnell, Flora *146:* 199, 200
McDonnell, Patrick *179:* 153, 154; *221:* 136, 137, 138
McDonough, Don *10:* 163
McElligott, Matt *196:* 147
McElmurry, Jill *137:* 148; *163:* 141; *202:* 186
McElrath-Eslick, Lori *129:* 145; *142:* 21; *173:* 123; *202:* 194; *204:* 88, 89
McEntee, Dorothy *37:* 124
McEwan, Keith *88:* 116; *165:* 122, 123
McEwen, Katharine *169:* 34
McFall, Christie *12:* 144
McFeely, Daniel *160:* 213
McGaw, Laurie *109:* 243; *143:* 216; *211:* 218
McGee, Barbara *6:* 165
McGee, Marni *163:* 153
McGillvray, Kim *158:* 171; *165:* 213; *186:* 183; *190:* 175
McGinley-Nally, Sharon *131:* 19
McGinnis, Robert *110:* 113; *177:* 80
McGovern, Tara *98:* 171
McGraw, Sheila *83:* 146
McGregor, Barbara *200:* 155
McGregor, Malcolm *23:* 27
McGrory, Anik *193:* 120
McGuiness, Dan *240:* 102
McGuire, Robert *204:* 57; *209:* 86
McGuirk, Leslie *152:* 159
McHale, John *138:* 190
McHenry, E.B. *193:* 122
McHugh, Tom *23:* 64
McIntosh, Jon *42:* 56
McKay, Donald *2:* 118; *32:* 157; *45:* 151, 152
McKean, Dave *150:* 71; *174:* 156; *197:* 83, 118; *229:* 45, 46
McKeating, Eileen *44:* 58
McKee, David *10:* 48; *21:* 9; *70:* 154, 155; *107:* 139, 140, 141; *134:* 218; *158:* 148, 149, 150, 151; *228:* 171
McKee, Diana *109:* 185
McKelvey, Patrick *164:* 141
McKendry, Joe *170:* 136
McKeveny, Tom *164:* 60; *173:* 79
McKie, Roy *7:* 44
McKie, Todd *205:* 181
McKillip, Kathy *30:* 153
McKinney, Ena *26:* 39
McKinnon, James *136:* 75
McKowen, Scott *172:* 63; *202:* 49
McLachlan, Edward *5:* 89
McLaren, Chesley *133:* 53; *213:* 112; *219:* 31
McLaren, Kirsty *123:* 99; *124:* 226
Mclean, Andrew *113:* 117, 118, 120, 121; *172:* 130, 131
Mclean, Janet *172:* 130
McLean, Meg *94:* 196
McLean, Sammis *32:* 197
McLean, Wilson *90:* 29; *113:* 195
McLoughlin, John C. *47:* 149
McLoughlin, Wayne *102:* 230; *134:* 178; *216:* 196
McMahon, Robert *36:* 155; *69:* 169
McManus, Shawn *85:* 71
McMenemy, Sarah *156:* 139; *211:* 93; *224:* 139; *226:* 152
McMillan, Bruce *22:* 184
McMullan, James *40:* 33; *67:* 172; *87:* 142; *99:* 63, 64; *189:* 133; *196:* 51
McMullen, Nigel *146:* 177
McNeely, Tom *162:* 55
McNaught, Harry *12:* 80; *32:* 136
McNaughton, Colin *39:* 149; *40:* 108; *92:* 144, 145, 146; *134:* 104, 106; *211:* 122, 123, 124
McNicholas, Maureen *38:* 148
McNicholas, Shelagh *173:* 61; *191:* 125, 126
McPhail, David *14:* 105; *23:* 135; *37:* 217, 218, 220,221; *47:* 151, 152, 153, 154, 155, 156, 158, 159, 160, 162, 163, 164; *71:* 211; *81:* 139, 140, 142; *86:* 123; *132:* 150; *140:* 129, 131, 132; *183:* 134, 135, 137; *189:* 132; *219:* 121, 122, 123, 124, 125; *231:* 158
McPhee, Richard B. *41:* 133
McPheeters, Neal *78:* 132; *86:* 90; *99:* 162; *111:* 141; *142:* 162; *231:* 146
McQuade, Jacqueline *124:* 223
McQueen, Lucinda *28:* 149; *41:* 249; *46:* 206; *53:* 103
McQuillan, Mary *153:* 97; *200:* 140
McVay, Tracy *11:* 68
McVicker, Charles *39:* 150
McWilliam, Howard *219:* 135
Mead, Ben Carlton *43:* 75
Meade, Holly *90:* 102; *94:* 101; *149:* 8; *151:* 107
Mecray, John *33:* 62
Meddaugh, Susan *20:* 42; *29:* 143; *41:* 241; *77:* 50; *84:* 173, 174, 175, 176, 177, 178; *125:* 160, 161, 162; *176:* 148, 149, 150, 151
Meehan, Dennis B. *56:* 144
Meents, Len W. *73:* 147, 150

Meers, Tony *99:* 113
Meisel, Paul *98:* 137; *124:* 18; *162:* 180; *179:* 16; *181:* 62; *194:* 154; *221:* 5; *224:* 100, 101, 102, 133; *231:* 25
Melanson, Luc *149:* 229; *198:* 97, 98; *221:* 166
Melendez, Francisco *72:* 180
Melling, David *202:* 199
Melnychuk, Monika *153:* 65
Melo, Esperança *196:* 90; *239:* 93, 94
Melo, John *16:* 285; *58:* 203
Meloni, Maria Teresa *98:* 62
Meltzer, Ericka
See O'Rourke, Ericka
Menasco, Milton *43:* 85
Menchin, Scott *188:* 129; *234:* 139
Mendelson, Steven T. *86:* 154
Mendelssohn, Felix *19:* 170
Mendola, Christopher *88:* 223
Meng, Heinz *13:* 158
Merian, Maria Sibylla *140:* 88
Mero, Lee *34:* 68
Merrell, David *205:* 3
Merrill, Frank T. *16:* 147; *19:* 71; *YABC 1:* 226, 229,273
Merriman, Rachel *98:* 108; *114:* 122; *149:* 142
Merveille, David *200:* 142
Meryman, Hope *27:* 41
Meryweather, Jack *10:* 179
Meseldzija, Petar *168:* 97
Meserve, Jessica *184:* 137; *211:* 127
Messick, Dale *64:* 150, 151, 152
Meth, Harold *24:* 203
Meyer, Alex Eben *226:* 60
Meyer, Herbert *19:* 189
Meyer, Renate *6:* 170
Meyers, Bob *11:* 136
Meyers, Nancy *172:* 124
Meynell, Louis *37:* 76
Micale, Albert *2:* 65; *22:* 185
Miccuci, Charles *82:* 163; *144:* 150
Micich, Paul *164:* 163
Middleton, Charlotte *230:* 81
Middleton, Jeffrey *177:* 173; *222:* 157
Middleton, Joshua *208:* 146; *219:* 24; *240:* 75
Middleton-Sandford, Betty *2:* 125
Mieke, Anne *45:* 74
Mighell, Patricia *43:* 134
Miglio, Paige *101:* 203; *151:* 223; *201:* 118, 119; *204:* 162
Mikec, Larry *204:* 125
Mikolaycak, Charles *9:* 144; *12:* 101; *13:* 212; *21:* 121; *22:* 168; *30:* 187; *34:* 103, 150; *37:* 183; *43:* 179; *44:* 90; *46:* 115, 118, 119; *49:* 25; *78:* 121, 122, 205, 207; *81:* 4
Milelli, Pascal *129:* 66; *135:* 153; *187:* 45; *235:* 47
Miles, Elizabeth *117:* 77
Miles, Jennifer *17:* 278
Milgrim, David *158:* 157; *187:* 125, 126, 128; *223:* 124, 125, 126, 127
Milhous, Katherine *15:* 193; *17:* 51
Milian, Tomaso *238:* 119
Millais, John E. *22:* 230, 231
Millar, H.R. *YABC 1:* 194, 195, 203
Millard, C.E. *28:* 186
Millard, Kerry *105:* 124; *204:* 93, 94
Miller, Don *15:* 195; *16:* 71; *20:* 106; *31:* 178
Miller, Edna *29:* 148
Miller, Edward *115:* 64; *183:* 140, 141; *218:* 129, 130, 131
Miller, Frank J. *25:* 94
Miller, Grambs *18:* 38; *23:* 16
Miller, Ian *99:* 128
Miller, Jane *15:* 196
Miller, Marcia *13:* 233
Miller, Marilyn *1:* 87; *31:* 69; *33:* 157
Miller, Mitchell *28:* 183; *34:* 207
Miller, Phil *175:* 150
Miller, Shane *5:* 140
Miller, Virginia *81:* 206
Miller, Woody *233:* 153; *236:* 146
Millman, Isaac *172:* 18
Mills, Elaine *72:* 181
Mills, Judith Christine *130:* 168, 169
Mills, Lauren *92:* 170
Mills, Yaroslava Surmach *35:* 169, 170; *46:* 114
Millsap, Darrel *51:* 102
Milone, Karen *89:* 169; *222:* 149
Milord, Susan *147:* 163, 164; *200:* 144
Milot, René *226:* 127
Milton, Debbie *162:* 161
Mims, Ashley *170:* 51
Min, Willemien *222:* 62
Miner, Julia *98:* 69
Minor, Wendell *39:* 188; *52:* 87; *56:* 171; *58:* 116; *62:* 56; *66:* 109; *74:* 93; *78:* 129; *94:* 67; *117:* 12, 13; *124:* 84, 86; *136:* 121; *164:* 168, 169; *170:* 71; *199:* 79, 80, 81, 82; *217:* 63; *223:* 149; *226:* 90, 91, 92
Minter, Daniel *176:* 154; *179:* 177
Mirocha, Paul *81:* 133; *192:* 148; *194:* 36
Misako Rocks! *192:* 149, 150
Mitchell, Judith *109:* 117
Mitchell, Mark *91:* 208
Mitchell, Tracy *190:* 15
Mitgutsch, Ali *76:* 161
Mitsuhashi, Yoko *45:* 153
Miyake, Yoshi *38:* 141
Mizumura, Kazue *10:* 143; *18:* 223; *36:* 159
Mochi, Ugo *8:* 122; *38:* 150
Mock, Paul *55:* 83; *123:* 32
Modarressi, Mitra *90:* 236; *126:* 168; *173:* 165, 166; *200:* 147, 148
Modell, Frank *39:* 152
Mogenson, Jan *74:* 183
Mohn, Susan *89:* 224
Mohr, Mark *133:* 201
Mohr, Nicholasa *8:* 139; *113:* 127
Molan, Christine *60:* 177; *84:* 183
Moldon, Peter L. *49:* 168
Molk, Laurel *92:* 150; *230:* 217, 219
Mollica, Gene *197:* 11
Momaday, N. Scott *48:* 159
Mombourquette, Paul *112:* 91; *126:* 142
Monk, Julie *165:* 231; *191:* 96
Monks, Lydia *189:* 136, 137
Monroe, Chris *219:* 133
Monroy, Manuel *199:* 192
Montalto, Luisa *233:* 79
Montgomery, Lucy *150:* 126
Montgomery, Michael G. *208:* 159
Montgomery-Higham, Amanda *169:* 131
Monteiel, David *201:* 95
Montiel, David *69:* 106; *84:* 145
Montijo, Rhode *193:* 164
Montresor, Beni *2:* 91; *3:* 138; *38:* 152, 153, 154,155, 156, 157, 158, 159, 160; *68:* 63
Montserrat, Pep *128:* 135; *181:* 119; *184:* 53
Moon, Carl *25:* 183, 184, 185
Moon, Eliza *14:* 40
Moon, Ivan *22:* 39; *38:* 140
Moore, Adrienne *67:* 147
Moore, Agnes Kay Randall *43:* 187
Moore, Cyd *117:* 107, 108; *159:* 137, 138; *186:* 148, 149, 151; *203:* 15; *214:* 138, 139; *233:* 111, 112, 113, 115
Moore, Gustav *127:* 181, 182; *170:* 162, 163
Moore, Jackie *128:* 79
Moore, Janet *63:* 153
Moore, Margie *176:* 156; *221:* 125; *224:* 106, 107
Moore, Mary *29:* 160
Moore, Patrick *184:* 121
Moore, Sean L. *237:* 98
Moore, Yvette *101:* 11, 12; *154:* 141
Mora, Giovanni *179:* 127; *184:* 11
Mora, Raul Mina *20:* 41
Moraes, Odilon *102:* 144
Morales, Magaly *225:* 137; *233:* 28
Morales, Yuyi *154:* 144; *226:* 120; *236:* 121; *241:* 105, 106, 107
Moran, Rosslyn *111:* 26
Moran, Tom *60:* 100
Mordan, C.B. *193:* 115
Mordvinoff, Nicolas *15:* 179
Moreno, René King *169:* 59; *190:* 133, 209; *212:* 52
Morgan, Barbara *169:* 116
Morgan, Jacqui *58:* 57
Morgan, Mary *114:* 133, 134, 135; *123:* 11; *213:* 115, 116, 117; *240:* 111
Morgan, Tom *42:* 157
Morgan, Pierr *173:* 148
Morgenstern, Michael *158:* 7, 57; *171:* 103; *174:* 60; *226:* 12; *233:* 5
Morice, Dave *93:* 142
Morin, Paul *73:* 132; *79:* 130; *88:* 140; *137:* 143
Moriuchi, Mique *177:* 203
Morozumi, Atsuko *110:* 155; *217:* 126, 127
Morrill, Leslie *18:* 218; *29:* 177; *33:* 84; *38:* 147; *42:* 127; *44:* 93; *48:* 164, 165, 167, 168, 169, 170,171; *49:* 162; *63:* 136, 180; *70:* 72; *71:* 70, 91,92; *72:* 228; *80:* 163, 164, 165; *90:* 121; *121:* 88; *178:* 117
Morrill, Rowena A. *84:* 16; *98:* 163
Morris *47:* 91
Morris, Frank *55:* 133; *60:* 28; *76:* 2
Morris, Harry O. *119:* 138
Morris, Jackie *128:* 194; *144:* 119; *151:* 146; *202:* 126, 127; *204:* 83; *211:* 80; *214:* 163
Morris, Jennifer E. *179:* 157
Morris, Oradel Nolen *128:* 180
Morris, Tony *62:* 146; *70:* 97
Morrison, Bill *42:* 116; *66:* 170; *69:* 40
Morrison, Gordon *87:* 150; *113:* 93; *128:* 181, 182; *183:* 144, 145, 146
Morrison, Frank *169:* 162; *205:* 156; *224:* 121; *226:* 154
Morrison, Taylor *159:* 144, 145; *187:* 131
Morrow, Gray *2:* 64; *5:* 200; *10:* 103, 114; *14:* 175
Morse, Joe *240:* 104
Morse, Scott *200:* 149, 150
Morstad, Julie *232:* 137
Morton, Lee Jack *32:* 140
Morton, Marian *3:* 185
Mosberg, Hilary *117:* 195; *118:* 164; *149:* 55
Moser, Barry *56:* 68, 117, 118, 119, 120, 121, 122, 123, 124; *59:* 141; *60:* 160; *79:* 91, 147, 149, 151, 152; *82:* 81; *90:* 118; *91:* 35; *95:* 210; *97:* 91, 93; *102:* 152; *126:* 4; *128:* 175; *133:* 141; *138:* 167, 171, 174; *153:* 205; *174:* 130; *185:* 152, 154; *195:* 163; *204:* 115; *209:* 201; *241:* 139
Moser, Cara *90:* 118; *138:* 167
Moses, Grandma *18:* 228
Moses, Will *178:* 170, 171
Moskof, Martin Stephen *27:* 152
Mosley, Francis *57:* 144
Moss, Donald *11:* 184
Moss, Geoffrey *32:* 198
Moss, Marissa *71:* 130; *104:* 127; *163:* 156; *216:* 164, 165, 166; *239:* 136
Most, Bernard *48:* 173; *91:* 142, 143; *134:* 120
Mourning, Tuesday *205:* 25; *220:* 68; *221:* 42; *236:* 91
Mowll, Joshua *188:* 133
Mowry, Carmen *50:* 62
Moxley, Sheila *96:* 174; *169:* 26; *206:* 16
Moyers, William *21:* 65
Moyler, Alan *36:* 142
Mozley, Charles *9:* 87; *20:* 176, 192, 193; *22:* 228; *25:* 205; *33:* 150; *43:* 170, 171, 172, 173, 174; *YABC2:* 89
Mueller, Hans Alexander *26:* 64; *27:* 52, 53
Mugnaini, Joseph *11:* 35; *27:* 52, 53; *35:* 62
Mujica, Rick *72:* 67; *88:* 95; *111:* 53; *180:* 185; *197:* 70
Mullen, Douglas *180:* 178; *239:* 105

Muller, Robin *86:* 161
Muller, Steven *32:* 167
Muller, Jorg *35:* 215; *67:* 138, 139
Mulock, Julie *163:* 112
Mullins, Edward S. *10:* 101
Mullins, Patricia *51:* 68
Multer, Scott *80:* 108
Munari, Bruno *15:* 200
Munch, Edvard *140:* 143
Munowitz, Ken *14:* 148; *72:* 178, 179
Muñoz, Claudio *208:* 161
Munoz, William *42:* 160
Munro, Roxie *58:* 134; *136:* 177; *137:* 218; *184:* 133, 134; *223:* 130, 132, 133
Munsinger, Lynn *33:* 161; *46:* 126; *71:* 92; *82:* 80; *89:* 218; *92:* 125; *94:* 157, 158, 159, 160; *98:* 196; *103:* 198; *142:* 143; *145:* 133, 134, 136; *153:* 203; *176:* 162; *177:* 140, 141, 142; *189:* 113, 114, 116, 117; *201:* 42; *221:* 148, 149,150
Munson, Russell *13:* 9
Munster, Sebastian *166:* 107
Munzar, Barbara *149:* 75
Murdocca, Salvatore *73:* 212; *98:* 132; *111:* 168; *157:* 228; *164:* 257
Murphy, Bill *5:* 138; *130:* 170
Murphy, Jill *37:* 142; *70:* 166; *142:* 132, 134
Murphy, Kelly *130:* 212; *143:* 119; *176:* 158; *190:* 135
Murphy, Liz *210:* 183; *212:* 157
Murphy, Mary *196:* 158
Murphy, Tom *192:* 40
Murphy, Yannick *240:* 107
Murr, Karl *20:* 62
Murray, Joe *175:* 37
Murray, Ossie *43:* 176
Mussino, Attilio *29:* 131; *100:* 164
Mutchler, Dwight *1:* 25
Myers, Bernice *9:* 147; *36:* 75; *81:* 146, 147, 148
Muth, Jon J. *165:* 169; *167:* 109; *190:* 227; *193:* 59; *228:* 206
Myers, Christopher *183:* 150; *193:* 139
Myers, Duane O. *99:* 145
Myers, Tim *147:* 168
Myers, V.G. *142:* 41
Myers, Lou *11:* 2

N

Na, Il Sung *231:* 136
Nachreiner, Tom *29:* 182
Nacht, Merle *65:* 49
Nadler, Ellis *88:* 91
Nagle, Shane *180:* 223
Nagy, Ian *195:* 64
Naifeh, Ted *236:* 34
Najaka, Marlies *62:* 101
Nakai, Michael *30:* 217; *54:* 29
Nakata, Hiroe *157:* 156; *162:* 30; *205:* 124, 125
Nakatani, Chiyoko *12:* 124
Narahashi, Keiko *77:* 188; *82:* 213; *115:* 142, 143, 144
Nascimbene, Yan *133:* 128; *173:* 132, 133
Nash, Lesa *87:* 135
Nash, Linell *46:* 175
Nash, Scott *130:* 36; *188:* 196; *224:* 180; *239:* 83
Naso, John *33:* 183
Nason, Thomas W. *14:* 68
Nasser, Muriel *48:* 74
Nast, Thomas *21:* 29; *28:* 23; *51:* 132, 133, 134, 135,136, 137, 138, 139, 141
Nasta, Vincent *78:* 185
Natale, Vincent *76:* 3; *78:* 125; *112:* 47; *166:* 81; *174:* 189; *185:* 212; *197:* 59; *218:* 35
Natchev, Alexi *96:* 177
Nathan, Charlott *125:* 151
Nathan, Cheryl *150:* 104; *186:* 112
Natti, Susanna *20:* 146; *32:* 141, 142; *35:* 178; *37:* 143; *71:* 49; *93:* 98; *125:* 166, 168; *126:* 228; *151:* 6; *178:* 8; *188:* 106; *231:* 10
Navarra, Celeste Scala *8:* 142
Naylor, Penelope *10:* 104
Nazz, James *72:* 8
Nebel, M. *45:* 154
Neebe, William *7:* 93
Needham, Dave *196:* 85
Needler, Jerry *12:* 93
Neel, Alice *31:* 23
Neely, Beth *119:* 184
Neely, Keith R. *46:* 124
Neff, Leland *78:* 74
Negri, Rocco *3:* 213; *5:* 67; *6:* 91, 108; *12:* 159
Negrin, Fabian *174:* 125; *175:* 15; *223:* 91; *240:* 22
Neidigh, Sherry *128:* 53; *204:* 101, 102, 103; *222:* 95
Neilan, Eujin Kim *180:* 241; *200:* 151, 152
Neill, John R. *18:* 8, 10, 11, 21, 30; *100:* 22
Neilsen, Cliff *158:* 131; *177:* 112, 121; *209:* 8; *215:* 150; *230:* 62
Neilsen, Terese *116:* 74
Nelson, Craig *62:* 151; 153; *183:* 86; *236:* 103
Nelson, Gail White *68:* 140
Nelson, Jennifer *129:* 152; *199:* 132; *239:* 145
Nelson, Kadir *151:* 185; *154:* 146, 147; *157:* 189, 222; *181:* 122, 124; *197:* 155; *213:* 122, 123, 124
Nelson, Melissa *224:* 87
Nelson, S.D. *131:* 34; *181:* 126, 127; *228:* 23
Ness, Evaline *1:* 164, 165; *2:* 39; *3:* 8; *10:* 147; *12:* 53; *26:* 150, 151, 152, 153; *49:* 30, 31, 32; *56:* 30; *60:* 113
Neubecker, Robert *170:* 143; *214:* 157; *233:* 25; *234:* 209; *238:* 93
Neville, Vera *2:* 182
Nevins, Daniel *191:* 173
Nevwirth, Allan *79:* 168
Newberry, Clare Turlay *1:* 170
Newbold, Greg *108:* 125; *145:* 199; *151:* 23; *193:* 178; *197:* 10; *199:* 92, 93
Newfeld, Frank *14:* 121; *26:* 154
Newhouse, Maxwell *232:* 144
Newland, Gillian *220:* 132
Newman, Andy *149:* 61; *195:* 63
Newman, Ann *43:* 90
Newman, Barbara Johansen *191:* 137, 138; *231:* 13; *240:* 114, 115
Newquist, H.P. *235:* 156
Newsham, Ian *143:* 162
Newsom, Carol *40:* 159; *44:* 60; *47:* 189; *65:* 29; *70:* 192; *80:* 36; *85:* 137, 138; *92:* 167; *191:* 82; *233:* 83
Newsom, Tom *49:* 149; *71:* 13, 62; *75:* 156; *91:* 113
Newton, Jill *83:* 105; *200:* 154
Newton, Vanessa Brantley *236:* 180
Nez, John *218:* 136
Ng, Michael *29:* 171
Ng, Simon *167:* 7
Ngui, Marc *229:* 50
Nguyen, Vincent *189:* 49; *226:* 160; *229:* 172
Nichols, Sandy *219:* 103
Nicholson, William *15:* 33, 34; *16:* 48
Nickens, Bessie *104:* 153
Nicklaus, Carol *45:* 194; *62:* 132, 133
Nickle, John *181:* 128
Nickless, Will *16:* 139
Nicholas, Corasue *154:* 20
Nicolas *17:* 130, 132, 133; *YABC 2:* 215
Niebrugge, Jane *6:* 118
Nielsen, Cliff *95:* 207, 208; *105:* 58; *114:* 112; *124:* 12; *125:* 91, 92; *132:* 224; *135:* 187; *136:* 40; *137:* 168; *145:* 54; *149:* 28; *158:* 129; *165:* 64, 158; *168:* 169; *170:* 6; *175:* 114, 116; *187:* 75, 76; *194:* 107; *197:* 172; *201:* 14; *208:* 192; *211:* 186; *216:* 215; *217:* 67; *224:* 61, 62; *230:* 21; *233:* 58, 59; *236:* 136; *238:* 47, 48; *239:* 164; *240:* 10, 181
Nielsen, Jon *6:* 100; *24:* 202
Nielsen, Kay *15:* 7; *16:* 211, 212, 213, 215, 217; *22:* 143; *YABC 1:* 32, 33
Niemann, Christoph *191:* 141; *238:* 123, 124
Nikola-Lisa, W. *180:* 180
Niland, Deborah *25:* 191; *27:* 156; *135:* 50; *172:* 143
Niland, Kilmeny *25:* 191; *75:* 143
Nino, Alex *59:* 145
Ninon *1:* 5; *38:* 101, 103, 108
Nissen, Rie *44:* 35
Nithael, Mark *158:* 237
Nivola, Claire A. *78:* 126; *140:* 147; *208:* 164
Nixon, K. *14:* 152
Nobati, Eugenia *194:* 118
Noble, Louise *61:* 170
Noble, Marty *97:* 168; *125:* 171
Noble, Trinka Hakes *39:* 162; *84:* 157
Nobles, Scott *226:* 159
Noda, Takayo *168:* 143
Noguchi, Yoshie *30:* 99
Nolan, Dennis *42:* 163; *67:* 163; *78:* 189; *82:* 225; *83:* 26; *92:* 169, 170; *103:* 166; *111:* 35; *112:* 213; *127:* 171; *166:* 161; *194:* 218
Noll, Sally *82:* 171
Nolte, Larry *121:* 63, 65
Nones, Eric Jon *61:* 111; *76:* 38; *77:* 177
Noonan, Daniel *100:* 224
Noonan, Julia *4:* 163; *7:* 207; *25:* 151; *91:* 29; *95:* 149; *231:* 163
Norcia, Ernie *108:* 155; *140:* 47
Nordenskjold, Birgitta *2:* 208
Noreika, Robert *173:* 20; *217:* 24
Norling, Beth *149:* 153, 154; *209:* 77
Norman, Elaine *77:* 72, 176; *94:* 35; *136:* 63; *178:* 42; *236:* 104
Norman, Mary *36:* 138, 147
Norman, Michael *12:* 117; *27:* 168
Normandin, Luc *227:* 180
Northway, Jennifer *85:* 96
Nostlinger, Christiana *162:* 131
Novak, Linda *166:* 205
Novak, Matt *104:* 132, 133; *165:* 173, 174; *204:* 104, 106
Novelli, Luca *61:* 137
Novgorodoff, Danica *215:* 133
Nugent, Cynthia *106:* 189; *205:* 126, 127; *209:* 180
Numberman, Neil *220:* 133
Numeroff, Laura Joffe *28:* 161; *30:* 177
Nurse, Chris *164:* 91
Nussbaumer, Paul *16:* 219; *39:* 117
Nutt, Ken *72:* 69; *97:* 170
Nyce, Helene *19:* 219
Nygren, Tord *30:* 148; *127:* 164

O

Oakley, Graham *8:* 112; *30:* 164, 165; *84:* 188,189, 190, 191, 192
Oakley, Thornton *YABC 2:* 189
Oberheide, Heide *118:* 37
Obligado, Lilian *2:* 28, 66, 67; *6:* 30; *14:* 179; *15:* 103; *25:* 84; *61:* 138, 139, 140, 141, 143
Oblinski, Rafael *190:* 139
Obrant, Susan *11:* 186
O'Brien, Anne Sibley *53:* 116, 117; *155:* 115; *213:* 127; *224:* 71; *227:* 9
O'Brien, John *41:* 253; *72:* 12; *89:* 59, 60; *98:* 16; *161:* 185; *169:* 16; *180:* 196; *228:* 38
O'Brien, Patrick *193:* 142, 143, 144
O'Brien, Teresa *87:* 89
O'Brien, Tim *93:* 25; *136:* 94; *164:* 57; *169:* 57; *173:* 55; *175:* 86; *184:* 192; *191:* 134; *193:* 137; *210:* 159; *224:* 28, 29; *229:* 140; *232:* 166; *239:* 123; *240:* 86

O'Clair, Dennis *127:* 25
O'Connor, George *183:* 153; *228:* 113, 114
Odell, Carole *35:* 47
Odem, Mel *99:* 164; *167:* 84, 87
O'Donohue, Thomas *40:* 89
Oechsli, Kelly *5:* 144, 145; *7:* 115; *8:* 83, 183; *13:* 117; *20:* 94; *81:* 199
Ofer, Avi *208:* 143
Offen, Hilda *42:* 207
Offermann, Andrea *233:* 108
Ogden, Bill *42:* 59; *47:* 55
Ogg, Oscar *33:* 34
Ogle, Nancy Gray *163:* 144
Ohi, Ruth *90:* 175, 177; *131:* 63; *135:* 106; *175:* 107; *179:* 55
Ohlsson, Ib *4:* 152; *7:* 57; *10:* 20; *11:* 90; *19:* 217; *41:* 246; *82:* 106; *92:* 213
Ohtomo, Yasuo *37:* 146; *39:* 212, 213
O'Keefe, Jennifer *136:* 184
O'Kelley, Mattie Lou *36:* 150
Olbinski, Rafal *149:* 27; *158:* 77; *203:* 36; *235:* 36
Oldland, Nicholas *223:* 136
O'Leary, Chris *208:* 166
Olander, Johan *231:* 138
Oleynikov, Igor *202:* 134
Oliver, Isaac *171:* 182
Oliver, Jenni *23:* 121; *35:* 112
Oliver, Narelle *152:* 192; *197:* 129, 130
Oller, Erika *128:* 186; *134:* 126; *234:* 146
Olschewski, Alfred *7:* 172
Olsen, Ib Spang *6:* 178, 179; *81:* 164
Olson, Alan *77:* 229
Olson, Julie *233:* 120
Olson-Brown, Ellen *183:* 154
Olugebefola, Ademola *15:* 205
O'Malley, Kevin *94:* 180; *106:* 8; *113:* 108; *136:* 70; *157:* 193; *191:* 146; *203:* 78; *217:* 84; *230:* 115, 117, 118
O'Neil, Dan IV *7:* 176
O'Neill, Catharine *72:* 113; *84:* 78; *134:* 153
O'Neill, Jean *22:* 146
O'Neill, Martin *187:* 39; *203:* 118
O'Neill, Michael J. *54:* 172
O'Neill, Rose *48:* 30, 31
O'Neill, Steve *21:* 118
Ono, Chiyo *7:* 97
Onoda, Yuta *237:* 136
Orbaan, Albert *2:* 31; *5:* 65, 171; *9:* 8; *14:* 241; *20:* 109
Orbach, Ruth *21:* 112
Orback, Craig *197:* 132
Orfe, Joan *20:* 81
Org, Ed *119:* 93
Ormai, Stella *72:* 129
Ormerod, Jan *55:* 124; *70:* 170, 171; *90:* 39; *132:* 172, 173, 174; *147:* 98
Ormsby, Virginia H. *11:* 187
O'Rourke, Ericka *108:* 216; *117:* 194; *111:* 142; *119:* 194; *137:* 152; *150:* 134; *167:* 64; *172:* 164; *188:* 163; *191:* 172; *201:* 15; *203:* 75; *209:* 130; *219:* 99
O'Rourke, Ericka Meltzer
See O'Rourke, Ericka
Orozco, Jose Clemente *9:* 177
Orr, Forrest W. *23:* 9
Orr, N. *19:* 70
Ortiz, Vilma *88:* 158
Osborn, Kathy *152:* 232; *199:* 101, 102; *206:* 67
Osborn, Robert *65:* 49
Osborne, Billie Jean *35:* 209
Osmond, Edward *10:* 111
Ostow, David *223:* 138
O'Sullivan, Tom *3:* 176; *4:* 55; *78:* 195
Otani, June *124:* 42; *156:* 53
Otis, Rebecca *185:* 92
Ottley, Matt *147:* 221; *171:* 133
Otto, Svend *22:* 130, 141; *67:* 188, 189
Oudry, J.B. *18:* 167
Oughton, Taylor *5:* 23; *104:* 136
Overeng, Johannes *44:* 36
Overlie, George *11:* 156
Owens, Carl *2:* 35; *23:* 521
Owens, Gail *10:* 170; *12:* 157; *19:* 16; *22:* 70; *25:* 81; *28:* 203, 205; *32:* 221, 222; *36:* 132; *46:* 40; *47:* 57; *54:* 66, 67, 68, 69, 70, 71, 72, 73; *71:* 100; *73:* 64; *77:* 157; *80:* 32; *82:* 3; *99:* 226; *224:* 198
Owens, Mary Beth *113:* 202, 203; *191:* 148, 149
Owens, Nubia *84:* 74
Oxenbury, Helen *3:* 150, 151; *24:* 81; *68:* 174, 175,176; *81:* 209; *84:* 213, 245; *129:* 56; *149:* 159; *184:* 181; *224:* 147
Oz, Robin *88:* 167; *185:* 181

P

Padgett, Jim *12:* 165
Page, Gail *205:* 128
Page, Homer *14:* 145
Page, Mark *162:* 70
Paget, Sidney *24:* 90, 91, 93, 95, 97
Paget, Walter *64:* 122
Paillot, Jim *173:* 89
Pajouhesh, Noushin *160:* 121
Pak *12:* 76
Pak, Yu Cha *86:* 174
Pal, Erika *239:* 112
Paladino, Lance *134:* 30
Palazzo, Tony *3:* 152, 153
Palecek, Josef *56:* 136; *89:* 158
Palen, Debbie *135:* 88; *195:* 148, 149
Palencar, John Jude *84:* 12, 45; *85:* 87; *92:* 187; *99:* 128; *110:* 204; *150:* 122; *171:* 86; *207:* 36
Palin, Nicki *81:* 201; *89:* 161
Palisi, Heather *231:* 109
Palladini, David *4:* 113; *40:* 176, 177, 178, 179, 181,224, 225; *50:* 138; *78:* 186
Pallarito, Don *43:* 36
Palmer, Carol *158:* 230; *195:* 187
Palmer, Gary *232:* 39
Palmer, Heidi *15:* 207; *29:* 102
Palmer, Jan *42:* 153; *82:* 161
Palmer, Judd *153:* 160, 161
Palmer, Juliette *6:* 89; *15:* 208
Palmer, Kate Salley *104:* 143; *154:* 169
Palmer, Lemuel *17:* 25, 29
Palmisciano, Diane *110:* 62; *162:* 26; *202:* 138, 139
Palmquist, Eric *38:* 133
Pamintuan, Macky *214:* 160
Panesis, Nicholas *3:* 127
Panter, Gary *182:* 191
Panton, Doug *52:* 99
Paparone, Pamela *129:* 174
Papas, William *11:* 223; *50:* 160
Papin, Joseph *26:* 113
Papish, Robin Lloyd *10:* 80
Papp, Robert *198:* 41; *205:* 130; *219:* 53
Paradis, Susan *40:* 216
Paraquin, Charles H. *18:* 166
Pardo DeLange, Alex *179:* 128; *211:* 135, 136
Paris, Peter *31:* 127
Parisi, Elizabeth B. *141:* 82; *164:* 57
Park, Nick *113:* 143
Park, Seho *39:* 110
Park, W.B. *22:* 189
Parker, Ant *82:* 87, 88; *104:* 121
Parker, Buzz *227:* 154
Parker, Jake *227:* 134
Parker, Lewis *2:* 179
Parker, Nancy Winslow *10:* 113; *22:* 164; *28:* 47, 144; *52:* 7; *69:* 153; *91:* 171, 174; *132:* 175
Parker, Robert *4:* 161; *5:* 74; *9:* 136; *29:* 39
Parker, Robert Andrew *11:* 81; *29:* 186; *39:* 165; *40:* 25; *41:* 78; *42:* 123; *43:* 144; *48:* 182; *54:* 140; *74:* 141; *91:* 24; *111:* 115; *151:* 201; *154:* 156; *200:* 163, 164; *211:* 67
Parker-Rees, Guy *149:* 145; *193:* 149, 150
Parkin, Trevor *140:* 151
Parkins, David *114:* 123; *146:* 176; *176:* 168; *192:* 107; *218:* 139, 140, 141, 148; *224:* 92
Parkinson, Kathy *71:* 143; *144:* 234
Parkinson, Keith *70:* 66; *241:* 18
Parks, Gordon, Jr. *33:* 228
Parlato, Stephen *222:* 137
Parnall, Peter *5:* 137; *16:* 221; *24:* 70; *40:* 78; *51:* 130; *69:* 17, 155; *136:* 22, 23, 24
Parnall, Virginia *40:* 78
Paros, Jennifer *210:* 197
Parow, Lorraine *158:* 127
Parr, Todd *134:* 139, 140; *179:* 163, 164, 165
Parra, John *225:* 150; *232:* 134
Parrish, Anne *27:* 159, 160
Parrish, Dillwyn *27:* 159
Parrish, Maxfield *14:* 160, 161, 164, 165; *16:* 109; *18:* 12, 13; *YABC 1:* 149, 152, 267; *2:* 146, 149
Parry, David *26:* 156
Parry, Marian *13:* 176; *19:* 179
Parsons, Garry *197:* 135
Partch, Virgil *45:* 163, 165
Pascal, David *14:* 174
Paschkis, Julie *177:* 153, 154; *220:* 140, 141; *231:* 64
Pasquier, J.A. *16:* 91
Pastel, Elyse *201:* 123
Pasternak, Robert *119:* 53
Paterson, Diane *13:* 116; *39:* 163; *59:* 164, 165, 166,167; *72:* 51, 53; *129:* 175; *177:* 156, 157
Paterson, Helen *16:* 93
Patkau, Karen *112:* 123
Paton, Jane *15:* 271; *35:* 176
Patricelli, Leslie *207:* 129; *236:* 155, 156
Patrick, John *139:* 190
Patrick, Pamela *90:* 160; *93:* 211; *105:* 12
Patrick, Tom *190:* 103
Patterson, Geoffrey *54:* 75
Patterson, Robert *25:* 118
Patti, Joyce *187:* 145, 146
Patz, Nancy *111:* 40; *154:* 161; *214:* 80
Paul, James *4:* 130; *23:* 161
Paul, Korky *102:* 85
Paull, Grace *24:* 157; *87:* 127
Paulsen, Ruth Wright *79:* 160, 164; *189:* 146; *231:* 150
Pavlov, Elena *80:* 49
Payne, Adam S. *135:* 166
Payne, C.F. *145:* 138, 140; *179:* 168
Payne, Joan Balfour *1:* 118
Payne, Tom *170:* 27
Payson, Dale *7:* 34; *9:* 151; *20:* 140; *37:* 22
Payzant, Charles *21:* 147
Peacock, Phyllis Hornung *230:* 124
Peacock, Ralph *64:* 118
Peake, Mervyn *22:* 136, 149; *23:* 162, 163, 164; *YABC2:* 307
Pearce, Carl *228:* 107; *229:* 148
Pearson, Larry *38:* 225
Pearson, Tracey Campbell *64:* 163, 164, 167, 168, 169; *118:* 51; *156:* 169, 171, 172; *163:* 140; *219:* 140, 141, 142, 143
Peat, Fern B. *16:* 115
Peck, Anne Merriman *18:* 241; *24:* 155
Peck, Beth *66:* 242; *79:* 166; *80:* 136; *91:* 34; *95:* 9; *101:* 77; *164:* 197; *190:* 170
Peddicord, Jane Ann *199:* 106
Pedersen, Janet *193:* 152; *217:* 57; *218:* 15; *228:* 85
Pedersen, Judy *66:* 217; *121:* 36; *172:* 67
Pedersen, Vilhelm *YABC 1:* 40
Pederson, Sharleen *12:* 92
Pedlar, Elaine *161:* 45
Peek, Merle *39:* 168

Peet, Bill *2:* 203; *41:* 159, 160, 161, 162, 163; *78:* 158, 159, 160, 161
Peguero, Adrian *116:* 133
Peguero, Gerard *116:* 133
Peirce, Lincoln *232:* 150
Pels, Winslow Pinney *55:* 126
Peltier, Leslie C. *13:* 178
Peltzer, Marc *202:* 92
Penberthy, Mark *171:* 78
Pendle, Alexy *7:* 159; *13:* 34; *29:* 161; *33:* 215; *86:* 62
Pendola, Joanne *76:* 203; *81:* 125; *105:* 181; *178:* 152, 153
Pene du Bois, William *4:* 70; *10:* 122; *26:* 61; *27:* 145, 211; *35:* 243; *41:* 216; *68:* 180, 181; *73:* 45
Penfound, David *102:* 185
Pennington, Eunice *27:* 162
Peot, Margaret *241:* 119
Peppe, Mark *28:* 142
Peppe, Rodney *4:* 164, 165; *74:* 187, 188, 189
Pepper, Hubert *64:* 143
Percy, Graham *63:* 2
Pericoli, Matteo *178:* 177
Perini, Ben *173:* 77
Perkins, David *60:* 68
Perkins, Lucy Fitch *72:* 199
Perkins, Lynne Rae *172:* 146; *212:* 153
Perl, Susan *2:* 98; *4:* 231; *5:* 44, 45, 118; *6:* 199; *8:* 137; *12:* 88; *22:* 193; *34:* 54, 55; *52:* 128; *YABC 1:* 176
Perlman, Janet *222:* 141
Perrone, Donna *78:* 166
Perry, Marie Fritz *165:* 180
Perry, Patricia *29:* 137; *30:* 171
Perry, Roger *27:* 163
Perske, Martha *46:* 83; *51:* 108, 147
Persson, Stina *175:* 166
Pesek, Ludek *15:* 237
Petach, Heidi *149:* 166; *200:* 207
Peters, David *72:* 205; *182:* 116
Petersen, Jeff *181:* 95
Petersham, Maud *17:* 108, 147, 148, 149, 150, 151, 152, 153
Petersham, Miska *17:* 108, 147, 148, 149, 150, 151, 152, 153
Peterson, Eric *109:* 125
Peterson, Nisse *99:* 27
Peterson, R.F. *7:* 101
Peterson, Russell *7:* 130
Petie, Haris *2:* 3; *10:* 41, 118; *11:* 227; *12:* 70
Petit-Roulet, Philippe *227:* 12
Petricic, Dusan *153:* 75, 76, 77; *170:* 12; *172:* 13; *176:* 170; *179:* 56
Petrides, Heidrun *19:* 223
Petrone, Valeria *159:* 160; *171:* 92; *186:* 173; *204:* 49; *216:* 208; *220:* 98; *233:* 126
Petrosino, Tamara *177:* 40; *193:* 154, 155
Petruccio, Steven James *67:* 159; *127:* 5
Pettingill, Ondre *64:* 181; *70:* 64; *222:* 167, 168
Peyo *40:* 56, 57
Peyton, K.M. *15:* 212
Pfeifer, Herman *15:* 262
Pfister, Marcus *83:* 165, 166, 167; *146:* 152; *150:* 160; *207:* 132, 134, 135, 136
Pfloog, Jan *124:* 60
Pham, LeUyen *160:* 48; *175:* 154, 156; *179:* 149; *201:* 124, 125, 126, 127; *204:* 28; *208:* 206; *217:* 92; *234:* 215; *237:* 110, 111, 112
Phelan, Matt *182:* 160; *184:* 222; *215:* 140, 141; *221:* 157; *231:* 28
Phillipps, J.C. *218:* 142
Phillips, Craig *70:* 151; *207:* 74; *221:* 159; *229:* 22
Phillips, Douglas *1:* 19
Phillips, F.D. *6:* 202
Phillips, Gary R. *223:* 23
Phillips, Louise *133:* 67
Phillips, Matt *184:* 173
Phillips, Thomas *30:* 55
Philpot, Glyn *54:* 46
Phiz
See Browne, Hablot K.
Piatti, Celestino *16:* 223
Pica, Steve *115:* 181
Picarella, Joseph *13:* 147
Picart, Gabriel *121:* 165; *201:* 169
Picasso, Pablo *228:* 131
Pichon, Liz *174:* 139
Pickard, Charles *12:* 38; *18:* 203; *36:* 152
Picken, George A. *23:* 150
Pickens, David *22:* 156
Pickering, Jimmy *195:* 152; *197:* 163; *238:* 71
Pien, Lark *222:* 143, 144
Pienkowski, Jan *6:* 183; *30:* 32; *58:* 140, 141, 142,143, 146, 147; *73:* 3; *87:* 156, 157; *131:* 189
Pieper, Christiane *200:* 168
Pignataro, Anna *163:* 220; *223:* 143 *Pile, Emma 218:* 156 *Pileggi, Steve 145:* 122
Pilkey, Dav *68:* 186; *115:* 164, 166; *166:* 173, 174, 175
Pimlott, John *10:* 205
Pincus, Harriet *4:* 186; *8:* 179; *22:* 148; *27:* 164, 165; *66:* 202
Pini, Wendy *89:* 166
Pinkett, Neil *60:* 8
Pinkney, Brian *81:* 184, 185; *94:* 107; *113:* 146, 147; *117:* 121, 166; *132:* 145; *158:* 108, 191; *160:* 189; *200:* 8
Pinkney, Jerry *8:* 218; *10:* 40; *15:* 276; *20:* 66; *24:* 121; *33:* 109; *36:* 222; *38:* 200; *41:* 165, 166, 167, 168, 169, 170, 171, 173, 174; *44:* 198; *48:* 51; *53:* 20; *56:* 61, 68; *58:* 184; *60:* 59; *61:* 91; *71:* 146, 148, 149; *72:* 17; *73:* 149; *74:* 159,192; *75:* 45; *80:* 206; *81:* 44; *85:* 144; *95:* 50; *107:* 158, 159, 160; *108:* 164; *112:* 114, 115; *133:* 58; *195:* 140; *227:* 131
Pinkwater, Daniel Manus *8:* 156; *46:* 180, 181, 182, 185, 188, 189, 190; *151:* 161 *76:* 178, 179, 180; *210:* 203
Pinkwater, Manus
See Pinkwater, Daniel Manus
Pinkwater, Jill *114:* 160, 161; *158:* 179; *188:* 143, 145, 146
Pinto, Ralph *10:* 131; *45:* 93
Pinto, Sara *200:* 165
Pinon, Mark *74:* 22
Piven, Hanoch *173:* 142; *236:* 157, 158, 159
Pistolesi *73:* 211
Pitcairn, Ansel *188:* 10; *227:* 20
Pittman, Helena Clare *71:* 151
Pitz, Henry C. *4:* 168; *19:* 165; *35:* 128; *42:* 80; *YABC 2:* 95, 176
Pitzenberger, Lawrence J. *26:* 94
Pitzer, Susanna *181:* 131
Place, François *218:* 42
Plant, Andrew *214:* 166
Player, Stephen *82:* 190
Plecas, Jennifer *84:* 201; *106:* 124; *149:* 168; *205:* 180; *220:* 81; *229:* 152, 153, 154
Ploog, Mike *180:* 19; *241:* 34
Plowden, David *52:* 135, 136
Plume, Ilse *170:* 149
Plummer, William *32:* 31
Podevin, Jean François *184:* 185
Podwal, Mark *56:* 170, 173; *101:* 154, 155, 157; *149:* 176; *160:* 194; *224:* 127, 128, 129
Pogany, Willy *15:* 46, 49; *19:* 222, 256; *25:* 214; *44:* 142, 143, 144, 145, 146, 147, 148
Pohrt, Tom *67:* 116; *104:* 80; *152:* 199; *195:* 154; *199:* 85
Poirson, V.A. *26:* 89
Polacco, Patricia *74:* 195, 196, 197, 198; *123:* 121, 122, 123; *180:* 189, 190, 191, 193, 194; *212:* 168, 170, 171
Polgreen, John *21:* 44
Polhemus, Coleman *210:* 209
Politi, Leo *1:* 178; *4:* 53; *21:* 48; *47:* 173,174, 176, 178, 179, 180, 181
Pollack, Barbara *219:* 60
Pollema-Cahill, Phyllis *123:* 126
Pollen, Samson *64:* 80
Polonsky, Arthur *34:* 168
Polseno, Jo *1:* 53; *3:* 117; *5:* 114; *17:* 154; *20:* 87; *32:* 49; *41:* 245
Pomaska, Anna *117:* 148
Pons, Bernadette *184:* 100
Ponter, James *5:* 204
Poole, Colin *111:* 27
Poortvliet, Rien *6:* 212; *65:* 165, 166, 167
Pope, Kevin *183:* 158
Popp, Wendy *72:* 122; *158:* 68
Poppel, Hans *71:* 154, 155
Porfirio, Guy *76:* 134
Portal, Colette *6:* 186; *11:* 203
Porter, George *7:* 181
Porter, Janice Lee *136:* 175; *164:* 37
Porter, John *113:* 47
Porter, Pat Grant *84:* 112; *125:* 101
Porter, Sue *146:* 246, 247; *213:* 139, 140, 141; *221:* 91
Porter, Walter *124:* 175
Porto, James *221:* 14
Posada, Mia *187:* 151
Posen, Michael *175:* 82
Post, R.K. *233:* 60
Posthuma, Sieb *150:* 163
Postier, Jim *202:* 140; *204:* 25
Postma, Lidia *79:* 17
Potter, Beatrix *100:* 194, 195; *132:* 179, 180, 181, 182; *YABC 1:* 208, 209, 210, 212, 213
Potter, Giselle *117:* 123; *143:* 44; *144:* 170, 197; *149:* 7; *150:* 165; *187:* 152, 153; *190:* 198; *196:* 152; *200:* 12; *225:* 60; *227:* 105; *235:* 150
Potter, Katherine *104:* 147; *171:* 135; *173:* 136; *217:* 130, 131
Potter, Miriam Clark *3:* 162
Poulin, Stephane *98:* 140, 141
Poullis, Nick *146:* 210
Powell, Constance Buffington *174:* 141
Powell, Gary *151:* 208
Powell, Ivan *67:* 219
Power, Margaret *105:* 122
Powers, Daniel *161:* 173
Powers, Richard M. *1:* 230; *3:* 218; *7:* 194; *26:* 186
Powledge, Fred *37:* 154
Powzyk, Joyce *74:* 214
Poydar, Nancy *96:* 149; *190:* 180, 181, 182; *240:* 84
Pracher, Richard *91:* 166
Prachaticka, Marketa *126:* 126
Prange, Beckie *181:* 169; *236:* 173, 175
Prap, Lila *177:* 165
Prater, John *103:* 142, 143, 144; *149:* 172
Pratt, Charles *23:* 29
Pratt, Christine Joy *214:* 167
Pratt, George *116:* 208; *212:* 37
Pratt, Pierre *150:* 73; *166:* 183; *168:* 172; *201:* 27; *208:* 171, 172, 173
Prebenna, David *73:* 174
Press, Jenny *116:* 95
Preston, Mark *152:* 162
Pretro, Korinna *91:* 126
Prevost, Mikela *209:* 111
Price, Christine *2:* 247; *3:* 163, 253; *8:* 166
Price, Cynthia *118:* 156
Price, Edward *33:* 34
Price, Garrett *1:* 76; *2:* 42
Price, Hattie Longstreet *17:* 13
Price, Nick *216:* 173; *220:* 7
Price, Norman *YABC 1:* 129
Price, Willard *48:* 184
Priceman, Marjorie *81:* 171; *136:* 169; *156:* 200; *168:* 153, 154; *188:* 45; *226:* 7; *234:* 160, 161, 163, 164; *235:* 74
Priestley, Alice *168:* 33; *227:* 142
Priestley, Chris *198:* 144
Prigmore, Shane *234:* 166; *238:* 156

Primavera, Elise *26:* 95; *58:* 151; *73:* 37; *80:* 79; *86:* 156; *105:* 161; *213:* 157; *230:* 132, 133, 134
Primrose, Jean *36:* 109
Prince, Alison *86:* 188, 189
Prince, Leonora E. *7:* 170
Pritchett, Shelley *116:* 148
Prittie, Edwin J. *YABC 1:* 120
Proimos, James *176:* 4; *217:* 132, 133, 134
Proimos, John *173:* 144
Prosmitsky, Jenya *132:* 33
Provensen, Alice *37:* 204, 215, 222; *70:* 176, 177, 178, 180, *71:* 213; *147:* 184; *191:* 190
Provensen, Martin *37:* 204, 215, 222; *70:* 176, 177, 178, 180; *71:* 213; *191:* 190
Pucci, Albert John *44:* 154
Pudlo *8:* 59
Puggaard, Ulla *196:* 25
Pullen, Zachary *211:* 161; *235:* 21
Pulver, Harry, Jr. *129:* 159
Pulver, Robin *160:* 4
Punchatz, Don *99:* 57
Purdy, Susan *8:* 162
Pursell, Weimer *55:* 18
Purston, Oliver *229:* 156
Purtscher, Alfons *97:* 6
Purvis, Leland *232:* 156
Puskas, James *5:* 141
Pyk, Jan *7:* 26; *38:* 123
Pyle, Charles S. *99:* 149; *191:* 83; *233:* 20, 21; *233:* 85
Pyle, Howard *16:* 225, 226, 227, 228, 230, 231, 232, 235; *24:* 27; *34:* 124, 125, 127, 128; *59:* 132; *100:* 198

Q

Quackenbush, Robert *4:* 190; *6:* 166; *7:* 175, 178; *9:* 86; *11:* 65, 221; *41:* 154; *43:* 157; *70:* 185, 186; *71:* 137; *85:* 47; *92:* 148; *133:* 154, 164, 169
Qualls, Sean *177:* 167, 168; *193:* 43; *228:* 108; *233:* 128, 129; *235:* 152
Quennell, Marjorie (Courtney) *29:* 163, 164
Quidor, John *19:* 82
Quirk, John *62:* 170
Quirk, Thomas *12:* 81

R

Rackham, Arthur *15:* 32, 78, 214-227; *17:* 105, 115; *18:* 233; *19:* 254; *20:* 151; *22:* 129, 131, 132, 133; *23:* 175; *24:* 161, 181; *26:* 91; *32:* 118; *64:* 18; *100:* 9, 16, 203, 204; *YABC 1:* 25, 45, 55, 147; *2:* 103, 142, 173, 210
Racz, Michael *56:* 134
Raczka, Bob *191:* 155, 156
Radcliffe, Andrew *82:* 215
Rader, Laura *101:* 219; *197:* 147; *203:* 53
Radunsky, Vladimir *177:* 170; *192:* 30; *238:* 140
Radzinski, Kandy *212:* 174
Rafilson, Sidney *11:* 172
Raglin, Tim *125:* 24
Raible, Alton *1:* 202, 203; *28:* 193; *35:* 181; *110:* 207
Raine, Patricia *82:* 74; *88:* 154
Ramá, Sue *173:* 45; *185:* 186; *190:* 184; *237:* 123
Ramhorst, John *117:* 11
Ramirez, Gladys *177:* 19
Ramirez, Jose *207:* 27
Ramsey, James *16:* 41
Ramsey, Marcy Dunn *82:* 11; *180:* 186
Ramus, Michael *51:* 171
Rand, Paul *6:* 188
Rand, Ted *67:* 9, 10, 121, 123; *74:* 190; *84:* 170; *103:* 170; *112:* 6; *114:* 73; *139:* 168; *143:* 194; *156:* 154; *161:* 9, 10; *200:* 38; *204:* 7
Randazzo, Tony *81:* 98
Randell, William *55:* 54
Rane, Walter *93:* 144; *143:* 109; *184:* 126
Rankin, Joan *163:* 40; *212:* 176
Rankin, Laura *176:* 173, 174; *179:* 150; *236:* 163
Ransome, Arthur *22:* 201
Ransome, James E. *74:* 137; *75:* 80; *84:* 181; *94:* 108; *117:* 115; *123:* 128, 129, 130; *158:* 101, 102; *159:* 205; *178:* 188, 189, 190; *216:* 114; *227:* 146, 148, 149, 150
Rantz, Don *119:* 184
Rao, Anthony *28:* 126
Raphael, Elaine *23:* 192; *71:* 24, 25
Rappaport, Eva *6:* 190
Raschka, Chris *80:* 187, 189, 190; *97:* 211; *115:* 210; *117:* 151, 152, 153, 154; *143:* 195; *145:* 153; *166:* 190, 191; *170:* 114; *207:* 140, 143, 144, 145; *208:* 82; *220:* 85
Rash, Andy *158:* 178; *162:* 172; *210:* 204; *219:* 145; *226:* 194
Raskin, Ellen *2:* 208, 209; *4:* 142; *13:* 183; *22:* 68; *29:* 139; *36:* 134; *38:* 173, 174, 175, 176, 177, 178,179, 180, 181; *60:* 163; *86:* 81
Rathmann, Peggy *93:* 32; *94:* 168; *157:* 212, 214
Ratkus, Tony *77:* 133
Rattray, Gail *227:* 96
Ratzkin, Lawrence *40:* 143
Rau, Margaret *9:* 157
Raverat, Gwen *YABC 1:* 152
Ravid, Joyce *61:* 73
Ravielli, Anthony *1:* 198; *3:* 168; *11:* 143
Ravilious, Robin *77:* 169
Rawlins, Donna *72:* 198; *73:* 15, 129
Rawlins, Janet *76:* 79
Rawlings, Steve *143:* 139; *151:* 54; *208:* 150
Rawlinson, Debbie *75:* 132
Ray, Deborah Kogan *8:* 164; *29:* 238; *50:* 112, 113; *62:* 119; *78:* 191; *203:* 149, 150, 151
Ray, Jane *96:* 166; *97:* 104; *152:* 208; *190:* 221; *196:* 165
Ray, Ralph *2:* 239; *5:* 73
Rayann, Omar *162:* 205; *186:* 29, 30
Rayevsky, Robert *64:* 17; *70:* 173; *80:* 204; *117:* 79; *190:* 187, 188
Raymond, Larry *31:* 108; *97:* 109
Rayner, Hugh *151:* 170
Rayner, Mary *22:* 207; *47:* 140; *72:* 191; *87:* 171, 172; *192:* 104
Rayner, Shoo
See Rayner, Hugh
Raynes, John *71:* 19
Raynor, Dorka *28:* 168
Raynor, Paul *24:* 73
Rayyan, Omar *110:* 222; *112:* 17; *125:* 131
Razzi, James *10:* 127
Read, Alexander D. *20:* 45
Reader, Dennis *71:* 157
Reasoner, Charles *53:* 33, 36, 37
Rebenshied, Shane *203:* 76; *215:* 124; *237:* 155
Reczuch, Karen *115:* 132; *145:* 131
Redlich, Ben *163:* 221; *198:* 193
Reddy, Mike *203:* 67
Reed, Joseph *116:* 139
Reed, Lynn Rowe *115:* 173; *171:* 146; *208:* 177; *215:* 144, 145
Reed, Mike *211:* 147; *215:* 131
Reed, Tom *34:* 171
Reeder, Colin *74:* 202; *77:* 113
Rees, Mary *134:* 219
Reese, Bob *60:* 135
Reeve, Philip *171:* 50
Reeves, Eira B. *130:* 173, 174; *141:* 151
Reeves, Rick *181:* 179
Reeves, Rosie *202:* 200
Regan, Dana *117:* 116
Regan, Laura *103:* 198; *153:* 206
Reichert, Renée *169:* 127
Reid, Barbara *82:* 178; *92:* 17; *93:* 169, 170; *222:* 45
Reid, Stephen *19:* 213; *22:* 89
Reim, Melanie *104:* 151; *150:* 98
Reinert, Kirk *89:* 138; *195:* 129
Reinertson, Barbara *44:* 150; *62:* 103
Reiniger, Lotte *40:* 185
Reisberg, Mira *119:* 2
Reisch, Jesse *158:* 130
Reiser, Lynn *81:* 175; *138:* 184; *180:* 200
Reiss, John J. *23:* 193
Relf, Douglas *3:* 63
Relyea, C.M. *16:* 29; *31:* 153
Remi, Georges *13:* 184
Remington, Frederic *19:* 188; *41:* 178, 179, 180, 181, 183,184, 185, 186, 187, 188; *62:* 197
Remkiewicz, Frank *67:* 102; *77:* 171; *80:* 130; *113:* 107; *152:* 116; *152:* 211, 212; *157:* 148; *217:* 120, 138, 139, 140, 141
Rendon, Maria *116:* 141; 192; *134:* 152
Renfro, Ed *79:* 176
Renier, Aaron *202:* 141; *207:* 119
Renlie, Frank *11:* 200
Reschofsky, Jean *7:* 118
Rethi *60:* 181
Rethi, Lili *2:* 153; *36:* 156
Reusswig, William *3:* 267
Revell, Cindy *195:* 93
Rex, Adam *156:* 172; *169:* 91; *186:* 178, 179; *215:* 103; *223:* 11; *225:* 154
Rex, Michael *157:* 147; *191:* 159, 160; *221:* 124
Rey, H.A. *1:* 182; *26:* 163, 164, 166, 167, 169; *69:* 172, 173, 174, 175; *86:* 195, 196, 197; *100:* 211; *YABC 2:* 17
Rey, Luis V. *201:* 162
Reynish, Jenny *222:* 155
Reynolds, Adrian *192:* 159, 160; *237:* 178
Reynolds, Doris *5:* 71; *31:* 77
Reynolds, Peter H. *142:* 12; *179:* 175, 176; *202:* 113, 114; *226:* 30, 166, 167; *228:* 132
Rhead, Louis *31:* 91; *100:* 228
Rhodes, Andrew *38:* 204; *50:* 163; *54:* 76; *61:* 123, 124; *87:* 200
Ribbons, Ian *3:* 10; *37:* 161; *40:* 76
Ricci, Regolo *93:* 22; *164:* 148
Rice, Elizabeth *2:* 53, 214
Rice, Eve *34:* 174, 175; *91:* 172
Rice, James *22:* 210; *93:* 173
Rich, Anna *212:* 180
Rich, Martha *195:* 16
Richards, Chuck *170:* 154
Richards, George *40:* 116, 119, 121; *44:* 179
Richards, Henry *YABC 1:* 228, 231
Richardson, Ernest *2:* 144
Richardson, Frederick *18:* 27, 31
Richardson, John *110:* 88
Richman, Hilda *26:* 132
Richmond, George *24:* 179
Riddell, Chris *114:* 170, 195; *166:* 179; *199:* 164, 166, 167; *218:* 146, 148; *219:* 149, 150, 152, 153; *228:* 125
Riddle, Tohby *74:* 204; *151:* 179; *223:* 154, 156
Riding, Peter *63:* 195
Rieniets, Judy King *14:* 28
Riger, Bob *2:* 166
Riggio, Anita *73:* 191; *85:* 63; *137:* 184; *172:* 165
Rigano, Giovanni *219:* 45
Riley, Jon *74:* 70
Riley, Kenneth *22:* 230
Riley, Terry *203:* 100
Riley-Webb, Charlotte *153:* 143; *235:* 14, 161, 162
Rim, Sujean *225:* 157

Rinaldi, Angelo *165:* 60, 69; *227:* 53
Ringgold, Faith *71:* 162; *114:* 173, 174, 176; *187:* 160, 161, 163
Ringi, Kjell *12:* 171
Rios, Tere
See Versace, Marie
Rioux, Jo *215:* 110; *226:* 170
Ripper, Charles L. *3:* 175
Ripplinger, Henry *117:* 31
Ritchie, Scot *217:* 145
Ritchie, William *74:* 183
Ritter, John *175:* 14; *240:* 21
Ritz, Karen *41:* 117; *72:* 239; *87:* 125; *102:* 7; *106:* 6
Rivas, Victor *209:* 193; *226:* 144; *241:* 120
Rivers, Ruth *178:* 193
Rivkin, Jay *15:* 230
Rivoche, Paul *45:* 125
Roach, Marilynne *9:* 158
Robbin, Jodi *44:* 156, 159
Robbins, Frank *42:* 167
Robbins, Ken *147:* 191, 192; *234:* 182
Robbins, Ruth *52:* 102
Roberton, Fiona *230:* 142
Roberts, Cliff *4:* 126
Roberts, David *154:* 4, 6; *191:* 162; *196:* 184; *197:* 105; *210:* 257
Roberts, Doreen *4:* 230; *28:* 105
Roberts, Jim *22:* 166; *23:* 69; *31:* 110
Roberts, Tony *109:* 195, 214
Roberts, W. *22:* 2, 3
Robertson, M.P. *197:* 153
Robins, Arthur *137:* 172; *151:* 225; *204:* 161
Robinson, Aminah Brenda Lynn *86:* 205; *103:* 55; *159:* 175
Robinson, Charles [1870-1937] *17:* 157, 171, 172, 173, 175, 176; *24:* 207; *25:* 204; *YABC 2:* 308, 309, 310, 331
Robinson, Charles *3:* 53; *5:* 14; *6:* 193; *7:* 150; *7:* 183; *8:* 38; *9:* 81; *13:* 188; *14:* 248, 249; *23:* 149; *26:* 115; *27:* 48; *28:* 191; *32:* 28; *35:* 210; *36:* 37; *48:* 96; *52:* 33; *53:* 157; *56:* 15; *62:* 142; *77:* 41; *111:* 148
Robinson, Fiona *225:* 158
Robinson, Jerry *3:* 262
Robinson, Joan G. *7:* 184
Robinson, Lolly *90:* 227
Robinson, T.H. *17:* 179, 181, 182, 183; *29:* 254
Robinson, W. Heath *17:* 185, 187, 189, 191, 193, 195, 197, 199, 202; *23:* 167; *25:* 194; *29:* 150; *YABC 1:* 44; *2:* 183
Rocco, John *187:* 4; *188:* 151; *208:* 180, 181, 182; *213:* 94; *222:* 34; *238:* 130, 131, 132
Roche, Christine *41:* 98
Roche, Denis *99:* 184; *180:* 32; *196:* 168
Roche, P.K. *57:* 151, 152
Rocker, Fermin *7:* 34; *13:* 21; *31:* 40; *40:* 190,191
Rocklen, Margot *101:* 181
Rockwell, Anne *5:* 147; *33:* 171, 173; *71:* 166, 167,168; *114:* 183, 184; *194:* 152, 155; *235:* 170
Rockwell, Gail *7:* 186
Rockwell, Harlow *33:* 171, 173, 175
Rockwell, Lizzy *114:* 182; *162:* 182; *185:* 189; *233:* 134, 135, 136; *235:* 171
Rockwell, Norman *23:* 39, 196, 197, 199, 200, 203, 204, 207; *41:* 140, 143; *123:* 47; *YABC 2:* 60
Rockwood, Richard *119:* 75
Rodanas, Kristina *156:* 183, 184; *221:* 127
Rodegast, Roland *43:* 100
Rodgers, Frank *69:* 177
Rodriguez, Albert G. *182:* 50
Rodriguez, Christina *184:* 12; *225:* 94
Rodriguez, Edel *204:* 86
Rodriguez, Joel *16:* 65
Rodriguez, Robert *145:* 145; *212:* 33
Rodriguez-Howard, Pauline *177:* 18
Roe, Monika *210:* 94
Roeckelein, Katrina *134:* 223
Roennfeldt, Robert *66:* 243
Roever, J.M. *4:* 119; *26:* 170
Roffey, Maureen *33:* 142, 176, 177
Rogasky, Barbara *46:* 90
Rogé *173:* 160; *233:* 138
Rogers, Carol *2:* 262; *6:* 164; *26:* 129
Rogers, Chris M. *150:* 59; *196:* 61
Rogers, Forest *87:* 160; *101:* 76
Rogers, Frances *10:* 130
Rogers, Gregory *104:* 76; *126:* 57; *171:* 26
Rogers, Jacqueline *78:* 249; *80:* 34; *86:* 54 *103:* 70; *115:* 72; *129:* 173; *131:* 57, 225; *143:* 211; *153:* 100; *193:* 186; *203:* 51; *213:* 144, 145, 146; *214:* 142; *234:* 173; *236:* 91
Rogers, Sherry *191:* 66
Rogers, Walter S. *31:* 135, 138; *67:* 65, 168; *100:* 81
Rogers, William A. *15:* 151, 153, 154; *33:* 35
Rogoff, Barbara *95:* 20
Rohmann, Eric *103:* 152; *198:* 151
Rojankovsky, Feodor *6:* 134, 136; *10:* 183; *21:* 128,129, 130; *25:* 110; *28:* 42; *68:* 120
Rolfsen, Alf *62:* 15
Rolston, Steve *209:* 154; *223:* 113
Romain, Trevor *134:* 157
Roman, Barbara J. *103:* 171
Romas *114:* 111; *165:* 63
Romano, Robert *64:* 68
Romero, Alejandro *187:* 185
Roos, Maryn *168:* 198; *225:* 160; *226:* 143
Root, Barry *80:* 212; *90:* 196; *146:* 78; *156:* 165; *159:* 161; *182:* 18, 172; *232:* 160, 161, 162; *240:* 15
Root, Kimberly Bulcken *86:* 72; *98:* 21; *108:* 111; *127:* 114; *159:* 162; *176:* 134; *192:* 163
Roper, Bob *65:* 153
Roraback, Robin *111:* 156
Rorer, Abigail *43:* 222; *85:* 155
Rosales, Melodye *80:* 35
Rosamilia, Patricia *36:* 120
Rose, Carl *5:* 62
Rose, David S. *29:* 109; *70:* 120
Rose, Gerald *68:* 200, 201; *86:* 48
Rose, Naomi C. *228:* 136
Rose, Ted *93:* 178
Rosen, Elizabeth *205:* 137
Rosenbaum, Jonathan *50:* 46
Rosenberg, Amye *74:* 207, 208
Rosenberry, Vera *87:* 22, 26; *144:* 212, 213; *158:* 120; *219:* 163, 164
Rosenblum, Richard *11:* 202; *18:* 18
Rosenstiehl, Agnès *203:* 153
Rosenstock, Jason *238:* 75
Rosier, Lydia *16:* 236; *20:* 104; *21:* 109; *22:* 125; *30:* 151, 158; *42:* 128; *45:* 214; *77:* 227, 228
Rosing, Jens *85:* 142
Ross
See Thomson, Ross
Ross, Christine *83:* 172, 173
Ross, Clare Romano *3:* 123; *21:* 45; *48:* 199
Ross, Dave *32:* 152; *57:* 108
Ross, Graham *199:* 4
Ross, Herbert *37:* 78
Ross, John *3:* 123; *21:* 45
Ross, Johnny *32:* 190
Ross, Larry *47:* 168; *60:* 62
Ross, Ruth *109:* 233
Ross, Tony *17:* 204; *56:* 132; *65:* 176, 177, 179; *90:* 123; *123:* 186, 187, 190; *130:* 188, 190, 191, 192; *132:* 242; *174:* 159; *176:* 181, 182, 183; *202:* 198; *225:* 168, 170; *237:* 176, 177
Rossetti, Dante Gabriel *20:* 151, 153
Rostant, Larry *180:* 221; *194:* 108; *195:* 96; *197:* 12; *207:* 53; *210:* 189; *226:* 22; *234:* 154; *239:* 82, 116
Roth, Arnold *4:* 238; *21:* 133
Roth, Julie Jersild *180:* 206
Roth, Marci *135:* 223
Roth, R.G. *184:* 50
Roth, Rob *105:* 98; *146:* 41
Roth, Robert *176:* 159
Roth, Roger *61:* 128; *190:* 192
Roth, Ruby *216:* 185
Roth, Susan L. *80:* 38; *93:* 78; *134:* 165, 166; *181:* 145, 146
Rothenberg, Joani Keller *162:* 190, 191
Rothman, Michael *139:* 62; *184:* 34 *Rotman, Jeffrey L. 145:* 30
Rotondo, Pat *32:* 158
Roughsey, Dick *35:* 186
Rouille, M. *11:* 96
Rounds, Glen *8:* 173; *9:* 171; *12:* 56; *32:* 194; *40:* 230; *51:* 161, 162, 166; *56:* 149; *70:* 198, 199; *YABC 1:* 1, 2, 3; *112:* 163
Roundtree, Katherine *114:* 88; *168:* 102
Rovetch, Lissa *201:* 164
Rowan, Evadne *52:* 51
Rowe, Eric *111:* 161
Rowe, Gavin *27:* 144; *72:* 47; *88:* 201
Rowe, John *132:* 70, 71; *180:* 126
Rowell, Kenneth *40:* 72
Rowen, Amy *52:* 143
Rowena *116:* 101
Rowland, Andrew *164:* 136
Rowland, Jada *83:* 73
Rowles, Daphne *58:* 24
Roy, Jeroo *27:* 229; *36:* 110
Royo *118:* 32; *144:* 105, 106, 108; *165:* 19; *166:* 166
Rubbino, Salvatore *220:* 147
Rubel, Nicole *18:* 255; *20:* 59; *81:* 66, 67; *95:* 169, 170; *119:* 60; *135:* 177, 179, 180; *169:* 68; *181:* 150
Rubel, Reina *33:* 217
Rud, Borghild *6:* 15
Ruddell, Gary *110:* 238; *116:* 207
Rudnicki, Richard *241:* 132
Rudolph, Norman Guthrie *17:* 13
Rue, Leonard Lee III *37:* 164
Rueda, Claudia *183:* 170, 171
Ruelle, Karen Gray *126:* 193
Ruff, Donna *50:* 173; *72:* 203; *78:* 49; *80:* 120,121; *93:* 162; *164:* 121
Ruffins, Reynold *10:* 134, 135; *41:* 191, 192, 193, 194, 195, 196; *125:* 187, 188, 189; *162:* 197; *239:* 153
Ruhlin, Roger *34:* 44
Rui, Paolo *217:* 115
Ruiz, Art *95:* 154; *110:* 91
Rumford, James *193:* 167
Runnerstroem, Bengt Arne *75:* 161
Runton, Andy *241:* 133
Ruse, Margaret *24:* 155
Rush, Ken *98:* 74
Rush, Peter *42:* 75
Russell, Charles M. *167:* 171
Russell, E.B. *18:* 177, 182
Russell, Jim *53:* 134
Russell, Natalie *218:* 170, 171
Russell, P. Craig *80:* 196; *146:* 102; *162:* 186
Russo, Marisabina *84:* 51; *106:* 164; *151:* 183; *188:* 153, 154, 155, 156
Russo, Susan *30:* 182; *36:* 144
Russon, Mary *87:* 145
Ruth, Greg *183:* 125
Ruth, Rod *9:* 161
Rutherford, Alexa *110:* 108
Rutherford, Jenny *78:* 5
Rutherford, Meg *25:* 174; *34:* 178, 179; *69:* 73; *72:* 31
Rutland, Jonathan *31:* 126
Ruurs, Margriet *147:* 195
Ruzzier, Sergio *159:* 176, 177; *163:* 184; *210:* 214, 216
Ryan, Amy *188:* 50
Ryan, Will *86:* 134
Rycroft, Nina *228:* 143
Ryden, Hope *8:* 176
Rylant, Cynthia *112:* 170, 172

Rymer, Alta M. *34:* 181
Ryniak, Christopher *178:* 11
Rystedt, Rex *49:* 80

S

Saaf, Chuck *49:* 179
Saaf, Donald *101:* 220; *124:* 180
Sabaka, Donna R. *21:* 172
Sabin, Robert *45:* 35; *60:* 30; *99:* 161; *223:* 29
Sabuda, Robert *170:* 166, 167, 168
Sacker, Amy *16:* 100
Sadler, Sonia Lynn *230:* 42, 163
Saelig, S.M. *129:* 73; *173:* 59
Saffioti, Lino *36:* 176; *48:* 60; *223:* 26
Saflund, Birgitta *94:* 2
Sagsoorian, Paul *12:* 183; *22:* 154; *33:* 106; *87:* 152
Sahara, Tony *168:* 106; *177:* 181; *178:* 228; *186:* 132; *207:* 89; *231:* 54; *236:* 107, 109
Sahlberg, Myron *57:* 165
Saidens, Amy *145:* 162; *191:* 131; *210:* 129
Saint Exupery, Antoine de *20:* 157
Saint James, Synthia *152:* 220; *188:* 90; *200:* 7
Sakai, Komako *213:* 148
Sakamoto, Miki *241:* 102
Saldutti, Denise *39:* 186; *57:* 178
Sale, Morton *YABC 2:* 31
Sale, Tim *153:* 177
Salerno, Steven *150:* 79; *176:* 188; *202:* 39; *216:* 190; *235:* 55
Salter, George *72:* 128, 130
Saltzberg, Barney *135:* 184, 185; *194:* 160; *233:* 147, 148
Saltzman, David *86:* 209
Salwowski, Mark *71:* 54
Salzman, Yuri *86:* 12
Sambourne, Linley *YABC 2:* 181
Sampson, Katherine *9:* 197
Samson, Anne S. *2:* 216
San Souci, Daniel *40:* 200; *96:* 199, 200; *113:* 171; *157:* 149; *170:* 69; *192:* 167, 168; *220:* 152; *221:* 126
Sancha, Sheila *38:* 185
Sanchez, Enrique O. *155:* 84
Sand, George X. *45:* 182
Sandberg, Lasse *15:* 239, 241
Sanders, Beryl *39:* 173
Sanderson, Ruth *21:* 126; *24:* 53; *28:* 63; *33:* 67; *41:* 48, 198, 199, 200, 201, 202, 203; *43:* 79; *46:* 36,44; *47:* 102; *49:* 58; *62:* 121, 122; *85:* 3; *109:* 207, 208, 209, 210; *172:* 157, 158; *223:* 85; *224:* 152, 153, 154
Sandia *119:* 74
Sandin, Joan *4:* 36; *6:* 194; *7:* 177; *12:* 145,185; *20:* 43; *21:* 74; *26:* 144; *27:* 142; *28:* 224, 225; *38:* 86; *41:* 46; *42:* 35; *59:* 6; *80:* 136; *94:* 188; *140:* 116; *153:* 179, 180; *197:* 168; *232:* 6
Sandland, Reg *39:* 215
Sandoz, Edouard *26:* 45, 47
Sanford, John *66:* 96, 97
Sanger, Amy Wilson *205:* 140
Sankey, Tom *72:* 103
Sano, Kazuhiko *153:* 208; *195:* 171; *203:* 21; *221:* 71
Santat, Dan *188:* 160; *221:* 62; *223:* 163; *224:* 157, 158, 159
Santiago, Wilfred *210:* 48
Santore, Charles *54:* 139; *200:* 171, 172
Santoro, Christopher *74:* 215
Santoro, Scott *236:* 166
Santos, Jesse J. *99:* 24
Sapieha, Christine *1:* 180
Saport, Linda *123:* 137, 138; *215:* 29
Sara
See De La Roche Saint Andre, Anne
Sarcone-Roach, Julia *215:* 158
Sardinha, Rick *175:* 151
Sarg, Tony *YABC 2:* 236
Sargent, Claudia *64:* 181
Sargent, Robert *2:* 217
Saris *1:* 33
Sarony *YABC 2:* 170
Saroff, Phyllis V. *202:* 160
Sasaki, Goro *170:* 46; *237:* 23
Sasaki, Ellen Joy *216:* 49
Sasek, Miroslav *16:* 239, 240, 241, 242
Sassman, David *9:* 79
Sattler, Jennifer Gordon *218:* 175
Satty *29:* 203, 205
Sauber, Robert *40:* 183; *76:* 256; *78:* 154; *87:* 92
Saunders, Dave *85:* 163, 164, 165
Savadier, Elivia *84:* 50; *145:* 45; *164:* 206; *228:* 146
Savage, Naomi *56:* 172
Savage, Steele *10:* 203; *20:* 77; *35:* 28
Savage, Stephen *174:* 182
Savio *76:* 4
Savitt, Sam *8:* 66, 182; *15:* 278; *20:* 96; *24:* 192; *28:* 98
Sawyer, Kem Knapp *84:* 228, 229
Sawyer, Odessa *239:* 117
Say, Allen *28:* 178; *69:* 182, 183, 232; *110:* 194, 195,196; *161:* 154, 155
Sayles, Elizabeth *82:* 93; *105:* 155; *109:* 116; *180:* 64; *220:* 160, 161; *232:* 177
Scabrini, Janet *13:* 191; *44:* 128
Scalora, Suza *224:* 160
Scanlan, Peter *83:* 27; *153:* 165; *187:* 149
Scanlon, Paul *83:* 87
Scannell, Reece *105:* 105
Scarry, Huck *35:* 204, 205
Scarry, Richard *2:* 220, 221; *18:* 20; *35:* 193, 194, 195,196, 197, 198, 199, 200, 201, 202; *75:* 165, 167, 168
Schachner, Judith Byron *88:* 180; *92:* 163; *93:* 102; *142:* 82; *178:* 199, 200; *190:* 140; *228:* 83
Schade, Susan *205:* 21
Schaeffer, Mead *18:* 81, 94; *21:* 137, 138, 139; *47:* 128
Schaffer, Amanda *90:* 206
Schallau, Daniel *222:* 164
Schanzer, Rosalyn *138:* 192, 193
Scharl, Josef *20:* 132; *22:* 128
Scharschmidt, Sherry *239:* 60; *240:* 131
Scheel, Lita *11:* 230
Scheffler, Axel *180:* 23, 24; *230:* 169, 170
Scheib, Ida *29:* 28
Schermer, Judith *30:* 184
Schick, Eleanor *82:* 210, 211; *144:* 222
Schick, Joel *16:* 160; *17:* 167; *22:* 12; *27:* 176; *31:* 147, 148; *36:* 23; *38:* 64; *45:* 116, 117; *52:* 5, 85; *104:* 159
Schields, Gretchen *75:* 171, 203
Schindelman, Joseph *1:* 74; *4:* 101; *12:* 49; *26:* 51; *40:* 146; *56:* 158; *73:* 40
Schindler, Edith *7:* 22
Schindler, S.D. *38:* 107; *46:* 196; *74:* 162; *75:* 172, 173; *99:* 133; *112:* 177; *118:* 185, 186; *121:* 71; *136:* 159; *143:* 45; *149:* 120; *156:* 30; *169:* 135; *171:* 161, 162, 163; *172:* 9; *186:* 163; *194:* 109; *195:* 35; *198:* 170, 171, 172; *237:* 121
Schlesinger, Bret *7:* 77
Schlossberg, Elisabeth *221:* 161
Schmid, Eleanore *12:* 188; *126:* 196, 197
Schmid, Paul *231:* 169
Schmiderer, Dorothy *19:* 224
Schmidt, Bill *73:* 34; *76:* 220, 222, 224
Schmidt, Elizabeth *15:* 242
Schmidt, George Paul *132:* 122
Schmidt, Karen Lee *54:* 12; *71:* 174; *92:* 56; *94:* 190, 191; *127:* 103
Schmidt, Lynette *76:* 205
Schmitz, Tamara *207:* 147
Schneider, Christine M. *171:* 165
Schneider, Howie *181:* 159
Schneider, Katy *237:* 128
Schneider, Rex *29:* 64; *44:* 171
Schnurr, Edward *170:* 62
Schoberle, Cecile *80:* 200; *92:* 134; *218:* 113
Schoenherr, Ian *32:* 83; *173:* 41; *235:* 174; *240:* 44
Schoenherr, John *1:* 146, 147, 173; *3:* 39, 139; *17:* 75; *29:* 72; *32:* 83; *37:* 168, 169, 170; *43:* 164, 165; *45:* 160, 162; *51:* 127; 66: 196, 197, 198; *68:* 83; *72:* 240; *75:* 225; *88:* 176
Scholder, Fritz *69:* 103
Schomburg, Alex *13:* 23
Schongut, Emanuel *4:* 102; *15:* 186; *47:* 218, 219; *52:* 147, 148, 149, 150; *185:* 27
Schoonover, Frank *17:* 107; *19:* 81, 190, 233; *22:* 88,129; *24:* 189; *31:* 88; *41:* 69; *YABC 2:* 282, 316
Schories, Pat *164:* 210; *232:* 170, 171, 172
Schottland, Miriam *22:* 172
Schramm, Ulrik *2:* 16; *14:* 112
Schreiber, Elizabeth Anne *13:* 193
Schreiber, Ralph W. *13:* 193
Schreiter, Rick *14:* 97; *23:* 171; *41:* 247; *49:* 131
Schroades, John *214:* 129
Schroeder, Binette *56:* 128, 129
Schroeder, E. Peter *12:* 112
Schroeder, Ted *11:* 160; *15:* 189; *30:* 91; *34:* 43
Schrotter, Gustav *22:* 212; *30:* 225
Schubert, Dieter *101:* 167, 168; *217:* 151, 152, 153, 155
Schubert, Ingrid *217:* 151, 152, 153, 155
Schubert-Gabrys, Ingrid *101:* 167, 168
Schucker, James *31:* 163
Schuett, Stacey *72:* 137; *208:* 204
Schulder, Lili *146:* 29
Schulke, Debra *57:* 167
Schulke, Flip *57:* 167
Schulz, Barbara *167:* 24
Schulz, Charles M. *10:* 137, 138, 139, 140, 141, 142; *118:* 192, 193, 194, 196, 199
Schutzer, Dena *109:* 32
Schwark, Mary Beth *51:* 155; *72:* 175
Schwartz, Amy *47:* 191; *82:* 100; *83:* 178, 179, 180,181; *129:* 107; *131:* 197, 198; *189:* 166, 168; *226:* 174
Schwartz, Carol *124:* 41; *130:* 199
Schwartz, Charles *8:* 184
Schwartz, Daniel *46:* 37
Schwartz, Joanie *124:* 170
Schwartzberg, Joan *3:* 208
Schwarz, Viviane *204:* 132
Schweitzer, Iris *2:* 137; *6:* 207
Schweninger, Ann *29:* 172; *82:* 246; *159:* 202; *168:* 166; *211:* 193
Schwinger, Laurence *84:* 44; *91:* 61
Scofield, Penrod *61:* 107; *62:* 160
Scott, Anita Walker *7:* 38
Scott, Art *39:* 41
Scott, Frances Gruse *38:* 43
Scott, Jane Wooster *226:* 181
Scott, Julian *34:* 126
Scott, Roszel *33:* 238
Scott, Sally *87:* 27
Scott, Steve *166:* 230, 231; *171:* 93
Scott, Trudy *27:* 172
Scotton, Rob *214:* 183
Scrace, Carolyn *143:* 95, 96
Scrambly, Crab *198:* 196
Scribner, Joanne *14:* 236; *29:* 78; *33:* 185; *34:* 208; *78:* 75; *164:* 237; *203:* 73
Scrofani, Joseph *31:* 65; *74:* 225
Scroggs, Kirk *187:* 169
Seaman, Mary Lott *34:* 64
Searle, Ronald *24:* 98; *42:* 172, 173, 174, 176, 177, 179; *66:* 73, 74; *70:* 205, 206, 207
Searle, Townley *36:* 85
Sebree, Charles *18:* 65

Sedacca, Joseph M. *11:* 25; *22:* 36
Seder, Jason *108:* 102
Seeger, Laura Vaccaro *172:* 162
Seegmiller, Don *174:* 57
Seely, David *164:* 173
Seeley, Laura L. *97:* 105
Segal, John *178:* 202
Segar, E.C. *61:* 179, 181
Segur, Adrienne *27:* 121
Seibold, J. Otto *83:* 188, 190, 191; *149:* 212, 214, 215, 216; *196:* 177, 179; *215:* 204
Seignobosc, Francoise *21:* 145, 146
Sejima, Yoshimasa *8:* 187
Selig, Sylvie *13:* 199
Seltzer, Isadore *6:* 18; *133:* 59
Seltzer, Meyer *17:* 214
Selven, Maniam *144:* 133
Selway, Martina *169:* 157
Selznick, Brian *79:* 192; *104:* 25; *117:* 175; *126:* 156; *134:* 171; *158:* 76, 78; *169:* 70; *171:* 172, 173; *191:* 106; *192:* 130; *197:* 158; *203:* 35; *205:* 92; *210:* 219, 220, 221, 222; *234:* 130
Sempe, Jean-Jacques *47:* 92; *YABC 2:* 109
Sendak, Maurice *1:* 135, 190; *3:* 204; *7:* 142; *15:* 199; *17:* 210; *27:* 181, 182, 183, 185, 186, 187, 189,190, 191, 192, 193, 194, 195, 197, 198, 199, 203; *28:* 181, 182; *32:* 108; *33:* 148, 149; *35:* 238; *44:* 180, 181; *45:* 97, 99; *46:* 174; *73:* 225; *91:* 10, 11 *YABC1:* 167; *113:* 163, 165, 167, 168; *118:* 153; *127:* 161
Senders, Marci *180:* 79
Sengler, Johanna *18:* 256
Senn, Steve *60:* 145
Seredy, Kate *1:* 192; *14:* 20, 21; *17:* 210
Sergeant, John *6:* 74
Serra, Sebastía *212:* 215
Servello, Joe *10:* 144; *24:* 139; *40:* 91; *70:* 130, 131; *146:* 159
Seton, Ernest Thompson *18:* 260-269, 271
Seuss, Dr.
See Geisel, Theodor
Severin, John Powers *7:* 62
Sewall, Marcia *15:* 8; *22:* 170; *37:* 171, 172, 173; *39:* 73; *45:* 209; *62:* 117; *69:* 185, 186; *71:* 212; *90:* 232; *96:* 127; *102:* 101; *107:* 129; *119:* 176, 177, 178, 180
Seward, James *70:* 35
Seward, Prudence *16:* 243
Sewell, Helen *3:* 186; *15:* 308; *33:* 102; *38:* 189, 190, 191, 192
Seymour, Stephen *54:* 21
Sfar, Joann *182:* 183
Shachat, Andrew *82:* 179
Shadbolt, Robert *203:* 68
Shahn, Ben *39:* 178; *46:* 193
Shalansky, Len *38:* 167
Shanks, Anne Zane *10:* 149
Shannon, David *57:* 137; *107:* 184; *112:* 216; *135:* 12; *152:* 223, 224, 225; *158:* 192; *212:* 159, 160, 163; *228:* 162, 163, 164, 165; *237:* 9; *238:* 152
Sharkey, Niamh *213:* 152
Sharp, Paul *52:* 60
Sharp, William *6:* 131; *19:* 241; *20:* 112; *25:* 141
Sharratt, Nick *102:* 207, 208; *104:* 163; *153:* 198; *175:* 176; *192:* 208; *199:* 141, 142, 143, 184, 187, 188
Shaw, Barclay *74:* 14, 16; *118:* 138
Shaw, Charles *21:* 135; *38:* 187; *47:* 124; *126:* 219
Shaw, Charles G. *13:* 200
Shaw, Hannah *227:* 163, 164
Shaw-Smith, Emma *144:* 117
Shea, Bob *231:* 170, 171
Shea, Edmund *56:* 19
Shearer, Ted *43:* 193, 194, 195, 196
Sheban, Chris *182:* 185; *190:* 102, 104; *202:* 28; *204:* 112, 114; *209:* 150; *210:* 107; *220:* 103; *224:* 185
Shecter, Ben *16:* 244; *25:* 109; *33:* 188, 191; *41:* 77
Shed, Greg *74:* 94; *84:* 204; *129:* 149, *167:* 91; *179:* 192; *223:* 104
Sheeban, Chris *144:* 190; *158:* 163
Shefcik, James *48:* 221, 222; *60:* 141
Shefelman, Karl *58:* 168
Shefelman, Tom *204:* 137
Shefts, Joelle *48:* 210
Shein, Bob *139:* 189
Sheinkin, Stephen *204:* 139
Shekerjian, Haig *16:* 245
Shekerjian, Regina *16:* 245; *25:* 73
Sheldon, David *184:* 174; *185:* 204; *211:* 189
Shelley, John *186:* 223
Shemie, Bonnie *96:* 207
Shenton, Edward *45:* 187, 188, 189; *YABC 1:* 218, 219, 221
Shepard, Ernest H. *3:* 193; *4:* 74; *16:* 101; *17:* 109; *25:* 148; *33:* 152, 199, 200, 201, 202, 203, 204, 205, 206,207; *46:* 194; *98:* 114; *100:* 111, 178, 179, 217, 219, 220,221; *YABC 1:* 148, 153, 174, 176, 180, 181
Shepard, Mary *4:* 210; *22:* 205; *30:* 132, 133; *54:* 150, 152, 153, 157, 158; *59:* 108, 109, 111; *100:* 246
Shepherd, Amanda *198:* 14
Shepherd, Irana *171:* 112
Sheppard, Kate *195:* 176
Shepperson, Rob *96:* 153; *177:* 163; *178:* 204; *197:* 34; *205:* 108; *240:* 136, 137
Sheridan, Brian *196:* 193
Sherman, Theresa *27:* 167
Sherwan, Earl *3:* 196
Shields, Charles *10:* 150; *36:* 63
Shields, Leonard *13:* 83, 85, 87
Shiffman, Lena *139:* 167; *168:* 136
Shiga, Jason *228:* 168
Shigley, Neil K. *66:* 219
Shillabeer, Mary *35:* 74
Shilston, Arthur *49:* 61; *62:* 58
Shimin, Symeon *1:* 93; *2:* 128, 129; *3:* 202; *7:* 85; *11:* 177; *12:* 139; *13:* 202, 203; *27:* 138; *28:* 65; *35:* 129; *36:* 130; *48:* 151; *49:* 59; *56:* 63, 65, 153
Shimizu, Yuko *215:* 197
Shine, Andrea *104:* 165; *128:* 34
Shinn, Everett *16:* 148; *18:* 229; *21:* 149, 150, 151; *24:* 218
Shinn, Florence Scovel *63:* 133, 135
Shore, Robert *27:* 54; *39:* 192, 193; *YABC 2:* 200
Shortall, Leonard *4:* 144; *8:* 196; *10:* 166; *19:* 227, 228, 229, 230; *25:* 78; *28:* 66, 167; *33:* 127; *52:* 125; *73:* 12, 212
Shortt, T.M. *27:* 36
Shpitalnik, Vladimir *83:* 194
Shroades, John *230:* 24
Shropshire, Sandy *170:* 191
Shtainments, Leon *32:* 161
Shulevitz, Uri *3:* 198, 199; *17:* 85; *22:* 204; *27:* 212; *28:* 184; *50:* 190, 191, 192, 193, 194, 195, 196,197, 198, 199, 201; *106:* 181, 182, 183; *165:* 203, 205; *166:* 138
Shulman, Dee *180:* 140
Shupe, Bobbi *139:* 80, 81
Shute, A.B. *67:* 196
Shute, Linda *46:* 59; *74:* 118
Siberell, Anne *29:* 193
Sibley, Don *1:* 39; *12:* 196; *31:* 47
Sibthorp, Fletcher *94:* 111, 112
Sidjakov, Nicolas *18:* 274
Siebel, Fritz *3:* 120; *17:* 145
Siebold, J. Otto *158:* 227
Siegel, Hal *74:* 246
Sieger, Ted *189:* 172
Siegl, Helen *12:* 166; *23:* 216; *34:* 185, 186
Siku *238:* 42
Silberberg, Alan *240:* 140
Silin-Palmer, Pamela *184:* 102
Sill, John *140:* 194; *141:* 157; *221:* 163; *222:* 171
Sills, Joyce *5:* 199
Silva, Simon *108:* 122
Silver, Maggie *85:* 210
Silveria, Gordon *96:* 44
Silverstein, Alvin *8:* 189
Silverstein, Shel *33:* 211; *92:* 209, 210
Silverstein, Virginia *8:* 189
Silvey, Joe *135:* 203
Simard, Rémy *95:* 156; *221:* 144
Siminovich, Laura *219:* 172
Simmons, Elly *110:* 2; *127:* 69; *134:* 181
Simon, Eric M. *7:* 82
Simon, Hilda *28:* 189
Simon, Howard *2:* 175; *5:* 132; *19:* 199; *32:* 163, 164, 165
Simont, Marc *2:* 119; *4:* 213; *9:* 168; *13:* 238,240; *14:* 262; *16:* 179; *18:* 221; *26:* 210; *33:* 189, 194; *44:* 132; *58:* 122; *68:* 117; *73:* 204, 205, 206; *74:* 221; *126:* 199, 200; *133:* 195; *163:* 40; *164:* 128; *223:* 28
Simpson, Martin *233:* 168; *241:* 109
Sims, Agnes *54:* 152
Sims, Blanche *44:* 116; *57:* 129; *75:* 179, 180; *77:* 92; *104:* 192; *152:* 117; *156:* 160; *160:* 70; *168:* 174, 175; *198:* 17; *236:* 54
Singer, Edith G. *2:* 30
Singer, Gloria *34:* 56; *36:* 43
Singer, Julia *28:* 190
Singh, Jen *178:* 146
Singh, Nikhil *234:* 54
Sinquette, Jaclyn *215:* 83
Siomades, Lorianne *134:* 45; *204:* 48; *217:* 157
Siracusa, Catherine *68:* 135; *82:* 218
Sisson, Stephanie Roth *136:* 171, 172; *237:* 131
Sís, Peter *67:* 179, 181, 183, 184, 185; *96:* 96, 98; *106:* 193, 194, 195; *149:* 224, 226; *180:* 177; *192:* 180, 182; *222:* 64; *239:* 104
Sivard, Robert *26:* 124
Sivertson, Liz *116:* 84
Skardinski, Stanley *23:* 144; *32:* 84; *66:* 122; *84:* 108
Slack, Michael *185:* 108; *189:* 173, 174
Slackman, Charles B. *12:* 201
Slade, Christian *193:* 187; *204:* 134; *234:* 59; *238:* 164, 165, 166
Slade, Paul *61:* 170
Slark, Albert *99:* 212; *205:* 161
Slater, Rod *25:* 167
Slavin, Bill *182:* 14, 15; *196:* 90; *199:* 148, 149, 150; *217:* 20; *235:* 45; *237:* 69; *239:* 93
Sloan, Joseph *16:* 68
Sloane, Eric *21:* 3; *52:* 153, 154, 155, 156, 157, 158, 160
Sloat, Teri *164:* 231
Slobodkin, Louis *1:* 200; *3:* 232; *5:* 168; *13:* 251; *15:* 13, 88; *26:* 173, 174, 175, 176, 178, 179; *60:* 180
Slobodkina, Esphyr *1:* 201
Slonim, David *166:* 167, 168
Small, David *50:* 204, 205; *79:* 44; *95:* 189, 190, 191; *126:* 203, 204; *136:* 119; *143:* 201, 202, 203; *144:* 246; *150:* 5; *161:* 176; *183:* 181, 182, 183, 184; *200:* 211; *212:* 86; *216:* 202, 203, 204; *230:* 222; *232:* 95
Small, W. *33:* 113
Smalley, Janet *1:* 154
Smath, Jerry *198:* 179, 180
Smedley, William T. *34:* 129
Smee, David *14:* 78; *62:* 30
Smee, Nicola *167:* 156
Smith, A.G., Jr. *35:* 182
Smith, Ali *204:* 68
Smith, Alvin *1:* 31, 229; *13:* 187; *27:* 216; *28:* 226; *48:* 149; *49:* 60
Smith, Andy *188:* 20; *207:* 151

Smith, Anne *194:* 147
Smith, Anne Warren *41:* 212
Smith, Barry *75:* 183
Smith, Brian *200:* 183
Smith, Carl *36:* 41
Smith, Cat Bowman *146:* 39; *164:* 219; *201:* 55, 184
Smith, Craig *97:* 197; *172:* 175; *206:* 40; *215:* 19; *217:* 129; *220:* 145
Smith, Donald A. *178:* 7
Smith, Doris Susan *41:* 139
Smith, Douglas *189:* 159; *213:* 170
Smith, Duane *171:* 152; *208:* 97
Smith, E. Boyd *19:* 70; *22:* 89; *26:* 63; *YABC 1:* 4, 5, 240, 248, 249
Smith, Edward J. *4:* 224
Smith, Elwood H. *157:* 231; *181:* 79; *203:* 160, 161, 162; *231:* 108; *236:* 176, 177, 178
Smith, Eunice Young *5:* 170
Smith, Gary *113:* 216
Smith, George *102:* 169
Smith, Howard *19:* 196
Smith, J. Gerard *95:* 42
Smith, Jacqueline Bardner *27:* 108; *39:* 197
Smith, Jay J. *61:* 119
Smith, Jeff *93:* 191
Smith, Jessie Willcox *15:* 91; *16:* 95; *18:* 231; *19:* 57, 242; *21:* 29, 156, 157, 158, 159, 160, 161; *34:* 65; *100:* 223; *YABC 1:* 6; *2:* 180, 185, 191, 311, 325
Smith, Jos. A. *52:* 131; *72:* 120; *74:* 151; *84:* 147, 148; *85:* 146; *87:* 96; *94:* 219; *96:* 97; *104:* 33; *108:* 126, 127, 128; *111:* 140; *136:* 145; *181:* 173; *200:* 213; *201:* 94; *231:* 148; *237:* 85
Smith, Kenneth R. *47:* 182
Smith, Keri *216:* 60
Smith, Kevin Warren *89:* 112
Smith, Kristin *209:* 197
Smith, L.H. *35:* 174
Smith, Lane *76:* 211, 213; *88:* 115; *105:* 202, 203,204, 205; *131:* 207; *160:* 217, 221; *179:* 183, 184, 185, 186; *199:* 122, 123, 124, 126; *224:* 164; *238:* 153, 154
Smith, Lee *29:* 32
Smith, Linell Nash *2:* 195
Smith, Maggie Kaufman *13:* 205; *35:* 191; *110:* 158; *178:* 226; *190:* 204; *209:* 145; *235:* 179, 180
Smith, Mavis *101:* 219
Smith, Moishe *33:* 155
Smith, Philip *44:* 134; *46:* 203
Smith, Ralph Crosby *2:* 267; *49:* 203
Smith, Robert D. *5:* 63
Smith, Sally J. *84:* 55
Smith, Susan Carlton *12:* 208
Smith, Terry *12:* 106; *33:* 158
Smith, Virginia *3:* 157; *33:* 72
Smith, William A. *1:* 36; *10:* 154; *25:* 65
Smith-Moore, J.J. *98:* 147
Smolinski, Dick *84:* 217
Smoljan, Joe *112:* 201
Smollin, Mike *39:* 203
Smyth, Iain *105:* 207
Smyth, M. Jane *12:* 15
Smythe, Fiona *151:* 213
Smythe, Theresa *141:* 37
Snair, Andy *176:* 4
Sneed, Brad *125:* 25; *191:* 175, 176; *211:* 194; *232:* 152
Snow, Sarah *228:* 47
Snyder, Andrew A. *30:* 212
Snyder, Betsy *230:* 173
Snyder, Jerome *13:* 207; *30:* 173
Snyder, Joel *28:* 163
So, Meilo *162:* 201; *208:* 188
Soentpiet, Chris K. *97:* 208; *110:* 33; *159:* 184; *161:* 10; *163:* 130
Sofia *1:* 62; *5:* 90; *32:* 166; *86:* 43
Sofilas, Mark *93:* 157
Sogabe, Aki *207:* 153; *221:* 110
Sohn, Jiho *182:* 78
Sokol, Bill *37:* 178; *49:* 23
Sokolov, Kirill *34:* 188
Solbert, Ronni *1:* 159; *2:* 232; *5:* 121; *6:* 34; *17:* 249
Solomon, Michael *174:* 115
Solonevich, George *15:* 246; *17:* 47
Soloviov, Michael *223:* 122
Soma, Liana *81:* 118
Soman, David *90:* 122; *102:* 126; *140:* 120; 93; *188:* 43, 89; *200:* 180, 181; *235:* 72
Sommer, Robert *12:* 211
Song, Jae *203:* 27
Soo, Kean *201:* 185
Sorel, Edward *4:* 61; *36:* 82; *65:* 191, 193; *126:* 214
Sorensen, Henri *196:* 58
Sorensen, Henrik *62:* 16
Sorensen, Svend Otto *22:* 130, 141; *67:* 188, 189
Sorra, Kristin *155:* 80; *229:* 85
Sosa, Hernan *198:* 66
Sostre, Maria *187:* 36
Sotomayor, Antonio *11:* 215
Souhami, Jessica *112:* 128; *176:* 193
Sousa, Natalie C. *209:* 89; *238:* 95
Souza, Diana *71:* 139
Sovak, Jan *115:* 190
Sowards, Ben *215:* 62
Soyer, Moses *20:* 177
Spaenkuch, August *16:* 28
Spafford, Suzy *160:* 228
Spain, Valerie *105:* 76
Spain, Sunday Sahara *133:* 204
Spalenka, Greg *149:* 69; *151:* 228; *184:* 195; *191:* 21; *196:* 12; *198:* 181, 182, 201; *208:* 92; *236:* 95
Spanfeller, James *1:* 72, 149; *2:* 183; *19:* 230, 231,232; *22:* 66; *36:* 160, 161; *40:* 75; *52:* 166; *76:* 37
Spangler, Brie *212:* 188
Sparks, Mary Walker *15:* 247
Spearing, Craig J. *228:* 172
Spears, Rick *182:* 187; *220:* 67
Speidel, Sandra *78:* 233; *94:* 178; *134:* 180; *210:* 67
Speirs, John *67:* 178
Spence, Geraldine *21:* 163; *47:* 196
Spence, Jim *38:* 89; *50:* 102
Spencer, Laurie *113:* 12
Spencer, Mark *57:* 170
Spengler, Kenneth J. *146:* 256
Sperling, Andrea *133:* 182
Spiegel, Beth *184:* 203
Spiegel, Doris *29:* 111
Spiegelman, Art *109:* 227
Spier, Jo *10:* 30
Spier, Peter *3:* 155; *4:* 200; *7:* 61; *11:* 78; *38:* 106; *54:* 120, 121, 122, 123, 124, 125, 126, 127, 128, 129, 130,131, 132, 133, 134
Spilka, Arnold *5:* 120; *6:* 204; *8:* 131
Spires, Ashley *231:* 96
Spirin, Gennady *95:* 196, 197; *113:* 172; *128:* 9; *129:* 49; *134:* 210; *153:* 9; *204:* 143, 144, 145; *220:* 153
Spiro, Ruth *208:* 197
Spivak, I. Howard *8:* 10; *13:* 172
Spohn, David *72:* 233
Spohn, Kate *87:* 195; *147:* 201, 202
Spollen, Christopher J. *12:* 214
Spooner, Malcolm *40:* 142
Spoor, Mike *220:* 92
Spowart, Robin *82:* 228; *92:* 149; *133:* 131; *176:* 163; *177:* 183, 184; *217:* 123, 124
Sprague, Kevin *150:* 60; *196:* 62
Spranger, Nina *201:* 199
Sprattler, Rob *12:* 176
Spring, Bob *5:* 60
Spring, Ira *5:* 60
Springer, Harriet *31:* 92
Spudvilas, Anne *110:* 74; *197:* 192; *199:* 154
Spurll, Barbara *78:* 199; *88:* 141, 142; *99:* 215
Spurrier, Steven *28:* 198
Spuvilas, Anne *85:* 114
Spy
See Ward, Leslie
Squires, Stuart *127:* 74
St. Aubin, Bruno *179:* 54
St. John, J. Allen *41:* 62
Staake, Bob *209:* 168, 169; *229:* 132
Stabin, Victor *101:* 131; *164:* 158
Stadler, John *62:* 33; *204:* 149
Stadnyk, Greg *212:* 55
Staffan, Alvin E. *11:* 56; *12:* 187
Stahl, Ben *5:* 181; *12:* 91; *49:* 122; *71:* 128; *87:* 206; *112:* 107
Stair, Gobin *35:* 214
Stallwood, Karen *73:* 126
Stamaty, Mark Alan *12:* 215; *230:* 175
Stammen, JoEllen McAllister *113:* 14
Stamp, Jørgen *225:* 184
Stampnick, Ken *51:* 142
Stanbridge, Joanne *150:* 91
Stanley, Diane *3:* 45; *37:* 180; *80:* 217, 219; *240:* 160, 161
Stanley, Sanna *145:* 228
Star, Lindsay *219:* 39
Starcke, Helmut *86:* 217
Stark, Ken *197:* 102
Starr, Branka *73:* 25
Stasiak, Krystyna *49:* 181; *64:* 194
Staub, Leslie *103:* 54
Stauffer, Brian *220:* 123
Staunton, Ted *112:* 192
Stawicki, Matt *164:* 250
Stead, Erin E. *232:* 179
Stead, L. *55:* 51, 56
Steadman, Broeck *97:* 185, 186; *99:* 56; *121:* 48; *208:* 190
Steadman, Henry *211:* 130
Steadman, Ralph *32:* 180; *123:* 143, 145
Stearn, Nick *183:* 26
Stearn, Todd *218:* 179
Steckler, June *90:* 178
Steele, Robert Gantt *169:* 174
Steichen, Edward *30:* 79
Steig, William *18:* 275, 276; *70:* 215, 216, 217, 218; *111:* 173, 174, 175, 176, 177
Stein, David Ezra *211:* 168
Stein, Harve *1:* 109
Steinberg, Saul *47:* 193
Steinel, William *23:* 146
Steiner, Charlotte *45:* 196
Steiner, Joan *110:* 219; *199:* 160, 161
Steirnagel, Michael *80:* 56
Stemp, Eric *60:* 184
Stengel, Christopher *229:* 200; *232:* 57; *237:* 135
Stephens, Alice Barber *66:* 208, 209
Stephens, Charles H. *YABC 2:* 279
Stephens, Pam *198:* 69
Stephens, Pat *126:* 110; *128:* 101
Stephens, William M. *21:* 165
Stephenson, Kristina *224:* 169
Steptoe, Javaka *151:* 203, 204; *190:* 169; *213:* 163, 164
Steptoe, John *8:* 197; *57:* 9; *63:* 158, 159, 160, 161,163, 164, 165, 166, 167; *96:* 4; *105:* 87; *240:* 4
Stern, Simon *15:* 249, 250; *17:* 58; *34:* 192, 193
Sterret, Jane *53:* 27
Stetsios, Debbie *165:* 108, 109
Steven, Kat *158:* 237
Stevens, David *62:* 44
Stevens, Helen *189:* 31; *207:* 83
Stevens, Janet *40:* 126; *57:* 10, 11; *80:* 112; *90:* 221, 222; *109:* 156; *130:* 34; *166:* 202; *176:* 53, 116; *193:* 199, 200, 202; *208:* 127; *212:* 182
Stevens, Mary *11:* 193; *13:* 129; *43:* 95

Stevenson, Harvey *66:* 143; *80:* 201, 221; *153:* 60; *191:* 166; *233:* 154
Stevenson, James *42:* 182, 183; *51:* 163; *66:* 184; *71:* 185, 187, 188; *78:* 262; *87:* 97; *113:* 182, 183,184, 185; *161:* 182, 183
Stevenson, Sucie *92:* 27; *104:* 194, 195; *112:* 168; *160:* 202; *194:* 172, 173; *195:* 166
Stewart, April Blair *75:* 210
Stewart, Arvis *33:* 98; *36:* 69; *60:* 118; *75:* 91; *127:* 4
Stewart, Charles *2:* 205
Stewart, Joel *151:* 205; *211:* 170, 171; *229:* 168
Stieg, William *172:* 58
Stiles, Fran *26:* 85; *78:* 56; *82:* 150
Stillman, Susan *44:* 130; *76:* 83
Stimpson, Tom *49:* 171
Stimson, James *208:* 46
Stinemetz, Morgan *40:* 151
Stinson, Paul *110:* 86
Stirnweis, Shannon *10:* 164
Stites, Joe *86:* 96
Stobbs, William *1:* 48, 49; *3:* 68; *6:* 20; *17:* 117, 217; *24:* 150; *29:* 250; *60:* 179; *87:* 204, 205,206
Stock, Catherine *37:* 55; *65:* 198; *72:* 7; *99:* 225; *114:* 197, 198, 199; *126:* 3; *145:* 161; *161:* 82; *173:* 149; *208:* 210; *214:* 192, 194; *224:* 196, 197
Stockman, Jack *113:* 24
Stoeke, Janet Morgan *90:* 225; *136:* 196; *202:* 182, 183
Stoerrle, Tom *55:* 147
Stolp, Jaap *49:* 98
Stolp, Todd *89:* 195
Stone, David L. *87:* 154
Stone, David *9:* 173
Stone, David K. *4:* 38; *6:* 124; *9:* 180; *43:* 182; *60:* 70
Stone, Helen V. *6:* 209
Stone, Helen *44:* 121, 122, 126
Stone, Kazuko G. *134:* 43; *241:* 57
Stone, Kyle M. *202:* 185
Stone, Phoebe *86:* 212; *134:* 213; *162:* 188; *205:* 145
Stone, Steve *166:* 213; *208:* 185; *220:* 57,58; *224:* 124
Stone, Tony *150:* 34, 35
Storms, Patricia *217:* 163
Storrings, Michael *191:* 108; *216:* 217
Stoud, Virginia A. *89:* 31
Stover, Jill *82:* 234
Stower, Adam *217:* 89; *227:* 53; *240:* 138
Strachan, Bruce *205:* 146
Stratton, Helen *33:* 151
Stratton-Porter, Gene *15:* 254, 259, 263, 264, 268, 269
Straub, Matt *192:* 176; *229:* 176
Straub, Phillip *197:* 22; *233:* 36
Streano, Vince *20:* 173
Street, Janet Travell *84:* 235
Streeter, Clive *121:* 2
Strickland, Shadra *209:* 179; *233:* 177
Stringer, Lauren *129:* 187; *154:* 172, 173; *161:* 127; *183:* 187, 188; *232:* 153
Strodl, Daniel *47:* 95
Strogart, Alexander *63:* 139
Stromoski, Rick *111:* 179; *124:* 161, 190
Strong, Joseph D., Jr. *YABC 2:* 330
Stroyer, Poul *13:* 221
Strugnell, Ann *27:* 38
Struzan, Drew *117:* 6
Stubbs, William *73:* 196
Stubis, Talivaldis *5:* 182, 183; *10:* 45; *11:* 9; *18:* 304; *20:* 127
Stubley, Trevor *14:* 43; *22:* 219; *23:* 37; *28:* 61; *87:* 26
Stuck, Marion *104:* 44
Stuecklen, Karl W. *8:* 34, 65; *23:* 103
Stull, Betty *11:* 46
Stutzman, Mark *119:* 99
Stutzmann, Laura *73:* 185
Suarez, Maribel *162:* 208; *200:* 202; *237:* 170
Suave, Gordon *209:* 66
Suba, Susanne *4:* 202, 203; *14:* 261; *23:* 134; *29:* 222; *32:* 30
Sue, Majella Lue *209:* 182; *212:* 146
Sueling, Barbara *98:* 185
Sueling, Gwenn *98:* 186
Sugarman, Tracy *3:* 76; *8:* 199; *37:* 181, 182
Sugimoto, Yugo *170:* 144; *223:* 137
Sugita, Yutaka *36:* 180, 181
Suh, John *80:* 157
Sullivan, Dorothy *89:* 113
Sullivan, Edmund J. *31:* 86
Sullivan, James F. *19:* 280; *20:* 192
Sully, Tom *104:* 199, 200; *182:* 77
Sumichrast, Jozef *14:* 253; *29:* 168, 213
Sumiko *46:* 57
Summers, Leo *1:* 177; *2:* 273; *13:* 22
Summers, Mark *118:* 144
Summers, Mike *190:* 176
Sutton, Judith *94:* 164
Svarez, Juan *56:* 113
Svendsen, Mark *181:* 176
Svolinsky, Karel *17:* 104
Swain, Carol *172:* 182
Swain, Su Zan Noguchi *21:* 170
Swan, Susan *22:* 220, 221; *37:* 66; *60:* 146; *145:* 205; *181:* 168; *236:* 172
Swann, Susan *86:* 55
Swanson, Karl *79:* 65; *89:* 186
Swarner, Kristina *203:* 62; *215:* 184
Swayne, Sam *53:* 143, 145
Swayne, Zoa *53:* 143, 145
Swearingen, Greg *152:* 56; *165:* 135; *173:* 2; *224:* 32; *225:* 188
Sweat, Lynn *25:* 206; *57:* 176; *73:* 184; *168:* 178
Sweet, Darrell K. *60:* 9; *69:* 86; *74:* 15; *75:* 215; *76:* 130, 131; *81:* 96, 122; *82:* 253; *83:* 11; *84:* 14; *85:* 37; *89:* 140; *90:* 6; *91:* 137,139; *95:* 160, 161; *126:* 25; *185:* 175; *195:* 132
Sweet, Darrell K. *1:* 163; *4:* 136; *164:* 175
Sweet, Melissa *71:* 94; *72:* 172; *111:* 82; *139:* 53, 58; *141:* 88; *142:* 231; *155:* 121; *159:* 121, 122; *172:* 185; *188:* 127; *209:* 81; *211:* 174, 175; *218:* 21; *235:* 54
Sweet, Ozzie *31:* 149, 151, 152
Sweetland, Robert *12:* 194
Swiatkowska, Gabi *132:* 43; *175:* 139; *180:* 218; *183:* 176
Swope, Martha *43:* 160; *56:* 86, 87, 89
Sylvada, Peter *154:* 174
Sylvester, Kevin *240:* 171
Sylvester, Natalie G. *22:* 222
Syme, Hugh *232:* 8
Szafran, Gene *24:* 144
Szasz, Susanne *13:* 55, 226; *14:* 48
Szekeres, Cyndy *2:* 218; *5:* 185; *8:* 85; *11:* 166; *14:* 19; *16:* 57, 159; *26:* 49, 214; *34:* 205; *60:* 150, 151, 152, 153, 154; *73:* 224; *74:* 218; *131:* 213, 215
Szpura, Beata *81:* 68; *119:* 65; *168:* 201
Szuc, Jeff *220:* 188

T

Taback, Simms *40:* 207; *52:* 120; *57:* 34; *80:* 241; *104:* 202, 203; *170:* 176, 177; *205:* 183
Taber, Patricia *75:* 124
Tabor, Nancy Maria Grande *89:* 210; *161:* 188
Taddei, Richard *112:* 13, 14
Tadgell, Nicole *150:* 77; *161:* 20; *177:* 186; *209:* 16; *220:* 190, 191; *235:* 90
Tadiello, Ed *133:* 200
Tafuri, Nancy *39:* 210; *75:* 199, 200; *92:* 75; *130:* 215, 216, 217
Tailfeathers, Gerald *86:* 85
Tait, Douglas *12:* 220; *74:* 105, 106
Takabayashi, Mari *113:* 112; *130:* 22; *156:* 169
Takahashi, Hideko *136:* 160; *187:* 6; *209:* 152, 187
Takakjian, Portia *15:* 274
Takashima, Shizuye *13:* 228
Talarczyk, June *4:* 173
Talbott, Hudson *84:* 240; *163:* 100; *212:* 191, 192, 193
Tallarico, Tony *116:* 197
Tallec, Olivier *218:* 4
Tallon, Robert *2:* 228; *43:* 200, 201, 202, 203, 204, 205,206, 207, 209
Tamaki, Jillian *201:* 188
Tamas, Szecsko *29:* 135
Tamburine, Jean *12:* 222
Tanaka, Yoko *215:* 187; *234:* 106
Tancredi, Sharon *215:* 127
Tandy, H.R. *13:* 69
Tandy, Russell H. *65:* 9; *100:* 30, 131
Tanenbaum, Robert *238:* 141
Tang, Charles *81:* 202; *90:* 192
Tang, Sandara *238:* 60
Tang, Susan *80:* 174; *108:* 158
Tang, You-shan *63:* 100
Tankersley, Paul *69:* 206; *133:* 219
Tannenbaum, Robert *48:* 181
Tanner, Jane *87:* 13; *97:* 37
Tanner, Tim *72:* 192; *84:* 35
Tanobe, Miyuki *23:* 221
Tarabay, Sharif *110:* 149; *113:* 123; *169:* 83
Tarkington, Booth *17:* 224, 225
Tarlow, Phyllis *61:* 198
Tate, Don *159:* 141, 191; *183:* 69; *186:* 120
Tauss, Herbert *95:* 179
Tauss, Marc *117:* 160; *126:* 155; *178:* 221; *197:* 7; *223:* 168; *238:* 109
Tavares, Matt *159:* 192, 193; *198:* 188, 189, 190; *199:* 86
Taxali, Gary *234:* 199
Taylor, Ann *41:* 226
Taylor, Dahl *129:* 157
Taylor, Geoff *93:* 156; *197:* 173, 175; *204:* 151, 152
Taylor, Isaac *41:* 228
Taylor, Jennifer *226:* 128; *232:* 154
Taylor, Mike *143:* 99, 100
Teague, Mark *83:* 6; *139:* 241; *170:* 180, 181; *205:* 150, 151
Teale, Edwin Way *7:* 196
Teason, James *1:* 14
Teckentrup, Britta *200:* 191, 192
Teeple, Lyn *33:* 147
Tee-Van, Helen Damrosch *10:* 176; *11:* 182
Teevee, Ningeokuluk *223:* 173
Teicher, Dick *50:* 211
Teichman, Mary *77:* 220; *124:* 208; *127:* 22; *197:* 33
Telgemeier, Raina *228:* 180, 181, 182
Temertey, Ludmilla *96:* 232; *104:* 43, 45; *109:* 244
Tempest, Margaret *3:* 237, 238; *88:* 200
Temple, Frances *85:* 185, 186, 187
Temple, Herbert *45:* 201
Templeton, Owen *11:* 77
ten Cate, Marijke *183:* 193
Tenggren, Gustaf *18:* 277, 278, 279; *19:* 15; *28:* 86; *YABC2:* 145
TenNapel, Doug *234:* 200
Tennent, Julie *81:* 105
Tenneson, Joyce *153:* 166
Tenney, Gordon *24:* 204
Tenniel, John *74:* 234, 235; *100:* 89; *YABC 2:* 99; *153:* 63
Teplin, Scott *231:* 180
Tepper, Matt *116:* 80
Terkel, Ari *103:* 162
Terry, Michael *180:* 209; *233:* 166
Terry, Will *131:* 73; *205:* 155; *223:* 105
Teskey, Donald *71:* 51
Tessler, Manya *200:* 193

Thacher, Mary M. *30:* 72
Thackeray, William Makepeace *23:* 224, 228
Thamer, Katie *42:* 187
Tharlet, Eve *146:* 149
Thelwell, Norman *14:* 201
Theobalds, Prue *40:* 23
Theurer, Marilyn Churchill *39:* 195
Thiesing, Lisa *89:* 134; *95:* 202; *156:* 190; *159:* 195
Thiewes, Sam *133:* 114
Thisdale, François *223:* 55
Thistlethwaite, Miles *12:* 224
Thollander, Earl *11:* 47; *18:* 112; *22:* 224
Thomas, Allan *22:* 13
Thomas, Art *48:* 217
Thomas, Eric *28:* 49
Thomas, Harold *20:* 98
Thomas, Jacqui *125:* 95
Thomas, Jan *197:* 180; *226:* 198
Thomas, Mark *42:* 136
Thomas, Martin *14:* 255
Thomas, Middy *177:* 114; *230:* 63
Thompson, Arthur *34:* 107
Thompson, Carol *85:* 189; *95:* 75; *102:* 86; *147:* 166; *189:* 179, 180, 181; *190:* 84; *207:* 18
Thompson, Colin *95:* 204
Thompson, Ellen *51:* 88, 151; *60:* 33; *67:* 42; *77:* 148; *78:* 75, 219; *79:* 122, 170; *84:* 219; *85:* 97; *87:* 37; *88:* 192, 194; *89:* 80; *93:* 37; *98:* 59; *132:* 14; *236:* 72, 73
Thompson, George W. *22:* 18; *28:* 150; *33:* 135
Thompson, John *58:* 201; *102:* 226; *124:* 154; *128:* 228; *129:* 157; *150:* 49; *185:* 160; *191:* 192; *224:* 110; *236:* 101
Thompson, Julie *44:* 158
Thompson, Katherine *132:* 146
Thompson, K. Dyble *84:* 6
Thompson, Miles *152:* 77
Thompson, Sharon *74:* 113; *158:* 60; *165:* 87
Thomson, Arline K. *3:* 264
Thomson, Bill *186:* 160
Thomson, Hugh *26:* 88
Thomson, Ross *36:* 179
Thorkelson, Gregg *95:* 183, 184; *98:* 58; *165:* 30, 31; *225:* 31, 32
Thorn, Lori *189:* 119
Thornberg, Dan *104:* 125
Thornburgh, Rebecca McKillip *143:* 37
Thorne, Diana *25:* 212
Thornhill, Jan *77:* 213
Thorpe, Peter *58:* 109
Thorvall, Kerstin *13:* 235
Threadgall, Colin *77:* 215
Thurber, James *13:* 239, 242, 243, 245, 248, 249
Thurman, Mark *63:* 173; *168:* 116
Tibbles, Jean-Paul *115:* 200
Tibbles, Paul *45:* 23
Tibo, Gilles *67:* 207; *107:* 199, 201
Tichenor, Tom *14:* 207
Tichnor, Richard *90:* 218
Tiegreen, Alan *36:* 143; *43:* 55, 56, 58; *77:* 200; *94:* 216, 217; *121:* 54, 59
Tierney, Tom *113:* 198, 200, 201
Tildes, Phyllis Limbacher *210:* 240
Tilley, Debbie *102:* 134; *133:* 226; *137:* 101; *159:* 96; *190:* 211, 212; *213:* 51
Tillman, Nancy *211:* 129, 178
Tillotson, Katherine *224:* 175
Tilney, F.C. *22:* 231
Timbs, Gloria *36:* 90
Timmins, Harry *2:* 171
Timmons, Bonnie *194:* 189
Tinkelman, Murray *12:* 225; *35:* 44
Titherington, Jeanne *39:* 90; *58:* 138; *75:* 79; *135:* 161
Tjader, Ella *209:* 14
Tobin, Nancy *145:* 197
Toddy, Irving *172:* 144
Tokunbo, Dimitrea *181:* 183; *187:* 182, 183; *226:* 209
Tolbert, Jeff *128:* 69
Toledo, Francisco *197:* 182; *198:* 199
Toledo, Natalia *197:* 182
Tolford, Joshua *1:* 221
Tolkien, J.R.R. *2:* 243; *32:* 215
Tolman, Marije *195:* 43
Tolmie, Ken *15:* 292
Tomei, Lorna *47:* 168, 171
Tomes, Jacqueline *2:* 117; *12:* 139
Tomes, Margot *1:* 224; *2:* 120, 121; *16:* 207; *18:* 250; *20:* 7; *25:* 62; *27:* 78, 79; *29:* 81, 199; *33:* 82; *36:* 186, 187, 188, 189, 190; *46:* 129; *56:* 71; *58:* 183; *70:* 228; *75:* 73, 75; *80:* 80; *83:* 97; *90:* 205
Tommaso, Rich *200:* 198
Tommorow, Tom *223:* 176
Toner, Raymond John *10:* 179
Tong, Gary *66:* 215
Tongier, Stephen *82:* 32
Tooke, Susan *173:* 162
Toothill, Harry *6:* 54; *7:* 49; *25:* 219; *42:* 192
Toothill, Ilse *6:* 54
Topaz, Ksenia *224:* 94
Topolski, Feliks *44:* 48
Torbert, Floyd James *22:* 226
Torgersen, Don *55:* 157
Torline, Kevin *169:* 171
Tormey, Bertram M. *75:* 3, 4
Torrecilla, Pablo *176:* 207
Torres, Leyla *156:* 199, 201
Torrey, Helen *87:* 41
Torrey, Marjorie *34:* 105
Torrey, Richard *189:* 182; *205:* 24
Toschik, Larry *6:* 102
Totten, Bob *13:* 93
Townsend, Michael *231:* 183
Toy, Julie *128:* 112
Trachok, Cathy *131:* 16; *228:* 10
Tracy, Libba *82:* 24
Trago, Keith *158:* 253
Trail, Lee *55:* 157
Trang, To Ngoc *167:* 180
Trang, Winson *89:* 151
Trapani, Iza *116:* 202; *214:* 203
Travers, Bob *49:* 100; *63:* 145
Treatner, Meryl *95:* 180
Tremain, Ruthven *17:* 238
Tresilian, Stuart *25:* 53; *40:* 212
Trez, Alain *17:* 236
Trezzo, Loretta *86:* 45
Trier, Walter *14:* 96
Trimby, Elisa *47:* 199
Trinkle, Sally *53:* 27
Triplett, Gina *182:* 193; *188:* 100; *198:* 38
Tripp, F.J. *24:* 167
Tripp, Wallace *2:* 48; *7:* 28; *8:* 94; *10:* 54,76; *11:* 92; *31:* 170, 171; *34:* 203; *42:* 57; *60:* 157; *73:* 182
Trivas, Irene *53:* 4; *54:* 168; *82:* 46, 101
Trnka, Jiri *22:* 151; *43:* 212, 213, 214, 215; *YABC 1:* 30, 31
Trondheim, Lewis *182:* 183
Troughton, Joanna *37:* 186; *48:* 72
Troyer, Johannes *3:* 16; *7:* 18
Trudeau, G.B. *35:* 220, 221, 222; *48:* 119, 123, 126, 127,128, 129, 133; *168:* 189
Trueman, Matthew *165:* 208; *183:* 191; *220:* 61; *222:* 174
Truesdell, Sue *55:* 142; *108:* 219, 220; *212:* 202; *220:* 78
Tryon, Leslie *84:* 7; *139:* 214; *143:* 10; *181:* 10
Tseng, Jean *72:* 195; *94:* 102; *119:* 126; *151:* 106; *173:* 138, 139; *200:* 158
Tseng, Mou-sien *72:* 195; *94:* 102; *119:* 126; *151:* 106; *173:* 138, 139; *200:* 158
Tsinajinie, Andy *2:* 62
Tsinganos, Jim *180:* 142
Tsugami, Kyuzo *18:* 198, 199
Tucker, Ezra *156:* 31
Tuckwell, Jennifer *17:* 205
Tudor, Bethany *7:* 103
Tudor, Tasha *18:* 227; *20:* 185, 186, 187; *36:* 111; *69:* 196, 198; *100:* 44; *YABC 2:* 46, 314; *160:* 234
Tuerk, Hanne *71:* 201
Tugeau, Jeremy *199:* 170; *203:* 96
Tulloch, Maurice *24:* 79
Tunis, Edwin *1:* 218, 219; *28:* 209, 210, 211, 212
Tunnicliffe, C.F. *62:* 176; 177; 178, 179; 181
Turkle, Brinton *1:* 211, 213; *2:* 249; *3:* 226; *11:* 3; *16:* 209; *20:* 22; *50:* 23; *67:* 50; *68:* 65; *79:* 205, 206, 207; *128:* 47; *YABC 1:* 79
Turnbull, Christopher J. *143:* 99, 100
Turner, Gwenda *59:* 195
Turner, Helen *203:* 154
Turska, Krystyna *12:* 103; *31:* 173, 174, 175; *56:* 32,34; *100:* 66
Tusa, Tricia *72:* 242; *111:* 180, 181; *157:* 165; *164:* 186; *189:* 40; *201:* 9; *207:* 163, 164; *233:* 132; *237:* 103
Tusan, Stan *6:* 58; *22:* 236, 237
Tuschman, Richard *219:* 100; *224:* 188; *225:* 175; *231:* 149; *238:* 138
Tworkov, Jack *47:* 207
Tyers, Jenny *89:* 220
Tylden-Wright, Jenny *114:* 119
Tyrol, Adelaide Murphy *103:* 27
Tyrrell, Frances *107:* 204
Tzimoulis, Paul *12:* 104

U

Uchida, Yoshiko *1:* 220
Uderzo *47:* 88
Udovic, David *189:* 185; *195:* 201
Ueno, Noriko *59:* 155
Ugliano, Natascia *196:* 186
Ulm, Robert *17:* 238
Ulrich, George *73:* 15; *75:* 136, 139; *99:* 150
Ulriksen, Mark *101:* 58; *182:* 43; *210:* 243; *240:* 33
Unada *84:* 67; *227:* 80
See Gliewe, Unada
Underhill, Liz *53:* 159
Underwood, Beck *192:* 36
Underwood, Clarence *40:* 166
Unger, Jim *67:* 208
Ungerer, Tomi *5:* 188; *9:* 40; *18:* 188; *29:* 175; *33:* 221, 222, 223, 225; *71:* 48; *106:* 209, 210, 211, 212
Unwin, Nora S. *3:* 65, 234, 235; *4:* 237; *44:* 173, 174; *YABC 1:* 59; *2:* 301
Unzner, Christa *230:* 186
Upitis, Alvis *145:* 179
Urban, Helle *149:* 243
Urbanovic, Jackie *86:* 86; *189:* 186, 187
Urberuaga, Emilio *219:* 110, 175
U'ren, Andrea *213:* 177; *232:* 175
Uris, Jill *49:* 188, 197
Ursell, Martin *50:* 51
Utpatel, Frank *18:* 114
Utz, Lois *5:* 190

V

Vagin, Vladimir *66:* 10; *142:* 215
Vaillancourt, Francois *107:* 199
Vainio, Pirkko *123:* 157, 158
Valério, Geraldo *180:* 225; *194:* 116
Valiant, Kristi *241:* 100
Vallejo, Boris *62:* 130; *72:* 212; *91:* 38; *93:* 61
Van Abbe, S. *16:* 142; *18:* 282; *31:* 90; *YABC 2:* 157, 161

Van Allsburg, Chris *37:* 205, 206; *53:* 161, 162, 163, 165,166, 167, 168, 169, 170, 171; *105:* 215, 216, 217, 218; *156:* 176, 177, 178
Vance, James *65:* 28
Van Der Linde, Henry *99:* 17
van der Meer, Ron *98:* 204, 205
van der Meer, Atie *98:* 204, 205
Vandivert, William *21:* 175
Van Dongen, H.R. *81:* 97
Van Dusen, Chris W. *173:* 169; *228:* 192
Vane, Mitch *210:* 160; *218:* 152
Van Everen, Jay *13:* 160; *YABC 1:* 121
Van Fleet, John *165:* 12, 13
Van Frankenhuyzen, Gijsbert *145:* 230; *149:* 164; *184:* 151; *210:* 248
van Genechten, Guido *165:* 226
van Haeringen, Annemarie *193:* 206
Van Horn, William *43:* 218
van Hout, Mies *195:* 191; *207:* 58
van Kampen, Vlasta *194:* 217
van Lawick, Hugo *62:* 76, 79
Van Lieshout, Maria *201:* 196; *223:* 119
Van Loon, Hendrik Willem *18:* 285, 289, 291
Van Munching, Paul *83:* 85
van Ommen, Sylvia *186:* 192
Van Patter, Bruce *183:* 195
Van Rynbach, Iris *102:* 192
Van Sciver, Ruth *37:* 162
VanSeveren, Joe *63:* 182
Van Stockum, Hilda *5:* 193
Van Vleet, John *213:* 180
Van Wassenhove, Sue *202:* 193
Van Wely, Babs *16:* 50; *79:* 16
Van Wright, Cornelius *72:* 18; *102:* 208; *116:* 107; *152:* 236; *173:* 170, 171; *199:* 185
Van Zyle, Jon *103:* 125; *160:* 181, 182; *176:* 199, 200; *221:* 128; *232:* 125
Vardzigulyants, Ruben *90:* 54
Varga, Judy *29:* 196
Vargo, Kurt *79:* 224
Varley, Susan *61:* 199; *63:* 176, 177; *101:* 148; *134:* 220
Varon, Sara *195:* 208
Vasconcellos, Daniel *80:* 42
Vasiliu, Mircea *2:* 166, 253; *9:* 166; *13:* 58; *68:* 42
Vaughn, Frank *34:* 157
Vavra, Robert *8:* 206
Vawter, Will *17:* 163
Vayas, Diana *71:* 61
Vazquez, Carlos *125:* 184
Veeder, Larry *18:* 4
Velasquez, Eric *45:* 217; *61:* 45; *63:* 110, 111; *88:* 162; *90:* 34, 144; *94:* 213; *107:* 147; *132:* 192; *138:* 213; *159:* 126; *181:* 184; *184:* 96; *191:* 16; *192:* 234; *208:* 37; *214:* 81; *226:* 201, 203, 212; *237:* 59; *239:* 165
Velasquez, Jose A. *63:* 73
Velez, Walter *71:* 75; *91:* 154; *121:* 181; *168:* 49; *207:* 52
Velthuijs, Max *110:* 228, 229
Vendrell, Carme Sole *42:* 205
Venezia, Mike *54:* 17
Venti, Anthony Bacon *124:* 103; *126:* 26
Venturo, Piero *61:* 194, 195
Ver Beck, Frank *18:* 16, 17
Verkaaik, Ben *110:* 209
Verling, John *71:* 27
Verney, John *14:* 225; *75:* 8
Vernon, Ursula *204:* 157; *240:* 177, 178
Verrier, Suzanne *5:* 20; *23:* 212
Verroken, Sarah *223:* 178
Versace, Marie *2:* 255
Verstraete, Randy *108:* 193
Vess, Charles *215:* 201; *233:* 182
Vestal, H.B. *9:* 134; *11:* 101; *27:* 25; *34:* 158
Vestergaard, Hope *190:* 203
Vicatan *59:* 146
Vickrey, Robert *45:* 59, 64
Victor, Joan Berg *30:* 193
Vieceli, Emma *210:* 245
Viereck, Ellen *3:* 242; *14:* 229
Vigna, Judith *15:* 293; *102:* 194, 195, 196, 197
Vila, Laura *207:* 172
Vilato, Gaspar E. *5:* 41
Villeneuve, Anne *230:* 189
Villiard, Paul *51:* 178
Vimnera, A. *23:* 154
Vincent, Eric *34:* 98
Vincent, Felix *41:* 237
Vincent, Gabrielle *121:* 175
Vip *45:* 164
Viskupic, Gary *83:* 48
Vitale, Stefano *109:* 71, 107; *114:* 219, 220; *123:* 106; *138:* 232; *180:* 228, 229; *212:* 38; *225:* 191, 192, 193
Vivas, Julie *51:* 67, 69; *96:* 225; *197:* 190; *199:* 71
Voake, Charlotte *114:* 221, 222; *180:* 232
Vo-Dinh, Mai *16:* 272; *60:* 191
Vogel, Ilse-Margret *14:* 230
Voigt, Erna *35:* 228
Vojnar, Kamil *95:* 31; *114:* 4; *115:* 62; *121:* 90; *124:* 72; *130:* 31; *141:* 81; *146:* 196; *150:* 123; *158:* 5, 6; *158:* 154; *171:* 119, 188; *179:* 15; *180:* 112; *203:* 74; *223:* 30; *229:* 43; *230:* 199; *231:* 53, 121, 122; *233:* 3, 4
Vojtech, Anna *42:* 190; *108:* 222, 223; *150:* 203; *174:* 173; *228:* 21; *234:* 181
von Buhler, Cynthia *149:* 237; *162:* 177; *177:* 205; *180:* 77; *185:* 214, 215, 216; *235:* 168; *237:* 144
von Roehl, Angela *126:* 191
von Schmidt, Eric *8:* 62; *50:* 209, 210
von Schmidt, Harold *30:* 80
Vosburgh, Leonard *1:* 161; *7:* 32; *15:* 295, 296; *23:* 110; *30:* 214; *43:* 181
Voss, Tom *127:* 104
Voter, Thomas W. *19:* 3, 9
Vroman, Tom *10:* 29
Vulliamy, Clara *72:* 65
Vyner, Tim *228:* 198

W

Waber, Bernard *47:* 209, 210, 211, 212, 213, 214; *95:* 215, 216, 217; *156:* 203, 205, 206, 207
Waber, Paulis *231:* 189
Wachenje, Benjamin *194:* 170
Wack, Jeff *95:* 140; *110:* 90
Wagner, John *8:* 200; *52:* 104
Wagner, Ken *2:* 59
Wagner, Michael *211:* 159
Wahman, Wendy *218:* 186
Waide, Jan *29:* 225; *36:* 139
Wainwright, Jerry *14:* 85
Waites, Joan *171:* 2; *226:* 184
Wakeen, Sandra *47:* 97
Wakiyama, Hanako *171:* 96; *192:* 236; *200:* 16
Waldherr, Kris *81:* 186
Waldman, Bruce *15:* 297; *43:* 178
Waldman, Neil *35:* 141; *50:* 163; *51:* 180; *54:* 78; *77:* 112; *79:* 162; *82:* 174; *84:* 5, 56, 106; *94:* 232, 233, 234; *96:* 41; *111:* 139; *113:* 9; *118:* 30; *142:* 220, 223; *203:* 173, 174; *238:* 147
Waldrep, Richard *111:* 147; *198:* 202
Waldron, Kevin *230:* 191
Walker, Brian *144:* 128
Walker, Charles *1:* 46; *4:* 59; *5:* 177; *11:* 115; *19:* 45; *34:* 74; *62:* 168; *72:* 218
Walker, Dugald Stewart *15:* 47; *32:* 202; *33:* 112
Walker, Gil *8:* 49; *23:* 132; *34:* 42
Walker, Jeff *55:* 154; *123:* 116
Walker, Jim *10:* 94
Walker, Mort *8:* 213
Walker, Norman *41:* 37; *45:* 58
Walker, Stephen *12:* 229; *21:* 174
Walker, Steve *231:* 119
Wallace, Beverly Dobrin *19:* 259
Wallace, Chad *229:* 198
Wallace, Cly *87:* 93
Wallace, Ian *53:* 176, 177; *56:* 165, 166; *58:* 4; *98:* 4; *101:* 191; *112:* 124; *141:* 197, 198, 199, 200; *151:* 212; *219:* 180, 182
Wallace, John *105:* 228
Wallace, Nancy Elizabeth *141:* 204; *186:* 195, 197, 199; *222:* 191, 192, 193, 194
Wallenta, Adam *123:* 180
Waller, S.E. *24:* 36
Wallner, Alexandra *15:* 120; *156:* 183
Wallner, John C. *9:* 77; *10:* 188; *11:* 28; *14:* 209; *31:* 56, 118; *37:* 64; *51:* 186, 187, 188, 189, 190, 191,192, 193, 194, 195; *52:* 96; *53:* 23, 26; *71:* 99; *73:* 158; *89:* 215; *141:* 9
Wallner, John *162:* 17
Wallower, Lucille *11:* 226
Walotsky, Ron *93:* 87
Walsh, Ellen Stoll *99:* 209; *147:* 219; *194:* 194, 195, 196
Walsh, Rebecca *158:* 193; *217:* 169, 170
Walsh, Vivian *149:* 215; *158:* 227
Walters, Anita *205:* 163
Walters, Audrey *18:* 294
Walther, Tom *31:* 179
Walton, Garry *69:* 149
Walton, Tony *11:* 164; *24:* 209; *153:* 8; *177:* 73; *237:* 50, 52
Waltrip, Lela *9:* 195
Waltrip, Mildred *3:* 209; *37:* 211
Waltrip, Rufus *9:* 195
Wan *12:* 76
Wan, Shelly *212:* 131
Wang, Lin *221:* 179
Wang, Shaoli *216:* 220
Wang, Suling *191:* 183; *213:* 194
Warburton, Sarah *154:* 187
Wappers, G. *121:* 40
Ward, Chad Michael *217:* 121
Ward, Fred *52:* 19
Ward, Helen *72:* 244; *144:* 240, 242
Ward, John *42:* 191; *96:* 54; *97:* 110; *123:* 105; *124:* 71; *173:* 66; *221:* 55
Ward, Keith *2:* 107; *132:* 69
Ward, Leslie *34:* 126; *36:* 87
Ward, Lynd *1:* 99, 132, 133, 150; *2:* 108, 158, 196, 259; *18:* 86; *27:* 56; *29:* 79, 187, 253, 255; *36:* 199,200, 201, 202, 203, 204, 205, 206, 207, 209; *43:* 34; *56:* 28; *60:* 116; *100:* 65
Ward, Peter *37:* 116
Waring, Geoff *172:* 84
Warhola, James *92:* 5; *115:* 85, 87; *118:* 174, 175, 177; *176:* 84; *187:* 189, 190; *223:* 102
Warner, Bob *230:* 5
Warner, Ben *159:* 171
Warner, Peter *14:* 87
Warner, Sally *214:* 210
Warnes, Tim *175:* 159; *202:* 188; *216:* 224
Warnick, Elsa *113:* 223
Warren, Betsy *2:* 101
Warren, Jim *85:* 81
Warren, Marion Cray *14:* 215
Warshaw, Jerry *30:* 197, 198; *42:* 165
Wasden, Kevin *102:* 162
Washington, Nevin *20:* 123
Washington, Phyllis *20:* 123
Wasserman, Amy L. *92:* 110; *209:* 95
Waterman, Stan *11:* 76
Watkins-Pitchford, D.J. *6:* 215, 217
Watling, James *67:* 210; *78:* 112; *101:* 81; *117:* 189, 190; *127:* 119, 120
Watson, Aldren A. *2:* 267; *5:* 94; *13:* 71; *19:* 253; *32:* 220; *42:* 193, 194, 195, 196, 197, 198, 199, 200, 201; *YABC 2:* 202
Watson, G. *83:* 162
Watson, Gary *19:* 147; *36:* 68; *41:* 122; *47:* 139

Watson, J.D. *22:* 86
Watson, Jesse Joshua *197:* 124; *199:* 181; *202:* 136
Watson, Karen *11:* 26
Watson, Mary *117:* 193
Watson, Richard Jesse *62:* 188, 189; *211:* 201
Watson, Wendy *5:* 197; *13:* 101; *33:* 116; *46:* 163; *64:* 12; *74:* 242, 243; *91:* 21; *142:* 228; *215:* 79; *241:* 166, 167, 168
Watt, Mélanie *136:* 206; *193:* 211
Wattenberg, Jane *174:* 200; *185:* 46; *187:* 108
Watterson, Bill *66:* 223, 225, 226
Watts, Bernadette *4:* 227; *103:* 182, 183; *230:* 193, 194, 195
Watts, James *59:* 197; *74:* 145; *86:* 124
Watts, John *37:* 149
Watts, Leslie Elizabeth *150:* 207; *165:* 106; *209:* 67
Watts, Sarah *234:* 115
Watts, Stan *116:* 205
Weatherby, Mark Alan *77:* 141
Web, Hannah *228:* 215
Webb, Jennifer *110:* 79
Webb, Lanny *142:* 175
Webb, Sophie *135:* 214
Webber, Helen *3:* 141
Webber, Irma E. *14:* 238
Weber, Erik *56:* 19, 20
Weber, Florence *40:* 153
Weber, Jill *127:* 227, 228; *189:* 163; *208:* 157; *209:* 190, 191; *216:* 46
Weber, Roland *61:* 204
Weber, Sam *190:* 227; *239:* 144
Weber, William J. *14:* 239
Webster, Jean *17:* 241
Weeks, Sarah *162:* 39
Wegman, William *78:* 243
Wegner, Fritz *14:* 250; *20:* 189; *44:* 165; *86:* 62
Weidenear, Reynold H. *21:* 122
Weigel, Jeff *170:* 193
Weihs, Erika *4:* 21; *15:* 299; *72:* 201; *107:* 207, 208
Weil, Lisl *7:* 203; *10:* 58; *21:* 95; *22:* 188,217; *33:* 193
Weiman, Jon *50:* 162, 165; *52:* 103; *54:* 78, 79, 81; *78:* 80; *82:* 107; *93:* 82; *97:* 69; *105:* 179; *193:* 65
Weiner, Greg *215:* 21
Weiner, Sandra *14:* 240
Weiner, Scott *55:* 27
Weinhaus, Karen Ann *53:* 90; *71:* 50; *86:* 124
Weinman, Brad *197:* 20; *233:* 35
Weinstock, Robert *204:* 165, 166
Weisgard, Leonard *1:* 65; *2:* 191, 197, 204, 264, 265; *5:* 108; *21:* 42; *30:* 200, 201, 203, 204; *41:* 47; *44:* 125; *53:* 25; *85:* 196, 198, 200, 201; *100:* 139,207; *YABC 2:* 13
Weisman, David *173:* 47
Weiss, Ellen *44:* 202
Weiss, Emil *1:* 168; *7:* 60
Weiss, Harvey *1:* 145, 223; *27:* 224, 227; *68:* 214; *76:* 245, 246, 247
Weiss, Nicki *33:* 229
Weissman, Bari *49:* 72; *90:* 125; *139:* 142
Weitzman, David L. *172:* 199
Welch, Sheila Kelly *130:* 221
Welkes, Allen *68:* 218
Wellington, Monica *99:* 223; *157:* 259, 260, 261; *222:* 197, 198, 199, 200
Welliver, Norma *76:* 94
Wellner, Fred *127:* 53
Wells, Frances *1:* 183
Wells, H.G. *20:* 194, 200
Wells, Haru *53:* 120, 121
Wells, Robert E. *184:* 208; *239:* 166, 167
Wells, Rosemary *6:* 49; *18:* 297; *60:* 32; *66:* 203; *69:* 215, 216; *114:* 227; *118:* 149, 150; *156:* 188, 189, 190, 191; *207:* 180, 181, 182, 183; *237:* 159, 161, 162
Wells, Rufus III *56:* 111, 113
Wells, Susan *22:* 43
Wendelin, Rudolph *23:* 234
Wengenroth, Stow *37:* 47
Weninger, Brigitte *189:* 192, 194
Werenskiold, Erik *15:* 6; *62:* 17
Werner, Honi *24:* 110; *33:* 41; *88:* 122
Werth, Kurt *7:* 122; *14:* 157; *20:* 214; *39:* 128
Wertz, Michael *240:* 184
Wesson,
West, Harry A. *124:* 38; *227:* 16
Westcott, Nadine Bernard *68:* 46; *84:* 49; *86:* 133; *106:* 199; *111:* 78; *113:* 111; *130:* 224; *139:* 54; *158:* 256; *194:* 199
Westerberg, Christine *29:* 226
Westerduin, Anne *105:* 229
Westerman, Johanna *162:* 206
Weston, Martha *29:* 116; *30:* 213; *33:* 85, 100; *53:* 181, 182, 183, 184; *77:* 95; *80:* 152; *119:* 196,197, 198, 199; *127:* 189; *133:* 196; *209:* 199
Wetherbee, Margaret *5:* 3
Wexler, Jerome *49:* 73; *150:* 129
Whalley, Peter *50:* 49
Whamond, Dave *222:* 203
Whatley, Bruce *186:* 93, 95; *207:* 127; *213:* 183, 184
Wheatley, Arabelle *11:* 231; *16:* 276
Wheeler, Cindy *49:* 205
Wheeler, Dora *44:* 179
Wheelright, Rowland *15:* 81; *YABC 2:* 286
Whelan, Michael *56:* 108; *70:* 27, 29, 67, 68, 148; *74:* 18; *84:* 14; *91:* 195, 196; *95:* 147; *98:* 150, 151; *106:* 157; *113:* 218, 220; *116:* 99, 100
Whelan, Patrick *135:* 145
Whistler, Rex *16:* 75; *30:* 207, 208
White, Beth *216:* 139
White, Craig *110:* 130; *119:* 193; *130:* 33; *179:* 31
White, David Omar *5:* 56; *18:* 6
White, Joan *83:* 225
White, Lee *221:* 176; *223:* 188, 189, 190
White, Martin *51:* 197; *85:* 127
Whitear *32:* 26
Whitehead, Beck *86:* 171
Whitehead, Jenny *221:* 16
Whitehead, S.B. *154:* 132
Whithorne, H.S. *7:* 49
Whitman, Candace *208:* 208
Whitney, George Gillett *3:* 24
Whitney, Jean *99:* 53
Whitson, Paul *102:* 161
Whittam, Geoffrey *30:* 191
Whyte, Mary *96:* 127; *232:* 39
Wiberg, Harald *38:* 127; *93:* 215
Wick, Walter *77:* 128
Wickstrom, Sylvie *106:* 87; *169:* 180; *214:* 110
Wickstrom, Thor *200:* 205
Widener, Terry *105:* 230; *106:* 7; *163:* 23; *200:* 17; *209:* 195; *231:* 12
Wiese, Kurt *3:* 255; *4:* 206; *14:* 17; *17:* 18, 19; *19:* 47; *24:* 152; *25:* 212; *32:* 184; *36:* 211,213, 214, 215, 216, 217, 218; *45:* 161; *100:* 92
Wiesner, David *33:* 47; *51:* 106; *57:* 67; *58:* 55; *64:* 78, 79, 81; *69:* 233; *72:* 247, 248, 249, 251,252, 253, 254; *83:* 134; *104:* 31; *117:* 197, 199, 200, 202; *139:* 223, 224; *151:* 51; *181:* 189, 190
Wiesner, William *4:* 100; *5:* 200, 201; *14:* 262
Wight, Eric *218:* 190; *232:* 195
Wiggins, George *6:* 133
Wijngaard, Juan *111:* 36; *114:* 124; *227:* 136; *230:* 202
Wikkelsoe, Otto *45:* 25, 26
Wikland, Ilon *5:* 113; *8:* 150; *38:* 124, 125, 130; *127:* 162
Wikler, Madeline *114:* 233
Wilbur, C. Keith, M.D. *27:* 228
Wilburn, Kathy *53:* 102; *68:* 234
Wilcox, Cathy *105:* 123
Wilcox, J.A.J. *34:* 122
Wilcox, Lydia *207:* 187
Wilcox, R. Turner *36:* 219
Wild, Jocelyn *46:* 220, 221, 222; *80:* 117
Wilde, George *7:* 139
Wildish, Lee *231:* 34, 193
Wildsmith, Brian *16:* 281, 282; *18:* 170, 171; *66:* 25; *69:* 224, 225, 227; *77:* 103; *83:* 218; *124:* 214,217, 219
Wildsmith, Mike *140:* 229
Wilhelm, Hans *58:* 189, 191; *73:* 157; *77:* 127; *135:* 229, 230, 233, 234; *196:* 209
Wilkin, Eloise *36:* 173; *49:* 208, 209, 210
Wilkinson, Barry *50:* 213
Wilkinson, Gerald *3:* 40
Wilkon, Jozef *31:* 183, 184; *71:* 206, 207, 209; *133:* 222
Wilks, Mike *34:* 24; *44:* 203; *224:* 193
Willems, Mo *154:* 245, 246, 247; *180:* 236, 237, 239; *228:* 204, 208
Willey, Bee *103:* 129; *139:* 159; *173:* 115
Willhoite, Michael A. *71:* 214
William, Maria *168:* 51
Williams, Berkeley, Jr. *64:* 75
Williams, Ferelith Eccles *22:* 238
Williams, Garth *1:* 197; *2:* 49, 270; *4:* 205; *15:* 198, 302, 304, 307; *16:* 34; *18:* 283, 298, 299, 300, 301; *29:* 177, 178, 179, 232, 233, 241, 242, 243, 244, 245, 248; *40:* 106; *66:* 229, 230, 231, 233, 234; *71:* 192; *73:* 218, 219, 220; *78:* 261; *100:* 251, 252, 255; *136:* 117; *YABC 2:* 15, 16, 19
Williams, J. Scott *48:* 28
Williams, Jennifer *102:* 201
Williams, Jenny *60:* 202; *81:* 21; *88:* 71
Williams, Kent *180:* 18; *241:* 33
Williams, Kit *44:* 206, 207, 208, 209, 211, 212
Williams, Marcia *97:* 214; *159:* 208, 209
Williams, Maureen *12:* 238
Williams, Patrick *14:* 218
Williams, Richard *44:* 93; *72:* 229; *74:* 133; *78:* 155, 237; *91:* 178; *110:* 212; *136:* 201, 202, 203; *152:* 115
Williams, Sam *124:* 222; *153:* 11; *177:* 201, 202; *180:* 34; *212:* 49; *232:* 155; *238:* 113
Williams, Sophy *135:* 236
Williams, Vera B. *53:* 186, 187, 188, 189; *102:* 201, 202, 203; *210:* 65
Williamson, Alex *177:* 180; *205:* 50
Williamson, Mel *60:* 9
Willingham, Fred *104:* 206; *154:* 157
Willis, Adam *181:* 75; *209:* 11
Willmore, J.T. *54:* 113, 114
Wilsdorf, Anne *180:* 122; *189:* 124; *191:* 195
Wilson, Anne *160:* 114; *224:* 199, 200
Wilson, Charles Banks *17:* 92; *43:* 73
Wilson, Connie *113:* 179
Wilson, Dagmar *10:* 47
Wilson, Dawn *67:* 161; *81:* 120; *113:* 158
Wilson, Edward A. *6:* 24; *16:* 149; *20:* 220, 221; *22:* 87; *26:* 67; *38:* 212, 214, 215, 216, 217
Wilson, Forrest *27:* 231
Wilson, Gahan *35:* 234; *41:* 136
Wilson, George *76:* 87
Wilson, Helen Miranda *140:* 61
Wilson, Jack *17:* 139
Wilson, Janet *77:* 154; *96:* 114; *99:* 219, 220; *153:* 64 *106:* 122; *130:* 210; *145:* 178; *173:* 64
Wilson, John *22:* 240
Wilson, Maurice *46:* 224
Wilson, Patten *35:* 61
Wilson, Peggy *15:* 4; *84:* 20
Wilson, Phil *181:* 29
Wilson, Rowland B. *30:* 170
Wilson, Sarah *50:* 215
Wilson, Tom *33:* 232
Wilson, W.N. *22:* 26
Wilson-Max, Ken *170:* 196; *180:* 181

Wilton, Nicholas *103:* 52; *183:* 111
Wilwerding, Walter J. *9:* 202
Wimmer, Mike *63:* 6; *70:* 121; *75:* 186; *76:* 21,22, 23; *91:* 114; *97:* 45, 68; *98:* 28; *107:* 130; *146:* 21; *149:* 47; *173:* 126; *193:* 21, 25; *194:* 204, 205
Winborn, Marsha *78:* 34; *99:* 70; *192:* 20
Winch, John *165:* 233
Winchester, Linda *13:* 231
Wind, Betty *28:* 158
Windham, Kathryn Tucker *14:* 260
Windham, Sophie *184:* 212
Winfield, Alison *115:* 78; *214:* 121
Winfield, Wayne *72:* 23
Wing, Gary *64:* 147
Wing, Ron *50:* 85
Wingerter, Linda S. *132:* 199; *174:* 181; *200:* 196
Winick, Judd *124:* 227, 228, 229
Winn-Lederer, Ilene *202:* 91
Winnick, Karen B. *211:* 207
Winslow, Will *21:* 124
Winstead, Rosie *180:* 243
Winsten, Melanie Willa *41:* 41
Winter, Jeanette *151:* 240, 241, 242; *184:* 215, 217, 218, 219
Winter, Milo *15:* 97; *19:* 221; *21:* 181, 203, 204, 205; *64:* 19; *YABC 2:* 144
Winter, Paula *48:* 227
Winter, Susan *163:* 177; *182:* 201; *226:* 173
Winters, Greg *70:* 117
Winters, Nina *62:* 194
Wise, Louis *13:* 68
Wiseman, Ann *31:* 187
Wiseman, B. *4:* 233
Wishnefsky, Phillip *3:* 14
Wiskur, Darrell *5:* 72; *10:* 50; *18:* 246
Wisnewski, Andrea *234:* 210
Wisniewski, David *95:* 220, 221
Wisniewski, Robert *95:* 10; *119:* 192
Withee, Maureen *225:* 42
Witschonke, Alan *153:* 149, 150
Witt, Dick *80:* 244
Wittmann, Patrick *162:* 204
Wittman, Sally *30:* 219
Wittner, Dale *99:* 43
Wittwer, Hala *158:* 267; *195:* 80
Woehr, Lois *12:* 5
Wohlberg, Meg *12:* 100; *14:* 197; *41:* 255
Wohnoutka, Mike *137:* 68; *190:* 199; *195:* 218; *205:* 132; *221:* 6; *230:* 206, 207
Wojtowycz, David *167:* 168
Woldin, Beth Weiner *34:* 211
Wolf, Elizabeth *133:* 151; *208:* 175
Wolf, J. *16:* 91
Wolf, Janet *78:* 254
Wolf, Linda *33:* 163
Wolfe, Corey *72:* 213
Wolfe, Frances *216:* 227
Wolfe, Gillian *199:* 193
Wolff, Ashley *50:* 217; *81:* 216; *156:* 216, 217; *170:* 57; *174:* 174; *184:* 72; *203:* 181, 182, 183, 184
Wolff, Glenn *178:* 230
Wolff, Jason *213:* 186
Wolfhard, Steve *235:* 199
Wolfsgruber, Linda *166:* 61
Wondriska, William *6:* 220
Wong, Janet S. *98:* 225; *152:* 43
Wong, Ken *224:* 23
Wong, Nicole *174:* 13; *214:* 216; *215:* 25
Wonsetler, John C. *5:* 168
Wood, Audrey *50:* 221, 222, 223; *81:* 219, 221; *198:* 206
Wood, Don *50:* 220, 225, 226, 228, 229; *81:* 218, 220; *139:* 239, 240
Wood, Grant *19:* 198
Wood, Heather *133:* 108
Wood, Ivor *58:* 17
Wood, Jakki *211:* 209
Wood, Muriel *36:* 119; *77:* 167; *171:* 55; *187:* 46; *235:* 49
Wood, Myron *6:* 220
Wood, Owen *18:* 187; *64:* 202, 204, 205, 206, 208, 210
Wood, Rob *193:* 48
Wood, Ruth *8:* 11
Woodbridge, Curtis *133:* 138; *204:* 113
Wooding, Sharon L. *66:* 237
Woodruff, Liza *132:* 239; *182:* 46, 204
Woodruff, Thomas *171:* 73
Woods, John, Jr. *109:* 142
Woods, Maria *227:* 69
Woodson, Jack *10:* 201
Woodson, Jacqueline *94:* 242
Woodward, Alice *26:* 89; *36:* 81
Wool, David *26:* 27
Wooley, Janet *112:* 75; *227:* 74
Woolman, Steven *106:* 47; *163:* 73
Wooten, Vernon *23:* 70; *51:* 170
Worboys, Evelyn *1:* 166, 167
Word, Reagan *103:* 204
Wormell, Christopher *154:* 251; *202:* 206
Worth, Jo *34:* 143
Worth, Wendy *4:* 133
Wosmek, Frances *29:* 251
Wrenn, Charles L. *38:* 96; *YABC 1:* 20, 21
Wright, Barbara Mullarney *98:* 161
Wright, Cliff *168:* 203
Wright, Dare *21:* 206
Wright-Frierson, Virginia *58:* 194; *110:* 246
Wright, George *YABC 1:* 268
Wright, Joseph *30:* 160
Wronker, Lili Cassel *3:* 247; *10:* 204; *21:* 10
Wu, Donald *200:* 18
Wummer, Amy *154:* 181; *168:* 150; *176:* 85; *201:* 202, 203; *218:* 154; *238:* 143; *241:* 177, 178
Wyant, Alexander Helwig *110:* 19
Wyatt, David *97:* 9; *101:* 44; *114:* 194; *140:* 20; *167:* 13; *188:* 48; *227:* 60; *241:* 126
Wyatt, Stanley *46:* 210
Wyeth, Andrew *13:* 40; *YABC 1:* 133, 134
Wyeth, Jamie *41:* 257
Wyeth, N.C. *13:* 41; *17:* 252, 253, 254, 255, 256, 257, 258, 259, 264, 265, 266, 267, 268; *18:* 181; *19:* 80, 191, 200; *21:* 57, 183; *22:* 91; *23:* 152; *24:* 28, 99; *35:* 61; *41:* 65; *100:* 206; *YABC1:* 133, 223; *2:* 53, 75, 171, 187, 317
Wyman, Cherie R. *91:* 42
Wynne, Patricia J. *210:* 260; *223:* 184

X

Xuan, YongSheng *119:* 202, 207, 208; *140:* 36; *187:* 21; *226:* 221, 227, 230, 232, 233

Y

Yaccarino, Dan *141:* 208, 209; *147:* 171; *192:* 244, 245; *207:* 168
Yakovetic, Joe *59:* 202; *75:* 85
Yalowitz, Paul *93:* 33; *211:* 92
Yamaguchi, Marianne *85:* 118
Yamasaki, James *167:* 93
Yang, Belle *170:* 198
Yang, Jay *1:* 8; *12:* 239
Yanok, Johnny *236:* 192
Yap, Weda *6:* 176
Yaroslava
See Mills, Yaroslava Surmach
Yashima, Taro *14:* 84
Yates, John *74:* 249, 250
Yates, Kelly *208:* 214
Yayo *178:* 88; *226:* 235
Yeatts, Tabatha *215:* 210
Yee, Cora *166:* 233
Yee, Wong Herbert *115:* 216, 217; *172:* 204, 205; *194:* 59
Yelchin, Eugene *204:* 4; *232:* 198
Yeo, Brad *135:* 121; *192:* 106
Yerxa, Leo *181:* 195
Yezerski, Thomas F. *162:* 29
Ylla
See Koffler, Camilla
Yohn, F.C. *23:* 128; *YABC 1:* 269
Yoo, Taeeun *191:* 198
Yorinks, Adrienne *144:* 248; *200:* 214
Yorke, David *80:* 178
Yoshida, Toshi *77:* 231
Yoshikawa, Sachiko *168:* 104; *177:* 28; *181:* 196, 197; *225:* 115
Youll, Paul *91:* 218
Youll, Stephen *92:* 227; *118:* 136, 137; *164:* 248; *202:* 92
Young, Amy L. *185:* 218; *190:* 46
Young, Cybéle *167:* 9
Young, Ed *7:* 205; *10:* 206; *40:* 124; *63:* 142; *74:* 250, 251, 252, 253; *75:* 227; *81:* 159; *83:* 98; *94:* 154; *115:* 160; *137:* 162; *YABC 2:* 242; *173:* 174, 175, 176; *205:* 29; *212:* 82; *221:* 72
Young, Karen Romano *237:* 184
Young, Mary O'Keefe *77:* 95; *80:* 247; *134:* 214; *140:* 213; *211:* 223, 225
Young, Ned *233:* 187
Young, Noela *8:* 221; *89:* 231; *97:* 195; *230:* 145, 146
Young, Paul *190:* 222; *225:* 38
Young, Selina *153:* 12; *201:* 204, 205
Yuen, Sammy, Jr. *223:* 46; *236:* 32; *241:* 19
Yum, Hyewon *211:* 228
Yun, Cheng Mung *60:* 143
Yung, Jennifer *220:* 136

Z

Zacharow, Christopher *88:* 98
Zacks, Lewis *10:* 161
Zadig *50:* 58
Zaffo, George *42:* 208
Zagwyn, Deborah Turney *138:* 227
Zahares, Wade *193:* 219
Zaid, Barry *50:* 127; *51:* 201
Zaidenberg, Arthur *34:* 218, 219, 220
Zahedi, Morteza *232:* 2
Zalben, Jane Breskin *7:* 211; *79:* 230, 231, 233; *170:* 202
Zallinger, Jean *4:* 192; *8:* 8, 129; *14:* 273; *68:* 36; *80:* 254; *115:* 219, 220, 222
Zallinger, Rudolph F. *3:* 245
Zakanitch, Robert Rahway *231:* 195
Zakrajsek, Molly *177:* 146
Zappa, Ahmet *180:* 250
Zebot, George *83:* 214
Zecca, Katherine *207:* 195
Zeck, Gerry *40:* 232
Zeff, Joe *181:* 98; *221:* 101
Zeifert, Harriet *154:* 265, 267
Zeiring, Bob *42:* 130
Zeldich, Arieh *49:* 124; *62:* 120
Zeldis, Malcah *86:* 239; *94:* 198; *146:* 265, 266
Zelinsky, Paul O. *14:* 269; *43:* 56; *49:* 218-223; *53:* 111; *68:* 195; *102:* 219, 222, 221, 222; *154:* 255, 256, 257; *171:* 141; *185:* 96
Zelvin, Diana *72:* 190; *76:* 101; *93:* 207
Zemach, Kaethe *149:* 250
Zemach, Margot *3:* 270; *8:* 201; *21:* 210, 211; *27:* 204, 205, 210; *28:* 185; *49:* 22, 183, 224; *53:* 151; *56:* 146; *70:* 245, 246; *92:* 74
Zeman, Ludmila *153* 212
Zemsky, Jessica *10:* 62

Zepelinsky, Paul *35:* 93
Zerbetz, Evon *127:* 34; *158:* 109
Zezejl, Daniel *197:* 74
Zhang, Ange *101:* 190; *172:* 41
Zhang, Son Nang *163:* 113; *170:* 206
Ziegler, Jack *84:* 134
Zimdars, Berta *129:* 155
Zimet, Jay *147:* 94; *152:* 74; *196:* 75
Zimic, Tricia *72:* 95
Zimmer, Dirk *38:* 195; *49:* 71; *56:* 151; *65:* 214; *84:* 159; *89:* 26; *147:* 224
Zimmer, Tracie Vaughn *169:* 183
Zimmerman, Andrea *192:* 49, 50
Zimmermann, H. Werner *101:* 223; *112:* 197
Zimnik, Reiner *36:* 224
Zingone, Robin *180:* 134; *236:* 147, 148
Zinkeisen, Anna *13:* 106
Zinn, David *97:* 97
Zoellick, Scott *33:* 231
Zollars, Jaime *190:* 190
Zonia, Dhimitri *20:* 234, 235
Zorn, Peter A., Jr. *142:* 157
Zudeck, Darryl *58:* 129; *63:* 98; *80:* 52
Zug, Mark *88:* 131; *204:* 169
Zulewski, Tim *164:* 95; *232:* 59
Zuma *99:* 36
Zvorykin, Boris *61:* 155
Zweifel, Francis *14:* 274; *28:* 187
Zwerger, Lisbeth *54:* 176, 178; *66:* 246, 247, 248; *130:* 230, 231, 232, 233; *181:* 92; *194:* 224, 225, 226
Zwinger, Herman H. *46:* 227
Zwolak, Paul *67:* 69, 71, 73, 74

Author Index

The following index gives the number of the volume in which an author's biographical sketch, Autobiography Feature, Brief Entry, or Obituary appears.

This index includes references to all entries in the following series, which are also published by The Gale Group.

YABC—*Yesterday's Authors of Books for Children: Facts and Pictures about Authors and Illustrators of Books for Young People from Early Times to 1960*
CLR—*Children's Literature Review: Excerpts from Reviews, Criticism, and Commentary on Books for Children*
SAAS—*Something about the Author Autobiography Series*

A

Aardema, Verna 1911-2000 ... *107*
Obituary ... *119*
Earlier sketches in SATA *4, 68*
See also CLR *17*
See also SAAS *8*
Aaron, Chester 1923- ... *216*
Autobiography Feature ... *216*
Earlier sketches in SATA *9, 74*
See also SAAS *12*
Aaseng, Nate
See Aaseng, Nathan
Aaseng, Nathan 1953- ... *236*
Autobiography Feature ... *236*
Brief entry ... *38*
Earlier sketches in SATA *51, 88, 172*
See also CLR *54*
See also SAAS *12*
Abadzis, Nick 1965- ... *193*
Abalos, Rafael 1956-
See Abalos, Rafael
Abalos, Rafael 1956- ... *197*
Abbas, Jailan 1952- ... *91*
Abbey, Lynn
See Abbey, Marilyn Lorraine
Abbey, Marilyn Lorraine 1948- ... *156*
Abbott, Alice
See Borland, Kathryn Kilby
and Speicher, Helen Ross S(mith)
Abbott, Jacob 1803-1879 ... *22*
Abbott, Manager Henry
See Stratemeyer, Edward L.
Abbott, R(obert) Tucker 1919-1995 ... *61*
Obituary ... *87*
Abbott, Sarah
See Zolotow, Charlotte
Abbott, Tony 1952- ... *205*
Earlier sketch in SATA *159*
Abdelsayed, Cindy 1962- ... *123*
Abdul, Raoul 1929- ... *12*
Abeele, Veronique van den ... *196*
Abel, Raymond 1911- ... *12*
Abell, Kathleen 1938- ... *9*
Abelove, Joan ... *110*
Abels, Harriette S(heffer) 1926- ... *50*
Abercrombie, Barbara 1939- ... *182*
Earlier sketch in SATA *16*
Abercrombie, Barbara Mattes
See Abercrombie, Barbara
Abercrombie, Lynn
See Sorrells, Walter
Abernethy, Robert G(ordon) 1927- ... *5*
Abisch, Roslyn Kroop 1927- ... *9*
Abisch, Roz
See Abisch, Roslyn Kroop
Ablow, Gail 1962- ... *198*
Abodaher, David J. (Naiph) 1919- ... *17*
Abolafia, Yossi 1944-
See Abulafia, Yossi
Abolivier, Aurelie ... *219*
Abouzeid, Chris ... *175*
Abrahall, Clare Hoskyns
See Hoskyns-Abrahall, Clare (Constance Drury)
Abrahams, Hilary (Ruth) 1938- ... *29*
Abrahams, Peter 1947- ... *194*
Abrahams, Robert David 1905-1998 ... *4*
Abramovitz, Anita (Zeltner Brooks) 1914- ... *5*
Abrams, Joy 1941- ... *16*
Abrams, Lawrence F. ... *58*
Brief entry ... *47*
Abramson, Andra Serlin ... *237*
Abrashkin, Raymond 1911-1960 ... *50*
Abulafia, Yossi 1944- ... *177*
Brief entry ... *46*
Earlier sketch in SATA *60*
Acampora, Paul ... *175*
Accardo, Anthony ... *191*
Acer, David ... *206*
Achebe, Albert Chinualumogu
See Achebe, Chinua
Achebe, Chinua 1930- ... *40*
Brief entry ... *38*
Earlier sketch in SATA *38*
See also CLR *156*
Acheson, Alison 1964- ... *222*
Ackerman, Diane 1948- ... *102*
Ackerman, Eugene (Francis) 1888-1974 ... *10*
Ackerman, Karen 1951- ... *126*
Ackerman, Peter ... *234*
Ackerman, Susan Yoder 1945- ... *92*
Ackison, Wendy Wassink 1956- ... *103*
Ackley, Peggy Jo 1955- ... *58*
Ackroyd, Peter 1949- ... *153*
Acorn, John (Harrison) 1958- ... *79*
Acredolo, Linda (Potter) 1947- ... *159*
Acs, Laszlo (Bela) 1931- ... *42*
Brief entry ... *32*
Acuff, Selma Boyd 1924- ... *45*
Ada, Alma Flor 1938- ... *222*
Autobiography Feature ... *222*
Earlier sketches in SATA *43, 84, 143, 181*
See also CLR *62*
Adair, Gilbert 1944-2011 ... *98*
Adair, Ian 1942- ... *53*
Adair, Margaret Weeks (?)-1971 ... *10*
Adam, Cornel
See Lengyel, Cornel Adam
Adam, Mark
See Alexander, Marc
Adam, Paul 1958- ... *231*
Adam, Robert 1948- ... *93*
Adams, Adrienne 1906- ... *90*
Earlier sketch in SATA *8*
See also CLR *73*
Adams, Andy 1859-1935
See YABC *1*
Adams, Barbara Johnston 1943- ... *60*
Adams, Beth ... *236*
Adams, Bruin
See Ellis, Edward S.
Adams, Captain Bruin
See Ellis, Edward S.
Adams, Captain J. F. C.
See Ellis, Edward S.
Adams, Dale
See Quinn, Elisabeth
Adams, Daniel
See Nicole, Christopher
Adams, Debra
See Speregen, Devra Newberger
Adams, Diane 1960- ... *217*
Adams, Douglas 1952-2001 ... *116*
Obituary ... *128*
Adams, Douglas Noel
See Adams, Douglas
Adams, Edith
See Shine, Deborah
Adams, Florence 1932- ... *61*
Adams, Georgie 1945- ... *216*
Adams, Harriet S(tratemeyer) 1892(?)-1982 ... *1*
Obituary ... *29*
Adams, Harrison
See Rathborne, St. George (Henry)
and Stratemeyer, Edward L.

Adams, Hazard 1926- *6*
Adams, Hazard Simeon
See Adams, Hazard
Adams, John Anthony 1944- *67*
Adams, Kathryn *224*
Adams, Laurie 1941- *33*
Adams, Lowell
See Joseph, James (Herz)
Adams, Nicholas
See Pine, Nicholas
Adams, Nicholas
See Smith, Sherwood
Adams, Nicholas
See Doyle, Debra
and Macdonald, James D.
Adams, Pam 1919- *112*
Adams, Pamela
See Adams, Pam
Adams, Richard 1920- *69*
Earlier sketch in SATA *7*
See also CLR *121*
Adams, Richard George
See Adams, Richard
Adams, Ruth Joyce *14*
Adams, S.J.
See Selzer, Adam
Adams, Tricia
See Kite, Pat
Adams, William Taylor 1822-1897 .... *28*
Adam Smith, Janet (Buchanan) 1905-1999 .. *63*
Adamson, Gareth 1925-1982(?) *46*
Obituary *30*
Adamson, George 1906-1989
Obituary *63*
Adamson, George (Worsley) 1913-2005 .... *30*
Adamson, Graham
See Groom, Arthur William
Adamson, Joy(-Friederike Victoria)
1910-1980 .... *11*
Obituary *22*
Adamson, Wendy Writson 1942- *22*
Addasi, Maha 1968- *205*
Addison, Kenneth 1949(?)-2005 .... *187*
Addison, Kenneth L.
See Addison, Kenneth
Addona, Angelo F. 1925- *14*
Addy, Sean 1976- *222*
Addy, Sharon Hart 1943- *192*
Earlier sketch in SATA *108*
Addy, Ted
See Winterbotham, R(ussell) R(obert)
Adelberg, Doris
See Orgel, Doris
Adelson, Leone 1908- *11*
Adinolfi, JoAnn *176*
Adkins, Jan 1944- *210*
Autobiography Feature *210*
Earlier sketches in SATA *8, 69, 144*
See also CLR *77*
See also SAAS *19*
Adl, Shirin 1975- *225*
Adler, C. S. 1932- *126*
Earlier sketches in SATA *26, 63, 102*
See also CLR *78*
See also SAAS *15*
Adler, Carole Schwerdtfeger
See Adler, C. S.
Adler, David A. 1947- *231*
Earlier sketches in SATA *14, 70, 106, 151, 178*
See also CLR *108*
Adler, Emily *230*
Adler, Irene
See Penzler, Otto
and Storr, Catherine (Cole)
Adler, Irving 1913- *29*
Autobiography Feature *164*
Earlier sketch in SATA *1*
See also CLR *27*
See also SAAS *15*
Adler, Larry 1939- *36*
Adler, Peggy *22*
Adler, Ruth 1915-1968 .... *1*
Adlerman, Daniel (Ezra) 1963- *163*
Earlier sketch in SATA *96*
Adlerman, Kim
See Adlerman, Kimberly M(arie)
Adlerman, Kimberly M(arie) 1964- *163*
Earlier sketch in SATA *96*
Adoff, Arnold 1935- *240*
Earlier sketches in SATA *5, 57, 96*
See also CLR *7*
See also SAAS *15*
Adoff, Jaime *163*
Adoff, Jaime Levi
See Adoff, Jaime
Adorjan, Carol (Madden) 1934- *71*
Earlier sketch in SATA *10*
Adornetto, Alexandra 1992- *236*
Adrian, Frances
See Polland, Madeleine A(ngela Cahill)
Adrian, Mary
See Jorgensen, Mary Venn
Adshead, Gladys L(ucy) 1896-1985 .... *3*
Aesop 620(?)B.C.-560(?)B.C. *64*
See also CLR *14*
Aesop, Abraham
See Newbery, John
Affabee, Eric
See Stine, R.L.
Agapida, Fray Antonio
See Irving, Washington
Agard, John 1949- *223*
Earlier sketch in SATA *138*
Agard, Nadema 1948- *18*
Agarwal, Deepa 1947- *141*
Agee, Jon 1960- *196*
Earlier sketches in SATA *116, 157*
Agell, Charlotte 1959- *214*
Earlier sketches in SATA *99, 150*
Agent Orange
See Moseley, James W(illett)
Aghill, Gordon
See Garrett, Randall
and Silverberg, Robert
Agle, Nan Hayden 1905- *3*
See also SAAS *10*
Agnew, Edith J(osephine) 1897-1988 .... *11*
Agnew, Lincoln *222*
Agonito, Joseph *177*
Agonito, Rosemary 1937- *177*
Aguilar, David *214*
Aguilar, David A.
See Aguilar, David
Ahearn, Janet Reed *236*
Ahern, Margaret McCrohan 1921- *10*
Ahl, Anna Maria 1926- *32*
Ahlberg, Allan 1938- *214*
Brief entry *35*
Earlier sketches in SATA *68, 120, 165*
See also CLR *18*
Ahlberg, Janet 1944-1994 .... *120*
Brief entry *32*
Obituary *83*
Earlier sketch in SATA *68*
See also CLR *18*
Ahlberg, Jessica 1980- *229*
Aho, Julia Kay
See Kay, Julia
Aichinger, Helga 1937- *4*
Aiken, Clarissa (M.) Lorenz 1899-1992 .... *12*
Obituary *109*
Aiken, Conrad 1889-1973 .... *30*
Earlier sketch in SATA *3*
Aiken, Conrad Potter
See Aiken, Conrad
Aiken, Joan 1924-2004 .... *73*
Autobiography Feature *109*
Obituary *152*
Earlier sketches in SATA *2, 30*
See also CLR *90*
See also SAAS *1*
Aiken, Joan Delano
See Aiken, Joan
Aillaud, Cindy Lou 1955- *184*
Ainsley, Alix
See Steiner, Barbara A(nnette)
Ainsworth, Catherine Harris 1910- *56*
Ainsworth, Norma 1911-1987 .... *9*
Ainsworth, Ruth (Gallard) 1908- *73*
Earlier sketch in SATA *7*
Ainsworth, William Harrison 1805-1882 .... *24*
Aistrop, Jack 1916- *14*
Aitken, Amy 1952- *54*
Brief entry *40*
Aitken, Dorothy 1916- *10*
Aitmatov, Chingiz 1928-2008 .... *56*
Aitmatov, Chingiz Torekulovich
See Aitmatov, Chingiz
Ajhar, Brian 1957- *220*
Akaba, Suekichi 1910- *46*
Akbarpour, Ahmad 1970- *232*
Akers, Floyd
See Baum, L. Frank
Akib, Jamel *181*
Akin, Sara Laux *236*
Aks, Patricia 1926-1994 .... *68*
al Abdullah, Rania
See Rania, Queen of Jordan
Alagoa, Ebiegberi Joe 1933- *108*
Alain
See Brustlein, Daniel
Alajalov, Constantin 1900-1987
Obituary *53*
Alalou, Ali *203*
Alalou, Elizabeth *203*
Alan, David
See Horsfield, Alan
Alan, Robert
See Silverstein, Robert Alan
Alarcon, Francisco X. 1954- *215*
Earlier sketch in SATA *104*
Alarcon, Francisco Xavier
See Alarcon, Francisco X.
Alarcon, Karen Beaumont
See Beaumont, Karen
Albarn, Jessica 1971- *238*
Albee, Sarah 1962- *231*
Albert, Burton 1936- *22*
Albert, Louise 1928- *157*
Albert, Michael 1966- *202*
Albert, Richard E. 1909-1999 .... *82*
Albert, Susan Wittig 1940- *107*
Alberts, Frances Jacobs 1907-1989 .... *14*
Albertson, Susan
See Wojciechowski, Susan
Albion, Lee Smith *29*
Alborough, Jez 1959- *149*
Earlier sketch in SATA *86*
Albrecht, Lillie (Vanderveer H.)
1894-1985 .... *12*
Albyn, Carole Lisa 1955- *83*
Alchemy, Jack
See Gershator, David
Alcock, Gudrun 1908- *56*
Brief entry *33*
Alcock, Vivien (Dolores) 1924-2003 .... *76*
Brief entry *38*
Obituary *148*
Earlier sketch in SATA *45*
See also CLR *26*
Alcorn, John 1935- *31*
Brief entry *30*
Alcorn, Stephen 1958- *207*
Earlier sketch in SATA *110*
Alcott, Louisa May 1832-1888 .... *100*
See also YABC *1*
See also CLR *109*
Alda, Arlene 1933- *205*
Brief entry *36*
Earlier sketches in SATA *44, 106, 158*
See also CLR *93*

Alden, Isabella (Macdonald) 1841-1930 ..... *115*
See also YABC *2*
Alden, Sue
See Francis, Dorothy
Alderman, Clifford Lindsey 1902-1988 .... *3*
Alderson, Sue Ann 1940- *59*
Brief entry *48*
Alding, Peter
See Jeffries, Roderic
Aldis, Dorothy (Keeley) 1896-1966 .... *2*
Aldiss, Brian W. 1925- *34*
Aldiss, Brian Wilson
See Aldiss, Brian W.
Aldon, Adair
See Meigs, Cornelia Lynde
Aldous, Allan (Charles) 1911- *27*
Aldrich, Ann
See Meaker, Marijane
Aldrich, Bess Streeter 1881-1954
See CLR *70*
Aldrich, Thomas (Bailey) 1836-1907 .... *114*
Earlier sketch in SATA *17*
Aldridge, (Harold Edward) James 1918- *87*
Aldridge, Josephine Haskell *14*
Aldridge, Sheila 1974- *192*
Aleas, Richard
See Ardai, Charles
Alegria, Malin 1974(?)- *190*
Alegria, Ricardo E(nrique) 1921- *6*
Aleksin, Anatolii Georgievich 1924- *36*
Alenov, Lydia 1948- *61*
Alex, Ben (a pseudonym) 1946- *45*
Alex, Marlee (a pseudonym) 1948- *45*
Alexander, Alma 1963- *217*
Alexander, Anna B(arbara Cooke) 1913- *1*
Alexander, Anne
See Alexander, Anna B(arbara Cooke)
Alexander, Claire *228*
Alexander, Ellen 1938- *91*
Alexander, Frances (Laura) 1888-1979 .... *4*
Alexander, Heather 1967- *232*
Alexander, Janet 1907-1994 .... *97*
Earlier sketch in SATA *1*
Alexander, Jill S. 1964- *223*
Alexander, Jill Shurbet
See Alexander, Jill S.
Alexander, Jocelyn Anne Arundel 1930- *22*
Alexander, Linda 1935- *2*
Alexander, Lloyd 1924-2007 .... *135*
Obituary *182*
Earlier sketches in SATA *3, 49, 81, 129*
See also CLR *48*
See also SAAS *19*
Alexander, Lloyd Chudley
See Alexander, Lloyd
Alexander, Marc 1929- *117*
Alexander, Martha 1920- *136*
Earlier sketches in SATA *11, 70*
Alexander, Rae Pace
See Alexander, Raymond Pace
Alexander, Raymond Pace 1898-1974 .... *22*
Alexander, R.C. *232*
Alexander, Robert *200*
Alexander, Robert C.
See Alexander, R.C.
Alexander, Rod
See Pellowski, Michael (Joseph)
Alexander, Sally Hobart 1943- *84*
Alexander, Sue 1933-2008 .... *136*
Obituary *195*
Earlier sketches in SATA *12, 89*
See also SAAS *15*
Alexander, Vincent Arthur 1925-1980
Obituary *23*
Alexeieff, Alexandre A. 1901-1979 .... *14*
Alger, Horatio, Jr.
See Stratemeyer, Edward L.
Alger, Horatio, Jr. 1832-1899 .... *16*
See also CLR *170*
Alger, Leclaire (Gowans) 1898-1969 .... *15*
Aliki
See Brandenberg, Aliki
Alkema, Chester Jay 1932- *12*
Al-Khalili, Jim 1962- *124*
Alkiviades, Alkis 1953- *105*
Alko, Selina 1968- *218*
Alkouatli, Claire *186*
Allaby, John Michael
See Allaby, Michael
Allaby, Michael 1933- *167*
Allamand, Pascale 1942- *12*
Allan, Mabel Esther 1915-1998 .... *75*
Earlier sketches in SATA *5, 32*
See also CLR *43*
See also SAAS *11*
Allan, Nicholas 1956- *123*
Earlier sketch in SATA *79*
Allan-Meyer, Kathleen 1918- *51*
Brief entry *46*
Allard, Harry, Jr. 1928- *216*
Earlier sketches in SATA *42, 102*
See also CLR *85*
Allard, Harry G.
See Allard, Harry, Jr.
Allee, Marjorie Hill 1890-1945 .... *17*
Allen, Adam
See Epstein, Beryl
and Epstein, Samuel
Allen, Alex B.
See Heide, Florence Parry
Allen, Allyn
See Eberle, Irmengarde
Allen, Betsy
See Harrison, Elizabeth (Allen) Cavanna
Allen, Bob 1961- *76*
Allen, Constance
See Albee, Sarah
Allen, Crystal *239*
Allen, Gertrude E(lizabeth) 1888-1984 .... *9*
Allen, Grace
See Hogarth, Grace (Weston Allen)
Allen, Jeffrey (Yale) 1948- *42*
Allen, John
See Perry, Ritchie (John Allen)
Allen, Jonathan 1957- *177*
Earlier sketch in SATA *131*
Allen, Jonathan Dean
See Allen, Jonathan
Allen, Joy 1948- *217*
Allen, Judy (Christina) 1941- *124*
Earlier sketch in SATA *80*
Allen, Kenneth S. 1913-1981 .... *56*
Allen, Leroy 1912- *11*
Allen, Linda 1925- *33*
Allen, Marjorie 1931- *22*
Allen, Maury 1932-2010 .... *26*
Allen, Merritt Parmelee 1892-1954 .... *22*
Allen, Nancy Kelly 1949- *171*
Earlier sketch in SATA *127*
Allen, Nina (Stroemgren) 1935- *22*
Allen, Pamela (Kay) 1934- *123*
Earlier sketches in SATA *50, 81*
See also CLR *44*
Allen, Raul *205*
Allen, Rodney F. 1938-1999 .... *27*
Allen, Roger MacBride 1957- *105*
Allen, Ruth
See Peterson, Esther (Allen)
Allen, Samuel W(ashington) 1917- *9*
Allen, T. D.
See Allen, Terril Diener
Allen, Terril Diener 1908- *35*
Allen, Terry D.
See Allen, Terril Diener
Allen, Thomas B. 1929- *193*
Earlier sketches in SATA *45, 140*
Allen, Thomas Benton
See Allen, Thomas B.
Allen, Tom
See Allen, Thomas B.
Allende, Isabel 1942- *163*
See also CLR *171*
Allerton, Mary
See Govan, (Mary) Christine Noble
Alley, Robert W.
See Alley, R.W.
Alley, R.W. *211*
Earlier sketch in SATA *169*
Alley, Zoe B. *214*
Alleyn, Ellen
See Rossetti, Christina
Allington, Richard L(loyd) 1947- *39*
Brief entry *35*
Allison, Amy 1956- *138*
Allison, Bob *14*
Allison, Diane Worfolk *78*
Allison, Jennifer *173*
Allison, Linda 1948- *43*
Allison, Margaret
See Klam, Cheryl
Allman, Barbara 1950- *137*
Allmendinger, David F(rederick), Jr. 1938- . *35*
Allred, Alexandra Powe 1965- *144*
Allred, Gordon T(hatcher) 1930- *10*
Allsop, Kenneth 1920-1973 .... *17*
Allsopp, Sophie *188*
Alma, Ann 1946- *201*
Almedingen, E. M.
See Almedingen, Martha Edith von
Almedingen, Martha Edith von 1898-1971 .... *3*
Almon, Russell
See Clevenger, William R.
and Downing, David A(lmon)
Almond, David 1951- *233*
Earlier sketches in SATA *114, 158*
See also CLR *168*
Almond, Linda Stevens 1881(?)-1987
Obituary *50*
Almquist, Don 1929- *11*
Alonzo, Sandra *199*
Alphin, Elaine Marie 1955- *232*
Autobiography Feature *139*
Earlier sketches in SATA *80, 130, 139*
Alsenas, Linas 1979- *186*
Alsop, Mary O'Hara 1885-1980 .... *34*
Obituary *24*
Earlier sketch in SATA *2*
Alter, Anna 1974- *206*
Earlier sketch in SATA *135*
Alter, Judith 1938- *101*
Earlier sketch in SATA *52*
Alter, Judith MacBain
See Alter, Judith
Alter, Judy
See Alter, Judith
Alter, Robert Edmond 1925-1965 .... *9*
Alter, Stephen 1956- *187*
Althea
See Braithwaite, Althea
Altman, Linda Jacobs 1943- *21*
Altman, Suzanne
See Orgel, Doris
and Schecter, Ellen
Alton, Steve *169*
Altschuler, Franz 1923- *45*
Altsheler, Joseph A(lexander) 1862-1919
See YABC *1*
Alvarez, John
See del Rey, Lester
Alvarez, Joseph A. 1930- *18*
Alvarez, Julia 1950- *129*
al-Windawi, Thura
See Windawi, Thura al-
Alyer, Philip A.
See Stratemeyer, Edward L.
Amado, Elisa *193*
Amann, Janet 1951- *79*
Amateau, Gigi 1964- *233*
Amato, Carol A. 1942- *92*
Amato, Mary 1961- *178*
Earlier sketch in SATA *140*

Ambrose, Stephen E. 1936-2002 ... *138*
Earlier sketch in SATA *40*
Ambrose, Stephen Edward
See Ambrose, Stephen E.
Ambrus, Gyozo Laszlo 1935- ... *1*
See also SAAS *4*
Ambrus, Victor G.
See Ambrus, Gyozo Laszlo
Amend, Bill 1962- ... *147*
Amerman, Lockhart 1911-1969 ... *3*
Ames, Evelyn 1908-1990 ... *13*
Obituary ... *64*
Ames, Gerald 1906-1993 ... *11*
Obituary ... *74*
Ames, Lee J. 1921-2011 ... *151*
Earlier sketch in SATA *3*
Ames, Lee Judah
See Ames, Lee J.
Ames, Mildred 1919-1994 ... *85*
Earlier sketches in SATA *22, 81*
Amico, Tom 1960(?)- ... *176*
Amini-Holmes, Liz ... *240*
Amit, Ofra 1966- ... *205*
Ammon, Richard 1942- ... *124*
Amon, Aline 1928- ... *9*
Amory, Jay
See Lovegrove, James
Amoss, Berthe 1925- ... *112*
Earlier sketch in SATA *5*
Amstutz, Andre 1925- ... *214*
Anastasio, Dina 1941- ... *94*
Brief entry ... *30*
Earlier sketch in SATA *37*
Anaya, Rudolfo 1937-
See CLR *129*
Anaya, Rudolfo A.
See Anaya, Rudolfo
Anaya, Rudolpho Alfonso
See Anaya, Rudolfo
Anckarsvard, Karin Inez Maria 1915-1969 ... *6*
Ancona, George 1929- ... *208*
Autobiography Feature ... *208*
Earlier sketches in SATA *12, 85, 145, 192*
See also SAAS *18*
Anders, C. J.
See Bennett, Cherie
Anders, Isabel 1946- ... *101*
Anders, Lou ... *176*
Andersdatter, Karla M. 1938- ... *34*
Andersen, Bethanne 1954- ... *191*
Andersen, Hans Christian 1805-1875 ... *100*
See also YABC *1*
See also CLR *113*
Andersen, Ted
See Boyd, Waldo T.
Andersen, Yvonne 1932- ... *27*
Anderson, Bernice G(oudy) 1894-1997 ... *33*
Anderson, Bob 1944- ... *139*
Earlier sketch in SATA *136*
Anderson, Brad 1924- ... *33*
Brief entry ... *31*
Anderson, Bradley Jay
See Anderson, Brad
Anderson, Brian 1974- ... *211*
Anderson, C. C.
See Anderson, Catherine Corley
Anderson, C(larence) W(illiam) 1891-1971 . *11*
Anderson, Carolyn Dunn
See Dunn, Carolyn
Anderson, Catherine C.
See Anderson, Catherine Corley
Anderson, Catherine Corley 1909-2001 ... *72*
See Lee, Cora
Anderson, Clifford
See Gardner, Richard (M.)
Anderson, Daryl Shon 1963- ... *93*
Anderson, Dave
See Anderson, David
Anderson, David 1929- ... *60*
Anderson, Derek 1969- ... *241*
Earlier sketch in SATA *169*
Anderson, Eloise Adell 1927- ... *9*
Anderson, George
See Groom, Arthur William
Anderson, Grace Fox 1932- ... *43*
Anderson, J(ohn) R(ichard) L(ane)
1911-1981 ... *15*
Obituary ... *27*
Anderson, Jessica Lee 1980- ... *224*
Anderson, Jodi Lynn ... *182*
Anderson, John David ... *197*
Anderson, John L. 1905- ... *2*
Anderson, Joy 1928- ... *1*
Anderson, Kevin J. 1962- ... *117*
Earlier sketch in SATA *74*
Anderson, Kevin James
See Anderson, Kevin J.
Anderson, Kirsty 1978- ... *108*
Anderson, K.J.
See Moesta, Rebecca
Anderson, K.J.
See Anderson, Kevin J.
Anderson, Laurie Halse 1961- ... *186*
Earlier sketches in SATA *95, 132*
See also CLR *138*
Anderson, LaVere Francis Shoenfelt
1907-1998 ... *27*
Anderson, Leone Castell 1923- ... *53*
Brief entry ... *49*
Anderson, Lisa G. 1963- ... *108*
Anderson, Lonzo
See Anderson, John L.
Anderson, Lucia (Lewis) 1922- ... *10*
Anderson, Madelyn Klein 1926-2005 ... *28*
Anderson, Margaret J. 1931- ... *234*
Autobiography Feature ... *234*
Earlier sketch in SATA *27*
See also SAAS *8*
Anderson, Marilyn D. 1943- ... *144*
Anderson, Mary 1939- ... *82*
Earlier sketch in SATA *7*
See also SAAS *23*
Anderson, Matthew Tobin
See Anderson, M.T.
Anderson, Mona 1910-2004 ... *40*
Anderson, Mrs. Melvin
See Anderson, Catherine Corley
Anderson, M.T. 1968- ... *182*
Earlier sketches in SATA *97, 146*
Anderson, Norman Dean 1928- ... *22*
Anderson, Peggy Perry 1953- ... *179*
Earlier sketch in SATA *84*
Anderson, Poul 1926-2001 ... *90*
Autobiography Feature ... *106*
Brief entry ... *39*
See also CLR *58*
Anderson, Poul William
See Anderson, Poul
Anderson, Rachel 1943- ... *86*
Earlier sketch in SATA *34*
See also SAAS *18*
Anderson, Rebecca J.
See Anderson, R.J.
Anderson, Rebecca M.
See Moesta, Rebecca
Anderson, Rebecca Moesta
See Moesta, Rebecca
Anderson, Richard
See Anderson, J(ohn) R(ichard) L(ane)
Anderson, R.J. 1970(?)- ... *216*
Anderson, Ryan G.
See Van Cleave, Ryan G.
Anderson, Sara ... *173*
Anderson, Scoular ... *201*
Anderson, (Tom) Scoular ... *138*
Anderson, Stephanie 1976- ... *225*
Anderson, Susan 1952- ... *90*
Anderson, Thomas Scoular
See Anderson, Scoular
Anderson, W. B.
See Schultz, James Willard
Anderson, Wayne 1946- ... *202*
Earlier sketches in SATA *56, 147*
Andersson, Kenneth 1970- ... *200*
Andre, Evelyn M. 1924- ... *27*
Andre, Evelyn Marie
See Andre, Evelyn M.
Andreasen, Dan ... *227*
Earlier sketch in SATA *186*
Andreassen, Karl
See Boyd, Waldo T.
Andreassi, K. Robert
See DeCandido, Keith R.A.
Andree, Louise
See Coury, Louise Andree
Andres, Kristina 1971- ... *233*
Andrew, Ian 1962- ... *166*
Earlier sketch in SATA *116*
Andrew, Ian Peter
See Andrew, Ian
Andrew, Prudence (Hastings) 1924- ... *87*
Andrews, Benny 1930-2006 ... *31*
Obituary ... *178*
Andrews, Eleanor Lattimore
See Lattimore, Eleanor Frances
Andrews, Elton V.
See Pohl, Frederik
Andrews, F(rank) Emerson 1902-1978 ... *22*
Andrews, J(ames) S(ydney) 1934- ... *4*
Andrews, Jan 1942- ... *167*
Brief entry ... *49*
Earlier sketches in SATA *58, 98*
Andrews, Julie 1935- ... *153*
Earlier sketch in SATA *7*
See also CLR *85*
Andrews, Laura
See Coury, Louise Andree
Andrews, Roy Chapman 1884-1960 ... *19*
Andrews, Tamra 1959- ... *129*
Andrews, V(irginia) C(leo) 1924(?)-1986
Obituary ... *50*
Andrews, Wendy
See Sharmat, Marjorie Weinman
Andrews, William G. 1930- ... *74*
Andrews, William George
See Andrews, William G.
Andrezel, Pierre
See Blixen, Karen
Andriani, Renee
See Williams-Andriani, Renee
Andriola, Alfred J. 1912-1983
Obituary ... *34*
Andrist, Ralph K. 1914-2004 ... *45*
Andronik, Catherine M. ... *189*
Andryszewski, Tricia 1956- ... *148*
Earlier sketch in SATA *88*
Anelli, Melissa 1979- ... *215*
Angaramo, Roberta 1974- ... *229*
Angel, Ann 1952- ... *192*
Angel, Carl ... *178*
Angel, Marie 1923- ... *47*
Angeles, Peter A. 1931- ... *40*
Angeletti, Roberta 1964- ... *124*
Angeli, Marguerite (Lofft) de
See de Angeli, Marguerite (Lofft)
Angell, Judie 1937- ... *78*
Earlier sketch in SATA *22*
See also CLR *33*
Angell, Madeline 1919- ... *18*
Angelo, Valenti 1897- ... *14*
Angelou, Maya 1928- ... *136*
Earlier sketch in SATA *49*
See also CLR *53*
Angier, Bradford -1997 ... *12*
Angle, Kimberly Greene ... *203*
Angle, Paul M(cClelland) 1900-1975
Obituary ... *20*
Anglund, Joan Walsh 1926- ... *2*
See also CLR *94*
Ango, Fan D.
See Longyear, Barry B(rookes)
Angrist, Stanley W(olff) 1933- ... *4*

Anhalt, Ariela 1990(?)- ... *227*
Anholt, Catherine 1958- ... *131*
Earlier sketch in SATA *74*
Anholt, Laurence 1959- ... *141*
Earlier sketch in SATA *74*
Aninno, J.G.
See Annino, Jan Godown
Anita
See Daniel, Anita
Anmar, Frank
See Nolan, William F.
Annett, Cora
See Scott, Cora Annett (Pipitone)
Annie-Jo
See Blanchard, Patricia
and Suhr, Joanne
Annino, Jan Godown 1952- ... *228*
Annixter, Jane
See Sturtzel, Jane Levington
Annixter, Paul
See Sturtzel, Howard A(llison)
Anno, Mitsumasa 1926- ... *157*
Earlier sketches in SATA *5, 38, 77*
See also CLR *122*
Anrooy, Francine Van
See Van Anrooy, Francine
Ansary, Mir Tamim 1948- ... *140*
Anstey, Caroline 1958- ... *81*
Antell, Will D. 1935- ... *31*
Anthony, Barbara
See Barber, Antonia
Anthony, C. L.
See Smith, Dorothy Gladys
Anthony, Edward 1895-1971 ... *21*
Anthony, Joelle ... *232*
Anthony, John
See Beckett, Ronald Brymer
and Ciardi, John (Anthony)
and Sabini, John Anthony
Anthony, Joseph Patrick 1964- ... *103*
Anthony, Patricia 1947- ... *109*
Anthony, Piers 1934- ... *129*
Autobiography Feature ... *129*
Earlier sketch in SATA *84*
See also CLR *118*
See also SAAS *22*
Anthony, Susan C(arol) 1953- ... *87*
Anticaglia, Elizabeth 1939- ... *12*
Antieau, Kim ... *214*
Antilles, Kem
See Moesta, Rebecca
Antle, Nancy 1955- ... *102*
Antolini, Margaret Fishback 1904-1985
Obituary ... *45*
Anton, Michael J(ames) 1940- ... *12*
Antonacci, Robert J(oseph) 1916- ... *45*
Brief entry ... *37*
Anvil, Christopher 1925-2009 ... *102*
Anzaldua, Gloria (Evanjelina) 1942-2004
Obituary ... *154*
Aoki, Hisako 1942- ... *45*
Aoyagi, Nora ... *229*
Apfel, Necia H(alpern) 1930- ... *51*
Brief entry ... *41*
Aphrodite, J.
See Livingston, Carole
Apikuni
See Schultz, James Willard
Apostolina, M. ... *184*
Apostolina, Michael
See Apostolina, M.
Apostolou, Christine Hale 1955- ... *179*
Earlier sketches in SATA *82, 128*
Appel, Allen (R.) 1945- ... *115*
Appel, Benjamin 1907-1977 ... *39*
Obituary ... *21*
Appel, Martin 1948- ... *45*
Appel, Martin Eliot
See Appel, Martin
Appel, Marty
See Appel, Martin
Appelbaum, Diana Muir Karter 1953- ... *132*
Appelbaum, Susannah ... *234*
Appelt, Kathi 1954- ... *190*
Earlier sketches in SATA *83, 129*
Apperley, Dawn 1969- ... *135*
Appiah, Peggy 1921-2006 ... *84*
Earlier sketch in SATA *15*
See also SAAS *19*
Apple, Margot ... *214*
Brief entry ... *42*
Earlier sketches in SATA *64, 152*
Applebaum, Stan 1922- ... *45*
Applegate, K.A.
See Applegate, Katherine
Applegate, Katherine 1956- ... *196*
Earlier sketches in SATA *109, 162*
See also CLR *90*
Applegate, Katherine Alice
See Applegate, Katherine
Appleton, Victor
See Barrett, Neal, Jr.
and Doyle, Debra
and Stratemeyer, Edward L.
and Vardeman, Robert E.
Appollo 1969- ... *214*
Appollodorus, Olivier
See Appollo
Apsler, Alfred 1907-1982 ... *10*
Aragones, Sergio 1937- ... *48*
Brief entry ... *39*
Arato, Rona ... *233*
Araujo, Frank P. 1937- ... *86*
Arbo, Cris 1950- ... *220*
Earlier sketch in SATA *103*
Arbuckle, Dorothy Fry 1910-1982
Obituary ... *33*
Arbuthnot, May Hill 1884-1969 ... *2*
Archambault, John ... *163*
Earlier sketches in SATA *67, 112*
Archambault, Matthew 1968- ... *219*
Archbold, Rick 1950- ... *97*
Archer, Colleen Rutherford 1949- ... *164*
Archer, Frank
See O'Connor, Richard
Archer, Jules 1915- ... *85*
Earlier sketch in SATA *4*
See also SAAS *5*
Archer, Lily 1981- ... *193*
Archer, Marion Fuller 1917- ... *11*
Archer, Nathan
See Watt-Evans, Lawrence
Archer, Peggy 1947- ... *199*
Archibald, Joe
See Archibald, Joseph S(topford)
Archibald, Joseph S(topford) 1898-1986 ... *3*
Obituary ... *47*
Ard, William
See Jakes, John
Ardagh, Philip 1961- ... *154*
Ardai, Charles 1969- ... *85*
Arden, Barbi
See Stoutenburg, Adrien (Pearl)
Arden, William
See Lynds, Dennis
Ardizzone, Edward (Jeffrey Irving)
1900-1979 ... *28*
Obituary ... *21*
Earlier sketch in SATA *1*
See also CLR *3*
Ardley, Neil 1937- ... *121*
Earlier sketch in SATA *43*
Ardley, Neil Richard
See Ardley, Neil
Arehart-Treichel, Joan 1942- ... *22*
Arena, Felice 1968- ... *151*
Arenella, Roy 1939- ... *14*
Arevamirp, Esile
See Primavera, Elise
Argent, Kerry 1960- ... *138*
Arguelles, Francisco Xavier
See Stork, Francisco X.
Argueta, Jorge ... *179*
Arihara, Shino 1973- ... *201*
Arkin, Alan 1934- ... *59*
Brief entry ... *32*
Arkin, Alan Wolf
See Arkin, Alan
Arksey, Neil ... *158*
Arlen, Leslie
See Nicole, Christopher
Arley, Robert
See Jackson, Mike
Armer, Alberta (Roller) 1904-1986 ... *9*
Armer, Laura Adams 1874-1963 ... *13*
Armistead, John 1941- ... *130*
Armitage, David 1943- ... *155*
Brief entry ... *38*
Earlier sketch in SATA *99*
Armitage, Frank
See Carpenter, John
Armitage, Ronda (Jacqueline) 1943- ... *155*
Brief entry ... *38*
Earlier sketches in SATA *47, 99*
Armour, Richard (Willard) 1906-1989 ... *14*
Obituary ... *61*
Armstrong, Alan 1939- ... *172*
Armstrong, Alan W.
See Armstrong, Alan
Armstrong, George D. 1927- ... *10*
Armstrong, Gerry (Breen) 1929- ... *10*
Armstrong, Jeannette (C.) 1948- ... *102*
Armstrong, Jennifer 1961- ... *165*
Autobiography Feature ... *120*
Earlier sketches in SATA *77, 111*
See also CLR *66*
See also SAAS *24*
Armstrong, Louise ... *43*
Brief entry ... *33*
Armstrong, Martin Donisthorpe
1882-1974 ... *115*
Armstrong, Matthew 1975- ... *188*
Armstrong, Matthew S.
See Armstrong, Matthew
Armstrong, Ralph Richard
See Armstrong, Richard
Armstrong, Richard 1903-1986 ... *11*
Armstrong, Shelagh 1961- ... *224*
Armstrong, William H(oward) 1914-1999 ... *4*
Obituary ... *111*
See also CLR *117*
See also SAAS *7*
Armstrong-Ellis, Carey (Fraser) 1956- ... *145*
Armstrong-Hodgson, Shelagh
See Armstrong, Shelagh
Arndt, Ursula (Martha H.) ... *56*
Brief entry ... *39*
Arneson, D(on) J(on) 1935- ... *37*
Arnett, Caroline
See Cole, Lois Dwight
Arnett, Jack
See Goulart, Ron
Arnette, Robert
See Silverberg, Robert
Arno, Enrico 1913-1981 ... *43*
Obituary ... *28*
Arnold, Ann 1953(?)- ... *207*
Arnold, Caroline 1944- ... *228*
Brief entry ... *34*
Earlier sketches in SATA *36, 85, 131, 174*
See also CLR *61*
See also SAAS *23*
Arnold, Elizabeth 1944- ... *164*
Arnold, Elliott 1912-1980 ... *5*
Obituary ... *22*
Arnold, Emily 1939- ... *210*
Autobiography Feature ... *134*
Earlier sketches in SATA *5, 50, 76, 110, 134*
See also CLR *46*
See also SAAS *7*
Arnold, Gillian Clare
See Cross, Gillian

Arnold, Katya 1947- *168*
Earlier sketches in SATA *82, 115*
Arnold, Louise *175*
Arnold, Louise Claire
See Arnold, Louise
Arnold, Marsha Diane 1948- *147*
Earlier sketch in SATA *93*
Arnold, Nick 1961- *113*
Arnold, Oren 1900-1980 .... *4*
Arnold, Susan (Riser) 1951- *58*
Arnold, Tedd 1949- *208*
Earlier sketches in SATA *69, 116, 160*
Arnoldy, Julie
See Bischoff, Julia Bristol
Arnosky, James Edward 1946- *189*
Earlier sketches in SATA *70, 118*
See also CLR *93*
Arnosky, Jim
See Arnosky, James Edward
Arnott, Kathleen 1914- *20*
Arnov, Boris, Jr. 1926- *12*
Arnow, Harriette (Louisa) Simpson
1908-1986 .... *42*
Obituary *47*
Arnsteen, Katy Keck 1934- *68*
Arnstein, Helene S(olomon) 1915- *12*
Arntson, Herbert E(dward) 1911-1982 .... *12*
Aroner, Miriam *82*
Aronin, Ben 1904-1980
Obituary *25*
Aronson, Marc 1950- *189*
Autobiography Feature *189*
Earlier sketches in SATA *126, 175*
Aronson, Marc Henry
See Aronson, Marc
Aronson, Sarah *196*
Aronson, Virginia 1954- *122*
Arora, Shirley (Lease) 1930- *2*
Arrasmith, Patrick *239*
Earlier sketch in SATA *176*
Arrick, Fran
See Angell, Judie
Arrigan, Mary 1943- *142*
Arrington, Aileen *183*
Arrington, Stephen L. 1948- *97*
Arrington, Stephen Lee
See Arrington, Stephen L.
Arrley, Richmond
See Delany, Samuel R., Jr.
Arrou-Vignod, Jean-Philippe 1958- *218*
Arrowood, (McKendrick Lee) Clinton
1939- *19*
Arrowsmith, Pat 1930- *59*
Arsenault, Isabelle 1978- *207*
Artell, Mike 1948- *183*
Earlier sketches in SATA *89, 134*
Arthur, A.C.
See Arthur, Artist
Arthur, Artist *235*
Arthur, Artist C.
See Arthur, Artist
Arthur, Robert (Andrew) 1909-1969
See Arthur, Robert, (Jr.)
Arthur, Robert, (Jr.) 1909-1969 .... *118*
Arthur, Ruth M(abel) 1905-1979 .... *26*
Earlier sketch in SATA *7*
Artis, Vicki Kimmel 1945- *12*
Artzybasheff, Boris (Miklailovich)
1899-1965 .... *14*
Aruego, Ariane
See Dewey, Ariane
Aruego, Jose 1932- *178*
Earlier sketches in SATA *6, 68, 125*
See also CLR *5*
Aruego, Jose Espiritu
See Aruego, Jose
Arundel, Honor (Morfydd) 1919-1973 .... *4*
Obituary *24*
See also CLR *35*
Arundel, Jocelyn
See Alexander, Jocelyn Anne Arundel
Arvey, Michael 1948- *79*
Arzoumanian, Alik *177*
Asare, Meshack (Yaw) 1945- *139*
Earlier sketch in SATA *86*
Asaro, Catherine 1955- *165*
Earlier sketch in SATA *101*
Asaro, Catherine Ann 1955-
See Asaro, Catherine
Asay, Donna Day 1945- *127*
Asbjornsen, Peter Christen 1812-1885 .... *15*
See also CLR *104*
Asch, Frank 1946- *154*
Earlier sketches in SATA *5, 66, 102*
Ash, Jutta 1942- *38*
Ashabranner, Brent 1921- *166*
Earlier sketches in SATA *1, 67, 130*
See also CLR *28*
See also SAAS *14*
Ashabranner, Brent Kenneth
See Ashabranner, Brent
Ashbless, William
See Blaylock, James P.
and Powers, Tim
Ashburn, Boni *241*
Ashby, Gil 1958- *146*
Ashby, Gwynneth 1922- *44*
Ashby, Ruth *170*
Ashby, Yvonne 1955- *121*
Ashe, Arthur (Robert, Jr.) 1943-1993 .... *65*
Obituary *87*
Ashe, Geoffrey (Thomas) 1923- *17*
Autobiography Feature *125*
Ashe, Mary Ann
See Lewis, Mary
Asher, Bridget
See Baggott, Julianna
Asher, Sandra Fenichel
See Asher, Sandy
Asher, Sandy 1942- *71*
Autobiography Feature *158*
Brief entry *34*
Earlier sketch in SATA *36*
See also SAAS *13*
Asheron, Sara
See Moore, Lilian
Ashey, Bella
See Breinburg, Petronella
Ashford, Daisy
See Ashford, Margaret Mary
Ashford, Jeffrey
See Jeffries, Roderic
Ashford, Margaret Mary 1881-1972 .... *10*
Ashland, Monk 1972- *207*
Ashley, Bernard (John) 1935- *155*
Brief entry *39*
Earlier sketches in SATA *47, 79*
See also CLR *4*
Ashley, Carol *238*
Ashley, Elizabeth
See Salmon, Annie Elizabeth
Ashley, Ray
See Abrashkin, Raymond
Ashman, Linda 1960- *203*
Earlier sketch in SATA *150*
Ashton, Lorayne
See Gottfried, Theodore Mark
Ashton, Warren T.
See Adams, William Taylor
Asimov, Isaac 1920-1992 .... *74*
Earlier sketches in SATA *1, 26*
See also CLR *79*
Asinof, Eliot 1919-2008 .... *6*
Asinof, Eliot Tager
See Asinof, Eliot
Aska, Warabe
See Masuda, Takeshi
Askani, Tanja 1962- *227*
Asprin, Robert 1946-2008 .... *92*
Asprin, Robert L.
See Asprin, Robert
Asprin, Robert Lynn
See Asprin, Robert
Asquith, Cynthia Mary Evelyn (Charteris)
1887-1960 .... *107*
Asquith, Ros *153*
Astley, Juliet
See Lofts, Norah (Robinson)
Aston, Dianna Hutts 1964- *176*
Aston, James
See White, T(erence) H(anbury)
Astor, Kristi
See Cook, Kristi
Ata, Te 1895-1995 .... *119*
Atene, Ann
See Atene, (Rita) Anna
Atene, (Rita) Anna 1922- *12*
Atheling, William, Jr.
See Blish, James
Atkins, Catherine *160*
Atkins, Jeannine 1953- *172*
Earlier sketch in SATA *113*
Atkinson, Allen G. 1953(?)-1987 .... *60*
Brief entry *46*
Obituary *55*
Atkinson, Elizabeth *215*
Atkinson, Elizabeth Jane
See Atkinson, Elizabeth
Atkinson, M. E.
See Frankau, Mary Evelyn Atkinson
Atkinson, Margaret Fleming *14*
Atteberry, Kevan J. *186*
Attema, Martha 1949- *156*
Earlier sketch in SATA *94*
Atticus
See Davies, Hunter
and Fleming, Ian
and Pawle, Gerald Strachan
and Wilson, (Thomas) Woodrow
Atwater, Florence 1896-1979 .... *66*
Earlier sketch in SATA *16*
See also CLR *19*
Atwater, Florence Hasseltine Carroll
See Atwater, Florence
Atwater, Montgomery Meigs 1904-1976 .... *15*
Atwater, Richard 1892-1948 .... *66*
Brief entry *27*
Earlier sketch in SATA *54*
See also CLR *19*
Atwater, Richard Tupper
See Atwater, Richard
Atwater-Rhodes, Amelia 1984- *240*
Earlier sketches in SATA *124, 170*
Atwell, Debby 1953- *150*
Earlier sketch in SATA *87*
Atwood, Ann (Margaret) 1913-1992 .... *7*
Atwood, Margaret 1939- *170*
Earlier sketch in SATA *50*
Atwood, Margaret Eleanor
See Atwood, Margaret
Aubrey, Meg Kelleher 1963- *83*
Aubry, Claude B. 1914-1984 .... *29*
Obituary *40*
Auch, Herm *173*
Auch, Mary Jane *173*
Earlier sketch in SATA *138*
Auch, M.J.
See Auch, Mary Jane
Auclair, Joan 1960- *68*
Auel, Jean
See Auel, Jean M.
Auel, Jean M. 1936- *91*
Auel, Jean Marie
See Auel, Jean M.
Auer, Martin 1951- *77*
Augarde, Steve 1950- *210*
Earlier sketches in SATA *25, 159*
Augarde, Steven Andre
See Augarde, Steve
Augelli, John P(at) 1921- *46*
Augustine, Mildred
See Benson, Mildred

Ault, Phil
See Ault, Phillip H(alliday)
Ault, Phillip H(alliday) 1914- *23*
Ault, Rosalie Sain 1942- *38*
Ault, Roz
See Ault, Rosalie Sain
Aung, (Maung) Htin 1909- *21*
Auntie Deb
See Coury, Louise Andree
Auntie Louise
See Coury, Louise Andree
Aunt Weedy
See Alcott, Louisa May
Auseon, Andrew 1976- *217*
Earlier sketch in SATA *166*
Austen, Carrie
See Bennett, Cherie
Austen, Catherine 1965- *223*
Austin, Carrie
See Seuling, Barbara
Austin, Elizabeth S. 1907-1977 .... *5*
Austin, Harry
See McInerny, Ralph
Austin, Margot 1909(?)-1990 .... *11*
Obituary *66*
Austin, Michael *178*
Austin, Oliver L(uther), Jr. 1903-1988 .... *7*
Obituary *59*
Austin, Patricia 1950- *137*
Austin, R. G.
See Gelman, Rita Golden
and Lamb, Nancy
Austin, Virginia 1951- *152*
Earlier sketch in SATA *80*
Auteur, Hillary
See Gottfried, Theodore Mark
Auth, Tony
See Auth, William Anthony, Jr.
Auth, William Anthony, Jr. 1942- *192*
Autry, Gloria Diener
See Allen, Terril Diener
Auvil, Peggy A 1954- *122*
Auvil, Peggy Appleby
See Auvil, Peggy A
Avasthi, Swati 1971- *231*
Aveni, Anthony F. 1938- *181*
Aveni, Anthony Francis
See Aveni, Anthony F.
Averbeck, Jim 1963- *201*
Averill, Esther (Holden) 1902-1992 .... *28*
Obituary *72*
Earlier sketch in SATA *1*
Avery, A. A.
See Montgomery, Rutherford George
Avery, Al
See Montgomery, Rutherford George
Avery, Gillian 1926- *137*
Autobiography Feature *137*
Earlier sketches in SATA *7, 75*
See also SAAS *6*
Avery, Gillian Elise
See Avery, Gillian
Avery, Kay 1908- *5*
Avery, Lorraine
See Older, Effin
and Older, Jules
Avery, Lynn
See Cole, Lois Dwight
Avi 1937- *226*
Earlier sketches in SATA *14, 71, 108, 156, 190*
See also CLR *68*
Aviles, Martha *218*
Avishai, Susan 1949- *82*
Avraham, Kate Aver *227*
Avril, Francois 1961- *191*
Avril, Lynne
See Cravath, Lynne W.
Awdry, Christopher Vere 1940- *67*
Awdry, Wilbert Vere 1911-1997 .... *94*
See also CLR *23*
Axelrod, Amy *131*
Axelsen, Stephen 1953- *165*
Axton, David
See Koontz, Dean
Ayars, James S(terling) 1898-1986 .... *4*
Aye, A. K.
See Edwards, Hazel (Eileen)
Ayer, Eleanor H. 1947-1998 .... *121*
Earlier sketch in SATA *78*
Ayer, Jacqueline 1930- *13*
Ayer, Margaret (?)-1981 .... *15*
Aylesworth, Jim 1943- *213*
Earlier sketches in SATA *38, 89, 139*
See also CLR *89*
Aylesworth, Thomas G(ibbons) 1927-1995 .. *88*
Earlier sketch in SATA *4*
See also CLR *6*
See also SAAS *17*
Ayliffe, Alex *190*
Aylward, Marcus
See Alexander, Marc
Aymar, Brandt 1911- *22*
Ayme, Marcel (Andre) 1902-1967 .... *91*
See also CLR *25*
Ayres, Becky
See Hickox, Rebecca (Ayres)
Ayres, Katherine 1947- *187*
Ayres, Pam 1947- *90*
Ayres, Patricia Miller 1923-1985
Obituary *46*
Aytmatov, Chingiz
See Aitmatov, Chingiz
Ayto, Russell 1960- *206*
Earlier sketches in SATA *111, 166*
Azaid
See Zaidenberg, Arthur
Azar, Penny 1952- *121*
Azarian, Mary 1940- *171*
Earlier sketch in SATA *112*
Azore, Barbara 1934- *188*

B

Baasansuren, Bolormaa 1982- *216*
Baastad, Babbis Friis
See Friis-Baastad, Babbis Ellinor
Bab
See Gilbert, W(illiam) S(chwenck)
Babbis, Eleanor
See Friis-Baastad, Babbis Ellinor
Babbitt, Lucy Cullyford 1960- *85*
Babbitt, Natalie 1932- *194*
Earlier sketches in SATA *6, 68, 106*
See also CLR *141*
See also SAAS *5*
Babbitt, Natalie Zane Moore
See Babbitt, Natalie
Babcock, Chris 1963- *83*
Babcock, Dennis 1948- *22*
Babcock, Dennis Arthur
See Babcock, Dennis
Baber, Carolyn Stonnell 1936- *96*
Baboni, Elena *198*
Baca, Ana 1967- *191*
Baca, Maria 1951- *104*
Baccalario, Pierdomenico 1974- *222*
Bach, Alice (Hendricks) 1942- *93*
Brief entry *27*
Earlier sketch in SATA *30*
Bach, Bellamy
See Windling, Terri
Bach, Mary 1960- *125*
Bach, Richard 1936- *13*
Bach, Richard David
See Bach, Richard
Bache, Ellyn 1942- *124*
Bachel, Beverly K. 1957- *142*
Bachelet, Gilles 1952- *196*
Bachem, Paul *231*
Bachman, Fred 1949- *12*
Bachman, Richard
See King, Stephen
Bachorz, Pam 1973- *226*
Bachrach, Deborah 1943- *80*
Bacigalupi, Paolo 1973- *230*
Backus, James Gilmore 1913-1989
Obituary *63*
Backus, Jim
See Backus, James Gilmore
Bacmeister, Rhoda W(arner) 1893-1991 .... *11*
Bacon, Betty
See Bacon, Elizabeth
Bacon, Elizabeth 1914-2001 .... *3*
Obituary *131*
Bacon, Joan Chase
See Bowden, Joan Chase
Bacon, Josephine Dodge (Daskam) 1876-1961 .... *48*
Bacon, Margaret Frances
See Bacon, Peggy
Bacon, Margaret Hope 1921- *6*
Bacon, Martha Sherman 1917-1981 .... *18*
Obituary *27*
See also CLR *3*
Bacon, Melvin 1950- *93*
Bacon, Melvin L.
See Bacon, Melvin
Bacon, Peggy 1895-1987 .... *50*
Bacon, R(onald) L(eonard) 1924- *84*
Earlier sketch in SATA *26*
Baddiel, Ivor 1963- *210*
Baden, Robert 1936- *70*
Baden-Powell, Robert (Stephenson Smyth) 1857-1941 .... *16*
Badoe, Adwoa *237*
Badt, Karin L(uisa) 1963- *91*
Bae, Hyun-Joo *186*
Baehr, Kingsley M. 1937- *89*
Baehr, Patricia 1952- *238*
Earlier sketch in SATA *65*
Baehr, Patricia Goehner
See Baehr, Patricia
Baek, Matthew J. 1971- *202*
Baer, Jill
See Gilbert, (Agnes) Joan (Sewell)
Baer, Judy 1951- *71*
Baer, Julie 1960- *161*
Baer-Block, Roxanna *172*
Baerg, Harry J(ohn) 1909-1996 .... *12*
Baeten, Lieve 1954-2001 .... *238*
Earlier sketch in SATA *83*
Bagert, Brod 1947- *191*
Earlier sketch in SATA *80*
Baggette, Susan K. 1942- *126*
Baggott, Julianna 1969- *197*
Bagnold, Enid 1889-1981 .... *25*
Earlier sketch in SATA *1*
Baguley, Elizabeth 1959- *199*
Bahlke, Valerie Worth -1994
See Worth, Valerie
Bahous, Sally 1939- *86*
Bahr, Mary (Madelyn) 1946- *95*
Bahr, Robert 1940- *38*
Bahti, Tom 1926-1972 .... *57*
Brief entry *31*
Bai, Durga *211*
Baicker-McKee, Carol 1958- *177*
Bailey, Alice Cooper 1890-1978 .... *12*
Bailey, Anne 1958- *71*
Bailey, Bernadine (Freeman) 1901-1995 .... *14*
Bailey, Carolyn Sherwin 1875-1961 .... *14*
Bailey, Debbie 1954- *123*
Bailey, Donna (Veronica Anne) 1938- *68*
Bailey, Jane H(orton) 1916- *12*
Bailey, John (Robert) 1940- *52*
Bailey, Len *193*
Bailey, Linda 1948- *217*
Earlier sketches in SATA *107, 182*
Bailey, Maralyn Collins (Harrison) 1941- *12*

Bailey, Matilda
See Radford, Ruby L(orraine)
Bailey, Maurice Charles 1932- ... *12*
Bailey, Pearl (Mae) 1918-1990 ... *81*
Bailey, Peter 1946- ... *194*
Bailey, Ralph Edgar 1893-1982 ... *11*
Bailey, Sheila (Lucas) 1960- ... *155*
Baillie, Allan 1943- ... *151*
Earlier sketch in SATA *87*
See also CLR *49*
See also SAAS *21*
Baillie, Allan Stuart
See Baillie, Allan
Baines, John (David) 1943- ... *71*
Bains, Larry
See Sabin, Louis
Baird, Alison 1963- ... *138*
Baird, Bil 1904-1987 ... *30*
Obituary ... *52*
Baird, Thomas (P.) 1923-1990 ... *45*
Brief entry ... *39*
Obituary ... *64*
Baird, William Britton
See Baird, Bil
Baity, Elizabeth Chesley 1907-1989 ... *1*
Baiul, Oksana 1977- ... *108*
Bajoria, Paul 1964- ... *187*
Bakeless, John (Edwin) 1894-1978 ... *9*
Bakeless, Katherine Little 1895-1992 ... *9*
Baker, Alan 1951- ... *146*
Earlier sketches in SATA *22, 93*
Baker, Augusta 1911-1998 ... *3*
Baker, Barbara 1947- ... *192*
Baker, Betty Lou 1928-1987 ... *73*
Obituary ... *54*
Earlier sketch in SATA *5*
Baker, Carin Greenberg 1959- ... *79*
Baker, Charlotte 1910- ... *2*
Baker, Christina
See Kline, Christina Baker
Baker, Christopher W. 1952- ... *144*
Baker, Deirdre 1955- ... *195*
Baker, E.D. ... *237*
Earlier sketch in SATA *190*
Baker, (Mary) Elizabeth (Gillette) 1923- ... *7*
Baker, Gayle Cunningham 1950- ... *39*
Baker, James W. 1924- ... *65*
Earlier sketch in SATA *22*
Baker, James W. 1926- ... *122*
Baker, Janice E(dla) 1941- ... *22*
Baker, Jeanette ... *178*
Baker, Jeannie 1950- ... *156*
Earlier sketches in SATA *23, 88*
See also CLR *28*
Baker, Jeffrey J(ohn) W(heeler) 1931- ... *5*
Baker, Jim
See Baker, James W.
Baker, Keith 1953- ... *222*
Earlier sketch in SATA *179*
Baker, Ken 1962- ... *133*
Baker, Laura Nelson 1911- ... *3*
Baker, Margaret 1890-1965 ... *4*
Baker, Margaret J(oyce) 1918- ... *12*
See also SAAS *8*
Baker, Mary Gladys Steel 1892-1974 ... *12*
Baker, (Robert) Michael (Graham) 1938- ... *4*
Baker, Nina (Brown) 1888-1957 ... *15*
Baker, Pamela J. 1947- ... *66*
Baker, Rachel 1904-1978 ... *2*
Obituary ... *26*
Baker, Roberta ... *206*
Baker, Rosalie F. 1945- ... *166*
Baker, Samm Sinclair 1909-1997 ... *12*
Obituary ... *96*
Baker, Sharon Reiss 1962- ... *207*
Baker, Susan (Catherine) 1942-1991 ... *29*
Baker-Smith, Grahame ... *223*
Balaam
See Lamb, G(eoffrey) F(rederick)
Balan, Bruce 1959- ... *113*
Balcavage, Dynise 1965- ... *137*
Balch, Glenn 1902-1989 ... *3*
Obituary ... *83*
See also SAAS *11*
Baldacci, David 1960- ... *184*
Baldacci, David G.
See Baldacci, David
and Baldacci, David
Balderose, Nancy Ward 1952- ... *93*
Balderson, Margaret 1935- ... *151*
Baldini, Michelle ... *205*
Baldry, Cherith 1947- ... *167*
Earlier sketch in SATA *72*
Balducci, Carolyn 1946- ... *5*
Balducci, Carolyn Feleppa
See Balducci, Carolyn
Baldwin, Alex
See Griffin, W. E. B.
Baldwin, Anne Norris 1938- ... *5*
Baldwin, Clara ... *11*
Baldwin, Gordo
See Baldwin, Gordon C(ortis)
Baldwin, Gordon C(ortis) 1908-1983 ... *12*
Baldwin, James 1841-1925 ... *24*
Baldwin, James 1924-1987 ... *9*
Obituary ... *54*
Baldwin, Louis 1919- ... *110*
Baldwin, Margaret
See Weis, Margaret
Baldwin, Stan(ley C.) 1929- ... *62*
Brief entry ... *28*
Bales, Carol Ann 1940- ... *57*
Brief entry ... *29*
Balet, Jan (Bernard) 1913- ... *11*
Balgassi, Haemi 1971- ... *131*
Balian, Lorna 1929- ... *91*
Earlier sketch in SATA *9*
Balit, Christina 1961- ... *212*
Earlier sketches in SATA *102, 159*
Ball, Duncan 1941- ... *73*
Ball, Zachary
See Janas, Frankie-Lee
and Masters, Kelly R(ay)
Ballantine, Lesley Frost
See Frost, Lesley
Ballantyne, R(obert) M(ichael) 1825-1894 ... *24*
See also CLR *137*
Ballard, James G.
See Ballard, J.G.
Ballard, James Graham
See Ballard, J.G.
Ballard, Jane
See Gorman, Carol
Ballard, J.G. 1930-2009 ... *93*
Obituary ... *203*
Ballard, Jim G.
See Ballard, J.G.
Ballard, John 1945- ... *110*
Ballard, Lowell C(lyne) 1904-1986 ... *12*
Obituary ... *49*
Ballard, (Charles) Martin 1929- ... *1*
Ballard, Mignon F. 1934- ... *64*
Brief entry ... *49*
Ballard, Mignon Franklin
See Ballard, Mignon F.
Ballard, Robert D(uane) 1942- ... *85*
See also CLR *60*
Ballard, Robin 1965- ... *126*
Balliett, Blue 1955- ... *239*
Earlier sketch in SATA *156*
Ballinger, Bryan 1968- ... *161*
Ballouhey, Pierre 1944- ... *90*
Balog, Cyn ... *221*
Balogh, Penelope 1916-1975 ... *1*
Obituary ... *34*
Balouch, Kristen ... *176*
Balow, Tom 1931- ... *12*
Baltazzi, Evan S(erge) 1921- ... *90*
Balterman, Marcia Ridlon 1942- ... *22*
Baltimore, J.
See Catherall, Arthur
Baltzer, Hans (Adolf) 1900- ... *40*
Balzano, Jeanne (Koppel) 1912- ... *7*
Bambara, Toni Cade 1939-1995 ... *112*
Bamfylde, Walter
See Bevan, Tom
Bamman, Henry A. 1918- ... *12*
Banat, D. R.
See Bradbury, Ray
Bancks, Tristan 1974- ... *231*
Bancroft, Bronwyn 1958- ... *216*
Bancroft, Griffing 1907-1999 ... *6*
Bancroft, Laura
See Baum, L. Frank
Bandel, Betty 1912- ... *47*
Baner, Skulda Vanadis 1897-1964 ... *10*
Banerjee, Anjali ... *174*
Banfill, A. Scott 1956- ... *98*
Bang, Betsy 1912- ... *48*
Brief entry ... *37*
Bang, Garrett
See Bang, Molly
Bang, Molly 1943- ... *215*
Earlier sketches in SATA *24, 69, 111, 158*
See also CLR *8*
Bang, Molly Garrett
See Bang, Molly
Bang-Campbell, Monika 1975(?)- ... *195*
Earlier sketch in SATA *140*
Banjo, The
See Paterson, A(ndrew) B(arton)
Banke, Cecile de
See de Banke, Cecile
Banks, Erin Bennett 1978- ... *211*
Banks, Kate 1960- ... *200*
Earlier sketches in SATA *134, 172*
Banks, Laura Stockton Voorhees 1908(?)-1980
Obituary ... *23*
Banks, Lynne Reid
See Reid Banks, Lynne
Banks, Merry ... *197*
Banks, Michael A. 1951- ... *101*
Banks, Paul 1952- ... *174*
Banks, Sara
See Harrell, Sara Gordon
Banks, Sara Jeanne Gordon Harrell
See Harrell, Sara Gordon
Bannatyne-Cugnet, Elizabeth Jo-Anne
See Bannatyne-Cugnet, Jo
Bannatyne-Cugnet, Jo 1951- ... *101*
Banner, Angela
See Maddison, Angela Mary
Bannerman, Helen (Brodie Cowan Watson)
1862(?)-1946 ... *19*
See also CLR *144*
Banning, Evelyn I. 1903-1993 ... *36*
Bannon, Laura (?)-1963 ... *6*
Bannor, Brett 1959- ... *143*
Bansch, Helga 1957- ... *224*
Banta, Susan ... *181*
Bantock, Nick 1950(?)- ... *95*
Banyai, Istvan ... *193*
Barakat, Ibtisam 1963- ... *186*
Barasch, Lynne 1939- ... *186*
Earlier sketches in SATA *74, 126*
Baratz-Logsted, Lauren ... *235*
Barbalet, Margaret 1949- ... *77*
Barbary, James
See Baumann, Amy Beeching
and Beeching, Jack
Barbash, Shepard 1957- ... *84*
Barbauld, Anna Laetitia 1743-1825
See CLR *160*
Barbe, Walter Burke 1926- ... *45*
Barber, Alison ... *222*
Barber, Antonia 1932- ... *163*
Earlier sketch in SATA *29*
Barber, Atiim Kiambu
See Barber, Tiki
Barber, Lynda
See Graham-Barber, Lynda
Barber, Lynda Graham
See Graham-Barber, Lynda

Barber, Richard (William) 1941- ... *35*
Barber, Ronde 1975- ... *240*
Earlier sketch in SATA *182*
Barber, Tiki 1975- ... *182*
Barbera, Joe 1911-2006 ... *51*
Obituary ... *179*
Barbera, Joseph
See Barbera, Joe
Barbera, Joseph Roland
See Barbera, Joe
Barberis, Juan C(arlos) 1920- ... *61*
Barbour, Karen 1956- ... *170*
Earlier sketches in SATA *63, 121*
Barbour, Ralph Henry 1870-1944 ... *16*
Barclay, Bill
See Moorcock, Michael
Barclay, Isabel
See Dobell, I(sabel) M(arian) B(arclay)
Barclay, William Ewert
See Moorcock, Michael
Barclay, William Ewert
See Moorcock, Michael
Bardhan-Quallen, Sudipta 1977- ... *214*
Earlier sketch in SATA *168*
Bardoe, Cheryl ... *181*
Bare, Arnold Edwin 1920- ... *16*
Bare, Colleen Stanley ... *32*
Bar-el, Dan ... *199*
Barenholtz, Bernard 1914-1989
Obituary ... *64*
Bargar, Gary W. 1947-1985 ... *63*
Barger, Jan 1948- ... *147*
Barish, Matthew 1907-2000 ... *12*
Barkan, Joanne ... *127*
Earlier sketch in SATA *77*
Barker, Albert W. 1900- ... *8*
Barker, Carol (Minturn) 1938- ... *31*
Barker, Cicely Mary 1895-1973 ... *49*
Brief entry ... *39*
See also CLR *88*
Barker, Claire 1969- ... *237*
Barker, Melvern 1907-1989 ... *11*
Barker, S. Omar 1894-1985 ... *10*
Barker, Squire Omar
See Barker, S. Omar
Barker, Will 1913-1983 ... *8*
Barkin, Carol 1944- ... *52*
Earlier sketch in SATA *42*
Barklem, Jill 1951- ... *96*
See also CLR *31*
Barkley, Brad ... *178*
Barkley, James Edward 1941- ... *6*
Barks, Carl 1901-2000 ... *37*
Barley, Janet Crane 1934- ... *95*
Barlow, Steve 1952- ... *211*
Barnaby, Ralph S(tanton) 1893-1986 ... *9*
Barnard, A. M.
See Alcott, Louisa May
Barnard, Bryn 1956- ... *169*
Earlier sketch in SATA *115*
Barne, Kitty
See Barne, Marion Catherine
Barne, Marion Catherine 1883-1957 ... *97*
Barneda, David ... *206*
Barner, Bob 1947- ... *238*
Earlier sketches in SATA *29, 136*
Barnes, Dawn 1957- ... *175*
Barnes, Derrick ... *191*
Barnes, Derrick D.
See Barnes, Derrick
Barnes, (Frank) Eric Wollencott 1907-1962 . *22*
Barnes, Joyce Annette 1958- ... *85*
Barnes, Laura T. 1958- ... *119*
Barnes, Loutricia
See Barnes-Svarney, Patricia L(ou)
Barnes, Malcolm 1909(?)-1984
Obituary ... *41*
Barnes, Michael 1934- ... *55*
Barnes-Murphy, Frances 1951- ... *88*
Barnes-Murphy, Rowan 1952- ... *88*
Barnes-Svarney, Patricia L(ou) 1953- ... *67*
Barnet, Nancy 1954- ... *84*
Barnett, Ivan 1947- ... *70*
Barnett, Lincoln (Kinnear) 1909-1979 ... *36*
Barnett, Mac ... *223*
Barnett, Moneta 1922-1976 ... *33*
Barnett, Naomi 1927- ... *40*
Barney, Maginel Wright 1881(?)-1966 ... *39*
Brief entry ... *32*
Barnhart, Clarence L(ewis) 1900-1993 ... *48*
Obituary ... *78*
Barnholdt, Lauren 1980(?)- ... *232*
Barnhouse, Rebecca 1961- ... *225*
Barnouw, Adriaan Jacob 1877-1968
Obituary ... *27*
Barnouw, Victor 1915-1989 ... *43*
Brief entry ... *28*
Barnstone, Willis 1927- ... *20*
Barnum, Jay Hyde 1888(?)-1962 ... *20*
Barnum, P. T., Jr.
See Stratemeyer, Edward L.
Barnum, Richard ... *67*
Earlier sketch in SATA *1*
Barnum, Theodore
See Stratemeyer, Edward L.
Barnwell, Ysaye M. 1946- ... *200*
Baron, Kathi 1956- ... *226*
Baron, Kathy 1954- ... *90*
Baron, Virginia Olsen 1931- ... *46*
Brief entry ... *28*
Barr, Donald 1921-2004 ... *20*
Obituary ... *152*
Barr, George 1907-1992 ... *2*
Barr, Jene 1922-1985 ... *16*
Obituary ... *42*
Barr, Nevada 1952- ... *126*
Earlier sketch in SATA *115*
Barragan, Paula 1963- ... *216*
Barratt, Mark 1954- ... *224*
Barrer, Gertrude
See Barrer-Russell, Gertrude
Barrer-Russell, Gertrude 1921- ... *27*
Barrett, Angela 1955- ... *223*
Barrett, Angela (Jane) 1955- ... *145*
Earlier sketch in SATA *75*
Barrett, Ethel ... *87*
Brief entry ... *44*
Barrett, Joyce Durham 1943- ... *138*
Barrett, Judi
See Barrett, Judith
Barrett, Judith 1941- ... *204*
Earlier sketch in SATA *26*
See also CLR *98*
Barrett, Robert T. 1949- ... *234*
Earlier sketch in SATA *92*
Barrett, Ron 1937- ... *14*
Barrett, Susan (Mary) 1938- ... *113*
Barrett, Tracy 1955- ... *207*
Earlier sketches in SATA *84, 115, 156*
Barrett, William E(dmund) 1900-1986
Obituary ... *49*
Barretta, Gene ... *214*
Earlier sketch in SATA *176*
Barretton, Grandall
See Garrett, Randall
Barrie, Baronet
See Barrie, J. M.
Barrie, J. M. 1860-1937 ... *100*
See also YABC *1*
See also CLR *124*
Barrie, James Matthew
See Barrie, J. M.
Barringer, William 1940-1996 ... *153*
Barrington, Michael
See Moorcock, Michael
Barris, George 1925- ... *47*
Barrol, Grady
See Bograd, Larry
Barron, Rex 1951- ... *84*
Barron, T.A. 1952- ... *192*
Earlier sketches in SATA *83, 126*
See also CLR *86*
Barron, Thomas Archibald
See Barron, T.A.
Barron, Tom
See Barron, T.A.
Barrow, Lloyd H. 1942- ... *73*
Barrows, Annie 1962- ... *241*
Earlier sketch in SATA *180*
Barry, Dan 1958- ... *177*
Barry, Dana (Marie Malloy) 1949- ... *139*
Barry, James P(otvin) 1918- ... *14*
Barry, Katharina Watjen 1936- ... *4*
Barry, Robert 1931- ... *6*
Barry, Robert Everett
See Barry, Robert
Barry, Scott 1952- ... *32*
Barry, Sheila Anne -2003 ... *91*
Barshaw, Ruth McNally ... *203*
Bartell, Susan S. ... *175*
Bartenbach, Jean 1918- ... *40*
Barth, Edna 1914-1980 ... *7*
Obituary ... *24*
Barth, Kelly L. 1964- ... *152*
Barthelme, Donald 1931-1989 ... *7*
Obituary ... *62*
Barth-Grozinger, Inge 1950- ... *185*
Bartholomew, Barbara 1941- ... *86*
Brief entry ... *42*
Bartholomew, Jean
See Beatty, Patricia (Robbins)
Bartlett, Alison ... *153*
Bartlett, Philip A. ... *1*
Bartlett, Robert Merrill 1899-1995 ... *12*
Bartoletti, Susan Campbell 1958- ... *237*
Earlier sketches in SATA *88, 129, 135, 173*
Barton, Byron 1930- ... *126*
Earlier sketches in SATA *9, 90*
Barton, Chris ... *224*
Barton, Jill(ian) 1940- ... *75*
Barton, May Hollis ... *67*
Earlier sketch in SATA *1*
Barton, Pat
See Arrowsmith, Pat
Barton, Patrice 1955- ... *226*
Bartos-Hoeppner, Barbara 1923- ... *5*
Bartram, Simon ... *218*
Earlier sketch in SATA *156*
Bartsch, Jochen 1906- ... *39*
Baruch, Dorothy W(alter) 1899-1962 ... *21*
Barunga, Albert 1912(?)-1977 ... *120*
Baryshnikov, Mikhail 1948- ... *192*
Bas, Rutger
See Rutgers van der Loeff-Basenau, An(na) Maria Margaretha
Base, Graeme 1958- ... *162*
Earlier sketches in SATA *67, 101*
See also CLR *22*
Base, Graeme Rowland
See Base, Graeme
Baseman, Gary 1960- ... *174*
Bash, Barbara 1948- ... *132*
Basher
See Basher, Simon
Basher, Simon ... *235*
Bashevis, Isaac
See Singer, Isaac Bashevis
Bashevis, Yitskhok
See Singer, Isaac Bashevis
Bashista, Adrienne Ehlert ... *203*
Basile, Gloria Vitanza 1929- ... *180*
Baskin, Leonard 1922-2000 ... *120*
Brief entry ... *27*
Earlier sketch in SATA *30*
Baskin, Nora Raleigh 1961- ... *189*
Earlier sketch in SATA *129*
Bason, Lillian 1913- ... *20*
Bass, Guy ... *241*
Bass, Hester 1956- ... *223*
Bass, L.G.
See Geringer, Laura
Bassett, Jeni 1959- ... *64*
Brief entry ... *43*

Bassett, John Keith
See Keating, Lawrence A.
Bassett, Lisa 1958- *61*
Bassil, Andrea
See Nilsen, Anna
Bastyra, Judy *108*
Basye, Dale E. *205*
Bataille, Marion 1963- *209*
Bat-Ami, Miriam 1950- *150*
Autobiography Feature *150*
Earlier sketches in SATA *82, 122*
Bate, Lucy 1939-1993 .... *18*
Bate, Norman (Arthur) 1916- *5*
Bateman, Colin 1962- *172*
Bateman, Donna M. *190*
Bateman, Teresa 1957- *216*
Earlier sketches in SATA *112, 168*
Bates, Amy June *239*
Earlier sketch in SATA *189*
Bates, Barbara S(nedeker) 1919- *12*
Bates, Betty
See Bates, Elizabeth
Bates, Dianne 1948- *147*
Bates, Elizabeth 1921- *19*
Bates, Ivan *175*
Bates, Katharine Lee 1859-1929 .... *113*
Bates, Martine
See Leavitt, Martine
Bateson, Catherine 1960- *197*
Earlier sketch in SATA *157*
Batey, Tom 1946- *52*
Brief entry *41*
Bath, Kevin P.
See Bath, K.P.
Bath, K.P. 1959- *171*
Batherman, Muriel
See Sheldon, Muriel
Batson, Larry 1930- *35*
Batt, Tanya Robyn 1970- *131*
Battaglia, Aurelius 1910- *50*
Brief entry *33*
Batten, H(arry) Mortimer 1888-1958 .... *25*
Batten, Mary 1937- *162*
Earlier sketches in SATA *5, 102*
Batterberry, Ariane Ruskin 1935- *13*
Batterberry, Michael Carver 1932-2010 .... *32*
Battle-Lavert, Gwendolyn 1951- *155*
Earlier sketches in SATA *85, 131*
Battles, (Roxy) Edith 1921- *7*
Baudouy, Michel-Aime 1909- *7*
Bauer, A.C.E. *201*
Bauer, Caroline Feller 1935- *98*
Brief entry *46*
Earlier sketch in SATA *52*
See also SAAS *24*
Bauer, Fred 1934- *36*
Bauer, Helen 1900-1988 .... *2*
Bauer, Joan 1951- *160*
Earlier sketch in SATA *117*
Bauer, Jutta 1955- *150*
Bauer, Marion Dane 1938- *192*
Autobiography Feature *144*
Earlier sketches in SATA *20, 69, 113, 144*
See also SAAS *9*
Bauer, Michael Gerard 1955(?)- *167*
Bauer, Steven 1948- *125*
Bauerschmidt, Marjorie 1926- *15*
Baughman, Dorothy 1940- *61*
Baum, Allyn Z(elton) 1924-1997 .... *98*
Earlier sketch in SATA *20*
Baum, L. Frank
See Thompson, Ruth Plumly
Baum, L. Frank 1856-1919 .... *100*
Earlier sketch in SATA *18*
See also CLR *175*
Baum, Louis 1948- *182*
Brief entry *52*
Earlier sketch in SATA *64*
Baum, Louis F.
See Baum, L. Frank
Baum, Lyman Frank
See Baum, L. Frank
Baum, Maxie *188*
Baum, Willi 1931- *4*
Bauman, Beth Ann 1964- *220*
Baumann, Amy Beeching 1922- *10*
Baumann, Amy Brown Beeching
See Baumann, Amy Beeching
Baumann, Hans 1914- *2*
See also CLR *35*
Baumann, Kurt 1935- *21*
Baumgartner, Barbara 1939- *86*
Baurys, Flo 1938- *122*
Baurys, Florence
See Baurys, Flo
Bausum, Ann *173*
Bawden, Nina 1925- *132*
Earlier sketches in SATA *4, 72*
See also CLR *51*
See also SAAS *16*
Bawden, Nina Mary Mabey
See Bawden, Nina
Baxter, Andy
See Dakin, Glenn
Baxter, Roberta 1952- *219*
Baxter, Valerie
See Meynell, Laurence Walter
Bay, Jeanette Graham 1928- *88*
Bayer, Harold
See Gregg, Andrew K.
Bayer, Jane E. (?)-1985
Obituary *44*
Bayley, Nicola 1949- *129*
Earlier sketches in SATA *41, 69*
Baylor, Byrd 1924- *136*
Earlier sketches in SATA *16, 69*
See also CLR *3*
Baynes, Pauline 1922-2008 .... *133*
Obituary *196*
Earlier sketches in SATA *19, 59*
Baynes, Pauline Diana
See Baynes, Pauline
Bayoc, Cbabi *186*
Bayrock, Fiona *215*
BB
See Watkins-Pitchford, Denys James
Beach, Charles
See Reid, (Thomas) Mayne
Beach, Charles Amory *1*
Beach, Edward L. 1918-2002 .... *12*
Obituary *140*
Beach, Edward Latimer
See Beach, Edward L.
Beach, Lisa 1957- *111*
Beach, Lynn
See Lance, Kathryn
Beach, Stewart T(aft) 1899-1979 .... *23*
Beachcroft, Nina 1931- *18*
Beagle, Peter S. 1939- *130*
Earlier sketch in SATA *60*
Beagle, Peter Soyer
See Beagle, Peter S.
Beaglehole, Helen 1946- *117*
Beake, Lesley 1949- *209*
Beaky, Suzanne 1971- *230*
Beale, Fleur *107*
Bealer, Alex W(inkler III) 1921-1980 .... *8*
Obituary *22*
Beales, Valerie 1915- *74*
Beals, Carleton 1893-1979 .... *12*
Beals, Frank Lee 1881-1972
Obituary *26*
Beam, Matt 1970- *187*
Beame, Rona 1934- *12*
Beamer, Charles 1942- *43*
Beamer, George Charles, Jr.
See Beamer, Charles
Bean, Jonathan 1979- *194*
Bean, Normal
See Burroughs, Edgar Rice
Beaney, Jan
See Udall, Jan Beaney
Beaney, Jane
See Udall, Jan Beaney
Bear, Carolyn
See Rayban, Chloe
Bear, Greg 1951- *105*
Earlier sketch in SATA *65*
See also CLR *175*
Bear, Gregory Dale
See Bear, Greg
Bearanger, Marie
See Messier, Claire
Beard, Alex 1970- *222*
Beard, Charles A(ustin) 1874-1948 .... *18*
Beard, Dan(iel Carter) 1850-1941 .... *22*
Beard, Darleen Bailey 1961- *96*
Bearden, Romare (Howard) 1914(?)-1988 ... *22*
Obituary *56*
Beardmore, Cedric
See Beardmore, George
Beardmore, George 1908-1979 .... *20*
Beardshaw, Rosalind 1969- *225*
Earlier sketch in SATA *190*
Beardsley, Martyn R. 1957- *150*
Bearman, Jane (Ruth) 1917- *29*
Bearn, Emily *220*
Beaton, Clare 1947- *220*
Earlier sketch in SATA *125*
Beatty, Elizabeth
See Holloway, Teresa (Bragunier)
Beatty, Hetty Burlingame 1907-1971 .... *5*
Beatty, Jerome, Jr. 1918- *5*
Beatty, John (Louis) 1922-1975 .... *6*
Obituary *25*
Beatty, Patricia (Robbins) 1922-1991 .... *73*
Obituary *68*
Earlier sketches in SATA *1, 30*
See also SAAS *4*
Beaty, Andrea *186*
Beaty, Mary (T.) 1947- *146*
Beaudoin, Sean *210*
Beauford, Jhenne Tyler
See Beauford, Tyler
Beauford, Tyler 1990- *225*
Beaufort, Simon
See Gregory, Susanna
and Riffenburgh, Beau
Beaumont, Karen 1954- *204*
Beavers, Ethen 1971- *225*
Beccia, Carlyn *189*
Bechard, Margaret 1953- *164*
Earlier sketch in SATA *85*
Bechtel, Louise Seaman 1894-1985 .... *4*
Obituary *43*
Bechtold, Lisze *208*
Beck, Andrea 1956- *226*
Beck, Barbara L. 1927- *12*
Beck, Ian 1947- *190*
Earlier sketch in SATA *138*
See Beck, Ian Archibald
Beck, Peggy 1949- *171*
Beck, Scott *197*
Becker, Beril 1901-1999 .... *11*
Becker, Bonny *184*
Becker, Deborah Zimmett 1955- *138*
Becker, Helaine 1961- *142*
Becker, John (Leonard) 1901- *12*
Becker, John E(mil) 1942- *148*
Becker, Joyce 1936- *39*
Becker, May Lamberton 1873-1958 .... *33*
Becker, Neesa 1951- *123*
Becker, Shari *174*
Beckerman, Chad W. *198*
Beckett, Sheilah 1913- *33*
Beckhorn, Susan Williams 1953- *189*
Beckles Willson, Robina 1930- *27*
Beckman, Delores 1914-1994 .... *51*
Beckman, Gunnel 1910- *6*
See also CLR *25*
See also SAAS *9*

Beckman, Kaj
 See Beckman, Karin
Beckman, Karin 1913- *45*
Beckman, Per (Frithiof) 1913- *45*
Bedard, Michael 1949- *154*
 Earlier sketch in SATA *93*
 See also CLR *35*
Beddor, Frank *194*
Beddows, Eric
 See Nutt, Ken
Bedford, A. N.
 See Watson, Jane Werner
Bedford, Annie North
 See Watson, Jane Werner
Bedford, David *224*
 Earlier sketch in SATA *159*
Bedford, David J.
 See Bedford, David
Bedoukian, Kerop 1907-1981 .... *53*
Bee, Jay
 See Brainerd, John W(hiting)
Bee, William *188*
Beebe, B. F.
 See Johnson, B. F.
Beebe, (Charles) William 1877-1962 .... *19*
Beeby, Betty 1923- *25*
Beech, Mark 1971- *191*
Beech, Webb
 See Griffin, W. E. B.
Beecham, Jahnna *161*
Beechcroft, William
 See Hallstead, William F(inn III)
Beeching, Jack 1922- *14*
Beeke, Tiphanie *219*
 Earlier sketch in SATA *163*
Beeler, Janet
 See Shaw, Janet
Beeler, Nelson F(rederick) 1910-1978 .... *13*
Beene, Jason *239*
Beere, Peter 1951- *97*
Beers, Dorothy Sands 1917- *9*
Beers, Lorna 1897-1989 .... *14*
Beers, V(ictor) Gilbert 1928- *130*
 Earlier sketch in SATA *9*
Beeton, Max
 See Redding, Robert Hull
Begay, Shonto 1954- *137*
Begaye, Lisa Shook
 See Beach, Lisa
Begin, Mary Jane 1963- *82*
Begin-Callanan, Mary Jane
 See Begin, Mary Jane
Begley, Kathleen A. 1948- *21*
Begley, Kathleen Anne
 See Begley, Kathleen A.
Beguine, Anna
 See Saintcrow, Lilith
Beha, Eileen *221*
Beha, Philippe *211*
Behan, Leslie
 See Gottfried, Theodore Mark
Behler, Deborah A. 1947- *145*
Behler, John L. 1943-2006 .... *145*
 Obituary *173*
Behler, John Luther
 See Behler, John L.
Behn, Harry 1898-1973 .... *2*
 Obituary *34*
Behnke, Frances L. *8*
Behr, Joyce 1929- *15*
Behrens, Andy *228*
Behrens, June York 1925- *19*
Behrman, Carol H(elen) 1925- *144*
 Earlier sketch in SATA *14*
Beifuss, John, (Jr.) 1959- *92*
Beil, Karen Magnuson 1950- *221*
 Earlier sketch in SATA *124*
Beil, Michael D. *226*
Beiler, Edna 1923- *61*
Beingessner, Laura 1965- *220*
Beinicke, Steve 1956- *69*
Beirne, Barbara 1933- *71*
Beiser, Arthur 1931- *22*
Beiser, Germaine 1931- *11*
Beitia, Sara 1977- *240*
Belair, Richard L. 1934- *45*
Belaney, Archibald Stansfeld 1888-1938 .... *24*
 See also CLR *32*
Belasen, Amy 1983- *213*
Belbin, David 1958- *164*
 Earlier sketch in SATA *106*
Belden, Wilanne Schneider 1925- *56*
Belford, Kevin *236*
Belfrage, Sally 1936-1994 .... *65*
 Obituary *79*
Belknap, B. H.
 See Ellis, Edward S.
Belknap, Boynton
 See Ellis, Edward S.
Belknap, Boynton M.D.
 See Ellis, Edward S.
Bell, Anthea 1936- *148*
 Earlier sketch in SATA *88*
Bell, Cathleen Davitt 1971- *203*
Bell, Cece *202*
Bell, Clare (Louise) 1952- *99*
Bell, Corydon Whitten 1894-1980 .... *3*
Bell, David Owen 1949- *99*
Bell, Emerson
 See Stratemeyer, Edward L.
Bell, Emily Mary
 See Cason, Mabel Earp
Bell, Frank
 See Benson, Mildred
Bell, Gertrude (Wood) 1911-1987 .... *12*
Bell, Gina
 See Balzano, Jeanne (Koppel)
Bell, Hilari 1958- *226*
 Earlier sketches in SATA *151, 197*
Bell, Jadrien
 See Golden, Christie
Bell, Janet
 See Clymer, Eleanor
Bell, Janet Cheatham 1937- *127*
Bell, Krista 1950- *215*
 Earlier sketch in SATA *126*
Bell, Krista Anne Blakeney
 See Bell, Krista
Bell, Margaret E(lizabeth) 1898-1990 .... *2*
Bell, Mary Reeves 1946- *88*
Bell, Norman (Edward) 1899- *11*
Bell, Raymond Martin 1907-1999 .... *13*
Bell, Siobhan *177*
Bell, Thelma Harrington 1896-1985 .... *3*
Bell, William 1945- *90*
 See also CLR *91*
Bellairs, John (Anthony) 1938-1991 .... *160*
 Obituary *66*
 Earlier sketches in SATA *2, 68*
 See also CLR *37*
Beller, Susan Provost 1949- *128*
 Earlier sketch in SATA *84*
 See also CLR *106*
Bellingham, Brenda 1931- *99*
 Brief entry *51*
Bello, Rosario de
 See De Bello, Rosario
Belloc, Hilaire 1870-1953 .... *112*
 See also YABC *1*
 See also CLR *102*
Belloc, Joseph Hilaire Pierre Sebastien Rene Swanton
 See Belloc, Hilaire
Belloc, Joseph Peter Rene Hilaire
 See Belloc, Hilaire
Belloc, Joseph Pierre Hilaire
 See Belloc, Hilaire
Belloli, Andrea P. A. 1947- *86*
Bell-Rehwoldt, Sheri 1962- *199*
Bellville, Cheryl Walsh 1944- *54*
 Brief entry *49*
Bell-Zano, Gina
 See Balzano, Jeanne (Koppel)
Belpre, Pura 1899-1982 .... *16*
 Obituary *30*
Belting, Natalia Maree 1915-1997 .... *6*
Belton, John Raynor 1931- *22*
Belton, Sandra 1939- *186*
 Earlier sketches in SATA *85, 134*
Belton, Sandra Yvonne
 See Belton, Sandra
Beltran, Alberto 1923- *43*
Beltran-Hernandez, Irene 1945- *74*
Belvedere, Lee
 See Grayland, Valerie (Merle Spanner)
Bemelmans, Ludwig 1898-1962 .... *100*
 Earlier sketch in SATA *15*
 See also CLR *93*
Bemis, John Claude 1972- *234*
Benander, Carl D. 1941- *74*
Benary, Margot
 See Benary-Isbert, Margot
Benary-Isbert, Margot 1889-1979 .... *2*
 Obituary *21*
 See also CLR *12*
Benasutti, Marion 1908-1992 .... *6*
Benatar, Raquel 1955- *167*
Benchley, Nathaniel (Goddard) 1915-1981 .. *25*
 Obituary *28*
 Earlier sketch in SATA *3*
Benchley, Peter 1940-2006 .... *164*
 Earlier sketches in SATA *3, 89*
Benchley, Peter Bradford
 See Benchley, Peter
Bendall-Brunello, John *185*
Bender, Edna 1941- *92*
Bender, Esther 1942- *88*
Bender, Lucy Ellen 1942- *22*
Bender, Robert 1962- *160*
 Earlier sketch in SATA *79*
Bendick, Jeanne 1919- *238*
 Autobiography Feature *238*
 Earlier sketches in SATA *2, 68, 135*
 See also CLR *5*
 See also SAAS *4*
Bendick, Robert L(ouis) 1917- *11*
Bendinger, Jessica 1966- *233*
Benedetto, William R. 1928- *180*
Benedetto, William Ralph
 See Benedetto, William R.
Benedict, Andrew
 See Arthur, Robert, (Jr.)
Benedict, Dorothy Potter 1889-1979 .... *11*
 Obituary *23*
Benedict, Lois Trimble 1902-1967 .... *12*
Benedict, Rex 1920-1995 .... *8*
Benedict, Stewart H(urd) 1924- *26*
Beneduce, Ann Keay *128*
Benet, Laura 1884-1979 .... *3*
 Obituary *23*
Benet, Stephen Vincent 1898-1943
 See YABC *1*
Benet, Sula 1906-1982 .... *21*
 Obituary *33*
Ben-Ezer, Ehud 1936- *122*
Benezra, Barbara (Beardsley) 1921- *10*
Benham, Leslie 1922- *48*
Benham, Lois (Dakin) 1924- *48*
Benham, Mary Lile 1914-1991 .... *55*
Benioff, Carol *232*
Benjamin, E. M. J.
 See Bache, Ellyn
Benjamin, Floella 1949- *206*
Benjamin, Nora
 See Kubie, Nora Gottheil Benjamin
Benjamin, Saragail Katzman 1953- *86*
Benner, Cheryl 1962- *80*
Benner, Judith Ann 1942- *94*
Bennett, Alice
 See Ziner, Florence
Bennett, Artie *227*

Bennett, Cherie 1960- 158
  Earlier sketch in SATA 97
Bennett, Dorothea
  See Young, Dorothea Bennett
Bennett, Erin Susanne
  See Banks, Erin Bennett
Bennett, Holly 1957- 181
Bennett, James (W.) 1942- 153
  Autobiography Feature 153
  Earlier sketches in SATA 93, 148
Bennett, Jay 1912- 87
  Brief entry 27
  Earlier sketch in SATA 41
  See also SAAS 4
Bennett, Jill (Crawford) 1934- 41
Bennett, John 1865-1956
  See YABC 1
Bennett, Kelly 1958- 231
Bennett, Kelly Goldman
  See Bennett, Kelly
Bennett, Penelope (Agnes) 1938- 94
Bennett, Rachel
  See Hill, Margaret (Ohler)
Bennett, Rainey 1907-1998 15
  Obituary 111
Bennett, Richard 1899- 21
Bennett, Russell H(oradley) 1896- 25
Bennett, Veronica 1953- 178
Bennett, William (John) 1943- 102
Benning, Elizabeth
  See Rice, Bebe Faas
Benny, Mike 1964- 203
Benson, Amber 1977- 235
Benson, Elizabeth P(olk) 1924- 65
Benson, Kathleen 1947- 183
  Earlier sketches in SATA 62, 111
Benson, Linda M(aria) 1959- 84
Benson, Mildred 1905-2002 100
  Obituary 135
  Earlier sketches in SATA 1, 65, 67
Benson, Mildred Augustine Wirt
  See Benson, Mildred
Benson, Mildred Wirt
  See Benson, Mildred
Benson, Millie
  See Benson, Mildred
Benson, Patrick 1956- 147
Benson, Sally 1900-1972 35
  Obituary 27
  Earlier sketch in SATA 1
Bentley, Judith (McBride) 1945- 89
  Earlier sketch in SATA 40
Bentley, Karen
  See Taschek, Karen
Bentley, Nancy (L.) 1946- 78
Bentley, Nicolas Clerihew 1907-1978
  Obituary 24
Bentley, Phyllis Eleanor 1894-1977 6
  Obituary 25
Bentley, Roy 1947- 46
Bentley, William (George) 1916- 84
Bently, Peter 1960- 221
Benton, Jim 1963- 172
ben Uzair, Salem
  See Horne, Richard Henry Hengist
Ben-Zvi, Rebeccca Tova
  See O'Connell, Rebecca
Bercaw, Edna Coe 1961- 124
Berck, Judith 1960- 75
Bereal, JaeMe 1959(?)- 228
Berelson, Howard 1940- 5
Berends, Polly Berrien 1939- 50
  Brief entry 38
Berenstain, Jan 1923- 135
  Earlier sketches in SATA 12, 64, 129
  See also CLR 150
  See also SAAS 20
Berenstain, Janice
  See Berenstain, Jan
Berenstain, Michael 1951- 220
  Earlier sketch in SATA 45
Berenstain, Mike
  See Berenstain, Michael
Berenstain, Stan 1923-2005 135
  Obituary 169
  Earlier sketches in SATA 12, 64, 129
  See also CLR 150
  See also SAAS 20
Berenstain, Stanley
  See Berenstain, Stan
Berenzy, Alix 1957- 168
  Earlier sketch in SATA 65
Beresford, Elisabeth 1928-2010 141
  Earlier sketches in SATA 25, 86
  See also SAAS 20
Berg, Adriane G(ilda) 1948- 152
Berg, Dave
  See Berg, David
Berg, David 1920-2002 27
  Obituary 137
Berg, Elizabeth 1948- 104
Berg, Jean Horton 1913-1995 6
Berg, Joan
  See Victor, Joan Berg
Berg, Ron 1952- 48
Bergaust, Erik 1925-1978 20
Bergel, Colin J. 1963- 137
Bergen, Joyce 1949- 95
Berger, Barbara (Helen) 1945- 77
Berger, Carin 232
  Earlier sketch in SATA 185
Berger, Gilda 1935- 88
  Brief entry 42
Berger, Joe 1970- 221
Berger, Josef 1903-1971 36
Berger, Lou 1950- 213
Berger, Melvin H. 1927- 158
  Autobiography Feature 124
  Earlier sketches in SATA 5, 88
  See also CLR 32
  See also SAAS 2
Berger, Phil 1942-2001 62
Berger, Samantha 1969- 140
Berger, Samantha Allison
  See Berger, Samantha
Berger, Terry 1933- 8
Bergey, Alyce 1934- 45
Bergey, Alyce Mae
  See Bergey, Alyce
Bergin, Mark 1961- 160
  Earlier sketch in SATA 114
Berglin, Ruth Marie 1970- 181
Bergman, Donna 1934- 73
Bergman, Mara 1956- 196
Bergman, Tamar 1939- 95
Bergren, Lisa T.
  See Bergren, Lisa Tawn
Bergren, Lisa Tawn 200
Bergsma, Jody Lynn 163
Bergstein, Rita M. 211
Bergum, Constance R. 1952- 208
  Earlier sketch in SATA 121
Berk, Ari 208
Berk, Josh 1976- 227
Berkebile, Fred D(onovan) 1900-1978
  Obituary 26
Berkeley, Jon 1962- 204
Berkes, Marianne 217
  Earlier sketch in SATA 173
Berkey, Barry Robert 1935- 24
Berkley, Elizabeth 1972- 241
Berkowitz, Freda Pastor 1908-1994 12
Berkus, Clara Widess 1909- 78
Berlan, Kathryn Hook 1946- 78
Berlfein, Judy Reiss 1958- 79
Berlin, Eric 1968- 195
Berliner, Don 1930- 33
Berliner, Franz 1930- 13
Berlitz, Charles (L. Frambach) 1914-2003 ... 32
  Obituary 151
Berman, Len 1947- 229
Berman, Linda 1948- 38
Berman, Paul (Lawrence) 1949- 66
Berman, Rachel 1946- 217
Berna, Paul 1910-1994 15
  Obituary 78
  See also CLR 19
Bernadette
  See Watts, Bernadette
Bernard, Bruce 1928-2000 78
  Obituary 124
Bernard, George I. 1949- 39
Bernard, Jacqueline (de Sieyes) 1921-1983 ... 8
  Obituary 45
Bernard, Patricia 1942- 181
  Earlier sketch in SATA 106
Bernard, Trish
  See Bernard, Patricia
Bernardin, James 1966- 227
  Earlier sketch in SATA 112
Bernardo, Anilu 184
Bernards, Neal 1963- 71
Bernasconi, Pablo 1973- 183
Bernays, Anne 1930- 32
Berne, Jennifer 238
Berner, Rotraut Susanne 1948- 214
Bernhard, Durga T. 1961- 80
Bernhard, Emery 1950- 80
Bernheimer, Kate 201
Bernier-Grand, Carmen T. 1947- 202
Bernstein, Daryl (Evan) 1976- 81
Bernstein, Joanne E(ckstein) 1943- 15
Bernstein, Jonathan 217
Bernstein, Margery 1933- 114
Bernstein, Nina 1949- 180
Bernstein, Theodore M(enline) 1904-1979 ... 12
  Obituary 27
Berrien, Edith Heal
  See Heal, Edith
Berrill, Jacquelyn (Batsel) 1905- 12
Berrington, John
  See Brownjohn, Alan
Berry, B. J.
  See Berry, Barbara J.
Berry, Barbara J. 1937- 7
Berry, Erick
  See Best, (Evangel) Allena Champlin
Berry, Holly 1957- 210
Berry, James 1924- 110
  Earlier sketch in SATA 67
  See also CLR 143
Berry, Jane Cobb 1915(?)-1979
  Obituary 22
Berry, Joy 1944- 58
  Brief entry 46
Berry, Joy Wilt
  See Berry, Joy
Berry, Julie 1974- 218
Berry, Lynne 190
Berry, William D(avid) 1926- 14
Bersani, Shennen 1961- 164
Berson, Harold 1926- 4
Bertagna, Julie 1962- 151
Bertholf, Bret 189
Bertin, Charles-Francois
  See Berlitz, Charles (L. Frambach)
Bertolet, Paul
  See McLaughlin, Frank
Berton, Pierre (Francis de Marigny)
  1920-2004 99
  Obituary 158
Bertrand, Cecile 1953- 76
Bertrand, Diane Gonzales 1956- 177
  Earlier sketch in SATA 106
Bertrand, Lynne 1963- 164
  Earlier sketch in SATA 81
Beskow, Elsa (Maartman) 1874-1953 20
  See also CLR 17
Bess, Clayton
  See Locke, Robert
Besson, Luc 1959- 199
Best, (Evangel) Allena Champlin 1892-1974 . 2
  Obituary 25

Best, Cari 1951- *200*
Earlier sketches in SATA *107, 149*
Best, (Oswald) Herbert 1894-1980 .... *2*
Bestall, A(lfred) E(dmeades) 1892-1986 .... *97*
Obituary *48*
Betancourt, Jeanne 1941- *148*
Brief entry *43*
Earlier sketches in SATA *55, 96*
Beth, Mary
See Miller, Mary Beth
Bethancourt, T. Ernesto
See Paisley, Tom
Bethel, Dell 1929- *52*
Bethell, Jean (Frankenberry) 1922- *8*
Bethers, Ray 1902-1973 .... *6*
Bethke, Bruce Raymond 1955- *114*
Bethlen, T.D.
See Silverberg, Robert
Bethune, J. G.
See Ellis, Edward S.
Bethune, J. H.
See Ellis, Edward S.
Betteridge, Anne
See Potter, Margaret
Betteridge, Deirdre *214*
Bettina
See Ehrlich, Bettina Bauer
Bettmann, Otto Ludwig 1903-1998 .... *46*
Bettoli, Delana *187*
Betts, James
See Haynes, Betsy
Betz, Eva Kelly 1897-1968 .... *10*
Bevan, Tom 1868-1930(?)
See YABC *2*
Bevis, Mary 1939- *202*
Bewick, Thomas 1753-1828 .... *16*
Beyer, Audrey White 1916- *9*
Beyer, Paul J. III 1950- *74*
Beynon, John
See Harris, John (Wyndham Parkes Lucas) Beynon
Bezencon, Jacqueline (Buxcel) 1924- *48*
Bhatia, Jamunadevi 1919-2011 .... *48*
Bhatia, June
See Bhatia, Jamunadevi
Bial, Morrison David 1917- *62*
Bial, Raymond 1948- *225*
Earlier sketches in SATA *76, 116, 165*
Biala
See Brustlein, Janice Tworkov
Biale, Rachel 1952- *99*
Bialk, Elisa
See Krautter, Elisa (Bialk)
Bianchi, John 1947- *91*
Bianchi, Robert S(teven) 1943- *92*
Bianco, Margery
See Bianco, Margery Williams
Bianco, Margery Williams 1881-1944 .... *15*
See also CLR *146*
Bianco, Pamela 1906- *28*
Bibby, Violet 1908-1996 .... *24*
Bible, Charles 1937- *13*
Bibo, Bobette
See Gugliotta, Bobette
Bice, Clare 1909-1976 .... *22*
Bick, Ilsa J. *238*
Bickerstaff, Isaac
See Swift, Jonathan
Bidner, Jenni 1963- *193*
Biedrzycki, David 1955- *219*
Biegel, Paul 1925- *79*
Earlier sketch in SATA *16*
See also CLR *27*
See also SAAS *18*
Biemiller, Carl L(udwig), Jr.) 1912-1979 .... *40*
Obituary *21*
Bienenfeld, Florence L(ucille) 1929- *39*
Bierhorst, John (William) 1936- *149*
Autobiography Feature *149*
Earlier sketches in SATA *6, 91*
See also SAAS *10*
Biggar, Joan R. 1936- *120*
Biggar, Joan Rawlins
See Biggar, Joan R.
Biggle, Lloyd, Jr. 1923-2002 .... *65*
Biggs, Brian 1968- *192*
Bilal, Abdel W(ahab) 1970- *92*
Bilbrough, Norman 1941- *111*
Bildner, Phil *230*
Earlier sketch in SATA *173*
Bileck, Marvin 1920- *40*
Bilibin, Ivan (Iakolevich) 1876-1942 .... *61*
Bill, Alfred Hoyt 1879-1964 .... *44*
Bill, Tannis *228*
Billam, Rosemary 1952- *61*
Billings, Charlene W(interer) 1941- *41*
Billingsley, Franny 1954- *235*
Earlier sketch in SATA *132*
Billington, Elizabeth T(hain) *50*
Brief entry *43*
Billout, Guy (Rene) 1941- *144*
Earlier sketch in SATA *10*
See also CLR *33*
Bilson, Geoffrey 1938-1987 .... *99*
Binch, Caroline (Lesley) 1947- *140*
Earlier sketch in SATA *81*
Bing, Christopher (H.) *126*
Bingham, Caroline 1962- *158*
Bingham, Jane M. 1941- *163*
Bingham, Jane Marie
See Bingham, Jane M.
Bingham, Janet 1959- *200*
Bingham, Kelly 1967- *207*
Bingham, Sam 1944- *96*
Bingham, Samuel A.
See Bingham, Sam
Bingley, Margaret (Jane Kirby) 1947- *72*
Binkley, Anne
See Rand, Ann (Binkley)
Binzen, Bill
See Binzen, William
Binzen, William *24*
Birch, David (W.) 1913-1996 .... *89*
Birch, Reginald B(athurst) 1856-1943 .... *19*
Birchman, David 1949- *72*
Birchmore, Daniel A. 1951- *92*
Bird, Carmel 1940- *124*
Bird, E(lzy) J(ay) 1911- *58*
Birdsall, Jeanne 1951- *231*
Birdsall, Jeanne 1952(?)- *170*
Birdseye, Tom 1951- *148*
Earlier sketches in SATA *66, 98*
Birenbaum, Barbara 1941- *65*
Birmingham, Christian 1970- *220*
Birmingham, Lloyd P(aul) 1924- *83*
Earlier sketch in SATA *12*
Birmingham, Ruth
See Sorrells, Walter
Birney, Betty G. 1947- *169*
Earlier sketch in SATA *98*
Biro, B.
See Biro, B. S.
Biro, B. S. 1921- *1*
See also CLR *28*
See also SAAS *13*
Biro, Val
See Biro, B. S.
Birtha, Becky 1948- *229*
Bischoff, Julia Bristol 1899-1970 .... *12*
Bishop, Bonnie 1943- *37*
Bishop, Claire Huchet 1899(?)-1993 .... *14*
Obituary *74*
See also CLR *80*
Bishop, Courtney
See Ruemmler, John D(avid)
Bishop, Curtis (Kent) 1912-1967 .... *6*
Bishop, Elizabeth 1911-1979
Obituary *24*
Bishop, Gavin 1946- *216*
Earlier sketches in SATA *97, 144*
Bishop, Kathleen Wong 1954- *120*
Bishop, Kathy
See Bishop, Kathleen Wong
Bishop, Nic 1955- *161*
Earlier sketch in SATA *107*
Bishop, Rudine Sims *224*
Bisset, Donald 1910-1995 .... *86*
Earlier sketch in SATA *7*
Bisson, Terry 1942- *99*
Bisson, Terry Ballantine
See Bisson, Terry
Bitter, Gary G(len) 1940- *22*
Bixby, William (Courtney) 1920-1986 .... *6*
Obituary *47*
Bjoerk, Christina 1938- *99*
Earlier sketch in SATA *67*
See also CLR *22*
Bjork, Christina
See Bjoerk, Christina
Bjorklund, Lorence F. 1913-1978 .... *35*
Brief entry *32*
Bjorkman, Lauren *222*
Bjorkman, Steve *223*
Earlier sketch in SATA *163*
Blabey, Aaron 1975(?)- *214*
Black, Algernon David 1900-1993 .... *12*
Obituary *76*
Black, Holly 1971- *236*
Earlier sketches in SATA *147, 210*
Black, Irma Simonton 1906-1972 .... *2*
Obituary *25*
Black, Jenna 1965- *239*
Black, Joe 1959- *224*
Black, Rabbi Joe
See Black, Joe
Black, Kat *217*
Black, Katherine
See Black, Kat
Black, Mansell
See Trevor, Elleston
Black, MaryAnn
See Easley, MaryAnn
Black, Susan Adams 1953- *40*
Blackaby, Susan 1953- *240*
Blackall, Bernie 1956- *126*
Blackall, Sophie *231*
Earlier sketch in SATA *182*
Blackburn, Claire
See Altman, Linda Jacobs
Blackburn, John(ny) Brewton 1952- *15*
Blackburn, Joyce Knight 1920- *29*
Blacker, Terence 1948- *194*
Blacker, Tina
See Louise, Tina
Blackett, Veronica Heath 1927- *12*
Blackie, Jean Cutler 1943- *79*
Blacklin, Malcolm
See Chambers, Aidan
Blacklock, Dyan 1951- *112*
Blackman, Malorie 1962- *196*
Earlier sketches in SATA *83, 128*
Blackton, Peter
See Wilson, Lionel
Blackwood, Alan 1932- *70*
Blackwood, Freya *199*
Blackwood, Gary
See Blackwood, Gary L.
Blackwood, Gary L. 1945- *226*
Earlier sketches in SATA *72, 118, 169*
Blade, Alexander
See Garrett, Randall
and Hamilton, Edmond
and Silverberg, Robert
Bladek, John 1963(?)- *237*
Blades, Ann (Sager) 1947- *69*
Earlier sketch in SATA *16*
See also CLR *15*
Bladow, Suzanne Wilson 1937- *14*
Blaine, Chris
See Gardner, Craig Shaw
Blaine, John
See Goodwin, Harold L(eland)

Blaine, Marge
See Blaine, Margery Kay
Blaine, Margery Kay 1937- *11*
Blair, Alison
See Lerangis, Peter
Blair, Anne Denton 1914-1993 .... *46*
Blair, David Nelson 1954- *80*
Blair, Eric
See Orwell, George
Blair, Jay 1953- *45*
Blair, Lucile
See Yeakley, Marjory Hall
Blair, Margaret Whitman 1951- *227*
Earlier sketch in SATA *124*
Blair, Mary 1911-1978 .... *195*
Blair, Pauline Hunter
See Clarke, Pauline
Blair, Ruth Van Ness 1912-1999 .... *12*
Blair, Shannon
See Kaye, Marilyn
Blair, Walter 1900-1992 .... *12*
Obituary *72*
Blaisdell, Bob
See Blaisdell, Robert
Blaisdell, Robert 1959- *105*
Blake, Bronwyn 1940- *149*
Blake, Francis *198*
Blake, Jon 1954- *171*
Earlier sketch in SATA *78*
Blake, Olive
See Supraner, Robyn
Blake, Quentin 1932- *211*
Earlier sketches in SATA *9, 52, 96, 125*
See also CLR *31*
Blake, Robert 1949- *42*
Blake, Robert J. *160*
Blake, Stephanie *233*
See Pearl, Jacques Bain
Blake, Walker E.
See Griffin, W. E. B.
Blake, William 1757-1827 .... *30*
See also CLR *52*
Blakely, Gloria 1950- *139*
Blakely, Roger K. 1922- *82*
Blakeney, Jay D.
See Chester, Deborah
Blakeslee, Lys 1985- *218*
Blakey, Nancy 1955- *94*
Blanc, Esther S. 1913-1997 .... *66*
Blanc, Mel 1908-1989
Obituary *64*
Blanchard, Patricia *125*
Blanchet, M(uriel) Wylie 1891-1961 .... *106*
Blanco, Richard L(idio) 1926- *63*
Bland, E.
See Nesbit, E.
Bland, Edith Nesbit
See Nesbit, E.
Bland, Fabian
See Nesbit, E.
Blane, Gertrude
See Blumenthal, Gertrude
Blank, Clarissa Mabel 1915-1965 .... *62*
Blankenship, LeeAnn 1944- *181*
Blassingame, Wyatt Rainey 1909-1985 .... *34*
Obituary *41*
Earlier sketch in SATA *1*
Blatchford, Claire H. 1944- *94*
Blau, Aljoscha 1972- *233*
Blauer, Ettagale 1940- *49*
Blecha, Aaron *233*
Bleck, Linda *207*
Bledsoe, Glen L. 1951- *108*
Bledsoe, Glen Leonard
See Bledsoe, Glen L.
Bledsoe, Karen E. 1962- *167*
Earlier sketch in SATA *108*
Bledsoe, Karen Elizabeth
See Bledsoe, Karen E.
Bledsoe, Lucy Jane 1957- *162*
Earlier sketch in SATA *97*
Bleeker, Sonia
See Zim, Sonia Bleeker
Blegen, Daniel M. 1950- *92*
Blegvad, Erik 1923- *132*
Earlier sketches in SATA *14, 66*
Blegvad, Lenore 1926- *176*
Earlier sketches in SATA *14, 66*
Bleiman, Andrew *237*
Blessing, Charlotte *223*
Bley, Anette 1967- *188*
Blish, James 1921-1975 .... *66*
Blish, James Benjamin
See Blish, James
Blishen, Edward (William) 1920-1996 .... *66*
Obituary *93*
Earlier sketch in SATA *8*
Bliss, Corinne Demas
See Demas, Corinne
Bliss, Frederick
See Card, Orson Scott
Bliss, Gillian
See Paton Walsh, Jill
Bliss, Harry 1964- *196*
Earlier sketch in SATA *156*
Bliss, Reginald
See Wells, H. G.
Bliss, Ronald G(ene) 1942- *12*
Blitt, Barry *187*
Bliven, Bruce, Jr. 1916-2002 .... *2*
Blixen, Karen 1885-1962 .... *44*
Blizzard, Gladys S. (?)-1992 .... *79*
Blobaum, Cindy 1966- *123*
Bloch, Lucienne 1909-1999 .... *10*
Bloch, Marie Halun 1910-1998 .... *6*
See also SAAS *9*
Bloch, Robert (Albert) 1917-1994 .... *12*
Obituary *82*
Bloch, Serge 1956- *213*
Blochman, Lawrence G(oldtree)
1900-1975 .... *22*
Block, Francesca Lia 1962- *213*
Earlier sketches in SATA *80, 116, 158*
See also CLR *116*
See also SAAS *21*
Block, Irvin 1917- *12*
Blomgren, Jennifer (Alice) 1954- *136*
Blonder, Terry Joyce
See Golson, Terry
Blood, Charles Lewis 1929- *28*
Bloom, Barbara Lee 1943- *146*
Bloom, Freddy 1914-2000 .... *37*
Obituary *121*
Bloom, Lloyd 1947- *108*
Brief entry *43*
Bloom, Suzanne 1950- *232*
Earlier sketch in SATA *172*
Bloomfield, Michaela 1966- *70*
Bloor, Edward 1950- *201*
Earlier sketches in SATA *98, 155*
Bloor, Edward William
See Bloor, Edward
Blos, Joan W. 1928- *153*
Autobiography Feature *153*
Brief entry *27*
Earlier sketches in SATA *33, 69, 109*
See also CLR *18*
See also SAAS *11*
Blos, Joan Winsor
See Blos, Joan W.
Bloss, Josie 1981- *232*
Blough, Glenn O(rlando) 1907-1995 .... *1*
Blue, Rose 1931- *166*
Autobiography Feature *117*
Earlier sketches in SATA *5, 91, 93*
See also SAAS *24*
Blue, Zachary
See Stine, R.L.
Bluemle, Elizabeth *209*
Bluggage, Oranthy
See Alcott, Louisa May
Blumberg, Leda 1956- *59*
Blumberg, Rhoda 1917- *123*
Earlier sketches in SATA *35, 70*
See also CLR *21*
Blume, Judy 1938- *195*
Earlier sketches in SATA *2, 31, 79, 142*
See also CLR *69*
Blume, Judy Sussman
See Blume, Judy
Blume, Lesley M.M. 1975- *180*
Blumenthal, Deborah *204*
Earlier sketch in SATA *161*
Blumenthal, Gertrude 1907-1971
Obituary *27*
Blumenthal, Shirley 1943- *46*
Blutig, Eduard
See Gorey, Edward (St. John)
Bly, Janet 1945- *43*
Bly, Janet Chester
See Bly, Janet
Bly, Stephen A(rthur) 1944- *116*
Earlier sketch in SATA *43*
Blyler, Allison Lee 1966- *74*
Blythe, Gary 1959- *185*
Blyton, Carey 1932-2002 .... *9*
Obituary *138*
Blyton, Enid 1897-1968 .... *25*
See also CLR *31*
Blyton, Enid Mary
See Blyton, Enid
Bo, Ben
See Richardson, V.A.
Boardman, Fon Wyman, Jr. 1911-2000 .... *6*
Boardman, Gwenn R.
See Petersen, Gwenn Boardman
Boase, Susan *226*
Boase, Wendy 1944-1999 .... *28*
Obituary *110*
Boatner, Mark Mayo III 1921- *29*
Bobbe, Dorothie de Bear 1905-1975 .... *1*
Obituary *25*
Bober, Natalie S. 1930- *134*
Earlier sketch in SATA *87*
See also SAAS *23*
Bobette, Bibo
See Gugliotta, Bobette
Bobri, Vladimir V. 1898-1986 .... *47*
Brief entry *32*
Bobritsky, Vladimir
See Bobri, Vladimir V.
Bochak, Grayce 1956- *76*
Bock, Hal
See Bock, Harold I.
Bock, Harold I. 1939- *10*
Bock, William Sauts Netamux'we 1939- *14*
Bodanis, David *179*
Bode, Janet 1943-1999 .... *96*
Obituary *118*
Earlier sketch in SATA *60*
Bode, N.E.
See Baggott, Julianna
Bodecker, N(iels) M(ogens) 1922-1988 .... *73*
Obituary *54*
Earlier sketch in SATA *8*
Bodeen, S. A. 1965- *158*
Earlier sketch in SATA *114*
See Stuve-Bodeen, Stephanie
Bodeen, S.A.
See Stuve-Bodeen, Stephanie
Boden, Hilda
See Bodenham, Hilda Morris
Bodenham, Hilda Morris 1901- *13*
Bodett, Thomas Edward 1955- *70*
Bodett, Tom
See Bodett, Thomas Edward
Bodie, Idella F(allaw) 1925- *89*
Earlier sketch in SATA *12*
Bodker, Cecil
See Bodker, Cecil
Bodker, Cecil 1927- *133*
Earlier sketch in SATA *14*
See also CLR *23*

Bodsworth, (Charles) Fred(erick) 1918- *27*
Boeckman, Charles 1920- *12*
Boegehold, Betty (Doyle) 1913-1985
Obituary *42*
Boelts, Maribeth 1964- *200*
Earlier sketches in SATA *78, 163*
Boerst, William J. 1939- *170*
Earlier sketch in SATA *121*
Boesch, Mark J(oseph) 1917- *12*
Boesen, Victor 1908- *16*
Bogacki, Tomek 1950- *214*
Earlier sketch in SATA *138*
Bogaerts, Gert 1965- *80*
Bogan, Paulette 1960- *201*
Earlier sketch in SATA *129*
Bogart, Jo Ellen 1945- *222*
Earlier sketch in SATA *92*
See also CLR *59*
Boggs, Ralph Steele 1901-1994 .... *7*
Bograd, Larry 1953- *89*
Earlier sketch in SATA *33*
See also SAAS *21*
Bogue, Gary 1938- *195*
Bogue, Gary L.
See Bogue, Gary
Bohdal, Susi 1951- *101*
Earlier sketch in SATA *22*
Bohlen, Nina 1931- *58*
Bohlmeijer, Arno 1956- *94*
Bohner, Charles (Henry) 1927- *62*
Bohnhoff, Maya Kaathryn 1954- *88*
Boie, Kirsten 1950- *221*
Boiger, Alexandra *178*
Boissard, Janine 1932- *59*
Bojunga, Lygia
See Nunes, Lygia Bojunga
Bojunga-Nunes, Lygia
See Nunes, Lygia Bojunga
Bok, Arthur
See Bok, Chip
Bok, Chip 1952- *205*
Bolam, Emily 1969- *206*
Boland, Janice *98*
Bolden, Tonya 1959- *227*
Earlier sketches in SATA *79, 138, 188*
Bolden, Tonya Wilyce
See Bolden, Tonya
Boles, Paul Darcy 1916-1984 .... *9*
Obituary *38*
Bolger, Kevin *233*
Bolian, Polly 1925- *4*
Bollen, Roger 1941(?)- *83*
Brief entry *29*
Bolliger, Max 1929- *7*
Bollinger, Max 1929- *167*
Bollinger, Peter *172*
Bolognese, Don(ald Alan) 1934- *129*
Earlier sketches in SATA *24, 71*
Bolognese, Elaine 1933- *23*
Bolotin, Norman (Phillip) 1951- *93*
Bolton, Carole 1926- *6*
Bolton, Elizabeth
See St. John, Nicole
Bolton, Evelyn
See Bunting, Eve
Bonar, Veronica
See Bailey, Donna (Veronica Anne)
Bond, B. J.
See Heneghan, James
Bond, Bruce 1939- *61*
Bond, Felicia 1954- *219*
Earlier sketches in SATA *49, 126*
Bond, Gladys Baker 1912- *14*
Bond, Higgins 1951- *220*
Earlier sketches in SATA *83, 177*
Bond, J. Harvey
See Winterbotham, R(ussell) R(obert)
Bond, (Thomas) Michael 1926- *157*
Earlier sketches in SATA *6, 58*
See also CLR *95*
See also SAAS *3*
Bond, Nancy 1945- *159*
Autobiography Feature *159*
Earlier sketches in SATA *22, 82*
See also CLR *11*
See also SAAS *13*
Bond, Nancy Barbara
See Bond, Nancy
Bond, Rebecca 1972- *214*
Earlier sketch in SATA *130*
Bond, Ruskin 1934- *87*
Earlier sketch in SATA *14*
See also CLR *171*
Bondie, J. D.
See Cunningham, Chet
Bondoux, Anne-Laure 1971- *240*
Earlier sketch in SATA *175*
Bone, Ian 1956- *158*
Earlier sketch in SATA *117*
Bone, J. *230*
Bone, Jason
See Bone, J.
Bonehill, Captain Ralph
See Stratemeyer, Edward L.
Bonestell, Chesley 1888-1986
Obituary *48*
Bonham, Barbara Thomas 1926- *7*
Bonham, Frank 1914-1989 .... *49*
Obituary *62*
Earlier sketch in SATA *1*
See also SAAS *3*
Boniface, William 1963- *182*
Earlier sketch in SATA *102*
Bonino, Louise
See Williams, Louise Bonino
Bonk, John J. *189*
Bonn, Pat
See Bonn, Patricia Carolyn
Bonn, Patricia Carolyn 1948- *43*
Bonner, Hannah *197*
Bonner, Mary Graham 1890-1974 .... *19*
Bonner, Mike 1951- *121*
Bonners, Susan 1947- *85*
Brief entry *48*
Bonnet, Rosalinde 1978- *226*
Bonnett-Rampersaud, Louise *173*
Bonning, Tony 1948- *169*
Bonsall, Crosby Barbara (Newell)
1921-1995 .... *23*
Obituary *84*
Bonsall, Joseph S. 1948- *119*
Bonsignore, Joan 1959- *140*
Bontemps, Arna 1902-1973 .... *44*
Obituary *24*
Earlier sketch in SATA *2*
See also CLR *6*
Bontemps, Arnaud Wendell
See Bontemps, Arna
Bonwill, Ann *238*
Bonzon, Paul-Jacques 1908-1978 .... *22*
Boock, Paula 1964- *134*
Booher, Dianna Daniels 1948- *33*
Book, Rick 1949- *119*
Book, Rita
See Holub, Joan
Bookman, Charlotte
See Zolotow, Charlotte
Boon, Debbie 1960- *103*
Boon, Emilie (Laetitia) 1958- *86*
Boone, Charles Eugene
See Boone, Pat
Boone, Pat 1934- *7*
Booraem, Ellen *211*
Boorman, Linda 1940- *46*
Boorman, Linda Kay
See Boorman, Linda
Boorstin, Daniel J(oseph) 1914-2004 .... *52*
Boos, Ben 1971- *206*
Booth, Coe *187*
Booth, Ernest Sheldon 1915-1984 .... *43*
Booth, George 1926- *191*
Booth, Graham (Charles) 1935- *37*
Bootman, Colin *239*
Earlier sketch in SATA *159*
Borden, Louise 1949- *190*
Autobiography Feature *141*
Earlier sketches in SATA *68, 104, 141*
Bordier, Georgette 1924- *16*
Borgman, James
See Borgman, Jim
Borgman, James Mark
See Borgman, Jim
Borgman, Jim 1954- *122*
Borgo, Lacy Finn 1972- *194*
Boring, Mel 1939- *168*
Earlier sketch in SATA *35*
Borja, Corinne 1929- *22*
Borja, Robert 1923- *22*
Borland, Hal
See Borland, Harold Glen
Borland, Harold Glen 1900-1978 .... *5*
Obituary *24*
Borland, Kathryn Kilby 1916- *16*
Borlenghi, Patricia 1951- *79*
Born, Adolf 1930- *49*
Bornstein, Ruth Lercher
See Bornstein-Lercher, Ruth
Bornstein-Lercher, Ruth 1927- *88*
Autobiography Feature *107*
Earlier sketch in SATA *14*
Borris, Albert *221*
Borski, Lucia Merecka *18*
Borten, Helen Jacobson 1930- *5*
Bortolotti, Dan 1969- *157*
Borton, Elizabeth
See Trevino, Elizabeth B(orton) de
Borton, Lady 1942- *98*
Borton de Trevino, Elizabeth
See Trevino, Elizabeth B(orton) de
Bortstein, Larry 1942-2010 .... *16*
Bortz, Alfred B(enjamin) 1944- *139*
Earlier sketch in SATA *74*
Bortz, Fred
See Bortz, Alfred B(enjamin)
Bosch, Pseudonymous *199*
Bosco, Jack
See Holliday, Joseph
Bose, Mitali
See Perkins, Mitali
Boshell, Gordon 1908-1991 .... *15*
Boshinski, Blanche 1922- *10*
Bosman, Paul 1929- *107*
Bosse, Malcolm (Joseph, Jr.) 1926-2002 .... *136*
Earlier sketch in SATA *35*
Bosserman, Charles Phillip
See Bosserman, Phillip
Bosserman, Phillip 1931- *84*
Bossley, Michele Martin 1969- *219*
Bossom, Naomi 1933- *35*
Bostock, Mike 1962- *114*
Boston, L(ucy) M(aria Wood) 1892-1990 .... *19*
Obituary *64*
See also CLR *3*
Bostrom, Kathleen (Susan) Long 1954- *139*
Bostrom, Kathy
See Bostrom, Kathleen (Susan) Long
Boswell, Addie *208*
Boswell, Addie Kay
See Boswell, Addie
Bosworth, J. Allan 1925- *19*
Bosworth, Lauren
See Bosworth, Lo
Bosworth, Lo 1986- *240*
Bothwell, Jean (?)-1977 .... *2*
Botkin, B(enjamin) A(lbert) 1901-1975 .... *40*
Botsford, Ward 1927-2004 .... *66*
Botting, Douglas (Scott) 1934- *43*
Bottner, Barbara 1943- *232*
Autobiography Feature *121*
Earlier sketches in SATA *14, 93, 170*
See also SAAS *26*
Bottone, Frank G., Jr. 1969- *141*

Bouchard, David 1952- *213*
Earlier sketch in SATA *117*
Boucher, (Clarence) Carter 1954- *129*
Boudelang, Bob
See Pell, Ed(ward)
Boudreau, Helene 1969- *238*
Boughton, Richard 1954- *75*
Boulet, Susan Seddon 1941- *50*
Boulle, Pierre 1912-1994 .... *22*
Obituary *78*
Boulle, Pierre Francois Marie-Louis
See Boulle, Pierre
Boulton, Jane 1921- *91*
Bouma, Paddy 1947- *128*
Bour, Daniele 1939- *62*
Bourbonniere, Sylvie 1966- *182*
Bourdon, David 1934-1998 .... *46*
Bourgeois, Paulette 1951- *153*
Bourne, Lesley
See Marshall, Evelyn
Bourne, Miriam Anne 1931-1989 .... *16*
Obituary *63*
Boutavant, Marc 1970- *200*
Boutet de Monvel, (Louis) M(aurice) 1850(?)-1913 .... *30*
See also CLR *32*
Bouwman, Heather M.
See Bouwman, H.M.
Bouwman, H.M. *209*
Bova, Ben 1932- *133*
Earlier sketches in SATA *6, 68*
See also CLR *96*
Bova, Benjamin William
See Bova, Ben
Bovaird, Anne E(lizabeth) 1960- *90*
Bow, Erin 1972- *237*
Bow, Patricia 1946- *168*
Bowden, Joan Chase 1925- *51*
Brief entry *38*
Bowe, Julie 1962- *194*
Bowen, Alexandria Russell *97*
Bowen, Andy Russell
See Bowen, Alexandria Russell
Bowen, Anne 1952- *202*
Earlier sketch in SATA *170*
Bowen, Betty Morgan
See West, Betty
Bowen, Catherine (Shober) Drinker 1897-1973 .... *7*
Bowen, David
See Bowen, Joshua David
Bowen, Fred 1953- *233*
Earlier sketch in SATA *136*
Bowen, Joshua David 1930- *22*
Bowen, Rhys
See Quin-Harkin, Janet
Bowen, Robert Sydney 1900-1977 .... *52*
Obituary *21*
Bowermaster, Jon 1954- *135*
Earlier sketch in SATA *77*
Bowers, Richard J.
See Bowers, Rick
Bowers, Rick 1952- *227*
Bowers, Terrell L. 1945- *101*
Bowers, Terry
See Bowers, Terrell L.
Bowers, Tim *218*
Earlier sketch in SATA *185*
Bowie, C. W.
See Old, Wendie C(orbin) and Wirths, Claudine (Turner) G(ibson)
Bowie, Jim
See Norwood, Victor G(eorge) C(harles) and Stratemeyer, Edward L.
Bowkett, Stephen 1953- *67*
Bowler, Jan Brett
See Brett, Jan
Bowler, Tim 1953- *209*
Earlier sketch in SATA *149*
Bowman, Catherine
See Smith, Cat Bowman
Bowman, Crystal 1951- *105*
Bowman, James Cloyd 1880-1961 .... *23*
Bowman, John S(tewart) 1931- *16*
Bowman, Kathleen (Gill) 1942- *52*
Brief entry *40*
Bowman, Leslie
See Bowman, Leslie W.
Bowman, Leslie W. *182*
Bowsher, Melodie *195*
Boxall, Ed *178*
Boyce, Frank Cottrell *182*
Boyce, George A(rthur) 1898- *19*
Boyd, Candy Dawson 1946- *72*
See also CLR *50*
Boyd, Pauline
See Schock, Pauline
Boyd, Selma
See Acuff, Selma Boyd
Boyd, Waldo T. 1918- *18*
Boyden, Linda 1948- *238*
Earlier sketch in SATA *143*
Boyer, Allen B. 1963- *153*
Boyer, Robert E(rnst) 1929- *22*
Boyes, Vivien 1952- *106*
Boyes, Vivien Elizabeth
See Boyes, Vivien
Boyle, Ann (Peters) 1916- *10*
Boyle, Bob *232*
Boyle, Eleanor Vere (Gordon) 1825-1916 .... *28*
Boyle, Robert II
See Boyle, Bob
Boyle, Robert H. 1928- *65*
Boylston, Helen Dore 1895-1984 .... *23*
Obituary *39*
Boyne, John 1971- *181*
Boynton, Sandra (Keith) 1953- *152*
Brief entry *38*
Earlier sketches in SATA *57, 107*
See also CLR *105*
Boz
See Dickens, Charles
Bozarth, Jan *227*
Braasch, Gary *201*
Bracegirdle, Paul
See Bracegirdle, P.J.
Bracegirdle, P.J. *236*
Bracken, Alexandra 1987- *233*
Bracken, Charles
See Pellowski, Michael (Joseph)
Brackers de Hugo, Pierre 1960- *115*
Brackett, Dolli Tingle 1911-1993 .... *137*
Brackett, Virginia 1950- *166*
Earlier sketch in SATA *121*
Brackett, Virginia Roberts Meredith
See Brackett, Virginia
Bradbury, Bianca (Ryley) 1908-1982 .... *56*
Earlier sketch in SATA *3*
Bradbury, Edward P.
See Moorcock, Michael
Bradbury, Ray 1920- *123*
Earlier sketches in SATA *11, 64*
See also CLR *174*
Bradbury, Ray Douglas
See Bradbury, Ray
Bradby, Marie *161*
Bradfield, Carl 1942- *91*
Bradford, Ann (Liddell) 1917- *56*
Brief entry *38*
Bradford, Barbara Taylor 1933- *66*
Bradford, Chris 1974- *215*
Bradford, Emma
See Perrin, Pat
Bradford, Karleen 1936- *96*
Earlier sketch in SATA *48*
Bradford, Lois J(ean) 1936- *36*
Bradford, Richard (Roark) 1932-2002 .... *59*
Obituary *135*
Bradford, Sally
See Bradford, Barbara Taylor
Bradley, Duane
See Sanborn, Duane
Bradley, Kimberly Brubaker 1967- *179*
Bradley, Marion Zimmer 1930-1999 .... *139*
Obituary *116*
Earlier sketch in SATA *90*
See also CLR *158*
Bradley, Timothy J. *193*
Bradley, Virginia 1912- *23*
Bradley, Will
See Strickland, Brad
Bradman, Tony 1954- *152*
Earlier sketch in SATA *81*
Bradshaw, Gillian (Joan) 1949- *118*
Bradshaw, Gillian 1956- *127*
Bradshaw, Gillian Marucha
See Bradshaw, Gillian
Bradstreet, T. J.
See Thesman, Jean
Brady, Esther Wood 1905-1987 .... *31*
Obituary *53*
Brady, Irene 1943- *4*
Brady, Kimberley S. 1953- *101*
Brady, Kimberley Smith
See Brady, Kimberley S.
Brady, Lillian 1902- *28*
Braeuner, Shellie 1966(?)- *233*
Bragdon, Elspeth MacDuffie 1897-1980 .... *6*
Bragdon, Lillian Jacot *24*
Brager, Bruce L. 1949- *146*
Bragg, Georgia *225*
Bragg, Mabel Caroline 1870-1945 .... *24*
Bragg, Michael 1948- *46*
Bragg, Ruth Gembicki 1943- *77*
Brahm, Sumishta 1954- *58*
Brailsford, Frances
See Wosmek, Frances
Brainerd, John W(hiting) 1918- *65*
Braithwaite, Althea 1940- *23*
Autobiography Feature *119*
See also SAAS *24*
Brallier, Jess M. 1953- *226*
Bram, Elizabeth 1948- *30*
Bramsen, Carin *227*
Bramsen, Kirsten *228*
Brancato, Robin F. 1936- *97*
See also CLR *32*
See also SAAS *9*
Brancato, Robin Fidler
See Brancato, Robin F.
Branch, Muriel Miller 1943- *152*
Earlier sketch in SATA *94*
Brand, Christianna
See Lewis, Mary
Brand, Rebecca
See Charnas, Suzy McKee
Brande, Robin *194*
Brandel, Marc 1919- *71*
Brandenberg, Alexa (Demetria) 1966- *97*
Brandenberg, Aliki 1929- *157*
Earlier sketches in SATA *2, 35, 75, 113*
See also CLR *71*
Brandenberg, Franz 1932- *75*
Earlier sketches in SATA *8, 35*
Brandenburg, Jim 1945- *87*
Brandhorst, Carl T(heodore) 1898-1988 .... *23*
Brandis, Marianne 1938- *149*
Earlier sketches in SATA *59, 96*
Brandon, Brumsic, Jr. 1927- *9*
Brandon, Curt
See Bishop, Curtis (Kent)
Brandreth, Gyles 1948- *28*
Brandreth, Gyles Daubeney
See Brandreth, Gyles
Brandt, Catharine 1905-1997 .... *40*
Brandt, Keith
See Sabin, Louis
Brandt, Sue R(eading) 1916- *59*
Branfield, John (Charles) 1931- *11*
Branford, Henrietta 1946-1999 .... *106*

Branley, Franklyn M(ansfield) 1915-2002 .. *136*
Earlier sketches in SATA *4, 68*
See also CLR *13*
See also SAAS *16*
Brannen, Sarah S. *202*
Branscum, Robbie (Tilley) 1937-1997 .... *72*
Obituary *96*
Earlier sketch in SATA *23*
See also SAAS *17*
Bransom, (John) Paul 1885-1979 .... *43*
Brashares, Ann 1967- *188*
Earlier sketch in SATA *145*
See also CLR *113*
Brassard, France 1963- *186*
Braswell, E.J.
See Lynn, Tracy
Braswell, Elizabeth J.
See Lynn, Tracy
Braswell, Liz
See Lynn, Tracy
Bratton, Helen 1899-1986 .... *4*
Bratun, Katy 1950- *160*
Earlier sketch in SATA *83*
Braude, Michael 1936- *23*
Braun, Lilian Jackson 1916(?)-2011 .... *109*
Brautigan, Richard 1935-1984 .... *56*
Brautigan, Richard Gary
See Brautigan, Richard
Bray, Libba 1964- *203*
Earlier sketch in SATA *159*
Bray, Martha E.
See Bray, Libba
Braymer, Marjorie Elizabeth 1911-1988 .... *6*
Brazil, Angela 1869(?)-1947
See CLR *157*
Breathed, Berke 1957- *161*
Earlier sketch in SATA *86*
See Breathed, Berkeley
Breathed, Berkeley *229*
See Breathed, Berke
Breathed, Guy Berkeley
See Breathed, Berke
Brecht, Edith 1895-1975 .... *6*
Obituary *25*
Breck, Vivian
See Breckenfeld, Vivian Gurney
Breckenfeld, Vivian Gurney 1895-1992 .... *1*
Breda, Tjalmar
See DeJong, David C(ornel)
Bredeson, Carmen 1944- *163*
Earlier sketch in SATA *98*
Breen, M.E. *216*
Breen, Molly
See Breen, M.E.
Breen, Steve 1970- *186*
Breinburg, Petronella 1927- *11*
See also CLR *31*
Breisky, William J(ohn) 1928- *22*
Brenaman, Miriam *172*
Brenna, Beverley 1962- *226*
Brennan, Caitlin
See Tarr, Judith
Brennan, Gale (Patrick) 1927- *64*
Brief entry *53*
Brennan, Herbie 1940- *214*
Autobiography Feature *214*
Earlier sketches in SATA *140, 183*
Brennan, J. H.
See Brennan, Herbie
Brennan, James Herbert
See Brennan, Herbie
Brennan, Jan
See Brennan, Herbie
Brennan, Joseph Lomas 1903-2000 .... *6*
Brennan, Linda Crotta 1952- *130*
Brennan, Sarah Rees 1983- *221*
Brennan, Tim
See Conroy, John Wesley
Brennan-Nelson, Denise *203*
Brenner, Anita 1905-1974 .... *56*
Brenner, Barbara (Johnes) 1925- *124*
Earlier sketches in SATA *4, 42, 76*
See also SAAS *14*
Brenner, Fred 1920- *36*
Brief entry *34*
Brent, Hope 1935(?)-1984
Obituary *39*
Brent, Stuart 1912-2010 .... *14*
Breskin, Jane
See Zalben, Jane Breskin
Breslin, Theresa *128*
Autobiography Feature *128*
Earlier sketch in SATA *70*
Breslow, Maurice 1935- *72*
Breslow, Maurice A
See Breslow, Maurice
Breslow, Susan 1951- *69*
Brett, Bernard 1925- *22*
Brett, Grace N(eff) 1900-1975 .... *23*
Brett, Jan 1949- *234*
Earlier sketches in SATA *42, 71, 130, 171*
See also CLR *27*
Brett, Jan Churchill
See Brett, Jan
Brett Bowler, Jan
See Brett, Jan
Brewer, Heather 1973- *196*
Brewer, James D. 1951- *108*
Brewer, Paul 1950- *230*
Brewer, Sally King 1947- *33*
Brewster, Benjamin
See Folsom, Franklin (Brewster)
Brewster, Hugh 1950- *191*
Earlier sketch in SATA *95*
Brewster, Patience 1952- *97*
Brewton, John E(dmund) 1898-1982 .... *5*
Brezenoff, Steve 1974- *236*
Brezenoff, Steven
See Brezenoff, Steve
Breznak, Irene *218*
Brian, Dennis 1971- *229*
Brian, Janeen (Paulette) 1948- *141*
Briant, Ed *218*
Earlier sketch in SATA *180*
Brick, John 1922-1973 .... *10*
Brickman, Robin D. 1954- *155*
Bride, Nadja
See Nobisso, Josephine
Bridgers, Sue Ellen 1942- *90*
Autobiography Feature *109*
Earlier sketch in SATA *22*
See also CLR *18*
See also SAAS *1*
Bridges, Laurie
See Bruck, Lorraine
Bridges, Ruby (Nell) 1954- *131*
Bridges, William (Andrew) 1901-1984 .... *5*
Bridwell, Norman (Ray) 1928- *138*
Earlier sketches in SATA *4, 68*
See also CLR *96*
Brier, Howard M(axwell) 1903-1969 .... *8*
Brierley, (Louise) 1958- *59*
Briggs, Katharine Mary 1898-1980 .... *101*
Obituary *25*
Briggs, Peter 1921-1975 .... *39*
Obituary *31*
Briggs, Raymond 1934- *184*
Earlier sketches in SATA *23, 66, 131*
See also CLR *168*
Briggs, Raymond Redvers
See Briggs, Raymond
Bright, Paul 1949- *231*
Earlier sketch in SATA *182*
Bright, Robert Sr.) 1902-1988 .... *63*
Obituary *60*
Earlier sketch in SATA *24*
Bright, Robert Douglas
See Bright, Robert Sr.)
Bright, Sarah
See Shine, Deborah
Brightfield, Richard 1927- *65*
Brief entry *53*
Brightfield, Rick
See Brightfield, Richard
Brighton, Catherine 1943- *206*
Earlier sketches in SATA *65, 107*
Brill, Marlene Targ 1945- *124*
Earlier sketch in SATA *77*
Brimberg, Stanlee 1947- *9*
Brimner, Larry Dane 1949- *232*
Autobiography Feature *112*
Earlier sketches in SATA *79, 170*
Brin, David 1950- *65*
Brin, Ruth Firestone 1921- *22*
Brinckloe, Julie 1950- *13*
Brinckloe, Julie Lorraine
See Brinckloe, Julie
Brindel, June (Rachuy) 1919- *7*
Brindle, Max
See Fleischman, Sid
Brindze, Ruth 1903-1984 .... *23*
Brink, Carol Ryrie 1895-1981 .... *100*
Obituary *27*
Earlier sketches in SATA *1, 31*
See also CLR *149*
Brinsmead, H. F.
See Brinsmead, H(esba) F(ay)
Brinsmead, H. F(ay)
See Brinsmead, H(esba) F(ay)
Brinsmead, H(esba) F(ay) 1922- *78*
Earlier sketch in SATA *18*
See also CLR *47*
See also SAAS *5*
Briquebec, John
See Rowland-Entwistle, (Arthur) Theodore (Henry)
Brisbane, Henry R.
See Ellis, Edward S.
Brisco, P. A.
See Matthews, Patricia
Brisco, Patty
See Matthews, Patricia
and Matthews, Clayton (Hartley)
Briscoe, Jill (Pauline) 1935- *56*
Brief entry *47*
Brisley, Joyce Lankester 1896-1978 .... *22*
Obituary *84*
Brissenden, Connie
See Brissenden, Constance
Brissenden, Constance 1947- *150*
Brisson, Pat 1951- *177*
Autobiography Feature *133*
Earlier sketches in SATA *67, 128, 133*
Bristow, David *237*
Bristow, David L.
See Bristow, David
Britt, Albert 1874-1969
Obituary *28*
Britt, Dell 1934- *1*
Brittain, Bill
See Brittain, William
Brittain, C. Dale 1948- *82*
Brittain, William 1930- *76*
Earlier sketch in SATA *36*
See also SAAS *7*
Brittingham, Geoffrey (Hugh) 1959- *76*
Brittney, L. *209*
Britton, Kate
See Stegeman, Janet Allais
Britton, Louisa
See McGuire, Leslie (Sarah)
Britton, Rick 1952- *82*
Bro, Margueritte (Harmon) 1894-1977 .... *19*
Obituary *27*
Broach, Elise 1963- *173*
Broadhead, Helen Cross 1913- *25*
Broadway, Hannah *208*
Brochmann, Elizabeth 1938- *41*
Brock, Betty (Carter) 1923-2003 .... *4*
Obituary *150*

Brock, C(harles) E(dmund) 1870-1938 .... *42*
Brief entry *32*
Brock, Delia
See Ephron, Delia
Brock, Emma L(illian) 1886-1974 .... *8*
Brock, H(enry) M(atthew) 1875-1960 .... *42*
Brockett, Eleanor Hall 1913-1967 .... *10*
Brockman, C(hristian) Frank 1902-1985 .... *26*
Brockmeier, Kevin 1972- *176*
Broda, Ron 1954- *209*
Broderick, Dorothy M. 1929- *5*
Brodeur, Ruth Wallace
See Wallace-Brodeur, Ruth
Brodie, Sally
See Cavin, Ruth
Brodien-Jones, Chris
See Brodien-Jones, Christine
Brodien-Jones, Christine 1950- *233*
Brodsky, Beverly
See McDermott, Beverly Brodsky
Brody, Wendy
See Staub, Wendy Corsi
Broekel, Rainer Lothar
See Broekel, Ray
Broekel, Ray 1923- *38*
Broekstra, Lorette 1964- *189*
Earlier sketch in SATA *124*
Brogden, Sherryl
See Jordan, Sherryl
Broger, Achim
See Broger, Achim
Broger, Achim 1944- *31*
Broida, Marian *154*
Brokamp, Marilyn 1920- *10*
Broman, Fred
See Moseley, James W(illett)
Bromely, Anne C. 1950- *234*
Bromhall, Winifred *26*
Brommer, Gerald F(rederick) 1927- *28*
Brondfield, Jerome 1913-1998 .... *22*
Brondfield, Jerry
See Brondfield, Jerome
Bronner, Stephen Eric 1949- *101*
Bronowski, Jacob 1908-1974 .... *55*
Bronson, Alice
See Watkins, Dawn L.
Bronson, Linda *203*
Bronson, Lynn
See Lampman, Evelyn Sibley
Bronson, Wilfrid Swancourt 1894-1985
Obituary *43*
Brook, Judith (Penelope) 1926- *59*
Brief entry *51*
Brook, Judy
See Brook, Judith (Penelope)
Brooke, L(eonard) Leslie 1862-1940 .... *17*
See also CLR *20*
Brooke, William J. 1946- *139*
Brooke-Haven, P.
See Wodehouse, P. G.
Brooker, Kyrsten *199*
Brookins, Dana 1931- *28*
Brooks, Anita
See Abramovitz, Anita (Zeltner Brooks)
Brooks, Bill 1939- *59*
Brooks, Bruce 1950- *112*
Brief entry *53*
Earlier sketch in SATA *72*
See also CLR *25*
Brooks, Caryl 1924- *84*
Brooks, Charlotte K(endrick) 1918-1998 .... *24*
Obituary *112*
Brooks, Erik 1972- *236*
Earlier sketches in SATA *152, 182*
Brooks, George
See Baum, L. Frank
Brooks, Gwendolyn 1917-2000 .... *6*
Obituary *123*
See also CLR *27*
Brooks, Gwendolyn Elizabeth
See Brooks, Gwendolyn
Brooks, Jerome 1931- *23*
Brooks, Kevin 1959- *197*
Earlier sketch in SATA *150*
Brooks, Kevin M.
See Brooks, Kevin
Brooks, Laurie *209*
Brooks, Lester 1924- *7*
Brooks, Martha 1944- *134*
Autobiography Feature *134*
Earlier sketches in SATA *68, 121*
Brooks, Maurice (Graham) 1900- *45*
Brooks, Polly Schoyer 1912- *12*
Brooks, Ron 1948- *212*
Brief entry *33*
Earlier sketch in SATA *94*
Brooks, Ronald George
See Brooks, Ron
Brooks, Terry 1944- *60*
Brooks, Walter R(ollin) 1886-1958 .... *17*
Brooks-Hill, Helen (Mason) 1908-1994 .... *59*
Broome, Errol 1937- *158*
Earlier sketch in SATA *105*
Brophy, Nannette 1963- *73*
Brosnan, James Patrick 1929- *14*
Brosnan, Jim
See Brosnan, James Patrick
Brostoff, Anita 1931- *132*
Brothers Grimm
See Grimm, Jacob Ludwig Karl
and Grimm, Wilhelm Karl
Brothers Hildebrandt, The
See Hildebrandt, Greg
and Hildebrandt, Tim
Brougham, Jason 1971(?)- *238*
Broun, Emily
See Sterne, Emma Gelders
Brouwer, S. W.
See Brouwer, Sigmund (W.)
Brouwer, Sigmund (W.) 1959- *109*
Brow, Thea 1934- *60*
Brower, Millicent *8*
Brower, Pauline 1929- *22*
Browin, Frances Williams 1898-1986 .... *5*
Brown, Alan
See Brown, Alan James
Brown, Alan James 1947- *232*
Brown, Alexis
See Baumann, Amy Beeching
Brown, Anne Ensign 1937- *61*
Brown, Beverly Swerdlow *97*
Brown, Bill
See Brown, William L(ouis)
Brown, Billye Walker
See Cutchen, Billye Walker
Brown, Bob
See Brown, Robert Joseph
Brown, Buck 1936- *45*
Brown, Calef *217*
Earlier sketch in SATA *179*
Brown, Cassie 1919-1986 .... *55*
Brown, Charlotte Lewis *181*
Brown, Conrad 1922- *31*
Brown, Craig 1947- *224*
Brown, Craig 1947- *224*
Earlier sketch in SATA *73*
Brown, Craig McFarland
See Brown, Craig
Brown, David
See Brown, David A(lan)
and Myller, Rolf
Brown, Dee 1908-2002 .... *110*
Obituary *141*
Earlier sketch in SATA *5*
Brown, Dee Alexander
See Brown, Dee
Brown, Don 1949- *200*
Earlier sketch in SATA *172*
Brown, Drew T. III 1955- *83*
Brown, Drollene P. 1939- *53*
Brown, Elbrite *198*
Brown, Eleanor Frances 1908-1987 .... *3*
Brown, Elizabeth Ferguson 1937- *153*
Brown, Elizabeth M(yers) 1915- *43*
Brown, Fern G. 1918- *34*
Brown, (Robert) Fletch 1923- *42*
Brown, Fornan 1901-1996 .... *71*
Obituary *88*
Brown, George Earl 1883-1964 .... *11*
Brown, George Mackay 1921-1996 .... *35*
Brown, Irene Bennett 1932- *3*
Brown, Irving
See Adams, William Taylor
Brown, Ivor (John Carnegie) 1891-1974 .... *5*
Obituary *26*
Brown, Jane Clark 1930- *81*
Brown, Janet Mitsui *87*
Brown, Jennifer 1972- *227*
Brown, Jo 1964- *170*
Brown, Joanne 1933- *147*
Brown, Joe David 1915-1976 .... *44*
Brown, Joseph E(dward) 1929- *59*
Brief entry *51*
Brown, Judith Gwyn 1933- *20*
Brown, Judy
See Chayil, Eishes
Brown, Kathryn 1955- *168*
Earlier sketch in SATA *98*
Brown, Kathy
See Brown, Kathryn
Brown, Ken (James) *129*
Brown, Kevin 1960- *101*
Brown, Laurene Krasny 1945- *99*
Earlier sketch in SATA *54*
Brown, Laurie Krasny
See Brown, Laurene Krasny
Brown, Leo *225*
Brown, Lisa *234*
Brown, Lloyd Arnold 1907-1966 .... *36*
Brown, Mahlon A.
See Ellis, Edward S.
Brown, Marc (Tolon) 1946- *145*
Earlier sketches in SATA *10, 53, 80*
See also CLR *29*
Brown, Marcia (Joan) 1918- *47*
Earlier sketch in SATA *7*
See also CLR *12*
Brown, Margaret Wise 1910-1952 .... *100*
See also YABC *2*
See also CLR *107*
Brown, Margery (Wheeler) *78*
Earlier sketch in SATA *5*
Brown, Marion Marsh 1908-2001 .... *6*
Brown, Monica 1969- *233*
Brown, Myra Berry 1918- *6*
Brown, Palmer 1919- *36*
Brown, Pamela (Beatrice) 1924-1989 .... *5*
Obituary *61*
Brown, Paul 1942- *221*
Brown, Peter 1979- *178*
Brown, Rachel W.N. 1947- *203*
Brown, Reeve Lindbergh
See Lindbergh, Reeve
Brown, Richard
See Brown, Rick
Brown, Richard E.
See Brown, Rick
Brown, Rick 1946- *226*
Earlier sketch in SATA *61*
Brown, Robert Joseph 1907-1989 .... *14*
Brown, Rod 1961- *232*
Brown, Roderick (Langmere) Haig-
See Haig-Brown, Roderick (Langmere)
Brown, Rosalie
See Moore, Rosalie (Gertrude)
Brown, Roswell
See Webb, Jean Francis (III)
Brown, Roy (Frederick) 1921-1982 .... *51*
Obituary *39*
Brown, Ruth 1941- *170*
Earlier sketch in SATA *105*
Brown, Scott 1971- *134*
Brown, Sue Ellen 1954- *81*

Brown, Tameka Fryer ... *235*
Brown, Tami Lewis ... *238*
Brown, Tricia 1954- ... *114*
Brown, Vinson 1912-1991 ... *19*
Brown, Walter R(eed) 1929- ... *19*
Brown, Will
See Ainsworth, William Harrison
Brown, William L(ouis) 1910-1964 ... *5*
Browne, Anthony 1946- ... *163*
Brief entry ... *44*
Earlier sketches in SATA *45, 61, 105*
See also CLR *156*
Browne, Anthony Edward Tudor
See Browne, Anthony
Browne, Dik
See Browne, Richard Arthur Allen
Browne, Hablot Knight 1815-1882 ... *21*
Browne, Matthew
See Rands, William Brighty
Browne, Nicki M.
See Browne, N.M.
Browne, Nicky Matthews
See Browne, N.M.
Browne, N.M. 1960- ... *167*
Browne, Richard Arthur Allen 1917-1989 ... *67*
Brief entry ... *38*
Browne, Vee F. 1956- ... *214*
Earlier sketch in SATA *90*
Browning, Diane ... *233*
Browning, Robert 1812-1889
See YABC *1*
See also CLR *97*
Browning, Tom 1949- ... *226*
Brownjohn, Alan 1931- ... *6*
Brownlee, Walter 1930- ... *62*
Brownlie, Betty 1946- ... *159*
Brownlow, Kevin 1938- ... *65*
Brownlow, Mike ... *183*
Brownridge, William R(oy) 1932- ... *94*
Broyles, Anne 1953- ... *201*
Bruce, Dorita Fairlie 1885-1970
Obituary ... *27*
Bruce, Harry 1934- ... *77*
Bruce, Mary 1927- ... *1*
Bruchac, Joseph III
See Bruchac, Joseph
Bruchac, Joseph 1942- ... *228*
Autobiography Feature ... *176*
Earlier sketches in SATA *42, 89, 131, 176*
See also CLR *46*
Bruchac, Margaret M.
See Bruchac, Marge
Bruchac, Marge ... *181*
Bruck, Lorraine 1921- ... *55*
Brief entry ... *46*
Bruel, Nick ... *205*
Earlier sketch in SATA *166*
Bruel, Robert O. 1929-2002 ... *189*
Bruemmer, Fred 1929- ... *47*
Brugman, Alyssa (F.) 1974- ... *152*
Brumbeau, Jeff 1955- ... *157*
Bruna, Dick 1927- ... *76*
Brief entry ... *30*
Earlier sketch in SATA *43*
See also CLR *7*
Brunelle, Lynn ... *233*
Brunhoff, Jean de 1899-1937 ... *24*
See also CLR *116*
Brunhoff, Laurent de 1925- ... *150*
Earlier sketches in SATA *24, 71*
See also CLR *116*
Brunkus, Denise ... *204*
Bruno, Elsa Knight 1935-2009 ... *221*
Brunskill, Elizabeth Ann Flatt
See Flatt, Lizann
Brush, Karen A(lexandra) 1960- ... *85*
Brussel-Smith, Bernard 1914- ... *58*
Brust, Steven 1955- ... *121*
Earlier sketch in SATA *86*
Brust, Steven Karl Zoltan
See Brust, Steven
Brustlein, Daniel 1904- ... *40*
Brustlein, Janice Tworkov -2000 ... *40*
Obituary ... *126*
Brutschy, Jennifer 1960- ... *84*
Bryan, Ashley 1923- ... *178*
Earlier sketches in SATA *31, 72, 132*
See also CLR *66*
Bryan, Ashley F.
See Bryan, Ashley
Bryan, Dorothy M. 1896(?)-1984
Obituary ... *39*
Bryan, Jennifer ... *190*
Bryan, Kathleen
See Tarr, Judith
Bryan, Sean ... *192*
Bryant, Bernice (Morgan) 1908-1976 ... *11*
Bryant, Jen 1960- ... *218*
Earlier sketches in SATA *94, 175*
Bryant, Jennifer
See Bryant, Jen
Bryant, Jennifer Fisher
See Bryant, Jen
Bryant, Laura J. ... *240*
Earlier sketch in SATA *176*
Brychta, Alex 1956- ... *21*
Brynie, Faith H. 1946- ... *113*
Brynie, Faith Hickman
See Brynie, Faith H.
Bryson, Bernarda 1903-2004 ... *9*
Buba, Joy Flinsch 1904- ... *44*
Buchan, Bryan 1945- ... *36*
Buchan, John 1875-1940
See YABC *2*
Buchan, Stuart 1942-1987
Obituary ... *54*
Buchanan, Debby 1952- ... *82*
Buchanan, Deborah Leevonne
See Buchanan, Debby
Buchanan, Jane 1956- ... *160*
Buchanan, Lang
See Buchanan, Michael
Buchanan, Lang
See Lang, Diane
Buchanan, Michael 1955- ... *235*
Buchanan, Michael David
See Buchanan, Michael
Buchanan, Paul 1959- ... *116*
Buchanan, Sue 1939- ... *139*
Buchheimer, Naomi Barnett
See Barnett, Naomi
Buchignani, Walter 1965- ... *84*
Buchmann, Stephen L. ... *194*
Buchwald, Art 1925-2007 ... *10*
Buchwald, Arthur
See Buchwald, Art
Buchwald, Emilie 1935- ... *7*
Buck, Gisela 1941- ... *101*
Buck, Lewis 1925- ... *18*
Buck, Margaret Waring 1905-1997 ... *3*
Buck, Nola
See Godwin, Laura
Buck, Pearl S. 1892-1973 ... *25*
Earlier sketch in SATA *1*
Buck, Pearl Sydenstricker
See Buck, Pearl S.
Buck, Siegfried 1941- ... *101*
Buckalew, Clare B.
See Dunkle, Clare B.
Buckeridge, Anthony (Malcolm) 1912-2004 ... *85*
Earlier sketch in SATA *6*
Buckholtz, Eileen (Garber) 1949- ... *54*
Brief entry ... *47*
Buckingham, Royce 1966- ... *210*
Buckingham, Royce Scott
See Buckingham, Royce
Buckler, Ernest 1908-1984 ... *47*
Buckless, Andrea K. 1968- ... *117*
Buckley, Helen E(lizabeth) 1918- ... *90*
Earlier sketch in SATA *2*
Buckley, James, Jr. 1963- ... *166*
Earlier sketch in SATA *114*
Buckley, Michael ... *229*
Earlier sketch in SATA *177*
Buckley, Susan ... *184*
Buckley, Susan Washburn
See Buckley, Susan
Buckley-Archer, Linda ... *185*
Buckmaster, Henrietta
See Stephens, Henrietta Henkle
Bucks, Brad
See Holub, Joan
Budd, E. S.
See Sirimarco, Elizabeth
Budd, Lillian (Peterson) 1897-1989 ... *7*
Budhos, Marina ... *236*
Earlier sketch in SATA *173*
Budhos, Marina Tamar
See Budhos, Marina
Buehler, Stephanie Jona 1956- ... *83*
Buehner, Caralyn 1963- ... *219*
Earlier sketches in SATA *104, 159*
Buehner, Mark 1959- ... *221*
Earlier sketches in SATA *104, 159*
Buehr, Walter Franklin 1897-1971 ... *3*
Buell, Ellen Lewis
See Cash, Ellen Lewis Buell
Buell, Janet 1952- ... *185*
Earlier sketch in SATA *106*
Buergel, Paul-Hermann H. 1949- ... *83*
Buettner, Dan 1960- ... *95*
Buff, Conrad 1886-1975 ... *19*
Buff, Mary (E. Marsh) 1890-1970 ... *19*
Buffett, Jimmy 1946- ... *110*
Earlier sketch in SATA *76*
Buffie, Margaret 1945- ... *161*
Earlier sketches in SATA *71, 107*
See also CLR *39*
Bugbee, Emma 1888(?)-1981
Obituary ... *29*
Bugni, Alice 1951- ... *122*
Bujold, Lois McMaster 1949- ... *136*
Bulfinch, Thomas 1796-1867 ... *35*
Bulion, Leslie 1958- ... *209*
Earlier sketch in SATA *161*
Bull, Angela (Mary) 1936- ... *45*
Bull, Emma 1954- ... *190*
Autobiography Feature ... *103*
Earlier sketch in SATA *99*
Bull, Norman John 1916- ... *41*
Bull, Peter (Cecil) 1912-1984
Obituary ... *39*
Bull, Schuyler M. 1974- ... *138*
Bulla, Clyde R. 1914-2007 ... *139*
Obituary ... *182*
Earlier sketches in SATA *2, 41, 91*
See also SAAS *6*
Bullard, Lisa 1961- ... *142*
Bullen, Alexandra ... *227*
Buller, Jon ... *205*
Bullock, Kathleen (Mary) 1946- ... *77*
Bullock, Robert (D.) 1947- ... *92*
Bulpin, (Barbara) Vicki ... *92*
Bulwer-Lytton, Edward 1803-1873 ... *23*
Bulwer-Lytton, Edward George Earle Lytton
See Bulwer-Lytton, Edward
Bumstead, Kathleen Mary 1918-1987 ... *53*
Bundles, A'Lelia Perry 1952- ... *76*
Bunge, Daniela 1973- ... *207*
Bunin, Catherine 1967- ... *30*
Bunin, Sherry 1925- ... *30*
Bunkers, Suzanne L. 1950- ... *136*
Bunting, A.E.
See Bunting, Eve
Bunting, Anne Evelyn
See Bunting, Eve
Bunting, Eve 1928- ... *235*
Earlier sketches in SATA *18, 64, 110, 158, 196*
See also CLR *82*
Bunting, Glenn (Davison) 1957- ... *22*

Bunyan, John 1628-1688
See CLR *124*
Bupp, Walter
See Garrett, Randall
Burack, Sylvia K. 1916-2003 .... *35*
Obituary *143*
Burbank, Addison (Buswell) 1895-1961 .... *37*
Burch, Joann J(ohansen) *75*
Burch, Robert J(oseph) 1925- *74*
Earlier sketch in SATA *1*
See also CLR *63*
Burchard, Peter Duncan 1921- *143*
Earlier sketches in SATA *5, 74*
See also SAAS *13*
Burchard, S. H.
See Burchard, Sue
Burchard, Sue 1937- *22*
Burchardt, Nellie 1921- *7*
Burckhardt, Marc 1962- *196*
Burden, Andrea 1969-2009 .... *227*
Burdett, Lois *117*
Burdick, Eugene (Leonard) 1918-1965 .... *22*
Burford, Eleanor
See Hibbert, Eleanor Alice Burford
Burg, Ann E. 1954- *217*
Burg, Shana 1968- *204*
Burgan, Michael 1960- *167*
Earlier sketch in SATA *118*
Burger, Carl 1888-1967 .... *9*
Burgess, Ann Marie
See Gerson, Noel Bertram
Burgess, Barbara Hood 1926- *69*
Burgess, Em
See Burgess, Mary Wyche
Burgess, (Frank) Gelett 1866-1951 .... *32*
Brief entry *30*
Burgess, Mark *157*
Burgess, Mary Wyche 1916- *18*
Burgess, Melvin 1954- *198*
Earlier sketches in SATA *96, 146*
Burgess, Michael
See Gerson, Noel Bertram
Burgess, Robert F(orrest) 1927- *4*
Burgess, Starling
See Tudor, Tasha
Burgess, Thornton Waldo 1874-1965 .... *17*
Burgess, Trevor
See Trevor, Elleston
Burgis, Stephanie *241*
Burgwyn, Mebane Holoman 1914-1992 .... *7*
Burke, David 1927- *46*
Burke, Diana G.
See Gallagher, Diana G.
Burke, Diana Gallagher
See Gallagher, Diana G.
Burke, Dianne O'Quinn 1940- *89*
Burke, Janine 1952- *139*
Burke, Jim 1973- *179*
Burke, John
See O'Connor, Richard
Burke, Katie 1953- *168*
Burke, Patrick 1958- *114*
Burke, Ralph
See Garrett, Randall
and Silverberg, Robert
Burkert, Nancy Ekholm 1933- *24*
See also SAAS *14*
Burkett, D. Brent *194*
Burke-Weiner, Kimberly 1962- *95*
Burks, Brian 1955- *95*
Burland, Brian (Berkeley) 1931- *34*
Burland, C. A.
See Burland, Cottie (Arthur)
Burland, Cottie (Arthur) 1905-1983 .... *5*
Burleigh, Robert 1936- *193*
Earlier sketches in SATA *55, 98, 146*
Burlingame, (William) Roger 1889-1967 .... *2*
Burman, Alice Caddy 1896(?)-1977
Obituary *24*
Burman, Ben Lucien 1896-1984 .... *6*
Obituary *40*
Burn, Doris 1923- *1*
Burn, Ted
See Burn, Thomas E.
Burn, Thomas E. 1940- *150*
Burnard, Damon 1963- *115*
Burne, Cristy *238*
Burnett, Constance Buel 1893-1975 .... *36*
Burnett, Frances Eliza Hodgson
See Burnett, Frances Hodgson
Burnett, Frances Hodgson 1849-1924 .... *100*
See also YABC *2*
See also CLR *122*
Burnett, Lindy *210*
Burnett Bossi, Lisa *193*
Burney, Anton
See Hopkins, (Hector) Kenneth
Burnford, Sheila (Philip Cochrane Every)
1918-1984 .... *3*
Obituary *38*
See also CLR *2*
Burnham, Gretchen
See Sprague, Gretchen
Burnham, Nicole 1970- *161*
Burnham, Niki
See Burnham, Nicole
Burnham, Sophy 1936- *65*
Burningham, John 1936- *225*
Earlier sketches in SATA *16, 59, 111, 160*
See also CLR *9*
Burningham, Robin Yoko
See Racoma, Robin Yoko
Burningham, Sarah O'Leary *216*
Burns, Diane L. 1950- *81*
See also SAAS *24*
Burns, Eloise Wilkin
See Wilkin, Eloise
Burns, Florence M. 1905-1988 .... *61*
Burns, Khephra 1950- *92*
Burns, Loree Griffin *193*
Burns, Marilyn 1941- *96*
Brief entry *33*
Burns, Olive Ann 1924-1990 .... *65*
Burns, Patrick 1968- *227*
Burns, Paul C. *5*
Burns, Ray
See Burns, Raymond (Howard)
Burns, Raymond (Howard) 1924- *9*
Burns, Theresa 1961- *84*
Burns, T.R.
See Rayburn, Tricia
Burns, William A. 1909-1999 .... *5*
Burr, Dan 1951- *65*
Burr, Dan 1960- *219*
Burr, Lonnie 1943- *47*
Burrell, Roy E(ric) C(harles) 1923- *72*
Burroughs, Edgar Rice 1875-1950 .... *41*
See also CLR *157*
Burroughs, Jean Mitchell 1908- *28*
Burroughs, Polly 1925- *2*
Burroway, Janet 1936- *23*
Burroway, Janet Gay
See Burroway, Janet
Burstein, Chaya M(alamud) 1923- *64*
Burstein, Fred 1950- *83*
Burstein, John 1949- *54*
Brief entry *40*
Burstein, Stanley M.
See Burstein, Stanley Mayer
Burstein, Stanley Mayer 1941- *175*
Bursztynski, Sue 1953- *114*
Burt, Jesse Clifton 1921-1976 .... *46*
Obituary *20*
Burt, Olive Woolley 1894-1981 .... *4*
Burtinshaw, Julie *185*
Burton, Gennett 1945- *95*
Burton, Hester (Wood-Hill) 1913-2000 .... *74*
Earlier sketch in SATA *7*
See also CLR *1*
See also SAAS *8*
Burton, Leslie
See McGuire, Leslie (Sarah)
Burton, Marilee Robin 1950- *82*
Earlier sketch in SATA *46*
Burton, Maurice 1898-1992 .... *23*
Burton, Rebecca 1970- *183*
Burton, Robert (Wellesley) 1941- *22*
Burton, Virginia Lee 1909-1968 .... *100*
Earlier sketch in SATA *2*
See also CLR *11*
Burton, William H(enry) 1890-1964 .... *11*
Busby, Ailie *192*
Busby, Cylin 1970- *118*
Busby, Edith (A. Lake) (?)-1964
Obituary *29*
Busby, John 1942- *209*
Buscaglia, (Felice) Leo(nardo) 1924-1998 .... *65*
Buscaglia, Leo F.
See Buscaglia, (Felice) Leo(nardo)
Buscema, Stephanie *232*
Busch, Phyllis S. 1909- *30*
Bush, Anne Kelleher
See Kelleher, Anne
Bush, Catherine 1961- *128*
Bush, Jenna 1981- *208*
Bush, Laura 1946- *208*
Bushmiller, Ernest Paul 1905-1982 .... *31*
Bushmiller, Ernie
See Bushmiller, Ernest Paul
Bushnell, Jack 1952- *86*
Busoni, Rafaello 1900-1962 .... *16*
Buss, Helen M.
See Clarke, Margaret
Busse, Sarah Martin *194*
Busselle, Rebecca 1941- *80*
Bustard, Anne 1951- *173*
Butcher, Kristin 1951- *140*
Butenko, Bohdan 1931- *90*
Butler, Beverly Kathleen 1932- *7*
Butler, Bill
See Butler, William Vivian
and Butler, Ernest Alton
and Butler, William Huxford
Butler, Charles 1963- *175*
Earlier sketch in SATA *121*
Butler, Charles Cadman
See Butler, Charles
Butler, Dori Hillestad 1965- *207*
Earlier sketch in SATA *164*
Butler, Dorothy 1925- *73*
Butler, Geoff 1945- *94*
Butler, John 1952- *225*
Butler, M. Christina 1934- *224*
Earlier sketches in SATA *72, 170*
Butler, Octavia 1947-2006 .... *84*
See also CLR *65*
Butler, Octavia E.
See Butler, Octavia
Butler, Octavia Estelle
See Butler, Octavia
Butler, Vivian
See Butler, William Vivian
Butler, William
See Butler, William Vivian
Butler, William Vivian 1927-1987 .... *79*
Butterfield, Moira 1960- *219*
Butters, Dorothy Gilman
See Gilman, Dorothy
Butterworth, Emma Macalik 1928- *43*
Butterworth, Nick 1946- *149*
Earlier sketch in SATA *106*
Butterworth, Oliver 1915-1990 .... *1*
Obituary *66*
Butterworth, W. E.
See Griffin, W. E. B.
Butterworth, William E.
See Griffin, W. E. B.
Butterworth, William Edmund III
See Griffin, W. E. B.
Button, Lana 1968- *229*
Butts, Ed 1951- *177*
Butts, Edward P.
See Butts, Ed

Butts, Ellen R. 1942- ... *93*
Butts, Ellen Rubinstein
See Butts, Ellen R.
Butzer, C. M. 1974- ... *212*
Buxton, Ralph
See Silverstein, Alvin
and Silverstein, Virginia B.
Buyea, Rob 1976- ... *238*
Buzzeo, Toni 1951- ... *215*
Earlier sketch in SATA *135*
Byalick, Marcia 1947- ... *141*
Earlier sketch in SATA *97*
Byard, Carole (Marie) 1941- ... *57*
Byars, Betsy 1928- ... *223*
Autobiography Feature ... *108*
Earlier sketches in SATA *4, 46, 80, 163*
See also CLR *72*
See also SAAS *1*
Byars, Betsy Cromer
See Byars, Betsy
Byfield, Barbara Ninde 1930-1988 ... *8*
Byman, Jeremy 1944- ... *129*
Bynum, Janie ... *133*
Byrd, Elizabeth 1912-1989 ... *34*
Byrd, Nicole
See Zach, Cheryl (Byrd)
Byrd, Robert 1942- ... *226*
Earlier sketches in SATA *33, 112, 158*
Byrd, Robert John
See Byrd, Robert
Byrd, Tim 1964- ... *216*
Byrne, Gayle ... *218*
Byrne, Mary Gregg 1951- ... *162*

C

C. 3. 3.
See Wilde, Oscar
C. E. M.
See Mastrangelo, Charles E(lmer)
Cabaniss, J(ames) Allen 1911-1997 ... *5*
Cabat, Erni 1914- ... *74*
Cabban, Vanessa 1971- ... *176*
Cable, Mary 1920- ... *9*
Cabot, Meg 1967- ... *217*
Earlier sketches in SATA *127, 175*
See also CLR *85*
Cabot, Meggin
See Cabot, Meg
Cabot, Meggin Patricia
See Cabot, Meg
Cabot, Patricia
See Cabot, Meg
Cabral, O. M.
See Cabral, Olga
Cabral, Olga 1909- ... *46*
Cabrera, Cozbi A. 1963- ... *177*
Cabrera, Jane 1968- ... *182*
Earlier sketches in SATA *103, 152*
Cabrera, Marcela 1966- ... *90*
Caddy, Alice
See Burman, Alice Caddy
Cade, Toni
See Bambara, Toni Cade
Cadena, Beth ... *222*
Cadmus and Harmonia
See Buchan, John
Cadnum, Michael 1949- ... *225*
Earlier sketches in SATA *87, 121, 165*
See also CLR *78*
Caduto, Michael J. 1955- ... *103*
Cadwallader, Sharon 1936- ... *7*
Cady, (Walter) Harrison 1877(?)-1970 ... *19*
Caffey, Donna (J.) 1954- ... *110*
Cagle, Malcolm W(infield) 1918- ... *32*
Cahn, Rhoda 1922- ... *37*
Cahn, William 1912-1976 ... *37*
Cain, Arthur H(omer) 1913-1981 ... *3*
Cain, Christopher
See Fleming, Thomas
Cain, Sheridan 1952- ... *186*
Caine, Geoffrey
See Walker, Robert W.
Caines, Jeannette (Franklin) 1938- ... *78*
Brief entry ... *43*
See also CLR *24*
Cairns, Julia 1960(?)- ... *239*
Cairns, Trevor 1922- ... *14*
Calabro, Marian 1954- ... *79*
Caldecott, Moyra 1927- ... *22*
Caldecott, Randolph (J.) 1846-1886 ... *100*
Earlier sketch in SATA *17*
See also CLR *110*
Calder, Charlotte 1952- ... *125*
Calder, David 1932-1997 ... *105*
Calder, Lyn
See Calmenson, Stephanie
Calder, Marie D(onais) 1948- ... *96*
Calderone-Stewart, Lisa
See Calderone-Stewart, Lisa-Marie
Calderone-Stewart, Lisa-Marie 1958- ... *123*
Caldwell, Ben 1973- ... *230*
Caldwell, Doreen (Mary) 1942- ... *71*
Caldwell, John C(ope) 1913-1984 ... *7*
Caletti, Deb 1963- ... *221*
Earlier sketch in SATA *171*
Calhoun, B. B. 1961- ... *98*
Calhoun, Chad
See Barrett, Neal, Jr.
and Cunningham, Chet
and Goulart, Ron
Calhoun, Dia 1959- ... *183*
Earlier sketch in SATA *129*
Calhoun, Mary
See Wilkins, Mary Huiskamp
Calhoun, T.B.
See Bisson, Terry
Cali, Davide 1972- ... *190*
Calif, Ruth 1922- ... *67*
Calkhoven, Laurie 1959- ... *229*
Calkins, Franklin
See Stratemeyer, Edward L.
Call, Greg ... *197*
Call, Hughie Florence 1890-1969 ... *1*
Callahan, Dorothy M. 1934- ... *39*
Brief entry ... *35*
Callahan, Dorothy Monahan
See Callahan, Dorothy M.
Callahan, Philip Serna 1923- ... *25*
Callahan, Sean 1965- ... *222*
Callan, Jamie 1954- ... *59*
Callan, Jim 1951- ... *181*
Callaway, Bernice (Anne) 1923- ... *48*
Callaway, Kathy 1943- ... *36*
Callen, Larry
See Callen, Lawrence Willard, Jr.
Callen, Lawrence Willard, Jr. 1927- ... *19*
Callen, Liz 1951- ... *231*
Callery, Sean ... *233*
Calley, Karin 1965- ... *92*
Calmenson, Stephanie 1952- ... *211*
Brief entry ... *37*
Earlier sketches in SATA *51, 84, 139*
Calonita, Jen ... *216*
Calvert, Elinor H.
See Lasell, Elinor H.
Calvert, John
See Leaf, (Wilbur) Munro
Calvert, Pam 1966- ... *205*
Calvert, Patricia 1931- ... *132*
Earlier sketches in SATA *45, 69*
See also SAAS *17*
Camburn, Carol A.
See Camburn-Bracalente, Carol A.
Camburn-Bracalente, Carol A. 1962- ... *118*
Cameron, Ann 1943- ... *129*
Earlier sketches in SATA *27, 89*
See also SAAS *20*
Cameron, Edna M. 1905-1999 ... *3*
Cameron, Eleanor (Frances) 1912-1996 ... *25*
Obituary ... *93*
Earlier sketch in SATA *1*
See also CLR *72*
See also SAAS *10*
Cameron, Elizabeth
See Nowell, Elizabeth Cameron
Cameron, Elizabeth Jane 1910-1976 ... *32*
Obituary ... *30*
Cameron, Ian
See Payne, Donald Gordon
Cameron, M(alcolm) G(ordon) Graham
See Graham-Cameron, M(alcolm) G(ordon)
Cameron, M. Graham
See Graham-Cameron, M(alcolm) G(ordon)
Cameron, Mike Graham
See Graham-Cameron, M(alcolm) G(ordon)
Cameron, Natalie Russell
See Russell, Natalie
Cameron, Polly 1928- ... *2*
Cameron, Scott 1962- ... *84*
Camp, Charles L. 1893-1975
Obituary ... *31*
Camp, Lindsay 1957- ... *133*
Camp, Madeleine L'Engle
See L'Engle, Madeleine
Camp, Walter (Chauncey) 1859-1925
See YABC *1*
Campbell, (Elizabeth) Andrea 1963- ... *50*
Campbell, Ann R. 1925- ... *11*
Campbell, Bill 1960- ... *89*
Campbell, Bruce
See Epstein, Samuel
Campbell, Camilla 1905-1992 ... *26*
Campbell, Carole R. 1939- ... *125*
Campbell, Hope 1925- ... *20*
Campbell, Hugh 1930- ... *90*
Campbell, Jane
See Edwards, Jane Campbell
Campbell, Julie
See Tatham, Julie Campbell
Campbell, Patricia J(ean) 1930- ... *45*
Campbell, Patty
See Campbell, Patricia J(ean)
Campbell, Peter A. 1948- ... *99*
Campbell, R. W.
See Campbell, Rosemae Wells
Campbell, Robin
See Strachan, Ian
Campbell, Rod 1945- ... *98*
Brief entry ... *44*
Earlier sketch in SATA *51*
Campbell, Rosemae Wells 1909- ... *1*
Campbell, Sarah C. 1966- ... *207*
Camper, Cathy 1956- ... *170*
Campion, Nardi Reeder 1917-2007 ... *22*
Campling, Elizabeth 1948- ... *53*
Campos, Maria de Fatima ... *229*
Campoy, F. Isabel 1946- ... *181*
Earlier sketch in SATA *143*
Camps, Luis 1928- ... *66*
Canales, Viola 1957- ... *141*
Candell, Victor 1903-1977
Obituary ... *24*
Canfield, Dorothea F.
See Fisher, Dorothy (Frances) Canfield
Canfield, Dorothea Frances
See Fisher, Dorothy (Frances) Canfield
Canfield, Dorothy
See Fisher, Dorothy (Frances) Canfield
Canfield, Jack 1944- ... *164*
Canfield, Jane White 1897-1984 ... *32*
Obituary ... *38*
Canfield, Muriel 1935- ... *94*
Canga, C.B. 1976- ... *216*
Canga, Chris
See Canga, C.B.
Caniff, Milton 1907-1988
Obituary ... *58*
Caniff, Milton Arthur Paul
See Caniff, Milton

Cann, Helen 1969- *179*
Earlier sketch in SATA *124*
Cann, Kate 1954- *152*
Earlier sketch in SATA *103*
Cannan, Joanna
See Pullein-Thompson, Joanna Maxwell
Cannell, Jon *196*
Cannell, Jonathan C.
See Cannell, Jon
Cannon, A.E. *202*
Earlier sketches in SATA *93, 163*
Cannon, Ann Edwards
See Cannon, A.E.
Cannon, Bettie (Waddell) 1922- *59*
Cannon, Curt
See Hunter, Evan
Cannon, Eileen E(mily) 1948- *119*
Cannon, Frank
See Mayhar, Ardath
Cannon, Janell 1957- *128*
Earlier sketch in SATA *78*
See also CLR *120*
Cannon, Marian G. 1923- *85*
Cannon, Taffy
See Cannon, Eileen E(mily)
Cantone, AnnaLaura *182*
Cantrell, Julie 1973- *217*
Canusi, Jose
See Barker, S. Omar
Canyon, Christopher 1966- *150*
Earlier sketch in SATA *104*
Caparo, Antonio
See Caparo, Antonio Javier
Caparo, Antonio Javier *205*
Capek, Michael 1947- *142*
Earlier sketch in SATA *96*
Capes, Bernard (Edward Joseph) 1854-1918 .... *116*
Caple, Kathy *193*
Caple, Laurie 1958- *201*
Caplin, Alfred Gerald 1909-1979 .... *61*
Obituary *21*
Caponigro, John Paul 1965- *84*
Capote, Truman 1924-1984 .... *91*
Capozzola, Michael *234*
Capp, Al
See Caplin, Alfred Gerald
Cappel, Constance 1936- *22*
Cappetta, Cynthia 1949- *125*
Cappo, Nan Willard 1955- *143*
Capps, Benjamin (Franklin) 1922- *9*
Cappy Dick
See Cleveland, George
Captain Kangaroo
See Keeshan, Robert J.
Captain Wheeler
See Ellis, Edward S.
Captain Young of Yale
See Stratemeyer, Edward L.
Capucilli, Alyssa Satin 1957- *203*
Earlier sketches in SATA *115, 163*
Capucine
See Mazille, Capucine
Carafoli, Marci
See Balterman, Marcia Ridlon
Caraher, Kim(berley Elizabeth) 1961- *105*
Caraker, Mary 1929- *74*
Caras, Roger A(ndrew) 1928-2001 .... *12*
Obituary *127*
Caravantes, Peggy 1935- *140*
Caraway, Caren 1939- *57*
Carbone, Elisa 1954- *173*
Earlier sketches in SATA *81, 137*
Carbone, Elisa Lynn
See Carbone, Elisa
Carbonnier, Jeanne 1894-1974 .... *3*
Obituary *34*
Card, Orson Scott 1951- *241*
Earlier sketches in SATA *83, 127*
See also CLR *116*
Cardinale, Christopher *231*
Cardon, Laurent 1962- *230*
Care, Felicity
See Coury, Louise Andree
Carew, Jan 1925- *51*
Brief entry *40*
Carew, Jan Rynveld
See Carew, Jan
Carey, Benedict 1960- *219*
Carey, Bonnie
See Marshall, Bonnie C.
Carey, Charles W., Jr. 1951- *170*
Carey, Ernestine Gilbreth 1908-2006 .... *2*
Obituary *177*
Carey, Janet Lee 1954(?)- *225*
Earlier sketch in SATA *185*
Carey, Lisa *110*
Carey, M. V.
See Carey, Mary V(irginia)
Carey, Mary V(irginia) 1925-1994 .... *44*
Brief entry *39*
Carey, Peter 1943- *94*
Carey, Peter Philip
See Carey, Peter
Carey, Valerie Scho 1949- *60*
Carheden, Goorel Kristina
See Naaslund, Goorel Kristina
Carigiet, Alois 1902-1985 .... *24*
Obituary *47*
See also CLR *38*
Carini, Edward 1923- *9*
Carkeet, David 1946- *75*
Carle, Eric 1929- *163*
Earlier sketches in SATA *4, 65, 120*
See also CLR *72*
See also SAAS *6*
Carleton, Captain L. C.
See Ellis, Edward S.
Carleton, Captain Latham C.
See Ellis, Edward S.
Carleton, Latham C.
See Ellis, Edward S.
Carley, V(an Ness) Royal 1906-1976
Obituary *20*
Carling, Amelia Lau 1949- *164*
Earlier sketch in SATA *119*
Carlisle, Carolyn
See Hawes, Louise
Carlisle, Clark
See Holding, James (Clark Carlisle, Jr.)
Carlisle, Olga Andreyev 1930- *35*
Carlock, Miriam
See Eyerly, Jeannette
Carls, Claudia 1978- *198*
Carlsen, G(eorge) Robert 1917- *30*
Carlsen, Ruth C(hristoffer) 1918- *2*
Carlson, Bernice Wells 1910- *8*
Carlson, Christopher C. *202*
Carlson, Dale (Bick) 1935- *1*
Carlson, Daniel (Bick) 1960- *27*
Carlson, Kirsten 1968- *192*
Carlson, Kirsten M.
See Carlson, Kirsten
Carlson, Laurie 1952- *173*
Earlier sketch in SATA *101*
Carlson, Laurie Winn
See Carlson, Laurie
Carlson, Melody 1956- *171*
Earlier sketch in SATA *113*
Carlson, Nancy 1953- *213*
Brief entry *45*
Earlier sketches in SATA *56, 90, 144*
Carlson, Nancy L.
See Carlson, Nancy
Carlson, Natalie Savage 1906-1997 .... *68*
Earlier sketch in SATA *2*
See also SAAS *4*
Carlson, Susan Johnston 1953- *88*
Carlson, Vada F. 1897- *16*
Carlstrom, Nancy White 1948- *215*
Brief entry *48*
Earlier sketches in SATA *53, 92, 156*
Carlton, Keith
See Robertson, Keith (Carlton)
Carlton, Susan 1960- *195*
Carluccio, Maria *236*
Carlyon, Richard *55*
Carman, Bill
See Carman, William
Carman, Patrick 1966- *233*
Earlier sketches in SATA *161, 197*
Carman, William *223*
Carmer, Carl (Lamson) 1893-1976 .... *37*
Obituary *30*
Carmer, Elizabeth Black 1904- *24*
Carmi, Giora 1944- *149*
Earlier sketch in SATA *79*
Carmichael, Carrie
See Carmichael, Harriet
Carmichael, Clay *218*
Carmichael, Harriet *40*
Carmody, Isobelle 1958- *191*
Earlier sketch in SATA *161*
Carmody, Isobelle Jane
See Carmody, Isobelle
Carney, Elizabeth 1981- *199*
Carney, Jeff 1962- *196*
Carney, Mary Lou 1949- *170*
Carol, Bill J.
See Knott, William C(ecil, Jr.)
Caron, Romi
See Caron-Kyselkova', Romana
Caron-Kyselkova', Romana 1967- *94*
Caroselli, Remus F(rancis) 1916- *36*
Carpelan, Bo 1926- *8*
Carpelan, Bo Gustaf Bertelsson
See Carpelan, Bo
Carpenter, (John) Allan 1917- *81*
Earlier sketch in SATA *3*
Carpenter, Angelica Shirley 1945- *153*
Earlier sketch in SATA *71*
Carpenter, Frances 1890-1972 .... *3*
Obituary *27*
Carpenter, John 1948- *58*
Carpenter, John Howard
See Carpenter, John
Carpenter, Johnny
See Carpenter, John
Carpenter, Nancy *215*
Carpenter, Nancy Sippel
See Carpenter, Nancy
Carpenter, Patricia (Healy Evans) 1920- *11*
Carr, Glyn
See Styles, (Frank) Showell
Carr, Harriett H(elen) 1899-1977 .... *3*
Carr, Jan 1953- *132*
Earlier sketch in SATA *89*
Carr, M. J.
See Carr, Jan
Carr, Mary Jane 1899-1988 .... *2*
Obituary *55*
Carr, Philippa
See Hibbert, Eleanor Alice Burford
Carr, Roger Vaughan 1937- *95*
Carrel, Annette Felder 1929- *90*
Carrick, Carol (Hatfield) 1935- *118*
Earlier sketches in SATA *7, 63*
See also SAAS *18*
Carrick, Donald (F.) 1929-1989 .... *63*
Earlier sketch in SATA *7*
Carrick, Malcolm 1945- *28*
Carrick, Paul 1972- *194*
Carrier, Lark 1947- *71*
Brief entry *50*
Carrier, Roch 1937- *166*
Earlier sketch in SATA *105*
Carrighar, Sally 1898-1985 .... *24*
Carrillo, Patricia S.
See Carrillo, P.S.
Carrillo, P.S. *209*
Carrington, G. A.
See Cunningham, Chet

Carrington, Marsha Gray 1954- *168*
Earlier sketch in SATA *111*
Carris, Joan 1938- *182*
Brief entry *42*
Earlier sketch in SATA *44*
Carris, Joan Davenport
See Carris, Joan
Carroll, Curt
See Bishop, Curtis (Kent)
Carroll, Elizabeth
See Barkin, Carol
and James, Elizabeth
Carroll, James Christopher 1960- *235*
Carroll, Jaye
See Carroll, Michael
Carroll, Jenny
See Cabot, Meg
Carroll, (Archer) Latrobe 1894-1996 .... *7*
Carroll, Laura
See Parr, Lucy
Carroll, Lewis 1832-1898 .... *100*
See also YABC *2*
See also CLR *108*
Carroll, Michael 1966- *203*
Carroll, Raymond 1924- *86*
Brief entry *47*
Carruth, Hayden 1921-2008 .... *47*
Obituary *197*
Carryl, Charles E. 1841-1920 .... *114*
Carryl, Charles Edward
See Carryl, Charles E.
Carse, Robert 1902-1971 .... *5*
Carson, J(ohn) Franklin 1920-1981 .... *1*
Obituary *107*
Carson, Mary Kay 1964- *200*
Earlier sketch in SATA *150*
Carson, Rachel 1907-1964 .... *23*
Carson, Rachel Louise
See Carson, Rachel
Carson, Rosalind
See Chittenden, Margaret
Carson, S. M.
See Gorsline, (Sally) Marie
Carson, William C. 1928- *154*
Carter, Abby *222*
Earlier sketch in SATA *184*
Carter, Alden R 1947- *137*
Earlier sketch in SATA *67*
See also CLR *22*
See also SAAS *18*
Carter, Alden Richardson
See Carter, Alden R
Carter, Andy 1948- *134*
Carter, Angela 1940-1992 .... *66*
Obituary *70*
Carter, Angela Olive
See Carter, Angela
Carter, Anne Laurel 1953- *209*
Earlier sketch in SATA *135*
Carter, Asa Earl
See Carter, Forrest
Carter, Avis Murton
See Allen, Kenneth S.
Carter, Bruce
See Hough, Richard (Alexander)
Carter, Carol S(hadis) 1948- *124*
Carter, David A. 1957- *228*
Earlier sketches in SATA *114, 170*
Carter, Don 1958- *192*
Earlier sketch in SATA *124*
Carter, Dorothy Sharp 1921- *8*
Carter, Forrest 1927(?)-1979 .... *32*
Carter, Helene 1887-1960 .... *15*
Carter, (William) Hodding, Jr. 1907-1972 .... *2*
Obituary *27*
Carter, James Earl, Jr.
See Carter, Jimmy
Carter, Jimmy 1924- *79*
Carter, Katharine J(ones) 1905-1984 .... *2*
Carter, Lin(wood Vrooman) 1930-1988 .... *91*
Carter, Mike 1936- *138*
Carter, Nick
See Avallone, Michael (Angelo, Jr.)
and Ballard, (Willis) Todhunter
and Crider, Bill
and Cassiday, Bruce (Bingham)
and Chastain, Thomas
and Dey, Frederic (Merrill) Van Rensselaer
and Garside, Jack
and Hayes, Ralph E(ugene)
and Henderson, M(arilyn) R(uth)
and Lynds, Dennis
and Lynds, Gayle (Hallenbeck)
and Randisi, Robert J.
and Rasof, Henry
and Stratemeyer, Edward L.
and Smith, Martin Cruz
and Swain, Dwight V(reeland)
and Vardeman, Robert E.
and Wallmann, Jeffrey M(iner)
and White, Lionel
Carter, Peter 1929- *57*
Carter, Phyllis Ann
See Eberle, Irmengarde
Carter, Samuel (Thomson) III 1904-1988 .... *37*
Obituary *60*
Carter, Scott William *231*
Carter, Timothy 1972- *224*
Carter, William E. 1926-1983 .... *1*
Obituary *35*
Cartlidge, Michelle 1950- *96*
Brief entry *37*
Earlier sketch in SATA *49*
Cartner, William Carruthers 1910- *11*
Cartwright, Ann 1940- *78*
Cartwright, Reg(inald Ainsley) 1938- *64*
Cartwright, Sally 1923- *9*
Carusone, Al 1949- *89*
Carvell, Marlene *172*
Carver, John
See Gardner, Richard (M.)
Carwell, L'Ann
See McKissack, Patricia C.
Cary
See Cary, Louis F(avreau)
Cary, Barbara Knapp 1912(?)-1975
Obituary *31*
Cary, Kate 1967(?)- *174*
Cary, Louis F(avreau) 1915- *9*
Caryl, Jean
See Kaplan, Jean Caryl Korn
Casanova, Mary 1957- *186*
Earlier sketches in SATA *94, 136*
Cascone, A.G.
See Cascone, Annette
and Cascone, Gina
Cascone, Annette 1960- *103*
Cascone, Gina 1955- *103*
Case, Chris 1976- *209*
Case, Marshal T(aylor) 1941- *9*
Case, Michael
See Howard, Robert West
Caseley, Judith 1951- *159*
Brief entry *53*
Earlier sketch in SATA *87*
Casewit, Curtis W(erner) 1922-2002 .... *4*
Casey, Barbara (Louise) 1944- *147*
Earlier sketch in SATA *79*
Casey, Brigid 1950- *9*
Casey, Tina 1959- *141*
Cash, Ellen Lewis Buell 1905-1989
Obituary *64*
Cash, John Carter 1970- *218*
Cash, Megan Montague *160*
Cashore, Kristin 1976(?)- *206*
Casilla, Robert 1959- *211*
Earlier sketches in SATA *75, 146*
Cason, Mabel Earp 1892-1965 .... *10*
Cass, Joan E(velyn) *1*
Cass-Beggs, Barbara 1904- *62*
Cassedy, Patrice (Rinaldo) 1953- *149*
Cassedy, Sylvia 1930-1989 .... *77*
Obituary *61*
Earlier sketch in SATA *27*
See also CLR *26*
Cassel, Lili
See Wronker, Lili Cassel
Cassels, Jean *173*
Cassidy, Anne 1952- *166*
Cassidy, Anne Josephine
See Cassidy, Anne
Cassidy, Cathy 1962- *183*
Cassidy, Kay *232*
Cassino, Mark *228*
Casson, Hugh Maxwell 1910-1999 .... *65*
Obituary *115*
Cassutt, Michael 1954- *78*
Cassutt, Michael Joseph
See Cassutt, Michael
Castaldi, Elicia *194*
Castaldo, Nancy Fusco 1962- *151*
Earlier sketch in SATA *93*
Castaneda, Omar S. 1954- *71*
Castell, Megan
See Williams, Jeanne
Castellanos, Jane Mollie Robinson
1913-2001 .... *9*
Castellon, Federico 1914-1971 .... *48*
Castellucci, Cecil 1969- *176*
Castillo, Edmund L. 1924-2005 .... *1*
Obituary *167*
Castillo, Lauren *195*
Castle, Lee
See Ogan, George F.
and Ogan, Margaret E. (Nettles)
Castle, Paul
See Howard, Vernon (Linwood)
Castle, Robert
See Hamilton, Edmond
Castro L., Antonio 1941- *226*
Castrovilla, Selene 1966- *186*
Caswell, Brian 1954- *171*
Earlier sketch in SATA *97*
Caswell, Deanna *223*
Caswell, Helen (Rayburn) 1923- *12*
Catalano, Dominic 1956- *163*
Earlier sketch in SATA *76*
Catalano, Grace (A.) 1961- *99*
Catalanotto, Peter 1959- *195*
Autobiography Feature *113*
Earlier sketches in SATA *70, 114, 159*
See also CLR *68*
See also SAAS *25*
Catanese, P.W. 1961- *227*
Earlier sketch in SATA *179*
Cate, Annette LeBlanc *196*
Cate, Dick
See Cate, Richard Edward Nelson
Cate, Richard Edward Nelson 1932- *28*
Cather, Willa 1873-1947 .... *30*
See also CLR *98*
Catherall, Arthur 1906-1980 .... *74*
Earlier sketches in SATA *3, 4*
Cathon, Laura E(lizabeth) 1908-1991 .... *27*
Catlett, Elizabeth 1919(?)- *82*
Catlin, Wynelle 1930- *13*
Catlow, Nikalas
See Catlow, Niki
Catlow, Niki 1975- *193*
Cato, Heather *105*
Cato, Sheila *114*
Catran, Ken 1944- *190*
Catrow, David
See Catrow, David J. III
Catrow, David J. III *206*
Earlier sketch in SATA *152*
Catt, Louis
See French, Vivian
Cattell, James 1954- *123*
Catton, (Charles) Bruce 1899-1978 .... *2*
Obituary *24*
Catusanu, Mircea *222*

Catz, Max
See Glaser, Milton
Caudell, Marian 1930- 52
Caudill, Rebecca 1899-1985 1
Obituary 44
Cauley, Lorinda Bryan 1951- 46
Brief entry 43
Caulfield, Peggy F. 1926-1987
Obituary 53
Cauman, Samuel 1910-1971 48
Causley, Charles (Stanley) 1917-2003 66
Obituary 149
Earlier sketch in SATA 3
See also CLR 30
Cavallaro, Ann (Abelson) 1918- 62
Cavallo, Diana 1931- 7
Cavanagh, Helen (Carol) 1939- 98
Brief entry 37
Earlier sketch in SATA 48
Cavanah, Frances 1899-1982 31
Earlier sketch in SATA 1
Cavanna, Betty
See Harrison, Elizabeth (Allen) Cavanna
Cavanna, Elizabeth
See Harrison, Elizabeth (Allen) Cavanna
Cave, Kathryn 1948- 123
Earlier sketch in SATA 76
Cave, Patrick 1965- 234
Cavendish, Grace
See Finney, Patricia
Cavendish, Peter
See Horler, Sydney
Caveney, Philip 1951- 219
Caveney, Philip Richard
See Caveney, Philip
Cavin, Ruth 1918-2011 38
Cavin, Ruth Brodie
See Cavin, Ruth
Cavoukian, Raffi 1948- 68
Cawley, Winifred 1915- 13
Cazeau, Charles J(ay) 1931- 65
Cazet, Denys 1938- 191
Brief entry 41
Earlier sketches in SATA 52, 99, 163
Cazzola, Gus 1934- 73
Cebulash, Mel 1937- 91
Earlier sketch in SATA 10
Ceccoli, Nicoletta 181
Cecil, Randy 1968- 223
Earlier sketch in SATA 187
Cecka, Melanie 199
Ceder, Georgiana Dorcas -1985 10
Celenza, Anna Harwell 133
Celestino, Martha Laing
See Laing, Martha
Cepeda, Joe 215
Earlier sketch in SATA 159
Cerf, Bennett (Alfred) 1898-1971 7
Cerf, Christopher (Bennett) 1941- 2
Cermak, Martin
See Duchacek, Ivo D(uka)
Cerullo, Mary M. 1949- 145
Earlier sketch in SATA 86
Cervantes, Jennifer 234
Cervon, Jacqueline
See Moussard, Jacqueline
Cetin, Frank Stanley 1921- 2
Chabon, Michael 1963- 145
Chabrian, Deborah
See Chabrian, Deborah L.
Chabrian, Deborah L. 212
Chaconas, D.J.
See Chaconas, Dori
Chaconas, Dori 1938- 208
Earlier sketches in SATA 145, 175
Chaconas, Doris J.
See Chaconas, Dori
Chadda, Sarwat 224
Chadwick, Lester 67
Earlier sketch in SATA 1
Chaffee, Allen 3
Chaffin, Lillie D(orton) 1925- 4
Chaikin, Miriam 1924- 152
Earlier sketches in SATA 24, 102
Chall, Marsha Wilson 150
Challand, Helen J(ean) 1921- 64
Challans, Mary
See Renault, Mary
Chalmers, Mary (Eileen) 1927- 6
See also SAAS 14
Chamberlain, Barbara A.
See Azore, Barbara
Chamberlain, Margaret 1954- 212
Earlier sketch in SATA 46
Chamberlin, Kate 1945- 105
Chamberlin, Mary 1960- 177
Chamberlin, Rich 177
Chamberlin, Richard
See Chamberlin, Rich
Chambers, Aidan 1934- 171
Earlier sketches in SATA 1, 69, 108
See also CLR 151
See also SAAS 12
Chambers, Bradford 1922-1984
Obituary 39
Chambers, Catherine E.
See St. John, Nicole
Chambers, John W. 1933- 57
Brief entry 46
Chambers, Kate
See St. John, Nicole
Chambers, Margaret Ada Eastwood 1911- 2
Chambers, Peggy
See Chambers, Margaret Ada Eastwood
Chambers, Robert W(illiam) 1865-1933 107
Chambliss, Maxie 186
Champlin, Susan 1961- 225
Chan, Gillian 1954- 147
Earlier sketch in SATA 102
Chan, Peter 1980(?)- 207
Chance, James T.
See Carpenter, John
Chance, John T.
See Carpenter, John
Chance, Stephen
See Turner, Philip (William)
Chandler, Caroline A(ugusta) 1906-1979 22
Obituary 24
Chandler, David P. 1933- 28
Chandler, David Porter
See Chandler, David P.
Chandler, Edna Walker 1908-1982 11
Obituary 31
Chandler, Jennifer
See Westwood, Jennifer
Chandler, Karen 1959- 122
Chandler, Kristen 230
Chandler, Linda S(mith) 1929- 39
Chandler, Pauline 175
Chandler, Robert 1953- 40
Chandler, Ruth Forbes 1894-1978 2
Obituary 26
Chandonnet, Ann F. 1943- 92
Chaney, Jill 1932- 87
Chang, Chih-Wei 1966- 111
Chang, Cindy 1968- 90
Chang, Grace 1961- 226
Chang, Margaret 1941- 71
Chang, Margaret Scrogin
See Chang, Margaret
Chang, Raymond 1939- 142
Earlier sketches in SATA 71, 142 PEN
Chanin, Michael 1952- 84
Channel, A. R.
See Catherall, Arthur
Chapian, Marie 1938- 29
Chapin, Alene Olsen Dalton 1915(?)-1986
Obituary 47
Chapin, Tom 1945- 83
Chapman, Allen 67
Earlier sketch in SATA 1
Chapman, Cheryl O(rth) 1948- 80
Chapman, (Constance) Elizabeth (Mann) 1919- 10
Chapman, Gaye 1970- 200
Chapman, Gaye Coralie
See Chapman, Gaye
Chapman, Gaynor 1935- 32
Chapman, Gillian 1955- 120
Chapman, Jane 1970- 212
Earlier sketches in SATA 122, 176
Chapman, Jean 104
Earlier sketch in SATA 34
See also CLR 65
Chapman, John Stanton Higham 1891-1972
Obituary 27
Chapman, Lee
See Bradley, Marion Zimmer
Chapman, Linda 1969- 223
Chapman, Lynne 1960- 197
Chapman, Lynne F(erguson) 1963- 150
Earlier sketch in SATA 94
Chapman, Maristan
See Chapman, John Stanton Higham
Chapman, Vera (Ivy May) 1898-1996 33
Chapman, Walker
See Silverberg, Robert
Chappell, Audrey 1954- 72
Chappell, Crissa-Jean 198
Chappell, Warren 1904-1991 68
Obituary 67
Earlier sketch in SATA 6
See also SAAS 10
Chapra, Mimi 182
Charbonneau, Eileen 1951- 118
Earlier sketch in SATA 84
Charbonnet, Gabrielle 1961- 227
Earlier sketch in SATA 81
Chardiet, Bernice 1927(?)- 27
Chardiet, Bernice Kroll
See Chardiet, Bernice
Charest, Emily MacLachlan 198
Charles, Donald
See Meighan, Donald Charles
Charles, Louis
See Stratemeyer, Edward L.
Charles, Nicholas
See Kuskin, Karla
Charles, Nicholas J.
See Kuskin, Karla
Charles, Norma 153
Charles, Veronika Martenova 182
Charlip, Remy 1929- 119
Earlier sketches in SATA 4, 68
See also CLR 8
Charlot, Jean 1898-1979 8
Obituary 31
Charlot, Martin 1944- 64
Charlot, Martin Day
See Charlot, Martin
Charlton, Michael (Alan) 1923- 34
Charlton-Trujillo, e.E. 189
Charmatz, Bill 1925-2005 7
Charnas, Suzy McKee 1939- 110
Earlier sketch in SATA 61
Charosh, Mannis 1906- 5
Chartier, Normand L. 1945- 66
Chase, Alice
See McHargue, Georgess
Chase, Alyssa 1965- 92
Chase, Andra 1942- 91
Chase, Emily
See Aks, Patricia
and Garwood, Julie
and Sachs, Judith
and White, Carol
Chase, Mary (Coyle) 1907-1981 17
Obituary 29
Chase, Mary Ellen 1887-1973 10
Chase, Paula 214
Chase, Richard 1904-1988 64
Obituary 56

Chase, Samantha
See Glick, Ruth
Chast, Roz 1954- ... *212*
Earlier sketch in SATA *97*
Chastain, Madye Lee 1908-1989 ... *4*
Chataway, Carol 1955- ... *140*
Chatterjee, Debjani 1952- ... *83*
Chatterton, Martin 1961- ... *225*
Chauncy, Nan(cen Beryl Masterman) 1900-1970 ... *6*
See also CLR *6*
Chaundler, Christine 1887-1972 ... *1*
Obituary ... *25*
Chavarri, Elisa ... *240*
Chayil, Eishes ... *240*
Chayka, Doug ... *196*
Chbosky, Stephen 1972- ... *164*
Cheaney, Janie B.
See Cheaney, J.B.
Cheaney, J.B. 1950- ... *188*
Chee, Cheng-Khee 1934- ... *79*
Cheese, Chloe 1952- ... *118*
Chekhonte, Antosha
See Chekhov, Anton
Chekhov, Anton 1860-1904 ... *90*
Chekhov, Anton Pavlovich
See Chekhov, Anton
Chelushkin, Kirill 1968- ... *186*
Chen, Anthony 1929- ... *6*
Chen, Chih-Yuan 1975- ... *216*
Earlier sketch in SATA *155*
Chen, Ju-Hong 1941- ... *78*
Chen, Pauline 1966- ... *202*
Chen, Sara
See Odgers, Sally Farrell
Chen, Tony
See Chen, Anthony
Chen, Yong 1963- ... *183*
Chen, Yuan-tsung 1932- ... *65*
Chen, Zhiyuan
See Chen, Chih-Yuan
Chenault, Nell
See Smith, Linell Nash
Chen Chih-Yuan
See Chen, Chih-Yuan
Chenery, Janet (Dai) 1923- ... *25*
Cheney, Cora 1916-1999 ... *3*
Obituary ... *110*
Cheney, Glenn (Alan) 1951- ... *99*
Cheney, Lynne V. 1941- ... *152*
Cheney, Lynne Vincent
See Cheney, Lynne V.
Cheney, Ted
See Cheney, Theodore Albert
Cheney, Theodore A. Rees
See Cheney, Theodore Albert
Cheney, Theodore Albert 1928- ... *11*
Cheng, Andrea 1957- ... *205*
Earlier sketches in SATA *128, 172*
Cheng, Christopher 1959- ... *173*
Earlier sketch in SATA *106*
Cheng, Judith 1955- ... *36*
Cheng, Shan
See Jiang, Cheng An
Cheripko, Jan 1951- ... *155*
Earlier sketch in SATA *83*
Chermayeff, Ivan 1932- ... *47*
Chernenko, Dan
See Turtledove, Harry
Chernett, Dan ... *224*
Chernoff, Dorothy A.
See Ernst, (Lyman) John
Chernoff, Goldie Taub 1909- ... *10*
Cherry, Carolyn Janice
See Cherryh, C.J.
Cherry, Lynne 1952- ... *99*
Earlier sketch in SATA *34*
Cherryh, C.J. 1942- ... *172*
Earlier sketch in SATA *93*
Cherryholmes, Anne
See Price, Olive
Cheshire, Simon ... *236*
Earlier sketch in SATA *172*
Chesler, Bernice 1932-2002 ... *59*
Chess, Victoria (Dickerson) 1939- ... *92*
Earlier sketch in SATA *33*
Chessa, Francesca ... *233*
Earlier sketch in SATA *191*
Chester, Deborah 1957- ... *85*
Chester, Kate
See Guccione, Leslie Davis
Chesterton, G. K. 1874-1936 ... *27*
Chesterton, Gilbert Keith
See Chesterton, G. K.
Chesworth, Michael ... *207*
Earlier sketch in SATA *160*
Chetin, Helen 1922- ... *6*
Chetwin, Grace ... *86*
Brief entry ... *50*
Chevalier, Christa 1937- ... *35*
Chevalier, Tracy 1962- ... *128*
Chew, Ruth 1920-2010 ... *7*
Chichester Clark, Emma 1955- ... *209*
Earlier sketches in SATA *117, 156, 69*
Chick, Bryan 1971- ... *239*
Chidsey, Donald Barr 1902-1981 ... *3*
Obituary ... *27*
Chiefari, Janet D. 1942- ... *58*
Chien, Catia ... *193*
Chien-min, Lin
See Rumford, James
Child, L. Maria
See Child, Lydia Maria
Child, Lauren 1965- ... *183*
Earlier sketches in SATA *119, 160*
Child, Lincoln 1957- ... *113*
Child, Lincoln B.
See Child, Lincoln
Child, Lydia Maria 1802-1880 ... *67*
Child, Mrs.
See Child, Lydia Maria
Child, Philip 1898-1978 ... *47*
Children's Shepherd, The
See Westphal, Arnold Carl
Childress, Alice 1920-1994 ... *81*
Earlier sketches in SATA *7, 48*
See also CLR *14*
Childs, H(alla) Fay (Cochrane) 1890-1971 ... *1*
Obituary ... *25*
Childs, Tera Lynn 1976- ... *235*
Chilton, Charles (Frederick William) 1917- ... *102*
Chima, Cinda Williams ... *226*
Earlier sketch in SATA *192*
Chimaera
See Farjeon, Eleanor
Chin, Jason 1978- ... *218*
Chin, Richard (M.) 1946- ... *52*
Chinery, Michael 1938- ... *26*
Chin-Lee, Cynthia 1958- ... *102*
Chin-Lee D., Cynthia
See Chin-Lee, Cynthia
Chippendale, Lisa A. ... *158*
Chipperfield, Joseph Eugene 1912-1980(?) .. *87*
Earlier sketch in SATA *2*
Chisholm, P. F.
See Finney, Patricia
Chislett, Gail (Elaine) 1948- ... *58*
Chittenden, Elizabeth F. 1903-1999 ... *9*
Chittenden, Margaret 1935- ... *28*
Chittum, Ida 1918- ... *7*
Chitwood, Suzanne Tanner 1958- ... *160*
Chmielarz, Sharon Lee 1940- ... *72*
Choat, Beth 1964- ... *238*
Choate, Judith (Newkirk) 1940- ... *30*
Chocolate, Debbi 1954- ... *223*
Earlier sketch in SATA *96*
Chocolate, Deborah H. Newton
See Chocolate, Debbi
Chodos-Irvine, Margaret ... *211*
Earlier sketch in SATA *152*
Choi, Sook Nyul 1937- ... *73*
Autobiography Feature ... *126*
See also CLR *53*
Choi, Yangsook ... *178*
Choksi, Nishant 1975- ... *222*
Choldenko, Gennifer 1957- ... *240*
Earlier sketches in SATA *135, 182*
Chorao, Kay 1936- ... *215*
Chorao, (Ann Mc)Kay (Sproat) 1936- ... *162*
Earlier sketches in SATA *8, 69*
Choron, Sandra (Zena Samelson) 1950- ... *146*
Choung, Eun-hee ... *199*
Chow, Cara 1972- ... *241*
Chown, Marcus 1959- ... *137*
Choyce, Lesley 1951- ... *165*
Earlier sketch in SATA *94*
Choyce, Lesley Willis
See Choyce, Lesley
Chrisman, Arthur Bowie 1889-1953 ... *124*
See also YABC *1*
Christelow, Eileen 1943- ... *184*
Autobiography Feature ... *120*
Brief entry ... *35*
Earlier sketches in SATA *38, 90*
Christensen, Bonnie 1951- ... *213*
Earlier sketches in SATA *110, 157*
Christensen, Gardell Dano 1907-1991 ... *1*
Christensen, Laurie
See Steding, Laurie
Christesen, Barbara 1940- ... *40*
Christgau, Alice Erickson 1902-1977 ... *13*
Christian, Mary Blount 1933- ... *9*
Christiana, David ... *195*
Christie, Agatha 1890-1976 ... *36*
Christie, Agatha Mary Clarissa
See Christie, Agatha
Christie, Ann Philippa
See Pearce, Philippa
Christie, Gregory
See Christie, R. Gregory
Christie, Peter 1962- ... *236*
Christie, Philippa
See Pearce, Philippa
Christie, R. Gregory 1971- ... *225*
Earlier sketches in SATA *127, 185*
Christopher, John
See Youd, Samuel
Christopher, Louise
See Hale, Arlene
Christopher, Matt(hew Frederick) 1917-1997 ... *80*
Obituary ... *99*
Earlier sketches in SATA *2, 47*
See also CLR *119*
See also SAAS *9*
Christopher, Milbourne 1914(?)-1984 ... *46*
Christy, Howard Chandler 1873-1952 ... *21*
Christy, Jana 1965- ... *239*
Chrustowski, Rick ... *176*
Chrystie, Frances N(icholson) 1904-1986 ... *60*
Chu, Daniel 1933- ... *11*
Chui, Vince 1975- ... *236*
Chukovsky, Kornei (Ivanovich) 1882-1969 . *34*
Earlier sketch in SATA *5*
Church, Caroline Jayne ... *219*
Earlier sketch in SATA *179*
Church, Richard 1893-1972 ... *3*
Churchill, E(lmer) Richard 1937- ... *11*
Churchill, Elizabeth
See Hough, Richard (Alexander)
Chute, B(eatrice) J(oy) 1913-1987 ... *2*
Obituary ... *53*
Chute, Marchette (Gaylord) 1909-1994 ... *1*
Chwast, Jacqueline 1932- ... *6*
Chwast, Seymour 1931- ... *146*
Earlier sketches in SATA *18, 96*
Ciardi, John (Anthony) 1916-1986 ... *65*
Obituary ... *46*
Earlier sketch in SATA *1*
See also CLR *19*
See also SAAS *26*

Ciccone, Madonna Louise Veronica
  See Madonna
Ciddor, Anna 1957- *213*
Ciment, James D. 1958- *140*
Cirrone, Dorian *182*
Cisneros, Sandra 1954-
  See CLR *123*
Citra, Becky 1954- *137*
Citrin, Michael 1965(?)- *183*
Claflin, Willy 1944- *208*
Clair, Andree *19*
Claire, Cassandra
  See Clare, Cassandra
Clampett, Bob 1914(?)-1985 .... *44*
  Obituary *38*
Clampett, Robert
  See Clampett, Bob
Clapp, John 1968- *109*
Clapp, Patricia 1912- *74*
  Earlier sketch in SATA *4*
  See also SAAS *4*
Clare, Cassandra 1973- *238*
Clare, Ellen
  See Sinclair, Olga
Clare, Helen
  See Clarke, Pauline
Claremont, Chris 1950- *87*
Claremont, Christopher Simon
  See Claremont, Chris
Clark, Ann Nolan 1896-1995 .... *82*
  Obituary *87*
  Earlier sketch in SATA *4*
  See also CLR *16*
  See also SAAS *16*
Clark, Champ 1923-2002 .... *47*
Clark, Christopher (Anthony) Stuart
  See Stuart-Clark, Christopher (Anthony)
Clark, Clara Gillow 1951- *154*
  Earlier sketch in SATA *84*
Clark, David
  See Hardcastle, Michael
Clark, David Allen
  See Ernst, (Lyman) John
Clark, Emma Chichester
  See Chichester Clark, Emma
Clark, Frank J(ames) 1922- *18*
Clark, Garel
  See Garelick, May
Clark, Halsey
  See Deming, Richard
Clark, Joan
  See Benson, Mildred
Clark, Joan 1934- *182*
  Earlier sketches in SATA *59, 96*
Clark, Karen Henry *237*
Clark, Leonard 1905-1981 .... *30*
  Obituary *29*
Clark, M. R.
  See Clark, Mavis Thorpe
Clark, Margaret (D.) 1943- *126*
Clark, Margaret Goff 1913- *82*
  Earlier sketch in SATA *8*
Clark, Mary Higgins 1929- *46*
Clark, Mavis Thorpe 1909-1999 .... *74*
  Earlier sketch in SATA *8*
  See also CLR *30*
  See also SAAS *5*
Clark, Merle
  See Gessner, Lynne
Clark, Patricia Denise
  See Robins, Patricia
Clark, Patricia Finrow 1929- *11*
Clark, Ronald Harry 1904-1999 .... *193*
Clark, Ronald William 1916-1987 .... *2*
  Obituary *52*
Clark, Sherryl 1956- *149*
Clark, Van D(eusen) 1909-1974 .... *2*
Clark, Virginia
  See Gray, Patricia (Clark)
Clark, Walter Van Tilburg 1909-1971 .... *8*
Clarke, Arthur
  See Clarke, Arthur C.
Clarke, Arthur C. 1917-2008 .... *115*
  Obituary *191*
  Earlier sketches in SATA *13, 70*
  See also CLR *119*
Clarke, Arthur Charles
  See Clarke, Arthur C.
Clarke, Clorinda 1917- *7*
Clarke, Elizabeth L. 1934- *103*
Clarke, Greg 1959- *215*
Clarke, Gus 1948- *134*
Clarke, J.
  See Clarke, Judith
Clarke, James Hall
  See Rowland-Entwistle, (Arthur) Theodore (Henry)
Clarke, Joan B. 1921- *42*
  Brief entry *27*
Clarke, John
  See Laklan, Carli
  and Sontup, Dan(iel)
Clarke, Judith 1943- *241*
  Earlier sketches in SATA *75, 110, 164*
  See also CLR *61*
Clarke, Julia 1950- *138*
Clarke, Kenneth 1957- *107*
Clarke, Lea
  See Rowland-Entwistle, (Arthur) Theodore (Henry)
Clarke, Margaret 1941-
  See CLR *99*
Clarke, Mary Stetson 1911-1994 .... *5*
Clarke, Michael
  See Newlon, (Frank) Clarke
Clarke, Pauline 1921- *131*
  Earlier sketch in SATA *3*
  See also CLR *28*
Clarkson, E(dith) Margaret 1915- *37*
Clarkson, Ewan 1929- *9*
Clarkson, Karen *233*
Claudia, Susan
  See Goulart, Ron
  and Johnston, William
Claverie, Jean 1946- *38*
Clay, Patrice 1947- *47*
Clay, Wil *203*
Clayman, Deborah Paula
  See Da Costa, Deborah
Claypool, Jane
  See Miner, Jane Claypool
Clayton, Elaine 1961- *209*
  Earlier sketches in SATA *94, 159*
Clayton, Lawrence (Otto, Jr.) 1945- *75*
Clayton, Sally Pomme *218*
Clayton, Sandra 1951- *110*
Cle, Troy *202*
Clea, Super
  See Hantman, Clea
Cleary, Beverly 1916- *121*
  Earlier sketches in SATA *2, 43, 79*
  See also CLR *72*
  See also SAAS *20*
Cleary, Beverly Atlee Bunn
  See Cleary, Beverly
Cleary, Brian P. 1959- *186*
  Earlier sketches in SATA *93, 132*
Cleaver, Bill
  See Cleaver, William J.
Cleaver, Carole 1934- *6*
Cleaver, Elizabeth (Ann Mrazik)
  1939-1985 .... *23*
  Obituary *43*
  See also CLR *13*
Cleaver, Hylton Reginald 1891-1961 .... *49*
Cleaver, Vera 1919-1993 .... *76*
  Earlier sketch in SATA *22*
  See also CLR *6*
Cleaver, Vera Allen
  See Cleaver, Vera
Cleaver, William J. 1920-1981 .... *22*
  Obituary *27*
  See also CLR *6*
Cleishbotham, Jebediah
  See Scott, Sir Walter
Cleland, Janet *226*
Cleland, Mabel
  See Widdemer, Mabel Cleland
Clem, Margaret H(ollingsworth) 1923- *90*
Clemens, James
  See Rollins, James
Clemens, Samuel
  See Twain, Mark
Clemens, Samuel Langhorne
  See Twain, Mark
Clemens, Virginia Phelps 1941- *35*
Clement, Gary *191*
Clement, Janet *182*
Clement, Nathan 1966- *200*
Clement, Priscilla Ferguson 1942- *171*
Clement, Rod *97*
Clement-Moore, Rosemary *229*
  Earlier sketch in SATA *188*
Clements, Andrew 1949- *235*
  Earlier sketches in SATA *104, 158, 203*
Clements, Bruce 1931- *178*
  Earlier sketches in SATA *27, 94*
Clemesha, David *192*
Cleminson, Katie *221*
Clemons, Elizabeth
  See Nowell, Elizabeth Cameron
Clerk, N. W.
  See Lewis, C. S.
Cleveland, Bob
  See Cleveland, George
Cleveland, George 1903(?)-1985
  Obituary *43*
Cleveland-Peck, Patricia *80*
Cleven, Cathrine
  See Cleven, Kathryn Seward
Cleven, Kathryn Seward *2*
Clevenger, William R. 1954- *84*
Clevenger, William Russell
  See Clevenger, William R.
Clevin, Joergen 1920- *7*
Clevin, Jorgen
  See Clevin, Joergen
Clewes, Dorothy (Mary) 1907-2003 .... *86*
  Obituary *138*
  Earlier sketch in SATA *1*
Clifford, David
  See Rosenberg, Eth Clifford
Clifford, Eth
  See Rosenberg, Eth Clifford
Clifford, Harold B(urton) 1893-1988 .... *10*
Clifford, Margaret Cort 1929- *1*
Clifford, Martin
  See Hamilton, Charles (Harold St. John)
Clifford, Mary Louise Beneway 1926- *23*
Clifford, Peggy
  See Clifford, Margaret Cort
Clifford, Rachel Mark
  See Lewis, Brenda Ralph
Clifton, Lucille 1936-2010 .... *128*
  Earlier sketches in SATA *20, 69*
  See also CLR *5*
Clifton, Thelma Lucille
  See Clifton, Lucille
Climo, Shirley 1928- *166*
  Autobiography Feature *110*
  Brief entry *35*
  Earlier sketches in SATA *39, 77*
  See also CLR *69*
Cline, Eric H. 1960- *240*
Cline-Ransome, Lesa *201*
Clinton, Catherine 1952- *203*
Clinton, Cathryn 1957- *136*
Clinton, Dirk
  See Silverberg, Robert
Clinton, Jon
  See Prince, J(ack) H(arvey)

Clippinger, Carol *193*
Clish, (Lee) Marian 1946- *43*
Clive, Clifford
See Hamilton, Charles (Harold St. John)
Clokey, Art 1921- *59*
Cloudsley-Thompson, J(ohn) L(eonard) 1921- *19*
Clouse, Nancy L. 1938- *78*
Clover, Peter 1952- *215*
Earlier sketch in SATA *152*
Clutha, Janet
See Frame, Janet
Clutha, Janet Paterson Frame
See Frame, Janet
Clymer, Eleanor 1906-2001 .... *85*
Obituary *126*
Earlier sketch in SATA *9*
See also SAAS *17*
Clyne, Patricia (Edwards) *31*
Cneut, Carll 1969- *197*
Coalson, Glo 1946- *94*
Earlier sketch in SATA *26*
Coates, Anna 1958- *73*
Coates, Belle 1896-1986 .... *2*
Coates, Ruth Allison 1915- *11*
Coats, Alice M(argaret) 1905-1976 .... *11*
Coatsworth, Elizabeth (Jane) 1893-1986 .... *100*
Obituary *49*
Earlier sketches in SATA *2, 56*
See also CLR *2*
Cobalt, Martin
See Mayne, William
Cobb, Jane
See Berry, Jane Cobb
Cobb, Mary 1931- *88*
Cobb, Vicki 1938- *136*
Autobiography Feature *136*
Earlier sketches in SATA *8, 69, 131*
See also CLR *2*
See also SAAS *6*
Cobbett, Richard
See Pluckrose, Henry
Cober, Alan E(dwin) 1935-1998 .... *7*
Obituary *101*
Cobham, Sir Alan
See Hamilton, Charles (Harold St. John)
Coburn, Jake 1978- *155*
Cocagnac, Augustin Maurice(-Jean) 1924- *7*
Cocca-Leffler, Maryann 1958- *194*
Earlier sketches in SATA *80, 136*
Cochran, Bill *187*
Cochran, Bobbye A. 1949- *11*
Cochran, Josh *221*
Cochran, Thomas 1955- *198*
Cochrane, Hamilton E.
See Cochrane, Mick
Cochrane, Mick 1956- *215*
Cockcroft, Jason *217*
Cockett, Mary *3*
Cocks, Peter *204*
Cocovini, Abby *202*
Coddell, Esme Raji
See Codell, Esme Raji
Codell, Esme Raji 1968- *160*
Cody, C. S.
See Waller, Leslie
Cody, Jess
See Cunningham, Chet
Cody, Matthew *229*
Coe, Anne (E.) 1949- *95*
Coe, Douglas
See Epstein, Beryl
and Epstein, Samuel
Coe, Lloyd 1899(?)-1976
Obituary *30*
Coen, Rena Neumann 1925- *20*
Coerr, Eleanor (Beatrice) 1922- *67*
Earlier sketch in SATA *1*
Cofer, Judith Ortiz 1952- *164*
Earlier sketch in SATA *110*
Coffelt, Nancy 1961- *189*
Coffey, Brian
See Koontz, Dean
Coffin, Geoffrey
See Mason, F(rancis) van Wyck
Coffin, M. T.
See Stanley, George Edward
Coffin, M.T.
See Stanley, George Edward
Coffman, Ramon Peyton 1896-1989 .... *4*
Cogan, Karen 1954- *125*
Coggins, Jack (Banham) 1911-2006 .... *2*
Cohagan, Carolyn 1972- *228*
Cohen, Barbara 1932-1992 .... *77*
Obituary *74*
Earlier sketch in SATA *10*
See also SAAS *7*
Cohen, Daniel (E.) 1936- *70*
Earlier sketch in SATA *8*
See also CLR *43*
See also SAAS *4*
Cohen, Deborah Bodin 1968- *240*
Earlier sketch in SATA *180*
Cohen, Jan Barger
See Barger, Jan
Cohen, Jene Barr
See Barr, Jene
Cohen, Joan Lebold 1932- *4*
Cohen, Joshua C. 1970- *241*
Cohen, Judith Love 1933- *78*
Cohen, Lisa 1963- *225*
Cohen, Miriam 1926-1955 .... *155*
Earlier sketches in SATA *29, 106*
See also SAAS *11*
Cohen, Nora *75*
Cohen, Paul 1945- *58*
Cohen, Paul S.
See Cohen, Paul
Cohen, Peter Zachary 1931- *150*
Earlier sketch in SATA *4*
Cohen, Robert Carl 1930- *8*
Cohen, Santiago 1954- *215*
Cohen, Sholom 1951- *94*
Cohn, Angelo 1914-1997 .... *19*
Cohn, Diana *194*
Cohn, Rachel 1968- *228*
Earlier sketch in SATA *161*
Coit, Margaret Louise 1922-2003 .... *2*
Obituary *142*
Colasanti, Susane 1973- *214*
Colato Lainez, Rene 1970- *226*
Earlier sketch in SATA *176*
Colbert, Anthony 1934-2007 .... *15*
Colbert, Nancy A. 1936- *139*
Colby, C(arroll) B(urleigh) 1904-1977 .... *35*
Earlier sketch in SATA *3*
Colby, Jean Poindexter 1909-1993 .... *23*
Cole, Annette
See Steiner, Barbara A(nnette)
Cole, Babette 1949- *155*
Earlier sketches in SATA *61, 96*
Cole, Betsy 1940- *83*
Cole, Brock 1938- *200*
Earlier sketches in SATA *72, 136*
See also CLR *18*
Cole, Davis
See Elting, Mary
Cole, Hannah 1954- *74*
Cole, Henry 1955- *213*
Earlier sketch in SATA *181*
Cole, Jack -1974
See Stewart, John
Cole, Jackson
See Curry, Thomas Albert
and Germano, Peter B.
and Heckelmann, Charles N(ewman)
and Newton, D(wight) B(ennett)
and Schisgall, Oscar
Cole, Jennifer
See Zach, Cheryl (Byrd)
Cole, Joanna 1944- *231*
Brief entry *37*
Earlier sketches in SATA *49, 81, 120, 168*
See also CLR *40*
Cole, Lois Dwight 1903-1979 .... *10*
Obituary *26*
Cole, Michael 1947- *59*
Cole, Samantha
See Cole, Stephen
Cole, Sheila 1939- *171*
Earlier sketches in SATA *24, 95*
Cole, Sheila R.
See Cole, Sheila
Cole, Sheila Rotenberg
See Cole, Sheila
Cole, Stephen 1971- *230*
Earlier sketch in SATA *161*
Cole, Steve
See Cole, Stephen
Cole, William (Rossa) 1919-2000 .... *71*
Earlier sketch in SATA *9*
See also SAAS *9*
Coleman, Andrew
See Pine, Nicholas
Coleman, Clare
See Bell, Clare (Louise)
and Easton, M(alcolm) Coleman
Coleman, Janet Wyman *184*
Coleman, Loren 1947- *164*
Coleman, Loren Elwood, Jr.
See Coleman, Loren
Coleman, Mary Ann 1928- *83*
Coleman, Michael
See Jones, Allan Frewin
Coleman, Michael 1946- *199*
Autobiography Feature *133*
Earlier sketches in SATA *108, 133*
Coleman, Rowan *187*
Coleman, William L(eRoy) 1938- *49*
Brief entry *34*
Coleman, Wim 1926- *212*
Coles, Robert 1929- *23*
Coles, Robert Martin
See Coles, Robert
Colfer, Eoin 1965- *197*
Earlier sketch in SATA *148*
See also CLR *112*
Colgan, Lynda 1953- *241*
Colin, Ann
See Ure, Jean
Collard, Sneed B. III 1959- *184*
Earlier sketches in SATA *84, 139*
Colledge, Anne 1939- *142*
Colley, Jacqui 1965- *202*
Collicott, Sharleen 1937- *143*
Earlier sketch in SATA *98*
Collicutt, Paul *229*
Collier, Bryan *204*
Earlier sketches in SATA *126, 174*
Collier, Christopher 1930- *70*
Earlier sketch in SATA *16*
See also CLR *126*
Collier, Ethel 1903-1999 .... *22*
Collier, James Lincoln 1928- *166*
Earlier sketches in SATA *8, 70*
See also CLR *126*
See also SAAS *21*
Collier, Jane
See Collier, Zena
Collier, Kristi *182*
Collier, Steven 1942- *61*
Collier, Zena 1926- *23*
Collings, Gillian 1939- *102*
Collington, Peter 1948- *99*
Earlier sketch in SATA *59*
Collins, Ace 1953- *82*
Collins, Andrew J.
See Collins, Ace
Collins, B. R. 1981- *214*
Collins, David R(aymond) 1940-2001 .... *121*
Earlier sketch in SATA *7*

Collins, Heather 1946- *81*
Collins, Hunt
See Hunter, Evan
Collins, Michael
See Lynds, Dennis
Collins, Michael 1930- *58*
Collins, Pat Lowery 1932- *217*
Earlier sketches in SATA *31, 151*
Collins, Paul 1954- *126*
Collins, Ross 1972- *239*
Earlier sketch in SATA *200*
Collins, Ruth Philpott 1890-1975
Obituary *30*
Collins, Suzanne 1963(?)- *224*
Earlier sketch in SATA *180*
Collins, Yvonne *194*
Collinson, A. S.
See Collinson, Alan S.
Collinson, Alan S. 1934- *80*
Collinson, Roger (Alfred) 1936- *133*
Collison, Linda 1953- *185*
Collodi, Carlo 1826-1890 .... *100*
Earlier sketch in SATA *29*
See also CLR *120*
Colloms, Brenda 1919- *40*
Colman, Hila 1909-2008 .... *53*
Earlier sketch in SATA *1*
See also SAAS *14*
Colman, Morris 1899(?)-1981
Obituary *25*
Colman, Penny (Morgan) 1944- *160*
Autobiography Feature *160*
Earlier sketches in SATA *77, 114*
Colman, Warren (David) 1944- *67*
Coloma, Cindy
See Martinusen-Coloma, Cindy
Colombo, John Robert 1936- *50*
Colon, Raul *156*
Colon, Raul 1952- *202*
Colonius, Lillian 1911-1992 .... *3*
Colorado, Antonio J.
See Colorado (Capella), Antonio J(ulio)
Colorado (Capella), Antonio J(ulio)
1903-1994 .... *23*
Obituary *79*
Colquhoun, Glenn 1964- *165*
Colston, Fifi E. 1960- *150*
Colt, Martin
See Epstein, Beryl
and Epstein, Samuel
Colum, Padraic 1881-1972 .... *15*
See also CLR *36*
Columbus, Chris 1959- *97*
Columbus, Christopher
See Columbus, Chris
Columella
See Moore, Clement Clarke
Colver, Anne 1908- *7*
Colvin, James
See Moorcock, Michael
Colwell, Eileen (Hilda) 1904-2002 .... *2*
Colwyn, Stewart
See Pepper, Frank S.
Coman, Carolyn 1951- *197*
Earlier sketch in SATA *127*
Combres, Elisabeth 1967- *226*
Combs, Lisa M.
See McCourt, Lisa
Combs, Robert
See Murray, John
Comfort, Jane Levington
See Sturtzel, Jane Levington
Comfort, Mildred Houghton 1886-1976 .... *3*
Comins, Ethel M(ae) *11*
Comins, Jeremy 1933- *28*
Commager, Henry Steele 1902-1998 .... *23*
Obituary *102*
Comora, Madeleine *190*
Compere, Mickie
See Davidson, Margaret
Compestine, Ying Chang 1963- *187*
Earlier sketch in SATA *140*
Comport, Sally Wern *190*
Compton, Patricia A. 1936- *75*
Comte, The Great
See Hawkesworth, Eric
Comus
See Ballantyne, R(obert) M(ichael)
Comyns, Nance
See Comyns-Toohey, Nantz
Comyns-Toohey, Nantz 1956- *86*
Conahan, Carolyn
See Conahan, Carolyn Digby
Conahan, Carolyn Digby 1961- *216*
Conan Doyle, Arthur
See Doyle, Sir Arthur Conan
Condie, Ally *204*
Condie, Allyson B.
See Condie, Ally
Condit, Martha Olson 1913- *28*
Condon, Bill 1949- *142*
Condon, Judith *83*
Condon, Ken *195*
Condy, Roy 1942- *96*
Cone, Ferne Geller 1921- *39*
Cone, Molly (Lamken) 1918- *151*
Autobiography Feature *151*
Earlier sketches in SATA *1, 28, 115*
See also SAAS *11*
Cone, Patrick 1954- *89*
Coney, Michael G. 1932-2005 .... *61*
Obituary *170*
Coney, Michael Greatrex
See Coney, Michael G.
Coney, Mike
See Coney, Michael G.
Conford, Ellen 1942- *162*
Earlier sketches in SATA *6, 68, 110*
See also CLR *71*
Conger, Lesley
See Suttles, Shirley (Smith)
Conklin, Gladys Plemon 1903- *2*
Conklin, Paul S. 1929(?)-2003 .... *43*
Brief entry *33*
Obituary *147*
Conkling, Hilda 1910-1986 .... *23*
Conlan, Kathleen Elizabeth 1950- *145*
Conlan, Kathy
See Conlan, Kathleen Elizabeth
Conley, Robyn 1963- *125*
Conley-Weaver, Robyn
See Conley, Robyn
Conlon-McKenna, Marita 1956- *71*
Conly, Jane Leslie 1948- *164*
Earlier sketches in SATA *80, 112*
Conly, Robert Leslie
See O'Brien, Robert C.
Connell, Kirk
See Chapman, John Stanton Higham
Connell, Tom *206*
Connelly, Gwen 1952- *212*
Connelly, Marc(us Cook) 1890-1980
Obituary *25*
Connolly, Jerome P(atrick) 1931- *8*
Connolly, Pat 1943- *74*
Connolly, Peter 1935- *105*
Earlier sketch in SATA *47*
Conover, Chris 1950- *213*
Earlier sketch in SATA *31*
Conquest, Owen
See Hamilton, Charles (Harold St. John)
Conrad, Joseph 1857-1924 .... *27*
Conrad, Pam 1947-1996 .... *133*
Brief entry *49*
Obituary *90*
Earlier sketches in SATA *52, 80*
See also CLR *18*
See also SAAS *19*
Conroy, Jack
See Conroy, John Wesley
Conroy, John Wesley 1899-1990 .... *19*
Obituary *65*
Conroy, Melissa 1969- *226*
Conroy, Robert
See Goldston, Robert (Conroy)
Constable, Kate 1966- *172*
Constant, Alberta Wilson 1908-1981 .... *22*
Obituary *28*
Constantin, Pascale *185*
Conway, Celeste *210*
Conway, David 1970- *213*
Conway, Diana C. 1943- *91*
Conway, Diana Cohen
See Conway, Diana C.
Conway, Gordon
See Hamilton, Charles (Harold St. John)
Cook, Ande *192*
Cook, Bernadine 1924- *11*
Cook, Fred J(ames) 1911-2003 .... *2*
Obituary *145*
Cook, Glen 1944- *171*
Earlier sketch in SATA *108*
Cook, Glen Charles
See Cook, Glen
Cook, Hugh 1956- *85*
Cook, Hugh, Walter Gilbert
See Cook, Hugh
Cook, Jean Thor 1930- *94*
Cook, Joel 1934- *79*
Cook, Joseph Jay 1924- *8*
Cook, Kristi *240*
Cook, Kristina
See Cook, Kristi
Cook, Lisa Broadie *157*
Cook, Lyn
See Waddell, Evelyn Margaret
Cook, Roy
See Silverberg, Robert
Cook, Sally *207*
Cook, Trish *175*
Cooke, Ann
See Cole, Joanna
Cooke, Arthur
See Lowndes, Robert A(ugustine) W(ard)
Cooke, Barbara
See Alexander, Anna B(arbara Cooke)
Cooke, David Coxe 1917- *2*
Cooke, Donald Ewin 1916-1985 .... *2*
Obituary *45*
Cooke, Frank E. 1920- *87*
Cooke, Jean (Isobel Esther) 1929- *74*
Cooke, John Estes
See Baum, L. Frank
Cooke, Trish 1962- *129*
Cookson, Catherine (McMullen) 1906-1998 .... *9*
Obituary *116*
Cooley, Beth *210*
Cooley, Elizabeth
See Cooley, Beth
Cooley, Regina Francoise 1940- *177*
Coolidge, Olivia E(nsor) 1908- *26*
Earlier sketch in SATA *1*
Cooling, Wendy *169*
Earlier sketch in SATA *111*
Coombs, Charles I(ra) 1914-1994 .... *43*
Earlier sketch in SATA *3*
See also SAAS *15*
Coombs, Chick
See Coombs, Charles I(ra)
Coombs, Jonathan *204*
Coombs, Kate *190*
Coombs, Patricia 1926- *51*
Earlier sketch in SATA *3*
See also SAAS *22*
Cooney, Barbara 1917-2000 .... *96*
Obituary *123*
Earlier sketches in SATA *6, 59*
See also CLR *23*

Cooney, Caroline B. 1947- ... *218*
Brief entry ... *41*
Earlier sketches in SATA *48, 80, 113, 130, 179*
Cooney, Doug ... *181*
Cooney, Nancy Evans 1932- ... *42*
Coontz, Otto 1946- ... *33*
Cooper, Ann (Catharine) 1939- ... *104*
Cooper, Dutch
See Kuyper, Sjoerd
Cooper, Elisha 1971- ... *234*
Earlier sketches in SATA *99, 157*
Cooper, Elizabeth Keyser -1992 ... *47*
Cooper, Floyd ... *227*
Earlier sketches in SATA *96, 144, 187*
See also CLR *60*
Cooper, Gordon 1932- ... *23*
Cooper, Helen 1963- ... *169*
Earlier sketch in SATA *102*
Cooper, Henry S. F., Jr. 1933- ... *65*
Cooper, Henry Spotswood Fenimore, Jr.
See Cooper, Henry S. F., Jr.
Cooper, Ilene 1948- ... *145*
Earlier sketches in SATA *66, 97*
Cooper, James Fenimore 1789-1851 ... *19*
See also CLR *105*
Cooper, John R. ... *1*
Cooper, Kay 1941- ... *11*
Cooper, Lee Pelham 1926- ... *5*
Cooper, Lester (Irving) 1919-1985 ... *32*
Obituary ... *43*
Cooper, Lettice (Ulpha) 1897-1994 ... *35*
Obituary ... *82*
Cooper, Louise 1952-2009 ... *152*
Cooper, Mark A. 1963- ... *235*
Cooper, M.E.
See Davis, Maggie S.
Cooper, M.E.
See Lerangis, Peter
Cooper, Melrose
See Kroll, Virginia L.
Cooper, Michael L. 1950- ... *181*
Earlier sketches in SATA *79, 117*
Cooper, Michelle 1969- ... *226*
Cooper, Patrick 1949- ... *134*
Cooper, Rose 1978- ... *240*
Cooper, Susan 1935- ... *151*
Earlier sketches in SATA *4, 64, 104*
See also CLR *161*
See also SAAS *6*
Cooper, Susan Mary
See Cooper, Susan
Cope, Jane U(rsula) 1949- ... *108*
Copeland, Helen 1920- ... *4*
Copeland, Mark 1956- ... *180*
Copeland, Paul W. ... *23*
Coplans, Peta 1951- ... *84*
Copley (Diana) Heather Pickering 1918- ... *45*
Coppard, A(lfred) E(dgar) 1878-1957
See YABC *1*
Copper, Melinda 1952- ... *172*
Copper, Melinda McConnaughey
See Copper, Melinda
Corace, Jen ... *208*
Coralie
See Anderson, Catherine Corley
Corbett, Grahame ... *43*
Brief entry ... *36*
Corbett, Scott 1913- ... *42*
Earlier sketch in SATA *2*
See also CLR *1*
See also SAAS *2*
Corbett, Sue ... *174*
Corbett, W(illiam) J(esse) 1938- ... *102*
Brief entry ... *44*
Earlier sketch in SATA *50*
See also CLR *19*
Corbin, Sabra Lee
See Malvern, Gladys
Corbin, William
See McGraw, William Corbin
Corbman, Marjorie 1987- ... *179*
Corby, Dan
See Catherall, Arthur
Corcoran, Barbara (Asenath) 1911-2003 ... *77*
Autobiography Feature ... *125*
Earlier sketch in SATA *3*
See also CLR *50*
See also SAAS *20*
Corcos, Lucille 1908-1973 ... *10*
Cordell, Alexander
See Graber, Alexander
Cordell, Matthew 1975- ... *238*
Earlier sketch in SATA *199*
Corder, Zizou
See Young, Louisa
Corderoy, Tracey ... *238*
Cordova, Amy ... *232*
Corella, Joseph
See Odgers, Sally Farrell
Coren, Alan 1938-2007 ... *32*
Obituary ... *187*
Corey, Dorothy ... *23*
Corey, Shana 1974- ... *219*
Earlier sketch in SATA *133*
Corfe, Thomas Howell 1928- ... *27*
Corfe, Tom
See Corfe, Thomas Howell
Corfield, Robin Bell 1952- ... *74*
Corke, Estelle 1969- ... *220*
Corlett, William 1938-2005 ... *46*
Brief entry ... *39*
Cormack, M(argaret) Grant 1913- ... *11*
Cormack, Maribelle B. 1902-1984 ... *39*
Cormier, Robert 1925-2000 ... *83*
Obituary ... *122*
Earlier sketches in SATA *10, 45*
See also CLR *167*
Cormier, Robert Edmund
See Cormier, Robert
Cornelius, Carol 1942- ... *40*
Cornelius, Kay 1933- ... *157*
Cornell, J.
See Cornell, Jeffrey
Cornell, James (Clayton, Jr.) 1938- ... *27*
Cornell, Jean Gay 1920- ... *23*
Cornell, Jeffrey 1945- ... *11*
Cornell, Kevin ... *241*
Cornell, Laura ... *189*
Cornish, D.M. 1972- ... *185*
Cornish, Sam(uel James) 1935- ... *23*
Cornwall, Nellie
See Sloggett, Nellie
Cornwell, Autumn ... *195*
Corr, Christopher 1955- ... *189*
Correa, E. Shan
See Correa, Shan
Correa, Shan ... *233*
Correy, Lee
See Stine, G(eorge) Harry
Corrick, James A. 1945- ... *76*
Corrigan, (Helen) Adeline 1909- ... *23*
Corrigan, Barbara 1922- ... *8*
Corrigan, Eireann 1977- ... *163*
Corrin, Sara 1918- ... *86*
Brief entry ... *48*
Corrin, Stephen ... *86*
Brief entry ... *48*
Corriveau, Art ... *231*
Corsi, Wendy
See Staub, Wendy Corsi
Cort, M. C.
See Clifford, Margaret Cort
Cort, Margaret
See Clifford, Margaret Cort
Corwin, Judith H(offman) 1946- ... *10*
Corwin, Oliver
See Corwin, Oliver J.
Corwin, Oliver J. ... *206*
Cory, Rowena
See Lindquist, Rowena Cory
Cosby, Bill 1937- ... *110*
Earlier sketch in SATA *66*
Cosby, William Henry, Jr.
See Cosby, Bill
and Cosby, Bill
Cosentino, Ralph ... *169*
Cosgrave, John O'Hara II 1908-1968
Obituary ... *21*
Cosgrove, Margaret (Leota) 1926- ... *47*
Cosgrove, Stephen E(dward) 1945- ... *53*
Brief entry ... *40*
Coskey, Evelyn 1932- ... *7*
Cosner, Shaaron 1940- ... *43*
Cossi, Olga 1921- ... *216*
Earlier sketches in SATA *67, 102*
Costa Bates, Janet 1959- ... *237*
Costabel, Eva Deutsch 1924- ... *45*
Costabel-Deutsch, Eva
See Costabel, Eva Deutsch
Costales, Amy 1974- ... *227*
Costanza, Stephen ... *238*
Coste, Marion 1938- ... *183*
Costello, David ... *174*
Costello, David F(rancis) 1904-1990 ... *23*
Cote, Genevieve 1964- ... *184*
Cote, Nancy 1952- ... *182*
Cott, Jonathan 1942- ... *23*
Cottam, Clarence 1899-1974 ... *25*
Cotten, Cynthia ... *188*
Cottin, Menena 1950- ... *213*
Cottle, Joan 1960- ... *135*
Cottler, Joseph 1899-1996 ... *22*
Cottonwood, Joe 1947- ... *92*
Cottrell, Leonard 1913-1974 ... *24*
Cottringer, Anne 1952- ... *150*
Earlier sketch in SATA *97*
Couch, Greg ... *199*
Coulman, Valerie 1969- ... *161*
Couloumbis, Akila 1932-2009 ... *225*
Couloumbis, Audrey ... *240*
Earlier sketch in SATA *173*
Counsel, June 1926- ... *70*
Countryman, The
See Whitlock, Ralph
Courlander, Harold 1908-1996 ... *6*
Obituary ... *88*
Coursen, Valerie 1965(?)- ... *102*
Courtis, Stuart Appleton 1874-1969
Obituary ... *29*
Courtland, Tyler
See Stevens, Serita
Courtney, Dayle
See Goldsmith, Howard
Coury, Louise Andree 1895(?)-1983
Obituary ... *34*
Cousins, Linda 1946- ... *90*
Cousins, Lucy 1964- ... *205*
Earlier sketch in SATA *172*
Cousins, Margaret 1905-1996 ... *2*
Obituary ... *92*
Cousteau, Jacques 1910-1997 ... *98*
Earlier sketch in SATA *38*
Cousteau, Jacques-Yves
See Cousteau, Jacques
Couture, Christin 1951- ... *73*
Couvillon, Alice ... *239*
Couvillon, Jacques ... *195*
Coventry, Susan ... *233*
Coverly, Dave 1964- ... *223*
Covert, Ralph 1968- ... *197*
Coville, Bruce 1950- ... *216*
Autobiography Feature ... *155*
Earlier sketches in SATA *32, 77, 118, 155*
Covington, Dennis ... *109*
Covington, Linda
See Windsor, Linda
Cowan, Catherine ... *121*
Cowan, Rebecca M.
See Moesta, Rebecca
Cowan, Rebecca Moesta
See Moesta, Rebecca

Coward, Fiona 1963- ... *178*
Cowdrey, Richard 1959- ... *204*
Cowell, Cressida 1966- ... *140*
Cowen, Eve
  See Werner, Herma
Cowen, Ida 1898-1993 ... *64*
Cowie, Leonard W(allace) 1919- ... *4*
Cowles, Kathleen
  See Krull, Kathleen
Cowley, Cassia Joy
  See Cowley, Joy
Cowley, Joy 1936- ... *164*
  Autobiography Feature ... *118*
  Earlier sketches in SATA *4, 90*
  See also CLR *55*
  See also SAAS *26*
Cowley, Marjorie 1925- ... *111*
Cox, (Christopher) Barry 1931- ... *62*
Cox, Clinton 1934- ... *108*
  Earlier sketch in SATA *74*
Cox, David 1933- ... *56*
Cox, David Dundas
  See Cox, David
Cox, Donald William 1921- ... *23*
Cox, Jack
  See Cox, John Roberts
Cox, John Roberts 1915-1981 ... *9*
Cox, Judy 1954- ... *236*
  Earlier sketches in SATA *117, 160, 198*
Cox, Marion Monroe 1898-1983
  Obituary ... *34*
Cox, Palmer 1840-1924 ... *24*
  See also CLR *24*
Cox, Paul 1957- ... *226*
Cox, Vic 1942- ... *88*
Cox, Vicki 1945- ... *158*
Cox, Victoria 1945- ... *44*
Cox, Wallace 1924-1973 ... *25*
Cox, Wally
  See Cox, Wallace
Cox, William R(obert) 1901-1988 ... *46*
  Brief entry ... *31*
  Obituary ... *57*
Coxe, Molly 1959- ... *101*
  Earlier sketch in SATA *69*
Coxon, Michele 1950- ... *158*
  Earlier sketch in SATA *76*
Coy, Harold 1902-1986 ... *3*
Coy, John 1958- ... *233*
  Earlier sketches in SATA *120, 171*
Craats, Rennay 1973- ... *131*
Crabtree, Judith 1928- ... *98*
  Earlier sketch in SATA *63*
Crabtree, Julie 1970- ... *214*
Cracker, Edward E.B.
  See Odgers, Sally Farrell
Craft, Elizabeth 1971(?)- ... *204*
Craft, K. Y.
  See Craft, Kinuko Y.
Craft, Kinuko Y. 1940- ... *127*
  Earlier sketch in SATA *65*
Craft, Kinuko Yamabe
  See Craft, Kinuko Y.
Craft, Ruth 1935- ... *87*
  Brief entry ... *31*
Craig, A. A.
  See Anderson, Poul
Craig, Alisa
  See MacLeod, Charlotte (Matilda)
Craig, David
  See James, Bill
Craig, Helen 1934- ... *213*
  Earlier sketches in SATA *46, 49, 94*
Craig, Joe 1979- ... *198*
Craig, Joe Alexander
  See Craig, Joe
Craig, John Eland
  See Chipperfield, Joseph Eugene
Craig, John Ernest 1921- ... *23*
Craig, Kit
  See Reed, Kit
Craig, M. F.
  See Craig, Mary (Francis) Shura
Craig, M. Jean ... *17*
Craig, M. S.
  See Craig, Mary (Francis) Shura
Craig, Margaret (Maze) 1911-1964 ... *9*
Craig, Mary
  See Craig, Mary (Francis) Shura
Craig, Mary Shura
  See Craig, Mary (Francis) Shura
Craig, Mary (Francis) Shura 1923-1991 ... *86*
  Obituary ... *65*
  Earlier sketch in SATA *6*
  See also SAAS *7*
Craig, Ruth 1922- ... *95*
Craik, Mrs.
  See Craik, Dinah Maria (Mulock)
Craik, Dinah Maria (Mulock) 1826-1887 ... *34*
Crandall, Court 1965- ... *175*
Crandell, Rachel 1943- ... *152*
Crane, Barbara (Joyce) 1934- ... *31*
Crane, Carol 1933- ... *232*
Crane, Caroline 1930- ... *11*
Crane, Jordan 1973- ... *174*
Crane, M. A.
  See Wartski, Maureen (Ann Crane)
Crane, Royston Campbell 1901-1977
  Obituary ... *22*
Crane, Stephen 1871-1900
  See YABC *2*
  See also CLR *132*
Crane, Stephen Townley
  See Crane, Stephen
Crane, Walter 1845-1915 ... *100*
  Earlier sketch in SATA *18*
  See also CLR *56*
Crane, William D(wight) 1892-1976 ... *1*
Cranfield, Ingrid 1945- ... *74*
Cranshaw, Stanley
  See Fisher, Dorothy (Frances) Canfield
Crary, Elizabeth (Ann) 1942- ... *99*
  Brief entry ... *43*
Crary, Margaret (Coleman) 1906-1986 ... *9*
Craste, Marc ... *201*
Cravath, Lynne Avril
  See Cravath, Lynne W.
Cravath, Lynne W. 1951- ... *182*
  Earlier sketches in SATA *98, 148*
Craven, Thomas 1889-1969 ... *22*
Crawford, Brent 1975- ... *220*
Crawford, Charles P. 1945- ... *28*
Crawford, Deborah 1922- ... *6*
Crawford, John E(dmund) 1904-1971 ... *3*
Crawford, K(aren) Michael 1959- ... *155*
Crawford, Laura 1977(?)- ... *227*
Crawford, Mel 1925- ... *44*
  Brief entry ... *33*
Crawford, Phyllis 1899- ... *3*
Crawley, Dave ... *177*
Cray, Roberta
  See Emerson, Ru
Crayder, Dorothy ... *7*
Crayder, Teresa
  See Colman, Hila
Crayon, Geoffrey
  See Irving, Washington
Craz, Albert G. 1926- ... *24*
Creagh, Kelly ... *234*
Crebbin, June 1938- ... *169*
  Earlier sketch in SATA *80*
Crecy, Jeanne
  See Williams, Jeanne
Credle, Ellis 1902-1998 ... *1*
Creech, Sharon 1945- ... *226*
  Earlier sketches in SATA *94, 139, 172*
  See also CLR *164*
Creeden, Sharon 1938- ... *91*
Creel, Ann Howard 1953- ... *187*
Creighton, (Mary) Helen 1899-1989
  Obituary ... *64*
Creighton, Jill 1949- ... *96*
Crelin, Bob 1959(?)- ... *221*
Cremer, Andrea 1978- ... *238*
Crenson, Victoria 1952- ... *159*
  Earlier sketch in SATA *88*
Cresp, Gael 1954- ... *119*
Crespo, George 1962- ... *82*
Cresswell, Helen 1934-2005 ... *79*
  Obituary ... *168*
  Earlier sketches in SATA *1, 48*
  See also CLR *18*
  See also SAAS *20*
Cressy, Michael 1955- ... *124*
Cressy, Mike
  See Cressy, Michael
Cretan, Gladys (Yessayan) 1921- ... *2*
Cretzmeyer, Stacy (Megan) 1959- ... *124*
Crew, Gary 1947- ... *163*
  Earlier sketches in SATA *75, 110*
  See also CLR *42*
Crew, Helen (Cecilia) Coale 1866-1941
  See YABC *2*
Crew, Linda (Jean) 1951- ... *137*
  Earlier sketch in SATA *71*
Crewe, Megan 1980- ... *225*
Crews, Donald 1938- ... *76*
  Brief entry ... *30*
  Earlier sketch in SATA *32*
  See also CLR *7*
Crews, Nina 1963- ... *158*
  Earlier sketch in SATA *97*
Crichton, John Michael
  See Crichton, Michael
Crichton, Michael 1942-2008 ... *88*
  Obituary ... *199*
  Earlier sketch in SATA *9*
Crider, Allen Billy
  See Crider, Bill
Crider, Bill 1941- ... *99*
Crilley, Mark 1966- ... *210*
  Autobiography Feature ... *148*
  Earlier sketches in SATA *120, 148*
Crilley, Paul 1975- ... *227*
Crimi, Carolyn 1959- ... *219*
  Earlier sketch in SATA *176*
Cripps, Enid Margaret
  See Appiah, Peggy
Crisler, Curtis L. ... *188*
Crisman, Ruth 1914- ... *73*
Crisp, Marta Marie
  See Crisp, Marty
Crisp, Marty 1947- ... *128*
Crispin, A(nn) C(arol) 1950- ... *86*
Crist, James J. 1961- ... *168*
Cristall, Barbara ... *79*
Crist-Evans, Craig 1954- ... *153*
Crocker, Carter ... *193*
Crocker, Nancy 1956- ... *185*
Crofford, Emily (Ardell) 1927- ... *61*
Crofut, William E. III 1934- ... *23*
Croggon, Alison 1962- ... *194*
Croll, Carolyn 1945- ... *102*
  Brief entry ... *52*
  Earlier sketch in SATA *56*
Croman, Dorothy Young
  See Rosenberg, Dorothy
Cromie, Alice Hamilton 1914-2000 ... *24*
Cromie, William J(oseph) 1930- ... *4*
Crompton, Anne Eliot 1930- ... *73*
  Earlier sketch in SATA *23*
Crompton, Richmal
  See Lamburn, Richmal Crompton
Cronbach, Abraham 1882-1965 ... *11*
Crone, Ruth 1919-2003 ... *4*
Cronin, A(rchibald) J(oseph) 1896-1981 ... *47*
  Obituary ... *25*
Cronin, Doreen (A.) ... *125*
Cronin, Doreen 1966(?)- ... *178*
  See also CLR *136*
Cronin, Doreen A.
  See Cronin, Doreen
Cronn-Mills, Kirstin 1968- ... *224*

Crook, Beverly Courtney ... *38*
Brief entry ... *35*
Crook, Connie Brummel 1930- ... *168*
Earlier sketch in SATA *98*
Crook, Constance
See Crook, Connie Brummel
Crosby, Alexander L. 1906-1980 ... *2*
Obituary ... *23*
Crosby, Harry C.
See Anvil, Christopher
Crosby, Margaret
See Rathmann, Peggy
Crosher, G. R. ... *14*
Cross, Gilbert B. 1939- ... *60*
Brief entry ... *51*
Cross, Gillian 1945- ... *178*
Autobiography Feature ... *178*
Earlier sketches in SATA *38, 71, 110, 165*
See also CLR *28*
Cross, Gillian Clare
See Cross, Gillian
Cross, Helen Reeder
See Broadhead, Helen Cross
Cross, Peter 1951- ... *95*
Cross, Sarah ... *216*
Cross, Shauna 1976(?)- ... *196*
Cross, Tom 1954- ... *146*
Cross, Verda 1914- ... *75*
Cross, Wilbur Lucius III 1918- ... *2*
Crossingham, John 1974- ... *226*
Crossland, Caroline 1964- ... *83*
Crossley-Holland, Kevin 1941- ... *165*
Earlier sketches in SATA *5, 74, 120*
See also CLR *84*
See also SAAS *20*
Crossley-Holland, Kevin John William
See Crossley-Holland, Kevin
Crossman, David A. 1951- ... *219*
Crouch, Karen Hillard
See Good, Karen Hillard
Crouch, Marcus 1913-1996 ... *4*
Crout, George C(lement) 1917- ... *11*
Crow, Donna Fletcher 1941- ... *40*
Crow, Francis Luther
See Luther, Frank
Crow, Kristyn ... *208*
Crowe, Andrew ... *111*
Crowe, Carole 1943- ... *204*
Crowe, Chris ... *206*
Crowe, Ellie ... *203*
Crowe, John
See Lynds, Dennis
Crowe, (Bettina) Peter Lum 1911- ... *6*
Crowell, Grace Noll 1877-1969 ... *34*
Crowell, Pers 1910-1990 ... *2*
Crowell, Robert Leland 1909-2001 ... *63*
Crowfield, Christopher
See Stowe, Harriet Beecher
Crowley, Arthur 1945- ... *38*
Crowley, Arthur McBlair
See Crowley, Arthur
Crowley, Cath 1971- ... *233*
Crowley, James 1969- ... *237*
Crowley, John 1942- ... *140*
Earlier sketch in SATA *65*
Crowley, Suzanne 1963- ... *196*
Crowley, Suzanne Carlisle
See Crowley, Suzanne
Crownfield, Gertrude 1867-1945
See YABC *1*
Crowther, James Gerald 1899-1983 ... *14*
Crowther, Kitty 1970- ... *220*
Crowther, Robert 1948- ... *163*
Croza, Laurel ... *233*
Cruikshank, George 1792-1878 ... *22*
See also CLR *63*
Cruise, Robin 1951- ... *179*
Crum, Shutta ... *192*
Earlier sketch in SATA *134*
Crummel, Susan Stevens 1949- ... *176*
Earlier sketch in SATA *130*
Crump, Fred H., Jr. 1931- ... *76*
Earlier sketch in SATA *11*
Crump, J(ames) Irving 1887-1979 ... *57*
Obituary ... *21*
Crump, William D(rake) 1949- ... *138*
Crunden, Reginald
See Cleaver, Hylton Reginald
Crunk, T.
See Crunk, Tony
Crunk, Tony 1956- ... *130*
Crutcher, Chris 1946- ... *196*
Earlier sketches in SATA *52, 99, 153*
See also CLR *159*
Crutcher, Christopher C.
See Crutcher, Chris
Cruz, Ray(mond) 1933- ... *6*
Cruz Martinez, Alejandro (?)-1987 ... *74*
Crystal, Billy 1947- ... *154*
Crystal, William
See Crystal, Billy
Ctvrtek, Vaclav 1911-1976
Obituary ... *27*
Cuate, Melodie A. ... *219*
Cuetara, Mittie 1957- ... *158*
Earlier sketch in SATA *106*
Cuffari, Richard 1925-1978 ... *66*
Obituary ... *25*
Earlier sketch in SATA *6*
Cuffe-Perez, Mary 1946- ... *199*
Culbertson, Kim 1974- ... *235*
Cullen, Countee 1903-1946 ... *18*
Cullen, Lynn 1955- ... *190*
Culliford, Pierre 1928-1992 ... *40*
Obituary ... *74*
Cullinan, Bernice E(llinger) 1926- ... *135*
Culp, Louanna McNary 1901-1965 ... *2*
Culper, Felix
See McCaughrean, Geraldine
Cumbaa, Stephen 1947- ... *72*
Cumming, Peter 1951- ... *168*
Cumming, Primrose Amy 1915- ... *24*
Cumming, Robert 1945- ... *65*
Cummings, Betty Sue 1918- ... *15*
See also SAAS *9*
Cummings, Gillian 1961- ... *233*
Cummings, John Michael 1963(?)- ... *216*
Cummings, Mary 1951- ... *185*
Cummings, Parke 1902-1987 ... *2*
Obituary ... *53*
Cummings, Pat 1950- ... *203*
Earlier sketches in SATA *42, 71, 107*
See also CLR *48*
See also SAAS *13*
Cummings, Phil 1957- ... *232*
Earlier sketches in SATA *74, 123*
Cummings, Priscilla 1951- ... *237*
Earlier sketches in SATA *129, 170*
Cummings, Richard
See Gardner, Richard (M.)
Cummings, Terrance ... *227*
Cummings, Troy ... *232*
Cummins, Julie ... *200*
Cummins, Maria Susanna 1827-1866
See YABC *1*
Cumpliano, Ina ... *207*
Cuneo, Mary Louise -2001 ... *85*
Cunliffe, John Arthur 1933- ... *86*
Earlier sketch in SATA *11*
Cunliffe, Marcus (Falkner) 1922-1990 ... *37*
Obituary ... *66*
Cunnane, Kelly ... *175*
Cunningham, Bob
See May, Julian
Cunningham, Captain Frank
See Glick, Carl (Cannon)
Cunningham, Cathy
See Cunningham, Chet
Cunningham, Chet 1928- ... *23*
Cunningham, Dale S(peers) 1932- ... *11*
Cunningham, Dru ... *91*
Cunningham, E. V.
See Fast, Howard
Cunningham, Julia (Woolfolk) 1916- ... *132*
Earlier sketches in SATA *1, 26*
See also SAAS *2*
Cunningham, Lawrence J. 1943- ... *125*
Cunningham, Virginia
See Holmgren, Virginia C(unningham)
Cunxin, Li 1961- ... *220*
Cupala, Holly ... *235*
Curiae, Amicus
See Fuller, Edmund (Maybank)
Curie, Eve 1904-2007 ... *1*
Obituary ... *188*
Curlee, Lynn 1947- ... *190*
Earlier sketches in SATA *98, 141*
Curley, Daniel 1918-1988 ... *23*
Obituary ... *61*
Curley, Marianne 1959- ... *175*
Earlier sketch in SATA *131*
Currey, Anna ... *194*
Currie, Robin 1948- ... *120*
Currie, Stephen 1960- ... *132*
Earlier sketch in SATA *82*
Curry, Ann (Gabrielle) 1934- ... *72*
Curry, Jane L(ouise) 1932- ... *138*
Autobiography Feature ... *138*
Earlier sketches in SATA *1, 52, 90*
See also CLR *31*
See also SAAS *6*
Curry, Peggy Simson 1911-1987 ... *8*
Obituary ... *50*
Curry, Tom ... *185*
Curtis, Bruce (Richard) 1944- ... *30*
Curtis, Chara M(ahar) 1950- ... *78*
Curtis, Christopher Paul 1953- ... *187*
Earlier sketches in SATA *93, 140*
See also CLR *172*
Curtis, Gavin 1965- ... *107*
Curtis, Jamie Lee 1958- ... *144*
Earlier sketch in SATA *95*
See also CLR *88*
Curtis, Jennifer Keats ... *185*
Curtis, Marci ... *160*
Curtis, Munzee
See Caseley, Judith
Curtis, Neil 1950-2006 ... *202*
Curtis, Patricia 1921- ... *101*
Earlier sketch in SATA *23*
Curtis, Peter
See Lofts, Norah (Robinson)
Curtis, Philip (Delacourt) 1920- ... *62*
Curtis, Richard 1937- ... *29*
Curtis, Richard Alan
See Curtis, Richard
Curtis, Richard Hale
See Deming, Richard
and Levinson, Leonard
and Rothweiler, Paul Roger
Curtis, Stacy ... *205*
Curtis, Wade
See Pournelle, Jerry
Curtiss, A(rlene) B. 1934- ... *90*
Cusack, Margaret 1945- ... *58*
Cushman, Doug 1953- ... *210*
Earlier sketches in SATA *65, 101, 157*
Cushman, Jerome ... *2*
Cushman, Karen 1941- ... *147*
Earlier sketch in SATA *89*
See also CLR *55*
Cusick, John M. ... *236*
Cusick, Richie Tankersley 1952- ... *231*
Earlier sketches in SATA *67, 140*
Cusimano, Maryann K.
See Love, Maryann Cusimano
Cutbill, Andy 1972- ... *201*
Cutchen, Billye Walker 1930- ... *15*
Cutchins, Judy 1947- ... *59*
Cutler, Daniel S. 1951- ... *78*
Cutler, Daniel Solomon
See Cutler, Daniel S.

Cutler, Ebbitt 1923- ... *9*
Cutler, Ivor 1923-2006 ... *24*
Obituary ... *174*
Cutler, Jane 1936- ... *162*
Earlier sketches in SATA *75, 118*
Cutler, May Ebbitt
See Cutler, Ebbitt
Cutler, Samuel
See Folsom, Franklin (Brewster)
Cutlip, Kimbra L(eigh-Ann) 1964- ... *128*
Cutrate, Joe
See Spiegelman, Art
Cutt, W(illiam) Towrie 1898-1981 ... *16*
Obituary ... *85*
Cuyler, Margery 1948- ... *229*
Earlier sketches in SATA *39, 99, 156, 195*
Cuyler, Margery Stuyvesant
See Cuyler, Margery
Cuyler, Stephen
See Bates, Barbara S(nedeker)
Cypess, Leah 1977- ... *233*
Cyrus, Kurt 1954- ... *236*
Earlier sketches in SATA *132, 179*
Czajkowski, James
See Rollins, James
Czekaj, Jef 1969- ... *217*
Czernecki, Stefan 1946- ... *178*

D

Daagnese, Joseph ... *228*
Dabba Smith, Frank ... *174*
Dabcovich, Lydia ... *99*
Brief entry ... *47*
Earlier sketch in SATA *58*
Dace, Dolores B(oelens) 1929- ... *89*
Da Costa, Deborah ... *193*
Daddo, Andrew 1967- ... *198*
Dadey, Debbie 1959- ... *217*
Earlier sketches in SATA *73, 136*
Dahl, Borghild (Margarethe) 1890-1984 ... *7*
Obituary ... *37*
Dahl, Roald 1916-1990 ... *73*
Obituary ... *65*
Earlier sketches in SATA *1, 26*
See also CLR *111*
Dahlberg, Maurine F. 1951- ... *171*
Dahlstedt, Marden (Stewart) 1921-1983 ... *8*
Obituary ... *110*
Dahme, Joanne ... *206*
Daigneault, Sylvie ... *236*
Dain, Martin J. 1924-2000 ... *35*
Dakin, Glenn 1960- ... *224*
Dakos, Kalli 1950- ... *115*
Earlier sketch in SATA *80*
Dale, Anna 1971- ... *170*
Dale, Gary
See Reece, Colleen L.
Dale, George E.
See Asimov, Isaac
Dale, Jack
See Holliday, Joseph
Dale, Kim 1957- ... *123*
Dale, Margaret J(essy) Miller 1911- ... *39*
Dale, Mitzi
See Hemstock, Gillian
Dale, Norman
See Denny, Norman (George)
Dale, Penny 1954- ... *151*
Earlier sketch in SATA *70*
Daley, Michael J. ... *170*
Dalgliesh, Alice 1893-1979 ... *17*
Obituary ... *21*
See also CLR *62*
Dalkey, Kara 1953- ... *132*
Dalkey, Kara Mia
See Dalkey, Kara
Dallas, Ruth 1919- ... *86*
Dalmas, John
See Jones, John R(obert)
Dalton, Alene
See Chapin, Alene Olsen Dalton
Dalton, Annie 1948- ... *140*
Earlier sketch in SATA *40*
Dalton, Kit
See Cunningham, Chet
Dalton, Max ... *234*
Dalton, Pamela
See Johnson, Pamela
Dalton, Sean
See Chester, Deborah
Dalton, Sheila 1949- ... *108*
D'Aluisio, Faith 1957- ... *205*
Daly, Cathleen ... *241*
Daly, James ... *217*
Daly, Jim
See Stratemeyer, Edward L.
Daly, Jude 1951- ... *222*
Earlier sketch in SATA *177*
Daly, Kathleen N(orah) ... *124*
Brief entry ... *37*
Daly, Maureen 1921-2006 ... *129*
Obituary ... *176*
Earlier sketch in SATA *2*
See also CLR *96*
See also SAAS *1*
Daly, Nicholas
See Daly, Niki
Daly, Niki 1946- ... *198*
Earlier sketches in SATA *37, 76, 114, 164*
See also CLR *41*
See also SAAS *21*
D'Amato, Alex 1919- ... *20*
D'Amato, Janet (Potter) 1925- ... *9*
Damerow, Gail 1944- ... *83*
Damerow, Gail Jane
See Damerow, Gail
D'Amico, Carmela ... *170*
D'Amico, Steve ... *170*
Damrell, Liz 1956- ... *77*
Damrosch, Helen
See Tee-Van, Helen Damrosch
Dana, Barbara 1940- ... *218*
Earlier sketch in SATA *22*
Dana, Richard Henry, Jr. 1815-1882 ... *26*
Danachair, Caoimhin O
See Danaher, Kevin
Danaher, Kevin 1913-2002 ... *22*
Danakas, John 1963- ... *94*
Danalis, John ... *236*
Dandi
See Mackall, Dandi Daley
D'Andrea, Kate
See Steiner, Barbara A(nnette)
Daneshvari, Gitty ... *236*
Dangerfield, Balfour
See McCloskey, (John) Robert
Daniel, Alan 1939- ... *76*
Brief entry ... *53*
Daniel, Anita 1893(?)-1978 ... *23*
Obituary ... *24*
Daniel, Anne
See Steiner, Barbara A(nnette)
Daniel, Becky 1947- ... *56*
Daniel, Claire 1949- ... *164*
Daniel, Colin
See Windsor, Patricia
Daniel, Hawthorne 1890- ... *8*
Daniel, (Donna) Lee 1944- ... *76*
Daniel, Rebecca
See Daniel, Becky
Daniels, Guy 1919-1989 ... *11*
Obituary ... *62*
Daniels, Kit
See Diver, Lucienne
Daniels, Lucy
See Oldfield, Jenny
Daniels, Max
See Gellis, Roberta
Daniels, Olga
See Sinclair, Olga
Daniels, Patricia 1955- ... *93*
Daniels, Zoe
See Laux, Constance
Dank, Gloria Rand 1955- ... *56*
Brief entry ... *46*
Dank, Leonard D(ewey) 1929- ... *44*
Dank, Milton 1920- ... *31*
Dann, Max 1955- ... *62*
Danneberg, Julie 1958- ... *173*
Dantz, William R.
See Philbrick, Rodman
Danzig, Dianne ... *213*
Danziger, Paula 1944-2004 ... *149*
Brief entry ... *30*
Obituary ... *155*
Earlier sketches in SATA *36, 63, 102*
See also CLR *20*
Darby, Gene Kegley
See Darby, Jean (Kegley)
Darby, J. N.
See Govan, (Mary) Christine Noble
Darby, Jean (Kegley) 1921- ... *68*
Darby, Patricia (Paulsen) ... *14*
Darby, Ray(mond) 1912-1982 ... *7*
Darbyshire, Kristen ... *218*
d'Arcy, Willard
See Cox, William R(obert)
Dare, Geena
See McNicoll, Sylvia (Marilyn)
D'arge, Mackie ... *218*
Darian, Shea 1959- ... *97*
Daringer, Helen Fern 1892-1986 ... *1*
Darke, Marjorie 1929- ... *87*
Earlier sketch in SATA *16*
Darley, F(elix) O(ctavius) C(arr) 1822-1888 ... *35*
Darling, David J. 1953- ... *60*
Brief entry ... *44*
Darling, Kathy
See Darling, Mary Kathleen
Darling, Lois (MacIntyre) 1917-1989 ... *3*
Obituary ... *64*
Darling, Louis, (Jr.) 1916-1970 ... *3*
Obituary ... *23*
Darling, Mary Kathleen 1943- ... *124*
Earlier sketches in SATA *9, 79*
Darling, Sandra Louise Woodward
See Day, Alexandra
Darnell, K(athryn) L(ynne) 1955- ... *150*
Darroll, Sally
See Odgers, Sally Farrell
Darrow, Sharon ... *181*
Darrow, Whitney, (Jr.) 1909-1999 ... *13*
Obituary ... *115*
Darwin, Len
See Darwin, Leonard
Darwin, Leonard 1916- ... *24*
Dasent, Sir George Webbe 1817-1896 ... *62*
Brief entry ... *29*
Dash, Joan 1925- ... *142*
Daskam, Josephine Dodge
See Bacon, Josephine Dodge (Daskam)
D'ath, Justin 1953- ... *174*
Earlier sketch in SATA *106*
Dauer, Rosamond 1934- ... *23*
Daugherty, Charles Michael 1914- ... *16*
Daugherty, James (Henry) 1889-1974 ... *13*
See also CLR *78*
Daugherty, Richard D(eo) 1922- ... *35*
Daugherty, Sonia Medwedeff (?)-1971
Obituary ... *27*
d'Aulaire, Edgar Parin 1898-1986 ... *66*
Obituary ... *47*
Earlier sketch in SATA *5*
See also CLR *21*
d'Aulaire, Ingri 1904-1980 ... *66*
Obituary ... *24*
Earlier sketch in SATA *5*
See also CLR *21*

d'Aulaire, Ingri Mortenson Parin
See d'Aulaire, Ingri
Dave, Dave
See Berg, David
Daveluy, Paule Cloutier 1919- *11*
Davenier, Christine 1961- *216*
Earlier sketches in SATA *127, 179*
Davenport, John 1960- *156*
Daves, Michael 1938- *40*
David, A. R.
See David, A(nn) Rosalie
David, A(nn) Rosalie 1946- *103*
David, Jonathan
See Ames, Lee J.
David, Keren 1963- *236*
David, Lawrence 1963- *165*
Earlier sketch in SATA *111*
David, Peter 1956- *72*
David, Peter Allen
See David, Peter
David, Rosalie
See David, A(nn) Rosalie
Davidson, Alice Joyce 1932- *54*
Brief entry *45*
Davidson, Basil 1914-2010 .... *13*
Davidson, (Marie) Diane 1924- *91*
Davidson, Hugh
See Hamilton, Edmond
Davidson, Jessica 1915-1986 .... *5*
Davidson, Judith 1953- *40*
Davidson, Lionel 1922-2009 .... *87*
Davidson, Margaret 1936- *5*
Davidson, Marion
See Garis, Howard R.
Davidson, Mary R. 1885-1973 .... *9*
Davidson, Mary S. 1940- *61*
Davidson, Mickie
See Davidson, Margaret
Davidson, Nicole
See Jensen, Kathryn
Davidson, R.
See Davidson, Raymond
Davidson, Raymond 1926- *32*
Davidson, Rosalie 1921- *23*
Davie, Helen K(ay) 1952- *148*
Earlier sketch in SATA *77*
Davies, Andrew (Wynford) 1936- *27*
Davies, Andy Robert *200*
Davies, Bettilu D(onna) 1942- *33*
Davies, Hunter 1936- *55*
Brief entry *45*
Davies, Jacqueline 1962- *186*
Earlier sketch in SATA *155*
Davies, Joan 1934- *50*
Brief entry *47*
Davies, Nicola 1958- *182*
Earlier sketches in SATA *99, 150*
Davies, Peter J(oseph) 1937- *52*
Davies, Stephen 1976- *239*
Davies, Sumiko 1942- *46*
Davis, (A.) Aubrey 1949- *153*
Davis, Barbara Steincrohn
See Davis, Maggie S.
Davis, Bette J. 1923- *15*
Davis, Burke 1913- *4*
Davis, Christopher 1928- *6*
Davis, D(elbert) Dwight 1908-1965 .... *33*
Davis, Daniel S(heldon) 1936- *12*
Davis, David R. 1948- *106*
Davis, Donald 1944- *169*
Earlier sketch in SATA *93*
Davis, Donald D.
See Davis, Donald
Davis, Eleanor 1983(?)- *209*
Davis, Emma
See Davis, Maggie S.
Davis, Gibbs 1953- *102*
Brief entry *41*
Earlier sketch in SATA *46*
Davis, Grania 1943- *88*
Brief entry *50*
Davis, H(arold) L(enoir) 1896-1960 .... *114*
Davis, Heather 1970- *221*
Davis, Hubert J(ackson) 1904-1997 .... *31*
Davis, Jack E. *210*
Davis, Jacky *204*
Davis, James Robert 1945- *32*
Davis, Jenny 1953- *74*
Davis, Jim
See Davis, James Robert
Davis, Julia 1900(?)-1993 .... *6*
Obituary *75*
Davis, Karen (Elizabeth) 1944- *109*
Davis, Katie 1959(?)- *208*
Earlier sketch in SATA *152*
Davis, Lambert *176*
Davis, Leslie
See Guccione, Leslie Davis
Davis, Louise Littleton 1921- *25*
Davis, Maggie S. 1943- *57*
Davis, Marguerite 1889- *34*
Davis, Mary L(ee) 1935- *9*
Davis, Mary Octavia 1901-1976 .... *6*
Davis, Nancy 1958(?)- *229*
Davis, Nelle 1958- *73*
Davis, Ossie 1917-2005 .... *81*
See also CLR *56*
Davis, Paxton 1925-1994 .... *16*
Davis, Rebecca Fjelland 1956- *240*
Davis, Rich 1958- *206*
Davis, Robert 1881-1949
See YABC *1*
Davis, Robin W(orks) 1962- *87*
Davis, Russell Gerard 1922- *3*
Davis, Tanita S. *212*
Davis, Tim(othy N.) 1957- *94*
Davis, Tony 1961- *222*
Davis, Verne Theodore 1889-1973 .... *6*
Davis, Yvonne 1927- *115*
Davol, Marguerite W. 1928- *146*
Earlier sketch in SATA *82*
DaVolls, Andy (P.) 1967- *85*
DaVolls, Linda 1966- *85*
Davys, Sarah
See Manning, Rosemary
Dawes, Claiborne 1935- *111*
Dawson, Arthur L. *207*
Dawson, Elmer A. *67*
Earlier sketch in SATA *1*
Dawson, Imogen (Zoe) 1948- *126*
Earlier sketch in SATA *90*
Dawson, Janine 1957- *196*
Dawson, Mary 1919- *11*
Dawson, Scott *233*
Dawson, Willow 1975- *208*
Day, A(rthur) Grove 1904-1994 .... *59*
Day, Alexandra 1941- *197*
Autobiography Feature *197*
Earlier sketches in SATA *67, 97, 169*
See also CLR *22*
See also SAAS *19*
Day, Beth (Feagles) 1924- *33*
Day, Donna
See Asay, Donna Day
Day, Edward C. 1932- *72*
Day, Jon 1936(?)- *79*
Day, Karen *187*
Day, Larry 1956- *227*
Earlier sketch in SATA *181*
Day, Nancy 1953- *140*
Day, Nancy Raines 1951- *148*
Earlier sketch in SATA *93*
Day, Shirley 1962- *94*
Day, Susie 1975- *231*
Day, Thomas 1748-1789
See YABC *1*
Day, Trevor 1955- *124*
Dazey, Agnes J(ohnston) *2*
Dazey, Frank M. *2*
Deacon, Alexis 1978- *139*
Deacon, Eileen
See Geipel, Eileen
Deacon, Richard
See McCormick, (George) Donald (King)
Deadman, Ronald 1919-1988(?)
Obituary *56*
Deak, Erzsi 1959- *152*
Dean, Anabel 1915- *12*
Dean, Carolee 1962- *148*
Dean, Claire *215*
Dean, David 1976- *192*
Dean, Karen Strickler 1923- *49*
Dean, Ruth (Brigham) 1947- *145*
Dean, Zoey
See Bennett, Cherie
de Angeli, Marguerite (Lofft) 1889-1987 ... *100*
Obituary *51*
Earlier sketches in SATA *1, 27*
See also CLR *1*
Deans, Karen *195*
Deans, Sis Boulos 1955- *136*
Earlier sketch in SATA *78*
DeArmand, Frances Ullmann 1904(?)-1984 . *10*
Obituary *38*
DeArmond, Dale 1914- *70*
DeArmond, Dale Burlison
See DeArmond, Dale
Deary, Terry 1946- *171*
Brief entry *41*
Earlier sketches in SATA *51, 101*
Deaver, Julie Reece 1953- *68*
de Banke, Cecile 1889-1965 .... *11*
De Bello, Rosario 1923- *89*
Debon, Nicolas *186*
Earlier sketch in SATA *151*
de Bono, Edward 1933- *66*
de Brissac, Malcolm
See Dickinson, Peter
de Brunhoff, Jean
See Brunhoff, Jean de
De Brunhoff, Laurent
See Brunhoff, Laurent de
De Bruyn, Monica G. 1952- *13*
De Bruyn, Monica Jean Grembowicz
See De Bruyn, Monica G.
DeBry, Roger K. 1942- *91*
de Camp, Catherine Crook 1907-2000 .... *83*
Earlier sketch in SATA *12*
de Camp, L. Sprague 1907-2000 .... *83*
Earlier sketch in SATA *9*
de Camp, Lyon Sprague
See de Camp, L. Sprague
DeCandido, Keith R.A. *112*
Dechausay, Sonia E. *94*
Decker, C.B. *172*
Decker, Cynthia B.
See Decker, C.B.
Decker, Duane 1910-1964 .... *5*
Decker, Timothy 1974- *197*
DeClements, Barthe 1920- *131*
Earlier sketches in SATA *35, 71*
See also CLR *23*
DeClements, Barthe Faith
See DeClements, Barthe
de Clercq Zubli, Rita la Fontaine 1929- *199*
de Conte, Sieur Louis
See Twain, Mark
Dedman, Stephen *108*
Dee, Barbara 1958- *220*
Dee, Catherine 1964- *138*
Dee, Ruby
See Wallace, Ruby Ann
Deeble, Jason 1979- *221*
Deedy, Carmen Agra 1960- *196*
Deedy, John 1923- *24*
Deegan, Paul Joseph 1937- *48*
Brief entry *38*
Deem, James M. 1950- *191*
Autobiography Feature *191*
Earlier sketches in SATA *75, 134*
Deem, James Morgan
See Deem, James M.
Deeter, Catherine 1947- *137*

Author Index

DeFelice, Cynthia 1951- 165
Earlier sketches in SATA 79, 121
DeFelice, Cynthia C.
See DeFelice, Cynthia
Defoe, Daniel 1660(?)-1731 22
See also CLR 164
de Fombelle, Timothee
See Fombelle, Timothee de
DeFord, Deborah H. 123
deFrance, Anthony
See DiFranco, Anthony (Mario)
Degen, Bruce 1945- 205
Brief entry 47
Earlier sketches in SATA 57, 97, 147
DeGering, Etta (Belle) Fowler 1898-1996 7
Degman, Lori 234
De Goldi, Kate 1959- 123
De Goldi, Kathleen Domenica
See De Goldi, Kate
de Goursac, Olivier 1959- 184
De Grazia, Ettore 1909-1982 39
De Grazia, Ted
See De Grazia, Ettore
deGroat, Diane 1947- 169
Earlier sketches in SATA 31, 90
deGros, J. H.
See Villiard, Paul
de Grummond, Lena Young 62
Earlier sketch in SATA 6
de Hamel, Joan Littledale 1924- 86
De Haven, Tom 1949- 72
de Hugo, Pierre
See Brackers de Hugo, Pierre
Deines, Brian 1955- 220
Deiss, Joseph Jay 1912-1999 12
de Jenkins, Lyll Becerra 1925-1997 102
DeJong, David C(ornel) 1905-1967 10
de Jong, Dola
See de Jong, Dorothea Rosalie
de Jong, Dorothea Rosalie 1911-2003 7
Obituary 149
DeJong, Meindert 1906-1991 2
Obituary 68
See also CLR 73
DeJonge, Joanne E. 1943- 56
Deka, Connie
See Laux, Constance
de Kay, Ormonde (Jr.) 1923-1998 7
Obituary 106
DeKeyser, Stacy 1959- 214
de Kiriline, Louise
See Lawrence, Louise de Kiriline
Dekker, Carl
See Laffin, John (Alfred Charles)
and Lynds, Dennis
deKruif, Paul (Henry) 1890-1971 50
Earlier sketch in SATA 5
Delacre, Lulu 1957- 209
Earlier sketches in SATA 36, 156
DeLaCroix, Alice 1940- 195
Earlier sketch in SATA 75
de la Cruz, Melissa 1971- 179
De la Garza, Phyllis 1942- 169
De Lage, Ida 1918- 11
de la Mare, Walter (John) 1873-1956 16
See also CLR 148
Delaney, Harry 1932- 3
Delaney, Joseph 1945- 172
Delaney, M.C.
See Delaney, Michael
Delaney, Michael 1955- 180
Earlier sketch in SATA 96
Delaney, Michael Clark
See Delaney, Michael
Delaney, Ned 1951- 28
Delaney, Thomas Nicholas III
See Delaney, Ned
DeLange, Alex Pardo
See Pardo DeLange, Alex
Delano, Hugh 1933- 20
Delano, Marfe Ferguson 215
Delany, Samuel R., Jr. 1942- 92
Delany, Samuel Ray
See Delany, Samuel R., Jr.
Delany, Shannon 239
de la Pena, Matt 205
De La Ramee, Marie Louise 1839-1908 20
de la Roche, Mazo 1879-1961 64
De La Roche Saint Andre, Anne 1950- 75
de Las Casas, Dianne 1970- 221
Delaune, (Jewel) Lynn (de Grummond) 7
DeLaurentis, Louise Budde 1920- 12
del Barco, Lucy Salamanca 1900(?)-1989
Obituary 64
Delderfield, Eric R(aymond) 1909-1995 14
Delderfield, Ronald Frederick 1912-1972 20
DeLeeuw, Adele (Louise) 1899-1988 30
Obituary 56
Earlier sketch in SATA 1
De Leon, Nephtali 1945- 97
Delessert, Etienne 1941- 179
Brief entry 27
Earlier sketches in SATA 46, 130
See also CLR 81
Delgado, James P. 1958- 122
Delinois, Alix 228
de Lint, Charles 1951- 207
Earlier sketches in SATA 115, 157
de Lint, Charles Henri Diederick Hofsmit
See de Lint, Charles
Delmar, Roy
See Wexler, Jerome (LeRoy)
Del Negro, Janice M. 197
Deloria, Vine, Jr. 1933-2005 21
Obituary 171
Deloria, Vine Victor, Jr.
See Deloria, Vine, Jr.
del Rey, Lester 1915-1993 22
Obituary 76
Delrio, Martin
See Doyle, Debra
and Macdonald, James D.
Delton, Judy 1931-2001 77
Obituary 130
Earlier sketch in SATA 14
See also SAAS 9
Delulio, John 1938- 15
Delvig, Lou
See Vigan, Delphine de
Delving, Michael
See Williams, Jay
de Marcken, Gail 186
Demarest, Chris L. 1951- 175
Brief entry 44
Earlier sketches in SATA 45, 82, 128
Demarest, Christopher Lynn
See Demarest, Chris L.
Demarest, Doug
See Barker, Will
De Mari, Silvana 1953- 193
Demas, Corinne 1947- 203
Earlier sketches in SATA 37, 131
Demas, Vida 1927- 9
Dematons, Charlotte 1957- 203
DeMatteis, J.M. 1953- 241
Earlier sketch in SATA 180
DeMatteis, John Marc
See DeMatteis, J.M.
De Mejo, Oscar 1911-1992 40
Demers, Dominique 1956- 177
de Messieres, Nicole 1930- 39
DeMeulemeester, Linda 1956- 230
Demi 1942- 210
Earlier sketches in SATA 11, 66, 102, 152
See also CLR 58
Demijohn, Thom
See Disch, Thomas M.
and Sladek, John
Deming, Richard 1915-1983 24
Deming, Sarah 191
de Monfreid, Dorothee 1973- 189
Dempsey, Kristy 238
Demuth, Patricia Brennan 1948- 84
Brief entry 51
De Muth, Roger 1948- 221
Dendinger, Roger E. 1952- 158
Denenberg, Barry 1940- 175
Dengler, Marianna (Herron) 1935- 103
Dengler, Sandy 1939- 54
Brief entry 40
Denim, Sue
See Pilkey, Dav
Denise, Anika 210
Denise, Christopher 1968- 193
Earlier sketch in SATA 147
Denman, K.L. 1957- 186
Denmark, Harrison
See Zelazny, Roger
Dennard, Deborah 1953- 136
Earlier sketch in SATA 78
Denney, Diana 1910-2000 25
Obituary 120
Dennis, Morgan 1891(?)-1960 18
Dennis, Wesley 1903-1966 18
Denniston, Elinore 1900-1978
Obituary 24
Denny, Norman (George) 1901-1982 43
Denos, Julia 202
Denslow, Sharon Phillips 1947- 142
Earlier sketch in SATA 68
Denslow, W(illiam) W(allace) 1856-1915 16
See also CLR 15
Dent, Grace 1973- 187
Denton, Kady MacDonald 181
Earlier sketches in SATA 66, 110
See also CLR 71
Denton, Terry 1950- 186
Denver, Walt
See Redding, Robert Hull
and Sherman, Jory (Tecumseh)
Denzel, Justin F(rancis) 1917-1999 46
Brief entry 38
Denzer, Ann Wiseman
See Wiseman, Ann (Sayre)
DePalma, Mary Newell 1961- 241
Earlier sketches in SATA 139, 185
De Palma, Toni 199
dePaola, Thomas Anthony 1934- 200
Earlier sketches in SATA 11, 59, 108, 155
See also CLR 81
See also SAAS 15
dePaola, Tomie
See dePaola, Thomas Anthony
deParrie, Paul 1949- 74
DePauw, Linda Grant 1940- 24
De Pretto, Lorenzo 1966- 225
de Quidt, Jeremy 237
DeRan, David 1946- 76
Derby, Ken 1956- 181
Derby, Kenneth R.
See Derby, Ken
Derby, Pat 1942- 172
Derby, Sally 1934- 189
Earlier sketches in SATA 89, 132
de Regniers, Beatrice Schenk (Freedman)
1914-2000 68
Obituary 123
Earlier sketch in SATA 2
See also SAAS 6
Dereske, Jo 1947- 72
Deriso, Christine Hurley 1961- 210
Derleth, August (William) 1909-1971 5
Derman, Martha (Winn) 74
Derman, Sarah Audrey 1915- 11
DeRoberts, Lyndon
See Silverstein, Robert Alan
Derom, Dirk 1980- 224
de Roo, Anne Louise 1931-1997 84
Earlier sketch in SATA 25
See also CLR 63
deRosa, Dee 70
Derrick, Lionel
See Cunningham, Chet

Derrickson, Jim 1959- ... 141
Derry Down Derry
See Lear, Edward
Derting, Kimberly 1968- ... 231
Dervaux, Isabelle 1961- ... 106
Derwent, Lavinia ... 14
Desai, Anita 1937- ... 126
Earlier sketch in SATA 63
DeSaix, Deborah Durland ... 188
De Saulles, Tony 1958- ... 119
Desbarats, Peter 1933- ... 39
de Selincourt, Aubrey 1894-1962 ... 14
de Seve, Peter 1958- ... 219
de Seve, Randall ... 198
Deshpande, Chris 1950- ... 69
Desimini, Lisa 1964- ... 216
Earlier sketches in SATA 86, 148
Desjarlais, John 1953- ... 71
Desjarlais, John J.
See Desjarlais, John
Desmoinaux, Christel 1967- ... 149
Earlier sketch in SATA 103
Desmond, Adrian 1947- ... 51
Desmond, Adrian J.
See Desmond, Adrian
Desmond, Adrian John
See Desmond, Adrian
Desmond, Alice Curtis 1897-1990 ... 8
Desnoettes, Caroline ... 183
Despain, Bree 1979- ... 239
DeSpain, Pleasant 1943- ... 87
Desputeaux, Helene 1959- ... 95
Dessen, Sarah 1970- ... 172
Earlier sketch in SATA 120
DeStefano, Lauren 1984- ... 241
Detine, Padre
See Olsen, Ib Spang
de Trevino, Elizabeth B.
See Trevino, Elizabeth B(orton) de
de Trevino, Elizabeth Borton
See Trevino, Elizabeth B(orton) de
Detwiler, Susan Dill 1956- ... 58
Deuker, Carl 1950- ... 196
Earlier sketches in SATA 82, 150
Deutsch, Babette 1895-1982 ... 1
Obituary ... 33
Deutsch, Barry ... 239
Deutsch, Eva Costabel
See Costabel, Eva Deutsch
Deutsch, Helen 1906-1992 ... 76
Deutsch, Kurt
See Singer, Kurt D.
De Valera, Sinead 1879(?)-1975
Obituary ... 30
Devaney, John 1926-1994 ... 12
de Varennes, Monique 1947- ... 168
de Varona, Frank J. 1943- ... 83
Devereux, Frederick L(eonard), Jr.
1914-1993 ... 9
Devi, Nila
See Woody, Regina Jones
DeVillers, Julia 1967- ... 227
deVinck, Christopher 1951- ... 85
DeVita, James ... 195
DeVito, Cara 1956- ... 80
Devlin, Dorothy Wende
See Devlin, Wende
Devlin, Harry 1918-2001 ... 136
Earlier sketches in SATA 11, 74
Devlin, Wende 1918-2002 ... 74
Earlier sketch in SATA 11
Devon, Paddie 1953- ... 92
Devons, Sonia 1974- ... 72
Devorah-Leah ... 111
de Vos, Gail 1949- ... 122
de Vries, Anke 1936- ... 222
DeVries, Douglas 1933- ... 122
De Waard, E(lliott) John 1935- ... 7
Dewan, Ted 1961- ... 226
Earlier sketches in SATA 108, 157
Dewdney, Anna ... 232
Earlier sketch in SATA 184
Dewdney, Selwyn (Hanington) 1909-1979 ... 64
DeWeese, Gene
See DeWeese, Thomas Eugene
DeWeese, Jean
See DeWeese, Thomas Eugene
DeWeese, Thomas Eugene 1934- ... 46
Brief entry ... 45
Dewey, Ariane 1937- ... 178
Earlier sketches in SATA 7, 109
Dewey, Jennifer (Owings) 1941- ... 103
Brief entry ... 48
Earlier sketch in SATA 58
Dewey, Kenneth Francis 1940- ... 39
Dewin, Howie
See Howie, Betsy
De Wire, Elinor 1953- ... 180
deWit, Dorothy (May Knowles) 1916-1980 . 39
Obituary ... 28
Dexter, Alison 1966- ... 125
Dexter, John
See Bradley, Marion Zimmer
Deyneka, Anita 1943- ... 24
Deyrup, Astrith Johnson 1923- ... 24
Dezern, Chad ... 201
de Zubizarreta, Alma
See Ada, Alma Flor
Dhami, Narinder 1958- ... 152
Dhondy, Farrukh 1944- ... 152
Earlier sketch in SATA 65
See also CLR 41
Diakite, Baba Wague 1961- ... 174
Diakite, Penda 1993(?)- ... 174
Diamand, Emily 1971- ... 227
Diamond, Arthur 1957- ... 76
Diamond, Donna 1950- ... 69
Brief entry ... 30
Earlier sketch in SATA 35
Diamond, Petra
See Sachs, Judith
Diamond, Rebecca
See Sachs, Judith
Dias, Earl Joseph 1916- ... 41
Dias, Ron 1937- ... 71
Diaz, David 1959(?)- ... 229
Earlier sketches in SATA 96, 150, 189
See also CLR 65
di Bartolo, Jim ... 225
Dibley, Glin ... 188
DiCamillo, Kate 1964- ... 202
Earlier sketches in SATA 121, 163
See also CLR 117
Di Certo, J(oseph) J(ohn) 1933- ... 60
DiCianni, Ron 1952- ... 107
Dick, Trella Lamson 1889-1974 ... 9
Dickens, Charles 1812-1870 ... 15
See also CLR 162
Dickens, Charles John Huffam
See Dickens, Charles
Dickens, Frank
See Huline-Dickens, Frank William
Dickens, Monica (Enid) 1915-1992 ... 4
Obituary ... 74
Dickerson, Roy Ernest 1886-1965
Obituary ... 26
Dickinson, Emily 1830-1886 ... 29
Dickinson, Emily Elizabeth
See Dickinson, Emily
Dickinson, Mary 1949- ... 48
Brief entry ... 41
Dickinson, Mary-Anne
See Rodda, Emily
Dickinson, Peter 1927- ... 229
Earlier sketches in SATA 5, 62, 95, 150
See also CLR 125
Dickinson, Peter Malcolm de Brissac
See Dickinson, Peter
Dickinson, Susan 1931- ... 8
Dickinson, Terence 1943- ... 102
Dickinson, W(illiam) Croft 1897-1963 ... 13
Dickson, Gordon R. 1923-2001 ... 77
Dickson, Gordon Rupert
See Dickson, Gordon R.
Dickson, Helen
See Reynolds, Helen Mary Greenwood Campbell
Dickson, Naida 1916- ... 8
Diehn, Gwen 1943- ... 80
Dierssen, Andreas 1962- ... 190
Diesen, Deborah 1967- ... 200
Dieterich, Michele M. 1962- ... 78
Dietz, David H(enry) 1897-1984 ... 10
Obituary ... 41
Dietz, Lew 1907-1997 ... 11
Obituary ... 95
Diffily, Deborah ... 159
Di Fiori, Larry
See Di Fiori, Lawrence
Di Fiori, Lawrence 1934- ... 130
DiFranco, Anthony (Mario) 1945- ... 42
Digby, Anne 1935- ... 72
Digges, Jeremiah
See Berger, Josef
Digman, Kristina 1959- ... 176
D'Ignazio, Fred 1949- ... 39
Brief entry ... 35
D'Ignazio, Frederick
See D'Ignazio, Fred
Di Grazia, Thomas (?)-1983 ... 32
Dijkstra, Lida 1961- ... 195
Dikty, Julian May
See May, Julian
Dillard, Annie 1945- ... 140
Earlier sketch in SATA 10
Dillard, Kristine 1964- ... 113
Dillard, Polly Hargis 1916- ... 24
Dillard, Sarah 1961- ... 217
Diller, Harriett 1953- ... 78
Dillon, Anna
See Scott, Michael
Dillon, Barbara 1927- ... 44
Brief entry ... 39
Dillon, Diane 1933- ... 194
Earlier sketches in SATA 15, 51, 106
See also CLR 44
Dillon, Diane Claire
See Dillon, Diane
Dillon, Eilis 1920-1994 ... 74
Autobiography Feature ... 105
Obituary ... 83
Earlier sketch in SATA 2
See also CLR 26
Dillon, Jana (a pseudonym) 1952- ... 117
Dillon, Leo 1933- ... 194
Earlier sketches in SATA 15, 51, 106
See also CLR 44
Dillon, Sharon Saseen
See Saseen, Sharon (Dillon)
Dils, Tracey E. 1958- ... 83
Dilson, Jesse 1914-1988 ... 24
Dinan, Carolyn ... 59
Brief entry ... 47
Dines, Carol 1956- ... 175
Dines, (Harry) Glen 1925-1996 ... 7
Dinesen, Isak
See Blixen, Karen
Dinessi, Alex
See Schembri, Jim
Dinneen, Betty 1929- ... 61
Dinnerstein, Harvey 1928- ... 42
Dinsdale, Tim(othy Kay) 1924-1987 ... 11
Dion, Nathalie 1964- ... 213
Dionne, Erin 1975- ... 217
Diop, Birago (Ismael) 1906-1989
Obituary ... 64
Diouf, Sylviane A. ... 168
Diouf, Sylviane Anna
See Diouf, Sylviane A.
DiPucchio, Kelly ... 204
Earlier sketch in SATA 159

Dirk
See Gringhuis, Richard H.
Dirks, Wilhelmina 1916- ... *59*
Dirks, Willy
See Dirks, Wilhelmina
Dirtmeister
See Tomecek, Steve
DiSalvo, DyAnne 1960- ... *144*
Earlier sketch in SATA *59*
DiSalvo-Ryan, DyAnne
See DiSalvo, DyAnne
Disch, Thomas M. 1940-2008 ... *92*
Obituary ... *195*
See also CLR *18*
See also SAAS *15*
Disch, Thomas Michael
See Disch, Thomas M.
Disch, Tom
See Disch, Thomas M.
Disher, Garry 1949- ... *125*
Earlier sketch in SATA *81*
Disney, Walt(er Elias) 1901-1966 ... *28*
Brief entry ... *27*
Ditchfield, Christin 1973- ... *226*
Earlier sketch in SATA *189*
DiTerlizzi, Tony 1969- ... *214*
Earlier sketch in SATA *154*
DiTerlooney, Tiny
See DiTerlizzi, Tony
Divakaruni, Chitra Banerjee 1956- ... *222*
Earlier sketch in SATA *160*
Di Valentin, Maria (Amelia) Messuri
1911-1985 ... *7*
Diver, Lucienne 1971- ... *218*
Divine, Arthur Durham 1904-1987
Obituary ... *52*
Divine, David
See Divine, Arthur Durham
Divine, L. ... *229*
Dixon, Ann 1954- ... *212*
Earlier sketches in SATA *77, 127*
Dixon, Ann Renee
See Dixon, Ann
Dixon, Dougal 1947- ... *190*
Earlier sketches in SATA *45, 127*
Dixon, Franklin W.
See Barrett, Neal, Jr.
and Goulart, Ron
and Lantz, Francess L(in)
and Lerangis, Peter
and McFarlane, Leslie
and Stanley, George Edward
and Stratemeyer, Edward L.
Dixon, Jeanne 1936- ... *31*
Dixon, Paige
See Corcoran, Barbara (Asenath)
Dixon, Peter L(ee) 1931- ... *6*
Dixon, Rachel 1952- ... *74*
Dizin, Pascal ... *230*
Djoleto, (Solomon Alexander) Amu 1929- ... *80*
d'Lacey, Chris 1949- ... *227*
Earlier sketch in SATA *165*
Doak, Annie
See Dillard, Annie
Doane, Pelagie 1906-1966 ... *7*
Dob, Bob ... *207*
Dobell, I(sabel) M(arian) B(arclay)
1909-1998 ... *11*
Dobie, J(ames) Frank 1888-1964 ... *43*
Dobkin, Alexander 1908-1975
Obituary ... *30*
Dobler, Lavinia G. 1910- ... *6*
Dobrin, Arnold 1928- ... *4*
Dobson, Jill 1969- ... *140*
Dobson, Julia 1941- ... *48*
Dobson, Mary 1954- ... *117*
DoCampo, Valeria 1976- ... *217*
Docherty, James
See Docherty, Jimmy
Docherty, Jimmy 1976- ... *204*
Docherty, Thomas 1955- ... *218*
Dockery, Wallene T. 1941- ... *27*
Dockray, Tracy 1962- ... *139*
Dockrey, Karen 1955- ... *103*
Doctor, Bernard
See Doctor, Bernard Aquina
Doctor, Bernard Aquina 1950- ... *81*
Doctor X
See Nourse, Alan E(dward)
Dodd, Ed(ward Benton) 1902-1991 ... *4*
Obituary ... *68*
Dodd, Emma 1969- ... *239*
Earlier sketch in SATA *203*
Dodd, Lynley (Stuart) 1941- ... *132*
Earlier sketches in SATA *35, 86*
See also CLR *62*
Dodd, Marty 1921- ... *142*
Dodd, Quentin 1972- ... *137*
Dodds, Bill 1952- ... *78*
Dodds, Dayle Ann 1952- ... *201*
Earlier sketches in SATA *75, 150*
Doder, Josh 1968- ... *187*
Dodge, Bertha S(anford) 1902-1995 ... *8*
Dodge, Fremont
See Grimes, Lee
Dodge, Gil
See Hano, Arnold
Dodge, Mary (Elizabeth) Mapes
1831(?)-1905 ... *100*
Earlier sketch in SATA *21*
See also CLR *62*
Dodgson, Charles Lutwidge
See Carroll, Lewis
Dodson, Emma ... *235*
Dodson, Kenneth MacKenzie 1907-1999 ... *11*
Dodson, Susan 1941- ... *50*
Brief entry ... *40*
Doerrfeld, Cori 1964- ... *214*
Dogar, Sharon 1962- ... *211*
Dogyear, Drew
See Gorey, Edward (St. John)
Doherty, Berlie 1943- ... *111*
Earlier sketch in SATA *72*
See also CLR *21*
See also SAAS *16*
Doherty, Charles Hugh 1913- ... *6*
Doherty, Craig A. 1951- ... *169*
Earlier sketch in SATA *83*
Doherty, Katherine M(ann) 1951- ... *83*
Doherty, Kieran 1945- ... *164*
Dokas, Dara 1968- ... *216*
Dokey, Cameron 1956- ... *97*
Dolamore, Jaclyn 1982- ... *227*
Dolan, Edward F(rancis), Jr. 1924- ... *94*
Brief entry ... *31*
Earlier sketch in SATA *45*
Dolan, Ellen M(eara) 1929-1998 ... *88*
Dolan, Sean J. 1958- ... *74*
Dolce, J. Ellen 1948- ... *75*
Dolch, Edward William 1889-1961 ... *50*
Dolch, Marguerite Pierce 1891-1978 ... *50*
Dollar, Diane (Hills) 1933- ... *57*
Dolson, Hildegarde
See Lockridge, Hildegarde (Dolson)
Domanska, Janina 1913(?)-1995 ... *68*
Obituary ... *84*
Earlier sketch in SATA *6*
See also CLR *40*
See also SAAS *18*
Dominguez, Angel 1953- ... *76*
Dominguez, Angela N. 1982- ... *219*
Domino, John
See Averill, Esther (Holden)
Domjan, Joseph (Spiri) 1907-1992 ... *25*
Domm, Jeffrey C. 1958- ... *84*
Donahue, Dorothy ... *178*
Donald, Rhonda Lucas 1962- ... *147*
Donalds, Gordon
See Shirreffs, Gordon D(onald)
Donaldson, Bryna
See Stevens, Bryna
Donaldson, Gordon 1913-1993 ... *64*
Obituary ... *76*
Donaldson, Joan 1953- ... *227*
Earlier sketch in SATA *78*
Donaldson, Julia 1948- ... *226*
Earlier sketches in SATA *82, 132, 180*
Donaldson, Stephen R. 1947- ... *121*
Donaldson, Stephen Reeder
See Donaldson, Stephen R.
Doner, Kim 1955- ... *208*
Earlier sketch in SATA *91*
Doney, Todd L. W. 1959- ... *104*
Dong-Sung, Kim 1970- ... *195*
Dong-Sung Kim
See Dong-Sung, Kim
Donkin, Andrew ... *219*
Donkin, Nance (Clare) 1915- ... *95*
Donna, Natalie 1934-1979 ... *9*
Donnelly, Elfie 1950-
See CLR *104*
Donnelly, Jennifer 1963- ... *154*
Donnelly, Matt 1972- ... *148*
Donnio, Sylviane ... *188*
Donofrio, Beverly 1950- ... *209*
Donoghue, Emma 1969- ... *101*
Donohue, Moira Rose 1954- ... *201*
Donoughue, Carol 1935- ... *139*
Donovan, Frank (Robert) 1906-1975
Obituary ... *30*
Donovan, Gail 1962- ... *217*
Donovan, Jane Monroe ... *237*
Donovan, John 1928-1992 ... *72*
Brief entry ... *29*
See also CLR *3*
Donovan, Mary Lee 1961- ... *86*
Donovan, William
See Berkebile, Fred D(onovan)
Donze, Mary Terese 1911- ... *89*
Doob, Leonard W(illiam) 1909-2000 ... *8*
Doodler, Todd H.
See Goldman, Todd Harris
Dooley, Norah 1953- ... *74*
Dooley, Sarah ... *236*
Dooling, Michael 1958- ... *220*
Earlier sketch in SATA *105*
Dor, Ana
See Ceder, Georgiana Dorcas
Doran, Colleen 1963- ... *211*
Dore, (Louis Christophe Paul) Gustave
1832-1883 ... *19*
Doremus, Robert 1913-2010 ... *30*
Doren, Marion (Walker) 1928- ... *57*
Dorenkamp, Michelle 1957- ... *89*
Dorflinger, Carolyn 1953- ... *91*
Dorfman, Joaquin 1979- ... *180*
Dorfman, Joaquin Emiliano
See Dorfman, Joaquin
Dorian, Edith M(cEwen) 1900-1983 ... *5*
Dorian, Harry
See Hamilton, Charles (Harold St. John)
Dorian, Marguerite ... *7*
Dorin, Patrick C(arberry) 1939- ... *59*
Brief entry ... *52*
Dorman, Brandon ... *194*
Dorman, Michael 1932- ... *7*
Dorman, N. B. 1927- ... *39*
Dormer, Frank W. ... *200*
Dorris, Michael 1945-1997 ... *75*
Obituary ... *94*
See also CLR *58*
Dorris, Michael A.
See Dorris, Michael
Dorris, Michael Anthony
See Dorris, Michael
Dorritt, Susan
See Schlein, Miriam
Dorros, Alex 1991- ... *194*
Dorros, Arthur 1950- ... *168*
Earlier sketches in SATA *78, 122*
See also CLR *42*
See also SAAS *20*

Dorros, Arthur M.
See Dorros, Arthur
Dorson, Richard M(ercer) 1916-1981 .... *30*
Doss, Helen (Grigsby) 1918- *20*
Doss, Margot Patterson *6*
dos Santos, Joyce Audy 1949- *57*
Brief entry *42*
Dothers, Anne
See Chess, Victoria (Dickerson)
Dotlich, Rebecca Kai 1951- *182*
Dottig
See Grider, Dorothy
Dotts, Maryann J. 1933- *35*
Doty, Jean Slaughter 1929- *28*
Doty, Roy 1922- *28*
Doubtfire, Dianne (Abrams) 1918- *29*
Doucet, Sharon Arms 1951- *144*
Autobiography Feature *144*
Earlier sketch in SATA *125*
Dougherty, Charles 1922- *18*
Dougherty, Terri (L.) 1964- *146*
Doughty, Rebecca 1955- *174*
Douglas, Allen *223*
Douglas, Blaise 1960- *101*
Douglas, Carole Nelson 1944- *73*
Douglas, David
See Tutt, Keith
Douglas, Garry
See Kilworth, Garry
Douglas, James McM.
See Griffin, W. E. B.
Douglas, Kathryn
See Ewing, Kathryn
Douglas, Leonard
See Bradbury, Ray
Douglas, Lola
See Zeises, Lara M.
Douglas, Marjory Stoneman 1890-1998 .... *10*
Douglas, Michael
See Bright, Robert Sr.)
Douglas, Michael
See Crichton, Michael
Douglas, Shirley Stewart
See Tepper, Sheri S.
Douglass, Barbara 1930- *40*
Douglass, Frederick 1817(?)-1895 .... *29*
Douglass, Keith
See Cunningham, Chet
Douty, Esther M(orris) 1909-1978 .... *8*
Obituary *23*
Dow, Emily R. 1904-1987 .... *10*
Dow, Vicki
See McVey, Vicki
Dowd, John David 1945- *78*
Dowd, Siobhan 1960-2007 .... *204*
Dowdell, Dorothy (Florence) Karns 1910- ... *12*
Dowden, Anne Ophelia Todd 1907-2007 .... *7*
Obituary *180*
See also SAAS *10*
Dowdey, Landon Gerald 1923- *11*
Dowdy, Mrs. Regera
See Gorey, Edward (St. John)
Dowell, Frances O'Roark 1964- *205*
Earlier sketch in SATA *157*
Dower, Laura 1967- *185*
Dowling, Terry 1947- *101*
Downard, Barry 1956- *202*
Downer, Ann 1960- *155*
Downer, Marion 1892(?)-1971 .... *25*
Downes, Belinda 1962- *180*
Downey, Fairfax D(avis) 1893-1990 .... *3*
Obituary *66*
Downey, Lisa *214*
Downey, Lynn 1961- *185*
Downham, Jenny 1964- *192*
Downie, John 1931- *87*
Downie, Mary Alice 1934- *171*
Earlier sketches in SATA *13, 87*
Downie, Mary Alice Dawe
See Downie, Mary Alice
Downing, David A(lmon) 1958- *84*
Downing, Erin 1976- *237*
Downing, Johnette *184*
Downing, Julie 1956- *148*
Earlier sketch in SATA *81*
Downing, Paula E. 1951- *80*
Downing, Warwick
See Downing, Wick
Downing, Wick 1931- *138*
Dowswell, Paul 1957- *184*
Doyle, A. Conan
See Doyle, Sir Arthur Conan
Doyle, Sir Arthur Conan 1859-1930 .... *24*
See also CLR *106*
Doyle, Brian 1935- *156*
Earlier sketches in SATA *67, 104*
See also CLR *22*
See also SAAS *16*
Doyle, Charlotte 1937- *178*
Earlier sketch in SATA *94*
Doyle, Charlotte Lackner
See Doyle, Charlotte
Doyle, Conan
See Doyle, Sir Arthur Conan
Doyle, Debra 1952- *165*
Earlier sketch in SATA *105*
Doyle, Donovan
See Boegehold, Betty (Doyle)
Doyle, Eugenie 1952- *225*
Doyle, John
See Graves, Robert
Doyle, Malachy 1954- *165*
Earlier sketch in SATA *120*
See also CLR *83*
Doyle, Richard 1824-1883 .... *21*
Doyle, Sir A. Conan
See Doyle, Sir Arthur Conan
Dr. A
See Asimov, Isaac
and Silverstein, Alvin
and Silverstein, Virginia B.
Dr. Alphabet
See Morice, Dave
Dr. Fred
See Bortz, Alfred B(enjamin)
Dr. Laura
See Schlessinger, Laura (Catherine)
Dr. Seuss 1904-1991 .... *100*
Obituary *67*
Earlier sketches in SATA *1, 28, 75*
See also CLR *100*
Dr. Zed
See Penrose, Gordon
Drabble, Margaret 1939- *48*
Drackett, Phil(ip Arthur) 1922- *53*
Draco, F.
See Davis, Julia
Dracup, Angela 1943- *74*
Dragisic, Patricia *116*
Dragonwagon, Crescent 1952- *186*
Autobiography Feature *186*
Earlier sketches in SATA *11, 41, 75, 133*
See also SAAS *14*
Drake, David 1945- *85*
Drake, David Allen
See Drake, David
Drake, Frank
See Hamilton, Charles (Harold St. John)
Drake, Jane 1954- *235*
Earlier sketch in SATA *82*
Drake, Salamanda
See Barlow, Steve
Drakeford, Dale B 1952- *113*
Drakeford, Dale Benjamin
See Drakeford, Dale B
Draper, Hastings
See Jeffries, Roderic
Draper, Sharon
See Draper, Sharon M.
Draper, Sharon M. 1948- *195*
Autobiography Feature *146*
Earlier sketches in SATA *98, 146*
See also CLR *57*
Draper, Sharon Mills
See Draper, Sharon M.
Drapier, M. B.
See Swift, Jonathan
Drawson, Blair 1943- *126*
Earlier sketch in SATA *17*
Dray, Matt 1967- *177*
Dray, Matthew Frederick
See Dray, Matt
Dresang, Eliza (Carolyn Timberlake) 1941- . *19*
Drescher, Henrik 1955- *172*
Earlier sketches in SATA *67, 105*
See also CLR *20*
Drescher, Joan E(lizabeth) 1939- *137*
Earlier sketch in SATA *30*
Dressen-McQueen, Stacey *191*
Dreves, Veronica R. 1927-1986
Obituary *50*
Drew, Patricia 1938- *15*
Drew, Patricia Mary
See Drew, Patricia
Drewery, Mary 1918- *6*
Drewery, Melanie 1970- *165*
Drewry, Henry N(athaniel) 1924- *138*
Dreyer, Ellen *177*
Drial, J. E.
See Laird, Jean E(louise)
Drimmer, Frederick 1916-2000 .... *60*
Obituary *124*
Driskill, J. Lawrence 1920- *90*
Driskill, Larry
See Driskill, J. Lawrence
Driving Hawk, Virginia
See Sneve, Virginia Driving Hawk
Dron, Laura
See Matthews, L. S.
Dronzek, Laura *199*
Drucker, Malka 1945- *214*
Brief entry *29*
Earlier sketches in SATA *39, 111*
Drucker, Olga Levy 1927- *79*
Druitt, Tobias
See Purkiss, Diane
Drummond, Allan 1957- *209*
Drummond, Karona 1965- *220*
Drummond, V(iolet) H(ilda) 1911-2000 .... *6*
Drummond, Walter
See Silverberg, Robert
Drury, Clare Marie
See Hoskyns-Abrahall, Clare (Constance Drury)
Drury, Roger W(olcott) 1914-1996 .... *15*
Druse, Eleanor
See King, Stephen
Dryden, Pamela
See St. John, Nicole
D.T., Hughes
See Hughes, Dean
Duane, Diane 1952- *233*
Brief entry *46*
Earlier sketches in SATA *58, 95, 145*
Dubanevich, Arlene 1950- *56*
Dubelaar, Thea 1947- *60*
Dubin, Jill *205*
du Blane, Daphne
See Groom, Arthur William
Duble, Kathleen Benner 1958- *164*
Dubois, Claude K. 1960- *196*
DuBois, Rochelle Holt 1946- *41*
Du Bois, Shirley Graham 1907(?)-1977 .... *24*
See Graham, Shirley
Du Bois, W. E. B. 1868-1963 .... *42*
Du Bois, William Edward Burghardt
See Du Bois, W. E. B.
du Bois, William Pene
See Pene du Bois, William (Sherman)
Duboise, Novella 1911-1999 .... *88*

Dubosarsky, Ursula 1961- *193*
Earlier sketches in SATA *107, 147*
DuBose, LaRocque (Russ) 1926- 2
Dubrovin, Vivian 1931- *139*
Earlier sketch in SATA *65*
DuBurke, Randy *224*
Earlier sketch in SATA *172*
Ducey, Jean Sparks 1915- *93*
Duchacek, Ivo D(uka) 1913-1988
Obituary *55*
Du Chaillu, Paul (Belloni) 1835(?)-1903 .... *26*
Ducharme, Dede Fox
See Ducharme, Lilian Fox
Ducharme, Lilian Fox 1950- *122*
Ducornet, Erica 1943- *7*
Ducornet, Rikki
See Ducornet, Erica
Duddle, Jonny 1971(?)- *219*
Duden, Jane 1947- *136*
Duder, Tessa 1940- *117*
Earlier sketch in SATA *80*
See also CLR *43*
See also SAAS *23*
Dudley, Helen
See Hope Simpson, Jacynth
Dudley, Martha Ward 1909(?)-1985
Obituary *45*
Dudley, Nancy
See Cole, Lois Dwight
Dudley, Robert
See Baldwin, James
Dudley, Ruth H(ubbell) 1905-2001 .... *11*
Dudley-Smith, T.
See Trevor, Elleston
Due, Linnea A. 1948- *64*
Dueck, Adele 1955- *97*
Dueland, Joy V(ivian) *27*
Duerr, Gisela 1968- *89*
Duey, Kathleen 1950- *238*
Earlier sketches in SATA *132, 199*
Dufault, Joseph Ernest Nephtali
See James, Will(iam Roderick)
Duff, Annis (James) 1904(?)-1986
Obituary *49*
Duff, Hilary 1987- *238*
Duff, Maggie
See Duff, Margaret K(app)
Duff, Margaret K(app) 1916-2003 .... *37*
Obituary *144*
Duffey, Betsy 1953- *236*
Earlier sketches in SATA *80, 131*
Duffie, Charles 1960- *144*
Duffield, Katy S. 1961- *147*
Duffy, Carol Ann 1955- *165*
Earlier sketch in SATA *95*
Duffy Stone, Heather *217*
Dugan, Jack
See Griffin, W. E. B.
Dugan, John Kevin
See Griffin, W. E. B.
Dugan, Karen *202*
Dugan, Karen M.
See Dugan, Karen
Dugan, Michael (Gray) 1947- *15*
Duggan, Alfred Leo 1903-1964 .... *25*
Duggan, Maurice 1922-1974 .... *40*
Obituary *30*
Duggan, Maurice Noel
See Duggan, Maurice
Dugger, Elizabeth L.
See Kanell, Beth
Duggleby, John 1952- *94*
Dugin, Andrej 1955- *77*
Dugina, Olga 1964- *77*
du Jardin, Rosamond Neal 1902-1963 .... *2*
Duka, Ivo
See Duchacek, Ivo D(uka)
Duke, Kate 1956- *192*
Earlier sketches in SATA *90, 148*
See also CLR *51*
Duke, Will
See Gault, William Campbell
Dulac, Edmund 1882-1953 .... *19*
Dumas, Alexandre (pere) 1802-1870 .... *18*
See also CLR *134*
Dumas, Jacqueline 1946- *55*
Dumas, Philippe 1940- *119*
Earlier sketch in SATA *52*
du Maurier, Daphne 1907-1989 .... *27*
Obituary *60*
Dumbleton, Mike 1948- *206*
Earlier sketches in SATA *73, 124*
Dunbar, Fiona 1961- *167*
Dunbar, Joyce 1944- *213*
Earlier sketches in SATA *76, 112, 162*
Dunbar, Paul Laurence 1872-1906 .... *34*
Dunbar, Polly 1980(?)- *211*
Earlier sketch in SATA *181*
Dunbar, Robert E(verett) 1926- *32*
Duncan, Alexandra
See Moore, Ishbel (Lindsay)
Duncan, Alice Faye 1967- *168*
Earlier sketch in SATA *95*
Duncan, Gregory
See McClintock, Marshall
Duncan, Jane
See Cameron, Elizabeth Jane
Duncan, Julia K.
See Benson, Mildred
Duncan, Lois 1934- *219*
Autobiography Feature *141*
Earlier sketches in SATA *1, 36, 75, 133, 141*
See also CLR *129*
See also SAAS *2*
Duncan, Norman 1871-1916
See YABC *1*
Duncan, Terence
See Nolan, William F.
Duncombe, Frances (Riker) 1900-1994 .... *25*
Obituary *82*
Dungy, Anthony
See Dungy, Tony
Dungy, Tony 1955- *206*
Dunham, Montrew 1919- *162*
Dunham, Montrew Goetz
See Dunham, Montrew
Dunkle, Clare B. 1964- *223*
Earlier sketch in SATA *155*
Dunlap, Julie 1958- *84*
Dunleavy, Deborah 1951- *133*
Dunlop, Agnes M. R. (?)-1982 .... *87*
Dunlop, Eileen (Rhona) 1938- *76*
Earlier sketch in SATA *24*
See also SAAS *12*
Dunmore, Helen 1952- *201*
Dunn, Anne M. 1940- *107*
Dunn, Carolyn 1965- *208*
Dunn, Harvey T(homas) 1884-1952 .... *34*
Dunn, Herb
See Gutman, Dan
Dunn, John M. (III) 1949- *93*
Dunn, Judy
See Spangenberg, Judith Dunn
Dunn, Mary Lois 1930- *6*
Dunnahoo, Terry Janson 1927- *7*
Dunne, Jeanette 1952- *72*
Dunne, Kathleen 1933- *126*
Dunne, Marie
See Clark, Ann Nolan
Dunne, Mary Collins 1914- *11*
Dunne, Mary Jo
See Dunne, Mary Collins
Dunnett, Kaitlyn
See Emerson, Kathy Lynn
Dunnett, Margaret (Rosalind) 1909-1977 .... *42*
Dunnick, Regan *178*
Dunning, John Harris 1974- *234*
Dunphy, Madeleine 1962- *219*
Dunrea, Olivier 1953- *233*
Brief entry *46*
Earlier sketches in SATA *59, 118, 160*
Dunrea, Olivier Jean-Paul Dominique
See Dunrea, Olivier
Dunstan Muller, Rachel *221*
Dunton, Dorothy 1912- *92*
Dupasquier, Philippe 1955- *151*
Earlier sketch in SATA *86*
duPont, Lindsay *207*
duPont, Lindsay Harper
See duPont, Lindsay
DuPrau, Jeanne 1944- *215*
Earlier sketch in SATA *144*
Dupuy, T(revor) N(evitt) 1916-1995 .... *4*
Obituary *86*
DuQuette, Keith 1960- *155*
Earlier sketch in SATA *90*
Duran, Gloria 1924- *171*
Duran, Gloria Bradley
See Duran, Gloria
Duranceau, Suzanne 1952- *162*
Durand, Delphine 1971- *200*
Durand, Hallie 1964(?)- *216*
Durango, Julia 1967- *215*
Earlier sketch in SATA *173*
Durant, Alan 1958- *214*
Earlier sketches in SATA *121, 165*
Durant, John 1902- *27*
Durbin, William 1951- *174*
Earlier sketch in SATA *143*
Durell, Ann 1930- *66*
Durkee, Sarah *173*
Durney, Ryan *205*
Durrant, Lynda 1954- *212*
Earlier sketches in SATA *96, 148*
Durrant, Sabine *210*
Durrell, Gerald (Malcolm) 1925-1995 .... *8*
Obituary *84*
Durrell, Julie 1955- *94*
Durrett, Deanne 1940- *144*
Earlier sketch in SATA *92*
Durst, Sarah Beth 1974- *203*
Dusikova, Maja 1946- *223*
Du Soe, Robert C. 1892-1958
See YABC *2*
Dussling, Jennifer 1970- *143*
Earlier sketch in SATA *96*
DuTemple, Lesley A. 1952- *113*
Dutton, Sandra *191*
Dutz
See Davis, Mary Octavia
Duval, Katherine
See James, Elizabeth
Duval, Kathy 1946- *181*
Duvall, Aimee
See Thurlo, Aimee
and Thurlo, David
Duvall, Evelyn Millis 1906- *9*
Duvall, Jill D. 1932- *102*
Duvall, Jill Donovan
See Duvall, Jill D.
Duvoisin, Roger (Antoine) 1904-1980 .... *30*
Obituary *23*
Earlier sketch in SATA *2*
See also CLR *23*
Dwiggins, Don(ald J.) 1913-1988 .... *4*
Obituary *60*
Dwight, Allan
See Cole, Lois Dwight
Dwyer, Deanna
See Koontz, Dean
Dwyer, K.R.
See Koontz, Dean
Dyck, Peter J. 1914- *75*
Dyer, Alan 1953- *218*
Dyer, Brooke *238*
Dyer, Hadley 1973- *229*
Dyer, James (Frederick) 1934- *37*
Dyer, Jane *191*
Earlier sketch in SATA *147*
Dyer, Sarah 1978- *212*
Dyer, Sarah L.
See Dyer, Sarah

Dyess, John (Foster) 1939- *76*
Dygard, Thomas J. 1931-1996 .... *97*
Obituary *92*
Earlier sketch in SATA *24*
See also SAAS *15*
Dyke, John 1935- *35*

E

E. V. L.
See Lucas, E(dward) V(errall)
Eagar, Frances (Elisabeth Stuart) 1940-1978 .... *11*
Obituary *55*
Eager, Edward (McMaken) 1911-1964 .... *17*
See also CLR *43*
Eager, George 1921- *56*
Eager, George B.
See Eager, George
Eagland, Jane *237*
Eagle, Ellen 1953- *61*
Eagle, Kin
See Adlerman, Daniel (Ezra) and Adlerman, Kimberly M(arie)
Eagle, Mike 1942- *11*
Eamer, Claire 1947- *222*
Earle, Olive L(ydia) 1888-1982 .... *7*
Earle, William
See Johns, W(illiam) E(arle)
Earls, Nick 1963- *156*
Earlier sketch in SATA *95*
Early, Jack
See Scoppettone, Sandra
Early, Jon
See Johns, W(illiam) E(arle)
Early, Margaret 1951- *72*
Earnest, Peter 1934- *222*
Earnshaw, Brian 1929- *17*
Earnshaw, Micky 1939- *88*
Earnshaw, Spencer Wright
See Earnshaw, Micky
Easley, MaryAnn *94*
Eason, Alethea 1957- *197*
East, Jacqueline *224*
Eastman, Charles A(lexander) 1858-1939
See YABC *1*
Eastman, P(hilip) D(ey) 1909-1986 .... *33*
Obituary *46*
Easton, Kelly 1960- *192*
Earlier sketch in SATA *141*
Eastwick, Ivy (Ethel) O(live) *3*
Eaton, Anne T(haxter) 1881-1971 .... *32*
Eaton, Anthony 1971- *167*
Eaton, George L.
See Verral, Charles Spain
Eaton, Janet
See Givens, Janet E(aton)
Eaton, Jeanette 1886-1968 .... *24*
Eaton, Maxwell III 1981- *199*
Eaton, Tom 1940- *22*
Ebbeler, Jeff
See Ebbeler, Jeffrey
Ebbeler, Jeffrey 1974- *206*
Ebbitt, Carolyn Q. 1974(?)- *225*
Ebel, Alex 1927- *11*
Eber, Dorothy (Margaret) Harley 1930- *27*
Eberhart, Sheri S.
See Tepper, Sheri S.
Eberle, Irmengarde 1898-1979 .... *2*
Obituary *23*
Eble, Diane 1956- *74*
Eboch, Chris *113*
Eccles Williams, Ferelith 1920- *22*
Echeverria-Bis, Olivia *217*
Echeverria Gyorkos, Charmaine *216*
Echlin, Kim 1955- *166*
Eckblad, Edith Berven 1923- *23*
Ecke, Wolfgang 1927-1983
Obituary *37*
Eckert, Allan W. 1931- *91*
Brief entry *27*
Earlier sketch in SATA *29*
See also SAAS *21*
Eckert, Horst 1931- *72*
Earlier sketch in SATA *8*
See also CLR *26*
Ecklar, Julia (Marie) 1964- *112*
Eddings, David 1931-2009 .... *91*
Eddings, David Carroll
See Eddings, David
Ede, Janina 1937- *33*
Edell, Celeste *12*
Edelman, Lily (Judith) 1915-1981 .... *22*
Edelson, Edward 1932- *51*
Edens, Cooper 1945- *166*
Earlier sketches in SATA *49, 112*
Edens, (Bishop) David 1926- *39*
Edey, Maitland A(rmstrong) 1910-1992 .... *25*
Obituary *71*
Edgerton, Perky *196*
Edgeworth, Maria 1768-1849 .... *21*
See also CLR *153*
Edgson, Alison *211*
Edgy, Wardore
See Gorey, Edward (St. John)
Edison, Theodore
See Stratemeyer, Edward L.
Edler, Tim(othy) 1948- *56*
Edmiston, Jim 1948- *80*
Edmonds, I(vy) G(ordon) 1917- *8*
Edmonds, Walter D(umaux) 1903-1998 .... *27*
Obituary *99*
Earlier sketch in SATA *1*
See also SAAS *4*
Edmund, Sean
See Pringle, Laurence
Edsall, Marian (Stickney) 1920- *8*
Edwards, Al
See Nourse, Alan E(dward)
Edwards, Anne 1927- *35*
Edwards, Audrey 1947- *52*
Brief entry *31*
Edwards, Becky (Jane) 1966- *125*
Edwards, Bertram
See Edwards, Herbert Charles
Edwards, Bronwen Elizabeth
See Rose, Wendy
Edwards, Cecile Pepin 1916- *25*
Edwards, David 1962- *198*
Edwards, Dorothy 1914-1982 .... *88*
Obituary *31*
Earlier sketch in SATA *4*
Edwards, F. E.
See Nolan, William F.
Edwards, Frank B. 1952- *93*
Edwards, Gunvor *32*
Edwards, Harvey 1929- *5*
Edwards, Hazel (Eileen) 1945- *135*
Edwards, Herbert Charles 1912- *12*
Edwards, Jane Campbell 1932- *10*
Edwards, Julia
See Stratemeyer, Edward L.
Edwards, Julie
See Andrews, Julie
Edwards, Julie Andrews
See Andrews, Julie
Edwards, June
See Bhatia, Jamunadevi
Edwards, Linda Strauss 1948- *49*
Brief entry *42*
Edwards, Margaret (Alexander) 1902-1988
Obituary *56*
Edwards, Michelle 1955- *152*
Earlier sketch in SATA *70*
Edwards, Monica le Doux Newton 1912-1998 .... *12*
Edwards, Olwen
See Gater, Dilys
Edwards, Page (Lawrence, Jr.) 1941-1999 .... *59*
Edwards, Pamela Duncan *189*
Edwards, R. T.
See Goulart, Ron
Edwards, Sally (Cary) 1929- *7*
Edwards, Samuel
See Gerson, Noel Bertram
Edwards, Wallace 1957(?)- *170*
Edwardson, Debby Dahl *223*
Eeckhout, Emmanuelle 1976- *208*
Egan, E. W. 1922- *35*
Egan, Edward Welstead
See Egan, E. W.
Egan, Kerry *175*
Egan, Lorraine Hopping 1960- *134*
Earlier sketch in SATA *91*
Egan, Tim 1957- *191*
Earlier sketches in SATA *89, 155*
Egermeier, Elsie E(milie) 1890-1986 .... *65*
Eggenberger, David 1918- *6*
Eggleston, Edward 1837-1902 .... *27*
Egielski, Richard 1952- *220*
Earlier sketches in SATA *11, 49, 106, 163*
Egypt, Ophelia Settle 1903-1984 .... *16*
Obituary *38*
Ehlert, Lois 1934- *237*
Earlier sketches in SATA *35, 69, 128, 172*
See also CLR *28*
Ehlert, Lois Jane
See Ehlert, Lois
Ehling, Katalin Olah 1941- *93*
Ehrenberg, Pamela 1972- *219*
Ehrenfreund, Norbert 1921- *86*
Ehrenhaft, Daniel 1970- *185*
Ehrenhaft, Daniel Parker
See Ehrenhaft, Daniel
Ehrhardt, Karen 1963- *184*
Ehrlich, Amy 1942- *217*
Earlier sketches in SATA *25, 65, 96, 132*
Ehrlich, Bettina Bauer 1903-1985 .... *1*
Ehrlich, Fred *205*
Ehrlich, Fred M.D.
See Ehrlich, Fred
Ehrlich, H. M.
See Ziefert, Harriet
Eichenberg, Fritz 1901-1990 .... *50*
Earlier sketch in SATA *9*
Eichler, Margrit 1942- *35*
Eichner, James A. 1927- *4*
Eidson, Thomas 1944- *112*
Eifert, Virginia (Louise) S(nider) 1911-1966 .... *2*
Eige, (Elizabeth) Lillian 1915- *65*
Eiken, J. Melia 1967- *125*
Einhorn, Edward 1970- *204*
Einsel, Naiad *10*
Einsel, Walter 1926- *10*
Einzig, Susan 1922- *43*
Eiseman, Alberta 1925- *15*
Eisenberg, Azriel (Louis) 1903-1985 .... *12*
Eisenberg, Lisa 1949- *155*
Brief entry *50*
Earlier sketch in SATA *57*
Eisenberg, Phyllis Rose 1924- *41*
Eisner, Vivienne
See Margolis, Vivienne
Eisner, Will 1917-2005 .... *165*
Earlier sketch in SATA *31*
Eisner, William Erwin
See Eisner, Will
Eitzen, Allan 1928- *9*
Eitzen, Ruth (Carper) 1924- *9*
Ekwensi, C. O. D.
See Ekwensi, Cyprian
Ekwensi, Cyprian 1921-2007 .... *66*
Ekwensi, Cyprian Odiatu Duaka
See Ekwensi, Cyprian
Elam, Richard M(ace, Jr.) 1920- *9*
Elborn, Andrew
See Clements, Andrew and Clements, Andrew
Elboz, Stephen 1956- *152*
Eldin, Peter 1939- *154*
Eldon, Kathy 1946- *107*

Eldridge, Marion *199*
Eley, Robin *219*
Elfman, Blossom 1925- *8*
Elgin, Kathleen 1923- *39*
Elia
See Lamb, Charles
Elio
See Eliopoulos, Chris
Eliopoulos, Chris *234*
Eliot, A. D.
See Jewett, Sarah Orne
Eliot, Alice
See Jewett, Sarah Orne
Eliot, Anne
See Cole, Lois Dwight
Eliot, Dan
See Silverberg, Robert
Elish, Dan 1960- *204*
Earlier sketches in SATA *68, 129*
Elisha, Ron 1951- *104*
Elisofon, Eliot 1911-1973
Obituary *21*
Elkeles, Simone 1970- *187*
Elkin, Benjamin 1911-1995 .... *3*
Elkins, Dov Peretz 1937- *5*
Ellacott, S(amuel) E(rnest) 1911- *19*
Elleman, Barbara 1934- *147*
Ellen, Jaye
See Nixon, Joan Lowery
Eller, Scott
See Holinger, William (Jacques)
and Shepard, Jim
Ellery, Amanda *216*
Ellestad, Myrvin
See Ellestad, Myrvin H.
Ellestad, Myrvin H. 1921- *120*
Elliot, Bruce
See Field, Edward
Elliot, David 1952- *208*
Earlier sketch in SATA *122*
Elliott, Bruce
See Field, Edward
Elliott, David 1947- *201*
Earlier sketch in SATA *163*
Elliott, Don
See Silverberg, Robert
Elliott, Elizabeth Shippen Green
See Green, Elizabeth Shippen
Elliott, Janice 1931-1995 .... *119*
Elliott, Joey
See Houk, Randy
Elliott, Laura Malone 1957- *197*
Elliott, L.M.
See Elliott, Laura Malone
Elliott, Louise *111*
Elliott, Mark 1949- *210*
Elliott, Odette 1939- *75*
Elliott, Patricia 1946- *176*
Elliott, Sarah M(cCarn) 1930- *14*
Elliott, (Robert) Scott 1970- *153*
Elliott, William
See Bradbury, Ray
Elliott, Zetta *206*
Ellis, (Mary) Amabel (Nassau Strachey) Williams
See Williams-Ellis, (Mary) Amabel (Nassau Strachey)
Ellis, Ann Dee *210*
Ellis, Anyon
See Rowland-Entwistle, (Arthur) Theodore (Henry)
Ellis, Carson 1975- *190*
Ellis, Carson Friedman
See Ellis, Carson
Ellis, Deborah 1960- *235*
Earlier sketches in SATA *129, 187*
Ellis, E. S.
See Ellis, Edward S.
Ellis, Edward S. 1840-1916
See YABC *1*
Ellis, Edward Sylvester
See Ellis, Edward S.
Ellis, Ella Thorp 1928- *127*
Earlier sketch in SATA *7*
See also SAAS *9*
Ellis, Harry Bearse 1921-2004 .... *9*
Ellis, Helen *232*
Ellis, Herbert
See Wilson, Lionel
Ellis, Julie 1961- *227*
Ellis, Mel(vin Richard) 1912-1984 .... *7*
Obituary *39*
Ellis, Richard 1938- *130*
Ellis, Sarah 1952- *179*
Earlier sketches in SATA *68, 131*
See also CLR *42*
Ellison, Chris *196*
Ellison, Elizabeth Stow 1970- *209*
Ellison, Emily *114*
Ellison, Lucile Watkins 1907(?)-1979 .... *50*
Obituary *22*
Ellison, Virginia H(owell) 1910- *4*
Ellsberg, Edward 1891-1983 .... *7*
Ellsworth, Loretta 1954- *199*
Ellsworth, Mary Ellen (Tressel) 1940- *146*
Ellwand, David 1965(?)- *213*
Elmer, Robert 1958- *154*
Earlier sketch in SATA *99*
Elmore, (Carolyn) Patricia 1933- *38*
Brief entry *35*
El-Moslimany, Ann P(axton) 1937- *90*
Elsammak, Ariane *236*
Elschner, Geraldine 1954- *183*
Elspeth
See Bragdon, Elspeth MacDuffie
Elster, Jean Alicia 1953- *150*
Elting, Mary 1906- *88*
Earlier sketch in SATA *2*
See also SAAS *20*
Elvgren, Jennifer Riesmeyer *179*
Elwart, Joan Potter 1927- *2*
Elwell, Peter *220*
Elwood, Ann 1931- *55*
Brief entry *52*
Elwood, Roger 1943-2007 .... *58*
Ely, Lesley *212*
Elya, Susan Middleton 1955- *235*
Earlier sketches in SATA *106, 159, 202*
Elzbieta *88*
Ember, Kathi *234*
Earlier sketch in SATA *190*
Emberley, Barbara A. 1932- *146*
Earlier sketches in SATA *8, 70*
See also CLR *5*
Emberley, Barbara Anne
See Emberley, Barbara A.
Emberley, Ed 1931- *146*
Earlier sketches in SATA *8, 70*
See also CLR *81*
Emberley, Edward Randolph
See Emberley, Ed
Emberley, Michael 1960- *232*
Earlier sketches in SATA *34, 80, 119, 189*
Emberley, Rebecca 1958- *218*
Embry, Margaret Jacob 1919-1975 .... *5*
Emecheta, Buchi 1944- *66*
See also CLR *158*
Emecheta, Florence Onye Buchi
See Emecheta, Buchi
Emerson, Alice B.
See Benson, Mildred
Emerson, Kate
See Emerson, Kathy Lynn
Emerson, Kathy Lynn 1947- *63*
Emerson, Kevin *209*
Emerson, Ru 1944- *107*
Earlier sketch in SATA *70*
Emerson, Sally 1952- *111*
Emerson, William K(eith) 1925- *25*
Emert, Phyllis R. 1947- *93*
Emert, Phyllis Raybin
See Emert, Phyllis R.
Emery, Anne (McGuigan) 1907- *33*
Earlier sketch in SATA *1*
Emmens, Carol Ann 1944- *39*
Emmett, Jonathan 1965- *188*
Earlier sketch in SATA *138*
Emmons, Della (Florence) Gould 1890-1983
Obituary *39*
Emond, Stephen 1979(?)- *231*
Emory, Jerry 1957- *96*
Emrich, Duncan (Black Macdonald) 1908-1970(?) *11*
Emshwiller, Carol 1921- *174*
Autobiography Feature *174*
Emshwiller, Carol Fries
See Emshwiller, Carol
Emslie, M. L.
See Simpson, Myrtle L(illias)
Ende, Michael (Andreas Helmuth) 1929-1995 .... *130*
Brief entry *42*
Obituary *86*
Earlier sketch in SATA *61*
See also CLR *138*
Enderle, Dotti 1954- *203*
Earlier sketch in SATA *145*
Enderle, Judith (Ann) Ross 1941- *89*
Autobiography Feature *114*
Earlier sketch in SATA *38*
See also SAAS *26*
Endle, Kate *207*
Enell, Trinka (Gochenour) 1951- *79*
Enfield, Carrie
See Smith, Susan Vernon
Engdahl, Sylvia Louise 1933- *4*
Autobiography Feature *122*
See also CLR *2*
See also SAAS *5*
Engel, Christiane *231*
Engel, Diana 1947- *70*
Engelbreit, Mary 1952- *169*
Engelhart, Margaret S. 1924- *59*
Engelmann, Kim (V.) 1959- *87*
England, George Allan 1877-1936 .... *102*
Englart, Mindi Rose 1965- *146*
Engle, Eloise
See Paananen, Eloise (Katherine)
Engle, Margarita 1951- *231*
Earlier sketch in SATA *193*
Englebert, Victor 1933- *8*
English, James W(ilson) 1915- *37*
English, Karen *202*
Engstrom, Elizabeth 1951- *110*
Enright, D(ennis) J(oseph) 1920-2002 .... *25*
Obituary *140*
Enright, Dominique *194*
Enright, Elizabeth (Wright) 1909-1968 .... *9*
See also CLR *4*
Ensor, Barbara *180*
Ensor, Robert (T.) 1922- *93*
Enthoven, Sam 1974- *187*
Entwistle, (Arthur) Theodore (Henry) Rowland
See Rowland-Entwistle, (Arthur) Theodore (Henry)
Enys, Sarah L.
See Sloggett, Nellie
Epanya, Christian A(rthur Kingue) 1956- *91*
Ephraim, Shelly S(chonebaum) 1952- *97*
Ephron, Delia 1944- *197*
Brief entry *50*
Earlier sketch in SATA *65*
Epler, Doris M. 1928- *73*
Epp, Margaret A(gnes) 1913- *20*
Eppenstein, Louise (Kohn) 1892-1987
Obituary *54*
Epple, Anne Orth 1927- *20*
Epstein, Adam Jay 1975- *235*
Epstein, Anne Merrick 1931- *20*

Epstein, Beryl 1910- ... *31*
Earlier sketch in SATA *1*
See also CLR *26*
See also SAAS *17*
Epstein, Beryl M. Williams
See Epstein, Beryl
Epstein, Perle S(herry) 1938- ... *27*
Epstein, Rachel S. 1941- ... *102*
Epstein, Robin 1972- ... *230*
Epstein, Samuel 1909-2000 ... *31*
Earlier sketch in SATA *1*
See also CLR *26*
See also SAAS *17*
Erdman, Loula Grace 1905(?)-1976 ... *1*
Erdoes, Richard 1912- ... *33*
Brief entry ... *28*
Erdogan, Buket ... *187*
Erdrich, Karen Louise
See Erdrich, Louise
Erdrich, Louise 1954- ... *141*
Earlier sketch in SATA *94*
Erickson, Betty J. 1923- ... *97*
Erickson, Betty Jean
See Erickson, Betty J.
Erickson, John R. 1943- ... *136*
Earlier sketch in SATA *70*
Erickson, Jon 1948- ... *141*
Erickson, Phoebe ... *59*
Erickson, Russell E(verett) 1932- ... *27*
Erickson, Sabra Rollins 1912-1995 ... *35*
Erickson, Walter
See Fast, Howard
Ericson, Walter
See Fast, Howard
Ericsson, Jennifer A. ... *170*
Erikson, Mel 1937- ... *31*
Eriksson, Eva 1949- ... *207*
Ering, Timothy Basil ... *176*
Erlanger, Baba
See Trahey, Jane
Erlbach, Arlene 1948- ... *160*
Earlier sketches in SATA *78, 115*
Erlbruch, Wolf 1948- ... *181*
Erlich, Lillian (Feldman) 1910-1983 ... *10*
Erlings, Fridrik 1962- ... *196*
Erlingsson, Friorik
See Erlings, Fridrik
Ermatinger, James W. 1959- ... *170*
Ernest, William
See Berkebile, Fred D(onovan)
Ernst, (Lyman) John 1940- ... *39*
Ernst, Kathleen
See Ernst, Kathleen
Ernst, Kathleen 1959- ... *162*
Ernst, Kathryn (Fitzgerald) 1942- ... *25*
Ernst, Lisa Campbell 1957- ... *212*
Brief entry ... *44*
Earlier sketches in SATA *55, 95, 154*
Erskine, Kathryn ... *193*
Ervin, Janet Halliday 1923- ... *4*
Erwin, Will
See Eisner, Will
Esbaum, Jill ... *213*
Earlier sketch in SATA *174*
Esbensen, Barbara J(uster) 1925-1996 ... *97*
Brief entry ... *53*
Earlier sketch in SATA *62*
Eschbacher, Roger ... *160*
Eschmeyer, R. E. 1898-1989 ... *29*
Escriva, Vivi ... *182*
Eseki, Bruno
See Mphahlele, Es'kia
Esekie, Bruno
See Mphahlele, Es'kia
Eshmeyer, Reinhart Ernst
See Eschmeyer, R. E.
Eskridge, Ann E. 1949- ... *84*
Espeland, Pamela (Lee) 1951- ... *128*
Brief entry ... *38*
Earlier sketch in SATA *52*
Espinosa, Laura ... *203*
Espinosa, Leo ... *203*
Espriella, Don Manuel Alvarez
See Southey, Robert
Espy, Willard R(ichardson) 1910-1999 ... *38*
Obituary ... *113*
Essakalli, Julie Klear ... *200*
Essrig, Harry 1912- ... *66*
Estep, Irene Compton ... *5*
Esterl, Arnica 1933- ... *77*
Estes, Eleanor (Ruth) 1906-1988 ... *91*
Obituary ... *56*
Earlier sketch in SATA *7*
See also CLR *70*
Estoril, Jean
See Allan, Mabel Esther
Estrada, Pau 1961- ... *200*
Earlier sketch in SATA *74*
Etchemendy, Nancy 1952- ... *166*
Earlier sketch in SATA *38*
Etchemendy, Nancy Elise Howell
See Etchemendy, Nancy
Etchison, Birdie L(ee) 1937- ... *38*
Etchison, Craig 1945- ... *133*
Etherington, Frank 1945- ... *58*
Etnier, Jennifer L. ... *227*
Eton, Robert
See Meynell, Laurence Walter
Ets, Marie Hall 1893-1984 ... *2*
See also CLR *33*
Ettlinger, Doris 1950- ... *173*
Eugenia, Maria ... *222*
Eulberg, Elizabeth 1975- ... *227*
Eunson, (John) Dale 1904-2002 ... *5*
Obituary ... *132*
Evan, Frances Y. 1951- ... *167*
Evanoff, Vlad 1916- ... *59*
Evans, Cambria 1981- ... *178*
Evans, Douglas 1953- ... *144*
Earlier sketch in SATA *93*
Evans, Eva (Knox) 1905-1998 ... *27*
Evans, Freddi Williams 1957- ... *211*
Earlier sketch in SATA *134*
Evans, Greg 1947- ... *143*
Earlier sketch in SATA *73*
Evans, Hubert Reginald 1892-1986 ... *118*
Obituary ... *48*
Evans, Katherine (Floyd) 1901-1964 ... *5*
Evans, Larry
See Evans, Laurence Chubb
Evans, Laurence Chubb 1939- ... *88*
Evans, Lawrence Watt
See Watt-Evans, Lawrence
Evans, Leslie 1953- ... *214*
Evans, Lezlie ... *180*
Evans, Mari 1923- ... *10*
Evans, Mark ... *19*
Evans, Nancy 1950- ... *65*
Evans, Nate ... *201*
Evans, Patricia Healy
See Carpenter, Patricia (Healy Evans)
Evans, (Alice) Pearl 1927- ... *83*
Evans, Shane W. ... *240*
Earlier sketch in SATA *189*
Evans, Shirlee 1931- ... *58*
Evans, Tabor
See Cameron, Lou
and Knott, William C(ecil, Jr.)
and Wallmann, Jeffrey M(iner)
and Whittington, Harry (Benjamin)
Evarts, Esther
See Benson, Sally
Evarts, Hal G., (Jr.) 1915-1989 ... *6*
Everett, Gail
See Hale, Arlene
Evernden, Margery 1916- ... *5*
Eversole, Robyn 1971- ... *74*
Eversole, Robyn H.
See Eversole, Robyn
Eversole, Robyn Harbert
See Eversole, Robyn
Evslin, Bernard 1922-1993 ... *83*
Brief entry ... *28*
Obituary ... *77*
Earlier sketch in SATA *45*
Ewart, Claire 1958- ... *145*
Earlier sketch in SATA *76*
Ewart, Franzeska G. 1950- ... *205*
Ewen, David 1907-1985 ... *4*
Obituary ... *47*
Ewing, Juliana (Horatia Gatty) 1841-1885 ... *16*
See also CLR *78*
Ewing, Kathryn 1921- ... *20*
Eyerly, Jeannette 1908-2008 ... *86*
Obituary ... *196*
Earlier sketch in SATA *4*
See also SAAS *10*
Eyerly, Jeannette Hyde
See Eyerly, Jeannette
Eyre, Dorothy
See McGuire, Leslie (Sarah)
Eyre, Frank 1910-1988
Obituary ... *62*
Eyre, Katherine Wigmore 1901-1970 ... *26*
Ezzell, Marilyn 1937- ... *42*
Brief entry ... *38*

F

Fabe, Maxene 1943- ... *15*
Faber, Doris (Greenberg) 1924- ... *78*
Earlier sketch in SATA *3*
Faber, Harold 1919-2010 ... *5*
Fabre, Jean Henri (Casimir) 1823-1915 ... *22*
Fabry, Glenn 1961- ... *205*
Facklam, Margaret
See Thomas, Peggy
Facklam, Margery (Metz) 1927- ... *132*
Earlier sketches in SATA *20, 85*
Fadden, David Kanietakeron ... *196*
Fadiman, Clifton (Paul) 1904-1999 ... *11*
Obituary ... *115*
Fagan, Cary 1957- ... *186*
Fagan, Deva ... *220*
Fahs, Sophia Blanche Lyon 1876-1978 ... *102*
Failing, Barbara Larmon ... *182*
Fain, Sarah 1971- ... *204*
Fair, David 1952- ... *96*
Fair, Sylvia 1933- ... *13*
Fairfax-Lucy, Brian (Fulke Cameron-Ramsay) 1898-1974 ... *6*
Obituary ... *26*
Fairfield, Flora
See Alcott, Louisa May
Fairlie, Gerard 1899-1983
Obituary ... *34*
Fairman, Joan A(lexandra) 1935- ... *10*
Faithfull, Gail 1936- ... *8*
Falcone, L.M. 1951- ... *231*
Earlier sketch in SATA *155*
Falcone, Lucy M.
See Falcone, L.M.
Falconer, Ian 1959- ... *179*
Earlier sketch in SATA *125*
See also CLR *146*
Falconer, James
See Kirkup, James
Falconer, Lee N.
See May, Julian
Falkner, Brian 1962- ... *206*
Falkner, Leonard 1900-1977 ... *12*
Fall, Andrew
See Arthur, Robert, (Jr.)
Fall, Thomas
See Snow, Donald Clifford
Faller, Regis 1968- ... *187*
Falls, C(harles) B(uckles) 1874-1960 ... *38*
Brief entry ... *27*
Falls, Kat ... *232*

Falls, Kathleen Moynihan
See Falls, Kat
Falstein, Louis 1909-1995 ... *37*
Falvey, David 1982- ... *222*
Falwell, Cathryn 1952- ... *196*
Fancher, Lou 1960- ... *228*
Earlier sketch in SATA *177*
Fanelli, Sara 1969- ... *126*
Earlier sketch in SATA *89*
Fanning, Leonard M(ulliken) 1888-1967 ... *5*
Fantaskey, Beth 1965- ... *217*
Faralla, Dana 1909- ... *9*
Faralla, Dorothy W.
See Faralla, Dana
Farb, Peter 1929-1980 ... *12*
Obituary ... *22*
Farber, Norma 1909-1984 ... *75*
Obituary ... *38*
Earlier sketch in SATA *25*
Fardell, John 1967- ... *195*
Fardell, John William
See Fardell, John
Faria, Rosana ... *213*
Farish, Terry 1947- ... *146*
Earlier sketch in SATA *82*
Farjeon, (Eve) Annabel 1919-2004 ... *11*
Obituary ... *153*
Farjeon, Eleanor 1881-1965 ... *2*
See also CLR *34*
Farley, Carol (J.) 1936- ... *137*
Earlier sketch in SATA *4*
Farley, Terri ... *165*
Farley, Walter (Lorimer) 1915-1989 ... *132*
Earlier sketches in SATA *2, 43*
Farlow, James O(rville, Jr.) 1951- ... *75*
Farmer, Jacqueline ... *210*
Farmer, Nancy 1941- ... *161*
Earlier sketches in SATA *79, 117*
Farmer, Patti 1948- ... *79*
Farmer, Penelope (Jane) 1939- ... *105*
Brief entry ... *39*
Earlier sketch in SATA *40*
See also CLR *8*
See also SAAS *22*
Farmer, Peter 1950- ... *38*
Farmer, Philip Jose
See Farmer, Philip Jose
Farmer, Philip Jose 1918-2009 ... *93*
Obituary ... *201*
Farmer, Philipe Jos
See Farmer, Philip Jose
Farnham, Burt
See Clifford, Harold B(urton)
Farnsworth, Bill 1958- ... *186*
Earlier sketches in SATA *84, 135*
Farooqi, Musharraf Ali 1968- ... *207*
Farquhar, Margaret C(utting) 1905-1988 ... *13*
Farquharson, Alexander 1944- ... *46*
Farquharson, Martha
See Finley, Martha
Farr, Diana ... *82*
Earlier sketch in SATA *3*
Farr, Finis (King) 1904-1982 ... *10*
Farr, Richard 1960- ... *209*
Farrar, Jill
See Morris, Jill
Farrar, Susan Clement 1917- ... *33*
Farrell, Ben
See Cebulash, Mel
Farrell, Darren ... *228*
Farrell, John 1951- ... *204*
Farrell, Patrick
See Odgers, Sally Farrell
Farrell, Sally
See Odgers, Sally Farrell
Farrer, Vashti ... *167*
Farrington, Benjamin 1891-1974
Obituary ... *20*
Farrington, S(elwyn) Kip, Jr. 1904-1983 ... *20*
Farris, Christine King 1927- ... *206*
Farshtey, Greg(ory T.) 1965- ... *148*
Farthing, Alison 1936- ... *45*
Brief entry ... *36*
Farthing-Knight, Catherine 1933- ... *92*
Fassler, Joan (Grace) 1931- ... *11*
Fast, Howard 1914-2003 ... *7*
Autobiography Feature ... *107*
Fast, Howard Melvin
See Fast, Howard
Fasulo, Michael 1963- ... *83*
Fatchen, Max 1920- ... *84*
Earlier sketch in SATA *20*
See also SAAS *20*
Fate, Marilyn
See Collins, Paul
Father Goose
See Ghigna, Charles
Fatigati, Evelyn 1948- ... *24*
Fatigati, Frances Evelyn
See Fatigati, Evelyn
Fatio, Louise 1904-1993 ... *6*
Fatus, Sophie 1957- ... *182*
Faulhaber, Martha 1926- ... *7*
Faulkner, Anne Irvin 1906- ... *23*
Faulkner, Frank
See Ellis, Edward S.
Faulkner, Nancy
See Faulkner, Anne Irvin
Faulknor, Cliff(ord Vernon) 1913- ... *86*
Faust, Anke 1971- ... *230*
Favole, Robert J(ames) 1950- ... *125*
Fawcett, Katie Pickard ... *229*
Fax, Elton Clay 1909-1993 ... *25*
Faxon, Lavinia
See Russ, Lavinia (Faxon)
Feagles, Anita M.
See Feagles, Anita MacRae
Feagles, Anita MacRae 1927- ... *9*
Feagles, Elizabeth
See Day, Beth (Feagles)
Feague, Mildred H. 1915- ... *14*
Fearing, Mark 1968- ... *224*
Fearnley, Jan 1965- ... *205*
Earlier sketch in SATA *153*
Fearrington, Ann (Peyton) 1945- ... *146*
Feasey, Steve ... *240*
Fecher, Constance
See Heaven, Constance (Christina)
Feder, Chris Welles 1938- ... *81*
Feder, Harriet K. 1928- ... *73*
Feder, Paula (Kurzband) 1935- ... *26*
Federici, Debbie 1965- ... *175*
Federici, Debbie Tanner
See Federici, Debbie
Feelings, Muriel 1938- ... *16*
See also CLR *5*
See also SAAS *8*
Feelings, Muriel Lavita Grey
See Feelings, Muriel
Feelings, Thomas 1933-2003 ... *69*
Obituary ... *148*
Earlier sketch in SATA *8*
See also CLR *58*
See also SAAS *19*
Feelings, Tom
See Feelings, Thomas
Fehler, Gene 1940- ... *201*
Earlier sketch in SATA *74*
Fehrenbach, T(heodore) R(eed, Jr.) 1925- ... *33*
Feiffer, Jules 1929- ... *201*
Earlier sketches in SATA *8, 61, 111, 157*
Feiffer, Jules Ralph
See Feiffer, Jules
Feiffer, Kate 1964- ... *206*
Earlier sketch in SATA *170*
Feig, Barbara Krane 1937- ... *34*
Feig, Paul ... *221*
Feikema, Feike
See Manfred, Frederick (Feikema)
Feil, Hila 1942- ... *12*
Feilen, John
See May, Julian
Feinberg, Barbara Jane 1938- ... *123*
Earlier sketch in SATA *58*
Feinberg, Barbara Silberdick
See Feinberg, Barbara Jane
Feinstein, John 1956- ... *239*
Earlier sketches in SATA *163, 195*
Feldman, Anne (Rodgers) 1939- ... *19*
Feldman, Elane ... *79*
Feldman, Eve B. ... *221*
Feldman, Jody ... *200*
Felin, M. Sindy ... *194*
Felix
See Vincent, Felix
Fell, Derek 1939- ... *167*
Fell, Derek John
See Fell, Derek
Fellowes, Julian 1950- ... *198*
Fellows, Muriel H. ... *10*
Fellows, Stan 1957- ... *177*
Fellows, Stanley
See Fellows, Stan
Felsen, Henry Gregor 1916-1995 ... *1*
See also SAAS *2*
Felstead, Cathie 1954- ... *192*
Feltenstein, Arlene 1934- ... *119*
Feltenstine, Arlene H.
See Feltenstein, Arlene
Felton, Harold William 1902-1991 ... *1*
Felton, Ronald Oliver 1909- ... *3*
Felts, Shirley 1934- ... *33*
Felts, Susannah 1973- ... *214*
Fenderson, Lewis H., Jr. 1907-1983 ... *47*
Obituary ... *37*
Fenner, Carol (Elizabeth) 1929-2002 ... *89*
Obituary ... *132*
Earlier sketch in SATA *7*
See also SAAS *24*
Fenner, Phyllis R(eid) 1899-1982 ... *1*
Obituary ... *29*
Fensham, Elizabeth ... *169*
Fenten, Barbara D(oris) 1935- ... *26*
Fenten, D(onald) X. 1932- ... *4*
Fenton, Carroll Lane 1900-1969 ... *5*
Fenton, Edward 1917-1995 ... *7*
Obituary ... *89*
Fenton, Joe ... *213*
Fenton, Mildred Adams 1899-1995 ... *21*
Fenwick, Patti
See Grider, Dorothy
Feravolo, Rocco Vincent 1922- ... *10*
Ferber, Brenda A. 1967- ... *184*
Ferber, Edna 1887-1968 ... *7*
Fergus, Charles ... *114*
Ferguson, Alane 1957- ... *182*
Earlier sketch in SATA *85*
Ferguson, Bob
See Ferguson, Robert Bruce
Ferguson, Cecil 1931- ... *45*
Ferguson, Pamela
See Ferguson, Pamela Ellen
Ferguson, Pamela Ellen 1943- ... *234*
Ferguson, Peter 1968- ... *199*
Ferguson, Robert Bruce 1927-2001 ... *13*
Ferguson, Sarah 1959- ... *180*
Earlier sketches in SATA *66, 110*
Ferguson, Sarah Margaret
See Ferguson, Sarah
Ferguson, Walter (W.) 1930- ... *34*
Fergusson, Erna 1888-1964 ... *5*
Fermi, Laura 1907-1977 ... *6*
Obituary ... *28*
Fern, Eugene A. 1919-1987 ... *10*
Obituary ... *54*
Fern, Tracey E. ... *202*
Fernandes, Eugenie 1943- ... *205*
Earlier sketches in SATA *77, 139*
Fernandez, Laura 1960- ... *171*
Ferraiolo, Jack D. ... *208*
Ferrari, Maria ... *123*
Ferrari, Michael ... *223*

Ferrari, Michael J.
See Ferrari, Michael
Ferreiro, Carmen 1958- *158*
Ferrell, Nancy Warren 1932- *70*
Ferrer, Barbara
See Ferrer, Caridad
Ferrer, Caridad *238*
Ferrer, Isabel
See Riu, Isabel Ferrer
Ferri, Giuliano 1965- *197*
Ferrier, Lucy
See Penzler, Otto
Ferris, Helen Josephine 1890-1969 .... *21*
Ferris, James Cody
See McFarlane, Leslie
Ferris, Jean 1939- *202*
Brief entry *50*
Earlier sketches in SATA *56, 105, 149*
Ferris, Jeri Chase 1937- *84*
Ferry, Charles 1927- *92*
Earlier sketch in SATA *43*
See also CLR *34*
See also SAAS *20*
Fetz, Ingrid 1915- *30*
Feydy, Anne Lindbergh
See Sapieyevski, Anne Lindbergh
Fiammenghi, Gioia 1929- *66*
Earlier sketch in SATA *9*
Fiarotta, Noel
See Ficarotta, Noel
Fiarotta, Phyllis
See Ficarotta, Phyllis
Ficarotta, Noel 1944- *15*
Ficarotta, Phyllis 1942- *15*
Fichter, George S. 1922-1993 .... *7*
Ficocelli, Elizabeth *189*
Fidler, Kathleen (Annie) 1899-1980 .... *87*
Obituary *45*
Earlier sketch in SATA *3*
Fiedler, Jean(nette Feldman) *4*
Fiedler, Joseph Daniel *159*
Fiedler, Lisa *185*
Field, Dorothy 1944- *97*
Field, Edward 1924- *109*
Earlier sketch in SATA *8*
Field, Elinor Whitney 1889-1980
Obituary *28*
Field, Eugene 1850-1895 .... *16*
Field, Gans T.
See Wellman, Manly Wade
Field, James 1959- *113*
Field, Peter
See Drago, Harry Sinclair
and Dresser, Davis
and Mann, E(dward) B(everly)
Field, Rachel (Lyman) 1894-1942 .... *15*
See also CLR *21*
Fielding, Kate
See Oldfield, Jenny
Fields, Bryan W. 1958(?)- *188*
Fields, Lisa 1984(?)- *216*
Fields, Terri 1948- *191*
Fields, T.S.
See Fields, Terri
Fienberg, Anna 1956- *183*
Earlier sketch in SATA *112*
Fiery, Ann
See Barrows, Annie
Fife, Dale (Odile Hollerbach) 1901- *18*
Fighter Pilot, A
See Johnston, H(ugh) A(nthony) S(tephen)
Figler, Jeanie 1949- *123*
Figley, Marty Rhodes 1948- *158*
Earlier sketch in SATA *88*
Figueredo, D(anilo) H. 1951- *155*
Figueroa, Pablo 1938- *9*
Fijan, Carol 1918- *12*
Filderman, Diane E(lizabeth) 1959- *87*
Files, Meg 1946- *107*
Fillmore, Parker H(oysted) 1878-1944
See YABC *1*
Filstrup, Chris
See Filstrup, E(dward) Christian
Filstrup, E(dward) Christian 1942- *43*
Filstrup, Janie
See Merrill, Jane
Finbarr, Desmond
See Zobel Nolan, Allia
Finchler, Judy 1943- *230*
Earlier sketch in SATA *93*
Finder, Martin
See Salzmann, Siegmund
Findlay, Jamieson 1958- *169*
Findon, Joanne 1957- *161*
Fine, Anne 1947- *197*
Earlier sketches in SATA *29, 72, 111, 160*
See also CLR *25*
See also SAAS *15*
Fine, Edith Hope *169*
Fine, Howard 1961- *181*
Fine, Jane
See Ziefert, Harriet
Finger, Charles J(oseph) 1869(?)-1941 .... *42*
Fink, William B(ertrand) 1916- *22*
Finke, Blythe Foote 1922- *26*
Finkel, George (Irvine) 1909-1975 .... *8*
Finkelstein, Norman H. 1941- *220*
Earlier sketches in SATA *73, 137*
Finkelstein, Norman Henry
See Finkelstein, Norman H.
Finlay, Alice Sullivan 1946- *82*
Finlay, Winifred Lindsay Crawford
(McKissack) 1910-1989 .... *23*
Finlayson, Ann 1925- *8*
Finley, Martha 1828-1909 .... *43*
See also CLR *148*
Finley, Mary Peace 1942- *83*
Finn, Mary *208*
Finney, Jack 1911-1995 .... *109*
Finney, Patricia 1958- *163*
Finney, Shan 1944- *65*
Finney, Walter Braden
See Finney, Jack
Firer, Ben Zion
See Firer, Benzion
Firer, Benzion 1914- *64*
Fireside, Bryna J. 1932- *73*
Firmin, Charlotte 1954- *29*
Firmin, Peter 1928- *58*
Earlier sketch in SATA *15*
Firth, Barbara *179*
Fischbach, Julius 1894-1988 .... *10*
Fischer, John
See Fluke, Joanne
Fischer, R.J.
See Fluke, Joanne
Fischer, Scott M. 1971- *195*
Fischer-Nagel, Andreas 1951- *56*
Fischer-Nagel, Heiderose 1956- *56*
Fischler, Shirley (Walton) *66*
Fischler, Stan(ley I.) *66*
Brief entry *36*
Fischtrom, Harvey 1933-1974 .... *3*
Fishback, Margaret
See Antolini, Margaret Fishback
Fishbone, Greg R. *195*
Fisher, Aileen (Lucia) 1906-2002 .... *73*
Obituary *143*
Earlier sketches in SATA *1, 25*
See also CLR *49*
Fisher, Barbara 1940- *44*
Brief entry *34*
Fisher, Carolyn 1968- *154*
Fisher, Catherine 1957- *241*
Earlier sketch in SATA *155*
Fisher, Chris 1958- *80*
Fisher, Clavin C(argill) 1912- *24*
Fisher, Cynthia *195*
Fisher, Dorothy (Frances) Canfield 1879-1958
See YABC *1*
See also CLR *71*
Fisher, Gary L. 1949- *86*
Fisher, John 1909-1996 .... *15*
Fisher, John Oswald Hamilton
See Fisher, John
Fisher, Laura Harrison 1934- *5*
Fisher, Leonard Everett 1924- *176*
Autobiography Feature *122*
Earlier sketches in SATA *4, 34, 73, 120*
See also CLR *18*
See also SAAS *1*
Fisher, Lois I. 1948- *38*
Brief entry *35*
Fisher, Margery (Turner) 1913-1992 .... *20*
Obituary *74*
Fisher, Marshall Jon 1963- *113*
Fisher, Nikki
See Strachan, Ian
Fisher, Robert (Tempest) 1943- *47*
Fisher, Suzanne
See Staples, Suzanne Fisher
Fisher, Valorie *214*
Earlier sketch in SATA *177*
Fishman, Cathy Goldberg 1951- *106*
Fisk, Nicholas
See Higginbottom, David
Fisk, Pauline 1948- *160*
Earlier sketch in SATA *66*
Fiske, Tarleton
See Bloch, Robert (Albert)
Fisscher, Catharina G. M. 1958- *142*
Fisscher, Tiny
See Fisscher, Catharina G. M.
Fitch, Clarke
See Sinclair, Upton
Fitch, John IV
See Cormier, Robert
Fitch, Sheree 1956- *178*
Earlier sketch in SATA *108*
Fitschen, Dale 1937- *20*
Fitzalan, Roger
See Trevor, Elleston
Fitzgerald, Captain Hugh
See Baum, L. Frank
FitzGerald, Cathleen 1932-1987
Obituary *50*
Fitzgerald, Dawn *175*
Fitzgerald, Edward Earl 1919-2001 .... *20*
Fitzgerald, F(rancis) A(nthony) 1940- *15*
Fitzgerald, Joanne 1956- *198*
Fitzgerald, John D(ennis) 1907(?)-1988 .... *20*
Obituary *56*
See also CLR *1*
Fitzgerald, Merni Ingrassia 1955- *53*
Fitzgibbon, Terry 1948- *121*
Fitzhardinge, Joan Margaret 1912- *73*
Earlier sketch in SATA *2*
See also CLR *5*
See also SAAS *3*
Fitzhugh, Louise (Perkins) 1928-1974 .... *45*
Obituary *24*
Earlier sketch in SATA *1*
See also CLR *72*
Fitzhugh, Percy Keese 1876-1950 .... *65*
Fitzmaurice, Kathryn *217*
Fitzpatrick, Becca 1979- *224*
Fitzpatrick, Marie-Louise 1962- *189*
Earlier sketch in SATA *125*
FitzRalph, Matthew
See McInerny, Ralph
Fitz-Randolph, Jane (Currens) 1915- *51*
Fitzsimons, Cecilia 1952- *97*
Fitzsimons, Cecilia A.L.
See Fitzsimons, Cecilia
Fixmer, Elizabeth *237*
Flack, Marjorie 1897-1958 .... *100*
See also YABC *2*
See also CLR *28*
Flack, Naomi John White -1999 .... *40*
Brief entry *35*
Flake, Sharon G. *166*
Flanagan, John 1944- *180*

Flanagan, John Anthony
See Flanagan, John
Flannery, Kate
See De Goldi, Kate
Flatt, Lizann 1966- *88*
Fleagle, Gail S(hatto) 1940- *117*
Fleetwood, Jenni 1947- *80*
Fleischer, Jane
See Oppenheim, Joanne
Fleischhauer-Hardt, Helga 1936- *30*
Fleischman, Albert Sidney
See Fleischman, Sid
Fleischman, John 1948- *145*
Fleischman, Paul 1952- *156*
Brief entry *32*
Earlier sketches in SATA *39, 72, 110*
See also CLR *66*
See also SAAS *20*
Fleischman, Sid 1920-2010 .... *185*
Earlier sketches in SATA *8, 59, 96, 148*
See also CLR *15*
Fleischner, Jennifer 1956- *188*
Earlier sketch in SATA *93*
Fleisher, Paul 1948- *132*
Earlier sketch in SATA *81*
Fleisher, Robbin 1951-1977 .... *52*
Brief entry *49*
Fleishman, Seymour 1918- *66*
Brief entry *32*
Fleming, A. A.
See Arthur, Robert, (Jr.)
Fleming, Alice Mulcahey 1928- *9*
Fleming, Candace 1962- *225*
Earlier sketches in SATA *94, 143, 190*
Fleming, Denise 1950- *241*
Earlier sketches in SATA *81, 126, 173*
Fleming, Elizabeth P. 1888-1985
Obituary *48*
Fleming, Ian 1908-1964 .... *9*
Fleming, Ian Lancaster
See Fleming, Ian
Fleming, Ronald Lee 1941- *56*
Fleming, Sally
See Walker, Sally M.
Fleming, Stuart
See Knight, Damon (Francis)
Fleming, Susan 1932- *32*
Fleming, Thomas 1927- *8*
Fleming, Thomas James
See Fleming, Thomas
Fleming, Virginia (Edwards) 1923- *84*
Flesch, Y.
See Flesch, Yolande
Flesch, Yolande 1950- *55*
Flesch, Yolande Catarina
See Flesch, Yolande
Fletcher, Charlie *220*
Fletcher, Charlie May Hogue 1897-1977 .... *3*
Fletcher, Colin 1922-2007 .... *28*
Fletcher, Dirk
See Cunningham, Chet
Fletcher, George U.
See Pratt, (Murray) Fletcher
Fletcher, Helen Jill 1910- *13*
Fletcher, Ralph 1953- *195*
Earlier sketches in SATA *105, 149*
See also CLR *104*
Fletcher, Ralph J.
See Fletcher, Ralph
Fletcher, Richard E. 1917(?)-1983
Obituary *34*
Fletcher, Rick
See Fletcher, Richard E.
Fletcher, Susan 1951- *181*
Earlier sketches in SATA *70, 110*
Fletcher, Susan Clemens
See Fletcher, Susan
Fleur, Paul
See Pohl, Frederik
Flexner, James Thomas 1908-2003 .... *9*
Fliess, Sue *241*
Flinn, Alex 1966- *198*
Earlier sketch in SATA *159*
Flint, Helen 1952- *102*
Flint, Russ 1944- *74*
Flitner, David, Jr. 1949- *7*
Flitner, David Perkins
See Flitner, David, Jr.
Floca, Brian *190*
Earlier sketch in SATA *155*
Floethe, Louise Lee 1913-1988 .... *4*
Floethe, Richard 1901-1998 .... *4*
Floherty, John Joseph 1882-1964 .... *25*
Flood, Bo
See Flood, Nancy Bo
Flood, Nancy Bo 1945- *233*
Earlier sketch in SATA *130*
Flood, Pansie Hart 1964- *140*
Flood, William 1942- *129*
Flooglebuckle, Al
See Spiegelman, Art
Flora, James (Royer) 1914-1998 .... *30*
Obituary *103*
Earlier sketch in SATA *1*
See also SAAS *6*
Flores-Galbis, Enrique 1952- *186*
Florian, Douglas 1950- *177*
Earlier sketches in SATA *19, 83, 125*
Flory, Jane Trescott 1917- *22*
Flournoy, Valerie 1952- *95*
Flournoy, Valerie Rose
See Flournoy, Valerie
Flowerdew, Phyllis -1994 .... *33*
Flowers, Pam 1946- *136*
Flowers, Sarah 1952- *98*
Floyd, Gareth 1940- *62*
Brief entry *31*
Fluchere, Henri 1914-1991 .... *40*
Fluke, Joanne 1943- *88*
Flutsztejn-Gruda, Ilona 1930- *170*
Flynn, Barbara 1928- *9*
Flynn, Jackson
See Bensen, Donald R.
and Shirreffs, Gordon D(onald)
Flynn, Nicholas
See Odgers, Sally Farrell
Flynn, Pat 1968- *214*
Flynn, Patrick
See Flynn, Pat
Flynn, Rachel 1953- *171*
Earlier sketch in SATA *109*
Flynn, Warren (G.) 1950- *154*
Fodor, R. V. 1944- *25*
Fodor, Ronald Victor
See Fodor, R. V.
Fogelin, Adrian 1951- *175*
Earlier sketch in SATA *129*
Foley, (Anna) Bernice Williams 1902-1987 . *28*
Foley, Greg E. 1969- *236*
Earlier sketch in SATA *190*
Foley, June 1944- *44*
Foley, (Mary) Louise Munro 1933- *106*
Brief entry *40*
Earlier sketch in SATA *54*
Foley, Rae
See Denniston, Elinore
Folke, Will
See Bloch, Robert (Albert)
Follett, Helen Thomas 1884(?)-1970
Obituary *27*
Folsom, Franklin (Brewster) 1907-1995 .... *5*
Obituary *88*
Folsom, Michael (Brewster) 1938-1990 .... *40*
Obituary *88*
Fombelle, Timothee de 1973- *218*
Fontenot, Mary Alice 1910-2003 .... *91*
Obituary *209*
Earlier sketch in SATA *34*
Fontes, Justine *172*
Fontes, Ron 1952- *183*
Foon, Dennis 1951- *119*
Fooner, Michael *22*
Foote, Timothy (Gilson) 1926- *52*
Forberg, Ati
See Forberg, Beate Gropius
Forberg, Beate Gropius 1925- *22*
Forbes, Anna 1954- *101*
Forbes, Bryan 1926- *37*
Forbes, Cabot L.
See Hoyt, Edwin P(almer), Jr.
Forbes, Esther 1891-1967 .... *100*
Earlier sketch in SATA *2*
See also CLR *147*
Forbes, Graham B. *1*
Forbes, Kathryn
See McLean, Kathryn (Anderson)
Forbes, Robert
See Arthur, Robert, (Jr.)
Ford, A.G. *231*
Ford, Albert Lee
See Stratemeyer, Edward L.
Ford, Barbara *56*
Brief entry *34*
Ford, Bernette *212*
Ford, Bernette G.
See Ford, Bernette
Ford, B.G.
See Ford, Bernette
Ford, Brian J(ohn) 1939- *49*
Ford, Carolyn 1938- *98*
Ford, Carolyn Mott
See Ford, Carolyn
Ford, Christine 1953- *176*
Ford, David
See Baldacci, David
and Baldacci, David
Ford, David B.
See Baldacci, David
Ford, David Baldacci
See Baldacci, David
Ford, Elbur
See Hibbert, Eleanor Alice Burford
Ford, Ellen 1949- *89*
Ford, George (Jr.) *31*
Ford, Hilary
See Youd, Samuel
Ford, Hildegarde
See Morrison, Velma Ford
Ford, Jerome W. 1949- *78*
Ford, Jerry
See Ford, Jerome W.
Ford, John C. 1971- *221*
Ford, Juwanda G(ertrude) 1967- *102*
Ford, Marcia
See Radford, Ruby L(orraine)
Ford, Nancy K(effer) 1906-1961
Obituary *29*
Ford, Peter 1936- *59*
Ford, S. M.
See Uhlig, Susan
Forde, Catherine 1961- *170*
Foreman, Mark *199*
Foreman, Michael 1938- *216*
Earlier sketches in SATA *2, 73, 129, 135, 184*
See also CLR *32*
See also SAAS *21*
Foreman, Wilmoth 1939- *153*
Forest, Antonia 1915-2003 .... *29*
Obituary *149*
Forest, Dial
See Gault, William Campbell
Forest, Heather 1948- *185*
Earlier sketch in SATA *120*
Forester, C. S. 1899-1966 .... *13*
Forester, Cecil Scott
See Forester, C. S.
Forester, Victoria *214*
Forler, Nan *223*
Forman, Brenda 1936- *4*
Forman, James
See Forman, James D.
Forman, James D. 1932-2009 .... *70*
Earlier sketch in SATA *8*

Forman, James Douglas
  See Forman, James D.
Forman, Mark L.
  See Forman, M.L.
Forman, M.L. 1964- *215*
Forman, Ruth 1970- *186*
Formento, Alison *228*
Forrest, Elizabeth
  See Salsitz, Rhondi Vilott
Forrest, Mary
  See Pausacker, Jenny
Forrest, Sybil
  See Markun, Patricia Maloney
Forrestal, Elaine 1941- *165*
  Earlier sketch in SATA *117*
Forrester, Frank H. 1919(?)-1986
  Obituary *52*
Forrester, Helen
  See Bhatia, Jamunadevi
Forrester, Jade
  See Pausacker, Jenny
Forrester, Marian
  See Schachtel, Roger
Forrester, Sandra 1949- *166*
  Earlier sketch in SATA *90*
Forrester, Victoria 1940- *40*
  Brief entry *35*
Forsee, (Frances) Aylesa -1986 .... *1*
Forsey, Chris 1950- *59*
Forshay-Lunsford, Cin 1965- *60*
Forster, E. M. 1879-1970 .... *57*
Forster, Edward Morgan
  See Forster, E. M.
Forsyth, Kate 1966- *154*
Fort, Paul
  See Stockton, Francis Richard
Forte, Maurizio 1961- *110*
Fortey, Richard 1946- *109*
Fortey, Richard A.
  See Fortey, Richard
Fortey, Richard Alan
  See Fortey, Richard
Forth, Melissa D(eal) *96*
Fortnum, Peggy
  See Nuttall-Smith, Margaret Emily Noel
Fortune, Eric *182*
Forward, Robert L(ull) 1932-2002 .... *82*
Fosberry, Jennifer *235*
Foster, Alan Dean 1946- *70*
Foster, Brad W. 1955- *34*
Foster, Doris Van Liew 1899-1993 .... *10*
Foster, E(lizabeth) C(onnell) 1902- *9*
Foster, Elizabeth 1902- *12*
Foster, Elizabeth 1905-1963 .... *10*
Foster, F. Blanche 1919- *11*
Foster, G(eorge) Allen 1907-1969 .... *26*
Foster, Genevieve (Stump) 1893-1979 .... *2*
  Obituary *23*
  See also CLR *7*
Foster, Gerald L. *198*
Foster, Hal
  See Foster, Harold
Foster, Harold 1892-1982 .... *31*
Foster, Jeanne
  See Williams, Jeanne
Foster, John
  See Foster, John L(ouis)
  and Furcolo, Foster
Foster, John (Thomas) 1925- *8*
Foster, John L(ouis) 1941- *102*
Foster, Juliana *196*
Foster, Laura Louise (James) 1918- *6*
Foster, Leila Merrell 1929- *73*
Foster, Lynne 1937- *74*
Foster, Margaret Lesser 1899(?)-1979
  Obituary *21*
Foster, Marian Curtis 1909-1978 .... *23*
Foster, Mark 1961- *197*
Foster, Sally *58*
Fotheringham, Edwin *201*
Foulds, E. V.
  See Foulds, Elfrida Vipont
Foulds, Elfrida Vipont 1902-1992 .... *52*
Fountas, Angela Jane *180*
Fourie, Corlia 1944- *91*
Fourth Brother, The
  See Aung, (Maung) Htin
Fowke, Edith (Margaret) 1913-1996 .... *14*
Fowles, John 1926-2005 .... *22*
  Obituary *171*
Fowles, John Robert
  See Fowles, John
Fowles, Shelley 1956- *205*
Fox, Aileen 1907-2005 .... *58*
  Obituary *170*
Fox, Aileen Mary
  See Fox, Aileen
Fox, Annie 1950- *175*
Fox, Charles Philip 1913-2003 .... *12*
  Obituary *150*
Fox, Christyan *188*
Fox, Diane *188*
Fox, Eleanor
  See St. John, Wylly Folk
Fox, Fontaine Talbot, Jr. 1884-1964
  Obituary *23*
Fox, Fred 1903(?)-1981
  Obituary *27*
Fox, Freeman
  See Hamilton, Charles (Harold St. John)
Fox, Geoffrey 1941- *73*
Fox, Grace
  See Anderson, Grace Fox
Fox, Helen 1962- *181*
Fox, Karen C. 1969- *229*
Fox, Larry *30*
Fox, Lee 1958- *227*
Fox, Lorraine 1922-1976 .... *27*
  Earlier sketch in SATA *11*
Fox, Louisa
  See Kroll, Virginia L.
Fox, Mary Virginia 1919- *152*
  Brief entry *39*
  Earlier sketches in SATA *44, 88*
Fox, Mem 1946- *211*
  Earlier sketches in SATA *51, 103, 155*
  See also CLR *80*
Fox, Merrion Frances
  See Fox, Mem
Fox, Michael W(ilson) 1937- *15*
Fox, Norma Diane
  See Mazer, Norma Fox
Fox, Paula 1923- *167*
  Earlier sketches in SATA *17, 60, 120*
  See also CLR *96*
Fox, Robert J. 1927- *33*
Fox, Robert Joseph
  See Fox, Robert J.
Fox-Davies, Sarah 1956- *199*
Foyt, Victoria .... *187.*
Fradin, Dennis
  See Fradin, Dennis Brindell
Fradin, Dennis Brindell 1945- *185*
  Earlier sketches in SATA *29, 90, 135*
Fradin, Judith Bloom 1945- *185*
  Earlier sketches in SATA *90, 152*
Frailey, Paige (Menefee) 1965- *82*
Frame, Janet 1924-2004 .... *119*
Frame, Janet Paterson
  See Frame, Janet
Frame, Paul 1913-1994 .... *60*
  Brief entry *33*
  Obituary *83*
Frances, Miss
  See Horwich, Frances R(appaport)
Franchere, Ruth *18*
Francis, Charles
  See Holme, Bryan
Francis, Dee
  See Haas, Dorothy F.
Francis, Dorothy 1926- *127*
  Earlier sketch in SATA *10*
Francis, Dorothy B.
  See Francis, Dorothy
Francis, Dorothy Brenner
  See Francis, Dorothy
Francis, Guy *225*
Francis, Jaye
  See Pausacker, Jenny
Francis, Pamela (Mary) 1926- *11*
Franck, Eddie
  See Cooke, Frank E.
Franco, Betsy *223*
  Earlier sketches in SATA *150, 188*
Franco, Eloise (Bauder) 1910- *62*
Franco, Johan (Henri Gustave) 1908-1988 ... *62*
Franco, Marjorie *38*
Franco, Tom *224*
Francois, Andre 1915-2005 .... *25*
Francoise
  See Seignobosc, Francoise
Frank, Anne 1929-1945 .... *87*
  Brief entry *42*
  See also CLR *101*
Frank, Annelies Marie
  See Frank, Anne
Frank, Daniel B. 1956- *55*
Frank, Emily R.
  See Frank, E.R.
Frank, E.R. 1967- *157*
Frank, Helene
  See Vautier, Ghislaine
Frank, Hillary 1976- *148*
Frank, John *199*
Frank, Josette 1893-1989 .... *10*
  Obituary *63*
Frank, Lucy 1947- *166*
  Earlier sketch in SATA *94*
Frank, Mary 1933- *34*
Frank, R., Jr.
  See Ross, Frank (Xavier), Jr.
Frankau, Mary Evelyn Atkinson 1899-1974 .. *4*
Frankel, Alona 1937- *66*
Frankel, Bernice *9*
Frankel, Edward 1910- *44*
Frankel, Ellen 1951- *78*
Frankel, Julie 1947- *40*
  Brief entry *34*
Frankenberg, Robert 1911- *22*
Frankland, David *207*
Franklin, Cheryl J. 1955- *70*
Franklin, Harold 1926- *13*
Franklin, Kristine L. 1958- *124*
  Earlier sketch in SATA *80*
Franklin, Lance
  See Lantz, Francess L(in)
Franklin, Madeleine
  See L'Engle, Madeleine
Franklin, Madeleine L'Engle
  See L'Engle, Madeleine
Franklin, Madeleine L'Engle Camp
  See L'Engle, Madeleine
Franklin, Max
  See Deming, Richard
Franklin, Steve
  See Stevens, Franklin
Franson, Leanne 1963- *223*
  Earlier sketch in SATA *111*
Franson, Scott E. 1966- *192*
Franzen, Nils-Olof 1916- *10*
Frascino, Edward *48*
  Brief entry *33*
  See also SAAS *9*
Frasconi, Antonio 1919- *131*
  Earlier sketches in SATA *6, 53*
  See also SAAS *11*
Fraser, Betty
  See Fraser, Elizabeth Marr
Fraser, Elizabeth Marr 1928- *31*
Fraser, Eric (George) 1902-1983 .... *38*

Fraser, Mary Ann 1959- *214*
Earlier sketches in SATA *76, 137*
See also SAAS *23*
Fraser, Wynnette (McFaddin) 1925- *90*
Frasier, Debra 1953- *182*
Earlier sketches in SATA *69, 112*
Fraustino, Lisa Rowe 1961- *146*
Autobiography Feature *146*
Earlier sketch in SATA *84*
Frazee, Marla 1958- *225*
Earlier sketches in SATA *105, 151, 187*
Frazer, Megan 1977- *221*
Frazetta, Frank 1928-2010 .... *58*
Frazier, Angie *234*
Frazier, Craig 1955- *221*
Earlier sketch in SATA *177*
Frazier, Neta (Osborn) Lohnes 1890-1990 .... *7*
Frazier, Sundee T. 1968- *198*
Frazier, Sundee Tucker
See Frazier, Sundee T.
Frederic, Mike
See Cox, William R(obert)
Frederick, Heather Vogel *207*
Fredericks, Anthony D. 1947- *113*
Freed, Alvyn M. 1913-1993 .... *22*
Freedman, Benedict 1919- *27*
Freedman, Claire *227*
Earlier sketch in SATA *185*
Freedman, Deborah 1960- *191*
Freedman, Jeff 1953- *90*
Freedman, Nancy 1920-2010 .... *27*
Freedman, Russell 1929- *235*
Earlier sketches in SATA *16, 71, 123, 175*
See also CLR *71*
Freedman, Russell Bruce
See Freedman, Russell
Freeman, Barbara C. 1906-1999 .... *28*
Freeman, Barbara Constance
See Freeman, Barbara C.
Freeman, Bill
See Freeman, William Bradford
Freeman, Don 1908-1978 .... *17*
See also CLR *90*
Freeman, Ira Maximilian 1905-1987 .... *21*
Freeman, Kimberley
See Wilkins, Kim
Freeman, Laura *200*
Freeman, Lucy (Greenbaum) 1916-2004 .... *24*
Freeman, Mae 1907-1985 .... *25*
Freeman, Mae Blacker
See Freeman, Mae
Freeman, Marcia S. 1937- *102*
Freeman, Marcia Sheehan
See Freeman, Marcia S.
Freeman, Martha 1956- *201*
Earlier sketches in SATA *101, 152*
Freeman, Nancy 1932- *61*
Freeman, Peter J.
See Calvert, Patricia
Freeman, Roy *235*
Freeman, Sarah (Caroline) 1940- *66*
Freeman, Tor 1977- *164*
Freeman, VicToria
See Freeman, Tor
Freeman, William Bradford 1938- *58*
Brief entry *48*
Fregosi, Claudia (Anne Marie) 1946- *24*
Freitas, Donna 1972- *205*
French, Allen 1870-1946
See YABC *1*
French, Dorothy Kayser 1926- *5*
French, Fiona 1944- *132*
Earlier sketches in SATA *6, 75*
See also CLR *37*
See also SAAS *21*
French, Jackie *186*
Autobiography Feature *139*
Earlier sketches in SATA *108, 139*
See French, Jackie Anne
and French, Jacqueline Anne
French, Kathryn
See Mosesson, Gloria R(ubin)
French, Martin *176*
French, Michael 1944- *49*
Brief entry *38*
French, Paul
See Asimov, Isaac
French, S. Terrell *216*
French, Simon 1957- *147*
Earlier sketch in SATA *86*
French, Vivian *209*
Earlier sketch in SATA *165*
French, Wendy 1972- *234*
Frenette, Liza *126*
Freschet, Gina 1960- *175*
Earlier sketch in SATA *139*
Frewer, Glyn (M.) 1931- *11*
Frey, Darcy *98*
Freymann, Saxton 1958(?)- *178*
Freymann-Weyr, Garret 1965- *145*
Freymann-Weyr, Rhoda Garret Michaela
See Freymann-Weyr, Garret
Freytes, Silvio 1971- *240*
Friar, Joanne *237*
Friar, Joanne H.
See Friar, Joanne
Frick, C. H.
See Irwin, Constance (H.) Frick
Frick, Constance
See Irwin, Constance (H.) Frick
Fricke, Aaron 1962- *89*
Fridell, Ron 1943- *124*
Fried, Janice *197*
Frieden, Sarajo *232*
Friedlander, Joanne K(ohn) 1930- *9*
Friedman, Aimee 1979- *189*
Friedman, D. Dina 1957- *180*
Friedman, Debra 1955- *150*
Friedman, Estelle (Ehrenwald) 1920- *7*
Friedman, Frieda 1905- *43*
Friedman, Hal *230*
See Friedman, Harold
Friedman, Ina R(osen) 1926- *136*
Brief entry *41*
Earlier sketch in SATA *49*
Friedman, Jerrold David
See Gerrold, David
Friedman, Judi 1935- *59*
Friedman, Laurie 1964- *219*
Earlier sketches in SATA *138, 179*
Friedman, Marvin 1930- *42*
Brief entry *33*
Friedman, Robin 1968- *219*
Earlier sketch in SATA *162*
Friedmann, Stan 1953- *80*
Friedrich, Otto (Alva) 1929-1995 .... *33*
Friedrich, Priscilla 1927- *39*
Friend, Catherine 1957(?)- *194*
Friend, David Michael 1975- *195*
Friend, Natasha 1972- *184*
Friendlich, Dick
See Friendlich, Richard J.
Friendlich, Richard J. 1909- *11*
Friermood, Elisabeth Hamilton 1903-1992 .... *5*
Friesen, Bernice (Sarah Anne) 1966- *105*
Friesen, Gayle 1960- *200*
Earlier sketch in SATA *109*
Friesen, Jonathan 1967(?)- *206*
Friesner, Esther 1951- *240*
Earlier sketches in SATA *71, 168, 207*
Friesner, Esther M.
See Friesner, Esther
Friis-Baastad, Babbis Ellinor 1921-1970 .... *7*
Frimmer, Steven 1928- *31*
Frischmuth, Barbara 1941- *114*
Friskey, Margaret (Richards) 1901-1995 .... *5*
Fritts, Mary Bahr
See Bahr, Mary (Madelyn)
Fritz, Jean (Guttery) 1915- *163*
Autobiography Feature *122*
Earlier sketches in SATA *1, 29, 72, 119*
See also CLR *96*
See also SAAS *2*
Froehlich, Margaret W(alden) 1930- *56*
Frois, Jeanne 1953- *73*
Froissart, Jean 1338(?)-1410(?) *28*
Froman, Elizabeth Hull 1920-1975 .... *10*
Froman, Robert (Winslow) 1917- *8*
Fromental, Jean-Luc 1950- *231*
Fromm, Lilo 1928- *29*
Frommer, Harvey 1937- *41*
Frossard, Claire *241*
Frost, A(rthur) B(urdett) 1851-1928 .... *19*
Frost, Elizabeth
See Frost-Knappman, Elizabeth
Frost, Erica
See Supraner, Robyn
Frost, Helen 1949- *194*
Autobiography Feature *194*
Earlier sketches in SATA *157, 183*
Frost, Helen Marie
See Frost, Helen
Frost, Lesley 1899-1983 .... *14*
Obituary *34*
Frost, Robert 1874-1963 .... *14*
See also CLR *67*
Frost, Robert Lee
See Frost, Robert
Frost, Shelley 1960- *138*
Frost-Knappman, Elizabeth 1943- *179*
Froud, Brian 1947- *150*
Fry, Annette R(iley) *89*
Fry, Christopher 1907-2005 .... *66*
Fry, Edward Bernard 1925- *35*
Fry, Rosalie Kingsmill 1911-1992 .... *3*
See also SAAS *11*
Fry, Virginia Lynn 1952- *95*
Frye, Sally
See Moore, Elaine
Fuchs, Bernie 1932- *162*
Earlier sketch in SATA *95*
Fuchs, Erich 1916- *6*
Fuchshuber, Annegert 1940- *43*
Fucile, Tony *221*
Fuerst, Jeffrey B. 1956- *143*
Fuertes, Gloria 1918-1998 .... *115*
Fuge, Charles 1966- *144*
Earlier sketch in SATA *74*
Fujikawa, Gyo 1908-1998 .... *76*
Brief entry *30*
Obituary *110*
Earlier sketch in SATA *39*
See also CLR *25*
See also SAAS *16*
Fujita, Tamao 1905-1999 .... *7*
Fujiwara, Kim 1957- *81*
Fujiwara, Michiko 1946- *15*
Fuka, Vladimir 1926-1977
Obituary *27*
Fulcher, Jennifer
See Westwood, Jennifer
Fuller, Catherine Leuthold 1916- *9*
Fuller, Edmund (Maybank) 1914- *21*
Fuller, Iola
See McCoy, Iola Fuller
Fuller, John G(rant, Jr.) 1913-1990 .... *65*
Fuller, Kathleen
See Gottfried, Theodore Mark
Fuller, Lois Hamilton 1915- *11*
Fuller, Margaret 1810-1850 .... *25*
Fuller, Maud
See Petersham, Maud
Fuller, Roy (Broadbent) 1912-1991 .... *87*
Fuller, Sarah Margaret
See Fuller, Margaret
Fults, John Lee 1932- *33*
Funk, Thompson 1911- *7*
Funk, Tom
See Funk, Thompson

Funke, Cornelia 1958- ... 209
Earlier sketches in SATA *154, 174*
See also CLR *145*
Funke, Cornelia Caroline
See Funke, Cornelia
Funke, Lewis 1912-1992 ... *11*
Fuqua, Jonathon Scott 1966- ... *141*
Furbee, Mary R.
See Furbee, Mary Rodd
Furbee, Mary Rodd 1954- ... *138*
Furchgott, Terry 1948- ... *29*
Furlong, Monica (Mavis) 1930-2003 ... *86*
Obituary ... *142*
Furlonger, Patricia
See Wrightson, Patricia
Furman, Gertrude Lerner Kerman 1909- ... *21*
Furniss, Tim 1948- ... *49*
Furrow, Robert 1985- ... *172*
Furukawa, Toshi 1924- ... *24*
Fusco, Kimberly Newton ... *236*
Fusillo, Archimede 1962- ... *137*
Fussell, Sandy 1960- ... *234*
Futcher, Jane P. 1947- ... *76*
Futehali, Zahida
See Whitaker, Zai
Fyleman, Rose (Amy) 1877-1957 ... *21*
Fyson, Jenny Grace
See Fyson, J.G.
Fyson, J.G. 1904-1998 ... *42*

G

Gaan, Margaret 1914- ... *65*
Gaber, Susan 1956- ... *169*
Earlier sketch in SATA *115*
Gaberman, Judie Angell
See Angell, Judie
Gabhart, Ann
See Gabhart, Ann H.
Gabhart, Ann H. 1947- ... *75*
Gable, Brian 1949- ... *195*
Gabler, Mirko 1951- ... *77*
Gabriel, Adriana
See Rojany, Lisa
Gabrys, Ingrid Schubert
See Schubert-Gabrys, Ingrid
Gackenbach, Dick 1927- ... *79*
Brief entry ... *30*
Earlier sketch in SATA *48*
Gadd, Jeremy 1949- ... *116*
Gaddis, Vincent H. 1913-1997 ... *35*
Gadler, Steve J. 1905-1985 ... *36*
Gaeddert, Lou Ann (Bigge) 1931- ... *103*
Earlier sketch in SATA *20*
Gaeddert, Louann
See Gaeddert, Lou Ann (Bigge)
Gaer, Joseph 1897-1969 ... *118*
Gaer, Yossef
See Gaer, Joseph
Gaetz, Dayle Campbell 1947- ... *138*
Gaffney, Timothy R. 1951- ... *170*
Earlier sketch in SATA *69*
Gaffron, Norma 1931- ... *97*
Gaffron, Norma Bondeson
See Gaffron, Norma
Gag, Flavia 1907-1979
Obituary ... *24*
Gag, Wanda (Hazel) 1893-1946 ... *100*
See also YABC *1*
See also CLR *150*
Gage, Brian ... *162*
Gage, Wilson
See Steele, Mary Q(uintard Govan)
Gagliano, Eugene M. 1946- ... *150*
Gagliardo, Ruth Garver 1895(?)-1980
Obituary ... *22*
Gagnon, Cecile 1936- ... *58*
Gaillard, Jason 1965- ... *200*
Gaiman, Neil 1960- ... *228*
Earlier sketches in SATA *85, 146, 197*
See also CLR *109*
Gaiman, Neil Richard
See Gaiman, Neil
Gainer, Cindy 1962- ... *74*
Gaines, Ernest J. 1933- ... *86*
See also CLR *62*
Gaines, Ernest James
See Gaines, Ernest J.
Gaither, Gloria 1942- ... *127*
Gal, Laszlo 1933- ... *96*
Brief entry ... *32*
Earlier sketch in SATA *52*
See also CLR *61*
Gal, Susan ... *228*
Galbraith, Ben 1980- ... *200*
Galbraith, Kathryn O. 1945- ... *219*
Earlier sketch in SATA *85*
Galbraith, Kathryn Osebold
See Galbraith, Kathryn O.
Galdone, Paul 1907(?)-1986 ... *66*
Obituary ... *49*
Earlier sketch in SATA *17*
See also CLR *16*
Galindo, Claudia 1979- ... *203*
Galinsky, Ellen 1942- ... *23*
Gall, Chris 1961- ... *176*
Gallagher, Diana G. 1946- ... *153*
Gallagher, Lurlene Nora
See McDaniel, Lurlene
Gallagher-Cole, Mernie 1958- ... *206*
Gallant, Roy A(rthur) 1924- ... *110*
Earlier sketches in SATA *4, 68*
See also CLR *30*
Gallardo, Evelyn 1948- ... *78*
Gallaz, Christophe 1948- ... *162*
See also CLR *126*
Gallego Garcia, Laura 1977- ... *173*
Gallico, Paul 1897-1976 ... *13*
Gallico, Paul William
See Gallico, Paul
Gallo, Donald R. 1938- ... *112*
Autobiography Feature ... *104*
Gallo, Donald Robert
See Gallo, Donald R.
Galloway, Owateka (S.) 1981- ... *121*
Galloway, Priscilla 1930- ... *227*
Earlier sketches in SATA *66, 112*
Gallup, Joan 1957- ... *128*
Galouchko, Annouchka Gravel 1960- ... *95*
Galt, Thomas Franklin, Jr. 1908-1989 ... *5*
Galt, Tom
See Galt, Thomas Franklin, Jr.
Galvin, Matthew R. 1950- ... *93*
Galvin, Matthew Reppert
See Galvin, Matthew R.
Gamble, Kim 1952- ... *183*
Earlier sketches in SATA *81, 124*
Gambrell, Jamey ... *82*
Gamerman, Martha 1941- ... *15*
Gammell, Stephen 1943- ... *226*
Earlier sketches in SATA *53, 81, 128*
See also CLR *83*
Ganly, Helen (Mary) 1940- ... *56*
Gann, Marjorie ... *239*
Gannett, Ruth Chrisman (Arens) 1896-1979 ... *33*
Gannett, Ruth Stiles 1923- ... *3*
Gannij, Joan ... *208*
Gannij, Joan Levine
See Gannij, Joan
Gannon, Ned 1974- ... *205*
Gannon, Robert Haines 1931- ... *8*
Gano, Lila 1949- ... *76*
Gans, Roma 1894-1996 ... *45*
Obituary ... *93*
Gant, Matthew
See Hano, Arnold
Gantner, Susan (Verble) 1939- ... *63*
Gantos, Jack 1951- ... *169*
Earlier sketches in SATA *20, 81, 119*
See also CLR *85*
Gantos, John Bryan, Jr.
See Gantos, Jack
Ganz, Yaffa 1938- ... *61*
Brief entry ... *52*
Garafano, Marie 1942- ... *84*
Garant, Andre J. 1968- ... *123*
Garbe, Ruth Moore
See Moore, Ruth (Ellen)
Garber, Esther
See Lee, Tanith
Garcia, Cristina 1958- ... *208*
Garcia, Emma 1969- ... *198*
Garcia, Geronimo 1960- ... *222*
Garcia, Kami 1972- ... *229*
Garcia, Yolanda P. 1952- ... *113*
Garcia, Yolanda Pacheco
See Garcia, Yolanda P.
Gard, Janice
See Latham, Jean Lee
Gard, Joyce
See Reeves, Joyce
Gard, Robert Edward 1910-1992 ... *18*
Obituary ... *74*
Gard, (Sanford) Wayne 1899-1986
Obituary ... *49*
Gardam, Jane 1928- ... *130*
Brief entry ... *28*
Earlier sketches in SATA *39, 76*
See also CLR *12*
See also SAAS *9*
Gardam, Jane Mary
See Gardam, Jane
Gardella, Tricia 1944- ... *96*
Garden, Nancy 1938- ... *147*
Autobiography Feature ... *147*
Earlier sketches in SATA *12, 77, 114*
See also CLR *51*
See also SAAS *8*
Gardiner, John Reynolds 1944-2006 ... *64*
Obituary ... *174*
Gardiner, Lindsey 1971- ... *144*
Gardner, Craig Shaw 1949- ... *99*
Gardner, Dic
See Gardner, Richard (M.)
Gardner, Graham ... *159*
Gardner, Hugh 1910-1986
Obituary ... *49*
Gardner, Jane Mylum 1946- ... *83*
Gardner, Jeanne LeMonnier 1925- ... *5*
Gardner, John, Jr. 1933-1982 ... *40*
Obituary ... *31*
Gardner, John Champlin, Jr.
See Gardner, John, Jr.
Gardner, John E(dward) 1917- ... *192*
Gardner, Lyn ... *192*
Gardner, Martin 1914-2010 ... *142*
Earlier sketch in SATA *16*
Gardner, Miriam
See Bradley, Marion Zimmer
Gardner, Richard (M.) 1931- ... *24*
Gardner, Richard A(lan) 1931-2003 ... *13*
Obituary ... *144*
Gardner, Sally ... *229*
Earlier sketch in SATA *177*
Gardner, Sandra 1940- ... *70*
Gardner, Scot 1968- ... *143*
Gardner, Sheldon 1934- ... *33*
Gardner, Ted
See Gardner, Theodore Roosevelt II
Gardner, Theodore Roosevelt
See Gardner, Theodore Roosevelt II
Gardner, Theodore Roosevelt II 1934- ... *84*
Garelick, May 1910-1989 ... *19*
Garfield, James B. 1881-1984 ... *6*
Obituary ... *38*

Garfield, Leon 1921-1996 ... *76*
Obituary ... *90*
Earlier sketches in SATA *1, 32*
See also CLR *166*
Garfinkle, Debra L.
See Garfinkle, D.L.
Garfinkle, D.L. ... *187*
Garis, Howard R. 1873-1962 ... *13*
Garis, Howard Roger
See Garis, Howard R.
Garland, Mark 1953- ... *79*
Garland, Mark A.
See Garland, Mark
Garland, Michael 1952- ... *208*
Earlier sketch in SATA *168*
Garland, Sarah 1944- ... *135*
Earlier sketch in SATA *62*
Garland, Sherry 1948- ... *145*
Autobiography Feature ... *145*
Earlier sketches in SATA *73, 114*
Garner, Alan 1934- ... *69*
Autobiography Feature ... *108*
Earlier sketch in SATA *18*
See also CLR *130*
Garner, David 1958- ... *78*
Garner, Eleanor Ramrath 1930- ... *122*
Garner, James Finn 1960(?)- ... *92*
Garnet, A. H.
See Slote, Alfred
Garnett, Eve C. R. 1900-1991 ... *3*
Obituary ... *70*
Garofoli, Viviana 1970- ... *186*
Garou, Louis P.
See Bowkett, Stephen
Garraty, John A. 1920-2007 ... *23*
Obituary ... *189*
Garraty, John Arthur
See Garraty, John A.
Garren, Devorah-Leah
See Devorah-Leah
Garret, Maxwell R. 1917- ... *39*
Garretson, Dee ... *236*
Garretson, Victoria Diane
See Cox, Victoria
Garrett, Helen 1895- ... *21*
Garrett, Randall 1927-1987 ... *180*
Garrett, Richard 1920- ... *82*
Garrigue, Sheila 1931- ... *21*
Garrison, Barbara 1931- ... *163*
Earlier sketch in SATA *19*
Garrison, Frederick
See Sinclair, Upton
Garrison, Mary 1952- ... *146*
Garrison, Peter
See Gardner, Craig Shaw
Garrison, Webb B(lack) 1919-2000 ... *25*
Garrity, Jennifer Johnson 1961- ... *124*
Garrity, Linda K. 1947- ... *128*
Garsee, Jeannine ... *199*
Garst, Doris Shannon 1894-1981 ... *1*
Garst, Shannon
See Garst, Doris Shannon
Garth, Will
See Hamilton, Edmond
and Kuttner, Henry
Garthwaite, Marion H(ook) 1893-1981 ... *7*
Garton, Malinda D(ean) (?)-1976
Obituary ... *26*
Garvie, Maureen 1944- ... *175*
Garvie, Maureen McCallum
See Garvie, Maureen
Garza, Carmen Lomas 1948- ... *182*
Garza, Xavier ... *184*
Gascoigne, Bamber 1935- ... *62*
Gaskins, Pearl Fuyo 1957- ... *134*
Gasperini, Jim 1952- ... *54*
Brief entry ... *49*
Gater, Dilys 1944- ... *41*
Gates, Doris 1901-1987 ... *34*
Obituary ... *54*
Earlier sketch in SATA *1*
See also SAAS *1*
Gates, Frieda 1933- ... *26*
Gates, Susan 1950- ... *153*
Gates, Viola R. 1931- ... *101*
Gathorne-Hardy, Jonathan G. 1933- ... *124*
Earlier sketch in SATA *26*
Gatti, Anne 1952- ... *103*
Gatty, Juliana Horatia
See Ewing, Juliana (Horatia Gatty)
Gauch, Patricia Lee 1934- ... *228*
Earlier sketches in SATA *26, 80*
See also CLR *56*
See also SAAS *21*
Gauch, Sarah ... *223*
Gaudasinska, Elzbieta 1943- ... *190*
Gaul, Randy 1959- ... *63*
Gault, Clare 1925- ... *36*
Gault, Frank 1926-1982 ... *36*
Brief entry ... *30*
Gault, William Campbell 1910-1995 ... *8*
Gauthier, Gail 1953- ... *203*
Earlier sketches in SATA *118, 160*
Gaver, Becky
See Gaver, Rebecca
Gaver, Rebecca 1952- ... *20*
Gavin, Jamila 1941- ... *223*
Earlier sketches in SATA *96, 125*
Gay, Amelia
See Hogarth, Grace (Weston Allen)
Gay, Francis
See Gee, H(erbert) L(eslie)
Gay, Kathlyn 1930- ... *144*
Earlier sketch in SATA *9*
Gay, Kelly
See Keaton, Kelly
Gay, Marie-Louise 1952- ... *179*
Earlier sketches in SATA *68, 126*
See also CLR *27*
See also SAAS *21*
Gay, Michel 1947- ... *162*
Gay, Zhenya 1906-1978 ... *19*
Gaze, Gillian
See Barklem, Jill
Gear, Kathleen M. O'Neal
See Gear, Kathleen O'Neal
Gear, Kathleen O'Neal 1954- ... *224*
Earlier sketches in SATA *71, 166*
Gear, W. Michael 1955- ... *224*
Earlier sketches in SATA *71, 166*
Geary, Rick 1946- ... *142*
Geason, Susan 1946- ... *122*
Gedalof, Robin
See McGrath, Robin
Gedge, Pauline (Alice) 1945- ... *101*
Gee, H(erbert) L(eslie) 1901-1977
Obituary ... *26*
Gee, Maurice 1931- ... *227*
Earlier sketches in SATA *46, 101*
See also CLR *56*
Gee, Maurice Gough
See Gee, Maurice
Geehan, Wayne (E.) 1947- ... *107*
Geer, Charles 1922- ... *42*
Brief entry ... *32*
Geeslin, Campbell 1925- ... *163*
Earlier sketch in SATA *107*
Gehman, Mary W. 1923- ... *86*
Gehr, Mary 1910(?)-1997 ... *32*
Obituary ... *99*
Geipel, Eileen 1932- ... *30*
Geis, Alissa Imre 1976- ... *189*
Geis, Darlene Stern 1918(?)-1999 ... *7*
Obituary ... *111*
Geisel, Helen 1898-1967 ... *26*
Geisel, Theodor Seuss
See Dr. Seuss
Geisert, Arthur 1941- ... *237*
Brief entry ... *52*
Earlier sketches in SATA *56, 92, 133, 171*
See also CLR *87*
See also SAAS *23*
Geisert, Arthur Frederick
See Geisert, Arthur
Geisert, Bonnie 1942- ... *165*
Earlier sketch in SATA *92*
Geist, Ken ... *191*
Gelber, Lisa ... *210*
Gelbwasser, Margie 1976- ... *241*
Geldart, William 1936- ... *15*
Gelinas, Paul J. 1904-1996 ... *10*
Gellis, Roberta 1927- ... *128*
Gellis, Roberta Leah Jacobs
See Gellis, Roberta
Gellman, Marc ... *112*
Gelman, Amy 1961- ... *72*
Gelman, Jan 1963- ... *58*
Gelman, Rita Golden 1937- ... *131*
Brief entry ... *51*
Earlier sketch in SATA *84*
Gelman, Steve 1934- ... *3*
Gemignani, Tony 1973- ... *220*
Gemming, Elizabeth 1932- ... *11*
Gendel, Evelyn W. 1916(?)-1977
Obituary ... *27*
Gennaro, Joseph F., Jr. 1924- ... *53*
Gennaro, Joseph Francis, Jr.
See Gennaro, Joseph F., Jr.
Gentieu, Penny ... *204*
Gentile, Petrina 1969- ... *91*
Gentle, Mary 1956- ... *48*
Gentleman, David (William) 1930- ... *7*
Gentry, Marita ... *215*
Geoghegan, Adrienne 1962- ... *143*
George, Barbara
See Katz, Bobbi
George, Emily
See Katz, Bobbi
George, Gail
See Katz, Bobbi
George, Jean
See George, Jean Craighead
George, Jean C.
See George, Jean Craighead
George, Jean Craighead 1919- ... *226*
Earlier sketches in SATA *2, 68, 124, 170*
See also CLR *136*
George, Jessica Day 1976- ... *210*
George, John L(othar) 1916- ... *2*
George, Kristine O'Connell 1954- ... *156*
Earlier sketch in SATA *110*
George, Lindsay Barrett 1952- ... *206*
Earlier sketches in SATA *95, 155*
George, S. C. 1898- ... *11*
George, Sally
See Orr, Wendy
George, Sidney Charles
See George, S. C.
George, Twig C. 1950- ... *114*
George, W(illiam) Lloyd 1900(?)-1975
Obituary ... *30*
Georgiou, Constantine 1927- ... *7*
Georgiou, Theo
See Odgers, Sally Farrell
Geraghty, Paul 1959- ... *130*
Gerard, Jean Ignace Isidore 1803-1847 ... *45*
Geras, Adele 1944- ... *180*
Autobiography Feature ... *180*
Earlier sketches in SATA *23, 87, 129, 173*
See also SAAS *21*
Geras, Adele Daphne Weston
See Geras, Adele
Gerber, Carole 1947- ... *207*
Gerber, Linda ... *213*
Gerber, Merrill Joan 1938- ... *170*
Autobiography Feature ... *170*
Earlier sketches in SATA *64, 127*
Gerber, Perren 1933- ... *104*

Gerberg, Mort 1931- ... *64*
Gergely, Tibor 1900-1978 ... *54*
Obituary ... *20*
Geringer, Laura 1948- ... *232*
Earlier sketches in SATA *29, 94, 164*
Gerler, William R(obert) 1917-1996 ... *47*
Gerrard, Jean 1933- ... *51*
Gerrard, Roy 1935-1997 ... *90*
Brief entry ... *45*
Obituary ... *99*
Earlier sketch in SATA *47*
See also CLR *23*
Gerritsen, Paula 1956- ... *177*
Gerrold, David 1944- ... *144*
Earlier sketch in SATA *66*
Gersh, A.
See Gersh, Amanda
Gersh, Amanda ... *235*
Gershator, David 1937- ... *180*
Gershator, Phillis 1942- ... *235*
Earlier sketches in SATA *90, 158, 188*
Gershon, Dann 1955- ... *187*
Gershon, Gina 1962- ... *187*
Gerson, Corinne 1927- ... *37*
Gerson, Mary-Joan ... *136*
Earlier sketch in SATA *79*
Gerson, Noel Bertram 1914-1988 ... *22*
Obituary ... *60*
Gerstein, Mordicai 1935- ... *222*
Brief entry ... *36*
Earlier sketches in SATA *47, 81, 142, 178*
See also CLR *102*
Gertridge, Allison 1967- ... *132*
Gervais, Bernadette 1959- ... *80*
Gervay, Susanne ... *183*
Gesner, Clark 1938-2002 ... *40*
Obituary ... *143*
Gessner, Lynne 1919- ... *16*
Geter, Tyrone ... *150*
Getz, David 1957- ... *91*
Getzinger, Donna 1968- ... *128*
Geus, Mireille 1964- ... *207*
Gevirtz, Eliezer 1950- ... *49*
Gevry, Claudine ... *188*
Gewe, Raddory
See Gorey, Edward (St. John)
Ghan, Linda (R.) 1947- ... *77*
Ghent, Natale 1962- ... *148*
Gherman, Beverly 1934- ... *123*
Earlier sketch in SATA *68*
Ghigna, Charles 1946- ... *153*
Earlier sketch in SATA *108*
Giacobbe, Beppe 1953- ... *174*
Giambastiani, Kurt R. A. 1958- ... *141*
Giannini, Enzo 1946- ... *68*
Gibala-Broxholm, Scott 1959(?)- ... *205*
Gibbons, Alan 1953- ... *198*
Earlier sketch in SATA *124*
Gibbons, Faye 1938- ... *103*
Earlier sketch in SATA *65*
Gibbons, Gail 1944- ... *201*
Earlier sketches in SATA *23, 72, 104, 160*
See also CLR *8*
See also SAAS *12*
Gibbons, Gail Gretchen
See Gibbons, Gail
Gibbons, Kaye 1960- ... *117*
Gibbs, Adrea 1960- ... *126*
Gibbs, Alonzo (Lawrence) 1915-1992 ... *5*
Gibbs, (Cecilia) May 1877-1969
Obituary ... *27*
Gibbs, Stuart 1969- ... *230*
Gibbs, Tony
See Gibbs, Wolcott, Jr.
Gibbs, Wolcott, Jr. 1935- ... *40*
Giblin, James Cross 1933- ... *197*
Earlier sketches in SATA *33, 75, 122*
See also CLR *29*
See also SAAS *12*
Gibson, Andrew (William) 1949- ... *72*
Gibson, Barbara L. ... *205*
Gibson, Barbara Leonard
See Gibson, Barbara L.
Gibson, Betty 1911- ... *75*
Gibson, Jo
See Fluke, Joanne
Gibson, Josephine
See Hine, Sesyle Joslin
and Hine, Al(fred Blakelee)
Gibson, Marley 1966- ... *225*
Gibson, Sarah P. 1962- ... *211*
Gibson, William 1914-2008 ... *66*
Obituary ... *199*
Gibson, William Ford
See Gibson, William
Gidal, Nachum
See Gidal, Tim Nachum
Gidal, Sonia (Epstein) 1922- ... *2*
Gidal, Tim Nachum 1909-1996 ... *2*
Gidalewitsch, Nachum
See Gidal, Tim Nachum
Gideon, Melanie 1963- ... *175*
Gidwitz, Adam 1982- ... *240*
Giegling, John A(llan) 1935- ... *17*
Gifaldi, David 1950- ... *209*
Earlier sketch in SATA *76*
Giff, Patricia Reilly 1935- ... *239*
Earlier sketches in SATA *33, 70, 121, 160, 203*
Giffard, Hannah 1962- ... *83*
Gifford, Carrie ... *224*
Gifford, Clive 1966- ... *198*
Gifford, Griselda 1931- ... *171*
Earlier sketch in SATA *42*
Gifford, Kerri 1961- ... *91*
Gifford, Peggy 1952- ... *191*
Gilani, Fawzia
See Gilani-Williams, Fawzia
Gilani-Williams, Fawzia 1967- ... *231*
Gilbert, Ann
See Taylor, Ann
Gilbert, Anne Yvonne 1951- ... *185*
Gilbert, Barbara Snow 1954- ... *97*
Gilbert, Catherine
See Murdock, Catherine Gilbert
Gilbert, Frances
See Collings, Gillian
Gilbert, Harriett 1948- ... *30*
Gilbert, (Agnes) Joan (Sewell) 1931- ... *10*
Gilbert, John (Raphael) 1926- ... *36*
Gilbert, Nan
See Gilbertson, Mildred Geiger
Gilbert, Roby Goodale 1966- ... *90*
Gilbert, Ruth Gallard Ainsworth
See Ainsworth, Ruth (Gallard)
Gilbert, Sara (Dulaney) 1943- ... *82*
Earlier sketch in SATA *11*
Gilbert, Sheri L. ... *157*
Gilbert, Suzie 1956- ... *97*
Gilbert, W(illiam) S(chwenck) 1836-1911 ... *36*
Gilbert, Yvonne
See Gilbert, Anne Yvonne
Gilbertson, Mildred Geiger 1908-1988 ... *2*
Gilbreath, Alice 1921- ... *12*
Gilbreth, Frank B., Jr. 1911-2001 ... *2*
Gilbreth, Frank Bunker
See Gilbreth, Frank B., Jr.
Gilchrist, Jan Spivey 1949- ... *130*
Earlier sketch in SATA *72*
Gilden, Mel 1947- ... *97*
Giles, Gail ... *196*
Earlier sketch in SATA *152*
Giles, Stephen M. ... *236*
Gilfond, Henry ... *2*
Gilge, Jeanette 1924- ... *22*
Gili, Phillida 1944- ... *70*
Gill, Derek (Lewis Theodore) 1919-1997 ... *9*
Gill, Margery Jean 1925- ... *22*
Gill, Shelley ... *176*
Gill, Stephen 1932- ... *63*
Gillespie, Carol Ann 1951- ... *158*
Gillett, Mary (Bledsoe) ... *7*
Gillette, Henry Sampson 1915- ... *14*
Gillette, J. Lynett 1946- ... *103*
Gillette, Jan Lynett
See Gillette, J. Lynett
Gilley, Jeremy 1969- ... *174*
Gillham, Bill
See Gillham, W(illiam) E(dwin) C(harles)
Gillham, W(illiam) E(dwin) C(harles) 1936- ... *42*
Gilliam, Stan 1946- ... *39*
Brief entry ... *35*
Gilliland, Alexis A. 1931- ... *72*
Gilliland, Alexis Arnaldus
See Gilliland, Alexis A.
Gilliland, (Cleburne) Hap 1918- ... *92*
Gilliland, Judith Heide ... *180*
Gillmor, Don 1954- ... *127*
Gilman, Dorothy 1923- ... *5*
Gilman, Esther 1925- ... *15*
Gilman, Laura Anne ... *178*
Gilman, Phoebe 1940-2002 ... *104*
Obituary ... *141*
Earlier sketch in SATA *58*
Gilmore, Iris 1900-1982 ... *22*
Gilmore, Kate 1931- ... *87*
Gilmore, Mary (Jean Cameron) 1865-1962 . *49*
Gilmore, Rachna 1953- ... *209*
Gilmore, Susan 1954- ... *59*
Gilpin, Stephen ... *213*
Earlier sketch in SATA *177*
Gilroy, Beryl (Agatha) 1924- ... *80*
Gilson, Barbara
See Gilson, Charles James Louis
Gilson, Charles James Louis 1878-1943
See YABC *2*
Gilson, Jamie 1933- ... *176*
Brief entry ... *34*
Earlier sketches in SATA *37, 91*
Gimpel, Carolyn
See Hart, Carolyn
Ginsberg, Blaze 1987- ... *222*
Ginsburg, Mirra 1909-2000 ... *92*
Earlier sketch in SATA *6*
See also CLR *45*
Giovanni, Nikki 1943- ... *208*
Earlier sketches in SATA *24, 107*
See also CLR *73*
Giovanni, Yolanda Cornelia
See Giovanni, Nikki
Giovanni, Yolande Cornelia
See Giovanni, Nikki
Giovanni, Yolande Cornelia, Jr.
See Giovanni, Nikki
Giovanopoulos, Paul (Arthur) 1939- ... *7*
Gipson, Billie
See Letts, Billie
Gipson, Fred(erick Benjamin) 1908-1973 ... *2*
Obituary ... *24*
Girard, Linda (Walvoord) 1942- ... *41*
Giraudon, David 1975- ... *215*
Girion, Barbara 1937- ... *78*
Earlier sketch in SATA *26*
See also SAAS *14*
Girl, Nerdy
See Castellucci, Cecil
Girouard, Patrick 1957- ... *155*
Girzone, Joseph F. 1930- ... *76*
Girzone, Joseph Francis
See Girzone, Joseph F.
Gise, Joanne
See Mattern, Joanne
Gist, E.M. ... *206*
Gittings, Jo (Grenville) Manton 1919- ... *3*
Gittings, Robert (William Victor) 1911-1992 . *6*
Obituary ... *70*
Givens, Janet E(aton) 1932- ... *60*
Givner, Joan 1936- ... *171*
Givner, Joan Mary
See Givner, Joan
Gladstone, Eve
See Werner, Herma

Gladstone, Gary 1935- 12
Gladstone, M(yron) J. 1923- 37
Glanville, Brian (Lester) 1931- 42
Glanzman, Louis S. 1922- 36
Glaser, Byron 1954- 154
Glaser, Dianne E(lizabeth) 1937- 50
Brief entry 31
Glaser, Isabel Joshlin 1929- 94
Glaser, Linda 225
Glaser, Milton 1929- 151
Earlier sketch in SATA *11*
Glaser, Shirley 151
Glaspell, Susan 1882(?)-1948
See YABC 2
Glass, Andrew 1949- 223
Brief entry 46
Earlier sketches in SATA *90, 150*
Glass, Linzi 175
Glass, Linzi Alex
See Glass, Linzi
Glasscock, Amnesia
See Steinbeck, John
Glasser, Robin Preiss 1956- 235
Glassman, Bruce 1961- 76
Glatt, Lisa 1963- 217
Glauber, Uta (Heil) 1936- 17
Glazer, Thomas (Zachariah) 1914-2003 9
Glazer, Tom
See Glazer, Thomas (Zachariah)
Gleasner, Diana (Cottle) 1936- 29
Gleason, Judith 1929- 24
Gleason, Katherine (A.) 1960- 104
Gleeson, Libby 1950- 142
Autobiography Feature 142
Earlier sketches in SATA *82, 118*
Gleiter, Jan 1947- 111
Gleitzman, Morris 1953- 234
Earlier sketches in SATA *88, 156*
See also CLR *88*
Glen, Maggie 1944- 88
Glendinning, Richard 1917-1988 24
Glendinning, Sally
See Glendinning, Sara W(ilson)
Glendinning, Sara W(ilson) 1913-1993 24
Glenn, John W. 195
Glenn, Mel 1943- 93
Brief entry 45
Earlier sketch in SATA *51*
See also CLR *51*
Glenn, Patricia Brown 1953- 86
Glenn, Sharlee 159
Glenn, Sharlee Mullins
See Glenn, Sharlee
Glennon, Karen M. 1946- 85
Gles, Margaret Breitmaier 1940- 22
Glick, Carl (Cannon) 1890-1971 14
Glick, Ruth 1942- 125
Glick, Ruth Burtnick
See Glick, Ruth
Glick, Virginia Kirkus 1893-1980
Obituary 23
Gliewe, Unada (Grace) 1927- 3
Glimmerveen, Ulco 1958- 85
Glines, Carroll V(ane), Jr. 1920- 19
Gliori, Debi 1959- 238
Earlier sketches in SATA *72, 138, 189*
Globe, Leah Ain 1900- 41
Glori Ann
See Blakely, Gloria
Glovach, Linda 1947- 105
Earlier sketch in SATA *7*
Glover, Denis (James Matthews) 1912-1980 . 7
Glubok, Shirley (Astor) 146
Autobiography Feature 146
Earlier sketches in SATA *6, 68*
See also CLR *1*
See also SAAS *7*
Gluck, Felix 1923-1981
Obituary 25
Glyman, Caroline A. 1967- 103
Glynne-Jones, William 1907-1977 11
Gobbato, Imero 1923- 39
Gobbletree, Richard
See Quackenbush, Robert M(ead)
Goble, Dorothy 26
Goble, Paul 1933- 131
Earlier sketches in SATA *25, 69*
See also CLR *21*
Goble, Warwick (?)-1943 46
Godden, (Margaret) Rumer 1907-1998 36
Obituary 109
Earlier sketch in SATA *3*
See also CLR *20*
See also SAAS *12*
Gode, Alexander
See Gode von Aesch, Alexander (Gottfried Friedrich)
Gode von Aesch, Alexander (Gottfried Friedrich) 1906-1970 14
Godfrey, Jane
See Bowden, Joan Chase
Godfrey, Martyn
See Godfrey, Martyn N.
and Godfrey, Martyn N.
Godfrey, Martyn N. 1949-2000 95
See also CLR *57*
Godfrey, William
See Youd, Samuel
Godkin, Celia 1948- 145
Earlier sketch in SATA *66*
Godkin, Celia Marilyn
See Godkin, Celia
Godon, Ingrid 1958- 186
Godown, Jan
See Annino, Jan Godown
Godwin, Laura 1956- 179
Godwin, Sam
See Pirotta, Saviour
Godwin, Sarah Massini
See Massini, Sarah
Goede, Irene 1966- 208
Goedecke, Christopher (John) 1951- 81
Goekler, Susan
See Wooley, Susan Frelick
Goembel, Ponder 204
Goertzen, Glenda 172
Goettel, Elinor 1930- 12
Goetz, Delia 1898-1996 22
Obituary 91
Goffe, Toni 1936- 61
Goffstein, Brooke
See Goffstein, Marilyn Brooke
Goffstein, M. B.
See Goffstein, Marilyn Brooke
Goffstein, Marilyn Brooke 1940- 70
Earlier sketch in SATA *8*
See also CLR *3*
Goforth, Ellen
See Francis, Dorothy
Gogol, Sara 1948-2004 80
Goh, Chan Hon 1969- 145
Going, Kelly L.
See Going, K.L.
Going, Kelly Louise
See Going, K.L.
Going, K.L. 199
Earlier sketch in SATA *156*
Golann, Cecil Paige 1921-1995 11
Golbin, Andree 1923- 15
Gold, Alison Leslie 1945- 104
Gold, August 1955- 215
Gold, Bernice 150
Gold, Phyllis
See Goldberg, Phyllis
Gold, Robert S(tanley) 1924- 63
Gold, Sharlya 9
Gold, Susan
See Gold, Susan Dudley
Gold, Susan Dudley 1949- 147
Goldbach, Veronica 1980- 220
Goldberg, Grace 1956- 78
Goldberg, Herbert S. 1926- 25
Goldberg, Jacob 1943- 94
Goldberg, Jake
See Goldberg, Jacob
Goldberg, Myla 1972(?)- 210
Goldberg, Phyllis 1941- 21
Goldberg, Stan J. 1939- 26
Goldberg, Susan 1948- 71
Goldberg, Whoopi 1955- 119
Goldberger, Judith M. 1948- 80
Goldblatt, Stacey 1969(?)- 191
Golden, Christie 1963- 167
Earlier sketch in SATA *116*
Goldentyer, Debra 1960- 84
Goldfeder, Cheryl
See Pahz, Cheryl Suzanne
Goldfeder, James
See Pahz, James Alon
Goldfeder, Jim
See Pahz, James Alon
Goldfinger, Jennifer P. 1963- 185
Goldfrank, Helen Colodny 1912- 6
Goldin, Augusta 1906-1999 13
Goldin, Barbara Diamond 1946- 129
Autobiography Feature 129
Earlier sketch in SATA *92*
See also SAAS *26*
Goldin, David 1963- 240
Earlier sketch in SATA *101*
Golding, Julia 1969- 188
Golding, Theresa Martin 1960- 150
Golding, William 1911-1993
See CLR *130*
Golding, William Gerald
See Golding, William
Goldman, Alex J. 1917- 65
Goldman, E. M. 1943- 103
Goldman, Eleanor Maureen
See Goldman, E. M.
Goldman, Elizabeth 1949- 90
Goldman, Judy 1955- 212
Goldman, Steven 1964- 207
Goldman, Todd Harris 221
Goldring, Ann 1937- 149
Golds, Cassandra 1962- 226
Goldsborough, June 1923- 19
Goldschmidt, Judy 202
Goldsmith, Connie 1945- 147
Goldsmith, Howard 1943- 108
Earlier sketch in SATA *24*
Goldsmith, John Herman Thorburn 1903-1987
Obituary 52
Goldsmith, Oliver 1730(?)-1774 26
Goldsmith, Ruth M. 1919- 62
Goldstein, Nathan 1927- 47
Goldstein, Philip 1910-1997 23
Goldston, Robert (Conroy) 1927- 6
Goldstone, Bruce 183
Goldstone, Lawrence A.
See Treat, Lawrence
Goldszmit, Henryk 1878-1942 65
See also CLR *152*
Golembe, Carla 1951- 79
Golenbock, Peter 1946- 99
Golio, Gary 241
Goll, Reinhold W(eimar) 1897-1993 26
Gollub, Matthew 1960- 241
Earlier sketches in SATA *83, 134*
Golson, Terry 213
Golson, Terry Blonder
See Golson, Terry
Gomes, Filomena 1965- 183
Gomez, Elena 191
Gomez, Elizabeth 133
Gomez-Freer, Elizabeth
See Gomez, Elizabeth
Gomi, Taro 1945- 103
Earlier sketch in SATA *64*
See also CLR *57*
Gondosch, Linda 1944- 58
Gonsalves, Rob 1959- 209

Gonyea, Mark *236*
Earlier sketch in SATA *194*
Gonzales, Chuck *230*
Gonzalez, Catherine Troxell 1917-2000 .... *87*
Gonzalez, Christina
See Gonzalez, Maya Christina
Gonzalez, Christina Diaz 1969- *231*
Gonzalez, Gloria 1940- *23*
Gonzalez, Julie 1958- *174*
Gonzalez, Julie Sehers
See Gonzalez, Julie
Gonzalez, Lucia M. 1957- *202*
Gonzalez, Maya
See Gonzalez, Maya Christina
Gonzalez, Maya Christina 1964- *175*
Earlier sketch in SATA *115*
Gonzalez, Rigoberto 1970- *147*
Gonzalez, Thomas 1959- *237*
Goobie, Beth 1959- *128*
Good, Alice 1950- *73*
Good, Clare
See Romano, Clare
Good, Karen Hillard *214*
Goodall, Daphne Machin
See Machin Goodall, Daphne (Edith)
Goodall, Jane 1934- *111*
Goodall, John S(trickland) 1908-1996 .... *66*
Obituary *91*
Earlier sketch in SATA *4*
See also CLR *25*
Goodbody, Slim
See Burstein, John
Goode, Diane 1949- *225*
Earlier sketches in SATA *15, 84, 114, 170*
Goode, Diane Capuozzo
See Goode, Diane
Goode, Stephen Ray 1943- *55*
Brief entry *40*
Goodenow, Earle 1913- *40*
Goodhart, Pippa 1958- *196*
Earlier sketch in SATA *153*
Goodhue, Thomas W. 1949- *143*
Goodin, Sallie (Brown) 1953- *74*
Goodman, Alison 1966- *111*
Goodman, Deborah Lerme 1956- *50*
Brief entry *49*
Goodman, Elaine 1930- *9*
Goodman, Emily *217*
Goodman, Joan Elizabeth 1950- *162*
Earlier sketches in SATA *50, 94*
Goodman, Shawn 1970- *238*
Goodman, Susan E. 1952- *181*
Goodman, Walter 1927-2002 .... *9*
Goodman Koz, Paula *211*
Goodrich, Carter 1959(?)- *221*
Goodrich, Samuel Griswold 1793-1860 .... *23*
Goodsell, Jane Neuberger 1921(?)-1988
Obituary *56*
Goodweather, Hartley
See King, Thomas
GoodWeather, Hartley
See King, Thomas
Goodwin, Hal
See Goodwin, Harold L(eland)
Goodwin, Harold L(eland) 1914-1990 .... *51*
Obituary *65*
Earlier sketch in SATA *13*
Goodwin, William 1943- *117*
Goor, Nancy (Ruth Miller) 1944- *39*
Brief entry *34*
Goor, Ron(ald Stephen) 1940- *39*
Brief entry *34*
Goossen, Agnes
See Epp, Margaret A(gnes)
Goossens, Philippe 1963- *195*
Gootman, Marilyn E. 1944- *179*
Gopnik, Adam 1956- *171*
Gorbachev, Valeri 1944- *222*
Autobiography Feature *143*
Earlier sketches in SATA *98, 143, 184*
Gordion, Mark
See Turtledove, Harry
Gordon, Ad
See Hano, Arnold
Gordon, Amy 1949- *197*
Earlier sketches in SATA *115, 156*
Gordon, Bernard Ludwig 1931-2010 .... *27*
Gordon, Colonel H. R.
See Ellis, Edward S.
Gordon, David
See Garrett, Randall
Gordon, Donald
See Payne, Donald Gordon
Gordon, Dorothy 1893-1970 .... *20*
Gordon, Esther S(aranga) 1935- *10*
Gordon, Frederick *1*
Gordon, Gaelyn 1939-1997
See CLR *75*
Gordon, Garrett
See Garrett, Randall
Gordon, Gary
See Edmonds, I(vy) G(ordon)
Gordon, Hal
See Goodwin, Harold L(eland)
Gordon, Jeffie Ross
See Enderle, Judith (Ann) Ross
and Gordon, Stephanie Jacob
Gordon, John
See Gesner, Clark
Gordon, John (William) 1925- *84*
Gordon, Lew
See Baldwin, Gordon C(ortis)
Gordon, Margaret (Anna) 1939- *9*
Gordon, Mike 1948- *101*
Gordon, Mildred 1912-1979
Obituary *24*
Gordon, Selma
See Lanes, Selma G.
Gordon, Sheila 1927- *88*
See also CLR *27*
Gordon, Shirley 1921- *48*
Brief entry *41*
Gordon, Sol 1923- *11*
Gordon, Stephanie Jacob 1940- *89*
Autobiography Feature *114*
Earlier sketch in SATA *64*
See also SAAS *26*
Gordon, Stewart
See Shirreffs, Gordon D(onald)
Gordons, The
See Gordon, Mildred
and Gordon, Gordon
Gore, Leonid *222*
Earlier sketch in SATA *185*
Gorelick, Molly C(hernow) 1920-2003 .... *9*
Obituary *153*
Gorey, Edward (St. John) 1925-2000 .... *70*
Brief entry *27*
Obituary *118*
Earlier sketch in SATA *29*
See also CLR *36*
Gorham, Charles Orson 1868-1936 .... *36*
Gorham, Michael
See Folsom, Franklin (Brewster)
Gorman, Carol *187*
Earlier sketch in SATA *150*
Gorman, Jacqueline Laks 1955- *148*
Gorman, Mike *206*
Gormley, Beatrice 1942- *202*
Brief entry *35*
Earlier sketches in SATA *39, 127*
Gormley, Greg 1966- *241*
Gorog, Judith (Katharine Allen) 1938- *75*
Earlier sketch in SATA *39*
Gorrell, Gena K. 1946- *170*
Gorsline, Douglas (Warner) 1913-1985 .... *11*
Obituary *43*
Gorsline, (Sally) Marie 1928- *28*
Gorsline, S. M.
See Gorsline, (Sally) Marie
Gorton, Julia *218*
Gorton, Kaitlyn
See Emerson, Kathy Lynn
Gorton, Kathy Lynn
See Emerson, Kathy Lynn
Goryan, Sirak
See Saroyan, William
Goschke, Julia 1973- *208*
Goscinny, Rene 1926-1977 .... *47*
Brief entry *39*
See also CLR *37*
Goss, Clay(ton E.) 1946- *82*
Goss, Gary 1947- *124*
Goss, Mini 1963- *186*
Gosselink, John 1967- *238*
Goto, Scott *203*
Gott, Barry *197*
Gottesman, S. D.
See Kornbluth, C(yril) M.
and Lowndes, Robert A(ugustine) W(ard)
and Pohl, Frederik
Gottfried, Ted
See Gottfried, Theodore Mark
Gottfried, Theodore Mark 1928- *150*
Earlier sketch in SATA *85*
Gottlieb, Gerald 1923- *7*
Gottlieb, William P. 1917-2006 .... *24*
Gottlieb, William Paul
See Gottlieb, William P.
Goudey, Alice E(dwards) 1898-1993 .... *20*
Goudge, Eileen 1950- *88*
Goudge, Elizabeth (de Beauchamp)
1900-1984 .... *2*
Obituary *38*
See also CLR *94*
Gough, Catherine
See Mulgan, Catherine
Gough, Philip 1908-1986 .... *45*
Gough, Sue 1940- *106*
Goulart, Ron 1933- *67*
Earlier sketch in SATA *1*
Goulart, Ronald Joseph
See Goulart, Ron
Gould, Alberta 1945- *96*
Gould, Chester 1900-1985 .... *49*
Obituary *43*
Gould, Jean R(osalind) 1909-1993 .... *11*
Obituary *77*
Gould, Lilian *6*
Gould, Marilyn 1928- *76*
Earlier sketch in SATA *15*
Gould, Robert *154*
Gould, Steven 1955- *95*
Gould, Steven Charles
See Gould, Steven
Gourlay, Candy *239*
Gourley, Catherine 1950- *190*
Earlier sketch in SATA *95*
Gourse, Leslie 1939-2004 .... *89*
Govan, (Mary) Christine Noble 1898-1985 .... *9*
Gove, Doris 1944- *72*
Govenar, Alan 1952- *189*
Govenar, Alan Bruce
See Govenar, Alan
Govern, Elaine 1939- *26*
Gow, Nancy *238*
Gowen, L. Kris 1968- *156*
Graaf, Peter
See Youd, Samuel
Grab, Daphne 1971- *233*
Grabenstein, Chris 1955- *238*
Graber, Alexander 1914-1997 .... *98*
Earlier sketch in SATA *7*
Graber, George Alexander
See Graber, Alexander
Graber, Janet 1942- *170*
Graber, Richard (Fredrick) 1927- *26*
Grabianski, Janusz 1928-1976 .... *39*
Obituary *30*
Graboff, Abner 1919-1986 .... *35*
Grace, Fran(ces Jane) *45*

Author Index

Grace, N.B.
See Harper, Suzanne
Grace, Theresa
See Mattern, Joanne
Gracza, Margaret Young 1928- *56*
Graduate of Oxford, A
See Ruskin, John
Grady, Denise 1952- *189*
Graeber, Charlotte Towner *106*
Brief entry *44*
Earlier sketch in SATA *56*
Graef, Renee 1956- *204*
Graeme, Roderic
See Jeffries, Roderic
Graf, Michael
See Graf, Mike
Graf, Mike 1960- *164*
Grafe, Max *198*
Graff, Lisa 1981- *235*
Earlier sketch in SATA *188*
Graff, Polly Anne Colver
See Colver, Anne
Graff, (S.) Stewart 1908-2009 .... *9*
Graham, Ada 1931- *11*
Graham, Alastair 1945- *74*
Graham, Arthur Kennon
See Harrison, David L.
Graham, Bob 1942- *187*
Earlier sketches in SATA *63, 101, 151*
See also CLR *31*
Graham, Brenda Knight 1942- *32*
Graham, Charlotte
See Bowden, Joan Chase
Graham, Christine 1952- *224*
Graham, Eleanor 1896-1984 .... *18*
Obituary *38*
Graham, Ennis
See Molesworth, Mary Louisa
Graham, Frank, Jr. 1925- *11*
Graham, Georgia 1959- *190*
Graham, Ian 1953- *229*
Earlier sketch in SATA *112*
Graham, John 1926-2007 .... *11*
Graham, Kennon
See Harrison, David L.
Graham, Larry
See Graham, Lawrence
Graham, Lawrence 1962- *63*
Graham, Lawrence Otis
See Graham, Lawrence
Graham, Linda
See Graham-Barber, Lynda
Graham, Lorenz (Bell) 1902-1989 .... *74*
Obituary *63*
Earlier sketch in SATA *2*
See also CLR *10*
See also SAAS *5*
Graham, Margaret Bloy 1920- *11*
Graham, Robin Lee 1949- *7*
Graham, Rosemary *236*
Graham, Shirley 1896(?)-1977
See Du Bois, Shirley Graham
Graham-Barber, Lynda 1944- *159*
Earlier sketch in SATA *42*
Graham-Cameron, M.
See Graham-Cameron, M(alcolm) G(ordon)
Graham-Cameron, M(alcolm) G(ordon)
1931- *53*
Brief entry *45*
Graham-Cameron, Mike
See Graham-Cameron, M(alcolm) G(ordon)
Grahame, Kenneth 1859-1932 .... *100*
See also YABC *1*
See also CLR *135*
Gralley, Jean *166*
Gramatky, Hardie 1907-1979 .... *30*
Obituary *23*
Earlier sketch in SATA *1*
See also CLR *22*
Grambling, Lois G. 1927- *206*
Earlier sketches in SATA *71, 148*
Grambo, Rebecca L(ynn) 1963- *109*
Grammer, June Amos 1927- *58*
Grand, Samuel 1912-1988 .... *42*
Grandits, John 1949- *192*
GrandPre, Mary 1954- *229*
Earlier sketch in SATA *184*
Grandville, J. J.
See Gerard, Jean Ignace Isidore
Grandville, Jean Ignace Isidore Gerard
See Gerard, Jean Ignace Isidore
Granfield, Linda 1950- *160*
Earlier sketch in SATA *96*
Grange, Peter
See Nicole, Christopher
Granger, Margaret Jane 1925(?)-1977
Obituary *27*
Granger, Michele 1949- *88*
Granger, Peggy
See Granger, Margaret Jane
Granowsky, Alvin 1936- *101*
Granstaff, Bill 1925- *10*
Granstrom, Brita 1969- *224*
Earlier sketches in SATA *111, 167*
Grant, Bruce 1893-1977 .... *5*
Obituary *25*
Grant, Cynthia D. 1950- *147*
Earlier sketches in SATA *33, 77*
Grant, Eva 1907-1996 .... *7*
Grant, Evva H. 1913-1977
Obituary *27*
Grant, Gordon 1875-1962 .... *25*
Grant, Gwen(doline Ellen) 1940- *47*
Grant, Judyann Ackerman *211*
Grant, Katie
See Grant, K.M.
Grant, Katie M.
See Grant, K.M.
Grant, Katy *238*
Grant, K.M. *230*
Earlier sketch in SATA *175*
Grant, (Alice) Leigh 1947- *10*
Grant, Matthew G.
See May, Julian
Grant, Maxwell
See Gibson, Walter B(rown)
and Lynds, Dennis
Grant, Melvyn *183*
Grant, Myrna (Lois) 1934- *21*
Grant, Neil 1938- *154*
Earlier sketch in SATA *14*
Grant, Nicholas
See Nicole, Christopher
Grant, Richard 1948- *80*
Grant, Skeeter
See Spiegelman, Art
Grater, Michael 1923- *57*
Gratz, Alan 1972- *212*
Graullera, Fabiola
See Graullera Ramirez, Fabiola
Graullera Ramirez, Fabiola *225*
Gravel, Fern
See Hall, James Norman
Gravelle, Karen 1942- *166*
Earlier sketch in SATA *78*
Graves, Charles Parlin 1911-1972 .... *4*
Graves, Keith *191*
Earlier sketch in SATA *156*
Graves, Robert 1895-1985 .... *45*
Graves, Robert von Ranke
See Graves, Robert
Graves, Valerie
See Bradley, Marion Zimmer
Gravett, Emily 1972(?)- *232*
Earlier sketch in SATA *189*
Gray, Betsy
See Poole, Gray Johnson
Gray, Caroline
See Nicole, Christopher
Gray, Claudia *213*
Gray, Dianne E. *183*
Gray, Elizabeth Janet
See Vining, Elizabeth Gray
Gray, Genevieve S(tuck) 1920-1995 .... *4*
Gray, Harold (Lincoln) 1894-1968 .... *33*
Brief entry *32*
Gray, Jenny
See Gray, Genevieve S(tuck)
Gray, John Lee
See Jakes, John
Gray, Judith A. 1949- *93*
Gray, Judith Anne
See Gray, Judith A.
Gray, Keith 1972- *151*
Gray, Kes 1960- *153*
Gray, Les 1929- *82*
Gray, Libba Moore 1937- *83*
Gray, Luli 1945- *149*
Earlier sketch in SATA *90*
Gray, Marian
See Pierce, Edith Gray
Gray, Nicholas Stuart 1922-1981 .... *4*
Obituary *27*
Gray, Nigel 1941- *104*
Earlier sketch in SATA *33*
Gray, (Lucy) Noel (Clervaux) 1898-1983 .... *47*
Gray, Patricia (Clark) *7*
Gray, Patsey
See Gray, Patricia (Clark)
Gray, Rita *184*
Gray, Serena
See Sheldon, Dyan
Gray, Steve 1950- *231*
Graydon, Shari 1958- *158*
Grayland, V. Merle
See Grayland, Valerie (Merle Spanner)
Grayland, Valerie (Merle Spanner) *7*
Grayson, Devin (Kalile) 1970- *119*
Grayson, Kristine
See Rusch, Kristine Kathryn
Grayson, Paul 1946- *79*
Graystone, Lynn
See Brennan, Joseph Lomas
Great Comte, The
See Hawkesworth, Eric
Greaves, Margaret 1914-1995 .... *87*
Earlier sketch in SATA *7*
Greaves, Nick 1955- *77*
Greban, Quentin 1977- *223*
Gree, Alain 1936- *28*
Green, Adam
See Weisgard, Leonard (Joseph)
Green, Anne Canevari 1943- *62*
Green, Brian
See Card, Orson Scott
Green, Cliff(ord) 1934- *126*
Green, Connie Jordan 1938- *80*
Green, D.
See Casewit, Curtis W(erner)
Green, Elizabeth Shippen 1871-1954 .... *139*
Green, Hannah
See Greenberg, Joanne (Goldenberg)
Green, Jane 1937- *9*
Green, Jessica *211*
Green, John 1977(?)- *235*
Earlier sketch in SATA *170*
Green, Mary Moore 1906- *11*
Green, Morton 1937- *8*
Green, Norma B(erger) 1925- *11*
Green, Phyllis 1932- *20*
Green, Roger (Gilbert) Lancelyn 1918-1987 . *2*
Obituary *53*
Green, (James Le)Roy 1948- *89*
Green, Sheila Ellen 1934- *148*
Earlier sketches in SATA *8, 87*
Green, Timothy 1953- *91*
Greenaway, Kate 1846-1901 .... *100*
See also YABC *2*
See also CLR *111*
Greenbank, Anthony Hunt 1933- *39*
Greenberg, David 1954- *171*

Greenberg, David T.
See Greenberg, David
Greenberg, Harvey R. 1935- *5*
Greenberg, Jan 1942- *211*
Earlier sketches in SATA *61, 125*
Greenberg, Joanne (Goldenberg) 1932- *25*
Greenberg, Melanie Hope 1954- *214*
Earlier sketch in SATA *72*
Greenberg, Polly 1932- *52*
Brief entry *43*
Greenblat, Rodney Alan 1960- *106*
Greenburg, Dan 1936- *175*
Earlier sketch in SATA *102*
Greene, Bette 1934- *161*
Earlier sketches in SATA *8, 102*
See also CLR *140*
See also SAAS *16*
Greene, Carla 1916- *67*
Earlier sketch in SATA *1*
Greene, Carol *102*
Brief entry *44*
Earlier sketch in SATA *66*
Greene, Constance C(larke) 1924- *72*
Earlier sketch in SATA *11*
See also CLR *62*
See also SAAS *11*
Greene, Edgar
See Papademetriou, Lisa
Greene, Ellin 1927- *23*
Greene, Graham 1904-1991 .... *20*
Greene, Graham Henry
See Greene, Graham
Greene, Jacqueline Dembar 1946- *212*
Earlier sketches in SATA *76, 131*
Greene, Laura Offenhartz 1935- *38*
Greene, Meg
See Malvasi, Meg Greene
Greene, Michele 1962- *178*
Greene, Michele Dominguez
See Greene, Michele
Greene, Rhonda Gowler 1955- *235*
Earlier sketches in SATA *101, 160*
Greene, Stephanie 1950- *221*
Earlier sketches in SATA *127, 173*
Greene, Wade 1933- *11*
Greene, Yvonne
See Flesch, Yolande
Greenfeld, Howard (Scheinman) 1928- *140*
Earlier sketch in SATA *19*
Greenfeld, Josh(ua Joseph) 1928- *62*
Greenfield, Eloise 1929- *155*
Earlier sketches in SATA *19, 61, 105*
See also CLR *38*
See also SAAS *16*
Greenhaus, Thelma Nurenberg 1903-1984
Obituary *45*
Greenhut, Josh
See Mercer, Sienna
Greening, Hamilton
See Hamilton, Charles (Harold St. John)
Greenlaw, M. Jean 1941- *107*
Greenleaf, Barbara Kaye 1942- *6*
Greenleaf, Peter 1910-1997 .... *33*
Greenlee, Sharon 1935- *77*
Greeno, Gayle 1949- *81*
Greenseid, Diane 1948- *178*
Earlier sketch in SATA *93*
Greenspun, Adele Aron 1938- *142*
Earlier sketch in SATA *76*
Greenstein, Elaine 1959- *150*
Earlier sketch in SATA *82*
Greenwald, Sheila
See Green, Sheila Ellen
Greenwood, Barbara 1940- *129*
Earlier sketch in SATA *90*
Greenwood, Mark 1958- *202*
Greenwood, Pamela D. 1944- *115*
Greer, Richard
See Garrett, Randall
and Silverberg, Robert
Gregg, Andrew K. 1929- *81*
Gregg, Charles T(hornton) 1927- *65*
Gregg, Walter H(arold) 1919- *20*
Gregor, Arthur 1923- *36*
Gregor, Lee
See Pohl, Frederik
Gregori, Leon 1919- *15*
Gregorian, Joyce Ballou 1946-1991 .... *30*
Obituary *83*
Gregorich, Barbara 1943- *184*
Earlier sketch in SATA *66*
Gregorowski, Christopher 1940- *30*
Gregory, Diana (Jean) 1933- *49*
Brief entry *42*
Gregory, Harry
See Gottfried, Theodore Mark
Gregory, Jean
See Ure, Jean
Gregory, Kristiana 1951- *212*
Earlier sketches in SATA *74, 136*
Gregory, Nan 1944- *192*
Earlier sketch in SATA *148*
Gregory, Philippa 1954- *122*
Gregory, Stephen
See Penzler, Otto
Gregory, Valiska 1940- *82*
Greif, Jean-Jacques 1944- *195*
Greisman, Joan Ruth 1937- *31*
Grendon, Stephen
See Derleth, August (William)
Grenville, Pelham
See Wodehouse, P. G.
Gretz, Susanna 1937- *7*
Gretzer, John *18*
Grewdead, Roy
See Gorey, Edward (St. John)
Grey, Carol
See Lowndes, Robert A(ugustine) W(ard)
Grey, Christopher *191*
Grey, Christopher Peter
See Grey, Christopher
Grey, Jerry 1926- *11*
Grey, Mini *239*
Earlier sketches in SATA *166, 205*
Greybeard the Pirate
See Macintosh, Brownie
Grey Owl
See Belaney, Archibald Stansfeld
Gri
See Denney, Diana
Gribbin, John 1946- *159*
Gribbin, John R.
See Gribbin, John
Grice, Frederick 1910-1983 .... *6*
Grider, Dorothy 1915- *31*
Gridley, Marion E(leanor) 1906-1974 .... *35*
Obituary *26*
Grieco-Tiso, Pina 1954- *108*
Grieder, Walter 1924- *9*
Griego, Tony A. 1955- *77*
Griese, Arnold A(lfred) 1921- *9*
Griessman, Annette 1962- *170*
Earlier sketch in SATA *116*
Grieve, James 1934- *146*
Grifalconi, Ann 1929- *210*
Earlier sketches in SATA *2, 66, 133*
See also CLR *35*
See also SAAS *16*
Griffin, Adele 1970- *236*
Earlier sketches in SATA *105, 153, 195*
Griffin, Elizabeth May 1985- *89*
Griffin, Gillett Good 1928- *26*
Griffin, Judith Berry *34*
Griffin, Kitty 1951- *137*
Griffin, Peni R. 1961- *193*
Earlier sketches in SATA *67, 99*
Griffin, Steven A. 1953- *89*
Griffin, Steven Arthur
See Griffin, Steven A.
Griffin, W. E. B. 1929- *5*
Griffith, Connie 1946- *89*
Griffith, Gershom 1960- *85*
Griffith, Helen V. 1934- *87*
Autobiography Feature *107*
Earlier sketch in SATA *39*
Griffith, Helen Virginia
See Griffith, Helen V.
Griffith, Jeannette
See Eyerly, Jeannette
Griffith, Saul 1974- *200*
Griffiths, Andy 1961- *196*
Earlier sketch in SATA *152*
Griffiths, G(ordon) D(ouglas) 1910-1973
Obituary *20*
Griffiths, Helen 1939- *86*
Earlier sketch in SATA *5*
See also CLR *75*
See also SAAS *5*
Grigsby, Susan *235*
Grigson, Jane (McIntire) 1928-1990 .... *63*
Grimes, Lee 1920- *68*
Grimes, Nikki 1950- *218*
Earlier sketches in SATA *93, 136, 174*
See also CLR *42*
Grimly, Gris *186*
Grimm, Jacob Ludwig Karl 1785-1863 .... *22*
See also CLR *112*
Grimm, Wilhelm Karl 1786-1859 .... *22*
See also CLR *112*
Grimm, William C(arey) 1907-1992 .... *14*
Grimm and Grim
See Grimm, Jacob Ludwig Karl
and Grimm, Wilhelm Karl
Grimm Brothers
See Grimm, Jacob Ludwig Karl
and Grimm, Wilhelm Karl
Grimsdell, Jeremy 1942- *83*
Grimshaw, Nigel (Gilroy) 1925- *23*
Grimsley, Gordon
See Groom, Arthur William
Grindley, Jane Sally
See Grindley, Sally
Grindley, Sally 1953- *148*
Gringhuis, Dirk
See Gringhuis, Richard H.
Gringhuis, Richard H. 1918-1974 .... *6*
Obituary *25*
Grinnell, David
See Wollheim, Donald A(llen)
Grinnell, George Bird 1849-1938 .... *16*
Grinspoon, David
See Grinspoon, David H.
Grinspoon, David H. 1959- *156*
Grinspoon, David Harry
See Grinspoon, David H.
Gripe, Maria 1923- *74*
Earlier sketch in SATA *2*
See also CLR *5*
Gripe, Maria Kristina
See Gripe, Maria
Gritton, Steve *223*
Grobler, Piet 1959- *201*
Groch, Judith (Goldstein) 1929- *25*
Grode, Redway
See Gorey, Edward (St. John)
Groener, Carl
See Lowndes, Robert A(ugustine) W(ard)
Groening, Matt 1954- *116*
Earlier sketch in SATA *81*
Grohmann, Susan 1948- *84*
Grohskopf, Bernice *7*
Grol, Lini R(icharda) 1913- *9*
Grollman, Earl A. 1925- *22*
Groom, Arthur William 1898-1964 .... *10*
Grooms, Duffy 1964- *169*
Gross, Alan 1947- *54*
Brief entry *43*
Gross, Ernie 1913- *67*
Gross, Philip 1952- *164*
Earlier sketch in SATA *84*
Gross, Philip John
See Gross, Philip
Gross, Ruth Belov 1929- *33*

Gross, Sarah Chokla 1906-1976 9
Obituary 26
Grosser, Morton 1931- 74
Grosser, Vicky 1958- 83
Grossman, Bill 1948- 126
Earlier sketch in SATA 72
Grossman, Nancy 1940- 29
Grossman, Patricia 1951- 73
Grossman, Robert 1940- 11
Grossmann-Hensel, Katharina 1973- 219
Grote, JoAnn A. 1951- 113
Groten, Dallas 1951- 64
Groth, John (August) 1908-1988 21
Obituary 56
Groth-Fleming, Candace
See Fleming, Candace
Grove, Vicki 1948- 151
Autobiography Feature 151
Earlier sketch in SATA 122
Grover, Lorie Ann 1964- 168
Grover, Wayne 1934- 69
Groves, Georgina
See Symons, (Dorothy) Geraldine
Groves, Maketa 1950- 107
Groves, Seli 77
Grubb, Lisa 160
Gruber, Michael 1940- 173
Gruber, Terry (deRoy) 1953- 66
Gruelle, John 1880-1938 35
Brief entry 32
See also CLR 34
Gruelle, Johnny
See Gruelle, John
Gruenberg, Sidonie Matsner 1881-1974 2
Obituary 27
Gruhzit-Hoyt, Olga (Margaret) 1922- 127
Earlier sketch in SATA 16
Grummer, Arnold E(dward) 1923- 49
Gruner, Jessica 233
Grunewalt, Pine
See Kunhardt, Edith
Grunwell, Jeanne Marie 1971- 147
Grupper, Jonathan 137
Gryski, Camilla 1948- 72
Guarino, Dagmar
See Guarino, Deborah
Guarino, Deborah 1954- 68
Guarnaccia, Steven 233
Guay, Georgette (Marie Jeanne) 1952- 54
Guay, Rebecca 209
Guay-Mitchell, Rebecca
See Guay, Rebecca
Guback, Georgia 88
Guccione, Leslie Davis 1946- 111
Earlier sketch in SATA 72
Guck, Dorothy 1913-2002 27
Gudeon, Karla 212
Guerny, Gene
See Gurney, Gene
Guest, Elissa Haden 1953- 218
Earlier sketch in SATA 125
Guest, Jacqueline 1952- 135
Guevara, Susan 167
Earlier sketch in SATA 97
Gugler, Laurel Dee 95
Gugliotta, Bobette 1918-1994 7
Guianan, Eve 1965- 102
Guiberson, Brenda Z. 1946- 211
Earlier sketches in SATA 71, 124
Guibert, Emmanuel 1964- 181
Guibord, Maurissa 1961- 240
Guile, Melanie 1949- 152
Earlier sketch in SATA 104
Guillaume, Jeanette G. Flierl 1899-1990 8
Guillot, Rene 1900-1969 7
See also CLR 22
Guisewite, Cathy 1950- 57
Guisewite, Cathy Lee
See Guisewite, Cathy
Gulbis, Stephen 1959- 142
Gulley, Judie 1942- 58
Gump, P.Q.
See Card, Orson Scott
Gundrey, Elizabeth 1924- 23
Gunn, James E. 1923- 35
Gunn, James Edwin
See Gunn, James E.
Gunn, Robin Jones 1955- 84
Gunnella 1956- 197
Gunning, Monica Olwen 1930- 161
Gunston, Bill
See Gunston, William Tudor
Gunston, William Tudor 1927- 9
Gunterman, Bertha Lisette 1886(?)-1975
Obituary 27
Gunther, John 1901-1970
Guravich, Dan 1918- 74
Gurko, Leo 1914- 9
Gurko, Miriam 1910(?)-1988 9
Obituary 58
Gurney, Gene 1924- 65
Gurney, James 1958- 120
Earlier sketch in SATA 76
Gurney, John Steven 1962- 227
Earlier sketches in SATA 75, 143
Gustafson, Sarah R.
See Riedman, Sarah R(egal)
Gustafson, Scott 1956- 34
Gustavson, Adam 1974- 214
Earlier sketch in SATA 176
Guthrie, A(lfred) B(ertram), Jr. 1901-1991 62
Obituary 67
Guthrie, Anne 1890-1979 28
Guthrie, Donna W. 1946- 105
Earlier sketch in SATA 63
Gutierrez, Akemi 172
Gutierrez, Rudy 203
Gutman, Bill 128
Brief entry 43
Earlier sketch in SATA 67
Gutman, Dan 1955- 221
Earlier sketches in SATA 77, 139, 188
Gutman, Naham 1899(?)-1981
Obituary 25
Gutmann, Bessie Pease 1876-1960 73
Guy, Geoffrey 1942- 153
Guy, Ginger Foglesong 1954- 171
Guy, Rosa 1925- 122
Earlier sketches in SATA 14, 62
See also CLR 137
Guy, Rosa Cuthbert
See Guy, Rosa
Guy, Susan 1948- 149
Guymer, (Wilhelmina) Mary 1909- 50
Guzman, Lila 1952- 168
Guzman, Rick 1957- 168
Gwaltney, Doris 1932- 181
Gwynne, Fred(erick Hubbard) 1926-1993 41
Brief entry 27
Obituary 75
Gwynne, Oscar A.
See Ellis, Edward S.
Gwynne, Oswald A.
See Ellis, Edward S.
Gyorkos, Charmaine Echeverria
See Echeverria Gyorkos, Charmaine

H

Haab, Sherri 1964- 169
Earlier sketch in SATA 91
Haar, Jaap ter
See ter Haar, Jaap
Haarsma, P.J. 183
Haas, Carolyn Buhai 1926- 43
Haas, Dan 1957- 105
Haas, Dorothy F. 46
Brief entry 43
See also SAAS 17
Haas, Irene 1929- 96
Earlier sketch in SATA 17
Haas, James E. 1943- 40
Haas, James Edward
See Haas, James E.
Haas, Jessie 1959- 215
Haas, (Katherine) Jessie 1959- 135
Autobiography Feature 135
Earlier sketch in SATA 98
Haas, Merle S. 1896(?)-1985
Obituary 41
Habenstreit, Barbara 1937- 5
Haber, Karen 1955- 78
Haber, Louis 1910-1988 12
Haber, Melissa Glenn 1969- 235
Hacker, Randi 1951- 185
Hacker, Randi Dawn
See Hacker, Randi
Hackett, John Winthrop 1910-1997 65
Hacks, Peter 1928-2003
Obituary 151
Hacohen, Dean 1958- 239
Haddix, Margaret Peterson 1964- 224
Earlier sketches in SATA 94, 125, 187
Haddon, Mark 1962- 223
Earlier sketch in SATA 155
Hader, Berta (Hoerner) 1891(?)-1976 16
Hader, Elmer (Stanley) 1889-1973 16
Hadithi, Mwenye
See Hobson, Bruce
Hadley, Franklin
See Winterbotham, R(ussell) R(obert)
Hadley, Lee 1934-1995 89
Brief entry 38
Obituary 86
Earlier sketch in SATA 47
See also CLR 40
See also SAAS 14
Haeffele, Deborah 1954- 76
Haenel, Wolfram 1956- 89
See also CLR 64
Hafner, Marylin 1925- 179
Earlier sketches in SATA 7, 121
Haft, Erin
See Ehrenhaft, Daniel
Hager, Alan 1940- 176
Hager, Alice Rogers 1894-1969
Obituary 26
Hager, Betty 1923- 89
Hager, Jenna Bush
See Bush, Jenna
Hager, Sarah 171
Hager, Thomas 1953- 119
Hager, Tom
See Hager, Thomas
Hagerup, Klaus 1946- 186
Haggard, H(enry) Rider 1856-1925 16
Haggerty, James J(oseph) 1920- 5
Hagon, Priscilla
See Allan, Mabel Esther
Hague, Kathleen 1949- 49
Brief entry 45
Hague, Michael 1948- 185
Brief entry 32
Earlier sketches in SATA 48, 80, 129
Hague, Michael R.
See Hague, Michael
Hague, Susan Kathleen
See Hague, Kathleen
Hahn, Emily 1905-1997 3
Obituary 96
Hahn, Hannelore 8
Hahn, James (Sage) 1947- 9
Hahn, Lynn 1949- 9
Hahn, Mary Downing 1937- 208
Autobiography Feature 157
Brief entry 44
Earlier sketches in SATA 50, 81, 138, 157
See also SAAS 12
Hahn, Michael T. 1953- 92

Hahn, Mona Lynn
See Hahn, Lynn
Haig, Matt 1975- ... *221*
Haig-Brown, Roderick (Langmere) 1908-1976 ... *12*
See also CLR *31*
Haight, Anne Lyon 1895-1977
Obituary ... *30*
Haight, Rip
See Carpenter, John
Haight, Sandy 1949- ... *79*
Haij, Vera
See Jansson, Tove (Marika)
Hailstone, Ruth ... *219*
Haines, Gail Kay 1943- ... *11*
Haines, Margaret Ann Beck
See Beck, Peggy
Haining, Peter 1940-2007 ... *14*
Obituary ... *188*
Haining, Peter Alexander
See Haining, Peter
Hains, Harriet
See Watson, Carol
Hajdusiewicz, Babs Bell ... *163*
Hakim, Joy 1931- ... *173*
Earlier sketch in SATA *83*
Halacy, D. S., Jr. 1919-2002 ... *36*
See also SAAS *8*
Halacy, Dan
See Halacy, D. S., Jr.
Halam, Ann
See Jones, Gwyneth A.
Haldane, Roger John 1945- ... *13*
Hale, Arlene 1924-1982 ... *49*
Hale, Bruce 1957- ... *203*
Earlier sketch in SATA *123*
Hale, Christy
See Apostolou, Christine Hale
Hale, Dean 1972- ... *227*
Hale, Edward Everett 1822-1909 ... *16*
Hale, Glenn
See Walker, Robert W.
Hale, Helen
See Mulcahy, Lucille Burnett
Hale, Irina 1932- ... *26*
Hale, Kathleen 1898-2000 ... *66*
Obituary ... *121*
Earlier sketch in SATA *17*
Hale, Linda (Howe) 1929- ... *6*
Hale, Lucretia P.
See Hale, Lucretia Peabody
Hale, Lucretia Peabody 1820-1900 ... *26*
See also CLR *105*
Hale, Marian ... *194*
Hale, Nancy 1908-1988 ... *31*
Obituary ... *57*
Hale, Nathan 1976- ... *210*
Hale, Shannon ... *200*
Earlier sketch in SATA *158*
Hale, Stephanie 1973- ... *232*
Haley, Amanda ... *205*
Haley, Gail E(inhart) 1939- ... *161*
Autobiography Feature ... *161*
Brief entry ... *28*
Earlier sketches in SATA *43, 78, 136*
See also CLR *21*
See also SAAS *13*
Haley, Neale ... *52*
Halfmann, Janet 1944- ... *208*
Hall, Adam
See Trevor, Elleston
Hall, Adele 1910- ... *7*
Hall, Anna Gertrude 1882-1967 ... *8*
Hall, August ... *207*
Hall, Barbara 1961- ... *68*
Hall, Becky 1950- ... *186*
Hall, Beverly B. 1918- ... *95*
Hall, Borden
See Yates, Raymond F(rancis)
Hall, Brian P(atrick) 1935- ... *31*
Hall, Cameron
See del Rey, Lester
Hall, Caryl
See Hansen, Caryl (Hall)
Hall, Donald 1928- ... *97*
Earlier sketch in SATA *23*
Hall, Donald Andrew, Jr.
See Hall, Donald
Hall, Douglas 1931- ... *43*
Hall, Elizabeth 1929- ... *77*
Hall, Elvajean 1910-1984 ... *6*
Hall, Francie 1940- ... *166*
Hall, James Norman 1887-1951 ... *21*
Hall, Jesse
See Boesen, Victor
Hall, Katy
See McMullan, Kate
Hall, Kirsten Marie 1974- ... *67*
Hall, Lynn 1937- ... *79*
Earlier sketches in SATA *2, 47*
See also SAAS *4*
Hall, Malcolm 1945- ... *7*
Hall, Marcellus ... *203*
Hall, Marjory
See Yeakley, Marjory Hall
Hall, Melanie 1949- ... *228*
Earlier sketches in SATA *78, 116, 169*
Hall, Michael 1954- ... *228*
Hall, Patricia 1940- ... *136*
Hall, Rosalys Haskell 1914- ... *7*
Hall, Teri ... *229*
Hall, Willis 1929-2005 ... *66*
Hallard, Peter
See Catherall, Arthur
Hallas, Richard
See Knight, Eric
Hall-Clarke, James
See Rowland-Entwistle, (Arthur) Theodore (Henry)
Hallensleben, Georg 1958- ... *173*
Haller, Dorcas Woodbury 1946- ... *46*
Hallett, Mark 1947- ... *220*
Earlier sketch in SATA *83*
Halliburton, Richard 1900-1939(?) ... *81*
Halliburton, Warren J. 1924- ... *19*
Halliday, Brett
See Dresser, Davis
and Johnson, (Walter) Ryerson
and Terrall, Robert
Halliday, William R(oss) 1926- ... *52*
Hallin, Emily Watson 1916-1995 ... *6*
Hallinan, P. K. 1944- ... *39*
Brief entry ... *37*
Hallinan, Patrick Kenneth
See Hallinan, P. K.
Hallman, Ruth 1929- ... *43*
Brief entry ... *28*
Hallowell, Tommy
See Hill, Thomas
Hall-Quest, (Edna) Olga W(ilbourne) 1899-1986 ... *11*
Obituary ... *47*
Halls, Kelly Milner 1957- ... *220*
Earlier sketch in SATA *131*
Hallstead, William F(inn III) 1924- ... *11*
Hallward, Michael 1889-1982 ... *12*
Halperin, Michael ... *156*
Halperin, Wendy Anderson 1952- ... *200*
Earlier sketches in SATA *80, 125*
Halpern, Julie 1975- ... *198*
Halpin, Abigail ... *236*
Halpin, Brendan 1968- ... *193*
Halpin, Marlene 1927- ... *88*
Halse, Laurie Beth
See Anderson, Laurie Halse
Halsell, Grace (Eleanor) 1923-2000 ... *13*
Halsey, Megan ... *185*
Halsted, Anna Roosevelt 1906-1975
Obituary ... *30*
Halter, Jon C(harles) 1941- ... *22*
Halverson, Deborah ... *202*
Halvorson, Adeline ... *218*
Halvorson, Marilyn 1948- ... *123*
Hamalian, Leo 1920- ... *41*
Hamberger, John 1934- ... *14*
Hamblin, Dora Jane 1920- ... *36*
Hambly, Barbara 1951- ... *108*
Hambly, Barbara Joan
See Hambly, Barbara
Hamer, Martyn
See Eldin, Peter
Hamerstrom, Frances 1907-1998 ... *24*
Hamil, Thomas Arthur 1928- ... *14*
Hamill, Ethel
See Webb, Jean Francis (III)
Hamilton, (John) Alan 1943- ... *66*
Hamilton, Alice
See Cromie, Alice Hamilton
Hamilton, Anita 1919- ... *92*
Hamilton, Barbara
See Hambly, Barbara
Hamilton, Buzz
See Hemming, Roy G.
Hamilton, Carol (Jean Barber) 1935- ... *94*
Hamilton, Charles (Harold St. John) 1876-1961 ... *13*
Hamilton, Charles 1913-1996 ... *65*
Obituary ... *93*
Hamilton, Clive
See Lewis, C. S.
Hamilton, Dorothy (Drumm) 1906-1983 ... *12*
Obituary ... *35*
Hamilton, Edith 1867-1963 ... *20*
Hamilton, Edmond 1904-1977 ... *118*
Hamilton, (Muriel) Elizabeth (Mollie) 1906- ... *23*
Hamilton, Emma Walton 1962- ... *237*
Earlier sketch in SATA *177*
Hamilton, Franklin
See Silverberg, Robert
Hamilton, Gail
See Corcoran, Barbara (Asenath)
and Dodge, Mary Abigail
Hamilton, Kersten 1958- ... *204*
Earlier sketch in SATA *134*
Hamilton, K.R.
See Hamilton, Kersten
Hamilton, Martha 1953- ... *183*
Earlier sketch in SATA *123*
Hamilton, Mary (E.) 1927- ... *55*
Hamilton, Meredith ... *233*
Hamilton, Mollie
See Kaye, M.M.
Hamilton, Morse 1943-1998 ... *101*
Earlier sketch in SATA *35*
Hamilton, Peter F. 1960- ... *109*
Hamilton, Priscilla
See Gellis, Roberta
Hamilton, Ralph
See Stratemeyer, Edward L.
Hamilton, Virginia 1936-2002 ... *123*
Obituary ... *132*
Earlier sketches in SATA *4, 56, 79*
See also CLR *127*
Hamilton, Virginia Esther
See Hamilton, Virginia
Hamilton-Paterson, James 1941- ... *82*
Hamlet, Ova
See Lupoff, Richard A.
Hamley, D. C.
See Hamley, Dennis
Hamley, Dennis 1935- ... *69*
Earlier sketch in SATA *39*
See also CLR *47*
See also SAAS *22*
Hamley, Dennis C.
See Hamley, Dennis
Hamlin, Peter J. 1970- ... *84*
Hamm, Diane Johnston 1949- ... *78*
Hammer, Charles 1934- ... *58*
Hammer, Richard 1928- ... *6*
Hammerman, Gay M(orenus) 1926- ... *9*

Author Index

Hammill, Matt 1982- *206*
Hammond, Andrew 1970- *181*
Hammond, Ralph
See Hammond Innes, Ralph
Hammond, Winifred G(raham) 1899-1992 ... *29*
Obituary *107*
Hammond Innes, Ralph 1913-1998 .... *116*
Hammontree, Marie (Gertrude) 1913- *13*
Hample, Zack 1977- *161*
Hampshire, Joyce Gregorian
See Gregorian, Joyce Ballou
Hampshire, Susan 1942- *98*
Hampson, (Richard) Denman 1929- *15*
Hampson, Frank 1918(?)-1985
Obituary *46*
Hampton, Wilborn 1940- *196*
Earlier sketch in SATA *156*
Hamre, Leif 1914- *5*
Hamsa, Bobbie 1944- *52*
Brief entry *38*
Han, Jenny 1981- *175*
Han, Lu
See Stickler, Soma Han
Han, Soma
See Stickler, Soma Han
Han, Suzanne Crowder 1953- *89*
Hancock, Mary A. 1923- *31*
Hancock, Sibyl 1940- *9*
Hand, Cynthia 1978- *241*
Hand, Elizabeth 1957- *167*
Earlier sketch in SATA *118*
Handford, Martin (John) 1956- *64*
See also CLR *22*
Handforth, Thomas (Schofield) 1897-1948 .. *42*
Handleman, Philip 1951- *222*
Handler, Daniel
See Snicket, Lemony
Handville, Robert (Tompkins) 1924- *45*
Hane, Roger 1940-1974
Obituary *20*
Hanel, Wolfram
See Haenel, Wolfram
Haney, Lynn 1941- *23*
Hanff, Helene 1916-1997 .... *97*
Earlier sketch in SATA *11*
Hanft, Josh 1956- *197*
Hanft, Joshua E.
See Hanft, Josh
Hanke, Karen *234*
Hanley, Boniface Francis 1924- *65*
Hanlon, Emily 1945- *15*
Hann, Jacquie 1951- *19*
Hann, Judith 1942- *77*
Hanna, Bill
See Hanna, William (Denby)
Hanna, Cheryl 1951- *84*
Hanna, Dan *200*
Hanna, Jack (Bushnell) 1947- *74*
Hanna, Nell(ie L.) 1908- *55*
Hanna, Paul R(obert) 1902-1988 .... *9*
Hanna, William (Denby) 1910-2001 .... *51*
Obituary *126*
Hannam, Charles 1925- *50*
Hannan, Peter 1954- *187*
Hannigan, Katherine *170*
Hannon, Ezra
See Hunter, Evan
Hann-Syme, Marguerite *127*
Hano, Arnold 1922- *12*
Hano, Renee Roth
See Roth-Hano, Renee
Hanover, Terri
See Huff, Tanya
Hansen, Amy S. *229*
Hansen, Ann Larkin 1958- *96*
Hansen, Brooks 1965- *104*
Hansen, Caryl (Hall) 1929- *39*
Hansen, Ian V. 1929- *113*
Hansen, Jennifer 1972- *156*
Hansen, Joyce 1942- *172*
Autobiography Feature *172*
Brief entry *39*
Earlier sketches in SATA *46, 101*
See also CLR *21*
See also SAAS *15*
Hansen, Joyce Viola
See Hansen, Joyce
Hansen, Mark Victor *112*
Hansen, Ron 1947- *56*
Hansen, Ronald Thomas
See Hansen, Ron
Hansen, Thore 1942- *224*
Hanser, Richard (Frederick) 1909-1981 .... *13*
Hanson, Joan 1938- *8*
Hanson, Joseph E. 1894(?)-1971
Obituary *27*
Hanson, Mary Elizabeth *188*
Hanson, Warren 1949- *239*
Earlier sketch in SATA *155*
Hansson, Gunilla 1939- *64*
Hantman, Clea *200*
Hapka, C.A.
See Hapka, Catherine
Hapka, Catherine *223*
Hapka, Cathy
See Hapka, Catherine
Harald, Eric
See Boesen, Victor
Harazin, S. A. *210*
Harbour, Elizabeth 1968- *221*
Harcourt, Ellen Knowles 1890(?)-1984
Obituary *36*
Hard, Charlotte (Ann) 1969- *98*
Hardcastle, Michael 1933- *216*
Brief entry *38*
Earlier sketch in SATA *47*
Harding, Lee 1937- *32*
Brief entry *31*
Hardinge, Frances 1973- *210*
Hardt, Helga Fleischhauer
See Fleischhauer-Hardt, Helga
Hardwick, Richard Holmes, Jr. 1923- *12*
Hardy, Alice Dale *67*
Earlier sketch in SATA *1*
Hardy, David A(ndrews) 1936- *9*
Hardy, Janice *222*
Hardy, Jon 1958- *53*
Hardy, LeAnne 1951- *154*
Hardy, Stuart
See Schisgall, Oscar
Hare, Norma Q(uarles) 1924- *46*
Brief entry *41*
Harel, Nira 1936- *154*
Harford, Henry
See Hudson, W(illiam) H(enry)
Hargis, Wes *219*
Hargrave, Leonie
See Disch, Thomas M.
Hargreaves, (Charles) Roger 1935-1988
Obituary *56*
Hargrove, James 1947- *57*
Brief entry *50*
Hargrove, Jim
See Hargrove, James
Harik, Elsa
See Marston, Elsa
Harik, Elsa M.
See Marston, Elsa
Harik, Elsa Marston
See Marston, Elsa
Hariton, Anca I. 1955- *79*
Hark, Mildred
See McQueen, Mildred Hark
Harkaway, Hal
See Stratemeyer, Edward L.
Harkins, Philip 1912-1997 .... *6*
Obituary *129*
Harlan, Elizabeth 1945- *41*
Brief entry *35*
Harlan, Glen
See Cebulash, Mel
Harlan, Judith 1949- *135*
Earlier sketch in SATA *74*
See also CLR *81*
Harland, Richard 1947- *152*
Harlee, J. V.
See Leese, Jennifer L.B.
Harler, Ann
See Van Steenwyk, Elizabeth (Ann)
Harley, Avis *183*
Harley, Bill 1954- *208*
Earlier sketch in SATA *87*
Harlow, Joan Hiatt 1932- *226*
Earlier sketch in SATA *157*
Harman, Fred 1902(?)-1982
Obituary *30*
Harman, Hugh 1903-1982
Obituary *33*
Harmelink, Barbara (Mary) *9*
Harmer, Mabel 1894-1992 .... *45*
Harmer, Wendy 1955- *241*
Harmon, Dan
See Harmon, Daniel E(lton)
Harmon, Daniel E(lton) 1949- *157*
Harmon, Kari Lee
See Townsend, Kari Lee
Harmon, Kate
See Gibson, Marley
Harmon, Margaret 1906- *20*
Harmon, Michael 1969- *189*
Harmon, Michael B.
See Harmon, Michael
Harmon, William (Ruth) 1938- *65*
Harnan, Terry 1920- *12*
Harness, Cheryl 1951- *178*
Earlier sketch in SATA *131*
Harnett, Cynthia (Mary) 1893-1981 .... *5*
Obituary *32*
Harper, Anita 1943- *41*
Harper, Betty 1946- *126*
Harper, Charise
See Harper, Charise Mericle
Harper, Charise Mericle *226*
Earlier sketch in SATA *179*
Harper, Elaine
See Hallin, Emily Watson
Harper, Ellen
See Noble, Marty
Harper, Jamie *241*
Earlier sketch in SATA *174*
Harper, Jessica 1949- *148*
Harper, Jo 1932- *169*
Earlier sketch in SATA *97*
Harper, Lee *201*
Harper, Mary Wood
See Dixon, Jeanne
Harper, Piers 1966- *161*
Earlier sketch in SATA *105*
Harper, Suzanne *194*
Harper, Wilhelmina 1884-1973 .... *4*
Obituary *26*
Harrah, Madge 1931- *154*
Harrah, Michael 1940- *41*
Harrah, Monique
See Harrah, Madge
Harrar, George E. 1949- *124*
Harrell, Beatrice Orcutt 1943- *93*
Harrell, Janice 1945- *70*
Harrell, Sara Gordon 1940- *26*
Harrell, Sara Jeanne Gordon
See Harrell, Sara Gordon
Harries, Joan 1922- *39*
Harrill, Ronald 1950- *90*
Harrington, Denis J(ames) 1932- *88*
Harrington, Evelyn Davis 1911- *5*
Harrington, Janice N. 1956- *187*
Harrington, Lyn
See Harrington, Evelyn Davis
Harris, Alan 1944- *71*

Harris, Aurand 1915-1996 ... *37*
Obituary ... *91*
Harris, Bob
See Harris, Robert J.
Harris, Carol Flynn 1933- ... *135*
Harris, Catherine
See Ainsworth, Catherine Harris
Harris, Christie
See Harris, Christie (Lucy) Irwin
Harris, Christie (Lucy) Irwin 1907-2002 ... *74*
Autobiography Feature ... *116*
Earlier sketch in SATA *6*
See also CLR *47*
See also SAAS *10*
Harris, Christine 1955- ... *105*
Harris, Colver
See Colver, Anne
Harris, David 1942- ... *118*
Harris, David William
See Harris, David
Harris, Dorothy Joan 1931- ... *153*
Earlier sketch in SATA *13*
Harris, Geraldine 1951- ... *54*
Harris, Geraldine Rachel
See Harris, Geraldine
Harris, Jacqueline L. 1929- ... *62*
Harris, Janet 1932-1979 ... *4*
Obituary ... *23*
Harris, Jesse
See Standiford, Natalie
Harris, Joan 1946- ... *146*
Harris, Joe 1928- ... *201*
Harris, Joel Chandler 1848-1908 ... *100*
See also YABC *1*
See also CLR *128*
Harris, John (Wyndham Parkes Lucas) Beynon 1903-1969 ... *118*
Harris, Johnson
See Harris, John (Wyndham Parkes Lucas) Beynon
Harris, Jonathan 1921-1997 ... *52*
Harris, Larry Vincent 1939- ... *59*
Harris, Lavinia
See St. John, Nicole
Harris, Leon A., Jr. 1926-2000 ... *4*
Harris, Lois V. ... *199*
Harris, Lorle K(empe) 1912-2001 ... *22*
Harris, Maria Guadalupe
See Harris, M.G.
Harris, Marilyn
See Springer, Marilyn Harris
Harris, Mark Jonathan 1941- ... *84*
Earlier sketch in SATA *32*
Harris, Mary K(athleen) 1905-1966 ... *119*
Harris, M.G. ... *231*
Harris, Robert J. 1955- ... *195*
Harris, Robie H. 1940- ... *203*
Brief entry ... *53*
Earlier sketches in SATA *90, 147*
Harris, Robin
See Shine, Deborah
Harris, Rosemary (Jeanne) ... *82*
Earlier sketch in SATA *4*
See also CLR *30*
See also SAAS *7*
Harris, Ruth Elwin 1935- ... *164*
Harris, Sherwood 1932-2009 ... *25*
Harris, Stephen 1959- ... *230*
Harris, Steven Michael 1957- ... *55*
Harris, Trudy 1949- ... *191*
Earlier sketch in SATA *128*
Harris-Filderman, Diane
See Filderman, Diane E(lizabeth)
Harrison, C(hester) William 1913-1994 ... *35*
Harrison, Carol
See Harrison, Carol Thompson
Harrison, Carol Thompson ... *113*
Harrison, David L. 1937- ... *186*
Earlier sketches in SATA *26, 92, 150*
Harrison, Deloris 1938- ... *9*
Harrison, Edward Hardy 1926- ... *56*
Harrison, Elizabeth (Allen) Cavanna 1909-2001 ... *30*
Earlier sketch in SATA *1*
See also SAAS *4*
Harrison, Harry 1925- ... *4*
Harrison, Harry Max
See Harrison, Harry
Harrison, Mette Ivie 1970- ... *236*
Earlier sketches in SATA *149, 202*
Harrison, Michael 1939- ... *106*
Harrison, Michelle 1979- ... *233*
Harrison, Molly (Hodgett) 1909-2002 ... *41*
Harrison, Sarah 1946- ... *63*
Harrison, Ted
See Harrison, Edward Hardy
Harsh, Fred (T.) 1925- ... *72*
Harshaw, Ruth H(etzel) 1890-1968 ... *27*
Harshman, Marc 1950- ... *109*
Earlier sketch in SATA *71*
Hart, Alexandra 1939- ... *14*
Hart, Alison
See Leonhardt, Alice
Hart, Bruce 1938-2006 ... *57*
Brief entry ... *39*
Hart, Carole 1943- ... *57*
Brief entry ... *39*
Hart, Carolyn 1936- ... *74*
Hart, Carolyn G.
See Hart, Carolyn
Hart, Carolyn Gimpel
See Hart, Carolyn
Hart, Jan Siegel 1940- ... *79*
Hart, Joyce 1954- ... *148*
Hart, Karen ... *185*
Hart, Lenore ... *171*
Hart, Philip S. 1944- ... *180*
Hart, Sam 1973- ... *241*
Hart, Virginia 1949- ... *83*
Harte, Bret 1836(?)-1902 ... *26*
Harte, Francis Brett
See Harte, Bret
Harter, Debbie 1963- ... *107*
Hartfield, Claire 1957- ... *147*
Hartinger, Brent 1964- ... *217*
Earlier sketches in SATA *145, 174*
Hartland, Jessie ... *171*
Hartley, Ellen (Raphael) 1915-1980 ... *23*
Hartley, Fred Allan III 1953- ... *41*
Hartley, William B(rown) 1913-1980 ... *23*
Hartling, Peter
See Hartling, Peter
Hartling, Peter 1933- ... *66*
See also CLR *29*
Hartman, Bob 1955- ... *224*
Hartman, Carrie ... *226*
Hartman, Cassie ... *202*
Hartman, Dan 1955- ... *202*
Hartman, Evert 1937- ... *38*
Brief entry ... *35*
Hartman, Jane E. 1928- ... *47*
Hartman, Jane Evangeline
See Hartman, Jane E.
Hartman, Louis F(rancis) 1901-1970 ... *22*
Hartman, Rachel ... *174*
Hartman, Victoria 1942- ... *91*
Hartnett, Sonya 1968- ... *176*
Earlier sketches in SATA *93, 130*
Hartry, Nancy ... *219*
Hartshorn, Ruth M. 1928- ... *11*
Hartt-Sussman, Heather ... *240*
Hartung, Susan Kathleen ... *192*
Earlier sketch in SATA *150*
Hartwig, Manfred 1950- ... *81*
Harvey, Alyxandra 1974- ... *227*
Earlier sketch in SATA *189*
Harvey, Brett 1936- ... *61*
Harvey, Edith 1908(?)-1972
Obituary ... *27*
Harvey, Gill ... *189*
Harvey, Karen D. 1935- ... *88*
Harvey, Roland 1945- ... *219*
Earlier sketches in SATA *71, 123, 179*
Harvey, Sarah N. 1950- ... *238*
Harvey-Fitzhenry, Alyxandra
See Harvey, Alyxandra
Harwick, B. L.
See Keller, Beverly L(ou)
Harwin, Brian
See Henderson, LeGrand
Harwood, Pearl Augusta (Bragdon) 1903-1998 ... *9*
Haseley, Dennis 1950- ... *221*
Brief entry ... *44*
Earlier sketches in SATA *57, 105, 157*
Hashmi, Kerri 1955- ... *108*
Haskell, Arnold L(ionel) 1903-1981(?) ... *6*
Haskins, James
See Haskins, James S.
Haskins, James S. 1941-2005 ... *132*
Autobiography Feature ... *132*
Earlier sketches in SATA *9, 69, 105*
See also CLR *39*
See also SAAS *4*
Haskins, Jim
See Haskins, James S.
Hasler, Eveline 1933- ... *181*
Hasler, Joan 1931- ... *28*
Hasler, Nikol 1979- ... *235*
Hasnat, Naheed
See Senzai, N.H.
Hass, Robert 1941- ... *94*
Hassall, Joan 1906-1988 ... *43*
Obituary ... *56*
Hassett, Ann 1958- ... *162*
Hassett, John ... *162*
Hassler, Jon 1933-2008 ... *19*
Obituary ... *191*
Hassler, Jon Francis
See Hassler, Jon
Hastings, Beverly
See Barkin, Carol
and James, Elizabeth
Hastings, Graham
See Jeffries, Roderic
Hastings, Ian 1912- ... *62*
Hastings, Victor
See Disch, Thomas M.
Haszard, Patricia Moyes 1923-2000 ... *63*
Hatch, Lynda S. 1950- ... *90*
Hathaway, Barbara ... *164*
Hathorn, Elizabeth
See Hathorn, Libby
Hathorn, Elizabeth Helen
See Hathorn, Libby
Hathorn, Libby 1943- ... *232*
Autobiography Feature ... *232*
Earlier sketches in SATA *74, 120, 156*
Hatke, Ben 1977- ... *240*
Hatkoff, Craig 1954- ... *192*
Hatlo, Jimmy 1898-1963
Obituary ... *23*
Hatton, Caroline 1957- ... *205*
Hauff, Wilhelm 1802-1827
See CLR *155*
Haugaard, Erik Christian 1923- ... *68*
Earlier sketch in SATA *4*
See also CLR *173*
See also SAAS *12*
Haugaard, Kay ... *117*
Hauge, Lesley ... *234*
Haugen, Hayley Mitchell 1968- ... *172*
Haugen, Tormod 1945- ... *66*
Hauman, Doris 1898-1984 ... *32*
Hauman, George 1890-1961 ... *32*
Hauptly, Denis J. 1945- ... *57*
Hauptly, Denis James
See Hauptly, Denis J.
Hauser, Jill Frankel 1950- ... *127*
Hauser, Margaret L(ouise) 1909- ... *10*
Hausherr, Rosmarie 1943- ... *86*

Hausman, Gerald 1945- *180*
Earlier sketches in SATA *13, 90, 132*
See also CLR *89*
Hausman, Gerry
See Hausman, Gerald
Hauth, Katherine B. 1940- *99*
Hautman, Pete 1952- *173*
Earlier sketches in SATA *82, 128*
Hautman, Peter Murray
See Hautman, Pete
Hautzig, Deborah 1956- *106*
Earlier sketch in SATA *31*
Hautzig, Esther Rudomin 1930-2009 .... *148*
Earlier sketches in SATA *4, 68*
See also CLR *22*
See also SAAS *15*
Havel, Geoff 1955- *152*
Havel, Jennifer
See Havill, Juanita
Havelin, Kate 1961- *143*
Haven, Paul 1971(?)- *213*
Haverfield, Mary *225*
Havighurst, Walter (Edwin) 1901-1994 .... *1*
Obituary *79*
Haviland, Virginia 1911-1988 .... *6*
Obituary *54*
Havill, Juanita 1949- *224*
Earlier sketches in SATA *74, 155*
Hawes, Judy 1913- *4*
Hawes, Louise 1943- *180*
Earlier sketch in SATA *60*
Hawk, Fran *222*
Hawke, Rosanne 1953- *165*
Earlier sketch in SATA *124*
Hawke, Rosanne Joy
See Hawke, Rosanne
Hawkes, Kevin 1959- *201*
Earlier sketches in SATA *78, 150*
Hawkes, Nigel 1943- *119*
Hawkesworth, Eric 1921- *13*
Hawking, Lucy 1969- *197*
Hawkins, Aaron R. *236*
Hawkins, Arthur 1903-1985 .... *19*
Hawkins, Colin 1945- *162*
Earlier sketch in SATA *112*
Hawkins, Jacqui *162*
Earlier sketch in SATA *112*
Hawkins, Jimmy 1941- *188*
Hawkins, Laura 1951- *74*
Hawkins, (Helena Ann) Quail 1905-2002 .... *6*
Obituary *141*
Hawkins, Rachel 1979- *228*
Hawkinson, John (Samuel) 1912-1994 .... *4*
Hawkinson, Lucy (Ozone) 1924-1971 .... *21*
Hawks, Robert 1961- *85*
Hawley, Mabel C. *67*
Earlier sketch in SATA *1*
Haworth, Danette *207*
Haworth-Attard, Barbara 1953- *215*
Hawthorne, Captain R. M.
See Ellis, Edward S.
Hawthorne, Nathaniel 1804-1864
See YABC *2*
See also CLR *163*
Hay, Jeff T. *154*
Hay, John 1915-2011 .... *13*
Hay, Samantha *213*
Hay, Timothy
See Brown, Margaret Wise
Hayashi, Leslie Ann 1954- *115*
Hayashi, Nancy 1939- *186*
Earlier sketch in SATA *80*
Haycak, Cara 1961- *180*
Haycock, Kate 1962- *77*
Haycraft, Howard 1905-1991 .... *6*
Obituary *70*
Haycraft, Molly Costain 1911- *6*
Hayden, Gwendolen Lampshire 1904- *35*
Hayden, Robert
See Hayden, Robert Earl
Hayden, Robert C(arter), Jr. 1937- *47*
Brief entry *28*
Hayden, Robert E.
See Hayden, Robert Earl
Hayden, Robert Earl 1913-1980 .... *19*
Obituary *26*
Hayden, Torey L. 1951- *163*
Earlier sketch in SATA *65*
Hayden, Torey Lynn
See Hayden, Torey L.
Hayes, Carlton J(oseph) H(untley)
1882-1964 .... *11*
Hayes, Daniel 1952- *109*
Earlier sketch in SATA *73*
Hayes, Geoffrey 1947- *207*
Earlier sketches in SATA *26, 91*
Hayes, Joe 1945- *131*
Earlier sketch in SATA *88*
Hayes, John F. 1904-1980 .... *11*
Hayes, Karel 1949- *207*
Hayes, Rosemary *227*
Earlier sketch in SATA *158*
Hayes, Sarah 1945- *208*
Hayes, Sheila 1937- *51*
Brief entry *50*
Hayes, Will *7*
Hayes, William D(imitt) 1913-1976 .... *8*
Haynes, Betsy 1937- *94*
Brief entry *37*
Earlier sketch in SATA *48*
See also CLR *90*
Haynes, David 1955- *97*
Haynes, Linda
See Swinford, Betty (June Wells)
Haynes, Mary 1938- *65*
Haynes, Max 1956- *72*
Hays, Anna Jane *214*
Hays, H(offmann) R(eynolds) 1904-1980 .... *26*
Hays, Thomas A.
See Hays, Tony
Hays, Thomas Anthony
See Hays, Tony
Hays, Tony 1957- *84*
Hays, Wilma Pitchford 1909- *28*
Earlier sketch in SATA *1*
See also CLR *59*
See also SAAS *3*
Hayter, Rhonda *233*
Hayward, Linda 1943- *185*
Brief entry *39*
Earlier sketch in SATA *101*
Haywood, Carolyn 1898-1990 .... *75*
Obituary *64*
Earlier sketches in SATA *1, 29*
See also CLR *22*
Hazelaar, Cor *217*
Hazell, Rebecca (Eileen) 1947- *141*
Hazen, Barbara Shook 1930- *178*
Earlier sketches in SATA *27, 90*
Hazen, Lynn E. *202*
Head, Gay
See Hauser, Margaret L(ouise)
Head, Tom 1978- *167*
Headley, Elizabeth
See Harrison, Elizabeth (Allen) Cavanna
Headley, Justina Chen 1968- *176*
Headstrom, (Birger) Richard 1902-1985 .... *8*
Heady, Eleanor B(utler) 1917-1979 .... *8*
Heagy, William D. 1964- *76*
Heal, Edith 1903-1995 .... *7*
Heal, Gillian 1934- *89*
Heale, Jay (Jeremy Peter Wingfield) 1937- *84*
Healey, Brooks
See Albert, Burton
Healey, Karen 1981- *230*
Healey, Larry 1927- *44*
Brief entry *42*
Heap, Sue 1954- *187*
Earlier sketch in SATA *150*
Heaps, Willard A(llison) 1908-1987 .... *26*
Hearn, Diane Dawson 1952- *209*
Earlier sketch in SATA *79*
Hearn, Emily
See Valleau, Emily
Hearn, Julie 1958- *212*
Earlier sketch in SATA *152*
Hearn, Lian
See Rubinstein, Gillian
Hearn, Sneed
See Gregg, Andrew K.
Hearne, Betsy 1942- *146*
Earlier sketches in SATA *38, 95*
Heasley, Gwendolyn *240*
Heath, Charles D(ickinson) 1941- *46*
Heath, Veronica
See Blackett, Veronica Heath
Heaven, Constance (Christina) 1911- *7*
Hebert-Collins, Sheila 1948- *111*
Hecht, George J(oseph) 1895-1980
Obituary *22*
Hecht, Henri Joseph 1922- *9*
Hechtkopf, Henryk 1910- *17*
Heck, Bessie (Mildred) Holland 1911-1995 . *26*
Heck, Ed 1963- *173*
Heckert, Connie K(aye Delp) 1948- *82*
Hector, Julian *205*
Hedderwick, Mairi 1939- *145*
Earlier sketches in SATA *30, 77*
Hedges, Sid(ney) G(eorge) 1897-1974 .... *28*
Hedrick, Irene Hope 1920- *175*
Heelan, Jamee Riggio 1965- *146*
Heerboth, Sharon
See Leon, Sharon
Heffernan, John 1949- *168*
Earlier sketch in SATA *121*
Heffron, Dorris 1944- *68*
Hefter, Richard 1942- *31*
Hegamin, Tonya C. 1975- *209*
Hegarty, Reginald Beaton 1906-1973 .... *10*
Hehenberger, Shelly 1968- *126*
Heidbreder, Robert 1947- *196*
Earlier sketch in SATA *130*
Heidbreder, Robert K.
See Heidbreder, Robert
Heide, Florence Parry 1919-2011 .... *192*
Earlier sketches in SATA *32, 69, 118*
See also CLR *60*
See also SAAS *6*
Heiderstadt, Dorothy 1907-2001 .... *6*
Heidi Louise
See Erdrich, Louise
Heidler, David S. 1955- *132*
Heidler, David Stephen
See Heidler, David S.
Heidler, Jeanne T. 1956- *132*
Heilbroner, Joan Knapp 1922- *63*
Heilbrun, Lois Hussey 1922(?)-1987
Obituary *54*
Heiligman, Deborah 1958- *193*
Earlier sketches in SATA *90, 144*
Heilman, Joan Rattner *50*
Heimann, Rolf 1940- *164*
Earlier sketch in SATA *120*
Heimberg, Justin *232*
Hein, Lucille Eleanor 1915-1994 .... *20*
Heine, Helme 1941- *135*
Earlier sketch in SATA *67*
See also CLR *18*
Heinlein, Robert A. 1907-1988 .... *69*
Obituary *56*
Earlier sketch in SATA *9*
See also CLR *75*
Heinlein, Robert Anson
See Heinlein, Robert A.
Heins, Ethel L(eah) 1918-1997 .... *101*
Heins, Paul 1909- *13*
Heintze, Carl 1922- *26*
Heinz, Bill
See Heinz, W. C.
Heinz, Brian J. 1946- *181*
Earlier sketch in SATA *95*

Heinz, Brian James
See Heinz, Brian J.
Heinz, W. C. 1915-2008 ... *26*
Heinz, Wilfred Charles
See Heinz, W. C.
Heinzen, Mildred
See Masters, Mildred
Heisel, Sharon E(laine) 1941- ... *125*
Earlier sketch in SATA *84*
Heitzmann, William Ray 1948- ... *73*
Heitzmann, Wm. Ray
See Heitzmann, William Ray
Helakoski, Leslie ... *238*
Earlier sketch in SATA *178*
Helberg, Shirley Adelaide Holden 1919- ... *138*
Heldring, Thatcher ... *229*
Helfer, Andrew ... *187*
Helfer, Ralph 1937- ... *177*
Helfman, Elizabeth S(eaver) 1911-2001 ... *3*
Helfman, Harry Carmozin 1910-1995 ... *3*
Helgerson, Joseph 1950- ... *181*
Hellard, Susan ... *232*
Earlier sketch in SATA *182*
Hellberg, Hans-Eric 1927- ... *38*
Heller, Linda 1944- ... *46*
Brief entry ... *40*
Heller, Mike
See Hano, Arnold
Heller, Ruth M. 1924- ... *112*
Earlier sketch in SATA *66*
Hellman, Hal
See Hellman, Harold
Hellman, Harold 1927- ... *4*
Helman, Andrea (Jean) 1946- ... *160*
Earlier sketch in SATA *107*
Helmer, Diana Star 1962- ... *86*
Helmer, Marilyn ... *160*
Earlier sketch in SATA *112*
Helps, Racey 1913-1971 ... *2*
Obituary ... *25*
Helquist, Brett ... *229*
Earlier sketches in SATA *146, 187*
Helweg, Hans H. 1917- ... *50*
Brief entry ... *33*
Helyar, Jane Penelope Josephine 1933- ... *5*
Autobiography Feature ... *138*
See also SAAS *2*
Hemingway, Edith M. 1950- ... *223*
Hemingway, Edith Morris
See Hemingway, Edith M.
Hemingway, Edward 1969(?)- ... *212*
Hemingway, Ernest 1899-1961
See CLR *168*
Hemingway, Ernest Miller
See Hemingway, Ernest
Hemmant, Lynette 1938- ... *69*
Hemming, Roy G. 1928-1995 ... *11*
Obituary ... *86*
Hemphill, Helen 1955- ... *179*
Hemphill, Kris (Harrison) 1963- ... *118*
Hemphill, Martha Locke 1904-1973 ... *37*
Hemphill, Michael ... *220*
Hemphill, Stephanie ... *190*
Hemstock, Gillian 1956- ... *173*
Henba, Bobbie 1926- ... *87*
Henbest, Nigel 1951- ... *55*
Brief entry ... *52*
Henderley, Brooks ... *1*
Henderson, Aileen Kilgore 1921- ... *178*
Henderson, Aileen Mary
See Fox, Aileen
Henderson, Gordon 1950- ... *53*
Henderson, Kathy 1949- ... *155*
Brief entry ... *53*
Earlier sketches in SATA *55, 95*
Henderson, Lauren 1966- ... *201*
Henderson, LeGrand 1901-1965 ... *9*
Henderson, Nancy Wallace 1916- ... *22*
Henderson, Zenna (Chlarson) 1917-1983 ... *5*
Hendra, Sue ... *235*
Hendrickson, Walter Brookfield, Jr. 1936- ... *9*
Hendrix, John 1976- ... *208*
Hendry, Diana 1941- ... *213*
Earlier sketches in SATA *68, 106*
Hendry, Frances Mary 1941- ... *171*
Earlier sketch in SATA *110*
Hendry, Linda (Gail) 1961- ... *83*
Heneghan, James 1930- ... *160*
Earlier sketches in SATA *53, 97*
Henkes, Kevin 1960- ... *207*
Earlier sketches in SATA *43, 76, 108, 154*
See also CLR *108*
Henn, Astrid ... *214*
Hennessy, Barbara G.
See Hennessy, B.G.
Hennessy, Barbara Gulbrandsen
See Hennessy, B.G.
Hennessy, B.G. 1951- ... *175*
Hennesy, Carolyn 1962- ... *221*
Henney, Carolee Wells 1928- ... *102*
Henriod, Lorraine 1925- ... *26*
Henriquez, Emile F. 1937- ... *170*
Earlier sketch in SATA *89*
Henry, April 1959- ... *235*
Earlier sketch in SATA *174*
Henry, Ernest 1948- ... *107*
Henry, Jed ... *239*
Henry, Joanne Landers 1927- ... *6*
Henry, Maeve 1960- ... *75*
Henry, Marguerite 1902-1997 ... *100*
Obituary ... *99*
See also CLR *4*
See also SAAS *7*
Henry, Marie H. 1935- ... *65*
Henry, Marilyn 1939- ... *117*
Henry, Marion
See del Rey, Lester
Henry, O. 1862-1910
See YABC *2*
Henry, Oliver
See Henry, O.
Henry, Rohan ... *217*
Henry, T. E.
See Rowland-Entwistle, (Arthur) Theodore (Henry)
Henschel, Elizabeth Georgie ... *56*
Henson, Heather ... *206*
Henson, James Maury
See Henson, Jim
Henson, Jim 1936-1990 ... *43*
Obituary ... *65*
Henstra, Friso 1928- ... *73*
Earlier sketch in SATA *8*
See also SAAS *14*
Hentoff, Nat(han Irving) 1925- ... *133*
Brief entry ... *27*
Earlier sketches in SATA *42, 69*
See also CLR *52*
Henty, G(eorge) A(lfred) 1832-1902 ... *64*
See also CLR *76*
Heo, Yumi 1964- ... *206*
Earlier sketches in SATA *94, 146*
Hepler, Heather ... *177*
Herald, Kathleen
See Peyton, Kathleen Wendy
Herb, Angela M. 1970- ... *92*
Herbert, Cecil
See Hamilton, Charles (Harold St. John)
Herbert, Don 1917-2007 ... *2*
Obituary ... *184*
Herbert, Donald Jeffrey
See Herbert, Don
Herbert, Frank 1920-1986 ... *37*
Obituary ... *47*
Earlier sketch in SATA *9*
Herbert, Frank Patrick
See Herbert, Frank
Herbert, Helen (Jean) 1947- ... *57*
Herbert, Janis 1956- ... *139*
Herbert, Wally 1934-2007 ... *23*
Herbert, Walter William
See Herbert, Wally
Herbst, Judith 1947- ... *74*
Herda, D.J. 1948- ... *80*
Herge
See Remi, Georges
Heritage, Martin
See Horler, Sydney
Herkimer, L(awrence) R(ussell) 1925(?)- ... *42*
Herlihy, Dirlie Anne 1935- ... *73*
Herlong, Madaline
See Herlong, M.H.
Herlong, M.H. ... *211*
Herman, Charlotte 1937- ... *203*
Earlier sketches in SATA *20, 99*
Hermanson, Dennis (Everett) 1947- ... *10*
Hermes, Jules 1962- ... *92*
Hermes, Patricia 1936- ... *233*
Earlier sketches in SATA *31, 78, 141, 191*
Hermes, Patricia Mary
See Hermes, Patricia
Hernandez, Natalie Nelson 1929- ... *123*
Herndon, Ernest ... *91*
Herold, Ann Bixby 1937- ... *72*
Herrera, Diego
See Yayo
Herrera, Juan Felipe 1948- ... *127*
Herrick, Steven 1958- ... *209*
Earlier sketches in SATA *103, 156*
Herriman, George (Joseph) 1880-1944 ... *140*
Herriot, James 1916-1995 ... *135*
Brief entry ... *44*
Earlier sketch in SATA *86*
See also CLR *80*
Herrmanns, Ralph 1933- ... *11*
Herrold, Tracey
See Dils, Tracey E.
Herron, Carolivia 1947- ... *203*
Herron, Edward A(lbert) 1912- ... *4*
Herschler, Mildred Barger ... *130*
Hersey, John 1914-1993 ... *25*
Obituary ... *76*
Hersey, John Richard
See Hersey, John
Hershberger, Priscilla (Gorman) 1951- ... *81*
Hershenhorn, Esther 1945- ... *151*
Hershey, Kathleen M. 1934- ... *80*
Hershey, Mary ... *173*
Hershey, Mary L.
See Hershey, Mary
Hersom, Kathleen 1911- ... *73*
Hertz, Grete Janus 1915- ... *23*
Herxheimer, Sophie 1963- ... *220*
Herzig, Alison Cragin 1935- ... *87*
Herzog, Brad 1968- ... *131*
Heshka, Ryan ... *236*
Heslewood, Juliet 1951- ... *82*
Hess, Lilo 1916- ... *4*
Hess, Paul 1961- ... *134*
Hesse, Hermann 1877-1962 ... *50*
Hesse, Karen 1952- ... *215*
Autobiography Feature ... *113*
Earlier sketches in SATA *74, 103, 158*
See also CLR *141*
See also SAAS *25*
Hest, Amy 1950- ... *193*
Earlier sketches in SATA *55, 82, 129*
Heuer, Karsten 1968(?)- ... *202*
Heuer, Kenneth John 1927- ... *44*
Heuman, William 1912-1971 ... *21*
Heuston, Kimberley 1960- ... *167*
Heuston, Kimberley Burton
See Heuston, Kimberley
Heuvel, Eric 1960- ... *224*
Hewes, Agnes Danforth 1874-1963 ... *35*
Hewett, Anita 1918-1989 ... *13*
Hewett, Joan 1930- ... *140*
Earlier sketch in SATA *81*
Hewett, Richard 1929- ... *81*
Hewitson, Jennifer 1961- ... *97*
Hewitt, Margaret 1961- ... *84*
Hewitt, Sally 1949- ... *231*
Earlier sketch in SATA *127*

Hext, Harrington
See Phillpotts, Eden
Hey, Nigel 1936- *20*
Hey, Nigel Stewart
See Hey, Nigel
Heyduck-Huth, Hilde 1929- *8*
Heyer, Carol 1950- *130*
Earlier sketch in SATA *74*
Heyer, Marilee 1942- *102*
Earlier sketch in SATA *64*
Heyerdahl, Thor 1914-2002 .... *52*
Earlier sketch in SATA *2*
Heyes, (Nancy) Eileen 1956- *150*
Earlier sketch in SATA *80*
Heyliger, William 1884-1955
See YABC *1*
Heyman, Ken(neth Louis) 1930- *114*
Earlier sketch in SATA *34*
Heyward, (Edwin) DuBose 1885-1940 .... *21*
Heywood, Karen 1946- *48*
Hezlep, William (Earl) 1936- *88*
Hiaasen, Carl 1953- *208*
Hiatt, Shelby *226*
Hibbert, Arthur Raymond
See Hibbert, Christopher
Hibbert, Christopher 1924-2008 .... *4*
Obituary *201*
Hibbert, Eleanor Alice Burford 1906-1993 .... *2*
Obituary *74*
Hickman, Estella (Lee) 1942- *111*
Hickman, Janet 1940- *127*
Earlier sketch in SATA *12*
Hickman, Martha Whitmore 1925- *26*
Hickman, Pamela 1958- *186*
Earlier sketch in SATA *128*
Hickock, Will
See Harrison, C(hester) William
Hickok, Lorena A. 1893-1968 .... *20*
Hickox, Rebecca (Ayres) *116*
Hicks, Barbara Jean 1953- *165*
Hicks, Betty *191*
Hicks, Clifford B. 1920- *50*
Hicks, Eleanor B.
See Coerr, Eleanor (Beatrice)
Hicks, Faith Erin *235*
Hicks, Harvey
See Stratemeyer, Edward L.
Hicks, Peter 1952- *111*
Hicyilmaz, Gaye 1947- *157*
Earlier sketch in SATA *77*
Hieatt, Constance B(artlett) 1928- *4*
Hiebert, Ray Eldon 1932- *13*
Hierstein, Judith *212*
Hierstein, Judy
See Hierstein, Judith
Higdon, Hal 1931- *4*
Higginbottom, David 1923- *87*
Earlier sketch in SATA *25*
Higginbottom, J(effrey) Winslow 1945- *29*
Higgins, Dalton *223*
Higgins, F.E. *219*
Higgins, Fiona
See Higgins, F.E.
Higgins, Joanna 1945- *125*
Higgins, Simon (Richard) 1958- *105*
Higginsen, Vy *79*
High, Linda Oatman 1958- *188*
Autobiography Feature *188*
Earlier sketches in SATA *94, 145*
High, Philip E. 1914- *119*
High, Philip Empson
See High, Philip E.
Higham, David 1949- *50*
Higham, David Michael
See Higham, David
Higham, Jon Atlas
See Higham, Jonathan Huw
Higham, Jonathan Huw 1960- *59*
Highet, Helen
See MacInnes, Helen (Clark)
Hightman, Jason 1971(?)- *189*
Hightman, J.P.
See Hightman, Jason
Hightower, Florence Cole 1916-1981 .... *4*
Obituary *27*
Highwater, Jamake (Mamake)
1942(?)-2001 .... *69*
Brief entry *30*
Earlier sketch in SATA *32*
See also CLR *17*
Hilb, Nora 1953- *178*
Hildebrandt, Greg, Jr. 1970- *228*
Hildebrandt, Greg 1939- *172*
Brief entry *33*
Earlier sketch in SATA *55*
Hildebrandt, Tim 1939-2006 .... *55*
Brief entry *33*
Hildebrandt, Timothy
See Hildebrandt, Tim
Hildebrandts, The
See Hildebrandt, Greg
and Hildebrandt, Tim
Hilder, Rowland 1905-1993 .... *36*
Obituary *77*
Hildick, E. W.
See Hildick, Wallace
Hildick, Wallace 1925-2001 .... *68*
Earlier sketch in SATA *2*
See also SAAS *6*
Hilgartner, Beth 1957- *58*
Hill, Alexis
See Craig, Mary (Francis) Shura
and Glick, Ruth
Hill, Anthony R. 1942- *164*
Earlier sketch in SATA *91*
Hill, Anthony Robert
See Hill, Anthony R.
Hill, David 1942- *152*
Earlier sketch in SATA *103*
Hill, Donna (Marie) 1921- *124*
Earlier sketch in SATA *24*
Hill, Douglas 1935-2007 .... *78*
Earlier sketch in SATA *39*
Hill, Douglas Arthur
See Hill, Douglas
Hill, Elizabeth Starr 1925- *143*
Earlier sketch in SATA *24*
Hill, Eric 1927- *133*
Brief entry *53*
Earlier sketch in SATA *66*
See also CLR *13*
Hill, Gordon
See Eldin, Peter
Hill, Grace Brooks *67*
Earlier sketch in SATA *1*
Hill, Grace Livingston 1865-1947
See YABC *2*
Hill, Helen M(orey) 1915- *27*
Hill, Isabel *225*
Hill, Isabel T.
See Hill, Isabel
Hill, John
See Koontz, Dean
Hill, Johnson
See Kunhardt, Edith
Hill, Judy I. R.
See Roberts, Judy I.
Hill, Kathleen Louise 1917- *4*
Hill, Kay
See Hill, Kathleen Louise
Hill, Kirkpatrick 1938- *188*
Earlier sketches in SATA *72, 126*
Hill, Laban
See Hill, Laban Carrick
Hill, Laban Carrick *170*
Hill, Lee Sullivan 1958- *96*
Hill, Lorna 1902-1991 .... *12*
Hill, Margaret (Ohler) 1915- *36*
Hill, Meg
See Hill, Margaret (Ohler)
Hill, Meredith
See Craig, Mary (Francis) Shura
Hill, Monica
See Watson, Jane Werner
Hill, Pamela Smith 1954- *112*
Hill, Ralph Nading 1917-1987 .... *65*
Hill, Robert W(hite) 1919-1982 .... *12*
Obituary *31*
Hill, Ruth A.
See Viguers, Ruth Hill
Hill, Ruth Livingston
See Munce, Ruth Hill
Hill, Stuart 1958- *186*
Hill, Susan 1942- *183*
Hill, Susan Elizabeth
See Hill, Susan
Hill, Susanna Leonard 1965- *193*
Hill, Thomas 1960- *82*
Hillcourt, William 1900-1992 .... *27*
Hillenbrand, Will 1960- *210*
Earlier sketches in SATA *84, 147*
Hiller, Ilo (Ann) 1938- *59*
Hillerman, Anthony Grove
See Hillerman, Tony
Hillerman, Tony 1925-2008 .... *6*
Obituary *198*
Hillert, Margaret 1920- *91*
Earlier sketch in SATA *8*
Hilliard, Richard *183*
Hillman, Ben 1957- *202*
Hillman, Elizabeth 1942- *75*
Hillman, John 1952- *120*
Hillman, Martin
See Hill, Douglas
Hillman, Priscilla 1940- *48*
Brief entry *39*
Hillman, Shane *200*
Hills, C.A.R. 1955- *39*
Hills, Charles Albert Reis
See Hills, C.A.R.
Hills, Lia *238*
Hills, Tad *237*
Earlier sketch in SATA *173*
Hilton, Irene Pothus -1979 .... *7*
Hilton, James 1900-1954 .... *34*
Hilton, Margaret Lynette 1946- *105*
Earlier sketch in SATA *68*
See also CLR *25*
See also SAAS *21*
Hilton, Nette
See Hilton, Margaret Lynette
Hilton, Ralph 1907-1982 .... *8*
Hilton, Suzanne 1922- *4*
Hilton-Bruce, Anne
See Hilton, Margaret Lynette
Him, George 1937-1982
Obituary *30*
Himelblau, Linda -2005 .... *179*
Himelstein, Shmuel 1940- *83*
Himler, Ann 1946- *8*
Himler, Ronald 1937- *234*
Earlier sketches in SATA *6, 92, 137, 183*
Himler, Ronald Norbert
See Himler, Ronald
Himmelman, John 1959- *221*
Earlier sketches in SATA *47, 94, 159*
Himmelman, John C.
See Himmelman, John
Hinckley, Helen
See Jones, Helen Hinckley
Hind, Dolores (Ellen) 1931- *53*
Brief entry *49*
Hindin, Nathan
See Bloch, Robert (Albert)
Hindley, Judy 1940- *179*
Earlier sketch in SATA *120*
Hinds, P. Mignon *98*
Hinds, Patricia Mignon
See Hinds, P. Mignon
Hine, Sesyle Joslin 1929- *2*

Hines, Anna Grossnickle 1946- *209*
Brief entry *45*
Earlier sketches in SATA *51, 95, 141*
See also SAAS *16*
Hines, Gary (Roger) 1944- *136*
Earlier sketch in SATA *74*
Hinman, Bonnie 1950- *216*
Hinojosa, Maria (de Lourdes) 1961- *88*
Hinton, Nigel 1941- *166*
Hinton, S. E. 1950- *160*
Earlier sketches in SATA *19, 58, 115*
See also CLR *23*
Hinton, Sam 1917-2009 .... *43*
Hinton, Susan Eloise
See Hinton, S. E.
Hintz, Martin 1945- *128*
Brief entry *39*
Earlier sketch in SATA *47*
Hintz, Stephen V. 1975- *129*
Hippopotamus, Eugene H.
See Kraus, (Herman) Robert
Hirano, Cathy 1957- *68*
Hirao, Amiko *203*
Hirsch, Karen 1941- *61*
Hirsch, Odo *157*
Earlier sketch in SATA *111*
Hirsch, Phil 1926- *35*
Hirsch, S. Carl 1913-1990 .... *2*
See also SAAS *7*
Hirschfelder, Arlene B. 1943- *227*
Earlier sketches in SATA *80, 138*
Hirschi, Ron 1948- *192*
Earlier sketches in SATA *56, 95*
Hirschmann, Linda (Ann) 1941- *40*
Hirsh, Marilyn 1944-1988 .... *7*
Obituary *58*
Hirshberg, Al(bert Simon) 1909-1973 .... *38*
Hische, Jessica 1984- *240*
Hiscock, Bruce 1940- *204*
Earlier sketches in SATA *57, 137*
Hiser, Constance 1950- *71*
Hiser, Iona Seibert -1998 .... *4*
Hislop, Julia Rose Catherine 1962- *74*
Hissey, Jane 1952- *130*
Autobiography Feature *130*
Earlier sketches in SATA *58, 103*
Hissey, Jane Elizabeth
See Hissey, Jane
Hitchcock, Alfred (Joseph) 1899-1980 .... *27*
Obituary *24*
Hite, Sid 1954- *175*
Earlier sketches in SATA *75, 136*
Hitte, Kathryn 1919- *16*
Hitz, Demi
See Demi
Hitzeroth, Deborah L. 1961- *78*
Hnizdovsky, Jacques 1915- *32*
Ho, Jannie *226*
Ho, Louise *185*
Ho, Minfong 1951- *151*
Earlier sketches in SATA *15, 94*
See also CLR *28*
Hoagland, Edward (Morley) 1932- *51*
Hoare, Robert J(ohn) 1921-1975 .... *38*
Hoban, Julia *217*
Hoban, Lillian 1925-1998 .... *69*
Obituary *104*
Earlier sketch in SATA *22*
See also CLR *67*
Hoban, Russell 1925-2011 .... *136*
Earlier sketches in SATA *1, 40, 78*
See also CLR *139*
Hoban, Russell Conwell
See Hoban, Russell
Hoban, Tana 1917(?)-2006 .... *104*
Obituary *173*
Earlier sketches in SATA *22, 70*
See also CLR *76*
See also SAAS *12*
Hobart, Lois (Elaine) *7*
Hobbie, Holly 1942- *225*
Earlier sketch in SATA *178*
See also CLR *88*
Hobbie, Jocelyn *190*
Hobbie, Nathaniel *196*
Hobbs, Leigh 1953- *166*
Hobbs, Valerie 1941- *193*
Autobiography Feature *145*
Earlier sketches in SATA *93, 145*
See also CLR *148*
Hobbs, Will 1947- *177*
Autobiography Feature *127*
Earlier sketches in SATA *72, 110*
See also CLR *59*
Hobbs, William Carl
See Hobbs, Will
Hoberman, Mary Ann 1930- *228*
Earlier sketches in SATA *5, 72, 111, 158*
See also CLR *22*
See also SAAS *18*
Hobson, Bruce 1950- *62*
Hobson, Burton (Harold) 1933- *28*
Hobson, Laura Z(ametkin) 1900-1986 .... *52*
Hobson, Sally 1967- *172*
Earlier sketch in SATA *84*
Hoce, Charley E. *174*
Hochman, David *202*
Hochschild, Arlie Russell 1940- *11*
Hockaby, Stephen
See Mitchell, Gladys (Maude Winifred)
Hockenberry, Hope
See Newell, Hope Hockenberry
Hodge, Deborah 1954- *163*
Earlier sketch in SATA *122*
Hodge, P. W.
See Hodge, Paul W(illiam)
Hodge, Paul W(illiam) 1934- *12*
Hodgell, P(atricia) C(hristine) 1951- *42*
Hodges, C. Walter 1909-2004 .... *2*
Obituary *158*
Hodges, Carl G. 1902-1964 .... *10*
Hodges, Cyril Walter
See Hodges, C. Walter
Hodges, Elizabeth Jamison *1*
Hodges, Margaret 1911-2005 .... *167*
Obituary *172*
Earlier sketches in SATA *1, 33, 75, 117*
See also SAAS *9*
Hodges, Margaret Moore
See Hodges, Margaret
Hodgetts, Blake Christopher 1967- *43*
Hodgkins, Fran 1964- *199*
Hodgkinson, Leigh 1975- *202*
Hodgman, Ann 1956- *198*
Hodgson, Harriet (W.) 1935- *84*
Hodson, Ben *241*
Hoehne, Marcia 1951- *89*
Hoellwarth, Cathryn Clinton
See Clinton, Cathryn
Hoestlandt, Jo 1948- *221*
Earlier sketch in SATA *94*
Hoestlandt, Jocelyne
See Hoestlandt, Jo
Hoexter, Corinne K. 1927- *6*
Hoeye, Michael 1947- *136*
Hof, Marjolijn 1956- *226*
Hoff, Carol 1900-1979 .... *11*
Hoff, Mary (King) 1956- *157*
Earlier sketch in SATA *74*
Hoff, Syd(ney) 1912-2004 .... *138*
Obituary *154*
Earlier sketches in SATA *9, 72*
See also CLR *83*
See also SAAS *4*
Hoffman, Edwin D. *49*
Hoffman, Elizabeth P(arkinson) 1921-2003
Obituary *153*
Hoffman, Mary 1945- *211*
Earlier sketches in SATA *59, 97, 144*
See also SAAS *24*
Hoffman, Mat 1972- *150*
Hoffman, Nina Kiriki 1955- *240*
Earlier sketch in SATA *160*
Hoffman, Phyllis M. 1944- *4*
Hoffman, Phyllis Miriam
See Hoffman, Phyllis M.
Hoffman, Rosekrans 1926- *15*
Hoffmann, E(rnst) T(heodor) A(madeus)
1776-1822 .... *27*
See also CLR *133*
Hoffmann, Felix 1911-1975 .... *9*
Hoffmann, Heinrich 1809-1894
See CLR *122*
Hoffmann, Margaret Jones 1910- *48*
Hoffmann, Peggy
See Hoffmann, Margaret Jones
Hofher, Catherine Baxley 1954- *130*
Hofher, Cathy
See Hofher, Catherine Baxley
Hofmeyr, Dianne (Louise) *138*
Hofsepian, Sylvia A. 1932- *74*
Hofsinde, Robert 1902-1973 .... *21*
Hogan, Bernice Harris 1929- *12*
Hogan, Inez 1895-1973 .... *2*
Hogan, James P. 1941-2010 .... *81*
Hogan, James Patrick
See Hogan, James P.
Hogan, Jamie *192*
Hogan, Linda 1947- *132*
Hogan, Mary 1957- *210*
Hogarth, Burne 1911-1996 .... *89*
Earlier sketch in SATA *63*
Hogarth, Grace (Weston Allen) 1905-1995 .. *91*
Hogarth, Jr.
See Kent, Rockwell
Hogarth, (Arthur) Paul 1917-2001 .... *41*
Hogg, Garry 1902-1976 .... *2*
Hogg, Gary 1957- *172*
Earlier sketch in SATA *105*
Hogner, Dorothy Childs *4*
Hogner, Nils 1893-1970 .... *25*
Hogrogian, Nonny 1932- *74*
Autobiography Feature *127*
Earlier sketch in SATA *7*
See also CLR *95*
See also SAAS *1*
Hoh, Diane 1937- *102*
Brief entry *48*
Earlier sketch in SATA *52*
Hoke, Helen
See Watts, Helen L. Hoke
Hoke, Helen L.
See Watts, Helen L. Hoke
Hoke, John 1925-2011 .... *7*
Hoke, John Lindsay
See Hoke, John
Hokenson, Terry 1948- *193*
Hol, Coby 1943- *126*
Holabird, Katharine 1948- *213*
Earlier sketches in SATA *62, 135*
Holaday, Bobbie 1922- *153*
Holbeach, Henry
See Rands, William Brighty
Holberg, Ruth L(angland) 1889-1984 .... *1*
Holbrook, Kathy 1963- *107*
Holbrook, Peter
See Glick, Carl (Cannon)
Holbrook, Sabra
See Erickson, Sabra Rollins
Holbrook, Sara *241*
Earlier sketch in SATA *131*
Holbrook, Stewart Hall 1893-1964 .... *2*
Holcomb, Jerry (Leona) Kimble 1927- *113*
Holcomb, Nan
See McPhee, Norma H.
Holdcroft, Tina *227*
Holden, Elizabeth Rhoda
See Lawrence, Louise
Holder, Jimmy 1962- *234*
Holding, James (Clark Carlisle, Jr.)
1907-1997 .... *3*
Hole, Stian 1969- *204*

Holeman, Linda 1949- *136*
Autobiography Feature *136*
Earlier sketch in SATA *102*
Holgate, Doug *225*
Holinger, William (Jacques) 1944- *90*
Holisher, Desider 1901-1972 .... *6*
Holl, Adelaide Hinkle 1910- *8*
Holl, Kristi
See Holl, Kristi D.
Holl, Kristi D. 1951- *51*
Holl, Kristi Diane
See Holl, Kristi D.
Holland, Gay W. 1941- *128*
Holland, Isabelle (Christian) 1920-2002 .... *70*
Autobiography Feature *103*
Obituary *132*
Earlier sketch in SATA *8*
See also CLR *57*
Holland, Janice 1913-1962 .... *18*
Holland, John L(ewis) 1919- *20*
Holland, Joyce
See Morice, Dave
Holland, Julia 1954- *106*
Holland, Lynda (H.) 1959- *77*
Holland, Lys
See Gater, Dilys
Holland, Marion 1908-1989 .... *6*
Obituary *61*
Holland, Richard 1976- *216*
Holland, Trish *221*
Hollander, John 1929- *13*
Hollander, Nicole 1940(?)- *101*
Hollander, Paul
See Silverberg, Robert
Hollander, Phyllis 1928- *39*
Hollander, Zander 1923- *63*
Holldobler, Turid 1939- *26*
Holliday, Joe
See Holliday, Joseph
Holliday, Joseph 1910- *11*
Hollihan, Kerrie Logan *235*
Holling, Holling C(lancy) 1900-1973 .... *15*
Obituary *26*
See also CLR *50*
Hollingsworth, Alvin C(arl) 1930- *39*
Hollingsworth, Mary 1947- *166*
Earlier sketch in SATA *91*
Holloway, Teresa (Bragunier) 1906- *26*
Hollyer, Beatrice 1957- *226*
Hollyer, Belinda *204*
Holm, (Else) Anne (Lise) 1922-1998 .... *1*
See also CLR *75*
See also SAAS *7*
Holm, Jennifer L. 1968(?)- *236*
Earlier sketches in SATA *120, 163, 183*
Holm, Matthew 1974- *174*
Holm, Sharon Lane 1955- *114*
Earlier sketch in SATA *78*
Holman, Felice 1919- *82*
Earlier sketch in SATA *7*
See also SAAS *17*
Holm and Hamel
See Holm, Jennifer L.
Holmberg, Bo R. 1945- *203*
Holme, Bryan 1913-1990 .... *26*
Obituary *66*
Holmes, Barbara Ware 1945- *127*
Earlier sketch in SATA *65*
Holmes, Elizabeth 1957- *191*
Holmes, Elizabeth Ann
See Holmes, Elizabeth
Holmes, John
See Souster, (Holmes) Raymond
Holmes, Liz
See Holmes, Elizabeth
Holmes, Marjorie (Rose) 1910-2002 .... *43*
Holmes, Martha 1961- *72*
Holmes, Mary Tavener 1954- *199*
Holmes, Mary Z(astrow) 1943- *80*
Holmes, Oliver Wendell 1809-1894 .... *34*
Holmes, Peggy 1898- *60*
Holmes, Raymond
See Souster, (Holmes) Raymond
Holmes, Rick
See Hardwick, Richard Holmes, Jr.
Holmes, Sara Lewis *186*
Holmgren, Helen Jean 1930- *45*
Holmgren, Sister George Ellen
See Holmgren, Helen Jean
Holmgren, Virginia C(unningham) 1909- *26*
Holmquist, Eve 1921- *11*
Holt, K.A.
See Roy, Kari Anne
Holt, Kimberly Willis 1960- *223*
Earlier sketches in SATA *122, 179*
Holt, Margaret 1937- *4*
Holt, Margaret Van Vechten (Saunders)
1899-1963 .... *32*
Holt, Michael (Paul) 1929- *13*
Holt, Rackham
See Holt, Margaret Van Vechten (Saunders)
Holt, Rochelle L.
See DuBois, Rochelle Holt
Holt, Stephen
See Thompson, Harlan
Holt, Victoria
See Hibbert, Eleanor Alice Burford
Holtei, Christa 1953- *214*
Holton, Leonard
See Wibberley, Leonard
Holtz, Thomas R., Jr. 1965- *203*
Holtze, Sally Holmes 1952- *64*
Holtzman, Jerome 1926-2008 .... *57*
Obituary *194*
Holub, Joan 1956- *229*
Earlier sketches in SATA *99, 149*
Holub, Josef 1926- *175*
Holubitsky, Katherine 1955- *165*
Earlier sketch in SATA *121*
Holyer, Erna Maria 1925- *22*
Holyer, Ernie
See Holyer, Erna Maria
Holyfield, John 1969- *227*
Holz, Loretta 1943- *17*
Holz, Loretta Marie
See Holz, Loretta
Homel, David 1952- *97*
Homze, Alma C. 1932- *17*
Honey, Elizabeth 1947- *137*
Autobiography Feature *137*
Earlier sketch in SATA *112*
Honeycutt, Natalie 1945- *97*
Hong, Lily Toy 1958- *76*
Hong, Maxine Ting Ting
See Kingston, Maxine Hong
Honig, Donald 1931- *18*
Honig, Donald Martin
See Honig, Donald
Honness, Elizabeth H. 1904- *2*
Hoobler, Dorothy 1941- *161*
Earlier sketches in SATA *28, 109*
Hoobler, Thomas *161*
Earlier sketches in SATA *28, 109*
Hood, Joseph F. 1925- *4*
Hood, Robert E. 1926- *21*
Hood, Sarah
See Killough, (Karen) Lee
Hook, Brendan 1963- *105*
Hook, Frances 1912-1983 .... *27*
Hook, Geoffrey R(aynor) 1928- *103*
Hook, Jeff
See Hook, Geoffrey R(aynor)
Hook, Martha 1936- *27*
Hooker, Richard
See Heinz, W. C.
Hooker, Ruth 1920-1998 .... *21*
hooks, bell 1952(?)- *170*
Earlier sketch in SATA *115*
Hooks, William H(arris) 1921- *94*
Earlier sketch in SATA *16*
Hoon, Patricia Easterly 1954- *90*
Hooper, Byrd
See St. Clair, Byrd Hooper
Hooper, Mary 1948- *205*
Earlier sketch in SATA *160*
Hooper, Maureen Brett 1927- *76*
Hooper, Meredith 1939- *159*
Earlier sketches in SATA *28, 101*
Hooper, Meredith Jean
See Hooper, Meredith
Hooper, Patricia 1941- *95*
Hoopes, Lyn Littlefield 1953- *49*
Brief entry *44*
Hoopes, Ned E(dward) 1932- *21*
Hoopes, Roy 1922-2009 .... *11*
Hoose, Phillip 1947- *215*
Earlier sketch in SATA *137*
Hoover, H(elen) M(ary) 1935- *132*
Brief entry *33*
Earlier sketches in SATA *44, 83*
See also SAAS *8*
Hoover, Helen (Drusilla Blackburn)
1910-1984 .... *12*
Obituary *39*
Hopcus, Anastasia *234*
Hope, Christopher 1944- *62*
Hope, Christopher David Tully
See Hope, Christopher
Hope, Laura Lee
See Goulart, Ron
and Stanley, George Edward
Hope Simpson, Jacynth 1930- *12*
Hopf, Alice (Martha) L(ightner) 1904-1988 .... *5*
Obituary *55*
Hopgood, Tim 1961- *224*
Hopkins, A. T.
See Turngren, Annette
Hopkins, C. M.
See Hopkins, Cathy
Hopkins, Cathy 1953- *165*
Hopkins, Cathy M.
See Hopkins, Cathy
Hopkins, Clark 1895-1976
Obituary *34*
Hopkins, Ellen 1955- *128*
Hopkins, Ellen L.
See Hopkins, Ellen
Hopkins, Jackie
See Hopkins, Jackie Mims
Hopkins, Jackie Mims 1952- *178*
Earlier sketch in SATA *92*
Hopkins, Joseph G(erard) E(dward) 1909- *11*
Hopkins, (Hector) Kenneth 1914-1988
Obituary *58*
Hopkins, Lee Bennett 1938- *215*
Earlier sketches in SATA *3, 68, 125, 168*
See also CLR *44*
See also SAAS *4*
Hopkins, Lyman
See Folsom, Franklin (Brewster)
Hopkins, Marjorie 1911-1999 .... *9*
Hopkins, Mary R(ice) 1956- *97*
Hopkinson, Amanda 1948- *84*
Hopkinson, Deborah 1952- *216*
Autobiography Feature *180*
Earlier sketches in SATA *76, 108, 159, 180*
See also CLR *118*
Hopman, Philip 1961- *177*
Hoppe, Joanne 1932- *42*
Hoppe, Matthias 1952- *76*
Hoppe, Paul *209*
Hopper, Nancy J. 1937- *38*
Brief entry *35*
Hoppey, Tim 1958- *225*
Hopping, Lorraine Jean
See Egan, Lorraine Hopping
Horacek, Judy 1961- *211*
Horacek, Petr *214*
Earlier sketch in SATA *163*
Horenstein, Henry 1947- *108*

Horgan, Paul (George Vincent O'Shaughnessy) 1903-1995 ... *13*
Obituary ... *84*
Horlak, E.E.
See Tepper, Sheri S.
Horler, Sydney 1888-1954 ... *102*
Horley, Alex 1970- ... *229*
Horn, Sandra Ann 1944- ... *154*
Hornblow, Arthur, Jr. 1893-1976 ... *15*
Hornblow, Leonora 1920-2005 ... *18*
Obituary ... *171*
Hornblow, Leonora Schinasi
See Hornblow, Leonora
Horne, Constance 1927- ... *149*
Horne, Richard 1960-2007 ... *169*
Obituary ... *180*
Earlier sketch in SATA *111*
Horne, Richard Henry Hengist 1802(?)-1884 ... *29*
Horner, Althea (Jane) 1926- ... *36*
Horner, Dave 1934- ... *12*
Horner, Emily 1982- ... *233*
Horner, Jack 1946- ... *106*
Horner, John R.
See Horner, Jack
Horner, John Robert
See Horner, Jack
Hornik, Laurie Miller ... *159*
Horniman, Joanne 1951- ... *167*
Earlier sketch in SATA *98*
Hornos, Axel 1907-1994 ... *20*
Hornstein, Reuben Aaron 1912- ... *64*
Horowitz, Anthony 1955- ... *236*
Earlier sketches in SATA *137, 195*
Horowitz, Dave 1970- ... *204*
Earlier sketch in SATA *172*
Horowitz, Eli ... *230*
Horowitz, Ruth 1957- ... *136*
Horrocks, Anita 1958- ... *169*
Horse, Harry
See Horne, Richard
Horsfield, Alan 1939- ... *153*
Horstman, Lisa 1964- ... *219*
Hort, Lenny ... *179*
Horton, James O. 1943- ... *173*
Horton, James Oliver
See Horton, James O.
Horton, Joan ... *217*
Horton, Madelyn (Stacey) 1962- ... *77*
Horvath, Betty 1927- ... *4*
Horvath, David 1972(?)- ... *192*
Horvath, Polly 1957- ... *194*
Earlier sketches in SATA *85, 140*
See also CLR *90*
Horwich, Frances R(appaport) 1908-2001 ... *11*
Obituary ... *130*
Horwitz, Elinor Lander ... *45*
Brief entry ... *33*
Horwood, William 1944- ... *85*
Hosford, Dorothy (Grant) 1900-1952 ... *22*
Hosford, Jessie 1892-1990 ... *5*
Hoshi, Shin'ichi 1926- ... *101*
Hoshino, Felicia 1968- ... *189*
Hoskyns-Abrahall, Clare (Constance Drury) ... *13*
Hosler, Danamarie 1978- ... *184*
Hossack, Sylvia 1939- ... *83*
Hossack, Sylvie Adams
See Hossack, Sylvia
Hosseini, Khaled 1965- ... *156*
Hossell, Karen Price
See Price, Karen
Hosta, Dar ... *192*
Hostetler, Marian 1932- ... *91*
Hostetter, Joyce Moyer 1952- ... *228*
Houck, Carter 1924- ... *22*
Houck, Colleen 1969- ... *239*
Hough, Charlotte 1924-2008 ... *9*
Obituary ... *202*
Hough, Helen Charlotte
See Hough, Charlotte
Hough, Judy Taylor 1932- ... *63*
Brief entry ... *51*
Earlier sketch in SATA *56*
Hough, Richard (Alexander) 1922-1999 ... *17*
Houghton, Eric 1930- ... *7*
Houk, Randy 1944- ... *97*
Houlehen, Robert J. 1918- ... *18*
Houlton, Peggy Mann 1925(?)-1990 ... *6*
Household, Geoffrey 1900-1988 ... *14*
Obituary ... *59*
Housman, Laurence 1865-1959 ... *25*
Houston, Dick 1943- ... *231*
Earlier sketch in SATA *74*
Houston, Gloria ... *138*
Autobiography Feature ... *138*
Earlier sketch in SATA *81*
Houston, James A(rchibald) 1921-2005 ... *74*
Obituary ... *163*
Earlier sketch in SATA *13*
See also CLR *3*
See also SAAS *17*
Houston, James D. 1933-2009 ... *78*
Obituary ... *203*
Houston, James Dudley
See Houston, James D.
Houston, James Dudley
See Houston, James D.
Houston, Jeanne Toyo Wakatsuki
See Houston, Jeanne Wakatsuki
Houston, Jeanne Wakatsuki 1934- ... *168*
Autobiography Feature ... *168*
Earlier sketch in SATA *78*
Houston, Juanita C. 1921- ... *129*
Houtman, Jacqueline 1960- ... *231*
Houtman, Jacqueline Jaeger
See Houtman, Jacqueline
Houton, Kathleen
See Kilgore, Kathleen
Houts, Amy F. ... *164*
Houts, Michelle ... *219*
Hovey, Kate ... *158*
Howard, Alan 1922- ... *45*
Howard, Alyssa
See Buckholtz, Eileen (Garber)
and Glick, Ruth
and Titchener, Louise
Howard, Arthur 1948- ... *212*
Earlier sketch in SATA *165*
Howard, Arthur Charles
See Howard, Arthur
Howard, Elizabeth Fitzgerald 1927- ... *119*
Earlier sketch in SATA *74*
Howard, Ellen 1943- ... *184*
Earlier sketches in SATA *67, 99*
Howard, Jane R(uble) 1924- ... *87*
Howard, Norman Barry 1949- ... *90*
Howard, P. M.
See Howard, Pauline Rodriguez
Howard, Paul 1967- ... *190*
Earlier sketch in SATA *118*
Howard, Pauline Rodriguez 1951- ... *124*
Howard, Prosper
See Hamilton, Charles (Harold St. John)
Howard, Robert West 1908-1988 ... *5*
Howard, Todd 1964- ... *135*
Howard, Tristan
See Currie, Stephen
Howard, Vernon (Linwood) 1918-1992 ... *40*
Obituary ... *73*
Howard, Warren F.
See Pohl, Frederik
Howarth, Daniel ... *222*
Earlier sketch in SATA *188*
Howarth, David (Armine) 1912-1991 ... *6*
Obituary ... *68*
Howarth, Lesley 1952- ... *94*
Howe, Deborah 1946-1978 ... *29*
Howe, James 1946- ... *224*
Earlier sketches in SATA *29, 71, 111, 161*
See also CLR *9*
Howe, John F. 1957- ... *79*
Howe, Norma 1930-2011 ... *126*
Howe, Peter 1942- ... *214*
Howell, Pat 1947- ... *15*
Howell, S.
See Styles, (Frank) Showell
Howell, Simmone 1971- ... *214*
Howell, Virginia
See Ellison, Virginia H(owell)
Howells, Amanda
See Gersh, Amanda
Howells, Tania ... *229*
Howes, Barbara 1914-1996 ... *5*
Howie, Betsy 1962- ... *215*
Howie, Diana 1945- ... *122*
Howie, Diana Melson
See Howie, Diana
Howker, Janni 1957- ... *72*
Brief entry ... *46*
See also CLR *14*
See also SAAS *13*
Howland, Ethan 1963- ... *131*
Howland, Naomi ... *232*
Hoxter, Holly Nicole 1983- ... *231*
Hoy, Linda 1946- ... *65*
Hoy, Nina
See Roth, Arthur J(oseph)
Hoyle, Geoffrey 1942- ... *18*
Hoyt, Ard ... *190*
Hoyt, Edwin P(almer), Jr. 1923- ... *28*
Hoyt, Erich 1950- ... *140*
Earlier sketch in SATA *65*
Hoyt, Olga
See Gruhzit-Hoyt, Olga (Margaret)
Hrdlitschka, Shelley 1956- ... *167*
Earlier sketch in SATA *111*
Hrdlitschka, Shelley Joanne
See Hrdlitschka, Shelley
Hromic, Alma A.
See Alexander, Alma
Htin Aung, U.
See Aung, (Maung) Htin
Hu, Ying-Hwa ... *173*
Huang, Benrei 1959- ... *86*
Huang, Nathan 1982(?)- ... *228*
Hubalek, Linda K. 1954- ... *111*
Hubbard, Crystal ... *209*
Hubbard, Jennifer R. ... *227*
Hubbard, Kirsten 1983- ... *241*
Hubbard, Margaret Ann
See Priley, Margaret (Ann) Hubbard
Hubbard, Michelle Calabro 1953- ... *122*
Hubbard, Patricia 1945- ... *124*
Hubbard, Woodleigh Marx ... *160*
Earlier sketch in SATA *98*
Hubbell, Patricia 1928- ... *186*
Earlier sketches in SATA *8, 132*
Hubery, Julia ... *195*
Hubley, Faith Elliot 1924-2001 ... *48*
Obituary ... *133*
Hubley, John 1914-1977 ... *48*
Obituary ... *24*
Huck, Charlotte S. 1922- ... *136*
Earlier sketch in SATA *82*
Hucke, Johannes 1966- ... *218*
Hudak, Michal 1956- ... *143*
Hudson, Cheryl Willis 1948- ... *237*
Earlier sketches in SATA *81, 160*
Hudson, Jan 1954-1990 ... *77*
See also CLR *40*
Hudson, Jeffery
See Crichton, Michael
Hudson, Jeffrey
See Crichton, Michael
Hudson, (Margaret) Kirsty 1947- ... *32*
Hudson, Margaret
See Shuter, Jane (Margaret)
Hudson, W(illiam) H(enry) 1841-1922 ... *35*
Hudson, Wade 1946- ... *162*
Earlier sketch in SATA *74*
Huelsmann, Eva 1928- ... *16*

Huerlimann, Bettina 1909-1983 ... *39*
Obituary ... *34*
Huerlimann, Ruth 1939- ... *32*
Brief entry ... *31*
Huff, Barbara A. 1929- ... *67*
Huff, Tanya 1957- ... *171*
Earlier sketch in SATA *85*
Huff, Tanya Sue
See Huff, Tanya
Huff, T.S.
See Huff, Tanya
Huff, Vivian 1948- ... *59*
Huffaker, Sandy 1943- ... *10*
Huffman, Tom ... *24*
Huggins, Nathan Irvin 1927-1989 ... *63*
Huggins, Peter 1951- ... *178*
Hughes, Carol 1955- ... *217*
Earlier sketch in SATA *108*
Hughes, Dean 1943- ... *235*
Earlier sketches in SATA *33, 77, 139*
See also CLR *76*
Hughes, D.T.
See Hughes, Dean
Hughes, Eden
See Griffin, W. E. B.
Hughes, Edward James
See Hughes, Ted
Hughes, James Langston
See Hughes, Langston
Hughes, Langston 1902-1967 ... *33*
Earlier sketch in SATA *4*
See also CLR *17*
Hughes, Libby ... *71*
Hughes, Mark Peter ... *238*
Hughes, Matilda
See MacLeod, Charlotte (Matilda)
Hughes, Monica 1925-2003 ... *162*
Earlier sketches in SATA *15, 70, 119*
See also CLR *60*
See also SAAS *11*
Hughes, Monica Ince
See Hughes, Monica
Hughes, Pat ... *197*
Hughes, Richard (Arthur Warren)
1900-1976 ... *8*
Obituary ... *25*
Hughes, Sara
See Saunders, Susan
Hughes, Shirley 1927- ... *159*
Earlier sketches in SATA *16, 70, 110*
See also CLR *15*
Hughes, Susan 1960- ... *216*
Hughes, Ted 1930-1998 ... *49*
Brief entry ... *27*
Obituary ... *107*
See also CLR *131*
Hughes, Thomas 1822-1896 ... *31*
See also CLR *160*
Hughes, Virginia
See Campbell, Hope
Hughes, Walter (Llewellyn) 1910-1993 ... *26*
Hughey, Roberta 1942- ... *61*
Hugo, Pierre Brackers de
See Brackers de Hugo, Pierre
Hugo, Victor 1802-1885 ... *47*
Hugo, Victor Marie
See Hugo, Victor
Huline-Dickens, Frank William 1931- ... *34*
Huling, Jan ... *172*
Huliska-Beith, Laura ... *232*
Earlier sketch in SATA *175*
Hull, Eleanor (Means) 1913- ... *21*
Hull, Eric Traviss
See Harnan, Terry
Hull, H. Braxton
See Jacobs, Helen Hull
Hull, Jesse Redding
See Hull, Jessie Redding
Hull, Jessie Redding 1932- ... *51*
Hull, Katharine 1921-1977 ... *23*
Hull, Lise (E.) 1954- ... *148*
Hull, Maureen 1949- ... *142*
Hulme, Joy N. 1922- ... *161*
Earlier sketches in SATA *74, 112*
Hults, Dorothy Niebrugge 1898-2000 ... *6*
Humble, Richard 1945- ... *60*
Hume, Lachie ... *189*
Hume, Lotta Carswell ... *7*
Hume, Ruth Fox 1922-1980 ... *26*
Obituary ... *22*
Hume, Stephen Eaton 1947- ... *136*
Hummel, Berta 1909-1946 ... *43*
Hummel, Sister Maria Innocentia
See Hummel, Berta
Hummon, Marcus 1960- ... *213*
Humphrey, Carol Sue 1956- ... *167*
Humphrey, Henry (III) 1930- ... *16*
Humphrey, Kate
See Forsyth, Kate
Humphrey, Sandra McLeod 1936- ... *95*
Humphreys, Martha 1943- ... *71*
Humphreys, Susan L.
See Lowell, Susan
Humphries, Tudor 1953- ... *226*
Hundal, Nancy 1957- ... *128*
Huneck, Stephen 1949- ... *183*
Earlier sketch in SATA *129*
Hungerford, Hesba Fay
See Brinsmead, H(esba) F(ay)
Hungerford, Pixie
See Brinsmead, H(esba) F(ay)
Hunkin, Tim 1950- ... *53*
Hunkin, Timothy Mark Trelawney
See Hunkin, Tim
Hunt, Angela Elwell 1957- ... *159*
Earlier sketch in SATA *75*
Hunt, Bernice 1920- ... *4*
Hunt, Charlotte Dumaresq
See Demi
Hunt, Francesca
See Holland, Isabelle (Christian)
Hunt, Irene 1907-2001 ... *91*
Earlier sketch in SATA *2*
See also CLR *1*
Hunt, Janie Louise 1963- ... *102*
Hunt, Jonathan 1966- ... *84*
Hunt, Joyce 1927- ... *31*
Hunt, Linda 1940- ... *39*
Hunt, Lisa B(ehnke) 1967- ... *84*
Hunt, Mabel Leigh 1892-1971 ... *1*
Obituary ... *26*
Hunt, Morton M(agill) 1920- ... *22*
Hunt, Nigel
See Greenbank, Anthony Hunt
Hunt, Peter (Leonard) 1945- ... *76*
Hunter, Anne B. 1966- ... *118*
Hunter, Bernice Thurman 1922-2002 ... *85*
Brief entry ... *45*
Hunter, Bobbi Dooley 1945- ... *89*
Hunter, Captain Marcy
See Ellis, Edward S.
Hunter, Chris
See Fluke, Joanne
Hunter, Clingham M.D.
See Adams, William Taylor
Hunter, Edith Fisher 1919- ... *31*
Hunter, Erin
See Cary, Kate
Hunter, Evan 1926-2005 ... *25*
Obituary ... *167*
Hunter, George E.
See Ellis, Edward S.
Hunter, Hilda 1921- ... *7*
Hunter, Jana
See Hunter, Jana Novotny
Hunter, Jana Novotny ... *190*
Hunter, Jim 1939- ... *65*
Hunter, Kristin
See Lattany, Kristin Hunter
Hunter, Leigh
See Etchison, Birdie L(ee)
Hunter, Lieutenant Ned
See Ellis, Edward S.
Hunter, Linzie 1979- ... *227*
Hunter, Mel 1927-2004 ... *39*
Hunter, Mollie 1922- ... *139*
Autobiography Feature ... *139*
Earlier sketches in SATA *2, 54, 106*
See also CLR *25*
See also SAAS *7*
Hunter, Ned
See Ellis, Edward S.
Hunter, Norman (George Lorimer)
1899-1995 ... *84*
Earlier sketch in SATA *26*
Hunter, Ryan Ann
See Greenwood, Pamela D.
and Macalaster, Elizabeth G.
Hunter, Sara Hoagland 1954- ... *98*
Hunter Blair, Pauline
See Clarke, Pauline
Huntington, Amy 1956- ... *180*
Earlier sketch in SATA *138*
Huntington, Geoffrey ... *145*
Huntington, Harriet E(lizabeth) 1909- ... *1*
Huntley, Amy ... *225*
Huntsberry, William E(mery) 1916- ... *5*
Hurd, Clement (G.) 1908-1988 ... *64*
Obituary ... *54*
Earlier sketch in SATA *2*
See also CLR *49*
Hurd, Edith Thacher 1910-1997 ... *64*
Obituary ... *95*
Earlier sketch in SATA *2*
See also CLR *49*
See also SAAS *13*
Hurd, John Thacher
See Hurd, Thacher
Hurd, Thacher 1949- ... *219*
Autobiography Feature ... *123*
Brief entry ... *45*
Earlier sketches in SATA *46, 94*
Hurley, Jo
See Dower, Laura
Hurley, Tonya ... *207*
Hurlimann, Bettina
See Huerlimann, Bettina
Hurlimann, Ruth
See Huerlimann, Ruth
Hurmence, Belinda 1921- ... *77*
See also CLR *25*
See also SAAS *20*
Hurst, Carol Otis 1933-2007 ... *185*
Earlier sketch in SATA *130*
Hurt-Newton, Tania 1968- ... *84*
Hurwin, Davida Wills 1950- ... *180*
Hurwitz, Johanna 1937- ... *175*
Earlier sketches in SATA *20, 71, 113*
See also SAAS *18*
Hurwood, Bernhardt J. 1926-1987 ... *12*
Obituary ... *50*
Husain, Shahrukh 1950- ... *108*
Huser, Glen 1943- ... *151*
Hutchens, Paul 1902-1977 ... *31*
Hutchins, Carleen M.
See Hutchins, Carleen Maley
Hutchins, Carleen Maley 1911-2009 ... *9*
Obituary ... *206*
Hutchins, Hazel J. 1952- ... *175*
Brief entry ... *51*
Earlier sketches in SATA *81, 135*
See also SAAS *24*
Hutchins, Pat 1942- ... *178*
Earlier sketches in SATA *15, 70, 111*
See also CLR *20*
See also SAAS *16*
Hutchins, Ross Elliott 1906- ... *4*
Hutchison, Linda 1942- ... *152*
Huthmacher, J. Joseph 1929- ... *5*
Hutto, Nelson (Allen) 1904-1985 ... *20*
Hutton, Kathryn 1915- ... *89*

Hutton, Sam
See Jones, Allan Frewin
Hutton, Warwick 1939-1994 ... *20*
Obituary ... *83*
See also SAAS *17*
Huxley, Aldous 1894-1963 ... *63*
See also CLR *151*
Huxley, Aldous Leonard
See Huxley, Aldous
Huxley, Elspeth (Josceline Grant) 1907-1997 ... *62*
Obituary ... *95*
Hyde, Catherine ... *232*
Hyde, Catherine R.
See Hyde, Catherine Ryan
Hyde, Catherine Ryan 1955- ... *224*
Earlier sketch in SATA *141*
Hyde, Dayton O(gden) ... *9*
Hyde, Hawk
See Hyde, Dayton O(gden)
Hyde, Jeannette
See Eyerly, Jeannette
Hyde, Margaret O. 1917- ... *139*
Earlier sketches in SATA *1, 42, 76*
See also CLR *23*
See also SAAS *8*
Hyde, Margaret Oldroyd
See Hyde, Margaret O.
Hyde, Shelley
See Reed, Kit
Hyde, Wayne Frederick 1922- ... *7*
Hylander, Clarence J(ohn) 1897-1964 ... *7*
Hyman, Miles 1962- ... *210*
Hyman, Paula Chase
See Chase, Paula
Hyman, Robin 1931- ... *12*
Hyman, Robin Phiilip
See Hyman, Robin
Hyman, Trina Schart 1939-2004 ... *95*
Obituary ... *158*
Earlier sketches in SATA *7, 46*
See also CLR *50*
Hymes, Lucia M(anley) 1907-1998 ... *7*
Hyndman, Jane Andrews Lee 1912-1978 ... *46*
Obituary ... *23*
Earlier sketch in SATA *1*
Hyndman, Robert Utley 1906-1973 ... *18*
Hynes, Pat ... *98*

I

Iannone, Jeanne
See Balzano, Jeanne (Koppel)
Ibatoulline, Bagram 1965(?)- ... *225*
Earlier sketch in SATA *174*
Ibbitson, John Perrie 1955- ... *102*
Ibbotson, Eva 1925-2010 ... *221*
Earlier sketches in SATA *13, 103, 156*
Ibbotson, M. C(hristine) 1930- ... *5*
Icenoggle, Jodi 1967- ... *168*
Icenoggle, Jodi O.
See Icenoggle, Jodi
Ichikawa, Satomi 1949- ... *208*
Brief entry ... *36*
Earlier sketches in SATA *47, 78, 146*
See also CLR *62*
Idle, Molly Schaar ... *223*
Iggulden, Hal 1972- ... *196*
Ignatow, Amy 1977- ... *233*
Ignoffo, Matthew 1945- ... *92*
Igus, Toyomi 1953- ... *112*
Earlier sketch in SATA *76*
Ihimaera, Witi (Tame) 1944- ... *148*
Ikeda, Daisaku 1928- ... *77*
Ilowite, Sheldon A. 1931- ... *27*
Ilsey, Dent
See Chapman, John Stanton Higham
Ilsley, Dent
See Chapman, John Stanton Higham
Ilsley, Velma (Elizabeth) 1918- ... *12*
Imai, Ayano 1980- ... *190*
Imai, Miko 1963- ... *90*
Imershein, Betsy 1953- ... *62*
Immel, Mary Blair 1930- ... *28*
Immell, Myra H. 1941- ... *92*
Impey, Rose 1947- ... *223*
Earlier sketches in SATA *69, 152*
Ingalls, Ann ... *227*
Ingelow, Jean 1820-1897 ... *33*
Ingermanson, Randall 1958- ... *134*
Ingermanson, Randy
See Ingermanson, Randall
Ingersoll, Norman 1928- ... *79*
Ingham, Colonel Frederic
See Hale, Edward Everett
Ingman, Bruce 1963- ... *182*
Earlier sketch in SATA *134*
Ingman, Nicholas 1948- ... *52*
Ingold, Jeanette ... *128*
Ingpen, Robert 1936- ... *166*
Earlier sketch in SATA *109*
Ingpen, Robert Roger
See Ingpen, Robert
Ingraham, Erick 1950- ... *145*
Ingraham, Leonard W(illiam) 1913-2003 ... *4*
Ingram, Scott 1948- ... *167*
Earlier sketch in SATA *92*
Ingram, W. Scott
See Ingram, Scott
Ingrams, Doreen 1906-1997 ... *97*
Earlier sketch in SATA *20*
Ingrid, Charles
See Salsitz, Rhondi Vilott
Ingves, Gunilla 1939- ... *101*
Ingves, Gunilla Anna Maria Folkesdotter
See Ingves, Gunilla
Inkpen, Mick 1952- ... *154*
Earlier sketch in SATA *99*
Innerst, Stacy ... *232*
Innes, (Ralph) Hammond
See Hammond Innes, Ralph
Innes, Ralph Hammond
See Hammond Innes, Ralph
Innes, Stephanie ... *220*
Innocenti, Roberto 1940- ... *159*
Earlier sketch in SATA *96*
See also CLR *126*
Innocenti and Gallaz
See Gallaz, Christophe
and Innocenti, Roberto
Inns, Chris ... *212*
Inyart, Gene
See Namovicz, Gene Inyart
Ionesco, Eugene 1909-1994 ... *7*
Obituary ... *79*
Ipcar, Dahlov (Zorach) 1917- ... *147*
Autobiography Feature ... *147*
Earlier sketches in SATA *1, 49*
See also SAAS *8*
Ireland, Karin ... *151*
Earlier sketch in SATA *101*
Ironside, Jetske 1940- ... *60*
Irvin, Fred 1914- ... *15*
Irvine, Georgeanne 1955- ... *72*
Irvine, Joan 1951- ... *80*
Irving, Alexander
See Hume, Ruth Fox
Irving, Robert
See Adler, Irving
Irving, Washington 1783-1859
See YABC *2*
See also CLR *97*
Irwin, Ann(abelle Bowen) 1915-1998 ... *89*
Brief entry ... *38*
Obituary ... *106*
Earlier sketch in SATA *44*
See also CLR *40*
See also SAAS *14*
Irwin, Constance (H.) Frick 1913-1995 ... *6*
Irwin, Hadley
See Hadley, Lee
and Irwin, Ann(abelle Bowen)
Irwin, Keith Gordon 1885-1964 ... *11*
Isaac, Joanne 1934- ... *21*
Isaacs, Anne 1949- ... *185*
Earlier sketch in SATA *90*
Isaacs, Jacob
See Kranzler, George G(ershon)
Isaacson, Philip M(arshal) 1924- ... *87*
Isadora, Rachel 1953(?)- ... *204*
Brief entry ... *32*
Earlier sketches in SATA *54, 79, 121, 165*
See also CLR *7*
Isbell, Rebecca T(emple) 1942- ... *125*
Isham, Charlotte H(ickock) 1912- ... *21*
Ishida, Jui ... *176*
Ish-Kishor, Judith 1892-1972 ... *11*
Ish-Kishor, Sulamith 1896-1977 ... *17*
Ishmael, Woodi 1914-1995 ... *31*
Obituary ... *109*
Isle, Sue 1963- ... *105*
Isol 1972- ... *220*
Israel, Elaine 1945- ... *12*
Israel, Marion Louise 1882-1973
Obituary ... *26*
Iterson, S(iny) R(ose) Van
See Van Iterson, S(iny) R(ose)
Ivanko, John D. 1966- ... *111*
Ivanko, John Duane
See Ivanko, John D.
Iversen, Jeremy 1980(?)- ... *174*
Iversen, Jeremy Watt
See Iversen, Jeremy
Iverson, Carol (L.) 1941- ... *145*
Iverson, Diane 1950- ... *122*
Iverson, Eric G.
See Turtledove, Harry
Ivery, Martha M. 1948- ... *124*
Ives, David 1951- ... *173*
Ives, Morgan
See Bradley, Marion Zimmer
Ives, Penny 1956- ... *215*
Iwai, Melissa ... *183*
Iwamatsu, Jun Atsushi 1908-1994 ... *81*
Earlier sketch in SATA *14*
See also CLR *4*
Iwamura, Kazuo 1939- ... *213*
Iwasaki (Matsumoto), Chihiro 1918-1974
See CLR *18*
Iyengar, Malathi Michelle 1954- ... *220*

J

Jabar, Cynthia ... *210*
Jablonski, Carla ... *184*
Jac, Lee
See Morton, Lee Jack, Jr.
Jack, Colin ... *234*
Jacka, Martin 1943- ... *72*
Jackson, Alison 1953- ... *228*
Earlier sketches in SATA *73, 108, 160*
Jackson, Anne 1896(?)-1984
Obituary ... *37*
Jackson, Barry
See Jackson, Barry E.
Jackson, Barry E. ... *200*
Jackson, C(aary) Paul 1902-1991 ... *6*
Jackson, Caary
See Jackson, C(aary) Paul
Jackson, Charlotte E. (Cobden) 1903(?)-1989
Obituary ... *62*
Jackson, Dave
See Jackson, J. David
Jackson, Donna M. 1959- ... *206*
Jackson, Ellen 1943- ... *214*
Earlier sketches in SATA *75, 115, 167*
Jackson, Ellen B.
See Jackson, Ellen

Jackson, Garnet Nelson 1944- *87*
Jackson, Geoffrey (Holt Seymour) 1915-1987
  Obituary *53*
Jackson, Gina
  See Fluke, Joanne
Jackson, Guida M. 1930- *71*
Jackson, J. David 1944- *91*
Jackson, Jacqueline 1928- *65*
Jackson, Jacqueline Dougan
  See Jackson, Jacqueline
Jackson, Jesse 1908-1983 .... *29*
  Obituary *48*
  Earlier sketch in SATA *2*
  See also CLR *28*
Jackson, Marjorie 1928- *127*
Jackson, Melanie 1956- *141*
Jackson, Mike 1946- *91*
Jackson, Neta J. 1944- *91*
Jackson, O. B.
  See Jackson, C(aary) Paul
Jackson, Rob 1961- *176*
Jackson, Robert B(lake) 1926- *8*
Jackson, Robert Bradley
  See Jackson, Rob
Jackson, Sally
  See Kellogg, Jean (Defrees)
Jackson, Shirley 1919-1965 .... *2*
Jackson, Woody 1948- *92*
Jackson Issa, Kai *205*
Jacob, Helen Pierce 1927- *21*
Jacobin
  See Bisson, Terry
Jacobs, Deborah Lynn *187*
Jacobs, Flora Gill 1918-2006 .... *5*
  Obituary *178*
Jacobs, Francine 1935- *150*
  Brief entry *42*
  Earlier sketch in SATA *43*
Jacobs, Frank 1929- *30*
Jacobs, Helen Hull 1908-1997 .... *12*
Jacobs, Joseph 1854-1916 .... *25*
Jacobs, Judy 1952- *69*
Jacobs, Laurie A. 1956- *89*
Jacobs, Leah
  See Gellis, Roberta
Jacobs, Lee
  See Stone, Tanya Lee
Jacobs, Leland Blair 1907-1992 .... *20*
  Obituary *71*
Jacobs, Linda
  See Altman, Linda Jacobs
Jacobs, Lou(is), Jr. 1921- *2*
Jacobs, Paul DuBois *235*
Jacobs, Shannon K. 1947- *77*
Jacobs, Susan
  See Quinn, Susan
Jacobs, William Jay 1933- *89*
  Earlier sketch in SATA *28*
Jacobsen, Laura *177*
Jacobson, Andrew *235*
Jacobson, Daniel 1923- *12*
Jacobson, Jennifer
  See Jacobson, Jennifer Richard
Jacobson, Jennifer Richard 1958- *233*
  Earlier sketch in SATA *170*
Jacobson, Morris K(arl) 1906- *21*
Jacobson, Rick *170*
Jacobus, Tim 1959- *234*
Jacopetti, Alexandra
  See Hart, Alexandra
Jacques, Brian 1939-2011 .... *176*
  Earlier sketches in SATA *62, 95, 138*
  See also CLR *21*
Jacques, Robin 1920-1995 .... *32*
  Brief entry *30*
  Obituary *86*
  See also SAAS *5*
Jaekel, Susan M. 1948- *89*
Jaffe, Michele *179*
Jaffe, Michele Sharon
  See Jaffe, Michele
Jaffee, Al(lan) 1921- *66*
  Earlier sketch in SATA *37*
Jagendorf, Moritz (Adolf) 1888-1981 .... *2*
  Obituary *24*
Jago 1979- *216*
Jahn, Joseph Michael
  See Jahn, Michael
Jahn, Michael 1943- *28*
Jahn, Mike
  See Jahn, Michael
Jahn-Clough, Lisa 1967- *193*
  Earlier sketches in SATA *88, 152*
Jahsmann, Allan Hart 1916- *28*
Jakes, John 1932- *62*
Jakes, John William
  See Jakes, John
Jalali, Reza *234*
James, Andrew
  See Kirkup, James
James, Ann 1952- *168*
  Earlier sketches in SATA *82, 117*
James, Betsy *183*
James, Bill 1929- *205*
James, B.J.
  See James, Brian
James, Brian 1976- *212*
  Earlier sketch in SATA *140*
James, Bronte
  See Nash, Renea Denise
James, Captain Lew
  See Stratemeyer, Edward L.
James, Charlie 1961- *185*
James, Curtis E. *182*
James, Dynely
  See Mayne, William
James, Edwin
  See Gunn, James E.
James, Elizabeth 1942- *97*
  Earlier sketches in SATA *39, 45, 52*
James, Emily
  See Standiford, Natalie
James, Gordon C. 1973- *195*
James, Harry Clebourne 1896-1978 .... *11*
James, J. Alison 1962- *146*
  Earlier sketch in SATA *83*
James, Josephine
  See Sterne, Emma Gelders
James, Kelle *241*
James, Mary
  See Meaker, Marijane
James, Matt *201*
James, Philip
  See del Rey, Lester
  and Moorcock, Michael
James, Rhian Nest *235*
James, Robin 1953- *50*
James, Robin Irene
  See James, Robin
James, Simon 1961- *202*
James, T. F.
  See Fleming, Thomas
James, Tegan
  See Odgers, Sally Farrell
James, Will(iam Roderick) 1892-1942 .... *19*
Jameson, W. C. 1942- *93*
Jamieson, Ian R.
  See Goulart, Ron
Jamieson, Victoria *218*
Jamiolkowski, Raymond M. 1953- *81*
Jane, Mary Childs 1909-1991 .... *6*
Jane, Pamela *158*
Janeczko, Paul B(ryan) 1945- *155*
  Earlier sketches in SATA *53, 98*
  See also CLR *47*
  See also SAAS *18*
Janes, Edward C. 1908-1984 .... *25*
Janes, Edward Clarence
  See Janes, Edward C.
Janes, J(oseph) Robert 1935- *148*
  Brief entry *50*
  Earlier sketch in SATA *101*
Janeway, Elizabeth (Hall) 1913-2005 .... *19*
Janger, Kathleen N. 1940- *66*
Jango-Cohen, Judith 1955- *208*
Janice
  See Brustlein, Janice Tworkov
Janisch, Heinz 1960- *181*
Janni, Rebecca *229*
Janosch
  See Eckert, Horst
Janover, Caroline (Davis) 1943- *141*
  Earlier sketch in SATA *89*
Janovitz, Marilyn *194*
Jansen, Jared
  See Cebulash, Mel
Janson, Dora Jane (Heineberg) 1916- *31*
Janson, H(orst) W(oldemar) 1913-1982 .... *9*
Jansson, Tove (Marika) 1914-2001 .... *41*
  Earlier sketch in SATA *3*
  See also CLR *125*
Janus, Grete
  See Hertz, Grete Janus
Jaques, Faith 1923-1997 .... *97*
  Earlier sketches in SATA *21, 69*
Jaquith, Priscilla 1908- *51*
Jaramillo, Mari-Luci 1928- *139*
Jarka, Jeff *221*
Jarman, Julia 1946- *198*
  Earlier sketch in SATA *133*
Jarman, Rosemary Hawley 1935- *7*
Jarrell, Mary Von Schrader 1914- *35*
Jarrell, Randall 1914-1965 .... *7*
  See also CLR *111*
Jarrett, Clare 1952- *201*
Jarrett, Roxanne
  See Werner, Herma
Jarrie, Martin 1953- *219*
Jarrow, Gail 1952- *185*
  Earlier sketch in SATA *84*
Jarvis, E.K.
  See Ellison, Harlan
  and Silverberg, Robert
Jarvis, Robin 1963- *181*
Jarzab, Anna 1984- *227*
Jaskol, Julie 1958- *127*
Jasner, W. K.
  See Watson, Jane Werner
Jassem, Kate
  See Oppenheim, Joanne
Jauss, Anne Marie 1902(?)-1991 .... *10*
  Obituary *69*
Javaherbin, Mina *230*
Javernick, Ellen 1938- *217*
  Earlier sketch in SATA *89*
Javins, Marie 1966- *212*
Jay, Alison *196*
Jay, Stacey 1978(?)- *231*
Jayne, Lieutenant R. H.
  See Ellis, Edward S.
Jaynes, Clare
  See Mayer, Jane Rothschild
Jeake, Samuel, Jr.
  See Aiken, Conrad
Jean-Bart, Leslie 1954- *121*
Jeapes, Ben 1965- *174*
Jecan, Gavriel 1962- *200*
Jefferds, Vincent H(arris) 1916- *59*
  Brief entry *49*
Jefferies, (John) Richard 1848-1887 .... *16*
Jeffers, Dawn *189*
Jeffers, Oliver 1977- *213*
  Earlier sketch in SATA *175*
Jeffers, Susan 1942- *202*
  Earlier sketches in SATA *17, 70, 129, 137*
  See also CLR *30*
Jefferson, Sarah
  See Farjeon, (Eve) Annabel
Jeffries, Roderic 1926- *4*
Jeffries, Roderic Graeme
  See Jeffries, Roderic
Jenkin-Pearce, Susie 1943- *80*
Jenkins, A. M. 1961- *174*

Jenkins, Amanda McRaney
See Jenkins, A. M.
Jenkins, Debra Reid
See Reid Jenkins, Debra
Jenkins, Emily 1967- *174*
Earlier sketch in SATA *144*
Jenkins, Jean *98*
Jenkins, Jerry B. 1949- *149*
Jenkins, Jerry Bruce
See Jenkins, Jerry B.
Jenkins, Leonard *189*
Jenkins, Marie M(agdalen) 1909- *7*
Jenkins, Martin 1959- *216*
Jenkins, M.D.
See Jenkins, Martin
Jenkins, Patrick 1955- *72*
Jenkins, Steve 1952- *218*
Earlier sketches in SATA *154, 188*
Jenkins, Ward 1968- *238*
Jenkins, William A(twell) 1922-1998 .... *9*
Jenkyns, Chris 1924- *51*
Jennewein, James *215*
Jennewein, Jim
See Jennewein, James
Jennings, Christopher S. 1971(?)- *201*
Jennings, Coleman A(lonzo) 1933- *64*
Jennings, C.S.
See Jennings, Christopher S.
Jennings, Dana Andrew 1957- *93*
Jennings, Elizabeth (Joan) 1926-2001 .... *66*
Jennings, Gary 1928-1999 .... *9*
Obituary *117*
Jennings, Gary Gayne
See Jennings, Gary
Jennings, Linda 1937- *211*
Jennings, Linda M.
See Jennings, Linda
Jennings, Patrick 1962- *205*
Earlier sketches in SATA *96, 160*
Jennings, Paul 1943- *165*
Earlier sketch in SATA *88*
See also CLR *40*
Jennings, Richard W. 1945- *185*
Earlier sketch in SATA *136*
Jennings, Robert
See Hamilton, Charles (Harold St. John)
Jennings, S. M.
See Meyer, Jerome Sydney
Jennings, Sharon 1954- *231*
Earlier sketch in SATA *95*
Jennings, Sharon Elizabeth
See Jennings, Sharon
Jennison, C. S.
See Starbird, Kaye
Jennison, Keith Warren 1911-1995 .... *14*
Jensen, Kathryn 1949- *81*
Jensen, Kristine Mary 1961- *78*
Jensen, Niels 1927- *25*
Jensen, Vickie (Dee) 1946- *81*
Jensen, Virginia Allen 1927- *8*
Jenson-Elliott, Cynthia L(ouise) 1962- *143*
Jeram, Anita 1965- *219*
Earlier sketches in SATA *71, 102, 154*
Jerman, Jerry 1949- *89*
Jernigan, E. Wesley 1940- *85*
Jernigan, Gisela (Evelyn) 1948- *85*
Jerome, Elaine *228*
Jeschke, Susan 1942- *42*
Brief entry *27*
Jessel, Camilla (Ruth) 1937- *143*
Earlier sketch in SATA *29*
Jessell, Tim *225*
Earlier sketch in SATA *177*
Jessey, Cornelia
See Sussman, Cornelia Silver
Jewel
See Kilcher, Jewel
Jewell, Nancy 1940- *109*
Brief entry *41*
Jewett, Eleanore Myers 1890-1967 .... *5*
Jewett, Sarah Orne 1849-1909 .... *15*
Jewett, Theodora Sarah Orne
See Jewett, Sarah Orne
Jezard, Alison 1919- *57*
Brief entry *34*
Jiang, Cheng An 1943- *109*
Jiang, Ji-li 1954- *101*
Jiang, Zheng An
See Jiang, Cheng An
Jiler, John 1946- *42*
Brief entry *35*
Jimenez, Francisco 1943- *219*
Earlier sketch in SATA *108*
Jinks, Catherine 1963- *207*
Earlier sketches in SATA *94, 155*
Jobb, Jamie 1945- *29*
Jobling, Curtis *131*
Jocelyn, Ann Henning 1948- *92*
Jocelyn, Marthe 1956- *198*
Earlier sketches in SATA *118, 163*
Joerns, Consuelo *44*
Brief entry *33*
Joey D
See Macaulay, Teresa
Johansen, Krista V.
See Johansen, K.V.
Johansen, K.V 1968- *186*
Johansen, K.V. 1968- *186*
Earlier sketch in SATA *129*
Johansson, Philip *163*
John, Antony 1972- *206*
John, Joyce *59*
Johns, Avery
See Cousins, Margaret
Johns, Elizabeth 1943- *88*
Johns, Janetta
See Quin-Harkin, Janet
Johns, Linda 1945- *173*
Johns, W(illiam) E(arle) 1893-1968 .... *55*
Johns, Captain W. E.
See Johns, W(illiam) E(arle)
Johnson, A.
See Johnson, Annabell
Johnson, A. E.
See Johnson, Annabell
and Johnson, Edgar (Raymond)
Johnson, Angela 1961- *188*
Earlier sketches in SATA *69, 102, 150*
See also CLR *33*
Johnson, Annabel
See Johnson, Annabell
Johnson, Annabell 1921- *72*
Earlier sketch in SATA *2*
Johnson, Art 1946- *123*
Johnson, B. F. 1920- *1*
Johnson, Benjamin F., of Boone
See Riley, James Whitcomb
Johnson, Bettye 1858-1919
See Rogers, Bettye
Johnson, Caryn
See Goldberg, Whoopi
Johnson, Caryn E.
See Goldberg, Whoopi
Johnson, Caryn Elaine
See Goldberg, Whoopi
Johnson, Charles R. 1925- *11*
Johnson, Charlotte Buel
See von Wodtke, Charlotte Buel Johnson
Johnson, Christine 1978- *232*
Johnson, Chuck
See Johnson, Charles R.
Johnson, Crockett
See Leisk, David (Johnson)
Johnson, D(ana) William 1945- *23*
Johnson, Daniel Shahid 1954- *73*
Johnson, David
See Johnson, David A.
Johnson, David A. 1951- *191*
Johnson, D.B. 1944- *183*
Earlier sketch in SATA *146*
Johnson, Dianne 1960- *130*
See Johnson, Dinah
Johnson, Dinah *231*
See Johnson, Dianne
Johnson, Dolores 1949- *69*
Johnson, Donald B.
See Johnson, D.B.
Johnson, Dorothy M(arie) 1905-1984 .... *6*
Obituary *40*
Johnson, E(ugene) Harper *44*
Johnson, Edgar (Raymond) 1912-1990 .... *72*
Earlier sketch in SATA *2*
Johnson, Eleanor Murdock 1892-1987
Obituary *54*
Johnson, Elizabeth 1911-1984 .... *7*
Obituary *39*
Johnson, Eric W(arner) 1918-1994 ....
Obituary *82*
Earlier sketch in SATA *8*
Johnson, Evelyne 1922- *20*
Johnson, Fred 19(?)-1982 .... *63*
Johnson, Gaylord 1884-1972 .... *7*
Johnson, Gerald White 1890-1980 .... *19*
Obituary *28*
Johnson, Gillian 1963- *215*
Johnson, Harper
See Johnson, E(ugene) Harper
Johnson, Harriett 1908-1987
Obituary *53*
Johnson, James Ralph 1922- *1*
Johnson, James Weldon 1871-1938 .... *31*
See also CLR *32*
Johnson, Jane 1951- *48*
Johnson, Jen Cullerton 1972- *230*
Johnson, Joan J. 1942- *59*
Johnson, John E(mil) 1929- *34*
Johnson, Johnny 1901-1995
See Johnson, (Walter) Ryerson
Johnson, Kathleen Jeffrie 1950- *186*
Johnson, Kathryn
See Jensen, Kathryn
Johnson, La Verne B(ravo) 1925- *13*
Johnson, Layne *222*
Earlier sketch in SATA *187*
Johnson, Lee Kaiser 1962- *78*
Johnson, Lissa H(alls) 1955- *65*
Johnson, Lois Smith 1894-1993 .... *6*
Johnson, Lois Walfrid 1936- *130*
Earlier sketches in SATA *22, 91*
Johnson, Margaret S(weet) 1893-1964 .... *35*
Johnson, Marguerite Annie
See Angelou, Maya
Johnson, Mary Frances K. 1929(?)-1979
Obituary *27*
Johnson, Maud Battle 1918(?)-1985
Obituary *46*
Johnson, Maureen 1973- *232*
Earlier sketch in SATA *200*
Johnson, Meredith Merrell 1952- *104*
Johnson, Milton 1932- *31*
Johnson, Mo 1966- *234*
Johnson, Neil 1954- *135*
Earlier sketch in SATA *73*
Johnson, Pamela 1949- *71*
Johnson, Patricia Polin 1956- *84*
Johnson, Paul Brett 1947- *132*
Earlier sketch in SATA *83*
Johnson, Rebecca L. 1956- *147*
Earlier sketch in SATA *67*
Johnson, Rick L. 1954- *79*
Johnson, (Walter) Ryerson 1901-1995 .... *10*
Obituary *106*
Johnson, Scott 1952- *119*
Earlier sketch in SATA *76*
Johnson, Sherrie 1948- *87*
Johnson, Shirley K(ing) 1927- *10*
Johnson, Siddie Joe 1905-1977
Obituary *20*
Johnson, Spencer 1938- *145*
Brief entry *38*
Johnson, Stacie
See Myers, Walter Dean

Johnson, Stephen T. 1964- *189*
Earlier sketches in SATA *84, 141*
Johnson, Steve 1960- *230*
Earlier sketch in SATA *177*
Johnson, Sue Kaiser 1963- *78*
Johnson, Sylvia A. *166*
Brief entry *52*
Earlier sketch in SATA *104*
Johnson, Varian 1977- *229*
Johnson, William R. *38*
Johnson, William Weber 1909-1992 .... *7*
Johnson-Feelings, Dianne
See Johnson, Dianne
Johnston, Agnes Christine
See Dazey, Agnes J(ohnston)
Johnston, Annie Fellows 1863-1931 .... *37*
Johnston, Dorothy Grunbock 1915-1979 .... *54*
Johnston, Ginny 1946- *60*
Johnston, H(ugh) A(nthony) S(tephen) 1913-1967 .... *14*
Johnston, Janet 1944- *71*
Johnston, Jeffry W. *188*
Johnston, Johanna 1914(?)-1982 .... *12*
Obituary *33*
Johnston, Julie 1941- *110*
Autobiography Feature *128*
Earlier sketch in SATA *78*
See also CLR *41*
See also SAAS *24*
Johnston, Lynn 1947- *216*
Earlier sketch in SATA *118*
Johnston, Lynn Beverley
See Johnston, Lynn
Johnston, Mark *194*
Johnston, Norma
See St. John, Nicole
Johnston, Portia
See Takakjian, Portia
Johnston, Susan Taylor 1942- *180*
Earlier sketches in SATA *8, 83, 128*
See Johnston, Tony
Johnston, Tim(othy Patrick) 1962- *146*
Johnston, Tony *226*
See Johnston, Susan Taylor
Joinson, Carla *160*
Jolin, Paula *186*
Jolivet, Joelle 1965- *221*
Jonas, Ann 1932- *135*
Brief entry *42*
Earlier sketch in SATA *50*
See also CLR *74*
Jonell, Lynne 1956- *196*
Earlier sketch in SATA *109*
Jones, Adrienne 1915-2000 .... *82*
Earlier sketch in SATA *7*
See also SAAS *10*
Jones, Allan Frewin 1954- *204*
Jones, Annabel
See Lewis, Mary
Jones, Betty Millsaps 1940- *54*
Jones, Carol 1942- *153*
Earlier sketch in SATA *79*
Jones, Carrie 1971- *229*
Earlier sketch in SATA *191*
Jones, Charles M.
See Jones, Chuck
Jones, Charlotte Foltz 1945- *122*
Earlier sketch in SATA *77*
Jones, Chuck 1912-2002 .... *53*
Obituary *133*
Jones, Constance *112*
Jones, Constance A.
See Jones, Constance
Jones, David 1956- *202*
Jones, Diana Wynne 1934-2011 .... *234*
Earlier sketches in SATA *9, 70, 108, 160*
See also CLR *120*
See also SAAS *7*
Jones, Douglas B. *202*
Jones, Douglas C(lyde) 1924-1998 .... *52*
Jones, Elizabeth McDavid *155*
Jones, Elizabeth Orton 1910-2005 .... *18*
Obituary *164*
Jones, Evan 1915-1996 .... *3*
Jones, Frewin
See Jones, Allan Frewin
Jones, Geraldine
See McCaughrean, Geraldine
Jones, Gillingham
See Hamilton, Charles (Harold St. John)
Jones, Gwyneth A. 1952- *159*
Jones, Gwyneth Ann
See Jones, Gwyneth A.
Jones, Harold 1904-1992 .... *14*
Obituary *72*
Jones, Helen Hinckley 1903-1991 .... *26*
Jones, Helen L(ouise) 1903-1973
Obituary *22*
Jones, Hettie 1934- *42*
Brief entry *27*
Jones, Hortense P. 1918- *9*
Jones, J. Sydney 1948- *101*
Jones, Jasmine
See Papademetriou, Lisa
Jones, Jennifer (Berry) 1947- *90*
Jones, Jessie Mae Orton 1887(?)-1983
Obituary *37*
Jones, John R(obert) 1926- *76*
Jones, Jon Sydney
See Jones, J. Sydney
Jones, Judith
See James, Bill
Jones, Kimberly K. 1957- *187*
Jones, Marcia Thornton 1958- *217*
Earlier sketches in SATA *73, 115*
Jones, Martha T(annery) 1931- *130*
Jones, Mary Alice 1898(?)-1980 .... *6*
Jones, McClure *34*
Jones, Noah Z. *182*
Jones, Patrick 1961- *210*
Earlier sketch in SATA *136*
Jones, Penelope 1938- *31*
Jones, Rebecca C(astaldi) 1947- *99*
Earlier sketch in SATA *33*
Jones, Robin D(orothy) 1959- *80*
Jones, Sanford W.
See Thorn, John
Jones, Sylvie *185*
Jones, Sylvie Michelle
See Jones, Sylvie
Jones, Terence Graham Parry 1942- *127*
Brief entry *51*
Earlier sketch in SATA *67*
Jones, Terry
See Jones, Terence Graham Parry
Jones, Tim *237*
Jones, Tim Wynne
See Wynne-Jones, Tim
Jones, Traci L. *186*
Jones, V. M. 1958- *147*
Jones, Veda Boyd 1948- *119*
Jones, Victoria Mary
See Jones, V. M.
Jones, Volcano
See Mitchell, Adrian
Jones, Weyman (B.) 1928- *4*
See also SAAS *11*
Jones, William Glynne
See Glynne-Jones, William
Jonk, Clarence 1906-1987 .... *10*
Jonsberg, Barry 1951- *168*
Joos, Francoise 1956- *78*
Joos, Frederic 1953- *78*
Joosse, Barbara 1949- *220*
Earlier sketches in SATA *52, 96, 164*
Joosse, Barbara M.
See Joosse, Barbara
Joosse, Barbara Monnot
See Joosse, Barbara
Jordan, Alexis Hill
See Glick, Ruth
and Titchener, Louise
Jordan, Anne Devereaux 1943- *80*
Jordan, Chris
See Philbrick, Rodman
Jordan, Deloris *191*
Jordan, Devin *221*
Jordan, Don
See Howard, Vernon (Linwood)
Jordan, Hope Dahle 1905-1995 .... *15*
Jordan, Jael (Michal) 1949- *30*
Jordan, June 1936-2002 .... *136*
Earlier sketch in SATA *4*
See also CLR *10*
Jordan, June Meyer
See Jordan, June
Jordan, Lee
See Scholefield, Alan
Jordan, Martin George 1944- *84*
Jordan, Robert 1948-2007 .... *95*
Jordan, Robert K.
See Jordan, Robert
Jordan, Rosa 1939- *191*
Jordan, Roslyn M. *189*
Jordan, Sherryl 1949- *122*
Earlier sketch in SATA *71*
See also SAAS *23*
Jordan, Shirley 1930- *154*
Jordan, Tanis 1946- *84*
Jordan-Fenton, Christy *239*
Jorgensen, Ivar
See Ellison, Harlan
and Garrett, Randall
Jorgensen, Mary Venn -1995 .... *36*
Jorgensen, Norman 1954- *157*
Jorgenson, Ivar
See Silverberg, Robert
Jorisch, Stephane *178*
Joseph, Anne
See Coates, Anna
Joseph, Danielle 1973- *235*
Joseph, James (Herz) 1924- *53*
Joseph, Joan 1939- *34*
Joseph, Joseph M(aron) 1903-1979 .... *22*
Joseph, Patrick
See O'Malley, Kevin
Josephs, Rebecca
See Talbot, Toby
Josephson, Judith Pinkerton 1943- *198*
Josephus Jitta, Ceseli 1952- *240*
Josh
See Twain, Mark
Joshua, Peter
See Stone, Peter
Joslin, Mary 1953- *176*
Joslin, Sesyle
See Hine, Sesyle Joslin
Joubert, Beverly 1957- *204*
Joubert, Dereck *204*
Journet, Mireille
See Marokvia, Mireille
Joyce, Bill
See Joyce, William
Joyce, J(ames) Avery 1902-1987 .... *11*
Obituary *50*
Joyce, Peter 1937- *127*
Joyce, William 1957- *118*
Brief entry *46*
Earlier sketch in SATA *72*
See also CLR *26*
Joyner, Jerry 1938- *34*
Juan, Ana 1961- *179*
Juarez, Fernando *230*
Juarez, Fernando Lopez
See Juarez, Fernando
Jubb, Sophie *210*
Jubert, Herve *185*
Juby, Susan 1969- *202*
Earlier sketch in SATA *156*
Jucker, Sita 1921- *5*
Judah, Aaron 1923- *118*

Judd, Cyril
See Kornbluth, C(yril) M.
and Merril, Judith
and Pohl, Frederik
Judd, Denis (O'Nan) 1938- ... *33*
Judd, Frances K.
See Benson, Mildred
Jude, Conny ... *81*
Judge, Lita ... *234*
Earlier sketch in SATA *192*
Judson, Clara Ingram 1879-1960 ... *38*
Brief entry ... *27*
Judy, Stephen
See Tchudi, Stephen N.
Judy, Stephen N.
See Tchudi, Stephen N.
Juhasz, Victor 1954- ... *177*
Jukes, Mavis 1947- ... *219*
Brief entry ... *43*
Earlier sketches in SATA *72, 111*
See also SAAS *12*
Jules, Jacqueline 1956- ... *218*
Earlier sketches in SATA *148, 183*
Julesberg, Elizabeth Rider Montgomery
1902-1985 ... *34*
Obituary ... *41*
Earlier sketch in SATA *3*
Julian, Jane
See Wiseman, David
Julian, Russell 1975- ... *237*
Julian, Sean ... *236*
Jumpp, Hugo
See MacPeek, Walter G.
Junco, Martha Aviles
See Aviles, Martha
Jungman, Ann ... *165*
Jupo, Frank J. 1904-1981 ... *7*
Jurmain, Suzanne 1945- ... *169*
Earlier sketch in SATA *72*
Jurmain, Suzanne Tripp
See Jurmain, Suzanne
Juster, Norton 1929- ... *220*
Earlier sketches in SATA *3, 132*
See also CLR *112*
Justus, May 1898-1989 ... *1*
Obituary ... *106*
Jutte, Jan 1953- ... *231*
Juvenilia
See Taylor, Ann

K

Kaaberbol, Lene
See Kaaberbol, Lene
Kaaberbol, Lene 1960- ... *159*
Kabdebo, Tamas
See Kabdebo, Thomas
Kabdebo, Thomas 1934- ... *10*
Kabibble, Osh
See Jobb, Jamie
Kacer, Kathy 1954- ... *184*
Earlier sketch in SATA *142*
Kaczman, James ... *156*
Kadair, Deborah Ousley ... *184*
Kade, Stacey ... *234*
Kadefors, Sara 1965- ... *218*
Kadesch, Robert R(udstone) 1922- ... *31*
Kadohata, Cynthia 1956(?)- ... *228*
Earlier sketches in SATA *155, 180*
See also CLR *121*
Kadohata, Cynthia L.
See Kadohata, Cynthia
Kaempfert, Wade
See del Rey, Lester
Kaestner, Erich 1899-1974 ... *14*
See also CLR *153*
Kagawa, Julie ... *228*
Kahl, Jonathan (D.) 1959- ... *77*
Kahl, M(arvin) P(hilip) 1934- ... *37*
Kahl, Virginia (Caroline) 1919-2004 ... *48*
Brief entry ... *38*
Obituary ... *158*
Kahn, Joan 1914-1994 ... *48*
Obituary ... *82*
Kahn, Katherine Janus 1942- ... *220*
Earlier sketches in SATA *90, 167*
Kahn, Peggy
See Katz, Bobbi
Kahn, Roger 1927- ... *37*
Kahukiwa, Robyn 1940- ... *134*
Kains, Josephine
See Goulart, Ron
Kaizuki, Kiyonori 1950- ... *72*
Kajikawa, Kimiko ... *212*
Kakimoto, Kozo 1915- ... *11*
Kalashnikoff, Nicholas 1888-1961 ... *16*
Kalb, Jonah 1926- ... *23*
Kalbacken, Joan 1925- ... *96*
Kalechofsky, Roberta 1931- ... *92*
Kaler, James Otis 1848-1912 ... *15*
Kalis, Jennifer ... *207*
Kalish, Claire M. 1947- ... *92*
Kallen, Stuart A. 1955- ... *126*
Earlier sketch in SATA *86*
Kallen, Stuart Arnold
See Kallen, Stuart A.
Kallevig, Christine Petrell 1955- ... *164*
Kalman, Bobbie 1947- ... *63*
Kalman, Maira 1949- ... *137*
Earlier sketch in SATA *96*
See also CLR *32*
Kalnay, Francis 1899-1992 ... *7*
Kaloustian, Rosanne 1955- ... *93*
Kalow, Gisela 1946- ... *32*
Kalstein, Dave ... *175*
Kamara, Mariatu ... *214*
Kamen, Gloria 1923- ... *98*
Earlier sketch in SATA *9*
Kamerman, Sylvia E.
See Burack, Sylvia K.
Kamm, Josephine (Hart) 1905-1989 ... *24*
Kammerman, Sylvia K.
See Burack, Sylvia K.
Kandel, Michael 1941- ... *93*
Kandell, Alice S. 1938- ... *35*
Kane, Bob 1916-1998 ... *120*
Kane, Henry Bugbee 1902-1971 ... *14*
Kane, Kim 1973(?)- ... *221*
Kane, L. A.
See Mannetti, Lisa
Kane, Robert W. 1910- ... *18*
Kane, Wilson
See Bloch, Robert (Albert)
Kanefield, Teri 1960- ... *135*
Kanell, Beth ... *215*
Kaner, Etta 1947- ... *198*
Earlier sketch in SATA *126*
Kanetzke, Howard W(illiam) 1932- ... *38*
Kangas, Juli 1958- ... *200*
Kann, Elizabeth ... *180*
Kann, Victoria ... *180*
Kanninen, Barbara ... *196*
Kanninen, Barbara J.
See Kanninen, Barbara
Kanoza, Muriel Canfield
See Canfield, Muriel
Kantner, Seth 1965- ... *179*
Kanzawa, Toshiko
See Furukawa, Toshi
Kanzler, John 1963- ... *188*
Kaplan, Andrew 1960- ... *78*
Kaplan, Anne Bernays
See Bernays, Anne
Kaplan, Bess 1927- ... *22*
Kaplan, Boche 1926- ... *24*
Kaplan, Elizabeth 1956- ... *83*
Kaplan, Elizabeth A.
See Kaplan, Elizabeth
Kaplan, Irma 1900- ... *10*
Kaplan, Jean Caryl Korn 1926- ... *10*
Kaplow, Robert 1954- ... *70*
Karageorge, Michael
See Anderson, Poul
Karas, G. Brian 1957- ... *222*
Earlier sketch in SATA *178*
Karas, George Brian
See Karas, G. Brian
Karasz, Ilonka 1896-1981
Obituary ... *29*
Karen, Ruth 1922-1987 ... *9*
Obituary ... *54*
Kark, Nina Mary
See Bawden, Nina
Karl, Herb 1938- ... *73*
Karl, Jean E(dna) 1927-2000 ... *122*
Earlier sketch in SATA *34*
See also SAAS *10*
Karlin, Bernie 1927- ... *68*
Karlin, Eugene 1918- ... *10*
Karlin, Nurit ... *103*
Earlier sketch in SATA *63*
Karlins, Mark 1947- ... *219*
Karnes, Frances A. 1937- ... *110*
Karp, Naomi J. 1926- ... *16*
Karpinski, J. Rick
See Karpinski, John Eric
Karpinski, John Eric 1952- ... *81*
Karpinski, Rick
See Karpinski, John Eric
Karr, Julia ... *239*
Karr, Kathleen 1946- ... *212*
Earlier sketches in SATA *82, 127*
Karr, Phyllis Ann 1944- ... *119*
Karwoski, Gail 1949- ... *127*
Karwoski, Gail Langer
See Karwoski, Gail
Kashiwagi, Isami 1925- ... *10*
Kaslik, Ibi
See Kaslik, Ibolya Emma
Kaslik, Ibolya Emma 1973- ... *185*
Kassem, Lou 1931- ... *62*
Brief entry ... *51*
Kastel, Warren
See Silverberg, Robert
Kastner, Erich
See Kaestner, Erich
Kastner, Jill (Marie) 1964- ... *117*
Earlier sketch in SATA *70*
Kasuya, Masahiro 1937- ... *51*
Kasza, Keiko 1951- ... *191*
Earlier sketch in SATA *124*
Kataphusin
See Ruskin, John
Katchen, Carole 1944- ... *9*
Katcher, Brian 1975- ... *203*
Kate, Lauren 1981- ... *237*
Kathryn
See Searle, Kathryn Adrienne
Kato, Aya 1982- ... *202*
Katona, Robert 1949- ... *21*
Katsarakis, Joan Harries
See Harries, Joan
Katz, Alan ... *231*
Earlier sketch in SATA *185*
Katz, Avi 1949- ... *199*
Katz, Avner 1939- ... *103*
Katz, Bobbi 1933- ... *217*
Earlier sketches in SATA *12, 179*
Katz, Fred(eric Phillip) 1938- ... *6*
Katz, Jane B(resler) 1934- ... *33*
Katz, Karen 1947- ... *232*
Earlier sketches in SATA *158, 195*
Katz, Marjorie P.
See Weiser, Marjorie P(hillis) K(atz)
Katz, Susan 1945- ... *156*
Katz, Welwyn Wilton 1948- ... *96*
Autobiography Feature ... *118*
Earlier sketch in SATA *62*
See also CLR *45*
Katz, William 1940- ... *98*
Katz, William Loren 1927- ... *13*

Kaufman, Bel ... *57*
Kaufman, Jeff 1955- ... *84*
Kaufman, Joe 1911-2001 ... *33*
Kaufman, Joseph
See Kaufman, Joe
Kaufman, Mervyn D. 1932- ... *4*
Kaufmann, Angelika 1935- ... *15*
Kaufmann, John 1931- ... *18*
Kaula, Edna Mason 1906-1987 ... *13*
Kaur Khalsa, Dayal
See Khalsa, Dayal Kaur
Kavaler, Lucy 1930- ... *23*
Kavanagh, Jack 1920- ... *85*
Kavanagh, P(atrick) J(oseph Gregory) 1931- ... *122*
Kavanaugh, Ian
See Webb, Jean Francis (III)
Kay, Alan N. 1965- ... *144*
Kay, Elizabeth 1949- ... *165*
Kay, Guy Gavriel 1954- ... *167*
Earlier sketch in SATA *121*
Kay, Helen
See Goldfrank, Helen Colodny
Kay, Jackie 1961- ... *165*
Earlier sketch in SATA *97*
Kay, Jacqueline Margaret
See Kay, Jackie
Kay, Julia ... *205*
Kay, Mara ... *13*
Kay, Verla 1946- ... *210*
Earlier sketch in SATA *120*
Kaye, Danny 1913-1987
Obituary ... *50*
Kaye, Geraldine (Hughesdon) 1925- ... *85*
Earlier sketch in SATA *10*
Kaye, Judy
See Baer, Judy
Kaye, Marilyn 1949- ... *230*
Earlier sketches in SATA *56, 110*
Kaye, Mary Margaret
See Kaye, M.M.
Kaye, M.M. 1908-2004 ... *62*
Obituary ... *152*
Kaye, Mollie
See Kaye, M.M.
Kaye, Peggy 1948- ... *143*
Keach, James P. 1950- ... *125*
Keams, Geri 1951- ... *117*
Keane, Bil 1922- ... *4*
Keane, Dave 1965- ... *216*
Keaney, Brian 1954- ... *188*
Earlier sketch in SATA *106*
Kearney, Meg 1964- ... *178*
Kearny, Jillian
See Goulart, Ron
Keat, Nawuth 1964- ... *222*
Keating, Bern
See Keating, Leo Bernard
Keating, Frank 1944- ... *143*
Keating, Lawrence A. 1903-1966 ... *23*
Keating, Leo Bernard 1915- ... *10*
Keaton, Kelly ... *241*
Keats, Emma 1899(?)-1979(?) ... *68*
Keats, Ezra Jack 1916-1983 ... *57*
Obituary ... *34*
Earlier sketch in SATA *14*
See also CLR *35*
Keefer, Catherine
See Ogan, George F.
and Ogan, Margaret E. (Nettles)
Keefer, Janice Kulyk
See Kulyk Keefer, Janice
Keegan, Marcia 1943- ... *104*
Earlier sketch in SATA *9*
Keehn, Sally M. 1947- ... *165*
Earlier sketch in SATA *87*
Keel, Frank
See Keeler, Ronald F(ranklin)
Keeler, Patricia ... *183*
Keeler, Patricia A.
See Keeler, Patricia
Keeler, Ronald F(ranklin) 1913-1983 ... *47*
Keely, Jack 1951- ... *119*
Keen, Martin L. 1913-1992 ... *4*
Keenan, Sheila 1953- ... *95*
Keene, Ann T. 1940- ... *86*
Keene, Ann Todd
See Keene, Ann T.
Keene, Carolyn
See Benson, Mildred
and Goulart, Ron
and Lerangis, Peter
and McFarlane, Leslie
and Stanley, George Edward
and Stratemeyer, Edward L.
Keens-Douglas, Richardo 1953- ... *154*
Earlier sketch in SATA *95*
Keep, Linda Lowery
See Lowery, Linda
Keep, Richard 1949- ... *170*
Keep, Richard Cleminson
See Keep, Richard
Keeping, Charles (William James) 1924-1988 ... *69*
Obituary ... *56*
Earlier sketch in SATA *9*
See also CLR *34*
Keeshan, Robert J. 1927-2004 ... *32*
Obituary ... *151*
Keeter, Susan ... *237*
Kehlenbeck, Angela 1959- ... *186*
Kehoe, Tim 1970- ... *224*
Kehret, Peg 1936- ... *212*
Autobiography Feature ... *149*
Earlier sketches in SATA *73, 108, 149*
Keillor, Garrison 1942- ... *58*
Keillor, Gary Edward
See Keillor, Garrison
Keir, Christine
See Pullein-Thompson, Christine
Keiser, Paige ... *220*
Keister, Douglas 1948- ... *88*
Keith, Doug 1952- ... *81*
Keith, Eros 1942- ... *52*
Keith, Hal 1934- ... *36*
Keith, Harold (Verne) 1903-1998 ... *74*
Earlier sketch in SATA *2*
Keith, Robert
See Applebaum, Stan
Keleinikov, Andrei 1924- ... *65*
Kelemen, Julie 1959- ... *78*
Kelen, Emery 1896-1978 ... *13*
Obituary ... *26*
Kelleam, Joseph E(veridge) 1913-1975 ... *31*
Kelleher, Anne 1959- ... *97*
Kelleher, Annette 1950- ... *122*
Kelleher, Daria Valerian 1955- ... *79*
Kelleher, Victor (Michael Kitchener) 1939- ... *129*
Brief entry ... *52*
Earlier sketch in SATA *75*
See also CLR *36*
Keller, Beverly L(ou) ... *91*
Earlier sketch in SATA *13*
Keller, Charles 1942- ... *82*
Earlier sketch in SATA *8*
Keller, Debra 1958- ... *94*
Keller, Dick 1923- ... *36*
Keller, Emily ... *96*
Keller, Gail Faithfull
See Faithfull, Gail
Keller, Holly 1942- ... *216*
Brief entry ... *42*
Earlier sketches in SATA *76, 108, 157*
See also CLR *45*
Keller, Irene (Barron) 1927-2002 ... *36*
Obituary ... *139*
Keller, Laurie 1961(?)- ... *196*
Kelley, Ann 1941- ... *217*
Kelley, Ellen A. ... *185*
Kelley, Ellen Chavez
See Kelley, Ellen A.
Kelley, Gary 1945- ... *217*
Earlier sketch in SATA *183*
Kelley, J.A.
See Kelley, Jane
Kelley, Jane 1954- ... *231*
Kelley, Leo P(atrick) 1928- ... *32*
Brief entry ... *31*
Kelley, Marty 1971- ... *211*
Kelley, Patrick (G.) 1963- ... *129*
Kelley, Patte 1947- ... *93*
Kelley, True 1946- ... *179*
Kelley, True (Adelaide) 1946- ... *130*
Brief entry ... *39*
Earlier sketches in SATA *41, 92*
Kelley, True Adelaide
See Kelley, True
Kellin, Sally Moffet 1932- ... *9*
Kelling, Furn L. 1914-2000 ... *37*
Kellogg, Gene
See Kellogg, Jean (Defrees)
Kellogg, Jean (Defrees) 1916-1978 ... *10*
Kellogg, Steven 1941- ... *177*
Earlier sketches in SATA *8, 57, 130*
See also CLR *6*
Kellogg, Steven Castle
See Kellogg, Steven
Kellow, Kathleen
See Hibbert, Eleanor Alice Burford
Kelly, C. M. O.
See Gibbs, (Cecilia) May
Kelly, Clint 1950- ... *140*
Kelly, Eric P(hilbrook) 1884-1960
See YABC *1*
Kelly, Fiona
See Coleman, Michael
and Hendry, Frances Mary
and Jones, Allan Frewin
and Oldfield, Jenny
and Welford, Sue
Kelly, Irene 1957- ... *210*
Earlier sketch in SATA *147*
Kelly, Jacqueline ... *216*
Kelly, Jeff
See Kelly, Jeffrey
Kelly, Jeffrey 1946- ... *65*
Kelly, Jenn 1973- ... *236*
Kelly, Jenn L.
See Kelly, Jenn
Kelly, Joanne (W.) 1934- ... *87*
Kelly, Kate 1958- ... *91*
Kelly, Kathleen M. 1964- ... *71*
Kelly, Katy 1955- ... *215*
Earlier sketch in SATA *169*
Kelly, Lauren
See Oates, Joyce Carol
Kelly, Laurene 1954- ... *123*
Kelly, Martha Rose 1914-1983 ... *37*
Kelly, Marty
See Kelly, Martha Rose
Kelly, Mij ... *166*
Kelly, Ralph
See Geis, Darlene Stern
Kelly, Regina Z(immerman) 1898-1986 ... *5*
Kelly, Rosalie (Ruth) ... *43*
Kelly, Tara ... *230*
Kelly, Tom 1961- ... *191*
Kelly, Walt(er Crawford) 1913-1973 ... *18*
Kelsey, Alice Geer 1896-1982 ... *1*
Kelsey, Elin 1961- ... *159*
Kelsey, Marybeth ... *216*
Kemly, Kathleen 1958- ... *197*
Kemnitz, Thomas Milton, Jr. 1984- ... *152*
Kemnitz, Tom, Jr.
See Kemnitz, Thomas Milton, Jr.
Kemp, Gene 1926- ... *75*
Earlier sketch in SATA *25*
See also CLR *29*
Kempner, Mary Jean 1913-1969 ... *10*
Kempter, Christa 1945- ... *187*
Kempton, Jean Welch 1914- ... *10*
Kenah, Katharine 1949- ... *182*

Kenda, Margaret 1942- *71*
Kendall, Carol (Seeger) 1917- *74*
Earlier sketch in SATA *11*
See also SAAS *7*
Kendall, Gideon 1966- *215*
Kendall, Katherine
See Applegate, Katherine
Kendall, Lace
See Stoutenburg, Adrien (Pearl)
Kendall, Martha E. *87*
Kendall, Russ 1957- *83*
Kenealy, James P. 1927- *52*
Brief entry *29*
Kenealy, Jim
See Kenealy, James P.
Kennaway, Adrienne 1945- *171*
Earlier sketch in SATA *60*
Kennedy, Anne 1955- *198*
Kennedy, Anne Vittur
See Kennedy, Anne
Kennedy, Brendan 1970- *57*
Kennedy, Dana Forrest 1917- *74*
Kennedy, Dorothy M(intzlaff) 1931- *53*
Kennedy, Doug 1963- *189*
Earlier sketch in SATA *122*
Kennedy, Frances 1937- *192*
Kennedy, James *214*
Kennedy, John F. 1917-1963 .... *11*
Kennedy, John Fitzgerald
See Kennedy, John F.
Kennedy, Joseph Charles
See Kennedy, X. J.
Kennedy, Kim *241*
Earlier sketch in SATA *189*
Kennedy, Marlane 1962- *210*
Kennedy, Pamela (J.) 1946- *87*
Kennedy, Paul E(dward) 1929- *113*
Earlier sketch in SATA *33*
Kennedy, Richard (Pitt) 1910-1989
Obituary *60*
Kennedy, (Jerome) Richard 1932- *22*
Kennedy, Robert 1938- *63*
Kennedy, T.A. 1953- *42*
Brief entry *35*
Kennedy, Teresa
See Kennedy, T.A.
Kennedy, Teresa A.
See Kennedy, T.A.
Kennedy, William 1928- *57*
Kennedy, William Joseph
See Kennedy, William
Kennedy, X. J. 1929- *130*
Autobiography Feature *130*
Earlier sketches in SATA *14, 86*
See also CLR *27*
See also SAAS *22*
Kennell, Ruth Epperson 1893-1977 .... *6*
Obituary *25*
Kennemore, Tim 1957- *220*
Earlier sketch in SATA *133*
Kennen, Ally *190*
Kennett, David 1959- *206*
Earlier sketch in SATA *121*
Kennison, Ruth *202*
Kenny, Ellsworth Newcomb 1909-1971
Obituary *26*
Kenny, Herbert Andrew 1912-2002 .... *13*
Kenny, Jude
See Daly, Jude
Kenny, Kathryn
See Bowden, Joan Chase
and Krull, Kathleen
and Sanderlin, Owenita (Harrah)
and Stack, Nicolete Meredith
Kenny, Kevin
See Krull, Kathleen
Kensinger, George
See Fichter, George S.
Kensington, Kathryn Wesley
See Rusch, Kristine Kathryn
Kent, Alexander
See Reeman, Douglas Edward
Kent, David
See Lambert, David
Kent, Deborah Ann 1948- *155*
Brief entry *41*
Earlier sketches in SATA *47, 104*
Kent, Jack
See Kent, John Wellington
Kent, John Wellington 1920-1985 .... *24*
Obituary *45*
Kent, Lisa 1942- *90*
Kent, Mallory
See Lowndes, Robert A(ugustine) W(ard)
Kent, Margaret 1894- *2*
Kent, Rockwell 1882-1971 .... *6*
Kent, Rose *188*
Kent, Sherman 1903-1986 .... *20*
Obituary *47*
Kenward, Jean 1920- *42*
Kenworthy, Leonard S. 1912-1991 .... *6*
Kenyon, Karen (Smith) 1938- *145*
Kenyon, Kate
See Adorjan, Carol (Madden)
and Ransom, Candice
Kenyon, Ley 1913-1990 .... *6*
Keown, Elizabeth *78*
Kepes, Juliet A(ppleby) 1919-1999 .... *13*
Kephart, Beth 1960- *196*
Keplinger, Kody 1991- *237*
Kerby, Johanna *235*
Kerby, Mona 1951- *202*
Earlier sketch in SATA *75*
Kerigan, Florence 1896-1984 .... *12*
Kerley, Barbara 1960- *191*
Earlier sketch in SATA *138*
Kerman, Gertrude
See Furman, Gertrude Lerner Kerman
Kerns, Thelma 1929- *116*
Kerr, Anne Louise
See Mackey, Weezie Kerr
Kerr, Bob 1951- *120*
Kerr, Jessica 1901-1991 .... *13*
Kerr, (Anne-)Judith 1923-1970 .... *24*
Kerr, M. E.
See Meaker, Marijane
Kerr, P.B.
See Kerr, Philip
Kerr, Philip 1956- *168*
Kerr, Phyllis Forbes 1942- *72*
Kerr, Tom 1950- *77*
Kerrin, Jessica Scott *174*
Kerry, Frances
See Kerigan, Florence
Kerry, Lois
See Duncan, Lois
Kershen, (L.) Michael 1982- *82*
Kerven, Rosalind 1954- *83*
Ker Wilson, Barbara 1929- *121*
Earlier sketches in SATA *20, 70*
See also SAAS *18*
Kerz, Anna 1947- *220*
Keselman, Gabriela 1953- *128*
Kesey, Ken 1935-2001 .... *66*
Obituary *131*
See also CLR *170*
Kesey, Ken Elton
See Kesey, Ken
Kesler, Jay 1935- *65*
Kessel, Joyce Karen 1937- *41*
Kessler, Cristina *190*
Kessler, Ethel 1922- *44*
Brief entry *37*
Kessler, Leonard P. 1921- *14*
Kessler, Liz 1966- *206*
Kest, Kristin 1967- *168*
Earlier sketch in SATA *118*
Kesteven, G. R.
See Crosher, G. R.
Ketcham, Hank
See Ketcham, Henry King
Ketcham, Henry King 1920-2001 .... *28*
Brief entry *27*
Obituary *128*
Ketcham, Sallie 1963- *124*
Ketchum, Liza 1946- *132*
Earlier sketch in SATA *78*
Ketner, Mary Grace 1946- *75*
Kettelkamp, Larry (Dale) 1933- *2*
See also SAAS *3*
Ketteman, Helen 1945- *223*
Earlier sketches in SATA *73, 115, 167*
Kettle, Peter
See Glover, Denis (James Matthews)
Kevles, Bettyann Holtzmann 1938- *23*
Key, Alexander (Hill) 1904-1979 .... *8*
Obituary *23*
Key, Samuel M.
See de Lint, Charles
Key, Watt 1970- *189*
Keyes, Daniel 1927- *37*
Keyes, Diane *207*
Keyes, Fenton 1915-1999 .... *34*
Keyes, Greg 1963- *116*
Keyes, J. Gregory
See Keyes, Greg
Keyes, Pamela 1962(?)- *238*
Keyser, Marcia 1933- *42*
Keyser, Sarah
See McGuire, Leslie (Sarah)
Khalid, Mohamed Nor
See Lat
Khalsa, Dayal Kaur 1943-1989 .... *62*
See also CLR *30*
Khan, Hena *214*
Khan, Rukhsana 1962- *231*
Earlier sketches in SATA *118, 165*
Khanshendel, Chiron
See Rose, Wendy
Kheirabadi, Masoud 1951- *158*
Khemir, Sabiha *87*
Kherdian, David 1931- *74*
Autobiography Feature *125*
Earlier sketch in SATA *16*
See also CLR *24*
Khing, T.T. 1933- *192*
Kibbe, Pat (Hosley) *60*
Kidd, Diana 1933-2000 .... *150*
Kidd, Richard 1952-2008 .... *152*
Obituary *194*
Kidd, Ronald 1948- *173*
Earlier sketches in SATA *42, 92*
Kiddell, John 1922- *3*
Kiddell-Monroe, Joan 1908-1972 .... *55*
Kidwell, Carl 1910- *43*
Kiefer, Irene 1926- *21*
Kiefer, Kathleen Balmes 1957- *142*
Kiepper, Shirley Morgan 1933- *10*
Kierstead, Vera M.
See Kierstead-Farber, Vera M.
Kierstead-Farber, Vera M. 1913- *121*
Kierstead-Farber, Vera May
See Kierstead-Farber, Vera M.
Kiesel, Stanley 1925- *35*
Kiesler, Kate (A.) 1971- *152*
Earlier sketch in SATA *90*
Kihn, Greg 1952- *110*
Kikukawa, Cecily H(arder) 1919- *44*
Brief entry *35*
Kilaka, John 1966- *223*
Kilcher, Jewel 1974- *109*
Kile, Joan 1940- *78*
Kilgore, Kathleen 1946- *42*
Kilian, Crawford 1941- *35*
Killdeer, John
See Mayhar, Ardath
Killen, Nicola *236*
Killien, Christi 1956- *73*
Killilea, Marie (Lyons) 1913-1991 .... *2*
Killingback, Julia 1944- *63*
Killough, (Karen) Lee 1942- *64*
Kilpatrick, Don *206*

Kilreon, Beth
See Walker, Barbara (Jeanne) K(erlin)
Kilworth, Garry 1941- 216
Earlier sketch in SATA *94*
Kilworth, Garry D.
See Kilworth, Garry
Kilworth, Garry Douglas
See Kilworth, Garry
Kim, David 1977- 201
Kim, Dong-hwa 1950- 225
Kim, Grace
See Maccarone, Grace
Kim, Helen 1899-1970 98
Kim, Joung Un 1970- 205
Kim, Susan 1958- 232
Kimball, Gayle 1943- 90
Kimball, Violet T(ew) 1932- 126
Kimball, Yeffe 1914-1978 37
Kimber, Murray 1964- 171
Kimble, Warren 176
Kimbrough, Emily 1899-1989 2
Obituary 59
Kimeldorf, Martin 1948- 121
Kimeldorf, Martin R.
See Kimeldorf, Martin
Kimenye, Barbara 1940(?)- 121
Kimmel, Elizabeth Cody 238
Earlier sketches in SATA *170, 209*
Kimmel, Eric A. 1946- 208
Earlier sketches in SATA *13, 80, 125, 176*
Kimmel, Margaret Mary 1938- 43
Brief entry 33
Kimmelman, Burt 1947- 180
Kimmelman, Leslie 1958- 211
Earlier sketches in SATA *85, 156*
Kincaid, Jamaica 1949-
See CLR *63*
Kinch, Michael 238
Kinch, Michael P.
See Kinch, Michael
Kincher, Jonni 1949- 79
Kincy, Karen 1986- 234
Kindl, Patrice 1951- 128
Earlier sketch in SATA *82*
See also CLR *132*
Kindred, Wendy (Good) 1937- 7
Kinerk, Robert 199
Kines, Pat Decker 1937- 12
King, Adam
See Hoare, Robert J(ohn)
King, Alison
See Martini, Teri
King, (Maria) Anna 1964- 72
King, A.S. 1970- 217
King, Billie Jean 1943- 12
King, Christine
See Farris, Christine King
King, Christopher (L.) 1945- 84
King, (David) Clive 1924- 144
Earlier sketch in SATA *28*
King, Colin 1943- 76
King, Cynthia 1925- 7
King, Daniel (John) 1963- 130
King, Daren 1972- 197
King, Elizabeth 1953- 83
King, Frank O. 1883-1969
Obituary 22
King, Frank R. 1904-1999 127
King, Jane
See Currie, Stephen
King, Jeanette (Margaret) 1959- 105
King, Larry L. 1929- 66
King, Laurie R. 1952- 88
King, Marian 1900(?)-1986 23
Obituary 47
King, Martin Luther, Jr. 1929-1968 14
King, Mary Ellen 1958- 93
King, M.G. 1968- 236
King, Paul
See Drackett, Phil(ip Arthur)
King, Paula
See Downing, Paula E.
King, Stephen 1947- 161
Earlier sketches in SATA *9, 55*
See also CLR *124*
King, Stephen Edwin
See King, Stephen
King, Stephen Michael 218
Earlier sketch in SATA *157*
King, Steve
See King, Stephen
King, Thomas 1943- 96
King, Thomas Hunt
See King, Thomas
King, Tony 1947- 39
King, Willie Christine
See Farris, Christine King
Kingfisher, Rupert 209
Kingman, Dong (Moy Shu) 1911-2000 44
Kingman, Lee
See Natti, Lee
Kingsbury, Evan
See Walker, Robert W.
Kingsland, Leslie William 1912- 13
Kingsley, Charles 1819-1875
See YABC *2*
See also CLR *167*
Kingsley, Emily Perl 1940- 33
Kingsley, Kaza 193
King-Smith, Dick 1922-2011 192
Brief entry 38
Earlier sketches in SATA *47, 80, 135*
See also CLR *40*
Kingston, Maxine Hong 1940- 53
Kingston, Maxine Ting Ting Hong
See Kingston, Maxine Hong
Kinkade, Sheila 1962- 229
Kinnaird, Ross 1954- 236
Kinney, C. Cle(land) 1915- 6
Kinney, Harrison 1921- 13
Kinney, Jean Stout 1912- 12
Kinney, Jeff 1971- 187
Kinsey, Elizabeth
See Clymer, Eleanor
Kinsey, Helen 1948- 82
Kinsey-Warnock, Natalie 1956- 167
Earlier sketches in SATA *71, 116*
Kinzel, Dorothy 1950- 57
Kinzel, Dottie
See Kinzel, Dorothy
Kipling, Joseph Rudyard
See Kipling, Rudyard
Kipling, Rudyard 1865-1936 100
See also YABC *2*
See also CLR *65*
Kippax, Frank
See Needle, Jan
Kirby, David 1944- 78
Kirby, David K.
See Kirby, David
Kirby, David Kirk
See Kirby, David
Kirby, Margaret
See Bingley, Margaret (Jane Kirby)
Kirby, Matthew J. 1976- 241
Kirby, Pamela F. 1952- 220
Kirby, Susan E. 1949- 62
Kirk, Connie Ann 1957- 167
Kirk, Daniel 1952- 196
Earlier sketches in SATA *107, 153*
Kirk, David 1955- 161
Earlier sketch in SATA *117*
Kirk, Heather 1949- 166
Kirk, Ruth (Kratz) 1925- 5
Kirkham, Dinah
See Card, Orson Scott
Kirkland, Will
See Hale, Arlene
Kirkpatrick, Katherine (Anne) 1964- 113
Kirkup, James 1918-2009 12
Kirkus, Virginia
See Glick, Virginia Kirkus
Kirkwood, Kathryn
See Fluke, Joanne
Kirsch, Vincent X. 211
Kirshenbaum, Binnie 79
Kirshner, David S. 1958- 123
Kirtland, G. B.
See Hine, Sesyle Joslin
and Hine, Al(fred Blakelee)
Kirwan, Wednesday 198
Kish, Eleanor M(ary) 1924- 73
Kish, Ely
See Kish, Eleanor M(ary)
Kishida, Eriko 1929- 12
Kisinger, Grace Gelvin (Maze) 1913-1965 10
Kissel, Richard 209
Kissin, Eva H. 1923- 10
Kissinger, Rosemary K.
See Updyke, Rosemary K.
Kistler, John M. 1967- 160
Kitamura, Satoshi 1956- 201
Earlier sketches in SATA *62, 98, 143*
See also CLR *60*
Kitanidis, Phoebe 1977- 230
Kitchen, Bert
See Kitchen, Herbert Thomas
Kitchen, Herbert Thomas 1940- 70
Kite, L. Patricia
See Kite, Pat
Kite, Pat 1940- 78
Kitt, Tamara
See de Regniers, Beatrice Schenk (Freedman)
Kittinger, Jo S(usenbach) 1955- 148
Earlier sketch in SATA *96*
Kittredge, Caitlin 1984- 239
Kituomba
See Odaga, Asenath (Bole)
Kitzinger, Sheila 1929- 57
Kiwak, Barbara 1966- 103
Kjelgaard, James Arthur 1910-1959 17
See also CLR *81*
Kjelgaard, Jim
See Kjelgaard, James Arthur
Kjelle, Marylou Morano 1954- 146
Klages, Ellen 1954- 196
Klagsbrun, Francine (Lifton) 36
Klaits, Barrie 1944- 52
Klam, Cheryl 191
Klaperman, Gilbert 1921- 33
Klaperman, Libby Mindlin 1921-1982 33
Obituary 31
Klass, David 1960- 207
Earlier sketches in SATA *88, 142*
Klass, Morton 1927-2001 11
Klass, Sheila Solomon 1927- 219
Autobiography Feature 126
Earlier sketches in SATA *45, 99*
See also SAAS *26*
Klassen, Jon 239
Klause, Annette Curtis 1953- 175
Earlier sketch in SATA *79*
See also CLR *104*
Klaveness, Jan O'Donnell 1939- 86
Kleberger, Ilse 1921- 5
Kleeberg, Irene (Flitner) Cumming 1932- 65
Klein, Aaron E. 1930-1998 45
Brief entry 28
Klein, Bill 1945- 89
Klein, David 1919-2001 59
Klein, Frederick C. 1938- 154
Klein, Gerda Weissmann 1924- 44
Klein, H(erbert) Arthur 8
Klein, James 1932- 115
Klein, Leonore (Glotzer) 1916- 6
Klein, Lisa 1958- 211
Klein, Lisa M.
See Klein, Lisa
Klein, Mina C(ooper) 1906-1979 8

Klein, Norma 1938-1989 ... *57*
Earlier sketch in SATA *7*
See also CLR *162*
See also SAAS *1*
Klein, Rachel S. 1953- ... *105*
Klein, Robin 1936- ... *164*
Brief entry ... *45*
Earlier sketches in SATA *55, 80*
See also CLR *21*
Klemin, Diana ... *65*
Klemm, Barry 1945- ... *104*
Klemm, Edward G., Jr. 1910-2001 ... *30*
Klemm, Roberta K(ohnhorst) 1884-1975 ... *30*
Klemstein, Stacey
See Kade, Stacey
Kleven, Elisa 1958- ... *217*
Earlier sketches in SATA *76, 173*
See also CLR *85*
Klevin, Jill Ross 1935- ... *39*
Brief entry ... *38*
Kliban, B(ernard) 1935-1990 ... *35*
Obituary ... *66*
Klier, Kimberly Wagner ... *208*
Klimo, Kate ... *214*
Klimowicz, Barbara 1927- ... *10*
Kline, Christina Baker 1964- ... *101*
Kline, James
See Klein, James
Kline, Jim
See Kline, Jim
Kline, Lisa Williams 1954- ... *143*
Kline, Suzy 1943- ... *193*
Autobiography Feature ... *193*
Brief entry ... *48*
Earlier sketches in SATA *67, 99, 152*
Kling, Heidi R. ... *233*
Klinger, Shula ... *230*
Kliros, Thea 1935- ... *106*
Klise, James 1967- ... *240*
Klise, Kate ... *221*
Earlier sketch in SATA *181*
Klise, M. Sarah 1961- ... *235*
Earlier sketches in SATA *128, 180*
Kloepfer, John ... *235*
Klots, Alexander Barrett 1903-1989
Obituary ... *62*
Klug, Ron(ald) 1939- ... *31*
Knaak, Richard A. 1961- ... *166*
Earlier sketch in SATA *86*
Knaak, Richard Allen
See Knaak, Richard A.
Knapman, Timothy ... *200*
Knapp, Edward
See Kunhardt, Edith
Knapp, Ron 1952- ... *34*
Knebel, Fletcher 1911-1993 ... *36*
Obituary ... *75*
Kneeland, Linda Clarke 1947- ... *94*
Kneen, Maggie 1957- ... *221*
Knickerbocker, Diedrich
See Irving, Washington
Knifesmith
See Cutler, Ivor
Knigge, Robert (R.) 1921(?)-1987 ... *50*
Knight, Anne (Katherine) 1946- ... *34*
Knight, Brenda ... *112*
Knight, Christopher G. 1943- ... *96*
Knight, Damon (Francis) 1922-2002 ... *9*
Obituary ... *139*
Knight, David C(arpenter) 1925-1984 ... *14*
See also CLR *38*
Knight, Eric 1897-1943 ... *18*
Knight, Eric Mowbray
See Knight, Eric
Knight, Francis Edgar 1905- ... *14*
Knight, Frank
See Knight, Francis Edgar
Knight, Hilary 1926- ... *132*
Earlier sketches in SATA *15, 69*
Knight, Joan
See Knight, Joan (MacPhail)
Knight, Joan (MacPhail) ... *159*
Earlier sketch in SATA *82*
Knight, Kathryn Lasky
See Lasky, Kathryn
Knight, Mallory T.
See Hurwood, Bernhardt J.
Knight, Ruth Adams 1898-1974
Obituary ... *20*
Knight, Steven 1959- ... *234*
Knight, Theodore O. 1946- ... *77*
Knobloch, Dorothea 1951- ... *88*
Knoepfle, John (Ignatius) 1923- ... *66*
Knorr, Laura 1971- ... *200*
Knott, Bill
See Knott, William C(ecil, Jr.)
Knott, William C(ecil, Jr.) 1927- ... *3*
Knotts, Howard (Clayton, Jr.) 1922- ... *25*
Knowles, Anne 1933- ... *37*
Knowles, Jo 1970- ... *197*
Knowles, Johanna Beth
See Knowles, Jo
Knowles, John 1926-2001 ... *89*
Obituary ... *134*
Earlier sketch in SATA *8*
See also CLR *98*
Knox, Calvin M.
See Silverberg, Robert
Knox, (Mary) Eleanor Jessie 1909-2000 ... *59*
Earlier sketch in SATA *30*
Knox, Elizabeth 1959- ... *176*
Knox, Elizabeth Fiona
See Knox, Elizabeth
Knox, James
See Brittain, William
Knox, Jolyne 1937- ... *76*
Knudsen, James 1950- ... *42*
Knudsen, Michelle 1974- ... *220*
Earlier sketch in SATA *171*
Knudson, Mike 1965- ... *209*
Knudson, R. R.
See Knudson, Rozanne
Knudson, Richard L(ewis) 1930- ... *34*
Knudson, Rozanne 1932-2008 ... *79*
Earlier sketch in SATA *7*
See also SAAS *18*
Knutson, Barbara 1959-2005 ... *166*
Knutson, Kimberley ... *115*
Knye, Cassandra
See Disch, Thomas M.
Kobayashi, Masako Matsuno 1935- ... *6*
Kober, Shahar 1979- ... *213*
Koch, Dorothy Clarke 1924- ... *6*
Koch, Kenneth 1925-2002 ... *65*
Koch, Kenneth Jay
See Koch, Kenneth
Koch, Phyllis (Mae) McCallum 1911- ... *10*
Kochalka, James 1967- ... *196*
Kocsis, J. C.
See Paul, James
Koda-Callan, Elizabeth 1944- ... *140*
Earlier sketch in SATA *67*
Kodera, Craig 1956- ... *222*
Kodman, Stanislawa ... *201*
Koehler, Phoebe 1955- ... *85*
Koehler-Pentacoff, Elizabeth 1957- ... *160*
Earlier sketch in SATA *96*
Koehn, Ilse
See Van Zwienen, Ilse Charlotte Koehn
Koeller, Carol ... *192*
Koenig, Viviane 1950- ... *80*
Koering, Ursula 1921-1976 ... *64*
Koerner, W(illiam) H(enry) D(avid)
1878-1938 ... *21*
Koertge, Ron 1940- ... *209*
Earlier sketches in SATA *53, 92, 131*
Koestler-Grack, Rachel A. 1973- ... *156*
Koff, Richard Myram 1926- ... *62*
Koffinke, Carol 1949- ... *82*
Kogan, Deborah
See Kogan Ray, Deborah
Kogan Ray, Deborah 1940- ... *203*
Earlier sketches in SATA *8, 50, 161*
Kogawa, Joy 1935- ... *99*
Kogawa, Joy Nozomi
See Kogawa, Joy
Kogler, Jennie
See Kogler, Jennifer Anne
Kogler, Jennifer Anne 1982(?)- ... *174*
Kohara, Kazuno ... *207*
Kohl, Herbert 1937- ... *47*
Kohl, Herbert R.
See Kohl, Herbert
Kohl, MaryAnn F(aubion) 1947- ... *144*
Earlier sketch in SATA *74*
Kohler, Dean Ellis 1947- ... *226*
Kohler, Julilly H(ouse) 1908-1976
Obituary ... *20*
Kohn, Bernice
See Hunt, Bernice
Kohn, Rita (T.) 1933- ... *89*
Kohner, Frederick 1905-1986 ... *10*
Obituary ... *48*
Koide, Tan 1938-1986 ... *50*
Koike, Kay 1940- ... *72*
Koja, Kathe 1960- ... *199*
Earlier sketch in SATA *155*
Koja, Stephan ... *198*
Kolar, Bob 1960(?)- ... *206*
Kolb, Larry J. 1953- ... *175*
Kolba, St. Tamara ... *22*
Kolibalova, Marketa
See Kolibalova, Marketa
Kolibalova, Marketa 1953- ... *126*
Koller, Jackie French 1948- ... *157*
Earlier sketches in SATA *72, 109*
See also CLR *68*
Kolodny, Nancy J. 1946- ... *76*
Kolosov, Jacqueline 1967- ... *199*
Komaiko, Leah 1954- ... *164*
Earlier sketch in SATA *97*
Komisar, Lucy 1942- ... *9*
Komiya, Teruyuki ... *239*
Komoda, Beverly 1939- ... *25*
Komoda, Kiyo 1937- ... *9*
Kompaneyets, Marc 1974- ... *169*
Komroff, Manuel 1890-1974 ... *2*
Obituary ... *20*
Konigsberg, Bill 1970- ... *207*
Konigsburg, E.L. 1930- ... *194*
Earlier sketches in SATA *4, 48, 94, 126*
See also CLR *81*
Konigsburg, Elaine Lobl
See Konigsburg, E.L.
Koning, Hans 1921-2007 ... *5*
Obituary ... *182*
Koningsberger, Hans
See Koning, Hans
Konkle, Janet Everest 1917- ... *12*
Kono, Erin Eitter 1973- ... *177*
Konrad, Marla Stewart ... *218*
Konzak, Burt 1946- ... *151*
Koob, Theodora (J. Foth) 1918- ... *23*
Kooiker, Leonie
See Kooyker-Romijn, Johanna Maria
Koons, James
See Pernu, Dennis
Koontz, Dean 1945- ... *165*
Earlier sketch in SATA *92*
See Koontz, Dean R.
Koontz, Dean R. ... *225*
See Koontz, Dean
Koontz, Dean Ray
See Koontz, Dean
Koontz, Robin Michal 1954- ... *136*
Earlier sketch in SATA *70*
Kooyker, Leonie
See Kooyker-Romijn, Johanna Maria
Kooyker-Romijn, Johanna Maria 1927- ... *48*
Kooyker-Romyn, Johanna Maria
See Kooyker-Romijn, Johanna Maria
Kopelke, Lisa 1963- ... *154*

Kopper, Lisa 1950- *105*
Brief entry *51*
Kopper, Lisa Esther
See Kopper, Lisa
Koppes, Steven N. 1957- *169*
Koppes, Steven Nelson
See Koppes, Steven N.
Korach, Mimi 1922- *9*
Koralek, Jenny 1934- *215*
Earlier sketches in SATA *71, 140*
Korczak, Janusz
See Goldszmit, Henryk
Koren, Edward (Benjamin) 1935- *148*
Earlier sketch in SATA *5*
Koren, Edward 1935- *206*
Korinets, Iurii Iosifovich
See Korinetz, Yuri (Iosifovich)
Korinetz, Yuri (Iosifovich) 1923- *9*
See also CLR *4*
Korman, Bernice 1937- *78*
Korman, Gordon 1963- *226*
Brief entry *41*
Earlier sketches in SATA *49, 81, 119, 167*
See also CLR *25*
Korman, Gordon Richard
See Korman, Gordon
Korman, Justine 1958- *70*
Kornblatt, Marc 1954- *147*
Earlier sketch in SATA *84*
Kornprobst, Jacques 1937- *177*
Korte, Gene J. 1950- *74*
Korthues, Barbara 1971- *203*
Korty, Carol 1937- *15*
Koscielniak, Bruce 1947- *153*
Earlier sketches in SATA *67, 99*
Koshin, Alexander (A.) 1952- *86*
Kositsky, Lynne 1947- *158*
Koskenmaki, Rosalie
See Maggio, Rosalie
Koss, Amy Goldman 1954- *158*
Earlier sketch in SATA *115*
Kossin, Sandy (Sanford) 1926- *10*
Kossman, Nina 1959- *84*
Kostecki-Shaw, Jenny Sue *203*
Kostick, Conor 1964- *186*
Kotzwinkle, William 1938- *146*
Earlier sketches in SATA *24, 70*
See also CLR *6*
Kouhi, Elizabeth 1917- *54*
Brief entry *49*
Kouts, Anne 1945- *8*
Koutsky, Jan Dale 1955- *146*
Kovacs, Deborah 1954- *132*
Earlier sketch in SATA *79*
Kovalski, Maryann 1951- *175*
Earlier sketches in SATA *58, 97*
See also CLR *34*
See also SAAS *21*
Kowalski, Kathiann M. 1955- *151*
Earlier sketch in SATA *96*
Koz, Paula G.
See Goodman Koz, Paula
Kozjan, Drazen *209*
Kraft, Betsy Harvey 1937- *157*
Kraft, Erik P. *193*
Krahn, Fernando 1935- *49*
Brief entry *31*
See also CLR *3*
Krakauer, Hoong Yee Lee 1955- *86*
Krakauer, Jon 1954- *108*
Krall, Dan 1970- *218*
Kramer, Andrew *237*
Kramer, George
See Heuman, William
Kramer, Nora 1896(?)-1984 .... *26*
Obituary *39*
Kramer, Remi (Thomas) 1935- *90*
Krantz, Hazel (Newman) *12*
Kranzler, George G(ershon) 1916- *28*
Kranzler, Gershon
See Kranzler, George G(ershon)
Krasilovsky, Phyllis 1926- *38*
Earlier sketch in SATA *1*
See also CLR *83*
See also SAAS *5*
Krasne, Betty
See Levine, Betty K(rasne)
Krasner, Steven 1953- *154*
Krasnesky, Thad 1969(?)- *224*
Krasno, Rena 1923- *104*
Kratman, Tom 1956- *175*
Kraus, Joanna Halpert 1937- *87*
Kraus, (Herman) Robert 1925-2001 .... *93*
Obituary *130*
Earlier sketches in SATA *4, 65*
See also SAAS *11*
Krauss, Ruth 1911-1993 .... *30*
Obituary *75*
Earlier sketch in SATA *1*
See also CLR *42*
Krauss, Ruth Ida
See Krauss, Ruth
Krautter, Elisa (Bialk) 1912(?)-1990 .... *1*
Obituary *65*
Krautwurst, Terry 1946- *79*
Kray, Robert Clement 1930- *82*
Krech, Bob 1956- *185*
Krech, Robert
See Krech, Bob
Kredel, Fritz 1900-1973 .... *17*
Kreikemeier, Gregory Scott 1965- *85*
Kreloff, Elliot *189*
Krementz, Jill 1940- *134*
Earlier sketches in SATA *17, 71*
See also CLR *5*
See also SAAS *8*
Kremer, Marcie
See Sorenson, Margo
Krenina, Katya 1968- *221*
Earlier sketch in SATA *101*
Krensky, Stephen 1953- *188*
Brief entry *41*
Earlier sketches in SATA *47, 93, 136*
Krensky, Stephen Alan
See Krensky, Stephen
Kresh, Paul 1919-1997 .... *61*
Obituary *94*
Kress, Nancy 1948- *147*
Autobiography Feature *147*
Earlier sketch in SATA *85*
Kricher, John C. 1944- *113*
Krieger, Melanie 1944- *96*
Krinitz, Esther Nisenthal 1927-2001 .... *194*
Kripke, Dorothy Karp *30*
Krisher, Trudy 1946- *160*
Earlier sketch in SATA *86*
Krisher, Trudy B.
See Krisher, Trudy
Krishnaswami, Uma 1956- *182*
Earlier sketch in SATA *144*
Kristiansen, Teddy 1964- *210*
Kristiansen, Teddy H.
See Kristiansen, Teddy
Kristof, Jane 1932- *8*
Kroeber, Theodora (Kracaw) 1897-1979 .... *1*
Kroeger, Mary Kay 1950- *92*
Krohn, Katherine E(lizabeth) 1961- *125*
Earlier sketch in SATA *84*
Kroll, Francis Lynde 1904-1973 .... *10*
Kroll, Steven 1941-2011 .... *212*
Autobiography Feature *135*
Earlier sketches in SATA *19, 66, 125, 135*
See also SAAS *7*
Kroll, Virginia L. 1948- *225*
Earlier sketches in SATA *76, 114, 168*
Kroll, Virginia Louisa
See Kroll, Virginia L.
Kromhout, Rindert 1958- *189*
Krommes, Beth 1956- *208*
Earlier sketches in SATA *128, 181*
Kronenwetter, Michael 1943- *62*
Kroniuk, Lisa
See Berton, Pierre (Francis de Marigny)
Kropp, Paul 1948- *38*
Brief entry *34*
See also CLR *96*
Kropp, Paul Stephan
See Kropp, Paul
Krosoczka, Jarrett J. 1977- *200*
Earlier sketch in SATA *155*
Krovatin, Christopher 1985- *171*
Krudop, Walter
See Krudop, Walter Lyon
Krudop, Walter Lyon 1966- *210*
Kruess, James
See Kruss, James
Krug, Nora 1977- *240*
Kruglik, Gerald *187*
Krull, Kathleen 1952- *229*
Autobiography Feature *106*
Brief entry *39*
Earlier sketches in SATA *52, 80, 149, 184*
See also CLR *44*
Krumgold, Joseph (Quincy) 1908-1980 .... *48*
Obituary *23*
Earlier sketch in SATA *1*
Krupinski, Loretta 1940- *161*
Earlier sketches in SATA *67, 102*
Krupnick, Karen 1947- *89*
Krupp, E. C. 1944- *123*
Earlier sketch in SATA *53*
Krupp, Edwin Charles
See Krupp, E. C.
Krupp, Robin Rector 1946- *53*
Krush, Beth 1918- *18*
Krush, Joe 1918-
See Krush, Joseph P.
Krush, Joseph P. 1918- *18*
Kruss, James 1926-1997 .... *8*
See also CLR *9*
Kruusval, Catarina 1951- *201*
Krykorka, Vladyana 1945- *96*
Krystoforski, Andrej 1943- *196*
Kubick, Dana *212*
Kubie, Eleanor Gottheil
See Kubie, Nora Gottheil Benjamin
Kubie, Nora Benjamin
See Kubie, Nora Gottheil Benjamin
Kubie, Nora Gottheil Benjamin 1899-1988 . *39*
Obituary *59*
Kubinyi, Laszlo 1937- *94*
Earlier sketch in SATA *17*
Kudlinski, Kathleen V. 1950- *213*
Earlier sketch in SATA *150*
Kuehnert, Stephanie 1979- *205*
Kuenstler, Morton 1927- *10*
Kuh, Charlotte 1892(?)-1985
Obituary *43*
Kuharski, Janice 1947- *128*
Kuhn, Dwight *199*
Kuijer, Guus 1942- *179*
Kujoth, Jean Spealman 1935-1975
Obituary *30*
Kuklin, Susan 1941- *163*
Earlier sketches in SATA *63, 95*
See also CLR *51*
Kulak, Jeff 1984(?)- *223*
Kulikov, Boris 1966- *205*
Earlier sketch in SATA *170*
Kulka, Joe *188*
Kulling, Monica 1952- *237*
Earlier sketch in SATA *89*
Kullman, Harry 1919-1982 .... *35*
Kulyk Keefer, Janice 1952- *132*
Kumin, Maxine 1925- *12*
Kumin, Maxine Winokur
See Kumin, Maxine
Kunhardt, Dorothy (Meserve) 1901-1979 .... *53*
Obituary *22*
Kunhardt, Edith 1937- *67*
Kunjufu, Jawanza 1953- *73*

Kunstler, Morton
See Kuenstler, Morton
Kuntz, J(ohn) L. 1947- ... *91*
Kuntz, Jerry 1956- ... *133*
Kunze, Lauren ... *240*
Kupferberg, Herbert 1918-2001 ... *19*
Kuratomi, Chizuko 1939- ... *12*
See also CLR *32*
Kurczok, Belinda 1978- ... *121*
Kurelek, William 1927-1977 ... *8*
Obituary ... *27*
See also CLR *2*
Kurian, George 1928- ... *65*
Kurilla, Renee 1981- ... *231*
Kurisu, Jane 1952- ... *241*
Kurjian, Judi(th M.) 1944- ... *127*
Kurland, Gerald 1942- ... *13*
Kurland, Michael 1938- ... *118*
Earlier sketch in SATA *48*
Kurland, Michael Joseph
See Kurland, Michael
Kuroi, Ken 1947- ... *120*
Kurokawa, Mitsuhiro 1954- ... *88*
Kurten, Bjorn (Olof) 1924-1988 ... *64*
Kurtz, Jane 1952- ... *139*
Earlier sketch in SATA *91*
See also CLR *123*
Kurtz, Katherine 1944- ... *182*
Earlier sketches in SATA *76, 126*
Kurtz, Katherine Irene
See Kurtz, Katherine
Kurusa 1942- ... *226*
Kurz, Rudolf 1952- ... *95*
Kushner, Donn (J.) 1927- ... *52*
See also CLR *55*
Kushner, Ellen 1955- ... *202*
Earlier sketch in SATA *98*
Kushner, Ellen Ruth
See Kushner, Ellen
Kushner, Jill Menkes 1951- ... *62*
Kushner, Lawrence 1943- ... *169*
Earlier sketch in SATA *83*
Kushner, Tony 1956- ... *160*
Kuskin, Karla 1932-2009 ... *164*
Obituary ... *206*
Earlier sketches in SATA *2, 68, 111*
See also CLR *4*
See also SAAS *3*
Kuskin, Karla Seidman
See Kuskin, Karla
Kusugak, Michael 1948- ... *143*
Kusugak, Michael Arvaarluk
See Kusugak, Michael
Kutner, Merrily 1948- ... *196*
Kuttner, Paul 1922- ... *18*
Kuyper, Sjoerd 1952- ... *177*
Kuzma, Kay 1941- ... *39*
Kvale, Velma R(uth) 1898-1979 ... *8*
Kvasnosky, Laura McGee 1951- ... *182*
Earlier sketches in SATA *93, 142*
Kwasney, Michelle D. 1960- ... *162*
Kyi, Tanya Lloyd 1973- ... *236*
Kyle, Benjamin
See Gottfried, Theodore Mark
Kyle, Elisabeth
See Dunlop, Agnes M. R.
Kyte, Kathy S. 1946- ... *50*
Brief entry ... *44*

L

L., Barry
See Longyear, Barry B(rookes)
L., Tommy
See Lorkowski, Thomas V(incent)
Labatt, Mary 1944- ... *215*
Labouisse, Eve Curie
See Curie, Eve
Labouisse, Eve Denise
See Curie, Eve
Lacamara, Laura ... *236*
Lace, William W. 1942- ... *126*
Lacey, Joshua
See Doder, Josh
Lachenmeyer, Nathaniel 1969- ... *221*
Lachner, Dorothea
See Knobloch, Dorothea
Lachtman, Ofelia Dumas 1919- ... *179*
Lackey, Mercedes ... *237*
See Lackey, Mercedes R.
Lackey, Mercedes R. 1950- ... *127*
Earlier sketch in SATA *81*
See Lackey, Mercedes
Lackey, Mercedes Ritchie
See Lackey, Mercedes R.
Lacoe, Addie ... *78*
Lacombe, Benjamin 1982- ... *198*
Lacome, Julie 1961- ... *174*
Earlier sketch in SATA *80*
LaCour, Nina 1982- ... *222*
Lacy, Leslie Alexander 1937- ... *6*
Lacy, Rick ... *231*
Ladd, Cheryl (Jean) 1951- ... *113*
Ladd, London 1972(?)- ... *206*
Ladd, Louise 1943- ... *97*
Ladd, Veronica
See Miner, Jane Claypool
Laden, Nina 1962- ... *148*
Earlier sketch in SATA *85*
Lader, Lawrence 1919-2006 ... *6*
Obituary ... *178*
LaDoux, Rita C. 1951- ... *74*
Ladwig, Tim 1952- ... *223*
Ladwig, Timothy
See Ladwig, Tim
Lady, A
See Taylor, Ann
Lady Mears
See Tempest, Margaret Mary
Lady of Quality, A
See Bagnold, Enid
La Farge, Oliver 1901-1963 ... *19*
La Farge, Oliver Hazard Perry
See La Farge, Oliver
La Farge, Phyllis ... *14*
LaFave, Kim ... *196*
LaFaye, A. 1970- ... *220*
Earlier sketches in SATA *105, 156*
LaFaye, Alexandria R.T.
See LaFaye, A.
LaFevers, R.L. ... *234*
Earlier sketch in SATA *191*
LaFevers, Robin
See LaFevers, R.L.
LaFevers, Robin L.
See LaFevers, R.L.
Lafferty, Mur 1973- ... *227*
Laffin, John (Alfred Charles) 1922- ... *31*
LaFleur, Suzanne 1983- ... *221*
LaFontaine, Bruce 1948- ... *176*
Earlier sketch in SATA *114*
La Fontaine, Jean de 1621-1695 ... *18*
Lafrance, Marie 1955- ... *197*
Lager, Claude
See Lapp, Christiane (Germain)
Lager, Marilyn 1939- ... *52*
Lagercrantz, Rose (Elsa) 1947- ... *39*
Lagerloef, Selma
See Lagerlof, Selma
Lagerlof, Selma 1858-1940 ... *15*
See also CLR *7*
Lagos, Alexander ... *232*
Lagos, Joseph ... *231*
Laguna, Sofie 1968- ... *158*
LaHaye, Tim 1926- ... *149*
LaHaye, Timothy F.
See LaHaye, Tim
Lai, Thanhha 1965- ... *239*
Laidlaw, Rob ... *205*
Laiken, Deirdre S. 1948- ... *48*
Brief entry ... *40*
Laiken, Deirdre Susan
See Laiken, Deirdre S.
Laimgruber, Monika 1946- ... *11*
Lain, Anna
See Lamb, Nancy
Laing, Alexander (Kinnan) 1903-1976 ... *117*
Laing, Martha 1951- ... *39*
Lairamore, Dawn ... *233*
Laird, Christa 1944- ... *108*
Autobiography Feature ... *120*
See also SAAS *26*
Laird, Elizabeth 1943- ... *228*
Earlier sketches in SATA *77, 114, 159*
See also CLR *65*
Laird, Elizabeth Mary Risk
See Laird, Elizabeth
Laird, Jean E(louise) 1930- ... *38*
Laite, Gordon 1925- ... *31*
Lake, Harriet
See Taylor, Paula (Wright)
Lake, Nick ... *227*
Lakeman, Victoria
See Forester, Victoria
Lakin, Patricia 1944- ... *190*
Laklan, Carli 1907-1988 ... *5*
Laliberte, Louise-Andree 1958- ... *169*
Lalicki, Barbara ... *61*
Lalicki, Tom 1949- ... *186*
Lally, Soinbhe 1945- ... *119*
LaMarche, Jim ... *239*
Earlier sketch in SATA *162*
Lamb, Albert ... *187*
Lamb, Beatrice Pitney 1904-1997 ... *21*
Lamb, Charles 1775-1834 ... *17*
Lamb, Elizabeth Searle 1917- ... *31*
Lamb, G(eoffrey) F(rederick) ... *10*
Lamb, Harold (Albert) 1892-1962 ... *53*
Lamb, Lynton (Harold) 1907-1977 ... *10*
Lamb, Mary Ann 1764-1847 ... *17*
Lamb, Nancy 1939- ... *80*
Lamb, Robert (Boyden) 1941- ... *13*
Lamba, Marie ... *195*
Lambert, David 1932- ... *84*
Brief entry ... *49*
Lambert, David Compton
See Lambert, David
Lambert, Janet 1895(?)-1973 ... *25*
Lambert, Martha L. ... *113*
Lambert, Saul 1928- ... *23*
Lambert, Stephen ... *174*
Lamburn, Richmal Crompton 1890-1969 ... *5*
Lamensdorf, Len 1930- ... *120*
Lamensdorf, Leonard
See Lamensdorf, Len
Laminack, Lester L. 1956- ... *163*
Earlier sketch in SATA *120*
Lammle, Leslie 1965- ... *213*
Lamont, Priscilla ... *200*
Lamorisse, Albert (Emmanuel) 1922-1970 ... *23*
Lampert, Emily 1951- ... *52*
Brief entry ... *49*
Lamplugh, Lois 1921- ... *17*
Lampman, Evelyn Sibley 1907-1980 ... *87*
Obituary ... *23*
Earlier sketch in SATA *4*
Lamprey, Louise 1869-1951
See YABC *2*
Lampton, Chris
See Lampton, Christopher F.
Lampton, Christopher
See Lampton, Christopher F.
Lampton, Christopher F. ... *67*
Brief entry ... *47*
Lamstein, Sarah 1943- ... *174*
Earlier sketch in SATA *126*
Lamstein, Sarah Marwil
See Lamstein, Sarah
Lamut, Sonja ... *241*

Lanagan, Margo 1960- ... *201*
Earlier sketch in SATA *163*
Lancaster, Bruce 1896-1963 ... *9*
Lancaster, Matthew 1973(?)-1983
Obituary ... *45*
Lance, Kathryn 1943- ... *76*
Land, Barbara (Neblett) 1923- ... *16*
Land, Jane
See Borland, Kathryn Kilby
and Speicher, Helen Ross S(mith)
Land, Myrick (Ebben) 1922-1998 ... *15*
Land, Ross
See Borland, Kathryn Kilby
and Speicher, Helen Ross S(mith)
Landa, Norbert 1952- ... *218*
Landau, Elaine 1948- ... *141*
Earlier sketches in SATA *10, 94*
Landau, Jacob 1917- ... *38*
Landeck, Beatrice 1904-1978 ... *15*
Landin, Les 1923- ... *2*
Landis, J. D. 1942- ... *60*
Brief entry ... *52*
Landis, James D.
See Landis, J. D.
Landis, James David
See Landis, J. D.
Landis, Jill Marie 1948- ... *101*
Landman, Tanya ... *207*
Landmann, Bimba 1968- ... *176*
Landon, Dena 1978(?)- ... *168*
Landon, Kristen 1966- ... *239*
Landon, Lucinda 1950- ... *56*
Brief entry ... *51*
Landon, Margaret (Dorothea Mortenson)
1903-1993 ... *50*
Landowne, Youme 1970- ... *211*
Landry, Leo ... *202*
Landshoff, Ursula 1908-1989 ... *13*
Landstrom, Lena 1943- ... *206*
Earlier sketch in SATA *146*
Landstrom, Olof 1943- ... *146*
Landy, Derek 1974- ... *210*
Lane, Alison Hoffman ... *215*
Lane, Andrew 1963- ... *239*
Lane, Andy
See Lane, Andrew
Lane, Carolyn 1926-1993 ... *10*
Lane, Connie
See Laux, Constance
Lane, Dakota 1959- ... *166*
Earlier sketch in SATA *105*
Lane, Jerry
See Martin, Patricia Miles
Lane, John (Richard) 1932- ... *15*
Lane, Leena ... *199*
Lane, Margaret 1907-1994 ... *65*
Brief entry ... *38*
Obituary ... *79*
Lane, Rose Wilder 1887-1968 ... *29*
Brief entry ... *28*
Lanes, Selma G. 1929- ... *3*
Lanes, Selma Gordon
See Lanes, Selma G.
Lanfredi, Judy 1964- ... *83*
Lang, Andrew 1844-1912 ... *16*
See also CLR *174*
Lang, Aubrey ... *169*
Lang, Diane ... *234*
Lang, Glenna 1951- ... *221*
Lang, Lang 1982- ... *208*
Lang, Paul 1948- ... *83*
Lang, Susan S. 1950- ... *68*
Lang, T.T.
See Taylor, Theodore
Langart, Darrell T.
See Garrett, Randall
Langdo, Bryan 1973- ... *233*
Earlier sketches in SATA *138, 191*
Lange, John
See Crichton, Michael
Lange, Karen E. ... *190*
Lange, Suzanne 1945- ... *5*
Langley, Andrew 1949- ... *166*
Earlier sketch in SATA *104*
Langley, Charles P(itman) III 1949- ... *103*
Langley, Jonathan 1952- ... *122*
Langley, Noel 1911-1980
Obituary ... *25*
Langley, Wanda ... *173*
Langner, Nola
See Malone, Nola Langner
Langone, John (Michael) 1929- ... *46*
Brief entry ... *38*
Langreuter, Jutta 1944- ... *122*
Langrish, Katherine ... *177*
Langsen, Richard C. 1953- ... *95*
Langstaff, John 1920-2005 ... *68*
Obituary ... *172*
Earlier sketch in SATA *6*
See also CLR *3*
Langstaff, John Meredith
See Langstaff, John
Langstaff, Launcelot
See Irving, Washington
Langston, Laura 1958- ... *186*
Langton, Jane 1922- ... *200*
Autobiography Feature ... *140*
Earlier sketches in SATA *3, 68, 129, 140*
See also CLR *33*
See also SAAS *5*
Lanier, Sidney 1842-1881 ... *18*
Lanier, Sterling E. 1927-2007 ... *109*
Lanier, Sterling Edmund
See Lanier, Sterling E.
Lanino, Deborah 1964- ... *123*
Lankford, Mary D. 1932- ... *112*
Earlier sketch in SATA *77*
Lannin, Joanne 1951- ... *121*
Lannin, Joanne A.
See Lannin, Joanne
Lansdale, Joe R. 1951- ... *116*
Lansdale, Joe Richard
See Lansdale, Joe R.
Lansing, Alfred 1921-1975 ... *35*
Lansing, Karen E. 1954- ... *71*
Lansky, Vicki 1942- ... *177*
Lanthier, Jennifer 1964- ... *204*
Lantier-Sampon, Patricia 1952- ... *92*
Lantz, Fran
See Lantz, Francess L(in)
Lantz, Francess L(in) 1952-2004 ... *153*
Autobiography Feature ... *153*
Obituary ... *159*
Earlier sketches in SATA *63, 109*
Lantz, Paul 1908- ... *45*
Lantz, Walter 1900-1994 ... *37*
Obituary ... *79*
Lanza, Barbara 1945- ... *101*
Lapp, Christiane (Germain) 1948- ... *74*
Lappin, Peter 1911-1999 ... *32*
Larbalestier, Justine ... *231*
Earlier sketch in SATA *178*
Lardy, Philippe 1963- ... *168*
LaReau, Jenna ... *181*
LaReau, Kara ... *181*
Larios, Julie 1949- ... *178*
Larios, Julie Hofstrand
See Larios, Julie
Larkin, Amy
See Burns, Olive Ann
Larkin, Maia
See Wojciechowska, Maia (Teresa)
Larkspur, Penelope
See Wyatt, Valerie
Laroche, Giles 1956- ... *221*
Earlier sketches in SATA *71, 126*
LaRochelle, David 1960- ... *171*
Earlier sketch in SATA *115*
Larom, Henry V. 1903(?)-1975
Obituary ... *30*
LaRose, Linda ... *125*
Larrabee, Lisa 1947- ... *84*
Larranaga, Ana Martin 1969- ... *229*
Larrecq, John M(aurice) 1926-1980 ... *44*
Obituary ... *25*
Larrick (Crosby), Nancy 1910-2004 ... *4*
Larsen, Anita 1942- ... *78*
Larsen, Egon 1904- ... *14*
Larsen, Rebecca 1944- ... *54*
Larson, Eve
See St. John, Wylly Folk
Larson, Gary 1950- ... *57*
Larson, Hope 1982- ... *205*
Larson, Ingrid D(ana) 1965- ... *92*
Larson, Jean Russell 1930- ... *121*
Larson, Kirby 1954- ... *240*
Earlier sketches in SATA *96, 181*
Larson, Norita D. 1944- ... *29*
Larson, Norita Dittberner
See Larson, Norita D.
Larson, William H. 1938- ... *10*
Larsson, Carl (Olof) 1853-1919 ... *35*
LaSalle, Charles A.
See Ellis, Edward S.
LaSalle, Charles E.
See Ellis, Edward S.
Lasell, Elinor H. 1929- ... *19*
Lasell, Fen H.
See Lasell, Elinor H.
Lasenby, Jack 1931- ... *172*
Earlier sketches in SATA *65, 103*
Laser, Michael 1954- ... *117*
Lash, Joseph P. 1909-1987 ... *43*
Lasher, Faith B. 1921- ... *12*
Lasker, David 1950- ... *38*
Lasker, Joe
See Lasker, Joseph Leon
Lasker, Joseph Leon 1919- ... *83*
Earlier sketch in SATA *9*
See also SAAS *17*
Laski, Marghanita 1915-1988 ... *55*
Laskin, Pamela L. 1954- ... *75*
Lasky, Kathryn 1944- ... *236*
Earlier sketches in SATA *13, 69, 112, 157, 210*
See also CLR *140*
Lasky Knight, Kathryn
See Lasky, Kathryn
Lass, Bonnie ... *131*
Lassalle, C. E.
See Ellis, Edward S.
Lassiter, Mary
See Hoffman, Mary
Lassiter, Rhiannon 1977- ... *157*
Lat 1951- ... *196*
Latham, Barbara 1896- ... *16*
Latham, Frank B(rown) 1910-2000 ... *6*
Latham, Irene 1971- ... *228*
Latham, Jean Lee 1902-1995 ... *68*
Earlier sketch in SATA *2*
See also CLR *50*
Latham, Mavis
See Clark, Mavis Thorpe
Latham, Philip
See Richardson, Robert S(hirley)
Lathrop, Dorothy P(ulis) 1891-1980 ... *14*
Obituary ... *24*
Lathrop, Francis
See Leiber, Fritz (Reuter, Jr.)
Latimer, Jim 1943- ... *80*
Latimer, Miriam ... *235*
Latta, Rich
See Latta, Richard
Latta, Richard 1946- ... *113*
Latta, Sara L. 1960- ... *174*
Lattany, Kristin
See Lattany, Kristin Hunter
Lattany, Kristin (Eggleston) Hunter 1931- . *154*
Autobiography Feature ... *154*
Earlier sketch in SATA *132*

Lattany, Kristin Hunter 1931-2008 .... *132*
Earlier sketch in SATA *12*
See also CLR *3*
See also SAAS *10*
Lattimore, Eleanor Frances 1904-1986 .... *7*
Obituary *48*
Lattin, Ann
See Cole, Lois Dwight
Latyk, Olivier 1976- *234*
Lauber, Patricia (Grace) 1924- *138*
Earlier sketches in SATA *1, 33, 75*
See also CLR *16*
Laugesen, Malene *207*
Laugesen, Malene Reynolds
See Laugesen, Malene
Laugesen, Mary E(akin) 1906-1995 .... *5*
Laughbaum, Steve 1945- *12*
Laughead, Mike 1978- *241*
Laughlin, Florence Young 1910-2001 .... *3*
Laughlin, Rosemary 1941- *123*
Launder, Sally *206*
Laure, Ettagale
See Blauer, Ettagale
Laure, Jason 1940- *50*
Brief entry *44*
Laurence, Ester Hauser 1935- *7*
Laurence, Jean Margaret Wemyss
See Laurence, Margaret
Laurence, Margaret 1926-1987
Obituary *50*
Laurie, Rona 1916- *55*
Laurie, Victoria *218*
Laurin, Anne
See McLaurin, Anne
Lauritzen, Jonreed 1902-1979 .... *13*
Lauscher, Hermann
See Hesse, Hermann
Lauture, Denize 1946- *86*
Laux, Connie
See Laux, Constance
Laux, Constance 1952- *97*
Laux, Dorothy 1920- *49*
Lavallee, Barbara 1941- *166*
Earlier sketch in SATA *74*
Lavau, Alexandra
See Watts, Frances
Lavender, David (Sievert) 1910-2003 .... *97*
Obituary *145*
Earlier sketch in SATA *64*
Lavender, William D. 1921- *143*
Laverne, Christine *175*
Lavert, Gwendolyn Battle 1951-
See Battle-Lavert, Gwendolyn
Laverty, Donald
See Blish, James
and Knight, Damon (Francis)
Lavigne, Louis-Dominique 1949- *107*
Lavine, David 1928- *31*
Lavine, Sigmund Arnold 1908-1986 .... *82*
Earlier sketch in SATA *3*
See also CLR *35*
Lavis, Steve *225*
Lavond, Paul Dennis
See Kornbluth, C(yril) M.
and Lowndes, Robert A(ugustine) W(ard)
and Pohl, Frederik
Law, Stephen *225*
Law, Stephen
See Law, Stephen
Lawford, Paula Jane 1960- *57*
Brief entry *53*
Lawhead, Stephen R. 1950- *109*
Lawhead, Steve
See Lawhead, Stephen R.
Lawler, Janet *222*
Lawlor, Laurie 1953- *235*
Earlier sketches in SATA *80, 137*
Lawlor, William
See Lawlor, William T.
Lawlor, William T. 1951- *183*
Lawrence, Ann (Margaret) 1942-1987 .... *41*
Obituary *54*
Lawrence, Caroline 1954- *203*
Lawrence, Iain 1955- *183*
Earlier sketch in SATA *135*
Lawrence, J. T.
See Rowland-Entwistle, (Arthur) Theodore (Henry)
Lawrence, Jerome 1915-2004 .... *65*
Lawrence, John 1933- *30*
Lawrence, Josephine 1890(?)-1978
Obituary *24*
Lawrence, Louise 1943- *119*
Earlier sketches in SATA *38, 78*
Lawrence, Louise de Kiriline 1894-1992 .... *13*
Lawrence, Lynn
See Garland, Sherry
Lawrence, Margery H. 1889-1969 .... *120*
Lawrence, Michael 1943- *132*
Lawrence, Mildred Elwood 1907-1997 .... *3*
Lawrence, R(onald) D(ouglas) 1921- *55*
Lawrinson, Julia 1969- *141*
Lawson, Amy
See Gordon, Amy
Lawson, Carol (Antell) 1946- *42*
Lawson, Don(ald Elmer) 1917-1990 .... *9*
Lawson, Joan 1906- *55*
Lawson, Julie 1947- *126*
Earlier sketch in SATA *79*
See also CLR *89*
Lawson, Marion Tubbs 1896-1994 .... *22*
Lawson, Robert 1892-1957 .... *100*
See also YABC *2*
See also CLR *73*
Lawton, Clive A. 1951- *145*
Laxdal, Vivienne 1962- *112*
Laybourn, Emma *193*
Layburn, Joe *228*
Laycock, George (Edwin) 1921- *5*
Layne, Laura
See Knott, William C(ecil, Jr.)
Layne, Steven L. *171*
Layson, Annelex Hofstra 1938(?)- *211*
Layton, Neal 1971- *187*
Earlier sketch in SATA *152*
Layton, Neal Andrew
See Layton, Neal
Lazare, Gerald John 1927- *44*
Lazare, Jerry
See Lazare, Gerald John
Lazarevich, Mila 1942- *17*
Lazarus, Keo Felker 1913-1993 .... *21*
Obituary *129*
Lea, Alec 1907- *19*
Lea, Bob 1952- *203*
Lea, Joan
See Neufeld, John (Arthur)
Leach, Maria 1892-1977 .... *39*
Brief entry *28*
Leacock, Elspeth 1946- *131*
Leacroft, Helen (Mabel Beal) 1919- *6*
Leacroft, Richard (Vallance Becher) 1914- *6*
Leaf, Margaret P. 1909(?)-1988
Obituary *55*
Leaf, (Wilbur) Munro 1905-1976 .... *20*
See also CLR *25*
Leaf, VaDonna Jean 1929- *26*
Leah, Devorah
See Devorah-Leah
Leakey, Richard E(rskine Frere) 1944- *42*
Leal, Ann Haywood *216*
Leander, Ed
See Richelson, Geraldine
Lear, Edward 1812-1888 .... *100*
Earlier sketch in SATA *18*
See also CLR *169*
Lears, Laurie 1955- *127*
Leasor, James 1923-2007 .... *54*
Leasor, Thomas James
See Leasor, James
Leavitt, Jerome E(dward) 1916- *23*
Leavitt, Martine 1953- *170*
LeBar, Mary E(velyn) 1910-1982 .... *35*
LeBlanc, Annette M. 1965- *68*
LeBlanc, L(ee) 1913- *54*
LeBox, Annette 1943- *145*
Lebrun, Claude 1929- *66*
Le Cain, Errol (John) 1941-1989 .... *68*
Obituary *60*
Earlier sketch in SATA *6*
Lechermeier, Philippe 1968- *235*
Lechner, Jack *201*
Lechner, John 1966- *200*
Leck, James 1973- *229*
Lecourt, Nancy (Hoyt) 1951- *73*
Ledbetter, Suzann 1953- *119*
Leder, Jane Mersky 1945- *61*
Brief entry *51*
Lederer, Muriel 1929- *48*
Lederer, William J. 1912-2009 .... *62*
Lederer, William Julius
See Lederer, William J.
Lee, Amanda
See Baggett, Nancy
and Buckholtz, Eileen (Garber)
and Glick, Ruth
Lee, Benjamin 1921- *27*
Lee, Betsy 1949- *37*
Lee, Carol
See Fletcher, Helen Jill
Lee, Carol Ann 1969- *185*
Lee, Chinlun *182*
Lee, Cora *223*
See Anderson, Catherine Corley
Lee, Dennis (Beynon) 1939- *102*
Earlier sketch in SATA *14*
See also CLR *3*
Lee, Dom 1959- *146*
Autobiography Feature *121*
Earlier sketch in SATA *83*
See also SAAS *26*
Lee, Doris Emrick 1905-1983 .... *44*
Obituary *35*
Lee, Edward
See Lee, J. Edward
Lee, Elizabeth Rogers 1940- *90*
Lee, Harper 1926- *11*
See also CLR *169*
Lee, Hector Viveros 1962- *115*
Lee, Howard N.
See Goulart, Ron
Lee, Huy Voun 1969- *217*
Earlier sketch in SATA *129*
Lee, Insu *213*
Lee, J. Edward 1953- *130*
Lee, Jared 1943- *215*
Lee, Jared D.
See Lee, Jared
Lee, Jeanne M. 1943- *138*
Lee, John R(obert) 1923-1976 .... *27*
Lee, Jordan
See Scholefield, Alan
Lee, Joseph Edward
See Lee, J. Edward
Lee, Julian
See Latham, Jean Lee
Lee, Linda
See Eyerly, Jeannette
Lee, Liz
See Lee, Elizabeth Rogers
Lee, Lucy
See Talbot, Charlene Joy
Lee, Lyn 1953- *128*
Lee, Manning de Villeneuve 1894-1980 .... *37*
Obituary *22*
Lee, Marian
See Clish, (Lee) Marian
Lee, Marie G. 1964- *178*
Earlier sketches in SATA *81, 130*
Lee, Marie Myung-Ok
See Lee, Marie G.

Lee, Mary Price 1934- ... *82*
 Earlier sketch in SATA *8*
Lee, Mildred
 See Scudder, Mildred Lee
Lee, Nelle Harper
 See Lee, Harper
Lee, Richard S. 1927- ... *82*
Lee, Robert C. 1931- ... *20*
Lee, Robert Edwin 1918-1994 ... *65*
 Obituary ... *82*
Lee, Robert J. 1921- ... *10*
Lee, Roy
 See Hopkins, Clark
Lee, Sally 1943- ... *67*
Lee, Suzy ... *193*
Lee, Tammie
 See Townsend, Thomas L.
Lee, Tanith 1947- ... *185*
 Earlier sketches in SATA *8, 88, 134*
Lee, Virginia 1976- ... *208*
Lee, Y.S. 1974- ... *232*
Leech, Ben
 See Bowkett, Stephen
Leeds, Contance ... *188*
Leedy, Loreen 1959- ... *238*
 Brief entry ... *50*
 Earlier sketches in SATA *54, 84, 128, 175*
Leedy, Loreen Janelle
 See Leedy, Loreen
Lee-Hostetler, Jeri 1940- ... *63*
Leekley, Thomas B(riggs) 1910-2001 ... *23*
Leeming, Jo Ann
 See Leeming, Joseph
Leeming, Joseph 1897-1968 ... *26*
Leemis, Ralph B. 1954- ... *72*
Leese, Jennifer L.B. 1970- ... *163*
Leeson, Muriel 1920- ... *54*
Leeson, R. A.
 See Leeson, Robert (Arthur)
Leeson, Robert (Arthur) 1928- ... *76*
 Earlier sketch in SATA *42*
Lee Tae-Jun 1904-1956(?) ... *194*
Lee-Tai, Amy 1964- ... *189*
Leffland, Ella 1931- ... *65*
Leffler, Silke ... *197*
Lefler, Irene (Whitney) 1917- ... *12*
LeFrak, Karen ... *182*
Le Gallienne, Eva 1899-1991 ... *9*
 Obituary ... *68*
Legg, Gerald 1947- ... *143*
Legg, Sarah Martha Ross Bruggeman (?)-1982
 Obituary ... *40*
LeGrand
 See Henderson, LeGrand
Le Guin, Ursula K. 1929- ... *194*
 Earlier sketches in SATA *4, 52, 99, 149*
 See also CLR *173*
Le Guin, Ursula Kroeber
 See Le Guin, Ursula K.
Legum, Colin 1919-2003 ... *10*
Lehman, Barbara 1963- ... *170*
 Earlier sketch in SATA *115*
Lehman, Bob ... *91*
Lehman, Elaine ... *91*
Lehmann, Debra Lynn
 See Vanasse, Deb
Lehman-Wilzig, Tami 1950- ... *224*
Lehn, Cornelia 1920- ... *46*
Lehne, Judith Logan 1947- ... *93*
Lehr, Delores 1920- ... *10*
Lehr, Norma 1930- ... *71*
Leiber, Fritz (Reuter, Jr.) 1910-1992 ... *45*
 Obituary ... *73*
Leibold, Jay 1957- ... *57*
 Brief entry ... *52*
Leichman, Seymour 1933- ... *5*
Leick, Bonnie ... *205*
Leigh, Nila K. 1981- ... *81*
Leigh, Tom 1947- ... *46*
Leigh-Pemberton, John 1911-1997 ... *35*
Leighton, Clare (Veronica Hope)
 1899-1989 ... *37*
Leighton, Margaret (Carver) 1896-1987 ... *1*
 Obituary ... *52*
Leijten, Aileen ... *216*
Leiner, Al(an) 1938- ... *83*
Leiner, Katherine 1949- ... *93*
Leipold, L. Edmond 1902-1983 ... *16*
Leisk, David (Johnson) 1906-1975 ... *30*
 Obituary ... *26*
 Earlier sketch in SATA *1*
 See also CLR *98*
Leist, Christina ... *226*
Leister, Mary 1917- ... *29*
Leitch, Patricia 1933- ... *98*
 Earlier sketch in SATA *11*
Leitner, Isabella 1924- ... *86*
Lekich, John ... *202*
Leland, Bob 1956- ... *92*
Leland, Robert E.
 See Leland, Bob
Leloup, Genevieve ... *230*
Lemaitre, Pascal 1967- ... *225*
 Earlier sketch in SATA *176*
Lember, Barbara Hirsch 1941- ... *92*
LeMieux, A.C. 1954- ... *125*
 Earlier sketch in SATA *90*
LeMieux, Anne
 See LeMieux, A.C.
LeMieux, Anne Connelly
 See LeMieux, A.C.
Lemieux, Michele 1955- ... *139*
Lemke, Horst 1922- ... *38*
Lemna, Don 1936- ... *216*
Lenain, Thierry 1959- ... *201*
Lenanton, Carola Mary Anima Oman
 See Oman, Carola (Mary Anima)
Lenard, Alexander 1910-1972
 Obituary ... *21*
Lendroth, Susan ... *207*
Leng, Qin ... *240*
Leng, Qin Chin
 See Leng, Qin
L'Engle, Madeleine 1918-2007 ... *128*
 Obituary ... *186*
 Earlier sketches in SATA *1, 27, 75*
 See also CLR *172*
 See also SAAS *15*
L'Engle, Madeleine Camp Franklin
 See L'Engle, Madeleine
Lengyel, Cornel Adam 1915- ... *27*
Lengyel, Emil 1895-1985 ... *3*
 Obituary ... *42*
Lennon, John 1940-1980 ... *114*
Lennon, John Ono
 See Lennon, John
Leno, Jay 1950- ... *154*
LeNoir, Janice 1941- ... *89*
Lens, Sidney 1912-1986 ... *13*
 Obituary ... *48*
Lenski, Lois 1893-1974 ... *100*
 Earlier sketches in SATA *1, 26*
 See also CLR *26*
Lent, Blair 1930-2009 ... *133*
 Obituary ... *200*
 Earlier sketch in SATA *2*
Lent, Henry Bolles 1901-1973 ... *17*
Lent, John 1948- ... *108*
Leodhas, Sorche Nic
 See Alger, Leclaire (Gowans)
Leokum, Arkady 1916(?)- ... *45*
Leon, Carol Boyd ... *212*
Leon, Sharon 1959- ... *79*
Leonard, Alison 1944- ... *70*
Leonard, Anna
 See Gilman, Laura Anne
Leonard, Constance (Brink) 1923- ... *42*
 Brief entry ... *40*
Leonard, Dutch
 See Leonard, Elmore
Leonard, Elmore 1925- ... *163*
Leonard, Elmore John, Jr.
 See Leonard, Elmore
Leonard, Jonathan N(orton) 1903-1975 ... *36*
Leonard, Laura 1923- ... *75*
Leonard, Tom 1955- ... *207*
Leonetti, Mike 1958- ... *202*
Leong, Gor Yun
 See Ellison, Virginia H(owell)
Leonhard, Herb ... *217*
Leonhardt, Alice 1950- ... *234*
 Earlier sketch in SATA *152*
Lerangis, Peter 1955- ... *171*
 Earlier sketch in SATA *72*
Lerman, Josh ... *215*
Lerner, Aaron 1920-2007 ... *35*
 Obituary ... *179*
Lerner, Aaron Bunsen
 See Lerner, Aaron
Lerner, Carol 1927- ... *86*
 Earlier sketch in SATA *33*
 See also CLR *34*
 See also SAAS *12*
Lerner, Gerda 1920- ... *65*
Lerner, Harriet 1944- ... *101*
Lerner, Marguerite Rush 1924-1987 ... *11*
 Obituary ... *51*
Lerner, Sharon (Ruth) 1938-1982 ... *11*
 Obituary ... *29*
Leroe, Ellen 1949- ... *99*
 Brief entry ... *51*
 Earlier sketch in SATA *61*
Leroe, Ellen W.
 See Leroe, Ellen
Leroe, Ellen Whitney
 See Leroe, Ellen
Leroux, Gaston 1868-1927 ... *65*
Leroux-Hugon, Helene 1955- ... *132*
LeRoy, Gen ... *52*
 Brief entry ... *36*
Lerrigo, Marion Olive 1898-1968
 Obituary ... *29*
LeShan, Eda J(oan) 1922-2002 ... *21*
 See also CLR *6*
Leshem, Yossi 1947- ... *222*
LeSieg, Theo.
 See Dr. Seuss
Lesinski, Jeanne M. 1960- ... *120*
Leslie, Robert Franklin 1911-1990 ... *7*
Leslie, Roger 1961- ... *168*
Leslie, Roger James
 See Leslie, Roger
Leslie, Sarah
 See McGuire, Leslie (Sarah)
LeSourd, Catherine
 See Marshall, (Sarah) Catherine (Wood)
Lessac, Frane
 See Lessac, Frane
Lessac, Frane 1954- ... *209*
 Earlier sketches in SATA *61, 148*
Lessem, Dino Don
 See Lessem, Don
Lessem, Don 1951- ... *182*
 Earlier sketches in SATA *97, 155*
Lesser, Margaret 1899(?)-1979
 Obituary ... *22*
Lesser, Rika 1953- ... *53*
Lester, Alison 1952- ... *218*
 Earlier sketches in SATA *50, 90, 129*
Lester, Helen 1936- ... *189*
 Earlier sketches in SATA *46, 92, 145*
Lester, Julius 1939- ... *157*
 Earlier sketches in SATA *12, 74, 112*
 See also CLR *143*
Lester, Julius Bernard
 See Lester, Julius
Lester, Mike 1955- ... *206*
 Earlier sketch in SATA *131*
Le Sueur, Meridel 1900-1996 ... *6*
Leszczynski, Diana ... *211*
Lethcoe, Jason ... *191*

Le Tord, Bijou 1945- *95*
Earlier sketch in SATA *49*
Letts, Billie 1938- *121*
Letts, Elizabeth
See Alalou, Elizabeth
Leuck, Laura 1962- *192*
Earlier sketches in SATA *85, 146*
Leung, Hilary 1975- *225*
Leutscher, Alfred (George) 1913- *23*
Levai, Blaise 1919- *39*
le Vann, Kate *237*
Levchuk, Lisa *215*
Leveen, Tom *230*
Levenkron, Steven 1941- *86*
Leverich, Kathleen 1948- *103*
LeVert, John 1946- *55*
Levert, Mireille 1956- *211*
LeVert, William John
See LeVert, John
Levete, Sarah 1961- *153*
Levin, Betty 1927- *201*
Earlier sketches in SATA *19, 84, 137*
See also SAAS *11*
Levin, Ira 1929-2007 ..... *66*
Obituary *187*
Levin, Ira Marvin
See Levin, Ira
Levin, Marcia Obrasky 1918- *13*
Levin, Meyer 1905-1981 ..... *21*
Obituary *27*
Levin, Miriam (Ramsfelder) 1962- *97*
Levine, Abby 1943- *54*
Brief entry *52*
Levine, Anna *212*
Levine, Betty K(rasne) 1933- *66*
Levine, David 1926-2009 ..... *43*
Brief entry *35*
Levine, Edna S(imon) *35*
Levine, Ellen 1939- *190*
Levine, Evan 1962- *77*
Earlier sketch in SATA *74*
Levine, Gail Carson 1947- *239*
Earlier sketches in SATA *98, 161, 195*
See also CLR *85*
Levine, I(srael) E. 1923-2003 ..... *12*
Obituary *146*
Levine, Joan Goldman *11*
Levine, Joseph 1910- *33*
Levine, Kristin 1974- *213*
Levine, Marge 1934- *81*
Levine, Rhoda *14*
Levine, Sarah 1970- *57*
Levine, Shar 1953- *131*
Levine-Freidus, Gail
See Provost, Gail Levine
Levinson, Nancy Smiler 1938- *211*
Earlier sketches in SATA *33, 80, 140*
Levinson, Riki *99*
Brief entry *49*
Earlier sketch in SATA *52*
Levithan, David 1972- *235*
Earlier sketch in SATA *166*
Levitin, Sonia 1934- *192*
Autobiography Feature *131*
Earlier sketches in SATA *4, 68, 119, 131*
See also CLR *53*
See also SAAS *2*
Levitt, Sidney (Mark) 1947- *68*
Levon, O. U.
See Kesey, Ken
Levoy, Myron 1930- *49*
Brief entry *37*
Levy, Barrie *112*
Levy, Constance 1931- *140*
Earlier sketch in SATA *73*
See also SAAS *22*
Levy, Debbie 1957- *232*
Levy, Deborah Marian
See Levy, Debbie
Levy, Elizabeth 1942- *169*
Earlier sketches in SATA *31, 69, 107*
See also SAAS *18*
Levy, Janice *172*
Levy, Marilyn 1937- *67*
Levy, Nathan 1945- *63*
Levy, Robert 1945- *82*
Lewees, John
See Stockton, Francis Richard
Lewin, Betsy 1937- *222*
Autobiography Feature *115*
Earlier sketches in SATA *32, 90, 169*
Lewin, Hugh 1939- *72*
Brief entry *40*
See also CLR *9*
Lewin, Ted 1935- *226*
Autobiography Feature *115*
Earlier sketches in SATA *21, 76, 119, 165, 195*
Lewis, Alice C. 1936- *46*
Lewis, Alice Hudson 1895(?)-1971
Obituary *29*
Lewis, Amanda 1955- *80*
Lewis, Anthony 1927- *27*
Lewis, Anthony 1966- *227*
Earlier sketch in SATA *120*
Lewis, Barbara A. 1943- *73*
Lewis, Beverly 1949- *80*
Lewis, Brenda Ralph 1932- *72*
Lewis, Brian 1963- *128*
Lewis, C. S. 1898-1963 ..... *100*
Earlier sketch in SATA *13*
See also CLR *173*
Lewis, Claudia (Louise) 1907-2001 ..... *5*
Lewis, Clive Staples
See Lewis, C. S.
Lewis, Cynthia Copeland 1960- *111*
Lewis, E. M. *123*
Earlier sketch in SATA *20*
Lewis, Earl Bradley
See Lewis, E.B.
Lewis, E.B. 1956- *211*
Earlier sketches in SATA *93, 124, 168*
Lewis, Elizabeth Foreman 1892-1958 ..... *121*
See also YABC *2*
Lewis, Francine
See Wells, Helen
Lewis, Harry Sinclair
See Lewis, Sinclair
Lewis, Hilda (Winifred) 1896-1974
Obituary *20*
Lewis, J. Patrick 1942- *205*
Earlier sketches in SATA *69, 104, 162*
Lewis, Jack P(earl) 1919- *65*
Lewis, Jean 1924- *61*
Lewis, Jon S.
See Lewis, J.S.
Lewis, Jon Samuel
See Lewis, J.S.
Lewis, Joseph Anthony
See Lewis, Anthony
Lewis, J.S. 1972- *238*
Earlier sketch in SATA *203*
Lewis, Julinda
See Lewis-Ferguson, Julinda
Lewis, Kevin *173*
Lewis, Kim 1951- *217*
Earlier sketches in SATA *84, 136*
Lewis, Linda (Joy) 1946- *67*
Lewis, Lucia Z.
See Anderson, Lucia (Lewis)
Lewis, Marjorie 1929- *40*
Brief entry *35*
Lewis, Mary 1907(?)-1988 ..... *64*
Obituary *56*
Lewis, Mervyn
See Frewer, Glyn (M.)
Lewis, Michael
See Untermeyer, Louis
Lewis, Naomi 1911-2009 ..... *144*
Earlier sketch in SATA *76*
Lewis, Paeony 1960- *173*
Lewis, Paul
See Gerson, Noel Bertram
Lewis, Richard 1935- *3*
Lewis, Richard 1956- *209*
Lewis, Rob 1962- *72*
Lewis, Roger
See Zarchy, Harry
Lewis, Rose *209*
Lewis, Rose A.
See Lewis, Rose
Lewis, Shannon
See Llywelyn, Morgan
Lewis, Shari 1934-1998 ..... *35*
Brief entry *30*
Obituary *104*
Lewis, Sylvan R.
See Aronson, Virginia
Lewis, Thomas P(arker) 1936- *27*
Lewis, Wendy A. 1966- *150*
Lewis-Ferguson, Julinda 1955- *85*
Lewison, Wendy Cheyette *177*
Lewiton, Mina 1904-1970 ..... *2*
Lew-Vriethoff, Joanne *186*
Lexau, Joan M. *130*
Earlier sketches in SATA *1, 36*
Ley, Willy 1906-1969 ..... *2*
Leydon, Rita (Floden) 1949- *21*
Leyland, Eric (Arthur) 1911- *37*
L'Hommedieu, Dorothy Keasley 1885-1961
Obituary *29*
Li, Xiao Jun 1952- *86*
Liao, Jimmy 1958- *202*
Liatsos, Sandra Olson 1942- *103*
Libby, Alisa M. *189*
Libby, Barbara M. *153*
Libby, Bill
See Libby, William M.
Libby, William M. 1927-1984 ..... *5*
Obituary *39*
Liberty, Gene 1924- *3*
Lichtenheld, Tom *208*
Earlier sketch in SATA *152*
Lichtman, Wendy 1946- *193*
Liddell, Kenneth 1912-1975 ..... *63*
Liddiment, Carol *224*
Lidz, Jane *120*
Lieb, Josh 1972- *224*
Lieberman, E(dwin) James 1934- *62*
Liebers, Arthur 1913-1984 ..... *12*
Lieblich, Irene 1923- *22*
Liers, Emil E(rnest) 1890-1975 ..... *37*
Lies, Brian 1963- *190*
Earlier sketch in SATA *131*
Lieshout, Elle van
See van Lieshout, Elle
Liestman, Vicki 1961- *72*
Lietz, Gerald S. 1918- *11*
Liew, Sonny 1974- *219*
Life, Kay (Guinn) 1930- *83*
Lifton, Betty Jean 1926-2010 ..... *118*
Earlier sketch in SATA *6*
Lifton, Robert Jay 1926- *66*
Light, Steve *237*
Lightburn, Ron 1954- *91*
Lightburn, Sandra 1955- *91*
Lightner, A. M.
See Hopf, Alice (Martha) L(ightner)
Lightner, Alice
See Hopf, Alice (Martha) L(ightner)
Lignell, Lois 1911- *37*
Liles, Maurine Walpole 1935- *81*
Lillegard, Dee *184*
Lilley, Stephen R. 1950- *97*
Lilley, Stephen Ray
See Lilley, Stephen R.
Lillington, Kenneth (James) 1916-1998 ..... *39*
Lilly, Nate *182*
Lilly, Ray
See Curtis, Richard
Lim, John 1932- *43*

Liman, Ellen (Fogelson) 1936- *22*
Limb, Sue 1946- *203*
Earlier sketch in SATA *158*
Limburg, Peter R(ichard) 1929- *13*
Lin, Grace 1974- *198*
Earlier sketches in SATA *111, 162*
Lincoln, C(harles) Eric 1924-2000 .... *5*
Lincoln, Christopher 1952- *208*
Lincoln, Hazel *187*
Lincoln, James
See Bates, Katharine Lee
Lindbergh, Anne
See Sapieyevski, Anne Lindbergh
Lindbergh, Anne Morrow 1906-2001 .... *33*
Obituary *125*
Lindbergh, Anne Spencer Morrow
See Lindbergh, Anne Morrow
Lindbergh, Charles A(ugustus, Jr.)
1902-1974 .... *33*
Lindbergh, Reeve 1945- *163*
Earlier sketch in SATA *116*
Lindblom, Steven (Winther) 1946- *94*
Brief entry *39*
Earlier sketch in SATA *42*
Linde, Gunnel 1924- *5*
Lindenbaum, Pija 1955- *183*
Earlier sketches in SATA *77, 144*
Lindgren, Astrid (Anna Emilia Ericsson)
1907-2002 .... *38*
Obituary *128*
Earlier sketch in SATA *2*
See also CLR *119*
Lindgren, Barbro 1937- *207*
Brief entry *46*
Earlier sketches in SATA *63, 120*
See also CLR *86*
Lindman, Maj (Jan) 1886-1972 .... *43*
Lindner, April 1962- *238*
Lindo, Elvira 1962- *219*
Lindop, Edmund 1925- *5*
Lindquist, Jennie Dorothea 1899-1977 .... *13*
Lindquist, Rowena Cory 1958- *98*
Lindquist, Willis 1908-1988 .... *20*
Lindsay, Nicholas Vachel
See Lindsay, Vachel
Lindsay, Norman Alfred William
1879-1969 .... *67*
See also CLR *8*
Lindsay, Vachel 1879-1931 .... *40*
Lindsey, Kathleen D(orothy) 1949- *153*
Line, David
See Davidson, Lionel
Line, Les 1935-2010 .... *27*
Lines, Kathleen Mary 1902-1988
Obituary *61*
Linfield, Esther *40*
Lingard, Joan (Amelia) 1932- *130*
Autobiography Feature *130*
Earlier sketches in SATA *8, 74, 114*
See also CLR *89*
See also SAAS *5*
Link, Martin 1934- *28*
Linn, Margot
See Ziefert, Harriet
Linnea, Sharon 1956- *82*
Lintern, Tom *228*
Lion, Melissa 1976- *176*
Lionni, Leo(nard) 1910-1999 .... *72*
Obituary *118*
Earlier sketch in SATA *8*
See also CLR *71*
Lipinsky de Orlov, Lino S. 1908- *22*
Lipkind, William 1904-1974 .... *15*
Lipman, David 1931-2008 .... *21*
Lipman, Matthew 1923-2010 .... *14*
Lipp, Frederick *204*
Lippincott, Bertram 1898(?)-1985
Obituary *42*
Lippincott, Gary A. 1953- *220*
Earlier sketches in SATA *73, 119*
Lippincott, Joseph W(harton) 1887-1976 .... *17*
Lippincott, Sarah Lee 1920- *22*
Lippman, Peter J. 1936- *31*
Lipsyte, Robert 1938- *198*
Earlier sketches in SATA *5, 68, 113, 161*
See also CLR *76*
Lipsyte, Robert Michael
See Lipsyte, Robert
Lisandrelli, Elaine Slivinski 1951- *94*
Lisker, Sonia O. 1933- *44*
Lisle, Holly 1960- *208*
Earlier sketch in SATA *98*
Lisle, Janet Taylor 1947- *150*
Brief entry *47*
Earlier sketches in SATA *59, 96*
See also SAAS *14*
Lisle, Rebecca *162*
Lisle, Seward D.
See Ellis, Edward S.
Lisowski, Gabriel 1946- *47*
Brief entry *31*
Liss, Howard 1922-1995 .... *4*
Obituary *84*
Lissiat, Amy
See Thompson, Colin
Lisson, Deborah 1941- *110*
Earlier sketch in SATA *71*
List, Ilka Katherine 1935- *6*
Liston, Robert A. 1927- *5*
Litchfield, Ada B(assett) 1916-1999 .... *5*
Litchfield, Jo 1973- *116*
Lithgow, John 1945- *145*
Lithgow, John Arthur
See Lithgow, John
Litowinsky, Olga 1936- *26*
Litowinsky, Olga Jean
See Litowinsky, Olga
Littke, Lael J. 1929- *140*
Earlier sketches in SATA *51, 83*
Little, A. Edward
See Klein, Aaron E.
Little, Douglas 1942- *96*
Little, (Flora) Jean 1932- *149*
Earlier sketches in SATA *2, 68, 106*
See also CLR *4*
See also SAAS *17*
Little, Lessie Jones 1906-1986 .... *60*
Obituary *50*
Little, Mary E. 1912-1999 .... *28*
Littlechild, George 1958- *85*
Littledale, Freya (Lota) 1929-1992 .... *74*
Earlier sketch in SATA *2*
Littlefield, Bill 1948- *83*
Littlefield, Holly 1963- *97*
Littlesugar, Amy 1953- *176*
Earlier sketch in SATA *122*
Littleton, Mark R. 1950- *142*
Earlier sketch in SATA *89*
Littlewood, Karin *211*
Littman, Sarah Darer *221*
Earlier sketch in SATA *175*
Litty, Julie 1971- *181*
Litwin, Mike *235*
Litzinger, Rosanne 1948- *196*
Liu, Cynthea *221*
Lively, Penelope 1933- *164*
Earlier sketches in SATA *7, 60, 101*
See also CLR *159*
Lively, Penelope Margaret
See Lively, Penelope
Liverakos, L. A.
See Gilman, Laura Anne
Liversidge, (Henry) Douglas 1913- *8*
Livesey, Claire (Warner) 1927- *127*
Livingston, Carole 1941- *42*
Livingston, (M.) Irene 1932- *150*
Livingston, Myra Cohn 1926-1996 .... *68*
Obituary *92*
Earlier sketch in SATA *5*
See also CLR *7*
See also SAAS *1*
Livingston, Richard R(oland) 1922- *8*
Livo, Norma J. 1929- *76*
Liwska, Renata *240*
Earlier sketch in SATA *199*
Ljungkvist, Laura *180*
Llerena Aguirre, Carlos 1952- *19*
Llerena Aguirre, Carlos Antonio
See Llerena Aguirre, Carlos
Llewellyn, Claire 1954- *196*
Earlier sketches in SATA *77, 143*
Llewellyn, Grace 1964- *110*
Llewellyn, Richard
See Llewellyn Lloyd, Richard Dafydd Vivian
Llewellyn, Sam 1948- *185*
Earlier sketch in SATA *95*
Llewellyn, Tom 1964- *234*
Llewellyn Lloyd, Richard Dafydd Vivian
1906-1983 .... *11*
Obituary *37*
Llewelyn, T. Harcourt
See Hamilton, Charles (Harold St. John)
Lloyd, Alan
See Lloyd, A.R.
Lloyd, Alan Richard
See Lloyd, A.R.
Lloyd, Alison 1966- *231*
Lloyd, A.R. 1927- *168*
Earlier sketch in SATA *97*
Lloyd, David
See Lloyd, David T.
Lloyd, David T. 1954- *167*
Lloyd, E. James
See James, Elizabeth
Lloyd, Errol 1943- *22*
Lloyd, Hugh
See Fitzhugh, Percy Keese
Lloyd, James
See James, Elizabeth
Lloyd, Megan 1958- *239*
Earlier sketches in SATA *77, 117, 189*
Lloyd, Norman 1909-1980
Obituary *23*
Lloyd, (Mary) Norris 1908-1993 .... *10*
Obituary *75*
Lloyd, Saci 1967- *220*
Lloyd, Sam *183*
Lloyd, Tanya
See Kyi, Tanya Lloyd
Lloyd-Jones, Sally 1960- *179*
Lloyd Webber, Andrew 1948- *56*
Llywelyn, Morgan 1937- *109*
Lo, Ginnie *165*
Lo, Malinda 1974- *222*
Lo, Virginia M.
See Lo, Ginnie
Lobato, Jose Bento Monteiro 1882-1948 .... *114*
Lobel, Anita 1934- *241*
Earlier sketches in SATA *6, 55, 96, 162*
Lobel, Arnold (Stark) 1933-1987 .... *55*
Obituary *54*
Earlier sketch in SATA *6*
See also CLR *5*
Lobel, Gillian *181*
Lobsenz, Amelia *12*
Lobsenz, Norman M(itchell) 1919- *6*
Lochak, Michele 1936- *39*
Lochlons, Colin
See Jackson, C(aary) Paul
Locke, Clinton W. *1*
Locke, Elsie (Violet) 1912-2001 .... *87*
Locke, Gary 1963- *197*
Locke, Lucie 1904-1989 .... *10*
Locke, Robert 1944- *63*
See also CLR *39*
Locker, Thomas 1937- *109*
Earlier sketch in SATA *59*
See also CLR *14*
Lockhart, E.
See Jenkins, Emily
Lockridge, Hildegarde (Dolson)
1908-1981 .... *121*
Earlier sketch in SATA *5*

Lockwood, Mary
See Spelman, Mary
Lodge, Bernard 1933- ... *215*
Earlier sketches in SATA *33, 107*
Lodge, Jo 1966- ... *173*
Earlier sketch in SATA *112*
Loeb, Jeffrey 1946- ... *57*
Loeb, Robert H., Jr. 1917- ... *21*
Loefgren, Ulf 1931- ... *3*
Loehfelm, Bill 1969- ... *153*
Loehr, Mallory ... *184*
Loehr, Patrick 1968(?)- ... *194*
Loeper, John J(oseph) 1929- ... *118*
Earlier sketch in SATA *10*
Loescher, Ann Dull 1942- ... *20*
Loescher, Gil 1945- ... *20*
Loescher, Gilburt Damian
See Loescher, Gil
Loewer, Jean Jenkins
See Jenkins, Jean
Loewer, (Henry) Peter 1934- ... *98*
LoFaro, Jerry 1959- ... *77*
Lofo
See Heimann, Rolf
Lofthouse, Liz ... *199*
Lofting, Hugh (John) 1886-1947 ... *100*
Earlier sketch in SATA *15*
See also CLR *143*
Lofts, Norah (Robinson) 1904-1983 ... *8*
Obituary ... *36*
Logan, Alysia
See Divine, L.
Logan, Bob 1968- ... *238*
Logan, Jake
See Knott, William C(ecil, Jr.)
and Krepps, Robert W(ilson)
and Pearl, Jacques Bain
and Riefe, Alan
and Rifkin, Shepard
and Smith, Martin Cruz
Logan, Laura ... *237*
Logan, Mark
See Nicole, Christopher
Logan, Rochelle 1954- ... *169*
Logsted, Greg ... *221*
Logston, Anne 1962- ... *112*
Logue, Christopher 1926-2011 ... *23*
Logue, Mary 1952- ... *161*
Earlier sketch in SATA *112*
Logue, Mary Louise
See Logue, Mary
Loh, Morag 1935- ... *73*
Lohans, Alison 1949- ... *101*
Loizeaux, William ... *185*
Loken, Newton Clayton 1919- ... *26*
Lomas, Steve
See Brennan, Joseph Lomas
Lomask, Milton (Nachman) 1909-1991 ... *20*
Lombard, Jenny ... *178*
Lombino, Salvatore
See Hunter, Evan
LoMonaco, Palmyra 1932- ... *102*
London, C. Alexander 1980(?)- ... *240*
London, Charles 1980-
See London, C. Alexander
London, Charles Alexander
See London, C. Alexander
London, Jack 1876-1916 ... *18*
See also CLR *108*
London, Jane
See Geis, Darlene Stern
London, John Griffith
See London, Jack
London, Jonathan 1947- ... *221*
Earlier sketches in SATA *74, 113, 157*
Lonergan, (Pauline) Joy (MacLean) 1909- ... *10*
Lonette, Reisie (Dominee) 1924- ... *43*
Long, Cathryn J. 1946- ... *89*
Long, Earlene (Roberta) 1938- ... *50*
Long, Emmett
See Leonard, Elmore
Long, Ethan 1968(?)- ... *223*
Earlier sketch in SATA *182*
Long, Helen Beecher ... *1*
Long, Judith Elaine 1953- ... *20*
Long, Judy
See Long, Judith Elaine
Long, Kim 1949- ... *69*
Long, Laura Mooney 1892-1967
Obituary ... *29*
Long, Laurel ... *203*
Long, Loren 1966(?)- ... *188*
Earlier sketch in SATA *151*
Long, Melinda 1960- ... *152*
Long, Sylvia 1948- ... *179*
Earlier sketch in SATA *120*
Longbeard, Frederick
See Longyear, Barry B(rookes)
Longfellow, Henry Wadsworth 1807-1882 ... *19*
See also CLR *99*
Longfellow, Layne 1937- ... *102*
Longfellow, Layne A.
See Longfellow, Layne
Longman, Harold S. 1919- ... *5*
Longsworth, Polly 1933- ... *28*
Longtemps, Kenneth 1933- ... *17*
Longway, A. Hugh
See Lang, Andrew
Longyear, Barry B(rookes) 1942- ... *117*
Look, Lenore ... *180*
Loomans, Diane 1955- ... *90*
Loomis, Christine ... *160*
Earlier sketch in SATA *113*
Loomis, Jennifer A. 1942- ... *101*
Loomis, Robert D. ... *5*
Lopez, Angelo (Cayas) 1967- ... *83*
Lopez, Antonio Castro
See Castro L., Antonio
Lopez, Barry 1945- ... *67*
Lopez, Barry Holstun
See Lopez, Barry
Lopez, Jack 1950- ... *178*
Lopez, Loretta 1963- ... *190*
Lopez, Lorraine 1956- ... *181*
Lopez, Lorraine M.
See Lopez, Lorraine
Lopez, Mario 1973- ... *226*
Lopez, Rafael 1961(?)- ... *198*
Lopshire, Robert 1927-2002 ... *233*
Earlier sketch in SATA *6*
Loraine, Connie
See Reece, Colleen L.
Lorbiecki, Marybeth 1959- ... *172*
Earlier sketch in SATA *121*
Lord, Athena V. 1932- ... *39*
Lord, Beman 1924-1991 ... *5*
Obituary ... *69*
Lord, Bette Bao 1938- ... *58*
See also CLR *151*
Lord, Cynthia ... *238*
Earlier sketch in SATA *182*
Lord, Doreen Mildred Douglas
See Lord, Douglas
Lord, Douglas 1904-1992 ... *12*
Lord, Janet ... *204*
Lord, John Vernon 1939- ... *21*
Lord, Michele ... *201*
Lord, Nancy J.
See Titus, Eve
Lord, Patricia C. 1927-1988
Obituary ... *58*
Lord, Walter 1917-2002 ... *3*
Lorde, Diana
See Reno, Dawn E(laine)
Lorenz, Albert 1941- ... *115*
Lorenzini, Carlo
See Collodi, Carlo
Lorey, Dean 1967- ... *193*
Lorimer, Janet 1941- ... *60*
Loring, Emilie (Baker) 1864(?)-1951 ... *51*
Lorkowski, Thomas V(incent) 1950- ... *92*
Lorkowski, Tom
See Lorkowski, Thomas V(incent)
Lorraine, Walter (Henry) 1929- ... *16*
Lorrimer, Claire
See Robins, Patricia
Loss, Joan 1933- ... *11*
Lothrop, Harriet Mulford Stone 1844-1924 . *20*
Lottridge, Celia Barker 1936- ... *157*
Earlier sketch in SATA *112*
LoTurco, Laura 1963- ... *84*
Lotz, Wolfgang 1912-1981 ... *65*
Loughridge, Stuart 1978- ... *214*
Louie, Ai-Ling 1949- ... *40*
Brief entry ... *34*
Louis, Catherine 1963- ... *186*
Louis, Pat
See Francis, Dorothy
Louisburgh, Sheila Burnford
See Burnford, Sheila (Philip Cochrane Every)
Louise, Anita
See Riggio, Anita
Louise, Tina 1934- ... *191*
Lourie, Helen
See Storr, Catherine (Cole)
Lourie, Peter 1952- ... *183*
Earlier sketches in SATA *82, 142*
Lourie, Peter King
See Lourie, Peter
Love, Ann 1947- ... *168*
Earlier sketch in SATA *79*
Love, D. Anne 1949- ... *180*
Earlier sketches in SATA *96, 145*
Love, Douglas 1967- ... *92*
Love, Judith Dufour
See Love, Judy
Love, Judy ... *188*
Love, Katherine (Isabel) 1907- ... *3*
Love, Kathleen Ann
See Love, Ann
Love, Maryann Cusimano ... *223*
Love, Sandra (Weller) 1940- ... *26*
Lovegrove, James 1965- ... *216*
Lovegrove, J.M.H.
See Lovegrove, James
Lovejoy, Jack 1937- ... *116*
Lovelace, Delos Wheeler 1894-1967 ... *7*
Lovelace, Maud Hart 1892-1980 ... *2*
Obituary ... *23*
Lovell, Ingraham
See Bacon, Josephine Dodge (Daskam)
Lovelock, Brian 1956- ... *214*
Loverseed, Amanda (Jane) 1965- ... *75*
Lovett, Margaret (Rose) 1915- ... *22*
Low, Alice 1926- ... *156*
Earlier sketches in SATA *11, 76*
Low, Elizabeth Hammond 1898-1991 ... *5*
Low, Joseph 1911-2007 ... *14*
Low, Penelope Margaret
See Lively, Penelope
Low, William ... *177*
Lowe, Helen 1961- ... *206*
Lowe, Jay, Jr.
See Loeper, John J(oseph)
Lowell, Pamela ... *187*
Lowell, Susan 1950- ... *206*
Earlier sketches in SATA *81, 127*
Lowenstein, Dyno 1914-1996 ... *6*
Lowenstein, Sallie 1949- ... *116*
Lowery, Linda 1949- ... *151*
Earlier sketch in SATA *74*
Lowery, Mike ... *227*
Lowitz, Anson C. 1901(?)-1978 ... *18*
Lowitz, Sadyebeth Heath 1901-1969 ... *17*
Lowndes, Robert A(ugustine) W(ard)
1916-1998 ... *117*
Lowrey, Janette Sebring 1892-1986 ... *43*
Lowry, Lois 1937- ... *230*
Autobiography Feature ... *127*
Earlier sketches in SATA *23, 70, 111, 177*
See also CLR *72*
See also SAAS *3*

Lowry, Lois Hammersberg
See Lowry, Lois
Lowry, Peter 1953- *7*
Lowther, George F. 1913-1975
Obituary *30*
Loxton, Daniel 1975- *229*
Loyie, Larry 1933- *150*
Lozansky, Edward D. 1941- *62*
Lozier, Herbert 1915- *26*
Lubar, David 1954- *190*
Earlier sketch in SATA *133*
Lubell, Cecil 1912-2000 .... *6*
Lubell, Winifred 1914- *6*
Lubell, Winifred A. Milius
See Lubell, Winifred
Lubin, Leonard
See Lubin, Leonard B.
Lubin, Leonard B. 1943-1994 .... *45*
Brief entry *37*
Lubka, S. Ruth 1948- *154*
Lubner, Susan *185*
Luby, Thia 1954- *124*
Lucado, Max 1955- *104*
Lucado, Max Lee
See Lucado, Max
Lucas, Cedric 1962- *101*
Lucas, David 1966- *208*
Lucas, E(dward) V(errall) 1868-1938 .... *20*
Lucas, Eileen 1956- *113*
Earlier sketch in SATA *76*
Lucas, George 1944- *56*
Lucas, Jerry 1940- *33*
Lucas, Margeaux *186*
Lucas, Victoria
See Plath, Sylvia
Lucashenko, Melissa 1967- *104*
Luccarelli, Vincent 1923- *90*
Luce, Celia (Geneva Larsen) 1914- *38*
Luce, Willard (Ray) 1914-1990 .... *38*
Lucht, Irmgard 1937- *82*
Lucke, Deb *202*
Luckett, Dave 1951- *220*
Earlier sketches in SATA *106, 167*
Luckhardt, Mildred Corell 1898-1990 .... *5*
Ludden, Allen (Ellsworth) 1918(?)-1981
Obituary *27*
Ludel, Jacqueline 1945- *64*
Ludlow, Geoffrey
See Meynell, Laurence Walter
Ludlum, Mabel Cleland
See Widdemer, Mabel Cleland
Ludwig, Helen *33*
Ludwig, Lyndell 1923- *63*
Ludwig, Trudy 1959- *209*
Earlier sketch in SATA *166*
Luebs, Robin 1949- *212*
Lueders, Edward (George) 1923- *14*
Luenn, Nancy 1954- *79*
Earlier sketch in SATA *51*
Lufkin, Raymond H. 1897- *38*
Lugard, Flora Louisa Shaw 1852-1929 .... *21*
Luger, Harriett Mandelay 1914- *23*
Luhrmann, Winifred B(ruce) 1934- *11*
Luis, Earlene W. 1929- *11*
Lujan, Jorge *201*
Lukas, Catherine
See Albee, Sarah
Luke, Pauline *178*
Luke, Pauline R.
See Luke, Pauline
Lum, Bernice *230*
Lum, Kate *229*
Lum, Peter
See Crowe, (Bettina) Peter Lum
Lumry, Amanda (R.) *159*
Luna, James 1962- *241*
Lund, Deb *157*
Lund, Doris Herold 1919- *12*
Lunde, Darrin *202*
Lundebrek, Amy 1975- *213*
Lundquist, David R. *239*
Lung, Chang
See Jordan, Robert
Lunge-Larsen, Lise 1955- *184*
Earlier sketch in SATA *138*
Lunn, Carolyn (Kowalczyk) 1960- *67*
Lunn, Janet (Louise Swoboda) 1928- *110*
Earlier sketches in SATA *4, 68*
See also CLR *18*
See also SAAS *12*
Lunsford, Cin Forshay
See Forshay-Lunsford, Cin
Lupica, Michael
See Lupica, Mike
Lupica, Michael Thomas
See Lupica, Mike
Lupica, Mike 1952- *236*
Earlier sketch in SATA *177*
Lupoff, Dick
See Lupoff, Richard A.
Lupoff, Richard A. 1935- *60*
Lupoff, Richard Allen
See Lupoff, Richard A.
Lurie, Alison 1926- *112*
Earlier sketch in SATA *46*
Lurie, Morris 1938- *72*
Lussert, Anneliese 1929- *101*
Lusted, Marcia Amidon 1962- *143*
Lustig, Arnost 1926-2011 .... *56*
Lustig, Loretta 1944- *46*
Lutes, Jason 1967- *210*
Luthardt, Kevin 1973- *172*
Luther, Frank 1905-1980
Obituary *25*
Luther, Rebekah (Lyn) S(tiles) 1960- *90*
Luttmann, Gail
See Damerow, Gail
Luttrell, Guy L. 1938- *22*
Luttrell, Ida (Alleene) 1934- *91*
Brief entry *35*
Earlier sketch in SATA *40*
Luttrell, William (J. III) 1954- *149*
Lutz, John 1939- *180*
Lutz, John Thomas
See Lutz, John
Lutz, Norma Jean 1943- *122*
Lutzeier, Elizabeth 1952- *72*
Lutzker, Edythe 1904-1991 .... *5*
Luxbacher, Irene 1970- *219*
Earlier sketch in SATA *153*
Luzadder, Patrick 1954- *89*
Luzzati, Emanuele 1921-2007 .... *7*
Luzzatto, Paola Caboara 1938- *38*
Ly, Many 1977- *208*
Lybbert, Tyler 1970- *88*
Lydon, Michael 1942- *11*
Lyfick, Warren
See Reeves, Lawrence F.
Lyle, Katie Letcher 1938- *8*
Lynch, Chris 1962- *209*
Earlier sketches in SATA *95, 131, 171*
See also CLR *58*
Lynch, Janet Nichols 1952- *221*
Lynch, Jay 1945- *204*
Lynch, Lorenzo 1932- *7*
Lynch, Marietta 1947- *29*
Lynch, Patricia (Nora) 1898-1972 .... *9*
See also CLR *167*
Lynch, Patrick James
See Lynch, P.J.
Lynch, P.J. 1962- *213*
Earlier sketches in SATA *79, 122*
Lynds, Dennis 1924-2005 .... *47*
Brief entry *37*
Lyne, Alison Davis *188*
Lyngseth, Joan
See Davies, Joan
Lynn, Elizabeth A(nne) 1946- *99*
Lynn, Mary
See Brokamp, Marilyn
Lynn, Patricia
See Watts, Mabel Pizzey
Lynn, Sarah *237*
Lynn, Tracy *175*
Lyon, Elinor 1921-2008 .... *6*
Obituary *192*
Lyon, Elinor Bruce
See Lyon, Elinor
Lyon, George Ella 1949- *207*
Autobiography Feature *148*
Earlier sketches in SATA *68, 119, 148*
Lyon, Lea 1945- *212*
Lyon, Lyman R.
See de Camp, L. Sprague
Lyons, Dorothy M(arawee) 1907-1997 .... *3*
Lyons, Grant 1941- *30*
Lyons, Jayne *226*
Lyons, Marcus
See Blish, James
Lyons, Mary E. 1947- *195*
Autobiography Feature *195*
Earlier sketches in SATA *93, 142*
Lyons, Mary Evelyn
See Lyons, Mary E.
Lystad, Mary (Hanemann) 1928- *11*
Lytle, Elizabeth Stewart 1949- *79*
Lytle, Robert A. 1944- *119*
Lyttle, Richard B(ard) 1927- *23*
Lytton, Deborah 1966- *218*
Lytton, Edward G.E.L. Bulwer-Lytton Baron
See Bulwer-Lytton, Edward
Lytton of Knebworth, Baron
See Bulwer-Lytton, Edward

M

Ma, Wenhai 1954- *84*
Maar, Leonard (Frank, Jr.) 1927- *30*
Maartens, Maretha 1945- *73*
Maas, Selve -1997 .... *14*
Maass, Robert *195*
Mabie, Grace
See Mattern, Joanne
Mac
See MacManus, Seumas
and Maccari, Ruggero
Macalaster, Elizabeth G. 1951- *115*
MacAlister, Katie *159*
MacAlister, V. A.
See McKernan, Victoria
MacAllan, Andrew
See Leasor, James
MacAodhagain, Eamon
See Egan, E. W.
MacArthur-Onslow, Annette Rosemary
1933- *26*
Macaulay, David (Alexander) 1946- *137*
Brief entry *27*
Earlier sketches in SATA *46, 72*
See also CLR *14*
Macaulay, Teresa 1947- *95*
Macauley, Theresa E.
See Macaulay, Teresa
Macavinta, Courtney *176*
MacBeth, George (Mann) 1932-1992 .... *4*
Obituary *70*
MacBride, Roger Lea 1929-1995 .... *85*
Maccarone, Grace *238*
MacCarter, Don 1944- *91*
MacClintock, Dorcas 1932- *8*
MacColl, Michaela *238*
MacCready, Robin Merrow 1959(?)- *190*
MacCullough, Carolyn *174*
MacDonald, Alan 1958- *192*
MacDonald, Amy 1951- *156*
Autobiography Feature *156*
Earlier sketches in SATA *76, 136*
MacDonald, Anne Elizabeth Campbell Bard
-1958
See MacDonald, Betty
MacDonald, Anne Louise 1955- *217*

MacDonald, Anson
See Heinlein, Robert A.
MacDonald, Betty 1908-1958
See YABC *1*
Macdonald, Blackie
See Emrich, Duncan (Black Macdonald)
Macdonald, Caroline 1948- *86*
Obituary *111*
See also CLR *60*
Macdonald, Dwight 1906-1982 .... *29*
Obituary *33*
MacDonald, George 1824-1905 .... *100*
Earlier sketch in SATA *33*
See also CLR *67*
MacDonald, Golden
See Brown, Margaret Wise
Macdonald, Guy *195*
Macdonald, James D. 1954- *67*
Earlier sketches in SATA *81, 114, 165, 1*
Macdonald, Marcia
See Hill, Grace Livingston
MacDonald, Margaret Read 1940- *194*
Earlier sketches in SATA *94, 164*
Macdonald, Marianne 1934- *113*
Macdonald, Mary
See Gifford, Griselda
Macdonald, Maryann 1947- *189*
Earlier sketch in SATA *72*
MacDonald, Ross 1957- *201*
Macdonald, Shelagh 1937- *25*
MacDonald, Suse 1940- *193*
Brief entry *52*
Earlier sketches in SATA *54, 109*
Macdonald, Wendy *217*
Macdonald, Wendy M.
See Macdonald, Wendy
Macdonald, Zillah K(atherine) 1885-1979 ... *11*
MacDonnell, Megan
See Stevens, Serita
MacDougal, John
See Blish, James
Mace, Elisabeth 1933- *27*
Mace, Varian 1938- *49*
MacEachern, Stephen *206*
MacEwen, Gwendolyn (Margaret) 1941-1987 .... *50*
Obituary *55*
Macfarlan, Allan A. 1892-1982 .... *35*
MacFarlane, Iris 1922- *11*
MacGill-Callahan, Sheila 1926-2000 .... *78*
MacGregor, Carol Lynn *153*
MacGregor, Ellen 1906-1954 .... *39*
Brief entry *27*
MacGregor-Hastie, Roy (Alasdhair Niall) 1929- *3*
MacGrory, Yvonne 1948- *142*
Machado, Ana Maria 1941- *150*
MacHale, D.J. 1956- *234*
Earlier sketch in SATA *175*
MacHale, Donald James
See MacHale, D.J.
Machetanz, Frederick 1908- *34*
Machin, Sue
See Williams, Sue
Machin Goodall, Daphne (Edith) *37*
Macht, Norm
See Macht, Norman L.
Macht, Norman L. 1929- *122*
Macht, Norman Lee
See Macht, Norman L.
Macht, Norman Lee
See Macht, Norman L.
MacInnes, Cat *236*
MacInnes, Helen (Clark) 1907-1985 .... *22*
Obituary *44*
Macintosh, Brownie 1950- *98*
MacIntyre, Elisabeth 1916- *17*
MacIntyre, Rod
See MacIntyre, R.P.
MacIntyre, R.P. 1947- *203*
MacIntyre, R.P. 1947- *203*
MacIntyre, Wendy 1947- *196*
Mack, Jeff *194*
Mack, L.V.
See Kimmelman, Burt
Mack, Stan(ley) *17*
Mack, Steve *241*
Mack, Todd *168*
Mack, Tracy 1968- *183*
Earlier sketch in SATA *128*
Mack, W.C.
See French, Wendy
Mack, Winnie
See French, Wendy
Mackall, Dandi D.
See Mackall, Dandi Daley
Mackall, Dandi Daley 1949- *218*
Earlier sketches in SATA *118, 177, 182*
Mackay, Claire 1930- *97*
Autobiography Feature *124*
Earlier sketch in SATA *40*
See also CLR *43*
Mackay, Constance D'Arcy (?)-1966 .... *125*
Mackay, Donald 1914-2005 .... *81*
Obituary *173*
Mackay, Donald Alexander
See Mackay, Donald
MacKaye, Percy (Wallace) 1875-1956 .... *32*
Mackel, Kathryn 1950- *162*
Mackel, Kathy
See Mackel, Kathryn
MacKellar, William 1914- *4*
Macken, JoAnn Early 1953- *201*
Macken, Walter 1915-1967 .... *36*
Mackenzie, Anna 1963- *212*
MacKenzie, Jill (Kelly) 1947- *75*
Mackenzie, Robert 1974- *204*
Mackey, Ernan
See McInerny, Ralph
Mackey, Weezie Kerr *188*
Mackie, Maron
See McNeely, Jeannette
Mackin, Edward
See McInerny, Ralph
MacKinnon, Bernie 1957- *69*
MacKinnon Groomer, Vera 1915- *57*
MacKinstry, Elizabeth 1879-1956 .... *42*
Mackler, Carolyn 1973- *231*
Earlier sketch in SATA *156*
MacLachlan, Emily
See Charest, Emily MacLachlan
MacLachlan, Patricia 1938- *229*
Brief entry *42*
Earlier sketches in SATA *62, 107, 168*
See also CLR *14*
MacLane, Jack
See Crider, Bill
MacLean, Alistair 1922(?)-1987 .... *23*
Obituary *50*
MacLean, Alistair Stuart
See MacLean, Alistair
Maclean, Art
See Shirreffs, Gordon D(onald)
MacLean, Christine Kole 1962- *177*
MacLean, Glynne 1964- *150*
MacLean, Jill 1941- *211*
MacLeod, Beatrice 1910- *162*
Earlier sketch in SATA *10*
MacLeod, Beatrice Beach
See MacLeod, Beatrice
MacLeod, Charlotte (Matilda) 1922-2005 .... *28*
Obituary *160*
MacLeod, Doug 1959- *201*
Earlier sketch in SATA *60*
MacLeod, Elizabeth *184*
Earlier sketch in SATA *158*
MacLeod, Ellen Jane (Anderson) 1916- *14*
MacManus, James
See MacManus, Seumas
MacManus, Seumas 1869-1960 .... *25*
MacMaster, Eve (Ruth) B(owers) 1942- *46*
MacMillan, Annabelle
See Quick, Annabelle
MacMillan, Dianne M(arie) 1943- *125*
Earlier sketch in SATA *84*
Macnaughton, Tina *218*
Earlier sketch in SATA *182*
Macneill, Janet
See McNeely, Jeannette
MacPeek, Walter G. 1902-1973 .... *4*
Obituary *25*
MacPhail, Catherine 1946- *197*
Earlier sketch in SATA *130*
MacPherson, Margaret 1908-2001 .... *9*
See also SAAS *4*
MacPherson, Thomas George 1915-1976
Obituary *30*
MacPherson, Winnie 1930- *107*
MacRae, Tom 1980- *181*
Macrae, Travis
See Feagles, Anita MacRae
MacRaois, Cormac 1944- *72*
Macumber, Mari
See Sandoz, Mari(e Susette)
Macy, Sue 1954- *227*
Earlier sketches in SATA *88, 134*
Madaras, Lynda 1947- *151*
Madden, Colleen *228*
Madden, Colleen M.
See Madden, Colleen
Madden, Don 1927- *3*
Madden, Kerry 1961- *168*
Madden-Lunsford, Kerry
See Madden, Kerry
Maddern, Eric 1950- *166*
Maddigan, Beth 1967- *174*
Maddison, Angela Mary 1923- *10*
See also CLR *24*
Maddock, Reginald (Bertram) 1912-1994 .... *15*
Maddox, Jake
See Trumbauer, Lisa
Madenski, Melissa (Ann) 1949- *77*
Madian, Jon 1941- *9*
Madigan, Lisa Kay
See Madigan, L.K.
Madigan, L.K. (?)-2011 .... *224*
Madison, Alan *182*
Madison, Arnold 1937- *6*
Madison, Bennett *220*
Madison, Winifred *5*
Madonna 1958- *149*
Madsen, Gunnar *171*
Madsen, Jim 1964- *202*
Madsen, Ross Martin 1946- *82*
Madsen, Susan A. 1954- *90*
Madsen, Susan Arrington
See Madsen, Susan A.
Maehlqvist, Stefan 1943- *30*
Maestro, Betsy (Crippen) 1944- *106*
Brief entry *30*
Earlier sketch in SATA *59*
See also CLR *45*
Maestro, Giulio 1942- *106*
Earlier sketches in SATA *8, 59*
See also CLR *45*
Maeterlinck, Maurice 1862-1949 .... *66*
Magee, Doug 1947- *78*
Magee, Wes 1939- *64*
Maggio, Rosalie 1943- *69*
Magid, Ken(neth Marshall) *65*
Magnus, Erica 1946- *77*
Magoon, Kekla 1980- *241*
Earlier sketch in SATA *213*
Magoon, Scott *222*
Earlier sketch in SATA *182*
Magorian, James 1942- *92*
Earlier sketch in SATA *32*
Magorian, Michelle 1947- *128*
Earlier sketch in SATA *67*
Magorian, Michelle Jane
See Magorian, Michelle
Magovern, Peg *103*

Magsamen, Sandra 1959- *213*
Maguire, Anne
See Nearing, Penny
Maguire, Eden *232*
Maguire, Gregory 1954- *200*
Autobiography Feature *200*
Earlier sketches in SATA *28, 84, 129*
See also SAAS *22*
Maguire, Gregory Peter
See Maguire, Gregory
Maguire, Jack 1920-2000 .... *74*
Maguire, Jesse
See Smith, Sherwood
Maguire, Jessie
See Smith, Sherwood
Maher, Ramona 1934- *13*
Mahlqvist, Stefan
See Maehlqvist, Stefan
Mahon, Julia C(unha) 1916- *11*
Mahoney, Karen *239*
Mahony, Elizabeth Winthrop
See Winthrop, Elizabeth
Mahood, Kenneth 1930- *24*
Mahy, Margaret 1936- *171*
Earlier sketches in SATA *14, 69, 119*
See also CLR *155*
Mahy, Margaret May
See Mahy, Margaret
Maiden, Cecil (Edward) 1902-1981 .... *52*
Maidoff, Ilka
See List, Ilka Katherine
Maifair, Linda Lee 1947- *83*
Maik, Henri
See Hecht, Henri Joseph
Maillu, David G(ian) 1939- *111*
Maine, Trevor
See Catherall, Arthur
Mains, Randolph P. 1946- *80*
Maione, Heather *189*
Maiorano, Robert 1946- *43*
Mair, J. Samia *237*
Mair, Julie Samia
See Mair, J. Samia
Maisner, Heather 1947- *89*
Maison, Della
See Katz, Bobbi
Maitland, Antony Jasper 1935- *25*
Maitland, Barbara *102*
Mai-Wyss, Tatjana 1972- *187*
Maizel, Rebecca 1980- *236*
Maizels, Jennie *210*
Major, Kevin (Gerald) 1949- *134*
Earlier sketches in SATA *32, 82*
See also CLR *11*
Majure, Janet 1954- *96*
Makhijani, Pooja *188*
Makie, Pam 1943- *37*
Makowski, Silk
See Sullivan, Silky
Makowski, Silvia Ann
See Sullivan, Silky
Malam, John 1957- *152*
Earlier sketch in SATA *89*
Maland, Nick *195*
Malaspina, Ann 1957- *222*
Malawer, Ted
See Michael, Ted
Malcolm, Dan
See Silverberg, Robert
Malcolm, Jahnna N.
See Beecham, Jahnna
Malcolmson, Anne
See von Storch, Anne B.
Malcolmson, David 1899-1978 .... *6*
Maletta, Dr. Arlene
See Feltenstein, Arlene
Maley, Carleen
See Hutchins, Carleen Maley
Mali, Jane Lawrence 1937-1995 .... *51*
Brief entry *44*
Obituary *86*
Malkin, Nina 1959(?)- *179*
Mallett, Jerry J. 1939- *76*
Malley, Gemma *198*
Malley, G.R.
See Malley, Gemma
Mallory, Kenneth 1945- *185*
Earlier sketch in SATA *128*
Mallowan, Agatha Christie
See Christie, Agatha
Malmberg, Carl 1904-1979 .... *9*
Malmgren, Dallin 1949- *65*
Malo, John W. 1911-2000 .... *4*
Malone, James Hiram 1930- *84*
Malone, Marianne *229*
Malone, Nola Langner 1930-2003 .... *8*
Obituary *151*
Malone, Patricia 1932- *155*
Malone, Peter 1953- *191*
Maloney, Pat
See Markun, Patricia Maloney
Malory, Sir Thomas 1410(?)-1471(?) *59*
Brief entry *33*
Maltbie, P.I. *237*
Maltbie, Priscilla
See Maltbie, P.I.
Maltese, Michael 1909(?)-1981
Obituary *24*
Malvasi, Meg Greene *143*
Malvern, Corinne 1905-1956 .... *34*
Malvern, Gladys (?)-1962 .... *23*
Mama G.
See Davis, Grania
Mammano, Julie 1962- *202*
Earlier sketch in SATA *107*
Mamonova, Tatyana 1943- *93*
Manchel, Frank 1935- *10*
Manchess, Gregory 1955- *203*
Manchester, William (Raymond)
1922-2004 .... *65*
Mandabach, Brian 1962(?)- *197*
Mandel, Brett H. 1969- *108*
Mandel, Peter 1957- *238*
Earlier sketch in SATA *87*
Mandel, Sally (Elizabeth) 1944- *64*
Mandell, Muriel (Hortense Levin) 1921- *63*
Manders, John 1957- *219*
Earlier sketch in SATA *175*
Mandine, Selma 1973- *228*
Manes, Stephen 1949- *99*
Brief entry *40*
Earlier sketch in SATA *42*
Manfred, Frederick (Feikema) 1912-1994 .... *30*
Mangin, Marie France 1940- *59*
Mangione, Gerlando 1909-1998 .... *6*
Obituary *104*
Mangione, Jerre
See Mangione, Gerlando
Mango, Karin N. 1936- *52*
Mangurian, David 1938- *14*
Mania, Cathy 1950- *102*
Mania, Robert 1952- *102*
Mania, Robert C., Jr.
See Mania, Robert
Maniatty, Taramesha 1978- *92*
Maniscalco, Joseph 1926- *10*
Manivong, Laura 1967- *229*
Manley, Deborah 1932- *28*
Manley, Seon 1921- *15*
See also CLR *3*
See also SAAS *2*
Mann, Elizabeth 1948- *153*
Mann, Josephine
See Pullein-Thompson, Josephine (Mary Wedderburn)
Mann, Kenny 1946- *91*
Mann, Pamela 1946- *91*
Mann, Patrick
See Waller, Leslie
Mann, Peggy
See Houlton, Peggy Mann
Mannetti, Lisa 1953- *57*
Brief entry *51*
Mannheim, Grete (Salomon) 1909-1986 .... *10*
Manniche, Lise 1943- *31*
Manning, Jane *233*
Earlier sketch in SATA *185*
Manning, Jane K.
See Manning, Jane
Manning, Maurie
See Manning, Maurie J.
Manning, Maurie J. *211*
Manning, Maurie Jo
See Manning, Maurie J.
Manning, Mick 1959- *176*
Manning, Rosemary 1911-1988 .... *10*
Manning, Sarra *162*
Manning-Sanders, Ruth (Vernon)
1895(?)-1988 .... *73*
Obituary *57*
Earlier sketch in SATA *15*
Mannion, Diane
See Paterson, Diane
Mannis, Celeste Davidson *173*
Mannon, Warwick
See Hopkins, (Hector) Kenneth
Manos, Helen *199*
Mansir, A. Richard 1932- *170*
Manson, Ainslie Kertland 1938- *115*
Manson, Beverlie 1945- *57*
Brief entry *44*
Mantchev, Lisa *221*
Mantha, John 1960- *217*
Manthorpe, Helen 1958- *122*
Mantinband, Gerda (B.) 1917- *74*
Manton, Jo
See Gittings, Jo (Grenville) Manton
Manuel, Lynn 1948- *179*
Earlier sketch in SATA *99*
Manushkin, Fran 1942- *205*
Earlier sketches in SATA *7, 54, 93, 166*
Manushkin, Frances
See Manushkin, Fran
Man Without a Spleen, A
See Chekhov, Anton
Many, Paul 1947- *210*
Many, Paul A.
See Many, Paul
Manzano, Sonia 1950- *167*
Mapes, Mary A.
See Ellison, Virginia H(owell)
Maple, Marilyn 1931- *80*
Mappin, Strephyn 1956- *109*
Mara, Barney
See Roth, Arthur J(oseph)
Mara, Jeanette
See Cebulash, Mel
Mara, Rachna
See Gilmore, Rachna
Marais, Josef 1905-1978
Obituary *24*
Marasmus, Seymour
See Rivoli, Mario
Marbach, Ethel
See Pochocki, Ethel (Frances)
Marcal, Annette B.
See Callaway, Bernice (Anne)
Marcelino
See Agnew, Edith J(osephine)
Marcellino, Fred 1939-2001 .... *118*
Obituary *127*
Earlier sketch in SATA *68*
March, Carl
See Fleischman, Sid
Marchant, Bessie 1862-1941
See YABC *2*
Marchant, Catherine
See Cookson, Catherine (McMullen)
Marcher, Marion Walden 1890-1987 .... *10*
Marchesi, Stephen 1951- *114*

Marchesi, Steve
See Marchesi, Stephen
and Older, Effin
and Older, Jules
Marchetta, Melina 1965- ... *170*
Marciano, John Bemelmans 1970- ... *240*
Earlier sketches in SATA *118, 167*
See also CLR *93*
Marco, Lou
See Gottfried, Theodore Mark
Marcus, Kimberly ... *240*
Marcus, Leonard S. 1950- ... *187*
Earlier sketch in SATA *133*
Marcus, Paul 1953- ... *82*
Marcus, Rebecca B(rian) 1907- ... *9*
Marcuse, Aida E. 1934- ... *89*
Marek, Margot L. 1934(?)-1987
Obituary ... *54*
Maren, Julie 1970- ... *199*
Margaret, Karla
See Andersdatter, Karla M.
Margolin, Harriet
See Ziefert, Harriet
Margolis, Jeffrey A. 1948- ... *108*
Margolis, Leslie ... *187*
Margolis, Richard J(ules) 1929-1991 ... *86*
Obituary ... *67*
Earlier sketch in SATA *4*
Margolis, Vivienne 1922- ... *46*
Mariana
See Foster, Marian Curtis
Marie, Geraldine 1949- ... *61*
Mariner, Scott
See Pohl, Frederik
Marino, Dorothy Bronson 1912- ... *14*
Marino, Gianna ... *231*
Marino, Jan 1936- ... *114*
Marino, Nan ... *216*
Marino, Nick
See Deming, Richard
Marino, Peter 1960- ... *179*
Marinsky, Jane ... *227*
Mario, Anna
See Odgers, Sally Farrell
Marion, Henry
See del Rey, Lester
Maris, Ron ... *71*
Brief entry ... *45*
Mariz, Rae 1981- ... *237*
Mark, Jan 1943-2006 ... *164*
Obituary ... *173*
Earlier sketches in SATA *22, 69, 114*
See also CLR *11*
Mark, Janet Marjorie
See Mark, Jan
Mark, Joan T. 1937- ... *122*
Mark, Pauline (Dahlin) 1913-1997 ... *14*
Mark, Polly
See Mark, Pauline (Dahlin)
Mark, Ted
See Gottfried, Theodore Mark
Markel, Michelle ... *169*
Marker, Sherry 1941- ... *76*
Markert, Jennifer 1965- ... *83*
Markert, Jenny
See Markert, Jennifer
Markey, Kevin 1965- ... *215*
Markham, Lynne 1947- ... *102*
Markham, Marion M. 1929- ... *60*
Markham, Wendy
See Staub, Wendy Corsi
Markins, W. S.
See Jenkins, Marie M(agdalen)
Markle, Sandra 1946- ... *218*
Brief entry ... *41*
Earlier sketches in SATA *57, 92, 148, 185*
Markle, Sandra L.
See Markle, Sandra
Marklew, Gilly ... *211*
Marko, Katherine D(olores) ... *28*
Markoosie
See Patsauq, Markoosie
Marks, Alan 1957- ... *187*
Earlier sketches in SATA *77, 151*
Marks, Burton 1930- ... *47*
Brief entry ... *43*
Marks, Graham ... *158*
Marks, Hannah K.
See Trivelpiece, Laurel
Marks, J.
See Highwater, Jamake (Mamake)
Marks, J(ames) M(acdonald) 1921- ... *13*
Marks, Laurie J. 1957- ... *68*
Marks, Margaret L. 1911(?)-1980
Obituary ... *23*
Marks, Mickey Klar -1986 ... *12*
Marks, Peter
See Smith, Robert Kimmel
Marks, Rita 1938- ... *47*
Marks, Stan(ley) ... *14*
Marks-Highwater, J.
See Highwater, Jamake (Mamake)
Markun, Patricia Maloney 1924- ... *15*
Markusen, Bruce (Stanley Rodriguez)
1965- ... *141*
Marley, Louise 1952- ... *173*
Earlier sketch in SATA *120*
Marlin, Hilda
See Van Stockum, Hilda
Marlow, Layne ... *204*
Marlow, Max
See Nicole, Christopher
Marlow, Susan K. 1953- ... *178*
Marlowe, Amy Bell ... *67*
Earlier sketch in SATA *1*
Marlowe, Jack
See Deary, Terry
Marlowe, Tess
See Glick, Ruth
Marney, Dean 1952- ... *90*
Marokvia, Artur 1909- ... *31*
Marokvia, Mireille 1908-2008 ... *5*
Obituary ... *197*
Marokvia, Mireille Journet
See Marokvia, Mireille
Marol, Jean-Claude 1946- ... *125*
Marr, John S(tuart) 1940- ... *48*
Marr, Melissa 1972- ... *189*
Marric, J. J.
See Butler, William Vivian
and Creasey, John
Marrin, Albert 1936- ... *193*
Brief entry ... *43*
Earlier sketches in SATA *53, 90, 126*
See also CLR *53*
Marriott, Alice Lee 1910-1992 ... *31*
Obituary ... *71*
Marriott, Janice 1946- ... *134*
Marriott, Pat(ricia) 1920- ... *35*
Marriott, Zoe 1982- ... *216*
Marriott, Zoe Davina
See Marriott, Zoe
Marroquin, Patricio
See Markun, Patricia Maloney
Mars, W. T.
See Mars, Witold Tadeusz J.
Mars, Witold Tadeusz J. 1912-1985 ... *3*
Marsden, Carolyn 1950- ... *212*
Autobiography Feature ... *212*
Earlier sketches in SATA *140, 175*
Marsden, John 1950- ... *146*
Earlier sketches in SATA *66, 97*
See also CLR *34*
See also SAAS *22*
Marsh, Carole 1946- ... *127*
Marsh, Dave 1950- ... *66*
Marsh, J. E.
See Marshall, Evelyn
Marsh, James 1946- ... *73*
Marsh, Jean
See Marshall, Evelyn
Marsh, Joan F. 1923- ... *83*
Marsh, Katherine 1974- ... *220*
Marsh, Paul
See Hopkins, (Hector) Kenneth
Marsh, Valerie 1954- ... *89*
Marshall, Anthony D(ryden) 1924- ... *18*
Marshall, Bonnie C. 1941- ... *141*
Earlier sketch in SATA *18*
Marshall, Bridget M(ary) 1974- ... *103*
Marshall, (Sarah) Catherine (Wood)
1914-1983 ... *2*
Obituary ... *34*
Marshall, Douglas
See McClintock, Marshall
Marshall, Edmund
See Hopkins, (Hector) Kenneth
Marshall, Edward
See Marshall, James
Marshall, Evelyn 1897-1991 ... *11*
Marshall, Felicity 1950- ... *116*
Marshall, Garry 1934- ... *60*
Marshall, H. H.
See Jahn, Michael
Marshall, James 1942-1992 ... *75*
Earlier sketches in SATA *6, 51*
See also CLR *21*
Marshall, James Edward
See Marshall, James
Marshall, James Vance
See Payne, Donald Gordon
Marshall, Janet (Perry) 1938- ... *97*
Marshall, Jeff
See Laycock, George (Edwin)
Marshall, Kim
See Marshall, Michael (Kimbrough)
Marshall, Michael (Kimbrough) 1948- ... *37*
Marshall, Percy
See Young, Percy M(arshall)
Marshall, S(amuel) L(yman) A(twood)
1900-1977 ... *21*
Marsoli, Lisa Ann 1958- ... *101*
Brief entry ... *53*
Marsten, Richard
See Hunter, Evan
Marston, Elsa 1933- ... *156*
Marston, Hope Irvin 1935- ... *127*
Earlier sketch in SATA *31*
Marszalek, John F. 1939- ... *167*
Marszalek, John Francis, Jr.
See Marszalek, John F.
Marszalek, John Francis 1939-
See Marszalek, John F.
Martchenko, Michael 1942- ... *154*
Earlier sketches in SATA *50, 95*
Martel, Aimee
See Thurlo, Aimee
and Thurlo, David
Martel, Suzanne 1924- ... *99*
Martignoni, Margaret E. 1908(?)-1974
Obituary ... *27*
Martin, Ann M. 1955- ... *234*
Brief entry ... *41*
Earlier sketches in SATA *44, 70, 126, 192*
See also CLR *32*
Martin, Bill, Jr. 1916-2004 ... *145*
Brief entry ... *40*
Earlier sketches in SATA *40, 67*
See also CLR *97*
Martin, Charles E(lmer)
See Mastrangelo, Charles E(lmer)
Martin, Christopher
See Hoyt, Edwin P(almer), Jr.
Martin, C.K. Kelly ... *207*
Martin, Claire 1933- ... *76*
Martin, Courtney Autumn 1984- ... *205*
Martin, David Stone 1913-1992 ... *39*
Martin, Donald
See Honig, Donald
Martin, Dorothy 1921- ... *47*
Martin, Dorothy McKay
See Martin, Dorothy

Martin, Eugene *1*
Martin, Eva M. 1939- *65*
Martin, Frances M(cEntee) 1906-1998 .... *36*
Martin, Francesca 1947- *101*
Martin, Fred 1948- *119*
Martin, Fredric
See Christopher, Matt(hew Frederick)
Martin, George Raymond Richard
See Martin, George R.R.
Martin, George R.R. 1948- *118*
Martin, J(ohn) P(ercival) 1880(?)-1966 .... *15*
Martin, Jacqueline Briggs 1945- *188*
Earlier sketches in SATA *98, 149*
Martin, Jane Read 1957- *84*
Martin, Jeremy
See Levin, Marcia Obrasky
Martin, Les
See Schulman, L(ester) M(artin)
Martin, Linda 1961- *82*
Martin, Lynne 1923- *21*
Martin, Marcia
See Levin, Marcia Obrasky
Martin, Marvin 1926- *126*
Martin, Melanie
See Pellowski, Michael (Joseph)
Martin, Nancy
See Salmon, Annie Elizabeth
Martin, Patricia *200*
Martin, Patricia A.
See Martin, Patricia
Martin, Patricia Miles 1899-1986 .... *43*
Obituary *48*
Earlier sketch in SATA *1*
Martin, Peter
See Chaundler, Christine
Martin, Rafe 1946- *175*
Martin, Rene 1891-1977 .... *42*
Obituary *20*
Martin, Rupert (Claude) 1905- *31*
Martin, S. R.
See Mappin, Strephyn
Martin, Stefan 1936- *32*
Martin, Vicky
See Storey, Victoria Carolyn
Martin, Webber
See Silverberg, Robert
Martin, Wendy
See Martini, Teri
Martin, William Ivan, Jr.
See Martin, Bill, Jr.
Martineau, Diane 1940- *178*
Martineau, Harriet 1802-1876
See YABC *2*
Martinet, Jeanne 1958- *80*
Martinez, Agnes *167*
Martinez, Arturo O. 1933- *192*
Martinez, Claudia Guadalupe 1978- *214*
Martinez, Ed(ward) 1954- *98*
Martinez, Elizabeth Coonrod 1954- *85*
Martinez, Rueben 1940- *232*
Martinez, Victor 1954-2011 .... *95*
Martini, Angela 1972(?)- *223*
Martini, Teri 1930- *3*
Martini, Therese
See Martini, Teri
Martino, Alfred C. 1964- *174*
Martinson, Janis
See Herbert, Janis
Martinusen, Cindy
See Martinusen-Coloma, Cindy
Martinusen, Cindy McCormick
See Martinusen-Coloma, Cindy
Martinusen-Coloma, Cindy 1970- *218*
Marton, Jirina 1946- *230*
Earlier sketches in SATA *95, 144*
Marton, Pierre
See Stone, Peter
Martson, Del
See Lupoff, Richard A.
Martyr, Paula (Jane)
See Lawford, Paula Jane
Maruki, Toshi 1912-2000 .... *112*
See also CLR *19*
Marvin, Isabel R(idout) 1924- *84*
Marx, Patricia Windschill
See Marx, Trish
Marx, Robert F(rank) 1936- *24*
Marx, Trish 1948- *202*
Earlier sketches in SATA *112, 160*
Marzani, Carl (Aldo) 1912-1994 .... *12*
Marzollo, Jean 1942- *190*
Autobiography Feature *190*
Earlier sketches in SATA *29, 77, 130*
See also SAAS *15*
Masefield, John (Edward) 1878-1967 .... *19*
See also CLR *164*
Masiello, Ralph 1961- *214*
Masoff, Joy 1951- *118*
Mason, Adrienne 1962- *163*
Mason, Cherie *170*
Mason, Edwin A. 1905-1979
Obituary *32*
Mason, Ernst
See Pohl, Frederik
Mason, F(rancis) van Wyck 1901-1978 .... *3*
Obituary *26*
Mason, Frank W.
See Mason, F(rancis) van Wyck
Mason, George Frederick 1904-2000 .... *14*
Mason, Margaret H. 1954- *241*
Mason, Miriam E(vangeline) 1900-1973 .... *2*
Obituary *26*
Mason, Prue *195*
Mason, Simon 1962- *178*
Mason, Tally
See Derleth, August (William)
Mason, Van Wyck
See Mason, F(rancis) van Wyck
Mass, Wendy 1967- *234*
Earlier sketches in SATA *158, 196*
Mass, William
See Gibson, William
Masse, Josee *221*
Masselman, George 1897-1971 .... *19*
Massey, Misty *212*
Massie, Dianne Redfield 1938- *125*
Earlier sketch in SATA *16*
Massie, Elizabeth *108*
Massini, Sarah *213*
Masson, Sophie 1959- *179*
Earlier sketch in SATA *133*
Masters, Anthony (Richard) 1940-2003 .... *112*
Obituary *145*
Masters, Kelly R(ay) 1897-1987 .... *3*
Masters, Mildred 1932- *42*
Masters, William
See Cousins, Margaret
Masters, Zeke
See Bensen, Donald R.
and Goulart, Ron
Mastrangelo, Charles E(lmer) 1910-1995 .... *70*
Earlier sketch in SATA *69*
Masuda, Takeshi 1944- *56*
Matas, Carol 1949- *194*
Autobiography Feature *112*
Earlier sketch in SATA *93*
See also CLR *52*
Matchette, Katharine E. 1941- *38*
Math, Irwin 1940- *42*
Mathabane, Mark 1960- *123*
Mather, Kirtley F(letcher) 1888-1978 .... *65*
Mathers, Petra 1945- *176*
Earlier sketch in SATA *119*
See also CLR *76*
Matheson, Richard (Christian) 1953- *119*
Matheson, Shirlee Smith 1942- *155*
Mathews, Eleanor
See Mathews, Ellie
Mathews, Ellie 1946(?)- *193*
Mathews, Janet 1914-1992 .... *41*
Mathews, Judith
See Goldberger, Judith M.
Mathews, Louise
See Tooke, Louise Mathews
Mathiesen, Egon 1907-1976
Obituary *28*
Mathieu, Joe 1949- *185*
Brief entry *36*
Earlier sketches in SATA *43, 94*
Mathieu, Joseph P.
See Mathieu, Joe
Mathis, Sharon Bell 1937- *58*
Earlier sketch in SATA *7*
See also CLR *147*
See also SAAS *3*
Matlin, Marlee 1965- *181*
Matlin, Marlee Beth
See Matlin, Marlee
Matloff, Gregory 1945- *73*
Matott, Justin 1961- *109*
Matranga, Frances Carfi 1922- *78*
Matray, James I. 1948- *161*
Matray, James Irving
See Matray, James I.
Matson, Emerson N(els) 1926- *12*
Matson, Morgan *230*
Matsui, Tadashi 1926- *8*
Matsuno, Masako
See Kobayashi, Masako Matsuno
Matsuoka, Mei 1981- *192*
Matte, (Encarnacion) L'Enc 1936- *22*
Mattern, Joanne 1963- *122*
Mattheson, Jenny *180*
Matthew, James
See Barrie, J. M.
Matthews, Aline
See De Wire, Elinor
Matthews, Andrew 1948- *138*
Matthews, Caitlin 1952- *122*
Matthews, Cecily 1945- *221*
Matthews, Downs 1925- *71*
Matthews, Elizabeth 1978- *194*
Matthews, Ellen
See Bache, Ellyn
Matthews, Ellen 1950- *28*
Matthews, Harold Downs
See Matthews, Downs
Matthews, Jacklyn Meek
See Meek, Jacklyn O'Hanlon
Matthews, John (Kentigern) 1948- *116*
Matthews, L. S. *183*
Matthews, Laura S.
See Matthews, L. S.
Matthews, Liz
See Pellowski, Michael (Joseph)
Matthews, Morgan
See Pellowski, Michael (Joseph)
Matthews, Nicola
See Browne, N.M.
Matthews, Patricia 1927-2006 .... *28*
Matthews, Patricia Anne
See Matthews, Patricia
Matthews, Tina 1961- *190*
Matthews, Tom L.
See Lalicki, Tom
Matthews, William Henry III 1919- *45*
Brief entry *28*
Matthies, Janna *241*
Matthiessen, Peter 1927- *27*
Mattingley, Christobel (Rosemary) 1931- *85*
Earlier sketch in SATA *37*
See also CLR *24*
See also SAAS *18*
Matulay, Laszlo 1912- *43*
Matus, Greta 1938- *12*
Matzigkeit, Philip *220*
Maugham, W. S.
See Maugham, W. Somerset
Maugham, W. Somerset 1874-1965 .... *54*
Maugham, William S.
See Maugham, W. Somerset
Maugham, William Somerset
See Maugham, W. Somerset

Maurer, Diane Philippoff
See Maurer-Mathison, Diane V(ogel)
Maurer, Diane Vogel
See Maurer-Mathison, Diane V(ogel)
Maurer-Mathison, Diane V(ogel) 1944- *89*
Mauser, Pat Rhoads
See McCord, Patricia
Mauser, Patricia Rhoads
See McCord, Patricia
Maves, Mary Carolyn 1916- *10*
Maves, Paul B(enjamin) 1913-1994 .... *10*
Mavor, Salley 1955- *125*
Mawicke, Tran 1911- *15*
Max 1906-1989
See Diop, Birago (Ismael)
Max, Jill
See Bennett, Kelly
Max, Peter 1939- *45*
Maxon, Anne
See Best, (Evangel) Allena Champlin
Maxwell, Arthur S. 1896-1970 .... *11*
Maxwell, B.E. 1957- *211*
Maxwell, Bruce E.
See Maxwell, B.E.
Maxwell, Edith 1923- *7*
Maxwell, Gavin 1914-1969 .... *65*
Maxwell, Katie
See MacAlister, Katie
Maxwell, William (Keepers, Jr.) 1908-2000
Obituary *128*
Maxwell-Hyslop, Miranda 1968- *154*
May, Charles Paul 1920- *4*
May, Elaine Tyler 1947- *120*
May, J. C.
See May, Julian
May, Julian 1931- *11*
May, Katie *225*
May, Robert Lewis 1905-1976
Obituary *27*
May, Robert Stephen 1929-1996 .... *46*
May, Robin
See May, Robert Stephen
Mayall, Beth *171*
Mayberry, Florence V(irginia) Wilson *10*
Maybury, Richard J. 1946- *72*
Maybury, Rick
See Maybury, Richard J.
Maydak, Michael S. 1952- *220*
Mayer, Agatha
See Maher, Ramona
Mayer, Albert Ignatius, Jr. 1906-1994
Obituary *29*
Mayer, Ann M(argaret) 1938- *14*
Mayer, Bill *200*
Mayer, Danuta 1958- *117*
Mayer, Hannelore Valencak 1929- *42*
Mayer, Jane Rothschild 1903-2001 .... *38*
Mayer, Marianna 1945- *132*
Earlier sketches in SATA *32, 83*
Mayer, Mercer 1943- *137*
Earlier sketches in SATA *16, 32, 73, 129*
See also CLR *11*
Mayerson, Charlotte Leon *36*
Mayerson, Evelyn Wilde 1935- *55*
Mayfield, Katherine 1958- *118*
Mayfield, Sue 1963- *146*
Earlier sketch in SATA *72*
Mayhar, Ardath 1930- *38*
Mayhew, James 1964- *204*
Earlier sketches in SATA *85, 149*
Maynard, Olga 1920- *40*
Mayne, William 1928-2010 .... *122*
Earlier sketches in SATA *6, 68*
See also CLR *123*
See also SAAS *11*
Mayne, William James Carter
See Mayne, William
Maynes, J. O. Rocky, Jr.
See Maynes, J. Oscar, Jr.
Maynes, J. Oscar, Jr. 1929- *38*
Mayo, Gretchen Will 1936- *163*
Earlier sketch in SATA *84*
Mayo, Margaret 1935- *165*
Earlier sketches in SATA *38, 96*
Mayo, Margaret Mary
See Mayo, Margaret
Mayr, Diane 1949- *197*
Mays, Lucinda L(a Bella) 1924- *49*
Mays, (Lewis) Victor (Jr.) 1927- *5*
Mazellan, Ron *210*
Mazer, Anne 1953- *235*
Earlier sketches in SATA *67, 105, 192*
Mazer, Harry 1925- *167*
Earlier sketches in SATA *31, 67, 105*
See also CLR *16*
See also SAAS *11*
Mazer, Norma Fox 1931-2009 .... *198*
Earlier sketches in SATA *24, 67, 105, 168*
See also CLR *23*
See also SAAS *1*
Mazille, Capucine 1953- *96*
Mazo, Michael *223*
Mazza, Adriana 1928- *19*
Mazzio, Joann 1926- *74*
Mbugua, Kioi Wa 1962- *83*
McAfee, Carol 1955- *81*
McAlister, Caroline 1960- *235*
McAllister, Amanda
See Dowdell, Dorothy (Florence) Karns
and Hager, Jean
and Meaker, Eloise
McAllister, Angela *225*
Earlier sketch in SATA *182*
McAllister, Margaret I. 1956- *169*
Earlier sketch in SATA *117*
McAllister, M.I.
See McAllister, Margaret I.
McArdle, Paula 1971- *198*
McArthur, Nancy *96*
McAvoy, Jim 1972- *142*
McBain, Ed
See Hunter, Evan
McBain, Georgina *189*
McBratney, Sam 1943- *203*
Earlier sketches in SATA *89, 164*
See also CLR *44*
McBride, Lish *237*
McBrier, Michael
See Older, Effin
and Older, Jules
McCafferty, Jim 1954- *84*
McCaffery, Janet 1936- *38*
McCaffrey, Anne 1926-2011 .... *152*
Autobiography Feature *152*
Earlier sketches in SATA *8, 70, 116*
See also CLR *130*
See also SAAS *11*
McCaffrey, Anne Inez
See McCaffrey, Anne
McCaffrey, Kate 1970- *228*
McCaffrey, Mary
See Szudek, Agnes S(usan) P(hilomena)
McCahan, Erin *234*
McCain, Becky Ray 1954- *138*
McCain, Murray (David, Jr.) 1926-1981 .... *7*
Obituary *29*
McCall, Bruce 1935(?)- *209*
McCall, Edith (Sansom) 1911- *6*
McCall, Virginia Nielsen 1909-2000 .... *13*
McCall, Wendell
See Pearson, Ridley
McCall Smith, Alexander
See Smith, Alexander McCall
McCallum, Phyllis
See Koch, Phyllis (Mae) McCallum
McCallum, Stephen 1960- *91*
McCampbell, Darlene Z. 1942- *83*
McCann, Edson
See del Rey, Lester
and Pohl, Frederik
McCann, Gerald 1916- *41*
McCann, Helen 1948- *75*
McCannon, Dindga *41*
McCants, William D. 1961- *82*
McCarter, Neely Dixon 1929- *47*
McCarthy, Agnes 1933- *4*
McCarthy, Colin (John) 1951- *77*
McCarthy, Mary 1951- *203*
McCarthy, Meghan *199*
Earlier sketch in SATA *168*
McCarthy, Ralph F. 1950- *139*
McCarthy-Tucker, Sherri N. 1958- *83*
McCarty, Peter 1966- *182*
McCarty, Rega Kramer 1904-1986 .... *10*
McCaslin, Nellie 1914-2005 .... *12*
McCaughrean, Geraldine 1951- *173*
Earlier sketches in SATA *87, 139*
See also CLR *38*
McCaughren, Tom 1936- *75*
McCauley, Adam 1965- *209*
Earlier sketch in SATA *128*
McCay, (Zenas) Winsor 1869-1934 .... *134*
Earlier sketch in SATA *41*
McClafferty, Carla Killough 1958- *137*
McClary, Jane Stevenson 1919-1990
Obituary *64*
McCleery, Patsy R. 1925- *133*
Earlier sketch in SATA *88*
McClelland, Susan *214*
McClements, George *196*
McClintock, Barbara 1955- *213*
Earlier sketches in SATA *57, 95, 146*
McClintock, Marshall 1906-1967 .... *3*
McClintock, May Garelick
See Garelick, May
McClintock, Mike
See McClintock, Marshall
McClintock, Norah *226*
Earlier sketch in SATA *178*
McClintock, Theodore 1902-1971 .... *14*
McClinton, Leon 1933- *11*
McCloskey, Kevin 1951- *79*
McCloskey, (John) Robert 1914-2003 .... *100*
Obituary *146*
Earlier sketches in SATA *2, 39*
See also CLR *7*
McCloy, James F(loyd) 1941- *59*
McClung, Robert M(arshall) 1916- *135*
Earlier sketches in SATA *2, 68*
See also CLR *11*
See also SAAS *15*
McClure, Gillian Mary 1948- *31*
McClure, Nikki *218*
McColley, Kevin 1961- *80*
See also SAAS *23*
McConduit, Denise Walter 1950- *89*
McConnell, James Douglas Rutherford
1915-1988 .... *40*
Obituary *56*
McCord, Anne 1942- *41*
McCord, David (Thompson Watson)
1897-1997 .... *18*
Obituary *96*
See also CLR *9*
McCord, Jean 1924- *34*
McCord, Pat Mauser
See McCord, Patricia
McCord, Patricia 1943- *159*
Earlier sketch in SATA *37*
McCord, Patricia Sue Rhoads Mauser
See McCord, Patricia
McCormack, Caren McNelly *217*
McCormick, Brooks
See Adams, William Taylor
McCormick, Dell J. 1892-1949 .... *19*
McCormick, (George) Donald (King)
1911-1998 .... *14*
McCormick, Edith (Joan) 1934- *30*
McCormick, Kimberly A. 1960- *153*
McCormick, Patricia 1956- *181*
Earlier sketch in SATA *128*

Author Index

McCourt, Edward (Alexander) 1907-1972
Obituary ... *28*
McCourt, Lisa 1964- ... *214*
Earlier sketches in SATA *117, 159*
McCourt, Malachy 1931- ... *126*
McCoy, Glenn 1965- ... *212*
McCoy, Iola Fuller ... *3*
McCoy, J(oseph) J(erome) 1917- ... *8*
McCoy, Karen Kawamoto 1953- ... *82*
McCoy, Lois (Rich) 1941- ... *38*
McCrady, Lady 1951- ... *16*
McCrea, James (Craig, Jr.) 1920- ... *3*
McCrea, Ruth (Pirman) 1921- ... *3*
McCreigh, James
See Pohl, Frederik
McCrumb, Sharyn 1948- ... *109*
McCue, Lisa 1959- ... *212*
Earlier sketches in SATA *65, 177*
McCue, Lisa Emiline
See McCue, Lisa
McCullen, Andrew
See Arthur, Robert, (Jr.)
McCullers, Carson 1917-1967 ... *27*
McCullers, Lula Carson Smith
See McCullers, Carson
McCulloch, Derek (Ivor Breashur) 1897-1967
Obituary ... *29*
McCulloch, John Tyler
See Burroughs, Edgar Rice
McCulloch, Sarah
See Ure, Jean
McCullough, David 1933- ... *62*
McCullough, David Gaub
See McCullough, David
McCullough, Frances Monson 1938- ... *8*
McCullough, Sharon Pierce 1943- ... *131*
McCully, Emily Arnold
See Arnold, Emily
McCune, Dan
See Haas, Dorothy F.
McCunn, Ruthanne Lum 1946- ... *63*
McCurdy, Michael 1942- ... *237*
Earlier sketches in SATA *13, 82, 147*
McCurdy, Michael Charles
See McCurdy, Michael
McCusker, Paul 1958- ... *220*
McCutcheon, Elsie (Mary Jackson) 1937- ... *60*
McCutcheon, John 1952- ... *97*
McDaniel, Becky Bring 1953- ... *61*
McDaniel, Lurlene 1944- ... *218*
Earlier sketches in SATA *71, 146*
McDaniels, Pellom III 1968- ... *121*
McDaniels, Preston 1952- ... *192*
McDearmon, Kay ... *20*
McDermott, Beverly Brodsky 1941- ... *11*
McDermott, Eleni ... *156*
McDermott, Gerald (Edward) 1941- ... *163*
Earlier sketches in SATA *16, 74*
See also CLR *9*
McDermott, Michael 1962- ... *76*
McDevitt, Jack 1935- ... *155*
Earlier sketch in SATA *94*
McDevitt, John Charles
See McDevitt, Jack
McDole, Carol
See Farley, Carol (J.)
McDonald, Candice Hartsough 1982- ... *225*
McDonald, Collin 1943- ... *79*
McDonald, Gerald D(oan) 1905-1970 ... *3*
McDonald, Jamie
See Heide, Florence Parry
McDonald, Janet 1953-2007 ... *204*
Earlier sketch in SATA *148*
McDonald, Jill (Masefield) 1927-1982 ... *13*
Obituary ... *29*
McDonald, Joyce 1946- ... *164*
Earlier sketch in SATA *101*
McDonald, Lucile Saunders 1898-1992 ... *10*
McDonald, Mary Ann 1956- ... *84*
McDonald, Megan 1958- ... *202*
Autobiography Feature ... *151*
Earlier sketches in SATA *67, 99, 148, 151*
See also CLR *94*
McDonald, Meme 1954- ... *112*
McDonald, Mercedes 1956- ... *169*
Earlier sketch in SATA *97*
McDonald, Rae A. 1952- ... *201*
McDonell, Chris 1960- ... *138*
McDonnell, Christine 1949- ... *225*
Earlier sketches in SATA *34, 115*
McDonnell, Flora (Mary) 1963- ... *146*
Earlier sketch in SATA *90*
McDonnell, Kathleen 1947- ... *186*
McDonnell, Lois Eddy 1914-2001 ... *10*
McDonnell, Patrick 1956- ... *221*
Earlier sketch in SATA *179*
McDonough, Yona Zeldis 1957- ... *73*
McDowell, Marilyn Taylor ... *217*
McElligott, Matt 1968- ... *196*
Earlier sketch in SATA *135*
McElligott, Matthew
See McElligott, Matt
McElmeel, Sharron L. 1942- ... *128*
McElmurry, Jill ... *198*
Earlier sketch in SATA *159*
McElrath, William N. 1932- ... *65*
McElrath-Eslick, Lori 1960- ... *204*
Earlier sketch in SATA *96*
McEntee, Dorothy (Layng) 1902- ... *37*
McEvoy, Anne ... *214*
McEwen, Katherine ... *183*
McEwen, Robert (Lindley) 1926-1980
Obituary ... *23*
McFadden, Kevin Christopher
See Pike, Christopher
McFall, Christie 1918- ... *12*
McFall, Gardner 1952- ... *183*
McFarlan, Donald M(aitland) 1915- ... *59*
McFarland, Henry "Hammer"
See McFarland, Henry O.
McFarland, Henry O. 1934- ... *143*
McFarland, Kenton D(ean) 1920- ... *11*
McFarland, Martha
See Smith-Ankrom, M. E.
McFarlane, Leslie 1902-1977 ... *100*
Earlier sketches in SATA *31, 1, 65, 67*
See also CLR *118*
McFarlane, Leslie Charles
See McFarlane, Leslie
McFarlane, Peter 1940- ... *95*
McFarlane, Peter William
See McFarlane, Peter
McFarlane, Sheryl P. 1954- ... *86*
McFarlane, Todd 1961- ... *117*
McFerrin, Grady ... *239*
McGaw, Jessie Brewer 1913-1997 ... *10*
McGee, Barbara 1943- ... *6*
McGee, Marni ... *163*
McGhee, Alison 1960- ... *231*
Earlier sketch in SATA *196*
McGhee, Alison R.
See McGhee, Alison
McGhee, Holly M.
See Durand, Hallie
McGiffin, (Lewis) Lee (Shaffer) 1908-1978 ... *1*
McGill, Alice ... *159*
McGill, Marci
See Balterman, Marcia Ridlon
McGill, Marci Ridlon
See Balterman, Marcia Ridlon
McGill, Ormond 1913- ... *92*
McGinley, Jerry 1948- ... *116*
McGinley, Phyllis 1905-1978 ... *44*
Obituary ... *24*
Earlier sketch in SATA *2*
McGinnis, Lila S(prague) 1924- ... *44*
McGinty, Alice B. 1963- ... *202*
Earlier sketch in SATA *134*
McGivern, Justin 1985- ... *129*
McGivern, Maureen Daly
See Daly, Maureen
McGivern, Maureen Patricia Daly
See Daly, Maureen
McGough, Elizabeth (Hemmes) 1934- ... *33*
McGovern, Ann 1930- ... *132*
Earlier sketches in SATA *8, 69, 70*
See also CLR *50*
See also SAAS *17*
McGowen, Thomas E. 1927- ... *109*
Earlier sketch in SATA *2*
McGowen, Tom
See McGowen, Thomas E.
McGrady, Mike 1933- ... *6*
McGrath, Barbara Barbieri 1953- ... *230*
Earlier sketches in SATA *108, 169*
McGrath, Robin 1949- ... *121*
McGrath, Thomas (Matthew) 1916-1990 ... *41*
Obituary ... *66*
McGraw, Eloise Jarvis 1915-2000 ... *67*
Obituary ... *123*
Earlier sketch in SATA *1*
See also SAAS *6*
McGraw, William Corbin 1916-1999 ... *3*
McGreal, Elizabeth
See Yates, Elizabeth
McGregor, Barbara 1959- ... *82*
McGregor, Craig 1933- ... *8*
McGregor, Iona 1929- ... *25*
McGrory, Anik ... *193*
McGuffey, Alexander Hamilton 1816-1896 . *60*
McGuigan, Mary Ann 1949- ... *228*
Earlier sketch in SATA *106*
McGuiness, Dan ... *240*
McGuire, Edna 1899- ... *13*
McGuire, Leslie (Sarah) 1945- ... *94*
Brief entry ... *45*
Earlier sketch in SATA *52*
McGuire, Robert ... *187*
McGuirk, Leslie (A.) 1960- ... *152*
McGurk, Slater
See Roth, Arthur J(oseph)
McHargue, Georgess 1941-2011 ... *77*
Earlier sketch in SATA *4*
See also CLR *2*
See also SAAS *5*
McHenry, E.B. 1963(?)- ... *193*
McHugh, (Berit) Elisabet 1941- ... *55*
Brief entry ... *44*
McIlvaine, Jane
See McClary, Jane Stevenson
McIlwraith, Maureen Mollie Hunter
See Hunter, Mollie
McInerney, Judith W(hitelock) 1945- ... *49*
Brief entry ... *46*
McInerny, Ralph 1929-2010 ... *93*
McInerny, Ralph Matthew
See McInerny, Ralph
McKaughan, Larry (Scott) 1941- ... *75*
McKay, Donald 1895- ... *45*
McKay, Hilary 1959- ... *208*
Earlier sketches in SATA *92, 145*
See also SAAS *23*
McKay, Hilary Jane
See McKay, Hilary
McKay, Lawrence, Jr. 1948- ... *114*
McKay, Robert W. 1921- ... *15*
McKay, Sharon E. 1954- ... *165*
McKay, Simon
See Nicole, Christopher
McKean, Dave 1963- ... *197*
McKean, David Jeff
See McKean, Dave
McKeating, Eileen 1957- ... *81*
McKee, David (John) 1935- ... *158*
Earlier sketches in SATA *70, 107*
See also CLR *38*
McKee, Tim 1970- ... *111*
McKeever, Marcia
See Laird, Jean E(louise)
McKellar, Danica 1975- ... *213*

McKelvey, Carole A. 1942- *78*
McKelvy, Charles 1950- *124*
McKendrick, Melveena (Christine) 1941- *55*
McKendry, Joe 1972- *170*
McKenna, Colleen O'Shaughnessy 1948- .. *136*
Earlier sketch in SATA *76*
McKenzie, Dorothy Clayton 1910-1981
Obituary *28*
McKenzie, Ellen Kindt 1928- *80*
McKernan, Victoria 1957- *171*
McKie, Robin *112*
McKillip, Patricia A. 1948- *174*
Earlier sketches in SATA *30, 80, 126*
McKillip, Patricia Anne
See McKillip, Patricia A.
McKim, Audrey Margaret 1909-1999 .... *47*
McKimmie, Chris *194*
McKinley, Jennifer Carolyn Robin
See McKinley, Robin
McKinley, Robin 1952- *229*
Brief entry *32*
Earlier sketches in SATA *50, 89, 130, 195*
See also CLR *127*
McKinney, Barbara Shaw 1951- *116*
McKinney, Nadine 1938- *91*
McKinty, Adrian *186*
McKissack, Fredrick L. 1939- *162*
Brief entry *53*
Earlier sketches in SATA *73, 117*
See also CLR *55*
McKissack, Fredrick Lemuel
See McKissack, Fredrick L.
McKissack, Patricia C. 1944- *195*
Earlier sketches in SATA *51, 73, 117, 162*
See also CLR *129*
McKissack, Patricia L'Ann Carwell
See McKissack, Patricia C.
McKissack and McKissack
See McKissack, Fredrick L.
and McKissack, Patricia C.
McKown, Robin (?)-1976 .... *6*
McKy, Katie 1956- *184*
McLaren, Chesley *213*
McLaren, Clemence 1938- *158*
Earlier sketch in SATA *105*
McLaughlin, Frank 1934- *73*
McLaughlin, Julie 1984- *226*
McLaughlin, Lauren *209*
McLaurin, Anne 1953- *27*
McLean, Andrew 1946- *172*
Earlier sketch in SATA *113*
McLean, Dirk 1956- *236*
McLean, J. Sloan
See Gillette, Virginia M(ary)
and Wunsch, Josephine (McLean)
McLean, Jacqueline
See Kolosov, Jacqueline
McLean, Janet 1946- *113*
McLean, Kathryn (Anderson) 1909-1966 .... *9*
McLean, Virginia Overton 1946- *90*
McLean-Carr, Carol 1948- *122*
McLeish, Kenneth 1940-1997 .... *35*
McLenighan, Valjean 1947- *46*
Brief entry *40*
McLennan, Connie *171*
McLennan, Will
See Wisler, G(ary) Clifton
McLeod, Bob 1951- *173*
McLeod, Chum 1955- *95*
McLeod, Emilie Warren 1926-1982 .... *23*
Obituary *31*
McLeod, Kirsty
See Hudson, (Margaret) Kirsty
McLeod, Margaret Vail
See Holloway, Teresa (Bragunier)
McLerran, Alice 1933- *137*
Earlier sketch in SATA *68*
McLimans, David 1949- *182*
McLoughlin, John C. 1949- *47*
McMahon, Bob 1956- *208*
McManus, Patrick F. 1933- *46*
McManus, Patrick Francis
See McManus, Patrick F.
McMeekin, Clark
See McMeekin, Isabel McLennan
McMeekin, Isabel McLennan 1895-1973 .... *3*
McMenemy, Sarah 1965- *226*
Earlier sketch in SATA *156*
McMillan, Bruce 1947- *192*
Earlier sketches in SATA *22, 70, 129*
See also CLR *47*
McMillan, Naomi
See Grimes, Nikki
McMorey, James L.
See Moyer, Terry J.
McMorrow, Annalisa 1969- *104*
McMullan, Jim 1934- *150*
Earlier sketch in SATA *87*
McMullan, K. H.
See McMullan, Kate
McMullan, Kate 1947- *189*
Brief entry *48*
Earlier sketches in SATA *52, 87, 132*
McMullan, Kate Hall
See McMullan, Kate
McMullan, Margaret 1960- *203*
McMurtrey, Martin A(loysias) 1921- *21*
McNabb, Linda 1963- *147*
McNair, Kate *3*
McNair, Sylvia 1924-2002 .... *74*
McNamara, Margaret C(raig) 1915-1981
Obituary *24*
McNaught, Harry *32*
McNaughton, Colin 1951- *211*
Earlier sketches in SATA *39, 92, 134*
See also CLR *54*
McNaughton, Janet 1953- *162*
Earlier sketch in SATA *110*
McNeal, Laura *194*
McNeal, Tom *194*
McNeely, Jeannette 1918- *25*
McNeer, May (Yonge) 1902-1994 .... *81*
Earlier sketch in SATA *1*
McNeese, Tim 1953- *139*
McNeill, Janet
See Alexander, Janet
McNicholas, Shelagh *191*
McNickle, D'Arcy 1904-1977
Obituary *22*
McNickle, William D'Arcy
See McNickle, D'Arcy
McNicoll, Sylvia (Marilyn) 1954- *113*
See also CLR *99*
McNulty, Faith 1918-2005 .... *168*
Earlier sketches in SATA *12, 84, 139*
McPhail, David 1940- *219*
Brief entry *32*
Earlier sketches in SATA *47, 81, 140, 183*
McPhail, David M.
See McPhail, David
McPhail, David Michael
See McPhail, David
McPhee, Norma H. 1928- *95*
McPhee, Peter 1957- *214*
McPhee, Richard B(yron) 1934- *41*
McPherson, James M. 1936- *141*
Earlier sketch in SATA *16*
McPherson, James Munro
See McPherson, James M.
McQueen, Lucinda 1950- *58*
Brief entry *48*
McQueen, Mildred Hark 1908-1978 .... *12*
McQuillan, Mary *200*
McRae, Russell (William) 1934- *63*
McShean, Gordon 1936- *41*
Mc Swigan, Marie 1907-1962 .... *24*
McTavish, Sandy
See Eyerly, Jeannette
McTighe, Carolyn *238*
McVeity, Jen *148*
McVey, Vicki 1946- *80*
McVicker, Charles (Taggart) 1930- *39*
McVicker, Chuck
See McVicker, Charles (Taggart)
McVoy, Terra Elan *220*
McWhirter, A(lan) Ross 1925-1975 .... *37*
Obituary *31*
McWhirter, Norris (Dewar) 1925-2004 .... *37*
McWilliam, Howard 1977- *219*
McWilliams, Karen 1943- *65*
Mdurvwa, Hajara E. 1962- *92*
Meacham, Margaret 1952- *203*
Earlier sketch in SATA *95*
Meachum, Virginia 1918- *133*
Earlier sketch in SATA *87*
Mead, Alice 1952- *146*
Earlier sketch in SATA *94*
Mead, Margaret 1901-1978
Obituary *20*
Mead, Russell (M., Jr.) 1935- *10*
Mead, Stella (?)-1981
Obituary *27*
Meade, Elizabeth Thomasina 1854(?)-1914(?)
See CLR *163*
Meade, Ellen
See Roddick, Ellen
Meade, Holly *207*
Meade, L. T.
See Meade, Elizabeth Thomasina
Meade, Marion 1934- *127*
Earlier sketch in SATA *23*
Meader, Stephen W(arren) 1892-1977 .... *1*
Meadmore, Susan
See Sallis, Susan (Diana)
Meadow, Charles T(roub) 1929- *23*
Meadowcroft, Enid LaMonte
See Wright, Enid Meadowcroft (LaMonte)
Meadows, Daisy
See Chapman, Linda
Meadows, Graham (W.) 1934- *161*
Meadows, Michelle *202*
Meaker, M. J.
See Meaker, Marijane
Meaker, Marijane 1927- *160*
Autobiography Feature *111*
Earlier sketches in SATA *20, 61, 99*
See also CLR *29*
See also SAAS *1*
Meaker, Marijane Agnes
See Meaker, Marijane
Means, Florence Crannell 1891-1980 .... *1*
Obituary *25*
See also CLR *56*
Mearian, Judy Frank 1936- *49*
Mebus, Scott 1974- *216*
Mecca, Judy Truesdell 1955- *127*
Mechling, Lauren 1978(?)- *194*
Mechling, Lauren 1978(?)- *194*
Mechner, Jordan 1964- *205*
Medary, Marjorie 1890-1980 .... *14*
Meddaugh, Susan 1944- *176*
Earlier sketches in SATA *29, 84, 125*
Medearis, Angela Shelf 1956- *123*
Earlier sketch in SATA *72*
Medearis, Mary 1915- *5*
Medina, Jane 1953- *167*
Earlier sketch in SATA *122*
Medina, Meg 1963- *212*
Medina, Nico 1982- *193*
Medlicott, Mary 1946- *88*
Mee, Charles L., Jr. 1938- *72*
Earlier sketch in SATA *8*
Meehan, Kierin *218*
Meehl, Brian *204*
Meek, Jacklyn O'Hanlon 1933- *51*
Brief entry *34*
Meek, S(terner St.) P(aul) 1894-1972
Obituary *28*
Meeker, Clare Hodgson 1952- *96*
Meeker, Oden 1919(?)-1976 .... *14*
Meeker, Richard
See Brown, Fornan
Meeks, Esther MacBain *1*

Author Index

Meggs, Libby Phillips 1943- *130*
Mehdevi, Alexander (Sinclair) 1947- *7*
Mehdevi, Anne (Marie) Sinclair 1947- *8*
Mehling, Carl 1969(?)- *237*
Meidell, Sherry 1951- *73*
Meier, Minta 1906- *55*
Meighan, Donald Charles 1929- *30*
Meigs, Cornelia Lynde 1884-1973 .... *6*
See also CLR *55*
Meilach, Dona Z(weigoron) 1926- *34*
Meilman, Philip W(arren) 1951- *79*
Meinstereifel, Ronald L. 1960- *134*
Meisel, Paul *224*
Earlier sketch in SATA *184*
Meister, Cari *204*
Melanson, Luc *198*
Melcher, Daniel 1912-1985
Obituary *43*
Melcher, Frederic Gershom 1879-1963
Obituary *22*
Melcher, Marguerite Fellows 1879-1969 .... *10*
Meldrum, Christina 1969(?)- *206*
Melendez, Francisco 1964- *72*
Melhuish, Eva *199*
Melin, Grace Hathaway 1892-1973 .... *10*
Mellersh, H(arold) E(dward) L(eslie) 1897- *10*
Melling, David *186*
Melmed, Laura Krauss *212*
Melmoth, Sebastian
See Wilde, Oscar
Melnikoff, Pamela (Rita) *97*
Melo, Esperanca *239*
Meltzer, Amy 1968- *202*
Meltzer, Milton 1915-2009 .... *201*
Autobiography Feature *124*
Earlier sketches in SATA *1, 50, 80, 128*
See also CLR *13*
See also SAAS *1*
Melville, Anne
See Potter, Margaret
Melville, Herman 1819-1891 .... *59*
Melwood, Mary
See Lewis, E. M.
Melzack, Ronald 1929- *5*
Memling, Carl 1918-1969 .... *6*
Menchin, Scott *234*
Earlier sketch in SATA *188*
Mendel, Jo
See Bond, Gladys Baker
and Gilbertson, Mildred Geiger
Mendelson, Steven T. 1958-1995 .... *86*
Mendelson-Stevens, Serita Deborah
See Stevens, Serita
Mendes, Valerie 1939- *157*
Mendez, Raymond A. 1947- *66*
Mendez, Simon 1975- *215*
Mendonca, Susan
See Smith, Susan Vernon
Mendoza, George 1934- *41*
Brief entry *39*
See also SAAS *7*
Menendez, Shirley (C.) 1937- *146*
Meng, Cece *194*
Meng, Heinz (Karl) 1924- *13*
Mennen, Ingrid 1954- *85*
Menotti, Gian Carlo 1911-2007 .... *29*
Obituary *180*
Menuhin, Sir Yehudi 1916-1999 .... *40*
Obituary *113*
Menville, Douglas 1935- *64*
Menzel, Barbara Jean 1946- *63*
Menzel, Peter 1948- *207*
Mercati, Cynthia *164*
Mercati, Cynthia J.
See Mercati, Cynthia
Mercer, Charles (Edward) 1917-1988 .... *16*
Obituary *61*
Mercer, Jessie *21*
Mercer, Sienna *192*
Meredith, Arnold
See Hopkins, (Hector) Kenneth
Meredith, David William
See Miers, Earl Schenck
Meringoff, Laurene Krasny
See Brown, Laurene Krasny
Meriwether, Louise 1923- *52*
Brief entry *31*
Merlin, Arthur
See Blish, James
Merlin, Christina
See Heaven, Constance (Christina)
Merola, Caroline 1962- *236*
Merrell, Billy 1982- *222*
Merriam, Eve 1916-1992 .... *73*
Earlier sketches in SATA *3, 40*
See also CLR *14*
Merrill, Jane 1946- *42*
Merrill, Jane Merrill
See Merrill, Jane
Merrill, Jean (Fairbanks) 1923- *82*
Earlier sketch in SATA *1*
See also CLR *52*
Merrill, Phil
See Merrill, Jane
Merriman, Alex
See Silverberg, Robert
Merriman, Rachel 1971- *149*
Earlier sketch in SATA *98*
Merrit, Elizabeth
See Goudge, Eileen
Merski, Patricia K.
See Merski, P.K.
Merski, P.K. *172*
Mertz, Barbara
See Peters, Elizabeth
Mertz, Barbara Gross
See Peters, Elizabeth
Merveille, David *200*
Merz, Jennifer J. *196*
Meschel, Susan V. 1936- *83*
Meschenmoser, Sebastian 1980- *229*
Meserve, Jessica *211*
Messenger, Charles (Rynd Milles) 1942- *59*
Messer, Stephen 1972- *231*
Messick, Dale 1906-2005 .... *64*
Brief entry *48*
Messier, Claire 1956- *103*
Messieres, Nicole de
See de Messieres, Nicole
Messinger, Carla *198*
Messmer, Otto 1892(?)-1983 .... *37*
Messner, Kate *224*
Mesta, Gabriel
See Anderson, Kevin J.
and Moesta, Rebecca
Metaxas, Eric 1963- *211*
Metcalf, Doris H(unter) *91*
Metcalf, Suzanne
See Baum, L. Frank
Metos, Thomas H(arry) 1932- *37*
Metter, Bert(ram Milton) 1927- *56*
Metzenthen, David 1958- *167*
Earlier sketch in SATA *106*
Metzger, Steve 1949- *241*
Meunier, Brian 1954- *195*
Meyer, Barbara 1939- *77*
Meyer, Carolyn 1935- *142*
Autobiography Feature *142*
Earlier sketches in SATA *9, 70, 118*
See also SAAS *9*
Meyer, Carolyn Mae
See Meyer, Carolyn
Meyer, Edith Patterson 1895-1993 .... *5*
Meyer, F(ranklyn) E(dward) 1932- *9*
Meyer, Jean Shepherd *11*
Meyer, Jerome Sydney 1895-1975 .... *3*
Obituary *25*
Meyer, June
See Jordan, June
Meyer, Kerstin 1966- *190*
Meyer, L.A. 1942- *221*
Earlier sketches in SATA *12, 144*
Meyer, Louis A.
See Meyer, L.A.
Meyer, Renate 1930- *6*
Meyer, Stephenie 1973- *193*
See also CLR *142*
Meyer, Susan E. 1940- *64*
Meyerhoff, Jenny 1972- *208*
Meyers, Susan 1942- *164*
Earlier sketches in SATA *19, 108*
Meynell, Laurence Walter 1899-1989
Obituary *61*
Meynier, Yvonne (Pollet) 1908- *14*
Mezey, Robert 1935- *33*
Micale, Albert 1913- *22*
Michael, James
See Scagnetti, Jack
Michael, Jan 1947- *216*
Michael, Livi 1960- *172*
Michael, Manfred
See Winterfeld, Henry
Michael, Olivia
See Michael, Livi
Michael, Ted 1984- *234*
Michaelis, Antonia 1979- *215*
Michaels, Barbara
See Peters, Elizabeth
Michaels, Jamie *195*
Michaels, Joanne Louise
See Teitelbaum, Michael
Michaels, Kristin
See Williams, Jeanne
Michaels, Molly
See Untermeyer, Louis
Michaels, Neal
See Teitelbaum, Michael
Michaels, Rune *194*
Michaels, Ski
See Pellowski, Michael (Joseph)
Michaels, Steve 1955- *71*
Michaels, William M. 1917- *77*
Michalak, Jamie 1973- *217*
Michel, Anna 1943- *49*
Brief entry *40*
Michel, Francois 1948- *82*
Michelin, Linda *183*
Michelson, Richard *198*
Earlier sketch in SATA *173*
Micich, Paul *74*
Mickelson, Scott 1963- *213*
Micklish, Rita 1931- *12*
Micklos, John, Jr. 1956- *173*
Earlier sketch in SATA *129*
Micklos J., John, Jr. 1956-
See Micklos, John, Jr.
Micucci, Charles (Patrick, Jr.) 1959- *144*
Earlier sketch in SATA *82*
Middleton, Charlotte *230*
Middleton, Haydn 1955- *152*
Earlier sketch in SATA *85*
Miers, Earl Schenck 1910-1972 .... *1*
Obituary *26*
Migdale, Lawrence 1951- *89*
Miglio, Paige 1966- *201*
Mikaelsen, Ben 1952- *173*
Earlier sketches in SATA *73, 107*
Mikaelsen, Benjamin John
See Mikaelsen, Ben
Miklowitz, Gloria D. 1927- *129*
Earlier sketches in SATA *4, 68*
See also SAAS *17*
Mikolaycak, Charles 1937-1993 .... *78*
Obituary *75*
Earlier sketch in SATA *9*
See also SAAS *4*
Mikulski, Keri 1977- *240*
Mild, Warren (Paul) 1922- *41*
Milelli, Pascal 1965- *135*

Miles, Betty 1928- ... *78*
Earlier sketch in SATA *8*
See also SAAS *9*
Miles, Miska
See Martin, Patricia Miles
Miles, (Mary) Patricia 1930- ... *29*
Miles, Patricia A.
See Martin, Patricia Miles
Miles, Victoria 1966- ... *188*
Milford, Kate 1976- ... *233*
Milgrim, David ... *223*
Earlier sketches in SATA *158, 187*
Milgrom, Harry 1912-1978 ... *25*
Milhous, Katherine 1894-1977 ... *15*
Milian, Tomaso ... *238*
Milich, Zoran ... *174*
Milios, Rita 1949- ... *79*
Militant
See Sandburg, Carl
Millais, Raoul 1901- ... *77*
Millar, Barbara F. 1924- ... *12*
Millar, Margaret (Ellis Sturm) 1915-1994 ... *61*
Obituary ... *79*
Millard, Glenda ... *203*
Millard, Kerry ... *204*
Millbank, Captain H. R.
See Ellis, Edward S.
Millen, C(ynthia) M. 1955- ... *114*
Miller, Albert G(riffith) 1905-1982 ... *12*
Obituary ... *31*
Miller, Alice Ann 1958- ... *150*
Miller, Alice P(atricia McCarthy) ... *22*
Miller, Allan 1978- ... *216*
Miller, Christopher 1976- ... *215*
Miller, Debbie 1951- ... *160*
Earlier sketch in SATA *103*
See Miller, Debbie S.
Miller, Debbie S. ... *232*
See Miller, Debbie
Miller, Deborah Uchill 1944- ... *61*
Miller, Don 1923- ... *15*
Miller, Doris R.
See Mosesson, Gloria R(ubin)
Miller, Eddie
See Miller, Edward
Miller, Edna Anita 1920- ... *29*
Miller, Edward 1905-1974 ... *8*
Miller, Edward 1964- ... *218*
Earlier sketch in SATA *183*
Miller, Elizabeth 1933- ... *41*
Miller, Ellanita 1957- ... *87*
Miller, Eugene 1925- ... *33*
Miller, Frances A. 1937- ... *52*
Brief entry ... *46*
Miller, Heather Lynn 1971- ... *214*
Miller, Helen M(arkley) -1984 ... *5*
Miller, Helen Topping 1884-1960
Obituary ... *29*
Miller, Jane (Judith) 1925-1989 ... *15*
Miller, Jewel 1956- ... *73*
Miller, John
See Samachson, Joseph
Miller, Judi ... *117*
Miller, Karen 1949- ... *210*
Miller, Karen Hokanson
See Miller, Karen
Miller, Kate 1948- ... *193*
Miller, Kirsten 1973- ... *185*
Miller, Louise (Rolfe) 1940- ... *76*
Miller, M. L. ... *85*
Miller, Madge 1918- ... *63*
Miller, Margaret J.
See Dale, Margaret J(essy) Miller
Miller, Marilyn (Jean) 1925- ... *33*
Miller, Marvin ... *65*
Miller, Mary
See Northcott, (William) Cecil
Miller, Mary Beth 1942- ... *9*
Miller, Mary Beth 1964- ... *185*
Miller, Maryann 1943- ... *73*
Miller, Natalie 1917-1976 ... *35*
Miller, Pat 1951- ... *214*
Miller, Robert H. 1944- ... *91*
Miller, Ron 1947- ... *185*
Miller, Ruth White
See White, Ruth
Miller, Sandra
See Miller, Sandy
Miller, Sandra Peden
See Miller, Sandy
Miller, Sandy 1948- ... *41*
Brief entry ... *35*
Miller, Sarah 1969- ... *175*
Miller, Virginia
See Austin, Virginia
Miller, William R. 1959- ... *116*
Miller, Woody ... *236*
Miller Brothers
See Miller, Allan
Milligan, Bryce 1953- ... *170*
Milligan, Spike
See Milligan, Terence Alan
Milligan, Terence Alan 1918-2002 ... *29*
Obituary ... *134*
See also CLR *92*
Millington, Ada
See Deyneka, Anita
Millman, Isaac 1933- ... *140*
Mills, Adam
See Stanley, George Edward
Mills, Claudia 1954- ... *191*
Brief entry ... *41*
Earlier sketches in SATA *44, 89, 145*
Mills, Elaine (Rosemary) 1941- ... *72*
Mills, G. Riley ... *196*
Mills, Joyce C. 1944- ... *102*
Mills, Judith Christine 1956- ... *130*
Mills, Yaroslava Surmach 1925-2008 ... *35*
Millspaugh, Ben P. 1936- ... *77*
Millstead, Thomas E. ... *30*
Millward, Gwen ... *202*
Milne, A. A. 1882-1956 ... *100*
See also YABC *1*
See also CLR *108*
Milne, Alan Alexander
See Milne, A. A.
Milne, Lorus J. ... *5*
See also CLR *22*
See also SAAS *18*
Milne, Margery ... *5*
See also CLR *22*
See also SAAS *18*
Milne, Terry
See Milne, Theresa Ann
Milne, Theresa Ann 1964- ... *84*
Milnes, Irma McDonough 1924- ... *101*
Milonas, Rolf
See Myller, Rolf
Milone, Karen
See Dugan, Karen
Milone-Dugan, Karen
See Dugan, Karen
Milord, Susan 1954- ... *200*
Earlier sketches in SATA *74, 147*
Milotte, Alfred G(eorge) 1904-1989 ... *11*
Obituary ... *62*
Milstein, Linda 1954- ... *80*
Milton, Ann ... *134*
Milton, Hilary (Herbert) 1920- ... *23*
Milton, John R(onald) 1924- ... *24*
Milton, Joyce 1946- ... *101*
Brief entry ... *41*
Earlier sketch in SATA *52*
Milusich, Janice ... *216*
Milverton, Charles A.
See Penzler, Otto
Milway, Alex 1978- ... *215*
Milway, Katie Smith 1960- ... *203*
Minahan, John A. 1956- ... *92*
Minar, Barbra (Goodyear) 1940- ... *79*
Minard, Rosemary 1939- ... *63*
Minarik, Else Holmelund 1920- ... *127*
Earlier sketch in SATA *15*
See also CLR *33*
Miner, Jane Claypool 1933- ... *103*
Brief entry ... *37*
Earlier sketch in SATA *38*
Miner, Lewis S. 1909-1971 ... *11*
Mines, Jeanette 1948- ... *61*
Mines, Jeanette Marie
See Mines, Jeanette
Minier, Nelson
See Stoutenburg, Adrien (Pearl)
Minnitt, Ronda Jacqueline
See Armitage, David
Minor, Wendell 1944- ... *199*
Earlier sketches in SATA *78, 109, 164*
Minter, Daniel 1961- ... *176*
Mintonye, Grace ... *4*
Miranda, Anne 1954- ... *109*
Earlier sketch in SATA *71*
Miranda, Inaki 1983(?)- ... *207*
Mirocha, Paul ... *192*
Mirsky, Jeannette 1903-1987 ... *8*
Obituary ... *51*
Mirsky, Reba Paeff 1902-1966 ... *1*
Misako Rocks! ... *192*
Misenta, Marisol
See Innes, Stephanie
Mishica, Clare 1960- ... *91*
Miskovits, Christine 1939- ... *10*
Miss Frances
See Horwich, Frances R(appaport)
Miss Read 1913-2012 ... *10*
Mister Rogers
See Rogers, Fred McFeely
Mitchard, Jacquelyn 1956- ... *219*
Earlier sketches in SATA *98, 168*
Mitchell, Adrian 1932-2008 ... *166*
Obituary ... *200*
Earlier sketch in SATA *104*
Mitchell, Allison
See Griffin, W. E. B.
Mitchell, Betty Jo
See Mitchell, B.J.
Mitchell, B.J. 1931- ... *120*
Mitchell, Clyde
See Ellison, Harlan
and Silverberg, Robert
Mitchell, Cynthia 1922- ... *29*
Mitchell, (Sibyl) Elyne (Keith) 1913- ... *10*
Mitchell, Gladys (Maude Winifred)
1901-1983 ... *46*
Obituary ... *35*
Mitchell, Jay
See Roberson, Jennifer
Mitchell, Joyce Slayton 1933- ... *142*
Brief entry ... *43*
Earlier sketch in SATA *46*
Mitchell, K. L.
See Lamb, Elizabeth Searle
Mitchell, Kathy 1948- ... *59*
Mitchell, Lori 1961- ... *128*
Mitchell, Margaree King 1953- ... *84*
Mitchell, Marianne 1947- ... *145*
Mitchell, Rhonda ... *89*
Mitchell, Saundra 1974(?)- ... *217*
Mitchell, Stephen 1943- ... *199*
Mitchell, Susan
See Mitchell, Susan K.
Mitchell, Susan K. 1972- ... *210*
Mitchell, Todd 1974- ... *191*
Mitchell, Yvonne 1925-1979
Obituary ... *24*
Mitchelson, Mitch
See Mitchelson, Peter Richard
Mitchelson, Peter Richard 1950- ... *104*
Mitchison, Naomi (Margaret Haldane)
1897-1999 ... *24*
Obituary ... *112*
Mitchnik, Helen 1901-1982 ... *41*
Brief entry ... *35*

Mitchum, Hank
See Knott, William C(ecil, Jr.)
and Murray, Stuart A. P.
and Newton, D(wight) B(ennett)
and Sherman, Jory (Tecumseh)
Mitgutsch, Ali 1935- ... *76*
Mitsuhashi, Yoko ... *45*
Brief entry ... *33*
Mitton, Jacqueline 1948- ... *162*
Earlier sketches in SATA *66, 115*
Mitton, Simon 1946- ... *66*
Mitton, Tony 1951- ... *235*
Earlier sketches in SATA *104, 149, 203*
Miura, Taro 1968- ... *181*
Mizner, Elizabeth Howard 1907- ... *27*
Mizumura, Kazue ... *18*
Mlynowski, Sarah 1977(?)- ... *236*
Earlier sketch in SATA *180*
Mobin-Uddin, Asma ... *216*
Earlier sketch in SATA *172*
Mobley, Joe A. 1945- ... *91*
Moche, Dinah (Rachel) L(evine) 1936- ... *44*
Brief entry ... *40*
Mochi, Ugo (A.) 1889-1977 ... *38*
Mochizuki, Ken 1954- ... *146*
Earlier sketch in SATA *81*
See also SAAS *22*
Modarressi, Mitra 1967- ... *200*
Earlier sketch in SATA *126*
Modell, Frank B. 1917- ... *39*
Brief entry ... *36*
Modesitt, Jeanne 1953- ... *217*
Earlier sketches in SATA *92, 143*
Modesitt, L.E., Jr. 1943- ... *164*
Earlier sketch in SATA *91*
Modesitt, Leland Exton, Jr.
See Modesitt, L.E., Jr.
Modrell, Dolores 1933- ... *72*
Moe, Barbara 1937- ... *20*
Moe, Jorgen (Ingebretsen) 1813-1882
See CLR *104*
Moed-Kass, Pnina ... *169*
Moerbeek, Kees 1955- ... *98*
Moeri, Louise 1924- ... *93*
Earlier sketch in SATA *24*
See also SAAS *10*
Moesta, Rebecca 1956- ... *182*
Moffett, Jami 1952- ... *84*
Moffett, Mark W. 1957(?)- ... *203*
Moffett, Martha (Leatherwood) 1934- ... *8*
Mogensen, Suzanne A(ncher) 1946- ... *129*
Mohammed, Khadra ... *197*
Mohanty, Raja ... *223*
Mohn, Peter B(urnet) 1934- ... *28*
Mohn, Viola Kohl 1914- ... *8*
Mohr, Nicholasa 1938- ... *97*
Autobiography Feature ... *113*
Earlier sketch in SATA *8*
See also CLR *22*
See also SAAS *8*
Mok, Esther 1953- ... *93*
Molan, Christine 1943- ... *84*
Molarsky, Osmond 1909- ... *16*
Moldon, Peter L(eonard) 1937- ... *49*
Mole, John 1941- ... *103*
Earlier sketch in SATA *36*
See also CLR *61*
Molesworth, Mary Louisa 1839-1921 ... *98*
See also CLR *166*
Molin, Charles
See Mayne, William
Molina, Silvia 1946- ... *97*
Molk, Laurel 1957- ... *162*
Earlier sketch in SATA *92*
Mollel, Tololwa M. 1952- ... *88*
Molloy, Anne Baker 1907-1999 ... *32*
Molloy, Michael (John) 1940- ... *162*
Molloy, Paul (George) 1924- ... *5*
Molnar, Haya Leah 1951(?)- ... *230*
Moloney, James 1954- ... *202*
Autobiography Feature ... *144*
Earlier sketches in SATA *94, 144*
Molski, Carol ... *215*
Momaday, N. Scott 1934- ... *48*
Brief entry ... *30*
Momaday, Navarre Scott
See Momaday, N. Scott
Monaco, Octavia 1963- ... *169*
Monagle, Bernie 1957- ... *121*
Moncure, Jane Belk 1926- ... *23*
Monjo, F(erdinand) N(icholas III)
1924-1978 ... *16*
See also CLR *2*
Monk, Isabell 1952- ... *136*
Monks, Lydia ... *189*
Monroe, Chris 1962- ... *219*
Monroe, Christine
See Monroe, Chris
Monroe, Lyle
See Heinlein, Robert A.
Monroe, Marion
See Cox, Marion Monroe
Monroy, Manuel 1970- ... *196*
Monsell, Helen Albee 1895-1971 ... *24*
Monson-Burton, Marianne 1975- ... *139*
Montalbano, Andrea ... *231*
Montana, Bob 1920-1975
Obituary ... *21*
Montanari, Eva 1977- ... *209*
Montecalvo, Janet ... *177*
Montenegro, Laura Nyman 1953- ... *95*
Montero, Gloria 1933- ... *109*
Montes, Marisa 1951- ... *144*
Montgomerie, Norah (Mary) 1913- ... *26*
Montgomery, Constance
See Cappel, Constance
Montgomery, Elizabeth
See Julesberg, Elizabeth Rider Montgomery
Montgomery, Elizabeth Rider
See Julesberg, Elizabeth Rider Montgomery
Montgomery, Hugh (Edward) 1962- ... *146*
Montgomery, L. M. 1874-1942 ... *100*
See also YABC *1*
See also CLR *145*
Montgomery, Lucy Maud
See Montgomery, L. M.
Montgomery, Michael G. 1952- ... *208*
Montgomery, Raymond A. (Jr.) 1936- ... *39*
Montgomery, Rutherford George 1894-1985 . *3*
Montgomery, Sy 1958- ... *184*
Autobiography Feature ... *132*
Earlier sketches in SATA *114, 132*
Montgomery, Vivian ... *36*
Monthei, Betty ... *179*
Montijo, Rhode ... *179*
Montileaux, Donald F. 1948- ... *183*
Montpetit, Charles 1958- ... *101*
Montresor, Beni 1926-2001 ... *38*
Earlier sketch in SATA *3*
See also SAAS *4*
Montserrat, Pep ... *181*
Monty Python
See Chapman, Graham
and Cleese, John (Marwood)
and Gilliam, Terry
and Idle, Eric
and Jones, Terence Graham Parry
and Palin, Michael
Moodie, Craig 1956- ... *172*
Moodie, Fiona 1952- ... *133*
Moody, Minerva
See Alcott, Louisa May
Moody, Ralph Owen 1898-1982 ... *1*
Moon, Carl 1879(?)-1948 ... *25*
Moon, Grace (Purdie) 1877(?)-1947 ... *25*
Moon, Lily
See Warnes, Tim
Moon, Nicola 1952- ... *147*
Earlier sketch in SATA *96*
Moon, Pat 1946- ... *113*
Moon, Sheila 1910-1991 ... *5*
Obituary ... *114*
Moon, Sheila Elizabeth
See Moon, Sheila
Mooney, Bel 1946- ... *95*
Mooney, Bill 1936- ... *122*
Mooney, Elizabeth C(omstock) 1918-1986
Obituary ... *48*
Mooney, Melissa Duke 1968-2009 ... *241*
Mooney, William
See Mooney, Bill
Moor, Emily
See Deming, Richard
Moorcock, Michael 1939- ... *166*
Earlier sketch in SATA *93*
Moorcock, Michael John
See Moorcock, Michael
Moorcock, Michael John
See Moorcock, Michael
Moore, Anne Carroll 1871-1961 ... *13*
Moore, Cheri
See Ladd, Cheryl (Jean)
Moore, Clement Clarke 1779-1863 ... *18*
Moore, Cyd 1957- ... *233*
Earlier sketches in SATA *83, 133, 186*
Moore, Don W. 1905(?)-1986
Obituary ... *48*
Moore, Elaine 1944- ... *86*
Moore, Eva 1942- ... *103*
Earlier sketch in SATA *20*
Moore, Ishbel (Lindsay) 1954- ... *140*
Moore, Jack (William) 1941- ... *46*
Brief entry ... *32*
Moore, Janet Gaylord 1905-1992 ... *18*
Moore, Jim 1946- ... *42*
Moore, John Travers 1908- ... *12*
Moore, Lilian 1909-2004 ... *137*
Obituary ... *155*
Earlier sketch in SATA *52*
See also CLR *15*
Moore, Liz
See Moore, M. Elizabeth
Moore, M. Elizabeth 1959- ... *156*
Moore, Margaret R(umberger) 1903- ... *12*
Moore, Margie ... *224*
Earlier sketch in SATA *176*
Moore, Marianne 1887-1972 ... *20*
Moore, Marianne Craig
See Moore, Marianne
Moore, Patrick (Alfred Caldwell) 1923- ... *49*
Brief entry ... *39*
See also SAAS *8*
Moore, Patrick 1959- ... *184*
Moore, Perry 1971-2011 ... *193*
Moore, Peter 1963- ... *175*
Moore, Peter G.
See Moore, Peter
Moore, Raina 1970- ... *212*
Moore, Ray (S.) 1905(?)-1984
Obituary ... *37*
Moore, Regina
See Dunne, Mary Collins
Moore, Rosalie (Gertrude) 1910-2001 ... *9*
Moore, Ruth (Ellen) 1908-1989 ... *23*
Moore, Ruth Nulton 1923- ... *38*
Moore, S(arah) E. ... *23*
Moore, Sarah Margaret
See Hodges, Margaret
Moore, Sean L. 1976- ... *237*
Moore, Stephanie Perry 1969(?)- ... *214*
Moore, Tara 1950- ... *61*
Moore, Yvette 1958- ... *154*
Earlier sketches in SATA *69, 70*
Moores, Dick
See Moores, Richard (Arnold)
Moores, Richard (Arnold) 1909-1986
Obituary ... *48*
Mooser, Stephen 1941- ... *75*
Earlier sketch in SATA *28*
Mora, Francisco X(avier) 1952- ... *90*

Mora, Pat 1942- *232*
Earlier sketches in SATA *92, 134, 186*
See also CLR *58*
Mora, Patricia
See Mora, Pat
Morais, Flavio *207*
Morales, Magaly *225*
Morales, Yuyi *241*
Earlier sketches in SATA *154, 180*
Moran, Tom 1943- *60*
Moranville, Sharelle Byars *196*
Earlier sketch in SATA *152*
Moray Williams, Ursula 1911-2006 .... *3*
Obituary *177*
See also SAAS *9*
Mordecai, Martin *220*
Morden, Simon 1966(?)- *211*
Mordhorst, Heidi 1964- *222*
Mordvinoff, Nicolas 1911-1973 .... *17*
More, Caroline
See Cone, Molly (Lamken)
and Strachan, Margaret Pitcairn
Moreau, Jean-Pierre
See Jarrie, Martin
Moreno, Rene King *190*
Moreton, Andrew Esq.
See Defoe, Daniel
Morey, Charles
See Fletcher, Helen Jill
Morey, Walt(er Nelson) 1907-1992 .... *51*
Obituary *70*
Earlier sketch in SATA *3*
See also SAAS *9*
Morgan, Alfred P(owell) 1889-1972 .... *33*
Morgan, Alison (Mary) 1930- *85*
Earlier sketch in SATA *30*
Morgan, Anne 1954- *121*
Morgan, Christopher 1956- *199*
Morgan, Clay 1950- *198*
Morgan, Douglas
See Macdonald, James D.
Morgan, Ellen
See Bumstead, Kathleen Mary
Morgan, Geoffrey 1916- *46*
Morgan, Helen (Gertrude Louise)
1921-1990 .... *29*
Morgan, Jane
See Cooper, James Fenimore
and Franklin, Jane (Morgan)
and Moren, Sally M(oore)
Morgan, Lenore H. 1908-1976 .... *8*
Morgan, Mary 1957- *213*
Earlier sketches in SATA *81, 114*
Morgan, McKayla
See Basile, Gloria Vitanza
Morgan, Michaela
See Basile, Gloria Vitanza
Morgan, Nicola 1961- *161*
Morgan, Nina 1953- *110*
Morgan, Pierr 1952- *122*
Earlier sketch in SATA *77*
Morgan, Robin (Evonne) 1941- *80*
Morgan, Roxanne
See Gentle, Mary
Morgan, Sarah (Nicola) 1959- *68*
Morgan, Shirley
See Kiepper, Shirley Morgan
Morgan, Stacy T(owle) 1959- *104*
Morgan, Stevie
See Davies, Nicola
Morgan, Tom 1942- *42*
Morgan, Wendy
See Staub, Wendy Corsi
Morgan-Vanroyen, Mary
See Morgan, Mary
Morgenstern, Susie Hoch 1945- *133*
Mori, Hana 1909-1990(?) *88*
Mori, Kyoko 1957- *122*
Autobiography Feature *126*
See also CLR *64*
See also SAAS *26*
Moriarty, Jaclyn 1968- *239*
Earlier sketch in SATA *162*
Moriarty, William J. 1930- *127*
Morice, Dave 1946- *93*
Morin, Isobel V. 1928- *110*
Morine, Hoder
See Conroy, John Wesley
Morley, Ben *228*
Morley, Taia *199*
Morley, Wilfred Owen
See Lowndes, Robert A(ugustine) W(ard)
Morningstar, Mildred (Whaley) 1912-1997 .. *61*
Obituary *114*
Morozumi, Atsuko *217*
Earlier sketch in SATA *110*
Morpurgo, Michael 1943- *225*
Earlier sketches in SATA *93, 143, 184*
See also CLR *51*
Morrah, Dave
See Morrah, David Wardlaw, Jr.
Morrah, David Wardlaw, Jr. 1914-1991 .... *10*
Morreale-de la Garza, Phyllis
See De la Garza, Phyllis
Morressy, John 1930-2006 .... *23*
Morrill, Leslie H(olt) 1934-2003 .... *48*
Brief entry *33*
Obituary *148*
See also SAAS *22*
Morris, Carla *210*
Morris, Carla D.
See Morris, Carla
Morris, Chris(topher Crosby) 1946- *66*
Morris, Deborah 1956- *91*
Morris, Desmond 1928- *14*
Morris, Desmond John
See Morris, Desmond
Morris, Don 1954- *83*
Morris, Gerald 1963- *207*
Earlier sketches in SATA *107, 150*
Morris, Gerald Paul
See Morris, Gerald
Morris, Gilbert (Leslie) 1929- *104*
Morris, Jackie *202*
Earlier sketch in SATA *151*
Morris, Janet (Ellen) 1946- *66*
Morris, Jay
See Tatham, Julie Campbell
Morris, (Margaret) Jean 1924- *98*
Morris, Jeffrey
See Morris, Jeffrey Brandon
Morris, Jeffrey B.
See Morris, Jeffrey Brandon
Morris, Jeffrey Brandon 1941- *92*
Morris, Jennifer E. 1969- *179*
Morris, Jill 1936- *165*
Earlier sketch in SATA *119*
Morris, Juddi *85*
Morris, Judy K. 1936- *61*
Morris, Oradel Nolen *128*
Morris, Richard 1969- *224*
Morris, Robert A(da) 1933- *7*
Morris, William 1913-1994 .... *29*
Morrison, Angela *218*
Morrison, Bill 1935- *66*
Brief entry *37*
Morrison, Chloe Anthony Wofford
See Morrison, Toni
Morrison, Dorothy Nafus *29*
Morrison, Frank 1971- *226*
Earlier sketch in SATA *185*
Morrison, Gordon 1944- *183*
Earlier sketches in SATA *87, 128*
Morrison, Joan 1922- *65*
Morrison, Lillian 1917- *108*
Earlier sketch in SATA *3*
Morrison, Lucile Phillips 1896- *17*
Morrison, Martha A. 1948- *77*
Morrison, Meighan 1966- *90*
Morrison, P.R. *196*
Morrison, Richard
See Lowndes, Robert A(ugustine) W(ard)
Morrison, Robert
See Lowndes, Robert A(ugustine) W(ard)
Morrison, Roberta
See Webb, Jean Francis (III)
Morrison, Slade 1964-2010 .... *228*
Morrison, Susan Dudley
See Gold, Susan Dudley
Morrison, Taylor 1971- *187*
Earlier sketches in SATA *95, 159*
Morrison, Toni 1931- *235*
Earlier sketches in SATA *57, 144*
See also CLR *99*
Morrison, Velma Ford 1909- *21*
Morrison, Wilbur Howard 1915- *64*
Morrison, William
See Samachson, Joseph
Morriss, James E(dward) 1932- *8*
Morrissey, Dean *183*
Morrow, Barbara Olenyik 1952- *167*
Morrow, Betty
See Bacon, Elizabeth
Morrow, Sue Anne 1966- *218*
Morse, C. Scott
See Morse, Scott
Morse, Carol
See Yeakley, Marjory Hall
Morse, C.S.
See Morse, Scott
Morse, Dorothy B(ayley) 1906-1979
Obituary *24*
Morse, Flo 1921- *30*
Morse, Joe *240*
Morse, Scott 1973- *200*
Morse, Tony 1953- *129*
Morstad, Julie *232*
Mort, Vivian
See Cromie, Alice Hamilton
Mortensen, Denise Dowling *179*
Mortensen, Lori 1955- *221*
Mortimer, Anne 1958- *206*
Earlier sketch in SATA *116*
Mortimer, Mary H.
See Coury, Louise Andree
Morton, Alexandra (Hubbard) 1957- *144*
Morton, Anthony
See Arthur, Robert, (Jr.)
Morton, Christine
See Morton-Shaw, Christine
Morton, Jane 1931- *50*
Morton, Joseph C. 1932- *156*
Morton, Lee Jack, Jr. 1928- *32*
Morton, Miriam 1918(?)-1985 .... *9*
Obituary *46*
Morton-Shaw, Christine 1957- *211*
Mosatche, Harriet 1949- *122*
Mosatche, Harriet S.
See Mosatche, Harriet
Moscow, Alvin 1925- *3*
Mosel, Arlene (Tichy) 1921-1996 .... *7*
Moseley, James W(illett) 1931- *139*
Moseng, Elisabeth 1967- *90*
Moser, Barry 1940- *185*
Earlier sketches in SATA *56, 79, 138*
See also CLR *49*
See also SAAS *15*
Moser, Don(ald Bruce) 1932- *31*
Moser, Laura *194*
Moser, Lisa *192*
Moses, Sheila P. 1961- *168*
Moses, Will 1956- *178*
Earlier sketch in SATA *120*
Mosesson, Gloria R(ubin) *24*
Mosher, Richard 1949- *120*
Moskin, Marietta D(unston) 1928- *23*
Moskof, Martin Stephen 1930- *27*
Mosley, Francis 1957- *57*
Moss, Don(ald) 1920- *11*
Moss, Elaine (Dora) 1924- *57*
Brief entry *31*
Moss, Jeff(rey) 1942-1998 .... *73*
Obituary *106*

Moss, Marissa 1959- *216*
Earlier sketches in SATA *71, 104, 163*
See also CLR *134*
Moss, Miriam 1955- *202*
Earlier sketches in SATA *76, 140*
Moss, Peggy 1966- *235*
Moss, Thylias 1954- *108*
Moss, Thylias Rebecca Brasier
See Moss, Thylias
Most, Bernard 1937- *134*
Brief entry *40*
Earlier sketches in SATA *48, 91*
Mosz, Gosia 1972- *194*
Mott, Evelyn Clarke 1962- *133*
Earlier sketch in SATA *75*
Motz, Lloyd 1909-2004 .... *20*
Mould, Chris *205*
Mould, Edwin
See Whitlock, Ralph
Moulton, Mark Kimball *212*
Mouly, Francoise *155*
Mountain, Robert
See Montgomery, Raymond A. (Jr.)
Mountfield, David
See Grant, Neil
Mourlevat, Jean-Claude 1952- *187*
Mourning, Tuesday *206*
Moussard, Jacqueline 1924- *24*
Mowat, Claire 1933- *123*
Mowat, Claire Angel Wheeler
See Mowat, Claire
Mowat, Farley 1921- *55*
Earlier sketch in SATA *3*
See also CLR *20*
Mowat, Farley McGill
See Mowat, Farley
Mowll, Joshua 1970(?)- *188*
Mowry, Jess 1960- *131*
Autobiography Feature *131*
Earlier sketch in SATA *109*
See also CLR *65*
Moxley, Sheila 1966- *96*
Moyer, Terry J. 1937- *94*
Moyes, Patricia
See Haszard, Patricia Moyes
Moyler, Alan (Frank Powell) 1926- *36*
Mozelle, Shirley *179*
Mozley, Charles 1915- *43*
Brief entry *32*
Mphahlele, Es'kia 1919-2008 .... *119*
Obituary *198*
Mphahlele, Ezekiel
See Mphahlele, Es'kia
Mphahlele, Zeke
See Mphahlele, Es'kia
Mr. McGillicuddy
See Abisch, Roslyn Kroop
Mr. Sniff
See Abisch, Roslyn Kroop
Mr. Tivil
See Lorkowski, Thomas V(incent)
Mr. Wizard
See Herbert, Don
Mraz, David 1947- *219*
Mrs. Fairstar
See Horne, Richard Henry Hengist
Muchamore, Robert 1972- *175*
Muchmore, Jo Ann 1937- *103*
Mude, O.
See Gorey, Edward (St. John)
Mudgeon, Apeman
See Mitchell, Adrian
Mueller, Jorg 1942- *67*
See also CLR *43*
Mueller, Miranda R. *201*
Mueller, Virginia 1924- *28*
Muggs
See Watkins, Lois
Muir, Diana
See Appelbaum, Diana Muir Karter
Muir, Frank (Herbert) 1920-1998 .... *30*
Muir, Helen 1937- *65*
Muirhead, Margaret *220*
Mukerji, Dhan Gopal 1890-1936 .... *40*
See also CLR *10*
Mulcahy, Lucille Burnett *12*
Muldrow, Diane *229*
Mulford, Philippa G. 1948- *112*
Earlier sketch in SATA *43*
Mulford, Philippa Greene
See Mulford, Philippa G.
Mulgan, Catherine 1931- *24*
Mulila, Vigad G.
See Maillu, David G(ian)
Mull, Brandon 1974- *190*
Mullen, Michael 1937- *122*
Muller, Billex
See Ellis, Edward S.
Muller, Birte 1973- *214*
Muller, Jorg
See Mueller, Jorg
Muller, (Lester) Robin 1953- *86*
Mulligan, Andy *238*
Mullin, Caryl Cude 1969- *130*
Mullins, Edward S(wift) 1922- *10*
Mullins, Hilary 1962- *84*
Mulock, Dinah Maria
See Craik, Dinah Maria (Mulock)
Mulvihill, William Patrick 1923- *8*
Mumford, Ruth
See Dallas, Ruth
Mumy, Bill 1954- *112*
Mun
See Leaf, (Wilbur) Munro
Munari, Bruno 1907-1998 .... *15*
See also CLR *9*
Munce, Ruth Hill 1898- *12*
Mundy, Simon 1954- *64*
Mundy, Simon Andrew James Hainault
See Mundy, Simon
Munger, Nancy *170*
Munowitz, Ken 1935-1977 .... *14*
Munoz, Claudio *208*
Munoz, William 1949- *92*
Earlier sketch in SATA *42*
Munro, Alice 1931- *29*
Munro, Alice Anne
See Munro, Alice
Munro, Eleanor 1928- *37*
Munro, Roxie 1945- *223*
Earlier sketches in SATA *58, 136, 184*
Munsch, Bob
See Munsch, Robert (Norman)
Munsch, Robert (Norman) 1945- *120*
Brief entry *48*
Earlier sketches in SATA *50, 83*
See also CLR *19*
Munsinger, Lynn 1951- *221*
Earlier sketches in SATA *33, 94, 177*
Munson, Derek 1970- *139*
Munson, R. W.
See Karl, Jean E(dna)
Munson-Benson, Tunie 1946- *15*
Munsterberg, Peggy 1921- *102*
Muntean, Michaela *182*
Munthe, Nelly 1947- *53*
Munves, James (Albert) 1922- *30*
Munzer, Martha E. 1899-1999 .... *4*
Murawski, Darlyne A. *193*
Murch, Mel
See Manes, Stephen
Murdoch, David H(amilton) 1937- *96*
Murdoch, Patricia 1957- *192*
Murdock, Catherine Gilbert *185*
Murhall, J(acqueline) J(ane) 1964- *143*
Murphy, Barbara Beasley 1933- *130*
Earlier sketch in SATA *5*
Murphy, Claire Rudolf 1951- *137*
Earlier sketch in SATA *76*
Murphy, E(mmett) Jefferson 1926- *4*
Murphy, Elizabeth Ann Maureen
See Murphy, Liz
Murphy, Jill 1949- *214*
Earlier sketches in SATA *37, 70, 142*
See also CLR *39*
Murphy, Jill Frances
See Murphy, Jill
Murphy, Jim 1947- *224*
Brief entry *32*
Earlier sketches in SATA *37, 77, 124, 185*
See also CLR *53*
Murphy, Joseph E., Jr. 1930- *65*
Murphy, Kelly 1977- *190*
Earlier sketch in SATA *143*
Murphy, Liz 1964- *210*
Murphy, Louise 1943- *155*
Murphy, Mary 1961- *196*
Murphy, Pat
See Murphy, E(mmett) Jefferson
Murphy, Patricia J. 1963- *132*
Murphy, Rita *180*
Murphy, Robert (William) 1902-1971 .... *10*
Murphy, Shirley Rousseau 1928- *126*
Earlier sketches in SATA *36, 71*
See also SAAS *18*
Murphy, Stuart J. 1942- *237*
Earlier sketches in SATA *115, 157*
Murphy, Thomas Basil, Jr. 1935- *191*
Murphy, Tim
See Murphy, Jim
Murphy, Tom
See Murphy, Thomas Basil, Jr.
Murphy, Yannick *240*
Murray, John 1923- *39*
Murray, Kirsty 1960- *165*
Earlier sketch in SATA *108*
Murray, Marguerite 1917- *63*
Murray, Marian *5*
Murray, Martine 1965- *125*
Murray, (Judith) Michele (Freedman) 1933-1974 .... *7*
Murray, Ossie 1938- *43*
Murray, Peter
See Hautman, Pete
Murrow, Liza Ketchum
See Ketchum, Liza
Musgrave, Florence 1902-1999 .... *3*
Musgrove, Margaret W(ynkoop) 1943- *124*
Earlier sketch in SATA *26*
Musgrove, Marianne *207*
Mussey, Virginia Howell
See Ellison, Virginia H(owell)
Mussey, Virginia T.H.
See Ellison, Virginia H(owell)
Mussi, Sarah *206*
Mutel, Cornelia F. 1947- *74*
Muth, Jon J. *206*
Earlier sketch in SATA *165*
Mutz
See Kuenstler, Morton
Mwangi, Meja 1948- *174*
My Brother's Brother
See Chekhov, Anton
Myers, Anna *220*
Earlier sketch in SATA *160*
Myers, Arthur 1917- *91*
Earlier sketch in SATA *35*
Myers, Bernice *81*
Earlier sketch in SATA *9*
Myers, Caroline Elizabeth Clark 1887-1980 .... *28*
Myers, Christopher 1975- *183*
See also CLR *97*
Myers, Edward 1950- *227*
Earlier sketches in SATA *96, 172*
Myers, Elisabeth P(erkins) 1918- *36*
Myers, (Mary) Hortense (Powner) 1913-1987 .... *10*
Myers, Jack 1913-2006 .... *83*
Obituary *178*
Myers, Jack Edgar
See Myers, Jack
Myers, Laurie *232*

Myers, Lou 1915-2005 .... *81*
Obituary *171*
Myers, Louis
See Myers, Lou
Myers, R.E. 1924- *119*
Myers, Robert Eugene
See Myers, R.E.
Myers, Tim 1953- *176*
Earlier sketch in SATA *147*
Myers, Timothy Joseph
See Myers, Tim
Myers, Walter Dean 1937- *229*
Brief entry *27*
Earlier sketches in SATA *41, 71, 109, 157, 193*
See also CLR *110*
See also SAAS *2*
Myers, Walter M.
See Myers, Walter Dean
Myklusch, Matt *236*
Myller, Rolf 1926-2006 .... *27*
Obituary *175*
Myra, Harold L(awrence) 1939- *46*
Brief entry *42*
Myracle, Lauren 1969- *204*
Earlier sketch in SATA *162*
Myrus, Donald (Richard) 1927- *23*
Mysterious Traveler, The
See Arthur, Robert, (Jr.)

N

Na, An *149*
Na, Il Sung *231*
Naaslund, Goorel Kristina 1940- *170*
Nadel, Laurie 1948- *74*
Naden, Corinne J. 1930- *166*
Earlier sketch in SATA *79*
Nadimi, Suzan *188*
Nadin, Joanna 1970- *239*
Nadol, Jen *228*
Nagda, Ann Whitehead *199*
Nagel, Andreas Fischer
See Fischer-Nagel, Andreas
Nagel, Heiderose Fischer
See Fischer-Nagel, Heiderose
Nagle, Shane *176*
Nahoko, Uehashi
See Uehashi, Nahoko
Naidoo, Beverley 1943- *180*
Earlier sketches in SATA *63, 135*
See also CLR *29*
Nails, Jennifer *213*
Naiyomah, Wilson Kimeli 1977- *226*
Nakae, Noriko 1940- *59*
Nakata, Hiroe *205*
Nakatani, Chiyoko 1930-1981 .... *55*
Brief entry *40*
See also CLR *30*
Nally, Susan W. 1947- *90*
Namioka, Lensey 1929- *157*
Autobiography Feature *116*
Earlier sketches in SATA *27, 89*
See also CLR *48*
See also SAAS *24*
Namovicz, Gene Inyart 1927- *6*
Nance, Andrew *210*
Nanji, Shenaaz 1954- *204*
Earlier sketch in SATA *131*
Nanogak Agnes 1925- *61*
Napier, Mark
See Laffin, John (Alfred Charles)
Napoli, Donna Jo 1948- *230*
Autobiography Feature *230*
Earlier sketches in SATA *92, 137, 190*
See also CLR *51*
See also SAAS *23*
Napp, Daniel 1974- *204*
Narahashi, Keiko 1959- *115*
Earlier sketch in SATA *79*
Narayan, R. K. 1906-2001 .... *62*
Narayan, Rasipuram Krishnaswami
See Narayan, R. K.
Nascimbene, Yan 1949- *173*
Earlier sketch in SATA *133*
Nascimbeni, Barbara 1969- *240*
Nash, Bruce M(itchell) 1947- *34*
Nash, Frediric Ogden
See Nash, Ogden
Nash, Linell
See Smith, Linell Nash
Nash, Mary (Hughes) 1925- *41*
Nash, Ogden 1902-1971 .... *46*
Earlier sketch in SATA *2*
Nash, Renea Denise 1963- *81*
Nast, Elsa Ruth
See Watson, Jane Werner
Nast, Thomas 1840-1902 .... *51*
Brief entry *33*
Nastick, Sharon 1954- *41*
Natale, Vince *196*
Natalini, Sandro 1970- *222*
Natarajan, Srividya *187*
Nathan, Adele (Gutman) 1900(?)-1986
Obituary *48*
Nathan, Amy *155*
Earlier sketch in SATA *104*
Nathan, Dorothy (Goldeen) (?)-1966 .... *15*
Nathan, Robert (Gruntal) 1894-1985 .... *6*
Obituary *43*
Nathanson, Laura Walther 1941- *57*
Nation, Kaleb 1988- *222*
Natti, Lee 1919- *67*
Earlier sketch in SATA *1*
See also SAAS *3*
Natti, Susanna 1948- *125*
Earlier sketch in SATA *32*
Nau, Thomas *186*
Naughtie, Eleanor
See Updale, Eleanor
Naughton, Bill
See Naughton, William John (Francis)
Naughton, James Franklin 1957- *85*
Naughton, Jim
See Naughton, James Franklin
Naughton, William John (Francis) 1910-1992 .... *86*
Navarra, John Gabriel 1927- *8*
Nayeri, Daniel *232*
Nayeri, Dina *226*
Naylor, Penelope 1941- *10*
Naylor, Phyllis 1933-
See Naylor, Phyllis Reynolds
Naylor, Phyllis Reynolds 1933- *209*
Autobiography Feature *152*
See also CLR *135*
See also SAAS *10*
Nazarian, Nikki
See Nichols, Cecilia Fawn
Nazaroff, Alexander I(vanovich) 1898-1981 .. *4*
Nazoa, Aquiles 1920-1976 .... *198*
Neal, Harry Edward 1906-1993 .... *5*
Obituary *76*
Neal, Michael
See Teitelbaum, Michael
Nearing, Penny 1916- *47*
Brief entry *42*
Nebel, Gustave E. *45*
Brief entry *33*
Nebel, Mimouca
See Nebel, Gustave E.
Nee, Kay Bonner *10*
Needham, Kate 1962- *95*
Needle, Jan 1943- *98*
Earlier sketch in SATA *30*
See also CLR *43*
See also SAAS *23*
Needleman, Jacob 1934- *6*
Neel, David 1960- *82*
Neel, Preston 1959- *93*
Neff, Henry H. 1973- *221*
Negri, Rocco 1932- *12*
Negrin, Fabian 1963- *189*
Neidigh, Sherry 1956- *204*
Neier, Aryeh 1937- *59*
Neigoff, Anne *13*
Neigoff, Mike 1920- *13*
Neilan, Eujin Kim 1969- *200*
Neilson, Frances Fullerton (Jones) 1910-2001 .... *14*
Neimark, Anne E. 1935- *145*
Earlier sketch in SATA *4*
Neimark, Paul G. 1934- *80*
Brief entry *37*
Neitzel, Shirley 1941- *134*
Earlier sketch in SATA *77*
Nell
See Hanna, Nell(ie L.)
Nelscott, Kris
See Rusch, Kristine Kathryn
Nelson, Blake 1960- *177*
Nelson, Catherine Chadwick 1926- *87*
Nelson, Cordner 1918-2009 .... *54*
Brief entry *29*
Nelson, Cordner Bruce
See Nelson, Cordner
Nelson, D.A. 1970- *215*
Nelson, Dawn Ann
See Nelson, D.A.
Nelson, Drew 1952- *77*
Nelson, Esther L. 1928- *13*
Nelson, Jandy *229*
Nelson, Jim A.
See Stotter, Mike
Nelson, Julie L. 1970- *117*
Nelson, Kadir *213*
Earlier sketches in SATA *154, 181*
Nelson, Kris
See Rusch, Kristine Kathryn
Nelson, Lawrence E(rnest) 1928-1977
Obituary *28*
Nelson, Marilyn 1946- *60*
Autobiography Feature *180*
Nelson, Mary Carroll 1929- *23*
Nelson, O. Terry 1941- *62*
Nelson, Peter 1953- *73*
Nelson, Peter N.
See Nelson, Peter
Nelson, R. A. *197*
Nelson, Richard K(ing) 1941- *65*
Nelson, Robin Laura 1971- *141*
Nelson, Roy Paul 1923- *59*
Nelson, S.D. *181*
Nelson, Sharlene (P.) 1933- *96*
Nelson, Suzanne 1976- *184*
Nelson, Ted (W.) 1931- *96*
Nelson, Theresa 1948- *143*
Autobiography Feature *143*
Earlier sketch in SATA *79*
Nelson, Vaunda Micheaux 1953- *220*
Nemeth, Sally *187*
Neri, G. *197*
Neri, Greg
See Neri, G.
Neri, Gregory
See Neri, G.
Nerlove, Miriam 1959- *53*
Brief entry *49*
Nesbit, E. 1858-1924 .... *100*
See also YABC *1*
See also CLR *70*
Nesbit, Edith
See Nesbit, E.
Nesbit, Troy
See Folsom, Franklin (Brewster)
Nesbitt, Kenn 1962- *239*
Nespojohn, Katherine V(eronica) 1912-1975 . *7*

Ness, Evaline (Michelow) 1911-1986 .... *26*
Obituary *49*
Earlier sketch in SATA *1*
See also CLR *6*
See also SAAS *1*
Ness, Patrick 1971- *207*
Nestor, Larry 1940- *149*
Nestor, William P(rodromos) 1947- *49*
Nethery, Mary *240*
Earlier sketch in SATA *93*
Neubecker, Robert *214*
Earlier sketch in SATA *170*
Neuberger, Julia (Babette Sarah) 1950- *142*
Earlier sketch in SATA *78*
Neufeld, John (Arthur) 1938- *131*
Autobiography Feature *131*
Earlier sketches in SATA *6, 81*
See also CLR *52*
See also SAAS *3*
Neuhaus, David 1958- *83*
Neumeyer, Peter F(lorian) 1929- *13*
Neurath, Marie (Reidemeister) 1898-1986 .... *1*
Neuschwander, Cindy 1953- *157*
Earlier sketch in SATA *107*
Neusner, Jacob 1932- *38*
Neville, Charles
See Bodsworth, (Charles) Fred(erick)
Neville, Emily Cheney 1919- *1*
See also SAAS *2*
Neville, Mary
See Woodrich, Mary Neville
Nevins, Albert (Francis) J(erome)
1915-1997 .... *20*
Nevius, Carol 1955- *186*
Newberger, Devra
See Speregen, Devra Newberger
Newberry, Clare Turlay 1903-1970 .... *1*
Obituary *26*
Newbery, John 1713-1767 .... *20*
See also CLR *147*
Newbery, Linda 1952- *184*
Earlier sketch in SATA *142*
Newbigging, Martha *198*
Newbold, Greg *199*
Newbound, Andrew 1969- *241*
Newcomb, Ellsworth
See Kenny, Ellsworth Newcomb
Newcombe, Eugene A. 1923-1990 .... *45*
Brief entry *33*
Newcombe, Jack
See Newcombe, Eugene A.
Newcome, Robert 1955- *91*
Newcome, Zita 1959- *88*
Newell, Crosby
See Bonsall, Crosby Barbara (Newell)
Newell, Edythe W(eatherford) 1910-1989 .... *11*
Newell, Hope Hockenberry 1896-1965 .... *24*
Newfeld, Frank 1928- *26*
Newgarden, Mark 1959- *194*
Newhouse, Maxwell 1947- *232*
Newland, Gillian *220*
Newlon, (Frank) Clarke 1905(?)-1982 .... *6*
Obituary *33*
Newman, Barbara Johansen *240*
Earlier sketch in SATA *191*
Newman, C.J.
See Newman, Coleman J.
Newman, Coleman J. 1935- *82*
Newman, Daisy 1904-1994 .... *27*
Obituary *78*
Newman, Gerald 1939- *46*
Brief entry *42*
Newman, Jeff 1976- *228*
Newman, Jerry
See Newman, Coleman J.
Newman, Leslea 1955- *234*
Earlier sketches in SATA *71, 128, 134*
Newman, Margaret
See Potter, Margaret
Newman, Marjorie *146*
Newman, Matthew (Harrison) 1955- *56*
Newman, Nanette 1934- *162*
Newman, Robert (Howard) 1909-1988 .... *87*
Obituary *60*
Earlier sketch in SATA *4*
Newman, Shirlee P(etkin) *144*
Earlier sketches in SATA *10, 90*
Newquist, Harvey
See Newquist, H.P.
Newquist, H.P. 1958- *235*
Newsom, Carol 1948- *92*
Earlier sketch in SATA *40*
Newsom, Tom 1944- *80*
Newsome, Richard 1964- *233*
Newth, Mette 1942- *140*
Newton, David E. 1933- *67*
Newton, David Edward
See Newton, David E.
Newton, James R(obert) 1935- *23*
Newton, Jill 1964- *200*
Newton, Robert 1965- *191*
Newton, Suzanne 1936- *77*
Earlier sketch in SATA *5*
Newton, Vanessa
See Newton, Vanessa Brantley
Newton, Vanessa Brantley 1962(?)- *206*
Ney, John 1923- *43*
Brief entry *33*
Nez, John *218*
Earlier sketch in SATA *155*
Nez, John Abbott
See Nez, John
Ng, Franklin *82*
Ngui, Marc 1972- *229*
Nguyen, Vincent *226*
Earlier sketch in SATA *187*
Nichol, B(arrie) P(hillip) 1944-1988 .... *66*
Nicholas, Louise D.
See Watkins, Dawn L.
Nicholls, Judith (Ann) 1941- *61*
Nicholls, Sally 1983- *209*
Nichols, Cecilia Fawn 1906-1987 .... *12*
Nichols, Grace 1950- *164*
Earlier sketch in SATA *98*
Nichols, Janet (Louise) 1952- *67*
Nichols, Judy 1947- *124*
Nichols, Leigh
See Koontz, Dean
Nichols, Michael 1952- *215*
Nichols, Nick
See Nichols, Michael
Nichols, Paul
See Hawks, Robert
Nichols, Peter
See Youd, Samuel
Nichols, (Joanna) Ruth 1948- *15*
See also CLR *149*
Nichols, Travis *206*
Nicholson, C. R.
See Nicole, Christopher
Nicholson, Christina
See Nicole, Christopher
Nicholson, Joyce Thorpe 1919-2011 .... *35*
Nicholson, Lois P. 1949- *88*
Nicholson, Robin
See Nicole, Christopher
Nicholson, William *239*
Earlier sketch in SATA *180*
Nicholson, William 1872-1949
See CLR *76*
Nickel, Barbara 1966- *188*
Nickell, Joe 1944- *167*
Earlier sketch in SATA *73*
Nickelsburg, Janet 1893-1983 .... *11*
Nickerson, Betty 1922- *14*
Nickerson, Elizabeth
See Nickerson, Betty
Nickl, Barbara (Elisabeth) 1939- *56*
Nicklaus, Carol *62*
Brief entry *33*
Nickle, John *181*
Nickless, Will 1902-1979(?) *66*
Nic Leodhas, Sorche
See Alger, Leclaire (Gowans)
Nicol, Ann
See Turnbull, Ann
Nicolas
See Mordvinoff, Nicolas
Nicolay, Helen 1866-1954
See YABC *1*
Nicole, Christopher 1930- *5*
Nicole, Christopher Robin
See Nicole, Christopher
Nicoll, Helen 1937- *87*
Nicolson, Cynthia Pratt 1949- *141*
Ni Dhuibhne, Eilis 1954- *91*
Niehaus, Paddy Bouma
See Bouma, Paddy
Nields, Nerissa 1967- *166*
Nielsen, Kay (Rasmus) 1886-1957 .... *16*
See also CLR *16*
Nielsen, Laura F. 1960- *93*
Nielsen, Laura Farnsworth
See Nielsen, Laura F.
Nielsen, Nancy J. 1951- *77*
Nielsen, Susin 1964- *195*
Nielsen, Virginia
See McCall, Virginia Nielsen
Nielsen-Fernlund, Susin
See Nielsen, Susin
Nielson, Sheila A. *234*
Niemann, Christoph 1970- *238*
Earlier sketch in SATA *191*
Nieuwsma, Milton J(ohn) 1941- *142*
Nightingale, Sandy 1953- *76*
Nikolajeva, Maria 1952- *127*
Nikola-Lisa, W. 1951- *180*
Earlier sketch in SATA *71*
Niland, Deborah 1951- *172*
Earlier sketch in SATA *27*
Niland, Kilmeny *75*
Nilsen, Anna 1948- *174*
Earlier sketch in SATA *96*
Nilsson, Eleanor 1939- *117*
Earlier sketch in SATA *81*
See also SAAS *23*
Nilsson, Per 1954- *159*
Nimmo, Jenny 1944- *144*
Earlier sketch in SATA *87*
See also CLR *44*
Nishimura, Kae *196*
Niven, Larry 1938- *171*
Earlier sketch in SATA *95*
Niven, Laurence Van Cott
See Niven, Larry
Niven, Laurence VanCott
See Niven, Larry
Nivola, Claire A. 1947- *208*
Earlier sketches in SATA *84, 140*
Nix, Garth 1963- *210*
Earlier sketches in SATA *97, 143*
See also CLR *68*
Nixon, Hershell Howard 1923- *42*
Nixon, Joan Lowery 1927-2003 .... *115*
Obituary *146*
Earlier sketches in SATA *8, 44, 78*
See also CLR *24*
See also SAAS *9*
Nixon, K.
See Nixon, Kathleen Irene (Blundell)
Nixon, Kathleen Irene (Blundell)
1894-1988(?) *14*
Obituary *59*
Nobati, Eugenia 1968- *201*
Nobisso, Josephine 1953- *121*
Earlier sketch in SATA *78*
Noble, Iris (Davis) 1922-1986 .... *5*
Obituary *49*
Noble, Marty 1947- *125*
Earlier sketch in SATA *97*
Noble, Trinka Hakes 1944- *197*
Brief entry *37*
Earlier sketch in SATA *123*

Nobleman, Marc Tyler 1972- 203
Noda, Takayo 1961- 168
Nodelman, Perry 1942- 101
Nodset, Joan L.
See Lexau, Joan M.
Noel Hume, Ivor 1927- 65
Noestlinger, Christine
See Nostlinger, Christine
Noguere, Suzanne 1947- 34
Nolan, Dennis 1945- 166
Brief entry 34
Earlier sketches in SATA *42, 92*
Nolan, Han 1956- 241
Earlier sketches in SATA *109, 157*
Nolan, Janet 1956- 191
Earlier sketch in SATA *145*
Nolan, Jeannette Covert 1897-1974 2
Obituary 27
Nolan, Lucy 215
Nolan, Paul T(homas) 1919- 48
Nolan, William F. 1928- 88
Brief entry 28
Nolan, William Francis
See Nolan, William F.
Nolen, Jerdine 1953- 157
Earlier sketch in SATA *105*
Noll, Amanda 219
Noll, Sally 1946- 82
Nolte, Jack
See Carter, Scott William
Noonan, Brandon 1979- 184
Noonan, Diana 1960- 146
Noonan, Julia 1946- 148
Earlier sketches in SATA *4, 95*
Norac, Carl 1960- 166
Norcliffe, James 1946- 234
Norcross, John
See Conroy, John Wesley
Nordan, Robert W(arren) 1934-2004 133
Nordhoff, Charles Bernard 1887-1947 23
Nordlicht, Lillian 29
Nordstrom, Ursula 1910-1988 3
Obituary 57
Nordtvedt, Matilda 1926- 67
Norling, Beth 1969- 149
Norman, Charles 1904-1996 38
Obituary 92
Norman, Geoffrey 223
Norman, Howard
See Norman, Howard A.
Norman, Howard A. 1949- 81
Norman, James
See Schmidt, James Norman
Norman, Jay
See Arthur, Robert, (Jr.)
Norman, Kim 241
Norman, Lilith 1927- 120
Earlier sketch in SATA *86*
Norman, Mary 1931- 36
Norman, Steve
See Pashko, Stanley
Norment, Lisa 1966- 91
Norris, Gunilla Brodde 1939- 20
North, Andrew
See Norton, Andre
North, Anthony
See Koontz, Dean
North, Captain George
See Stevenson, Robert Louis
North, Captain George
See Stevenson, Robert Louis
North, Howard
See Trevor, Elleston
North, Joan 1920- 16
North, Milou
See Erdrich, Louise
North, Robert
See Withers, Carl A.
North, Sara
See Bonham, Barbara Thomas and Hager, Jean
North, Sherry 201
North, Sterling 1906-1974 45
Obituary 26
Earlier sketch in SATA *1*
Northcott, (William) Cecil 1902-1987
Obituary 55
Northeast, Brenda V(ictoria) 1948- 106
Northmore, Elizabeth Florence 1906-1974 . 122
Norton, Alice Mary
See Norton, Andre
Norton, Andre 1912-2005 91
Earlier sketches in SATA *1, 43*
See also CLR *50*
Norton, Browning
See Norton, Frank R. B(rowning)
Norton, Frank R. B(rowning) 1909-1989 10
Norton, Mary 1903-1992 60
Obituary 72
Earlier sketch in SATA *18*
See also CLR *140*
Nosredna, Trebor
See Anderson, Bob
Nostlinger, Christine 1936- 162
Brief entry 37
Earlier sketch in SATA *64*
See also CLR *12*
Noteboom, Erin
See Bow, Erin
Nourse, Alan E(dward) 1928-1992 48
See also CLR *33*
Novak, Matt 1962- 204
Brief entry 52
Earlier sketches in SATA *60, 104, 165*
Novelli, Luca 1947- 61
Novesky, Amy 241
Novgorodoff, Danica 1982(?)- 215
Nowell, Elizabeth Cameron 12
Noyes, Deborah 1965- 194
Earlier sketch in SATA *145*
Nugent, Cynthia 1954- 205
Nugent, Nicholas 1949- 73
Numberman, Neil 1981(?)- 220
Numeroff, Laura 1953- 206
Earlier sketches in SATA *28, 90, 142*
See also CLR *85*
Numeroff Joffe, Laura
See Numeroff, Laura
Nunes, Lygia Bojunga 1932- 154
Earlier sketch in SATA *75*
Nunn, Laura (Donna) Silverstein 1968- 124
Nurenberg, Thelma
See Greenhaus, Thelma Nurenberg
Nurnberg, Maxwell 1897-1984 27
Obituary 41
Nussbaumer, Paul (Edmund) 1934- 16
Nutt, Ken 1951- 163
Earlier sketch in SATA *97*
Nuttall-Smith, Margaret Emily Noel 1919- .. 26
Nuygen, Mathieu 1967- 80
Nuzum, K. A. 195
Nuzum, Kathy A.
See Nuzum, K. A.
Nwapa, Flora (Nwanzuruaha) 1931-1993
See CLR *162*
Nyberg, (Everett Wayne) Morgan 1944- 87
Nyce, (Nellie) Helene von Strecker 1885-1969 19
Nyce, Vera 1862-1925 19
Nye, Naomi Shihab 1952- 198
Earlier sketches in SATA *86, 147*
See also CLR *59*
Nye, Robert 1939- 6
Nyeu, Tao 206
Nyikos, Stacy A. 1969- 164
Nystrom, Carolyn 1940- 130
Earlier sketch in SATA *67*

O

O. Henry
See Henry, O.
Oakes, Elizabeth H. 1964- 132
Oakes, Vanya 1909-1983 6
Obituary 37
Oakley, Don(ald G.) 1927- 8
Oakley, Graham 1929- 84
Earlier sketch in SATA *30*
See also CLR *7*
Oakley, Helen (McKelvey) 1906- 10
Oaks, J. Adams 220
Oana, Katherine 1929- 53
Brief entry 37
Oates, Eddie H. 1943- 88
Oates, Joyce Carol 1938- 159
Oates, Stephen B(aery) 1936- 59
Obed, Ellen Bryan 1944- 74
Oberdieck, Bernhard 1949- 230
Oberle, Joseph 1958- 69
Oberman, Sheldon 1949-2004 85
Autobiography Feature 114
Obituary 153
See also CLR *54*
See also SAAS *26*
Obligado, Lilian (Isabel) 1931- 61
Brief entry 45
Obrant, Susan 1946- 11
O'Brian, E.G.
See Clarke, Arthur C.
O'Brien, Anne Sibley 1952- 213
Brief entry 48
Earlier sketches in SATA *53, 80*
O'Brien, Caragh M. 232
O'Brien, E.G.
See Clarke, Arthur C.
O'Brien, Esse Forrester 1895(?)-1975
Obituary 30
O'Brien, Johnny 222
O'Brien, Patrick 1960- 193
O'Brien, Robert C. 1918-1973 23
See also CLR *2*
O'Brien, Thomas C. 1938-2010 29
O'Brien, Thomas Clement
See O'Brien, Thomas C.
O'Callaghan, Julie 1954- 113
O'Callahan, Jay 1938- 88
O'Carroll, Ryan
See Markun, Patricia Maloney
Ochiltree, Dianne 1953- 117
Ockham, Joan Price
See Price, Joan
Ockler, Sarah 239
O'Connell, Margaret F(orster) 1935-1977 30
Obituary 30
O'Connell, Peg
See Ahern, Margaret McCrohan
O'Connell, Rebecca 1968- 212
Earlier sketch in SATA *130*
O'Connor, Barbara 1950- 193
Earlier sketch in SATA *154*
O'Connor, Francine M(arie) 1930- 90
O'Connor, Genevieve A. 1914- 75
O'Connor, George 228
Earlier sketch in SATA *183*
O'Connor, Ian 1965- 188
O'Connor, Jane 1947- 186
Brief entry 47
Earlier sketches in SATA *59, 103, 150*
O'Connor, Karen 1938- 89
Earlier sketch in SATA *34*
O'Connor, Patrick
See Wibberley, Leonard
O'Connor, Richard 1915-1975
Obituary 21
O'Conor, Jane 1958- 78
Odaga, Asenath (Bole) 1937- 130
Earlier sketch in SATA *67*
See also SAAS *19*

O Danachair, Caoimhin
See Danaher, Kevin
Odanaka, Barbara *159*
O'Daniel, Janet 1921- *24*
O'Day, Cathy
See Crane, Barbara (Joyce)
O'Dell, Scott 1898-1989 .... *134*
Earlier sketches in SATA *12, 60*
See also CLR *126*
Odenwald, Robert P(aul) 1899-1965 .... *11*
Odgers, Sally
See Odgers, Sally Farrell
Odgers, Sally Farrell 1957- *139*
Earlier sketch in SATA *72*
Odone, Jamison 1980- *209*
O'Donnell, Dick
See Lupoff, Richard A.
and Thompson, Don(ald Arthur)
O'Donnell, Liam 1970- *209*
Odriozola, Elena *186*
Oechsli, Kelly 1918-1999 .... *5*
Oertel, Andreas 1966- *230*
Oesterle, Virginia Rorby
See Rorby, Ginny
Ofek, Uriel 1926- *36*
See also CLR *28*
Ofer, Avi 1975- *207*
Offenbacher, Ami 1958- *91*
Offermann, Andrea *231*
Offill, Jenny 1968- *211*
Offit, Sidney 1928- *10*
Ofosu-Appiah, L(awrence) H(enry) 1920- ... *13*
Ogan, George F. 1912-1983 .... *13*
Ogan, M. G.
See Ogan, George F.
and Ogan, Margaret E. (Nettles)
Ogan, Margaret E. (Nettles) 1923-1979 .... *13*
Ogburn, Charlton (Jr.) 1911-1998 .... *3*
Obituary *109*
Ogburn, Jacqueline K. *162*
Ogilvie, Elisabeth May 1917-2006 .... *40*
Brief entry *29*
Obituary *176*
Ogilvy, Gavin
See Barrie, J. M.
Ogilvy, Ian 1943- *177*
Ogilvy, Ian Raymond
See Ogilvy, Ian
Ogle, Lucille Edith 1904-1988
Obituary *59*
Ogletree, Charles J. 1952- *175*
O'Green, Jennifer
See Roberson, Jennifer
O'Green, Jennifer Roberson
See Roberson, Jennifer
O'Hagan, Caroline 1946- *38*
O'Hanlon, Jacklyn
See Meek, Jacklyn O'Hanlon
O'Hara, Elizabeth
See Ni Dhuibhne, Eilis
O'Hara, Kenneth
See Morris, (Margaret) Jean
O'Hara, Mary
See Alsop, Mary O'Hara
O'Hara (Alsop), Mary
See Alsop, Mary O'Hara
O'Hare, Jeff(rey A.) 1958- *105*
O'hearn, Kate *225*
Ohi, Ruth 1964- *95*
Ohiyesa
See Eastman, Charles A(lexander)
Ohlsson, Ib 1935- *7*
Ohmi, Ayano 1959- *115*
Ohtomo, Yasuo 1946- *37*
o huigin, sean 1942- *138*
See also CLR *75*
Oiseau
See Moseley, James W(illett)
Oke, Janette 1935- *97*
O'Keefe, Susan Heyboer *176*
Earlier sketch in SATA *133*
O'Keeffe, Frank 1938- *99*
O'Kelley, Mattie Lou 1908-1997 .... *97*
Earlier sketch in SATA *36*
Okimoto, Jean Davies 1942- *103*
Earlier sketch in SATA *34*
Okomfo, Amasewa
See Cousins, Linda
olafsdottir, Gudrun Elin
See Gunnella
Olaleye, Isaac O. 1941- *96*
See also SAAS *23*
Olander, Johan 1967- *231*
Olcott, Frances Jenkins 1872(?)-1963 .... *19*
Old, Wendie C(orbin) 1943- *154*
Old Boy
See Hughes, Thomas
Oldenburg, E(gbert) William 1936-1974 ...... *35*
Older, Effin 1942- *114*
Older, Jules 1940- *156*
Earlier sketch in SATA *114*
Oldfield, Jenny 1949- *140*
Oldfield, Margaret J(ean) 1932- *56*
Oldfield, Pamela 1931- *86*
Oldham, June *70*
Oldham, Mary 1944- *65*
Oldland, Nicholas 1972- *223*
Olds, Elizabeth 1896-1991 .... *3*
Obituary *66*
Olds, Helen Diehl 1895-1981 .... *9*
Obituary *25*
Oldstyle, Jonathan
See Irving, Washington
O'Leary, Brian (Todd) 1940- *6*
O'Leary, Chris *208*
O'Leary, Patsy B. 1937- *97*
O'Leary, Patsy Baker
See O'Leary, Patsy B.
Oleynikov, Igor 1953- *202*
Oliphant, B.J.
See Tepper, Sheri S.
Oliver, Burton
See Burt, Olive Woolley
Oliver, Chad
See Oliver, Symmes C.
Oliver, Jana
See Oliver, Jana G.
Oliver, Jana G. *240*
Oliver, John Edward 1933- *21*
Oliver, Lauren 1982- *228*
Oliver, Lin *202*
Oliver, Marilyn Tower 1935- *89*
Oliver, Mark 1960- *214*
Oliver, Narelle 1960- *197*
Earlier sketch in SATA *152*
Oliver, Shirley (Louise Dawkins) 1958- *74*
Oliver, Symmes C. 1928-1993 .... *101*
Oliviero, Jamie 1950- *84*
Olmsted, Lorena Ann 1890-1989 .... *13*
Olney, Ross R. 1929- *13*
Olschewski, Alfred (Erich) 1920- *7*
Olsen, Barbara *148*
Olsen, Carol 1945- *89*
Olsen, Ib Spang 1921- *81*
Earlier sketch in SATA *6*
Olsen, Violet (Mae) 1922-1991 .... *58*
Olson, Arielle North 1932- *67*
Olson, David J. 1974- *198*
Olson, Gene 1922- *32*
Olson, Gretchen *187*
Olson, Helen Kronberg *48*
Olson, Julie 1976- *233*
Olson, Kay Melchisedech 1948- *175*
Olson, Marianne
See Mitchell, Marianne
Olson-Brown, Ellen 1967- *183*
Olten, Manuela 1970- *197*
Olugebefola, Ademole 1941- *15*
Oluonye, Mary N(kechi) 1955- *111*
Om
See Gorey, Edward (St. John)
O'Malley, Donough *208*
O'Malley, Kevin 1961- *230*
Earlier sketches in SATA *157, 191*
Oman, Carola (Mary Anima) 1897-1978 ..... *35*
O'Mara, Carmel 1965- *166*
O'Mara-Horwitz, Carmel
See O'Mara, Carmel
O'Meara, Walter (Andrew) 1897-1989 .... *65*
Ommanney, F(rancis) D(ownes) 1903-1980 . *23*
Omololu, Cynthia Jaynes *222*
O Mude
See Gorey, Edward (St. John)
Oneal, Elizabeth 1934- *82*
Earlier sketch in SATA *30*
See also CLR *169*
O'Neal, Katherine Pebley 1957- *204*
O'Neal, Reagan
See Jordan, Robert
O'Neal, Regan
See Jordan, Robert
Oneal, Zibby
See Oneal, Elizabeth
O'neill, Alexis 1949- *220*
O'Neill, Amanda 1951- *111*
O'Neill, Catharine *203*
O'Neill, Gerard K(itchen) 1927-1992 .... *65*
O'Neill, Judith (Beatrice) 1930- *34*
O'Neill, Mary L(e Duc) 1908(?)-1990 .... *2*
Obituary *64*
O'Neill, Reagan
See Jordan, Robert
Onslow, Annette Rosemary MacArthur
See MacArthur-Onslow, Annette Rosemary
Onslow, John 1906-1985
Obituary *47*
Onyefulu, Ifeoma 1959- *157*
Earlier sketches in SATA *81, 115*
Opie, Iona (Margaret Balfour) 1923- *118*
Earlier sketches in SATA *3, 63*
See also SAAS *6*
Opie, Peter (Mason) 1918-1982 .... *118*
Obituary *28*
Earlier sketches in SATA *3, 63*
Oppel, Kenneth 1967- *199*
Earlier sketches in SATA *99, 153*
Oppel, Kenneth Kerry
See Oppel, Kenneth
Oppenheim, Joanne 1934- *174*
Earlier sketches in SATA *5, 82, 136*
Oppenheim, Shulamith Levey 1928- *177*
Oppenheimer, Joan L(etson) 1925- *28*
Oppong, Joseph Ransford 1953- *160*
Optic, Oliver
See Adams, William Taylor
and Stratemeyer, Edward L.
Oram, Hiawyn 1946- *101*
Earlier sketch in SATA *56*
Orbach, Ruth Gary 1941- *21*
Orback, Craig *197*
Orczy, Emma
See Orczy, Baroness Emmuska
Orczy, Emma Magdalena Rosalia Maria Josefa
See Orczy, Baroness Emmuska
Orczy, Emmuska
See Orczy, Baroness Emmuska
Orczy, Baroness Emmuska 1865-1947 .... *40*
Orde, A.J.
See Tepper, Sheri S.
O'Reilly, Jackson
See Jordan, Robert
Orenstein, Denise Gosliner 1950- *157*
Orgad, Dorit 1936- *199*
Orgel, Doris 1929- *148*
Earlier sketches in SATA *7, 85*
See also CLR *48*
See also SAAS *19*
Orgill, Roxane *198*
Oriolo, Joe
See Oriolo, Joseph D.
Oriolo, Joseph D. 1913-1985
Obituary *46*

Orlandelli, Alessandro
See Horley, Alex
Orlean, Susan 1955- *209*
Orleans, Ilo 1897-1962 *10*
Orlev, Uri 1931- *135*
Earlier sketch in SATA *58*
See also CLR *30*
See also SAAS *19*
Orloff, Karen Kaufman *236*
Ormai, Stella *57*
Brief entry *48*
Ormerod, Jan 1946- *210*
Brief entry *44*
Earlier sketches in SATA *55, 70, 132*
See also CLR *20*
Ormerod, Janette Louise
See Ormerod, Jan
Ormes, Jackie
See Ormes, Zelda J.
Ormes, Zelda J. 1914-1986
Obituary *47*
Ormondroyd, Edward 1925- *14*
Ormsby, Virginia H(aire) 1906-1990 *11*
Oron, Judie *239*
Orona-Ramirez, Kristy 1964- *189*
Orozco, Jose-Luis 1948- *179*
Orr, Katherine S(helley) 1950- *72*
Orr, Wendy 1953- *206*
Earlier sketches in SATA *90, 141*
Orris
See Ingelow, Jean
Orth, Richard
See Gardner, Richard (M.)
Ortiz Cofer, Judith
See Cofer, Judith Ortiz
Orwell, George 1903-1950 *29*
See also CLR *171*
Orwin, Joanna 1944- *141*
Os, Eric van
See van Os, Erik
Osborn, Elinor 1939- *145*
Osborn, Jacob 1981(?)- *215*
Osborn, Kathy 1955(?)- *199*
Osborn, Lois D(orothy) 1915- *61*
Osborne, Charles 1927- *59*
Osborne, Chester G(orham) 1915-1987 *11*
Osborne, David
See Silverberg, Robert
Osborne, George
See Silverberg, Robert
Osborne, Leone Neal 1914-1996 *2*
Osborne, Linda Barrett 1949- *215*
Osborne, Mary Pope 1949- *144*
Earlier sketches in SATA *41, 55, 98*
See also CLR *88*
Osceola
See Blixen, Karen
Osgood, William E(dward) 1926- *37*
O'Shaughnessy, Darren
See Shan, Darren
O'Shaughnessy, Ellen Cassels 1937- *78*
O'shaughnessy, Tam 1951- *221*
O'Shea, Catherine Patricia Shiels
See O'Shea, Pat
O'Shea, Pat 1931-2007 *87*
See also CLR *18*
Osmond, Edward 1900- *10*
Ossoli, Sarah Margaret
See Fuller, Margaret
Ostendorf, (Arthur) Lloyd, (Jr.) 1921-2000 .. *65*
Obituary *125*
Osterweil, Adam 1972- *217*
Ostow, Micol 1976- *223*
Earlier sketch in SATA *170*
Otfinoski, Steven 1949- *116*
Earlier sketch in SATA *56*
Otis, James
See Kaler, James Otis
O'Toole, Thomas 1941- *71*
O'Trigger, Sir Lucius
See Horne, Richard Henry Hengist
Otten, Charlotte
See Otten, Charlotte F.
Otten, Charlotte F. 1926- *98*
Otten, Charlotte Fennema
See Otten, Charlotte F.
Ottley, Matt 1962- *171*
Earlier sketch in SATA *102*
Ottley, Reginald Leslie 1909-1985 *26*
See also CLR *16*
Otto, Margaret Glover 1909-1976
Obituary *30*
Otto, Svend
See Soerensen, Svend Otto
Ouellet, Debbie 1954- *219*
Oughton, Jerrie (Preston) 1937- *131*
Earlier sketch in SATA *76*
Oughton, (William) Taylor 1925- *104*
Ouida
See De La Ramee, Marie Louise
Ousley, Odille 1896-1976 *10*
Outcalt, Todd 1960- *123*
Overmyer, James E. 1946- *88*
Overton, Jenny (Margaret Mary) 1942- *52*
Brief entry *36*
Owen, Ann
See Qualey, Marsha
Owen, Annie 1949- *75*
Owen, Caroline Dale
See Snedeker, Caroline Dale (Parke)
Owen, Clifford
See Hamilton, Charles (Harold St. John)
Owen, Dilys
See Gater, Dilys
Owen, (Benjamin) Evan 1918-1984 *38*
Owen, (John) Gareth 1936-2002 *162*
Earlier sketch in SATA *83*
See also CLR *31*
See also SAAS *14*
Owen, James A. *185*
Owens, Bryant 1968- *116*
Owens, Dana Elaine
See Queen Latifah
Owens, Gail 1939- *54*
Owens, Mary Beth *191*
Owens, Thomas S(heldon) 1960- *86*
Owens, Tom
See Owens, Thomas S(heldon)
Oxenbury, Helen 1938- *149*
Earlier sketches in SATA *3, 68*
See also CLR *70*
Oxendine, Bess Holland 1933- *90*
Oz, Frank (Richard) 1944- *60*
Ozer, Jerome S. 1927- *59*

P

Paananen, Eloise (Katherine) 1923-1993 *9*
Pace, Lorenzo 1943- *131*
Pace, Mildred Mastin 1907- *46*
Brief entry *29*
Pachter, Hedwig (?)-1988 *63*
Pack, Janet 1952- *77*
Pack, Robert 1929- *118*
Packard, Edward 1931- *148*
Earlier sketches in SATA *47, 90*
Packer, Kenneth L. 1946- *116*
Packer, Vin
See Meaker, Marijane
Pad, Peter
See Stratemeyer, Edward L.
Page, Eileen
See Heal, Edith
Page, Eleanor
See Coerr, Eleanor (Beatrice)
Page, Gail 1950- *205*
Page, Jake 1936- *81*
Page, James Keena, Jr.
See Page, Jake
Page, Lou Williams 1912-1997 *38*
Page, Mary
See Heal, Edith
Page, Robin 1943- *154*
Pagliarulo, Antonio 1977(?)- *212*
Pagnucci, Susan 1944- *90*
Pahlen, Kurt 1907-2003
Obituary *147*
Pahz, Cheryl
See Pahz, Cheryl Suzanne
Pahz, Cheryl Suzanne 1949- *11*
Pahz, James Alon 1943- *11*
Paice, Margaret 1920- *10*
Paige, Harry W(orthington) 1922- *41*
Brief entry *35*
Paige, Richard
See Koontz, Dean
Paige, Robin
See Albert, Susan Wittig
Paillot, Jim *230*
Paine, Penelope Colville 1946- *87*
Paine, Roberta M. 1925- *13*
Paisley, Tom 1932- *11*
See also CLR *3*
Pal, Erika *239*
Palatini, Margie *207*
Earlier sketches in SATA *134, 174*
Palazzo, Anthony D.
See Palazzo, Tony
Palazzo, Tony 1905-1970 *3*
Palder, Edward L. 1922- *5*
Palecek, Josef 1932- *56*
Palecek, Libuse 1937- *89*
Palen, Debbie *195*
Palin, Michael 1943- *67*
Palin, Michael Edward
See Palin, Michael
Palladini, David (Mario) 1946- *40*
Brief entry *32*
Pallas, Norvin 1918-1983 *23*
Pallister, John C(lare) 1891-1980
Obituary *26*
Pallotta, Gerard Larry
See Pallotta, Jerry
Pallotta, Jerry 1953- *186*
Pallotta-Chiarolli, Maria 1960- *117*
Palmer, Bernard (Alvin) 1914-1998 *26*
Palmer, C. Everard 1930- *14*
Palmer, (Ruth) Candida 1926- *11*
Palmer, Cyril Everard
See Palmer, C. Everard
Palmer, Don
See Benson, Mildred
Palmer, Gary 1968- *231*
Palmer, Hap 1942- *68*
Palmer, Heidi 1948- *15*
Palmer, Helen Marion
See Geisel, Helen
Palmer, Jessica 1953- *120*
Palmer, Judd 1972- *153*
Palmer, Juliette 1930- *15*
Palmer, Kate Salley 1946- *97*
Palmer, Maria
See Strachan, Ian
Palmer, Maria
See Brennan, Herbie
Palmer, Robin 1909-2000 *43*
Palmer, Robin 1969- *232*
Palmero Caceres, Ana *198*
Palmisciano, Diane *202*
Paltrowitz, Donna 1950- *61*
Brief entry *50*
Paltrowitz, Donna Milman
See Paltrowitz, Donna
Paltrowitz, Stuart 1946- *61*
Brief entry *50*
Pamela, Todd 1950- *124*
Pamintuan, Macky *214*
Earlier sketch in SATA *178*
Panagopoulos, Janie Lynn *149*
Panati, Charles 1943- *65*
Panchyk, Richard 1970- *138*

Panetta, George 1915-1969 .... *15*
Panetta, Joseph N. 1953- *96*
Pang, YaWen Ariel *206*
Panik, Sharon 1952- *82*
Panowski, Eileen Thompson 1920- *49*
Pansy
See Alden, Isabella (Macdonald)
Pantell, Dora (Fuchs) *39*
Panter, Carol 1936- *9*
Paolini, Christopher 1983- *157*
See also CLR *102*
Papademetriou, Lisa *175*
Paparone, Pam *185*
Paparone, Pamela
See Paparone, Pam
Papas, Bill
See Papas, William
Papas, William 1927-2000 .... *50*
Papashvily, George 1898-1978 .... *17*
Papashvily, Helen (Waite) 1906-1996 .... *17*
Pape, D. L.
See Pape, Donna (Lugg)
Pape, Donna (Lugg) 1930- *82*
Earlier sketch in SATA *2*
Paperny, Myra (Green) 1932- *51*
Brief entry *33*
Papineau, Lucie 1962- *224*
Papp, Robert 1967- *205*
Paradis, Adrian A(lexis) 1912- *67*
Earlier sketch in SATA *1*
See also SAAS *8*
Paradis, Marjorie Bartholomew 1886(?)-1970 .... *17*
Paradiz, Valerie 1963- *176*
Paratore, Coleen
See Paratore, Coleen Murtagh
Paratore, Coleen Murtagh 1958- *200*
Pardo DeLange, Alex *211*
Parenteau, Shirley 1935- *199*
Brief entry *40*
Earlier sketch in SATA *47*
Parish, Margaret 1927-1988 .... *73*
Obituary *59*
Earlier sketch in SATA *17*
See also CLR *22*
Parish, Margaret Holt
See Holt, Margaret
Parish, Peggy
See Parish, Margaret
Park, Barbara 1947- *123*
Brief entry *35*
Earlier sketches in SATA *40, 78*
See also CLR *34*
Park, Bill
See Park, W(illiam) B(ryan)
Park, Frances 1955- *171*
Park, Ginger *173*
Park, Janie Jaehyun *150*
Park, Jordan
See Kornbluth, C(yril) M.
and Pohl, Frederik
Park, Linda Sue 1960- *200*
Earlier sketches in SATA *127, 173*
See also CLR *84*
Park, Nick 1958- *113*
Park, Rosina Ruth Lucia
See Park, Ruth
Park, Ruth 1917(?)-2010 .... *93*
Earlier sketch in SATA *25*
See also CLR *51*
Park, W(illiam) B(ryan) 1936- *22*
Parke, Marilyn 1928- *82*
Parker, Barbara Keevil 1938- *157*
Parker, Daniel
See Ehrenhaft, Daniel
Parker, Elinor Milnor 1906- *3*
Parker, Jake 1977- *227*
Parker, Julie F. 1961- *92*
Parker, Kim 1963- *174*
Parker, Kristy 1957- *59*
Parker, Lois M(ay) 1912-1996 .... *30*
Parker, Margot M. 1937- *52*
Parker, Marjorie Blain 1960- *205*
Earlier sketch in SATA *145*
Parker, Mary Jessie 1948- *71*
Parker, Nancy Winslow 1930- *132*
Earlier sketches in SATA *10, 69*
See also SAAS *20*
Parker, Richard 1915-1990 .... *14*
Parker, Robert
See Boyd, Waldo T.
and Parker, Robert Andrew
Parker, Robert Andrew 1927- *200*
Parker, Steve 1954- *213*
Parker, Tom S. *215*
Parker, Toni Trent 1947-2005 .... *142*
Obituary *169*
Parker-Rees, Guy *193*
Parker-Rock, Michelle *214*
Parkes, Lucas
See Harris, John (Wyndham Parkes Lucas) Beynon
Parkhill, John
See Cox, William R(obert)
Parkins, David 1955- *218*
Earlier sketch in SATA *176*
Parkinson, Curtis *219*
Parkinson, Ethelyn M(inerva) 1906-1999 .... *11*
Parkinson, Kathryn N. 1954- *71*
Parkinson, Kathy
See Parkinson, Kathryn N.
Parkinson, Siobhan
See Parkinson, Siobhan
Parkinson, Siobhan 1954- *178*
Parks, Deborah A. 1948- *133*
Earlier sketch in SATA *91*
Parks, Edd Winfield 1906-1968 .... *10*
Parks, Gordon 1912-2006 .... *108*
Obituary *175*
Earlier sketch in SATA *8*
Parks, Gordon Roger Alexander
See Parks, Gordon
Parks, Peggy J. 1951- *143*
Parks, PJ
See Parks, Peggy J.
Parks, Rosa 1913-2005 .... *83*
Obituary *169*
Parks, Rosa Louise Lee
See Parks, Rosa
Parks, Van Dyke 1943- *62*
Parlato, Stephen 1954- *222*
Parley, Peter
See Goodrich, Samuel Griswold
Parlin, John
See Graves, Charles Parlin
Parme, Fabrice 1966- *191*
Parnall, Peter 1936- *69*
Earlier sketch in SATA *16*
See also SAAS *11*
Paros, Jennifer *210*
Parotti, Phillip (Elliott) 1941- *109*
Parr, Ann 1943- *144*
Parr, Danny
See Parr, Ann
Parr, Letitia (Evelyn) 1906-1985(?) *37*
Parr, Lucy 1924- *10*
Parr, Todd *179*
Earlier sketch in SATA *134*
Parra, John 1972- *225*
Parrish, Anne 1888-1957 .... *27*
Parrish, Mary
See Cousins, Margaret
Parrish, Maxfield
See Parrish, (Frederick) Maxfield
Parrish, (Frederick) Maxfield 1870-1966 .... *14*
Parry, Marian 1924- *13*
Parry, Rosanne *212*
Parson Lot
See Kingsley, Charles
Parsons, Alexandra 1947- *92*
Parsons, Ellen
See Dragonwagon, Crescent
Parsons, Garry *197*
Parsons, Martin 1951- *116*
Parsons, Martin Leslie
See Parsons, Martin
Parsons, Tom
See MacPherson, Thomas George
Parsons-Yazzi, Evangeline *172*
Partch, Virgil Franklin II 1916-1984 .... *39*
Obituary *39*
Parton, Dolly 1946- *94*
Parton, Dolly Rebecca
See Parton, Dolly
Partridge, Benjamin W., Jr. 1915-2005 .... *28*
Obituary *163*
Partridge, Benjamin Waring, Jr.
See Partridge, Benjamin W., Jr.
Partridge, Cora Cheney
See Cheney, Cora
Partridge, Elizabeth *216*
Earlier sketch in SATA *134*
Partridge, Jenny (Lilian) 1947- *52*
Brief entry *37*
Pasachoff, Naomi 1947- *147*
Pascal, David 1918- *14*
Pascal, Francine 1938- *143*
Brief entry *37*
Earlier sketches in SATA *51, 80*
See also CLR *25*
Paschal, Nancy
See Trotter, Grace V(iolet)
Paschkis, Julie 1957- *220*
Earlier sketch in SATA *177*
Pascudniak, Pascal
See Lupoff, Richard A.
Pashko, Stanley 1913-1982 .... *29*
Pasqualotto, Chiara 1976- *228*
Passailaigue, Thomas E.
See Paisley, Tom
Pastel, Elyse *201*
Pateman, Robert 1954- *84*
Patent, Dorothy Hinshaw 1940- *162*
Autobiography Feature *162*
Earlier sketches in SATA *22, 69, 120*
See also CLR *19*
See also SAAS *13*
Paterson, A(ndrew) B(arton) 1864-1941 .... *97*
Paterson, Banjo
See Paterson, A(ndrew) B(arton)
Paterson, Diane 1946- *177*
Brief entry *33*
Earlier sketch in SATA *59*
Paterson, John (Barstow) 1932- *114*
Paterson, Katherine 1932- *204*
Earlier sketches in SATA *13, 53, 92, 133*
See also CLR *127*
Paterson, Katherine Womeldorf
See Paterson, Katherine
Patience, John 1949- *90*
Patneaude, David 1944- *233*
Earlier sketches in SATA *85, 159*
Paton, Alan 1903-1988 .... *11*
Obituary *56*
Paton, Alan Stewart
See Paton, Alan
Paton, Jane (Elizabeth) 1934- *35*
Paton, Priscilla 1952- *98*
Paton Walsh, Gillian
See Paton Walsh, Jill
Paton Walsh, Jill 1937- *190*
Autobiography Feature *190*
Earlier sketches in SATA *4, 72, 109*
See also CLR *128*
See also SAAS *3*
Patricelli, Leslie *236*
Earlier sketch in SATA *207*
Patrick, Susan
See Robins, Patricia
Patron, Susan 1948- *182*
Earlier sketch in SATA *76*
Patsauq, Markoosie 1942-
See CLR *23*

Patschke, Steve 1955- *125*
Patt, Beverly *231*
Patten, Brian 1946- *152*
Earlier sketch in SATA *29*
Patterson, Charles 1935- *59*
Patterson, Geoffrey 1943- *54*
Brief entry *44*
Patterson, James 1947- *234*
Earlier sketches in SATA *164, 197*
Patterson, James B.
See Patterson, James
Patterson, Lillie G. -1999 .... *88*
Earlier sketch in SATA *14*
Patterson, Nancy Ruth 1944- *148*
Earlier sketch in SATA *72*
Patterson, Valerie O. *223*
Pattison, Darcy (S.) 1954- *126*
Earlier sketch in SATA *72*
Pattou, Edith *164*
Patz (Blaustein), Nancy *154*
Paul, Aileen 1917- *12*
Paul, Alison *196*
Paul, Ann Whitford 1941- *209*
Earlier sketches in SATA *76, 110, 168*
Paul, Chris 1985- *224*
Paul, David (Tyler) 1934-1988
Obituary *56*
Paul, Dominique 1973- *184*
Paul, Elizabeth
See Crow, Donna Fletcher
Paul, Hamish Vigne Christie 1951- *151*
See also CLR *87*
Paul, James 1936- *23*
Paul, Korky
See Paul, Hamish Vigne Christie
Paul, Robert
See Roberts, John G(aither)
Paul, Tessa 1944- *103*
Pauley, Kimberly 1973- *208*
Pauli, Hertha (Ernestine) 1909-1973 .... *3*
Obituary *26*
Paull, Grace A. 1898- *24*
Paulsen, Gary 1939- *231*
Earlier sketches in SATA *22, 50, 54, 79, 111, 158, 189*
See also CLR *82*
Paulson, Jack
See Jackson, C(aary) Paul
Pauquet, Gina Ruck
See Ruck-Pauquet, Gina
Pausacker, Jenny 1948- *72*
See also SAAS *23*
Pausewang, Gudrun 1928- *165*
Earlier sketch in SATA *104*
Pavel, Frances 1907- *10*
Paver, Michelle *215*
Earlier sketch in SATA *170*
Paxton
See Barr, Nevada
Paxton, Thomas R. 1937- *70*
Paxton, Tom
See Paxton, Thomas R.
Paye, Won-Ldy *185*
Payne, Alan
See Jakes, John
Payne, Bernal C., Jr. 1941- *60*
Payne, C. Douglas
See Payne, C.D.
Payne, C.D. 1949- *133*
Payne, C.F. 1956- *179*
Payne, Chris Fox
See Payne, C.F.
Payne, Donald Gordon 1924- *37*
Payne, Emmy
See West, Emily Govan
Payne, Nina *135*
Payne, Rachel Ann
See Jakes, John
Payson, Dale 1943- *9*
Payzant, Charles *18*
Paz, A.
See Pahz, James Alon
Paz, Natalia Toledo
See Toledo, Natalia
Paz, Zan
See Pahz, Cheryl Suzanne
Peace, Mary
See Finley, Mary Peace
Peacock, Louise *210*
Peacock, Phyllis Hornung 1977- *230*
Peacock, Shane 1957- *192*
Peake, Mervyn 1911-1968 .... *23*
Peale, Norman Vincent 1898-1993 .... *20*
Obituary *78*
Pearce, Ann Philippa
See Pearce, Philippa
Pearce, Carl *229*
Pearce, Emily Smith 1975- *199*
Pearce, Jackson 1984- *235*
Pearce, Jacqueline 1962- *146*
Pearce, Margaret *104*
Pearce, Philippa 1920-2006 .... *129*
Obituary *179*
Earlier sketches in SATA *1, 67*
See also CLR *9*
Peare, Catherine Owens 1911- *9*
Pearle, Ida *207*
Pearsall, Shelley 1966- *190*
Pearson, Gayle 1947- *119*
Earlier sketch in SATA *53*
Pearson, Jean Mary
See Gardam, Jane
Pearson, Kit 1947- *77*
Autobiography Feature *117*
See also CLR *26*
Pearson, Mary E. 1955- *211*
Earlier sketch in SATA *134*
Pearson, Michael Parker
See Pearson, Mike Parker
Pearson, Mike Parker 1957- *228*
Pearson, Ridley 1953- *182*
Pearson, Susan 1946- *166*
Brief entry *27*
Earlier sketches in SATA *39, 91*
Pearson, Tracey Campbell 1956- *219*
Earlier sketches in SATA *64, 155*
Pease, (Clarence) Howard 1894-1974 .... *2*
Obituary *25*
Peavy, Linda 1943- *54*
Peck, Anne Merriman 1884-1976 .... *18*
Peck, Beth 1957- *190*
Earlier sketch in SATA *79*
Peck, Jan *159*
Peck, Jeanie J. 1967- *147*
Peck, Marshall III 1951- *92*
Peck, Richard 1934- *228*
Autobiography Feature *110*
Earlier sketches in SATA *18, 55, 97, 110, 158, 190*
See also CLR *142*
See also SAAS *2*
Peck, Richard Wayne
See Peck, Richard
Peck, Robert Newton 1928- *156*
Autobiography Feature *108*
Earlier sketches in SATA *21, 62, 111*
See also CLR *163*
See also SAAS *1*
Peck, Sylvia 1953- *133*
Peck-Whiting, Jeanie J.
See Peck, Jeanie J.
Peddicord, Jane Ann *199*
Pedersen, Janet *193*
Pederson, Sharleen
See Collicott, Sharleen
Pedler, Caroline *197*
Peebles, Anne
See Galloway, Priscilla
Peek, Merle 1938- *39*
Peel, John 1954- *79*
Peel, Norman Lemon
See Hirsch, Phil
Peeples, Edwin A(ugustus, Jr.) 1915-1994 .... *6*
Peers, Judi 1956- *119*
Peers, Judith May West
See Peers, Judi
Peet, Bill
See Peet, William Bartlett
Peet, Creighton B. 1899-1977 .... *30*
Peet, Mal *227*
Earlier sketch in SATA *171*
Peet, Malcolm
See Peet, Mal
Peet, William Bartlett 1915-2002 .... *78*
Obituary *137*
Earlier sketches in SATA *2, 41*
See also CLR *12*
Peete, Holly Robinson 1964- *229*
Peguero, Leone *116*
Peirce, Lincoln *232*
Pelaez, Jill 1924- *12*
Pelham, David 1938- *70*
Pelikan, Judy 1941- *219*
Pell, Ed(ward) 1950- *157*
Pelletier, Andrew T. *195*
Pelletier, Andrew Thomas
See Pelletier, Andrew T.
Pellowski, Anne 1933- *20*
Pellowski, Michael (Joseph) 1949- *151*
Brief entry *48*
Earlier sketch in SATA *88*
Pellowski, Michael Morgan
See Pellowski, Michael (Joseph)
Pelta, Kathy 1928- *18*
Peltier, Leslie C(opus) 1900-1980 .... *13*
Pemberton, Bonnie *191*
Pemberton, John Leigh
See Leigh-Pemberton, John
Pembury, Bill
See Groom, Arthur William
Pemsteen, Hans
See Manes, Stephen
Pendennis, Arthur Esquir
See Thackeray, William Makepeace
Pender, Lydia Podger 1907- *61*
Pendery, Rosemary (Schmitz) *7*
Pendle, Alexy 1943- *29*
Pendle, George 1906-1977
Obituary *28*
Pendleton, Don
See Cunningham, Chet
and Garside, Jack
and Jagninski, Tom
and Krauzer, Steven M(ark)
and Obstfeld, Raymond
Pendleton, Thomas 1965- *206*
Pendziwol, Jean E. 1965- *177*
Pene du Bois, William (Sherman) 1916-1993 .... *68*
Obituary *74*
Earlier sketch in SATA *4*
See also CLR *1*
Penn, Audrey 1947- *212*
Penn, Audrey 1950- *22*
Penn, Ruth Bonn
See Rosenberg, Eth Clifford
Pennac, Daniel 1944- *155*
Pennage, E. M.
See Finkel, George (Irvine)
Penner, Fred 1946- *169*
Earlier sketch in SATA *67*
Penner, Frederick Ralph Cornelius
See Penner, Fred
Penner, Lucille Recht 1942- *226*
Penney, Grace Jackson 1904-2000 .... *35*
Penney, Ian 1960- *76*
Penney, Sue 1957- *152*
Earlier sketch in SATA *102*
Pennington, Eunice 1923- *27*
Pennington, Lillian Boyer 1904-2003 .... *45*
Pennypacker, Sara 1951- *187*

Penrose, Gordon 1925- ... *66*
Penson, Mary E. 1917- ... *78*
Penzler, Otto 1942- ... *38*
Peot, Margaret ... *241*
Pepe, Phil 1935- ... *20*
Pepe, Philip
See Pepe, Phil
Peppe, Rodney (Darrell) 1934- ... *74*
Earlier sketch in SATA *4*
See also SAAS *10*
Pepper, Frank S. 1910-1988
Obituary ... *61*
Percy, Charles Henry
See Smith, Dorothy Gladys
Percy, Rachel 1930- ... *63*
Perdomo, Willie ... *228*
Perdrizet, Marie-Pierre 1952- ... *79*
Perenyi, Constance 1954- ... *93*
Perenyi, Constance Marie
See Perenyi, Constance
Perera, Hilda 1926- ... *105*
Perera, Thomas Biddle 1938- ... *13*
Peretti, Frank E. 1951- ... *141*
Earlier sketch in SATA *80*
Perez, L. King 1940- ... *199*
Perez, Lana
See Perez, Marlene
Perez, Lucia Angela 1973- ... *182*
Perez, Marlene ... *170*
Pericoli, Matteo 1968- ... *178*
Perkins, Al(bert Rogers) 1904-1975 ... *30*
Perkins, Dan
See Tomorrow, Tom
Perkins, Lucy Fitch 1865-1937 ... *72*
Perkins, Lynne Rae 1956- ... *212*
Earlier sketches in SATA *131, 172*
Perkins, (Richard) Marlin 1905-1986 ... *21*
Obituary ... *48*
Perkins, Mitali 1963- ... *237*
Earlier sketches in SATA *88, 188*
Perkins, Stephanie ... *240*
Perks, Anne-Marie 1955- ... *122*
Perl, Erica S. ... *222*
Earlier sketch in SATA *188*
Perl, Lila ... *72*
Earlier sketch in SATA *6*
Perl, Susan 1922-1983 ... *22*
Obituary ... *34*
Perlman, Janet 1954- ... *222*
Perlman, Rhea 1948- ... *183*
Perlmutter, O(scar) William 1920-1975 ... *8*
Pernu, Dennis 1970- ... *87*
Perrault, Charles 1628-1703 ... *25*
See also CLR *134*
Perret, Delphine 1980- ... *190*
Perret, Gene (Richard) 1937- ... *76*
Perriman, Cole
See Perrin, Pat
Perriman, Cole
See Coleman, Wim
and Perrin, Pat
Perrin, Pat ... *212*
Perrine, Mary 1913-1976 ... *2*
Perrins, Lesley 1953- ... *56*
Perro
See Perro, Bryan
Perro, Bryan 1968- ... *239*
Perrow, Angeli 1954- ... *121*
Perry, Andrea 1956- ... *190*
Earlier sketch in SATA *148*
Perry, Barbara Fisher
See Fisher, Barbara
Perry, Elizabeth 1959- ... *174*
Perry, Elizabeth Goodwin
See Perry, Elizabeth
Perry, John 1967- ... *223*
Perry, M. LaVora ... *232*
Perry, Marie Fritz ... *165*
Perry, Patricia 1949- ... *30*
Perry, Phyllis J(ean) 1933- ... *152*
Earlier sketches in SATA *60, 101*
Perry, Ritchie (John Allen) 1942- ... *105*
Perry, Roger 1933- ... *27*
Perry, Steve(n Carl) 1947- ... *76*
Pershall, Mary K. 1951- ... *172*
Earlier sketch in SATA *70*
Pershing, Marie
See Schultz, Pearle Henriksen
Perske, Robert 1927- ... *57*
Persun, Morgan Reed
See Watkins, Dawn L.
Perversi, Margaret ... *213*
Petach, Heidi ... *149*
Peter
See Stratemeyer, Edward L.
Peters, Alexander
See Hollander, Zander
Peters, Andrew Fusek 1965- ... *169*
Earlier sketch in SATA *107*
Peters, Bernadette 1948- ... *212*
Peters, Caroline
See Betz, Eva Kelly
Peters, David
See David, Peter
Peters, Elizabeth 1927- ... *49*
Peters, Emma
See Price, Karen
Peters, Gabriel
See Matott, Justin
Peters, Julie Anne 1952- ... *197*
Earlier sketches in SATA *82, 128*
Peters, Linda
See Catherall, Arthur
Peters, Lisa Westberg 1951- ... *232*
Earlier sketches in SATA *74, 115, 161*
Peters, Patricia 1953- ... *84*
Peters, Russell M. 1929- ... *78*
Peters, S. H.
See Henry, O.
and Proffitt, Nicholas
Peters, Stephanie True 1965- ... *224*
Petersen, David 1946- ... *109*
Earlier sketch in SATA *62*
Petersen, Gwenn Boardman 1924- ... *12*
Petersen, P(eter) J(ames) 1941- ... *118*
Brief entry ... *43*
Earlier sketches in SATA *48, 83*
Petersen, Palle 1943- ... *85*
Petersham, Maud 1890-1971 ... *17*
See also CLR *24*
Petersham, Maud Sylvia Fuller
See Petersham, Maud
Petersham, Miska 1888-1960 ... *17*
See also CLR *24*
Peterson, Cris 1952- ... *174*
Earlier sketches in SATA *84, 145*
Peterson, Dawn 1934- ... *86*
Peterson, Esther (Allen) 1934- ... *35*
Peterson, Hans 1922- ... *8*
Peterson, Harold L(eslie) 1922-1978 ... *8*
Peterson, Helen Stone 1910- ... *8*
Peterson, Jean Sunde 1941- ... *108*
Peterson, Jeanne Whitehouse 1939- ... *159*
Earlier sketch in SATA *29*
Peterson, John 1924-2002 ... *233*
Peterson, Kathleen B. 1951- ... *119*
Peterson, Lorraine 1940- ... *56*
Brief entry ... *44*
Peterson, Mary ... *215*
Peterson, Shelley 1952- ... *146*
Peterson, Will
See Cocks, Peter
Petie, Haris
See Petty, Roberta
Petricic, Dusan 1946- ... *176*
Petrides, Heidrun 1944- ... *19*
Petrie, Catherine 1947- ... *52*
Brief entry ... *41*
Petrone, Valeria ... *233*
Earlier sketch in SATA *186*
Petrosino, Tamara ... *193*
Petroski, Catherine (Ann Groom) 1939- ... *48*
Petrovich, Michael B(oro) 1922- ... *40*
Petrovskaya, Kyra
See Wayne, Kyra Petrovskaya
Petruccio, Steven James 1961- ... *67*
Petrucha, Stefan 1959- ... *213*
Petry, Ann 1908-1997 ... *5*
Obituary ... *94*
See also CLR *12*
Petry, Ann Lane
See Petry, Ann
Pettit, Jayne 1932- ... *108*
Petty, J.T. 1977- ... *189*
Petty, Kate 1951-2007 ... *204*
Petty, Roberta 1915- ... *10*
Pevsner, Stella ... *131*
Earlier sketches in SATA *8, 77*
See also SAAS *14*
Peyo
See Culliford, Pierre
Peyton, K. M.
See Peyton, Kathleen Wendy
Peyton, Kathleen Wendy 1929- ... *157*
Earlier sketches in SATA *15, 62*
See also CLR *3*
See also SAAS *17*
Pfanner, (Anne) Louise 1955- ... *68*
Pfeffer, Susan Beth 1948- ... *180*
Earlier sketches in SATA *4, 83*
See also CLR *11*
See also SAAS *17*
Pfeffer, Wendy 1929- ... *204*
Earlier sketches in SATA *78, 142*
Pfeiffer, Janet (B.) 1949- ... *96*
Pfister, Marcus ... *207*
Earlier sketches in SATA *83, 150*
See also CLR *42*
Pfitsch, Patricia Curtis 1948- ... *148*
Pfitzenmaier, Audrey 1959- ... *220*
Pflieger, Pat 1955- ... *84*
Pham, LeUyen 1973- ... *237*
Earlier sketches in SATA *175, 201*
Phelan, Mary Kay 1914- ... *3*
Phelan, Matt 1970- ... *215*
Earlier sketch in SATA *172*
Phelan, Terry Wolfe 1941- ... *56*
Phelps, Ethel Johnston 1914-1984 ... *35*
Philbrick, Rodman 1951- ... *163*
Philbrick, W. Rodman
See Philbrick, Rodman
Philbrick, W.R.
See Philbrick, Rodman
Philbrook, Clem(ent E.) 1917- ... *24*
Phillipps, J.C. ... *218*
Phillipps, Julie Christine
See Phillipps, J.C.
Phillips, Aileen Paul
See Paul, Aileen
Phillips, Betty Lou
See Phillips, Elizabeth Louise
Phillips, Bob 1940- ... *95*
Phillips, Douglas A. 1949- ... *161*
Phillips, Elizabeth Louise ... *58*
Brief entry ... *48*
Phillips, Gary R. ... *225*
Phillips, Irv(ing W.) 1905-2000 ... *11*
Obituary ... *125*
Phillips, Jack
See Sandburg, Carl
Phillips, Leon
See Gerson, Noel Bertram
Phillips, Loretta (Hosey) 1893-1987 ... *10*
Phillips, Louis 1942- ... *102*
Earlier sketch in SATA *8*
Phillips, Mark
See Garrett, Randall
and Janifer, Laurence M(ark)
Phillips, Mary Geisler 1881-1964 ... *10*
Phillips, Michael
See Nolan, William F.
Phillips, (Woodward) Prentice 1894-1981 ... *10*
Phillpotts, Eden 1862-1960 ... *24*

Phin
See Thayer, Ernest Lawrence
Phipson, Joan
See Fitzhardinge, Joan Margaret
Phiz
See Browne, Hablot Knight
Phleger, Fred B. 1909-1993 .... *34*
Phleger, Marjorie Temple 1908(?)-1986 .... *1*
Obituary *47*
Piaget, Jean 1896-1980
Obituary *23*
Piatti, Celestino 1922- *16*
Picard, Barbara Leonie 1917- *89*
Earlier sketch in SATA *2*
See also SAAS *10*
Pichon, Liz *174*
Pickard, Charles 1932- *36*
Pickering, James Sayre 1897-1969 .... *36*
Obituary *28*
Pickering, Jimmy *195*
Pickering, Robert B. 1950- *93*
Pielichaty, Helena 1955- *142*
Pien, Lark *222*
Pienkowski, Jan (Michal) 1936- *131*
Earlier sketches in SATA *6, 58*
See also CLR *6*
Pierce, Edith Gray 1893-1977 .... *45*
Pierce, Katherine
See St. John, Wylly Folk
Pierce, Meredith Ann 1958- *127*
Brief entry *48*
Earlier sketch in SATA *67*
See also CLR *20*
Pierce, Ruth (Ireland) 1936- *5*
Pierce, Sharon
See McCullough, Sharon Pierce
Pierce, Tamora 1954- *187*
Brief entry *49*
Earlier sketches in SATA *51, 96, 153*
Pierce, Terry *178*
Pierik, Robert 1921- *13*
Piernas-Davenport, Gail *199*
Piers, Robert
See Anthony, Piers
Pig, Edward
See Gorey, Edward (St. John)
Pignataro, Anna 1965- *223*
Pike, Aprilynne *218*
Pike, Bob
See Pike, Robert W.
Pike, Christopher 1954(?)- *239*
Earlier sketches in SATA *68, 156*
See also CLR *29*
Pike, Deborah 1951- *89*
Pike, E(dgar) Royston 1896-1980 .... *22*
Obituary *56*
Pike, R. William 1956- *92*
Pike, Robert
See Pike, Robert W.
Pike, Robert W. 1931- *102*
Pike, Robert Wilson
See Pike, Robert W.
Pilarski, Laura 1926- *13*
Pilgrim, Anne
See Allan, Mabel Esther
Pilkey, Dav 1966- *166*
Earlier sketches in SATA *68, 115*
See also CLR *160*
Pilkey, David Murray, Jr.
See Pilkey, Dav
Pilkington, Francis Meredyth 1907-1993 .... *4*
Pilkington, Roger (Windle) 1915-2003 .... *10*
Obituary *144*
Pilutti, Deb *208*
Pin, Isabel 1975- *183*
Pinchot, David 1914(?)-1983
Obituary *34*
Pincus, Harriet 1938- *27*
Pinczes, Elinor J(ane) 1940- *81*
Pine, Nicholas 1951- *91*
Pine, Tillie S(chloss) 1896-1999 .... *13*
Pini, Richard (Alan) 1950- *89*
Pini, Wendy 1951- *89*
Pinkerton, Kathrene Sutherland (Gedney) 1887-1967
Obituary *26*
Pinkett, Jada
See Smith, Jada Pinkett
Pinkney, Andrea Davis 1963- *160*
Earlier sketch in SATA *113*
Pinkney, Brian 1961- *206*
Earlier sketches in SATA *74, 148*
See also CLR *54*
Pinkney, Gloria Jean 1941- *212*
Earlier sketch in SATA *85*
Pinkney, J. Brian
See Pinkney, Brian
Pinkney, Jerry 1939- *198*
Autobiography Feature *198*
Brief entry *32*
Earlier sketches in SATA *41, 71, 107, 151*
See also CLR *43*
See also SAAS *12*
Pinkney, John *97*
Pinkney, Sandra L. *193*
Earlier sketch in SATA *128*
Pinkwater, D. Manus
See Pinkwater, Daniel
Pinkwater, Daniel 1941- *210*
Earlier sketches in SATA *8, 46, 76, 114, 158*
See also CLR *175*
See also SAAS *3*
Pinkwater, Daniel M.
See Pinkwater, Daniel
Pinkwater, Daniel Manus
See Pinkwater, Daniel
Pinkwater, Jill *188*
Pinkwater, Manus
See Pinkwater, Daniel
Pinner, Joma
See Werner, Herma
Pinto, Sara *200*
Pioneer
See Yates, Raymond F(rancis)
Piowaty, Kim Kennelly 1957- *49*
Piper, Roger
See Fisher, John
Pirner, Connie White 1955- *72*
Piro, Richard 1934- *7*
Pirot, Alison Lohans
See Lohans, Alison
Pirotta, Saviour *184*
Pirsig, Robert M(aynard) 1928- *39*
Pita
See Rendon, Maria
Pitcher, C.
See Pitcher, Caroline
Pitcher, Caroline 1948- *214*
Earlier sketch in SATA *128*
Pitcher, Caroline Nell
See Pitcher, Caroline
Pitman, (Isaac) James 1901-1985
Obituary *46*
Pitre, Felix 1949- *84*
Pitrone, Jean Maddern 1920- *4*
Pittman, Helena Clare 1945- *71*
Pittman, Rickey E. *241*
Pitz, Henry C(larence) 1895-1976 .... *4*
Obituary *24*
Pitzer, Susanna 1958- *181*
Piven, Hanoch 1963- *236*
Earlier sketch in SATA *173*
Pixley, Marcella *194*
Pizer, Vernon 1918- *21*
Place, Francois 1957- *234*
Place, Marian T(empleton) 1910- *3*
Place, Robin (Mary) 1926- *71*
Plaidy, Jean
See Hibbert, Eleanor Alice Burford
Plain, Belva 1919-2010 .... *62*
Plaine, Alfred R. 1898(?)-1981
Obituary *29*
Plant, Andrew *214*
Plath, Sylvia 1932-1963 .... *96*
Platt, Chris 1959- *185*
Platt, Kin 1911- *86*
Earlier sketch in SATA *21*
See also SAAS *17*
Platt, Randall 1948- *95*
Platt, Randall Beth
See Platt, Randall
Platt, Richard 1953- *218*
Earlier sketches in SATA *120, 166*
Playfellow, Robin
See Ellis, Edward S.
Playsted, James
See Wood, James Playsted
Plecas, Jennifer 1966- *229*
Earlier sketches in SATA *84, 149*
Plimpton, George 1927-2003 .... *10*
Obituary *150*
Plimpton, George Ames
See Plimpton, George
Plomer, William Charles Franklin 1903-1973 .... *24*
Plotz, Helen Ratnoff 1913-2000 .... *38*
Plourde, Lynn 1955- *218*
Earlier sketches in SATA *122, 168*
Plowden, David 1932- *52*
Plowden, Martha Ward 1948- *98*
Plowhead, Ruth Gipson 1877-1967 .... *43*
Plowman, Stephanie 1922- *6*
Pluckrose, Henry 1931-2011 .... *141*
Earlier sketch in SATA *13*
Pluckrose, Henry Arthur
See Pluckrose, Henry
Plum, J.
See Wodehouse, P. G.
Plum, Jennifer
See Kurland, Michael
Plumb, Charles P. 1900(?)-1982
Obituary *29*
Plume, Ilse *170*
Brief entry *43*
Plumme, Don E.
See Katz, Bobbi
Plummer, Margaret 1911- *2*
Plum-Ucci, Carol 1957- *184*
Poblocki, Dan 1981- *224*
Pochocki, Ethel (Frances) 1925- *76*
Podendorf, Illa (E.) 1903(?)-1983 .... *18*
Obituary *35*
Podwal, Mark 1945- *224*
Earlier sketches in SATA *101, 160*
Podwal, Mark H.
See Podwal, Mark
Poe, Edgar Allan 1809-1849 .... *23*
Poe, Ty (Christopher) 1975- *94*
Pogany, William Andrew 1882-1955 .... *44*
Brief entry *30*
Pogany, Willy
See Pogany, William Andrew
Pogue, Carolyn 1948- *223*
Pogue, David 1963- *231*
Pohl, Frederik 1919- *24*
Pohlmann, Lillian (Grenfell) 1902-1997 .... *11*
Pohrt, Tom 1953- *195*
Earlier sketches in SATA *67, 152*
Pointon, Robert
See Rooke, Daphne
Points, Larry G. 1945- *177*
Earlier sketch in SATA *133*
Points, Larry Gene
See Points, Larry G.
Pokeberry, P.J.
See Mitchell, B.J.
Pokiak-Fenton, Margaret *239*
POLA
See Watson, Pauline
Polacco, Patricia 1944- *212*
Earlier sketches in SATA *74, 123, 180*
See also CLR *40*

Polacco, Patricia Ann
See Polacco, Patricia
Polak, Monique 1960- ... *230*
Earlier sketch in SATA *178*
Polatnick, Florence T. 1923- ... *5*
Polcovar, Jane 1948- ... *211*
Polder, Markus
See Kruss, James
Polenghi, Evan 1961- ... *225*
Polese, Carolyn 1947- ... *58*
Polese, James 1914- ... *87*
Polette, Nancy (Jane) 1930- ... *42*
Polhamus, Jean Burt 1928- ... *21*
Polhemus, Coleman ... *210*
Policoff, Stephen Phillip 1948- ... *77*
Polikoff, Barbara G. 1929- ... *162*
Earlier sketch in SATA *77*
Polikoff, Barbara Garland
See Polikoff, Barbara G.
Polisar, Barry Louis 1954- ... *134*
Earlier sketch in SATA *77*
Politi, Leo 1908-1996 ... *47*
Obituary ... *88*
Earlier sketch in SATA *1*
See also CLR *29*
Polking, Kirk 1925- ... *5*
Pollack, Jill S. 1963- ... *88*
Pollack, Merrill S. 1924-1988
Obituary ... *55*
Polland, Barbara K(ay) 1939- ... *44*
Polland, Madeleine A(ngela Cahill) 1918- ... *68*
Earlier sketch in SATA *6*
See also SAAS *8*
Pollema-Cahill, Phyllis 1958- ... *123*
Pollock, Bruce 1945- ... *46*
Pollock, Mary
See Blyton, Enid
Pollock, Penny 1935- ... *137*
Brief entry ... *42*
Earlier sketch in SATA *44*
Pollowitz, Melinda Kilborn 1944- ... *26*
Polner, Murray 1928- ... *64*
Polonsky, Arthur 1925- ... *34*
Polseno, Jo ... *17*
Pomaska, Anna 1946- ... *117*
Pomerantz, Charlotte 1930- ... *177*
Earlier sketches in SATA *20, 80*
Pomeroy, Pete
See Roth, Arthur J(oseph)
Pon, Cindy 1973- ... *216*
Pon, Cynthia ... *229*
Pond, Alonzo W(illiam) 1894-1986 ... *5*
Pontiflet, Ted 1932- ... *32*
Poole, Gray Johnson 1906- ... *1*
Poole, Josephine
See Helyar, Jane Penelope Josephine
Poole, (Jane Penelope) Josephine
See Helyar, Jane Penelope Josephine
Poole, Lynn 1910-1969 ... *1*
Poole, Peggy 1925- ... *39*
Pooler, Paige ... *235*
Poon, Janice ... *228*
Poortvliet, Rien 1932- ... *65*
Brief entry ... *37*
Pope, Elizabeth Marie 1917-1992 ... *38*
Brief entry ... *36*
Pope, Kevin 1958- ... *183*
Popescu, Christine
See Pullein-Thompson, Christine
Poploff, Michelle 1956- ... *67*
Popp, K. Wendy ... *91*
Poppel, Hans 1942- ... *71*
Porfirio, Guy 1958- ... *197*
Portal, Colette 1936- ... *6*
Porte, Barbara Ann 1943- ... *152*
Brief entry ... *45*
Earlier sketches in SATA *57, 93*
Porter, A(nthony) P(eyton) 1945- ... *68*
Porter, Connie (Rose) 1959(?)- ... *129*
Earlier sketch in SATA *81*
Porter, Donald Clayton
See Gerson, Noel Bertram
Porter, Eleanor H(odgman) 1868-1920
See CLR *110*
Porter, Gene Stratton
See Stratton-Porter, Gene
Porter, Janice Lee 1953- ... *108*
Earlier sketch in SATA *68*
Porter, Katherine Anne 1890-1980 ... *39*
Obituary ... *23*
Porter, Kathryn
See Swinford, Betty (June Wells)
Porter, Pamela 1956- ... *193*
Porter, Sheena 1935- ... *24*
See also SAAS *10*
Porter, Sue
See Limb, Sue
Porter, Sue 1951- ... *213*
Earlier sketch in SATA *76*
Porter, Tracey ... *191*
Porter, William Sydney
See Henry, O.
Portis, Antoinette ... *189*
Porto, Tony 1960- ... *153*
Portteus, Eleanora Marie Manthei (?)-1983
Obituary ... *36*
Posada, Mia ... *187*
Posell, Elsa Z(eigerman) -1995 ... *3*
Posesorski, Sherie ... *216*
Posten, Margaret L(ois) 1915- ... *10*
Postgate, Daniel 1964- ... *216*
Posthuma, Sieb 1960- ... *150*
Postier, Jim 1965- ... *202*
Potok, Chaim 1929-2002 ... *106*
Obituary ... *134*
Earlier sketch in SATA *33*
See also CLR *92*
Potok, Herbert Harold
See Potok, Chaim
Potok, Herman Harold
See Potok, Chaim
Potter, Alicia ... *216*
Potter, Beatrix 1866-1943 ... *132*
Earlier sketch in SATA *100*
See also YABC *1*
See also CLR *165*
Potter, Ellen 1973- ... *218*
Potter, Giselle ... *187*
Earlier sketch in SATA *150*
Potter, Helen Beatrix
See Potter, Beatrix
Potter, Katherine ... *217*
Potter, Margaret 1926-1998 ... *21*
Obituary ... *104*
Potter, Marian 1915- ... *9*
Potter, Miriam Clark 1886-1965 ... *3*
Potter, Ryan ... *230*
Poulin, Stephane 1961- ... *98*
See also CLR *28*
Poulton, Kimberly 1957(?)- ... *136*
Pournelle, Jerry 1933- ... *161*
Earlier sketches in SATA *26, 91*
Pournelle, Jerry Eugene
See Pournelle, Jerry
Povelite, Kay 1955- ... *102*
Pow, Tom 1950- ... *163*
Powe-Allred, Alexandra
See Allred, Alexandra Powe
Powell, A. M.
See Morgan, Alfred P(owell)
Powell, Consie ... *174*
Powell, E. Sandy 1947- ... *72*
Powell, E.S.
See Powell, E. Sandy
Powell, Pamela 1960- ... *78*
Powell, Patricia Hruby 1951- ... *136*
Powell, Randy 1956- ... *118*
Powell, Richard Stillman
See Barbour, Ralph Henry
Powell, Robert (Stephenson Smyth) Baden
See Baden-Powell, Robert (Stephenson Smyth)
Powell, Stephanie 1953- ... *93*
Power, Margaret (M.) 1945- ... *125*
Earlier sketch in SATA *75*
Power, Timothy 1960- ... *241*
Powers, Anne
See Schwartz, Anne Powers
Powers, Bill 1931- ... *52*
Brief entry ... *31*
Powers, Daniel 1959- ... *164*
Powers, J. L. ... *195*
Powers, Jessica
See Powers, J. L.
Powers, Jessica Lynn
See Powers, J. L.
Powers, Margaret
See Heal, Edith
Powers, Tim 1952- ... *107*
Powers, Timothy Thomas
See Powers, Tim
Powledge, Fred 1935- ... *37*
Poydar, Nancy ... *190*
Poynter, Margaret 1927- ... *27*
Prachaticka, Marketa
See Kolibalova, Marketa
Prachatika, Marketa
See Kolibalova, Marketa
Prager, Arthur ... *44*
Prager, Ellen J. 1962- ... *136*
Prange, Beckie ... *172*
Prap, Lila 1955- ... *177*
Praprotnik-Zupancic, Lilijana
See Prap, Lila
Pratchett, Terence David John
See Pratchett, Terry
Pratchett, Terry 1948- ... *185*
Earlier sketches in SATA *82, 139*
See also CLR *64*
Prater, John 1947- ... *149*
Earlier sketches in SATA *72, 103*
Prato, Rodica ... *184*
Pratt, Christine Joy ... *214*
Pratt, (Murray) Fletcher 1897-1956 ... *102*
Pratt, Kristin Joy 1976- ... *87*
Pratt, Pierre 1962- ... *208*
Earlier sketches in SATA *95, 166*
Preble, Joy ... *240*
Preiss, Byron 1953-2005 ... *166*
Brief entry ... *42*
Earlier sketch in SATA *47*
Preiss, Byron Cary
See Preiss, Byron
Preller, James 1961- ... *209*
Earlier sketch in SATA *88*
Prelutsky, Jack 1940- ... *171*
Earlier sketches in SATA *22, 66, 118*
See also CLR *115*
Prentice, Amy
See Kaler, James Otis
Prescott, Casey
See Morris, Chris(topher Crosby)
Presnall, Judith (Ann) Janda 1943- ... *96*
Pressler, Mirjam 1940- ... *155*
Preston, Douglas 1956- ... *113*
Preston, Edna Mitchell ... *40*
Preston, Lillian Elvira 1918- ... *47*
Preus, Margi ... *209*
Preussler, Otfried 1923- ... *24*
Prevert, Jacques 1900-1977
Obituary ... *30*
Prevert, Jacques Henri Marie
See Prevert, Jacques
Prevost, Guillaume 1964- ... *192*
Prevost, Mikela ... *203*
Price, Beverley Joan 1931- ... *98*
Price, Charlie ... *237*
Earlier sketch in SATA *187*
Price, Christine (Hilda) 1928-1980 ... *3*
Obituary ... *23*

Price, Garrett 1896-1979
  Obituary ... *22*
Price, Jennifer
  See Hoover, Helen (Drusilla Blackburn)
Price, Joan 1931- ... *124*
Price, Jonathan (Reeve) 1941- ... *46*
Price, Karen 1957- ... *125*
Price, Kathy Z. 1957- ... *172*
Price, Lucie Locke
  See Locke, Lucie
Price, Mara ... *240*
Price, Olive 1903-1991 ... *8*
Price, Susan 1955- ... *128*
  Earlier sketches in SATA *25, 85*
Price, Willard 1887-1983 ... *48*
  Brief entry ... *38*
Price-Groff, Claire ... *127*
Priceman, Marjorie 1958- ... *234*
  Earlier sketches in SATA *81, 120, 168*
Prichard, Katharine Susannah 1883-1969 ... *66*
Priddy, Roger ... *227*
Prideaux, Tom 1908-1993 ... *37*
  Obituary ... *76*
Priestley, Alice 1962- ... *227*
  Earlier sketch in SATA *95*
Priestley, Chris 1958- ... *198*
Priestley, Lee (Shore) 1904-1999 ... *27*
Priestly, Doug 1954- ... *122*
Priestly, Douglas Michael
  See Priestly, Doug
Prieto, Mariana Beeching 1912-1999 ... *8*
Prigmore, Shane 1977- ... *234*
Priley, Margaret (Ann) Hubbard 1909-1992
  Obituary ... *130*
Primavera, Elise 1954- ... *230*
  Brief entry ... *48*
  Earlier sketches in SATA *58, 109, 185*
Prime, Derek (James) 1931- ... *34*
Prince, Alison (Mary) 1931- ... *86*
  Earlier sketch in SATA *28*
Prince, April Jones 1975- ... *180*
Prince, J(ack) H(arvey) 1908- ... *17*
Prince, Joshua ... *188*
Prince, Maggie ... *102*
Prineas, Sarah ... *204*
Pringle, Eric ... *138*
Pringle, Laurence 1935- ... *201*
  Autobiography Feature ... *201*
  Earlier sketches in SATA *4, 68, 104, 154*
  See also CLR *57*
  See also SAAS *6*
Pringle, Laurence Patrick
  See Pringle, Laurence
Prinz, Yvonne 1960- ... *175*
Prior, Natalie Jane 1963- ... *106*
Pritchett, Elaine H(illyer) 1920- ... *36*
Pritchett, Laura 1971- ... *178*
Pritchett, Laura Rose
  See Pritchett, Laura
Pritts, Kim Derek 1953- ... *83*
Prochazkova, Iva 1953- ... *68*
Proctor, Everitt
  See Montgomery, Rutherford George
Proeysen, Alf 1914-1970 ... *67*
  See also CLR *24*
Professor Scribbler
  See Hollingsworth, Mary
Proimos, James 1955- ... *217*
  Earlier sketch in SATA *173*
Promitzer, Rebecca ... *229*
Prose, Francine 1947- ... *198*
  Earlier sketches in SATA *101, 149*
Prosek, James 1975- ... *216*
Protopopescu, Orel ... *186*
Protopopescu, Orel Odinov
  See Protopopescu, Orel
Provensen, Alice 1918- ... *147*
  Earlier sketches in SATA *9, 70*
  See also CLR *11*
Provensen, Martin 1916-1987 ... *70*
  Obituary ... *51*
  Earlier sketch in SATA *9*
  See also CLR *11*
Provensen, Martin Elias
  See Provensen, Martin
Provenzo, Eugene (F., Jr.) 1949- ... *142*
  Earlier sketch in SATA *78*
Provist, d'Alain 1906-1989
  See Diop, Birago (Ismael)
Provost, Gail Levine 1944- ... *65*
Provost, Gary (Richard) 1944-1995 ... *66*
Proysen, Alf
  See Proeysen, Alf
Pruett, Candace (J.) 1968- ... *157*
Pryor, Bonnie H. 1942- ... *69*
Pryor, Boori (Monty) 1950- ... *112*
Pryor, Helen Brenton 1897-1972 ... *4*
Pryor, Michael 1957- ... *153*
Pucci, Albert John 1920- ... *44*
Pudney, John (Sleigh) 1909-1977 ... *24*
Pugh, Ellen (Tiffany) 1920- ... *7*
Pullein-Thompson, Christine 1925-2005 ... *82*
  Obituary ... *172*
  Earlier sketch in SATA *3*
Pullein-Thompson, Diana
  See Farr, Diana
Pullein-Thompson, Joanna Maxwell
  1898-1961 ... *82*
Pullein-Thompson, Josephine (Mary
  Wedderburn) ... *82*
  Earlier sketch in SATA *3*
Pullen, Zachary ... *189*
Pullman, Philip 1946- ... *198*
  Earlier sketches in SATA *65, 103, 150*
  See also CLR *84*
  See also SAAS *17*
Pullman, Philip Nicholas
  See Pullman, Philip
Pulver, Harry, Jr. 1960- ... *129*
Pulver, Robin 1945- ... *208*
  Earlier sketches in SATA *76, 133*
Puner, Helen W(alker) 1915-1989 ... *37*
  Obituary ... *63*
Purdy, Carol 1943- ... *120*
  Earlier sketch in SATA *66*
Purdy, Susan G(old) 1939- ... *8*
Purkiss, Diane 1961- ... *194*
Purmell, Ann 1953- ... *206*
  Earlier sketch in SATA *147*
Purnell, Idella 1901-1982 ... *120*
Purscell, Phyllis 1934- ... *7*
Purtill, Richard L. 1931- ... *53*
Purvis, Leland ... *232*
Pushker, Gloria 1927- ... *162*
  Earlier sketch in SATA *75*
Pushker, Gloria Teles
  See Pushker, Gloria
Pushkin, Aleksandr Sergeevich
  See Pushkin, Alexander
Pushkin, Alexander 1799-1837 ... *61*
Putnam, Alice 1916- ... *61*
Putnam, Arthur Lee
  See Alger, Horatio, Jr.
Putnam, Peter B(rock) 1920-1998 ... *30*
  Obituary ... *106*
Puttapipat, Niroot ... *199*
Puttock, Simon ... *178*
Puvilland, Alex ... *205*
Puvilland, Alexandre
  See Puvilland, Alex
Puybaret, Eric 1976- ... *299*
  Earlier sketch in SATA *195*
Pyle, Charles S. 1954(?)- ... *229*
Pyle, Chuck
  See Pyle, Charles S.
Pyle, Howard 1853-1911 ... *100*
  Earlier sketch in SATA *16*
  See also CLR *117*
Pyle, Katharine 1863-1938 ... *66*
Pyne, Mable Mandeville 1903-1969 ... *9*
Pyrnelle, Louise-Clarke 1850-1907 ... *114*

Q

Quackenbush, Robert M(ead) 1929- ... *133*
  Autobiography Feature ... *133*
  Earlier sketches in SATA *7, 70*
  See also CLR *122*
  See also SAAS *7*
Qualey, Marsha 1953- ... *124*
  Earlier sketch in SATA *79*
Qualls, Sean ... *233*
  Earlier sketch in SATA *177*
Quammen, David 1948- ... *7*
Quark, Jason
  See Eldin, Peter
Quarles, Benjamin 1904-1996 ... *12*
Quarles, Benjamin Arthur
  See Quarles, Benjamin
Quatermass, Martin
  See Carpenter, John
Quattlebaum, Mary 1958- ... *185*
  Earlier sketches in SATA *88, 134*
Quay, Emma ... *173*
  Earlier sketch in SATA *119*
Queen, Ellery
  See Deming, Richard
  and Dannay, Frederic
  and Davidson, Avram (James)
  and Fairman, Paul W.
  and Flora, Fletcher
  and Holding, James (Clark Carlisle, Jr.)
  and Hoch, Edward D.
  and Kane, Henry
  and Lee, Manfred B.
  and Marlowe, Stephen
  and Powell, (Oval) Talmage
  and Sheldon, Walter J(ames)
  and Sturgeon, Theodore (Hamilton)
  and Tracy, Don(ald Fiske)
  and Vance, Jack
Queen Latifah 1970- ... *185*
Quennell, Marjorie Courtney 1884-1972 ... *29*
Quentin
  See Sheldon, David
Quentin, Brad
  See Bisson, Terry
Quest, (Edna) Olga W(ilbourne) Hall
  See Hall-Quest, (Edna) Olga W(ilbourne)
Quick, Annabelle 1922-1986 ... *2*
Quigg, Jane (Hulda) (?)-1986
  Obituary ... *49*
Quigley, Sarah 1976- ... *220*
Quill, Monica
  See McInerny, Ralph
Quimby, Laura ... *237*
Quin-Harkin, Janet 1941- ... *165*
  Earlier sketches in SATA *18, 90, 119*
Quin-Harkin, Janet Elizabeth
  See Quin-Harkin, Janet
Quinlan, Susan E. 1954- ... *88*
Quinlan, Susan Elizabeth
  See Quinlan, Susan E.
Quinn, Elisabeth 1881-1962 ... *22*
Quinn, Pat 1947- ... *130*
Quinn, Patrick 1950- ... *73*
Quinn, Rob 1972- ... *138*
Quinn, Spencer
  See Abrahams, Peter
Quinn, Susan 1940- ... *30*
Quinn, Susan Taft
  See Quinn, Susan
Quinn, Theodora K.
  See Kroeber, Theodora (Kracaw)
Quinn, Vernon
  See Quinn, Elisabeth

Quintano, D.M.
See Sheldon, Dyan
Quirk, Anne (E.) 1956- ... *99*
Quixley, Jim 1931- ... *56*
Quyth, Gabriel
See Jennings, Gary

R

Ra, Carol F. 1939- ... *76*
Raab, Evelyn 1951- ... *129*
Rabb, Margo 1972- ... *188*
Rabb, M.E.
See Rabb, Margo
Rabe, Berniece (Louise) 1928- ... *148*
Autobiography Feature ... *148*
Earlier sketches in SATA *7, 77*
See also SAAS *10*
Rabe, Olive H(anson) (?)-1968 ... *13*
Rabin, Staton 1958- ... *162*
Earlier sketch in SATA *84*
Rabinowich, Ellen 1946- ... *29*
Rabinowitz, Sandy 1954- ... *52*
Brief entry ... *39*
Rachlin, Carol K(ing) 1919- ... *64*
Rachlin, Harvey 1951- ... *47*
Rachlin, Harvey Brant
See Rachlin, Harvey
Rachlin, Nahid ... *64*
Rachlis, Eugene (Jacob) 1920-1986
Obituary ... *50*
Rackham, Arthur 1867-1939 ... *100*
Earlier sketch in SATA *15*
See also CLR *57*
Racoma, Robin Yoko 1953- ... *207*
Raczka, Bob 1963- ... *228*
Earlier sketches in SATA *163, 191*
Radencich, Marguerite C. 1952-1998 ... *79*
Rader, Laura ... *197*
Radford, Ruby L(orraine) 1891-1971 ... *6*
Radin, Ruth Yaffe 1938- ... *107*
Brief entry ... *52*
Earlier sketch in SATA *56*
Radlauer, David 1952- ... *28*
Radlauer, Edward 1921- ... *15*
Radlauer, Ruth Shaw 1926- ... *98*
Earlier sketch in SATA *15*
Radley, Gail 1951- ... *112*
Earlier sketch in SATA *25*
Radunsky, Vladimir ... *177*
Radzinski, Kandy 1948- ... *212*
Rae, Gwynedd 1892-1977 ... *37*
Raebeck, Lois 1921- ... *5*
Rael, Elsa Okon 1927-
See CLR *84*
Raffi
See Cavoukian, Raffi
Raftery, Gerald (Bransfield) 1905-1986 ... *11*
Ragan-Reid, Gale 1956- ... *90*
Rahaman, Vashanti 1953- ... *98*
Rahn, Joan Elma 1929- ... *27*
Rai, Bali 1971- ... *152*
Raible, Alton (Robert) 1918- ... *35*
Raiff, Stan 1930- ... *11*
Railsback, Lisa ... *230*
Raines, Shirley C(arol) 1945- ... *128*
Rainey, W. B.
See Blassingame, Wyatt Rainey
Rake, Jody 1961- ... *157*
Rallison, Janette 1966- ... *238*
Earlier sketch in SATA *183*
Ralston, Jan
See Dunlop, Agnes M. R.
Rama, Sue ... *190*
Ramal, Walter
See de la Mare, Walter (John)
Ramanujan, A(ttipat) K(rishnaswami)
1929-1993 ... *86*
Rame, David
See Divine, Arthur Durham
Ramirez, Jose 1967- ... *198*
Ramirez, Orlando L. 1972- ... *194*
Ramos, Jorge 1958- ... *205*
Ramsey, Calvin Alexander ... *239*
Ramstad, Ralph L. 1919- ... *115*
Ramthun, Bonnie ... *214*
Rana, Indi
See Rana, Indira Higham
Rana, Indira Higham 1944- ... *82*
Rana, J.
See Bhatia, Jamunadevi
Ranadive, Gail 1944- ... *10*
Rand, Ann (Binkley) ... *30*
Rand, Gloria 1925- ... *156*
Earlier sketch in SATA *101*
Rand, Paul 1914-1996 ... *6*
Randall, Carrie
See Ransom, Candice
Randall, David 1972- ... *167*
Randall, Florence Engel 1917-1997 ... *5*
Randall, Janet
See Young, Janet Randall
and Young, Robert W(illiam)
Randall, Robert
See Garrett, Randall
and Silverberg, Robert
Randall, Ruth (Elaine) Painter 1892-1971 ... *3*
Randell, Beverley
See Price, Beverley Joan
Randle, Kristen D. 1952- ... *92*
Autobiography Feature ... *119*
See also SAAS *24*
Randle, Kristen Downey
See Randle, Kristen D.
Randolph, Boynton M.D.
See Ellis, Edward S.
Randolph, Ellen
See Rawn, Melanie
Randolph, Geoffrey
See Ellis, Edward S.
Randolph, J. H.
See Ellis, Edward S.
Randolph, Lieutenant J. H.
See Ellis, Edward S.
Rands, William Brighty 1823-1882 ... *17*
Raney, Ken 1953- ... *74*
Rania, Queen of Jordan 1970- ... *233*
Rankin, Joan 1940- ... *212*
Earlier sketches in SATA *88, 148*
Rankin, Laura 1953(?)- ... *236*
Earlier sketch in SATA *176*
Ranney, Agnes V. 1916-1985 ... *6*
Ransom, Candice 1952- ... *222*
Brief entry ... *49*
Earlier sketches in SATA *52, 89, 135, 183*
Ransom, Jeanie Franz 1957- ... *187*
Ransome, Arthur (Michell) 1884-1967 ... *22*
See also CLR *8*
Ransome, James E. 1961- ... *227*
Earlier sketches in SATA *76, 123, 178*
See also CLR *86*
Rant, Tol E.
See Longyear, Barry B(rookes)
Rao, Rohitash ... *218*
Raphael, Elaine
See Bolognese, Elaine
Raposo, Joseph Guilherme 1938-1989
Obituary ... *61*
Rapp, Adam 1968- ... *148*
Rappaport, Doreen ... *211*
Earlier sketch in SATA *151*
Rappaport, Eva 1924- ... *6*
Rappoport, Ken 1935- ... *167*
Earlier sketch in SATA *89*
Rarick, Carrie 1911-2002 ... *41*
Raschka, Chris 1959- ... *207*
Earlier sketches in SATA *80, 117, 166*
Raschka, Christopher
See Raschka, Chris
Rascol, Sabina I. ... *159*
Rash, Andy ... *219*
Earlier sketch in SATA *162*
Raskin, Edith Lefkowitz 1908-1987 ... *9*
Raskin, Ellen 1928-1984 ... *139*
Earlier sketches in SATA *2, 38*
See also CLR *12*
Raskin, Joseph 1897-1982 ... *12*
Obituary ... *29*
Rathjen, Carl Henry 1909-1984 ... *11*
Rathmann, Peggy 1953- ... *157*
Earlier sketch in SATA *94*
See also CLR *77*
Ratliff, Thomas M. 1948- ... *118*
Ratner, Sue Lynn
See Alexander, Sue
Rattigan, Jama Kim 1951- ... *99*
Ratto, Linda Lee 1952- ... *79*
Rattray, Simon
See Trevor, Elleston
Ratz de Tagyos, Paul 1958- ... *198*
Earlier sketch in SATA *76*
Rau, Dana Meachen 1971- ... *218*
Earlier sketches in SATA *94, 167*
Rau, Margaret 1913- ... *168*
Earlier sketch in SATA *9*
See also CLR *8*
Rauch, Mabel Thompson 1888-1972
Obituary ... *26*
Raucher, Herman 1928- ... *8*
Raude, Karina ... *199*
Rauh, Sherry
See North, Sherry
Raum, Elizabeth 1949- ... *155*
Rausch, Molly ... *240*
Raut, Radhashyam ... *222*
Rave, Friederike 1970- ... *231*
Raven, Margot Theis ... *184*
RavenWolf, Silver 1956- ... *155*
Ravielli, Anthony 1916-1997 ... *3*
Obituary ... *95*
Ravilious, Robin 1944- ... *77*
Ravishankar, Anushka 1961- ... *200*
Rawding, F(rederick) W(illiam) 1930- ... *55*
Rawlings, Marjorie Kinnan 1896-1953 ... *100*
See also YABC *1*
See also CLR *63*
Rawlins, Donna 1956- ... *206*
Rawlinson, Julia ... *212*
Earlier sketch in SATA *175*
Rawls, (Woodrow) Wilson 1913-1984 ... *22*
See also CLR *81*
Rawlyk, George Alexander 1935- ... *64*
Rawn, Melanie 1954- ... *98*
Rawn, Melanie Robin
See Rawn, Melanie
Rawson, Katherine 1955- ... *190*
Ray, Carl 1943-1978 ... *63*
Ray, Deborah
See Kogan Ray, Deborah
Ray, Delia 1963- ... *179*
Earlier sketch in SATA *70*
Ray, Irene
See Sutton, Margaret Beebe
Ray, Jane 1960- ... *196*
Earlier sketches in SATA *72, 152*
Ray, JoAnne 1935- ... *9*
Ray, Mary (Eva Pedder) 1932- ... *127*
Earlier sketch in SATA *2*
Ray, Mary Lyn 1946- ... *154*
Earlier sketch in SATA *90*
Rayban, Chloe 1944- ... *167*
Rayburn, Tricia ... *234*
Rayevsky, Robert 1955- ... *190*
Earlier sketch in SATA *81*
Raymond, James Crossley 1917-1981
Obituary ... *29*
Raymond, Robert
See Alter, Robert Edmond
Rayner, Catherine ... *204*
Rayner, Hugh ... *151*

Rayner, Mary 1933- 87
Earlier sketch in SATA *22*
See also CLR *41*
Rayner, Shoo
See Rayner, Hugh
Rayner, William 1929- 55
Brief entry 36
Raynor, Dorka 28
Raynor, Gemma 1985- 216
Rayson, Steven 1932- 30
Rayyan, Omar 1968- 216
Razzell, Arthur (George) 1925- 11
Razzell, Mary (Catherine) 1930- 102
Razzi, James 1931- 10
Read, Elfreida 1920- 2
Read, Nicholas 1956- 146
Read, Piers Paul 1941- 21
Reade, Deborah 1949- 69
Reader, Dennis 1929- 71
Reading, Richard P(atrick) 1962- 161
Readman, Jo 1958- 89
Ready, Kirk L(ewis) 1943- 39
Reaney, James 1926-2008 43
Reaney, James Crerar
See Reaney, James
Reardon, Joyce
See Pearson, Ridley
Reaver, Chap 1935-1993 69
Obituary 77
Reaver, Herbert R.
See Reaver, Chap
Reaves, J. Michael
See Reaves, (James) Michael
Reaves, (James) Michael 1950- 99
Reber, Deborah 189
Recorvits, Helen 191
Redding, Robert Hull 1919- 2
Redekopp, Elsa 61
Redlich, Ben 1977- 181
Redsand, Anna 1948- 184
Redway, Ralph
See Hamilton, Charles (Harold St. John)
Redway, Ridley
See Hamilton, Charles (Harold St. John)
Reece, Colleen L. 1935- 116
Reece, Gabrielle 1970- 108
Reed, Amy 1979- 223
Reed, Betty Jane 1921- 4
Reed, Dallas
See Pendleton, Thomas
Reed, E.
See Evans, Mari
Reed, Gwendolyn E(lizabeth) 1932- 21
Reed, Kit 1932- 184
Autobiography Feature 184
Earlier sketches in SATA *34, 116*
Reed, Lynn Rowe 215
Earlier sketch in SATA *171*
Reed, Mike 1951- 211
Reed, Neil 1961- 99
Reed, Talbot Baines 1852-1893
See CLR *76*
Reed, Thomas (James) 1947- 34
Reed, William Maxwell 1871-1962 15
Reeder, Carolyn 1937- 97
Earlier sketch in SATA *66*
See also CLR *69*
Reeder, Colin (Dawson) 1938- 74
Reeder, Colonel Red
See Reeder, Russell P(otter), Jr.
Reeder, Russell P(otter), Jr. 1902-1998 4
Obituary 101
Reeder, Stephanie Owen 1951- 102
Reed-Jones, Carol 1955- 112
Reedy, Trent 1979(?)- 239
Reef, Catherine 1951- 223
Earlier sketches in SATA *73, 128, 189*
Reekie, Jocelyn (Margaret) 1947- 145
Reeman, Douglas Edward 1924- 63
Brief entry 28
Rees, Celia 1949- 124
Rees, David (Bartlett) 1936-1993 69
Obituary 76
Earlier sketch in SATA *36*
See also SAAS *5*
Rees, Douglas 1947- 237
Earlier sketch in SATA *169*
Rees, Ennis (Samuel, Jr.) 1925-2009 3
Rees, (George) Leslie (Clarence) 1905-2000 105
Obituary 135
Reese, Bob
See Reese, Robert A.
Reese, Carolyn Johnson 1938- 64
Reese, Della 1931(?)- 114
Reese, Lyn
See Reese, Carolyn Johnson
Reese, Robert A. 1938- 60
Brief entry 53
Reese, (John) Terence 1913-1996 59
Reeve, Joel
See Cox, William R(obert)
Reeve, Kirk 1934- 117
Reeve, Philip 1966- 241
Earlier sketches in SATA *170, 201*
Reeve, Rosie 188
Earlier sketch in SATA *186*
Reeves, Dia 1977- 227
Reeves, Faye Couch 1953- 76
Reeves, James
See Reeves, John Morris
Reeves, Jeni 1947- 111
Reeves, John Morris 1909-1978 87
Earlier sketch in SATA *15*
Reeves, Joyce 1911- 17
Reeves, Lawrence F. 1926- 29
Reeves, Ruth Ellen
See Ranney, Agnes V.
Regan, Dian Curtis 1950- 224
Autobiography Feature 149
Earlier sketches in SATA *75, 133, 149*
Regehr, Lydia 1903-1991 37
Reger, James P. 1952- 106
Reger, Rob 1969- 227
Reggiani, Renee 1925- 18
Rehm, Karl M. 1935- 72
Reibstein, Mark 211
Reich, Ali
See Katz, Bobbi
Reich, Susanna 1954- 214
Earlier sketch in SATA *113*
Reiche, Dietlof 1941- 159
Reichert, Edwin C(lark) 1909-1988
Obituary 57
Reichert, Mickey Zucker
See Reichert, Miriam Zucker
Reichert, Miriam Zucker 1962- 85
Reichert, Renee 172
Reichhold, Jane(t E.) 1937- 147
Reid, Alastair 1926- 46
Reid, Barbara 1922- 21
Reid, Barbara (Jane) 1957- 93
See also CLR *64*
Reid, Desmond
See Moorcock, Michael
and McNeilly, Wilfred (Glassford)
Reid, Eugenie Chazal 1924- 12
Reid, John Calvin 21
Reid, (Thomas) Mayne 1818-1883 24
Reid, Meta Mayne 1905-1991 58
Brief entry 36
Reid, Robin (Nicole) 1969- 145
Reid Banks, Lynne 1929- 165
Earlier sketches in SATA *22, 75, 111*
See also CLR *86*
Reider, Katja 1960- 126
Reid Jenkins, Debra 1955- 87
Reidy, Jean 228
Reiff, Stephanie Ann 1948- 47
Brief entry 28
Reig, June 1933- 30
Reigot, Betty Polisar 1924- 55
Brief entry 41
Reilly, Joan 195
Reim, Melanie (K.) 1956- 104
Reinach, Jacquelyn (Krasne) 1930-2000 28
Reiner, Carl 1922- 151
Reiner, William B(uck) 1910-1976 46
Obituary 30
Reinfeld, Fred 1910-1964 3
Reinhardt, Dana 1971- 240
Earlier sketch in SATA *175*
Reinhart, Matthew 1971- 197
Earlier sketch in SATA *161*
Reiniger, Lotte 1899-1981 40
Obituary 33
Reinsma, Carol 1949- 91
Reinstedt, Randall A. 1935- 101
Reinstedt, Randy
See Reinstedt, Randall A.
Reisberg, Mira 1955- 82
Reisberg, Veg
See Reisberg, Mira
Reiser, Lynn 1944- 180
Earlier sketches in SATA *81, 138*
Reiser, Lynn Whisnant
See Reiser, Lynn
Reisgies, Teresa (Maria) 1966- 74
Reiss, Johanna 1929(?)- 18
See also CLR *19*
Reiss, Johanna de Leeuw
See Reiss, Johanna
Reiss, John J. 23
Reiss, Kathryn 1957- 144
Earlier sketch in SATA *76*
Reit, Seymour Victory 1918-2001 21
Obituary 133
Reit, Sy
See Reit, Seymour Victory
Relf, Patricia 1954- 134
Earlier sketch in SATA *71*
Remark, Erich Paul
See Remarque, Erich Maria
Remarque, Erich Maria 1898-1970
See CLR *159*
Remi, Georges 1907-1983 13
Obituary 32
See also CLR *114*
Remington, Frederic S(ackrider) 1861-1909 41
Remkiewicz, Frank 1939- 217
Earlier sketches in SATA *77, 152*
Rempt, Fiona 1973- 198
Remy, Georges
See Remi, Georges
Renaud, Anne 1957- 211
Renaud, Bernadette 1945- 66
Renault, Mary 1905-1983 23
Obituary 36
Rendell, Joan 28
Rendina, Laura (Jones) Cooper 1902- 10
Rendon, Marcie R. 1952- 97
Rendon, Maria 1965- 116
Renee, Janina 1956- 140
Renfro, Ed 1924- 79
Renick, Marion (Lewis) 1905-1983 1
Renier, Aaron 1977- 202
Renken, Aleda 1907- 27
Renlie, Frank H. 1936- 11
Rennert, Laura Joy 224
Rennert, Richard Scott 1956- 67
Rennison, Louise 1951- 149
Reno, Dawn E(laine) 1953- 130
Rensie, Willis
See Eisner, Will
Renton, Cam
See Armstrong, Richard
Renvoize, Jean 5
Resau, Laura 1973- 230
Earlier sketch in SATA *190*
Resciniti, Angelo G. 1952- 75

Resnick, Michael David
See Resnick, Mike
Resnick, Mike 1942- *159*
Earlier sketches in SATA *38, 106*
Resnick, Seymour 1920- *23*
Restrepo, Bettina 1972- *241*
Retla, Robert
See Alter, Robert Edmond
Rettig, Liz *199*
Rettstatt, Chris
See Ashland, Monk
Reuter, Bjarne (B.) 1950- *142*
Earlier sketch in SATA *68*
Reuter, Carol (Joan) 1931- *2*
Revena
See Wright, Betty Ren
Revis, Beth *240*
Revsbech, Vicki
See Liestman, Vicki
Rex, Adam *225*
Earlier sketch in SATA *186*
Rex, Michael *191*
Rey, H. A. 1898-1977 .... *100*
Earlier sketches in SATA *1, 26, 69*
See also CLR *93*
Rey, Hans Augusto
See Rey, H. A.
Rey, Luis V. 1955- *201*
Rey, Margret 1906-1996 .... *86*
Obituary *93*
Earlier sketch in SATA *26*
See also CLR *93*
Rey, Margret Elisabeth
See Rey, Margret
Reyher, Becky
See Reyher, Rebecca Hourwich
Reyher, Rebecca Hourwich 1897-1987 .... *18*
Obituary *50*
Reynish, Jenny *222*
Reynold, Ann
See Bernardo, Anilu
Reynolds, Aaron 1970- *197*
Reynolds, Adrian 1963- *192*
Reynolds, C. Buck 1957- *107*
Reynolds, Dickson
See Reynolds, Helen Mary Greenwood Campbell
Reynolds, Helen Mary Greenwood Campbell 1884-1969
Obituary *26*
Reynolds, Jan 1956- *180*
Reynolds, John
See Whitlock, Ralph
Reynolds, Madge
See Whitlock, Ralph
Reynolds, Malvina 1900-1978 .... *44*
Obituary *24*
Reynolds, Marilyn 1935- *121*
See also SAAS *23*
Reynolds, Marilyn M.
See Reynolds, Marilyn
Reynolds, Marilynn 1940- *141*
Earlier sketch in SATA *80*
Reynolds, Pamela 1923- *34*
Reynolds, Peter H. 1961- *226*
Earlier sketch in SATA *128*
Reynolds, Peter J. 1961- *179*
Reynolds, Susan *179*
Rhine, Richard
See Silverstein, Alvin
and Silverstein, Virginia B.
Rhoades, Diane 1952- *90*
Rhodes, Bennie (Loran) 1927- *35*
Rhodes, Donna McKee 1962- *87*
Rhodes, Frank Harold Trevor 1926- *37*
Rhuday-Perkovich, Olugbemisola *227*
Rhue, Morton
See Strasser, Todd
Rhyne, Nancy 1926- *66*
Rhynes, Martha E. 1939- *141*
Ribbons, Ian 1924- *37*
Brief entry *30*
See also SAAS *3*
Ricciuti, Edward R(aphael) 1938- *10*
Rice, Alice (Caldwell) Hegan 1870-1942 .... *63*
Rice, Bebe Faas 1932- *89*
Rice, Charles D(uane) 1910-1971
Obituary *27*
Rice, Dale R. 1948- *42*
Rice, Dale Richard
See Rice, Dale R.
Rice, Dick
See Rice, R. Hugh
Rice, Earle (Wilmont), Jr. 1928- *151*
Earlier sketch in SATA *92*
Rice, Edward 1918-2001 .... *47*
Brief entry *42*
Rice, Elizabeth 1913-1976 .... *2*
Rice, Eve 1951- *91*
Earlier sketch in SATA *34*
Rice, Eve Hart
See Rice, Eve
Rice, Inez 1907- *13*
Rice, James 1934- *93*
Earlier sketch in SATA *22*
Rice, John F. 1958- *82*
Rice, R. Hugh 1929- *115*
Rice, Richard H.
See Rice, R. Hugh
Rich, Anna 1956- *212*
Rich, Barbara
See Graves, Robert
Rich, Elaine Sommers 1926- *6*
Rich, Josephine Bouchard 1912- *10*
Rich, Louise Dickinson 1903-1991 .... *54*
Obituary *67*
Rich, Naomi *217*
Richard, Adrienne 1921- *5*
See also SAAS *9*
Richard, James Robert
See Bowen, Robert Sydney
Richards, Chuck 1957- *170*
Richards, Frank
See Hamilton, Charles (Harold St. John)
Richards, Hilda
See Hamilton, Charles (Harold St. John)
Richards, Jackie 1925- *102*
Richards, Jame *230*
Richards, Jean 1940- *135*
Richards, Justin *169*
Richards, Kay
See Baker, Susan (Catherine)
Richards, Laura E(lizabeth Howe) 1850-1943
See YABC *1*
See also CLR *54*
Richards, Leigh
See King, Laurie R.
Richards, Marlee
See Brill, Marlene Targ
Richards, Norman 1932- *48*
Richards, R(onald) C(harles) W(illiam) 1923- *59*
Brief entry *43*
Richards, Scott
See Card, Orson Scott
Richards, Walter Alden (Jr.) 1907-1988
Obituary *56*
Richardson, Andrew (William) 1986- *120*
Richardson, Carol 1932- *58*
Richardson, Frank Howard 1882-1970
Obituary *27*
Richardson, Grace Lee
See Dickson, Naida
Richardson, Jean (Mary) *59*
Richardson, Judith Benet 1941- *77*
Richardson, Nigel 1957- *187*
Richardson, Robert S(hirley) 1902-1981 .... *8*
Richardson, Sandy 1949- *116*
Richardson, V.A. *189*
Richardson, Willis 1889-1977 .... *60*
Richelson, Geraldine 1922- *29*
Richemont, Enid 1940- *82*
Richler, Mordecai 1931-2001 .... *98*
Brief entry *27*
Earlier sketch in SATA *44*
See also CLR *17*
Richman, Sophia 1941- *142*
Rich-McCoy, Lois
See McCoy, Lois (Rich)
Richmond, Robin 1951- *75*
Richoux, Pat(ricia) 1927- *7*
Richter, Alice 1941- *30*
Richter, Conrad (Michael) 1890-1968 .... *3*
Richter, Hans Peter 1925-1993 .... *6*
See also CLR *21*
See also SAAS *11*
Richter, Jutta 1955- *184*
Rickard, Graham 1949- *71*
Rico, Don(ato) 1917-1985
Obituary *43*
Riddell, Chris 1962- *219*
Earlier sketches in SATA *114, 166*
Riddell, Christopher Barry
See Riddell, Chris
Riddell, Edwina 1955- *82*
Ridden, Brian 1934- *123*
See Ridden, Brian John
Riddle, Tohby 1965- *223*
Earlier sketches in SATA *74, 151*
Riddleburger, Sam *202*
Riddles, Libby 1956- *140*
Ride, Sally 1951- *219*
Ride, Sally Kristen
See Ride, Sally
Rideout, Sandy *194*
Rider, D. F.
See Perrin, Pat
Rider, David F.
See Perrin, Pat
Ridge, Antonia (Florence) (?)-1981 .... *7*
Obituary *27*
Ridge, Martin 1923-2003 .... *43*
Ridley, Philip *171*
Earlier sketch in SATA *88*
Ridlon, Marci
See Balterman, Marcia Ridlon
Riedman, Sarah R(egal) 1902-1995 .... *1*
Riehecky, Janet 1953- *164*
Ries, Lori *237*
Earlier sketch in SATA *185*
Riesenberg, Felix, Jr. 1913-1962 .... *23*
Rieu, E(mile) V(ictor) 1887-1972 .... *46*
Obituary *26*
Riffenburgh, Beau 1955- *175*
Rigg, Sharon
See Creech, Sharon
Riggenbach, Holly
See Black, Holly
Riggio, Anita 1952- *148*
Earlier sketch in SATA *73*
Riggs, Shannon *190*
Riggs, Sidney Noyes 1892-1975
Obituary *28*
Riggs, Stephanie 1964- *138*
Riglietti, Serena 1969- *189*
Rigney, James Oliver, Jr.
See Jordan, Robert
Rikhoff, Jean 1928- *9*
Rikki
See Ducornet, Erica
Riley, James A. 1939- *97*
Riley, James Whitcomb 1849-1916 .... *17*
Riley, Jocelyn 1949- *60*
Brief entry *50*
Riley, Jocelyn Carol
See Riley, Jocelyn
Riley, Linda Capus 1950- *85*
Riley, Martin 1948- *81*
Riley-Webb, Charlotte 1948- *235*
Rim, Sujean *225*
Rimbauer, Steven
See Pearson, Ridley

Rimes, (Margaret) LeAnn 1982- *154*
Rinaldi, Ann 1934- *202*
Brief entry *50*
Earlier sketches in SATA *51, 78, 117, 161*
See also CLR *46*
Rinard, Judith E(llen) 1947- *140*
Earlier sketch in SATA *44*
Rinck, Maranke 1976- *214*
Rinder, Lenore 1949- *92*
Ring, Elizabeth 1920- *79*
Ringdalh, Mark
See Longyear, Barry B(rookes)
Ringgold, Faith 1930- *187*
Earlier sketches in SATA *71, 114*
See also CLR *174*
Ringi, Kjell (Arne Soerensen) 1939- *12*
Rinkoff, Barbara Jean (Rich) 1923-1975 .... *4*
Obituary *27*
Rinn, Miriam 1946- *127*
Riordan, James 1936- *95*
Riordan, Rick *238*
Earlier sketches in SATA *174, 208*
Rios, Tere
See Versace, Marie Teresa Rios
Rioux, Jo *226*
Rioux, Jo-Anne
See Rioux, Jo
Ripken, Cal, Jr. 1960- *215*
Earlier sketch in SATA *114*
Ripken, Calvin Edward, Jr.
See Ripken, Cal, Jr.
Ripley, Catherine 1957- *82*
Ripley, Elizabeth Blake 1906-1969 .... *5*
Ripper, Charles L(ewis) 1929- *3*
Ripper, Chuck
See Ripper, Charles L(ewis)
Rippin, Sally *220*
Riq
See Atwater, Richard
Rish, David 1955- *110*
Riskind, Mary 1944- *60*
Rissinger, Matt 1956- *93*
Rissman, Art
See Sussman, Susan
Rissman, Susan
See Sussman, Susan
Ritchie, Barbara Gibbons *14*
Ritchie, Scot 1954- *217*
Ritter, Felix
See Kruss, James
Ritter, John H. 1951- *215*
Earlier sketches in SATA *129, 137*
Ritter, Lawrence S(tanley) 1922-2004 .... *58*
Obituary *152*
Ritthaler, Shelly 1955- *91*
Ritts, Paul 1920(?)-1980
Obituary *25*
Ritz, Karen 1957- *202*
Earlier sketch in SATA *80*
Riu, Isabel Ferrer 1969- *222*
Rivera, Geraldo (Miguel) 1943- *54*
Brief entry *28*
Rivera, Guadalupe
See Rivera Marin, Guadalupe
Rivera Marin, Guadalupe 1924- *224*
Rivers, Elfrida
See Bradley, Marion Zimmer
Rivers, Karen 1970- *131*
Riverside, John
See Heinlein, Robert A.
Rivkin, Ann 1920- *41*
Rivoli, Mario 1943- *10*
Roach, Marilynne K. 1946- *9*
Roach, Marilynne Kathleen
See Roach, Marilynne K.
Roach, Portia
See Takakjian, Portia
Robb, Don 1937- *194*
Robb, Laura 1937- *95*
Robberecht, Thierry 1960- *182*
Robbins, Frank 1917-1994(?) *42*
Brief entry *32*
Robbins, Jacqui *221*
Robbins, Ken 1945- *219*
Brief entry *53*
Earlier sketches in SATA *94, 147*
Robbins, Raleigh
See Hamilton, Charles (Harold St. John)
Robbins, Ruth 1917(?)- *14*
Robbins, Tony
See Pashko, Stanley
Robbins, Wayne
See Cox, William R(obert)
Robel, S. L.
See Fraustino, Lisa Rowe
Roberson, Jennifer 1953- *72*
Roberson, John R(oyster) 1930- *53*
Robert, Adrian
See St. John, Nicole
Roberton, Fiona *230*
Roberts, Bethany *202*
Earlier sketch in SATA *133*
Roberts, Bruce (Stuart) 1930- *47*
Brief entry *39*
Roberts, Charles G(eorge) D(ouglas)
1860-1943 .... *88*
Brief entry *29*
See also CLR *33*
Roberts, David
See Cox, John Roberts
Roberts, David 1970- *191*
Roberts, Diane 1937- *184*
Roberts, Elizabeth 1944- *80*
Roberts, Elizabeth Madox 1886-1941 .... *33*
Brief entry *27*
See also CLR *100*
Roberts, Jim
See Bates, Barbara S(nedeker)
Roberts, Jody *218*
Roberts, John G(aither) 1913-1993 .... *27*
Roberts, Judy I. 1957- *93*
Roberts, Katherine 1962- *152*
Roberts, Ken *223*
See Lake, Kenneth R(obert)
Roberts, Laura Peyton *232*
Roberts, M. L.
See Mattern, Joanne
Roberts, Marion 1966- *212*
Roberts, Nancy Correll 1924- *52*
Brief entry *28*
Roberts, Priscilla 1955- *184*
Roberts, Terence
See Sanderson, Ivan T(erence)
Roberts, Willo Davis 1928-2004 .... *150*
Autobiography Feature *150*
Obituary *160*
Earlier sketches in SATA *21, 70, 133*
See also CLR *95*
See also SAAS *8*
Robertson, Barbara (Anne) 1931- *12*
Robertson, Don 1929-1999 .... *8*
Obituary *113*
Robertson, Dorothy Lewis 1912- *12*
Robertson, Ellis
See Ellison, Harlan
and Silverberg, Robert
Robertson, James I., Jr. 1930- *182*
Robertson, James Irvin
See Robertson, James I., Jr.
Robertson, Janet (E.) 1935- *68*
Robertson, Jennifer Sinclair 1942-1998 .... *12*
Robertson, Jenny
See Robertson, Jennifer Sinclair
Robertson, Keith (Carlton) 1914-1991 .... *85*
Obituary *69*
Earlier sketch in SATA *1*
See also SAAS *15*
Robertson, Mark
See Robertson, M.P.
Robertson, M.P. 1965- *197*
Robertson, Stephen
See Walker, Robert W.
Robertus, Polly M. 1948- *212*
Earlier sketch in SATA *73*
Robeson, Kenneth
See Dent, Lester
and Goulart, Ron
Robeson, Kenneth
See Johnson, (Walter) Ryerson
Robinet, Harriette Gillem 1931- *104*
Earlier sketch in SATA *27*
See also CLR *64*
Robins, Deri 1958- *166*
Earlier sketch in SATA *117*
Robins, Patricia 1921- *117*
Robins, Rollo, Jr.
See Ellis, Edward S.
Robins, Seelin
See Ellis, Edward S.
Robinson, Adjai 1932- *8*
Robinson, Aminah Brenda Lynn 1940- *159*
Earlier sketch in SATA *77*
Robinson, Barbara (Webb) 1927- *84*
Earlier sketch in SATA *8*
Robinson, C(harles) A(lexander), Jr.
1900-1965 .... *36*
Robinson, Charles 1870-1937 .... *17*
Robinson, Charles 1931- *6*
Robinson, Dorothy W. 1929- *54*
Robinson, Elizabeth Keeler 1959- *204*
Robinson, Eve
See Tanselle, Eve
Robinson, Fiona 1965- *225*
Robinson, Glen 1953- *92*
Robinson, Glendal P.
See Robinson, Glen
Robinson, Jan M. 1933- *6*
Robinson, Jean O. 1934- *7*
Robinson, Joan (Mary) G(ale Thomas)
1910-1988 .... *7*
Robinson, Kim Stanley 1952- *109*
Robinson, Lee 1948- *110*
Robinson, Lloyd
See Silverberg, Robert
Robinson, Lynda S(uzanne) 1951- *107*
Robinson, Marileta 1942- *32*
Robinson, Maudie Millian Oller 1914- *11*
Robinson, Maurice R(ichard) 1895-1982
Obituary *29*
Robinson, Nancy K(onheim) 1942-1994 .... *91*
Brief entry *31*
Obituary *79*
Earlier sketch in SATA *32*
Robinson, Ray 1920- *23*
Robinson, Raymond Kenneth
See Robinson, Ray
Robinson, Shari
See McGuire, Leslie (Sarah)
Robinson, Sharon 1950- *197*
Earlier sketch in SATA *162*
Robinson, Spider 1948- *118*
Robinson, Sue
See Robinson, Susan Maria
Robinson, Susan Maria 1955- *105*
Robinson, Susan Patricia
See Gates, Susan
Robinson, Suzanne
See Robinson, Lynda S(uzanne)
Robinson, T(homas) H(eath) 1869-1950 .... *17*
Robinson, Tim 1963- *205*
Robinson, (Wanda) Veronica 1926- *30*
Robinson, W(illiam) Heath 1872-1944 .... *17*
Robison, Bonnie 1924- *12*
Robison, Nancy L(ouise) 1934- *32*
Robles, Harold E. 1948- *87*
Robottom, John 1934- *7*
Robson, Eric 1939- *82*
Roca, Francois 1971- *200*
Rocco, John 1967- *188*

Roche, A. K.
See Abisch, Roslyn Kroop
and Kaplan, Boche
Roche, Denis 1967- *196*
Earlier sketch in SATA *99*
Roche, Denis Mary
See Roche, Denis
Roche, Luane 1937- *170*
Roche, P(atricia) K. 1935- *57*
Brief entry *34*
Roche, Terry
See Poole, Peggy
Rochman, Hazel 1938- *105*
Rock, Lois
See Joslin, Mary
Rock, Maxine 1940- *108*
Rocker, Fermin 1907- *40*
Rockliff, Mara *224*
Rocklin, Joanne 1946- *134*
Earlier sketch in SATA *86*
Rockwell, Anne 1934- *235*
Earlier sketches in SATA *33, 71, 114, 162, 194*
See also SAAS *19*
Rockwell, Anne F.
See Rockwell, Anne
Rockwell, Anne Foote
See Rockwell, Anne
Rockwell, Bart
See Pellowski, Michael (Joseph)
Rockwell, Harlow 1910-1988 .... *33*
Obituary *56*
Rockwell, Lizzy 1961- *233*
Earlier sketch in SATA *185*
Rockwell, Norman (Percevel) 1894-1978 .... *23*
Rockwell, Thomas 1933- *231*
Earlier sketches in SATA *7, 70*
See also CLR *6*
Rockwood, Joyce 1947- *39*
Rockwood, Roy
See McFarlane, Leslie
and Stratemeyer, Edward L.
Rodanas, Kristina 1952- *155*
Rodari, Gianni 1920-1980
See CLR *24*
Rodd, Kathleen Tennant
See Rodd, Kylie Tennant
Rodd, Kylie Tennant 1912-1988 .... *57*
Obituary *55*
Earlier sketch in SATA *6*
Rodda, Emily 1948- *230*
Earlier sketches in SATA *97, 146*
See also CLR *32*
Roddenberry, Eugene Wesley 1921-1991 .... *45*
Obituary *69*
Roddenberry, Gene
See Roddenberry, Eugene Wesley
Roddick, Ellen 1936- *5*
Roddie, Shen *153*
Roddy, Lee 1921- *57*
Rodenas, Paula *73*
Rodgers, Frank 1944- *69*
Rodgers, Mary 1931- *130*
Earlier sketch in SATA *8*
See also CLR *20*
Rodman, Emerson
See Ellis, Edward S.
Rodman, Eric
See Silverberg, Robert
Rodman, Maia
See Wojciechowska, Maia (Teresa)
Rodman, Mary Ann *185*
Rodman, (Cary) Selden 1909-2002 .... *9*
Rodowsky, Colby 1932- *164*
Earlier sketches in SATA *21, 77, 120*
See also SAAS *22*
Rodowsky, Colby F.
See Rodowsky, Colby
Rodriguez, Alejo 1941- *83*
Rodriguez, Alex 1975- *189*
Rodriguez, Beatrice 1969- *230*
Rodriguez, Christina 1981- *177*
Rodriguez, Edel 1971- *196*
Rodriguez, Luis J. 1954- *125*
Rodriguez, Rachel *180*
Rodriguez, Rachel Victoria
See Rodriguez, Rachel
Roeder, Virginia Marsh 1926- *98*
Roehrig, Catharine H. 1949- *67*
Roennfeldt, Robert 1953- *78*
Roessel-Waugh, C. C.
See Waugh, Carol-Lynn Rossel
and Waugh, Charles G(ordon)
Roets, Lois F. 1937- *91*
Roever, J(oan) M(arilyn) 1935- *26*
Rofes, Eric 1954-2006 .... *52*
Rofes, Eric Edward 1954-2006
See Rofes, Eric
Roffey, Maureen 1936- *33*
Rogak, Lisa 1962- *80*
Rogak, Lisa Angowski
See Rogak, Lisa
Rogan, S. Jones *199*
Rogan, Sally Jones
See Rogan, S. Jones
Rogasky, Barbara 1933- *144*
Earlier sketch in SATA *86*
Roge 1972- *233*
Rogers, (Thomas) Alan (Stinchcombe) 1937- *81*
Earlier sketch in SATA *2*
Rogers, Bettye 1858-1919 .... *103*
Rogers, Cindy 1950- *89*
Rogers, Emma 1951- *74*
Rogers, Frances 1888-1974 .... *10*
Rogers, Fred McFeely 1928-2003 .... *33*
Obituary *138*
Rogers, Gregory 1957- *211*
Rogers, Hal
See Sirimarco, Elizabeth
Rogers, Jacqueline 1958- *213*
Rogers, Jean 1919- *55*
Brief entry *47*
Rogers, Matilda 1894-1976 .... *5*
Obituary *34*
Rogers, Pamela 1927- *9*
Rogers, Paul 1950- *98*
Earlier sketch in SATA *54*
Rogers, Robert
See Hamilton, Charles (Harold St. John)
Rogers, Sherry *193*
Rogers, W(illiam) G(arland) 1896-1978 .... *23*
Rohan, M. S.
See Rohan, Michael Scott
Rohan, Michael Scott 1951- *98*
Rohan, Mike Scott
See Rohan, Michael Scott
Rohmann, Eric 1957- *239*
Earlier sketch in SATA *171*
See also CLR *100*
Rohmer, Harriet 1938- *56*
Rohrer, Doug 1962- *89*
Rojan
See Rojankovsky, Feodor (Stepanovich)
Rojankovsky, Feodor (Stepanovich) 1891-1970 .... *21*
Rojany, Lisa *94*
Rokeby-Thomas, Anna E(lma) 1911- *15*
Roland, Albert 1925-2002 .... *11*
Roland, Mary
See Lewis, Mary
Roleff, Tamara L. 1959- *143*
Rolerson, Darrell A(llen) 1946- *8*
Roll, Winifred 1909-1998 .... *6*
Rollins, Charlemae Hill 1897-1979 .... *3*
Obituary *26*
Rollins, James 1961- *216*
Rollock, Barbara T(herese) 1924- *64*
Rolston, Steve 1978- *209*
Romack, Janice Reed
See LeNoir, Janice
Romain, Trevor *134*
Romanenko, Vitaliy 1962- *101*
Romano, Christy
See Romano, Christy Carlson
Romano, Christy Carlson 1984- *210*
Romano, Clare 1922- *111*
Earlier sketch in SATA *48*
Romano, Louis G. 1921- *35*
Romano, Melora A. 1966- *118*
Romano, Ray 1957- *170*
Romano, Raymond
See Romano, Ray
Romijn, Johanna Maria Kooyker
See Kooyker-Romijn, Johanna Maria
Romyn, Johanna Maria Kooyker
See Kooyker-Romijn, Johanna Maria
Rong, Yu 1970- *174*
Rongen, Bjoern 1906- *10*
Rongen, Bjorn
See Rongen, Bjoern
Ronson, Mark
See Alexander, Marc
Rood, Ronald (N.) 1920- *12*
Rook, Sebastian
See Jeapes, Ben
Rooke, Daphne 1914-2009 .... *12*
Rooke, Daphne Marie
See Rooke, Daphne
Rooney, Ronnie 1970- *212*
Roop, Connie 1951- *167*
Brief entry *49*
Earlier sketches in SATA *54, 116*
Roop, Constance Betzer
See Roop, Connie
Roop, Peter 1951- *167*
Brief entry *49*
Earlier sketches in SATA *54, 116*
Roop, Peter G.
See Roop, Peter
Roop, Peter Geiger
See Roop, Peter
Roos, Maryn *225*
Roos, Stephen 1945- *128*
Brief entry *41*
Earlier sketches in SATA *47, 77*
Roosa, Karen 1961- *218*
Roose-Evans, James 1927- *65*
Roosevelt, Eleanor 1884-1962 .... *50*
Root, Barry *232*
Earlier sketch in SATA *182*
Root, Betty *84*
Root, Kimberly Bulcken *192*
Root, Phyllis 1949- *224*
Brief entry *48*
Earlier sketches in SATA *55, 94, 145, 184*
Root, Shelton L., Jr. 1923-1986
Obituary *51*
Roper, Laura (Newbold) Wood 1911-2003 .... *34*
Obituary *150*
Roper, Robert 1946- *142*
Earlier sketch in SATA *78*
Roraback, Robin (Ellan) 1964- *111*
Rorby, Ginny 1944- *238*
Earlier sketch in SATA *94*
Rorer, Abigail 1949- *85*
Rosaler, Maxine *208*
Rosamel, Godeleine de 1968- *151*
Roscoe, D(onald) T(homas) 1934- *42*
Rose, Anne *8*
Rose, Deborah Lee 1955- *185*
Earlier sketches in SATA *71, 124*
Rose, Elizabeth (Jane Pretty) 1933- *68*
Brief entry *28*
Rose, Florella
See Carlson, Vada F.
Rose, Gerald (Hembdon Seymour) 1935- *68*
Brief entry *30*
Rose, Malcolm 1953- *168*
Earlier sketch in SATA *107*
Rose, Nancy A.
See Sweetland, Nancy A(nn)
Rose, Naomi C. *228*

Rose, Ted 1940- *93*
Rose, Wendy 1948- *12*
Rosen, Elizabeth 1961- *205*
Rosen, Lillian (Diamond) 1928- *63*
Rosen, Marvin 1933- *161*
Rosen, Michael 1946- *229*
Brief entry *40*
Earlier sketches in SATA *48, 84, 137, 181*
See also CLR *45*
Rosen, Michael J. 1954- *199*
Earlier sketch in SATA *86*
Rosen, Michael Wayne
See Rosen, Michael
Rosen, Sidney 1916- *1*
Rosen, Winifred 1943- *8*
Rosenbaum, Maurice 1907-1987 .... *6*
Rosenberg, Amye 1950- *74*
Rosenberg, Dorothy 1906- *40*
Rosenberg, Eth Clifford 1915- *92*
See also SAAS *22*
Rosenberg, Jane 1949- *58*
Rosenberg, Liz 1958- *129*
Earlier sketch in SATA *75*
Rosenberg, Maxine B(erta) 1939- *93*
Brief entry *47*
Earlier sketch in SATA *55*
Rosenberg, Nancy 1931- *4*
Rosenberg, Sharon 1942- *8*
Rosenberry, Vera 1948- *219*
Earlier sketches in SATA *83, 144*
Rosenblatt, Arthur
See Rosenblatt, Arthur S.
Rosenblatt, Arthur S. 1938- *68*
Brief entry *45*
Rosenblatt, Lily 1956- *90*
Rosenbloom, Joseph 1928- *21*
Rosenblum, Richard 1928- *11*
Rosenburg, John M. 1918- *6*
Rosenfeld, Dina 1962- *99*
Rosenstiehl, Agnes 1941- *203*
Rosenstock, Barb 1960- *241*
Rosenstock, Jason 1978- *238*
Rosenthal, Amy Krouse 1965- *222*
Earlier sketch in SATA *177*
Rosenthal, Betsy R. 1957- *178*
Rosenthal, Eileen *239*
Rosenthal, Harold 1914-1999 .... *35*
Rosenthal, M(acha) L(ouis) 1917-1996 .... *59*
Rosenthal, Marc 1949- *193*
Rosenthal, Mark A(lan) 1946- *64*
Rosing, Norbert 1953- *196*
Rosman, Steven M 1956- *81*
Rosman, Steven Michael
See Rosman, Steven M
Rosoff, Meg 1956- *209*
Earlier sketch in SATA *160*
Ross, Alan
See Warwick, Alan R(oss)
Ross, Christine 1950- *172*
Earlier sketch in SATA *83*
Ross, Clare
See Romano, Clare
Ross, Dana Fuller
See Cockrell, Amanda
and Gerson, Noel Bertram
Ross, Dave
See Ross, David
Ross, David 1896-1975 .... *49*
Obituary *20*
Ross, David 1949- *133*
Earlier sketch in SATA *32*
Ross, Deborah J.
See Wheeler, Deborah
Ross, Diana
See Denney, Diana
Ross, Edward S(hearman) 1915- *85*
Ross, Eileen 1950- *115*
Ross, Frank (Xavier), Jr. 1914- *28*
Ross, Jane 1961- *79*
Ross, John 1921- *45*
Ross, Judy 1942- *54*
Ross, Katharine Reynolds
See Ross, Kathy
Ross, Kathy 1948- *169*
Earlier sketch in SATA *89*
Ross, Kent 1956- *91*
Ross, Lillian Hammer 1925- *72*
Ross, Michael Elsohn 1952- *170*
Earlier sketches in SATA *80, 127*
Ross, Pat(ricia Kienzle) 1943- *53*
Brief entry *48*
Ross, Ramon R(oyal) 1930- *62*
Ross, Stewart 1947- *134*
Earlier sketch in SATA *92*
See also SAAS *23*
Ross, Sylvia 1937- *231*
Ross, Tom 1958- *84*
Ross, Tony 1938- *225*
Earlier sketches in SATA *17, 65, 130, 176*
Ross, Wilda 1915- *51*
Brief entry *39*
Rossel, Seymour 1945- *28*
Rossell, Judith 1953- *187*
Rossel-Waugh, C. C.
See Waugh, Carol-Lynn Rossel
Rossetti, Christina 1830-1894 .... *20*
See also CLR *115*
Rossetti, Christina Georgina
See Rossetti, Christina
Rossi, Joyce 1943- *116*
Rossotti, Hazel Swaine 1930- *95*
Rostkowski, Margaret I. 1945- *59*
Rostoker-Gruber, Karen *229*
Roth, Arnold 1929- *21*
Roth, Arthur J(oseph) 1925-1993 .... *43*
Brief entry *28*
Obituary *75*
See also SAAS *11*
Roth, Carol *222*
Roth, David 1940- *36*
Roth, Julie Jersild *180*
Roth, Matthue 1978(?)- *174*
Roth, R.G.
See Roth, Robert
Roth, Rob
See Roth, Robert
Roth, Robert 1965- *230*
Roth, Roger *190*
Roth, Ruby 1983(?)- *216*
Roth, Stephanie
See Sisson, Stephanie Roth
Roth, Susan L. *181*
Earlier sketch in SATA *134*
Roth, Ty 1962- *239*
Rothberg, Abraham 1922-2011 .... *59*
Roth-Hano, Renee 1931- *85*
Rothkopf, Carol Z. 1929- *4*
Rothman, Joel 1938- *7*
Rotner, Shelley 1951- *169*
Earlier sketch in SATA *76*
Rottman, S.L. 1970- *157*
Earlier sketch in SATA *106*
Rottman, Susan Lynn
See Rottman, S.L.
Roueche, Berton 1911-1994 .... *28*
Roughsey, Dick 1921(?)-1985 .... *35*
See also CLR *41*
Roughsey, Goobalathaldin
See Roughsey, Dick
Rounds, Glen (Harold) 1906-2002 .... *112*
Obituary *141*
Earlier sketches in SATA *8, 70*
Rourke, Constance Mayfield 1885-1941
See YABC *1*
Rouss, Sylvia *211*
Rovetch, Gerda 1925(?)- *202*
Rovetch, L. Bob
See Rovetch, Lissa
Rovetch, Lissa *201*
Rowan, Deirdre
See Williams, Jeanne
Rowe, Jennifer
See Rodda, Emily
Rowe, John A. 1949- *198*
Earlier sketch in SATA *146*
Rowe, Viola Carson 1903-1969
Obituary *26*
Rowh, Mark 1952- *90*
Rowland, Florence Wightman 1900-1997 .... *8*
Obituary *108*
Rowland-Entwistle, (Arthur) Theodore (Henry) 1925- *94*
Earlier sketch in SATA *31*
Rowling, J.K. 1965- *174*
Earlier sketch in SATA *109*
See also CLR *112*
Rowling, Joanne Kathleen
See Rowling, J.K.
Rowsome, Frank (Howard), Jr. 1914-1983 .. *36*
Roy, Gabrielle 1909-1983 .... *104*
Roy, Jacqueline 1954- *74*
Roy, James 1968- *218*
Roy, Jennifer
See Roy, Jennifer Rozines
Roy, Jennifer Rozines 1967- *178*
Roy, Jessie Hailstalk 1895-1986
Obituary *51*
Roy, Kari Anne 1977(?)- *221*
Roy, Lena *238*
Roy, Liam
See Scarry, Patricia (Murphy)
Roy, Ron 1940- *228*
Brief entry *35*
Earlier sketches in SATA *40, 110*
Roybal, Laura 1956- *85*
Roybal, Laura Husby
See Roybal, Laura
Royds, Caroline 1953- *55*
Royston, Angela 1945- *230*
Earlier sketches in SATA *120, 169*
Rozakis, Laurie E. 1952- *84*
Rozen, Anna 1960- *206*
Rubbino, Salvatore 1970- *220*
Rubel, David 1961- *223*
Rubel, Nicole 1953- *181*
Earlier sketches in SATA *18, 95, 135*
Rubin, Eva Johanna 1925- *38*
Rubin, Susan Goldman 1939- *182*
Earlier sketches in SATA *84, 132*
Rubin, Vicky 1964- *193*
Rubinetti, Donald 1947- *92*
Rubinger, Ami 1953- *225*
Rubinstein, Gillian 1942- *158*
Autobiography Feature *116*
Earlier sketches in SATA *68, 105*
See also CLR *35*
See also SAAS *25*
Rubinstein, Gillian Margaret
See Rubinstein, Gillian
Rubinstein, Patricia -2003
See Forest, Antonia
Rubinstein, Patricia Giulia Caulfield Kate
See Forest, Antonia
Rubinstein, Robert E(dward) 1943- *49*
Rublowsky, John M(artin) 1928- *62*
Rubright, Lynn 1936- *171*
Ruby, Laura *227*
Earlier sketches in SATA *155, 181*
Ruby, Lois 1942- *184*
Autobiography Feature *105*
Brief entry *34*
Earlier sketches in SATA *35, 95*
Ruby, Lois F.
See Ruby, Lois
Ruchlis, Hy(man) 1913-1992 .... *3*
Obituary *72*
Ruckdeschel, Liz *214*
Rucker, Mike 1940- *91*
Ruckman, Ivy 1931- *93*
Earlier sketch in SATA *37*
Ruck-Pauquet, Gina 1931- *40*
Brief entry *37*

Ruddell, Deborah 1949- *210*
Ruditis, Paul *190*
Rudley, Stephen 1946- *30*
Rudnicki, Richard *241*
Rudolph, Marguerita 1908- *21*
Rudomin, Esther
See Hautzig, Esther Rudomin
Rue, Ginger *236*
Rue, Leonard Lee III 1926- *142*
Earlier sketch in SATA *37*
Rue, Nancy 1951- *233*
Rue, Nancy N.
See Rue, Nancy
Rue, Nancy Naylor
See Rue, Nancy
Rueda, Claudia *183*
Ruedi, Norma Paul
See Ainsworth, Norma
Ruelle, Karen Gray 1957- *209*
Earlier sketches in SATA *84, 126*
Ruemmler, John D(avid) 1948- *78*
Ruepp, Krista 1947- *143*
Ruffell, Ann 1941- *30*
Ruffins, Reynold 1930- *125*
Earlier sketch in SATA *41*
Rugg, Jim *206*
Ruggles, Lucy
See Williams, Kathryn
Rugoff, Milton 1913- *30*
Ruhen, Olaf 1911-1989 .... *17*
Rui, Paolo 1962- *217*
Rukeyser, Muriel 1913-1980
Obituary *22*
Rumbaut, Hendle 1949- *84*
Rumford, James 1948- *193*
Earlier sketch in SATA *116*
Rumsey, Marian (Barritt) 1928- *16*
Rumstuckle, Cornelius
See Brennan, Herbie
Runholt, Susan *216*
Runnerstroem, Bengt Arne 1944- *75*
Runton, Andy *241*
Runyan, John
See Palmer, Bernard (Alvin)
Runyon, Brent *217*
Runyon, Catherine 1947- *62*
Ruoff, A. LaVonne Brown 1930- *76*
Rupp, Rebecca *239*
Earlier sketch in SATA *185*
Rusch, Elizabeth 1966- *198*
Rusch, Kris
See Rusch, Kristine Kathryn
Rusch, Kristine Kathryn 1960- *113*
Rush, Alison 1951- *41*
Rush, Peter 1937- *32*
Rushdie, Ahmed Salman
See Rushdie, Salman
Rushdie, Salman 1947-
See CLR *125*
Rushford, Patricia H(elen) 1943- *134*
Rushmore, Helen 1898-1994 .... *3*
Rushmore, Robert (William) 1926-1986 .... *8*
Obituary *49*
Ruskin, Ariane
See Batterberry, Ariane Ruskin
Ruskin, John 1819-1900 .... *24*
Russ, Lavinia (Faxon) 1904-1992 .... *74*
Russell, Charlotte
See Rathjen, Carl Henry
Russell, Ching Yeung 1946- *107*
Russell, Don(ald Bert) 1899-1986
Obituary *47*
Russell, Franklin (Alexander) 1926- *11*
Russell, Gertrude Barrer
See Barrer-Russell, Gertrude
Russell, Helen Ross 1915- *8*
Russell, James 1933- *53*
Russell, Jim
See Russell, James
Russell, Joan Plummer 1930- *139*
Russell, Natalie 1972- *218*
Russell, P(hilip) Craig 1951- *162*
Earlier sketch in SATA *80*
Russell, Patrick
See Sammis, John
Russell, Paul (Gary) 1942- *57*
Russell, Sarah
See Laski, Marghanita
Russell, Sharman Apt 1954- *123*
Russell, Solveig Paulson 1904-1985 .... *3*
Russo, Marisabina 1950- *188*
Earlier sketches in SATA *106, 151*
Russo, Monica J. 1950- *83*
Russo, Susan 1947- *30*
Russon, Penni 1974- *179*
Rutgers van der Loeff, An
See Rutgers van der Loeff-Basenau, An(na) Maria Margaretha
Rutgers van der Loeff-Basenau, An(na) Maria Margaretha 1910- *22*
Ruth, Rod 1912-1987 .... *9*
Rutherford, Douglas
See McConnell, James Douglas Rutherford
Rutherford, Meg 1932- *34*
Ruthin, Margaret
See Catherall, Arthur
Rutkoski, Marie 1977- *219*
Rutland, J. *232*
Rutland, Jarrett
See Rutland, J.
Rutledge, Jill Zimmerman 1951- *155*
Rutz, Viola Larkin 1932- *12*
Ruurs, Margriet 1952- *215*
Earlier sketches in SATA *97, 147*
Ruzicka, Rudolph 1883-1978
Obituary *24*
Ruzzier, Sergio 1966- *210*
Earlier sketch in SATA *159*
Ryan, Betsy
See Ryan, Elizabeth (Anne)
Ryan, Candace *234*
Ryan, Cheli Duran *20*
Ryan, Darlene 1958- *176*
Ryan, Elizabeth (Anne) 1943- *30*
Ryan, Jeanette
See Mines, Jeanette
Ryan, John 1921-2009 .... *22*
Ryan, John Gerald Christopher
See Ryan, John
Ryan, Margaret 1950- *166*
Earlier sketch in SATA *78*
Ryan, Mary E. 1953- *61*
Ryan, Mary Elizabeth
See Ryan, Mary E.
Ryan, Pam Munoz 1951- *197*
Earlier sketch in SATA *134*
Ryan, Patrick 1957- *138*
Ryan, Peter (Charles) 1939- *15*
Ryan, Rob 1962- *237*
Ryan-Lush, Geraldine 1949- *89*
Rybakov, Anatoli (Naumovich) 1911-1998 .. *79*
Obituary *108*
Rybakov, Anatolii (Naumovich)
See Rybakov, Anatoli (Naumovich)
Rybolt, Thomas R. 1954- *62*
Rybolt, Thomas Roy
See Rybolt, Thomas R.
Rybolt, Tom
See Rybolt, Thomas R.
Rycroft, Nina *228*
Rydberg, Ernest E(mil) 1901-1993 .... *21*
Rydberg, Lou(isa Hampton) 1908- *27*
Rydell, Katy 1942- *91*
Rydell, Wendell
See Rydell, Wendy
Rydell, Wendy *4*
Ryden, Hope *91*
Earlier sketch in SATA *8*
Ryder, Joanne 1946- *226*
Brief entry *34*
Earlier sketches in SATA *65, 122, 163*
See also CLR *37*
Ryder, Pamela
See Lamb, Nancy
Rye, Anthony
See Youd, Samuel
Rylander, Chris *239*
Rylant, Cynthia 1954- *241*
Brief entry *44*
Earlier sketches in SATA *50, 76, 112, 160, 195*
See also CLR *86*
See also SAAS *13*
Rymer, Alta May 1925- *34*
Rymond, Lynda Gene *199*

S

S. L. C.
See Twain, Mark
S., Svend Otto
See Soerensen, Svend Otto
Saaf, Donald W(illiam) 1961- *124*
Saal, Jocelyn
See Sachs, Judith
Sabbeth, Carol (Landstrom) 1957- *125*
Saberhagen, Fred 1930-2007 .... *89*
Obituary *184*
Earlier sketch in SATA *37*
Saberhagen, Fred T.
See Saberhagen, Fred
Saberhagen, Fred Thomas
See Saberhagen, Fred
Saberhagen, Frederick Thomas
See Saberhagen, Fred
Sabin, Edwin L(egrand) 1870-1952
See YABC *2*
Sabin, Francene *27*
Sabin, Lou
See Sabin, Louis
Sabin, Louis 1930- *27*
Sabre, Dirk
See Laffin, John (Alfred Charles)
Sabuda, Robert (James) 1965- *120*
Earlier sketch in SATA *81*
Sabuda, Robert 1965- *170*
Sabuda, Robert James
See Sabuda, Robert
Sachar, Louis 1954- *238*
Brief entry *50*
Earlier sketches in SATA *63, 104, 154*
See also CLR *161*
Sachs, Elizabeth-Ann 1946- *48*
Sachs, Judith 1947- *52*
Brief entry *51*
Sachs, Marilyn 1927- *164*
Autobiography Feature *110*
Earlier sketches in SATA *3, 68*
See also CLR *2*
See also SAAS *2*
Sachs, Marilyn Stickle
See Sachs, Marilyn
Sackett, S(amuel) J(ohn) 1928- *12*
Sackson, Sid 1920- *16*
Sacre, Antonio 1968- *152*
Saddler, Allen
See Richards, R(onald) C(harles) W(illiam)
Saddler, K. Allen
See Richards, R(onald) C(harles) W(illiam)
Sadie, Stanley 1930-2005 .... *14*
Sadie, Stanley John
See Sadie, Stanley
Sadiq, Nazneen
See Sheikh, Nazneen
Sadler, Catherine Edwards 1952- *60*
Brief entry *45*
Sadler, Marilyn (June) 1950- *79*
Sadler, Mark
See Lynds, Dennis
Sadler, Sonia Lynn *230*
Saffer, Barbara *144*

Sagan, Carl 1934-1996 ... *58*
Obituary ... *94*
Sagan, Carl Edward
See Sagan, Carl
Sage, Angie 1952- ... *197*
Sage, Juniper
See Brown, Margaret Wise
and Hurd, Edith Thacher
Sagsoorian, Paul 1923- ... *12*
Said, S.F. 1967- ... *174*
Saidman, Anne 1952- ... *75*
Saint, Dora Jessie
See Miss Read
St. Anthony, Jane ... *175*
St. Antoine, Sara L. 1966- ... *84*
St. Clair, Byrd Hooper 1905-1976
Obituary ... *28*
St. Crow, Lili
See Saintcrow, Lilith
Saintcrow, Lilith 1976- ... *221*
Saint-Exupery, Antoine de 1900-1944 ... *20*
See also CLR *142*
Saint-Exupery, Antoine Jean Baptiste Marie Roger de
See Saint-Exupery, Antoine de
St. George, Judith 1931- ... *161*
Earlier sketches in SATA *13, 99*
See also CLR *57*
See also SAAS *12*
St. George, Judith Alexander
See St. George, Judith
St. James, Blakely
See Gottfried, Theodore Mark
and Platt, Charles
St. James, Blakely
See Griffin, W. E. B.
St. James, Sierra
See Rallison, Janette
Saint James, Synthia 1949- ... *152*
Earlier sketch in SATA *84*
St. John, Lauren 1966- ... *214*
St. John, Nicole ... *143*
Autobiography Feature ... *143*
Earlier sketches in SATA *29, 89*
See also CLR *46*
See also SAAS *7*
St. John, Patricia Mary 1919-1993
Obituary ... *79*
St. John, Philip
See del Rey, Lester
St. John, Wylly Folk 1908-1985 ... *10*
Obituary ... *45*
St. Max, E. S.
See Ellis, Edward S.
St. Meyer, Ned
See Stratemeyer, Edward L.
St. Mox, E. A.
See Ellis, Edward S.
St. Myer, Ned
See Stratemeyer, Edward L.
St. Tamara
See Kolba, St. Tamara
Saito, Michiko
See Fujiwara, Michiko
Sakai, Komako 1966- ... *213*
Sakaki, Ichiro 1969- ... *192*
Sakamoto, Miki ... *198*
Sakers, Don 1958- ... *72*
Sakharnov, S.
See Sakharnov, Svyatoslav
Sakharnov, Svyatoslav 1923- ... *65*
Sakharnov, Svyatoslav Vladimirovich
See Sakharnov, Svyatoslav
Saksena, Kate ... *148*
Sakurai, Gail 1952- ... *153*
Earlier sketch in SATA *87*
Salamanca, Lucy
See del Barco, Lucy Salamanca
Salas, Laura Purdie 1966- ... *216*
Salassi, Otto R(ussell) 1939-1993 ... *38*
Obituary ... *77*
Salat, Cristina ... *82*
Saldana, Rene, Jr. ... *186*
Saldutti, Denise 1953- ... *39*
Sale, Tim 1956- ... *153*
Salem, Kay 1952- ... *92*
Salerni, Dianne K. ... *231*
Salerno, Steven ... *176*
Sales, Leila 1984- ... *241*
Salinger, J.D. 1919-2010 ... *67*
See also CLR *18*
Salinger, Jerome David
See Salinger, J.D.
Salisbury, Graham 1944- ... *234*
Earlier sketches in SATA *76, 108, 161, 195*
Salisbury, Joyce E(llen) 1944- ... *138*
Salkey, (Felix) Andrew (Alexander) 1928-1995 ... *118*
Earlier sketch in SATA *35*
Salley, Coleen ... *166*
Sallis, Susan (Diana) 1929- ... *55*
Salmieri, Daniel 1983- ... *208*
Salmon, Annie Elizabeth 1899- ... *13*
Salmon, Dena K. 1959(?)- ... *219*
Salonen, Roxane Beauclair 1968- ... *184*
Salsi, Lynn 1947- ... *130*
Salsitz, R. A. V.
See Salsitz, Rhondi Vilott
Salsitz, Rhondi Vilott ... *115*
Salten, Felix
See Salzmann, Siegmund
Salter, Cedric
See Knight, Francis Edgar
Salter, Sydney ... *220*
Saltman, Judith 1947- ... *64*
Saltzberg, Barney 1955- ... *233*
Earlier sketches in SATA *135, 194*
Saltzman, David (Charles Laertes) 1967-1990 ... *86*
Salvadori, Mario (George) 1907-1997 ... *97*
Earlier sketch in SATA *40*
Salwood, F.K.
See Kilworth, Garry
Salzer, L. E.
See Wilson, Lionel
Salzman, Marian 1959- ... *77*
Salzmann, Siegmund 1869-1945 ... *25*
Samachson, Dorothy (Mirkin) 1914-1997 ... *3*
Samachson, Joseph 1906-1980 ... *3*
Obituary ... *52*
Sammis, John 1942- ... *4*
Sampson, Emma (Keats) Speed 1868-1947 . *68*
Sampson, Fay 1935- ... *151*
Brief entry ... *40*
Earlier sketch in SATA *42*
Sampson, Fay Elizabeth
See Sampson, Fay
Sampson, Jeff 1982- ... *232*
Sampson, Michael 1952- ... *143*
Earlier sketch in SATA *95*
Samson, Anne S(tringer) 1933- ... *2*
Samson, Joan 1937-1976 ... *13*
Samson, Suzanne M. 1959- ... *91*
Samuels, Barbara ... *199*
Samuels, Charles 1902-1982 ... *12*
Samuels, Cynthia K(alish) 1946- ... *79*
Samuels, Gertrude 1910(?)-2003 ... *17*
Obituary ... *147*
Sanborn, Duane 1914-1996 ... *38*
Sancha, Sheila 1924- ... *38*
Sanchez, Alex 1957- ... *151*
Sanchez, Anita 1956- ... *209*
Sanchez, Sonia 1934- ... *136*
Earlier sketch in SATA *22*
See also CLR *18*
Sanchez-Silva, Jose Maria 1911- ... *132*
Earlier sketch in SATA *16*
See also CLR *12*
Sand, George X. ... *45*
Sandak, Cass R(obert) 1950-2001 ... *51*
Brief entry ... *37*
Sandberg, (Karin) Inger 1930- ... *15*
Sandberg, Karl C. 1931- ... *35*
Sandberg, Lasse (E. M.) 1924- ... *15*
Sandburg, Carl 1878-1967 ... *8*
See also CLR *67*
Sandburg, Carl August
See Sandburg, Carl
Sandburg, Charles
See Sandburg, Carl
Sandburg, Charles A.
See Sandburg, Carl
Sandburg, Helga 1918- ... *3*
See also SAAS *10*
Sandell, Lisa Ann 1977- ... *175*
Sandemose, Iben 1950- ... *211*
Sander, Heather L. 1947- ... *157*
Sanderlin, George 1915- ... *4*
Sanderlin, Owenita (Harrah) 1916- ... *11*
Sanders, Betty Jane
See Monthei, Betty
Sanders, Nancy I. 1960- ... *141*
Earlier sketch in SATA *90*
Sanders, Scott Russell 1945- ... *109*
Earlier sketch in SATA *56*
Sanders, Winston P.
See Anderson, Poul
Sanderson, Irma 1912- ... *66*
Sanderson, Ivan T(erence) 1911-1973 ... *6*
Sanderson, Margaret Love
See Keats, Emma
and Sampson, Emma (Keats) Speed
Sanderson, Ruth 1951- ... *224*
Earlier sketches in SATA *41, 109, 172*
Sanderson, Ruth L.
See Sanderson, Ruth
Sanders-Wells, Linda ... *220*
Sand-Eveland, Cyndi ... *211*
Sandin, Joan 1942- ... *197*
Earlier sketches in SATA *12, 94, 153*
Sandison, Janet
See Cameron, Elizabeth Jane
Sandler, Martin W. ... *216*
Earlier sketch in SATA *160*
Sandom, J. Gregory
See Welsh, T.K.
Sandom, J.G.
See Welsh, T.K.
Sandoz, Mari(e Susette) 1900-1966 ... *5*
Sanford, Agnes (White) 1897-1976 ... *61*
Sanford, Doris 1937- ... *69*
Sanford, Rose
See Simmonds, Posy
Sanger, Amy Wilson 1967- ... *205*
Sanger, Marjory Bartlett 1920- ... *8*
San Jose, Christine 1929- ... *167*
Sankey, Alice (Ann-Susan) 1910- ... *27*
Sansone, Adele 1953- ... *230*
San Souci, Daniel ... *192*
Earlier sketch in SATA *96*
San Souci, Robert D. 1946- ... *220*
Earlier sketches in SATA *40, 81, 117, 158*
See also CLR *43*
Santamaria, Benjamin 1955- ... *184*
Santat, Dan ... *224*
Earlier sketch in SATA *188*
Santesson, Hans Stefan 1914(?)-1975
Obituary ... *30*
Santiago, Esmeralda 1948- ... *129*
Santopolo, Jill ... *214*
Santore, Charles 1935- ... *200*
Santoro, C.
See Santoro, Christopher
Santoro, Christopher ... *218*
Santoro, Scott 1956- ... *236*
Santos, Helen
See Griffiths, Helen
Santrey, Louis
See Sabin, Louis
Santucci, Barbara 1948- ... *130*
Sapergia, Barbara 1943- ... *181*
Sapet, Kerrily 1972- ... *214*

Sapieyevski, Anne Lindbergh 1940-1993 ..... *81*
Brief entry *32*
Earlier sketches in SATA *35, 78*
Saport, Linda 1954- *123*
Sapp, Allen 1929- *151*
Sarac, Roger
See Caras, Roger A(ndrew)
Sarah, Duchess of York
See Ferguson, Sarah
Sarasin, Jennifer
See Sachs, Judith
Sarcone-Roach, Julia *215*
Sardinha, Rick *192*
Sarg, Anthony Frederick
See Sarg, Tony
Sarg, Tony 1882-1942
See YABC *1*
Sargent, Pamela 1948- *78*
Earlier sketch in SATA *29*
Sargent, Robert 1933- *2*
Sargent, Sarah 1937- *44*
Brief entry *41*
Sargent, Shirley 1927-2004 ..... *11*
Sarnoff, Jane 1937- *10*
Saroff, Phyllis V. *202*
Saroyan, William 1908-1981 ..... *23*
Obituary *24*
Sartell, Debra *229*
Sarton, Eleanor May
See Sarton, May
Sarton, May 1912-1995 ..... *36*
Obituary *86*
Sasaki, Chris *182*
Sasaki, Ellen Joy *206*
Saseen, Sharon (Dillon) 1949- *59*
Sasek, Miroslav 1916-1980 ..... *16*
Obituary *23*
See also CLR *4*
Sasso, Sandy Eisenberg 1947- *162*
Earlier sketches in SATA *86, 116*
Sathre, Vivian 1952- *133*
Earlier sketch in SATA *79*
Satterfield, Charles
See del Rey, Lester
and Pohl, Frederik
Sattgast, L. J.
See Sattgast, Linda J.
Sattgast, Linda J. 1953- *91*
Sattler, Helen Roney 1921-1992 ..... *74*
Earlier sketch in SATA *4*
See also CLR *24*
Sattler, Jennifer
See Sattler, Jennifer Gordon
Sattler, Jennifer Gordon *218*
Sauer, Julia Lina 1891-1983 ..... *32*
Obituary *36*
Sauer, Tammi 1972- *223*
Sauerwein, Leigh 1944- *155*
Saul, Carol P. 1947- *117*
Earlier sketch in SATA *78*
Saul, John 1942- *98*
Saul, John W.
See Saul, John
Saul, John Woodruff III
See Saul, John
Saul, (Ellen) Wendy 1946- *42*
Saulnier, Karen Luczak 1940- *80*
Saunders, Caleb
See Heinlein, Robert A.
Saunders, Dave 1939- *85*
Saunders, Julie 1939- *85*
Saunders, (William) Keith 1910-1994 ..... *12*
Saunders, Rubie (Agnes) 1929- *21*
Saunders, Steven
See Jones, Allan Frewin
Saunders, Susan 1945- *96*
Brief entry *41*
Earlier sketch in SATA *46*
Saunders-Smith, Gail 1952- *169*
Sauvain, Philip Arthur 1933- *111*
Savadier, Elivia 1950- *228*
Earlier sketches in SATA *79, 164*
Savage, Alan
See Nicole, Christopher
Savage, Blake
See Goodwin, Harold L(eland)
Savage, Candace 1949- *142*
Savage, Deborah 1955- *76*
Savage, Jeff 1961- *97*
Savage, Katharine James 1905-1989
Obituary *61*
Savage, Stephen 1965- *194*
Savage, Thomas 1915-2003
Obituary *147*
Savageau, Cheryl 1950- *96*
Savery, Constance (Winifred) 1897-1999 ..... *1*
Saville, Andrew
See Taylor, Andrew
Saville, (Leonard) Malcolm 1901-1982 ..... *23*
Obituary *31*
Saviozzi, Adriana
See Mazza, Adriana
Savitt, Sam 1917-2000 ..... *8*
Obituary *126*
Savitz, Harriet May 1933-2008 ..... *72*
Earlier sketch in SATA *5*
See also SAAS *26*
Sawicki, Mary 1950- *90*
Sawyer, (Frederick) Don(ald) 1947- *72*
Sawyer, Kem Knapp 1953- *84*
Sawyer, Kim Vogel *233*
Sawyer, Robert J. 1960- *149*
Earlier sketch in SATA *81*
Sawyer, Robert James
See Sawyer, Robert J.
Sawyer, Ruth 1880-1970 ..... *17*
See also CLR *36*
Saxby, H.M.
See Saxby, (Henry) Maurice
Saxby, (Henry) Maurice 1924- *71*
Saxon, Andrew
See Arthur, Robert, (Jr.)
Saxon, Antonia
See Sachs, Judith
Say, Allen 1937- *161*
Earlier sketches in SATA *28, 69, 110*
See also CLR *135*
Sayers, Frances Clarke 1897-1989 ..... *3*
Obituary *62*
Sayles, Elizabeth 1956- *220*
Earlier sketches in SATA *108, 163*
Saylor-Marchant, Linda 1963- *82*
Sayre, April Pulley 1966- *233*
Earlier sketches in SATA *88, 131, 191*
Sazer, Nina 1949- *13*
Scabrini, Janet 1953- *13*
Scagell, Robin 1946- *107*
Scagnetti, Jack 1924- *7*
Scales, Simon *241*
Scaletta, Kurtis 1968- *215*
Scalora, Suza *224*
Scamander, Newt
See Rowling, J.K.
Scamell, Ragnhild 1940- *180*
Earlier sketch in SATA *77*
Scandiffio, Laura *227*
Scanlon, Elizabeth Garton
See Scanlon, Liz Garton
Scanlon, Liz Garton *226*
Scanlon, Marion Stephany *11*
Scannel, John Vernon
See Scannell, Vernon
Scannell, Vernon 1922-2007 ..... *59*
Obituary *188*
Scarborough, Elizabeth
See Scarborough, Elizabeth Ann
Scarborough, Elizabeth Ann 1947- *171*
Earlier sketch in SATA *98*
Scarf, Maggi
See Scarf, Maggie
Scarf, Maggie 1932- *5*
Scariano, Margaret M. 1924- *86*
Scarlett, Susan
See Streatfeild, Noel
Scarrow, Alex 1966- *236*
Scarry, Huck
See Scarry, Richard McClure, Jr.
Scarry, Patricia (Murphy) 1924- *2*
Scarry, Patsy
See Scarry, Patricia (Murphy)
Scarry, Richard (McClure) 1919-1994 ..... *75*
Obituary *90*
Earlier sketches in SATA *2, 35*
See also CLR *41*
Scarry, Richard McClure, Jr. 1953- *35*
Schachner, Judith Byron 1951- *178*
Earlier sketch in SATA *88*
Schachner, Judy
See Schachner, Judith Byron
Schachtel, Roger 1949- *38*
Schachtel, Roger Bernard
See Schachtel, Roger
Schade, Susan *189*
Schaedler, Sally *116*
Schaefer, Carole Lexa *173*
Schaefer, Jack (Warner) 1907-1991 ..... *66*
Obituary *65*
Earlier sketch in SATA *3*
Schaefer, Lola M. 1950- *183*
Earlier sketches in SATA *91, 144*
Schaeffer, Mead 1898- *21*
Schaeffer, Susan Fromberg 1940-2011 ..... *22*
Schaer, Brigitte 1958- *112*
Schallau, Daniel 1966- *222*
Schaller, George
See Schaller, George B.
Schaller, George B. 1933- *30*
Schaller, George Beals
See Schaller, George B.
Schanzer, Rosalyn (Good) 1942- *138*
Earlier sketch in SATA *77*
Scharschmidt, Sherry 1957- *240*
Schatell, Brian *66*
Brief entry *47*
Schechter, Betty (Goodstein) 1921- *5*
Schechter, Simone
See Elkeles, Simone
Schecter, Ellen 1944- *85*
Scheeder, Louis 1946- *141*
Scheer, Julian (Weisel) 1926-2001 ..... *8*
Scheerger, Sarah Lynn
See Lynn, Sarah
Scheffer, Victor B(lanchard) 1906- *6*
Scheffler, Axel 1957- *230*
Earlier sketch in SATA *180*
Scheffler, Ursel 1938- *81*
Scheffrin-Falk, Gladys 1928- *76*
Scheidl, Gerda Marie 1913- *85*
Scheier, Michael 1943- *40*
Brief entry *36*
Schell, Mildred 1922- *41*
Schell, Orville (Hickok) 1940- *10*
Scheller, Melanie 1953- *77*
Schellie, Don 1932- *29*
Schembri, Jim 1962- *124*
Schembri, Pamela 1969- *195*
Schemm, Mildred Walker 1905-1998 ..... *21*
Obituary *103*
Schenker, Dona 1947- *133*
Earlier sketch in SATA *68*
Scher, Paula 1948- *47*
Scherer, Jeffrey *194*
Scherf, Margaret 1908-1979 ..... *10*
Schermer, Judith (Denise) 1941- *30*
Schertle, Alice 1941- *231*
Earlier sketches in SATA *36, 90, 145, 192*
Schick, Alice 1946- *27*
Schick, Eleanor 1942- *144*
Earlier sketches in SATA *9, 82*
Schick, Joel 1945- *31*
Brief entry *30*
Schields, Gretchen 1948- *75*

Schiff, Ken(neth Roy) 1942- ... *7*
Schiller, Andrew 1919- ... *21*
Schiller, Barbara (Heyman) 1928- ... *21*
Schiller, Pamela (Byrne) ... *127*
Schindel, John 1955- ... *213*
Earlier sketches in SATA *77, 115*
Schindelman, Joseph 1923- ... *67*
Brief entry ... *32*
Schindler, S.D. 1952- ... *198*
Brief entry ... *50*
Earlier sketches in SATA *75, 118, 171*
Schindler, Steven D.
See Schindler, S.D.
Schinto, Jeanne 1951- ... *93*
Schisgall, Oscar 1901-1984 ... *12*
Obituary ... *38*
Schlaepfer, Gloria G. 1931- ... *154*
Schlee, Ann 1934- ... *44*
Brief entry ... *36*
Schleichert, Elizabeth 1945- ... *77*
Schlein, Miriam 1926-2004 ... *130*
Obituary ... *159*
Earlier sketches in SATA *2, 87*
See also CLR *41*
Schlesinger, Arthur M., Jr. 1917-2007 ... *61*
Obituary ... *181*
See Schlesinger, Arthur Meier
Schlesinger, Arthur Meier 1888-1965
Schlessinger, Laura (Catherine) 1947- ... *160*
Earlier sketch in SATA *110*
Schlitz, Laura Amy ... *232*
Earlier sketch in SATA *184*
Schloat, G. Warren, Jr. 1914-2000 ... *4*
Schlossberg, Elisabeth ... *221*
Schmais, Libby ... *227*
Schmatz, Pat ... *197*
Schmid, Eleonore 1939- ... *126*
Earlier sketches in SATA *12, 84*
Schmid, Paul ... *231*
Schmid, Susan Maupin ... *208*
Schmiderer, Dorothy 1940- ... *19*
Schmidt, Annie M. G. 1911-1995 ... *67*
Obituary ... *91*
See also CLR *22*
Schmidt, C.A. ... *196*
Schmidt, Diane 1953- ... *70*
Schmidt, Elizabeth 1915- ... *15*
Schmidt, Gary D. 1957- ... *193*
Earlier sketches in SATA *93, 135*
Schmidt, James Norman 1912-1983 ... *21*
Schmidt, Karen Lee 1953- ... *185*
Earlier sketch in SATA *94*
Schmidt, Lynette 1952- ... *76*
Schmitz, Tamara ... *207*
Schneider, Antonie 1954- ... *167*
Earlier sketch in SATA *89*
Schneider, Christine M. 1972(?)- ... *171*
Earlier sketch in SATA *120*
Schneider, Dick
See Schneider, Richard H.
Schneider, Elisa
See Kleven, Elisa
Schneider, Herman 1905-2003 ... *7*
Obituary ... *148*
Schneider, Howie -2007 ... *181*
Schneider, Josh 1980- ... *196*
Schneider, Katy ... *237*
Schneider, Laurie
See Adams, Laurie
Schneider, Nina 1913-2007 ... *2*
Obituary ... *186*
Schneider, Nina Zimet
See Schneider, Nina
Schneider, Rex 1937- ... *44*
Schneider, Richard H. 1922- ... *171*
Schneider, Richard Henry
See Schneider, Richard H.
Schneider, Robyn 1986- ... *187*
Schnirel, James R. 1931- ... *14*
Schnitter, Jane T. 1958- ... *88*
Schnitzlein, Danny ... *134*
Schnur, Steven 1952- ... *144*
Earlier sketch in SATA *95*
Schnurre, Wolfdietrich 1920-1989
Obituary ... *63*
Schoberle, Cecile 1949- ... *80*
Schock, Pauline 1928- ... *45*
Schoell, William 1951- ... *160*
Schoen, Barbara (Taylor) 1924-1993 ... *13*
Schoenherr, Ian ... *235*
Earlier sketch in SATA *177*
Schoenherr, John 1935-2010 ... *66*
Earlier sketch in SATA *37*
See also SAAS *13*
Schoenherr, John Carl
See Schoenherr, John
Schofield, Sandy
See Rusch, Kristine Kathryn
Scholastica, Sister Mary
See Jenkins, Marie M(agdalen)
Scholefield, A. T.
See Scholefield, Alan
Scholefield, Alan 1931- ... *66*
Scholefield, Edmund O.
See Griffin, W. E. B.
Scholey, Arthur 1932- ... *28*
Scholz, Jackson Volney 1897-1986
Obituary ... *49*
Schon, Nick 1955- ... *223*
Schone, Virginia ... *22*
Schongut, Emanuel 1936- ... *184*
Brief entry ... *36*
Earlier sketch in SATA *52*
Schoonmaker, Elizabeth ... *239*
Schoonover, Frank (Earle) 1877-1972 ... *24*
Schoor, Gene 1921- ... *3*
Schories, Pat 1952- ... *232*
Earlier sketches in SATA *116, 164*
Schorr, Melissa 1972- ... *194*
Schorr, Melissa Robin
See Schorr, Melissa
Schott, Jane A. 1946- ... *172*
Schotter, Roni ... *190*
Earlier sketches in SATA *105, 149*
Schrader, Dave 1967(?)- ... *225*
Schraff, Anne E(laine) 1939- ... *92*
Earlier sketch in SATA *27*
Schram, Penninah 1934- ... *219*
Earlier sketch in SATA *119*
Schrank, Joseph 1900-1984
Obituary ... *38*
Schrecengost, Maity 1938- ... *118*
Schrecengost, S. Maitland
See Schrecengost, Maity
Schreck, Karen
See Schreck, Karen Halvorsen
Schreck, Karen Halvorsen 1962- ... *185*
Schrecker, Judie 1954- ... *90*
Schreiber, Elizabeth Anne (Ferguson) 1947- ... *13*
Schreiber, Ellen ... *241*
Schreiber, Ralph W(alter) 1942- ... *13*
Schreiner, Samuel A(gnew), Jr. 1921- ... *70*
Schroades, John ... *214*
Schroder, Monika 1965- ... *229*
Schroeder, Alan 1961- ... *98*
Earlier sketch in SATA *66*
Schroeder, Binette
See Nickl, Barbara (Elisabeth)
Schroeder, Russell (K.) 1943- ... *146*
Schroeder, Ted 1931(?)-1973
Obituary ... *20*
Schubert, Dieter 1947- ... *217*
Earlier sketches in SATA *62, 101*
Schubert, Ingrid 1953- ... *217*
Schubert, Leda 1945(?)- ... *232*
Earlier sketch in SATA *181*
Schubert, Leda Deirdre
See Schubert, Leda
Schubert-Gabrys, Ingrid 1953- ... *101*
Earlier sketch in SATA *62*
Schuelein-Steel, Danielle
See Steel, Danielle
Schuelein-Steel, Danielle Fernande
See Steel, Danielle
Schuerger, Michele R. ... *110*
Schuett, Stacey 1960- ... *168*
Earlier sketch in SATA *75*
Schulke, Flip Phelps Graeme 1930- ... *57*
Schulman, Arlene 1961- ... *105*
Schulman, Janet 1933- ... *208*
Earlier sketches in SATA *22, 137*
Schulman, L(ester) M(artin) 1934- ... *13*
Schulte, Elaine L(ouise) 1934- ... *36*
Schultz, Betty K(epka) 1932- ... *125*
Schultz, Gwendolyn ... *21*
Schultz, James Willard 1859-1947
See YABC *1*
Schultz, Pearle Henriksen 1918- ... *21*
Schulz, Charles M. 1922-2000 ... *10*
Obituary ... *118*
Schulz, Charles Monroe
See Schulz, Charles M.
Schumacher, Julie 1958- ... *191*
Schumaker, Ward 1943- ... *96*
Schuman, Michael A. 1953- ... *134*
Earlier sketch in SATA *85*
Schur, Maxine
See Schur, Maxine Rose
Schur, Maxine Rose 1948- ... *135*
Autobiography Feature ... *135*
Brief entry ... *49*
Earlier sketches in SATA *53, 98*
Schurfranz, Vivian 1925- ... *13*
Schutzer, A. I. 1922- ... *13*
Schuyler, Pamela R. 1948- ... *30*
Schwabach, Karen ... *185*
Schwager, Tina 1964- ... *110*
Schwandt, Stephen (William) 1947- ... *61*
Schwark, Mary Beth 1954- ... *51*
Schwartz, Alvin 1927-1992 ... *56*
Obituary ... *71*
Earlier sketch in SATA *4*
See also CLR *89*
Schwartz, Amy 1954- ... *189*
Brief entry ... *41*
Earlier sketches in SATA *47, 83, 131*
See also CLR *25*
See also SAAS *18*
Schwartz, Anne Powers 1913-1987 ... *10*
Schwartz, Carol 1954- ... *77*
Schwartz, Charles W(alsh) 1914- ... *8*
Schwartz, David M. 1951- ... *239*
Earlier sketches in SATA *59, 110*
Schwartz, David Martin
See Schwartz, David M.
Schwartz, Elizabeth Reeder 1912- ... *8*
Schwartz, Ellen 1949- ... *117*
Schwartz, Howard 1945- ... *238*
Schwartz, Jerome L.
See Lawrence, Jerome
Schwartz, Joanne 1960- ... *220*
Schwartz, Joel L. 1940- ... *54*
Brief entry ... *51*
Schwartz, John 1957- ... *232*
Schwartz, Joyce R. 1950- ... *93*
Schwartz, Julius 1907-2004 ... *45*
Schwartz, Perry 1942- ... *75*
Schwartz, Sheila (Ruth) 1929- ... *27*
Schwartz, Stephen (Lawrence) 1948- ... *19*
Schwartz, Virginia Frances 1950- ... *184*
Earlier sketch in SATA *131*
Schwarz, Silvia Tessa Viviane
See Schwarz, Viviane
Schwarz, Viviane 1977- ... *204*
Schwarz, (Silvia Tessa) Viviane 1977- ... *141*
Schweitzer, Byrd Baylor
See Baylor, Byrd
Schweitzer, Iris ... *59*
Brief entry ... *36*
Schweninger, Ann 1951- ... *168*
Earlier sketches in SATA *29, 98*

Schwerin, Doris H(alpern) 1922- *64*
Schy, Yael *197*
Scieszka, Casey 1984- *241*
Scieszka, Jon 1954- *238*
Earlier sketches in SATA *68, 105, 160, 199*
See also CLR *107*
Scillian, Devin *199*
Earlier sketch in SATA *128*
Scioscia, Mary (Hershey) 1926- *63*
Sciurba, Katie 1957- *196*
Scofield, Penrod 1933- *62*
Obituary *78*
Scoggin, Margaret C(lara) 1905-1968 .... *47*
Brief entry *28*
Scoltock, Jack 1942- *141*
Earlier sketch in SATA *72*
Scoppettone, Sandra 1936- *92*
Earlier sketch in SATA *9*
Scot, Michael
See Rohan, Michael Scott
Scot-Bernard, P.
See Bernard, Patricia
Scotland, Jay
See Jakes, John
Scott, Alastair
See Allen, Kenneth S.
Scott, Ann Herbert 1926- *140*
Autobiography Feature *140*
Brief entry *29*
Earlier sketches in SATA *56, 94*
Scott, Bill
See Scott, William N(eville)
Scott, Bill 1920(?)-1985
Obituary *46*
Scott, Cora Annett (Pipitone) 1931- *11*
Scott, Dan
See Barker, S. Omar
Scott, Elaine 1940- *198*
Earlier sketches in SATA *36, 90, 164*
Scott, Elizabeth 1972- *240*
Earlier sketch in SATA *194*
Scott, Inara *236*
Scott, Jack Denton 1915-1995 .... *83*
Earlier sketch in SATA *31*
See also CLR *20*
See also SAAS *14*
Scott, Jane (Harrington) 1931- *55*
Scott, Jane Wooster 1939- *226*
Scott, Jennifer Power 1968- *230*
Scott, Jessica
See De Wire, Elinor
Scott, John 1912-1976 .... *14*
Scott, John Anthony 1916- *23*
Scott, John M(artin) 1913- *12*
Scott, Mary
See Mattern, Joanne
Scott, Melissa 1960- *109*
Scott, Michael 1959- *211*
Scott, Michael Peter
See Scott, Michael
Scott, Mike
See Scott, Michael
Scott, Richard
See Rennert, Richard Scott
Scott, Roney
See Gault, William Campbell
Scott, Sally 1909-1978 .... *43*
Scott, Sally 1948- *44*
Scott, Sally Elisabeth
See Scott, Sally
Scott, W. N.
See Scott, William N(eville)
Scott, Sir Walter 1771-1832
See YABC *2*
See also CLR *154*
Scott, Warwick
See Trevor, Elleston
Scott, William N(eville) 1923- *87*
Scotti, Anna
See Coates, Anna
Scotton, Rob 1960- *214*
Earlier sketch in SATA *177*
Scribner, Charles, Jr. 1921-1995 .... *13*
Obituary *87*
Scribner, Joanne L. 1949- *33*
Scribner, Kimball 1917- *63*
Scrimger, Richard 1957- *164*
Earlier sketch in SATA *119*
Scrimsher, Lila Gravatt 1897-1974
Obituary *28*
Scroder, Walter K. 1928- *82*
Scroggs, Kirk *187*
Scruggs, Sandy 1961- *89*
Scudder, Brooke 1959- *154*
Scudder, Mildred Lee 1908- *6*
See also SAAS *12*
Scull, Marie-Louise 1943-1993 .... *77*
Scuro, Vincent 1951- *21*
Seabrooke, Brenda 1941- *148*
Earlier sketches in SATA *30, 88*
Seagraves, D.B.
See Seagraves, Donny Bailey
Seagraves, Donny
See Seagraves, Donny Bailey
Seagraves, Donny Bailey 1951- *224*
Seaman, Augusta Huiell 1879-1950 .... *31*
Seamands, Ruth 1916- *9*
Searcy, Margaret Zehmer 1926- *54*
Brief entry *39*
Searight, Mary W(illiams) 1918- *17*
Searle, Kathryn Adrienne 1942- *10*
Searle, Ronald 1920- *70*
Earlier sketch in SATA *42*
Searle, Ronald William Fordham
See Searle, Ronald
Sears, Stephen W. 1932- *4*
Seaskull, Cecil
See Castellucci, Cecil
Sebastian, Lee
See Silverberg, Robert
Sebestyen, Igen
See Sebestyen, Ouida
Sebestyen, Ouida 1924- *140*
Earlier sketch in SATA *39*
See also CLR *17*
See also SAAS *10*
Sebrey, Mary Ann 1951- *62*
Sechrist, Elizabeth Hough 1903-1991 .... *2*
Sederman, Marty *211*
Sedges, John
See Buck, Pearl S.
Sedgwick, Marcus 1968- *197*
Earlier sketch in SATA *160*
Sedita, Francesco 1974- *235*
Seed, Cecile Eugenie 1930- *86*
Earlier sketch in SATA *8*
See also CLR *76*
Seed, Jenny
See Seed, Cecile Eugenie
Seed, Sheila Turner 1937(?)-1979
Obituary *23*
Seeger, Elizabeth 1889-1973
Obituary *20*
Seeger, Laura Vaccaro *200*
Earlier sketch in SATA *172*
Seeger, Pete 1919- *139*
Earlier sketch in SATA *13*
Seeger, Peter R.
See Seeger, Pete
Seeley, Laura L. 1958- *71*
Seever, R.
See Reeves, Lawrence F.
Sefozo, Mary 1925- *82*
Sefton, Catherine
See Waddell, Martin
Segal, John *178*
Segal, Joyce 1940- *35*
Segal, Lore 1928- *228*
Autobiography Feature *228*
Earlier sketches in SATA *4, 66, 163*
See also SAAS *11*
Segal, Lore Groszmann
See Segal, Lore
Segar, E(lzie) C(risler) 1894-1938 .... *61*
Segovia, Andres 1893(?)-1987
Obituary *52*
Segovia, Carmen 1978- *240*
Seguin, Marilyn W(eymouth) 1951- *91*
Seguin-Fontes, Marthe 1924- *109*
Seibold, J. Otto 1960- *196*
Earlier sketches in SATA *83, 149*
See also SAAS *22*
Seidel, Ross *95*
Seidelman, James Edward 1926- *6*
Seiden, Art(hur) *107*
Brief entry *42*
Seidensticker, John 1944- *200*
Seidler, Ann (G.) 1925- *131*
Seidler, Tor 1952- *149*
Brief entry *46*
Earlier sketches in SATA *52, 98*
Seidman, Karla
See Kuskin, Karla
Seidman, Laurence Ivan 1925- *15*
Seigel, Kalman 1917-1998 .... *12*
Obituary *103*
Seignobosc, Francoise 1897-1961 .... *21*
Seinfeld, Jerry 1954- *146*
Seitz, Jacqueline 1931- *50*
Seixas, Judith S. 1922- *17*
Sejima, Yoshimasa 1913- *8*
Selberg, Ingrid (Maria) 1950- *68*
Selden, George
See Thompson, George Selden
Selden, Neil R(oy) 1931- *61*
Self, Margaret Cabell 1902-1996 .... *24*
Selfors, Suzanne 1963- *193*
Selick, Henry 1952- *183*
Selig, Sylvie 1942- *13*
Selkirk, Jane
See Chapman, John Stanton Higham
Sellers, Naomi
See Flack, Naomi John White
Sellier, Marie 1953- *212*
Selman, LaRue W. 1927- *55*
Selsam, Millicent E(llis) 1912-1996 .... *29*
Obituary *92*
Earlier sketch in SATA *1*
See also CLR *1*
Seltzer, Meyer 1932- *17*
Seltzer, Richard 1946- *41*
Seltzer, Richard Warren, Jr.
See Seltzer, Richard
Selvadurai, Shyam 1965(?)- *171*
Selway, Martina 1940- *169*
Earlier sketch in SATA *74*
Selzer, Adam 1980- *229*
Earlier sketch in SATA *192*
Selznick, Brian 1966- *210*
Earlier sketches in SATA *79, 117, 171*
Semel, Nava 1954- *107*
Semloh
See Holmes, Peggy
Sendak, Jack 1924(?)-1995 .... *28*
Sendak, Maurice 1928- *165*
Earlier sketches in SATA *1, 27, 113*
See also CLR *131*
Sendak, Maurice Bernard
See Sendak, Maurice
Sender, Ruth M(insky) 1926- *62*
Sengler, Johanna 1924- *18*
Senir, Mirik
See Snir, Mirik
Senisi, Ellen B. 1951- *116*
Senisi, Ellen Babinec
See Senisi, Ellen B.
Senn, J(oyce) A(nn) 1941- *115*
Senn, Steve 1950- *60*
Brief entry *48*
Sensel, Joni 1962- *204*
Senzai, N.H. *233*
Serafini, Frank *201*

Serage, Nancy 1924- *10*
Seredy, Kate 1899-1975 .... *1*
Obituary *24*
See also CLR *10*
Serfozo, Mary 1925- *194*
Serlin, Andra
See Abramson, Andra Serlin
Seroff, Victor I(ilyitch) 1902-1979 .... *12*
Obituary *26*
Serra, Sebastia 1966- *202*
Serraillier, Ian (Lucien) 1912-1994 .... *73*
Obituary *83*
Earlier sketch in SATA *1*
See also CLR *2*
See also SAAS *3*
Serres, Alain 1956- *239*
Serros, Michele *175*
Serros, Michele M.
See Serros, Michele
Servello, Joe 1932- *10*
Service, Pamela F. 1945- *222*
Earlier sketch in SATA *64*
Service, Robert
See Service, Robert W.
Service, Robert W. 1874(?)-1958 .... *20*
Serwadda, W(illiam) Moses 1931- *27*
Serwer-Bernstein, Blanche L(uria) 1910-1997 .... *10*
Sescoe, Vincent E. 1938- *123*
Seskin, Steve 1953- *211*
Seth, Mary
See Lexau, Joan M.
Seton, Anya 1904(?)-1990 .... *3*
Obituary *66*
Seton, Ernest (Evan) Thompson 1860-1946 . *18*
See also CLR *59*
Seton-Thompson, Ernest
See Seton, Ernest (Evan) Thompson
Seuling, Barbara 1937- *220*
Autobiography Feature *220*
Earlier sketches in SATA *10, 98, 145, 193*
See also SAAS *24*
Seuss, Dr.
See Dr. Seuss
Severn, Bill
See Severn, William Irving
Severn, David
See Unwin, David S.
Severn, William Irving 1914- *1*
Sewall, Marcia 1935- *119*
Earlier sketches in SATA *37, 69*
Seward, Prudence 1926- *16*
Sewell, Anna 1820-1878 .... *100*
Earlier sketch in SATA *24*
See also CLR *17*
Sewell, Helen (Moore) 1896-1957 .... *38*
Sexton, Anne 1928-1974 .... *10*
Sexton, Anne Harvey
See Sexton, Anne
Sexton, Brenda 1957- *237*
Seymour, Alta Halverson *10*
Seymour, Jane 1951- *139*
Seymour, Tres 1966- *164*
Earlier sketch in SATA *82*
Sfar, Joann 1971- *182*
Shachtman, Tom 1942- *49*
Shackleton, C.C.
See Aldiss, Brian W.
Shader, Rachel
See Sofer, Barbara
Shadow, Jak
See Sutherland, Jon
Shadyland, Sal
See Cooper, Louise
Shafer, Audrey *183*
Shafer, Robert E(ugene) 1925- *9*
Shaffer, Terea 1968- *79*
Shahan, Sherry 1949- *216*
Earlier sketches in SATA *92, 134*
Shahn, Ben(jamin) 1898-1969
Obituary *21*
Shahn, Bernarda Bryson
See Bryson, Bernarda
Shaik, Fatima *114*
Shalant, Phyllis 1949- *150*
Shan, Darren 1972- *239*
Earlier sketches in SATA *129, 168, 199*
Shan, D.B.
See Shan, Darren
Shanahan, Lisa *199*
Shanberg, Karen
See Shragg, Karen (I.)
Shane, Harold Gray 1914-1993 .... *36*
Obituary *76*
Shange, Ntozake 1948- *157*
Shanks, Ann Zane (Kushner) *10*
Shannon, David 1959- *228*
Earlier sketches in SATA *107, 152*
See also CLR *87*
Shannon, George 1952- *202*
Earlier sketches in SATA *35, 94, 143*
Shannon, George William Bones
See Shannon, George
Shannon, Jacqueline *63*
Shannon, Margaret
See Silverwood, Margaret Shannon
Shannon, Monica 1905(?)-1965 .... *28*
Shannon, Terry
See Mercer, Jessie
Shannon, Terry Miller 1951- *148*
Shapiro, Irwin 1911-1981 .... *32*
Shapiro, Jody Fickes 1940- *193*
Shapiro, Karen Jo 1964- *186*
Shapiro, Michelle 1961- *196*
Shapiro, Milton J. 1926- *32*
Shapiro, Tricia
See Andryszewski, Tricia
Shapiro, Zachary 1970- *213*
Shapp, Charles M(orris) 1906-1989
Obituary *61*
Shapp, Martha Glauber 1910- *3*
Sharenow, Robert *193*
Sharfman, Amalie *14*
Sharkey, Niamh *213*
Sharma, Partap 1939- *15*
Sharma, Rashmi
See Singh, Rashmi Sharma
Sharman, Alison
See Leonard, Alison
Sharmat, Marjorie Weinman 1928- *133*
Earlier sketches in SATA *4, 33, 74*
Sharmat, Mitchell 1927- *127*
Earlier sketch in SATA *33*
Sharp, Anne Wallace 1947- *144*
Sharp, Luke
See Alkiviades, Alkis
Sharp, Margery 1905-1991 .... *29*
Obituary *67*
Earlier sketch in SATA *1*
See also CLR *27*
Sharp, Zerna A. 1889-1981
Obituary *27*
Sharpe, Jon
See Duncan, Alice
and Knott, William C(ecil, Jr.)
and Messman, Jon
Sharpe, Mitchell R(aymond) 1924- *12*
Sharpe, Susan 1946- *71*
Sharratt, Nick 1962- *199*
Earlier sketches in SATA *104, 153*
Shasha, Mark 1961- *80*
Shattuck, Roger 1923-2005 .... *64*
Obituary *174*
Shattuck, Roger Whitney
See Shattuck, Roger
Shaw, Arnold 1909-1989 .... *4*
Obituary *63*
Shaw, Carolyn V. 1934- *91*
Shaw, Charles (Green) 1892-1974 .... *13*
Shaw, Evelyn S. 1927- *28*
Shaw, Flora Louisa
See Lugard, Flora Louisa Shaw
Shaw, Hannah 1982(?)- *227*
Shaw, Janet 1937- *146*
Earlier sketch in SATA *61*
See also CLR *96*
Shaw, Janet Beeler
See Shaw, Janet
Shaw, Liane 1959- *222*
Shaw, Lisa
See Rogak, Lisa
Shaw, Margret 1940- *68*
Shaw, Mary 1965- *180*
Shaw, Nancy 1946- *162*
Earlier sketch in SATA *71*
Shaw, Ray *7*
Shaw, Richard 1923- *12*
Shawn, Frank S.
See Goulart, Ron
Shay, Art
See Shay, Arthur
Shay, Arthur 1922- *4*
Shay, Lacey
See Shebar, Sharon Sigmond
Shea, Bob *231*
Earlier sketch in SATA *188*
Shea, George 1940- *54*
Brief entry *42*
Shea, Pegi Deitz 1960- *172*
Earlier sketches in SATA *77, 137*
Shearer, Alex 1949- *204*
Shearer, John 1947- *43*
Brief entry *27*
See also CLR *34*
Shearer, Ted 1919- *43*
Shearing, Leonie 1972- *184*
Sheban, Chris *182*
Shebar, Sharon Sigmond 1945- *36*
Shecter, Ben 1935- *16*
Shecter, Vicky Alvear 1961- *234*
Shedd, Warner 1934- *147*
Earlier sketch in SATA *87*
Sheedy, Alexandra Elizabeth 1962- *39*
Earlier sketch in SATA *19*
Sheehan, Ethna 1908-2000 .... *9*
Sheehan, Patty 1945- *77*
Sheehan, Sean 1951- *154*
Earlier sketch in SATA *86*
Sheen, Barbara 1949- *143*
Shefelman, Janice 1930- *205*
Earlier sketches in SATA *58, 129*
Shefelman, Janice Jordan
See Shefelman, Janice
Shefelman, Tom 1927- *204*
Earlier sketch in SATA *58*
Sheffer, H. R.
See Abels, Harriette S(heffer)
Sheffield, Charles 1935-2002 .... *109*
Sheffield, Janet N. 1926- *26*
Sheikh, Nazneen 1944- *101*
Sheinkin, Steve 1968- *204*
Sheinmel, Alyssa B. *233*
Sheinmel, Courtney 1977- *211*
Shekerjian, Regina Tor *16*
Shelby, Anne 1948- *85*
Autobiography Feature *121*
See also SAAS *26*
Sheldon, Ann
See Antle, Nancy
Sheldon, Ann *67*
Earlier sketch in SATA *1*
Sheldon, Aure 1917-1976 .... *12*
Sheldon, David *185*
Sheldon, Deyan *181*
Sheldon, Dyan *238*
Sheldon, John
See Bloch, Robert (Albert)
Sheldon, Muriel 1926- *45*
Brief entry *39*
Shell, Barry 1951- *176*
Shelley, Frances
See Wees, Frances Shelley
Shelley, John 1959- *202*

Shelley, Mary
 See Shelley, Mary Wollstonecraft
Shelley, Mary Wollstonecraft 1797-1851 ..... *29*
 See also CLR *133*
Shelton, Paula Young 1961- *227*
Shelton, William Roy 1919-1995 ..... *5*
 Obituary *129*
Shemie, Bonnie (Jean Brenner) 1949- *96*
Shemin, Margaretha (Hoeneveld) 1928- *4*
Shen, Michele 1953- *173*
Shenker, Michele
 See Shen, Michele
Shenton, Edward 1895-1977 ..... *45*
Shepard, Aaron 1950- *187*
 Earlier sketches in SATA *75, 113*
Shepard, Ernest Howard 1879-1976 ..... *100*
 Obituary *24*
 Earlier sketches in SATA *3, 33*
 See also CLR *27*
Shepard, James R.
 See Shepard, Jim
Shepard, Jim 1956- *164*
 Earlier sketch in SATA *90*
Shepard, Mary
 See Knox, (Mary) Eleanor Jessie
Shephard, Esther 1891-1975 ..... *5*
 Obituary *26*
Shepherd, Amanda *201*
Shepherd, Donna Walsh
 See Walsh Shepherd, Donna
Shepherd, Elizabeth *4*
Shepherd, Irana *173*
Shepherd, Nicole Leigh
 See Mikulski, Keri
Shepherd, Roni
 See Shepherd, Irana
Sheppard, Kate *195*
Shepperson, Rob *240*
 Earlier sketch in SATA *178*
Sherburne, Zoa (Lillian Morin) 1912-1995 .... *3*
 See also SAAS *18*
Sherk-Savage, Candace
 See Savage, Candace
Sherlock, Patti *71*
Sherman, D(enis) R(onald) 1934- *48*
 Brief entry *29*
Sherman, Diane (Finn) 1928- *12*
Sherman, Elizabeth
 See Friskey, Margaret (Richards)
Sherman, Harold (Morrow) 1898-1987 ..... *37*
 Obituary *137*
Sherman, Josepha *163*
 Earlier sketch in SATA *75*
Sherman, Michael
 See Lowndes, Robert A(ugustine) W(ard)
Sherman, Nancy
 See Rosenberg, Nancy
Sherman, Pat *174*
Sherman, Peter Michael
 See Lowndes, Robert A(ugustine) W(ard)
Sherrard, Valerie 1957- *141*
Sherrard, Valerie Anne
 See Sherrard, Valerie
Sherrod, Jane
 See Singer, Jane Sherrod
Sherry, Clifford J. 1943- *84*
Sherry, Maureen 1964(?)- *240*
Sherry, (Dulcie) Sylvia 1932- *122*
 Earlier sketch in SATA *8*
Sherwan, Earl 1917- *3*
Sherwood, Jonathan
 See London, Jonathan
Sheth, Kashmira *186*
Shetterly, Will 1955- *78*
 Autobiography Feature *106*
Shetterly, William Howard
 See Shetterly, Will
Shiefman, Vicky 1942- *22*
Shields, Brenda Desmond (Armstrong)
 1914- *37*
Shields, Carol Diggory *174*
Shields, Charles 1944- *10*
Shields, Gillian *203*
Shiels, Barbara
 See Adams, Barbara Johnston
Shiffman, Lena 1957- *101*
Shiga, Jason 1976- *228*
Shiina, Makoto 1944- *83*
Shimin, Symeon 1902-1984 ..... *13*
Shimko, Bonnie 1941- *191*
Shine, Andrea 1955- *104*
Shine, Deborah 1932- *71*
Shinn, Everett 1876-1953 ..... *21*
Shinn, Sharon 1957- *229*
 Earlier sketches in SATA *110, 164*
Shipp, Josh 1982- *236*
Shippen, Katherine B(inney) 1892-1980 ..... *1*
 Obituary *23*
 See also CLR *36*
Shippey, T. A. 1943- *143*
Shippey, Thomas Alan
 See Shippey, T. A.
Shipton, Eric Earle 1907-1977 ..... *10*
Shipton, Jonathan 1948- *215*
Shipton, Paul 1963- *196*
Shiraz, Yasmin *173*
Shirer, William L. 1904-1993 ..... *45*
 Obituary *78*
 See Shirer, William Lawrence
Shirley, Debra *203*
Shirley, Gayle C 1955- *96*
Shirley, Gayle Corbett
 See Shirley, Gayle C
Shirley, Jean 1919- *70*
Shirreffs, Gordon D(onald) 1914-1996 ..... *11*
Shirts, Morris A(lpine) 1922- *63*
Shlichta, Joe 1968- *84*
Shmurak, Carole B. 1944- *118*
Sholokhov, Mikhail 1905-1984
 Obituary *36*
Sholokhov, Mikhail Aleksandrovich
 See Sholokhov, Mikhail
Shore, Diane Z. *215*
 Earlier sketch in SATA *179*
Shore, Diane ZuHone
 See Shore, Diane Z.
Shore, June Lewis *30*
Shore, Nancy 1960- *124*
Shore, Robert 1924- *39*
Short, Michael 1937- *65*
Short, Roger
 See Arkin, Alan
Shortall, Leonard W. *19*
Shortt, Tim(othy Donald) 1961- *96*
Shotwell, Louisa Rossiter 1902-1993 ..... *3*
Shoulders, Michael 1954- *216*
Shoup, Barbara 1947- *156*
 Earlier sketch in SATA *86*
 See also SAAS *24*
Shoveller, Herb *184*
Showalter, Jean B(reckinridge) *12*
Showell, Ellen Harvey 1934- *33*
Showers, Paul C. 1910-1999 ..... *92*
 Obituary *114*
 Earlier sketch in SATA *21*
 See also CLR *6*
 See also SAAS *7*
Shpakow, Tanya 1959(?)- *94*
Shpitalnik, Vladimir 1964- *83*
Shragg, Karen (I.) 1954- *142*
Shreeve, Elizabeth 1956- *156*
Shreve, Susan
 See Shreve, Susan Richards
Shreve, Susan Richards 1939- *152*
 Brief entry *41*
 Earlier sketches in SATA *46, 95*
Shriver, Jean Adair 1932- *75*
Shriver, Maria 1955- *134*
Shriver, Maria Owings
 See Shriver, Maria
Shrode, Mary
 See Hollingsworth, Mary
Shtainmets, Leon *32*
Shub, Elizabeth 1915(?)-2004 ..... *5*
Shuken, Julia 1948- *84*
Shulevitz, Uri 1935- *165*
 Earlier sketches in SATA *3, 50, 106*
 See also CLR *61*
Shulman, Alix Kates 1932- *7*
Shulman, Dee 1957- *146*
Shulman, Irving 1913-1995 ..... *13*
Shulman, Lisa *202*
Shulman, Mark 1962- *184*
Shulman, Max 1919-1988
 Obituary *59*
Shulman, Milton 1913-2004
 Obituary *154*
Shulman, Neil B(arnett) 1945- *89*
Shulman, Polly *235*
Shumsky, Zena
 See Collier, Zena
Shura, Mary Francis
 See Craig, Mary (Francis) Shura
Shusterman, Neal 1962- *201*
 Autobiography Feature *140*
 Earlier sketches in SATA *85, 121, 140*
Shuter, Jane (Margaret) 1955- *151*
 Earlier sketch in SATA *90*
Shuttlesworth, Dorothy Edwards *3*
Shwartz, Susan (Martha) 1949- *94*
Shyer, Christopher 1961- *98*
Shyer, Marlene Fanta *13*
Siberell, Anne *29*
Sibley, Don 1922- *12*
Siburt, Ruth 1951- *121*
Siculan, Daniel 1922- *12*
Siddals, Mary McKenna *232*
Siddon, Barbara
 See Bradford, Barbara Taylor
Sidgwick, Ethel 1877-1970 ..... *116*
Sidjakov, Nicolas 1924- *18*
Sidman, Joyce 1956- *236*
 Earlier sketches in SATA *145, 181*
Sidney, Frank
 See Warwick, Alan R(oss)
Sidney, Margaret
 See Lothrop, Harriet Mulford Stone
Siebert, Diane 1948- *189*
Siegal, Aranka 1930- *88*
 Brief entry *37*
Siegel, Beatrice *36*
Siegel, Helen
 See Siegl, Helen
Siegel, Randolph
 See Siegel, Randy
Siegel, Randy *234*
Siegel, Robert 1939- *39*
Siegel, Robert Harold
 See Siegel, Robert
Siegel, Siena Cherson 1967(?)- *185*
Siegelson, Kim L. 1962- *114*
Sieger, Ted 1958- *189*
Siegl, Helen 1924- *34*
Siepmann, Mary Aline
 See Wesley, Mary (Aline)
Sierra, Judy 1945- *239*
 Earlier sketches in SATA *104, 162, 195*
Sieswerda, Paul L. 1942- *147*
Sievert, Terri
 See Dougherty, Terri (L.)
Sigsawa, Keiichi 1972- *211*
Silas
 See McCay, (Zenas) Winsor
Silberberg, Alan *240*
Silcock, Sara Lesley 1947- *12*
Silin-Palmer, Pamela *184*
Sill, Cathryn 1953- *221*
 Earlier sketches in SATA *74, 141*
Sill, John 1947- *222*
 Earlier sketches in SATA *74, 140*
Sillitoe, Alan 1928-2010 ..... *61*
Sills, Leslie (Elka) 1948- *129*

Silly, E. S.
See Kraus, (Herman) Robert
Silsbe, Brenda 1953- ... *73*
Silva, Joseph
See Goulart, Ron
Silvano, Wendi 1962- ... *223*
Silver, Jago
See Jago
Silver, Maggie ... *216*
Silver, Ruth
See Chew, Ruth
Silverberg, Robert 1935- ... *91*
Autobiography Feature ... *104*
Earlier sketch in SATA *13*
See also CLR *59*
Silverman, Erica 1955- ... *222*
Earlier sketches in SATA *78, 112, 165*
Silverman, Janis L. 1946- ... *127*
Silverman, Mel(vin Frank) 1931-1966 ... *9*
Silverman, Robin L. 1954- ... *96*
Silverman, Robin Landew
See Silverman, Robin L.
Silverstein, Alvin 1933- ... *124*
Earlier sketches in SATA *8, 69*
See also CLR *25*
Silverstein, Herma 1945- ... *106*
Silverstein, Robert Alan 1959- ... *124*
Earlier sketch in SATA *77*
Silverstein, Shel 1932-1999 ... *92*
Brief entry ... *27*
Obituary ... *116*
Earlier sketch in SATA *33*
See also CLR *96*
Silverstein, Sheldon Allan
See Silverstein, Shel
Silverstein, Virginia B. 1937- ... *124*
Earlier sketches in SATA *8, 69*
See also CLR *25*
Silverstein, Virginia Barbara Opshelor
See Silverstein, Virginia B.
Silverthorne, Elizabeth 1930- ... *35*
Silverwood, Margaret Shannon 1966- ... *137*
Earlier sketch in SATA *83*
Silvey, Diane F. 1946- ... *135*
Sim, David 1953- ... *162*
Sim, Dorrith M. 1931- ... *96*
Simak, Clifford D(onald) 1904-1988
Obituary ... *56*
Simard, Remy 1959- ... *168*
Siminovich, Lorena 1976(?)- ... *219*
Simmie, Lois (Ann) 1932- ... *106*
Simmonds, Posy 1945- ... *130*
See also CLR *23*
Simmonds, Rosemary Elizabeth
See Simmonds, Posy
Simmons, Andra 1939- ... *141*
Simmons, Elly 1955- ... *134*
Simmons, Michael 1970- ... *185*
Simms, Laura 1947- ... *117*
Simner, Janni Lee ... *113*
Simon, Charlie May
See Fletcher, Charlie May Hogue
Simon, Francesca 1955- ... *111*
Simon, Gabriel 1972- ... *118*
Simon, Hilda Rita 1921- ... *28*
See also CLR *39*
Simon, Howard 1903-1979 ... *32*
Obituary ... *21*
Simon, Joe
See Simon, Joseph H.
Simon, Joseph H. 1913-2011 ... *7*
Simon, Martin P(aul William) 1903-1969 ... *12*
Simon, Mina Lewiton
See Lewiton, Mina
Simon, Norma (Feldstein) 1927- ... *129*
Earlier sketches in SATA *3, 68*
Simon, Seymour 1931- ... *202*
Earlier sketches in SATA *4, 73, 138*
See also CLR *63*
Simon, Shirley (Schwartz) 1921- ... *11*
Simon, Solomon 1895-1970 ... *40*
Simone, Ni-Ni ... *241*
Simonetta, Linda 1948- ... *14*
Simonetta, Sam 1936- ... *14*
Simons, Barbara B(rooks) 1934- ... *41*
Simont, Marc 1915- ... *126*
Earlier sketches in SATA *9, 73*
Simpson, Colin 1908-1983 ... *14*
Simpson, Harriette
See Arnow, Harriette (Louisa) Simpson
Simpson, Jacynth Hope
See Hope Simpson, Jacynth
Simpson, Lesley 1963- ... *150*
Simpson, Margaret 1943- ... *128*
Simpson, Myrtle L(illias) 1931- ... *14*
Sims, Blanche ... *168*
Earlier sketch in SATA *75*
Sims, Blanche L.
See Sims, Blanche
Sims, Rudine
See Bishop, Rudine Sims
Simundsson, Elva 1950- ... *63*
Sinclair, Clover
See Gater, Dilys
Sinclair, Emil
See Hesse, Hermann
Sinclair, Jeff 1958- ... *77*
Sinclair, Olga 1923- ... *121*
Sinclair, Rose
See Smith, Susan Vernon
Sinclair, Upton 1878-1968 ... *9*
Sinclair, Upton Beall
See Sinclair, Upton
Singer, A.L.
See Lerangis, Peter
Singer, Arthur 1917-1990 ... *64*
Singer, Isaac
See Singer, Isaac Bashevis
Singer, Isaac Bashevis 1904-1991 ... *27*
Obituary ... *68*
Earlier sketch in SATA *3*
See also CLR *1*
Singer, Jane Sherrod 1917-1985 ... *4*
Obituary ... *42*
Singer, Julia 1917- ... *28*
Singer, Kurt D. 1911-2005 ... *38*
Obituary ... *172*
Singer, Marilyn 1948- ... *234*
Autobiography Feature ... *158*
Brief entry ... *38*
Earlier sketches in SATA *48, 80, 125, 158, 201*
See also CLR *48*
See also SAAS *13*
Singer, Muff 1942-2005 ... *104*
Obituary ... *160*
Singer, Nicky 1956- ... *194*
Singer, Susan (Mahler) 1941- ... *9*
Singh, Rashmi Sharma 1952- ... *90*
Singleton, Linda Joy 1957- ... *166*
Earlier sketch in SATA *88*
Singleton, L.J.
See Singleton, Linda Joy
Singleton, Sarah 1966- ... *214*
Sinykin, Sheri
See Sinykin, Sheri Cooper
Sinykin, Sheri Cooper 1950- ... *142*
Autobiography Feature ... *142*
Earlier sketches in SATA *72, 133*
Sinykin, Sheril Terri Cooper
See Sinykin, Sheri Cooper
Siomades, Lorianne ... *217*
Sipiera, Paul P., (Jr.) 1948- ... *144*
Earlier sketch in SATA *89*
Siracusa, Catherine (Jane) 1947- ... *82*
Sirett, Dawn (Karen) 1966- ... *88*
Sirimarco, Elizabeth 1966- ... *158*
Sirof, Harriet 1930- ... *94*
Earlier sketch in SATA *37*
Sirois, Allen L. 1950- ... *76*
Sirvaitis (Chernyaev), Karen (Ann) 1961- ... *79*
Sis, Peter 1949- ... *192*
Earlier sketch in SATA *149*
See also CLR *110*
Sisson, Rosemary Anne 1923- ... *11*
Sisson, Stephanie Roth ... *237*
Earlier sketch in SATA *202*
Sister Mary Terese
See Donze, Mary Terese
Sita, Lisa 1962- ... *87*
Sitarski, Anita ... *200*
Sitomer, Alan Lawrence ... *174*
Sitomer, Harry 1903-1985 ... *31*
Sitomer, Mindel 1903-1987 ... *31*
Sittenfeld, Curtis 1975(?)- ... *164*
Sive, Helen R(obinson) 1951- ... *30*
Sivulich, Sandra (Jeanne) Stroner 1941- ... *9*
Siy, Alexandra ... *193*
Skarmeta, Antonio 1940- ... *57*
Skeers, Linda 1958- ... *207*
Skelly, James R(ichard) 1927- ... *17*
Skelton, Matthew 1971- ... *185*
Skinner, Constance Lindsay 1877-1939
See YABC *1*
Skinner, Cornelia Otis 1901-1979 ... *2*
Skipper, G. C. 1939- ... *46*
Brief entry ... *38*
Sklansky, Amy E(dgar) 1971- ... *145*
Sklansky, Amy E. 1971- ... *204*
Skofield, James ... *95*
Brief entry ... *44*
Skold, Betty Westrom 1923- ... *41*
Skorpen, Liesel Moak 1935- ... *3*
Skott, Maria
See Nikolajeva, Maria
Skovron, Jon 1976- ... *229*
Skrypuch, Marsha Forchuk 1954- ... *134*
Skultety, Nancy Laney 1960- ... *175*
Skurzynski, Gloria 1930- ... *145*
Autobiography Feature ... *145*
Earlier sketches in SATA *8, 74, 122*
See also SAAS *9*
Skurzynski, Gloria Joan
See Skurzynski, Gloria
Skutch, Robert 1925- ... *89*
Skye, Maggie
See Werner, Herma
Skye, Obert ... *200*
Earlier sketch in SATA *170*
Slack, Michael 1969- ... *189*
Slackman, Charles B. 1934- ... *12*
Slade, Arthur G. 1967- ... *221*
Earlier sketches in SATA *106, 149*
Slade, Arthur Gregory
See Slade, Arthur G.
Slade, Christian 1974- ... *238*
Earlier sketch in SATA *193*
Slade, Richard 1910-1971 ... *9*
Slade, Suzanne 1964- ... *226*
Slangerup, Erik Jon 1969- ... *130*
Slate, Joseph 1928- ... *174*
Earlier sketches in SATA *38, 122*
Slate, Joseph Frank
See Slate, Joseph
Slater, Dashka 1963- ... *179*
Slater, David Michael 1970- ... *212*
Slater, Ray
See Lansdale, Joe R.
Slaughter, Hope 1940- ... *84*
Slaughter, Jean
See Doty, Jean Slaughter
Slaughter, Tom 1955- ... *152*
Slavicek, Louise Chipley 1956- ... *144*
Slavin, Bill 1959- ... *199*
Earlier sketches in SATA *76, 148*
Slaymaker, Melissa Eskridge 1958- ... *158*
Slayton, Fran Cannon ... *221*
Sleator, William 1945-2011 ... *208*
Earlier sketches in SATA *3, 68, 118, 161*
See also CLR *128*
Sleator, William Warner III
See Sleator, William

Slegers, Liesbet 1975- ... *154*
Sleigh, Barbara 1906-1982 ... *86*
Obituary ... *30*
Earlier sketch in SATA *3*
Slepian, Jan 1921- ... *85*
Brief entry ... *45*
Earlier sketch in SATA *51*
See also SAAS *8*
Slepian, Janice B.
See Slepian, Jan
Slicer, Margaret O. 1920- ... *4*
Slier, Debby
See Shine, Deborah
Sloan, Brian 1966- ... *172*
Sloan, Carolyn 1937- ... *116*
Earlier sketch in SATA *58*
Sloan, Glenna 1930- ... *120*
Sloan, Glenna Davis
See Sloan, Glenna
Sloane, Eric 1910(?)-1985 ... *52*
Obituary ... *42*
Sloane, Todd 1955- ... *88*
Sloat, Teri 1948- ... *164*
Earlier sketches in SATA *70, 106*
Slobodkin, Florence Gersh 1905-1994 ... *5*
Obituary ... *107*
Slobodkin, Louis 1903-1975 ... *26*
Earlier sketch in SATA *1*
Slobodkina, Esphyr 1908-2002 ... *1*
Obituary ... *135*
See also SAAS *8*
Sloggett, Nellie 1851-1923 ... *44*
Slonim, David 1966- ... *207*
Sloss, Lesley Lord 1965- ... *72*
Slote, Alfred 1926- ... *72*
Earlier sketch in SATA *8*
See also CLR *4*
See also SAAS *21*
Slote, Elizabeth 1956- ... *80*
Small, Charlie
See Ward, Nick
Small, David 1945- ... *216*
Brief entry ... *46*
Earlier sketches in SATA *50, 95, 126, 183*
See also CLR *53*
Small, Ernest
See Lent, Blair
Small, Mary 1932- ... *165*
Small, Terry 1942- ... *75*
Smallcomb, Pam 1954- ... *159*
Smallman, Steve ... *227*
Earlier sketch in SATA *197*
Smalls, Irene
See Smalls-Hector, Irene
Smalls-Hector, Irene 1950- ... *146*
Earlier sketch in SATA *73*
See also CLR *103*
Smallwood, Norah (Evelyn) 1910(?)-1984
Obituary ... *41*
Smaridge, Norah (Antoinette) 1903-1994 ... *6*
Smath, Jerry 1933- ... *198*
Smee, Nicola 1948- ... *167*
Earlier sketch in SATA *76*
Smiley, Virginia Kester 1923- ... *2*
Smit, Noelle 1972- ... *199*
Smith, Alexander McCall 1948- ... *179*
Earlier sketch in SATA *73*
Smith, Andrew 1959- ... *209*
Smith, Andrew Anselmo
See Smith, Andrew
Smith, Andy J. 1975- ... *207*
Smith, Anne Warren 1938- ... *41*
Brief entry ... *34*
Smith, Barry (Edward Jervis) 1943- ... *75*
Smith, Beatrice S(chillinger) ... *12*
Smith, Betsy Covington 1937- ... *55*
Earlier sketch in SATA *43*
Smith, Betty (Wehner) 1904-1972 ... *6*
Smith, Bradford 1909-1964 ... *5*
Smith, Brenda 1946- ... *82*
Smith, C. Pritchard
See Hoyt, Edwin P(almer), Jr.
Smith, Caesar
See Trevor, Elleston
Smith, Cat Bowman 1939- ... *201*
Smith, Charles R., Jr. 1969- ... *203*
Earlier sketch in SATA *159*
Smith, Craig 1955- ... *172*
Earlier sketches in SATA *81, 117*
Smith, Cynthia Leitich 1967- ... *215*
Earlier sketch in SATA *152*
Smith, D. James 1955- ... *176*
Smith, Danna ... *216*
Smith, Danna Kessimakis
See Smith, Danna
Smith, Datus C(lifford), Jr. 1907-1999 ... *13*
Obituary ... *116*
Smith, Debra 1955- ... *89*
Smith, Derek 1943- ... *141*
Smith, Dick King
See King-Smith, Dick
Smith, D.J.
See Smith, D. James
Smith, Dodie
See Smith, Dorothy Gladys
Smith, Doris Buchanan 1934-2002 ... *75*
Obituary ... *140*
Earlier sketch in SATA *28*
See also SAAS *10*
Smith, Dorothy Gladys 1896-1990 ... *82*
Obituary ... *65*
Smith, Dorothy Stafford 1905- ... *6*
Smith, Duane 1974- ... *202*
Smith, E(lmer) Boyd 1860-1943
See YABC *1*
Smith, E(dric) Brooks 1917- ... *40*
Smith, Elwood H. 1941- ... *236*
Earlier sketch in SATA *203*
Smith, Emily Wing 1980- ... *215*
Smith, Emma 1923- ... *52*
Brief entry ... *36*
Smith, (Katherine) Eunice (Young) 1902-1993 ... *5*
Smith, Frances C(hristine) 1904-1986 ... *3*
Smith, Gary R. 1932- ... *14*
Smith, Geof 1969- ... *102*
Smith, George Harmon 1920- ... *5*
Smith, Gordon 1951- ... *184*
Smith, Greg Leitich ... *152*
Smith, H(arry) Allen 1907-1976
Obituary ... *20*
Smith, Helene 1937- ... *142*
Smith, Hope Anita ... *202*
Smith, Howard E(verett), Jr. 1927- ... *12*
Smith, Hugh L(etcher) 1921-1968 ... *5*
Smith, Icy 1966- ... *228*
Smith, Imogene Henderson 1922- ... *12*
Smith, Jacqueline B. 1937- ... *39*
Smith, Jada Pinkett 1971- ... *161*
Smith, James Noel 1950- ... *193*
Smith, Janet (Buchanan) Adam
See Adam Smith, Janet (Buchanan)
Smith, Janice Lee 1949- ... *155*
Earlier sketch in SATA *54*
Smith, Jean
See Smith, Frances C(hristine)
Smith, Jean Pajot 1945- ... *10*
Smith, Jeff 1958- ... *161*
Earlier sketch in SATA *93*
Smith, Jeff Allen
See Smith, Jeff
Smith, Jeffrey Alan
See Smith, Jeff
Smith, Jenny 1963- ... *90*
Smith, Jessie
See Kunhardt, Edith
Smith, Jessie Willcox 1863-1935 ... *21*
See also CLR *59*
Smith, Jim W.W. ... *231*
Smith, Joan (Mary) 1933- ... *54*
Brief entry ... *46*
Smith, Johnston
See Crane, Stephen
Smith, Jos A. 1936- ... *181*
Earlier sketches in SATA *73, 120*
Smith, Joseph Arthur
See Smith, Jos A.
Smith, Judie R. 1936- ... *80*
Smith, Kirsten 1970- ... *210*
Smith, Lafayette
See Higdon, Hal
Smith, Lane 1959- ... *224*
Earlier sketches in SATA *76, 131, 179*
See also CLR *47*
Smith, Lee
See Albion, Lee Smith
Smith, Lendon H(oward) 1921- ... *64*
Smith, Lillian H(elena) 1887-1983
Obituary ... *32*
Smith, Linda 1949- ... *177*
Smith, Linell Nash 1932- ... *2*
Smith, Lucia B. 1943- ... *30*
Smith, Maggie 1965- ... *235*
Earlier sketch in SATA *190*
Smith, Margaret Emily Noel Nuttall
See Nuttall-Smith, Margaret Emily Noel
Smith, Marion Hagens 1913- ... *12*
Smith, Marion Jaques 1899-1987 ... *13*
Smith, Mary Ellen ... *10*
Smith, Marya 1945- ... *78*
Smith, Mike
See Smith, Mary Ellen
Smith, Nancy Covert 1935- ... *12*
Smith, Norman F. 1920- ... *70*
Earlier sketch in SATA *5*
Smith, Patricia Clark 1943- ... *96*
Smith, Pauline C.
See Arthur, Robert, (Jr.)
Smith, Pauline C(oggeshall) 1908-1994 ... *27*
Smith, Philip Warren 1936- ... *46*
Smith, R. Alexander McCall
See Smith, Alexander McCall
Smith, Rebecca 1946- ... *123*
Smith, Robert Kimmel 1930- ... *77*
Earlier sketch in SATA *12*
Smith, Robert Paul 1915-1977 ... *52*
Obituary ... *30*
Smith, Roland 1951- ... *193*
Earlier sketches in SATA *115, 161*
Smith, Rosamond
See Oates, Joyce Carol
Smith, Ruth Leslie 1902- ... *2*
Smith, Samantha 1972-1985
Obituary ... *45*
Smith, Sandra Lee 1945- ... *75*
Smith, Sarah Stafford
See Smith, Dorothy Stafford
Smith, Sharon 1947- ... *82*
Smith, Sherri L. 1971- ... *156*
Smith, Sherwood 1951- ... *206*
Autobiography Feature ... *206*
Earlier sketches in SATA *82, 140*
Smith, Shirley Raines
See Raines, Shirley C(arol)
Smith, Susan Carlton 1923- ... *12*
Smith, Susan Mathias 1950- ... *43*
Brief entry ... *35*
Smith, Susan Vernon 1950- ... *48*
Brief entry ... *45*
Smith, Tim(othy R.) 1945- ... *151*
Smith, Ursula 1934- ... *54*
Smith, Vian (Crocker) 1920-1969 ... *11*
Smith, Wanda VanHoy 1926- ... *65*
Smith, Ward
See Goldsmith, Howard
Smith, Wendy
See French, Wendy
Smith, William A. 1918- ... *10*
Smith, William Jay 1918- ... *154*
Autobiography Feature ... *154*
Earlier sketches in SATA *2, 68*
See also SAAS *22*

Smith, Winsome 1935- *45*
Smith, Z.Z.
See Westheimer, David
Smith-Ankrom, M. E. 1942- *130*
Smith-Griswold, Wendy 1955- *88*
Smith Hernandez, Duncan Tonatiuh
See Tonatiuh, Duncan
Smith-Rex, Susan J. 1950- *94*
Smithsen, Richard
See Pellowski, Michael (Joseph)
Smithson, Ryan 1985- *216*
Smits, Teo
See Smits, Theodore R(ichard)
Smits, Theodore R(ichard) 1905-1996 .... *45*
Brief entry *28*
Smolinski, Dick 1932- *86*
Smothers, Ethel Footman 1944- *149*
Earlier sketch in SATA *76*
Smucker, Anna Egan 1948- *209*
Smucker, Barbara 1915-2003 .... *130*
Earlier sketches in SATA *29, 76*
See also CLR *10*
See also SAAS *11*
Smucker, Barbara Claassen
See Smucker, Barbara
Smy, Pam *240*
Smyth, Iain 1959- *105*
Snedeker, Caroline Dale (Parke) 1871-1956
See YABC *2*
Sneed, Brad *191*
Sneider, Marian 1932-2005 .... *197*
Snell, Gordon 1933(?)- *228*
Snell, Nigel (Edward Creagh) 1936- *57*
Brief entry *40*
Snellgrove, L(aurence) E(rnest) 1928- *53*
Snelling, Dennis (Wayne) 1958- *84*
Sneve, Virginia Driving Hawk 1933- *95*
Earlier sketch in SATA *8*
See also CLR *2*
Snicket, Lemony 1970- *215*
Earlier sketches in SATA *126, 187*
See also CLR *79*
Sniegoski, Thomas E. 1962- *195*
Sniegoski, Tom
See Sniegoski, Thomas E.
Snir, Eleyor *225*
Snir, Mirik 1948- *226*
Snodgrass, Mary Ellen 1944- *75*
Snodgrass, Quentin Curtius
See Twain, Mark
Snodgrass, Thomas Jefferson
See Twain, Mark
Snook, Barbara (Lillian) 1913-1976 .... *34*
Snow, Alan 1959- *190*
Snow, Carol 1965- *208*
Snow, Donald Clifford 1917-1979 .... *16*
Snow, Dorothea J(ohnston) 1909- *9*
Snow, Richard F. 1947- *52*
Brief entry *37*
Snow, Richard Folger
See Snow, Richard F.
Snow, Sarah *229*
Snyder, Anne 1922-2001 .... *4*
Obituary *125*
Snyder, Bernadette McCarver 1930- *97*
Snyder, Betsy *230*
Snyder, Carol 1941- *35*
Snyder, Gerald S(eymour) 1933- *48*
Brief entry *34*
Snyder, Jerome 1916-1976
Obituary *20*
Snyder, Laurel 1974- *209*
Snyder, Midori 1954- *106*
Snyder, Paul A. 1946- *125*
Snyder, Zilpha Keatley 1927- *226*
Autobiography Feature *163*
Earlier sketches in SATA *1, 28, 75, 110, 163*
See also CLR *121*
See also SAAS *2*
Snyderman, Reuven K. 1922- *5*
So, Meilo *162*
Sobel, June 1950- *149*
Soble, Jennie
See Cavin, Ruth
Sobol, Donald J. 1924- *132*
Earlier sketches in SATA *1, 31, 73*
See also CLR *4*
Sobol, Harriet Langsam 1936- *47*
Brief entry *34*
Sobol, Richard *211*
Sobol, Rose 1931- *76*
Sobott-Mogwe, Gaele 1956- *97*
Soderberg, Erin Kate
See Downing, Erin
Soderlind, Arthur E(dwin) 1920- *14*
Soentpiet, Chris K. 1970- *159*
Earlier sketch in SATA *97*
Soerensen, Svend Otto 1916- *67*
Sofer, Barbara 1949- *109*
Sofer, Rachel
See Sofer, Barbara
Softly, Barbara Frewin 1924- *12*
Sogabe, Aki *207*
Soglow, Otto 1900-1975
Obituary *30*
Sohl, Frederic J(ohn) 1916- *10*
Sohr, Daniel 1973- *190*
Sokol, Bill
See Sokol, William
Sokol, William 1923- *37*
Sokolov, Kirill 1930- *34*
Solbert, Romaine G. 1925- *2*
Solbert, Ronni
See Solbert, Romaine G.
Solheim, James *233*
Earlier sketch in SATA *133*
Solomon, Heather M. *188*
Solomon, Joan 1930- *51*
Brief entry *40*
Solomons, Ikey Esquir
See Thackeray, William Makepeace
Solonevich, George 1915-2003 .... *15*
Solot, Mary Lynn 1939- *12*
Solov'ev, Mikhail
See Soloviov, Michael
Soloviov, Michael 1972- *222*
Soman, David 1965- *200*
Somerlott, Robert 1928-2001 .... *62*
Somers, Kevin *205*
Somervill, Barbara A(nn) 1948- *140*
Sommer, Angela
See Sommer-Bodenburg, Angela
Sommer, Carl 1930- *175*
Earlier sketch in SATA *126*
Sommer, Elyse 1929- *7*
Sommer, Robert 1929- *12*
Sommer-Bodenburg, Angela 1948- *113*
Earlier sketch in SATA *63*
Sommerdorf, Norma 1926- *131*
Sommerdorf, Norma Jean
See Sommerdorf, Norma
Sommerfelt, Aimee 1892-1975 .... *5*
Son, John *160*
Sones, Sonya 1953(?)- *131*
Sonneborn, Ruth (Cantor) 1899-1974 .... *4*
Obituary *27*
Sonnenblick, Jordan 1969- *223*
Earlier sketch in SATA *185*
See also CLR *144*
Sonnenmark, Laura A. 1958- *73*
Soo, Kean *201*
Sopko, Eugen 1949- *58*
Sorel, Edward 1929- *126*
Brief entry *37*
Earlier sketch in SATA *65*
Sorensen, Henri 1950- *115*
Earlier sketch in SATA *77*
Sorensen, Svend Otto
See Soerensen, Svend Otto
Sorensen, Virginia 1912-1991 .... *2*
Obituary *72*
See also SAAS *15*
Sorenson, Jane 1926- *63*
Sorenson, Margo 1946- *96*
Sorley Walker, Kathrine *41*
Sorra, Kristin *185*
Sorrells, Walter *177*
Sorrentino, Joseph N. 1937- *6*
Sortor, June Elizabeth 1939- *12*
Sortor, Toni
See Sortor, June Elizabeth
Sosa, Hernan 1977- *203*
Soskin, V. H.
See Ellison, Virginia H(owell)
Soto, Gary 1952- *174*
Earlier sketches in SATA *80, 120*
See also CLR *38*
Sotomayor, Antonio 1902-1985 .... *11*
Souci, Robert D. San
See San Souci, Robert D.
Souders, Taryn 1977- *237*
Soudley, Henry
See Wood, James Playsted
Souhami, Jessica *176*
Soule, Gardner (Bosworth) 1913-2000 .... *14*
Soule, Jean Conder 1919- *10*
Soup, Cuthbert
See Swallow, Gerry
Souster, (Holmes) Raymond 1921- *63*
South, Sheri Cobb 1959- *82*
Southall, Ivan 1921-2008 .... *134*
Autobiography Feature *134*
Earlier sketches in SATA *3, 68*
See also CLR *165*
See also SAAS *3*
Southall, Ivan Francis
See Southall, Ivan
Southey, Robert 1774-1843 .... *54*
Southgate, Vera *54*
Souza, Janet
See Tashjian, Janet
Sovak, Jan 1953- *115*
Sowden, Celeste
See Walters, Celeste
Sowter, Nita *69*
Spafford, Suzy 1945- *160*
Spagnoli, Cathy 1950- *134*
Earlier sketch in SATA *79*
Spain, Sahara Sunday 1991- *133*
Spain, Susan Rosson *185*
Spalding, Andrea 1944- *150*
Earlier sketch in SATA *101*
Spalenka, Greg 1958- *198*
Spanfeller, James J. 1930- *19*
See also SAAS *8*
Spanfeller, Jim
See Spanfeller, James J.
Spangenberg, Judith Dunn 1942- *5*
Spangler, Brie *212*
Spanyol, Jessica 1965- *206*
Earlier sketch in SATA *137*
Spar, Jerome 1918- *10*
Sparks, Barbara 1942- *78*
Sparks, Beatrice (Mathews) 1918- *44*
Brief entry *28*
See also CLR *139*
Sparks, Mary W. 1920- *15*
Spaulding, Douglas
See Bradbury, Ray
Spaulding, Leonard
See Bradbury, Ray
Spaulding, Norma *107*
Speare, Elizabeth George 1908-1994 .... *62*
Obituary *83*
Earlier sketch in SATA *5*
See also CLR *8*
Spearing, Craig J. *228*
Spearing, Judith (Mary Harlow) 1922- *9*
Spears, Rick *182*
Speck, Katie *196*
Speck, Nancy 1959- *104*
Specking, Inez 1890-1960(?) *11*

Speed, Nell
See Keats, Emma
and Sampson, Emma (Keats) Speed
Speed, Nell (Ewing) 1878-1913 .... *68*
Speer, Bonnie Stahlman 1929- *113*
Speer-Lyon, Tammie L. 1965- *89*
Speicher, Helen Ross S(mith) 1915- *8*
Speir, Nancy 1958- *210*
Earlier sketch in SATA *81*
Spelling, Tori 1973- *236*
Spelling, Victoria Davey
See Spelling, Tori
Spellman, John W(illard) 1934- *14*
Spellman, Roger G.
See Cox, William R(obert)
Spelman, Cornelia Maude 1946- *144*
Earlier sketch in SATA *96*
Spelman, Mary 1934- *28*
Spelvin, George
See Lerangis, Peter
and Phillips, David Atlee
Spence, Cynthia
See Eble, Diane
Spence, Eleanor (Rachel) 1928- *21*
See also CLR *26*
Spence, Geraldine 1931- *47*
Spencer, Ann 1918- *10*
Spencer, Britt *206*
Spencer, Cornelia
See Yaukey, Grace S(ydenstricker)
Spencer, Donald D(ean) 1931- *41*
Spencer, Elizabeth 1921- *14*
Spencer, Leonard G.
See Garrett, Randall
and Silverberg, Robert
Spencer, William 1922- *9*
Spencer, Zane A(nn) 1935- *35*
Spengler, Margaret *223*
Sper, Emily 1957- *142*
Speregen, Devra Newberger 1964- *84*
Sperling, Dan(iel Lee) 1949- *65*
Sperry, Armstrong W. 1897-1976 .... *1*
Obituary *27*
Sperry, Raymond
See Garis, Howard R.
Sperry, Raymond, Jr. *1*
Spetter, Jung-Hee 1969- *134*
Spicer, Dorothy Gladys -1975 .... *32*
Spiegel, Beth *184*
Spiegelman, Art 1948- *158*
Earlier sketch in SATA *109*
Spiegelman, Judith M. *5*
Spielberg, Steven 1947- *32*
Spier, Peter (Edward) 1927- *54*
Earlier sketch in SATA *4*
See also CLR *5*
Spilhaus, Athelstan (Frederick) 1911-1998 .. *13*
Obituary *102*
Spilka, Arnold 1917- *6*
Spillane, Frank Morrison
See Spillane, Mickey
Spillane, Mickey 1918-2006 .... *66*
Obituary *176*
Spillebeen, Geert 1956- *225*
Spinelli, Eileen 1942- *225*
Earlier sketches in SATA *38, 101, 150, 186*
Spinelli, Jerry 1941- *195*
Earlier sketches in SATA *39, 71, 110, 158*
See also CLR *82*
Spink, Reginald (William) 1905-1994 .... *11*
Spinka, Penina Keen 1945- *72*
Spinner, Stephanie 1943- *234*
Earlier sketches in SATA *38, 91, 132*
Spinossimus
See White, William, Jr.
Spiotta-DiMare, Loren *173*
Spires, Ashley 1978- *183*
Spires, Elizabeth 1952- *215*
Earlier sketches in SATA *71, 111*
Spiridellis, Gregg 1971(?)- *199*
Spirin, Gennadii
See Spirin, Gennady
Spirin, Gennadij
See Spirin, Gennady
Spirin, Gennady 1948- *204*
Earlier sketches in SATA *95, 134*
See also CLR *88*
Spiro, Ruth *208*
Spivak, Dawnine *101*
Spizman, Robyn Freedman *194*
Spohn, David 1948- *72*
Spohn, Kate 1962- *147*
Earlier sketch in SATA *87*
Spollen, Christopher 1952- *12*
Spooner, Michael (Tim) 1954- *92*
Spoor, Mike *218*
Spowart, Robin 1947- *177*
Earlier sketch in SATA *82*
Spradlin, Michael P. *235*
Earlier sketch in SATA *204*
Sprague, Gretchen 1926-2003 .... *27*
Spranger, Nina 1969- *203*
Spratt, R.A. *235*
Spratt, Rachel
See Spratt, R.A.
Sprengel, Artie
See Lerangis, Peter
Sprigge, Elizabeth (Miriam Squire)
1900-1974 .... *10*
Spring, (Robert) Howard 1889-1965 .... *28*
Springer, Kristina *226*
Springer, Margaret 1941- *78*
Springer, Marilyn Harris 1931- *47*
Springer, Nancy 1948- *222*
Earlier sketches in SATA *65, 110, 172*
Springstubb, Tricia 1950- *78*
Brief entry *40*
Earlier sketch in SATA *46*
Spudvilas, Anne 1951- *199*
Earlier sketch in SATA *94*
Spurll, Barbara 1952- *78*
Spurr, Elizabeth *172*
Spykman, E(lizabeth) C(hoate) 1896-1965 .. *10*
See also CLR *35*
Spyri, Johanna (Heusser) 1827-1901 .... *100*
Earlier sketch in SATA *19*
See also CLR *115*
Squires, Janet *215*
Squires, Phil
See Barker, S. Omar
Srba, Lynne *98*
Sreenivasan, Jyotsna 1964- *101*
S-Ringi, Kjell
See Ringi, Kjell (Arne Soerensen)
Staake, Bob 1957- *209*
Stacey, Cherylyn 1945- *96*
Stacy, Donald
See Pohl, Frederik
Stadler, John *204*
Stadtler, Bea 1921- *17*
Stafford, Jean 1915-1979
Obituary *22*
Stafford, Liliana 1950- *141*
Stafford, Paul 1966- *116*
Stahl, Ben(jamin) 1910-1987 .... *5*
Obituary *54*
Stahl, Hilda 1938-1993 .... *48*
Obituary *77*
Stahler, David, Jr. *218*
Earlier sketch in SATA *162*
Staib, Walter *233*
Staines, Bill 1949- *213*
Stainton, Sue *187*
Stair, Gobin (John) 1912- *35*
Stalder, Valerie *27*
Stamaty, Mark Alan 1947- *230*
Earlier sketch in SATA *12*
Stambler, Irwin 1924- *5*
Stamp, Jorgen 1969- *225*
Stampler, Ann Redisch *209*
Standiford, Natalie 1961- *169*
Earlier sketch in SATA *81*
Stanek, Lou Willett 1931- *63*
Stang, Judit 1921-1977 .... *29*
Stang, Judy
See Stang, Judit
Stangl, (Mary) Jean 1928- *67*
Stanhope, Eric
See Hamilton, Charles (Harold St. John)
Stankevich, Boris 1928- *2*
Stanley, Diane 1943- *240*
Autobiography Feature *240*
Brief entry *32*
Earlier sketches in SATA *37, 80, 115, 164, 213*
See also CLR *46*
See also SAAS *15*
Stanley, Elizabeth 1947- *206*
Stanley, George Edward 1942-2011 .... *228*
Earlier sketches in SATA *53, 111, 157, 1, 67*
Stanley, Jerry 1941- *127*
Earlier sketch in SATA *79*
Stanley, Mandy *165*
Stanley, Robert
See Hamilton, Charles (Harold St. John)
Stanley, Sanna 1962- *145*
Stanli, Sue
See Meilach, Dona Z(weigoron)
Stanstead, John
See Groom, Arthur William
Stanton, Karen 1960- *190*
Stanton, Schuyler
See Baum, L. Frank
Staples, Suzanne Fisher 1945- *207*
Earlier sketches in SATA *70, 105, 151*
See also CLR *137*
Stapleton, Marjorie (Winifred) 1932- *28*
Stapp, Arthur D(onald) 1906-1972 .... *4*
Starbird, Kaye 1916- *6*
See also CLR *60*
Stark, Evan 1942- *78*
Stark, James
See Goldston, Robert (Conroy)
Stark, Ken 1943- *199*
Stark, Ulf 1944- *124*
Starke, Ruth (Elaine) 1946- *129*
Starkey, Marion L(ena) 1901-1991 .... *13*
Starmer, Aaron 1976- *226*
Starr, Ward
See Manes, Stephen
Starret, William
See McClintock, Marshall
Starr Taylor, Bridget 1959- *99*
Stasiak, Krystyna *49*
Staub, Frank 1949- *116*
Staub, Frank Jacob
See Staub, Frank
Staub, Wendy Corsi 1964- *114*
Stauffacher, Sue 1961- *236*
Earlier sketches in SATA *155, 199*
Stauffer, Don
See Berkebile, Fred D(onovan)
Staunton, Schuyler
See Baum, L. Frank
Staunton, Ted 1956- *167*
Earlier sketch in SATA *112*
Stead, Erin E. 1982- *232*
Stead, Judy *210*
Stead, Philip C.
See Stringer, Helen
Stead, Philip Christian *225*
Stead, Rebecca 1968(?)- *228*
Earlier sketch in SATA *188*
Steadman, Ralph 1936- *123*
Earlier sketch in SATA *32*
Steadman, Ralph Idris
See Steadman, Ralph
Stearman, Kaye 1951- *118*
Stearn, Ted 1961- *218*
Stearns, Monroe (Mather) 1913-1987 .... *5*
Obituary *55*

Steckler, Arthur 1921-1985 .... *65*
Steding, Laurie 1953- *119*
Steel, Danielle 1947- *66*
Steel, Danielle Fernande
See Steel, Danielle
Steele, Addison II
See Lupoff, Richard A.
Steele, Alexander 1958- *116*
Steele, Henry Maxwell
See Steele, Max
Steele, Mary 1930- *94*
Steele, Mary Q(uintard Govan) 1922-1992 .. *51*
Obituary *72*
Earlier sketch in SATA *3*
Steele, Max 1922-2005 .... *168*
Earlier sketch in SATA *10*
Steele, Philip 1948- *140*
Earlier sketch in SATA *81*
Steele, William O(wen) 1917-1979 .... *51*
Obituary *27*
Earlier sketch in SATA *1*
Steelhammer, Ilona 1952- *98*
Steelsmith, Shari 1962- *72*
Stefanik, Alfred T. 1939- *55*
Steffanson, Con
See Cassiday, Bruce (Bingham)
and Goulart, Ron
Steffens, Bradley 1955- *166*
Earlier sketch in SATA *77*
Steffensmeier, Alexander 1977- *195*
Stegeman, Janet Allais 1923- *49*
Brief entry *49*
Steggall, Susan 1967- *182*
Steig, William 1907-2003 .... *111*
Obituary *149*
Earlier sketches in SATA *18, 70*
See also CLR *103*
Steig, William H.
See Steig, William
Stein, David Ezra *211*
Earlier sketch in SATA *180*
Stein, Janet 1955- *218*
Stein, M(eyer) L(ewis) 1920- *6*
Stein, Mathilde 1969- *195*
Stein, Mini *2*
Stein, R(ichard) Conrad 1937- *154*
Earlier sketches in SATA *31, 82*
Stein, Tammar 1979(?)- *240*
Stein, Wendy 1951- *77*
Steinbeck, John 1902-1968 .... *9*
See also CLR *172*
Steinbeck, John Ernst
See Steinbeck, John
Steinberg, Alfred 1917-1995 .... *9*
Steinberg, David 1962- *200*
Steinberg, D.J.
See Steinberg, David
Steinberg, Don 1962- *239*
Steinberg, Fannie 1899-1990 .... *43*
Steinberg, Fred J. 1933- *4*
Steinberg, Phillip Orso 1921- *34*
Steinberg, Rafael (Mark) 1927- *45*
Steinberg, Saul 1914-1999 .... *67*
Steincrohn, Maggie
See Davis, Maggie S.
Steiner, Barbara A(nnette) 1934- *83*
Earlier sketch in SATA *13*
See also SAAS *13*
Steiner, Charlotte 1900-1981 .... *45*
Steiner, George 1929- *62*
Steiner, Joan *199*
Earlier sketch in SATA *110*
Steiner, Jorg
See Steiner, Jorg
Steiner, Jorg 1930- *35*
Steiner, K. Leslie
See Delany, Samuel R., Jr.
Steiner, Stan(ley) 1925-1987 .... *14*
Obituary *50*
Steinmetz, Karen *235*
Steins, Richard 1942- *79*
Stem, Jacqueline 1931- *110*
Stemple, Heidi E.Y. 1966- *214*
Stemple, Jason *179*
Steneman, Shep 1945- *132*
Stengel, Joyce A. 1938- *158*
Stephanie, Gordon
See Gordon, Stephanie Jacob
Stephens, Alice Barber 1858-1932 .... *66*
Stephens, Casey
See Wagner, Sharon B.
Stephens, Helen 1972- *234*
Stephens, Henrietta Henkle 1909-1993 .... *6*
Stephens, J.B.
See Lynn, Tracy
Stephens, Mary Jo 1935- *8*
Stephens, Rebecca 1961- *141*
Stephens, Reed
See Donaldson, Stephen R.
Stephens, Suzanne
See Kirby, Susan E.
Stephens, William M(cLain) 1925- *21*
Stephensen, A. M.
See Manes, Stephen
Stephenson, Kristina *224*
Stephenson, Lynda 1941- *179*
Stephenson, Lynda A.
See Stephenson, Lynda
Stepp, Ann 1935- *29*
Stepto, Michele 1946- *61*
Steptoe, Javaka 1971- *213*
Earlier sketch in SATA *151*
Steptoe, John (Lewis) 1950-1989 .... *63*
Earlier sketch in SATA *8*
See also CLR *12*
Sterling, Brett
See Bradbury, Ray
and Hamilton, Edmond
and Samachson, Joseph
Sterling, Dorothy 1913-2008 .... *83*
Autobiography Feature *127*
Obituary *200*
Earlier sketch in SATA *1*
See also CLR *1*
See also SAAS *2*
Sterling, Helen
See Watts, Helen L. Hoke
Sterling, Philip 1907-1989 .... *8*
Obituary *63*
Sterling, Shirley (Anne) 1948- *101*
Stern, Ellen Norman 1927- *26*
Stern, Judith M. 1951- *75*
Stern, Madeleine
See Stern, Madeleine B.
Stern, Madeleine B. 1912-2007 .... *14*
Stern, Madeleine Bettina
See Stern, Madeleine B.
Stern, Maggie 1953- *156*
Stern, Philip Van Doren 1900-1984 .... *13*
Obituary *39*
Stern, Simon 1943- *15*
Sterne, Emma Gelders 1894- *6*
Steurt, Marjorie Rankin 1888-1978 .... *10*
Stevens, April 1963- *208*
Stevens, Bryna 1924- *65*
Stevens, Carla M(cBride) 1928- *13*
Stevens, Chambers 1968- *128*
Stevens, Diane 1939- *94*
Stevens, Franklin 1933- *6*
Stevens, Greg
See Cook, Glen
Stevens, Gwendolyn 1944- *33*
Stevens, Helen *209*
Stevens, Jan Romero 1953- *95*
Stevens, Janet 1953- *193*
Earlier sketches in SATA *90, 148*
Stevens, Kathleen 1936- *49*
Stevens, Leonard A. 1920- *67*
Stevens, Lucile Vernon 1899-1994 .... *59*
Stevens, Margaret Dean
See Aldrich, Bess Streeter
Stevens, Patricia Bunning 1931- *27*
Stevens, Peter
See Geis, Darlene Stern
Stevens, Serita 1949- *70*
Stevens, Serita Deborah
See Stevens, Serita
Stevens, Serita Mendelson
See Stevens, Serita
Stevens, Shira
See Stevens, Serita
Stevenson, Anna (M.) 1905- *12*
Stevenson, Augusta 1869(?)-1976 .... *2*
Obituary *26*
Stevenson, Burton Egbert 1872-1962 .... *25*
Stevenson, Drew 1947- *60*
Stevenson, Emma *207*
Stevenson, Harvey 1960- *148*
Earlier sketch in SATA *80*
Stevenson, James 1929- *195*
Brief entry *34*
Earlier sketches in SATA *42, 71, 113, 161*
See also CLR *17*
Stevenson, Janet 1913- *8*
Stevenson, Robert Louis 1850-1894 .... *100*
See also YABC *2*
See also CLR *107*
Stevenson, Robert Louis Balfour
See Stevenson, Robert Louis
Stevenson, Sarah Jamila 1977- *241*
Stevenson, Sucie
See Stevenson, Sucie
Stevenson, Sucie 1956- *194*
Earlier sketch in SATA *104*
Stewart, A(gnes) C(harlotte) *15*
Stewart, Amber *181*
Stewart, Chantal 1945- *173*
Earlier sketch in SATA *121*
Stewart, Charles
See Zurhorst, Charles (Stewart, Jr.)
Stewart, Eleanor
See Porter, Eleanor H(odgman)
Stewart, Elisabeth J(ane) 1927- *93*
Stewart, Elizabeth Laing 1907- *6*
Stewart, Gail B. 1949- *141*
Stewart, George Rippey 1895-1980 .... *3*
Obituary *23*
Stewart, Jennifer J. 1960- *128*
Stewart, Jennifer Jenkins
See Stewart, Jennifer J.
Stewart, Joel *211*
Earlier sketch in SATA *151*
Stewart, John 1920- *14*
Stewart, Mary (Florence Elinor) 1916- *12*
Stewart, Mary Rainbow
See Stewart, Mary (Florence Elinor)
Stewart, Melissa 1968- *209*
Earlier sketches in SATA *111, 167*
Stewart, Paul 1955- *199*
Earlier sketches in SATA *114, 163*
Stewart, Robert Neil 1891-1972 .... *7*
Stewart, Sarah *143*
Stewart, Scott
See Zaffo, George J.
Stewart, Trenton Lee 1970- *216*
Stewart, W(alter) P. 1924- *53*
Stewart, Whitney 1959- *167*
Earlier sketch in SATA *92*
Stewig, John Warren 1937- *162*
Earlier sketches in SATA *26, 110*
Stickler, Soma Han 1942- *128*
Stidworthy, John 1943- *63*
Stiefvater, Maggie 1981- *237*
Stiegemeyer, Julie *180*
Stier, Catherine *198*
Stiles, Martha Bennett *108*
Earlier sketch in SATA *6*
Still, James 1906-2001 .... *29*
Obituary *127*
Stille, Darlene R. 1942- *170*
Earlier sketch in SATA *126*
Stille, Darlene Ruth
See Stille, Darlene R.

Stillerman, Marci ... *104*
Stillerman, Robbie 1947- ... *12*
Stilley, Frank 1918- ... *29*
Stilton, Geronimo ... *158*
Stimpson, Gerald
See Mitchell, Adrian
Stimson, James 1964- ... *213*
Stine, Catherine ... *165*
Stine, G(eorge) Harry 1928-1997 ... *136*
Earlier sketch in SATA *10*
Stine, Jovial Bob
See Stine, R.L.
Stine, R.L. 1943- ... *194*
Earlier sketches in SATA *31, 76, 129*
See also CLR *111*
Stine, Robert Lawrence
See Stine, R.L.
Stinetorf, Louise (Allender) 1900-1992 ... *10*
Stinson, Kathy 1952- ... *98*
Stirling, Arthur
See Sinclair, Upton
Stirling, Ian 1941- ... *77*
Stirling, Nora B(romley) 1900-1997 ... *3*
Stirnweis, Shannon 1931- ... *10*
Stobbs, William 1914-2000 ... *17*
Obituary ... *120*
Stock, Carolmarie 1951- ... *75*
Stock, Catherine 1952- ... *214*
Earlier sketches in SATA *65, 114, 158*
Stockdale, Susan 1954- ... *206*
Earlier sketch in SATA *98*
Stockham, Peter (Alan) 1928- ... *57*
Stockton, Francis Richard 1834-1902 ... *44*
Brief entry ... *32*
Stockton, Frank R.
See Stockton, Francis Richard
Stockwell-Moniz, Marc J. 1954- ... *164*
Stoddard, Edward G. 1923- ... *10*
Stoddard, Hope 1900-1987 ... *6*
Stoddard, Sandol 1927- ... *98*
Earlier sketch in SATA *14*
Stoehr, Shelley 1969- ... *107*
Stoeke, Janet Morgan 1957- ... *202*
Earlier sketches in SATA *90, 136*
Stohl, Margaret ... *227*
Stohner, Anu 1952- ... *179*
Stoiko, Michael 1919- ... *14*
Stojic, Manya 1967- ... *156*
Stoker, Abraham
See Stoker, Bram
Stoker, Bram 1847-1912 ... *29*
Stokes, Cedric
See Beardmore, George
Stokes, Jack (Tilden) 1923- ... *13*
Stokes, Olivia Pearl 1916- ... *32*
Stolarz, Laurie Faria 1972- ... *203*
Stolz, Mary 1920-2006 ... *133*
Obituary ... *180*
Earlier sketches in SATA *10, 71*
See also SAAS *3*
Stolz, Mary Slattery
See Stolz, Mary
Stone, Alan
See Svenson, Andrew E(dward)
Stone, David K(arl) 1922- ... *9*
Stone, David Lee 1978- ... *166*
Stone, Eugenia 1879-1971 ... *7*
Stone, Gene
See Stone, Eugenia
Stone, Helen V(irginia) ... *6*
Stone, Idella Purnell
See Purnell, Idella
Stone, Ikey
See Purnell, Idella
Stone, Irving 1903-1989 ... *3*
Obituary ... *64*
Stone, Jeff ... *178*
Stone, Jon 1931-1997 ... *39*
Obituary ... *95*
Stone, Josephine Rector
See Dixon, Jeanne
Stone, Kyle M. 1972- ... *202*
Stone, Lesley
See Trevor, Elleston
Stone, Mary Hanlon ... *231*
Stone, Peter 1930-2003 ... *65*
Obituary ... *143*
Stone, Phoebe ... *205*
Earlier sketch in SATA *134*
Stone, Raymond ... *1*
Stone, Rosetta
See Dr. Seuss
Stone, Tanya Lee 1965- ... *217*
Earlier sketch in SATA *182*
Stonehouse, Bernard 1926- ... *140*
Earlier sketches in SATA *13, 80*
Stones, (Cyril) Anthony 1934- ... *72*
Stong, Phil(ip Duffield) 1899-1957 ... *32*
Stoops, Erik D(aniel) 1966- ... *142*
Earlier sketch in SATA *78*
Stoppelmoore, Cheryl Jean
See Ladd, Cheryl (Jean)
Stops, Sue 1936- ... *86*
Storace, Patricia ... *193*
Storad, Conrad J. 1957- ... *119*
Storey, Margaret 1926- ... *9*
Storey, Victoria Carolyn 1945- ... *16*
Stork, Francisco
See Stork, Francisco X.
Stork, Francisco X. 1953- ... *210*
Storme, Peter
See Stern, Philip Van Doren
Storms, Patricia 1963- ... *217*
Storr, Catherine (Cole) 1913-2001 ... *87*
Obituary ... *122*
Earlier sketch in SATA *9*
Story, Josephine
See Loring, Emilie (Baker)
Stotko, Mary-Ann 1960- ... *154*
Stott, Ann ... *219*
Stott, Dorothy (M.) 1958- ... *99*
Earlier sketch in SATA *67*
Stott, Dot
See Stott, Dorothy (M.)
Stotter, Mike 1957- ... *108*
Stotts, Stuart ... *227*
Stout, Shawn K. ... *226*
Stout, William 1949- ... *132*
Stoutenburg, Adrien (Pearl) 1916-1982 ... *3*
Stoutland, Allison 1963- ... *130*
Stover, Allan C(arl) 1938- ... *14*
Stover, Jill (Griffin) 1958- ... *82*
Stover, Marjorie Filley 1914- ... *9*
Stowe, Harriet Beecher 1811-1896
See YABC *1*
See also CLR *131*
Stowe, Harriet Elizabeth Beecher
See Stowe, Harriet Beecher
Stowe, Leland 1899-1994 ... *60*
Obituary ... *78*
Stowe, Rosetta
See Ogan, George F.
and Ogan, Margaret E. (Nettles)
Stower, Adam ... *229*
Earlier sketch in SATA *195*
Strachan, Bruce 1959- ... *205*
Strachan, Ian 1938- ... *85*
Strachan, Linda ... *167*
Strachan, Margaret Pitcairn 1908-1998 ... *14*
Strahinich, H. C.
See Strahinich, Helen C.
Strahinich, Helen C. 1949- ... *78*
Strait, Treva Adams 1909-2002 ... *35*
Strand, Mark 1934- ... *41*
Strange, Philippa
See Coury, Louise Andree
Stranger, Joyce
See Wilson, Joyce M.
Strangis, Joel 1948- ... *124*
Strannigan, Shawn 1956- ... *93*
Strannigan, Shawn Alyne
See Strannigan, Shawn
Strasnick, Lauren ... *222*
Strasser, Todd 1950- ... *215*
Earlier sketches in SATA *41, 45, 71, 107, 153*
See also CLR *11*
Stratemeyer, Edward L. 1862-1930 ... *100*
Earlier sketches in SATA *1, 67*
See also CLR *166*
See Adams, Harrison
Stratford, Philip 1927- ... *47*
Stratton, Allan 1951- ... *178*
Stratton, J. M.
See Whitlock, Ralph
Stratton, Thomas
See Coulson, Robert S(tratton)
and DeWeese, Thomas Eugene
Stratton-Porter, Gene 1863-1924 ... *15*
See also CLR *87*
Strauss, Gwen 1963- ... *77*
Strauss, Joyce 1936- ... *53*
Strauss, Linda Leopold 1942- ... *127*
Strauss, Susan (Elizabeth) 1954- ... *75*
Strayer, E. Ward
See Stratemeyer, Edward L.
Streano, Vince(nt Catello) 1945- ... *20*
Streatfeild, Mary Noel
See Streatfeild, Noel
Streatfeild, Noel 1897(?)-1986 ... *20*
Obituary ... *48*
See also CLR *83*
Street, Janet Travell 1959- ... *84*
Street, Julia Montgomery 1898-1993 ... *11*
Streissguth, Thomas 1958- ... *116*
Strelkoff, Tatiana 1957- ... *89*
Stren, Patti 1949- ... *88*
Brief entry ... *41*
See also CLR *5*
Strete, Craig Kee 1950- ... *96*
Earlier sketch in SATA *44*
Stretton, Barbara (Humphrey) 1936- ... *43*
Brief entry ... *35*
Strevens-Marzo, Bridget ... *238*
Strickland, Brad 1947- ... *200*
Earlier sketches in SATA *83, 137, 142*
Strickland, Craig (A.) 1956- ... *102*
Strickland, Dorothy S(alley) 1933- ... *89*
Strickland, Michael R. 1965- ... *144*
Earlier sketch in SATA *83*
Strickland, Shadra ... *209*
Strickland, Tessa ... *173*
Strickland, William Bradley
See Strickland, Brad
Striegel, Jana 1955- ... *140*
Striegel-Wilson, Jana
See Striegel, Jana
Striker, Lee
See Clark, Margaret (D.)
Striker, Susan 1942- ... *63*
Stringam, Jean 1945- ... *233*
Stringer, Helen ... *225*
Stringer, Lauren 1957- ... *183*
Earlier sketch in SATA *129*
Stroeyer, Poul 1923- ... *13*
Stromoski, Rick 1958- ... *111*
Strong, Charles
See Epstein, Beryl
and Epstein, Samuel
Strong, David
See McGuire, Leslie (Sarah)
Strong, Jeremy 1949- ... *175*
Earlier sketches in SATA *36, 105*
Strong, J.J.
See Strong, Jeremy
Strong, Pat
See Hough, Richard (Alexander)
Strong, Stacie 1965- ... *74*
Stroud, Bettye 1939- ... *165*
Earlier sketch in SATA *96*
Stroud, Jonathan 1970- ... *213*
Earlier sketches in SATA *102, 159*
See also CLR *134*

Stroyer, Poul
See Stroeyer, Poul
Strug, Kerri 1977- *108*
Stryer, Andrea Stenn 1938- *192*
Stryker, Daniel
See Morris, Chris(topher Crosby)
and Stump, Jane Barr
Stuart, David
See Hoyt, Edwin P(almer), Jr.
Stuart, Derek
See Foster, John L(ouis)
Stuart, Forbes 1924- *13*
Stuart, Ian
See MacLean, Alistair
Stuart, Jesse (Hilton) 1906-1984 .... *2*
Obituary *36*
Stuart, Ruth McEnery 1849(?)-1917 .... *116*
Stuart, Sheila
See Baker, Mary Gladys Steel
Stuart-Clark, Christopher (Anthony) 1940- .. *32*
Stuber, Barbara 1951- *234*
Stubis, Talivaldis 1926- *5*
Stubley, Trevor (Hugh) 1932- *22*
Stuchner, Joan Betty *209*
Stucky, Naomi R. 1922- *72*
Stucley, Elizabeth
See Northmore, Elizabeth Florence
Stultifer, Morton
See Curtis, Richard
Sture-Vasa, Mary
See Alsop, Mary O'Hara
Sturges, Philemon *174*
Sturman, Jennifer *237*
Sturtevant, Katherine 1950- *180*
Earlier sketch in SATA *130*
Sturton, Hugh
See Johnston, H(ugh) A(nthony) S(tephen)
Sturtzel, Howard A(llison) 1894-1985 .... *1*
Sturtzel, Jane Levington 1903-1996 .... *1*
Stutley, D(oris) J(ean) 1959- *142*
Stutson, Caroline 1940- *234*
Earlier sketch in SATA *104*
Stuve-Bodeen, Stephanie *240*
See Bodeen, S. A.
Stux, Erica 1929- *140*
Styles, (Frank) Showell 1908- *10*
Stynes, Barbara White *133*
Suarez, Maribel 1952- *201*
Suba, Susanne *4*
Suber, Melissa *213*
Subond, Valerie
See Grayland, Valerie (Merle Spanner)
Sudbery, Rodie 1943- *42*
Sudyka, Diana *208*
Sue, Majella Lue *209*
Suen, Anastasia 1956(?)- *157*
Sufrin, Mark 1925- *76*
Sugarman, Joan G. 1917- *64*
Sugarman, Tracy 1921- *37*
Sugita, Yutaka 1930- *36*
Suhl, Yuri (Menachem) 1908-1986 .... *8*
Obituary *50*
See also CLR *2*
See also SAAS *1*
Suhr, Joanne *129*
Suid, Murray 1942- *27*
Sullivan, Edward T. *206*
Sullivan, George (Edward) 1927- *147*
Earlier sketches in SATA *4, 89*
Sullivan, Jacqueline Levering *203*
Sullivan, Jody
See Rake, Jody
Sullivan, Kathryn A. 1954- *141*
Sullivan, Mary Ann 1954- *63*
Sullivan, Mary W(ilson) 1907- *13*
Sullivan, Pat
See Messmer, Otto
Sullivan, Paul 1939- *106*
Sullivan, Sarah G. 1953- *179*
Sullivan, Silky 1940- *101*
Sullivan, Sue
See Sullivan, Susan E.
Sullivan, Susan E. 1962- *123*
Sullivan, Thomas Joseph, Jr. 1947- *16*
Sullivan, Tom
See Sullivan, Thomas Joseph, Jr.
Sully, Tom 1959- *104*
Suma, Nova Ren *223*
Sumichrast, Jozef 1948- *29*
Sumiko
See Davies, Sumiko
Summerforest, Ivy B.
See Kirkup, James
Summers, Barbara 1944- *182*
Summers, Cassia Joy
See Cowley, Joy
Summers, James L(evingston) 1910-1973 .... *57*
Brief entry *28*
Summertree, Katonah
See Windsor, Patricia
Summy, Barrie *208*
Sumner, William 1971- *229*
Sun, Chyng Feng 1959- *90*
Sunderlin, Sylvia (S.) 1911-1997 .... *28*
Obituary *99*
Sung, Betty Lee *26*
Supeene, Shelagh Lynne 1952- *153*
Supplee, Suzanne *204*
Supraner, Robyn 1930- *101*
Earlier sketch in SATA *20*
Supree, Burt(on) 1941-1992 .... *73*
Surface, Mary Hall 1958- *126*
Surge, Frank 1931- *13*
Susac, Andrew 1929- *5*
Susi, Geraldine Lee 1942- *98*
Sussman, Cornelia Silver 1914-1999 .... *59*
Sussman, Irving 1908-1996 .... *59*
Sussman, Michael 1953- *217*
Sussman, Michael B.
See Sussman, Michael
Sussman, Susan 1942- *48*
Sutcliff, Rosemary 1920-1992 .... *78*
Obituary *73*
Earlier sketches in SATA *6, 44*
See also CLR *138*
Sutcliffe, Jane 1957- *138*
Sutherland, Colleen 1944- *79*
Sutherland, Efua (Theodora Morgue)
1924-1996 .... *25*
Sutherland, Jon 1958- *167*
Sutherland, Jonathan D.
See Sutherland, Jon
Sutherland, Jonathan David
See Sutherland, Jon
Sutherland, Margaret 1941- *15*
Sutherland, Zena Bailey 1915-2002 .... *37*
Obituary *137*
Suttles, Shirley (Smith) 1922- *21*
Sutton, Ann (Livesay) 1923- *31*
Sutton, Eve(lyn Mary) 1906-1992 .... *26*
Sutton, Felix 1910(?)-1973 .... *31*
Sutton, Jane 1950- *52*
Brief entry *43*
Sutton, Larry M(atthew) 1931- *29*
Sutton, Margaret Beebe 1903-2001 .... *1*
Obituary *131*
Sutton, Myron Daniel 1925- *31*
Sutton, Roger 1956- *93*
Sutton, Sally 1973- *214*
Suzanne, Jamie
See Hawes, Louise
and Lantz, Francess L(in)
and Singleton, Linda Joy
and Zach, Cheryl (Byrd)
Suzuki, David 1936- *138*
Suzuki, David Takayoshi
See Suzuki, David
Svendsen, Mark 1962- *181*
Earlier sketch in SATA *120*
Svendsen, Mark Nestor
See Svendsen, Mark
Svenson, Andrew E(dward) 1910-1975 .... *2*
Obituary *26*
Swaab, Neil 1978- *191*
Swaim, Jessica 1950- *202*
Swain, Carol 1962- *172*
Swain, Gwenyth 1961- *134*
Earlier sketch in SATA *84*
Swain, Ruth
See Swain, Ruth Freeman
Swain, Ruth Freeman 1951- *161*
Earlier sketch in SATA *119*
Swain, Su Zan (Noguchi) 1916- *21*
Swain, Wilson 1976- *225*
Swallow, Gerry *227*
Swallow, Pamela Curtis *178*
Swamp, Jake 1941- *98*
Swan, Susan 1944- *108*
Earlier sketch in SATA *22*
Swann, Brian (Stanley Frank) 1940- *116*
Swann, E.L.
See Lasky, Kathryn
Swann, Ruth Rice 1920- *84*
Swanson, Diane 1944- *203*
Swanson, Helen M(cKendry) 1919- *94*
Swanson, June 1931- *76*
Swanson, Susan Marie *209*
Swanson, Wayne 1942- *167*
Swarner, Kristina 1965- *215*
Swarthout, Glendon (Fred) 1918-1992 .... *26*
Swarthout, Kathryn 1919- *7*
Swayne, Sam(uel F.) 1907- *53*
Swayne, Zoa (Lourana) 1905- *53*
Swearingen, Greg 1976- *225*
Sweat, Lynn 1934- *168*
Earlier sketch in SATA *57*
Swede, George 1940- *67*
Sweeney, James B(artholomew) 1910-1999 . *21*
Sweeney, Joyce 1955- *167*
Earlier sketches in SATA *65, 68, 108*
Sweeney, Joyce Kay
See Sweeney, Joyce
Sweeney, Karen O'Connor
See O'Connor, Karen
Sweeney, Matthew (Gerard) 1952- *156*
Sweet, Melissa 1956- *211*
Earlier sketch in SATA *172*
Sweet, Sarah C.
See Jewett, Sarah Orne
Sweetland, Nancy A(nn) 1934- *48*
Swender, Jennifer *235*
Swenson, Allan A(rmstrong) 1933- *21*
Swenson, May 1919-1989 .... *15*
Swentzell, Rina 1939- *79*
Swiatkowska, Gabi 1971(?)- *180*
Swift, Bryan
See Knott, William C(ecil, Jr.)
Swift, David
See Kaufmann, John
Swift, Hildegarde Hoyt 1890(?)-1977
Obituary *20*
Swift, Jonathan 1667-1745 .... *19*
See also CLR *161*
Swift, Merlin
See Leeming, Joseph
Swiger, Elinor Porter 1927- *8*
Swinburne, Laurence (Joseph) 1924- *9*
Swinburne, Stephen R. 1952- *231*
Earlier sketches in SATA *150, 188*
Swinburne, Steve
See Swinburne, Stephen R.
Swindells, Robert (Edward) 1939- *150*
Brief entry *34*
Earlier sketches in SATA *50, 80*
See also SAAS *14*
Swinford, Betty (June Wells) 1927- *58*
Swinford, Bob
See Swinford, Betty (June Wells)
Swithen, John
See King, Stephen
Switzer, Ellen 1923- *48*
Swope, Sam *156*

Swope, Samuel
See Swope, Sam
Sybesma, Jetske
See Ironside, Jetske
Sydney, Frank
See Warwick, Alan R(oss)
Sydor, Colleen 1960- *207*
Sykes, Julie 1963- *202*
Sylvada, Peter 1964- *202*
Sylver, Adrienne *230*
Sylvester, Kevin *240*
Sylvester, Natalie G(abry) 1922- *22*
Syme, (Neville) Ronald 1913-1992 ..... *87*
Earlier sketch in SATA *2*
Symes, R. F. *77*
Symes, Ruth Louise 1962- *179*
Symons, (Dorothy) Geraldine 1909- *33*
Symons, Stuart
See Stanley, George Edward
Symynkywicz, Jeffrey B. 1954- *87*
Symynkywicz, Jeffrey Bruce
See Symynkywicz, Jeffrey B.
Synge, (Phyllis) Ursula 1930- *9*
Sypher, Lucy Johnston 1907- *7*
Szasz, Suzanne (Shorr) 1915-1997 ..... *13*
Obituary *99*
Szekeres, Cyndy 1933- *157*
Autobiography Feature *157*
Earlier sketches in SATA *5, 60, 131*
See also SAAS *13*
Szekessy, Tanja *98*
Szpirglas, Jeff *241*
Szpura, Beata 1961- *93*
Szuc, Jeff 1975- *220*
Szudek, Agnes S(usan) P(hilomena) *57*
Brief entry *49*
Szulc, Tad 1926-2001 ..... *26*
Szydlow, Jarl
See Szydlowski, Mary Vigliante
Szydlowski, Mary Vigliante 1946- *94*
Szymanski, Lois 1957- *91*

T

Taback, Simms 1932- *170*
Brief entry *36*
Earlier sketches in SATA *40, 104*
See also CLR *100*
Taber, Gladys (Bagg) 1899-1980
Obituary *22*
Tabor, Nancy Maria Grande 1949- *161*
Earlier sketch in SATA *89*
Tabrah, Ruth Milander 1921- *14*
Tacang, Brian *213*
Tackach, James 1953- *123*
Tackach, James M.
See Tackach, James
Tadgell, Nicole 1969- *220*
Earlier sketch in SATA *177*
Tafolla, Carmen 1951- *220*
Tafolla, Mary Carmen
See Tafolla, Carmen
Tafuri, Nancy 1946- *192*
Autobiography Feature *192*
Earlier sketches in SATA *39, 75, 130*
See also CLR *74*
See also SAAS *14*
Tagg, Christine Elizabeth 1962- *138*
Tagliaferro, Linda *173*
Taha, Karen T(erry) 1942- *156*
Earlier sketch in SATA *71*
Tai, Sharon O. 1963- *153*
Tait, Douglas 1944- *12*
Takabayashi, Mari 1960- *156*
Earlier sketch in SATA *115*
Takahashi, Hideko *209*
Takahashi, Rumiko 1957- *163*
Takakjian, Portia 1930- *15*
Takashima, Misako
See Misako Rocks!
Takashima, Shizuye 1928- *13*
Takayama, Sandi 1962- *106*
Takeda, Pete(r M.) 1964- *148*
Tal, Eve 1947- *176*
Talbert, Marc (Alan) 1953- *154*
Autobiography Feature *154*
Earlier sketches in SATA *68, 99*
Talbot, Charlene Joy 1928- *10*
Talbot, Toby 1928- *14*
Talbott, Hudson 1949- *212*
Earlier sketches in SATA *84, 131*
Talifero, Gerald 1950- *75*
Talker, T.
See Rands, William Brighty
Tallarico, Tony 1933- *116*
Tallcott, Emogene *10*
Tallec, Olivier 1970- *197*
Tallis, Robyn
See Smith, Sherwood
Tallon, Robert 1939- *43*
Brief entry *28*
Talmadge, Marian *14*
Tamaki, Jillian 1980- *201*
Tamar, Erika 1934- *150*
Earlier sketches in SATA *62, 101*
Tamarin, Alfred H. 1913-1980 ..... *13*
Tamburine, Jean 1930- *12*
Tames, Richard (Lawrence) 1946- *102*
Earlier sketch in SATA *67*
Tamminga, Frederick W(illiam) 1934- *66*
Tammuz, Benjamin 1919-1989
Obituary *63*
Tan, Amy 1952- *75*
Tan, Amy Ruth
See Tan, Amy
Tan, Shaun 1974- *198*
Tanaka, Beatrice 1932- *76*
Tanaka, Shelley *214*
Earlier sketch in SATA *136*
Tanaka, Yoko 1947- *215*
Tang, Charles 1948- *81*
Tang, Greg *172*
Tang, You-Shan 1946- *53*
Tania B.
See Blixen, Karen
Tankard, Jeremy 1973- *191*
Tannen, Mary 1943- *37*
Tannenbaum, Beulah Goldstein 1916- *3*
Tannenbaum, D(onald) Leb 1948- *42*
Tanner, Jane 1946- *74*
Tanner, Lian 1951- *237*
Tanner, Louise S(tickney) 1922-2000 ..... *9*
Tanobe, Miyuki 1937- *23*
Tanselle, Eve 1933- *125*
Tapio, Pat Decker
See Kines, Pat Decker
Tapp, Kathy Kennedy 1949- *88*
Brief entry *50*
Tarbescu, Edith 1939- *107*
Tarkington, (Newton) Booth 1869-1946 ..... *17*
Tarpley, Natasha A(nastasia) 1971- *147*
Tarr, Judith 1955- *237*
Earlier sketches in SATA *64, 149*
Tarry, Ellen 1906-2008 ..... *16*
See also CLR *26*
See also SAAS *16*
Tarshis, Jerome 1936- *9*
Tarshis, Lauren *187*
Tarsky, Sue 1946- *41*
Taschek, Karen 1956- *185*
Tashjian, Jake 1994- *234*
Tashjian, Janet 1956- *238*
Earlier sketches in SATA *102, 151*
Tashjian, Virginia A. 1921-2008 ..... *3*
Tasker, James 1908- *9*
Tate, Don(ald E.) *159*
Tate, Eleanora E. 1948- *191*
Earlier sketches in SATA *38, 94*
See also CLR *37*
Tate, Eleanora Elaine
See Tate, Eleanora E.
Tate, Ellalice
See Hibbert, Eleanor Alice Burford
Tate, Joan 1922- *86*
Earlier sketch in SATA *9*
See also SAAS *20*
Tate, Mary Anne
See Hale, Arlene
Tate, Nikki *134*
Tate, Richard
See Masters, Anthony (Richard)
Tate, Suzanne 1930- *91*
Tatham, Betty *142*
Tatham, Campbell
See Elting, Mary
Tatham, Julie
See Tatham, Julie Campbell
Tatham, Julie Campbell 1908-1999 ..... *80*
Tavares, Matt *198*
Earlier sketch in SATA *159*
Tavares, Victor 1971- *176*
Taves, Isabella 1915- *27*
Taxali, Gary 1968- *234*
Tayleur, Karen 1961- *213*
Taylor, Alastair 1959- *130*
Taylor, Andrew 1951- *70*
Taylor, Andrew John Robert
See Taylor, Andrew
Taylor, Ann 1782-1866 ..... *41*
Brief entry *35*
Taylor, Audilee Boyd 1931- *59*
Taylor, Barbara J. 1927- *10*
Taylor, Ben
See Strachan, Ian
Taylor, Brooke *205*
Taylor, Carl 1937-2010 ..... *14*
Taylor, Carrie-Jo
See Taylor, C.J.
Taylor, Cheryl Munro 1957- *96*
Taylor, C.J. 1952- *224*
Taylor, Cora (Lorraine) 1936- *103*
Earlier sketch in SATA *64*
See also CLR *63*
Taylor, Dave 1948- *78*
Taylor, David
See Taylor, Dave
Taylor, David 1900-1965 ..... *10*
Taylor, Debbie A. 1955- *169*
Taylor, Eleanor 1969- *206*
Taylor, Elizabeth 1912-1975 ..... *13*
Taylor, Florance Walton *9*
Taylor, Florence M(arian Tompkins)
1892-1983 ..... *9*
Taylor, Gage 1942-2000 ..... *87*
Taylor, Geoff 1946- *204*
Taylor, G.P. 1958(?)- *216*
Earlier sketch in SATA *156*
Taylor, Graham Peter
See Taylor, G.P.
Taylor, Greg 1951- *221*
Taylor, Herb(ert Norman, Jr.) 1942-1987 ..... *22*
Obituary *54*
Taylor, J. David
See Taylor, Dave
Taylor, Jane 1783-1824 ..... *41*
Brief entry *35*
Taylor, Jerry D(uncan) 1938- *47*
Taylor, John Robert
See Taylor, Andrew
Taylor, Judy
See Hough, Judy Taylor
Taylor, Kenneth N. 1917-2005 ..... *26*
Taylor, Kenneth Nathaniel
See Taylor, Kenneth N.
Taylor, Kim *180*
Taylor, L(ester) B(arbour), Jr. 1932- *27*
Taylor, Lois Dwight Cole
See Cole, Lois Dwight
Taylor, Louise Todd 1939- *47*
Taylor, Margaret 1950- *106*

Taylor, Mark 1927- ... *32*
Brief entry ... *28*
Taylor, Mildred D. 1943- ... *135*
See also CLR *144*
See also SAAS *5*
Taylor, Mildred Delois
See Taylor, Mildred D.
Taylor, Paula (Wright) 1942- ... *48*
Brief entry ... *33*
Taylor, Peter Lane ... *210*
Taylor, Robert Lewis 1912-1998 ... *10*
Taylor, Sean 1965- ... *192*
Taylor, Susan Champlin
See Champlin, Susan
Taylor, Sydney (Brenner) 1904(?)-1978 ... *28*
Obituary ... *26*
Earlier sketch in SATA *1*
Taylor, Theodore 1921-2006 ... *128*
Obituary ... *177*
Earlier sketches in SATA *5, 54, 83*
See also CLR *30*
See also SAAS *4*
Taylor, William 1938- ... *164*
Earlier sketches in SATA *78, 113*
See also CLR *63*
Taylor-Butler, Christine 1959- ... *218*
Tazewell, Charles 1900-1972 ... *74*
Tchana, Katrin
See Tchana, Katrin Hyman
Tchana, Katrin H.
See Tchana, Katrin Hyman
Tchana, Katrin Hyman 1963- ... *177*
Earlier sketch in SATA *125*
Tchekhov, Anton
See Chekhov, Anton
Tchen, Richard ... *120*
Tchudi, Stephen N. 1942- ... *55*
Teague, Bob
See Teague, Robert
Teague, David ... *235*
Teague, Mark 1963- ... *205*
Earlier sketches in SATA *68, 99, 170*
Teague, Mark Christopher
See Teague, Mark
Teague, Robert 1929- ... *32*
Brief entry ... *31*
Teal, Val 1902-1997 ... *10*
Obituary ... *114*
Teal, Valentine M.
See Teal, Val
Teale, Edwin Way 1899-1980 ... *7*
Obituary ... *25*
Teasdale, Sara 1884-1933 ... *32*
Tebbel, John (William) 1912-2004 ... *26*
Teckentrup, Britta 1969- ... *200*
Tedesco, P.R.
See Naylor, Phyllis Reynolds
Teensma, Lynne Bertrand
See Bertrand, Lynne
Tee-Van, Helen Damrosch 1893-1976 ... *10*
Obituary ... *27*
Teevee, Ningeokuluk 1963- ... *223*
Tegner, Bruce 1928- ... *62*
Teitelbaum, Michael 1953- ... *116*
Earlier sketch in SATA *59*
Tejima
See Tejima, Keizaburo
Tejima, Keizaburo 1931- ... *139*
See also CLR *20*
Telander, Todd (G.) 1967- ... *88*
Teleki, Geza 1943- ... *45*
Telemaque, Eleanor Wong 1934- ... *43*
Telescope, Tom
See Newbery, John
Telgemeier, Raina 1977- ... *228*
Tellegen, Toon 1941- ... *229*
Teller, Janne 1964- ... *230*
Tellis, Annabel 1967- ... *191*
Temkin, Sara Anne Schlossberg 1913-1996 . *26*
Temko, Florence ... *13*
Tempest, Margaret Mary 1892-1982
Obituary ... *33*
Templar, Maurice
See Groom, Arthur William
Temple, Arthur
See Northcott, (William) Cecil
Temple, Charles 1947- ... *79*
Temple, Frances (Nolting) 1945-1995 ... *85*
Temple, Herbert 1919- ... *45*
Temple, Paul
See McConnell, James Douglas Rutherford
Temple, William F(rederick) 1914-1989 .... *107*
Tenggren, Gustaf 1896-1970 ... *18*
Obituary ... *26*
Tennant, Kylie
See Rodd, Kylie Tennant
Tennant, Veronica 1947- ... *36*
TenNapel, Doug 1966- ... *234*
Tenneshaw, S.M.
See Beaumont, Charles
and Garrett, Randall
and Silverberg, Robert
Tenniel, John 1820-1914 ... *74*
Brief entry ... *27*
See also CLR *146*
Teplin, Scott ... *231*
Tepper, Sheri S. 1929- ... *113*
Tepper, Yona 1941- ... *228*
Terada, Alice M. 1928- ... *90*
Terban, Marvin 1940- ... *54*
Brief entry ... *45*
Teresi, Judith M.
See Goldberger, Judith M.
ter Haar, Jaap 1922- ... *6*
See also CLR *15*
Terhune, Albert Payson 1872-1942 ... *15*
Terkel, Susan N(eiburg) 1948- ... *103*
Earlier sketch in SATA *59*
Terlouw, Jan (Cornelis) 1931- ... *30*
Terrazzini, Daniela Jaglenka ... *218*
Terrell, John Upton 1900-1988
Obituary ... *60*
Terrill, Beth ... *198*
Terrill, Elizabeth
See Terrill, Beth
Terris, Susan 1937- ... *77*
Earlier sketch in SATA *3*
Terry, Luther L(eonidas) 1911-1985 ... *11*
Obituary ... *42*
Terry, Margaret
See Dunnahoo, Terry Janson
Terry, Michael 1947- ... *233*
Terry, Walter 1913-1982 ... *14*
Terry, Will 1966- ... *205*
Terzian, James P. 1915- ... *14*
Tessendorf, K(enneth) C(harles) 1925-2003 . *75*
Obituary ... *142*
Tessler, Manya ... *200*
Tessler, Stephanie Gordon
See Gordon, Stephanie Jacob
Testa, Dom ... *208*
Tester, Sylvia Root 1939- ... *64*
Brief entry ... *37*
Tether, (Cynthia) Graham 1950- ... *46*
Brief entry ... *36*
Tetzner, Lisa 1894-1963 ... *169*
Thach, James Otis 1969- ... *195*
Thacher, Mary McGrath 1933- ... *9*
Thackeray, William Makepeace 1811-1863 .. *23*
Thake, Richard 1938- ... *237*
Thaler, Michael C.
See Thaler, Mike
Thaler, Mike 1936- ... *215*
Brief entry ... *47*
Earlier sketches in SATA *56, 93*
Thaler, Shmuel 1958- ... *126*
Earlier sketch in SATA *72*
Thamer, Katie 1955- ... *42*
Thane, Elswyth 1900-1984(?) ... *32*
Tharp, Louise (Marshall) Hall 1898-1992 ...... *3*
Obituary ... *129*
Tharp, Tim 1957- ... *189*
Thayer, Ernest Lawrence 1863-1940 ... *60*
Thayer, Jane
See Woolley, Catherine
Thayer, Marjorie 1908-1992 ... *74*
Brief entry ... *37*
Thayer, Peter
See Wyler, Rose
Thelwell, Norman 1923-2004 ... *14*
Themerson, Stefan 1910-1988 ... *65*
Thermes, Jennifer 1966- ... *155*
Theroux, Paul 1941- ... *109*
Earlier sketch in SATA *44*
Theroux, Paul Edward
See Theroux, Paul
Thesman, Jean ... *124*
Earlier sketch in SATA *74*
The Tjong-Khing
See Khing, T.T.
Thieda, Shirley Ann 1943- ... *13*
Thiele, Colin 1920-2006 ... *125*
Earlier sketches in SATA *14, 72*
See also CLR *27*
See also SAAS *2*
Thiele, Colin Milton
See Thiele, Colin
Thiesing, Lisa 1958- ... *159*
Earlier sketch in SATA *95*
Thimmesh, Catherine ... *189*
Thiry, Joan (Marie) 1926- ... *45*
Thisdale, Francois 1964- ... *222*
Thistlethwaite, Miles 1945- ... *12*
Thollander, Earl 1922- ... *22*
Thomas, Abigail 1941- ... *112*
Thomas, Andrea
See Hill, Margaret (Ohler)
Thomas, Art(hur Lawrence) 1952- ... *48*
Brief entry ... *38*
Thomas, Carroll
See Ratliff, Thomas M.
and Shmurak, Carole B.
Thomas, Cassia ... *236*
Thomas, Dylan 1914-1953 ... *60*
Thomas, Dylan Marlais
See Thomas, Dylan
Thomas, Egbert S.
See Ellis, Edward S.
Thomas, Estelle Webb 1899-1982 ... *26*
Thomas, Frances 1943- ... *171*
Earlier sketch in SATA *92*
Thomas, Garen ... *213*
Thomas, H. C.
See Keating, Lawrence A.
Thomas, Ianthe 1951- ... *139*
Brief entry ... *42*
See also CLR *8*
Thomas, J. F.
See Fleming, Thomas
Thomas, Jan 1958- ... *226*
Earlier sketch in SATA *197*
Thomas, Jane Resh 1936- ... *171*
Earlier sketches in SATA *38, 90*
Thomas, Jerry D. 1959- ... *91*
Thomas, Joan Gale
See Robinson, Joan (Mary) G(ale Thomas)
Thomas, Joyce Carol 1938- ... *210*
Autobiography Feature ... *137*
Earlier sketches in SATA *40, 78, 123, 137*
See also CLR *19*
See also SAAS *7*
Thomas, Lee
See Floren, Lee
and Pendleton, Thomas
Thomas, Lowell Jackson, Jr. 1923- ... *15*
Thomas, Margaret
See Thomas, Peggy
Thomas, Meredith 1963- ... *119*
Thomas, Michael
See Wilks, Michael Thomas
Thomas, Middy 1931- ... *191*

Thomas, Patricia 1934- ... *199*
Earlier sketch in SATA *51*
Thomas, Peggy ... *174*
Thomas, Rob 1965- ... *97*
Thomas, Scott 1959- ... *147*
Thomas, Velma Maia 1955- ... *171*
Thomas, Vernon (Arthur) 1934- ... *56*
Thomas, Victoria
See DeWeese, Thomas Eugene
and Kugi, Constance Todd
Thomasma, Kenneth R. 1930- ... *90*
Thomason, Mark ... *215*
Thomassie, Tynia 1959- ... *92*
Thompson, Alicia 1984- ... *224*
Thompson, Brenda 1935- ... *34*
Thompson, Carol 1951- ... *189*
Earlier sketch in SATA *85*
Thompson, China
See Lewis, Mary
Thompson, Colin 1942- ... *198*
Earlier sketches in SATA *95, 163*
Thompson, David H(ugh) 1941- ... *17*
Thompson, Eileen
See Panowski, Eileen Thompson
Thompson, George Selden 1929-1989 ... *73*
Obituary ... *63*
Earlier sketch in SATA *4*
See also CLR *8*
Thompson, Harlan 1894-1987 ... *10*
Obituary ... *53*
Thompson, Hilary 1943- ... *56*
Brief entry ... *49*
Thompson, Holly 1959- ... *239*
Thompson, Joanna Maxwell Pullein
See Pullein-Thompson, Joanna Maxwell
Thompson, Julian F(rancis) 1927- ... *155*
Brief entry ... *40*
Earlier sketches in SATA *55, 99*
See also CLR *24*
See also SAAS *13*
Thompson, K(athryn Carolyn) Dyble
1952- ... *82*
Thompson, Kate 1956- ... *241*
Earlier sketch in SATA *204*
Thompson, Kay 1912(?)-1998 ... *16*
See also CLR *22*
Thompson, Keith 1982- ... *238*
Thompson, Lauren 1962- ... *200*
Earlier sketches in SATA *132, 174*
Thompson, Lauren Stevens
See Thompson, Lauren
Thompson, Megan Lloyd
See Lloyd, Megan
Thompson, Richard 1951- ... *184*
Thompson, Ruth Plumly 1891-1976 ... *66*
Thompson, Sharon 1952- ... *119*
Thompson, Sharon Elaine
See Thompson, Sharon
Thompson, Stith 1885-1976 ... *57*
Obituary ... *20*
Thompson, Vivian L(aubach) 1911- ... *3*
Thomson, Bill 1963- ... *187*
Thomson, Celia
See Lynn, Tracy
Thomson, David (Robert Alexander)
1914-1988 ... *40*
Obituary ... *55*
Thomson, Melissa 1979- ... *205*
Thomson, Pat 1939- ... *122*
Earlier sketch in SATA *77*
Thomson, Peggy 1922- ... *31*
Thomson, Sarah L. ... *212*
Earlier sketch in SATA *178*
Thon, Melanie Rae 1957- ... *132*
Thong, Roseanne ... *174*
Thor, Annika 1950- ... *222*
Thorburn, John
See Goldsmith, John Herman Thorburn
Thorn, John 1947- ... *59*
Thorndyke, Helen Louise
See Benson, Mildred
Thorne, Ian
See May, Julian
Thorne, Jean Wright
See May, Julian
Thornhill, Jan 1955- ... *148*
Earlier sketch in SATA *77*
Thornton, Hall
See Silverberg, Robert
Thornton, W. B.
See Burgess, Thornton Waldo
Thornton, Yvonne S. 1947- ... *96*
Thornton, Yvonne Shirley
See Thornton, Yvonne S.
Thorpe, E(ustace) G(eorge) 1916- ... *21*
Thorpe, J. K.
See Nathanson, Laura Walther
Thorvall, Kerstin 1925- ... *13*
Thorvall-Falk, Kerstin
See Thorvall, Kerstin
Thrasher, Crystal (Faye) 1921- ... *27*
Threadgall, Colin 1941- ... *77*
Three Little Pigs
See Lantz, Francess L(in)
Thum, Gladys 1920- ... *26*
Thum, Marcella ... *28*
Earlier sketch in SATA *3*
Thundercloud, Katherine
See Witt, Shirley Hill
Thurber, James 1894-1961 ... *13*
Thurber, James Grover
See Thurber, James
Thurlo, Aimee ... *161*
Thurlo, David ... *161*
Thurman, Judith 1946- ... *33*
Thurman, Mark (Gordon Ian) 1948- ... *63*
Thwaite, Ann (Barbara Harrop) 1932- ... *14*
Tibbetts, Peggy ... *127*
Tibbles, Jean-Paul 1958- ... *115*
Tibo, Gilles 1951- ... *107*
Earlier sketch in SATA *67*
Tiburzi, Bonnie 1948- ... *65*
Ticheburn, Cheviot
See Ainsworth, William Harrison
Tichenor, Tom 1923-1992 ... *14*
Tichnor, Richard 1959- ... *90*
Tichy, William 1924- ... *31*
Tickle, Jack
See Chapman, Jane
Tidholm, Anna-Clara 1946- ... *223*
Tiegreen, Alan F. 1935- ... *94*
Brief entry ... *36*
Tierney, Fiona ... *229*
Tierney, Frank M. 1930- ... *54*
Tierney, Tom 1928- ... *113*
Tiffault, Benette W. 1955- ... *77*
Tildes, Phyllis Limbacher 1945- ... *210*
Tiller, Ruth L. 1949- ... *83*
Tilley, Debbie ... *190*
Tillman, Nancy ... *211*
Tillotson, Katherine ... *224*
Tilly, Nancy 1935- ... *62*
Tilton, Madonna Elaine 1929- ... *41*
Tilton, Rafael
See Tilton, Madonna Elaine
Timberlake, Amy ... *156*
Timberlake, Carolyn
See Dresang, Eliza (Carolyn Timberlake)
Timmers, Leo 1970- ... *190*
Timmins, Jeffrey Stewart 1979- ... *227*
Timmins, William F(rederick) ... *10*
Tinbergen, Niko(laas) 1907-1988
Obituary ... *60*
Tincknell, Cathy ... *194*
Tiner, John Hudson 1944- ... *32*
Tingle, Dolli (?)-
See Brackett, Dolli Tingle
Tingle, Rebecca ... *174*
Tingle, Tim ... *208*
Tingum, Janice 1958- ... *91*
Tinkelman, Murray 1933- ... *12*
Tinkham, Kelly A. ... *188*
Tinkle, (Julien) Lon 1906-1980 ... *36*
Tinling, Marion (Rose) 1904- ... *140*
Tipene, Tim 1972- ... *141*
Tippett, James S(terling) 1885-1958 ... *66*
Tirone Smith, Mary-Ann 1944- ... *143*
Titcomb, Gordon ... *237*
Titlebaum, Ellen ... *195*
Titler, Dale M(ilton) 1926- ... *35*
Brief entry ... *28*
Titmarsh, Michael Angelo
See Thackeray, William Makepeace
Titus, Eve 1922- ... *2*
Tjia, Sherwin 1975- ... *204*
Tjong Khing, The 1933- ... *76*
Tobia, Lauren ... *240*
Tobias, Katherine
See Gottfried, Theodore Mark
Tobias, Tobi 1938- ... *82*
Earlier sketch in SATA *5*
See also CLR *4*
Tobin, James ... *226*
Tocci, C. Lee 1958- ... *220*
Tocci, Cynthia Lee
See Tocci, C. Lee
Tocher, Timothy ... *228*
Todd, Anne Ophelia
See Dowden, Anne Ophelia Todd
Todd, Barbara 1961- ... *173*
Todd, Barbara K(eith) 1917- ... *10*
Todd, Chuck ... *195*
Todd, H(erbert) E(atton) 1908-1988 ... *84*
Earlier sketch in SATA *11*
Todd, Loreto 1942- ... *30*
Todd, Pamela ... *212*
Todd, Peter
See Hamilton, Charles (Harold St. John)
Toews, Miriam 1964- ... *165*
Tofel, Richard J. 1957- ... *140*
Toffler-Corrie, Laura ... *237*
Toft, Di 1958- ... *233*
Toft, Kim Michelle 1960- ... *170*
Tokunbo, Dimitrea ... *187*
Tolan, Stephanie S. 1942- ... *142*
Earlier sketches in SATA *38, 78*
Toland, John (Willard) 1912-2004 ... *38*
Tolbert, Steve 1944- ... *143*
Toledo, Francisco 1940- ... *198*
Toledo, Natalia 1967- ... *197*
Tolkien, J. R. R. 1892-1973 ... *100*
Obituary ... *24*
Earlier sketches in SATA *2, 32*
See also CLR *152*
Tolkien, John Ronald Reuel
See Tolkien, J. R. R.
Toll, Emily
See Cannon, Eileen E(mily)
Toll, Nelly S. 1935- ... *78*
Tolland, W. R.
See Heitzmann, William Ray
Tolles, Martha 1921- ... *76*
Earlier sketch in SATA *8*
Tolliver, Ruby C(hangos) 1922- ... *110*
Brief entry ... *41*
Earlier sketch in SATA *55*
Tolmie, Kenneth Donald 1941- ... *15*
Tolstoi, Lev
See Tolstoy, Leo
Tolstoy, Leo 1828-1910 ... *26*
Tolstoy, Count Leo
See Tolstoy, Leo
Tolstoy, Leo Nikolaevich
See Tolstoy, Leo
Tomalin, Ruth ... *29*
Tomaselli, Rosa
See Pausacker, Jenny
Tomecek, Steve ... *172*
Tomes, Margot (Ladd) 1917-1991 ... *70*
Brief entry ... *27*
Obituary ... *69*
Earlier sketch in SATA *36*
Tomey, Ingrid 1943- ... *77*

Tomfool
See Farjeon, Eleanor
Tomic, Tomislav 1977- ... *202*
Tomkins, Jasper
See Batey, Tom
Tomline, F. Latour
See Gilbert, W(illiam) S(chwenck)
Tomlinson, Heather ... *192*
Tomlinson, Jill 1931-1976 ... *3*
Obituary ... *24*
Tomlinson, Reginald R(obert) 1885-1979(?)
Obituary ... *27*
Tomlinson, Theresa 1946- ... *165*
Earlier sketch in SATA *103*
See also CLR *60*
Tommaso, Rich 1970(?)- ... *200*
Tomorrow, Tom 1961- ... *223*
Tompert, Ann 1918- ... *139*
Earlier sketches in SATA *14, 89*
Tompkins, Troy
See Cle, Troy
Tonatiuh, Duncan ... *231*
Toner, Raymond John 1908-1986 ... *10*
Tong, Gary S. 1942- ... *66*
Tong, Paul ... *188*
Took, Belladonna
See Chapman, Vera (Ivy May)
Tooke, Louise Mathews 1950- ... *38*
Tooke, Susan ... *173*
Toonder, Martin
See Groom, Arthur William
Toothaker, Roy Eugene 1928- ... *18*
Tooze, Ruth (Anderson) 1892-1972 ... *4*
Topaz, Ksenia ... *212*
Topek, Susan Remick 1955- ... *78*
Topping, Audrey R(onning) 1928- ... *14*
Tor, Regina
See Shekerjian, Regina Tor
Torbert, Floyd James 1922- ... *22*
Torgersen, Don Arthur 1934- ... *55*
Brief entry ... *41*
Torley, Luke
See Blish, James
Torrecilla, Pablo 1967- ... *206*
Torres, Andres Segovia
See Segovia, Andres
Torres, Daniel 1958- ... *102*
Torres, J. 1969- ... *230*
Torres, John A. 1965- ... *163*
Earlier sketch in SATA *94*
Torres, John Albert
See Torres, John A.
Torres, Joseph
See Torres, J.
Torres, Laura 1967- ... *146*
Earlier sketch in SATA *87*
Torres, Leyla 1960- ... *155*
Torrey, Michele 1960(?)- ... *238*
Torrey, Rich
See Torrey, Richard
Torrey, Richard ... *189*
Torrie, Malcolm
See Mitchell, Gladys (Maude Winifred)
Toten, Teresa 1955- ... *99*
Totham, Mary
See Breinburg, Petronella
Touponce, William F. 1948- ... *114*
Tournier, Michel 1924- ... *23*
Tournier, Michel Edouard
See Tournier, Michel
Towle, Ben 1970- ... *228*
Towle, Wendy 1963- ... *79*
Towne, Mary
See Spelman, Mary
Townley, Rod
See Townley, Roderick
Townley, Roderick 1942- ... *177*
Townsend, Brad W. 1962- ... *91*
Townsend, John Rowe 1922- ... *132*
Autobiography Feature ... *132*
Earlier sketches in SATA *4, 68*
See also CLR *2*
See also SAAS *2*
Townsend, Kari Lee 1968- ... *240*
Townsend, Michael 1981- ... *231*
Earlier sketch in SATA *194*
Townsend, Sue 1946- ... *93*
Brief entry ... *48*
Earlier sketch in SATA *55*
Townsend, Susan Lilian
See Townsend, Sue
Townsend, Thomas L. 1944- ... *59*
Townsend, Tom
See Townsend, Thomas L.
Townsend, Wendy 1962- ... *201*
Townson, Hazel ... *134*
Toye, William Eldred 1926- ... *8*
Trafton, Jennifer ... *239*
Traherne, Michael
See Watkins-Pitchford, Denys James
Trahey, Jane 1923-2000 ... *36*
Obituary ... *120*
Trapani, Iza 1954- ... *214*
Earlier sketches in SATA *80, 116*
Trapp, Maria Augusta von
See von Trapp, Maria Augusta
Travers, P(amela) L(yndon) 1899-1996 ... *100*
Obituary ... *90*
Earlier sketches in SATA *4, 54*
See also CLR *93*
See also SAAS *2*
Travis, Lucille ... *133*
Earlier sketch in SATA *88*
Treadgold, Mary 1910-2005 ... *49*
Trease, (Robert) Geoffrey 1909-1998 ... *60*
Obituary ... *101*
Earlier sketch in SATA *2*
See also CLR *42*
See also SAAS *6*
Treat, Lawrence 1903-1998 ... *59*
Tredez, Alain 1926- ... *17*
Tredez, Denise 1930- ... *50*
Treece, Henry 1912-1966 ... *2*
See also CLR *2*
Tregarthen, Enys
See Sloggett, Nellie
Tregaskis, Richard 1916-1973 ... *3*
Obituary ... *26*
Treherne, Katie Thamer 1955- ... *76*
Trell, Max 1900-1996 ... *14*
Obituary ... *108*
Tremain, Ruthven 1922- ... *17*
Trembath, Don 1963- ... *168*
Earlier sketch in SATA *96*
Tremens, Del
See MacDonald, Amy
Trent, Robbie 1894-1988 ... *26*
Trent, Timothy
See Malmberg, Carl
Treseder, Terry Walton 1956- ... *68*
Tresilian, (Cecil) Stuart 1891-(?) ... *40*
Tresselt, Alvin 1916-2000 ... *7*
See also CLR *30*
Trevino, Elizabeth B(orton) de 1904- ... *29*
Earlier sketch in SATA *1*
See also SAAS *5*
Trevor, Elleston 1920-1995 ... *28*
Trevor, Frances
See Teasdale, Sara
Trevor, Glen
See Hilton, James
Trevor, (Lucy) Meriol 1919-2000 ... *113*
Obituary ... *122*
Earlier sketch in SATA *10*
Trewellard, J.M. ... *195*
Trewellard, Juliet
See Trewellard, J.M.
Trez, Alain
See Tredez, Alain
Trez, Denise
See Tredez, Denise
Trezise, Percy 1923-
See CLR *41*
Trezise, Percy James
See Trezise, Percy
Triggs, Tony D. 1946- ... *70*
Trimble, Marshall I(ra) 1939- ... *93*
Trimby, Elisa 1948- ... *47*
Brief entry ... *40*
Trine, Greg ... *238*
Tring, A. Stephen
See Meynell, Laurence Walter
Triplett, Gina ... *229*
Tripp, Eleanor B(aldwin) 1936- ... *4*
Tripp, Janet 1942- ... *108*
Tripp, Jenny ... *188*
Tripp, John
See Moore, John Travers
Tripp, Nathaniel 1944- ... *101*
Tripp, Paul 1916-2002 ... *8*
Obituary ... *139*
Tripp, Valerie 1951- ... *168*
Earlier sketch in SATA *78*
Tripp, Wallace (Whitney) 1940- ... *31*
Trivelpiece, Laurel 1926- ... *56*
Brief entry ... *46*
Trivett, Daphne Harwood 1940- ... *22*
Trivizas, Eugene 1946- ... *84*
Trnka, Jiri 1912-1969 ... *43*
Brief entry ... *32*
Trollope, Anthony 1815-1882 ... *22*
Trost, Lucille W(ood) 1938- ... *149*
Earlier sketch in SATA *12*
Trott, Betty 1933- ... *91*
Trotter, Deborah W. ... *184*
Trotter, Grace V(iolet) 1900-1991 ... *10*
Trottier, Maxine 1950- ... *175*
Earlier sketch in SATA *131*
Troughton, Joanna (Margaret) 1947- ... *37*
Trout, Kilgore
See Farmer, Philip Jose
Trout, Richard E. ... *123*
Trudeau, Garretson Beekman
See Trudeau, G.B.
Trudeau, Garry
See Trudeau, G.B.
Trudeau, Garry B.
See Trudeau, G.B.
Trudeau, G.B. 1948- ... *168*
Earlier sketch in SATA *35*
Trueit, Trudi
See Trueit, Trudi Strain
Trueit, Trudi Strain 1963- ... *179*
Trueman, Matthew ... *183*
Trueman, Terry 1947- ... *178*
Earlier sketch in SATA *132*
Truesdell, Judy
See Mecca, Judy Truesdell
Truesdell, Sue
See Truesdell, Susan G.
Truesdell, Susan G. ... *212*
Brief entry ... *45*
Earlier sketch in SATA *108*
Trumbauer, Lisa 1963- ... *228*
Earlier sketch in SATA *149*
Trumbauer, Lisa Trutkoff
See Trumbauer, Lisa
Truss, Jan 1925- ... *35*
Truss, Lynne 1955(?)- ... *194*
Tryon, Leslie ... *194*
Earlier sketch in SATA *139*
Tsiang, Sarah ... *239*
Tsiang, Yi-Mei
See Tsiang, Sarah
Tubb, Jonathan N. 1951- ... *78*
Tubb, Kristin O'Donnell 1971- ... *209*
Tubby, I. M.
See Kraus, (Herman) Robert
Tucker, Allan James
See James, Bill

Tucker, Caroline
See Nolan, Jeannette Covert
Tucker, James
See James, Bill
Tudor, Edward
See Browne, Anthony
Tudor, Tasha 1915-2008 .... *160*
Obituary *205*
Earlier sketches in SATA *20, 69*
See also CLR *13*
Tuerk, Hanne 1951- *71*
Tugeau, Jeremy *199*
Tulloch, Richard 1949- *180*
Earlier sketch in SATA *76*
Tulloch, Richard George
See Tulloch, Richard
Tulloch, Shirley *169*
Tully, John (Kimberley) 1923- *14*
Tumanov, Vladimir A. 1961- *138*
Tung, Angela 1972- *109*
Tunis, Edwin (Burdett) 1897-1973 .... *28*
Obituary *24*
Earlier sketch in SATA *1*
See also CLR *2*
Tunis, John R(oberts) 1889-1975 .... *37*
Brief entry *30*
Tunnell, Michael
See Tunnell, Michael O.
Tunnell, Michael O. 1950- *157*
Earlier sketch in SATA *103*
Tunnell, Michael O'Grady
See Tunnell, Michael O.
Tunnicliffe, C(harles) F(rederick)
1901-1979 .... *62*
Turck, Mary C. 1950- *144*
Turk, Hanne
See Tuerk, Hanne
Turk, Ruth 1917- *82*
Turkle, Brinton 1915- *79*
Earlier sketch in SATA *2*
Turlington, Bayly 1919-1977 .... *5*
Obituary *52*
Turnbull, Agnes Sligh 1888-1982 .... *14*
Turnbull, Ann 1943- *160*
Earlier sketch in SATA *18*
Turnbull, Ann Christine
See Turnbull, Ann
Turnbull, Susan *222*
Turner, Alice K. 1940- *10*
Turner, Ann 1945- *188*
Autobiography Feature *188*
Earlier sketches in SATA *14, 77, 113, 178*
Turner, Ann Warren
See Turner, Ann
Turner, Bonnie 1932- *75*
Turner, Elizabeth 1774-1846
See YABC *2*
Turner, Glennette Tilley 1933- *183*
Earlier sketch in SATA *71*
Turner, Josie
See Crawford, Phyllis
Turner, Megan Whalen 1965- *174*
Earlier sketch in SATA *94*
Turner, Pamela S. 1957- *211*
Turner, Philip (William) 1925- *83*
Earlier sketch in SATA *11*
See also CLR *89*
See also SAAS *6*
Turner, Robyn 1947- *77*
Turner, Sheila R.
See Seed, Sheila Turner
Turngren, Annette 1902(?)-1980
Obituary *23*
Turngren, Ellen (?)-1964 .... *3*
Turska, Krystyna (Zofia) 1933- *31*
Brief entry *27*
Turteltaub, H. N.
See Turtledove, Harry
Turtledove, Harry 1949- *166*
Earlier sketch in SATA *116*
Turtledove, Harry Norman
See Turtledove, Harry
Tusa, Tricia 1960- *207*
Earlier sketches in SATA *72, 111*
Tusiani, Joseph 1924- *45*
Tutt, Keith 1959- *238*
Tuttle, Cameron *237*
Tuxbury, Larry 1969- *235*
Twain, Mark 1835-1910 .... *100*
See also YABC *2*
See also CLR *156*
Tweit, Susan J 1956- *94*
Tweit, Susan Joan
See Tweit, Susan J
Tweton, D. Jerome 1933- *48*
Twinem, Neecy 1958- *92*
Twohill, Maggie
See Angell, Judie
Tworkov, Jack 1900-1982 .... *47*
Obituary *31*
Tyche
See Papademetriou, Lisa
Tyers, Jenny 1969- *89*
Tyers, Kathy 1952- *82*
Tyler, Anne 1941- *173*
Earlier sketches in SATA *7, 90*
Tyler, Linda
See Tyler, Linda W(agner)
Tyler, Linda W(agner) 1952- *65*
Tyler, Vicki 1952- *64*
Tyne, Joel
See Schembri, Jim
Tyrrell, Frances 1959- *107*

U

Ubell, Earl 1926-2007 .... *4*
Obituary *182*
Uchida, Yoshiko 1921-1992 .... *53*
Obituary *72*
Earlier sketch in SATA *1*
See also CLR *56*
See also SAAS *1*
Udall, Jan Beaney 1938- *10*
Uden, (Bernard Gilbert) Grant 1910- *26*
Uderzo, Albert 1927-
See CLR *37*
Udovic, David 1950- *189*
Udovic, Jane Morris 1947- *224*
Udry, Janice May 1928- *152*
Earlier sketch in SATA *4*
Uegaki, Chieri 1969- *211*
Earlier sketch in SATA *153*
Uehashi, Nahoko 1962- *215*
Ueno, Noriko
See Nakae, Noriko
Ugliano, Natascia *196*
Uhlberg, Myron *174*
Uhlig, Richard 1970- *195*
Uhlig, Susan 1955- *129*
Ulam, S(tanislaw) M(arcin) 1909-1984 .... *51*
Ullman, Barb Bentler *210*
Ullman, James Ramsey 1907-1971 .... *7*
Ulm, Robert 1934-1977 .... *17*
Ulmer, Louise 1943- *53*
Ulmer, Wendy K. 1950- *201*
Ulrich, Maureen 1958- *206*
Ulriksen, Mark 1957- *210*
Ulyatt, Kenneth 1920- *14*
Umansky, Kaye 1946- *224*
Earlier sketches in SATA *158, 188*
Unada
See Gliewe, Unada (Grace)
Uncle Carter
See Boucher, (Clarence) Carter
Uncle Eric
See Maybury, Richard J.
Uncle Gus
See Rey, H. A.
Uncle Mac
See McCulloch, Derek (Ivor Breashur)
Uncle Ray
See Coffman, Ramon Peyton
Uncle Shelby
See Silverstein, Shel
Underhill, Alice Mertie (Waterman)
1900-1971 .... *10*
Underhill, Liz 1948- *53*
Brief entry *49*
Underwood, Deborah 1962- *206*
Unger, Harlow G. 1931- *75*
Unger, Harlow Giles
See Unger, Harlow G.
Unger, Jim 1937- *67*
Ungerer, (Jean) Thomas 1931- *106*
Earlier sketches in SATA *5, 33*
See also CLR *77*
Ungerer, Tomi 1931-
See Ungerer, (Jean) Thomas
Unkelbach, Kurt 1913-1992 .... *4*
Unnerstad, Edith (Totterman) 1900-1982 .... *3*
See also CLR *36*
Unobagha, Uzo *139*
Unrau, Ruth 1922- *9*
Unstead, R(obert) J(ohn) 1915-1988 .... *12*
Obituary *56*
Unsworth, Walt(er) 1928- *4*
Untermeyer, Bryna Ivens 1909-1985 .... *61*
Untermeyer, Louis 1885-1977 .... *37*
Obituary *26*
Earlier sketch in SATA *2*
Unwin, David S. 1918-2010 .... *14*
Unwin, David Storr
See Unwin, David S.
Unwin, Nora S(picer) 1907-1982 .... *3*
Obituary *49*
Unzner, Christa 1958- *230*
Earlier sketches in SATA *80, 141*
Unzner-Fischer, Christa
See Unzner, Christa
Updale, Eleanor 1953- *175*
Updyke, Rosemary K. 1924- *103*
Upitis, Alvis *109*
Upjohn, Rebecca 1962- *238*
Urbain, Cat 1956- *211*
Urbain, Catherine
See Urbain, Cat
Urban, Helle (Denise) 1957- *149*
Urban, Linda *199*
Urbanovic, Jackie *189*
Urberuaga, Emilio 1954- *219*
Urbigkit, Cat 1965- *196*
Urdahl, Catherine *215*
Ure, Jean 1943- *192*
Autobiography Feature *192*
Earlier sketches in SATA *48, 78, 129*
See also CLR *34*
See also SAAS *14*
U'Ren, Andrea 1968- *213*
Earlier sketch in SATA *142*
Uris, Leon 1924-2003 .... *49*
Obituary *146*
Uris, Leon Marcus
See Uris, Leon
Ursu, Anne *177*
Ury, Allen B. 1954- *98*
Uschan, Michael V. 1948- *129*
Usher, Margo Scegge
See McHargue, Georgess
Usher, Mark David
See Usher, M.D.
Usher, M.D. 1966- *221*
Uslan, Michael E. 1951- *169*
Uston, Ken(neth Senzo) 1935-1987 .... *65*

Uttley, Alice Jane 1884-1976 .... *88*
Obituary *26*
Earlier sketch in SATA *3*
Uttley, Alison
See Uttley, Alice Jane
Utz, Lois (Marie) 1932-1986 .... *5*
Obituary *50*

V

Vaeth, J. Gordon 1921- *17*
Vaeth, Joseph Gordon
See Vaeth, J. Gordon
Vagin, Vladimir (Vasilevich) 1937- *142*
Vail, Rachel 1966- *201*
Earlier sketches in SATA *94, 163*
Vainio, Pirkko 1957- *123*
Earlier sketch in SATA *76*
Valen, Nanine 1950- *21*
Valencak, Hannelore
See Mayer, Hannelore Valencak
Valens, Amy 1946- *70*
Valens, E(vans) G(ladstone), Jr. 1920-1992 ... *1*
Valentine, Johnny *72*
Valentine, Madeline *236*
Valerio, Geraldo 1970- *180*
Valgardson, W. D. 1939- *151*
Earlier sketch in SATA *101*
Valgardson, William Dempsey
See Valgardson, W. D.
Valleau, Emily 1925- *51*
Vamos, Samantha R. *215*
Van Abbe, Salaman 1883-1955 .... *18*
Van Allsburg, Chris 1949- *156*
Earlier sketches in SATA *37, 53, 105*
See also CLR *113*
Van Anrooy, Francine 1924- *2*
Van Anrooy, Frans
See Van Anrooy, Francine
Vanasse, Deb 1957- *170*
Van Buren, David *203*
Van Camp, Katie 1981- *222*
Vance, Cynthia *207*
Vance, Eleanor Graham 1908-1985 .... *11*
Vance, Gerald
See Garrett, Randall
and Silverberg, Robert
Vance, Marguerite 1889-1965 .... *29*
Vance-Abrams, Cynthia
See Vance, Cynthia
VanCleave, Janice 1942- *116*
Autobiography Feature *123*
Earlier sketch in SATA *75*
Van Cleave, Ryan G. 1972- *241*
Vandenburg, Mary Lou 1943- *17*
Vander Boom, Mae M. *14*
Vander-Els, Betty 1936- *63*
van der Heide, Iris 1970- *183*
van der Linde, Laurel 1952- *78*
van der Linden, Martijn 1979- *214*
van der Meer, Ron 1945- *98*
Vanderpool, Clare 1964- *232*
van de Ruit, John 1975- *199*
Van der Veer, Judy 1912-1982 .... *4*
Obituary *33*
Vanderwal, Andrew H. 1956- *219*
Vanderwerff, Corrine 1939- *117*
Vander Zee, Ruth *199*
Earlier sketch in SATA *159*
Vande Velde, Vivian 1951- *211*
Earlier sketches in SATA *62, 95, 141*
See also CLR *145*
Vandivert, Rita (Andre) 1905-1986 .... *21*
Van Draanen, Wendelin *207*
Earlier sketch in SATA *122*
Van Dusen, Chris *228*
Earlier sketch in SATA *173*
Van Duyn, Janet 1910- *18*
Van Dyne, Edith
See Baum, L. Frank
and Sampson, Emma (Keats) Speed
and van Zantwijk, Rudolf (Alexander Marinus)
Vane, Mitch
See Vane, Mitchelle
Vane, Mitchelle *176*
van Eekhout, Greg *232*
van Etten, David
See Levithan, David
van Frankenhuyzen, Gijsbert 1951- *132*
Van Genechten, Guido 1957- *165*
van Haeringen, Annemarie *193*
Van Hook, Beverly 1941- *99*
Van Hook, Beverly H.
See Van Hook, Beverly
Van Hook, Beverly Hennen
See Van Hook, Beverly
Van Horn, William 1939- *43*
van Hout, Mies 1962- *178*
Van Iterson, S(iny) R(ose) *26*
Van Kampen, Vlasta 1943- *163*
Earlier sketch in SATA *54*
Van Laan, Nancy 1939- *214*
Earlier sketch in SATA *105*
van Lawick-Goodall, Jane
See Goodall, Jane
Van Leeuwen, Jean 1937- *211*
Autobiography Feature *141*
Earlier sketches in SATA *6, 82, 132, 141*
See also SAAS *8*
van Lhin, Erik
See del Rey, Lester
van Lieshout, Elle 1963- *217*
van Lieshout, Maria *201*
Van Loon, Hendrik Willem 1882-1944 .... *18*
van Ommen, Sylvia 1978- *186*
VanOosting, James 1951- *170*
Van Orden, M(erton) D(ick) 1921- *4*
van Os, Erik 1963- *217*
Van Patter, Bruce *183*
Van Reek, Wouter *204*
Van Rensselaer, Alexander (Taylor Mason) 1892-1962 .... *14*
Van Riper, Guernsey, Jr. 1909-1995 .... *3*
van Rossum, Heleen 1962- *174*
Van Rynbach, Iris 1952- *102*
Vansant, Rhonda Joy Edwards 1950- *92*
Van Steenwyk, Elizabeth (Ann) 1928- *89*
Earlier sketch in SATA *34*
Van Stockum, Hilda 1908-2006 .... *5*
Obituary *179*
van Straaten, Harmen 1961- *218*
Earlier sketch in SATA *195*
Van Tuyl, Barbara 1940- *11*
van Vogt, A(lfred) E(lton) 1912-2000 .... *14*
Obituary *124*
Van Wassenhove, Sue 1951- *202*
Van Woerkom, Dorothy (O'Brien) 1924-1996 .... *21*
Van Wormer, Joe
See Van Wormer, Joseph Edward
Van Wormer, Joseph Edward 1913-1998 .... *35*
Van Wright, Cornelius *173*
Van Zwienen, Ilse Charlotte Koehn 1929-1991 .... *34*
Brief entry *28*
Obituary *67*
Van Zyle, Jon 1942- *176*
Earlier sketch in SATA *84*
Varela, Barry *180*
Varga, Judy
See Stang, Judit
Varley, Dimitry V. 1906-1984 .... *10*
Varley, Susan 1961- *134*
Earlier sketch in SATA *63*
Varon, Sara *195*
Vasileva, Tatiana
See Wassiljewa, Tatjana
Vasiliev, Valery 1949- *80*
Vasilieva, Tatiana
See Wassiljewa, Tatjana
Vasiliu, Mircea 1920- *2*
Vass, George 1927- *57*
Brief entry *31*
Vaughan, Carter A.
See Gerson, Noel Bertram
Vaughan, Harold Cecil 1923- *14*
Vaughan, Marcia (K.) 1951- *159*
Earlier sketches in SATA *60, 95*
Vaughan, Richard 1947- *87*
Vaughan, Sam 1928- *14*
Vaughn, Ruth 1935- *14*
Vaught, Susan 1965- *195*
Vaupel, Robin *198*
Vautier, Ghislaine 1932- *53*
Vavra, Robert James 1935- *8*
Vecsey, George Spencer 1939- *9*
Vedral, Joyce L(auretta) 1943- *65*
Vega, Denise *216*
Earlier sketch in SATA *174*
Vega, Denise B.
See Vega, Denise
Vega, Diego
See Adkins, Jan
Veglahn, Nancy (Crary) 1937- *5*
Vejjajiva, Jane 1963- *189*
Velasquez, Crystal *228*
Velasquez, Eric *226*
Earlier sketch in SATA *192*
Velasquez, Gloria 1949- *229*
Earlier sketch in SATA *113*
Velthuijs, Max 1923-2005 .... *110*
Obituary *160*
Earlier sketch in SATA *53*
Venable, Alan (Hudson) 1944- *8*
Venable, Colleen A.F. 1980- *233*
Venezia, Mike 1945- *150*
Venner, Grace Chang
See Chang, Grace
Ventura, Anthony
See Pellowski, Michael (Joseph)
Ventura, Piero (Luigi) 1937- *61*
Brief entry *43*
See also CLR *16*
Venuti, Kristin Clark *237*
Vequin, Capini
See Quinn, Elisabeth
Verba, Joan Marie 1953- *78*
Verboven, Agnes 1951- *103*
verDorn, Bethea (Stewart) 1952- *76*
Vere, Ed *197*
Verissimo, Erico (Lopes) 1905-1975 .... *113*
Verne, Jules 1828-1905 .... *21*
See also CLR *88*
Verne, Jules Gabriel
See Verne, Jules
Verner, Gerald 1897(?)-1980
Obituary *25*
Verney, John 1913-1993 .... *14*
Obituary *75*
Verniero, Joan C. 1949- *181*
Vernon, (Elda) Louise A(nderson) 1914- *14*
Vernon, Rosemary
See Smith, Susan Vernon
Vernon, Ursula *204*
Vernor, D.
See Casewit, Curtis W(erner)
Verr, Harry Coe
See Kunhardt, Edith
Verral, Charles Spain 1904-1990 .... *11*
Obituary *65*
Verrillo, Erica 1953- *199*
Verrillo, Erica F.
See Verrillo, Erica
Verroken, Sarah 1982- *223*
Verrone, Robert J. 1935(?)-1984
Obituary *39*
Versace, Marie Teresa Rios 1917- *2*
Vertreace, Martha M(odena) 1945- *78*
Vesey, A(manda) 1939- *62*

Vesey, Mark (David) 1958- *123*
Vesey, Paul
  See Allen, Samuel W(ashington)
Vess, Charles 1951- *215*
Vestergaard, Hope *178*
Vestly, Anne-Cath(arina) 1920-2008 .... *14*
  See also CLR *99*
Vevers, (Henry) Gwynne 1916-1988 .... *45*
  Obituary *57*
Viator, Vacuus
  See Hughes, Thomas
Viau, Nancy *208*
Vicar, Henry
  See Felsen, Henry Gregor
Vick, Helen Hughes 1950- *88*
Vicker, Angus
  See Felsen, Henry Gregor
Vickers, Sheena 1960- *94*
Vickery, Kate
  See Kennedy, T.A.
Victor, Edward 1914- *3*
Victor, Joan Berg 1942- *30*
Vidrine, Beverly Barras 1938- *188*
  Earlier sketch in SATA *103*
Vieceli, Emma 1979- *210*
Viereck, Ellen K. 1928- *14*
Viereck, Phillip 1925- *3*
Viergutz, Dina Nayeri
  See Nayeri, Dina
Viertel, Janet 1915- *10*
Vigan, Delphine de 1966- *236*
Vigilante, Danette *240*
Vigliante, Mary
  See Szydlowski, Mary Vigliante
Vigna, Judith 1936- *102*
  Earlier sketch in SATA *15*
Viguers, Ruth Hill 1903-1971 .... *6*
Vila, Laura *207*
Vilela, Fernando 1973- *216*
Villareal, Ray *187*
Villasenor, Edmund
  See Villasenor, Victor E.
Villasenor, Edmundo
  See Villasenor, Victor E.
Villasenor, Victor
  See Villasenor, Victor E.
Villasenor, Victor E. 1940- *171*
Villasenor, Victor Edmundo
  See Villasenor, Victor E.
Villeneuve, Anne *230*
Villiard, Paul 1910-1974 .... *51*
  Obituary *20*
Villiers, Alan (John) 1903-1982 .... *10*
Vilott, Rhondi
  See Salsitz, Rhondi Vilott
Vincent, Amy
  See Gray, Claudia
Vincent, Eric Douglas 1953- *40*
Vincent, Erin 1969- *188*
Vincent, Felix 1946- *41*
Vincent, Gabrielle 1928-2000 .... *121*
  Earlier sketch in SATA *61*
  See also CLR *13*
Vincent, Mary Keith
  See St. John, Wylly Folk
Vincent, Rachel 1978- *222*
Vincent, William R.
  See Heitzmann, William Ray
Vinegar, Tom
  See Gregg, Andrew K.
Vinest, Shaw
  See Longyear, Barry B(rookes)
Vinge, Joan (Carol) D(ennison) 1948- *113*
  Earlier sketch in SATA *36*
Vining, Elizabeth Gray 1902-1999 .... *6*
  Obituary *117*
Vinson, Kathryn 1911-1995 .... *21*
Vinton, Iris 1906(?)-1988 .... *24*
  Obituary *55*
Viola, Herman J(oseph) 1938- *126*
Viorst, Judith 1931- *172*
  Earlier sketches in SATA *7, 70, 123*
  See also CLR *90*
Vip
  See Partch, Virgil Franklin II
Vipont, Charles
  See Foulds, Elfrida Vipont
Vipont, Elfrida
  See Foulds, Elfrida Vipont
Viramontes, Helena Maria 1954-
  See CLR *285*
Viscott, David S(teven) 1938-1996 .... *65*
Visser, W(illem) F(rederik) H(endrik)
  1900-1968 .... *10*
Vitale, Stefano 1958- *225*
  Earlier sketches in SATA *114, 180*
Vivas, Julie 1947- *96*
Vivelo, Jackie 1943- *63*
Vivelo, Jacqueline J.
  See Vivelo, Jackie
Vivelo, Jacqueline Jean
  See Vivelo, Jackie
Vivian, Siobhan 1979(?)- *215*
Vizzini, Ned 1981- *179*
  Earlier sketch in SATA *125*
Vlahos, Olivia 1924- *31*
Vlasic, Bob
  See Hirsch, Phil
Voake, Charlotte *180*
  Earlier sketch in SATA *114*
Voake, Steve 1961- *178*
Vo-Dinh, Mai 1933- *16*
Voelkel, J&P
  See Voelkel, Pamela
Voelkel, J&P
  See Voelkel, Jon
Voelkel, Jon *239*
Voelkel, Pamela *240*
Vogel, Carole Garbuny 1951- *231*
  Earlier sketches in SATA *70, 105*
Vogel, Ilse-Margret 1914-2001 .... *14*
  See also CLR *170*
Vogel, John H., Jr. 1950- *18*
Vogt, Esther Loewen 1915-1999 .... *14*
Vogt, Gregory L. *94*
Vogt, Marie Bollinger 1921- *45*
Vohwinkel, Astrid 1969- *207*
Voight, Virginia Frances 1909-1989 .... *8*
Voigt, Cynthia 1942- *160*
  Brief entry *33*
  Earlier sketches in SATA *48, 79, 116*
  See also CLR *141*
Voigt, Erna 1925- *35*
Voigt-Rother, Erna
  See Voigt, Erna
Vojtech, Anna 1946- *108*
  Earlier sketch in SATA *42*
Vollstadt, Elizabeth Weiss 1942- *121*
Volponi, Paul *228*
  Earlier sketch in SATA *175*
Volting, Dr. R.E.
  See Lerangis, Peter
Von Ahnen, Katherine 1922- *93*
von Buhler, Cynthia *185*
Vondra, J. Gert
  See Vondra, Josef
Vondra, Josef 1941- *121*
Vondra, Josef Gert
  See Vondra, Josef
Von Gunden, Kenneth 1946- *113*
Von Hagen, Victor Wolfgang 1908-1985 .... *29*
von Klopp, Vahrah
  See Malvern, Gladys
von Schmidt, Eric 1931-2007 .... *50*
  Brief entry *36*
  Obituary *181*
von Storch, Anne B. 1910- *1*
von Trapp, Maria Augusta 1905-1987 .... *16*
von Wodtke, Charlotte Buel Johnson
  1918-1982 .... *46*
von Ziegesar, Cecily 1970- *161*
Vos, Ida 1931-2006 .... *121*
  Earlier sketch in SATA *69*
  See also CLR *85*
Vosburgh, Leonard (W.) 1912- *15*
Votaw, Carol 1961- *201*
Voyle, Mary
  See Manning, Rosemary
Vrettos, Adrienne Maria *187*
Vriens, Jacques 1946- *151*
Vugteveen, Verna Aardema
  See Aardema, Verna
Vulture, Elizabeth T.
  See Gilbert, Suzie
Vuong, Lynette Dyer 1938- *110*
  Earlier sketch in SATA *60*
Vyner, Tim 1963- *228*

W

Waas, Uli
  See Waas-Pommer, Ulrike
Waas-Pommer, Ulrike 1949- *85*
Waber, Bernard 1924- *155*
  Brief entry *40*
  Earlier sketches in SATA *47, 95*
  See also CLR *55*
Waber, Paulis *231*
Wachtel, Shirley Russak 1951- *88*
Wachter, Oralee (Roberts) 1935- *61*
  Brief entry *51*
Waddell, Evelyn Margaret 1918- *10*
Waddell, Martin 1941- *232*
  Autobiography Feature *129*
  Earlier sketches in SATA *43, 81, 127, 129*
  See also CLR *31*
  See also SAAS *15*
Waddy, Lawrence 1912-2010 .... *91*
Waddy, Lawrence Heber
  See Waddy, Lawrence
Wade, Mary Dodson 1930- *151*
  Earlier sketch in SATA *79*
Wade, Suzanne
  See Kirby, Susan E.
Wade, Theodore E., Jr. 1936- *37*
Wademan, Peter John 1946- *122*
Wademan, Spike
  See Wademan, Peter John
Wadsworth, Ginger 1945- *223*
  Earlier sketches in SATA *103, 157*
Wagenheim, Kal 1935- *21*
Wagner, Hilary *237*
Wagner, Michele R. 1975- *157*
Wagner, Sharon B. 1936- *4*
Wagoner, David (Russell) 1926- *14*
Wahl, Jan (Boyer) 1933- *132*
  Earlier sketches in SATA *2, 34, 73*
  See also SAAS *3*
Wahl, Mats 1945- *186*
Wahman, Wendy *218*
Waide, Jan 1952- *29*
Wainscott, John Milton 1910-1981 .... *53*
Wainwright, Debra *218*
Wainwright, Richard M. 1935- *91*
Wainwright, Ruth
  See Symes, Ruth Louise
Wait, Lea 1946- *137*
Waite, Judy *174*
Waite, Judy Bernard
  See Bernard, Patricia
Waite, Michael
  See Waite, Michael P.
Waite, Michael P. 1960- *101*
Waite, P(eter) B(usby) 1922- *64*
Waites, Joan C. *187*
Waitley, Douglas 1927- *30*
Wakefield, Jean L.
  See Laird, Jean E(louise)
Wakin, Daniel (Joseph) 1961- *84*
Wakin, Edward 1927- *37*

Wakiyama, Hanako 1966- *192*
Walck, Henry Z. 1908(?)-1984
Obituary *40*
Walden, Amelia Elizabeth *3*
Walden, Mark *188*
Waldherr, Kris 1963- *76*
Waldman, Bruce 1949- *15*
Waldman, Neil 1947- *203*
Earlier sketches in SATA *51, 94, 142*
Waldrep, Richard *198*
Waldron, Ann Wood 1924-2010 *16*
Waldron, Kathleen Cook *176*
Waldron, Kevin 1979- *230*
Wales, Dirk 1931- *205*
Walgren, Judy 1963- *118*
Walker, Addison
See Walker, Mort
Walker, Addison Mort
See Walker, Mort
Walker, Alice 1944- *31*
Walker, Alice Malsenior
See Walker, Alice
Walker, Anna *223*
Walker, Barbara (Jeanne) K(erlin) 1921- *80*
Earlier sketch in SATA *4*
Walker, Barbara M(uhs) 1928- *57*
Walker, (James) Braz(elton) 1934-1983 *45*
Walker, David 1965- *197*
Walker, David G(ordon) 1926- *60*
Walker, David Harry 1911-1992 *8*
Obituary *71*
Walker, Diana 1925- *9*
Walker, Diane Marie Catherine
See Walker, Kate
Walker, Dick
See Pellowski, Michael (Joseph)
Walker, Frank 1931-2000 *36*
Walker, Holly Beth
See Bond, Gladys Baker
Walker, Kate 1950- *165*
Earlier sketch in SATA *82*
Walker, Kathrine Sorley
See Sorley Walker, Kathrine
Walker, Kristin *228*
Walker, Lou Ann 1952- *66*
Brief entry *53*
Walker, Louise Jean 1891-1976
Obituary *35*
Walker, Mary Alexander 1927- *61*
Walker, Mildred
See Schemm, Mildred Walker
Walker, Mort 1923- *8*
Walker, Pamela 1948- *142*
Earlier sketch in SATA *24*
Walker, Paul Robert 1953- *154*
Walker, Robert W. 1948- *66*
Walker, Robert Wayne
See Walker, Robert W.
Walker, Sally M. 1954- *221*
Earlier sketch in SATA *135*
Walker, Stephen J. 1951- *12*
Walker, Steve *232*
Walker-Blondell, Becky 1951- *89*
Wallace, Barbara Brooks 1922- *136*
Earlier sketches in SATA *4, 78*
See also CLR *150*
See also SAAS *17*
Wallace, Beverly Dobrin 1921- *19*
Wallace, Bill 1947- *169*
Brief entry *47*
Earlier sketches in SATA *53, 101*
Wallace, Carol 1948- *218*
Wallace, Chad *229*
Wallace, Daisy
See Cuyler, Margery
Wallace, Ian 1950- *219*
Earlier sketches in SATA *53, 56, 141*
See also CLR *37*
Wallace, John 1966- *155*
Earlier sketch in SATA *105*
Wallace, John A(dam) 1915-2004 *3*
Obituary *155*
Wallace, Karen 1951- *188*
Earlier sketches in SATA *83, 139*
Wallace, Nancy Elizabeth 1948- *222*
Earlier sketches in SATA *141, 186*
Wallace, Nigel
See Hamilton, Charles (Harold St. John)
Wallace, Paula S. *153*
Wallace, Rich 1957- *233*
Earlier sketches in SATA *117, 158, 196*
Wallace, Robert 1932-1999 *47*
Brief entry *37*
Wallace, Ruby Ann 1923(?)- *77*
Wallace, Sandra Neil *236*
Wallace, William Keith
See Wallace, Bill
Wallace-Brodeur, Ruth 1941- *169*
Brief entry *41*
Earlier sketches in SATA *51, 88*
Wallenfels, Stephen *232*
Wallenta, Adam 1974- *123*
Waller, Leslie 1923-2007 *20*
Walley, Byron
See Card, Orson Scott
Walliams, David 1971- *227*
Wallis, Diz 1949- *77*
Wallis, G. McDonald
See Campbell, Hope
Wallner, Alexandra 1946- *156*
Brief entry *41*
Earlier sketches in SATA *51, 98*
Wallner, John C. 1945- *133*
Earlier sketches in SATA *10, 51*
Wallower, Lucille *11*
Walrod, Amy 1973(?)- *182*
Walsh, Ann 1942- *176*
Earlier sketch in SATA *62*
Walsh, Ellen Stoll 1942- *194*
Earlier sketches in SATA *49, 99, 147*
Walsh, George Johnston 1889-1981 *53*
Walsh, Gillian Paton
See Paton Walsh, Jill
Walsh, Jill Paton
See Paton Walsh, Jill
Walsh, Joanna 1970- *182*
Walsh, Lawrence 1942- *170*
Walsh, Marissa 1972- *195*
Walsh, Mary Caswell 1949- *118*
Walsh, Mitzy
See Walsh, Marissa
Walsh, Pat 1954- *237*
Walsh, Rebecca *217*
Walsh, Suella *170*
Walsh, V. L.
See Walsh, Vivian
Walsh, Vivian 1960- *120*
Walsh Shepherd, Donna 1948- *78*
Walter, Frances V. 1923- *71*
Walter, Mildred Pitts 1922- *133*
Brief entry *45*
Earlier sketch in SATA *69*
See also CLR *61*
See also SAAS *12*
Walter, Villiam Christian
See Andersen, Hans Christian
Walter, Virginia
See Walter, Virginia A.
Walter, Virginia A. *134*
Walters, Audrey 1929- *18*
Walters, Celeste 1938- *126*
Walters, Eric 1957- *205*
Earlier sketches in SATA *99, 155*
Walters, Eric Robert
See Walters, Eric
Walters, Gregory 1964- *213*
Walters, Helen B. (?)-1987
Obituary *50*
Walters, Hugh
See Hughes, Walter (Llewellyn)
Walther, Thomas A. 1950- *31*
Walther, Tom
See Walther, Thomas A.
Waltner, Elma 1912-1987 *40*
Waltner, Willard H. 1909- *40*
Walton, Darwin McBeth 1926- *119*
Walton, Fiona L. M. 1959- *89*
Walton, Richard J. 1928- *4*
Walton, Rick 1957- *204*
Earlier sketches in SATA *101, 151*
Waltrip, Lela (Kingston) 1904-1995 *9*
Waltrip, Mildred 1911- *37*
Waltrip, Rufus (Charles) 1898-1988 *9*
Walworth, Nancy Zinsser 1917- *14*
Wang, Gabrielle *212*
Wang, Lin 1973- *221*
Wang, Shaoli *216*
Wangerin, Walter, Jr. 1944- *98*
Brief entry *37*
Earlier sketch in SATA *45*
Waniek, Marilyn
See Nelson, Marilyn
Waniek, Marilyn Nelson 1946-
See Nelson, Marilyn
Wannamaker, Bruce
See Moncure, Jane Belk
Warbler, J. M.
See Cocagnac, Augustin Maurice(-Jean)
Warburg, Sandol Stoddard
See Stoddard, Sandol
Warburton, Tom 1968(?)- *218*
Ward, David 1967- *213*
Ward, E. D.
See Gorey, Edward (St. John)
and Lucas, E(dward) V(errall)
Ward, Ed
See Stratemeyer, Edward L.
Ward, Helen 1962- *206*
Earlier sketches in SATA *72, 144*
Ward, Jay 1920-1989
Obituary *63*
Ward, Jennifer 1963- *226*
Earlier sketch in SATA *146*
Ward, John (Stanton) 1917- *42*
Ward, Jonas
See Ard, William
and Cox, William R(obert)
and Garfield, Brian (Francis Wynne)
Ward, Lindsay M. *236*
Ward, Lynd (Kendall) 1905-1985 *36*
Obituary *42*
Earlier sketch in SATA *2*
Ward, Martha (Eads) *5*
Ward, Melanie
See Curtis, Richard
and Lynch, Marilyn
Ward, Nicholas John
See Ward, Nick
Ward, Nick 1955- *190*
Ward, Rachel 1964- *229*
Ward, Tom
See Stratemeyer, Edward L.
Wardell, Dean
See Prince, J(ack) H(arvey)
Wardlaw, Lee 1955- *115*
Earlier sketch in SATA *79*
Ware, Cheryl 1963- *101*
Ware, Chris 1967- *140*
Ware, Leon (Vernon) 1909-1976 *4*
Wargin, Kathy-jo 1964- *210*
Earlier sketch in SATA *145*
Warhola, James 1955- *187*
Waring, Geoff *238*
Warman, Jessica 1981- *225*
Warner, Frank A. *67*
Earlier sketch in SATA *1*
Warner, Gertrude Chandler 1890-1979 *9*
Obituary *73*
Warner, J(ohn) F. 1929- *75*
Warner, Lucille Schulberg *30*
Warner, Marsha *232*

Warner, Matt
See Fichter, George S.
Warner, Oliver (Martin Wilson) 1903-1976 . *29*
Warner, Sally 1946- *214*
Earlier sketch in SATA *131*
Warner, Sunny (B.) 1931- *108*
Warnes, Tim 1971- *216*
Earlier sketches in SATA *116, 166*
Warnes, Timothy
See Warnes, Tim
Warnick, Elsa 1942- *113*
Warren, Andrea 1946- *98*
Warren, Betsy
See Warren, Elizabeth Avery
Warren, Billy
See Warren, William Stephen
Warren, Cathy 1951- *62*
Brief entry *46*
Warren, Elizabeth
See Supraner, Robyn
Warren, Elizabeth Avery 1916- *46*
Brief entry *38*
Warren, Jackie M. 1953- *135*
Warren, Joshua P(aul) 1976- *107*
Warren, Joyce W(illiams) 1935- *18*
Warren, Mary Phraner 1929- *10*
Warren, Robert Penn 1905-1989 .... *46*
Obituary *63*
Warren, Scott S. 1957- *79*
Warren, William Stephen 1882-1968 .... *9*
Warrick, Patricia Scott 1925- *35*
Warriner, John 1907(?)-1987
Obituary *53*
Warsh
See Warshaw, Jerry
Warshaw, Jerry 1929- *30*
Warshaw, Mary 1931- *89*
Warshofsky, Fred 1931- *24*
Warshofsky, Isaac
See Singer, Isaac Bashevis
Wartski, Maureen (Ann Crane) 1940- *50*
Brief entry *37*
Warwick, Alan R(oss) 1900-1973 .... *42*
Wa-Sha-Quon-Asin
See Belaney, Archibald Stansfeld
Wa-sha-quon-asin
See Belaney, Archibald Stansfeld
Washburn, Bradford 1910-2007 .... *38*
Obituary *181*
Washburn, Henry Bradford, Jr.
See Washburn, Bradford
Washburn, Jan(ice) 1926- *63*
Washburn, Lucia *193*
Washburne, Carolyn Kott 1944- *86*
Washburne, Heluiz Chandler 1892-1970 ...... *10*
Obituary *26*
Washington, Booker T. 1856-1915 .... *28*
Washington, Donna L. 1967- *159*
Earlier sketch in SATA *98*
Wasserman, Robin 1978- *207*
Wasserstein, Wendy 1950-2006 .... *94*
Obituary *174*
Wassiljewa, Tatjana 1928- *106*
Watanabe, Etsuko 1968- *219*
Watanabe, Shigeo 1928- *131*
Brief entry *32*
Earlier sketch in SATA *39*
See also CLR *8*
Waters, John F(rederick) 1930- *4*
Waters, Summer
See Sykes, Julie
Waters, Tony 1958- *75*
Waterton, Betty 1923- *99*
Brief entry *34*
Earlier sketch in SATA *37*
Waterton, Betty Marie
See Waterton, Betty
Watkins, Angela Farris *239*
Watkins, Dawn L. *126*
Watkins, Gloria Jean
See hooks, bell
Watkins, Lis
See Watkins, Liselotte
Watkins, Liselotte 1971- *215*
Watkins, Lois 1930- *88*
Watkins, Peter 1934- *66*
Watkins, Yoko Kawashima 1933- *93*
Watkins-Pitchford, Denys James
1905-1990 .... *87*
Obituary *66*
Earlier sketch in SATA *6*
See also SAAS *4*
Watling, James 1933- *117*
Earlier sketch in SATA *67*
Watson, Aldren A(uld) 1917- *42*
Brief entry *36*
Watson, Amy Zakrzewski 1965- *76*
Watson, B. S.
See Teitelbaum, Michael
Watson, Carol 1949- *78*
Watson, C.G. *193*
Watson, Clyde 1947- *68*
Earlier sketch in SATA *5*
See also CLR *3*
Watson, Geoff 1978- *237*
Watson, Helen Orr 1892-1978
Obituary *24*
Watson, James 1936- *106*
Earlier sketch in SATA *10*
Watson, Jane Werner 1915- *54*
Earlier sketch in SATA *3*
Watson, Jesse Joshua *199*
Watson, John H.
See Farmer, Philip Jose
Watson, Mary 1953- *117*
Watson, N. Cameron 1955- *81*
Watson, Nancy Dingman *32*
Watson, Pauline 1925- *14*
Watson, Renee 1978- *233*
Watson, Richard F.
See Silverberg, Robert
Watson, Richard Jesse 1951- *211*
Earlier sketch in SATA *62*
Watson, Sally (Lou) 1924- *3*
Watson, Sasha *211*
Watson, Stephanie 1979- *237*
Watson, Wendy 1942- *241*
Earlier sketches in SATA *5, 74, 142*
Watson Taylor, Elizabeth 1915- *41*
Watt, Melanie 1975- *193*
Earlier sketch in SATA *136*
Watt, Thomas 1935- *4*
Wattenberg, Jane *174*
Watterson, Bill 1958- *66*
Watt-Evans, Lawrence 1954- *121*
Watts, Bernadette 1942- *230*
Earlier sketches in SATA *4, 103*
Watts, Ephraim
See Horne, Richard Henry Hengist
Watts, Frances *240*
Watts, Franklin (Mowry) 1904-1978 .... *46*
Obituary *21*
Watts, Helen L. Hoke 1903-1990
Obituary *65*
Watts, Irene N(aemi) 1931- *111*
Earlier sketch in SATA *56*
Watts, Isaac 1674-1748 .... *52*
Watts, James K(ennedy) M(offitt) 1955- *59*
Watts, Jeri Hanel 1957- *170*
Watts, Julia 1969- *103*
Watts, Leander 1956- *146*
Watts, Leslie Elizabeth 1961- *168*
Watts, Mabel Pizzey 1906-1994 .... *11*
Watts, Nigel 1957-1999 .... *121*
Watts, Sarah 1986- *234*
Waugh, C. C. Roessel
See Waugh, Carol-Lynn Rossel
and Waugh, Charles G(ordon)
Waugh, Carol-Lynn Rossel 1947- *41*
Waugh, Dorothy -1996 .... *11*
Waugh, Sylvia 1935- *169*
Waugh, Virginia
See Sorensen, Virginia
Wax, Wendy A. 1963- *219*
Earlier sketches in SATA *73, 163*
Wayland, April Halprin 1954- *143*
Earlier sketch in SATA *78*
See also SAAS *26*
Wayland, Patrick
See O'Connor, Richard
Wayne, (Anne) Jenifer 1917-1982 .... *32*
Wayne, Kyra Petrovskaya 1918- *8*
Wayne, Richard
See Decker, Duane
Wayshak, Deborah Noyes
See Noyes, Deborah
Waystaff, Simon
See Swift, Jonathan
Weales, Gerald (Clifford) 1925- *11*
Weary, Ogdred
See Gorey, Edward (St. John)
Weatherford, Carole Boston 1956- *226*
Earlier sketches in SATA *138, 181*
Weatherill, Cat *203*
Weatherly, Lee 1967- *192*
Weatherly, Myra 1926- *130*
Weatherly, Myra S.
See Weatherly, Myra
Weaver, Brian M.
See Numberman, Neil
Weaver, Harriett E. 1908-1993 .... *65*
Weaver, Janice *236*
Weaver, John L. 1949- *42*
Weaver, Robyn
See Conley, Robyn
Weaver, Robyn M.
See Conley, Robyn
Weaver, Tess *197*
Weaver, Ward
See Mason, F(rancis) van Wyck
Weaver, Will 1950- *217*
Earlier sketches in SATA *88, 109, 161*
Weaver, William Weller
See Weaver, Will
Weaver-Gelzer, Charlotte 1950- *79*
Webb, Christopher
See Wibberley, Leonard
Webb, Jacqueline
See Pearce, Margaret
Webb, Jacquelyn
See Pearce, Margaret
and Pearce, Margaret
Webb, Jean Francis (III) 1910-1991 .... *35*
Webb, Kaye 1914- *60*
Webb, Lois Sinaiko 1922- *82*
Webb, Margot 1934- *67*
Webb, Sarah *235*
Webb, Sharon 1936-2010 .... *41*
Webb, Sophie 1958- *135*
Webber, Andrew Lloyd
See Lloyd Webber, Andrew
Webber, Desiree Morrison 1956- *170*
Webber, Irma E(leanor Schmidt)
1904-1995 .... *14*
Weber, Alfons 1921- *8*
Weber, Bruce 1942- *120*
Earlier sketch in SATA *73*
Weber, Debora 1955- *58*
Weber, Dennis J. 1951- *234*
Weber, EdNah New Rider 1919(?)- *168*
Weber, Elka 1968- *219*
Weber, Jill 1950- *209*
Earlier sketch in SATA *127*
Weber, Judith E(ichler) 1938- *64*
Weber, Ken(neth J.) 1940- *90*
Weber, Lenora Mattingly 1895-1971 .... *2*
Obituary *26*
Weber, Lisa K. *217*
Weber, Lori 1959- *220*
Weber, Michael 1945- *87*
Weber, Penny *235*
Weber, Sandra 1961- *158*

Weber, William J(ohn) 1927- *14*
Webster, Alice Jane Chandler 1876-1916 ..... *17*
Webster, David 1930- *11*
Webster, Frank V. *67*
Earlier sketch in SATA *1*
Webster, Gary
See Garrison, Webb B(lack)
Webster, James 1925-1981 .... *17*
Obituary *27*
Webster, Jean
See Webster, Alice Jane Chandler
Wechsler, Doug *189*
Wechsler, Herman J. 1904-1976
Obituary *20*
Wechter, Nell (Carolyn) Wise 1913-1989 .. *127*
Earlier sketch in SATA *60*
Weck, Thomas L. 1942- *62*
Wedd, Kate
See Gregory, Philippa
Weddle, Ethel Harshbarger 1897-1996 .... *11*
Wedekind, Annie *204*
Weeks, Sarah *194*
Earlier sketch in SATA *158*
Weems, David B(urnola) 1922- *80*
Wees, Frances Shelley 1902-1982 .... *58*
Weevers, Peter 1944- *59*
Wegen, Ronald 1946-1985 .... *99*
Wegman, William (George) 1943- *135*
Earlier sketches in SATA *78, 129*
Wegner, Fritz 1924- *20*
Wehrman, Vicki *223*
Weidhorn, Manfred 1931- *60*
Weidt, Maryann N. 1944- *85*
Weigel, Jeff 1958- *170*
Weigelt, Udo 1960- *201*
Earlier sketch in SATA *168*
Weihs, Erika 1917-2010 .... *107*
Earlier sketch in SATA *15*
Weik, Mary Hays 1898(?)-1979 .... *3*
Obituary *23*
Weil, Ann Yezner 1908-1969 .... *9*
Weil, Lisl 1910- *7*
Weilerstein, Sadie Rose 1894-1993 .... *3*
Obituary *75*
Weill, Cynthia 1959- *167*
Wein, Elizabeth E. 1964- *151*
Earlier sketch in SATA *82*
Wein, Elizabeth Eve
See Wein, Elizabeth E.
Wein, Hallie
See Zobel Nolan, Allia
Weinberg, Larry
See Weinberg, Lawrence (E.)
Weinberg, Lawrence (E.) *92*
Brief entry *48*
Weinberger, Tanya 1939- *84*
Weiner, Sandra 1922- *14*
Weingarten, Lynn *217*
Weingarten, Violet (Brown) 1915-1976 .... *3*
Obituary *27*
Weingartner, Charles 1922- *5*
Weinheimer, Beckie 1958- *186*
Weinstein, Bruce 1960- *220*
Weinstein, Bruce M.
See Weinstein, Bruce
Weinstein, Ellen Slusky 1959- *200*
Weinstein, Muriel Harris *215*
Weinstein, Nina 1951- *73*
Weinstock, Robert 1967- *204*
Weir, Bob 1947- *76*
Weir, Diana (R.) Loiewski 1958- *111*
Weir, Joan S(herman) 1928- *99*
Weir, LaVada *2*
Weir, Rosemary (Green) 1905-1994 .... *21*
Weir, Wendy 1949- *76*
Weis, Margaret 1948- *164*
Earlier sketches in SATA *38, 92*
Weisberger, Bernard A(llen) 1922- *21*
Weisburd, Stefi 1957- *202*
Weise, Patty *236*
Weiser, Marjorie P(hillis) K(atz) 1934- *33*
Weisgard, Leonard (Joseph) 1916-2000 .... *85*
Obituary *122*
Earlier sketches in SATA *2, 30*
See also SAAS *19*
Weiss, Adelle 1920- *18*
Weiss, Ann E(dwards) 1943- *69*
Earlier sketch in SATA *30*
See also SAAS *13*
Weiss, Edna
See Barth, Edna
Weiss, Ellen 1953- *44*
Weiss, Harvey 1922- *76*
Earlier sketches in SATA *1, 27*
See also CLR *4*
See also SAAS *19*
Weiss, Jaqueline Shachter 1926- *65*
Weiss, Malcolm E. 1928- *3*
Weiss, Margaret Edith
See Weis, Margaret
Weiss, Miriam
See Schlein, Miriam
Weiss, Mitch 1951- *183*
Earlier sketch in SATA *123*
Weiss, Nicki 1954- *86*
Earlier sketch in SATA *33*
Weiss, Renee Karol 1923- *5*
Weissberger, Ela 1930- *181*
Weissberger, Ela Stein
See Weissberger, Ela
Weissenborn, Hellmuth 1898-1982
Obituary *31*
Weissman, Elissa Brent *217*
Weitzman, David L. 1936- *172*
Earlier sketch in SATA *122*
Wekesser, Carol A. 1963- *76*
Welber, Robert *26*
Welch, Amanda (Jane) 1945- *75*
Welch, D'Alte Aldridge 1907-1970
Obituary *27*
Welch, Holly *206*
Welch, Jean-Louise
See Kempton, Jean Welch
Welch, Pauline
See Bodenham, Hilda Morris
Welch, Ronald
See Felton, Ronald Oliver
Welch, Sheila Kelly 1945- *130*
Welch, Willy 1952- *93*
Weldin, Frauke 1969- *188*
Welford, Sue 1942- *75*
Weller, George 1907-2002 .... *31*
Obituary *140*
Weller, George Anthony
See Weller, George
Welling, Peter J. 1947- *135*
Wellington, Monica 1957- *222*
Earlier sketches in SATA *67, 99, 157*
Wellman, Alice 1900-1984 .... *51*
Brief entry *36*
Wellman, Manly Wade 1903-1986 .... *6*
Obituary *47*
Wellman, Paul I. 1898-1966 .... *3*
Wellman, Paul Iselin
See Wellman, Paul I.
Wellman, Sam 1939- *122*
Wellman, Samuel
See Wellman, Sam
Wells, H. G. 1866-1946 .... *20*
See also CLR *133*
Wells, Helen
See Campbell, Hope
Wells, Helen 1910-1986 .... *49*
Earlier sketch in SATA *2*
Wells, Herbert George
See Wells, H. G.
Wells, J. Wellington
See de Camp, L. Sprague
Wells, June
See Swinford, Betty (June Wells)
Wells, Robert
See Welsch, Roger L(ee)
Wells, Robert E. *239*
Earlier sketch in SATA *184*
Wells, Rosemary 1943- *237*
Earlier sketches in SATA *18, 69, 114, 156, 207*
See also CLR *69*
See also SAAS *1*
Wells, Susan (Mary) 1951- *78*
Wels, Byron G(erald) 1924-1993 .... *9*
Welsbacher, Anne 1955- *89*
Welsch, Roger L(ee) 1936- *82*
Welsh, C.E.L. *234*
Welsh, Chris
See Welsh, C.E.L.
Welsh, David
See Hills, C.A.R.
Welsh, Mary Flynn 1910(?)-1984
Obituary *38*
Welsh, T.K. 1956- *184*
Weltevrede, Pieter 1957- *228*
Weltner, Linda R(iverly) 1938- *38*
Welton, Jude 1955- *143*
Earlier sketch in SATA *79*
Welty, S. F.
See Welty, Susan F.
Welty, Susan F. 1905- *9*
Wemmlinger, Raymond *190*
Wendelin, Rudolph 1910-2000 .... *23*
Weninger, Brigitte 1960- *189*
Wensell, Ulises 1945- *229*
Wentworth, Robert
See Hamilton, Edmond
Werlin, Nancy 1961- *161*
Earlier sketches in SATA *87, 119*
Werner, Elsa Jane
See Watson, Jane Werner
Werner, Herma 1926- *47*
Brief entry *41*
Werner, Jane
See Watson, Jane Werner
Werner, K.
See Casewit, Curtis W(erner)
Wersba, Barbara 1932- *58*
Autobiography Feature *103*
Earlier sketch in SATA *1*
See also CLR *78*
See also SAAS *2*
Werstein, Irving 1914(?)-1971 .... *14*
Werth, Kurt 1896-1983 .... *20*
Wertz, Michael *240*
Wesley, Alison
See Barnes, Michael
Wesley, Kathryn
See Rusch, Kristine Kathryn
Wesley, Mary (Aline) 1912-2002 .... *66*
Wesley, Valerie Wilson 1947- *168*
Earlier sketch in SATA *106*
Wesselhoeft, Conrad 1953- *237*
West, Andrew
See Arthur, Robert, (Jr.)
West, Anna 1938- *40*
West, Barbara
See Price, Olive
West, Betty 1921- *11*
West, Bruce 1951- *63*
West, C. P.
See Wodehouse, P. G.
West, Dorothy
See Benson, Mildred
West, Emily Govan 1919- *38*
West, Emmy
See West, Emily Govan
West, Jacqueline 1979- *235*
West, James
See Withers, Carl A.
West, Jerry
See Svenson, Andrew E(dward)
West, (Mary) Jessamyn 1902-1984
Obituary *37*
West, John
See Arthur, Robert, (Jr.)

West, Owen
See Koontz, Dean
West, Ward
See Borland, Harold Glen
Westall, Robert (Atkinson) 1929-1993 .... *69*
Obituary *75*
Earlier sketch in SATA *23*
See also CLR *13*
See also SAAS *2*
Westaway, Jane 1948- *121*
Westcott, Nadine Bernard 1949- *130*
Westera, Marleen 1962- *187*
Westerberg, Christine 1950- *29*
Westerduin, Anne 1945- *105*
Westerfeld, Scott 1963- *230*
Earlier sketch in SATA *161*
Westervelt, Virginia Veeder 1914-2005 .... *10*
Westheimer, David 1917-2005 .... *14*
Obituary *170*
Westheimer, David Kaplan
See Westheimer, David
Westmacott, Mary
See Christie, Agatha
Westman, Barbara *70*
Westman, Paul (Wendell) 1956- *39*
Westmoreland, William C. 1914-2005 .... *63*
Westmoreland, William Childs
See Westmoreland, William C.
Weston, Allen
See Hogarth, Grace (Weston Allen) and Norton, Andre
Weston, Carol 1956- *135*
Weston, Carrie *190*
Weston, John (Harrison) 1932- *21*
Weston, Martha 1947- *119*
Earlier sketch in SATA *53*
Weston, Robert Paul *209*
Westphal, Arnold Carl 1897- *57*
Westrup, Hugh *102*
Westwood, Jennifer 1940-2008 .... *10*
Obituary *192*
Wexler, Jerome (LeRoy) 1923- *14*
Weyland, Jack 1940- *81*
Weyn, Suzanne 1955- *220*
Earlier sketches in SATA *63, 101, 164*
Weyr, Garret
See Freymann-Weyr, Garret
Wezyk, Joanna 1966- *82*
Whaley, Joyce Irene 1923- *61*
Whalin, W. Terry 1953- *93*
Whamond, Dave *222*
Wharf, Michael
See Weller, George
Wharmby, Margot *63*
Wharton, Edith 1862-1937
See CLR *136*
Wharton, Edith Newbold Jones
See Wharton, Edith
Wharton, Thomas 1963- *223*
Whatley, Bruce 1954- *213*
Earlier sketch in SATA *177*
Wheat, Chris 1949- *238*
Wheatley, Arabelle 1921- *16*
Wheatley, Nadia 1949- *147*
Wheeler, Cindy 1955- *49*
Brief entry *40*
Wheeler, Deborah 1947- *83*
Wheeler, Janet D. *1*
Wheeler, Jill C. 1964- *136*
Earlier sketch in SATA *86*
Wheeler, Jody 1952- *148*
Earlier sketch in SATA *84*
Wheeler, Lisa 1963- *237*
Earlier sketches in SATA *162, 200*
Wheeler, Opal 1898- *23*
Whelan, Elizabeth M(urphy) 1943- *14*
Whelan, Gloria 1923- *224*
Earlier sketches in SATA *85, 128, 178*
See also CLR *90*
Whelan, Gloria Ann
See Whelan, Gloria
Whelan, Kat *238*
Whinnem, Reade Scott *224*
Whipple, A(ddison) B(eecher) C(olvin) 1918- *64*
Whipple, Cal
See Whipple, A(ddison) B(eecher) C(olvin)
Whisp, Kennilworthy
See Rowling, J.K.
Whistler, Reginald John 1905-1944 .... *30*
Whistler, Rex
See Whistler, Reginald John
Whitaker, Zai *183*
Whitcher, Susan (Godsil) 1952- *96*
Whitcomb, Jon 1906-1988 .... *10*
Obituary *56*
Whitcomb, Laura 1958- *214*
Earlier sketch in SATA *171*
White, Amy Brecount *228*
White, Anne Terry 1896-1980 .... *2*
White, Bessie (Felstiner) 1892(?)-1986
Obituary *50*
White, Carolyn 1948- *130*
White, Dale
See Place, Marian T(empleton)
White, Dori 1919- *10*
White, E. B. 1899-1985 .... *100*
Obituary *44*
Earlier sketches in SATA *2, 29*
See also CLR *107*
White, Eliza Orne 1856-1947
See YABC *2*
White, Elwyn Brooks
See White, E. B.
White, Florence M(eiman) 1910- *14*
White, Kathryn 1956- *234*
White, Kathryn Ivy
See White, Kathryn
White, K.I.
See White, Kathryn
White, Kiersten 1983(?)- *241*
White, Laurence B(arton), Jr. 1935- *10*
White, Lee *223*
Earlier sketch in SATA *176*
White, Linda
See White, Linda Arms
White, Linda Arms *238*
White, Martin 1943- *51*
White, Nancy 1942- *126*
White, Ramy Allison *67*
Earlier sketch in SATA *1*
White, Robb 1909-1990 .... *83*
Earlier sketch in SATA *1*
See also CLR *3*
See also SAAS *1*
White, Ruth 1942- *186*
Autobiography Feature *186*
Earlier sketches in SATA *39, 117, 165*
White, Ruth C.
See White, Ruth
White, T(erence) H(anbury) 1906-1964 .... *12*
See also CLR *139*
White, Tekla N. 1934- *115*
White, Timothy (Thomas Anthony) 1952-2002 .... *60*
White, Tom 1923- *148*
White, Tracy *235*
White, Tracy A.
See White, Tracy
White, William, Jr. 1934- *16*
Whitehead, Don(ald) F. 1908-1981 .... *4*
Whitehead, Jenny 1964- *191*
Whitehead, Kathy 1957- *176*
Whitehouse, Arch
See Whitehouse, Arthur George Joseph
Whitehouse, Arthur George Joseph 1895-1979 .... *14*
Obituary *23*
Whitehouse, Elizabeth S(cott) 1893-1968 .... *35*
Whitehouse, Jeanne
See Peterson, Jeanne Whitehouse
Whitelaw, Nancy 1933- *166*
Earlier sketch in SATA *76*
Whitesel, Cheryl Aylward *162*
Whiting, Sue 1960- *205*
Whiting, Susan Allana
See Whiting, Sue
Whitinger, R. D.
See Place, Marian T(empleton)
Whitley, David 1984- *225*
Whitley, Mary Ann
See Sebrey, Mary Ann
Whitley, Peggy 1938- *140*
Whitlock, Pamela 1921(?)-1982
Obituary *31*
Whitlock, Ralph 1914-1995 .... *35*
Whitman, Alice
See Marker, Sherry
Whitman, Candace 1958- *208*
Whitman, Emily *238*
Whitman, Sylvia (Choate) 1961- *135*
Earlier sketch in SATA *85*
Whitman, Walt 1819-1892 .... *20*
Whitman, Walter
See Whitman, Walt
Whitmore, Arvella 1922- *125*
Whitmore, Benette 1955- *203*
Whitney, Alex(andra) 1922- *14*
Whitney, David C(harles) 1921- *48*
Brief entry *29*
Whitney, Kim Ablon *162*
Whitney, Phyllis A. 1903-2008 .... *30*
Obituary *189*
Earlier sketch in SATA *1*
See also CLR *59*
Whitney, Phyllis Ayame
See Whitney, Phyllis A.
Whitney, Sharon 1937- *63*
Whitney, Thomas P. 1917-2007 .... *25*
Obituary *189*
Whitney, Thomas Porter
See Whitney, Thomas P.
Whittemore, Jo 1977- *241*
Whittington, Mary K(athrine) 1941- *75*
Whitworth, John 1945- *123*
Whybrow, Ian *202*
Earlier sketch in SATA *132*
Whyte, Mal(colm Kenneth, Jr.) 1933- *62*
Whyte, Mary 1953- *148*
Earlier sketch in SATA *94*
Whyte, Ron 1942(?)-1989
Obituary *63*
Whytock, Cherry *177*
Wiater, Stanley 1953- *84*
Wibbelsman, Charles J(oseph) 1945- *59*
Wibberley, Leonard 1915-1983 .... *45*
Obituary *36*
Earlier sketch in SATA *2*
See also CLR *3*
Wibberley, Leonard Patrick O'Connor
See Wibberley, Leonard
Wiberg, Harald (Albin) 1908- *93*
Brief entry *40*
Wick, Walter 1953- *148*
Wickberg, Susan
See Rottman, S.L.
Wickens, Elaine *86*
Wicker, Ireene 1905(?)-1987
Obituary *55*
Wickstrom, Sylvie 1960- *169*
Wickstrom, Thor 1960- *200*
Widdemer, Mabel Cleland 1902-1964 .... *5*
Widener, Terry 1950- *209*
Earlier sketch in SATA *105*
Widerberg, Siv 1931- *10*
Wiebe, Rudy 1934- *156*
Wiebe, Rudy Henry
See Wiebe, Rudy
Wieler, Diana (Jean) 1961- *109*
Wiener, Lori 1956- *84*
Wier, Ester (Alberti) 1910-2000 .... *3*

Wiese, Kurt 1887-1974 .... *36*
Obituary *24*
Earlier sketch in SATA *3*
See also CLR *86*
Wiesel, Elie 1928- *56*
Wiesel, Eliezer
See Wiesel, Elie
Wiesner, David 1956- *181*
Earlier sketches in SATA *72, 117, 139*
See also CLR *84*
Wiesner, Portia
See Takakjian, Portia
Wiesner, William 1899-1984 .... *5*
Wiewandt, Thomas 1945- *231*
Wiggers, Raymond 1952- *82*
Wiggin, Eric E. 1939- *167*
Earlier sketch in SATA *88*
Wiggin, Eric Ellsworth 1939-
See Wiggin, Eric E.
Wiggin (Riggs), Kate Douglas (Smith) 1856-1923
See YABC *1*
See also CLR *52*
Wiggins, VeraLee (Chesnut) 1928-1995 .... *89*
Wight, Eric 1974- *232*
Earlier sketch in SATA *218*
Wight, James Alfred
See Herriot, James
Wignell, Edel 1936- *69*
Wijnberg, Ellen *85*
Wijngaard, Juan 1951- *230*
Wikland, Ilon 1930- *93*
Brief entry *32*
Wikler, Madeline 1943- *114*
Wilber, Donald N(ewton) 1907-1997 .... *35*
Wilbur, C. Keith 1923- *27*
Wilbur, Frances 1921- *107*
Wilbur, Helen L. 1948- *204*
Wilbur, Richard 1921- *108*
Earlier sketch in SATA *9*
Wilbur, Richard Purdy
See Wilbur, Richard
Wilburn, Kathy 1948- *68*
Wilcox, Charlotte 1948- *72*
Wilcox, Leah 1975(?)- *207*
Wilcox, R(uth) Turner 1888-1970 .... *36*
Wilcox, Roger
See Collins, Paul
Wild, Jocelyn 1941- *46*
Wild, Kate 1954- *192*
Wild, Margaret 1948- *197*
Earlier sketch in SATA *151*
Wild, Robin (Evans) 1936- *46*
Wild, Robyn 1947- *117*
Wilde, D. Gunther
See Hurwood, Bernhardt J.
Wilde, Oscar 1854(?)-1900 .... *24*
See also CLR *114*
Wilde, Oscar Fingal O'Flahertie Willis
See Wilde, Oscar
Wilder, Buck
See Smith, Tim(othy R.)
Wilder, Laura Elizabeth Ingalls
See Wilder, Laura Ingalls
Wilder, Laura Ingalls 1867-1957 .... *100*
Earlier sketches in SATA *15, 29*
See also CLR *111*
Wildish, Lee *231*
Wildsmith, Brian 1930- *124*
Earlier sketches in SATA *16, 69*
See also CLR *52*
See also SAAS *5*
Wiles, Deborah *171*
Wilhelm, Doug 1952- *190*
Wilhelm, Hans 1945- *196*
Autobiography Feature *196*
Earlier sketches in SATA *58, 135*
See also CLR *46*
See also SAAS *21*
Wilkie, Katharine E(lliott) 1904-1980 .... *31*
Wilkin, Eloise 1904-1987 .... *49*
Obituary *54*
Wilkins, Ebony Joy *234*
Wilkins, Frances 1923- *14*
Wilkins, Kim *147*
Wilkins, Marilyn (Ruth) 1926- *30*
Wilkins, Marne
See Wilkins, Marilyn (Ruth)
Wilkins, Mary Huiskamp 1926- *2*
See also CLR *42*
Wilkins, Mary Huiskamp Calhoun
See Wilkins, Mary Huiskamp
Wilkins, Rose *180*
Wilkinson, (Thomas) Barry 1923- *50*
Brief entry *32*
Wilkinson, Beth 1925- *80*
Wilkinson, Brenda 1946- *91*
Earlier sketch in SATA *14*
See also CLR *20*
Wilkinson, (John) Burke 1913-2000 .... *4*
Wilkinson, Carole 1950- *210*
Wilkinson, Lili 1981- *240*
Wilkinson, Sylvia 1940- *56*
Brief entry *39*
Wilkon, Jozef 1930- *133*
Earlier sketches in SATA *31, 71*
Wilkowski, Sue *193*
Wilks, Michael Thomas 1947- *44*
See Wilks, Mike
Wilks, Mike *224*
See Wilks, Michael Thomas
Will
See Lipkind, William
Willard, Barbara (Mary) 1909-1994 .... *74*
Earlier sketch in SATA *17*
See also CLR *2*
See also SAAS *5*
Willard, Elizabeth Kimmel
See Kimmel, Elizabeth Cody
Willard, Mildred Wilds 1911-1978 .... *14*
Willard, Nancy 1936- *191*
Brief entry *30*
Earlier sketches in SATA *37, 71, 127*
See also CLR *5*
Willcox, Isobel 1907-1996 .... *42*
Willems, Mo *228*
Earlier sketches in SATA *154, 180*
See also CLR *114*
Willen, Janet *240*
Willett, Edward 1959- *115*
Willett, Edward C.
See Willett, Edward
Willey, Bee *184*
Willey, Margaret 1950- *226*
Earlier sketch in SATA *86*
Willey, Robert
See Ley, Willy
Willhoite, Michael A. 1946- *71*
William, Kate
See Armstrong, Jennifer
Williams, Alex 1969- *209*
Williams, Arlene *171*
Williams, Barbara 1925- *107*
Earlier sketch in SATA *11*
See also CLR *48*
See also SAAS *16*
Williams, Barbara 1937- *62*
Williams, Beryl
See Epstein, Beryl
Williams, Brian (Peter) 1943- *54*
Williams, Carol Lynch 1959- *212*
Earlier sketch in SATA *110*
Williams, Charles
See Collier, James Lincoln
Williams, Clyde C. 1881-1974 .... *8*
Obituary *27*
Williams, Coe
See Harrison, C(hester) William
Williams, Colleen Madonna Flood 1963- .. *156*
Williams, Cynthia G. 1958- *123*
Williams, Dar 1967- *168*
Williams, Donna Reilly 1945- *83*
Williams, Dorothy
See Williams, Marcia
Williams, Dorothy Snowden
See Williams, Dar
Williams, Eric (Ernest) 1911-1983 .... *14*
Obituary *38*
Williams, Ferelith Eccles
See Eccles Williams, Ferelith
Williams, Frances B.
See Browin, Frances Williams
Williams, Gabrielle *238*
Williams, Garth (Montgomery) 1912-1996 .. *66*
Obituary *90*
Earlier sketch in SATA *18*
See also CLR *57*
See also SAAS *7*
Williams, Guy R(ichard) 1920- *11*
Williams, Hawley
See Heyliger, William
Williams, Helen 1948- *77*
Williams, J. R.
See Williams, Jeanne
Williams, J. Walker
See Wodehouse, P. G.
Williams, Jay 1914-1978 .... *41*
Obituary *24*
Earlier sketch in SATA *3*
See also CLR *8*
Williams, Jeanne 1930- *5*
Williams, Jenny 1939- *60*
Williams, Karen Lynn 1952- *224*
Earlier sketches in SATA *66, 99*
Williams, Kathryn 1981- *222*
Williams, Katie 1978- *235*
Williams, Kit 1946(?)- *44*
See also CLR *4*
Williams, L. E.
See Williams, Laura E.
Williams, Laura E.
See Williams, Laura Ellen
Williams, Laura Ellen *180*
Williams, Leslie 1941- *42*
Williams, Linda 1948- *59*
Williams, Louise Bonino 1904(?)-1984
Obituary *39*
Williams, Lynn
See Hale, Arlene
Williams, Maiya 1962- *230*
Williams, Marcia 1945- *159*
Earlier sketches in SATA *71, 97*
Williams, Marcia Dorothy
See Williams, Marcia
Williams, Margery
See Bianco, Margery Williams
Williams, Mark
See Arthur, Robert, (Jr.)
Williams, Mark London 1959- *140*
Williams, Maureen 1951- *12*
Williams, Michael
See St. John, Wylly Folk
Williams, Patrick J.
See Griffin, W. E. B.
Williams, Paulette Linda
See Shange, Ntozake
Williams, Pete
See Faulknor, Cliff(ord Vernon)
Williams, Richard Treat
See Williams, Treat
Williams, S. P.
See Hart, Virginia
Williams, Sam *177*
Earlier sketch in SATA *124*
Williams, Selma R(uth) 1925- *14*
Williams, Sherley Anne 1944-1999 .... *78*
Obituary *116*
Williams, Sheron 1955- *77*
Williams, Shirley
See Williams, Sherley Anne
Williams, Slim
See Williams, Clyde C.

Williams, Sophy 1965- ... *135*
Williams, Sue 1948-2007 ... *208*
Williams, Susan
 See Beckhorn, Susan Williams
Williams, Suzanne
 See Williams, Suzanne Morgan
Williams, Suzanne 1953- ... *202*
 Earlier sketch in SATA *71*
Williams, Suzanne M.
 See Williams, Suzanne Morgan
Williams, Suzanne Morgan 1949- ... *207*
Williams, Treat 1951- ... *234*
Williams, Ursula Moray
 See Moray Williams, Ursula
Williams, Vera B(aker) 1927- ... *102*
 Brief entry ... *33*
 Earlier sketch in SATA *53*
 See also CLR *9*
Williams-Andriani, Renee 1963- ... *98*
Williams-Ellis, (Mary) Amabel (Nassau Strachey) 1894-1984 ... *29*
 Obituary ... *41*
Williams-Garcia, Rita 1957- ... *160*
 Earlier sketch in SATA *98*
 See also CLR *36*
Williamson, Gwyneth 1965- ... *109*
Williamson, Henry (William) 1895-1977 ... *37*
 Obituary ... *30*
Williamson, Joanne S(mall) 1926- ... *122*
 Earlier sketch in SATA *3*
Williamson, Kate T. 1979- ... *215*
Williamson, Melanie ... *196*
Williamson, Pete ... *241*
Willis, Charles
 See Clarke, Arthur C.
Willis, Connie 1945- ... *110*
 See also CLR *66*
Willis, Cynthia Chapman ... *215*
Willis, Jeanne 1959- ... *237*
 Earlier sketches in SATA *61, 123, 195*
Willis, Jeanne Mary
 See Willis, Jeanne
Willis, Meredith Sue 1946- ... *101*
Willis, Nancy Carol 1952- ... *139*
 Earlier sketch in SATA *93*
Willis, Paul J. 1955- ... *113*
Willms, Russ ... *95*
Willner-Pardo, Gina 1957- ... *235*
Willoughby, Lee Davis
 See Avallone, Michael (Angelo, Jr.)
 and Brandner, Gary (Phil)
 and Deming, Richard
 and DeAndrea, William L(ouis)
 and Laymon, Richard (Carl)
 and Streib, Dan(iel Thomas)
 and Toombs, John
 and Webb, Jean Francis (III)
Willson, Robina Beckles
 See Beckles Willson, Robina
Willson, Sarah
 See Albee, Sarah
Wilma, Dana
 See Faralla, Dana
Wilsdorf, Anne 1954- ... *191*
Wilson, Anne 1974- ... *224*
Wilson, April ... *80*
Wilson, Barbara Ker
 See Ker Wilson, Barbara
Wilson, Beth P(ierre) ... *8*
Wilson, Budge 1927- ... *55*
 Brief entry ... *51*
Wilson, Carletta 1951- ... *81*
Wilson, Carter 1941- ... *6*
Wilson, Charles Morrow 1905-1977 ... *30*
Wilson, Christopher B. 1910(?)-1985
 Obituary ... *46*
Wilson, Daniel H. 1978- ... *239*
Wilson, Darryl B(abe) 1939- ... *90*
Wilson, Diane Lee ... *172*
Wilson, Dirk
 See Pohl, Frederik
Wilson, Dorothy Clarke 1904-2003 ... *16*
Wilson, Edward A(rthur) 1886-1970 ... *38*
Wilson, Ellen (Janet Cameron) (?)-1976 ... *9*
 Obituary ... *26*
Wilson, Eric (H.) 1940- ... *34*
 Brief entry ... *32*
Wilson, Erica 1928-2011 ... *51*
Wilson, Forrest 1918- ... *27*
Wilson, Gahan 1930- ... *35*
 Brief entry ... *27*
Wilson, Gina 1943- ... *85*
 Brief entry ... *34*
 Earlier sketch in SATA *36*
Wilson, (Leslie) Granville 1912- ... *14*
Wilson, Hazel (Hutchins) 1898-1992 ... *3*
 Obituary ... *73*
Wilson, J(erry) M. 1964- ... *121*
Wilson, Jacqueline 1945- ... *199*
 Brief entry ... *52*
 Earlier sketches in SATA *61, 102, 153*
Wilson, John 1922- ... *22*
Wilson, John 1951- ... *227*
 Earlier sketch in SATA *182*
Wilson, John Alexander
 See Wilson, John
Wilson, Johnniece Marshall 1944- ... *75*
Wilson, Jonathan 1950- ... *181*
Wilson, Joyce M. ... *84*
 Earlier sketch in SATA *21*
 See also SAAS *24*
Wilson, Karma ... *221*
 Earlier sketch in SATA *174*
Wilson, Leslie 1952- ... *166*
Wilson, Linda Miller 1936- ... *116*
Wilson, Lionel 1924-2003 ... *33*
 Brief entry ... *31*
 Obituary ... *144*
Wilson, Marjorie
 See Wilson, Budge
Wilson, Martin 1973- ... *205*
Wilson, Maurice (Charles John) 1914- ... *46*
Wilson, Nancy Hope 1947- ... *138*
 Earlier sketch in SATA *81*
Wilson, Nathan D.
 See Wilson, N.D.
Wilson, N.D. 1978- ... *194*
Wilson, Nick
 See Ellis, Edward S.
Wilson, Phil 1948- ... *181*
Wilson, Ron(ald William) 1941- ... *38*
Wilson, Sarah 1934- ... *208*
 Earlier sketches in SATA *50, 142*
Wilson, Tom 1931-2011 ... *33*
 Brief entry ... *30*
Wilson, Troy 1970- ... *169*
Wilson, Walt(er N.) 1939- ... *14*
Wilson-Max, Ken 1965- ... *170*
 Earlier sketch in SATA *93*
Wilton, Elizabeth 1937- ... *14*
Wilton, Hal
 See Pepper, Frank S.
Wilwerding, Walter Joseph 1891-1966 ... *9*
Wimmer, Mike 1961- ... *194*
 Earlier sketch in SATA *70*
Winborn, Marsha (Lynn) 1947- ... *75*
Winch, John 1944- ... *165*
 Earlier sketch in SATA *117*
Winchester, James H(ugh) 1917-1985 ... *30*
 Obituary ... *45*
Winchester, Stanley
 See Youd, Samuel
Windawi, Thura al- 1983(?)- ... *165*
Winders, Gertrude Hecker -1987 ... *3*
Windham, Basil
 See Wodehouse, P. G.
Windham, Kathryn T. 1918-2011 ... *14*
Windham, Kathryn Tucker
 See Windham, Kathryn T.
Windham, Sophie ... *184*
Windling, Terri 1958- ... *233*
 Earlier sketch in SATA *151*
Windrow, Martin
 See Windrow, Martin Clive
Windrow, Martin C.
 See Windrow, Martin Clive
Windrow, Martin Clive 1944- ... *68*
Windsor, Claire
 See Hamerstrom, Frances
Windsor, Linda 1950- ... *124*
Windsor, Patricia 1938- ... *78*
 Earlier sketch in SATA *30*
 See also SAAS *19*
Wineman-Marcus, Irene 1952- ... *81*
Winer, Yvonne 1934- ... *120*
Winerip, Michael ... *175*
Winfield, Arthur M.
 See Stratemeyer, Edward L.
Winfield, Edna
 See Stratemeyer, Edward L.
Winfield, Julia
 See Armstrong, Jennifer
Wing, Natasha 1960- ... *200*
 Earlier sketch in SATA *82*
Wingerter, Linda S. 1973(?)- ... *207*
Winget, Susan ... *211*
Winick, Judd 1970- ... *124*
Winks, Robin William 1930-2003 ... *61*
Winn, Alison
 See Wharmby, Margot
Winn, Chris 1952- ... *42*
Winn, Janet Bruce 1928- ... *43*
Winn, Marie 1936(?)- ... *38*
Winnick, Karen B. 1946- ... *211*
Winnick, Karen B(eth) B(inkoff) 1946- ... *51*
Winn-Lederer, Ilene ... *198*
Winslow, Barbara 1947- ... *91*
Winstead, Rosie ... *180*
Winston, Clara 1921-1983 ... *54*
 Obituary ... *39*
Winston, Richard 1917-1979 ... *54*
Winston, Sherri 1964(?)- ... *201*
Winter, Janet 1926- ... *126*
Winter, Jeanette 1939- ... *184*
 Earlier sketch in SATA *151*
Winter, Jonah 1962- ... *225*
 Earlier sketch in SATA *179*
Winter, Milo (Kendall) 1888-1956 ... *21*
Winter, Paula Cecelia 1929- ... *48*
Winter, R. R.
 See Winterbotham, R(ussell) R(obert)
Winter, Susan ... *182*
Winterbotham, R(ussell) R(obert) 1904-1971 ... *10*
Winterbotham, Russ
 See Winterbotham, R(ussell) R(obert)
Winterfeld, Henry 1901-1990 ... *55*
Winters, J. C.
 See Cross, Gilbert B.
Winters, Jon
 See Cross, Gilbert B.
Winters, Katherine
 See Winters, Kay
Winters, Kay 1936- ... *153*
 Earlier sketch in SATA *103*
Winters, Nina 1944- ... *62*
Winters, Paul A. 1965- ... *106*
Winterson, Jeanette 1959- ... *190*
Winterton, Gayle
 See Adams, William Taylor
Winthrop, Elizabeth 1948- ... *164*
 Autobiography Feature ... *116*
 Earlier sketches in SATA *8, 76*
 See also CLR *89*
Winton, Ian (Kenneth) 1960- ... *76*
Winton, Tim 1960- ... *98*
Wintz-Litty, Julie
 See Litty, Julie
Wirt, Ann
 See Benson, Mildred
Wirt, Mildred A.
 See Benson, Mildred
Wirtenberg, Patricia Z. 1932-2007 ... *10*

Wirtenberg, Patricia Zarrella
See Wirtenberg, Patricia Z.
Wirth, Beverly 1938- *63*
Wirths, Claudine (Turner) G(ibson)
1926-2000 .... *104*
Earlier sketch in SATA *64*
Wise, Bill 1958- *191*
Wise, Lenny
See Wise, Leonard
Wise, Leonard 1940- *167*
Wise, Leonard A.
See Wise, Leonard
Wise, Leonard Allan
See Wise, Leonard
Wise, William 1923- *163*
Earlier sketch in SATA *4*
Wise, Winifred E. *2*
Wiseman, Ann (Sayre) 1926- *31*
Wiseman, B(ernard) 1922-1995 .... *4*
Wiseman, David 1916- *43*
Brief entry *40*
Wiseman, Eva 1947- *210*
Wishinsky, Frieda 1948- *166*
Earlier sketches in SATA *70, 112*
Wisler, G(ary) Clifton 1950- *103*
Brief entry *46*
Earlier sketch in SATA *58*
Wismer, Donald (Richard) 1946- *59*
Wisner, Bill
See Wisner, William L.
Wisner, William L. 1914(?)-1983 .... *42*
Wisnewski, Andrea *234*
Wisnewski, David 1953-2002
See Wisniewski, David
Wisniewski, David 1953-2002 .... *95*
Obituary *139*
See also CLR *51*
Wister, Owen 1860-1938 .... *62*
Witham, (Phillip) Ross 1917- *37*
Withers, Carl A. 1900-1970 .... *14*
Withers, Pam 1956- *182*
Withrow, Sarah 1966- *199*
Earlier sketch in SATA *124*
Witt, Dick 1948- *80*
Witt, Shirley Hill 1934- *17*
Wittanen, Etolin 1907- *55*
Wittels, Harriet Joan 1938- *31*
Wittenstein, Vicki Oransky 1954- *228*
Wittig, Susan
See Albert, Susan Wittig
Wittlinger, Ellen 1948- *189*
Autobiography Feature *128*
Earlier sketches in SATA *83, 122*
Wittman, Sally (Anne Christensen) 1941- *30*
Witty, Paul 1898-1976 .... *50*
Obituary *30*
Wodehouse, P. G. 1881-1975 .... *22*
Wodehouse, Pelham Grenville
See Wodehouse, P. G.
Wodge, Dreary
See Gorey, Edward (St. John)
Woelfle, Gretchen 1945- *145*
Wohlberg, Meg 1905-1990 .... *41*
Obituary *66*
Wohlrabe, Raymond A. 1900-1977 .... *4*
Wohnoutka, Mike *230*
Earlier sketch in SATA *195*
Wojciechowska, Maia (Teresa) 1927-2002 ... *83*
Autobiography Feature *104*
Obituary *134*
Earlier sketches in SATA *1, 28*
See also CLR *1*
See also SAAS *1*
Wojciechowski, Susan *126*
Earlier sketch in SATA *78*
Wojnarowski, Adrian 1970- *190*
Wojtowycz, David 1969- *236*
Wojtusik, Elizabeth *208*
Wolcott, Patty 1929- *14*
Wold, Allen L. 1943- *64*
Wold, Jo Anne 1938- *30*
Woldin, Beth Weiner 1955- *34*
Wolf, Allan 1963- *192*
Wolf, Bernard 1930- *102*
Brief entry *37*
Wolf, Erica (Van Varick) 1978- *156*
Wolf, Gita 1956- *238*
Earlier sketch in SATA *101*
Wolf, J. M.
See Wolf, Joan M.
Wolf, Janet 1957- *78*
Wolf, Joan M. 1966- *193*
Wolf, Sallie 1950- *205*
Earlier sketch in SATA *80*
Wolfe, Art 1952- *76*
Wolfe, Burton H. 1932- *5*
Wolfe, Frances *216*
Wolfe, Gene 1931- *165*
Earlier sketch in SATA *118*
Wolfe, Gene Rodman
See Wolfe, Gene
Wolfe, Gillian *199*
Wolfe, Louis 1905-1985 .... *8*
Obituary *133*
Wolfe, Rinna (Evelyn) 1925- *38*
Wolfenden, George
See Beardmore, George
Wolfer, Dianne 1961- *167*
Autobiography Feature *117*
Earlier sketch in SATA *104*
Wolfermann, Iris 1972- *240*
Wolff, Alexander (Nikolaus) 1957- *137*
Earlier sketch in SATA *63*
Wolff, Ashley 1956- *203*
Earlier sketches in SATA *50, 81, 155*
Wolff, Diane 1945- *27*
Wolff, Ferida 1946- *164*
Earlier sketch in SATA *79*
Wolff, Jason 1972- *213*
Wolff, Jennifer Ashley
See Wolff, Ashley
Wolff, Nancy *202*
Wolff, Robert Jay 1905-1977 .... *10*
Wolff, Sonia
See Levitin, Sonia
Wolff, Virginia Euwer 1937- *137*
Earlier sketch in SATA *78*
See also CLR *62*
Wolfhard, Steve *235*
Wolfman, Judy 1933- *138*
Wolf-Sampath, Gita
See Wolf, Gita
Wolfson, Evelyn 1937- *62*
Wolitzer, Hilma 1930- *31*
Wolkoff, Judie (Edwards) *93*
Brief entry *37*
Wolkstein, Diane 1942- *138*
Earlier sketches in SATA *7, 82*
Wollheim, Donald A(llen) 1914-1990
Obituary *69*
Wolny, P.
See Janeczko, Paul B(ryan)
Wolters, Richard A. 1920-1993 .... *35*
Wondriska, William 1931- *6*
Wong, Jade Snow 1922-2006 .... *112*
Obituary *175*
Wong, Janet S. 1962- *210*
Earlier sketches in SATA *98, 148*
See also CLR *94*
Wong, Marissa Lopez *226*
Wong, Nicole *214*
Woo, Howie 1974- *207*
Wood, Addie Robinson
See Wiggin, Eric E.
Wood, Anne (Savage) 1937- *64*
Wood, Audrey *198*
Brief entry *44*
Earlier sketches in SATA *50, 81, 139*
See also CLR *26*
Wood, Catherine
See Etchison, Birdie L(ee)
Wood, David 1944- *212*
Earlier sketch in SATA *87*
Wood, Don 1945- *50*
Brief entry *44*
See also CLR *26*
Wood, Douglas 1951- *234*
Earlier sketches in SATA *81, 132, 180*
Wood, Douglas Eric
See Wood, Douglas
Wood, Edgar A(llardyce) 1907-1998 .... *14*
Wood, Esther
See Brady, Esther Wood
Wood, Frances Elizabeth *34*
Wood, Frances M. 1951- *241*
Earlier sketch in SATA *97*
Wood, Jacqueline
See Wood, Jakki
Wood, Jakki 1957- *211*
Wood, James Playsted 1905- *1*
Wood, Jenny 1955- *88*
Wood, John Norris 1930- *85*
Wood, June Rae 1946- *120*
Earlier sketch in SATA *79*
See also CLR *82*
Wood, Kerry
See Wood, Edgar A(llardyce)
Wood, Kim Marie *134*
Wood, Laura N.
See Roper, Laura (Newbold) Wood
Wood, Linda C(arol) 1945- *59*
Wood, Marcia 1956- *80*
Wood, Marcia Mae
See Wood, Marcia
Wood, Michele *239*
Wood, Nancy
See Wood, Nancy C.
Wood, Nancy C. 1936- *178*
Earlier sketch in SATA *6*
Wood, Nuria
See Nobisso, Josephine
Wood, Owen 1929- *64*
Wood, Phyllis Anderson 1923- *33*
Brief entry *30*
Wood, Richard 1949- *110*
Wood, Tim(othy William Russell) 1946- *88*
Wood, Wallace 1927-1981
Obituary *33*
Woodard, Carol 1929- *14*
Woodburn, John Henry 1914- *11*
Woodbury, David Oakes 1896-1981 .... *62*
Woodford, Peggy 1937- *25*
Woodhouse, Barbara (Blackburn)
1910-1988 .... *63*
Woodhull, Ann Love *194*
Wooding, Chris 1977- *166*
Wooding, Sharon
See Wooding, Sharon L(ouise)
Wooding, Sharon L(ouise) 1943- *66*
Woodman, Allen 1954- *76*
Woodrich, Mary Neville 1915- *2*
Woodruff, Elvira 1951- *211*
Earlier sketches in SATA *70, 106, 162*
Woodruff, Joan Leslie 1953- *104*
Woodruff, Liza 1971(?)- *182*
Woodruff, Marian
See Goudge, Eileen
Woodruff, Noah 1977- *86*
Woods, George A(llan) 1926-1988 .... *30*
Obituary *57*
Woods, Geraldine 1948- *111*
Brief entry *42*
Earlier sketch in SATA *56*
Woods, Harold 1945- *56*
Brief entry *42*
Woods, Lawrence
See Lowndes, Robert A(ugustine) W(ard)
Woods, Margaret 1921- *2*
Woods, Nat
See Stratemeyer, Edward L.
Woods, Titania
See Weatherly, Lee

Woodson, Jack
See Woodson, John Waddie Jr.
Woodson, Jacqueline 1964- *189*
Earlier sketches in SATA *94, 139*
See also CLR *49*
Woodson, Jacqueline Amanda
See Woodson, Jacqueline
Woodson, John Waddie Jr. 1913- *10*
Woodtor, Dee
See Woodtor, Delores Parmer
Woodtor, Dee Parmer 1945(?)-2002
See Woodtor, Delores Parmer
Woodtor, Delores Parmer 1945-2002 .... *93*
Wood-Trost, Lucille
See Trost, Lucille W(ood)
Woodward, (Landon) Cleveland 1900-1986 . *10*
Obituary *48*
Woodworth, Chris 1957- *168*
Woodworth, Viki 1952- *127*
Woody, Regina Jones 1894-1983 .... *3*
Woodyadd, Charlotte
See Hough, Charlotte
Woog, Adam 1953- *125*
Earlier sketch in SATA *84*
Wooldridge, Connie Nordhielm 1950- *143*
Earlier sketch in SATA *92*
Wooldridge, Frosty 1947- *140*
Wooldridge, Rhoda 1906-1988 .... *22*
Wooley, Susan Frelick 1945- *113*
Woolf, Paula 1950- *104*
Woolfe, Angela 1976- *169*
Woolley, Catherine 1904-2005 .... *3*
Obituary *166*
Woolman, Steven 1969-2004 .... *163*
Earlier sketch in SATA *90*
Woolsey, Janette 1904-1989 .... *3*
Obituary *131*
Woon, Yvonne 1984- *240*
Worcester, Donald E(mmet) 1915- *18*
Word, Reagan 1944- *103*
Work, Virginia 1946- *57*
Brief entry *45*
Worline, Bonnie Bess 1914- *14*
Wormell, Christopher 1955- *154*
Earlier sketch in SATA *103*
Wormell, Mary 1959- *96*
Wormser, Richard 1933- *106*
Autobiography Feature *118*
See also SAAS *26*
Wormser, Sophie 1897-1979 .... *22*
Worth, Richard
See Wiggin, Eric E.
Worth, Richard 1945- *59*
Brief entry *46*
Worth, Valerie 1933-1994 .... *81*
Earlier sketches in SATA *8, 70*
See also CLR *21*
Worthington, Leonie 1956- *200*
Wortis, Avi
See Avi
Wortis, Edward Irving
See Avi
Wosmek, Frances 1917- *29*
Woychuk, Denis 1953- *71*
Wrede, Patricia C(ollins) 1953- *146*
Earlier sketch in SATA *67*
Wriggins, Sally Hovey 1922- *17*
Wright, Alexandra 1979- *103*
Wright, Betty Ren 1927- *109*
Brief entry *48*
Earlier sketch in SATA *63*
Wright, Cliff 1963- *168*
Earlier sketch in SATA *76*
Wright, Courtni
See Wright, Courtni C(rump)
Wright, Courtni C(rump) 1950- *84*
Wright, Courtni Crump
See Wright, Courtni C(rump)
Wright, Dare 1914(?)-2001 .... *21*
Obituary *124*
Wright, David K. 1943- *112*
Earlier sketch in SATA *73*
Wright, Elinor
See Lyon, Elinor
Wright, Enid Meadowcroft (LaMonte)
1898-1966 .... *3*
Wright, Esmond 1915-2003 .... *10*
Wright, Frances Fitzpatrick 1897-1982 .... *10*
Wright, J. B.
See Barkan, Joanne
Wright, Johanna *220*
Wright, Judith 1915-2000 .... *14*
Obituary *121*
Wright, Judith Arundell
See Wright, Judith
Wright, Katrina
See Gater, Dilys
Wright, Kenneth
See del Rey, Lester
Wright, Kit 1944- *87*
Wright, Leslie B(ailey) 1959- *91*
Wright, Maureen 1961- *233*
Wright, Michael 1954- *198*
Wright, Nancy Means *38*
Wright, R(obert) H(amilton) 1906- *6*
Wright, Rachel *220*
Earlier sketch in SATA *134*
Wright, Simeon 1942- *232*
Wright, Susan Kimmel 1950- *97*
Wrightfrierson
See Wright-Frierson, Virginia (Marguerite)
Wright-Frierson, Virginia (Marguerite)
1949- *110*
Earlier sketch in SATA *58*
Wrightson, Alice Patricia
See Wrightson, Patricia
Wrightson, Patricia 1921-2010 .... *112*
Obituary *215*
Earlier sketches in SATA *8, 66*
See also CLR *154*
See also SAAS *4*
Wroble, Lisa A. 1963- *134*
Wrongo, I.B.
See Katz, Alan
Wronker, Lili
See Wronker, Lili Cassel
Wronker, Lili Cassel 1924- *10*
Wryde, Dogear
See Gorey, Edward (St. John)
Wu, Donald *212*
Wu, Elizabeth
See Wu, Liz
Wu, Liz *184*
Wu, Norbert 1961- *155*
Earlier sketch in SATA *101*
Wulf, Linda Press *205*
Wulffson, Don 1943- *155*
Earlier sketches in SATA *32, 88*
Wulffson, Don L.
See Wulffson, Don
Wummer, Amy 1955- *241*
Earlier sketch in SATA *201*
Wunderli, Stephen 1958- *79*
Wunsch, Josephine (McLean) 1914- *64*
Wunsch, Marjory 1942- *220*
Earlier sketch in SATA *82*
Wuorio, Eva-Lis 1918- *34*
Brief entry *28*
Wurts, Janny 1953- *98*
Wyatt, B. D.
See Robinson, Spider
Wyatt, David 1968- *185*
Wyatt, Jane
See Bradbury, Bianca (Ryley)
Wyatt, Melissa 1963- *177*
Wyatt, Valerie *209*
Wyeth, Betsy James 1921- *41*
Wyeth, N(ewell) C(onvers) 1882-1945 .... *17*
See also CLR *106*
Wyler, Rose 1909-2000 .... *18*
Obituary *121*
Wylie, Betty Jane *48*
Wylie, Laura
See Matthews, Patricia
Wylie, Laurie
See Matthews, Patricia
Wyllie, Stephen *86*
Wyman, Andrea *75*
Wyman, Carolyn 1956- *83*
Wymer, Norman (George) 1911- *25*
Wynard, Talbot
See Hamilton, Charles (Harold St. John)
Wyndham, John
See Harris, John (Wyndham Parkes Lucas) Beynon
Wyndham, Lee
See Hyndman, Jane Andrews Lee
Wyndham, Robert
See Hyndman, Robert Utley
Wynne, Patricia J. *210*
Wynne-Jones, Tim 1948- *186*
Autobiography Feature *136*
Earlier sketches in SATA *67, 96, 136*
See also CLR *58*
Wynne-Jones, Timothy
See Wynne-Jones, Tim
Wynter, Edward (John) 1914- *14*
Wynyard, Talbot
See Hamilton, Charles (Harold St. John)
Wyshynski, Sue *233*
Wyss, Johann David Von 1743-1818 .... *29*
Brief entry *27*
See also CLR *92*
Wyss, Thelma Hatch 1934- *202*
Earlier sketches in SATA *10, 140*

X

Xavier, Father
See Hurwood, Bernhardt J.
Xuan, YongSheng 1952- *226*
Autobiography Feature *226*
Earlier sketch in SATA *116*

Y

Yaccarino, Dan *192*
Earlier sketch in SATA *141*
Yadin, (Rav-Aloof) Yigael 1917-1984 .... *55*
Yaffe, Alan
See Yorinks, Arthur
Yagher, Kevin 1962- *143*
Yakovetic, (Joseph Sandy) 1952- *59*
Yakovetic, Joe
See Yakovetic, (Joseph Sandy)
Yamada, Utako 1963- *188*
Yamaguchi, Marianne (Illenberger) 1936- *7*
Yamaka, Sara 1978- *92*
Yamanaka, Lois-Ann 1961- *166*
Yamasaki, Katie *206*
Yancey, Diane 1951- *138*
Earlier sketch in SATA *81*
Yancey, Richard
See Yancey, Rick
Yancey, Rick *193*
Yang, Belle 1960- *170*
Yang, Dori Jones 1954- *239*
Yang, James 1960- *190*
Yang, Jay 1941- *12*
Yang, Mingyi 1943- *72*
Yankovic, Al 1959- *239*
Yankovic, Weird Al
See Yankovic, Al
Yanok, Johnny *236*
Yarbrough, Camille 1938- *79*
See also CLR *29*
Yarbrough, Ira 1910(?)-1983
Obituary *35*

Yaroslava
See Mills, Yaroslava Surmach
Yarrow, Peter 1938- *195*
Yashima, Taro
See Iwamatsu, Jun Atsushi
Yates, Elizabeth 1905-2001 ..... *68*
Obituary *128*
Earlier sketch in SATA *4*
See also SAAS *6*
Yates, Janelle K(aye) 1957- *77*
Yates, John 1939- *74*
Yates, Kelly 1971- *208*
Yates, Louise 1983(?)- *218*
Yates, Philip 1956- *212*
Earlier sketches in SATA *92, 149*
Yates, Raymond F(rancis) 1895-1966 ..... *31*
Yaukey, Grace S(ydenstricker) 1899-1994 ... *80*
Earlier sketch in SATA *5*
Yayo 1961- *226*
Yazzie, Johnson 1946- *205*
Ye, Ting-xing 1952- *106*
Yeahpau, Thomas M. 1975- *187*
Yeakley, Marjory Hall 1908- *21*
Yeates, Thomas 1955- *230*
Yeatman, Linda 1938- *42*
Yeatts, Tabatha 1970- *215*
Yee, Brenda Shannon *133*
Yee, Lisa 1959- *218*
Earlier sketch in SATA *160*
Yee, Paul 1956- *211*
Earlier sketches in SATA *67, 96, 143*
See also CLR *44*
Yee, Tammy *206*
Yee, Wong Herbert 1953- *172*
Earlier sketches in SATA *78, 115*
Yee, Ying S.
See Lee, Y.S.
Yeh, Chun-Chan 1914- *79*
Ye Junjian
See Yeh, Chun-Chan
Yelchin, Eugene 1956- *232*
Earlier sketch in SATA *196*
Yenawine, Philip 1942- *85*
Yensid, Retlaw
See Disney, Walt(er Elias)
Yeo, Wilma (Lethem) 1918-1994 ..... *81*
Earlier sketch in SATA *24*
Yeoman, John 1934- *80*
Earlier sketch in SATA *28*
See also CLR *46*
Yep, Kathleen S. *203*
Yep, Laurence 1948- *213*
Earlier sketches in SATA *7, 69, 123, 176*
See also CLR *132*
Yep, Laurence Michael
See Yep, Laurence
Yepsen, Roger B(ennet), Jr. 1947- *59*
Yerian, Cameron John *21*
Yerian, Margaret A. *21*
Yerxa, Leo 1947- *181*
Yetska
See Ironside, Jetske
Yezerski, Thomas F. 1969- *190*
Yin *194*
Ylvisaker, Anne 1965(?)- *172*
Yoder, Carolyn P. 1953- *149*
Yoder, Carolyn Patricia
See Yoder, Carolyn P.
Yoder, Dorothy Meenen 1921- *96*
Yoder, Dot
See Yoder, Dorothy Meenen
Yoder, Walter D. 1933- *88*
Yohalem, Eve *219*
Yolen, Jane 1939- *230*
Autobiography Feature *111*
Earlier sketches in SATA *4, 40, 75, 112, 158, 194*
See also CLR *149*
See also SAAS *1*
Yolen, Jane Hyatt
See Yolen, Jane
Yonezu, Yusuke *196*
Yonge, Charlotte 1823-1901 ..... *17*
Yonge, Charlotte Mary
See Yonge, Charlotte
Yoo, Paula 1969(?)- *174*
Yoo, Taeeun *191*
Yoon, Salina 1972- *204*
Yorinks, Adrienne 1956- *171*
Yorinks, Arthur 1953- *200*
Earlier sketches in SATA *33, 49, 85, 144*
See also CLR *20*
York, Alison
See Nicole, Christopher
York, Andrew
See Nicole, Christopher
York, Carol Beach 1928- *77*
Earlier sketch in SATA *6*
York, Rebecca
See Buckholtz, Eileen (Garber) and Glick, Ruth
York, Simon
See Heinlein, Robert A.
Yoshida, Toshi 1911- *77*
Yoshikawa, Sachiko *181*
Yost, Edna 1889-1971
Obituary *26*
Youd, C. S.
See Youd, Samuel
Youd, Samuel 1922- *135*
Brief entry *30*
Earlier sketch in SATA *47*
See also CLR *2*
See also SAAS *6*
Youme
See Landowne, Youme
Young, Amy L. *185*
Young, Anne Mortimer
See Mortimer, Anne
Young, Bob
See Young, Robert W(illiam) and Young, James Robert
Young, Carol 1945- *102*
Young, Catherine
See Olds, Helen Diehl
Young, Clarence
See Garis, Howard R. and Stratemeyer, Edward L.
Young, Collier
See Bloch, Robert (Albert)
Young, Dan 1952- *126*
Young, Dianne 1959- *88*
Young, Dorothea Bennett 1924- *31*
Young, Ed 1931- *211*
Earlier sketches in SATA *10, 74, 122, 173*
See also CLR *27*
Young, Ed Tse-chun
See Young, Ed
Young, Edward
See Reinfeld, Fred
Young, E.L. 1973- *219*
Young, Elaine L.
See Schulte, Elaine L(ouise)
Young, Emma L.
See Young, E.L.
Young, James
See Graham, Ian
Young, Jan
See Young, Janet Randall
Young, Janet 1957- *188*
Young, Janet Randall 1919-1994 ..... *3*
Young, Janet Ruth
See Young, Janet
Young, Jeff C. 1948- *132*
Young, John
See Macintosh, Brownie
Young, Judy 1956- *207*
Earlier sketch in SATA *155*
Young, Judy (Elaine) Dockrey 1949- *72*
Young, Karen Romano 1959- *237*
Earlier sketches in SATA *116, 168*
Young, Ken 1956- *86*
Young, Lois Horton 1911-1981 ..... *26*
Young, Louisa *161*
Young, Louise B. 1919- *64*
Young, Margaret B. 1922-2009 ..... *2*
Young, Margaret Buckner
See Young, Margaret B.
Young, Mary 1940- *89*
Young, Miriam 1913-1974 ..... *7*
Young, Ned *233*
Young, Noela 1930- *89*
Young, (Rodney Lee) Patrick (Jr.) 1937- *22*
Young, Percy M(arshall) 1912-2004 ..... *31*
Obituary *154*
Young, Richard Alan 1946- *72*
Young, Robert W(illiam) 1916-1969 ..... *3*
Young, Ross B. 1955- *150*
Young, Ruth 1946- *67*
Young, Sara
See Pennypacker, Sara
Young, Scott A. 1918-2005 ..... *5*
Young, Scott Alexander
See Young, Scott A.
Young, Selina 1971-2006 ..... *201*
Young, Vivien
See Gater, Dilys
Younger, Barbara 1954- *108*
Youngs, Betty 1934-1985 ..... *53*
Obituary *42*
Younkin, Paula 1942- *77*
Yount, Lisa (Ann) 1944- *124*
Earlier sketch in SATA *74*
Yourgrau, Barry *179*
Yovanoff, Brenna 1979- *239*
Yuditskaya, Tatyana 1964- *75*
Yue, Stephanie 1984- *231*
Yum, Hyewon *211*
Yumoto, Kazumi 1959- *153*

Z

Zach, Cheryl (Byrd) 1947- *98*
Brief entry *51*
Earlier sketch in SATA *58*
See also SAAS *24*
Zacharias, Gary L. 1946- *153*
Zadoff, Allen 1967- *224*
Zaffo, George J. (?)-1984 ..... *42*
Zagarenski, Pamela 1969(?)- *183*
Zagwyn, Deborah Turney 1953- *138*
Earlier sketch in SATA *78*
Zahares, Wade *193*
Zahedi, Morteza 1978- *233*
Zahidi, Murtiza
See Zahedi, Morteza
Zahler, Diane *228*
Zahn, Timothy 1951- *156*
Earlier sketch in SATA *91*
Zaid, Barry 1938- *51*
Zaidenberg, Arthur 1908(?)-1990 ..... *34*
Obituary *66*
Zakanitch, Robert Rahway 1935- *231*
Zakanitch, Robert S.
See Zakanitch, Robert Rahway
Zalben, Jane Breskin 1950- *170*
Earlier sketches in SATA *7, 79, 120*
See also CLR *84*
Zallinger, Jean (Day) 1918- *115*
Earlier sketches in SATA *14, 80*
Zallinger, Peter Franz 1943- *49*
Zambreno, Mary Frances 1954- *140*
Earlier sketch in SATA *75*
Zanderbergen, George
See May, Julian
Zappa, Ahmet 1974- *180*
Zappa, Ahmet Emuukha Rodan
See Zappa, Ahmet
Zappitello, Beth *237*
Zappler, Lisbeth 1930- *10*
Zarchy, Harry 1912-1987 ..... *34*

Zarin, Cynthia 1959- *192*
Earlier sketch in SATA *108*
Zaring, Jane (Thomas) 1936- *40*
Zarins, Joyce Audy
See dos Santos, Joyce Audy
Zaslavsky, Claudia 1917- *36*
Zaugg, Sandra L. 1938- *118*
Zaugg, Sandy
See Zaugg, Sandra L.
Zaunders, Bo 1939- *137*
Zawadzki, Marek 1958- *97*
Zebra, A.
See Scoltock, Jack
Zebrowski, George 1945- *67*
Zebrowski, George T.
See Zebrowski, George
Zecca, Katherine *207*
Zeck, Gerald Anthony 1939- *40*
Zeck, Gerry
See Zeck, Gerald Anthony
Zed, Dr.
See Penrose, Gordon
Zei, Alki 1925- *24*
See also CLR *6*
Zeier, Joan T(heresa) 1931- *81*
Zeinert, Karen 1942-2002 .... *137*
Earlier sketch in SATA *79*
Zeises, Lara M. 1976- *184*
Earlier sketch in SATA *145*
Zelazny, Roger 1937-1995 .... *57*
Brief entry *39*
Zelazny, Roger Joseph
See Zelazny, Roger
Zeldis, Malcah 1931- *146*
Earlier sketch in SATA *86*
Zelinsky, Paul O. 1953- *154*
Brief entry *33*
Earlier sketches in SATA *49, 102*
See also CLR *55*
Zellan, Audrey Penn
See Penn, Audrey
Zemach, Harve
See Fischtrom, Harvey
Zemach, Kaethe 1958- *149*
Brief entry *39*
Earlier sketch in SATA *49*
Zemach, Margot 1931-1989 .... *70*
Obituary *59*
Earlier sketch in SATA *21*
Zemach-Bersin, Kaethe
See Zemach, Kaethe
Zeman, Ludmila 1947- *153*
Zepeda, Gwendolyn 1971- *206*
Zephaniah, Benjamin 1958- *189*
Earlier sketches in SATA *86, 140*
Zephaniah, Benjamin Obadiah Iqbal
See Zephaniah, Benjamin
Zephaniah, Benjamin Pbadiah Iqubal
See Zephaniah, Benjamin
Zerman, Melvyn Bernard 1930-2010 .... *46*
Zettner, Pat 1940- *70*
Zevin, Gabrielle 1977- *176*
Zhang, Christopher Zhong-Yuan 1954- *91*
Zhang, Song Nan 1942- *170*
Earlier sketch in SATA *85*
Ziefert, Harriet 1941- *205*
Earlier sketches in SATA *101, 154*
Ziegler, Jack (Denmore) 1942- *60*
Ziemienski, Dennis (Theodore) 1947- *10*
Ziliox, Marc
See Fichter, George S.
Zillah
See Macdonald, Zillah K(atherine)
Zim, Herbert S(pencer) 1909-1994 .... *30*
Obituary *85*
Earlier sketch in SATA *1*
See also CLR *2*
See also SAAS *2*
Zim, Sonia Bleeker 1909-1971 .... *2*
Obituary *26*
Zima, Gordon 1920- *90*
Zimelman, Nathan 1921- *65*
Brief entry *37*
Zimmer, Dirk 1943- *147*
Earlier sketch in SATA *65*
Zimmer, Tracie Vaughn *169*
Zimmerman, Andrea 1950- *192*
Earlier sketch in SATA *123*
Zimmerman, Andrea Griffing
See Zimmerman, Andrea
Zimmerman, H. Werner 1951- *101*
Zimmerman, Heinz Werner
See Zimmerman, H. Werner
Zimmerman, Naoma 1914-2004 .... *10*
Zimmermann, Arnold E. 1909- *58*
Zimmermann, Karl 1943- *211*
Zimmermann, Karl R.
See Zimmermann, Karl
Zimmett, Debbie
See Becker, Deborah Zimmett
Zimmy
See Stratemeyer, Edward L.
Zimnik, Reiner 1930- *36*
See also CLR *3*
Zindel, Bonnie 1943- *34*
Zindel, Lizabeth *187*
Zindel, Paul 1936-2003 .... *102*
Obituary *142*
Earlier sketches in SATA *16, 58*
See also CLR *85*
Ziner, Feenie
See Ziner, Florence
Ziner, Florence 1921- *5*
Zingara, Professor
See Leeming, Joseph
Zinger, Yitskhok
See Singer, Isaac Bashevis
Zink, Michelle 1969- *220*
Zion, Eugene 1913-1975 .... *18*
Zion, Gene
See Zion, Eugene
Zobel, Allia
See Zobel Nolan, Allia
Zobel Nolan, Allia *218*
Zoehfeld, Kathleen Weidner 1954- *193*
Zohorsky, Janet R. 1958- *148*
Zolkower, Edie Stoltz *171*
Zolkowski, Cathy (A.) 1969- *121*
Zollars, Jaime *191*
Zolotow, Charlotte 1915- *138*
Earlier sketches in SATA *1, 35, 78*
See also CLR *77*
Zolotow, Charlotte Gertrude Shapiro
See Zolotow, Charlotte
Zolotow, Ellen
See Dragonwagon, Crescent
Zonderman, Jon 1957- *92*
Zonia, Dhimitri 1921- *20*
Zonta, Pat 1951- *143*
Zubrowski, Bernard 1939- *90*
Earlier sketch in SATA *35*
Zubrowski, Bernie
See Zubrowski, Bernard
Zucker, Jonny *228*
Zucker, Miriam S.
See Reichert, Miriam Zucker
Zuckerman, Amy *217*
Zuckerman, Andrew 1977- *224*
Zuckerman, Linda *190*
Zudeck, Darryl 1961- *61*
Zug, Mark *204*
Zulkey, Claire 1979- *225*
Zupa, G. Anthony
See Zeck, Gerald Anthony
Zupancic, Lilijana Praprotnik
See Prap, Lila
Zurbo, Matt(hew) 1967- *98*
Zurhorst, Charles (Stewart, Jr.) 1913-1989 .. *12*
Zurlo, Tony 1941- *145*
Zuromskis, Diane
See Stanley, Diane
Zuromskis, Diane Stanley
See Stanley, Diane
Zusak, Markus 1975- *149*
Zwahlen, Diana 1947- *88*
Zweifel, Frances W. 1931- *14*
Zwerger, Lisbeth 1954- *194*
Earlier sketches in SATA *66, 130*
See also CLR *46*
See also SAAS *13*
Zwinger, Ann (H.) 1925- *46*
Zymet, Cathy Alter 1965- *121*